Tropical Rainforests

Tropical

Rainforests

PAST, PRESENT & FUTURE

Edited by ELDREDGE BERMINGHAM,
CHRISTOPHER W. DICK, and CRAIG MORITZ

The University of Chicago Press CHICAGO & LONDON

ELDREDGE BERMINGHAM is a staff scientist and deputy director of the Smithsonian Tropical Research Institute in Panama and associate professor in the biology departments of the University of Missouri and McGill University.
CHRISTOPHER W. DICK is assistant professor in the Department of Ecology and Evolutionary Biology at the University of Michigan and assistant curator of the University of Michigan Herbarium.
CRAIG MORITZ is director of the Museum of Vertebrate Zoology, chairman of the Berkeley Natural History Museums, and professor in the Department of Integrative Biology at the University of California, Berkeley. He is coeditor of *Molecular Systematics* (1990, with D. M. Hillis) and *Conservation Biology in Australia and Oceania* (1994, with J. Kikkawa).

The editors are listed on the title page in alphabetical order.

The University of Chicago Press, Chicago 60637
The University of Chicago Press, Ltd., London
 Published 2005
Printed in the United States of America

14 13 12 11 10 09 08 07 06 05 1 2 3 4 5

ISBN: 0-226-04466-1 (cloth)
ISBN: 0-226-04468-8 (paper)

Library of Congress
Cataloging-in-Publication Data
Tropical rainforests : past, present, and future / edited by Eldredge Bermingham, Christopher W. Dick, and Craig Moritz.
p. cm.
Edited and updated papers from a symposium held in Cairns, Australia, April 1998.
Includes bibliographical references and index.
ISBN 0-226-04466-1 (cloth)—
ISBN 0-226-04468-8 (pbk.)
1. Rain forests—Congresses. 2. Rain forest ecology—Congresses. 3. Rain forest conservation—Congresses. I. Bermingham, Eldredge. II. Dick, Christopher W. III. Moritz, Craig.
QH86.T764 2005
577.34—dc22

2004019348

This book is printed on acid-free paper.

CONTENTS

PART III. RAINFOREST FUTURES

ACKNOWLEDGMENTS

We are grateful to the Australian Cooperative Research Centre for Tropical Rainforest Ecology and Management and the Smithsonian Tropical Research Institute for funding the *Rainforests: Past and Future* symposium leading to the publication of this book, and to James Cook University, Cairns, Australia, for hosting the symposium. Partial support for the editing of the volume was provided by a grant from the National Science Foundation to CM, a Smithsonian Tupper Fellowship to CD, and a Smithsonian Mellon Foundation grant to EB and CD. We thank the Smithsonian Tropical Research Institute for providing general support for preparation of the volume and funds for the indexing of the book. We thank University of Chicago Press editor Christie Henry and associate editor Jennifer Howard for their expert counsel at every step of the book's development. Our copyeditor, Norma Roche, provided careful appraisal and refinement of the entire volume, and the production editor, Leslie Keros, deftly coordinated the book's publication. We wish to especially acknowledge and thank the contributors and our families for their exceptional patience and support.

1

From the Past to the Future: Evolution, Ecology, and Conservation of Tropical Rainforests

CRAIG MORITZ, CHRISTOPHER W. DICK, AND ELDREDGE BERMINGHAM

The idea for this book arose from our conviction that there is much to be gained by increasing the level of communication and collaboration between the evolutionary biologists and ecologists engaged in the study of tropical rainforest communities. That knowledge of history and evolution should inform ecology, and vice versa, is hardly a new idea (Ricklefs and Schluter 1993a). Likewise, previous works have dealt explicitly with the effects of history on diversity in rainforests (Flenley 1979; Prance 1982a; Morley 2000). What is new is that we are reaching a sufficient understanding of ecological and evolutionary processes and, for some places, of patterns of local and regional diversity to attempt an integrative approach to the analysis of species-rich tropical rainforests.

As several contributions in this volume make clear, there is much still to be done by way of basic description of species, let alone their ranges, interactions, and phylogenetic relationships. However, the past few years have seen great advances in basic knowledge of tropical rainforests, resulting from, among other things, the establishment of networks of permanent tree inventory plots (Condit 1995), increasing knowledge of the paleoecological history of tropical regions (Morley 2000), the capacity for large-scale sequence-based analysis of phylogenetic and biogeographic history (Moritz et al. 2000), and the acquisition of fine-grained environmental data via remote sensing (Saatchi et al. 2000). These advances are moving us toward a deeper understanding of the origin and maintenance of species diversity in tropical rainforests.

Of course, the glue needed to bind these somewhat disparate fields is theory—specifically, theory that combines ecological and evolutionary approaches. The traditional view can be paraphrased as "ecological processes—productivity, demographics, and species interactions—determine local species richness, while evolutionary processes leading to speciation and extinction set species numbers at regional scales." A newer view, exemplified by Hubbell's neutral theory of biodiversity and biogeography (Hubbell 2001; Hubbell, chap.

4 in this volume), is that local community structure is determined by *both* ecological (productivity, J_M) and evolutionary (speciation rate, v) dynamics, moderated by dispersal limitation, and, as a deviation from the Hubbell model, species interactions. While far from universally accepted (Nee and Stone 2003) and subject to refinement, Hubbell's theory and other attempts to combine ecological and evolutionary theory (e.g., Rosenzweig 1995) provide a promising direction for integrative studies of rainforest diversity at varying spatial and temporal scales.

A principal aim of this book is to showcase the Australian Wet Tropics, because the history of this region has been more thoroughly reconstructed through geological, climatological, and molecular genetic records than that of other rainforest regions. As evolutionary biologists, the editors of this volume have looked at rainforest communities principally through a historical lens, and we felt that the integrated evolutionary and ecological research in the Wet Tropics provides a useful case study. Therefore, this book couples an integrated view of research in the Australian Wet Tropics to chapters focusing on rainforests in Africa, Southeast Asia, and the Neotropics. All of these rainforests have distinct evolutionary and biogeographic histories (Morley 2000), which have undoubtedly had a profound influence on regional differences in alpha and beta diversity (Richards 1973; Condit et al. 2002; Dick, Abdul-Salim, and Bermingham 2003).

The book also aims to provide an improved scientific basis for conservation that we hope will serve as one more resource in the battle to retard, and in some cases reverse, the steady clearing and degradation of rainforests worldwide. While the drivers of rainforest destruction are economic and political, it is up to biologists studying rainforests to develop an understanding of rainforest community dynamics across varying spatial and temporal scales and to communicate their observations and knowledge at multiple levels in order to develop effective conservation strategies. As D. H. Janzen (1986) has written, "Engineers build bridges, writers weave words, and biologists are the representatives of the natural world." The contributors to this volume lucidly represent rainforest biomes around the world, offering suggestions about how their science might lead to improved stewardship of tropical forests.

This volume is divided into three parts. Part I presents a series of contributions spanning general evolutionary and ecological influences on the species diversity of rainforest biotas, and includes approaches referencing different temporal and geographic scales. Part II focuses on the Australian Wet Tropics, with the aim of bringing together evolutionary, paleoecological, and ecological perspectives on the only region of the world's tropics where the rainforest is adequately protected by legal and cultural stewardship. Although human effects on tropical rainforests are not the principal theme of this volume, part III closes the book with four chapters that recognize that the future of tropical rainforests will depend on human behavior and political decisions.

The concept for the book arose in connection with the symposium *Rainforests: Past and Future,* held in Cairns, Australia, in April 1998, cosponsored by the Cooperative Research Centre for Tropical Rainforest Ecology and Management and the Smithsonian Tropical Research Institute. The volume in your hands, however, includes chapters by authors who were recruited after the Cairns symposium, and all contributions were updated prior to their final submission in May 2003.

With so many new sources of information and theoretical understanding, this is an exciting time to be a rainforest biologist. Given the ongoing threat to this biologically rich biome, it is a critical time to be engaged in the study of rainforests. We hope that this volume will stimulate investigators, old hands and newcomers alike, to think broadly about how evolutionary and ecological factors interact to promote or maintain tropical diversity, and how this understanding can be used to better protect the integrity of rainforests around the world.

Part I

EVOLUTIONARY AND ECOLOGICAL DETERMINANTS OF TROPICAL RAINFOREST DIVERSITY

2
Overview: The History and Ecology of Tropical Rainforest Communities

ELDREDGE BERMINGHAM
AND CHRISTOPHER W. DICK

The biologists and natural historians of the nineteenth century had a prescient fascination with the species richness of lowland tropical forests (Bates 1864; Belt 1874; Wallace 1878). More than a hundred years later, we remain fascinated, yet not sufficiently close to understanding the origins and long-term maintenance of high species diversity in the tropical forest biome. Thus, a principal aim of this volume is to accelerate the understanding of tropical rainforests through increased recognition that evolutionary processes, in addition to ecological ones, strongly influence the species composition of local communities. As we will see in the chapters of part I, questions regarding the relative roles that ecology and evolution play in the assembly and persistence of tropical forest communities are deeply intertwined, and at a time when biodiversity is being lost at an unprecedented rate, they are among the most important questions in biology.

Although attitudes are changing rapidly, many ecologists have argued that history can be safely ignored. Simply put, because species interactions—principally competition—have rapid dynamics relative to climatic or geologic change, communities reach local equilibria fast enough to overwrite the trace of history (MacArthur 1965; Ricklefs 1989). However, diversity differences among communities occupying similar habitats in different regions (so-called diversity anomalies) provide a strong indication that history has a lasting effect on the species richness of local communities. For example, diversity anomalies between local tree communities in the rainforests of Africa and the Neotropics indicate that regional differences in species richness translate into differences in local species richness. As Richards (1952) noted, "whatever the true explanation for the poverty of the African rain forest, it can hardly be due to any ecological factor operating at the present day."

Diversity anomalies indicate that historical factors reach down through time, interacting with ecological processes to determine patterns of local diversity. But a strong role for historical/regional processes is difficult to reconcile with local processes operating on time scales several orders of magnitude shorter in duration. Ricklefs (1989) pointed out that the putatively weak force of historical/regional processes might be reconciled with their apparent imprint on local diversity if the outcomes of competitive exclusion were prolonged to evolutionary time scales. The experiments of Gause (1934) and others notwithstanding, it may be rare in nature that one species excludes another in ecological time. The competitive equivalence of species is a principal assumption of Stephen Hubbell's neutral theory of biodiversity and biogeography (2001; Hubbell, chap. 4 in this volume). Under the neutral theory, species characterized by even modest population sizes persist for long periods of evolutionary history. Furthermore, even a small increase in the time course of competitive exclusion beyond the tens of generations often considered by ecologists (Ricklefs 1989, table 3) brings this local community process into temporal register with the regional process of dispersal, and even with speciation under Hubbell's (2001) point mutation mode of species formation.

Ricklefs (1987, 1989; Ricklefs and Schluter 1993b) has long argued that a major synthesis of ecology and evolution is necessary to adequately interpret the development of biological communities. Although we are still a long way from the desired synthesis, part I of this volume fosters a more dualistic approach to the investigation of tropical rainforest assembly, maintenance, and conservation. It is fitting that Ricklefs leads off part I, and the book, with a chapter presenting two phylogenetic methods aimed at providing insight into the role that historical factors have played in establishing regional and local differences in species richness. Phylogenetic analysis of species production, dispersal, ecological adaptation, and extinction in relation to geologic, geographic, and environmental history is key to understanding regional differences in diversity and, in turn, local diversity anomalies. Sister-taxon phylogenetic analysis provides one profitable direction of investigation because differences in the contemporary species richness of sister clades located in different regions must have resulted from differences in the net rate of diversification (speciation minus extinction). Thus, sister-taxon phylogenetic comparison provides a means for identifying differences in morphology, ecology, or geographic distribution that set regional differences in species number. The second method advocated by Ricklefs is increased use of phylogenetic analysis to separate the contributions of time and speciation rate to species diversity in order to determine the relative ages of clades constituting regional species pools or local ecological communities.

Phylogeny and species identification (taxonomy) also play a role in assessing the relative importance of ecological drift in establishing species richness and relative abundance. According to Hubbell's neutral theory (2001), described in chapter 4, local diversity is controlled primarily by rates of species diversification and by the size of the metacommunity, defined as the "evolutionary-biogeographic unit within which most member species spend their entire evolutionary lifetimes" (Hubbell 2003). But this is a challenging area of inquiry, particularly to the degree that species form according to the point mutation mode, thus yielding species that are not sufficiently divergent from their parent to be recognizable. The evolutionary unit is the individual, and lineages have no assigned probabilities of speciating or going extinct, as in conventional neutral models of phylogenetic reconstruction (Raup et al. 1973; Gould et al. 1977; Nee, Mooers, and Harvey 1992; Nee, May, and Harvey 1994). Rather, the probability of speciating or going extinct is determined by the relative abundance of a lineage, leading to the prediction that most regionally abundant species are old compared with rare species, and are far more likely to have produced daughter species. Thus, the loss of species through competitive exclusion might not occur much more rapidly than the gain of new species in a community, and both of these processes might occur on much longer time scales than apparent in simplified model systems or microcosms.

Because ecological drift is a stochastic process, samples of local communities separated in time (or space) should have low correlations between their species compositions. In the absence of changes in metacommunity size or in the speciation rate, local species richness should stay the same and should represent a genuine steady state between speciation and extinction (Hubbell 2003). Assessments of temporal changes in species diversity and community membership based on the fossil record are often faulted owing to holes in the record. In chapter 5, John Flenley presents a simple but useful test of the quality of plant pollen and spore fossil data by establishing that the well-documented increase in tree species diversity with decline in latitude can be recovered with a high degree of reliability from the arboreal pollen record. This is a fair test of palynological data quality, given that the latitudinal diversity gradient must be a relatively persistent feature of earth history because it is expressed at multiple taxonomic levels (species, genera, and families). Having verified that the pollen record provides a reasonable proxy for species richness, Flenley sets out to test whether tropical rainforest tree species diversity has increased or decreased during the Pleistocene. Such a test can falsify diversification hypotheses predicting either positive or negative change in species diversity due to climatic fluctuations.

Pollen records from only two sites, Borneo and Amazonia, meet the sedimentary and chronological criteria necessary to assess changes in local species number over time. The Borneo site showed virtually no change in species number over time, and the pollen taxa in the Miocene and Holocene pollen records were almost identical, whereas the Amazonian site revealed that palynological richness was approximately halved in the Holocene compared with the Miocene. Keeping in mind caveats regarding taxonomic resolution and sample quality between time intervals, the apparent lack of species turnover between the Miocene and Holocene records at the Borneo site falsifies ecological drift and suggests that non-stochastic processes (e.g., niche assembly) have stabilized community composition. A similar pattern of community stability for a temperate forest was observed across a 10,000-year pollen record of red maple, birch, beech, ash, oak, hemlock, and elm trees from cores of lake sediments in southern Ontario (Clark and McLachlan 2003). If the time scale of species turnover through ecological drift is generally longer than the time scale of environmental change at a particular location (Ricklefs 2003), it follows that the palynological record can more easily be used to reject the neutral theory than to support it. Thus, the decline in species number at the Amazonian site documented by Flenley could be considered evidence of ecological drift only in the absence of environmental change over the time interval assessed by the pollen record.

In chapter 6, Paul Colinvaux holds our focus on the Amazon basin during a period of dynamic environmental change and marshals pollen, temperature, CO_2, and geomorphological evidence to advance two important points. The first is that the lowland South American rainforest was a stable formation in the face of Pleistocene climate change. In other words, the forest was never fragmented into the refugia envisioned by Haffer (1969). Second, both species composition and species population sizes varied with climate in Amazonian rainforests. The Amazon pollen record demonstrates the penetration of some montane tree species into the lowland rainforest and hints at changes in the relative abundances of lowland species. Thus, the detailed species composition of Neotropical lowland plant communities varied, but there was no community-level replacement, and what is forested now was forested during the Pleistocene glacial periods. The evidence of changes in species composition and relative abundance presented by Colinvaux is consistent with the species turnover predicted by Hubbell's ecological drift model, but environmental fluctuations can produce the same patterns.

In any event, Colinvaux's stated objective was to write the requiem for Haffer's (1969) extraordinarily resilient refuge theory. A growing body of evidence, including a number of molecular systematic studies (reviewed in Moritz et al. 2000), discounts the importance of forest refugia in increasing the rate of speciation across the Pleistocene ice ages (Bermingham and Dick 2001). Of course, palynological studies, such as those presented here and in part II of this volume (chapters 18 and 19) and by Morley (2000), paint history with a very broad brush; finer brushstrokes will undoubtedly be required to represent the history of tropical forests that cover regions as large and complex as Amazonia.

Palynology profits from reliable dating techniques and the long-term integration of pollen and spores into the sedimentary records of catchment basins, and thus provides well-dated snapshots of species richness. The small number of sedimentary records and the coarse taxonomic scale of palynomorph identification at present, however, permit only a first impression of historical change across tropical environments. Second impressions of the evolutionary dynamics of the tropics are being formed, at an increasing pace, from the phylogenetic reconstruction of relationships—most often based on DNA molecules—between geographic populations, species, and higher taxa. The molecular phylogenetic approach suffers from uncertain dating techniques based on molecular clocks and the considerable effort required to accumulate sufficient phylogenetic information to permit integration at the community level (Ricklefs and Bermingham 2001), but gains considerably from the accessibility of a historical record carried in the genome of every member of the contemporary tropical fauna and flora.

The advantage of being able to choose both organisms and locations for study has promoted a growing body of phylogenetic data and analysis that not only establishes a refined evolutionary understanding of tropical species and their distributions, but also permits alternative models of speciation to be tested for any given group of organisms and for any specific geographic region. This approach is epitomized by the studies of Jim Patton and his students, who have enriched our understanding of the species relationships and distribution patterns of Neotropical forest mammals while utilizing explicit analytical methods to tease population history from population structure in order to adequately test speciation models. In chapter 7, Patton and da Silva present an overview and synthesis of the phylogeographic patterns exhibited by Amazonian mammals, which discount the importance of Wallace's (1852) riverine hypothesis. The relatively high levels of genetic divergence documented between populations of Amazonian mammals suggest that these population divergences precede the Pleistocene, and thus also cast doubt on theories such as Haffer's (1969) that posit increased rates of Pleistocene speciation. Rather, the data suggest a deep history that is concordant with, and may have resulted from, episodes of Andean uplift and changes in paleodrainages.

The temporal dimension of regional biodiversity assessment is possible mainly because the basic description of the tropical flora and fauna increasingly incorporates molecular systematic analysis alongside natural history observation. In turn, molecular divergence, particularly accumulated changes in DNA sequences among contemporary members of the tropical community, provides considerable insight into the ages of species and the timing of their expansions across tropical landscapes (Bermingham and Martin 1998; Perdices et al. 2002; Dick, Abdul-Salim, and Bermingham 2003). As we learn more about the temporal and geographic origins of species, it becomes possible to design conservation strategies that steward not only the biodiversity of today, but also the evolutionary processes that have generated it.

This point is clearly demonstrated in chapter 8 by Fjeldså and coauthors' molecular study of greenbuls, common African forest birds, and galagos, nocturnal African forest and savanna mammals. The study found that in both groups the oldest taxa were widespread in lowland rainforests, while more recently diverged taxa inhabited ecotonal montane habitats in eastern Africa, suggesting a species source/sink relationship between tropical mountains and lowland rainforests. In the framework of conservation strategy, this result indicates that altitudinal habitat gradients represent an important cradle of diversification that needs to be protected.

Ecotonal speciation, the idea that divergent natural selection across environmental transitions might drive phenotypic change and diversification (Endler 1977), presumably results in sufficient character differentiation to permit sympatry of sister species and thus elevated levels of alpha diversity. However, natural selection is usually assumed to be too weak to cause morphological change in the absence of barriers to gene flow. In chapter 9, Smith and co-workers focus attention on the vast African forest-savanna mosaic between contiguous rainforest and savanna, suggesting that the ecotonal speciation model might explain the widespread occurrence of ecotonal populations that are phenotypically differentiated from their central forest relatives. For many rainforest bird species, food quality and habitat structure differ dramatically between ecotones and the central forest, suggesting that selection might explain the observed phenotypic divergence. Smith and colleagues set out to test this hypothesis by estimating levels of gene flow and divergent selection in populations of black-bellied seedcrackers, olive sunbirds, and little greenbuls existing in ecotonal forest patches and in central rainforest areas. Their results provide a tantalizing suggestion that phenotypic diversification can occur in the face of significant gene flow, but they have yet to document the reproductive isolation necessary to support the ecotonal speciation model. But they lay out methods—one intraspecific assay of reproductive divergence and one sister-species test based on distribution patterns—to more generally assess the role that ecotonal speciation has played in the dramatic diversification of tropical species.

Several chapters in this book discount the idea that speciation rates were especially high during the Pleistocene, although these authors remain neutral regarding the existence of rainforest refugia during that time. Colinvaux (chapter 6) rejects the very notion of rainforest refugia in the Amazon. We support a healthy skepticism about their existence. Nevertheless, we also recognize that the patterns of endemism that initially swayed biologists to the side of the refuge hypothesis still require explanation. In chapter 10, Keith Brown expands his survey of the geographic distribution of Neotropical butterflies, a pivotal data set presented in support of the refuge hypothesis in Prance's *Biological Diversification in the Tropics* (1982a). The new data suggest at least forty-seven regions of subspecies endemism, many of which strongly overlap with paleoecological forest refugia proposed on the basis of geologic and climatic data. As Nelson and colleagues (1990) pointed out with regard to Amazon refugia, caution is required to ensure that endemism and collecting intensity are not conflated. In addition, species richness is highest at the peripheries of the areas of endemism, presumably because these areas represent zones of contact between species originating in different refugia. Under a refuge model, the lower species richness within refugia would suggest elevated extinction rates during the Pleistocene.

Owing to the rich species diversity of tropical landscapes, empirical approaches to understanding distribution patterns are painstaking. Computer simulations that mimic natural landscape dynamics provide one means for deciphering contemporary distribution patterns of forest organisms. Mackey and Su (chap. 11) provide such a model in order to predict the spatial scales over which phenomena such as disturbance responses are more or less likely to occur. But even at very limited spatial scales, the challenge for meaningful simulations is formidable, and, as the authors note, considerable development is required before dynamic landscape models can be routinely applied to tropical rainforest systems. If successful, however, such models have the potential to guide exploration of the relative roles of stochastic (e.g., ecological drift, disturbance) and deterministic (e.g., niche assembly) processes in establishing species richness and relative abundances at different spatial scales, as well as to provide heuristic models for land managers.

A single contentious assumption of the neutral theory—competitive equivalence among species—raises the hackles of many biologists who strive to explain species richness and coexistence with reference to adaptation. Leigh and Rubinoff, in chapter 12, provide a sweeping overview of the ecological interactions, life history trade-offs, and population regulatory mechanisms that underpin ecologically complex rainforests. The authors consider the dynamics of ecological interactions as the species composition of local communities passes through climatic oscillations, continental drift, and mass extinctions. In contrast to the neutral theory of chapter 4, Leigh and Rubinoff emphasize the life histories of species, and their ecological interactions with mutualists and pests, as fundamental forces underlying the structure of local rainforest (and coral reef) communities.

The need to gain improved knowledge of the roles that the regional driving force of species production and the local constraining force of competition play in tropical diversity points to increased study of beta diversity, or the turnover in species between communities. Ruokolainen, Tuomisto, and Kalliola (chap. 13) discuss an intriguing paradox from western Amazonia; namely, the discrepancy between high local and low regional species diversity. Western Amazonia harbors some of the most species-rich tropical forests in the world, with over 900 vascular plant species documented in a single hectare of Ecuadorian forest (Balslev et al. 1998). Yet its regional diversity is unremarkable. Renner, Balslev, and Holm-Nielsen (1990) documented a total of 3,100 flowering plant species in the lowlands of Ecuador and estimated that a total of 4,000 might be expected for the entire area (71,000 km^2). This implies that a single 1 ha plot harbors nearly a quarter of all the species known for an area 7 million times larger. Ruokolainen and colleagues evaluate this paradox in a detailed spatial analysis of ferns and small trees in the family Melastomataceae in sample sites spanning Ecuador and Peru, and conclude that the anomaly merely reflects our incomplete taxonomic description of tropical plant diversity, rather than a true pattern of low species turnover across the western Amazon. Widespread, common, and easily recognized species in tropical rainforests are typically the first to be named, either because the investigator is already familiar with them or because they are abundantly represented in herbaria and therefore easy to match. Rare and more cryptic species may be identified eventually, but, as the authors suggest, a high percentage (20%–30% of tree species) are likely to remain unidentified. The authors conclude that our current knowledge of Amazonian plant taxonomy, ecology, and biogeography is inadequate for answering even rudimentary questions regarding the spatial scale of species turnover in tropical forests, a point that, taken more generally, resonates across many of the book's chapters.

Condit and colleagues (chap. 14) have had the good fortune to study the less diverse but much better described flora of central Panama. Using inventory plots scattered along the drainage system of the Panama Canal, the authors examine the tree species composition of Panamanian forests along soil substrate and climatic gradients. The authors document high levels of species turnover among plots and little correlation in species assemblages across habitats marked by similar rainfall or soils. This result implies that conservation planning cannot be based on habitat selection alone. Condit and colleagues liken this problem to the debate about using "indicator" groups to designate conservation areas, since many studies find poor correlations between the distribution patterns of species in different groups of higher taxa (Moritz et al. 2001).

As we saw in chapter 6 by Paul Colinvaux, climate change can measurably alter the species composition of rainforest tree communities over geologic time scales. Climatic dynamics that act over ecological time scales can regulate the demographic success of tropical rainforest trees and thereby contribute to changes in community structure. Models of anthropogenic climate change stemming from CO_2 emissions and regional deforestation predict decreased precipitation, increased temperatures, and more intense seasonality in the tropics. As Joe Wright observes in chapter 15, El Niño events share these attributes and provide a window on the future for many tropical rainforests.

The El Niño Southern Oscillation (ENSO) alters cloud cover, rainfall, and temperature in ways that directly limit plant function and the resources available for reproduction. Climatic anomalies may have different effects on different plant guilds and growth forms within a single forest. For example, susceptibility to drought is greatest among epiphytes, intermediate among shallowly rooted herbs and shrubs, and least among deeply rooted trees and lianas. Some changes in temperature and moisture availability, as well as changes in day length, appear to act as proximate cues to initiate reproduction in rainforest trees (Ashton, Givnish, and Appanah 1988). Wright evaluates the hypothesis that tree performance is enhanced during mild El Niño events and reduced during very strong El Niño events, and he finds supporting evidence in his examination of seed set, radial growth, and mortality in the Barro Colorado Island tree community. The ecological effects of El Niño events have broad implications as we face the prospect of managing remnant tropical forests that are subject to drought, fire, and flooding (Laurance, Williamson et al. 2001; Cochrane and Laurance 2002). This study further indicates that even the best-protected rainforests should be expected to experience profound ecological changes resulting from global climate change.

The chapters in part I are first steps toward characterizing the history and geography of members of regional tropical species pools and local communities and establishing the temporal and spatial dimensions of species production and extinction. These diverse chapters cover every major tropical rainforest biome. Their subject matter sets the stage for the integrated historical and ecological analysis of the Australian Wet Tropics rainforests presented in part II and for the assessment of tropical rainforest futures in part III.

3
Phylogenetic Perspectives on Patterns of Regional and Local Species Richness

ROBERT E. RICKLEFS

ABSTRACT

Comparative studies of community diversity have revealed substantial contributions of regional processes, geography, and unique historical events to global patterns in the size of regional species pools and in the species richness of local ecological communities. Understanding how such large-scale factors influence diversity requires historical analysis of species production, ecological adaptation, and extinction in relation to differences between regions with respect to the historical record of geologic, geographic, and environmental change. Two phylogenetically based approaches can provide insight into these processes. Sister-taxon comparison allows one to contrast the attributes of lineages (e.g., frequency of branching) that exhibit different traits ("key innovations") or occur in different regions or under different ecological conditions (e.g., temperate vs. tropical). Phylogenetic reconstruction allows one to determine the origins and relative ages of clades included in regional species pools or local ecological communities and thus to separate the contributions to species diversity of ecological history, time, and rate of cladogenesis. Calibration of divergence with respect to time allows one to link the development of biotas to geologic and climatic history. Examples are drawn from plants with disjunct distributions in eastern Asia and eastern North America, from the global mangrove flora, from island avifaunas, and from tropical-temperate comparisons of regional species pools of birds. In general, age promotes diversity. The ability of lineages to cross adaptation barriers appears to limit species pools under stressful conditions such as those occurring, for example, in saline environments and frost zones. Such evolutionary constraints have a characteristic phylogenetic signature, with the taxa in the more diverse region being paraphyletic with respect to the smaller number of derived taxa in the less diverse region. Historical differences between regions in climatic stability and geographic configuration also may have long-lasting effects on the diversity of regional species pools through speciation and extinction. These effects cannot be appreciated until membership in species pools and ecological communities is examined in a phylogenetic framework.

INTRODUCTION

Many spatial patterns in taxonomic diversity, such as the pervasive increase in number of species and higher taxonomic groups from the poles to the equator, can be related to variation in the physical environment (Pianka 1966; Currie 1991; Rohde 1992; Badgley and Fox 2000; O'Brien, Field, and Whittaker 2000; Roy, Jablonski, and Valentine 2000). For this reason, ecologists have generally viewed variation in diversity as reflecting the different outcomes of local species interactions in different ecological settings (MacArthur 1972; Cody 1975; Brown 1981). In addition, because local interactions between species have fast dynamics compared with the slow pace of climatic and geologic change, ecologists have for the most part considered communities to be approximately in equilibrium with the physical environment (MacArthur 1965; Ricklefs 1989).

In spite of the traditional focus of ecologists on local, contemporary processes and phenomena, community ecology has recently drawn increasing inspiration from historical analysis (Ricklefs and Schluter 1993a; Webb et al. 2002). Comparisons of the diversity of communities occupying similar habitats in different regions indicate strong effects of unique history and geography at both regional and local levels. Even patterns of diversity attributed to local ecological equilibria attained under different environmental conditions—for example, latitudinal gradients in species diversity and species-energy relationships—might have largely historical origins. Different climate zones and habitats have different ages and areas of extent, which can result in different rates of species production and extinction in their biotas. Differences in diversity between environments can reflect physiological barriers requiring evolutionary adaptation to cross.

It has been claimed that historical explanations cannot be tested because they cannot be subjected to experimental analysis (Francis and Currie 1998). Even if this were a valid reason to exclude history from science—and it is not—some regional/historical configurations have been repeated often enough, or present a sufficient array of natural "treatments," that the outcomes of certain processes occurring within these settings are predictable, and they are therefore both testable and generalizable. This comparative approach making use of "natural experiments" has a long tradition in ecology where historical or geographic circumstances can be ascertained, as in the comparison of diversity between oceanic islands and otherwise similar land-bridge islands isolated by rising sea levels during the past 20,000 years (Diamond 1972; Terborgh 1974; Wilcox 1978). Phylogenetic analyses can reveal the historical and geographic connections of individual ecological communities and allow us to assess historical and regional influences on their attributes (Webb et al. 2002).

Here I suggest ways in which phylogenetic analyses can be used to characterize large-scale processes related to community development and to evaluate the contributions of local and regional processes to spatial patterns of biodiversity. Such approaches include comparing the diversities of sister taxa, analyzing the phylogenetic positions of the taxa constituting regional biotas and local communities, and characterizing the diversity of monophyletic lineages. Sister-taxon comparisons allow one to examine net rates of lineage proliferation associated with shifts in morphology, local ecological relationships, or regional distributions—essentially, the influence of key innovations and entry into new adaptive zones (Mitter, Farrell, and Weigmann 1988; Farrell and Mitter 1993; Slowinski and Guyer 1993; Heard and Hauser 1995; Givnish 1997; Savolainen et al. 2002). Examination of the phylogenetic positions of taxa allows one to separate differences in diversity into those components related to the antiquity of the taxa within biotas or communities, and hence to the origin of new clades, and those related to the net rate of proliferation of lineages within a region, habitat, or guild. Finally, the overall conformation of a clade may provide information about the relative roles of lineage diversification and extinction in molding contemporary diversity (Harvey, May, and Nee 1994; Mooers and Heard 1997; Nee 2001; Heard and Mooers 2002).

GLOBAL PATTERNS OF DIVERSITY

One of the legacies of the work of Robert H. MacArthur (e.g., MacArthur 1965, 1972) was the conceptual separation of regional species pools and local ecological communities (Kingsland 1985; Ricklefs 1987). Regional species pools are built up over long periods by speciation and the mixing of regional biotas, processes that, by their nature, have large dimensions in time and space (Vermeij 1991; Webb 1991). In contrast, many ecologists have argued that species membership in ecological communities is regulated locally by environmental filters reinforced by interactions between species (Brown 1981; Zobel 1992; Weiher and Keddy 1999). Species interactions presumably cause community species richness to reach local equilibrium in tens or hundreds of generations—fast enough to wipe clean the imprint of history (Ricklefs 1989). Discrepancies between the regional driving force of species production and the local constraining force of competition can be adjusted by the degree of turnover, or replacement, of species between habitats, the so-called "beta" component of diversity (Whittaker 1972; Cody 1975).

MacArthur's insight allowed ecologists to study diversity on ecological scales and ignore history and geography. More recently, however, doubts concerning the statistical validity of perceived patterns in communities (Connor and Simberloff 1979), combined with increasing access to phylogenetic and historical information (Ricklefs and Schluter 1993a), have led many ecologists to reconsider regional and historical explanations for diversity patterns (Ricklefs 1987; Rosenzweig 1995). At the extreme, Hubbell's (2001, chap. 4 in this volume) theory of ecological drift denies a role for species interactions altogether and sees patterns in community diversity as being established through variation in rates of species production and dispersal.

THE EVIDENCE FOR REGIONAL AND HISTORICAL INFLUENCES ON LOCAL DIVERSITY

Local ecological regulation of diversity is suggested by a close correlation between diversity and conditions of the environment. The pervasive decrease in diversity with distance from the equator (Stevens 1989), and the general correlation between diversity and biological productivity or local physical conditions of the environment (Currie 1991; Rosenzweig and Abramsky 1993; Wright, Currie, and Maurer 1993; Badgley and Fox 2000; O'Brien, Field, and Whittaker 2000), are accepted as evidence of local determination. A fundamental prediction of the hypothesis of local determinism is that independently derived communities occupying similar habitats should have similar structure—specifically, similar diversity. Tests of this prediction of community convergence reveal many cases in which local diversity differs markedly among communities occupying similar habitats in different regions. Such "diversity anomalies" may be as large as a factor of 2 or 3, as in the case of mangrove vegetation (Ricklefs and Latham 1993; Ellison, Farnsworth, and Merkt 1999). Differences in local diversity between regions average about 1.4- to 1.7-fold over a wide range of comparisons (Orians and Paine 1983; Schluter and Ricklefs 1993a; Westoby 1993). Assuming that environments are well matched in these comparisons, local diversity clearly bears the imprint of the size of the regional pool of species.

The hypothesis of local determinism also predicts that local diversity is independent of regional diversity (community saturation: Terborgh and Faaborg 1980), but many analyses suggest that local communities sample their regional pools proportionately (Terborgh and Faaborg 1980; Cornell and Lawton 1992; Cornell 1993; Caley 1997; Srivastava 1999; Loreau 2000; Ricklefs 2000). Available evidence now strongly supports the idea that regional and local diversity are directly connected and that variation in the former is translated to the local level, as well as to the turnover of species between localities. For example, differences in the sizes of island avifaunas in the West Indies are reflected about equally in local, within-habitat diversity and in turnover of species between habitats (Ricklefs and Schluter 1993b; Ricklefs 2000).

It is ironic that ecologists adhered to local determinism as persistently as they did, because diversity anomalies were regularly reported in the literature of the 1970s, and regional processes and regional history were proposed to explain some of them (e.g., Karr 1976; Pearson 1977, 1982). The most famous regional hypothesis in community ecology is MacArthur and Wilson's "equilibrium" theory of island biogeography (MacArthur and Wilson 1967), in which the regional process of colonization played a dominant role. One can also point to the related "peninsula effect" hypothesis, which portrayed the low diversity of the ends of peninsulas, such as southern Florida and southern Baja California, as the result of limited dispersal of continental populations to such peripheral areas (Simpson 1964; Brown and Opler 1990; Rapoport 1994), although alternative explanations based on changes in local ecological conditions also were proposed (Busack and Hedges 1984; Means and Simberloff 1987). The Pleistocene refuge hypothesis to account for high diversity in the Amazon basin and in certain North Temperate groups (Mengel 1964; Haffer 1969; Simpson and Haffer 1978; Prance 1982a) also received considerable attention, but not uniform acceptance (Endler 1982b; 1982c; Ricklefs 1989; Bermingham et al. 1992; Klicka and Zink 1997; Lovette and Bermingham 1999).

Regional thinking on a smaller scale has been assimilated into ecology in the guise of metapopulation ecology (Hanski 1997) and landscape ecology (Shmida and Wilson 1985; Turner 1989; Kareiva and Wennergren 1995; Wiens 1997; Whittaker, Willis, and Field 2001). However, like MacArthur and Wilson's theory of diversity on islands, these remain equilibrium ideas, albeit placed in spatially complex ecological settings. Whether regional species pools and local communities are in equilibrium remains a pressing issue for ecologists (Jablonski 1998, 2002; Ricklefs and Bermingham 2001). But this issue is independent of the distinction between local and regional determinism, as either type of system may or may not have reached equilibrium under long-term, constant conditions.

Assuming that large-scale regional processes and historical events are important, how can phylogenetic approaches help to resolve their effects on the development of regional biotas and, especially, the assembly of local communities? Species production takes place over large dimensions of time and space, and it has long been argued that more time and more space result in more species (Wallace 1876; Willis 1922; Fischer 1960; Whittaker 1972; Rosenzweig 1995). In addition, species production itself has both temporal and spatial dimensions that enter as coefficients into the equation relating diversity to age and area. Thus, our challenge is to characterize the history and geography of members of the regional species pool and the local community, and to establish the temporal and spatial dimensions of species production and extinction (Losos 1996; Richman 1996; Losos et al. 1998; Price et al. 2000).

SISTER-TAXON COMPARISONS

By definition, sister taxa are identical in age, having descended from the same ancestral taxon as the result of the splitting of a lineage (fig. 3.1). Thus, differences in the contemporary diversity of sister taxa must result from differences in the net rate of diversification (speciation − extinction). When sister taxa differ in some aspect of their morphology, ecology, or geographic distribution, one can estimate the effect of such a difference on diversification (Barraclough, Nee, and Harvey 1998; Barraclough, Vogler, and Harvey 1998). As Slowinski and Guyer (1993) have pointed out, when rates of cladogenesis are the same in both clades, the expected proportion (P) of species in one of the sister clades is uniformly distributed between 0 and 1. Thus, only the most extremely unbalanced comparisons (e.g., $P < 0.025$ or $P > 0.975$) are individually indicative of differences in proliferation rates. However, the null hypothesis for the expected proportions in several independent comparisons of sister pairs has a binomial distribution, with $p = 0.5$. Several studies have used the method of independent sister-taxon comparisons to assess the association of lineage diversification with "key innovations" (Heard and Hauser 1995; Barraclough, Nee, and Harvey 1998; Hunter 1998), including herbivory in insects (Mitter, Farrell, and Weigmann 1988), egg structure in terrestrial arthropods (Zeh, Zeh, and Smith 1989), plant defenses against herbivores (Farrell, Doussourd, and Mitter 1991), floral spurs (Hodges and Arnold 1995; Hodges 1997), colonial breeding in birds (Mooers and Møller 1996), sexual selection in birds (Barraclough, Harvey, and Nee 1995; Mitra, Landel, and Pruett-Jones 1996; Møller and Cuervo 1998; Owens, Bennett, and Harvey 1999), and pollination and dispersal mechanisms in plants (Dodd, Silvertown, and Chase 1999; Ricklefs and Renner 2000).

Few of these studies have analyzed sister groups occupying different habitats or geographic regions. Farrell and Mitter (1993) compared the numbers of species in five pairs of sister genera in the Coleoptera (beetles) and Lepidoptera (moths) in which one member was tropical in distribution and the other temperate. In two cases, the tropical member of the pair was more diverse; in three cases, the temperate member was. In only one case was the proportion of spe-

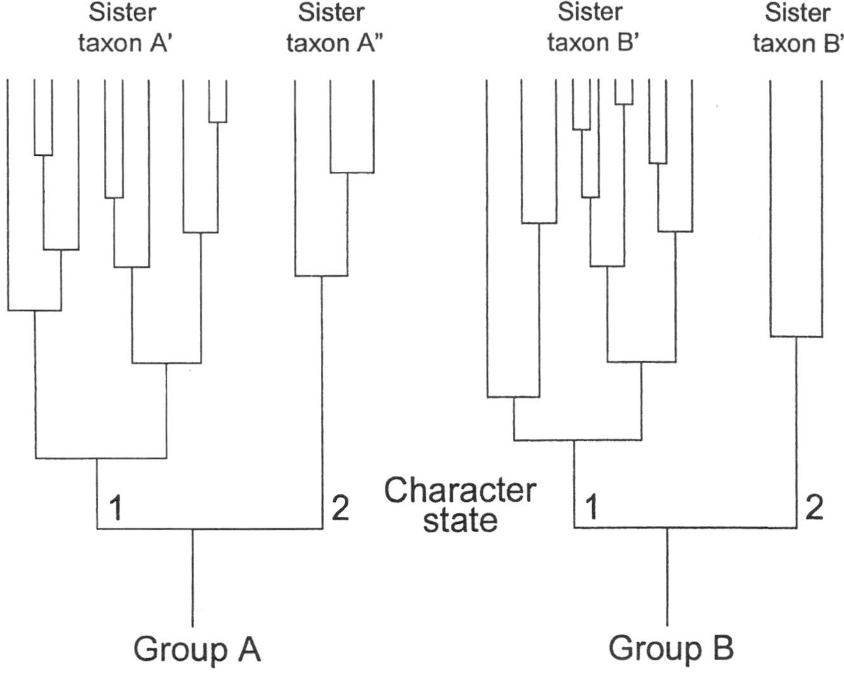

Figure 3.1 Diagrammatic representation of the technique of sister-taxon comparison. Numbers of species are compared across several pairs of sister taxa (group A, group B, etc.) in which the members are distinguished by the same character difference (character state 1 versus character state 2; e.g., tropical versus temperate). When there is no difference in the proliferation rate with respect to the character, the number of clades with character state 1 having the greater diversity will be binomially distributed. Thus, statistically significant biases in diversification rate can be detected when one of the character states is associated with higher diversity in a large proportion of cases. Additional tests based on tree balance are discussed by Slowinski and Guyer (1993), Mooers and Heard (1997), Chan and Moore (2002), and Agapow and Purvis (2002).

cies in the tropical clade extreme (0.978). Although this particular example was inconclusive, similar latitudinal comparisons have suggested higher rates of lineage proliferation in the tropics (e.g., Cardillo 1999).

The taxonomic richness of most groups of organisms is higher in tropical than in temperate and boreal regions. This pattern is exhibited at both regional and local scales, suggesting that its basis lies in large-scale processes that determine regional diversity (Ricklefs and Schluter 1993b). Accordingly, differences in diversity can result from differences in net rates of species proliferation (speciation − extinction), ages of lineages, or both. Tropical-temperate differences in diversity appear at all levels of the taxonomic hierarchy (Ricklefs 1989), suggesting that the origins of these diversity patterns are either very old or, if these patterns have been produced by differences in extinction rates, that lineages have disappeared more or less at random rather than unduly favoring a smaller number of higher taxa.

In a survey of species richness in families of flowering plants, Ricklefs and Renner (1994) found that the average number of species per family was 5.6 times greater in families with exclusively tropical distributions (geometric mean = 52 species) than in those with exclusively temperate distributions (8 species), and even higher yet in cosmopolitan families (293 species). This effect was independent of variation in pollination mode, dispersal mode, and growth form. In addition, the number of families restricted to the tropics, about half the total, exceeded the number of families with exclusively temperate distributions by a factor of almost 4 (191 versus 53).

Ricklefs and Renner's analysis did not use sister-taxon comparisons, primarily because the phylogenetic positions of the recognized families were poorly known and few unambiguous tropical-temperate sister-taxon relationships could be identified. Many long-recognized sister pairs of angiosperm families have not withstood phylogenetic scrutiny (Judd, Sanders, and Donoghue 1994). Frequently, one of the families has proved to be paraphyletic, with the second family nested within it. Judd, Sanders, and Donoghue (1994, 1) concluded that "in most of these cases the paraphyletic group is best developed in the tropics, with groups that are more widespread in temperate regions evolving later. With a few exceptions, members of the paraphyletic group are mostly woody plants, while members of the derived temperate lines are mostly herbaceous. In general, it appears that the distinctive morphological specializations of the more temperate lines can be traced to related tropical plants." As phylogenies become better resolved (e.g., Soltis, Soltis, and Chase et al. 2000), sister-taxon comparisons will become a more powerful tool for historical analysis (e.g., Dodd, Silvertown, and Chase 1999; Heilbuth 2000).

DIVERSITY ANOMALIES

One of the most prominent diversity anomalies is the sixfold greater species richness and fourfold greater genus richness of mangrove plants in the Indo-West Pacific (IWP) region than in the Atlantic-Caribbean-Eastern Pacific (ACEP) region (Saenger, Hegerl, and Davie 1983; Duke 1992; Ricklefs and Latham 1993; Duke et al. 1998; Plaziat et al. 2001). This anomaly appears as a two- to threefold difference in diversity at the local level. Because the areas of mangrove habitat and the mangrove habitats themselves are so similar in the two regions (Saenger, Hegerl, and Davie 1983; cf. Ellison, Farnsworth, and Merkt 1999), this marked difference in diversity presumably has regional or historical origins that cannot be perceived in the local environment.

Most mangrove taxa are derived from larger, otherwise terrestrial, clades. Lineages of mangrove plants have originated fifteen times; at present, four of these lineages are cosmopolitan, one (*Pelliciera*) is now restricted to the ACEP region, and ten are restricted to the IWP region (Ricklefs and Latham 1993). Currently postulated taxonomic affinities are consistent with the origins of six of the IWP endemics in the IWP region; in the other four cases, these relationships convey no information with respect to region of origin. Although *Pelliciera* now occurs only in the Caribbean, the earliest fossils are from the Mediterranean (central Tethys Sea) region (Cavagnetto and Anadón 1995), which does not exclude a Tethyan rather than a Caribbean origin.

In the case of one of the cosmopolitan mangrove lineages, the Rhizophoreae, the sister taxon (Gynotrocheae) is currently restricted to the IWP region. Thus, it is most parsimonious to assume that the Rhizophoreae also arose within this region. Of this tribe, only *Rhizophora* also occurs in the ACEP region, and the ACEP species *R. mangle* is closely related to the IWP species *R. racemosa*. Apparently, Paleogene fossils of *Rhizophora* from the Caribbean region (Muller 1981; Graham 1985) refer to a lineage that is now extinct, and *R. mangle* is a recent colonist of the region (Schwarzbach and Ricklefs 2000). It would appear that most contemporary mangrove lineages arose in the IWP region, and therefore that the mangrove diversity anomaly reflects a difference between the IWP and ACEP regions in the likelihood of transitions of terrestrial lineages into the mangrove environment. Although mangrove environments themselves probably have not differed between regions, the juxtaposition of terrestrial and mangrove habitats may well have differed, owing to variations in precipitation and other climatic factors and to differences in the configuration of landmasses.

Several lineages of plants appear to have proliferated within the mangrove habitat. The most diverse exclusively mangrove lineage is the Rhizophoreae, with approximately 15 species in four genera. The number of species in a lineage and the level at which it is endemic to the mangrove environment (that is, species, genus, tribe, or family) are positively correlated (Ricklefs and Latham 1993). This observation suggests that the diversity of mangrove clades increases with time; whether species production in mangroves slows as diversity builds cannot yet be determined. Andrea Schwarzbach and I are investigating the phylogenetic relationships of the mangrove lineages, and one goal of our work is to determine whether the rate of species proliferation is affected by transition to the mangrove

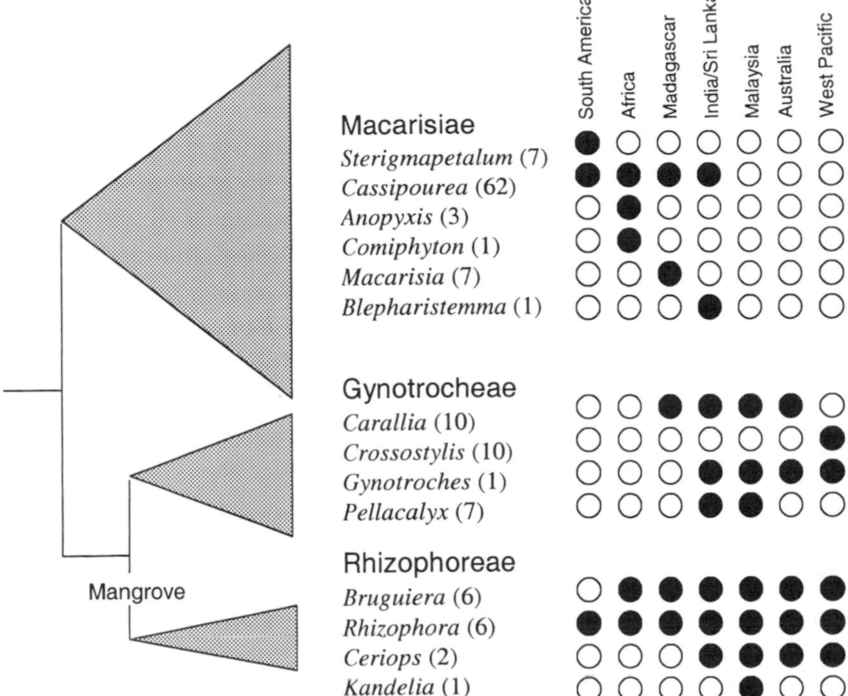

Figure 3.2 Species diversity and geographic distribution of the tribes of the Rhizophoreae. The width of the shaded area is proportional to the species diversity of each group. The African distribution of the mangrove *Bruguiera* is restricted to the coasts of the Indian Ocean. Number of species per genus does not differ significantly among tribes (Kruskal-Wallis $c^2 = 1.67$, df = 2, $P = 0.43$).

environment. In the case of the mangrove tribe Rhizophoreae, its sister taxon, the terrestrial Gynotrocheae, has almost twice as many species, and the sister taxon to both of these, the Macarisiae, has almost twice again as many species (fig. 3.2). By themselves, these numbers are not instructive because they could have resulted by chance under homogeneous rates of diversification in both clades. However, when comparisons can be made among a large number of sister-taxon pairs, it may be possible to test the hypothesis that invasion of the mangrove environment, or any other environment or region, either accelerates or suppresses the rate of diversification.

Temperate Asia supports a more diverse flora than comparable areas of North America (White 1983; Latham and Ricklefs 1993b; Li and Adair 1994; Guo, Ricklefs, and Cody 1998; Qian and Ricklefs 1999; Guo and Ricklefs 2000), revealing a pattern similar to that of mangrove floras. By one account, fifty-six genera or

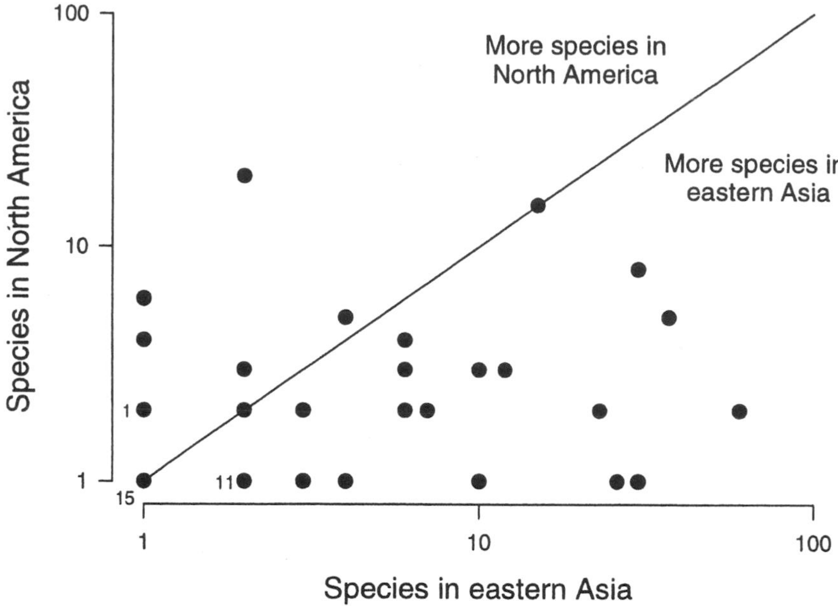

Figure 3.3 The number of species in eastern Asia and North America in genus-level sister-taxon pairs of plants with disjunct distributions between eastern Asia and North America (after data in Li 1952). The solid line represents equal number of species in each region. Small numbers next to symbols indicate the number of cases.

genus pairs of plants have disjunct ranges between eastern Asia and eastern North America (Li 1952). If we assume that the members of a disjunct genus in one region form a sister clade with respect to those in the other region, we can ask whether diversification has been more rapid in Asia or in North America (Ricklefs 1989). According to Li (1952), these disjunct genera include 366 species in Asia and 132 in North America. Fifteen of the pairs of clades have one species in each region. Of the twelve pairs with a total of 3 species, eleven had 2 species in Asia and only one had 2 species in North America (binomial test; $P = 0.003$). Of the remaining pairs with more than 3 species, twenty-four were more diverse in eastern Asia and five were more diverse in eastern North America ($P < 0.001$); one was tied. The distribution of the species between the regions (fig. 3.3) shows a strong skew toward higher diversity in eastern Asia, which is exaggerated in taxa whose distributions extend into the tropics in Southeast Asia (see also Qian and Ricklefs 2000). The diversity anomaly is reversed only in genera whose distributions in North America extend to the western part of the continent (Qian and Ricklefs 2000). One can conclude that the net rate of species proliferation has been higher in eastern Asia than in eastern North America during the period over which these pairs of sister clades have been isolated, probably the last 5–30 million years (Qiu, Parks, and Chase 1995; Lee et al. 1996; Wen, Jansen, and Kilgore 1996; Wen 1999).

Among temperate trees, fossil data indicate that extinction has not been an important factor influencing diversity at the genus level in either region, but especially in eastern Asia, where most Tertiary fossil genera are represented in the extant flora (Latham and Ricklefs 1993b). Because taxonomic richness is higher in Asia than in North America at the genus and family levels in ferns, gymnosperms, and angiosperms (Guo, Ricklefs, and Cody 1998), we can infer that the diversity difference between the regions is old and that net diversification rates have favored Asia for a long time. Several explanations for this difference seem reasonable, including a persistent, broad land connection between temperate Asia and tropical environments in Southeast Asia and the great topographic diversity of eastern Asia (Guo and Ricklefs 2000). Qian and Ricklefs (2000) emphasized the role of topographic and climatic heterogeneity combined with sea-level changes in promoting higher rates of allopatric speciation in eastern Asia. Eastern Asian–North American disjunct genera that include the heterogeneous region of western North America in their distributions are as diverse in North America as in Asia.

USING PHYLOGENETIC TREES TO CHARACTERIZE THE HISTORY OF COMMUNITY ASSEMBLY

Phylogenetic trees reveal the history of the living members of monophyletic groups. By comparing the members of two biotas or communities having different diversities, one may determine the relative ages and geographic extents of the monophyletic groups represented in each (Richman 1996). Such descriptive characterization cannot reject the hypothesis of local determinism, but it can support historical explanations for variation in regional species pools. For example, Ricklefs and Schluter (1993b) compared the relative ages of clades (determined by DNA-DNA hybridization; Sibley and Ahlquist 1990) represented by passerine birds in forested communities in Panama (41 species) and Illinois (23 species). The tropical clades were 2.6 times older on average than the temperate clades.

A comparison of the passerine birds of South America (approximately 1,668 species in 471 genera; Meyer de Schauensee 1966) with those of North America north of Mexico (approximately 257 species in 101 genera; American Ornithologists' Union 1998) reveals both more ancient roots and more rapid diversifica-

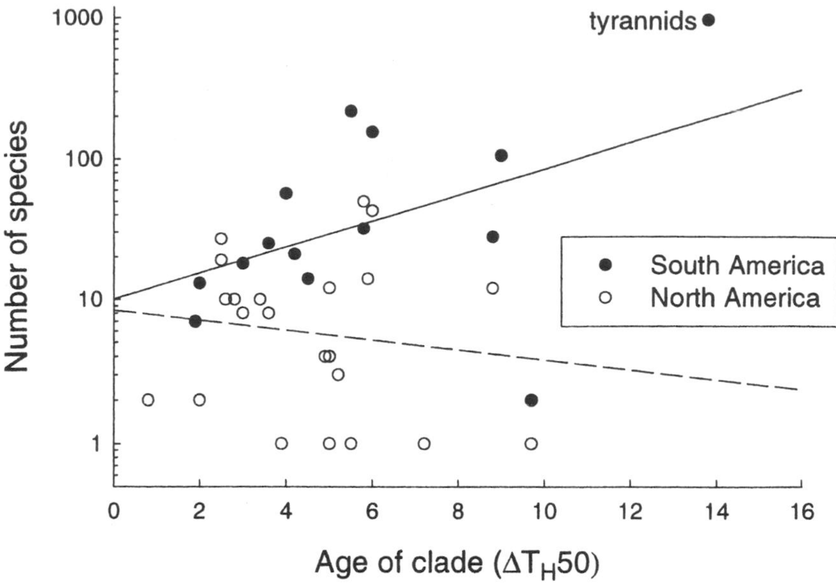

Figure 3.4 The relationship of number of species to relative age of clades among passerine birds in North America (north of Mexico) and South America. The tyrannids are an old endemic clade in South America that constitutes most of the regional passerine diversity. Age and diversity of clades are positively correlated in South America (solid line). North American clades of passerine birds have in general experienced lower diversification rates than their counterparts in South America and exhibit no significant relationship between age and diversity.

tion in the regional avifauna of South America (fig. 3.4). Fifty-eight percent of the passerine species in South America belong to the endemic tyrannid radiation (966 species in 291 genera), whose root in South America corresponds to a DNA heteroduplex melting temperature (ΔT_H50) of 13.8°C (the greater the temperature difference, the greater the genetic distance or age). North American flycatchers (27 species in 6 genera) are relatively recent offshoots of this South American radiation (ΔT_H50 2.3°C–4.1°C). Passerine birds have experienced two additional major radiations: the Corvida, with roots in Australasia, and the Passerida, with roots in the Northern Hemisphere and Africa. Members of these clades in South America (ΔT_H50 1.9°C–9.7°C) are derived from secondary invasions of that continent, probably mostly from North America. Nonetheless, South America still has many more species of Passerida (667) than North America (204). Furthermore, in the cases of the Certhiidae (wrens), Thraupini (tanagers), and Icterini (orioles), the basal lineages among extant taxa are localized in South America, and the contemporary North American species are probably secondarily derived from South America.

Table 3.1 Numbers of species, relative ages of clades, and relative rates of diversification of passerine birds in three continental regions

	Number of species (N)	Average relative divergence time ($\Delta T_H 50$)[a]	Relative rate of diversification[b]
South America			
Tyrannida radiation	966	13.8	0.50
14 additional clades	702	5.3	0.61
North America			
23 clades	257	4.6	0.38
Australia			
Corvida radiation	241	11.7	0.47
15 additional clades	76	(2.0)[c]	0.54

[a]$\Delta T_H 50$ is the difference in melting temperature between homoduplex DNA and heteroduplex DNA formed between members of a clade and the clade's closest sister taxon.
[b]The rate (S) is calculated as if the number of species increases exponentially, according to $S = \ln(N)/\Delta T_H 50$.
[c]The relative ages of these clades are estimated because they are so recent that their origins are poorly resolved in the Sibley and Ahlquist (1990) phylogeny.

Comparing clades within the Passerida that occur more or less as sister taxa in North America and in South America, the diversification rate (ln[species]/$\Delta T_H 50$) has been greater in South America in six cases (Muscicapidae, 0.38 vs. 0.28; Certhiidae, 0.52 vs. 0.50; Hirundinidae, 0.96 vs. 0.69; Emberizini, 0.84 vs. 0.63; Thraupini, 0.98 vs. 0.28; and Cardinalini, 0.89 vs. 0.58) and in North America in one case (Parulini, 0.67 vs. 0.60). This general discrepancy is not surprising, considering the greater range of environments and topographic heterogeneity in South America. This example tells us that the greater diversity of the more tropical regional avifauna of South America compared with the more temperate avifauna of North America reflects both the greater age of the avifauna and higher rates of diversification (table 3.1). These data do not allow us to determine whether the contrast between tropical and temperate/boreal environments has played a significant role in this diversity pattern.

Australia provides an interesting contrast with both North and South America. Like South America, Australia was an isolated island continent throughout much of the Tertiary and developed an endemic and highly successful radiation of birds, the Corvida. Of the 317 species of passerines in Australia (Simpson and Day 1984), 241 belong to this clade, which has its root at a DNA hybridization value of $\Delta T_H 50 = 11.7°C$. The resulting average exponential rate of proliferation of the Corvida within Australia has been $0.47°C^{-1}$, which compares favorably with the long-term average for the Tyrannida in South America (0.50). An additional 76 species (24% of the total) in Australia were derived more recently from perhaps fifteen clades that have invaded the continent. This finding suggests more isolation in Australia than in South America, where 40% of the species belong to perhaps fourteen older clades that invaded from elsewhere. Thus, the difference in diversity between Australia and South America would appear to reflect primarily the somewhat older endemic radiation in South America and the greater isolation of Australia, and not a difference in the rate of proliferation of existing clades.

A lineage-through-time plot, which portrays the number of ancestral lineages of contemporary species as a function of time in the past (Nee, Mooers, and Harvey 1992; Nee, Barraclough, and Harvey 1996; Nee 2001), provides more information on the history of diversification of a clade. A lineage-through-time plot is constructed from a phylogenetic tree, such as the ones portrayed in figure 3.1, by counting the number of lineages present in successive time slices from the origin of a clade to the present. New nodes are the most convenient time points, as each represents the addition of a single lineage. Lineage-through-time plots based on DNA-DNA hybridization phylogenies (Sibley and Ahlquist 1990) are compared for the South American Tyrannida and Australasian (including New Guinea) Corvida in figure 3.5. These plots indicate a relatively constant rate of diversification for the Tyrannida throughout its history. The curve levels off toward the present owing to incomplete sampling of taxa. The contemporary diversity lies above the extrapolation of the diversification line to the present because few recently formed branches have had time to go extinct (Nee, Barraclough, and Harvey 1996; Mooers and Heard 1997). The pattern for the Corvida differs in that the rate of proliferation of lineages appears to have slowed throughout the history of the clade, perhaps owing to a general drying of the climate of Australia during the latter part of the Tertiary, which reduced the area of wet habitat that can support a high diversity of species.

A picture that is beginning to emerge from phylogenetic investigations of regional biotas is that the latitudinal gradient in diversity reflects the history of major climate regions rather than, or in addition to, local contemporary ecology (Farrell, Mitter, and Futuyma 1992; Farrell and Mitter 1993; Latham and Ricklefs 1993b). This conclusion may apply to other patterns in communities conspicuously related to variation in the physical environment as well. Tropical environments have a greater age and extent than temperate environments, and perhaps the majority of contemporary lineages originated in the tropics (see Crane and Lidgard 1990 for angiosperms) and are excluded from temperate regions owing to such physiological barriers as frost. Few representatives of the dominant suboscine passerine radiation in South America have colonized temperate North

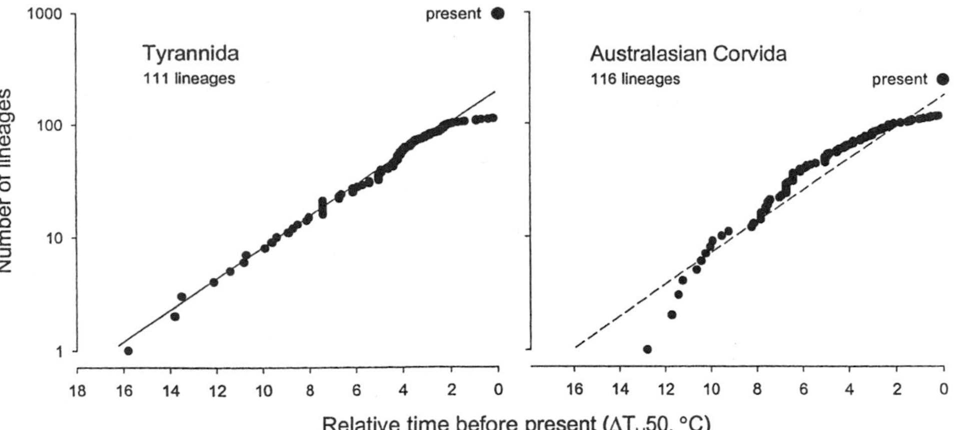

Figure 3.5 Lineage-by-time plots for the endemic radiations of South American and Australian passerine birds. The solid line at left approximates the relatively constant exponential rate of increase of lineages in the South American Tyrannida. It is replicated by the dashed line at right for comparison with the Australian Corvida. (Based on phylogenies in Sibley and Ahlquist 1990.)

America. Indeed, suboscine and oscine passerines largely segregate by habitat and microhabitat where they do co-occur, the suboscines dominating forest interiors and the oscines, especially fringillid lineages, dominating open habitats and the forest canopy (Ricklefs and Schluter 1993b; Ricklefs 2002).

The derivation of mangrove floras from adjoining terrestrial floras, which requires taxa to cross salinity and anoxia barriers (Hutchings and Saenger 1987), provides a good model of the effect of physiological barriers on diversity (Ricklefs and Latham 1993). The evolutionary change required for a lineage to extend its distribution ecologically could result in a gradient of increasing diversity between recently or sporadically colonized environments and the environments under which most lineages arose—for terrestrial organisms, generally warm and moist ones. This gradient would create a correlation between diversity and ecological conditions based on history rather than on the direct influence of ecological conditions on the regulation of community properties (Latham and Ricklefs 1993a; Schluter and Ricklefs 1993a).

HISTORY AND EQUILIBRIUM IN ISLAND BIOTAS

The avifaunas of both South America and Australia are dominated by large, old endemic radiations. However, additional clades have invaded the continents from elsewhere more recently and diversified. In contrast, many elements of the biotas of small islands differ from those of continents in that they arrive from elsewhere and do not proliferate in situ. Thus, diversity is determined primarily by the balance between rates of colonization and extinction, and the history of diversity is revealed to some extent by the distribution of colonization times. According to the MacArthur and Wilson (1967) model of island diversity, loss of species through extinction is balanced by colonization at equilibrium. Accordingly, the distribution of colonization times should be exponential, and a cumulative plot of taxa with progressively older age on the island should approach the equilibrium number of species exponentially.

Ricklefs and Bermingham (2001) tested this prediction with birds of the Lesser Antilles and found, instead, little evidence for recurring extinction within the archipelago as a whole, no indication that the avifauna of the Lesser Antilles has reached an equilibrium, and a suggestion of either marked heterogeneity in the rate of colonization or a mass extinction event approximately 0.7 million years ago (fig. 3.6). However, to emphasize the difficulty of inferring process from history, Cherry, Adler, and Johnson (2002) pointed out that the same pattern of colonization times could result from the prevention of genetic divergence from the continental source of colonists by continuing migration and gene flow until a reproductive barrier had formed (Johnson, Adler, and Cherry 2000). That model can be fit to the data as well as a homogeneous colonization/extinction event model (Ricklefs and Bermingham, unpublished data). Additional information on the geographic structure of genetic diversity within the archipelago (Ricklefs and Bermingham 2002b) or additional genetic markers will be required to distinguish between these hypotheses.

HISTORIES OF INDIVIDUAL TAXA

Because the taxa that constitute regional biotas and local communities have individual histories, we may ask whether the ecological position of a taxon depends in some way on its relative age or history (Cavender-Bares and Holbrook 2001; Webb et al. 2002). In this context, the concepts of the taxon cycle, as developed by Wilson (1961) and Ricklefs and Cox (1972), and the related taxon pulse of Erwin (1981) view the ecological positions of island species as changing over time from coastal, lowland habitats occupied by recent colonists to inland, montane habitats attained by older lineages (Ricklefs and Bermingham 2002a).

Ricklefs and Cox (1972) divided species into four categories depending on distribution and taxonomic differentiation (table 3.2). Species having patterns 3 and

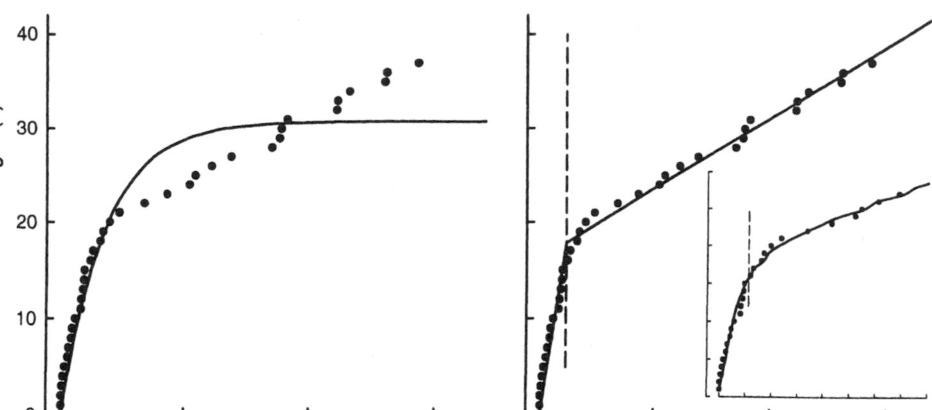

Figure 3.6 The cumulative distribution of colonization times among small land birds of the Lesser Antilles. Genetic distance (d_A), which is roughly proportional to time, is measured as the sequence divergence in the mitochondrial ATPase 6 and ATPase 8 genes. Under time-homogeneous colonization and extinction rates, the cumulative curve should approach an equilibrium number of species exponentially, as shown by the solid curve at the left. At the right, models with an abrupt increase in colonization rate or a mass extinction event at a genetic distances of about 0.011 fit the data well, and even better when the models incorporate the stochasticity of nucleotide substitution (inset). Johnson, Adler, and Cherry's (2000) speciation threshold model, which is based on processes having constant rates, fits the data equally well, however (Ricklefs and Bermingham, unpublished data). (After Ricklefs and Bermingham 2001.)

4 tended to have narrower habitat distributions, shifted toward montane forest habitats, and lower population densities than species having patterns 1 and 2 (Ricklefs and Cox 1978). Ricklefs and Cox inferred that patterns 1 through 4 represented stages in a temporal sequence; this has now been confirmed by mtDNA sequence analysis (Ricklefs and Bermingham 1999, table 3.2 and fig. 3.7). The relationship between habitat breadth and taxon cycle stage (fig. 3.8) suggests that habitat breadth decreases with the age of a population and that distributions shift toward tall forest and montane habitats. It is also clear that older taxa may undergo new phases of expansion within an archipelago, as inferred from the absence of differentiation between island populations of endemic species. Such recently expanded taxa tend to have broader habitat distributions and densities within occupied habitats than old endemics, emphasizing the close connection between local ecology and geography (Ricklefs and Bermingham 1999). It is not surprising that old endemic populations have been more vulnerable to extinction resulting from human activities (Ricklefs and Bermingham 1999).

Table 3.2 Four patterns of geographic distribution and taxonomic differentiation recognized by Ricklefs and Cox (1972) in the avifauna of the West Indies

Pattern	Geographical distribution	Taxonomic differentiation	Examples from the Lesser Antilles	Maximum genetic differentiation[a]
1	Widespread	Undifferentiated	*Elaenia martinica*	0.002
			Tiaris bicolor	0.002
2	Widespread	Differentiated	*Coereba flaveola*	0.009
			Loxigilla noctis	0.005
3	Fragmented	Differentiated	*Dendroica adelaidae*	0.031
			Cichlherminia lherminieri	0.067
			Icterus [dominicensis]	0.082
4	Single-island endemic		*Melanospiza richardsoni*	0.087[b]
			Catheropeza bishopi	0.130[c]

Source: E. Bermingham and R. E. Ricklefs, unpublished data.

[a]Maximum genetic distance for the mitochondrial ATPase 6 and ATPase 8 gene sequences among island populations in the Lesser Antilles.

[b]Distance to *Tiaris fuliginosa*.

[c]Distance to *Dendroica angelae*.

The ecological positions of plants within the mangrove environment also appear to be related to the history of taxa in the mangroves. Duke (1992) classified mangrove species according to their height in the intertidal zone (low, middle, and high) and their distance from the mouth of the estuary (downriver, intermediate, and upriver). As shown in table 3.3, the diverse species in older mangrove clades occupy most of the ecological space available, whereas those taxa that are endemic to mangroves at the species level (i.e., with terrestrial congeners) appear to be restricted to the higher part of the intertidal range. Use of the lower level of the tidal range within the mangrove environment (greatest relative inundation) appears to require a longer history of evolutionary adaptation to its saline, anoxic conditions. More detailed phylogenetic analyses (A. E. Schwarzbach and R. E. Ricklefs, unpublished data) will permit a closer examination of ecological shifts during the diversification of lineages in this environment.

TOPOLOGY OF PHYLOGENETIC TREES AND RATES OF SPECIATION AND EXTINCTION

One of the difficulties of using phylogenetic trees based on genetic relationships among contemporary organisms is that extinct lineages cannot be

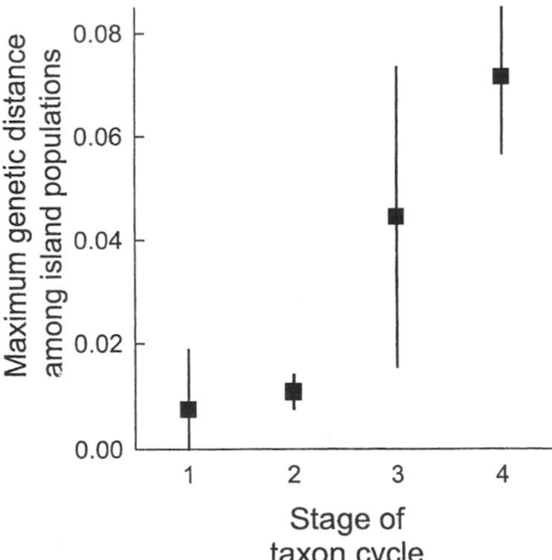

Figure 3.7 Genetic distances representing the initiation of the most recent expansion phases of species grouped according to stage of taxon cycle. Genetic distances are based on mtDNA ATPase 6 and ATPase 8 gene sequences. In the case of stage 4 species, the distance is to the closest sister taxon. Data are presented as means and standard deviations. Means differ significantly among stages ($F = 8.35$, df = 3, 21, $P = 0.0008$, $R^2 = 0.54$). (After Ricklefs and Bermingham 1999.)

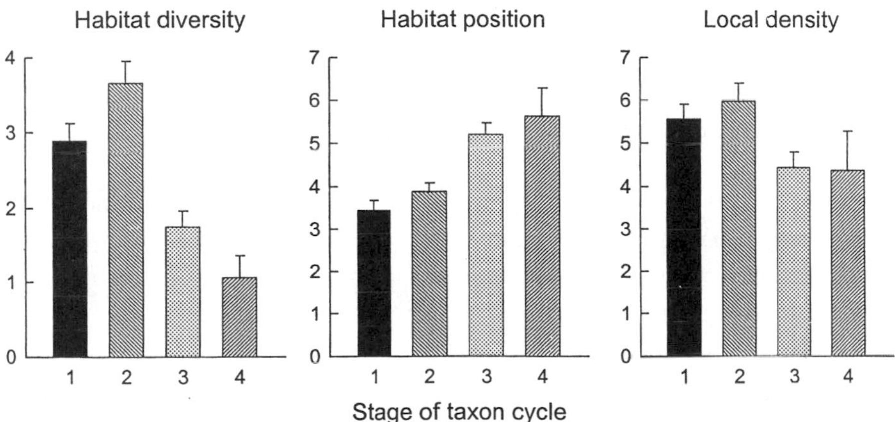

Figure 3.8 Average values of habitat diversity, habitat position, and local density as a function of stage of taxon cycle. Data are presented as means and standard errors. Statistical tests were determined in nested ANOVAs based on the *F*-ratio of stage/species (stage): diversity ($F = 5.2$, df = 3, 49, $P = 0.0035$); position ($F = 4.6$, df = 3, 36, $P = 0.0065$); density ($F = 2.1$, df = 3, 46, $P = 0.12$). *t*-tests of least-squares means identified the following significant differences: diversity (stages 1 and 2 vs. 3 and 4); position (1 vs. 2 vs. 3, 4); density (1, 2 vs. 3, 4). (After Ricklefs and Bermingham 1999.)

sampled. Extinction has had an important influence on the development of regional biotas. Differences in rates of extinction, or even unique catastrophic extinction events, might have caused some geographic and ecological patterns in taxonomic diversity. For example, the relatively depauperate flora of central Europe is thought to have resulted from the extinction of cold-intolerant plants

Table 3.3 Distribution of mangrove species in the Indo–West Pacific region with respect to tidal height and position within the estuary

Tribal- and family-level endemics[a]

Tidal height	Downriver	Both	Intermediate	Both	Upriver
High	A, S	C	B	B	
Both		B, C	C	B	
Middle		B	R		
Both	A	A, R		R	S
Low	K, S		A		N, S

Position in estuary

Genus- and species-level endemics[b]

Tidal height	Downriver	Both	Intermediate	Both	Upriver
High	S		S		S, S
Both	G, G, G	S	S		
Middle			G		
Both		G			
Low				G	

Position in estuary

Source: Data from Duke 1992.

Note: Taxa that occur in more than one stratum are placed in the "Both" categories. Tidal height (Wilcoxon rank sum test, $c^2 = 6.1$, $p = 0.013$) but not position in estuary ($p > 0.05$) differ significantly between older (tribal, family, and genus) and younger (species) mangrove taxa.

[a]A, *Avicennia* spp. (Avicenniaceae); B, *Bruguiera* spp. (Rhizophoreae); C, *Ceriops* spp. (Rhizophoreae); K, *Kandelia candel* (Rhizophoreae); N, *Nypa fructicans* (Palmae); R, *Rhizophora* spp. (Rhizophoreae); S, *Sonneratia* spp. (Sonneratiaceae).

[b]Distribution of species endemic to the mangroves at either the species (S) or genus (G) levels. Shaded area indicates restriction of recent (species-level) clades to higher part of the tidal range.

during the latter part of the Tertiary (Sauer 1988). Taxa in mid-Tertiary fossil assemblages are as diverse as those in similar assemblages in eastern Asia, in spite of the fact that eastern Asia has nearly five times as many living species of trees (Latham and Ricklefs 1993a).

Harvey, May, and Nee (1994) have shown how constant extinction and speciation rates can be estimated from the curve of reconstructed numbers of taxa in a phylogeny as a function of time prior to the present (see fig. 3.5). Of course, extinct lineages are not represented in such a reconstruction, and over most of the history of the clade, the slope of the taxa-versus-time regression will equal the net rate of proliferation (speciation − extinction). As one gets closer to the present, however, fewer new lineages will have gone extinct, and the curve will asymptotically approach a line whose slope is equal to the speciation rate. If one can estimate the speciation rate, the extinction rate can be estimated by subtraction. This technique can also reveal episodes of mass extinction or changes in speciation and extinction rates in the history of a monophyletic group, although the size of the clade required for reasonable resolution is large (Nee, Barraclough, and Harvey 1996; Mooers and Heard 1997; Lovette and Bermingham 1999; Heard and Mooers 2002).

Although it may not be possible to estimate speciation and extinction rates, tree topologies make us aware of the heterogeneous histories of many taxa (Price et al. 2000). Similar tree topologies shared independently by different taxa having similar ecologies and distributions would strengthen the idea that global patterns of taxonomic diversity have regional/historical as well as local/contemporary (ecological) causes (Cracraft 1982; Losos et al. 1998; Price et al. 2000).

CONCLUSIONS

Comparisons of communities and regional species pools in different parts of the world suggest that regional processes, unique geographic and climatic circumstances, and historical events may help to shape geographic and ecological patterns of taxonomic diversity. Phylogenetic reconstruction provides a window on history and helps us to interpret patterns of diversity within a regional/historical context. Knowledge of phylogenetic relationships makes possible two kinds of analyses. First, sister-taxon comparisons allow us to assess the effects on rates of diversification of single factors that differentiate sister taxa. Second, analysis of the historical development of regional species pools and local ecological communities allows us to estimate the relative ages and net proliferation rates of clades, as well as to infer the ecological origins of species pools (Losos 1996; Losos et al. 1998). Such analyses are beginning to reveal a pattern in which the contemporary diversity of a region is determined primarily by the age and frequency of origination of clades within the region, whether by immigration over a geographic distance or by adaptive shifts over an ecological distance.

Extinctions and differential rates of proliferation of clades within regions also can be important effects. From this perspective, species production drives species diversity, and ecological interactions sort out local and regional patterns of distribution to accommodate the regional species pool. Increasingly comprehensive phylogenetic analyses will be needed to characterize the historical development of regional species pools and local ecological communities and to test the effects of key innovations and ecological shifts on rates of species proliferation.

The analyses discussed here raise a number of crucial questions that have not yet been addressed to any extent in the literature. First, why do historical processes seem to be so important when ecological processes come to equilibrium so quickly by comparison? The answer to this question would seem to lie in a mistaken perception of the rate of equilibration in natural systems. Competition in model systems and microcosms usually leads to exclusion within a few tens of generations. However, such simplified and homogeneous systems exaggerate competitive asymmetries among species. Hubbell (2001, chap. 4 in this volume) suggests that when species are competitively equivalent, diversity is controlled primarily by rates of species diversification and by the size of the community and of the metacommunity within which it is imbedded. I suspect that competitive equivalence or near-equivalence is generally the rule in ecological communities, leading to long persistence times of species, but that this equivalence is achieved by evolutionary or ecological adjustment of habitat distribution, which balances average population growth rate against the diversity of habitats occupied. Moreover, new species sometimes enter a "community" by dispersal from a distance ("invasion"), but more frequently by adaptive shift from adjacent "communities." Thus, the loss of species through competitive exclusion may not occur much more rapidly than the gain of new species in a community, and both of these processes may occur on much longer time scales than apparent in simplified model systems or microcosms.

A second question concerns the direction of influence of diversity. One might reasonably view regional diversity as the product of ecologically constrained local diversity and habitat variation within a region; thus, regional diversity is scaled-up local diversity. Alternatively, the regional production of species might drive diversity within a local community in a manner analogous to the influence of colonization rate on island diversity. The test of convergence in local diversity between regions having different regional diversity can resolve this question to some extent. However, a more general test may be applied to the pattern of beta diversity, or turnover of species composition over ecological gradients. When diversity is controlled at a local level by species interactions, beta diversity should not vary between regions, and differences in diversity between regions should reflect only the regional ecological diversity. When diversity is driven by regional processes, the packing of species into the regional-local ecological space, which includes the range of habitats within the region as well as the range of ecological space within habitats, should affect both local and beta diversity. We have seen this effect, for example, in the ecological distributions of birds on West Indian islands. Testing the sensitivity of beta diversity to regional diversity requires that habitat variation be either controlled (i.e., matched) or fully characterized; that is, beta diversity must be quantified with respect to habitat change, and not simply distance (Schluter and Ricklefs 1993b).

The most basic issue concerns our concept of the community. In the development of population concepts of community ecology, the idea of community became associated with a fixed boundary enclosing an ecologically uniform area within which individuals of many species interacted with each other freely, either directly through antagonistic and mutualistic encounters or indirectly through their effects on mutual resources or consumers. It is ironic that this concept disregarded the increasingly accepted open view of species distributions over habitat gradients (Gleason 1926; Whittaker 1953, 1956) in favor of the more circumscribed and homogeneous concept of the community matrix (Vandermeer 1972; May 1975b).

From the standpoint of the relationship between local and regional diversity, it may be more appropriate to view the "community" as the entire region, within which species specialize ecologically with respect to both habitat and position within habitat (J. H. Brown 1984). Their distributions are continually adjusted according to ecological conditions within the region and evolutionary relationships between species, including predators and their prey and parasites and their hosts. This continual readjustment is responsible for maintaining the competitive equivalence of most populations, as decreases in average population productivity are balanced by contraction of ecological distribution (Ricklefs and Cox 1972), leading to a high species-level component of variance for ecological distribution, range size, and total population abundance (Gaston 1998). Essentially, we cannot understand "community" diversity until our concept of the community matches the scale in space and time over which the processes that influence diversity act.

ACKNOWLEDGMENTS

I am grateful to E. Bermingham, J. H. Connell, S. B. Heard, and J. L. Patton for comments on an earlier draft of this chapter. My work in community ecology in collaboration with E. Bermingham and A. E. Schwarzbach has been supported by the National Geographic Society, the Smithsonian Institution, the National Science Foundation, and the University of Missouri Research Board.

4
Large-Scale Diversity and Species-Area Relationships in Tropical Tree Communities under the Neutral Theory

STEPHEN P. HUBBELL

ABSTRACT

The incorporation of speciation into the theory of island biogeography unexpectedly results in a powerful neutral theory of biogeography and biodiversity in homogeneous landscapes. This formal theory generates a fundamental biodiversity number that quantitatively predicts not only species richness, but also patterns of local and regional relative species abundance, as well as species-area relationships. The theory is applied with remarkable success to tropical tree communities in Panama. The neutral theory of biodiversity and biogeography is analogous to neutral theory in population genetics, and it is hoped the theory will stimulate new questions and rigor in community ecology.

INTRODUCTION

Neutral theories in population genetics, beginning with classic ideas about genetic drift, have had a profound effect on the intellectual growth of population genetics (Crow and Kimura 1970; Kimura and Ohta 1971; Ewens 1979; Nei 1987). Sadly, the same cannot be said for neutral theories in community ecology, which have had a decidedly checkered history of generating more heat than light (Strong et al. 1984). This is unfortunate, because a well-formulated neutral theory would be enormously beneficial to ecology (Caswell 1976; Gotelli and Graves 1996). A foundation for such a theory has already been laid by the theory of island biogeography (MacArthur and Wilson 1963, 1967). Although it is not always appreciated as such, the theory of island biogeography is a neutral theory that asserts that species are ecologically equivalent in their probabilities of immigration and extinction and that communities are assembled purely by random dispersal.

The assumption of species equivalence led MacArthur and Wilson to a nonequilibrium view of community organization and to the conclusion that natural communities are in diversity equilibrium, but not in taxonomic equilibrium.

This and similar theories of community organization constitute the *dispersal-assembly perspective* (Hubbell 1997a). In contrast, the *niche-assembly perspective,* the current paradigm in community ecology, asserts that ecological communities are in taxonomic as well as diversity equilibrium. In this view, member species are assumed to be in adaptive and competitive equipoise with other species in the community; and because of the complete partitioning of limiting resources among the niche-differentiated species, the community is resistant to invasion by nonmember species (i.e., limited species membership). Reconciling these two perspectives, both of which have strong elements of truth, is by no means trivial. However, the theory developed here, it is hoped, will provide a fresh point of departure for attempting to unify these perspectives into an improved theoretical framework for community ecology. The unified neutral theory of biodiversity and biogeography (hereafter referred to simply as the neutral theory) is developed fully in Hubbell 2001 and briefly outlined in Hubbell 1995 and 1997b.

Three modifications to the original theory of island biogeography were essential to successfully developing the neutral theory. First, speciation is incorporated. The original theory of island biogeography is conceptually incomplete in this regard because it lacks a mechanism of speciation. Although species can go extinct, there is no provision for the origination of new species, either on islands or on the mainland. Second, a dynamic theory of relative species abundance is also incorporated. The neutral theory predicts the distribution of local and mainland ("metacommunity") species abundances as well as species-area relationships. Island biogeography theory does not predict the relative abundances of species, only species richness. Relative abundance is briefly mentioned in MacArthur and Wilson's (1967) monograph in relation to the species-area relationship. However, the expected species-area relationship and the equilibrium distribution of relative species abundances on islands or on the mainland are not derivable from the first principles of the theory. Finally, the neutral theory is based on a core principle that is absent from the original theory, namely, that the dynamics of ecological communities are a stochastic, zero-sum game. This principle states that community drift occurs under the dynamic constraint that for any species to increase in abundance, all other species collectively must decrease by an approximately equal and opposite amount, so that community size remains constant, or nearly so. This principle is formally captured in the equation $J = \rho A$, where J is the number of individuals of all species in the community occurring at density ρ in area A.

As I will endeavor to show, a pure dispersal-assembly theory of relative species abundance is not only possible, but does as good, if not a better, job of predicting relative species abundance than current niche-assembly theory does. In order for the theory to do so, however, it is necessary to modify the level of biological organization on which the neutrality assumption is made. In the theory of island biogeography, neutrality is defined at the species level. In the "neutral" theory, neutrality is defined at the per capita or *individual* level. This distinction may not seem important, but in fact it is fundamental to building a successful dispersal-assembly theory of relative species abundance. One of the primary ways in which species are not dynamically equivalent is a result of their differing abundances. Because it assumed the dynamic equivalence of species, the theory of island biogeography was unable to explain differences in rates of immigration and extinction due to species differences in population size. Under neutral theory, large differences in relative species abundance arise, and common and rare species have very different dynamics—even though the theory is completely neutral. This change effectively eliminates one of the most serious objections to the original theory.

Many predictions can be made from neutral theory, but in this chapter, I focus mainly on large landscape spatial scales. In particular, I examine the self-organization of landscape-level patterns of species richness and relative species abundance, as well as species-area relationships, in communities undergoing zero-sum drift. I illustrate the application of the theory to closed-canopy tropical tree communities, mainly using data from the tree flora of Panama. Before discussing these landscape-level patterns, however, it is helpful to give a brief synopsis of the theory. Applications of the theory to relative species abundance and phylogenetic reconstruction are discussed fully elsewhere (Hubbell 1997b, 2001).

BRIEF SYNOPSIS OF THE THEORY

The neutral theory was developed in two phases. In phase one, a spatially implicit theory was developed for the classic island-mainland biogeography problem posed by MacArthur and Wilson (1967). The problem is analyzed at two spatiotemporal scales: local communities, which have fast dynamics, and the metacommunity—the source area or "mainland"—which has much slower dynamics (Hubbell 1997b). The drift theory of relative species abundance, which predicts the existence of a fundamental biodiversity number θ, is a set of theorems based on this spatially implicit theory (Hubbell 1998). In phase two, a spatially explicit version of the theory was developed to study species-area relationships on continuous landscapes. This theory, formulated as a contact-process model, has fewer analytical results; however, the simulation-based results of phase two are fully consistent with the analytical results of phase one.

The engine of the spatially implicit theory is a Markovian model of the population dynamics of arbitrary species i embedded in a local community, all of whose member species obey zero-sum dynamics. Let N_i be the current size of the population of the ith species, and let J be the size of the local community, $J = \sum N_i$. Let m be the probability that a death in the local community is replaced by an immigrant from the metacommunity source area. Let P_i be the relative abundance of the ith species in the metacommunity, $0 < P_i < 1$. Then the transition probabilities for the population decreasing in size by one individual, for staying the same size, and for increasing by one individual in the next time step are given by

$$\Pr\{N_i - 1 | N_i\} = \frac{N_i}{J}\left[m(1 - P_i) + (1 - m)\left(\frac{J - N_i}{J - 1}\right)\right], \tag{4.1}$$

$$\Pr\{N_i | N_i\} = \frac{N_i}{J}\left[mP_i + (1 - m)\left(\frac{N_i - 1}{J - 1}\right)\right]$$
$$+ \left(\frac{J - N_i}{J}\right)\left[m(1 - P_i) + (1 - m)\left(\frac{J - N_i - 1}{J - 1}\right)\right],$$

$$\Pr\{N_i + 1 | N_i\} = \left(\frac{J - N_i}{J}\right)\left[mP_i + (1 - m)\left(\frac{N_i}{J - 1}\right)\right].$$

The first equation, for example, gives the transition probability of the ith species declining in abundance by one individual. For this to happen, a death must occur in the ith species, N_i/J, and the birth must be in some other species. The first probability inside the square brackets is that of an immigration event of some species other than i: $m(1 - P_i)$. The second probability is that of having no immigration event and a local birth in a species other than i: $(1 - m)\,(J - N_i)/(J - 1)$.

Species i can drift to zero abundance ($N_i = 0$) and become extinct in the local community, or become monodominant ($N_i = J$), but the probabilities of these two outcomes are rarely equal. We can calculate the exact probability of the ith species being in any particular abundance state from 0 to J by solving for the eigenvector of the transition matrix for equation (4.1) for arbitrary J, m, and P_i (Hubbell 1998). From this eigenvector, we obtain the mean (E) and variance (Var) of the local abundance of the ith species:

$$\mathrm{E}\{N_i\} = \sum_{k=0}^{J} \psi(k) \cdot k = JP_i, \tag{4.2}$$

$$\mathrm{Var}\{N_i\} = \sum_{k=1}^{J} (k - E\{N_i\})^2 \cdot \psi(k),$$

$$= \frac{\sum_{k=0}^{J}\left[C(J, m, P_i, k) \cdot \prod_{x=1}^{k-1} H(J, m, P_i, x) \cdot \prod_{x=k}^{J-2} G(J, m, P_i, x)\right]}{\prod_{x=1}^{J-2}[(J-1) - x(1-m)]}$$

where

$$C(J, m, P_i, k) = \begin{cases} \binom{J}{k}(JP_i)^2(1 - P_i)(1 - mP_i) & \text{for} \quad k = 0 \\ \binom{J}{k}(k - JP_i)^2(1 - P_i)mP_i & \text{for} \quad k = 1, \ldots, J-1 \\ \binom{J}{k}(k - JP_i)^2 P_i[1 - m(1 - P_i)] & \text{for} \quad k = J \end{cases}$$

$$\prod_{x>k-1}^{k-1} H(J, m, P_i, x) = 1,$$

and

$$\prod_{x>J-2}^{J-2} G(J, m, P_i, x) = 1.$$

Thus, the equilibrium abundance of the *i*th species in the local community is simply the size of the local community *J*, times the metacommunity relative abundance of the *i*th species, P_i. The variance in local abundance of the *i*th species is a more complex function of the parameters, including the probability of immigration per birth, *m*.

Speciation is incorporated into the theory of the metacommunity. In the original theory of island biogeography, the metacommunity, or mainland source area, was treated as a permanent pool of potential immigrant species to islands. In reality, all species ultimately go extinct in the source area, though usually at slower rates than on islands because of larger population sizes. In the metacommunity, speciation is analogous to immigration into a local community or onto islands. A steady-state species richness and relative species abundance will arise in the metacommunity at equilibrium between speciation and extinction. Let J_M be the metacommunity size, such that $J_M = \sum J$, the sum of all the local community sizes; and let ν be the probability per birth of a speciation event.

To solve for the equilibrium in the metacommunity, we need to calculate the unconditional equilibrium probability of every possible configuration of relative species abundance in a sample of *J* individuals drawn randomly from the metacommunity (Hubbell 1997b, 1998). Let $\theta = 2J_M \nu$. Then the probability of obtaining S species with $n_1, n_2, \ldots, n_S$ individuals, respectively, where $J = \sum n_i$, is

$$\Pr\{S, n_1, n_2, \ldots, n_S\} = \frac{J!\theta^S}{1^{\phi_1}2^{\phi_2} \ldots J^{\phi_J}\phi_1!\phi_2! \ldots \phi_J!\prod_{k=1}^{J}(q + k - 1)}, \quad (4.3)$$

where ϕ_i is the number of species that have i individuals in the sample of size J. Those familiar with neutral theory in population genetics will recognize a similar expression from the infinite allele case analyzed by Ewens (1972) and Karlin and MacGregor (1972). We can order species in each configuration by rank, from commonest to rarest. Then the expected abundance, r_i, of the ith-ranked species in the equilibrium rank-ordered relative abundance distribution for a random sample of size J individuals from the metacommunity is

$$\mathrm{E}\{r_i|J\} = \sum_{k=1}^{C} r_i(k) \cdot \Pr\{S, r_1, r_2, \ldots, r_S, 0, 0, \ldots, 0\}_k, \quad (4.4)$$

where C is the total number of configurations, $r_i(k)$ is the abundance of the ith-ranked species in the kth configuration, and $\Pr\{S, r_1, r_2, \ldots, r_S, 0, 0, \ldots, 0\}_k$ is the probability of the kth configuration. Equation (4.4) yields the expected dominance-diversity curve for the metacommunity at equilibrium between speciation and extinction. (Analytical details are given in Hubbell 1998.) The expected metacommunity abundance of the ith species is now predicted by $P_i = \mathrm{E}\{r_i|J\}$. Thus, by combining the results of local community and metacommunity dynamics [equations (4.1) and (4.4)], we eliminate the need for any species-specific parameters in the final theory.

In neutral theory, θ is a dimensionless number that completely specifies the steady-state species richness and relative species abundance in the source metacommunity. Because of its importance in controlling relative species abundance, species-area relationships, and equilibrium metacommunity diversity, θ is appropriately named the *fundamental biodiversity number* (Hubbell 1997b, 1998, 2001). This number is equal to twice the product of the metacommunity size and the speciation rate, and it varies from zero to positive infinity. When $\theta = 0$, the metacommunity equilibrium is a single monodominant species everywhere. When $\theta = +\infty$, species diversity is "infinite," and every individual sampled is of a new and different species. Figure 4.1 shows the changing shape of the theoretical dominance-diversity curve of relative species abundance in the metacommunity for various values of θ when $m = 1$ for a sample of sixty-four individuals.

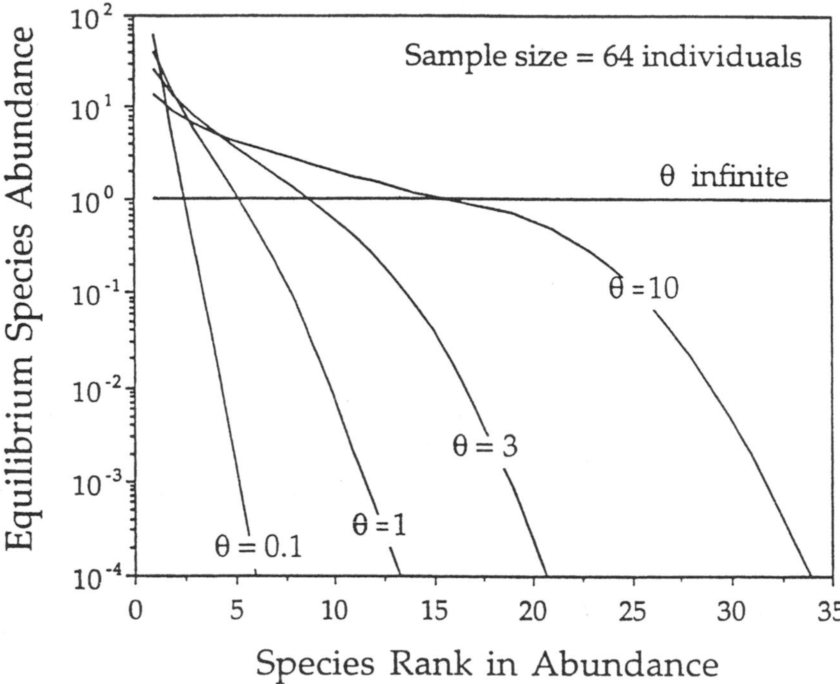

Figure 4.1 Expected metacommunity dominance-diversity distributions for a sample of sixty-four individuals, for various values of the fundamental biodiversity number, θ. When θ is small, the expected dominance-diversity curve is geometric. As θ becomes larger, the expected dominance-diversity curve becomes S-shaped. As $\theta \rightarrow +\infty$, the distribution approaches a horizontal line. In the limit, when θ is infinite, every individual in the sample is a new and different species, however large a sample is taken ("infinite diversity").

Together with the dispersal parameter, m, the biodiversity number θ also controls relative species abundance in the local community of size J, as well as the shape and slope of the species-area curve. Fits of the theoretical distribution to data on relative tree species abundances from temperate and tropical closed-canopy tree communities are consistently good to excellent. For example, figure 4.2 shows the theoretical distribution with dispersal limitation fitted to relative tree species abundances in the 50 ha Forest Dynamics Plot on Barro Colorado island (BCI), Panama ($\theta = 50$, $m = 0.10$). Figure 4.3 illustrates the fit to relative tree species abundances in the 50 ha plot in Pasoh Forest Reserve, Peninsular Malaysia ($\theta = 180$, $m = 0.15$). In both figures, the dashed diagonal line extending down and to the right is the expected metacommunity distribution without dispersal limitation ($m = 1$). Estimates of the fundamental biodiversity number θ from data on other forests range from a low of about 0.1 for boreal spruce-fir

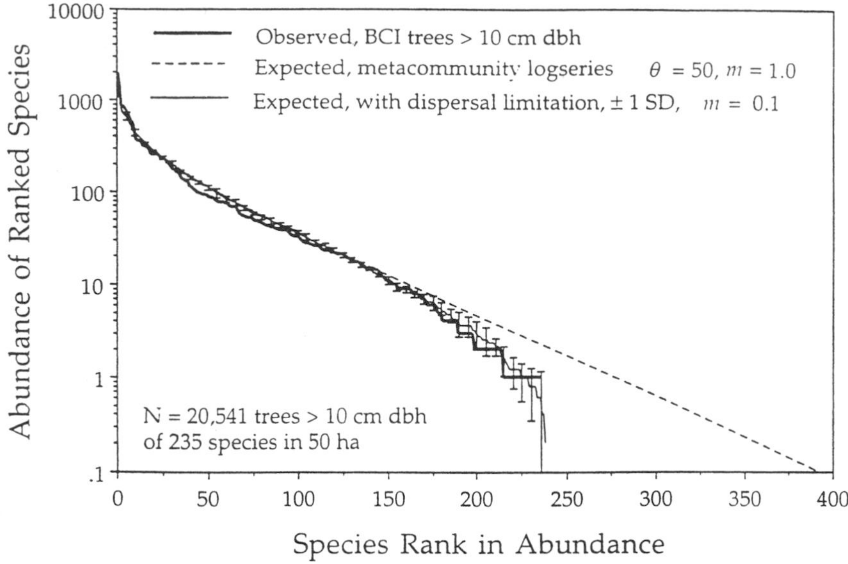

Figure 4.2 Fitted and observed dominance-diversity distributions for trees greater than 10 cm DBH in the 50 ha Forest Dynamics Plot on Barro Colorado Island, Panama. The best fit θ had a value of 50. Note the departure of the metacommunity logseries-like distribution for very rare species, but that the observed distribution is fit well once dispersal limitation ($m = 0.10$) is taken into account. The error bars are ±1 standard deviation.

forests to a high of about 200 for the most diverse tropical wet forest tree communities known (Hubbell 1998).

The metacommunity relative abundance distribution given by equations (4.3) and (4.4) is derived under a model of speciation in which new species arise like rare point mutations. Under this mode of speciation, the equilibrium metacommunity distribution of relative species abundance (with no dispersal limitation) is asymptotically identical to Fisher's logseries distribution (Fisher, Corbet, and Williams 1943) for large J_M (Watterson 1974; Hubbell 1998). This "point mutation" model of speciation is probably a reasonable representation for many speciation events, particularly in plants, in which new species can arise by sudden changes in ploidy number or hybridization (Arnold 1997).

On the other hand, if new species arise through a process of random fission of preexisting species populations, then a different equilibrium metacommunity distribution of relative species abundance arises—a new statistical distribution called a zero-sum multinomial (Hubbell 1998). This "random fission" mode is probably more appropriate as a model of allopatric speciation (Mayr

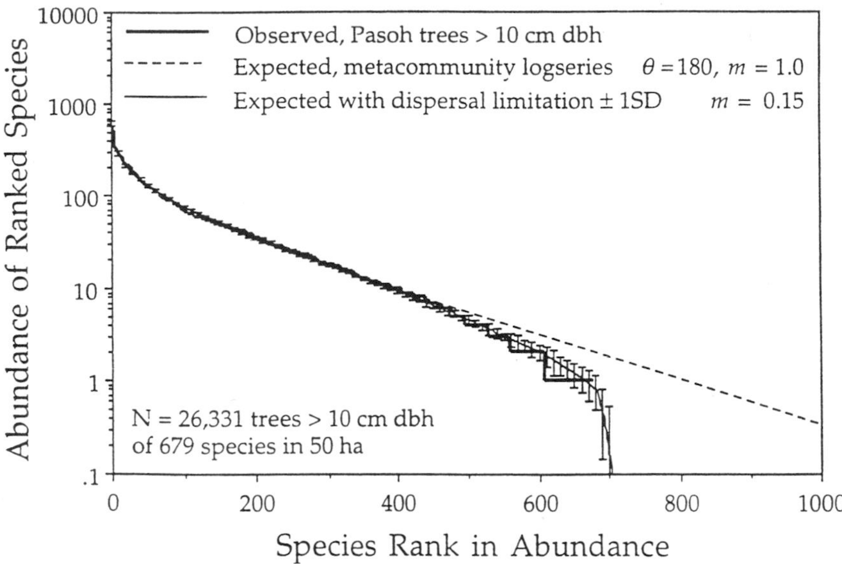

Figure 4.3 Fitted and observed dominance-diversity distributions for trees greater than 10 cm DBH in the 50 ha plot in Pasoh Forest Reserve, Malaysia. The best fit θ had a value of 180. Again note the departure of the metacommunity logseries-like distribution for very rare species, but that the observed distribution is fit well once dispersal limitation ($m = 0.15$) is taken into account. The error bars are ±1 standard deviation.

1963). In this case, the equilibrium metacommunity relative species abundance distribution is qualitatively more similar to the lognormal distribution of Preston (1948, 1962) than to Fisher's logseries. However, it differs in having a long asymmetric tail of very rare species (Hubbell 1995).

In either case, under the point mutation or the random fission mode of speciation, the same fundamental biodiversity number θ exists. A remarkable finding is that θ is asymptotically identical to the diversity parameter α of Fisher's logseries distribution for large J_M. Fisher's α is one of the most widely used statistical measures of species diversity in collections of individuals (Magurran 1988). The equilibrium metacommunity distribution of relative species abundance is strongly affected by the mode of speciation. Under the point mutation mode, each new species is very rare at origination and has a high probability of early extinction. However, under the random fission mode, many species are abundant at origination, which means that they have much longer expected times to extinction (Hubbell 1998). The result is that steady-state metacommunity diversity is much higher under the random fission than under the point

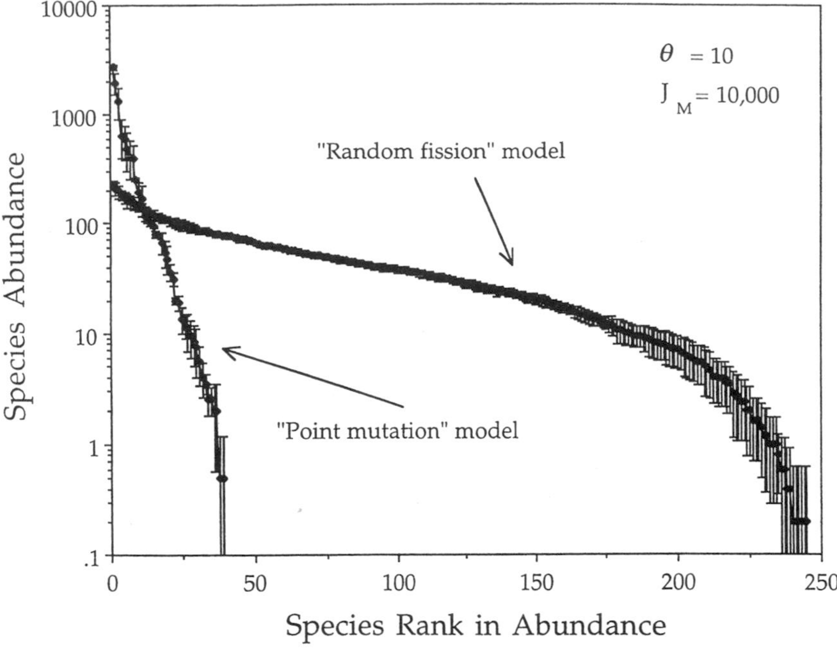

Figure 4.4 Comparison of steady-state metacommunity diversity under the "point mutation" model of speciation and under the "random fission" model, for a metacommunity size $J_M = 10{,}000$. Both curves have the same value of the fundamental biodiversity number ($\theta = 10$), but the steady-state species richness under random fission is about seven times greater in this example. The error bars are ±1 standard deviation.

mutation model of speciation for a given value of θ (fig. 4.4). Note that the distributions that were fit to the data for the BCI and Pasoh tree communities assumed the point mutation mode of speciation.

On islands or in local communities, the distribution of relative species abundance is a zero-sum multinomial, regardless of the mode of speciation (point mutation or random fission). The predicted relative species abundance distribution for the local community is not the same as a random subsample of the metacommunity distribution. As in the theory of island biogeography, the neutral theory predicts a reduction in species richness on islands relative to same-sized areas on the mainland. However, the neutral theory also predicts that dominance will increase on islands. Common species will be too common, and rare species too rare, on islands. Rare species will be less abundant on islands than expected from their mainland abundance because they are more extinction-prone on islands, and once locally extinct, they re-immigrate less often than do common species (Hubbell 1998).

A DYNAMIC THEORY OF SPECIES-AREA RELATIONSHIPS

Thus far, I have discussed the self-organization of local community and metacommunity relative species abundance according to the spatially implicit version of neutral theory. The theory of island biogeography also treats space implicitly. This treatment is adequate when discussing migration from a mainland metacommunity to islands whose dynamics occur on very different spatial and temporal scales. But it is no longer acceptable in a general theory of biogeography on continuous landscapes—the kind of theory needed to achieve deeper understanding of species-area relationships.

I now explore the spatially explicit version of the neutral theory. The metacommunity is modeled as a large but finite plain, gridded into many local communities. The spatially explicit model differs from the implicit theory somewhat in that only immediately adjacent communities can exchange migrants in one time step. This change results in small quantitative differences in the predicted equilibrium distribution of relative species abundance in the metacommunity. To analyze species-area relationships, I simulated the dynamics of a metacommunity consisting of 201^2 local communities. I restricted the analysis of species-area relationships to the central block of 181^2 communities, after determining that this central subarea was free of detectable edge effect dynamics.

The inevitability of a positive species-area relationship has led some ecologists to suggest that it is a static sampling phenomenon of little biological interest (e.g., Connor and McCoy 1979; Gilbert 1980). However, the species-area problem is far deeper than it might at first seem. One must explain why species-area relationships show strong and recurrent qualitative and quantitative patterns (Johnson and Raven 1973; Connor and Simberloff 1979; McGuinness 1984; Williamson 1988), as has been abundantly documented recently by Rosenzweig (1995). I now explore the neutral theory's explanations for these recurrent patterns.

The most common species-area relationship found at intermediate spatial scales in relatively homogeneous landscapes is a linear relationship between the logarithm of the number of species present and the logarithm of the area sampled. For example, Watson (1859, cited in Rosenzweig 1995) found this relationship for the vascular plants of Great Britain, on spatial scales ranging from a square mile to all of Great Britain (fig. 4.5). The relationship is given by $S = cA^z$, where S is the total number of species encountered in geographic area A, and c and z are fitted constants. This equation has come to be known as the Arrhenius species-area relationship, after its most ardent champion (Arrhenius 1921), and is certainly now the most widely accepted relationship (Kilburn 1966;

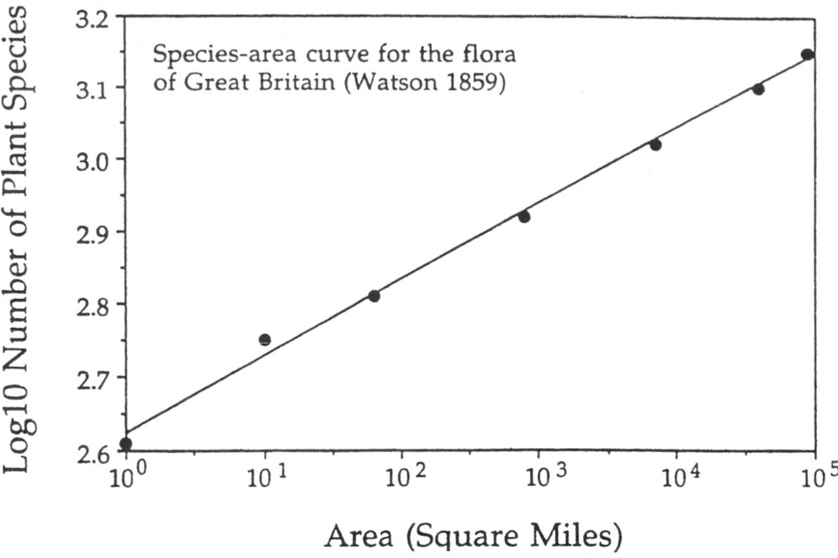

Figure 4.5 Watson's species-area curve for the vascular plants of Great Britain, accumulating species from a starting point in Surrey. (After Williams 1964 and Rosenzweig 1995.)

MacArthur and Wilson 1967; May 1975a; Connor and McCoy 1979). Note that if we let the constant $c = r^z$, where r is the mean density of individuals per unit area, then from our first principle, we also obtain the number of species as a simple power function of the number of individuals J sampled: $S = J^z$. The Arrhenius relationship can be linearized by log transformation: $\ln S = \ln c + z \ln A$.

In a review of species-area relationships, Williamson (1988) posed four questions about observed patterns. First, why is the Arrhenius relationship so common? Second, why do some surveys clearly not fit the Arrhenius relationship? Third, why is the z parameter of the Arrhenius relationship generally between 0.15 and 0.40? Finally, why is there so much variation in z among surveys? Williamson's second question has been empirically, if not theoretically, answered by Rosenzweig (1995), who found a quite general result; namely, that species-area relationships are triphasic on local to global spatial scales. The Arrhenius relationship holds only for intermediate spatial scales; it does not hold on very local scales, and on very large scales the slope gradually steepens.

Shmida and Wilson (1985), for example, obtained a triphasic curve for the world's flora when they plotted the plant species-area relationship on local to global scales (fig. 4.6). Shmida and Wilson argued that the change in the form of the curve was due to scale-dependent changes in the biological determinants of

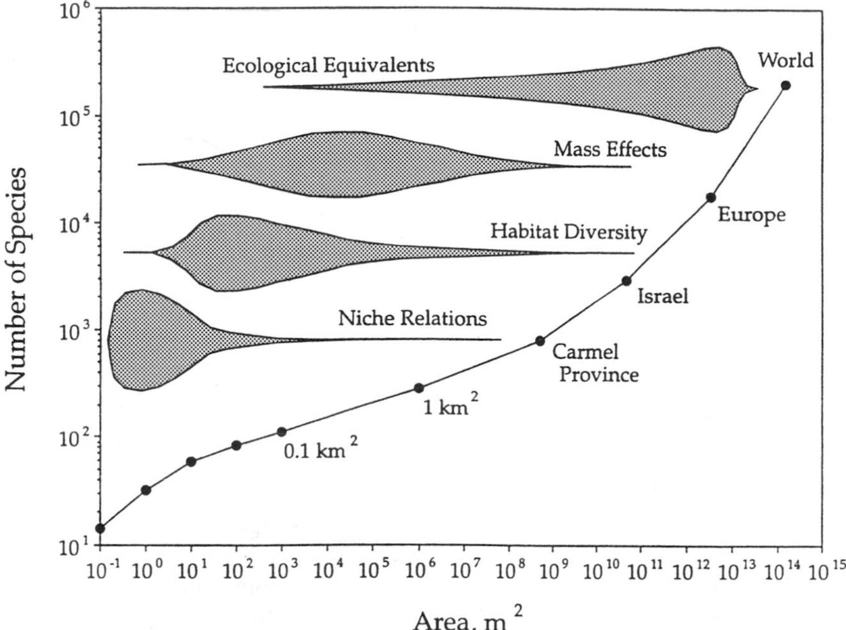

Figure 4.6 Shmida and Wilson's (1985) hypothesis for the control of vascular plant species diversity on different spatial scales, in relation to a species-area curve drawn from a local area in Israel (the mattoral region) to the entire world. Shmida and Wilson proposed that the biological determinants of species diversity change from niche assembly on local scales to mass effects and habitat diversity on intermediate scales, and finally to ecological equivalency on the largest spatial scales. The neutral theory predicts similar qualitative changes in the species-area relationship without positing any niche-assembly rules.

plant species richness. They suggested that on very local scales, niche-assembly rules would dominate community assembly. On somewhat larger spatial scales, mass effects and habitat diversity would become important. They defined mass-effect species as being sink populations that are present in local communities due to continual immigration and whose local populations would go extinct in the absence of this immigration subsidy. Finally, they proposed that at very large scales, there are many "ecologically substitutable" species. However, as I will show, a completely neutral dynamic theory of species-area relationships is fully capable of explaining such triphasic species-area curves without invoking any niche-assembly rules whatsoever.

Taking a dynamic perspective, one realizes that the species-area relationship must represent a steady-state phenomenon, just like the steady-state species richness on islands in the theory of island biogeography. Every species originates at some point or in some region on the landscape, disperses out from that point or region of origin, and ultimately goes extinct. The neutral theory predicts a triphasic species-area curve that will be a function of the fundamental biodiversity number θ and the dispersal rate m. Even under neutral dynamics, the triphasic nature of the species-area curve indicates that changes in the sampling units occur as the spatial scale increases. At very local spatial scales, the species-area curve is very sensitive to the local commonness and rarity of species, as individuals are collected one by one. However, on regional to subcontinental spatial scales, the rate of encounter of new species depends much less on relative species abundance and more on rates of speciation and dispersal and the resulting steady-state geographic ranges of species. If species disperse over the geographic region quickly relative to speciation and extinction, then the regional species-area curve will have a shallow slope. Conversely, if species disperse slowly relative to rates of speciation and extinction, then the regional species-area curve will be steep. At very large, intercontinental scales, the species-area curve will steepen as the spatial scale exceeds the correlation length of regional biogeographic processes, such that biogeographic events become independent and uncorrelated. Durrett and Levin (1996) analyzed species-area relationships for a very similar contact-process model and proved that the slope of the species-area curve approaches unity for length scales much larger than the correlation length.

Consider first local spatial scales—the scales on which local relative species abundance matters. In the discussion that follows, I use species-individual curves interchangeably with species-area curves because it is always possible to convert one to the other by our first principle: $J = \rho A$ and $q = 2\rho A_M \nu$, where A_M is the area occupied by the metacommunity. Under the case of no dispersal limitation ($m = 1$), the theory predicts that the species-individual curve will simply be a function of θ. The expected number of species in a sample of size J with a given value of θ is given by (Hubbell 1998):

$$\mathrm{E}\{S \mid \theta, J\} = \frac{\theta}{\theta} + \frac{\theta}{\theta + 1} + \frac{\theta}{\theta + 2} + \cdots + \frac{\theta}{\theta + J - 1}. \tag{4.5}$$

Figure 4.7 illustrates the expected local species-individual curves for various values of θ; the faster the speciation rate or the larger the metacommunity size, the faster the rise in the local species-individual curve.

This pattern is expected under the point mutation speciation mode when individuals are well mixed or when the sampling regime compensates for dispersal limitation. For example, Saunders (1968) compared benthic marine invertebrate diversity in samples from four sites across a broad latitudinal range, each collected with many scattered trawls, from which species-individual curves were

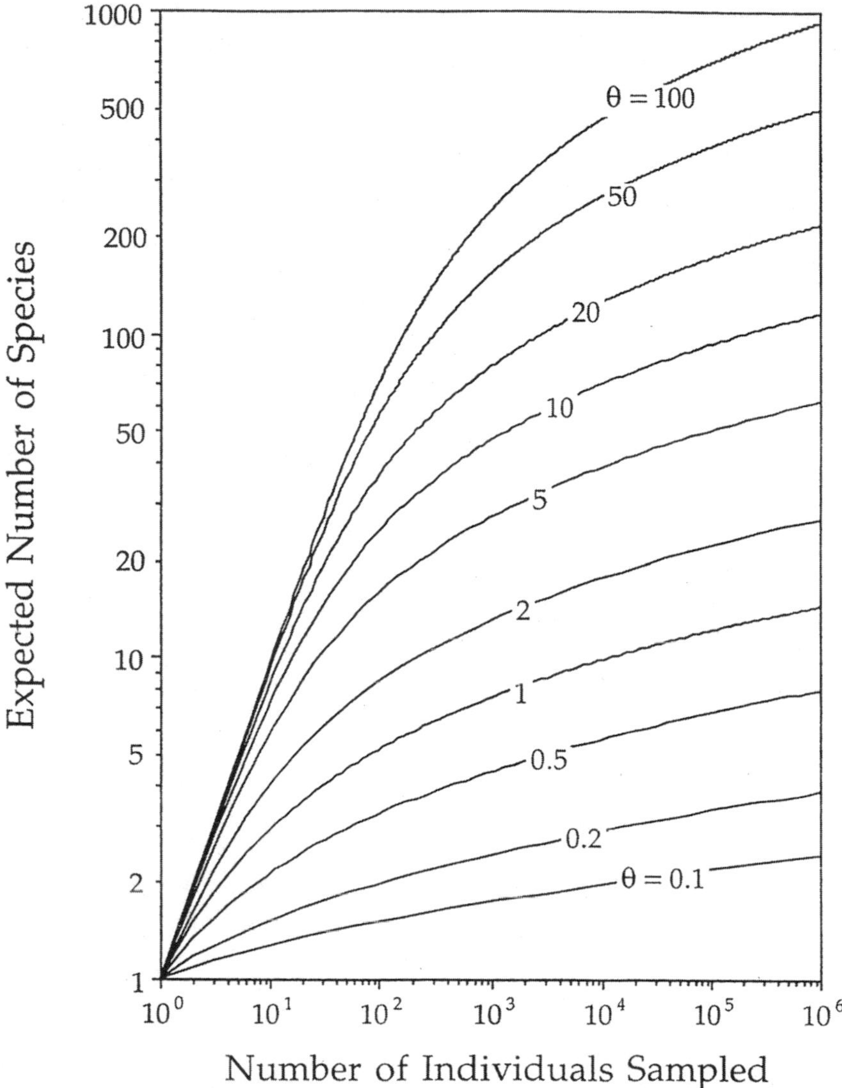

Figure 4.7 Expected species-individual curves for various values of the fundamental biodiversity number θ ranging over three orders of magnitude from 0.1 to 100. Note the double log scales. These are expectations for a random sample of individuals from the metacommunity (no dispersal limitation).

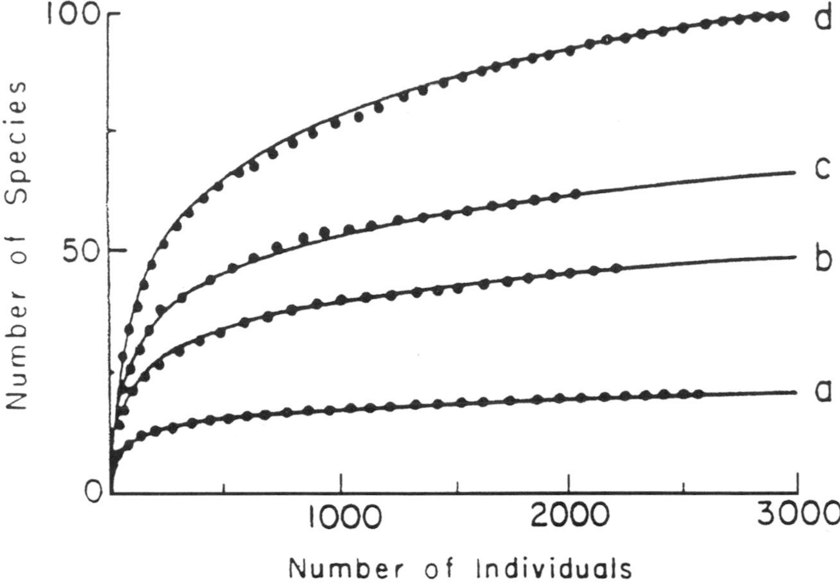

Figure 4.8 Species-individual curves for benthic invertebrate communities at four sites spanning a broad latitudinal range. Dots are Saunders's observations; solid lines are the expected curves. a, boreal shallow water ($\theta = 3.0$); b, deep water off southern New England ($\theta = 6\ 8.2$); c, Valvis Bay, South Africa ($\theta = 0\ 12.0$); d, tropical shallow water ($\theta = 0\ 20.0$). (After May 1975.)

calculated by a random bootstrap method. The results are well fit by equation (4.5) (fig. 4.8). More generally, however, dispersal limitation almost always reduces the rate of encounter of species below that expected from equation (4.5). Including the effect of dispersal limitation in equation (4.5), we obtain the approximation (Hubbell 1998)

$$E\{S|\theta, J\} \approx \frac{\theta \cdot 1^{-\omega}}{\theta} + \frac{\theta \cdot 2^{-\omega}}{\theta + 1} + \cdots + \frac{\theta \cdot J^{-\omega}}{\theta + J - 1} \qquad (4.6)$$

or

$$E\{S|\theta, J\} = \sum_{i=1}^{J} \frac{\theta \cdot i^{-\omega}}{\theta + i - 1},$$

where the dispersal limitation parameter $\omega \geq 0$. Note that when $\omega = 0$, equation (4.6) reduces to the limiting metacommunity case of no dispersal limitation [equation (4.5)]. Equations (4.5) and (4.6) are appropriate only at local spatial scales, but also note that the log-log linear Arrhenius equation fails at these local

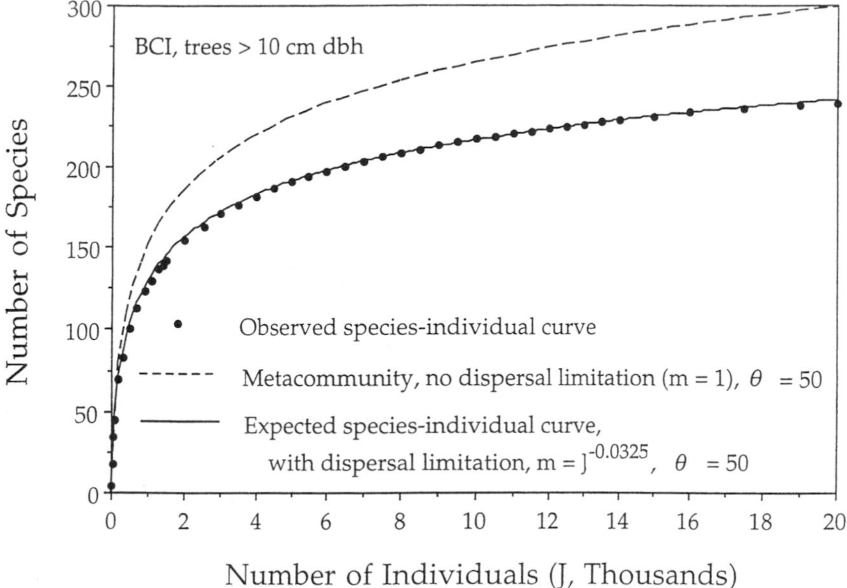

Figure 4.9 Species-individual curve for trees greater than 10 cm DBH in the 50 ha Forest Dynamics Plot on Barro Colorado Island, Panama. The observed curve (dots) was obtained by averaging species richness in randomly chosen contiguous areas containing a given number of individual trees. The metacommunity species-individual curve overestimates the number of species in the plot by sixty-five species (28%). The parameters of the species-individual curve under dispersal limitation were estimated by maximum likelihood and yielded $\theta = 50$ and $\omega = 0.0325$.

spatial scales. Figure 4.9 shows the excellent fit of equation (4.6) to the species-individual curve for trees greater than 10 cm DBH in the 50 ha plot on BCI with a maximum likelihood estimate of 0.0325 for $\theta = 50$. Note that if we assume no dispersal limitation, the expected species-individual curve rises too quickly.

At regional and larger scales, however, dispersal limitation is predicted to increase, rather than decrease, the slope of the species-area curve. This effect becomes increasingly important as the spatial sampling scale exceeds the steady-state range sizes of more and more species, increasing the encounter rate of previously untallied, dispersal-limited species. Therefore, the neutral theory's explanation for the triphasic form of the species-area curve is that the effect of dispersal limitation on the rate of species addition changes from being negative to positive with increasing spatial scale. The theory predicts linear log-log species-individual and species-area curves on intermediate spatial scales when sampling falls within a single metacommunity with its dynamic equilibrium logseries relative abundance distribution. At larger scales, however, when

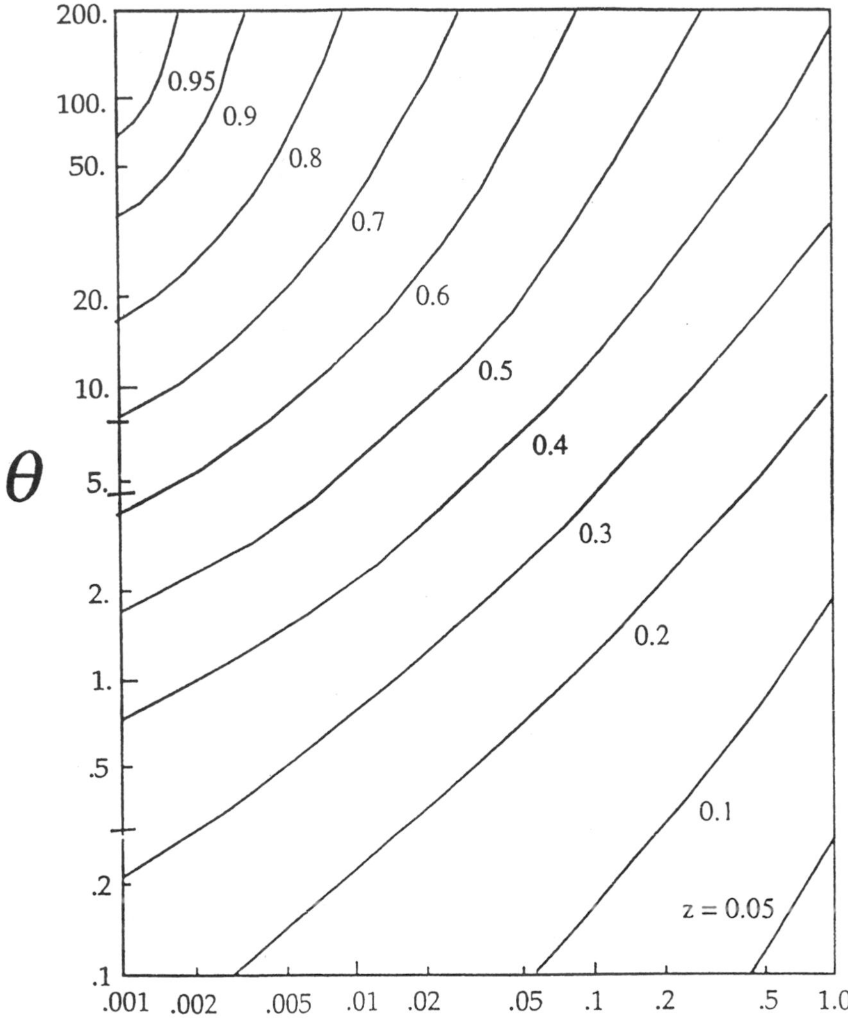

Figure 4.10 The effect of varying the fundamental biodiversity number θ and the dispersal parameter m on the slope (z value) of the Arrhenius species-area curve at regional spatial scales, according to the unified neutral theory. Note that $z \rightarrow 1$ as $\theta \rightarrow \infty$, and that z becomes smaller as $m \rightarrow 1$. It should also be noted that $m = 1$ in the spatially explicit model does not correspond to infinite dispersal, as in the spatially implicit theory, but rather to a case in which all local community deaths are replaced by immigrants from immediately adjacent local communities. Results are from simulations of the spatially explicit model.

sampling crosses a boundary between metacommunities having long separate evolutionary histories, the curves will steepen to an asymptotic slope of 1.0 at infinite area (Hubbell 1998) as the processes of speciation, dispersal, and extinction become increasingly independent and uncoupled dynamically in different metacommunities. Realized species-area curves will seldom achieve a slope of unity, however, because they are curves for biogeographic regions of finite size.

Figure 4.10 shows the influence of the fundamental biodiversity number θ and the dispersal rate m on the slope of the log-log species-individual curve at the intermediate spatial scales over which the Arrhenius relationship holds. In the figure, I have varied θ over slightly more than three orders of magnitude, from 0.1 to 200, the range observed in nature—at least for closed-canopy tree communities. I have also varied the immigration rate m over three orders of magnitude, from 0.001 to 1.0. The z values are predicted to be steep for large θ and small m and shallow for small θ and large m. These results make intuitive sense. When the mean dispersal rate is low and the speciation rate is high, the equilibrium slope of the species-area curve will be steep because new species arise quickly relative to their rates of dispersal over the metacommunity landscape. Conversely, when the dispersal rate is high and the speciation rate is low, the equilibrium slope of the species-area curve is shallow because most species have time to disperse over the metacommunity landscape before the next species originates.

Figure 4.10 also allows us to answer the remaining questions posed by Williamson (1988) according to the neutral theory. The answer to Williamson's first question, namely, why the Arrhenius relationship is so common, is that on regional spatial scales, a log-log relationship is always expected from sampling within a single metacommunity. The answer to the third question, namely, why the slopes tend to lie between $z = 0.15$ and $z = 0.40$, is that there is a very broad region of parameter space for variation in θ and m for which z is between 0.15 and 0.40. The answer to Williamson's fourth question, namely, why there is so much variation in the slopes of observed species-area curves, is that the steady-state z value is a function of the speciation rate, the metacommunity size, and the dispersal rate, all of which may vary from one taxon to another. Thus, a given z value defines a unique functional isocline in θ, m space that should provide some avenues for testing the predictions of neutral theory.

Figure 4.11 illustrates a sample theoretical species-area curve for intermediate and large spatial scales. In this case I simulated a metacommunity of 40,401 local communities each of size $J = 4$ for $\theta = 1.0$ and $m = 0.5$. The figure shows the characteristic inflection point of the species-area curve. It occurs at that area (number of individuals) equal to the logarithm of the squared correlation length L of the dynamic biogeographic process. We use the tangents to the species-area

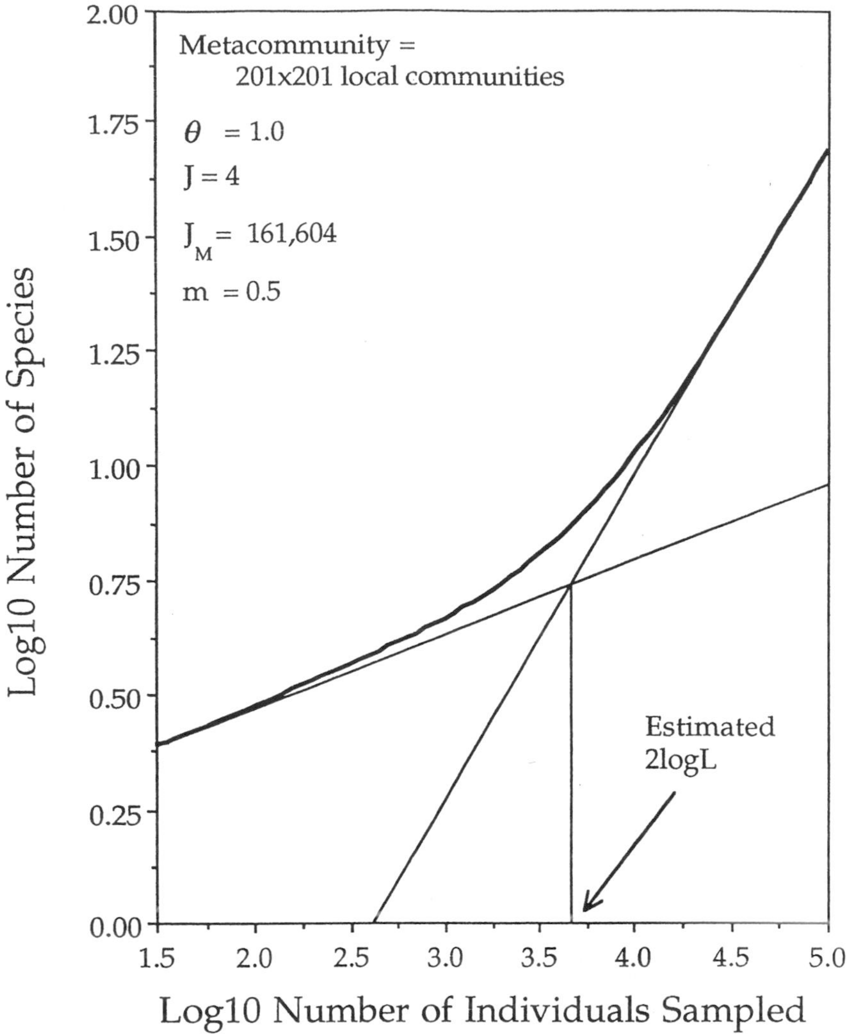

Figure 4.11 The increase in the slope of the species-area relationship at large spatial scales, illustrated for the case of a metacommunity of 201^2 local communities each of size $J = 4$, for $\theta = 1.0$ and $m = 0.5$. The inflection point defined by the intersecting tangents of the curve for intermediate and large areas yields an estimate of $2 \log L = 3.67$, which gives an estimated correlation length, L, of 68.4 individuals (mean of 100 simulation runs).

curve at intermediate and large spatial scales to estimate the inflection point in the curve and thence the correlation length of the process. In this numerical example, $2 \log L = 3.67$, so that $L = 68.4$ individuals. This correlation length corresponds to a biogeographic region measuring 17.1 local communities on a side, or a total of 292 local communities.

According to the neutral theory, the correlation length, L, is an important number because it measures and defines the natural length scale of a biogeographic process below which metacommunity events are expected to be correlated. The correlation length is also potentially important for conservation biology because it quantifies the size of biogeographic region within which most of the observed biodiversity of the region evolved. Although this prediction is not illustrated here, the theory predicts that correlation lengths will become smaller with increasing speciation rate (increasing θ) and larger with increasing m, which again makes intuitive sense.

SPECIES-AREA RELATIONSHIPS FOR PANAMANIAN TREES

We can apply this theory to interpreting the species-area curves and estimating the correlation lengths of the tree flora of Panama. I compiled species range data for twenty-seven families of Panamanian trees and shrubs from checklists in *Flora of Panama* (D'Arcy 1987). Species-area curves were constructed for trees and shrubs greater than 1 cm DBH. The areas sampled ranged from the 50 ha Forest Dynamics Plot (0.5 km^2) on Barro Colorado Island (BCI), at the low end, to all of BCI (15 km^2), to the area of the former Canal Zone (10^3 km^2), to the Province of Panama ($2 \cdot 10^4$ km^2), and finally, to the entire country of Panama ($7.5 \cdot 10^4$ km^2). From these data, I computed the z values of the species-area curves for each family on intermediate spatial scales.

Figure 4.12 shows the species-area curves for a representative sample of six families. In the flora of Panama, three of these are primarily families of the main canopy or are midstory trees (Bombacaceae, Myristicaceae, and Lecythidaceae), and three are generally shrubs or understory treelets (Melastomataceae, Piperaceae, and Rubiaceae). All six curves are log-log linear up to a spatial scale of approximately 10^3 km^2, the area of the former Canal Zone, and z values were calculated up to this area. Then the curves all begin to bend upward, more or less at the same spatial scale, steepening for the area of the Province of Panama, and steepening once again for the area representing the entire country of Panama. Note that the curves, although they become steeper, do not attain a slope of unity at the spatial scale of the country of Panama.

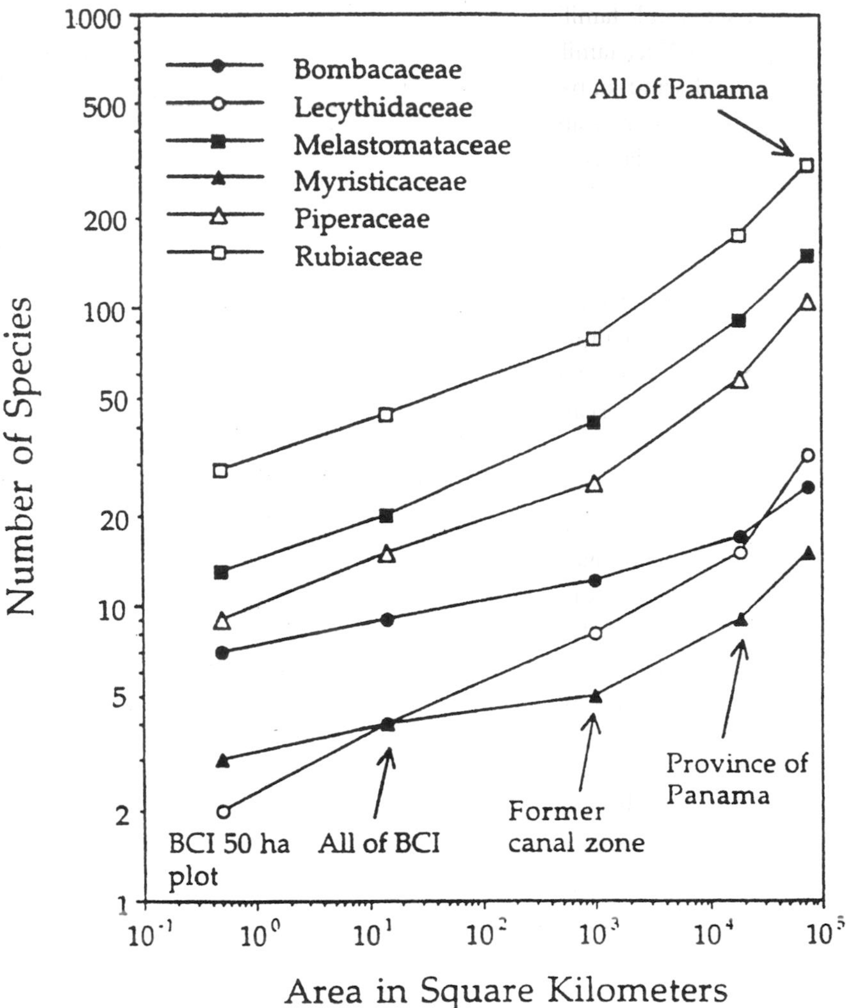

Figure 4.12 Species-area curves for trees and shrubs greater than 1 cm DBH in six plant families in the flora of Panama, over a range of spatial scales from the 50 ha Forest Dynamics Plot on BCI to all of Panama. Note the log-log linear curves at intermediate scales (small scales less than 50 ha are not shown; for smaller scales, see fig. 4.9) and the upturn at large sample areas that represent a significant fraction of the total area of Panama. The upturn in the curves occurs when sample areas exceed the squared correlation length of the speciation-dispersal-extinction process.

Of the six sample families, the lowest z value occurred in the family Bombacaceae ($z = 0.097$), a family of mainly emergent, late secondary heliophilic species with small wind- or bat-dispersed seeds. Steeper curves were found in families of understory trees and shrubs (Melastomataceae, $z = 0.201$, Piperaceae, $z = 0.195$, and Rubiaceae, $z = 0.190$). Even steeper curves were found in the New World nutmeg family, Myristicaceae ($z = 0.215$), and in the Brazil nut family, Lecythidaceae ($z = 0.262$). Myristicacs have large arillate seeds dispersed by large frugivorous birds, but seldom far. Lecythidacs are a family of mainly midstory tree species in Panama with relatively poor seed dispersal. They have very heavy seedpods containing large seeds that are eaten and scatter-hoarded by ground-foraging mammals. The diversity of the species-area curves in figure 4.12 implies that, at least among families, the assumption of equal per capita dispersal and speciation probabilities has been violated. However, as it turns out, the neutral theory is quite robust to violations of this assumption, provided that zero-sum dynamics still apply (Hubbell 1998).

The historical, ecological, and evolutionary explanations for the variation in species-area curves among Panamanian tree and shrub families are currently unknown. Speciation rates aside, however, one might expect that dispersal rates would be affected by plant growth form. Other things being equal, canopy trees might be expected to disperse seeds, on average, farther and faster than small-stature understory shrubs or herbs. Therefore, plant families that contain mainly canopy or emergent tree species might be expected to have shallower species-area curves than families that contain mainly shrubs or herbs. The species-area data for the twenty-seven Panamanian tree and shrub families show surprisingly good agreement with this prediction (fig. 4.13). At intermediate spatial scales, families made up mainly or exclusively of canopy or emergent tree species exhibited species-area curves with consistently lower z values than families made up mainly of understory trees, treelets, or shrubs.

We can return to the species-area curves in figure 4.12 to estimate the natural correlation lengths for each family, using the tangent line method to find the inflection point in each species-area curve. I used the smallest three sample areas for each family to fit the lower tangent line and the two largest sample areas, the Province of Panama and all of Panama, to fit the upper tangent fine. This method yielded the following estimates for L^2 and for the correlation length L for each of the six families: Bombacaceae, $L^2 = 11{,}000$ km^2, $L = 105$ km; Lecythidaceae, $L^2 = 16{,}000$ km^2, $L = 126$ km; Melastomataceae, $L^2 = 5{,}700$ km^2, $L = 75$ km; Myristicaceae, $L^2 = 7{,}000$ km^2, $L = 84$ km; Piperaceae, $L^2 = 6{,}800$ km^2, $L = 82$ km; and Rubiaceae, $L^2 = 4{,}600$ km^2, $L = 68$ km. It is interesting that all of the estimated correlation lengths are small and relatively similar, varying over only

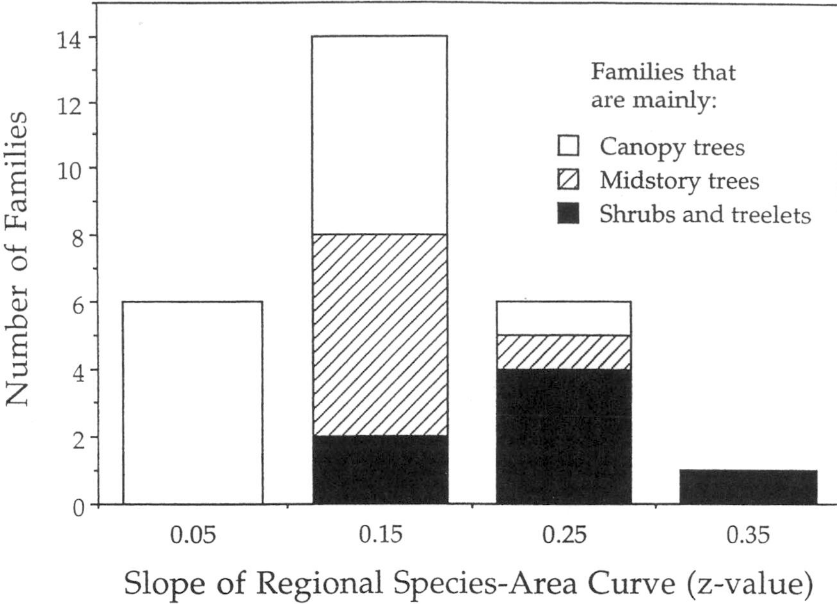

Figure 4.13 Relationship between the characteristic stature of species in twenty-seven tropical tree and shrub families in the flora of Panama and the slope (z value) of the Arrhenius log-log linear species-area curves for those families at intermediate spatial scales in Panama. Families made up mainly of small-stature species have steeper species-area curves than families of large-stature species.

about a twofold range, from 68 km to 126 km. The small sizes and similarity of L values among these plant families may reflect strong biogeographic constraints on the evolution of metacommunity tree diversity in Panama, a country that is a long, narrow isthmus only about 70 km wide at its narrowest point. The three plant families that are primarily understory shrubs and treelets (Melastomataceae, Piperaceae, and Rubiaceae) had the smallest correlation lengths. Low dispersal rates are expected from the theory to be associated with high z values and small correlation lengths.

When we examine the species-area curve for the complete native tree and shrub flora of Panama, we see a similar upturn in the species-area curve at about the same spatial scale (fig. 4.14). Drawing the upper and lower tangents to the species-area curve yields an L^2 of 4,300 km^2 and a correlation length of 65.6 km, which once again is commensurate with the width of the Panamanian isthmus and in good agreement with the results from individual families. As mentioned, correlation lengths are expected to be short and similar in size for different taxa in Panama because of the geographic shape of the country, which presumably

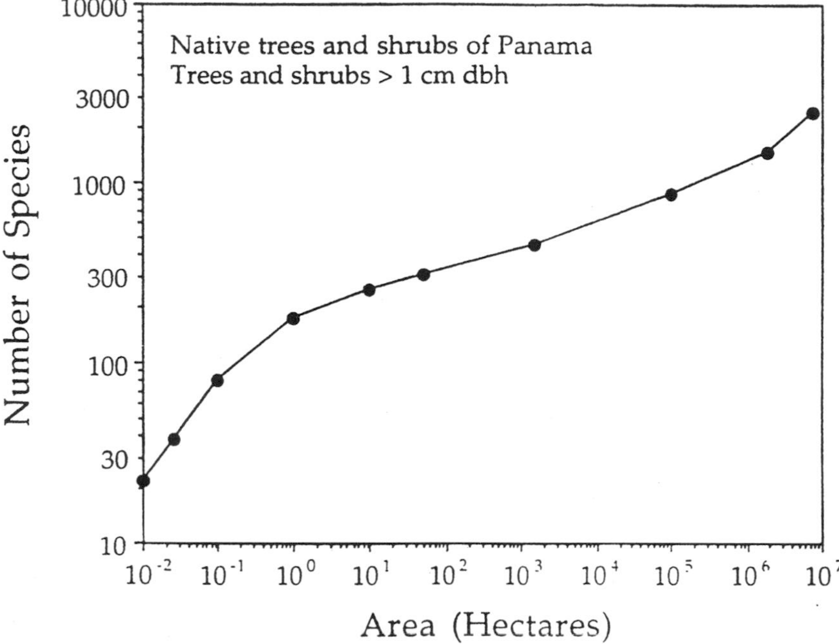

Figure 4.14 Species-area curve for the entire native tree and shrub flora of Panama, over a range of spatial scales from 10^{-2} ha (a 10×10 m quadrat within the 50 ha Forest Dynamics Plot) to all of Panama. In Panama, the range of intermediate spatial scales over which the log-log linear Arrhenius relationship applies is approximately from 1 ha to 10^5 ha. The estimated correlation length for the tree and shrub flora of Panama is 65.6 km. Note that the qualitative triphasic shape is similar to Shmida and Wilson's (1985) species-area curve for the flora of the world (see fig. 4.6). (Species range data from D'Arcy 1987.)

strongly restricts the two-dimensional migration of species. This conclusion is suggested by the fact that the correlation length for the entire vascular flora of the world, which we can estimate from figure 4.6 (Shmida and Wilson 1985), is more than an order of magnitude larger. The value of the squared correlation length is about $7 \cdot 10^{11}$ km^2, yielding an estimated correlation length L of $8.4 \cdot 10^5$ m, or 837 km, for the world's vascular flora.

CONCLUSIONS

In this chapter I have discussed the predictions of the neutral theory for biogeographic patterns of relative species abundance and species-area relationships, and I have applied the theory to tropical tree communities in Panama. The theory asserts that species-area curves are not simply static sampling patterns, but in fact represent the spatially distributed steady state of a dynamic speciation-dispersal-extinction process playing out on a metacommunity landscape. The theory gives a neutral explanation for the triphasic shape of the species-area relationship from very local spatial scales to regional scales and finally to global scales. On local scales, on a double log plot of log species number against log area or log individuals sampled, the theoretical species-area relationship is curvilinear, reflecting the differential rates of collecting common versus rare species. The expected curve fits the observed species-area curve for tree species in the 50 ha Forest Dynamics Plot on BCI very well. At larger spatial scales in a biogeographic region, the effects of speciation, migration, and range dominate over the effects of relative species abundance in controlling the species-area curve, and the theory predicts log-log linear relationships whose slopes are determined by the fundamental biodiversity number θ and the dispersal rate m. The theory further predicts that there exists a natural length scale of the biogeographic process, the correlation length L, again determined by θ and m, that defines the spatial scale of the region within which biogeographic processes will be correlated. At very large spatial scales, approaching and then exceeding the correlation length of the speciation-dispersal-extinction process, the species-area curve steepens and the species-area slope approaches unity. Thus, the theory suggests that species-area relationships contain useful information about broad patterns of speciation, dispersal, and extinction rates that warrants further exploration.

ADDENDUM

This chapter represents the written version of only the third public presentation of the unified neutral theory of biodiversity and biogeography, three years before publication of the neutral theory in book form (Hubbell 2001). In the two years since publication of the book, there have been several thoughtful critiques, and responses to them, as well as several important theoretical advances. A number of papers have argued that the neutral theory is not the only theory that can successfully describe patterns of relative species abundance in ecological communities of trophically similar species (e.g., Chave, Muller-Landau, and Levin 2002; McGill 2003; Sugihara et al. 2003). Also, Ricklefs (2003) has written a critique of the speciation modes in the neutral theory, to which I have responded (Hubbell 2003). Here I shall comment briefly mainly on one paper (McGill 2003) and report a few of our most exciting new analytical results (Volkov et al. 2003).

McGill (2003) suggested that the lognormal distribution is a more parsimonious null hypothesis for describing relative species abundance than the neutral theory. He asserted that the lognormal fits the data from the BCI plot better than the neutral theory does. McGill encountered problems with those simulations, particularly in knowing when the stochastic equilibrium distribution of relative species abundance had been reached.

Recent advances in the neutral theory make all problems with simulations moot because an analytical solution is now available for the distribution of relative species abundance in local communities undergoing immigration from the metacommunity (Volkov et al. 2003). Moreover, the new solution demonstrates some other remarkable results. First, it confirms that Fisher's logseries is the expected distribution of relative species abundance in the metacommunity. Second, and more importantly, it shows that Fisher's logseries implies density independence in the birth and death rates of species in the communities. Finally, in the specific instance of BCI, the analytical solution to the neutral theory actually fits the BCI data better than the lognormal does.

The analytical solution was found by taking a new approach and simplifying the fundamental stochastic equation for changes in abundance of a given species (Volkov et al. 2003). Let $b_{n,k}$ and $d_{n,k}$ be the probabilities of birth and death of an arbitrary species k at abundance n at time t. Let $p_{n,k}(t)$ be the probability that species k is at abundance n at time t. Then the derivative of this probability is given by

$$\frac{\mathrm{d}p_{n,k}(t)}{\mathrm{d}t} = p_{n+1,k}(t)d_{n+1} + p_{n-1,k}(t)b_{n-1} - p_{n,k}(t)(b_{n,k} + d_{n,k}). \tag{4.7}$$

The first term on the right represents the transition from abundance $n + 1$ to n, accompanying a death. The second term is the transition from abundance $n - 1$ to n with a birth. The last two terms are losses to $p_{n,k}(t)$ because they represent transitions from abundance n to either $n + 1$ or $n - 1$ through a birth or death, respectively. Although at first sight, equation (4.7) appears to be little more than a bookkeeping exercise, it is actually much more. It is a recursive function on abundance that allows for the equilibrium solution to be found. When all derivatives at all abundances are set equal to 0, then the solution satisfies "detailed balance," which means that each abundance transition is in equilibrium. Let uppercase $P_{n,k}$ denote this equilibrium. Then

$$P_{n,k} = P_{n-1,k} \cdot [b_{n-1,k}/d_{n,k}].$$

More generally, this equation corresponds to an equilibrium solution for the metacommunity

$$P_{n,k} = P_{0,k} \prod_{i=0}^{n-1} \frac{b_{i,k}}{d_{i+1,k}}. \tag{4.8}$$

Note that the probability of being at abundance n is a function of the product of birth rate to death rate ratios over all abundances. Because the $P_{n,k}$'s must sum to unity, we can find the value of $P_{0,k}$ from this sum, and therefore all other terms as well.

Now consider a neutral community of S species that are all alike on a demographic basis, such that they all have the same birth rates and death rates; that is, $b_{n,k} \equiv b_n$ and $d_{n,k} \equiv d_n$ (i.e., the species identifier k doesn't matter). Speciation is introduced by considering a special "birth rate" in this general metacommunity solution; that is, $b_0 = \nu$, the speciation rate. The mean number of species with n individuals, $\langle \phi_n \rangle$, in a community of S identical species is simply proportional to P_n:

$$\langle \phi_n \rangle = SP_0 \prod_{i=0}^{n-1} \frac{b_i}{d_{i+1}}. \tag{4.9}$$

Another theoretical advance of the new theoretical formations represented by equations (4.7)–(4.9) is that we have relaxed the assumption of perfect zero-sum dynamics. The elimination of the theoretical requirement for total community size constancy is certainly more in agreement with actual ecological data. This said, because all species are identical demographically on a per capita basis, the size of the metacommunity and of local communities will not fluctuate too much, so the assumption of constant community size will be a good and reasonable approximation. That is why the theoretical results obtained under zero-sum dynamics are essentially in full agreement with the results of the new theoretical formulation of neutral theory. The only difference is that, in the new formulation, when $\theta = 0$, all species eventually go extinct, and the metacommunity becomes empty. In contrast, under the zero-sum formulation, when $\theta = 0$, there is one surviving species everywhere in the metacommunity.

From equation (4.9) we are now in a position to derive Fisher's logseries. (Fisher, Corbet, and Williams 1943). Suppose that the birth rate of a species with current abundance n is simply n times the birth rate of a species with abundance 1; that is, $b_n = nb_1$, or density independence. Similarly, suppose that death rates are also density-independent, $d_n = nd_1$. Substituting these expressions into equation (4.10), we directly obtain Fisher's logseries:

$$\langle \phi_n \rangle_{\mathrm{M}} = S_{\mathrm{M}} P_0 \frac{b_0 b_1 \ldots b_{n-1}}{d_1 d_2 \ldots d_n} = \theta \frac{x^n}{n}, \tag{4.10}$$

where the subscript M refers to the metacommunity, $x = b_1/d_1 = b/d$, $b_0 = \nu$, and $\theta = S_{\mathrm{M}} P_0 \nu / b = \alpha$ of Fisher's logseries. This derivation reveals that the mysterious parameter x of the logseries is, in fact, biologically interpretable as the ratio of the density-independent per capita birth rate to death rate. Note that when one introduces speciation, parameter x must be less than 1 to maintain a finite metacommunity size. Thus, we have a complete derivation of the logseries and its parameters from the neutral theory. We can now say that the logseries arises in the metacommunity when birth and death rates are density-independent and all species share the same per capita rates.

An analytical solution for the distribution of relative species abundance in a local community undergoing immigration from a much larger metacommunity, the classic problem of island biogeography theory, is now available. Once again, let $\langle \phi_n \rangle$ be the mean number of species with n individuals. Then

$$\langle \phi_n \rangle = \theta \frac{J!}{n!(J-n)!} \frac{\Gamma(\gamma)}{\Gamma(J+\gamma)} \int_0^{\gamma} \frac{\Gamma(n+y)}{\Gamma(1+y)} \frac{\Gamma(J-n+\gamma-y)}{\Gamma(\gamma-y)} \exp\left(\frac{-\gamma\theta}{\gamma}\right) dy \tag{4.11}$$

where

$$\Gamma(z) = \int_0^{\infty} t^{z-1} e^{-t} dt,$$

which is equal to $(z-1)!$ for integer z, and

$$\gamma = \frac{m(J-1)}{1-m}.$$

This expression can be solved numerically quite accurately. For the derivation, the reader should consult Volkov et al. (2003). The behavior of equation (4.11) is such that the distribution of relative species abundance becomes progressively more skewed as the immigration rate decreases, confirming the simulation-based results in my book (Hubbell 2001). Thus, as islands or local communities become more isolated, rare species become rarer, and common species become commoner.

I conclude this addendum with several comments on the use of the lognormal distribution to describe relative species abundance patterns. McGill (2003) claimed that he had tested the neutral theory and found it wanting, and he argued that the lognormal was a better and more parsimonious null model. On the other hand, Sugihara el al. (2003) argued that the lognormal is derivable from a model of hierarchically niche-assembled communities; in other words, that the lognormal is, in fact, not null at all. Beyond the fact that these statements are contradictory, the quality of a fit to the lognormal, to the neutral theory, or to any other distribution does not, by itself, constitute an adequate test of the underlying theory. Adequate tests will require evaluating the numerous qualitative and quantitative predictions of the neutral theory in many different ecological communities. For example, holding all else equal, does reducing the immigration rate decrease the frequency of rare species, as predicted?

Second, the lognormal is not predictive. Fitting a lognormal does not lead directly to further hypotheses to test. One reason for this is that the parameters of the lognormal do not have any straightforward biological interpretation, even in the case of niche-hierarchy theory (Sugihara et al. 2003). In contrast, the parameters of the neutral theory are all readily interpretable in biological terms, and are things like birth and death rates, immigration rates, sizes of local communities and of the metacommunity, and speciation rates.

Finally, there are mathematical reservations regarding use of the lognormal. It is unlikely that the lognormal can ever be developed as the foundation for a dynamic hypothesis of community assembly unless one very serious problem is overcome. That problem is the fact that, in the time evolution of the multiplicative processes underlying a lognormal, the variance of the distribution increases without bound. The lognormal has been successfully fit to relative abundance data from communities, but to my knowledge, it has been fit only to static sample data for which there is a fixed variance, not to dynamic data. Actual ecological communities must obviously have finite variance, but whatever processes regulate that variance, they are not embodied in a lognormal. To attempt to address this problem, Preston (1962) and Sugihara et al. (2003) have argued in favor of a special class of lognormals, so-called canonical lognormals, which have a constant variance in log abundance. However, I know of almost no studies reporting that, if sample sizes are increased, the variance in log species abundance does not also increase, implying that the data are not canonical. I am not saying that ecologists should never fit lognormals to relative abundance data. However, I am saying that if ecologists want to test additional hypotheses about dynamic community assembly rules, they will need to think beyond the lognormal. The neutral theory of biodiversity and biogeography may be of some utility in such exercises.

ACKNOWLEDGMENTS

I thank the Smithsonian Tropical Research Institute and the Center for Tropical Forest Science for logistical and financial support of the BCI Forest Dynamics Project, and the Forest Research Institute Malaysia for support of the Pasoh

Forest Dynamics Project. I also thank the National Science Foundation, the John D. and Katherine T. MacArthur Foundation, the Pew Charitable Trusts, the Andrew Mellon Foundation, and numerous other private donors for their support. I thank Robin Foster, Rick Condit, Liz Losos, and Ira Rubinoff for support and collaboration.

5

Palynological Richness and the Tropical Rainforest

JOHN R. FLENLEY

ABSTRACT

This chapter argues that the numerous hypotheses that have been proposed to explain taxonomic richness (and the related concept of biodiversity) may be classified into those that predict a finding of increasing richness during the Quaternary and those that predict the reverse. The concept of palynological richness (the taxonomic richness in a pollen/spore assemblage) is then introduced, and palynological richness is shown statistically to be a suitable proxy for taxonomic richness of plant formations, provided the study is restricted to woody taxa. Evidence is then adduced to indicate that palynological richness has probably declined during the Quaternary. Thus, those hypotheses that predict increasing richness during the Quaternary are not supported.

INTRODUCTION

The high taxonomic richness characteristic of the tropical rainforest and of other tropical environments is one end of a global latitudinal trend, the other end being the lower taxonomic richness toward the poles (Whittaker 1977; Isawa, Kubo, and Sato 1995; Givnish 1999). This trend is not followed equally by all structural forms or by all taxonomic groups, however. For instance, species of herbaceous plants and of the family Poaceae are most numerous at intermediate latitudes. For trees and shrubs, however, taxonomic richness does decline fairly uniformly with increasing latitude. The related concept of taxonomic diversity is more rigidly defined, and therefore is not discussed in this chapter.

Many hypotheses have been advanced to explain the high taxonomic richness of the tropics (Hill and Hill 2001). Several of these hypotheses are not mutually exclusive, so the true answer may be a multivariate one, in which many causal factors are operating together. It would, however, be a good scientific strategy to try to identify those factors that are not operating, or are less significant. One way to do this would be to investigate the changes in taxonomic richness through geologic time in relation to environmental changes, especially Quaternary climatic fluctuations.

Table 5.1 A classification of some hypotheses proposed to explain high taxonomic richness in the tropics

1. Hypotheses predicting increasing taxonomic richness during the Quaternary
   - Refuge hypothesis (Prance 1973)
   - Intermediate disturbance hypothesis (Connell 1978)
   - Nonequilibrium hypothesis (Wallace 1878)
2. Hypotheses predicting decreasing taxonomic richness during the Quaternary
   - Increased speciation rates in the tropics resulting from greater productivity, greater turnover, more rapid reproduction, etc. (Connell and Orias 1964)
   - Increased importance of biological factors such as predation, thus promoting isolation (the pest pressure hypothesis of Gillett 1962 and Janzen, 1970)
   - Decreased extinction, resulting from climatic and/or seasonal stability, thus allowing smaller populations to persist (Sanders 1968)
   - Increased number of niches, resulting from the combined effect of the above three factors (Hutchinson 1959)

In an attempt to move toward such a strategy, I have developed a classification of hypotheses proposed to explain taxonomic richness, dividing them into those that predict an increase in richness during the variable climates of the Quaternary and those that predict the reverse. This classification, partly based on that of Ricklefs (1973), is shown in table 5.1. The hypotheses predicting an increase in richness during the Quaternary include the well-known refuge hypothesis (Haffer 1969; Prance 1973), which argues that isolation of rainforest islands during Pleistocene dry phases would have promoted allopatric speciation. In addition, the nonequilibrium hypothesis of Wallace (1878) must be included here, since it proposes continuous increases in richness through time.

Most of the other hypotheses relate to the idea of long-term stability and favorable conditions in the tropics, and are thus included under the heading of those that predict decreasing richness during the Quaternary, when climatic stability and favorability were reduced, compared with the late Tertiary. The idea of increased control by predators, otherwise known as pest pressure (Gillett 1962; Janzen 1970), seems to me to be also one that would predict a Quaternary decline in richness, since insect predators are known to be at their most abundant in everwet forests (Gentry 1982; Clinebell et al. 1995).

PALYNOLOGICAL RICHNESS

If we had a measure of taxonomic richness in the past, we could now test these hypotheses. If richness increased during the Quaternary, then the hypotheses predicting increased richness during the Quaternary would be supported, and vice versa. We do in fact have a proxy measure of richness in the past: palynological richness. By "palynological richness," I mean the taxonomic richness of fossil pollen and spore types in an assemblage.

If palynological richness is capable of being in any way a proxy for taxonomic richness in living plant formations, then it should follow the same major geographic trends the latter does; that is, we should be able to detect the same latitudinal trend in richness for tree and shrub taxa, from high in the tropics to low near the poles, in assemblages of the same age. To test this idea, I assembled data from published late Quaternary (usually Holocene and late Pleistocene) pollen/spore diagrams from a range of latitudes in both hemispheres. I admitted only lowland sites (plus lower montane sites in the tropics), and included only tree and shrub taxa. I plotted number of taxa against latitude N or S. The result gave a good regression fit (fig. 5.1), with 83% of the variance explained. Such a result will come as no surprise to palynologists, who have become used to encountering many more taxa (at least from trees and shrubs) in tropical than in temperate research. I therefore conclude that there is a relationship between palynological richness (of woody taxa) and latitude, and thus between palynological richness and the taxonomic richness of parent assemblages. This conclusion is similar to the conclusion reached by Odgaard (1999).

PALYNOLOGICAL RICHNESS IN THE PAST

How has palynological richness varied in the geologic past? It is difficult to assemble useful data on this topic because palynological assemblages differ so much from place to place and from time to time, depending on local environmental factors. There is also considerable variation in the taxonomic differentiation practiced by different palynologists. Some indication of the fluctuation through time may, however, be obtained from the data provided by Morley (2000; see especially his figs. 5.15a for South America, 5.15b for Africa, and 9.13 for Borneo). Unfortunately, none of his diagrams include data for the Pleistocene. Both Africa and South America seem to have lost taxa at the end of the Eocene. In South America and Borneo, a peak is reached in the Mio-Pliocene. The point at issue, however, is whether such levels of richness were increased or

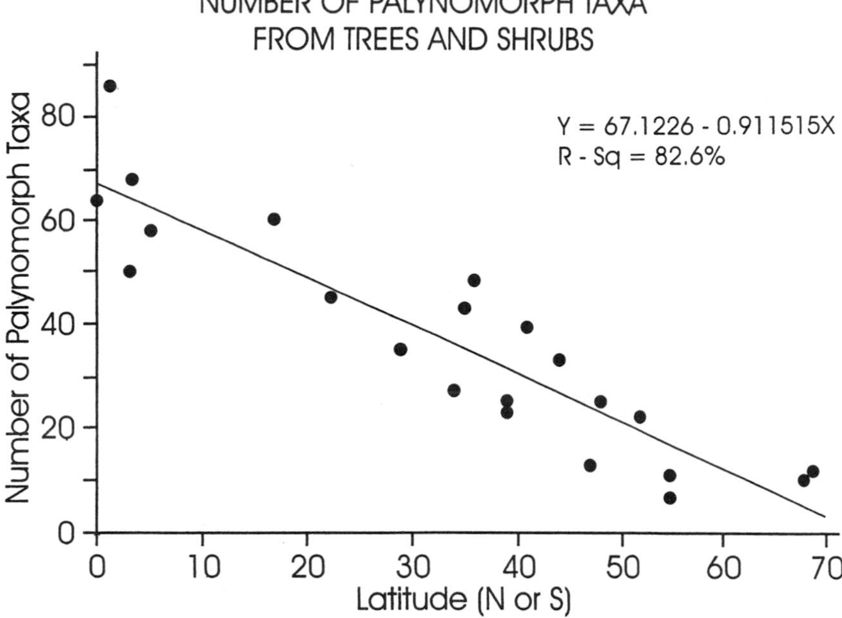

Figure 5.1 Palynological richness (trees and shrubs) plotted against latitude for late Quaternary pollen/spore diagrams. (Data from Absy 1979; Bennett 1983; Colinvaux 1981; Elenga, Vincens, and Schwartz 1991; Hyvärinen and Ritchie 1975; Janssen 1967; Kendall 1969; Kershaw 1976; Lloyd and Kershaw 1997; Mohammed, Bonnefille, and Johnson 1995; Newsome and Flenley 1988; Oldfield 1968; Parkes, Teller, and Flenley 1992; Ritchie 1977; van Zeist and van der Spoel-Walvius 1980; van Zeist and Woldring 1980; Walker 1966; Watts 1969, 1970.)

reduced during the Quaternary. To address this question, we need to find situations in which a direct comparison has been made between deposits in near-identical sedimentary situations in the same region, but of two distinct ages, preferably late Tertiary and late Quaternary.

I know of two such comparisons. The first is that by Anderson and Muller (1975) between a Miocene brown coal and a Holocene peat swamp in Borneo. They show clearly that the former is simply a buried version of the latter, and that both exhibit similar successions, forming on top of mangrove swamps. The palynological richness is almost identical in the two sequences (52 woody taxa in the Holocene and 51 in the Miocene), and many of the pollen taxa show little or no morphological change. The reason for this stability may be that the peat swamp habitat is so extreme, with almost continuously waterlogged peat soil and pH values as low as 2.0 at the center of the swamp, that relatively few taxa have been able to invade the niche. Thus, it is not surprising that there has been little change in the flora over a long period of time. This lack of change in richness argues neither for nor against any particular hypothesis of richness generation.

The second example is that given by Absy and van der Hammen (1976), who compared alluvial sediments of Miocene and Holocene age from Amazonia. Their results indicate that the palynological richness was approximately halved in the Holocene compared with the Miocene. These data seem to me more likely to be indicative of the trend in richness over a whole landscape, since the alluvial situation integrates pollen assemblages from an entire catchment. It may therefore be tentatively concluded that the climatic fluctuations of the Quaternary caused extinction on a grand scale, leading to the observed decline in palynological richness in Amazonia.

These data, therefore, do not conflict with the idea that the factors proposed by the three hypotheses listed in the first part of table 5.1 are unlikely to be operating effectively. They may not be totally ineffective, but their total effect is more than outweighed by other processes. This conclusion is in agreement with the mtDNA evidence from 35 species of small mammals in Amazonia, which appear to have diverged in the Pliocene, not the Quaternary (Da Silva and Patton 1998; Hewitt 2000; see also Moritz et al. 2000).

THE QUATERNARY CATASTROPHE

The exact mechanism for such a reduction in taxonomic richness during the Quaternary needs to be investigated. At present, the greatest richness, at least of trees and shrubs, occurs in the lowland rainforest. This formation extends, in the everwet tropics, to ca. 1000 m altitude. Above this, there is a progressive decline in taxonomic richness, analogous to the latitudinal decline (Flenley 1979; Givnish 1999). This decline has generally been related to the lapse-rate decline of temperatures with increasing altitude (van Steenis 1934–1936). At higher altitudes the decline could also be related to increased ultraviolet insolation (Flenley 1996), or to reduced partial pressure of carbon dioxide (Street-Perrott 1994).

It is now generally accepted that the lowland tropics were cooler at the last glacial maximum (LGM), ca.18,000 BP. Although initial studies based on marine Foraminifera suggested rather little cooling (ca.2°C: CLIMAP 1976), more recent evidence based on oxygen isotope ratios in tropical corals suggests 5°C–6°C cooling (Guilderson, Fairbanks, and Rubenstone 1994). This evidence conforms with palynological evidence for the penetration of montane forest elements into the lowlands at the LGM in all three main areas of tropical rainforest: Africa, Latin America, and Southeast Asia (Flenley 1998). There is also abundant evidence for increased aridity at the LGM in many tropical areas (Flenley 1998). The Quaternary extinctions may be regarded, therefore, as a direct response to the cold and arid phases of the Pleistocene, bringing the taxonomic richness into line with the ambient temperatures and moisture availabilities.

CONCLUSIONS

It is provisionally concluded that, at least in the case of woody plant taxa, those hypotheses that predict a finding of increasing taxonomic richness during the Quaternary (i.e., the refuge theory, the intermediate disturbance hypothesis, and the nonequilibrium hypothesis) are not supported by the evidence described above. This does not necessarily mean that these factors are completely inoperative. For instance, the general increase in palynological richness in the Mahakam Delta during the Miocene-Pliocene (Morley 2000) could support the nonequilibrium hypothesis. Likewise, there is some evidence that disturbance of some kinds, at some scales and in some locations, may promote, maintain, or at least only slightly diminish taxonomic or palynological richness (Charles-Dominique et al. 1998; Burslem and Whitmore 1999; Hamer and Hill 2000; Flenley and Butler 2001). Nevertheless, the evidence presented here suggests that the major climatic shifts of the Quaternary could be associated with a decline in taxonomic richness in the tropical rainforest. In the future it may even prove possible to use changes in palynological richness over limited time spans as a measure of paleoclimatic fluctuation (Flenley 2003).

ACKNOWLEDGMENTS

I thank Richard Heerdegen for assistance with computing and Karen Puklowski for drawing the diagram. I am also grateful to several referees for helpful comments.

6
The Pleistocene Vector of Neotropical Diversity

PAUL COLINVAUX

ABSTRACT

Pleistocene climatic changes as vectors of speciation are customarily invoked to explain the evolution of phenomenally high diversity in Amazonia. The most extreme scenario of ice age Amazonia is the refuge hypothesis, which postulates Pleistocene fragmentation of the forest by more arid vegetation, such as savanna. This postulate can be tested by paleoecological means, whether by using geologic or paleobiological data. The geologic data now available, without exception, exclude the possibility of widespread aridity in the Amazon Pleistocene. The prevailing impression to the contrary has been the result of erroneous interpretations of sparse observations, often influenced by the expectations of the refuge hypothesis itself. For example, Amazonian stone lines and steeply dissected soils are not arid land signals, as often claimed, but the familiar result of long-continued humid weathering under intact forest canopies. A history of less severe, but equally misleading, wrong interpretation of scanty data led to mistakes in pollen reconstructions of vegetation. Errors of palynological interpretation came most widely from applying temperate-zone experience to pollen from complex, zoophilous vegetation; for instance, assigning successional peaks in grass pollen to the sought-after savanna. The pollen data now available all agree with the geologic data, again without exception, in excluding the possibility of widespread drought sufficient to invoke biome change. Pollen data from both Amazonian lakes and the deep sea fan show that closed-canopy forest, comparable to that of the present day, occupied the Amazon lowlands for at least two complete glacial cycles, and by extrapolation, for the whole of the Pleistocene. The only vector of Pleistocene climatic change to affect community structure so far detected is modest cooling at glacial maxima, which resulted in population expansions of more stenothermic taxa within the forest. The original problem of explaining speciation within the great forest remains. Apparently, Amazonian speciation requires less geographic isolation than is allowed by classic vicariance theory.

PREAMBLE

The Pleistocene ice ages necessarily altered the distribution and abundance of life on earth, even in the tropics, and the last ice age was very recent. In round numbers, we date the end of it to 10,000 years ago. This is only 40 lifetimes for a tree, if you grant an old tree in the forest a span of 250 years. For comparison,

40 human lifetimes ago (letting us have 50 years each) takes us back only to the times of Julius Caesar, a man so nearly our contemporary that we can read his memoirs. If the climate of that most recent ice age in the Amazon was sufficiently different from the modern climate to alter the vegetation, then the Amazon forests are probably still re-forming, and possibly will still be re-forming when the next glaciation begins to drive the changes in a new direction.

Thus, glacial and interglacial periods should act as vectors of change in plant communities. The word "vector" is an agent noun derived from the Latin *vehere*, "to carry." The mathematical meaning for "vector" of "direction and length" came through the astronomical concept of "vector radius" of a planet. I take the phrase "Pleistocene vector of diversity" in my title to mean the forcing and direction of community change imposed on tropical diversity by the climatic changes of a glacial cycle.

EPHEMERAL COMMUNITIES OF ORGANISMS

In reconstructing the consequences of vectors of climatic change on the plant communities of the past, it is essential to recognize that plant communities are ephemeral associations of species populations. We should expect the communities of ice age time to be more or less unlike those with which we are familiar on the contemporary earth. Most, possibly all, Pleistocene communities should have no direct modern analogue.

One of the most persistent fallacies of ecological thought requires communities to exist as concrete entities that are duplicated in time and space. The fallacy comes in various degrees, but most versions have their origin in plant ecological observations of the early twentieth century as botanists tried to describe and classify plant communities. Familiar vegetation of North America or Europe was subjectively easy to classify—oak woodland, beech-maple forest, prairie—all of them existing in familiar array for longer than the lifetime of an ecologist. Schemes of classification of these units of vegetation took the form of a new discipline called phytosociology, whose practitioners dominated ecology teaching for several decades. Eventually the near-legendary struggle between the individualist arguments of Gleason and the superorganism views of Clements was settled within the ecological profession in favor of the individualistic model (Whittaker 1956, 1969; Colinvaux 1973, 1978).

Since the late 1960s the ecology mainstream has abandoned the concept of the permanent plant community as being inconsistent with both data and the working of natural selection. The more metaphysical arguments of phytosociology gave birth instead to Tansley's (1935) mechanistic, and highly useful, concept of the ecosystem. But the metaphysical lure remains: apparently the idea that whole groups of unrelated species have a common destiny is as fascinating to the human mind as is astrology, but the fallacy has moved away from plant ecology and now mainly obstructs thought in the branches of geology that believe in the God Gaia. Except among paleoecologists—notably those who reconstruct predator-dominated communities such as coral reefs, but also including some palynologists tempted to reconstruct past vegetation in terms of modern plant communities.

Pollen analysis was invented early in the twentieth century as a stratigraphic tool that supplied both time-stratigraphic markers and gross indexes of climatic change for the European Holocene. The European pollen flora was simple, consisting of the wind-dispersed pollen of a few tree genera plus grass and weed pollen for the treeless regions. It was convenient for palynologists to interpret their pollen histories in terms of the plant associations that their phytosociological colleagues were describing: grass and weed pollen close to glaciers meant tundra, abundant pine or spruce pollen meant the boreal forest, oak pollen meant the deciduous forest associations of warmer times, and so on. Those early practices of palynology became standard procedures, so that some pollen diagrams continued to group pollen taxa as elements of this association or that, even as ecological theory buried the concept of the permanent association. And this is doubly strange, given that the most decisive evidence against the persistence of plant communities through time and space came from pollen data.

Margaret Davis and Tom Webb independently reviewed the history of the vegetation of eastern North America since the glacial retreat as depicted in pollen diagrams accumulated over the preceding 50 years (Davis 1986; Webb 1987). They found that none of the classic plant associations known from eastern North America could be traced back more than two or three thousand years. During marine isotope stage two time (MIS 2) and before, in the last glacial period, the trees of what are now the eastern forests lived in various southern places in various communities, but not in communities like those with which we associate them now. Afterward, with the glacial retreat, began the long, independent migrations, which had reached the present pattern of distribution and abundance shortly before the Yankee settlers arrived with their axes to cut the forest down. What look to us like ancient, settled communities of plants are ephemera on ecological time scales, mere temporary accommodations in ever-shifting alliance. Similar studies reveal parallel developments in Europe (Huntley and Webb 1988; Prentice, Bartlein, and Webb 1991).

It is a prudent working hypothesis that the same essential truths hold for the tropics as for the temperate regions, and that the fallacy of concrete communities is no less a fallacy in the Neotropics than in North America or Europe. We should not look to wholesale replacements of tropical plant communities in the Pleistocene, but rather to more subtle changes in community composition.

THE NEOTROPICAL POLLEN RECORD

Pollen analysts came late to the Neotropics, the Amazon in particular, partly due to the forbidding size of the pollen flora, or practical difficulties of working in tropical forests. More important, however, was the fact that the vast majority of Neotropical trees are pollinated by insects, birds, or bats, suggesting a pollen rain so incomplete as to make the pollen nearly useless (Faegri and van der Pilj 1979). Fortunately, we can now set this pessimistic idea aside. Pollen accumulation in Neotropical lake sediments turns out to be large, diverse, and informative. In the sediments of Amazon Lake Pata, for instance, mean pollen concentrations are in the 100,000–200,000 grains/ml range, which is comparable to the figure for Mirror Lake in New Hampshire (Colinvaux, De Oliveira et al. 1996; Davis, Moeller, and Ford 1984).

Tropical vegetation includes representatives of families, particularly grasses and herbs, that are both wind-pollinated and familiar to pollen analysts of temperate zones. Savannas, the typical grasslands of dry regions in the tropics, characteristically yield pollen rains with some 80% of the total pollen being windblown grasses and herbs, mostly grass. But these taxa, though present in the Amazon forest, contribute very little to the total Amazon pollen rain; at Lake Pata, in lowland Amazon forest, only 3% of the total pollen comes from grass and other wind-pollinated herbs (Colinvaux, De Oliveira et al. 1996). In lakes with floating grass mats or emergent aquatic grasses, the contribution of grass pollen can be higher due to local overrepresentation, a circumstance easily recognized from the pollen company the grass keeps.

To these globally present wind-pollinated taxa, the tropics add a few wind-pollinated taxa of their own. In Amazonia the most notable are many trees of the family Moraceae, particularly its colonizing genera such as *Cecropia.* Urticaceae and Euphorbiaceae are predominantly wind-pollinated also, and some forest habitats have tropical genera of the elm family, Ulmaceae, which retain that family's wind-pollinated trait. Some tropical families with tiny flowers, particularly Melastomataceae, produce pollen in comparable quantities, suggesting anemophily also. In Amazonian forests these anemophilous pollen taxa combined serve roughly the function that pollen clouds of tree pollen do in temperate forests: they are the principal ingredients of the regional pollen rain, wafted high in the air, drifting far and wide, finally to be washed out of the air into lakes or bogs by rain. In our pollen samples from Amazon rainforest lakes, these taxa together make up about half of the total pollen accumulation.

The other half of the take is the animal-dispersed pollen of rainforest trees. This pollen is highly diverse, with taxa often turning up as only one or two grains in total pollen counts of 300. In tackling the identity and significance of these taxa, pollen analysts encounter the real difficulties of the tropical record: What are they? How did they get there? What do they mean?

Satisfactory general answers to those questions took years of effort. The regional part of the pollen rain was mastered in the conventional way: unremitting collection of surface samples, core tops, surface mud from any impoundment, moss polsters (an unsatisfactory source in tropical forest), even soil pinches (more unsatisfactory still). These yielded mostly an understanding of regional pollen rains (Bush 1991). The three questions set by the diverse array of animal-dispersed (zoophilous) pollen taxa required a different approach: pollen trapping.

At Mark Bush's instigation, we set out "funnel" pollen traps in large arrays (up to an hundred) in places where intensive botanical surveys had been done, preferably in actual botanical plots. We left them out for at least a year, longer when possible, monitoring and changing filters every 6 months where practicable. The results were a wonderful aid to taxonomy, since the pollen had to be compared only to reference pollen from the known taxon list of the local forest patch or quadrat. Rapidly the unknowns in our pollen counts fell from greater than 40% to less than 5%, eventually enabling the compilation of an Amazon pollen manual (Colinvaux, De Oliveira, and Moreno 1999).

But the trapped pollen was more usefully informative even than this, for it revealed which taxa in the forest dropped measurable amounts of pollen on the forest floor, thus revealing the subset of the local flora that we might expect in a lake (we did not have to know the others, phew!). Further, the data demonstrated the limits to air transport for these pollen types: 25 m for most of them, with an extreme airborne range of 40 m for some. These findings essentially supplied the answers to the last two questions. The pollen, for the most part, "got there" over land, obviously in runoff water after it was dropped on the soil surface. What the pollen meant was that these taxa actually lived on the lake's catchment (watershed). Our understanding of Amazonian pollen assemblies is based on these data (Bush 1991, 2000; Bush and Rivera 1998; Bush et al. 2001).

The two parts of the Amazonian pollen record, the regional signal and the taxon list from the watershed, potentially make pollen analysis an even more useful tool than it has been in temperate lands. Answering questions such as, "were there biome replacements in the Pleistocene?" is easy (there were no biome replacements). That is because biome types such as savanna, caatinga, and tall lowland forest have starkly different regional pollen rains (80% grass in savanna; less grass, different herbs in caatinga; 3% grass and a characteristic anemophilous tree assemblage in the forest). In addition, it should be possible to use the taxon list from the watershed to plot community changes within stable biomes on ecological time scales.

A first use has been to test hypotheses of climate change. Climatic forcing of plant communities in the tropics over the course of a glacial cycle might be expected to work through temperature, precipitation, or the carbon dioxide (CO_2) concentration of the air. Pollen analysis in this role yields direct, though rough, measures of temperature or precipitation. In this way, the paleoecological data have been vital for reconstructing the environments of the ice age Amazon, and thus the vectors of diversity.

Yet to a card-carrying ecologist, this is a prostitution of pollen data. Better to infer the forcing from other evidence, then use the pollen data to reconstruct the response of plant communities to that forcing. This essay seeks to use pollen data, as far as possible, to infer community response rather than climatic forcing, though sometimes the pollen data allow both inferences with the minimum of circularity in the reasoning.

AIR STARVED OF CARBON DIOXIDE

Of the three most likely climatic changes of glacial times—temperature, precipitation, and CO_2—we know most certainly the changes in CO_2. Data from the Antarctic ice cores demonstrate that the global atmospheric CO_2 concentration in glacial times was generally only two-thirds of the concentration maintained throughout the Holocene: 0.02% by volume, as opposed to our 0.03% (Neftel et al. 1982; Sundquist and Broecker 1985). This is a profound difference, as CO_2 is the prime raw material of growth for all green plants.

The distribution and abundance of species populations cannot have been the same in a world with a CO_2 concentration only two-thirds of that with which we are familiar, but we are nowhere near being able to predict the changes in community composition that should have resulted. Speculation inevitably turns on the properties of the different enzymes used to fix CO_2 by C_4 and C_3 plants, because the PEP carboxylase used to absorb CO_2 through the stomata by C_4 and CAM (crassulacean acid metabolism) plants demonstrably can extract more

CO_2 at low concentrations than can the rubisco enzyme used for that purpose by the rest of the plant kingdom. The generality of plant species of lowland tropical forests, however, including all the trees, are C_3: they surely survived glacial episodes. In forests, therefore, the reshuffling of relative abundance derived from alternative photosynthetic pathways should have been expressed mostly through herbs or understory plants. If forest floor bromeliads such as *Ananas*, or opportunistically CAM shrubs such as *Clusia*, maintained larger populations on forest floors, the boundary conditions for competition among tree seedlings conceivably could have been altered sufficiently to have affected the relative abundance of canopy species.

It has also been suggested that forest-savanna ecotones might have been influenced (Street-Perrott et al. 1997). At an ecotone between tropical forest and savanna, the C_3 trees of a forest are immediately adjacent to the C_4 grasses of a savanna, letting in the hypothesis that the forest edge might retreat in low-CO_2 times. But can a photosynthetic pathway more suited to ambient CO_2 concentration give a grass the edge in competition with a tree? The forest-savanna boundary is known to be critically dependent on water, particularly on the effects of dry seasons and the savanna fires they make possible. Forests maintain their own moister microclimates. The boundary is typically in constant flux, depending on vagaries of the weather. That a superior photosynthetic pathway for the herbs on the dry side of the forest-savanna divide should be decisive in moving the boundary seems questionable.

More speculation about the effects of low CO_2, however, has been concerned with the plant communities of high altitudes, where the low atmospheric pressure might make the availability of CO_2 critical in glacial times. Because alpine trees are all C_3, might the tree line on high mountains have been depressed in glacial times not so much by glacial cold as by reduced CO_2? Two recent modeling exercises have suggested that this might be so (Jolly and Haxeltine 1997; Street-Perrott et al. 1997). These models are too recent for proper evaluation, but there are reasons to doubt the conclusion. The position of the tree line, as currently understood, is a function of temperature acting in two ways, by subjecting young leaves to freeze-drying (Tranquillini 1979) or by preventing the maintenance of a positive heat budget beyond some critical chill factor (Gates 1968). Postulating a carbon balance model invokes a fundamentally different mechanism for the establishment of tree lines. Paleoecological data for tree line depression (summarized under "cooling" below) are more parsimoniously explained as a response to reduced temperature than to reduced CO_2.

Suggestions that either forest-savanna boundaries or alpine tree lines should be sensitive to reduced CO_2 are in part related to the fallacy of permanent associations. Community boundaries are seen to be paramount, with the forcing that sets the position of those inviolate boundaries being allowed to change. That the first modeling efforts should be directed to tree lines almost certainly reflects the difficulty of accepting tree line depressions as evidence for glacial cooling while at same time accepting the CLIMAP inference of almost constant sea surface temperature (Rind and Peteet 1985). Models based on CO_2 concentration remove the apparent paradox of cool highlands over warm lowlands, albeit at some insult to the principles of uniformity and parsimony. With the more recent acceptance of tropical cooling by the paleooceanographic community and climate modelers, enthusiasm for CO_2-based explanations of Pleistocene tree line depressions is likely to wane.

The true effects of reduced CO_2 concentration in glacial times on the distribution and abundance of species in diverse tropical forests remain unknown. We must surely expect that taxa that have existed through many glacial cycles are not without adaptive responses to changed concentrations of CO_2. Without experimental data, the best we can say is that the effects on relative abundance, though present, were probably minor, since diversity remains great throughout the Amazon basin so soon after the last major change in CO_2 concentration.

COOLING OF AMAZON LOWLANDS

For two decades after the CLIMAP (1976) reconstruction of sea surface temperatures (SST) for the world oceans was first published, the prevailing paradigm was that the tropics cooled little, if at all, in times of global glaciation. The thermometer used by CLIMAP was assemblies of Foraminifera in deep-sea cores, calibrated against the presence of living Foraminifera in surface water masses of known temperature. According to these calculations, cooling of SST at high latitudes was generally large, in the range of 6°C–9°C, but cooling in equatorial latitudes was almost everywhere no more than 1°C–2°C. These estimates of glacial SST then became boundary conditions for climate models of the past, a use that tended to encourage widespread acceptance of the paradigm of minimal tropical cooling.

The concept of tropical lands without significant cooling in glacial times was always problematic for many glacial geologists and paleoecologists because of evidence that both tropical glaciers and tropical montane tree lines had descended on all continents. The idea of cold mountaintops poised over relatively warm oceans presented what Broecker and Denton (1989) were to call "an enigma for which they had no explanation."

The first direct evidence that the Amazon lowlands might have cooled significantly came from their western periphery, on the flank of the Ecuadorian Andes at a place called Mera. Mera is at 1,100 m elevation, just within the upper boundary of lowland tropical rainforest. Old lacustrine deposits, rich in both pollen and macrofossils, are exposed by a road cut. Radiocarbon dating of wood samples gave ages of close to 30,000 BP, an isotope stage 3 (MIS 3) of the last glaciation. Pollen analysis suggested large local populations of *Podocarpus* and other plants, comparable populations of which now occupy elevations many hundreds of meters higher in the Andes. Based on these data, we suggested cooling on the order of 4°C (Liu and Colinvaux 1985).

Kam-biu Liu had found the Mera sample site by inspired serendipity on a day when our field party was stranded at Mera by bad flying weather. A second site at San Juan Bosco (SJB), 160 km from Mera, was found by Mark Bush and Paulo De Oliveira after a prolonged search of the foothills of the Ecuadorian Andes. This exposure of old lacustrine deposits was in a face exposed by stream incision. Radiocarbon dates on wood spanned 26,000–30,000 BP. Pollen, phytolith, and macrofossil data again demonstrated significant populations of Andean plants at low elevations. Notable among the low-elevation populations, in addition to *Podocarpus,* were *Hedyosmum, Alnus,* Ericaceae, *Weinmannia,* and *Magnolia.* On the assumption of downslope migration from present centers of population, and using measured contemporary lapse rates, we calculated cooling on the order of 7°C (Bush et al. 1990).

We were subsequently able to demonstrate comparable low-elevation populations of what are now thought of as montane species at two sites between 7° and 8° N latitude in Panama (Bush and Colinvaux 1990; Bush et al. 1992). These Panama records were in well-dated, continuously deposited lake sediments. thus corroborating the dating of the SJB and Mera results, the dates of which suffered by being near the limit of beta-decay radiocarbon dating.

Southeast of the periphery of the Amazon basin, pollen evidence suggested a northward advance of stands of the temperature-sensitive tree *Araucaria angustifolium* on the order of 700 km, to place the edge of *Araucaria* woodland north of the Tropic of Capricorn (De Oliveira 1992; Ledru 1993), a range change that suggested cooling of at least 6°C. In the Amazon lowlands themselves, the appearance of significant percentages of pollen of *Podocarpus, Myrsine* (ex *Rapanea*), *Weinmannia,* and others at the last glacial maximum (LGM) of Lake Pata brought the pollen evidence of cooling, as it were, to the heartlands (Colinvaux, De Oliveira et al. 1996).

These conclusions of glacial cooling suffered, however, from the uncertainties of our pollen thermometers. Except for the *Araucaria* study, which was fortified by reliable data on the thermal tolerances of *Araucaria* (the trees need frost to break seed dormancy, for instance), our thermometers were decidedly crude. We had to assume that temperature was decisive in setting the altitudinal ranges of species populations for which we had essentially no physiological data.

It should be evident that this conclusion, to the extent that it relies on pollen, involves prostituting paleoecological data to infer climatic parameters in the way that I castigated in my introductory remarks. However, the cooling of the equatorial tropics in glacial times has now been established independently of the pollen data. Leyden et al. (1993) interpreted $\delta^{18}O$ data from Central American lakes as requiring cooling on the order of 8°C. Of more direct importance to evaluating the Amazon botanical data was the study of fossil groundwater in northeastern Brazil by Stute et al. (1995), who used ratios of noble gases in solution as their thermometer to show cooling in the range of 5°C during MIS 2, a conclusion in striking agreement with our general interpretation of the paleobotanical data (Colinvaux, Liu et al. 1996).

Since then, the CLIMAP descriptions of glacial SSTs at low latitudes have been significantly revised by the use of chemical thermometers on paleooceanographic data in place of relative abundances of Foraminifera. First to appear was the study by Guilderson, Fairbanks, and Rubenstone (1994) of fossil Barbados coral reefs, using $\delta^{18}O$ and strontium/calcium ratios to infer local depression of SST on the order of 4°C in glacial times. Later, the development of magnesium/calcium ratios as paleothermometers are leading to some revisionism of the CLIMAP measures of tropical SST, suggesting differential cooling of tropical SSTs in glacial periods, both in time and space (Curry and Oppo 1997; Bard 2001). At the same time, new climate models began to include cooling of the tropics among their results (Webb et al. 1997; Ganopolski et al. 1998).

These developments have now led to a climate of opinion in which modest cooling of low latitudes is a respectable assumption. It is, for instance, no longer necessary to explain away the large descents of low-latitude montane glaciers by manipulation of lapse rates or water budget scenarios for glacial advance, as was briefly the fashion. Another example is the surprise report of a rise in *Podocarpus* in the Carajas, Amazon pollen record, previously published with *Podocarpus* omitted from both data and mention (possibly on the assumption that it was a windblown contaminant) (Absy et al. 1991). The new paper admits *Podocarpus* pollen to the Carajas record, correlates it with the record at Lake Pata, and interprets it, together with *Myrsine* (ex *Rapanea*), as evidence for cooling (Ledru et al. 2001).

To an evolutionary ecologist, however, it is more productive to concede cooling as an established physical condition and to use the pollen of *Podocarpus*,

Myrsine, and others as evidence of forest changes in response to the forcing of glacial climates, of which cooling was a major vector.

THE EFFECT OF COOLING ON DIVERSE LOWLAND AMAZON FOREST COMMUNITIES

The most complete pollen record of lowland Amazon forest is from the Hill of Six Lakes (Serra dos Seis Lagos), a low inselberg near zero latitude in the west central lowlands of Amazonia. The combined pollen record from three closed-basin lakes on the inselberg provides an unbroken history of forest back through MIS 6, which is to say two complete glacial cycles (as dated by an internal record of Milankovitch forcing: Bush et al. 2002). A rich array of pollen types in the sediments was resolved into more than 400 pollen taxa at generic or family rank, accounting for more than 95% of all pollen types encountered, with more than 100 taxa counted at each level (Colinvaux, De Oliveira, and Moreno 1999). The most detailed pollen analysis is from the last 40,000 years of radiocarbon time at Lake Pata (Colinvaux, De Oliveira et al. 1996). This has now been supplemented by continuation of the Pata record through MIS 6 (160,000–170,000 BP) and by parallel records from the other two lakes, Verde and Dragão (Bush et al., forthcoming).

The Lake Pata record of MIS 2 (including the LGM) is comparable to the glacial record in all three lakes in both glacial periods. The overriding pollen signature in each is of forest stability, the species assembly of the Holocene remaining throughout glacial episodes with only minor changes in relative importance. Diversity of pollen types remains high throughout, spectacularly so by the standards of temperate-zone pollen analysis. There was never an incursion of herb taxa, or significant change in herb and forest ratios that might suggest biome changes, such as wholesale replacement of forest type. This history is one of forest continuity through glacial and interglacial periods alike; it is the continuous history of a single biome.

Yet there is that one qualification to this history of community stability: the appearance or prominence of *Podocarpus* and *Myrsine* (ex *Rapanea*) in glacial times only, in all three lake cores, in both glacial periods. These two taxa were sometimes accompanied as intruders by *Weinmannia, Alnus, Hedyosmum, Humiria, Eugenia,* or Ericaceae, the exact assemblage being site-specific. Even in aggregate, the total pollen percentage of these taxa is small, in the range of 5%–10%. They represent a small pollen incursion into what is basically a stable pollen matrix. They do not discredit or diminish the conclusion of no biome change. What they do supply is evidence for community adjustments resulting from the secular climatic change of glacial episodes.

Collectively, these taxa are associated in the minds of modern botanists with higher elevations, and by inference, with cooler temperatures. But a few are plants known to be present, though rare, in the modern Amazon lowlands. This is particularly true of one species of *Podocarpus, P. lambertii.* I was made vividly aware of this fact after the first publication of the Mera results in 1985 by a letter from Alwyn Gentry, saying that "*Podocarpus* is very definitely *not* restricted to the high altitude Andes, as you suggest. I have collected *Podocarpus* at 140 m altitude on white sands near Iquitos." There was more, but those two sentences give the gist of the correction.

Gentry's experience has been shared by many botanists of the Neotropics: *Podocarpus* can be found even down to sea level, though usually in places like the white sands near Iquitos. So, certainly, can *Hedyosmum.* No one, to my knowledge, has found *Weinmannia* except at high elevations, but I have myself seen *Alnus* trees 10 m tall lining a Panamanian stream at 900 m, close to the elevation of the Ecuadorian fossil sites (Mera and SJB). Altitude, and hence temperature, therefore, is not an absolute criterion setting distribution limits to these pollen taxa.

The critical statistic, however, is that none of these intruding taxa of glacial times are common enough in modern Amazon forests for significant representation in the modern pollen rain. Most, including *Podocarpus,* are never present in surface (or Holocene) samples at all (Bush and Rivera 1998; Bush 2000). The pollen data thus show that in glacial periods, populations of these plants in the Amazon lowlands expanded from trivial or nonexistent to be of sufficient density for their pollen to become statistically visible. First seen at Mera, then expanded with the finds on the Hill of Six Lakes and confirmed at Carajas, in lake sediments on the east-central inselberg of Maicuru, and elsewhere, a similar response is now known from throughout the Amazon lowlands (Colinvaux et al. 2001; Bush et al., forthcoming).

The parsimonious explanation of these population expansions is that the rare became common as scattered populations of rare individuals confined in interglacial times to particularly favored habitats were able to compete on more reasonable terms with other species in the highly diverse forests of Amazonia in the changed ambience of glacial times. In this event, no actual invasion downslope is required, and the pollen data are explained by population dynamics within the forest.

Paulo De Oliveira and Mark Bush, however, have reexamined the *Podocarpus* pollen in the Hill of Six Lakes records, finding that they can identify many

Podocarpus pollen grains to species rank (Bush et al., forthcoming). Some of the fossil pollen grains belong to *Podocarpus* species that really are limited in modern times to high elevations, locally to the upper reaches of a mountain some 200 km away. It seems inescapable that populations of these species did indeed expand "downslope" to become part of the lowland forest of glacial times. This finding makes it plausible that taxa such as *Weinmannia* and *Alnus* in the lowland forest represent populations that had also expanded "downslope" to suitable habitats.

Whether the parents of these lowland populations of "montane" species were forest rarities or immigrants from on high is probably irrelevant. The essential observation is that the one measurable change in lowland forest communities that we know about is a modest increase in the populations of these taxa within an unchanging forest biome. That, and no more, is what the pollen record shows.

The ecological inference is clear: the modest cooling of glacial times was within the tolerance of the plants of the highly diverse flora that we know from modern tropical lowland forest, so that the forest species are able to persist throughout glacial cycles. But the warming of an interglacial like the present, although still within the tolerance of most of the forest flora, was intolerable to a small subset of species that can now maintain viable populations only outside the lowland forest at high elevations or where particularly favored by local circumstance (perhaps the white sands near Iquitos). These elements of the modern montane forest are best thought of as refugees from the interglacial warming of the lowlands.

WAS THE AMAZON EVER ARID?

For more than three decades, biogeographers and paleoclimatologists have taken as a working hypothesis that the Neotropics were much drier, or even actually arid, at the time of the last glaciation. One recent manifestation of this belief is a reconstruction of forest history that sees much of the lowlands occupied by dry woodland or caatinga in glacial times (Pennington, Prado, and Pendry 2000). More extreme is the celebrated "refuge hypothesis" of Jurgen Haffer, who postulates lowland forest replaced by savanna, with forest confined to patches in elevated spots with orographic rainfall (Haffer 1969, 1974). And a modern geologic treatise sees the Amazon basin lowlands as truly arid, with the Amazon River carrying water from the Andes to the Atlantic Ocean through a great gorge (Clapperton 1993). All these models or speculations imply massive extinctions, invasions, and replacements—true biome changes not evident in the pollen record.

The hypothesis of Amazonian aridity was inspired by early reports of glacial aridity in East Africa—reports based on hard evidence of drying lakes and falling water levels, well dated to the last glacial period by radiocarbon (Livingstone 1975; Street and Grove 1979). If East Africa, then why not the Amazon? Were the East African data the whole story, the answer to "Why not the Amazon?" should have been short and decisive. East Africa has a monsoonal climate and an elevated land surface on a continent that has its mountains flanking the east side. Amazonia is an immense lowland close to sea level, on the east side of a continent that has its mountains in the west. Amazonia has a much wetter climate, with the high basic precipitation enhanced by recycling of water in the transpiration streams of lowland forests, and with short or minimal dry seasons. The comparison with Africa should have collapsed at once.

It lingered because of serial misinterpretation of soil and landform data that were extremely few, or even anecdotal, coming from a vast, little-known wilderness. Dissected land surface under the trees, buried stone lines, sand dunes or heaps of sand at the periphery, dunes in the celebrated white sands of the interior, aragonite or gypsum chunks in old river deposits, arcosic sands in the Amazon fan, and sorted fine-grained deposits on floodplains all were interpreted (wrongly) as being relics of an episode of aridity in the distant past, for which the ice age was inevitably the candidate time.

The provenance of all these claims has been comprehensively investigated by a team charged by the journal *Amazoniana* to review the paleoecological data underlying controversial reconstructions of the ice age Amazon, critical analyses of the geologic claims being by Georg Irion of the Senckenberg Institute in Germany and Matti Räsänen of Turku University in Finland. The details, together with reviews of the relevant literature, are given in the published results (Colinvaux et al. 2001). What follows is a brief summary.

Most catchy have been the twin observations of a dissected land surface under the central Amazon forest and buried stone lines in those same soils. These bear a superficial similarity to gullied soils of semiarid places like Arizona, with the stone lines likened to the stone pavements left behind when fine particles are removed by wind. The superficial became reality to those without experience of tropical soils on other continents, where these phenomena had long been known as the products of prolonged humid weathering under tropical forest cover.

Accurate, though widely ignored, interpretations of these phenomena have long been available (Irion 1978; Irion et al. 1995). Immensely deep weathering of the lateritic soils, the particular clay minerals remaining, the imprints of the soil profiles on different regoliths, even the steep dissection itself, are all known characteristics of ancient and continuous weathering under warm humid environments. The stone lines are concretionary layers deep within lateritic soil profiles, again well known as properties of soils of the humid tropics on other continents. Far from being evidence of past aridity or savanna climates, these phenomena demonstrate that the land has been subjected to uninterrupted humid weathering under an intact forest canopy for a span of years probably measured in the millions.

A quote from an unsolicited letter from a geographer commenting on the *Amazoniana* paper describes succinctly the scale of error involved in linking these phenomena to aridity: "having seen so many lateritic soils, stone lines and concretion lines in Africa (I worked in Uganda for 14 years as a forester before I became an academic geographer), I find it almost incredible that similar soil horizons could have been so persistently misinterpreted in S. America" (Henry Osmaston, Bristol University, personal communication).

On fossil sand dunes, the errors in misinterpretation have been both various and different. The undoubted dune fields of northeastern Brazil, called "little Sahara" in the vernacular, were merely wrongly assigned to the glacial period; radiocarbon dating has now shown that they were active until at least the late Holocene (De Oliveira, Barreto, and Suguio 1999).

The huge fossil dune fields reported in central Brazil at the periphery of the Amazon basin appeared from the published accounts to be known only from remote sensing data, being not only without radiometric dating but with no ground truth that we could discover. Georg Irion went with J. Nunes de Mello to examine the reported dunes on the ground, finding only the sandbanks of old river systems. The great fossil dune fields of central Brazil do not exist; they are a chimera of misinterpretation of early remote sensing data.

Dunes do exist, however, on the white sands in central parts of the Amazon lowlands. The ground-truth team found that some are still active. They are not, therefore, fossil relics of Pleistocene aridity. Rather, they are a feature, probably permanent, of these huge Cretaceous sand deposits, with their edaphically constrained, fire-prone vegetation. As such, they are an illustration, comparable to the classic dunes on the south shore of Lake Michigan, of the well-known fact that thick sand deposits get blown about, particularly when disturbance breaks the frail edaphic vegetation cover.

The aragonite and gypsum chunks dug out of riverbanks are of Miocene age, relics associated with the retreat of the mid-Tertiary marine incursion, but wrongly dated by association with young debris in riverine mud or trace contamination by modern carbon (Räsänen et al. 1995). Arcosic sands in the fan deposits are of Andean origin, transported to the Pleistocene ocean in rivers downcutting their channels in response to the lowered sea level. Thus, the "geologic evidence" used to support the extrapolation of aridity has, without exception, resulted from mistakes made when data were few and the land remote. In many instances, however, mistaken inference would not have been possible without a climate of opinion that expected to find evidence for aridity; data were fitted to hypothesis.

Dispassionate interpretation of the geologic data strongly argues that the Amazon lowlands have never been arid, or even semiarid, since at least Miocene times (Colinvaux et al. 2001).

MILANKOVITCH OVER THE AMAZON: EVIDENCE OF LAKE LEVELS

Water levels in closed-basin lakes fell, apparently in synchrony, over a huge area of the Amazon basin. The first critical report was from a small pseudokarst lake on the Carajas plateau of southeastern Amazonia, where changes in gross core stratigraphy were shown by mineral analysis to represent very shallow water, fluctuating water levels, or actual drying with marsh formation. Radiocarbon dating assigned low water to glacial times (Soubies, Suguio, and Martin 1991). Soon various reports of low lake levels estimated by radiocarbon dating to be of glacial age were collected to show that the phenomenon was widespread across the Amazon basin and beyond (Ledru et al. 1998). At last, dated evidence for reduced precipitation in glacial times!

But this was not the long-coveted record of aridity. It was something at once more modest and far more interesting. The lessened precipitation implied turned out to be minor, well within the tolerance of the forest biome. Whether it was sufficient to drain a closed-basin lake depended on the properties of the lake basin itself. Of far more importance, it was the first hint of what would be shown to be a direct signal for Milankovitch forcing in the Amazon lowlands. The long record of fluctuating water levels from three of the lakes on the Hill of Six Lakes demonstrates what happened.

Measurements by Michael Miller of total sedimentary potassium and sodium at 10 cm intervals in the Lake Pata cores produced a surprising result: potassium fluctuated through wide amplitudes with regularity suggestive of true rhythm, whereas sodium remained almost constant throughout the sediment body. Usually these two monovalent ions are eroded, and move, in parallel, but at Pata, potassium was periodically enriched by a process that ignored sodium. The inevitably preferred hypothesis was biological enrichment.

Lake Pata, like most pseudokarst lakes, is strongly oligotrophic; it is a blackwater system with poor light penetration, low redox potential at the sediment surface, low nutrients, and low pH. Only when they are so shallow that light and oxygen reach the bottom can these systems support algal blooms. Each of the potassium-rich layers in the Pata sediments had massive concentrations of algal (*Scenedesmus*) fossils, explaining the potassium enrichment as the result of algal concentration at a time of shallow water. The presence of nodular clays rich in siderite confirm that the potassium-rich layers represent times of low water with high algal productivity and intermittent oxidation of the mud surface.

Mark Bush compared the apparent periodicity of the potassium maxima with Milankovitch insolation departure curves calculated for zero degrees latitude. The Pata chronology was directly established by AMS (accelerator mass spectrometry) radiocarbon dates for the last fifty thousand years, then extrapolated assuming constant sedimentation rates for the remainder of the cores. A very good match to the precession component of the forcing for June-July-August (JJA) was obtained (Bush et al. 2002). This correlation shows that the cores span about 170,000 years, or two complete glacial cycles, beginning at MIS 6–7. Precipitation, therefore, tracks the modest insolation changes associated with the 22,000-year precession cycle, within glacial time as well as with the glacial-interglacial rhythm.

The lake level effect is not a simple function of changes in the precipitation/evaporation ratio. Like the Carajas lake, the three lakes from the Hill of Six Lakes are pseudokarst lakes on inselbergs, all occupying solution basins that leak. Like those of the eponymous karst lakes of limestone formations, these solution basins in silicate rocks can be connected to underlying water tables through solution channels. The level of one of our three lakes, Dragão, fell more than a meter in the 10 days that we camped on its rim, and Brazilian survey parties have found it to be totally without water in other years. Shoreline features show less violent fluctuations in Pata, and less still in our third lake, Verde. Not surprisingly, the most extreme record of prolonged low water or drying is from Dragão, whereas deep Lake Verde showed little fluctuation in potassium/sodium ratios (Bush et al. 2004). The three lakes lie within a few hundred meters of each other. Clearly their leak rates are different, suggesting that relative leak rate is more important to water level in these lakes than is evaporation. Water level is maintained in these lakes, when it is maintained, only because precipitation balances leakage.

Low water levels correlated with insolation departures associated with precessional forcing, therefore, represent failures of precipitation to balance leakage. Whether this matters to the lake ecosystem depends on the properties of the individual lake, particularly its leak rate, but also its water volume. In all lakes, the greatest lowering should be in the dry season, when all pseudokarst lakes lose water; hence the JJA correlation with the precession signal.

Pollen data from all three lakes show continuous forest cover independent of lake state. The record is particularly clear at Lake Pata, where the intermediate leak rate provided a sedimentary record uninterrupted by gaps representing sediment lost through oxidation. Pollen is preserved at Pata continuously through the Milankovitch cycles, even in the time of most greatly reduced precipitation 22,000 to 32,000 calendar years ago. The pollen is unequivocal in showing that forest persisted, unaltered except for the expansion of some cool-adapted taxa, as already noted. Reductions in rains, therefore, were minor, with remaining precipitation ample to maintain the lowland rainforest biome.

The logic of this conclusion applies also to the Carajas history. The shallow Carajas lake obviously has a high leak rate, since most of its glacial history was marshlike or dry. The Carajas pollen assemblage is unique. It clearly signals the peculiar wet "altitude" savanna, not forest, that has surrounded the lake throughout its history—a vegetation type dependent both on the relatively high altitude (700 m) and the edaphic constraints of the ironstone formation of the Carajas inselberg. The incomplete published pollen diagram (the same one that failed to include the observed influx of *Podocarpus* in glacial times) lists only thirteen pollen taxa, all common in the surrounding wet savanna vegetation. But there is a percentage increase in grass and shoreline herbs in glacial times. This grass increase has been the prime datum for those claiming pollen evidence for savanna, with the reasoning that the extra grass pollen must have blown up from true savannas expected by the refuge hypothesis to have replaced the lowland forests in the bottom lands (Absy et al. 1991; Van der Hammen and Absy 1994). The much more parsimonious, and frankly obvious, explanation for the modest grass and herb rise is local overrepresentation of herbs growing on the drained lakebed and encroaching shorelines (Colinvaux, De Oliveira, and Bush 2000).

The measurable effects of Milankovitch forcing on Amazonian biomes have thus been uninterestingly small. Precipitation was affected, but only marginally, detected only by the sensitive indicators of closed-basin lakes that leak. The periodicity of precipitation reduction is that of the 22,000-year precession cycle, not the glacial to interglacial cycle. Any effect of changed precipitation on diversity in the lowland forests was too small to be measured by present paleoecological means. Temperature fluctuations have been larger, with measurable effects on species composition within the established forest biome and being expressed with glacial to interglacial periodicity, not just with the shorter precession component of the Milankovitch cycle.

The overriding conclusion from the paleoecological data from lake sediments is that there was no biome replacement in the Amazon lowlands due to Milankovitch forcing at any time in the last two glacial cycles covered by the record.

POLLEN HISTORY OF THE AMAZONIAN LOWLANDS

All the pollen data available from the Amazon basin are, without exception, consistent with the conclusion from geomorphology of no biome changes. The forest occupied its great hinterland through all the secular climatic changes of the Pleistocene. Only at the forest periphery, near ecotones in flux between biomes, can vegetation changes on biome scales be detected. Whether a pollen diagram suggests biome change, as some have, depends on whether the site is close to the peripheral ecotones (change likely) or from within the great forested lowlands themselves (no change).

Only three long pollen histories of the forested interior are available. Two are from the sediments of pseudokarst lakes, one west (the Hill of Six Lakes inselberg), one east (the Maicuru inselberg). The third is from sediments of the Amazon river system accumulated at the mouth of the Amazon, either on the continental shelf or in the Amazon fan. The remaining long history of the interior, from the Carajas inselberg, is in edaphically constrained, altitudinal savanna land that was never covered with closed-canopy forest.

The records from the Hill of Six Lakes, at 0°16′ N, 66°41′ W, are described above; the three lakes sampled together provide a rich and detailed history of forest, in both glacials and interglacials, over two complete glacial cycles. Combining the three records leaves no gaps. Forest spectra from each of the three lakes show slight differences, reflecting the different habitat properties of the three different watersheds. The resolution of these subtle differences is possible only because a significant proportion of the pollen sum is made up of pollen of zoophilous trees that does not become airborne, but works its way into lakes through movements of surface water, thus recording the presence of trees actually growing in the immediate watershed. Sediments from glacial intervals at each lake reveal an influx of taxa favored by cooling into otherwise stable communities (Colinvaux, De Oliveira et al. 1996; Colinvaux, De Oliveira, and Moreno 1999; Bush et al. 2002, 2004).

The Maicuru inselberg, at 0°30′ S, 54°15′ W, is physically similar to the Hill of Six Lakes, though the sampled lake, at 500 m, is 200 m higher in elevation. It provides a comparable forest history from the eastern Amazon lowlands. Unlike Carajas (also in the eastern Amazon, at 6°20′ S, 50°25′ W and 700 m high), the less elevated Maicuru watershed holds tall lowland forest, with trees up to 2 m DBH growing on one half of the watershed and an edaphically constrained but dense scrub forest (*Clusia, Psidium, Miconia,* etc.) on the rocky surface of the rest. The pseudokarst Maicuru lake differs from the three on the Hill of Six Lakes in having extensive shallows with dense stands of emergent aquatic grasses.

The richly diverse forest pollen signal at Maicuru is comparable to that at Lake Pata, more than a thousand miles to the west, although with its own local watershed stamp, particularly some 5% *Clusia* pollen from the edaphic forest component. The presence of emergent aquatic grasses is recorded by grass pollen fluctuating around the 10% range in all samples back to 15,000 BP (radiocarbon years). Interestingly, grass pollen is back to the familiar trace in samples earlier than 30,000 BP and back through the more than 40,000 years of the record, though the diverse assemblage of forest pollen persists. Experience with the Hill of Six Lakes suggests that this reduction of grass pollen in the early (MIS 3–4) samples is a signal of changes in lake level and hence in the population of emergent aquatic grasses; alternatively, the later grass expansion could record a local colonization event unrelated to climate change.

Close-interval AMS dating demonstrates an interval of no sediment accumulation correlating with the latest (MIS 2) interval of low sedimentation at Lake Pata due to a time of low water and oxidation of organic sediment. At Maicuru this process was particularly devastating because the sediment is virtually without mineral components. Oxic conditions at this period resulted in a completely closed carbon cycle and hence no accumulation of organic sediment, a condition that we have frequently encountered in very shallow modern lakes. The forest pollen signal is unaltered on either side of this gap, which could not have been discovered without the dating of adjacent samples. As elsewhere in Amazonia, pollen of *Podocarpus* is detectable only in samples of glacial age (close to the gap). A pollen percentage diagram is given by Colinvaux et al. (2001); complete pollen data are being prepared for publication by Paulo De Oliveira and Jason Curtis. Like the Hill of Six Lakes pollen records, the Maicuru record reveals a history of strong biome stability, subtle community reshuffling to accommodate Pleistocene cooling without biome change, and forests essentially immune to the modest precipitation changes measured by the levels of lakes that leak.

The third long record of forest pollen, from the deposits of the great river system, gives generality and areal spread to the Pleistocene forest reconstruction. This is because by far the largest part of the Amazon basin is drained by streams that anastomose into the single outlet of the Amazon River. Except for small areas of internal drainage, the rivers and streams of the Amazon river system collect runoff water from every watershed in the huge basin. Streams and rivers everywhere receive their share of the regional portion of the pollen rain, which is blown by wind from miles around, then washed down in rainstorms to the water or land surface below. The pollen rain that falls directly on the water surface becomes part of the sediment load of rivers as they blend gradually into one giant river on their way to the distant ocean.

Not all the pollen in rivers should come from the pollen rain, as some will be contributed in runoff. To some limited extent, the runoff component should be skewed toward stream bank communities, because poorly dispersed zoophilous pollen from inland communities might be filtered out during its passage over the land surface. That this effect is both real and strictly limited is the experience of pollen analysts of estuarine deposits in other river systems. The large pollen rain component could not be masked, particularly if it were to come from vegetation dominated by anemophilous plants such as grasses.

For the purpose of testing hypotheses of biome change in the Amazon basin as a whole, the river-borne pollen record should be ideal. The theoretically possible biome changes all involve increases in the proportion of regional (windblown) pollen. Pollen from a tropical savanna, for instance, is known from surface sampling and fossil histories to be on the order of 80% grass (Gramineae/Poaceae) pollen, with much of the remaining 20% also windblown (Ferraz-Vicentini and Salgado-Labouriau 1996). Pollen from caatinga is also heavily skewed toward grass and other windblown pollen. Were any biome other than lowland forest to occupy significant portions of the Amazon lowlands, therefore, it should leave an unequivocal pollen signal in deposits at the river mouth.

In interglacial times like the present, the massive sediment load of the Amazon is mostly dumped on the broad continental shelf. In glacial times of low sea level, however, the bulk of the sediment load is carried in turbidity currents through canyons across the shelf to fall into the deep sea, here 4,000 m deep, where deposits have collected as the Amazon fan. The international Ocean Drilling Program (ODP) raised long cores from the fan. Together with cores from the continental shelf, these allowed the reconstruction of a continuous record of the sediment load of the Amazon River for the last two glacial cycles and beyond (Flood et al. 1997).

Simon Haberle undertook the pollen analysis of core samples spanning two glacial cycles, working in the laboratory with Paulo De Oliveira and Enrique

Moreno while they were refining pollen taxonomy for our Amazon atlas to ensure comparability of results. Haberle also made his own surface samples, boating down the Amazon to collect buckets of water from which to filter the sediment load. Also available was our collection of sediments from mudflats in the central Amazon. Haberle's analysis counted eighty-three pollen taxa, not including cryptogam spores and ancient pollen types reworked from sedimentary rocks. The pollen spectra included a signal for shoreline communities, as expected; pollen from the true mangrove *Rhizophora*, for instance, did not come from interior forests. Grass pollen in the 15% range was present alike in surface samples, in our cores of the last 3,000 years from a river diverticulum, in postglacial sediments from the shelf, and in glacial period sediments from the fan. This grass pollen, being present in the modern system, could only have come from the extensive grass meadows on mudflats, seasonal várzea lakes, floating mats, and shoreline communities generally of the riverine system itself.

But the bulk of the pollen, and most of the pollen diversity, is of the familiar assemblage of the lowland tropical forest. This is true for the whole reconstructed sedimentary sequence for the last two complete glacial cycles. Not only does this analysis show an uninterrupted history of diverse tropical lowland forest, but it even shows the now familiar events of glacial cooling, with the modest appearance of *Podocarpus* and other cool-adapted taxa synchronously with their invasions of the Hill of Six Lakes, Maicuru, Carajas, and the Andean foothills at Mera and SJB (Haberle 1997; Haberle and Maslin 1999).

As a test of hypotheses of biome changes, pollen from these river deposits is even more potent than a bald conclusion of a forest history implies. The vital datum is that at no time in the last two glacial cycles was there more grass pollen coming down the Amazon River than is present in either the modern or Holocene deposits of the river. This result should be impossible if a significant part of the Amazon basin had ever been given over to savanna or caatinga, with their suppression of the zoophilous pollen component of lowland forests and their immense signals of grass pollen dominating regional pollen rains. Pollen clouds from the interior are not filtered through stands of trees along riverbanks; they blow over the trees until falling rain washes them out. Suggestions sometimes made (e.g., Haffer and Prance 2001; Hooghiemstra and van der Hammen 1998) that the fan pollen record can be discounted as merely a riverbank record should be seen as absurd.

The savanna and caatinga hypotheses are also disqualified by measures of carbon isotope ratios in fan deposits (Kastner and Goñi 2003). These measures show that there has not been a proportional increase in plants using C_4 photosynthesis (tropical grasses) over those using C_3 photosynthesis (all forest trees, etc.) at any time in the last glacial cycle, in any of the landscapes drained by the Amazon river system. From this observation, Kastner and Goñi conclude that the forest was never replaced by tropical grasslands of any sort, thus confirming the stability of forest cover deduced from the pollen data.

The dynamic stability of Amazon vegetation as a whole is confirmed by the pollen history from the nonforest site at Carajas. Located as it is in edaphically constrained vegetation, variously called wet savanna, altitudinal savanna, or campo rupestre, the Carajas pollen diagram shows how an Amazonian community within the basin but outside the predominant forest responded to Milankovitch forcing (demonstrated by Bush et al. 2002). With the fluctuations in grass and herb pollen coincident with changes in water level seen for what they are—pollen overrepresentation of the waxing and waning of marsh flat communities around the lake—the remaining Carajas pollen describes the persistence of the altitudinal savanna community (Colinvaux et al. 2001). Yet even at Carajas the expansion of cool-adapted populations in response to glacial cooling can be detected as *Podocarpus* and *Myrsine* pollen become significant in the pollen sum (Colinvaux et al. 2001).

Thus, all paleoecological data yet available to us from deep within the Amazon basin describe vegetation that has persisted, in situ, through glacials and interglacials alike, for at least two complete glacial cycles. This is true from forested bottom lands through a nonforest community high on an inselberg to the forested foothills of the Andes. The implied community stability is dynamic, able to respond to glacial cooling by accommodating populations of more stenothermic species without basic alterations in community structure.

A prime test of biome stability is, "what happens at the boundaries?" A biome, as originally conceived by Shelford and Clements, has its boundaries set by the underlying plant formation. These formations were described long ago by de Candolle, refined by Schimper, and used by Koeppen to establish the basic modern climate maps (Colinvaux 1973). Biomes so defined have boundaries set by the meetings of air masses. These boundaries are as fluid as the air masses themselves, moving with the mean positions of air mass fronts, but with inertias that are functions of tree lifetimes and dispersal rates. With secular climate change, there should be movements of biome boundaries that could be detected by pollen analysis.

Detected they have been. Indeed, many pollen studies of ice age Amazonia purporting to describe the ice age Amazon actually describe movements at the boundaries, nowadays called ecotones. By an ugly chance, the first ancient samples from Amazonia given to a pollen analyst came from close to an ecotone. The pollen suggested savanna, the atlas suggested forest, the conclusion ought to have been, "here is the moving ecotone," but the conclusion, as published, can be paraphrased as, "this is the replacement of lowland forest by dry savanna as predicted by the refuge hypothesis" (Absy and van der Hammen 1976).

The genesis of that earliest analysis was a series of drill cores of valley fill from Katira, Rondônia, collected by a geologist. Five samples were sent to pollen analysts, who had apparently not seen the site. All five spectra are dominated by grass pollen, except that the bottom sample has about 45% of pollen of the marsh palm *Mauritia*. In aggregate, the drill cores represent a 13 m accumulation of colluvium. Two radiocarbon dates at 7 m and 13 m are in the 40,000–50,000 BP range. The pollen spectra are grass-dominated, with essentially no tree taxa suggestive of closed-canopy forest. The sample with *Mauritia* was originally mistaken for forest, but can now be seen to represent a marshy area in savanna (Ferraz-Vicentini and Salgado-Labouriau 1996; Colinvaux et al. 2001). Although no surface samples or vegetation maps are available for the site, the geographic location puts it close to, perhaps 100 km from, the modern forest-savanna ecotone at the biome boundary. Scanty though the data are, they are good evidence that the boundary shifted at some time in the last glacial cycle, as should be expected at the borders of a biome, but that is all they show.

Sadly, the Katira data are still cited as evidence for biome replacement across Amazonia. The unjustified inference that they signaled the replacement of Amazon forests with savanna contributed heavily to the mistaken interpretation of the Carajas data and lingers on in interpretations of pollen diagrams and in review writings (Van der Hammen and Absy 1994; van der Hammen and Hooghiemstra 2000).

Movement of the ecotone in southwestern Amazonia, showing a local advance of the savanna, has now been confirmed by pollen in lake sediments from northern Bolivia (Mayle, Burbridge, and Killeen 2000). These data suggest that the forest has been advancing into the local savanna throughout much of the Holocene, with the forest edge reaching its present position only three or four thousand years ago. Like many an ecotone, the one in Bolivia is a mosaic of vegetation patterns, rather than a continuous line. The local geography is complex, and the sedimentary sequence, although containing older sediments, is not continuous before 10,000 BP. Because of this, it is not yet possible to deduce the mean distance moved by the ecotone, but it seems unlikely to have been more than a few tens of kilometers.

Thus, these data from ecotones show that plant formation (biome) boundaries moved on Pleistocene time scales, as they should. These ecotones are also air mass boundaries whose movements were inevitably driven by global secular events, perhaps not least as a sort of domino effect of the presence of Northern

Hemisphere ice sheets. What is striking, however, is that the boundaries did not move very far. The climate, environment, and vegetation of the vast Amazon basin was largely unchanged by the advent of northern ice sheets.

PALEOECOLOGICAL SUMMARY: THE MUTED PLEISTOCENE VECTOR

The outline of possible environmental limits in Amazonia is now clear, as are the limits to vegetation and community responses. The history of the Pleistocene Amazon is one of stability—dynamic stability, certainly, but still stability. There never was fragmentation of the forest into refugia; there never was a conversion of the lowlands to savanna or caatinga; there never was significant aridity. In ecological language, there never was replacement of biomes.

The actual changes in climate, environment, or community, though present, were far more muted. None were of a scale to suggest early vicariance opportunities not present in contemporary Amazonia. That said, changes in all three Pleistocene atmospheric variants—temperature, water budgets, and CO_2—can be detected or inferred.

Water budgets were marginally altered as a function of solar insolation changes driven by the precession parameter of Milankovitch forcing. This was so mild an environmental change that it is recognized only in the enhanced dry-season lowering of levels in pseudokarst lakes whose leaking basins have always lost water in dry seasons throughout their long histories. No measurable effects of changed water budgets on regional vegetation cover can be detected in the pollen record.

Measurable, but not extreme, cooling was certainly associated with times of global glaciation, though we do not yet have a detailed chronology for cooling comparable to that for changes in the water budget. Since it is temperature that is most directly influenced by the insolation changes of Milankovitch forcing, and because the effects of precession are most pronounced at low latitudes, it is tempting to suggest that cooling cycles should be synchronized with reduced water budget cycles. But this would be arguing ahead of the data. It is perhaps more likely that mean annual temperature is directly related to the larger cooling, on longer time scales than precession, of high latitudes by teleconnection. It has, however, been demonstrated that the vegetation response to cooling was modest, merely an expansion of stenothermic plant populations into diverse communities that were otherwise unchanged.

It may be assumed that CO_2 concentrations were lowered in synchrony with the full 100,000-year Milankovitch cycle. This assumption is based on extrapolation from Antarctic ice cores, though with some support from ice cores nearer the equator. No direct evidence of such lowering is available from the Amazon basin, and no Amazonian plant responses can be attributed to this factor. Speculations that tree lines were forced downslope, or that savannas occupied the lowlands, because of CO_2 shortage are disqualified by paleoecological data: tree line descents are correlated with temperature lowering and glacial descent; the savannas never existed. So the CO_2 event happened, but no Amazonian data confirm it, and no measurable effect on plant populations or species diversity has been found.

So there is the dread conclusion: the biogeography of Amazonia was not greatly altered by the Pleistocene ice ages. The great forest occupied the lowlands then as now, without dry causeways for passage of woodland species (*sensu* Pennington, Prado, and Pendry 2000). Nor can there be much comfort in projecting the postulated causeways into some remote past of the Tertiary: the geomorphological evidence shows that humid weathering under trees has worked its will without a break since well into the Tertiary.

These data strongly suggest that the links between disjunct populations on far sides of the forest should be sought in outlying populations of low density occupying, at different times, locally favorable habitats within the forest. The diversity data, both pollen and taxonomic, demonstrate how massive is the tolerance of Amazonian ecosystems for vast arrays of specialized species. The Pleistocene history of *Podocarpus, Myrsine,* and other taxa that flourished in the lowland forest whenever ambient temperatures fell show what can happen. In interglacials these populations are so rare as to be scarcely visible. Lives at similar population densities for the presumptive woodland migrants, perhaps in locally ephemeral populations, could provide the "stepping-stone" links between population centers divided by the great reach of the Amazon forests.

One thing is now certain for biogeography: the lowland Amazon forest has been present, intact and undivided, throughout the Pleistocene. But a great range of lifestyles is permitted within it, as shown by its prodigious diversity. Among those myriad lifestyles can be the rare or marginal, so why not the occasional immigrant? All evidence of disjunction across the great forest implies that, huge though it is, the forest is permeable to transients, if only at rates suggestive of osmosis. Speed does not matter because the forest has been there for a very long time, and the transients are of ancient lineage.

A LICENSE FOR EVOLUTIONARY PLAYWRIGHTS

The refuge hypothesis, with its imaginary fragmentation of the forest by savannas, attracted so many for so long because it conformed to the vicariance paradigm. The lowland forest of the Amazon basin had no duplicates, it was a single entity, yet it had collected more species than anywhere on earth. Were we to abandon the stipulation of complete geographic isolation for Amazonian speciation, or was the concept of the unitary forest to go? This was the central dilemma for those of us who were puzzled to explain the spectacular richness of the Amazon landscape. Refugial thinking resolved this dilemma by abolishing the unitary forest.

The hypothesis then provided the Amazon with its own species pump, driven by ice ages, regulated by the astronomical forcing of climatic change. With every successive glacial advance, the forest was disrupted, and savannas flooded in to leave only vicariant islands of forest. In this archipelago of forest refugia, speciation worked its isolated will, before the sea of savanna ebbed with the tide of the next interglacial. The waxing and waning of forest refugia pumped out species with the timeless rhythms of astronomical cycles.

This solution to the speciation dilemma effectively raised the refuge hypothesis to the status of a theory, one of that select group called "beautiful." Ernst Mayr once said to me that if my investigations of lake sediments should show that the Amazon was never arid, no one would believe me because the refuge theory was so beautiful.

The species pump was part of the beauty growing out of the refuge hypothesis. I doubt if many of us agonized over Haffer's endemic birds (though see Mayr and O'Hara 1986 for an alternative view). Brown's heliconid butterflies, the second best known "refugial" distributions, gripped from the sheer scale of his data set, but his maps closely mirror relief maps of the Amazon suggesting very local origins, like those of the swarms of orchid species in parts of the Andes or cichlid fishes in African lakes (Brown 1987a). The heliconids of Brown's research, with their spectacular coloring, are familiar friends to wanderers in the forest; they float above you with all the volant dynamism of a hot air balloon on a calm day. Hard to believe that they require an ocean of savanna to ensure vicariance.

Biogeographers themselves loved the hypothesis for a different reason: as a new working tool to explain difficult distributions. Disjunctions across Amazonia? Merge them in the Pleistocene when the forest was not there. Disjunctions on other tropical continents? Think Pleistocene refugia first. It was, after all, a hypothesis built on biogeographic data. The hypothesis provided barriers where other barriers were hard to find.

But it is in refuge "theory" as the provider of ancient vicariance that we found greatest beauty. We needed reproductive isolation to make sense of species. Ours has been a generation unable to agree on widely applicable mechanisms of rigorous reproductive isolation without geographic isolation. Speciation is necessarily allopatric; sympatric speciation is an interesting idea not usually taken seriously. Without Amazonian refugia we should have to face explaining that astonishing diversity of a mighty unbroken, continuously connected forest without convincing allopatry for species to emerge. Rivers as barriers?—perhaps; critical steepness of clines?—show me. But a forested archipelago in a sea of savanna! That was vicariance.

Geomorphological and paleoecological data now demonstrate, I think beyond peradventure, that the predictions of the refuge hypothesis cannot be met. The Pleistocene vector of Amazonian environments was stability, not the alternation of environments required by refuge theory. Savanna never cut up the forest. For 170,000 years (demonstrated) and a million years (by reasonable extrapolation) forest has continuously occupied the Amazon lowlands. Whatever speciation has occurred in this vast forest in that long period, therefore, was in some sense sympatric.

This is an opportunity for evolutionary playwrights. The Amazon theater of the evolutionary play has been extraordinarily stable, because the Pleistocene vectors of environmental change have been gentle to it. Some wafts of cool air quite tolerable to most, shorter commons of CO_2 such as the whole earth endured with little effect for most of the 100,000 years of each glacial cycle, and marginally reduced precipitation, well within the tolerances of lowland forest, on a roughly 22,000-year precession cycle was all that glacial periods could offer Amazonia. Indeed, the most striking vector of Pleistocene climates in the Amazon was the warming that came with each interglacial. For warming, at least, we are able to record ecological effects as a cohort of stenothermic forest plants became rare or extinct in the lowlands, leaving the competitive field to the great majority for whom the heat of the kitchen was no problem.

The evolutionary play performed in the Amazon these last million years has of necessity been even more confined by its ecological stage than most such plays. The vicariance of an archipelago seems not, after all, to have been part of the theater. Instead, an immense stage, in continuous shades of green, allowed the playwright unlimited time, but no intermissions. The play performed in this ecological theater was the greatest evolutionary extravaganza of them all.

Wanted! a playwright to reconstruct the ecological stage directions, given little vicariance and much sympatry.

ACKNOWLEDGMENTS

The revision of geomorphological and soils data is based on the work of Georg Irion of the Senckenberg Institute and Matti Räsänen of Turku University. Together they brought enlightenment to the Pleistocene geology of Amazonia. Georg Irion also undertook the crucial ground-truth investigations of claims for the existence or antiquity of fossil dune systems.

The efforts of my laboratory in Amazonia spanned a quarter-century and represent the work of many daring and perceptive students and colleagues. The beginning in Ecuador depended on the acumen and resourcefulness of Miriam Steinitz-Kannan, native of Quito, now Regents Professor at Northern Kentucky University. In Brazil our operations, and the discovery of the critical ancient lakes, were masterminded by Paulo De Oliveira, now of the Institute of Botany in São Paulo. Without the remarkable flair, industry, and local knowledge of Steinitz-Kannan and De Oliveira, these studies would not have been possible. Both began as students and later became indispensable professional colleagues.

Mark Bush of the Florida Institute of Technology (FIT) has been a principal colleague in both field and laboratory, contributing a large share of the intellectual strength of our research. Among the accomplishments that were peculiarly his were understanding the significance of zoophilous pollen as watershed records (leading to new protocols for the interpretation of Neotropical pollen) and the spectacular discovery of the precession signal in the core logs of lakes on the Hill of Six Lakes. Bush's FIT laboratory is now expanding Amazon paleoecological studies in ways of which I could only dream. Kam-biu Liu, now of Louisiana State University, then a postdoctoral fellow, found and developed the critical Pleistocene forest record from Mera in Ecuador and nudged our thinking toward cooling as the principal vector of Pleistocene climate change.

In nearly all the difficult field operations I had the high good fortune to have at my side Michael Miller of the University of Cincinnati, whose sagacity, experience, toughness, and unfailing composure are all a man needs to lean on when an expedition is stressed. I have a great debt to his friendship. We were accompanied by a splendid succession of student companions in Amazonia, most of whom were on their way to advanced degrees: Melanie Riedinger, Mark Scheutzow, Eduardo Asanza, Ana Cristina Sosa-Asanza, Chela Vasquez, Kris Olson, Nicholas Carter, Ian Frost, Shana Weber, Melissa Carter, and Jason Curtis. The principal funding source throughout has been the U.S. National Science Foundation.

7
The History of Amazonian Mammals: Mechanisms and Timing of Diversification

JAMES L. PATTON AND
MARIA NAZARETH F. DA SILVA

ABSTRACT

We summarize the limited molecular phylogeographic data available for small, nonvolant mammals of the lowland rainforests of Amazonia, including eight species of didelphid marsupials, eleven species of murid rodents, and twelve species of echimyid rodents. We use these data to examine the temporal depth of lineages as well as to test hypotheses that have been proposed to account for the high species diversity in this region. Many of the data are based on a detailed sampling protocol carried out along the 1,000 km length of the Rio Juruá of western Brazil, one of the major whitewater drainages of Amazonia. This sampling program was designed to examine the role of large rivers as barriers to dispersal, and thus as potential causal agents in vicariant divergence, a hypothesis originally proposed by Alfred Russel Wallace in the early 1800s. Nearly every species of marsupial and rodent examined is strongly structured geographically across Amazonia, and divergences among reciprocally monophyletic haplotype lineages of what are currently considered single species range as high as 14% in the mitochondrial cytochrome *b* gene. The great depth of these lineages argues against recency in the diversification of these taxa, as has been often assumed by those who believe that possible forest refugia in the Pleistocene, especially the late Pleistocene, were a driving force in speciation. Moreover, expectations of a population genetic signature indicating relatively recent expansion from presumptive forest refugia are not met by the data available. Finally, our data from the Rio Juruá do not support a significant role for current rivers as barriers in generating diversity, but do suggest a link with tectonic events during Andean uplift of the Miocene and Pliocene and the shifting drainages within Amazonia that resulted. Each of these results must be considered preliminary at best, given the large number of taxa and huge geographic areas within Amazonia that have yet to be sampled.

INTRODUCTION

The mammalian fauna of the lowland Neotropical forests is among the richest in the world, whether measured at the level of single localities (alpha diversity) or across geography (gamma diversity). Over 430 species are currently recognized, including more than 135 endemics (Mares 1992). Despite this richness, our knowledge of this fauna remains extremely limited (Voss and Emmons 1996). The dearth of information encompasses the entire biological spectrum, including the basics of species boundaries, geographic and habitat ranges, phylogenetic relationships, and population ecologies. In many ways, this is surprising, since worldwide mammalian diversity (approximately 4,600 species: Wilson and Reeder 1993) is limited in comparison to that of many other animal groups, and because we have traditionally expressed an inherent interest in those taxa closest to ourselves. As a consequence, and with the exception of Alfred Russel Wallace's (1852) emphasis on riverine barriers and primate distribution patterns within Amazonia, mammals have not figured importantly in debates concerning either the origin or the maintenance of Neotropical diversity.

In this chapter we evaluate some of the proposed mechanisms of evolutionary divergence as they relate to Amazonian mammals using our documentation of the geographic and phylogenetic relationships of extant populations of nonvolant and small-bodied species. This combination of geography and genealogy is the emergent field of "phylogeography," as defined by Avise and his coworkers over a decade ago (Avise et al. 1987; Avise 1989a), and reviewed in full in Avise's (2000) recent book. This field describes the spatial distribution and genealogical propinquity of individual genes and attempts to separate the effects of population structure from those of population history by explicit analytical methods (e.g., Templeton, Routman, and Phillips 1995). Using such approaches, it is often possible to test alternative models of speciation and to search for generality in any given group of organisms, or in any specific geographic region, in ways not previously possible.

While we emphasize the utility of the phylogeographic perspective as a test for these specific diversification models, we also recognize that data for Amazonian mammals remain too sparse for generalizations. Nevertheless, patterns are emerging that question current dogma regarding the recency of and mechanism of Amazonian diversification of mammals, and potentially of other organisms as well. The patterns we are beginning to uncover instead suggest a deep history, one that is concordant with, and perhaps resulting from, episodes of Andean uplift and changes in paleodrainages within the Amazon basin.

THE PHYLOGEOGRAPHIC APPROACH

Phylogeography is based on the principles and processes governing the geographic distributions of genealogical lineages. Importantly, these lineages include those identifiable at the intraspecific level, for it is through the reconstruction of ancestral patterns from current ones that explicit models of diversification can be falsified.

Three generalized phylogeographic patterns are observed at the intraspecific level (Avise 1994; Riddle 1996). First, in most species, single populations are likely to contain unrelated molecular haplotypes for any given gene; that is, a phylogeny of the haplotypes of a single species is often polyphyletic or paraphyletic with respect to the populations in which they occur. This observation extends to the interspecific level, since gene trees do not necessarily mirror the relationships of the organisms that contain those genes (Avise 1989a; Pamilo and Nei 1988; Tajima 1983). While this lack of monophyly might be considered problematic for the phylogeographic approach, in fact the combination of the phyletic and geographic distributions of alleles (or haplotypes) among populations and closely related species can be used to infer both the geographic relationships of ancestral populations prior to divergence (Harrison 1991) and the sequence of historical gene flow events (Slatkin and Maddison 1989; Slatkin 1994). Put another way, each of the geographic models of species formation (allopatric, parapatric, or sympatric) makes explicit predictions relative to any given gene tree in the descendant units (daughter populations or species: see Moritz et al. 2000). Moreover, while polyphyletic or paraphyletic relationships of haplotypes among descendant taxa are expected immediately following speciation, reciprocal monophyly is usually obtained with time (Neigel and Avise 1986; Moore 1995). Observations of reciprocal monophyly in the gene trees of related species thus imply a substantial time depth to their divergences.

The second observation of molecular phylogeography is that species that exhibit little phylogeographic structure are those expected to have substantial dispersal capabilities that can readily overcome geographic barriers representing impediments to gene flow in other organisms. Gene flow retards divergence because it makes effective population sizes much larger. Consequently, the lack of phylogeographic structure for some taxa might not be due to recency of origin, but rather to the historical maintenance of large effective population sizes and high gene flow through dispersal. These taxa are of interest in an ecological and metapopulation context, but may offer little or no insight into historical processes in the regions that they inhabit.

The third observation, and the most important to this chapter, is that monophyletic groups distinguished by phylogenetic gaps are likely to result from extrinsic barriers to gene flow. There are two corollaries to this observation, namely, that the geographic placement of phylogenetic gaps tends to be concordant among different species, and that these concordant phylogenetic gaps signal common historical vicariant events. Thus, the presence of reciprocal monophyletic haplotype lineages for a number of independent taxa signals a congruent history, and the common placement of those lineages in space suggests the presence of a vicariant event causal to the diversification pattern observed.

AMAZONIAN DIVERSIFICATION: MODELS AND PROBLEMS

The high species diversity encountered in the lowland tropical forests of Amazonia has been hypothesized to result from riverine barriers (Wallace 1852), Pleistocene forest refugia (Haffer 1969; Vanzolini and Williams 1970), parapatric divergence across sharp ecological gradients (Endler 1977, 1982b, 1982c), long-term paleoclimatic shifts (Bush 1994) or cycles (Haffer 1993), floodplain dynamics (Salo 1988), and ecological heterogeneity (Tuomisto et al. 1995). There is no general consensus as to the validity of any of these processes. The lack of such consensus should not be unexpected, however (see Haffer 2001 and Ron 2001 for a general overview of models of diversification and how they have been applied to various taxonomic groups). For one thing, all taxa have inherently different population structures, and thus may respond uniquely even to the same historical event, be it the formation of a river or the physical isolation of populations on habitat islands. Moreover, none of these hypotheses are mutually exclusive; each process could have acted in concert with another, and all are thus of potential importance for any given set of taxa.

One of the major obstacles to the achievement of any consensus on diversification processes in Amazonia, or elsewhere, has been the difficulty of falsifying any specific hypothesis. However, some speciation models are amenable to falsification by phylogenetic methodologies. The gradient hypothesis, for example, is falsified if the requisite phylogenetic propinquity of the taxa located on either side of an identifiable gradient is not verified by robust phylogenetic analysis (Aleixo 2002; Moritz et al. 2000; Patton and Smith 1992). Similarly, the riverine hypothesis requires that differentiation patterns be partitioned to opposite-bank populations. If such is not the case for a given taxon, then riverine diversification is falsified (Patton, da Silva, and Malcolm 2000). Unfortunately, while some models can be evaluated by a strictly phylogeographic approach, others cannot. As we describe below, this is true of the refuge hypothesis, at least as it applies to the lowland forests of Amazonia.

In this chapter we focus on our tests of Alfred Russel Wallace's riverine hypothesis and, to a lesser extent, Haffer's refuge hypothesis. We illustrate the expectations of both models and detail the patterns of phylogeography and population expansion exhibited by our sample of small, nonvolant terrestrial and arboreal mammals, designed to test Wallace's model. Work on selected anurans collected at the same time by our colleague Claude Gascon (Gascon, Lougheed, and Bogart 1996, 1998; Lougheed et al. 1999) has proceeded in parallel with our analyses of riverine diversification in mammals. We also use our samples of a few western Amazonian small mammal species to describe past population histories of these taxa based on population genetic and coalescent methodologies, and we show how these historical patterns can be used to evaluate the likelihood of the refuge hypothesis. Finally, we show that the patterns exhibited in our tests of both riverine and refuge models, with minor exceptions, do not conform to the expectations of those hypotheses, but suggest deeper historical processes that appear linked to Andean tectonic events. We then place these localized results in the larger context of the broader Amazon basin. Many of the data used in our analyses here have been published elsewhere, as have some of the major conclusions (da Silva and Patton 1993, 1998; Patton, da Silva, and Malcolm 1994, 1996, 2000; Patton and da Silva 1998, 2001).

The Refuge Hypothesis

The suggestion that the lowland rainforests of Amazonia experienced cyclic contraction and expansion coincident with Pleistocene glacial cycles was almost globally accepted by both botanists and zoologists in the two decades following Haffer's (1969) original proposal (Prance 1982a; Whitmore and Prance 1987). Indeed, the refuge hypothesis became the paradigm of a global explanation for tropical diversification. In the past decade or so, however, the generality of this hypothesis has been challenged from several different directions (see reviews by Bush 1994, Burnham and Graham 1999, and Moritz et al. 2000). Specific criticisms related to Amazonia have included lack of palynological evidence for savanna vegetation in the core of Amazonia (Colinvaux 1996 and chap. 7 in this volume; Colinvaux, De Oliveira et al. 1996), ignorance of landscape changes from the late Tertiary to the Recent (Salo 1987), concerns about sampling bias in identifying refuge locations even if the refugia did exist (Nelson et al. 1990), debate over whether contact zones between presumed sister taxa are appropriately located (Endler 1982b), increased complexity (and reduced testability) as additional refugia are proposed (Lynch 1988), and the argument that alternative mechanisms provide equally good explanations for the patterns observed (Endler 1982b, 1982c).

Unfortunately, phylogeography per se does not provide a means to evaluate the refuge hypothesis, at least for the lowland forests of Amazonia. The hypothesis does not specify any explicit hierarchical temporal division of refugia that can be tracked by concordant taxon-splitting events (Patton and da Silva 1998). Moreover, because the glacial cycles of the Pleistocene were repeated numerous times, each successive one would potentially override or erase the phylogeographic signal of previous ones, leaving a record impossible to decipher. This is also a major problem with Haffer's (1993) more recent emphasis on long-term paleoclimatic cycles driven by Milankovitch oscillations. While we cannot evaluate the hypothesis of Amazonian refugia by phylogeographic methodology, population genetic approaches do offer a potential test, based on expectations of the theoretical genetic diversity in populations expanding from hypothesized refugial areas (Moritz et al. 2000).

The refuge hypothesis argues that taxa became restricted to, and diverged within, geographically isolated forest patches. Such a scenario, therefore, predicts that populations expanded outward from these patches as the forest itself expanded when glacial maxima gave way to the ameliorated climate of interglacial periods. Population expansion affects a number of parameters of DNA sequences, resulting in a predicted starlike phylogeny and a Poisson distribution of pairwise differences between haplotypes due to increased retention of gene lineages. Stable populations, on the other hand, are likely to have strongly structured haplotype phylogenies with multimodal distributions of pairwise differences (Slatkin and Hudson 1991; Rogers and Harpending 1992). These pairwise distributions have been termed "mismatch" distributions and have figured importantly in interpreting the history of the spread of human populations (e.g., Harpending et al. 1998).

In the case of Amazonia, species of small mammals whose distributions include Peru, Bolivia, and western Brazil south of the Amazon would probably have been restricted to the east Peru-Acre refuge (Prance 1982b) (fig. 7.1), if such a refuge in fact existed. The mismatch distributions of four species of small mammals within this range for which we had adequate data are illustrated in figure 7.2. In each case, the pattern of pairwise differences is highly erratic and significantly different from the unimodal expected signature of a recent expansion (Rogers and Harpending 1992). Consequently, while we are unable to provide a test of the refuge hypothesis as it applies to the whole of Amazonia from phylogeographic patterns, the data in figure 7.2 suggest that the hypothesis can be rejected based on population genetic expectations. At the very least, populations of four species appear to have been stable throughout the latest Pleistocene glacial cycle, and probably even longer, rather than expanding, as would be predicted by the refuge model.

The Riverine Hypothesis

One of the many observations Alfred Russel Wallace made during his years of travel in Amazonia was the relationship between primate distributions and river systems:

> During my residence in the Amazon district, I took every opportunity of determining the limits of species, and I soon found that the Amazon, the Rio Negro and the Madeira formed the limits beyond which certain species never passed. . . . On approaching the sources of the rivers they cease to be a boundary, and most of the species are found on both sides of them. Thus several Guiana species come up to the Rio Negro and Amazon, but do not pass them; Brazilian species on the contrary reach but do not pass the Amazon to the north. Several Ecuador species from the east of the Andes reach down into the tongue on land between the Rio Negro and Upper Amazon, but pass neither of those rivers, and others from Peru are bounded on the north by the Upper Amazon, and on the east by the Madeira. Thus there are four districts, the Guiana, the Ecuador, the Peru and the Brazil districts, whose boundaries on one side are determined by the rivers I have mentioned. (Wallace 1852, 110)

Two separate but equally important evolutionary components are contained within Wallace's writings. First, rivers mark the boundaries of geographic areas, each of which contains a similar community of species, but between which species compositions differ. Second, the strength of any barrier potentially decreases toward a river's headwaters, such that sharing of species by opposite-bank communities is more likely where the channel is narrower. Both of these predictions are supported by the recent analysis of Ayres and Clutton-Brock (1992), who showed that primate community similarity on opposite sides of rivers within Amazonia decreased as a function of river size and that communities became progressively more similar toward the headwaters of the Amazon itself.

Wallace's hypothesis was based solely on distribution patterns, yet its clear corollary is that rivers within Amazonia not only separate distinct faunas, but also serve as barriers to gene flow and thus have promoted species divergence. This idea has been termed the "riverine barrier hypothesis" in the recent literature, and it has been invoked as an alternative to the refuge hypothesis and other models proposed to explain Amazonian diversification (reviewed in Haffer 2001). Empirical support for the riverine hypothesis comes from the commonly observed pattern of organismal distribution in which the boundaries of closely

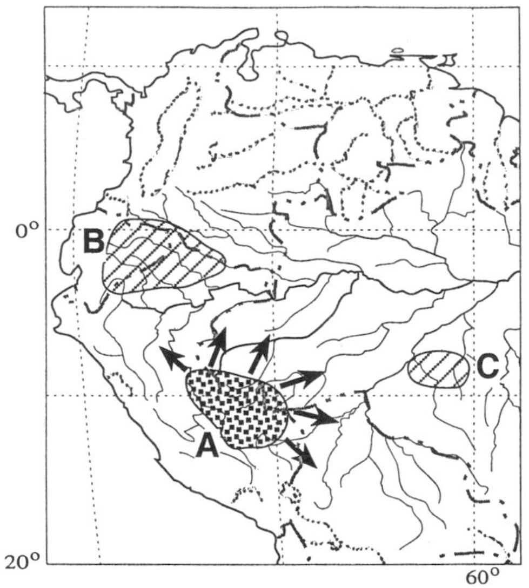

Figure 7.1 Western Amazonia, showing the location of three putative Pleistocene refugia: A, east Peru-Acre; B, Napo; and C, Rondônia-Aripuanã. Arrows indicate the direction of likely population expansion from the east Peru-Acre refuge following the last glacial maximum. (From Prance 1982b.)

related species or subspecies often coincide with the major rivers of Amazonia. One need only look at the distribution maps in Hershkovitz (1977) for tamarins and marmosets, those for various birds published by Haffer (1974, 1978), or those for Amazonian lizard species (Ávila-Pires 1995) for examples. Despite its intuitive appeal, given the obvious size and number of fluvial systems in lowland Amazonia, this hypothesis has received only limited attention in the 150 years since the publication of Wallace's original observations.

As appealing as the riverine hypothesis might be in the case of Amazonian organisms, its efficacy as a mode of species formation has remained poorly documented. For one thing, it is difficult to distinguish between rivers as primary barriers in the diversification process versus the simple secondary meeting point of taxa that diverged elsewhere (Simpson and Haffer 1978; Haffer 1992, 1997). A second problem is the way in which riverine effects have been typically measured. The most common approach to date has been to examine the degree of genetic differentiation between opposite-bank and same-bank populations, using distance methodology derived from protein electrophoretic data (e.g., Capparella 1988, 1992; Gascon, Lougheed, and Bogart 1996, 1998). These types of approaches, however, suffer from two fundamental problems. For one, because of isolation-by-distance phenomena, samples must be geographically placed so that genetic and geographic distances are not confounded. And, more importantly, these methods cannot distinguish between alternative hypotheses underlying the divergence pattern observed because an explicit phylogenetic

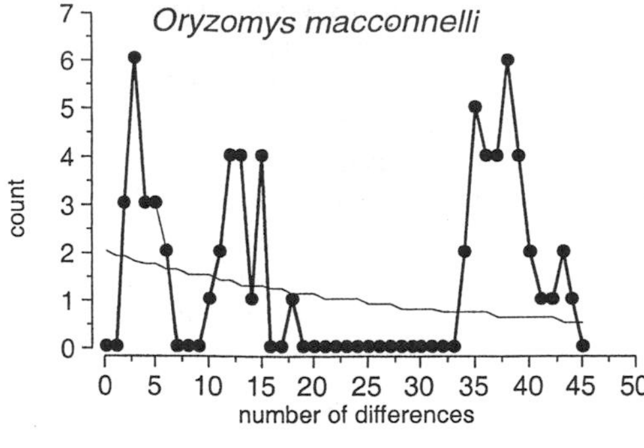

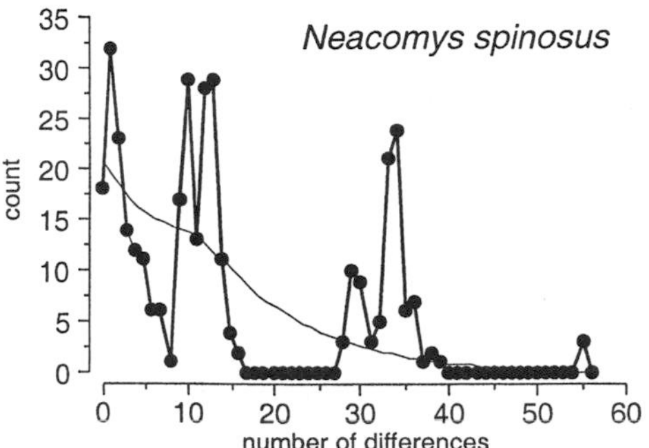

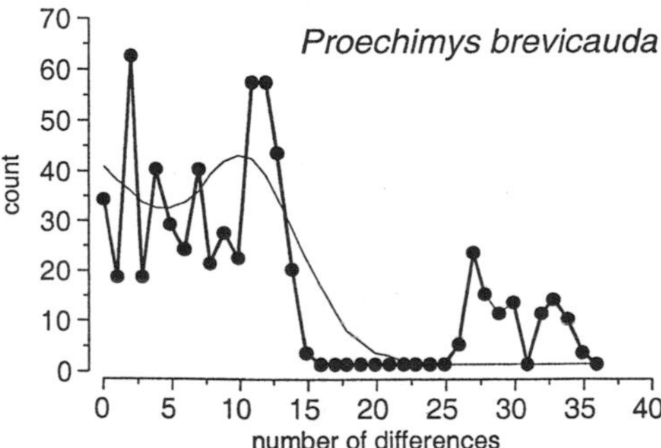

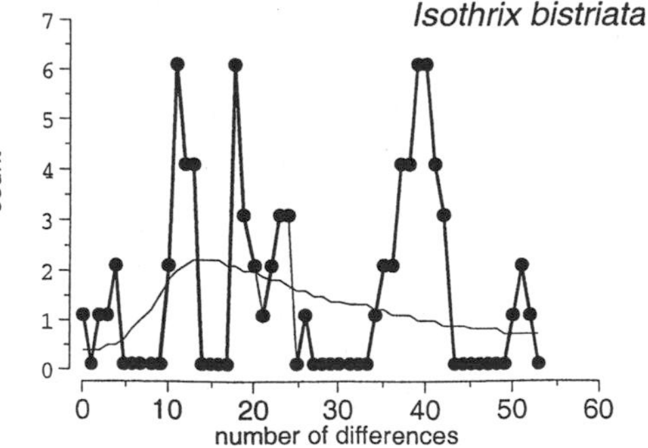

Figure 7.2 Observed distributions (solid circles and thick lines) of pairwise differences among all haplotypes and distributions predicted by a model of population expansion (thin lines) from ten or more separate population samples for four species of rodents whose distributions have been sampled in eastern Peru, western Brazil, and northern Bolivia and which presumably would have expanded from the putative east Peru-Acre refuge following the last glacial maximum. The multimodal empirical distributions for all species are inconsistent with an expansion model in each case ($p < 0.01$).

hypothesis does not extend from phenetic distance approaches (Patton, da Silva, and Malcolm 2000).

PHYLOGEOGRAPHY AND RIVERINE DIVERSIFICATION: MAMMALS OF THE RIO JURUÁ

To circumvent problems presented in other attempts to examine riverine diversification in Amazonia, we used a phylogeographic approach to study mammals of the Rio Juruá in the western Brazilian Amazon. This river is one of the major whitewater tributaries of the Amazon itself, extending from the border of Brazil and Peru to enter the Rio Solimões on its right (= south) bank some 1,000 km to the northeast. Our sample sites consisted of two pairs of across-river localities in each of four regions of the river, from near the mouth to its headwaters. Descriptions of localities and sampling effort, as well as taxonomic and phylogeographic details, can be found in Patton, da Silva, and Malcolm (2000); we provide only summaries here.

We have examined sequence differentiation in the mitochondrial DNA cytochrome *b* gene for eight species of marsupials, eleven murid rodents, and twelve echimyid rodents, as well as one tamarin. Several of the species examined exhibit little or no differentiation along the Rio Juruá (e.g., the marsupials *Metachirus nudicaudatus* and *Didelphis marsupialis* and the murid rodents *Oryzomys perenensis* and *Oligoryzomys microtis*), although these species may exhibit deep divergences elsewhere in Amazonia (Patton, da Silva, and Malcolm 2000; Patton and Costa 2003). However, a substantial number of species, or species pairs, exhibit strong phylogeographic partitioning along the Rio Juruá, with levels of sequence divergence (Kimura two-parameter distances) ranging from approximately 4% to nearly 15% between regionally defined clades (fig. 7.3). These species are divided into geographic segments within the Rio Juruá basin, each of which has been substantially isolated with respect to historical and present-day gene flow. Among the thirty-two taxa we examined, two broadly generalized phylogeographic patterns are apparent. One of these illustrates aspects of riverine diversification; the second points to a previously unrecognized history of western Amazonia.

Riverine Phylogeographic Patterns

Phylogeographic analysis can do more than simply identify taxa that are structured geographically; it can also distinguish between alternative historical

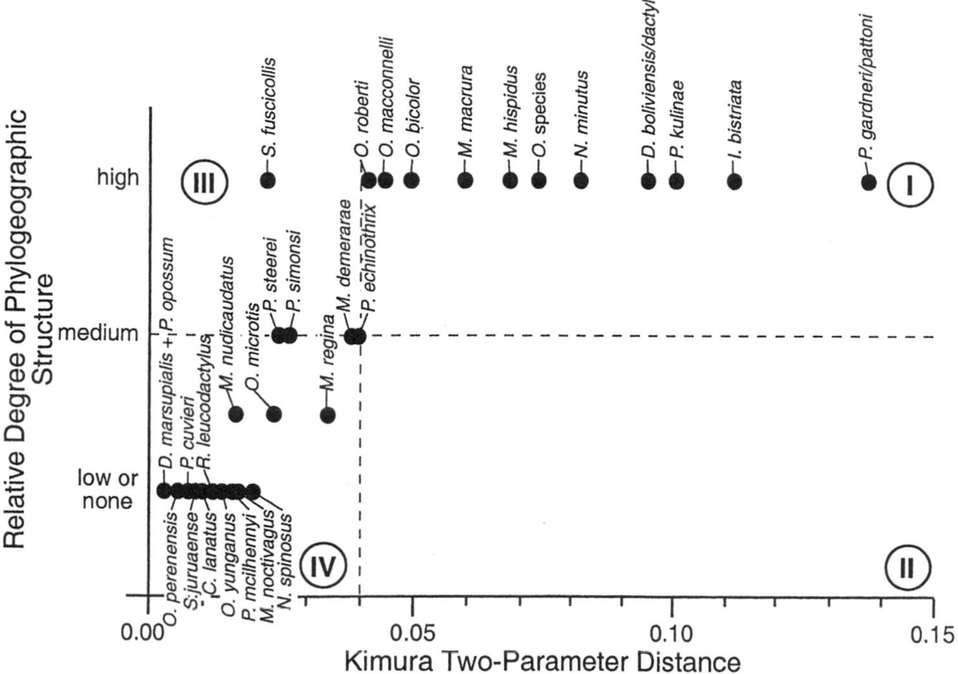

Figure 7.3 The relationship between average sequence divergence (Kimura two-parameter distances) for the mitochondrial cytochrome *b* gene and the relative degree of phylogeographic partitioning in thirty species or species pairs of nonvolant mammals of the Rio Juruá (following Avise et al. 1987). A high degree of phylogeographic structure indicates that haplotype lineages are confined to particular sections along the river, showing either a left- versus right-bank pattern or some other pattern of regional partitioning. Medium structure occurs when some haplotype lineages are confined to single geographic areas while others are not. Finally, low or no structure characterizes those taxa in which there is no relationship between haplotype lineages and geography. The four phylogeographic categories of Avise et al. (1987) (I–IV) are indicated.

hypotheses underlying patterns of differentiation (Harrison 1991; Lynch 1988; Patton and da Silva 1998). As examples, three different hypotheses for riverine divergence are presented in figure 7.4. In the first of these (fig. 7.4A), a river has been imposed on an existing taxon range, dividing it into two parts. If the river has formed a complete barrier, then with time, opposite-bank populations will become reciprocally monophyletic haplotype lineages that will remain sisters with regard to any haplotypes outside of the geographic area of interest. This pattern, then, represents primary riverine diversification, and is readily distinguishable phylogenetically from secondary contact resulting from range expan-

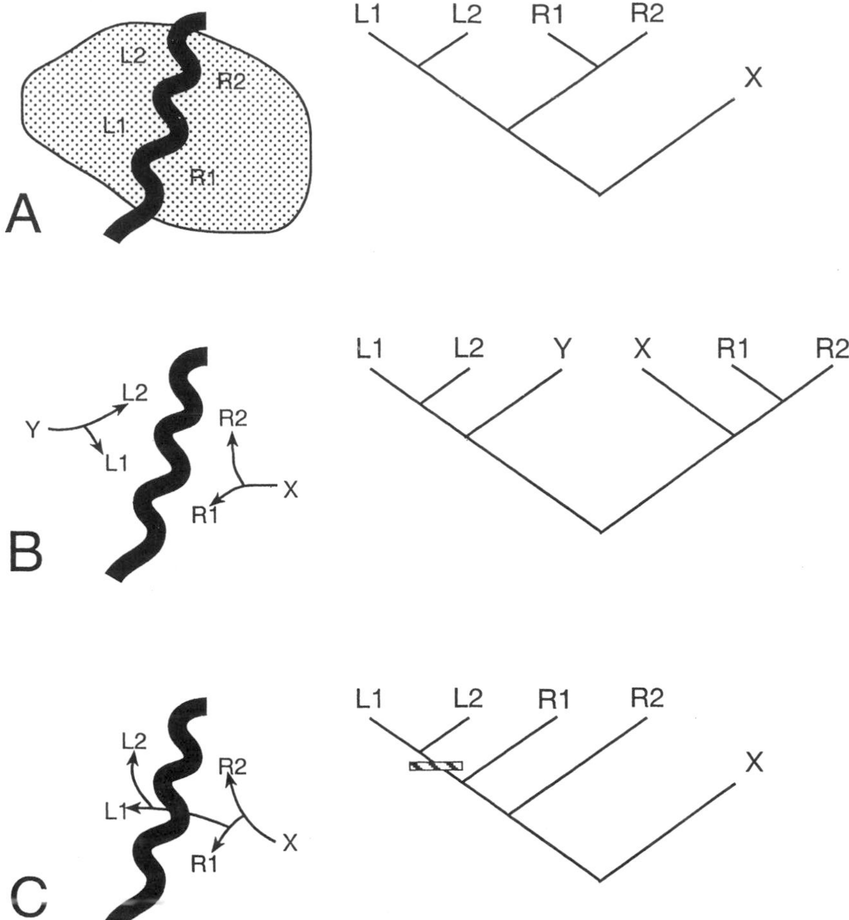

Figure 7.4 Three alternative phylogeographic hypotheses for riverine diversification. (A) Primary diversification: reciprocally monophyletic sister clades are bounded by a river that imposed itself on an existing species range. (B) Secondary contact: reciprocally monophyletic, but nonsister clades are bounded by a river that served as the secondary meeting point of clades that evolved elsewhere. (C) Overwater dispersal: right-bank and left-bank haplotypes show a paraphyletic relationship due to one episode of across-river transfer.

sions where the river forms only a common meeting place (fig. 7.4B). Phylogeography may also uncover clear instances of dispersal, with overwater transfer from established populations on the opposite side (fig. 7.4C). We offer these patterns as exemplars only, stressing that, in the early stages of divergence, gene genealogies may not be sufficiently robust to falsify one or more competing historical hypotheses. Given adequate time, however, hypotheses such as primary diversification versus secondary contact may be distinguishable by phylogeographic methodologies.

Phylogeographic analyses can not only be used to test alternative hypotheses of diversification, but can also offer a temporal window into the timing of differentiation. For example, in the riverine model, both the extant distributions of single haplotypes and their phylogenetic linkage provide evidence for across-river transfers. The former signals relatively recent, and potentially ongoing, dispersal movements across and along the river, while genealogical evidence suggests deeper historical dispersal events. The coalescence methodology of Slatkin and Maddison (1989) permits one to estimate the numbers of both types of across-river haplotype transfers.

We have data for six species of small mammals for which adequate geographic and population sampling is available. Data for all six species have been published (the spiny tree rat *Mesomys hispidus* [Patton, da Silva, and Malcolm 1994], the rice rats *Oligoryzomys microtis* and *Oryzomys perenensis* [Patton, da Silva, and Malcolm 1996], the saddleback tamarin *Saguinus fuscicollis* [Peres, Patton, and da Silva 1996], and the terrestrial spiny rats *Proechimys simonsi* and *P. steerei* [Matocq, Patton, and da Silva 2000]). While each of these species exhibits somewhat different patterns, all provide important insights into the general divergence patterns and processes for the nonvolant mammals of the Rio Juruá, and elsewhere within Amazonia.

PATTERN 1: WALLACEAN BARRIER

Only one species exhibits clear patterns of haplotype distribution expected from riverine diversification: the saddleback tamarin, *Saguinus fuscicollis* (see Peres, Patton, and da Silva 1996). The level of cytochrome *b* sequence differentiation among samples of tamarins is limited (an average of 2.3% among the eight haplotypes recovered), but the pattern of divergence matches both predictions of Wallace's model. Molecularly differentiated populations are separated on opposite sides of the river, concordant with the morphologically based subspecies *S. f. fuscicollis* and *S. f. melanoleucus* (see Hershkovitz 1977 for complete taxon descriptions and distributions), and evidence of across-river gene flow is present in, but limited to, localities in the headwaters region (Peres, Patton, and da Silva 1996). This species is a terra firme specialist, so populations along the middle and lower sections of the river are separated not only by the width of the water channel, but also by the extensive lateral expanse of floodplain várzea forest. However, while the phylogeographic pattern exhibited by this tamarin conforms to riverine expectations, the Rio Juruá has apparently not served as a primary barrier in the evolutionary development of the subspecies occurring on opposite banks. Phylogenetic analysis of the entire species complex (Jacobs, Larson, and Cheverud 1995) does not support a sister relationship between the two subspecies that contact each other along the Rio Juruá, as would be required if the river was a primary barrier (that is, the phyletic pattern for these tamarins is that of fig. 7.4B, not 7.4A).

PATTERN 2: LEAKY, OR NO BARRIER

Unlike the tamarins, the other five species share a substantial number of haplotypes among localities, with numerous examples of across-river sharing. Some taxa, such as the rice rat *Oryzomys perenensis*, the pygmy rice rat *Oligoryzomys microtis*, and the spiny rat *Proechimys steerei*, exhibit little structure throughout their distributions along the river, having either the same haplotypes shared among populations on both banks along most of the river or showing clear phyletic linkages of haplotypes among those populations (Matocq, Patton, and da Silva 2000; Patton, da Silva, and Malcolm 1996). Other taxa, however, display substantial geographic structure, but with that structure opposite of that expected from riverine diversification. For example, *M. hispidus* exhibits a reverse riverine pattern, with the number of haplotypes shared by across-river pairs of localities increasing from the headwaters toward the mouth of the Rio Juruá (Patton, da Silva, and Malcolm 1994). Since this species is an arboreal member of both terra firme and várzea forests (Patton, da Silva, and Malcolm 2000), the distribution of haplotypes (and the degree of across-river exchange) is generally related to the amount and rapidity of habitat transfer due to the dynamic nature of channel meanders, which increases successively downriver.

Non-Riverine Patterns

The geographic structure present among haplotypes of *Mesomys hispidus* does identify two deeply divergent clades (6.8% divergence, on average), although they do not correspond to opposite-bank groupings. Rather, these clades delimit upriver and downriver units that overlap at one central locality (Patton, da Silva, and Malcolm 1994). This phylogeographic pattern was an unexpected discovery. However, and equally unexpectedly, it is a pattern shared by essentially all taxa of nonvolant mammals of the Rio Juruá that exhibit deeply divergent mtDNA genomes (Patton and da Silva 1998; Patton, da Silva, and Malcolm 2000). Even more surprisingly, it is also a pattern shared by nonmammalian terrestrial vertebrates, such as the poison-dart frog *Epipedobates femoralis* (Lougheed et al. 1999). Furthermore, it is a pattern exhibited at the community level by both mammals and amphibians (Gascon, Malcolm et al. 2000; J. R. Malcolm, personal communication). Mammal species that exhibit this upriver-downriver divergence pattern include both terrestrial and arboreal, upland (terra firme) and floodplain (várzea) forest representatives. Each species comprises reciprocally monophyletic lineages co-distributed into upriver and downriver clades, with the points of contact between clades in each case in a similar position along the river (Patton, da Silva, and Malcolm 2000). These patterns cannot be explained by direct effects of the Rio Juruá itself, yet their commonality suggests a single underlying historical explanation, following phylogeographic expectations. What, then, might be this historical event?

LANDFORM EVOLUTION AND AMAZONIAN DIVERSIFICATION

A central tenet of phylogeography is that shared distribution patterns among diverse clades of organisms are more parsimoniously explained by the occurrence of extrinsic geologic or climatic events, which affected all groups in the same way, than by the intrinsic characteristics of each taxon independently. Concordant distributions may thus be used as evidence to infer biogeographic history.

The region between our upper and lower midriver sampling sites (fig. 7.5) coincides with the phytogeographic transitional boundary between Floresta Ombrofila Densa (downriver) and Floresta Ombrofila Aberta (upriver), major terra firme plant formations that sit on different underlying soil formations (RADAMBRASIL 1977). Positioned underneath this transition point is a geologic feature, the Iquitos Arch, a Precambrian zone of prior uplift within the western Amazon (Putzer 1984), one of several deep-basin features that generally delimit broad phytogeographic units across Amazonia (Daly and Prance 1989). Although this feature is not part of the contemporary topography of western Amazonia, it marks the boundary between the pre-Pleistocene Acre and Central Amazon fluvial deposition systems (Räsänen, Salo, and Kalliola 1987; Räsänen et al. 1990, 1992). The Acre basin, at least, apparently underwent impressive successive subsidence, beginning with the last major episode of Andean uplift during the Late Miocene and Pliocene, but continuing into the Pleistocene (Lundberg et al. 1998).

The topographic and consequent ecological effects of landform changes resulting from Andean tectonic events are unknown, nor is it understood whether,

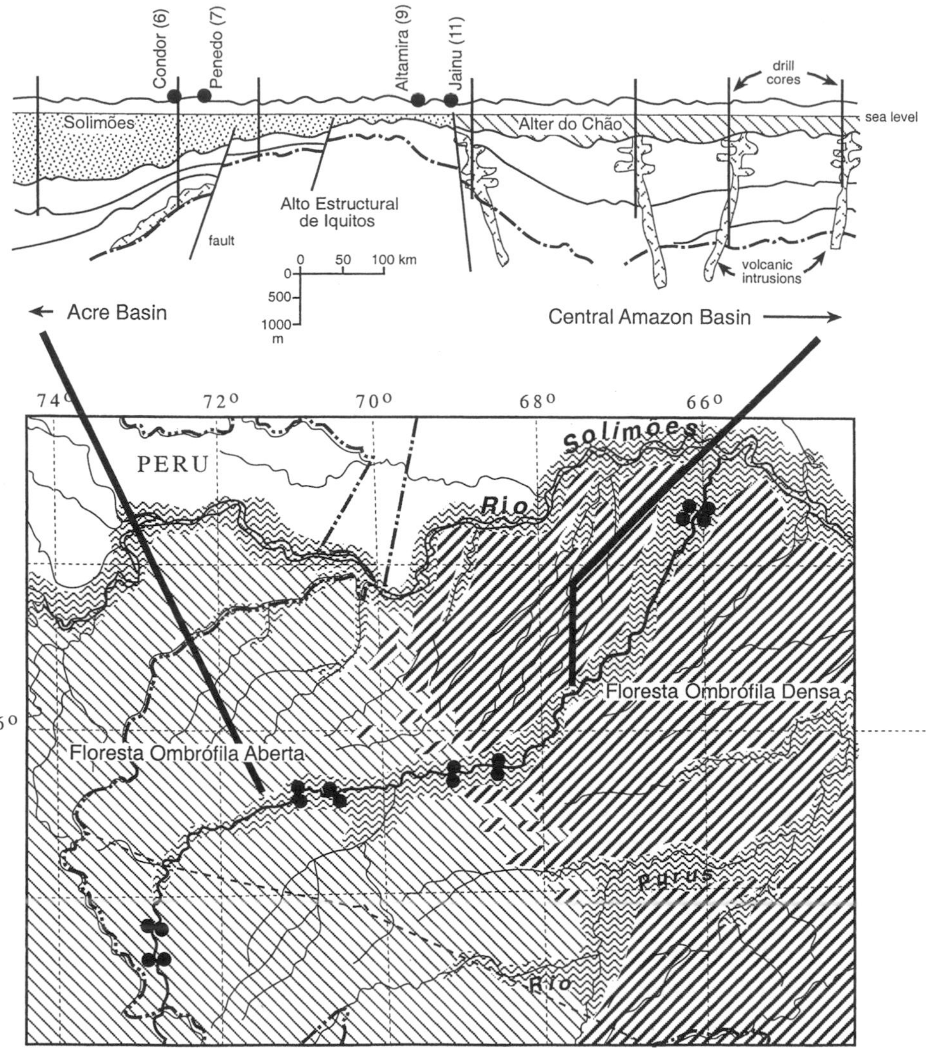

Figure 7.5 Map of Rio Juruá basin (below) with sample sites (solid circles) indicated. Wavy lines indicate approximate extent of the seasonally flooded forest, or várzea; diagonal lines give the approximate distribution of the two phytogeographic upland forest types (Floresta Ombrofila Aberta and Floresta Ombrofila Densa; from Daly and Prance 1989). A geologic cross-section (above) along the central Rio Juruá indicates the position of the submerged Iquitos Arch ("Alto Estructural de Iquitos") and the midriver sets of sample localities. Upriver from the Iquitos Arch is the Acre sub-basin; downriver is the Central Amazon sub-basin (from RADAMBRASIL 1977). Most phylogeographic boundaries between clades of marsupials and rodents are coincident with the position of the Iquitos Arch (da Silva and Patton 1998; Patton, da Silva, and Malcolm 2000; see also Lougheed et al. 1999 for similar pattern for frogs).

much less how, such events might be related causally to the phylogeographic patterns we observe. However, the concordance of phylogeographic breaks with geologic structures suggests a relationship between landform evolution in western Amazonia and these phylogeographic patterns. The potential importance of an active tectonic history within Amazonia has been little appreciated by most students of organismal diversification until quite recently. Its importance cannot be underestimated, as summarized by Räsänen et al.:

> The late Cenozoic foreland dynamics partitioning the western Amazon lowlands into more distinct intraforeland basins is the latest phase in the relief evolution which changed the Tertiary Neotropical lowlands into the present Andes. . . . Instead of reflecting locations of isolated Pleistocene broad-leaved forests (climatic refugia), modern species distributions in the western Amazon may be a result of historical species dynamics controlled by landscape evolution. Owing to late Cenozoic palaeogeographical changes in relief evolution, the forest biota of the western Amazon have probably alternated between allopatry and sympatry, commonness and rarity, and continuous distribution and fragmentation. (Räsänen et al. 1990, 330–331)

The linkage between late Cenozoic landform changes and the diversification of nonvolant mammals within the Rio Juruá basin, and elsewhere within Amazonia, is strengthened by estimates of the timing of lineage splits generated from the molecular sequence data. While any such estimates are necessarily very approximate, and with large errors (Hillis, Mable, and Moritz 1996), sequence divergences calculated from third position transversions of the cytochrome *b* gene (following Irwin, Kocher, and Wilson 1991) all suggest divergence times ranging from greater than 1 to at least 3 million years (da Silva and Patton 1993; Patton and da Silva 1998). Summaries of sequence divergence values between sister species in molecular phylogenies available to date for Amazonian didelphid marsupials, as well as murid and echimyid rodents, also suggest deep divergences of the lineages leading to the modern fauna (fig. 7.6). For each group, the average Kimura two-parameter distance is approximately 15%, and the mode is well above that expected for divergences within the past 1–2 million years. Similar deep divergence values have been observed for other Amazonian taxa for which molecular data are available, such as howler monkeys (Cortés-Ortiz et al. 2003), antbirds (Bates, Hackett, and Goerck 1999), and, importantly, *Anolis* lizards (Glor, Vitt, and Larson 2001), one of the taxa on which the original refuge model was built (Vanzolini and Williams 1970). Consequently, even given the uncertainties regarding rates of molecular evolution and the uniform time kept by any molecular clock (Arbogast et al. 2002), or even the fact that molecular lineage

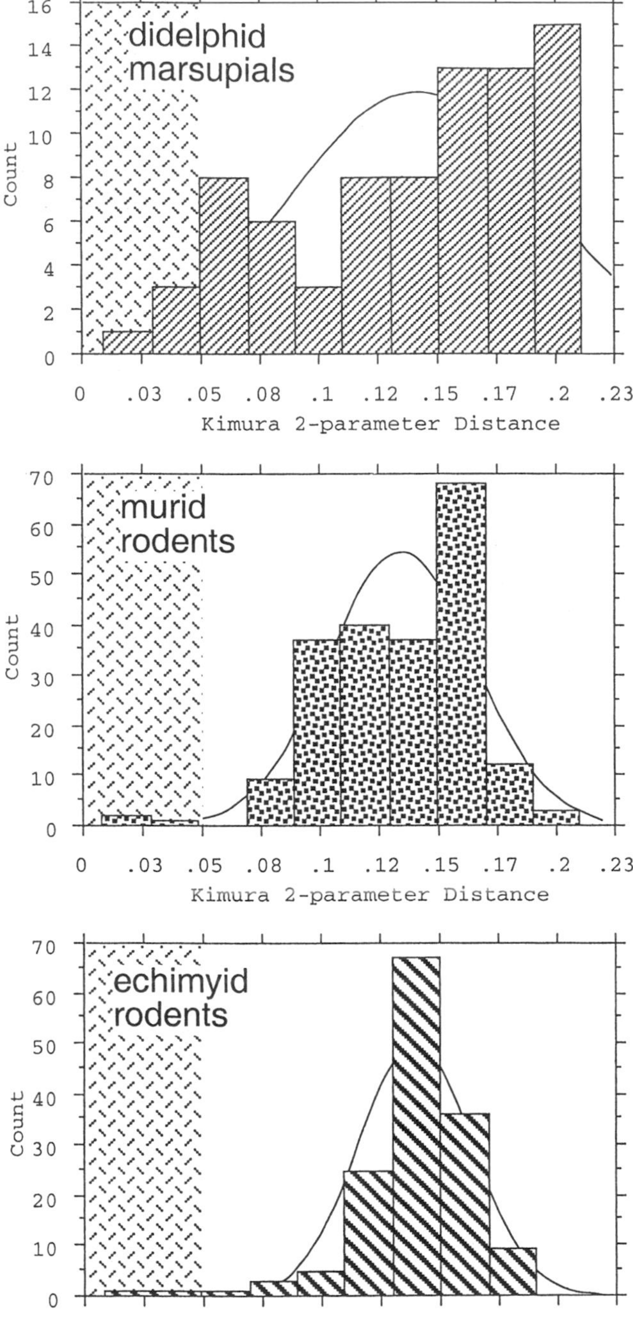

Figure 7.6 Histograms of Kimura two-parameter distances between sister species or clades for eight species of didelphid marsupials, eleven species of murid rodents, and twelve species of echimyid rodents. Cross-hatching on the left of each diagram indicates the approximate level of divergence expected for the last 0.5–1.0 million years, based on third position transversions (Irwin, Kocher, and Wilson 1991).

splits must necessarily predate speciation events (Edwards and Beerli 2000), the extensive divergence values between so many taxa suggest cladistic events much more ancient than have been commonly invoked for forest refuge formation in the late Pleistocene (Haffer 1969; but see Haffer 1993).

The hypothesis of a linkage between landform change and lineage diversification can be verified, in part, by examining the pattern of phylogeographic differentiation at other points where the Iquitos Arch underlies the western Amazon basin. If it is verified, then the positions of paleobasins may signal present-day centers of endemism and diversity more than the putative Pleistocene refugia suggested by other workers (review in Brown 1987b). This perspective reinforces the recent view (Bush 1994) that Amazonian speciation, and thus geographic patterns of species diversity, cannot be explained entirely by any single model of vicariance or climate change. Rather, it is quite likely that pre- or early Quaternary events established the major regional divisions of species complexes as well as a substantial portion of the modern fauna. Subsequent events, be they forest refugia (Haffer 1969), floodplain dynamics (Salo 1987, 1988), or ecological heterogeneity (Tuomisto et al. 1995), have more than likely acted only to redistribute the extant species into different community matrices, which have been superimposed on the earlier landscape pattern.

CONCLUSIONS AND PROSPECTUS

Bush (1994, 15) concludes his review of speciation processes in Amazonian organisms with the statement that "the need for a new biogeographic appraisal of the Amazon basin using paleoecological and modern phylogenetic [*sic*] techniques is clear." He goes on to suggest that "the history we reveal will almost certainly be complex and to some extent species-specific . . . with enough detail, the factors forcing speciation, and the timing of those events may help to resolve the riddle of tropical species richness."

The history of the Amazon basin is complex, with periods of Andean uplift and marine incursions, and the fluvial system has clearly undergone major changes in extent and direction (Hoorn 1993, 1994a, 1994b; Lundberg et al. 1998; Räsänen et al. 1995). Nevertheless, common patterns of geographic positioning of phylogenetic units suggest the importance of single vicariant events in the evolution of organismal diversity. Thus, the coincidental positions of phylogeographic breaks among extant mammals along the Rio Juruá in western Brazil and the Iquitos Arch, a structure that underlies and runs perpendicular to the present river basin, supports a causal linkage between them. This linkage is strengthened by consideration of the timing of arch formation (somewhere between the Middle Miocene and the Pliocene) and that of clade formation, as estimated from molecular divergences.

Regardless of the validity of Andean tectonic events as potential triggers for biotic diversification within greater Amazonia, our data from the Rio Juruá cannot be explained by any of the major hypotheses currently proposed to underlie that diversification. It seems clear, therefore, that a better understanding of the geologic history of Amazonia, including changes in both the placement of paleodrainages and their directions of flow, will be critical in achieving broader understanding. We have argued here that both phylogeographic and population genetic approaches can provide means to test explicit diversification models, through the delineation of common patterns of geographic and phyletic sharing of molecular haplotypes among groups of unrelated taxa, and to estimate the temporal depths of focal lineages. The area to be covered is huge and the number of potential taxa staggering, yet clear answers will come only from a combination of broad-scale and defined geographic sampling designed to examine particular models of diversification. We look forward to a rich future of exciting research.

ACKNOWLEDGMENTS

We thank our co-workers on the Projeto Juruá (Claude Gascon, Jay R. Malcolm, and Carlos Peres), through whose collective efforts the materials that form the basis for this chapter were collected and analyzed. Our work in Brazil has been under the auspices of the Conselho Nacional de Desenvolvimento Científico e Tecnológico (CNPq), the Instituto Brasileiro do Meio Ambiente e dos Recursos Naturais Renovavais (IBAMA), and the Instituto Nacional de Pesquisas da Amazônia (INPA); we are exceedingly grateful to each. Fieldwork was generously supported by grants from the National Geographic Society, the Wildlife Conservation Society, and the Museum of Vertebrate Zoology of the University of California; laboratory analyses were underwritten by grants from the National Science Foundation. Drs. Elizabeth Hadly, Márcia Lara, Meika Mustrangi, and Albert Ditchfield helped us develop much of the content of this chapter. Finally, we thank the editors of this volume for important insights that, we hope, have made this chapter a stronger contribution.

8
Biogeography and Diversification of African Forest Faunas: Implications for Conservation

JON FJELDSÅ, MICHELLE K. BAYES,
MICHAEL W. BRUFORD, AND MICHAEL S. ROY

ABSTRACT

It has been widely assumed that the species richness of tropical rainforest biota reflects speciation driven by Pleistocene climatic-vegetational cycles. However, an analysis of published DNA hybridization data suggested that the main tracts of lowland rainforest are inhabited mainly by forms that speciated much earlier. Using mtDNA sequence data, we studied the biogeography of two groups of Afrotropical vertebrates (diurnal birds of the family Pycnonotidae, genus *Andropadus*, and two genera of the nocturnal primate family Galagidae, *Galagoides* and *Otolemur*). In both groups we found that the Guineo-Congolian rainforest was inhabited by widespread species representing deep lineages, while speciation during the later Tertiary and Pleistocene mainly occurred in the more patchy forests elsewhere, especially in the montane "archipelagoes" of eastern Africa. In the case of the primate group, eastern Africa also appeared to be the site of an adaptive shift to savanna woodlands. Adaptive redistribution driven by the functional heterogeneity of lowland rainforests may have obscured the signals concerning initial speciation events in this biome. Certain montane areas harbor some relict species, but also gave rise to successful colonization and new speciation events. These observations suggest that management actions to protect unique biological communities and maintain the diversification process can be targeted most precisely in the ecotonal and montane areas. Since the most important montane areas for speciation are under strong human pressure, intensive support for sustainable land use may be more essential here than traditional reserves. The species of the Guineo-Congolian rainforest are well covered by the existing reserve network, and it is suggested that biodiversity conservation now depends mainly on regional development policies and other macroeconomic decisions.

INTRODUCTION

Most actions undertaken to conserve global biodiversity are local. However, macroeconomic decisions affecting regional development and resource management policies may be more important (Kahn and McDonald 1997; Oates 1999). There is no "correct" scale for biodiversity management, as there is no "correct" scale for studying the processes that cause variations in biodiversity (Levin 1992). To develop the predictive models that are needed to design local and regional management strategies, we must learn how to integrate the disparate scales of interest of scientists studying these problems. In this chapter we examine macroscale patterns of species richness among African forest biota, and we use two case studies based on DNA sequence data to evaluate some hypotheses concerning the geographic origin of species and their persistence in a changing world. Our findings then serve as a background for discussing how to focus conservation action.

Since Moreau (1963), the diversification of African rainforest biota has often been interpreted in terms of Pleistocene climatic-vegetational changes. These changes are now explained as the combined effect of a general global cooling (Shackleton, Berger, and Peltier 1990) and orbital forcing (Berger et al. 1984; deMenocal 1995; Kennett 1995) causing cyclic changes in the impact of polar air masses on the tropics (Servant et al. 1993). It is widely believed that the repeated isolation of forest-dependent species in those forest refugia that remained during cold and dry episodes was a principal cause of speciation (Haffer 1974; Diamond and Hamilton 1980; see Kingdon 1989 for a popular overview). Wet periods provided a vehicle for the new species to be redistributed (Diamond and Hamilton 1980; Prigogine 1987) and become sympatric.

In contrast to this view, the relatively poor biological diversity of the African humid forests, compared with other continents (Richards 1973) and with the Tertiary pan-African "Super Rainforest" (Axelrod and Raven 1978; Flenley, chap. 5 in this volume), would suggest that the forest biota was impoverished, not diversified, during the Pleistocene. Regional variation in species richness could therefore reflect how ancient species survived despite the Pleistocene ecoclimatic changes, instead of reflecting a Pleistocene speciation burst (see Williams and Pearson 1997).

Using DNA hybridization data (from Sibley and Ahlquist 1990), Fjeldså (1994) and Fjeldså and Lovett (1997) demonstrated that the Guineo-Congolian rainforest is dominated by species that represent lineages of pre-Pleistocene age, while species representing more recent proliferations dominate in the ecotonal regions and in "montane forest islands" outside the main rainforest tracts. This generalization needs to be carefully evaluated: we need well-resolved phylogenies (Roy et al. 1997), and we also need to consider to what extent biogeographic patterns simply reflect random distribution constrained by physical boundaries (Jetz and Rahbek 2001) and modified by current ecology (net primary production, habitat complexity, etc.: Jetz and Rahbek 2002).

By using phylogenetic data for one group of forest birds and one group of forest mammals, we will examine the extent to which the fairly similar macroscale patterns of mammal and bird diversity reflect similar speciation histories (however, it falls outside the scope of this chapter to evaluate speciation mechanisms; see Patton and da Silva, chap. 7 in this volume; Smith et al., chap. 9 in this volume). The alternative to a speciation-driven pattern would be that variation in species richness simply reflects adaptive redistribution (and extinction) of species over long periods of time and in relation to physical parameters.

The birds under study are the greenbuls (Passeriformes, Pycnonotidae), a species-rich group of African and Oriental birds of forest and thickets. We will focus on members of the genus *Andropadus,* which are common birds of forest mid-strata all over tropical Africa, from lowlands up to the tree line. Of the eleven to eighteen species (see Roy, Arctander, and Fjeldså 1998), seven are widespread in lowland forest, and six of these are widely sympatric in the Guineo-Congolian forest, while the rest are montane.

The mammals under study are the galagos or bush babies (Primates, Strepsirrhini, Galaginae), which are nocturnal primates of forest and savanna. Traditionally they were divided into six or seven species (Hill 1953; Kingdon 1971), but new bioacoustic and morphological data (Olson 1979; Zimmermann 1990; Bearder, Honess, and Ambrose 1995; Honess 1996; Honess and Bearder 1998) suggest that the number of species may be at least twice as high. This is especially true for the focal group of our chapter, the "dwarf galagos," previously all placed in one species, *Galagoides demidoff* (often referred to as *Galago demidovi*). These are among the smallest primates known, with some forms weighing as little as 60 g. They are now known to comprise several species, which are virtually indistinguishable by external morphology, but show complex parapatric replacement patterns in eastern Africa and some sympatry.

BIOGEOGRAPHIC PATTERNS

Development of Distributional Databases

Distributional databases have been compiled jointly by the Percy FitzPatrick Institute in South Africa and the Danish Centre for Tropical Biodiversity, using published literature and information from numerous specialists (see Burgess et al. 2000; de Klerk et al. 2002). Distributions were digitized within the computer program WorldMap (Version 4.0 for Windows '95, 1996), developed by Paul Williams of the Natural History Museum in London. This is a specialized platform for compiling distributional data and for investigating conservation priorities using a variety of algorithms (P. H. Williams et al. 1996). Distributional data were studied at the scale of a one-degree square (approx. 110 km × 110 km) and at 15 minutes for forest birds of eastern Africa. These scales were chosen after considering the quality of the data in the most poorly known districts, where we aim to make range maps, assuming that species are continuously distributed between collecting points in areas with fairly uniform habitats, except where the data suggest range disjunctions or a very local occurrence.

Congruent Species Richness Patterns for Forest Mammals and Forest Birds

Color plate 1/figure 8.1 (A, B) illustrate the patterns of species richness and endemism (sum of inverse range sizes of all species present) for birds and mammals of evergreen and semi-evergreen forest habitats (see Williams 1998 for techniques). These figures comprise 391 resident forest birds and 183 mammals (Burgess et al. 2000) (excluding some groups of rodents and bats, for which systematic relationships and species distributions are poorly understood). Similar patterns are described for many other taxonomic groups (White 1983; Lovett and Wasser 1993; Barthlott, Lauer, and Placke 1996; Stattersfield et al. 1998; T. Brooks et al. 2001).

In general, African forests are species-poor compared with rainforests of other continents (Richards 1973) and with the habitat mosaics of eastern Africa (T. Brooks et al. 2001; de Klerk et al. 2002). Plate 1/figure 8.1 (A, B) show a particularly impoverished fauna (80–110 forest birds and 35–40 forest mammals per cell) in the western and central parts of the Congo basin. This is not just an artifact of poor sampling, since the inclusion of data from some detailed new studies (e.g., Dowsett and Dowsett-Lemaire 1997) had little effect on the pattern. The low species richness may reflect flat terrain with swamp formations, some notoriously oligotrophic areas, and relatively little habitat heterogeneity (Grove 1978), in addition to the general relationship between species richness and climate (Jetz and Rahbek 2002). The highest species richness is found in areas that are topographically more complex; at the eastern edge of the Congo basin there are up to 183 forest birds and 55 forest mammals. In the west, the Mount Cameroon cell has up to 167 birds and 54 mammals, and for Gabon there are up to 152 birds and 59 mammals. Fairly high values are also found along the southern boundary of the Congo basin and locally in the Guinea highland. The richest areas correspond well with the postulated Pleistocene forest refugia (Diamond and Hamilton 1980). For the Guineo-Congolian rainforest as a whole, cell-by-cell comparisons demonstrate that endemism correlates very closely with species richness (Spearman, r_s 0.944, $P \ll .001$ for birds, r_s 0.715, $P \ll .001$

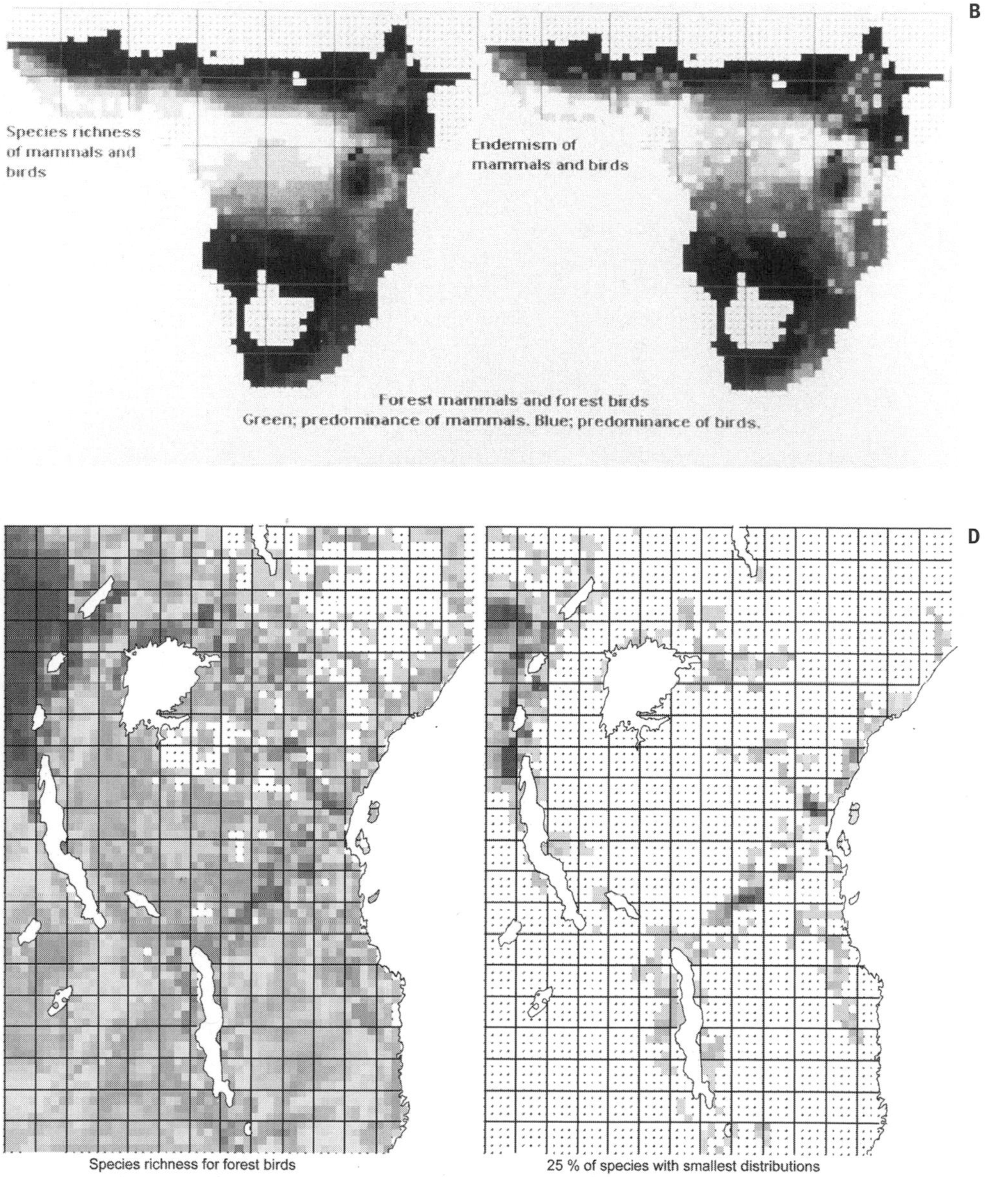

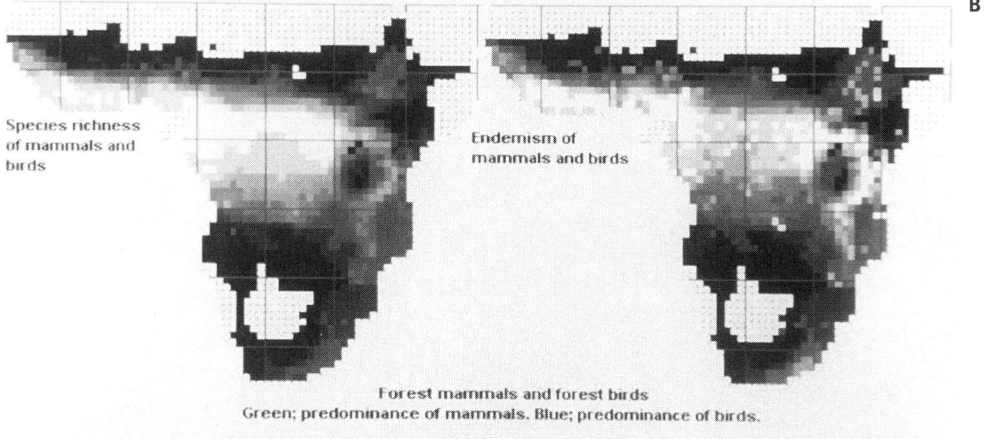

Figure 8.1 Species richness and endemism in Africa. Maps A and B compare patterns for forest birds and forest mammals, on a 1° spatial resolution. Species richness (A) and endemism (B) are expressed as brightness, with areas with the highest richness of both groups appearing white, a bias toward birds shown in green, and a bias toward mammals in blue (see Williams 1998). Maps C and D are focused on eastern Africa (15′ resolution) and show species richness and narrow (lower quartile) endemism (richness peaks are hot red, poor areas are bold blue). See plate 1.

Table 8.1 Distributional data for species of greenbuls (*Andropadus*) and galagos (*Galagoides, Otolemur*)

Species	Distribution[a]	Range (No. cells)[b]	Range Areas[c]
	Greenbuls		
Andropadus masukuensis	Nyasa-Tanzania montane forests	12	1
A. m. kakamegae	Albertine Rift Mts	15	4
A. montanus	Cameroon Mts	7	0
A. tephrolaemus	Cameroon Mts	7	0
A. t. kikuyensis	Albertine Mts to Kenya highland	19	8
A. t. "nigriceps/ usambarae"	Southern Kenya to Usambara Mts	8	2
A. t. fusciceps	Nyasa Rift Mts	4	1
A. t. chlorigula	Udzungwa to Nguru Mts	9	1
A. t. neumanni	Uluguru Mts	2	0
A. milanjensis	Montane forests from E Zimbabwe to S Kenya	33	5
A. virens	Guineo-Congolian forest (G IG NCG WC CC UC U K Z NT)	427	71
"A." gracilis	Guineo-Congolian forest (G IG NCG WC CC UC U)	305	52
"A." ansorgei	Guineo-Congolian forest (G IG NCG CC UC K)	143	29
A. curvirostris	Guineo-Congolian forest (G IG NCG CC UC K)	288	50
"A." gracilirostris	Guineo-Congolian forest (G IG NCG WC CC UC K U)	354	53
A. latirostris	Guineo-Congolian forest (G IG NCG CC UC K U)	327	55
A. importunus	Eastern African coastal zone	152	25

(continued)

for mammals, $N = 316$; the rather low value for mammals is mainly a sampling artifact caused by species known from single collections).

The forests of eastern Africa create a "montane circle" (clockwise, the Albertine Rift Mountains, Mount Elgon, the Kenya highlands, the Eastern Arc crystalline fault-block mountains and the mountains north of Lake Malawi, and the scarps of the Rukwa and southern Tanganyika rifts) (plate 1B, C/fig. 8.1B, C). While species richness is fairly uniform in the eastern mountain ranges (peak values 105 species in the Kenya highlands and 97 in the Eastern Arc), the number of narrow endemics shows a very localized pattern (plate 1D/fig. 8.1D; de Klerk et al. 2002; Fjeldså 2003), with marked peaks in the Eastern Arc (Udzungwa, Uluguru, and Usambara mountains) and in some coastal forests, but very few narrow endemics in the Kenya highland forests. The endemism is well marked also in the Ethiopian highland and along the southeastern coast of Africa (color plate 1B/fig. 8.1B). The peaks of endemism include species representing recently radiated groups as well as ancient relict taxa whose nearest relatives sometimes live on other continents (Fjeldså and Lovett 1997).

Table 8.1 *(continued)*

Species	Distribution[a]	Range (No. cells)[b]	Areas[c]
	Galagos		
Otolemur crassicaudatus	Eastern Africa and southern savanna belt	401	47
O. argentatus	Savannas SE of Lake Victoria	15?	5
O. garnettii	Coastal and submontane forests of Tanzania and Kenya	69	20
Galagoides rondoensis	Rondo/Litipo plateaus, SE Tanzania	1	0
G. udzungwensis	Foothills of Udzungwas and Ulugurus	4	1
G. "orinus"	Disjunct in Eastern Arc Mts, Tanzania	5	1
G. zanzibaricus	Coastal forests of Tanzania/Kenya N Rufiji River	20	4
G. granti	Coastal forests S Rufiji River	46	6
G. demidoff	Guineo-Congolian forest (G IG NCG WC CC UC K)	323	52
G. thomasi	Guineo-Congolian forest (G IG NCG WC? CC? UC K U)	296	45

Note: For a more precise overview, we have separated here some taxa that are regarded as subspecies in the currently accepted classification, but which represent well-marked lineages with no documented intergradation.

[a]Geographic subdivisions of the Guineo-Congolian forest are as follows (* marking assumed refuge areas): G, Guinea*; IG, Ivory Coast and Ghana*; NCG, Nigeria-Cameroon-Gabon*; WC, western Congo Basin; CC, central Congo Basin*; UC, upper Congo Basin.* Range extensions into adjacent areas are U, Uganda lowland forest to Kenya; K, Katanga hills; Z, Zambian woodlands; NT, Nyasa-Tanganyika Mountains*).

[b]Range size expressed as the number of 1° cells occupied.

[c]Number of occupied cells containing more than 100 km² of conservation areas (as recorded in the databases of the World Conservation Monitoring Centre), except if these definitely do not cover the species' habitat.

Bird and mammal patterns were compared visually and cell by cell (Spearman, r_s 0.877 for species richness, 0.814 for endemism scores; $P < .001$ in both cases). The differences, especially in endemism, may to some extent reflect the less complete sampling of mammals than of birds, as some potentially fairly widespread mammals are known from only one or a very few collections—for example, in the Congo basin and along the Congo/Zambezi watershed. East of the Albertine Rift, the peak site for avian endemism (Udzungwa Mountains, with six narrow endemics) is also known as the peak site for primates (ten species, four of them narrow endemics) (Kingdon 1997). On the other hand, no narrowly endemic forest mammals have been recorded (yet) for the Angola Scarp (plate 1B/fig. 8.1B).

The distributional data for *Andropadus* greenbuls (reviewed in table 8.1) conform to the general pattern in terms of maxima and minima of species richness. In view of the recent revisions of dwarf galagos, we will review their distributions in more detail. All dwarf galagos inhabit various kinds of evergreen forest habitat, with a complex geographic replacement pattern in eastern Africa and a broad overlap in the Guineo-Congolian area of two ecologically and vocally distinctive species. *G. demidoff* and *G. thomasi* (table 8.1). The latter may be somewhat local and associated with mature forest in submontane areas, and it extends into Uganda north of Lake Victoria; an isolated population on Mount Marsabit in northern Kenya may represent this or an unnamed species. Eastern Africa is inhabited by widespread as well as local (relictual) species. Two "incremental callers," *G. zanzibaricus* and *G. granti,* inhabit the Zanzibar-Inhabane coastal forest mosaic north and south of the Rufiji River, respectively. Three relictual species are the poorly known *G. orinus* of Eastern Arc highland forests (East Usambara, Nguru, Mkungwe, Uluguru, and Udzungwa mountains, apparently with some population differentiation) and two "roller-callers" (Honess 1996; Honess and Bearder 1998), *G. udzungwensis* from the foothill forests of the Uluguru and Udzungwa mountains and *G. rondoensis* from the Rondo and Litipo plateaus near the coast of southern Tanzania. As will be shown below, the dwarf galagos are a paraphyletic group with respect to the large *Otolemur* species, which comprise *O. garnettii* in eastern coastal forests and *O. crassicaudatus,* which inhabits a wide range of woodland habitats in eastern and southern Africa. Weighing up to 2 kg, the latter species represents a major evolutionary shift compared with the dwarf galagos. The populations of the savannas southeast of Lake Victoria may be a good species, *O. argentatus,* and other populations may also qualify for species rank.

STUDIES USING MTDNA SEQUENCE DATA

Greenbuls

Blood and feather samples were taken from mist-netted birds. We included members of all species (except the two tiny, slender-billed and rather atypical species *A. gracilis* and *A. ansorgei,* for which we had no samples). Two individuals of each population were analyzed (although fig. 8.2 shows only those that had dissimilar sequences), with several populations included for some montane species. Standard procedures were used for cell lysis, proteinase digestion in SDS-based extraction buffer, organic purification using phenol/chloroform, ethanol precipitation in the presence of ammonium acetate, and PCR sequencing (Roy, Arctander, and Fjeldså 1998). We partially sequenced two mitochon-

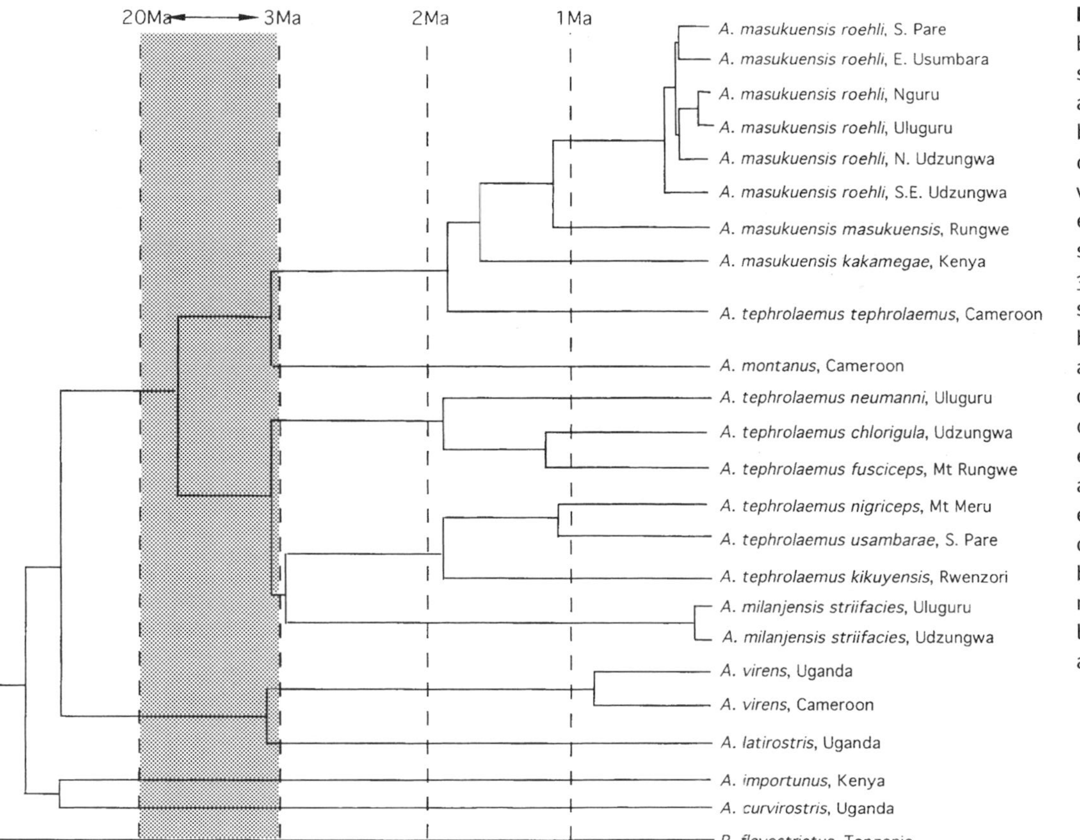

Figure 8.2 A maximum parsimony–based topology for *Andropadus* using sequences of *Cytochrome b* (575 bp) and *ND2* (296 bp) combined, and branch lengths according to sequence divergence (see Roy 1997 for bootstrap values and a full evaluation). A time estimate is given assuming 10% sequence divergence per MYA up until 3 MYA. Because of transition saturation, there is a lack of linearity between overall divergence and time, and we therefore used transversions only below 3 MYA, assuming a rate of 0.5% per MYA. However, at this level of evolutionary divergence transversion accumulation between clades and time estimation had a high variance, which decreased above 12 MYA. The split between highland and lowland forms may have been 18–32 MYA, and the lowland forms diverged from one another 12–28 MYA (Roy 1997).

drial (mt) genes, Cytochrome *b* (575 bp, primer pairs L14841/H15149 and L15546/H15915) and *ND2* (296 bp, primer pair H5578/L5215). Sequences were aligned by eye, and parsimony analysis was carried out using the "branch and bound" option of PAUP for Macintosh (version 3.1.1: Swofford 1991).

Sequence divergence in *Andropadus* (combined for the two genes) ranged from 0.2% for geographically close (montane) intraspecific comparisons to 17.6% between species, with the largest variation among the lowland species (Roy 1997). The highest values are extreme for intrageneric comparisons in birds (Moore and DeFilippis 1997). *A. gracilirostris* was found to be even more divergent from montane *Andropadus* (*ND2* gives 20% average divergence) than was the defined outgroup (*Phyllastrephus flavostriatus,* 14.9% divergence; see also Beresford 2002). We do not find it justified to keep *A. gracilirostris* in *Andropadus,* and we exclude it from figure 8.2 and from further discussions.

One hundred seventy-seven out of 575 and 117 out of 296 sites were parsimony informative for Cyt *b* and *ND2* respectively. Individual phylogenetic analyses of the two genes were carried out weighting transversions 10:1 over transitions. Consensus trees from the two genes were similar, and in a strict consensus tree, only a few nodes within *A. masukuensis roehli* and the relationship between *A. curvirostris* and *importunus* were unresolved (see Roy, Arctander, and Fjeldså 1998 for a detailed evaluation). The tree topology is not affected by the much denser sampling of montane than lowland taxa, since the deep branches are robust to changes in the number of montane specimens. Figure 8.2 shows an estimated time schedule for the diversification, using all substitutions in the top branches and transversions alone below 3 MYA (because of the saturation for third codon position transitions).

The lowland species represent a paraphyletic assemblage of deep branches. They comprise the widely sympatric Guineo-Congolian species *A. curvirostris, A. virens,* and *A. latirostris* (and the "dwarf" species *A. gracilis* and *A. ansorgei,* for which we had no tissue; the first resembles *A. curvirostris* by plumage colors, but is ecologically and vocally quite different from it), and *A. importunus* along the African east coast (table 8.1). These taxa are all fully compatible species. Each of them has two or more subspecies, but the variation (color hues, size) is subtle, overall, and does not indicate gene flow breaks.

The montane taxa form a monophyletic group, perhaps with an early separation of populations in the Cameroon and East African mountains, followed by a separation of populations in the Albertine Rift area and nearer to the east coast. The populations inhabiting the Tanzania-Malawi mountains present a complex case. Those traditionally referred to *A. tephrolaemus* represent two lineages: the northeastern *usambarae* (Usambara and Pare mountains), which is linked, through *nigriceps*, to *kikuyensis* of the northern Kenya and Albertine Rift mountains, and the southern forms *fusciceps, chlorigula,* and *neumanni,* representing a deep branch (11% average sequence divergence from the other taxa and 9% internal subdivision). While the concordance between phenetic and genetic divergence is good, overall, a strong element of randomness in evolution of pigment saturation is found among different isolates of the *A. tephrolaemus* complex (Roy, Arctander, and Fjeldså 1998). Unfortunately, we did not have samples for resolving the internal structure of *A. milanjensis.* In *A. masukuensis,* the progressively shorter branches in the east suggest a recent colonization from mountain to mountain across Tanzania.

Galagos

We used tissue (including samples from museum specimens) from five populations referred to as *G. demidoff* and two populations from the Udzungwa Mountains of Tanzania (the low-altitude *G. udzungwensis* and a highland form that we refer to as *G. orinus*). Because a more comprehensive analysis (Bayes 1998) revealed that the dwarf galagos are paraphyletic with respect to the large *Otolemur* species, these were also included in our analysis.

Due to the deep branching patterns within this group (Seiffert, Simons, and Attia 2003), a relatively constrained mitochondrial gene was chosen for analysis, 12S rRNA. Whole genomic DNA was extracted using standard methods, as described for *Andropadus.* All sequences were aligned using the program Sequencher 3.0, then entered into the program MacClade (Maddison and Swofford 1992), exported into ClustalW (Thompson, Higgins, and Gibson 1994), and then checked by eye with respect to the secondary structure model of the mitochondrial 12S rRNA gene. Trees were calculated using the maximum likelihood method with settings that correspond to the HKY85+γ model of nucleotide substitution (Hasegawa, Kishino, and Yano 1985), and bootstrap analysis was carried out using the fast method and 100 replicates. The maximum likelihood tree was calculated using starting branch lengths obtained using the Rogers-Swofford approximation method, two substitution types, a transition/transversion ratio of 3.5 ($\kappa = 7.3627593$), assumed nucleotide frequencies set to empirical frequencies ($A = .35728$, $C = .24526$, $G = .18359$, $T = .21387$), and a shape parameter (α) of 0.156242, with four rate categories and the mean average rate for each category.

Sequence divergence for the 12S rRNA gene was corrected for multiple hits using the Kimura two-parameter model. The galagos differed by 14%–17% from the defined outgroup (*Loris tardigradus*), and the variation ranged up to 13%

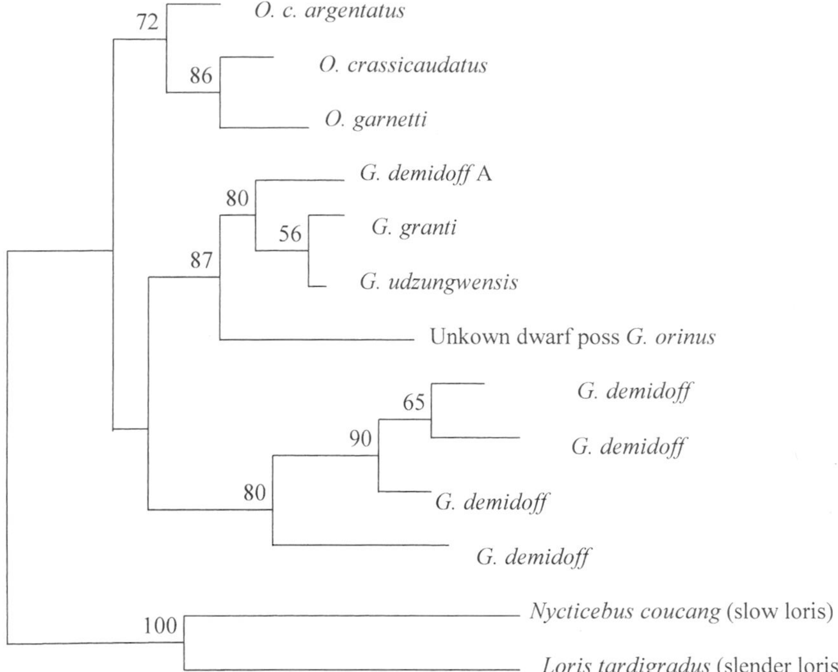

Figure 8.3 Maximum likelihood tree (−ln likelihood = 3203.35223) of dwarf galagos, genus *Galagoides*, and two large bush babies, genus *Otolemur*. Numbers beside nodes indicate bootstrap support from 100 resampling replicates using the branch and bound algorithm and maximum likelihood analysis. The "unknown dwarf galago" (Udekwa in the Udzungwa Mountains) is best referred to *G. orinus*, although the differentiation of populations inhabiting different montane forests in the Eastern Arc is not yet fully understood.

between dwarf galagos from the Guineo-Congolian forest. A lower level of divergence, 5%, was seen between the two *Otolemur* species, and intermediate levels among all eastern populations. This result is remarkable in view of the subtle morphological differentiation among the dwarf galagos and the enormous morphological change in *Otolemur*.

Maximum likelihood analysis produced 227 distinct data patterns; the log likelihood of the best tree (fig. 8.3) was −3203.35. The topology of the tree did not change when using either parsimony or distance algorithms. Some species are missing from this analysis, so it should be noted that, based on vocalizations and penile morphology, we expect *G. rondoensis* to cluster with *G. udzungwensis* and *G. zanzibaricus*.

Curiously, *G. demidoff* A from Franceville in Gabon was genetically nearest to *G. udzungwensis* and *G. granti* (3% sequence divergence) and clustered with it in figure 8.3. It should be noted that reliable identification of dwarf galago voucher specimens is very difficult due to lack of data on penile morphology and calls. Because of poor access to reliably identified fresh specimens (for which the above-mentioned data are available), our study can only be regarded as tentative. Clearly, the *G. demidoff* A specimen is specifically distinct from other members of *G. demidoff* and could well represent *G. thomasi.*

DISCUSSION

Cryptic Biodiversity Revealed by New Data

The genetic variation observed among the galagos supports the views (e.g., Bearder, Honess, and Ambrose 1995) that many populations of very similar-looking dwarf galagos qualify for species rank. Although tissue samples have been analyzed across the range for other galago species (Bayes 1998), the result for the dwarf galagos remains unique in terms of deep genetic subdivision of what was traditionally considered a single species. Considering the sequence divergence from the outgroup, the variation represents an enormous time span. Yoder (1997) estimates that the split between lorises and galagos was as early as the late Paleocene, around 55 MYA. An early date of divergence has also recently found support in the discovery of fossils believed to be ancestral to the galago and loris groups, dating from the Middle Eocene (Seiffert, Simons, and Attia 2003). This time scale seems to be accepted by many primatologists, although Purvis (1995) suggests a younger age. Compared with the 14%–17% sequence divergence between *Loris* and dwarf galagos, the early divergence among dwarf galagos would be approximately 45 MYA, in the Middle Eocene, with *Otolemur* diverging in the Miocene. Irrespective of the uncertainties involved in such estimates, we can assume that the Guineo-Congolian subspecies of *G. demidoff* represent an enormous level of genetic diversity. Yet there is no definite evidence of breaks in gene flow among populations (subspecies) currently referred to as *G. demidoff.*

Species rank is confirmed for the eastern forms, as two dwarfs and one *Otolemur* have been found together in several places (Honess 1996). Our *G. udzungwensis* sample was collected in foothill forest closely below the collecting site for the *G. orinus* sample, and farther south along the Udzungwa scarp J. Fjeldså has found the two only 2 kilometers apart (at different altitudes). It seems that the eastern populations comprise a range of adaptations, as some "relict dwarf galagos" survived over long geologic periods in some places, which had humid forest permanently, while others are widespread in the coastal forest patchwork, with the "greater galagos" having undergone significant adaptive change and successfully spread through various woodland habitats.

The association of *G. demidoff* A from Gabon with the eastern African group, closest to *G. udzungwensis*, provides support for the idea (Roy et al. 1997) that the Guineo-Congolian fauna can be enriched by colonization from other parts of the continent where there are more opportunities for speciation. Prigogine (1987) suggested that suitable conditions for dispersal along the northern "rim" of the Congo basin to Cameroon-Gabon would exist during humid climatic episodes.

For greenbuls, the sequence divergence data seem consistent with the DNA hybridization evidence (Sibley and Ahlquist 1990, 865) and other molecular data (Beresford 2002) in suggesting a rapid mid-Tertiary radiation of the Pycnonotidae. Beresford (2002) demonstrated that Guineo-Congolian species of the genera *Bleda* and *Criniger* show considerable phylogeographic structure and that this differentiation took place long before the Pleistocene. For the widespread *A. virens*, Smith et al. (1997) demonstrated that, despite significant gene flow in marginal ecotonal habitat mosaics, there is sufficient isolation by distance and selective pressures to produce morphologically divergent populations. However, whether such processes lead to speciation is an open question. Despite the significant age of the lowland species, and some subspecific variation, the morphological variation does not indicate gene flow breaks or raise doubt about the monophyly of currently recognized species. However, a more comprehensive sampling is desirable to reexamine the subdivision of lowland species and the phylogeographic structure within them.

Among the montane forms, the initial split was in the later Miocene, while the further differentiation happened after the Plio-Pleistocene transition (Roy et al. 1998). Many allopatric montane populations referred to as the same species in the current classification differ to a degree (6%–12% sequence divergence) that is similar to that between fully compatible species and not analogous to that of interbreeding populations (Arctander and Fjeldså 1994; Moore and DeFilippis 1997). The traditional taxonomy apparently failed in this respect because of the implicit assumption under the biological species concept (Mayr 1982) that taxa replacing each other in adjacent and ecologically similar areas must be closely related and are therefore best treated as subspecies (Bock 1986; Amadon and Short 1992). We assume that local populations subject to uniform selection pressures on permanently forested slopes will mainly be subject to neutral drift (as suggested by the pattern of variation in pigment saturations; see García-Moreno and Fjeldså 1999 for another example). Despite considerable genetic divergence, they therefore apparently remain "the same species" for long periods of time (Walter 1988), but as independent evolutionary trajectories, they should be accepted as species (Corbet 1997; Johnson, Remsen, and Cicero 1999). Transient hybrid zones are unrecorded in the montane greenbuls.

The current research on parapatric birds is dominated by demonstration of limited interbreeding and replacement where paraspecies meet (Gill 1998), suggesting that they represent mutually exclusive species rather than subspecies. Strong selective pressures are also sometimes involved, as suggested, for example, by the dramatic adaptive shift in *Otolemur* (possibly in response to the gradual aridification in eastern Africa since the Miocene) and by indications of sympatric divergence (see below).

The Distinction between Guineo-Congolian and Peripheral Forest Biota

Although species richness peaks (see plate 1/fig. 8.1) correspond to the hypothesized Pleistocene refugia, our phylogenetic data provide no evidence for Pleistocene speciation centered in the lowland rainforests. One possible case is provided, however, of a late Tertiary colonization of the Guineo-Congolian rainforest from eastern Africa (*G. demidoff* A). Similarly, new molecular data for *Phyllastrephus* greenbuls suggest a late Tertiary colonist from eastern Africa, *P. scandens* (B. Slikas, personal communication). Most of the Guineo-Congolian species are widespread and broadly sympatric across the biome (table 8.1, fig. 8.4), as suggested already by other data (Fjeldså 1994; Fjeldså and Lovett 1997). Since every lowland *Andropadus* species (apart from *A. importunus*) inhabits all the assumed refugia within the Guineo-Congolian region, it seems that all biogeographic signals concerning the initial speciation events have been obliterated. Also, data for other Guineo-Congolian greenbuls suggest that most speciation events, and even the differentiation of "subspecies" east and west of the Dahomey Gap, are ancient events (Beresford 2002). It is worth noting that, because of the position of Africa relative to the equator, the cold Benguela Current may have excluded warm equatorial waters from the Gulf of Guinea up until the end of the Miocene (Smith, Smith, and Funnell 1994), and we may infer from this that speciation was linked with an enormous savanna gap separating the Cameroon and Guinea forests at this time, rather than with Pleistocene forest cover changes.

Throughout the Guineo-Congolian rainforest, the variation in endemism reflects the species richness closely, and there is also a close correlation with environmental parameters such as topographic complexity, vegetation index, and rainfall (de Klerk et al. 2002; Jetz and Rahbek 2002). Given the empirically documented variation in abundance rank relationships and range sizes in

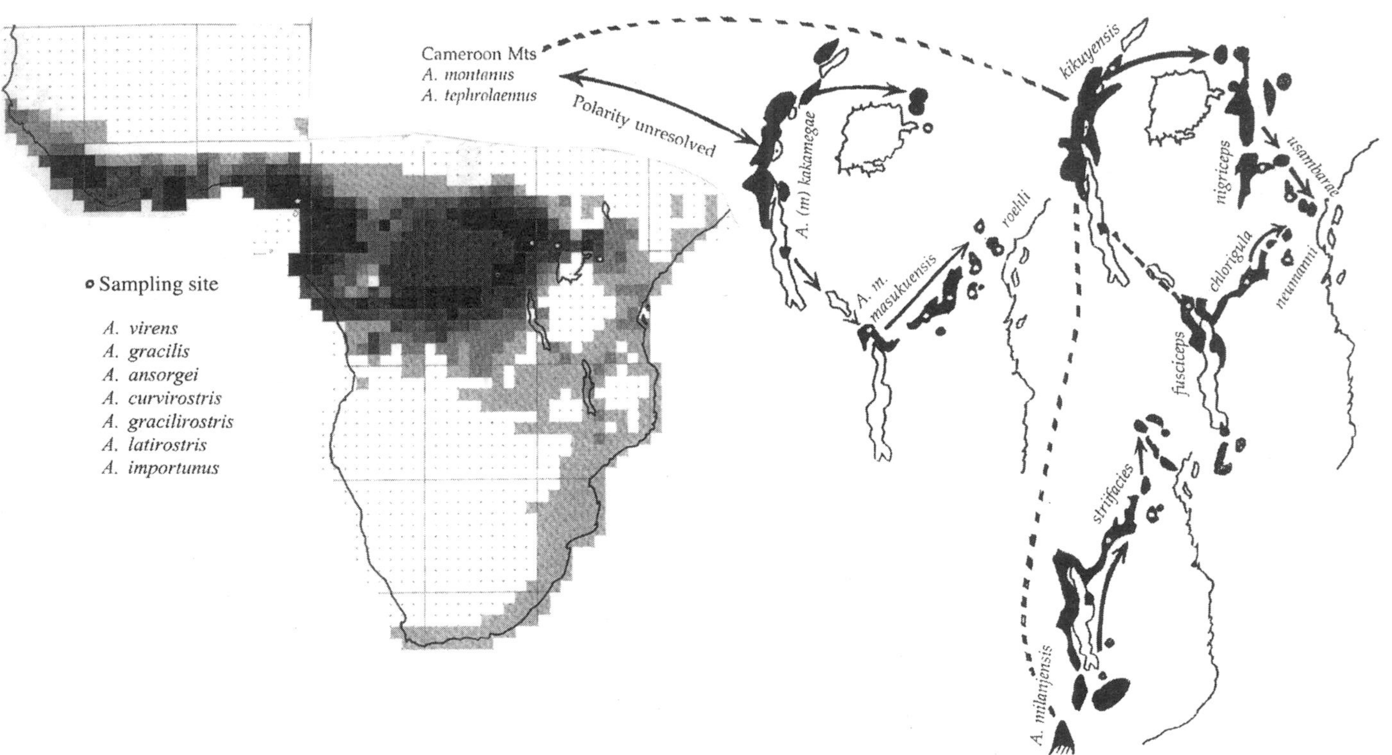

Figure 8.4 A simplified model of diversification of *Andropadus* greenbuls. The left map illustrates the variation in richness of species representing deep (Miocene) lineages. All species except the eastern *A. importunus* are present in all assumed Pleistocene "refuge areas" within the Guineo-Congolian rainforest, which therefore appear black. The other three maps (of eastern Africa) show distribution patterns of the major lineages of the monophyletic group of montane species. Broken lines illustrate early vicariance and arrows illustrate later dispersal.

communities (Hubbell 2001), some species must necessarily, at any time, be restricted to the most species-rich parts of a biome. So the raised endemism observable in certain parts of the Guineo-Congolian forests can be explained by a neutral community drift model (Hubbell 2001 and chap. 4 in this volume), with no need to invoke recent speciation. The model would predict the rare "specialists" to be found mainly in the most complex and productive areas (in the Upper Guinea forest, Cameroon-Gabon, and along the eastern boundary of the Congo basin). Other species may, as a consequence of the instability of Pleistocene habitats and fast dynamics on the local level, have become widespread, even reaching eastern Africa (e.g., *A. curvirostris, gracilis, latirostris,* and *virens*).

Although the instability of African climates is indisputable (Livingstone 1993; Nicholson 1994), the location of forest refugia is undocumented, and in fact inferred from present-day distribution patterns. If forest refugia existed, they may have functioned as dynamic networks rather than as isolates (see Hopkins et al. 1993), and were not the cause of much speciation. The Guineo-Congolian rainforest could instead be regarded as an evolutionary "sink" where the species of the Miocene Super Rainforest persisted up until the present, according to current ecology.

Our two case studies suggest that diversification in the late Tertiary and Pleistocene happened mainly in the montane areas, especially in eastern Africa. This result is not just an artifact of the denser sampling in the East African mountains, and it is corroborated by other, more recent molecular studies (Bowie 2003). Unlike the Guineo-Congolian rainforest, this region is characterized by several sharp geographic replacements. Certain mountains are as rich in species as many parts of the Guineo-Congolian rainforest, despite the very small forest area. Our mammal data suggest a long persistence of some relict taxa, as well as a marked adaptive shift in *Otolemur. O. garnettii* is most typical of semi-evergreen lowland forest, but *O. crassicaudatus* is found in a wide range of habitats, from coastal and montane forests to savanna woodland and plantations all over eastern Africa and across the southern savannas to Angola.

A fairly detailed biogeographic reconstruction is possible for the montane greenbuls. The early events have several possible interpretations (figs. 8.2 and 8.4). An early separation of pre-*kakamegae* and pre-*kikuyensis* in central Africa may have been followed by two colonizations along the northern rim of the Congo basin (Prigogine 1987) to the Cameroon Mountains. This interpretation does not explain the initial separation of *kakamegae* and *kikuyensis* within central Africa, where they are now fully sympatric. Alternatively, an early separation of populations in eastern Africa and in the Cameroon Mountains may have been followed by a dispersal from the Cameroon Mountains to the Albertine Rift

Mountains (pre-*kakamegae*) and then back to the Cameroon Mountains (as *tephrolaemus*, now specifically distinct from the earlier resident *A. montanus*). For the remaining eastern African lineages, the most conservative interpretation would be to suggest an early trichotomy (of the *kikuyensis* group, the *neumanni* group, and *milanjensis*). The morphocline within *A. milanjensis* (from "plesiomorphic" *kikuyensis*-like birds in the far south to the rich greenish subspecies *striifacies* in Tanzania and Kenya) would suggest that it originated as a southern isolate, then spread into the areas occupied by its northern relatives (fig. 8.4) and changed because of altered selective pressures.

A. (masukuensis) kakamegae became sympatric with *kikuyensis* along the length of the Albertine Rift, and the Malawi Rift population (*masukuensis*) gave rise to a quite recent (Pleistocene) dispersal along the Eastern Arc mountains of Tanzania. It is tempting to associate the specialized scansorial habits of the Tanzanian birds (Dinesen 1995) with selective pressures caused by sympatry with two congeners in the east.

The isolating effects of distance and intermittent forest contractions have, together with at least three successful colonizations along the Eastern Arc (including submontane populations of *A. virens*), contributed to the development of a complex guild of *Andropadus* greenbuls here. By using rapidly evolving genes, large numbers of samples, and coalescence methods, more detailed information will certainly be obtained about dispersal and gene flow. Such studies are now in progress (Bowie 2003) and suggest that many bird "species" inhabiting these "islands in the sky" are in fact species groups, and that some populations have persisted for long periods of time, especially in Tanzania, while others have rapidly expanded to other highlands, and in one case (*Nectarinia olivacea*) has fairly recently spread across all evergreen parts of the Afrotropics.

Conservation Perspectives

Two important messages can be taken from our study. First, the biodiversity of the lowland rainforests has been maintained over enormous periods of time and reflects the slow dynamics on the metacommunity level (Hubbell 2001 and chap. 4 in this volume), rather than Pleistocene speciation. Since the species are generally widespread across a wide range of forest types and in many protected areas (table 8.1), the risks of global extinctions are low. Second, there is a high level of cryptic biodiversity, in terms of evolutionarily significant units (ESUs), that was overlooked by past systematists, who mainly examined museum specimens. Many of these ESUs are found at the periphery of, or outside, the main rainforest blocks, and they are concentrated in quite specific places. Because of the cryptic nature of many species, there is a risk that genetically distinct forms will be lost in these places by lack of taxonomic recognition (Avise 1989b; Smith et al., chap. 9 in this volume; Moritz and McDonald, chap. 26 in this volume). The dwarf galago of Mount Marsabit may already be extinct (L. Borghesio, personal communication). We are also concerned that these places are important for maintaining the speciation process.

A nested structure of local avian communities in eastern Africa (Cordeiro 1998; see also Wright and Reeves 1992 and Schneider and Williams, chap. 20 in this volume) is consistent with a high level of local extinction. However, this does not mean that these communities are "doomed to extinction." As demonstrated by Johnson (1998), old relict species are often common within their tiny geographic ranges. Apparently, a few places support viable relict populations of plants and animals over enormous evolutionary time spans (Fjeldså and Lovett 1997): the East Usambara and Uluguru mountains, the eastern scarp of the Udzungwa highland, the coastal forests of southern Kenya, the East Usambara foothills, and the Rondo Plateau (plate 1D/fig. 8.1D). In some of these areas it is still possible to maintain a certain connectivity of forest patches and fairly intact altitudinal habitat gradients, which is essential for conserving these communities. Being biologically unique, and potential sources for recruitment to the regional species pool, these places should be top priorities for conservation action. Unfortunately, they are covered very poorly by the existing protected areas network (see table 8.1).

The nested pattern of species distributions indicates that endemism is more than just a consequence of isolating barriers. It reflects special local conditions that allow relict populations to persist. The essential feature could be the constantly humid climate on certain escarpments facing the Indian Ocean (Lovett and Wasser 1993). Data derived from long time series of satellite imagery suggest that local peaks of endemism correlate with high levels of interannual stability (Fjeldså et al. 1997; Fjeldså, Lambin, and Mertens 1999; de Klerk et al. 2002). This orographic climatic moderation will probably persist despite shifting global climates (at least near the equator). Theoretical considerations linking speciation with local environments that exhibit few effects of orbitally forced climate change have recently been presented by Jansson and Dynesius (2002).

Across Africa, biological species richness and human population density show parallel responses to net primary productivity, meaning that the biologically richest areas also are the most densely populated (Balmford et al. 2001; Moore et al. 2002). It is even more worrying that the local peaks of endemism are often immediately adjacent to cultural centers where human civilizations have flourished over long periods of time. This is the case for the lowlands adjacent to the Cameroon Mountains (Igbo and Benin cultures) and the Albertine Rift (Nkena, Rwanda, Burundi, and Buganda), in the Nyasa-Tanganyika Mountains (Kliwa, Fipa, Hehe) and adjacent coast (Swahili), in eastern Zimbabwe (Great Zimbabwe), and in Ethiopia (Aksum). We suggest that the long human history in areas with high endemism is related to resource predictability caused by the orographic climatic moderation and a steady water supply from the mountain ridges, where mossy and microphyllic vegetation "combs" moisture out of the wind-driven mist. Fertile soils develop locally on the transition to rain shadow areas, where there is a balance between rainfall and evaporation (Holdridge 1967), and in volcanic areas.

The unique biodiversity of these places is threatened by dense rural populations that have few alternatives to unsustainable land use practices (as exemplified by the overpopulation in Rwanda-Burundi and on the slopes of the Uluguru Mountains). Many areas that may initially have been covered by species-rich montane forests have now been turned into eroded and dry wastelands. In some districts, so little cloud forest is left that important water catchment functions may have been lost. Although the cost of developing fully representative networks of conservation areas will be high, investments to protect "hotspots of endemism" are indeed relevant, since they will maintain ecosystem services that are essential in the long-term for human livelihood in these places. Instead of traditional reservations, the most efficient approach may be to help local communities abandon unsustainable and devastating land use practices and adopt more area-intensive methods (see Johansson 2001 for a practical example from eastern Africa). These actions can be targeted quite precisely as we shift our focus from regional to local planning of conservation efforts.

Traditional conservation strategies for Africa (e.g., Stuart, Adams, and Jenkins 1990) did not take into account the correlation between endemism and human pressures. Instead, they focused on regional species richness and on ad hoc reservation of areas where there were few people and low conflict levels (Pressey and Tully 1994: Fjeldså and Rahbek 1998). To a large extent, reservation of areas with few people leads to redundant conservation of the widespread and adaptable species that are characteristic of ecologically unstable regions (Balmford et al. 2001). Apart from some of the megafauna, these areas have few species to lose.

We will not dispute the uniqueness of large tracts of lowland rainforests, their climatic effect, or the fact that they maintain high levels of genetic diversity. However, because these species pools are partly a consequence of area, floodplain dynamics, and other aspects of functional heterogeneity acting over wide areas, global persistence of species is indeed possible despite considerable amounts of local elimination. While human habitat disturbance has had marked negative effects in centers of endemism in Africa (e.g., Newmark 1991; Fjeldså 1999), the effects are unclear in some areas characterized by high levels of floodplain or forest-savanna dynamics (see examples in Danielsen 1997 and Laurance and Bierregaard 1997). For many areas of lowland rainforest, macropolitical decisions based on principles of sustainability may be more important, overall, than traditional protection of isolated reserves (Oates 1999). Improving international agreements on climate, tariffs, and trade (notably of timber) and removing perverse subsidies should therefore be a high priority. On the more local scale, economic planning that helps people establish stable communities with access to predictable external markets should be promoted, as opposed to uncontrolled and opportunistic colonization following the construction of new roads into the rainforest.

We suggest that much more attention be paid to the relationships between large-scale patterns of biodiversity and human pressures on nature. Development of good management strategies, with balanced attention to macropolitical and local actions, will require that we understand the local and regional processes that govern species richness, endemism, and speciation, as well as human population patterns.

ACKNOWLEDGMENTS

The Danish Center for Tropical Biodiversity (Danish Natural Science Research Council grant 11-0390) provided a good environment for interdisciplinary studies. The grant provided salaries and working budgets for the DNA work by Mike Roy, for fieldwork, and for the development of the African distributional databases, organized by Neil Burgess together with Carsten Rahbek and J. Fjeldså. The bird databases were developed jointly with Helen de Klerk and Tim Crowe of the Percy FitzPatrick Institute of Cape Town University. The following persons have assisted with data entry for birds and mammals: Louis A. Hansen, Jesper B. Larsen, Steffan Galster, and Andy Jacobsen. Galago work was carried out by M. Bayes, who was funded by a dev-R grant from Oxford Brookes University. We thank the National Museum of Kenya, Uganda National Parks, Dr. T. Smith, and Copenhagen University field teams for collection of tissue samples. Neil Burgess, Niels Krabbe, Chris Schneider, and Tom B. Smith made comments on the manuscript.

9

Evaluating the Divergence-with-Gene-Flow Model in Natural Populations: The Importance of Ecotones in Rainforest Speciation

THOMAS B. SMITH, ROBERT K. WAYNE,
DEREK GIRMAN, AND MICHAEL W. BRUFORD

ABSTRACT

Decades of often intense debate have not produced a comprehensive explanation for the high biodiversity of tropical rainforests. Most theories require physical isolation of populations and cessation of gene flow for speciation to occur. However, there is frequently a lack of concordance between species boundaries and hypothesized geographic barriers. Studies of species distributions have suggested that transition zones (or ecotones) between central African rainforest and savanna mark the boundaries between many avian taxa, suggesting that these regions may be important in generating the high species richness of African rainforests. However, explanations of exactly how they might be important, and specific data on the evolutionary processes responsible, have been lacking. Over the last decade, the divergence-with-gene-flow model of speciation has received strong support from laboratory studies of *Drosophila.* Studies show that if populations are experiencing strong divergent selection, they may diverge and become reproductively isolated even if some genetic exchange occurs between them. Using one of the central predictions of the model—that morphological divergence resulting from divergent selection should increase as gene flow decreases—we examine the role of ecotones between central African rainforest and savanna in promoting divergence. We show that populations of three rainforest passerines that exist in forest patches in ecotones are highly divergent from central forest populations in characters important to fitness, despite high rates of genetic exchange. Our results provide evidence and a mechanism for previous assertions that transitional regions at the periphery of rainforests may be instrumental in generating the high biodiversity of tropical rainforests.

INTRODUCTION

Most theories of speciation have focused on isolated small populations in which founder effects, drift, inbreeding, and natural selection interact to cause evolutionary change free from the homogenizing effects of gene flow (Mayr 1963;

Templeton 1987). Frequently, natural selection has been assumed to be too weak to cause morphological change given modest rates of gene flow (Endler 1977; Rice and Hostert 1993). However, few studies have estimated levels of gene flow and divergent selection simultaneously (Endler 1977).

In Africa, the vast forest-savanna mosaic existing between contiguous rainforest and savanna (Millington, Styles, and Critchley 1992) offers a unique model system to test ideas about the influence of selection and gene flow on phenotypic divergence and speciation. Populations existing in forest patches in ecotones should experience divergent selection relative to central rainforest populations because these regions have lower levels of rainfall and experience greater annual fluctuations in environmental variables (Longman and Jenik 1992). For many rainforest bird species, food quality and habitat structure differ dramatically between ecotones and the central forest (Chapin 1954; Smith 1993), suggesting that selection might explain the widespread occurrence of phenotypically unique ecotone populations and races (Chapin 1932, 1954; Endler 1982b, 1982c). However, phenotypic divergence in ecotones may have a variety of causes. If ecotone forests have been genetically isolated, then phylogenetic history, founder effects, genetic drift, and inbreeding could have contributed substantially to the observed pattern of divergence. In contrast, if gene flow has been high, in excess of a few migrants per generation (Slatkin 1987), then selection is strongly implicated as the cause of phenotypic divergence. Our research has focused on understanding the importance of these factors in promoting phenotypic divergence and speciation in ecotones and in other ecological transition zones.

EMPIRICAL EVIDENCE THAT DIVERSIFICATION OCCURS IN ECOTONES

Considerable empirical evidence suggests that the forest-savanna mosaics that form the ecotone between contiguous rainforest and savanna may be important areas of divergence in Africa. Comprising over 3,000 square kilometers of the African continent and often greater than 1,000 kilometers wide, the forest-savanna ecotone contains forest fragments of varying size and degree of isolation (Millington, Styles, and Critchley 1992). Ecotone forests often have populations whose phenotypes diverge from those of central rainforest populations in characters important to fitness (Smith 1997; Smith et al. 1997). These differences were first noted by Chapin (1932), who described distinctive differences in morphology between central rainforest and ecotone populations of over 60 species and subspecies of birds. Later studies confirmed this pattern by showing that high subspecific diversity was concentrated in ecotones around the Congo forest (Chapin 1954; Crowe and Crowe 1982; Endler 1982b; Hall and Moreau 1970). Endler (1982b, 1982c), in particular, called attention to these regions. Using atlases of avian species distributions, he estimated that 52% of the contact zones between sister species in Africa occurred between forest and savanna, 39% within hypothesized refugia, and only 9% between ancient refugia as predicted by the forest refuge hypothesis. Finally, recent support for ecotones as areas of rapid morphological divergence was provided by Fjeldså (1994), who analyzed avian phylogenies based on DNA-DNA hybridization data (Sibley and Ahlquist 1990). Fjeldså found that more deeply rooted species were concentrated in the forest zone, whereas more recently evolved species were characteristic of transitional habitats and mountains.

The ecology of ecotone forest fragments differs in numerous ways from that of the central rainforest. Rainfall is lower and more variable annually (Longman and Jenik 1992), habitats are more open, and there are differences in food quality and abundance (Chapin 1924, 1932, 1954; Hall and Moreau 1970; Smith 1997). Consequently, the different selective regimes of ecotones cause morphological divergence when the two habitats are compared. For example, ecotone birds have longer wing lengths, which may reflect increased predation risk in open habitats, and show different bill morphologies reflecting differences in food habits (Benkman 1991; Schluter and Repasky 1991; Smith 1997; Smith, Schneider, and Holder 2001). Yet, despite these characteristics, little attention has been given to the importance of habitat differences in speciation (Endler 1977, 1982b, 1982c). The divergence-with-gene-flow model of speciation provides a theoretical framework for the study of divergence in ecotones (Endler 1977; Rice and Hostert 1993; Schluter 2000).

THE DIVERGENCE-WITH-GENE-FLOW MODEL IN ECOTONES

The divergence-with-gene-flow model was based on an analysis of 40 years of laboratory experiments on *Drosophila* (Endler 1977; Rice and Hostert 1993). This analysis showed that populations that experience divergent selection on several phenotypic traits are more likely to develop reproductive isolation, even in the presence of some gene flow. To explain this association, Rice and Hostert (1993) suggested that characters experiencing divergent selection might be linked to those affecting reproduction either by genetic hitchhiking or pleiotropy. Consequently, intense divergent selection on specific traits leads to diver-

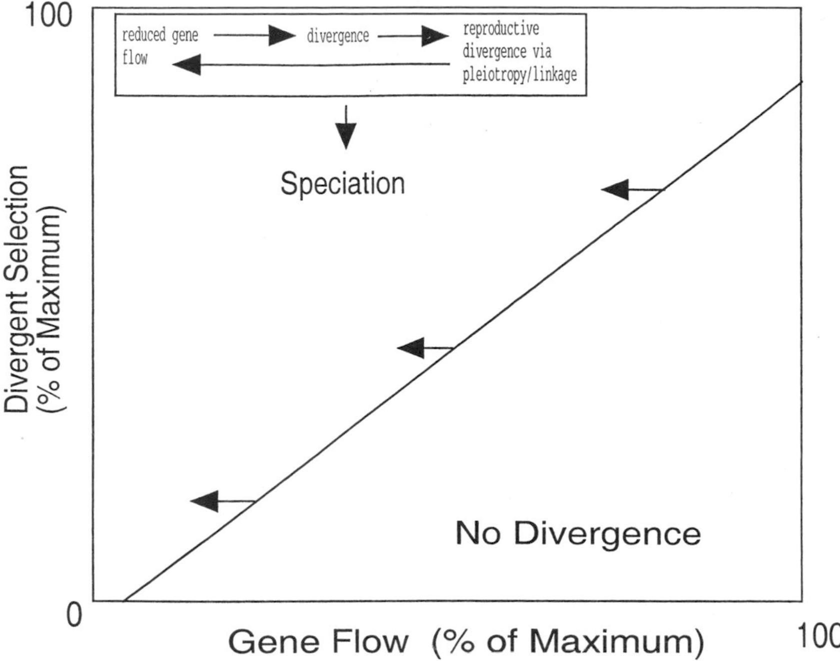

Figure 9.1 The divergence-with-gene-flow model, based on over 40 years of laboratory studies of *Drosophila*. Horizontal arrows point toward the region of the figure where speciation is most likely to occur. The upper box indicates the feedback loop by which divergent selection may lead to speciation (Rice and Hostert 1993). The model predicts that as divergent selection on many characters increases and gene flow decreases, the likelihood of speciation increases. Under this model, reproductive isolation is predicted to evolve via pleiotropy or hitchhiking.

gence in reproductive characteristics. The latter reduces gene flow, thus allowing for more rapid evolution in less intensely selected characters, increasing reproductive divergence and the probability of speciation (fig. 9.1).

Under the divergence-with-gene-flow model, speciation can occur if natural selection is intense and the nature of selection differs among populations. The probability of speciation also is increased if selection acts on many characters. Rice and Hostert have labeled this condition multifarious divergent natural selection. Importantly, under the divergence-with-gene-flow model, speciation does not require complete genetic isolation, but rather depends on the relative magnitudes of selection and gene flow. Speciation may still occur, even in the face of significant gene flow, if selection is strong enough, or with little or no gene flow if selection is weak (see fig. 9.1). In this way, the divergence-with-gene-flow model may encompass instances of allopatry, parapatry, and sympatry.

The ecotone hypothesis posits that divergent natural selection in ecotones has resulted in speciation through the association of traits under selection and those affecting reproduction. A prerequisite of the ecotone hypothesis is that phenotypic divergence should occur despite gene flow and should increase with decreasing gene flow. More precisely, we predict that morphological divergence (as an indicator of divergent selection) between forest and ecotone habitats per unit gene flow should be greater than that between populations in the same habitats (fig. 9.2A). Comparisons of populations from the same habitats should reveal little morphological divergence because the direction and intensity of natural selection are similar and gene flow is high. A qualitative expression of these ideas is the slope of the line relating morphological divergence and gene flow. For between-habitat comparisons, the slope should be significantly negative and larger than that for within-habitat comparisons. The negative slope reflects the homogenizing effect of gene flow on morphological divergence as gene flow increases.

The level of gene flow can be estimated using neutral molecular genetic markers (Slatkin 1993), and morphological divergence can be estimated by measuring characters that typically show a close correlation with feeding ecology,

Figure 9.2 (A) Predicted relationships between gene flow and morphological divergence. Horizontal arrows point toward the region of the figure where speciation is most likely to occur. The *x*-axis represents gene flow and the *y*-axis phenotypic divergence (an index of divergent selection) between pairs of populations. The forest-forest/ecotone-ecotone oval contains gene flow and phenotypic divergence estimates for comparisons between continuous lowland rainforest populations or between ecotone populations; the comparisons are predicted to show a slightly negative slope due to the interaction of drift and gene flow. The ecotone versus contiguous forest oval contains estimates for comparisons of ecotone populations with those in the contiguous rainforest. Our prediction is that ecotone versus contiguous rainforest comparisons will show a strong negative slope and much higher levels of morphological divergence per unit gene flow. (After Rice and Hostert 1993.) (B) The relationship between gene flow and morphological divergence in *A. virens*. Open circles represent pairwise comparisons between populations in forest patches occurring in ecotones and contiguous forest populations; solid triangles, populations occurring in forest patches within ecotone; and solid squares, populations occurring in contiguous rainforest. Morphological divergence (estimated by the Euclidean distance between population means of normalized measurements of five characters) between ecotone and forest populations is two to three times greater than that between ecotone or forest populations when gene flow is low ($Nm < 2$ migrants per generation), but decreases to a similar value when gene flow is high ($Nm > 6$ migrants per generation). The correlation between Nm and morphological divergence is significant for ecotone-forest comparisons ($r = .48$, $p < .05$, Mantel's test), but nonsignificant for forest-forest and ecotone-ecotone comparisons ($r = .02$ and $.04$, respectively, $p > .10$, Mantel's test). (Data from Smith et al. 1997.)

Phenotypic divergence

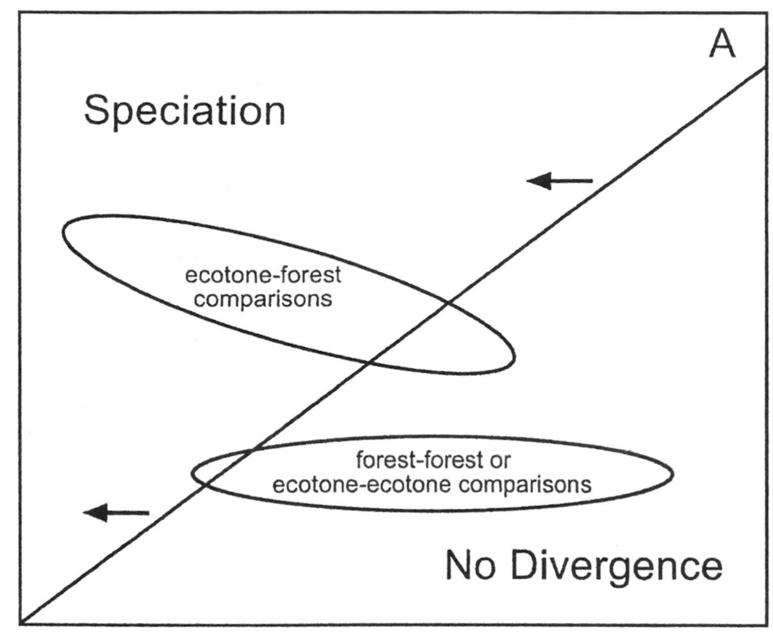
A
Speciation
ecotone-forest
comparisons
forest-forest or
ecotone-ecotone comparisons
No Divergence
Gene Flow

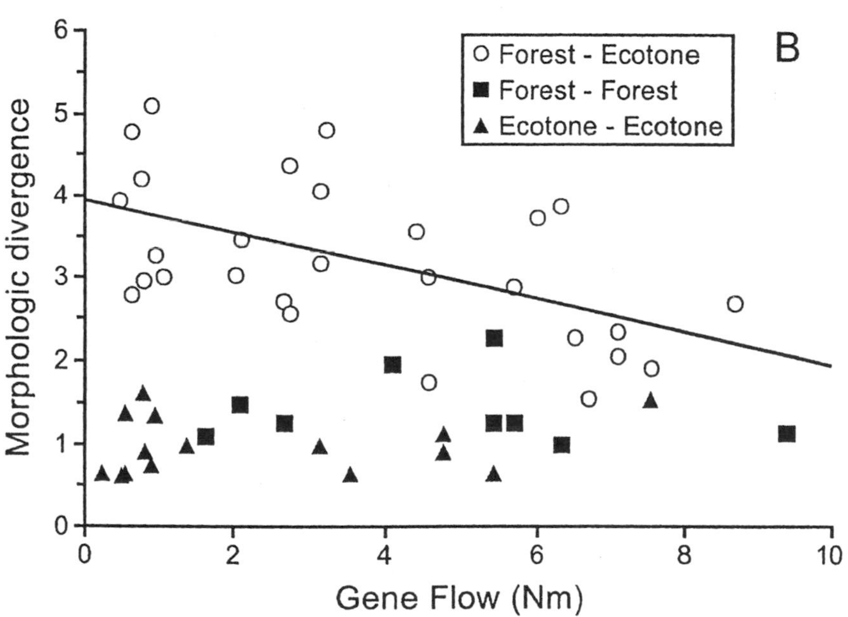
B
Forest - Ecotone
Forest - Forest
Ecotone - Ecotone
Morphologic divergence
Gene Flow (Nm)
0
1
2
3
4
5
6
0
2
4
6
8
10

performance, and fitness. A central prediction of the model would be supported if comparisons between populations in ecotone forest fragments and those in contiguous rainforest showed significantly more divergence per unit gene flow than analogous comparisons of populations within habitats (forest-forest or ecotone-ecotone). Obtaining accurate estimates of *Nm* from F_{st} is problematic (Whitlock and McCauley 1999). In evaluating the model, however, we are interested only in the overall pattern of correspondence between *Nm* and morphological divergence, not the exact magnitude of *Nm*.

EVALUATING THE DIVERGENCE-WITH-GENE-FLOW MODEL IN THREE AFRICAN BIRD SPECIES

To evaluate the divergence-with-gene-flow model, we examined three widely distributed and phylogenetically distinct species of passerine birds in central Africa. We compared levels of morphological divergence within and between habitats and, for one species, levels of genetic divergence. Our three target species were the little greenbul (*Andropadus virens*), the olive sunbird (*Nectarinia olivacea*), and the black-bellied seedcracker (*Pyrenestes ostrinus*). The little greenbul is a common forest bulbul that reaches its highest densities in secondary forest, but is also found in mature forest and ecotone forest fragments. Little greenbuls are omnivores, feeding on both invertebrates and fruit (Chapin 1954; Keith, Urban, and Fry 1992; Louette 1981; Mackworth-Praed and Grant 1973; Serle, Morel, and Hartwig 1977). The olive sunbird, a common forest sunbird that feeds on both nectar and insects, occurs in both mature and secondary forest (Louette 1981; Mackworth-Praed and Grant 1973; Serle, Morel, and Hartwig 1977). The black-bellied seedcracker, an estrildid finch, has been the subject of intensive research for many years (Smith 1987, 1990a, 1990b, 1991, 1993, 1997; Smith and Girman 2000; Smith, Schneider, and Holder 2001). Seedcrackers feed primarily on sedge seeds and occur in all forest types, reaching their highest densities in seasonally flooded forests (Smith 1987, 1990a, 1990b). *Pyrenestes ostrinus* is unusual in showing a polymorphism in bill size (Smith 1987). Small- and large-billed morphs interbreed throughout their range and differ in their ecologies (Smith 1990a, 1991). Breeding experiments indicate that the polymorphism is determined by a single diallelic locus of large effect, with the allele for large bill dominant (Smith 1993). Bill morphs also differ in diet and feeding efficiencies on sedges, resulting in disruptive selection on bill size (Smith 1993).

Field research took place between 1990 and 1997 at selected sites in Cameroon (fig. 9.3). Sites included forest, ecotone, and mountain habitats (Smith 1997;

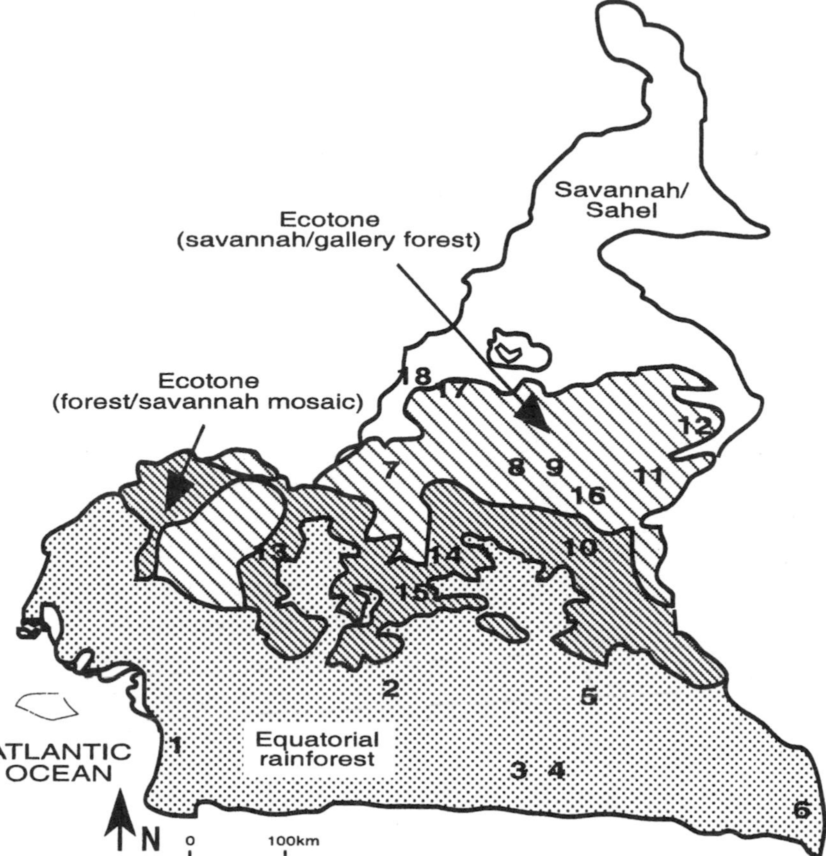

Figure 9.3 Map of Cameroon, showing ecotone and forest habitats (Letouzey 1968) and locations of the eighteen sampling sites. Forest populations are those existing in contiguous equatorial rainforest. Sampling sites in contiguous forest were at least 10 km from major roads or large human settlements. Sampling sites in ecotone consisted of patches of rainforest surrounded by savanna. These patches often, but not exclusively, consist of gallery forest (Smith et al. 1997, Smith, Schneider, and Holder 2001). Sites 17 and 18 are mountain sites.

Smith and McNiven 1993; Smith et al. 1997). Details on field methods are described elsewhere (Smith 1990a, 1993).

Little Greenbuls

In little greenbuls, the relationship between gene flow and morphological divergence supports the central prediction of the divergence-with-gene-flow model (fig. 9.2B). Estimates of gene flow are based on allele frequencies of presumed selectively neutral microsatellite loci (Slatkin 1993). Morphological divergence is estimated by the Euclidean distance between population means of normalized measurements of five characters. Ecotone-forest comparisons were more divergent per unit gene flow than within-habitat comparisons, except for comparisons in which gene flow was exceptionally high (Smith et al. 1997). Ecotone-forest comparisons showed high levels of morphological divergence, even when compared with that among widely separated populations of the same habitat type (fig. 9.4A). Central forest and ecotone populations of *A. virens* were found to differ significantly in all but one morphological character (table 9.1), whereas only one character differed significantly in comparisons between ecotone sites, and two differed significantly between forest sites (Smith et al. 1997). Furthermore, analysis shows significant differences for adult males and females when the sexes were separated (Smith, Schneider, and Holder 2001, T. B. Smith, R. K. Wayne, and N. Manoukis, unpublished data). In addition, the direction of morphological change in some characters in ecotones is consistent with selection pressures hypothesized for those habitats. For example, ecotone populations have significantly longer wings than forest populations, a characteristic consistent with the need for greater aerodynamic efficiency in more open habitats because of increased predation by aerial predators (Benkman 1991; Schluter and Repasky 1991). Also, bill depth, a character often closely related to feeding performance and fitness (Smith 1993), is larger in ecotones, a finding that is consistent with trends seen in other species, suggesting that differences in the types of available foods have resulted in directional selection on bill characters (Smith 1993).

The magnitude of the morphological differences between ecotone and forest populations is as large as that found between sympatric congeneric species of

Figure 9.4 (A) Plot of morphological divergence against geographic distance for populations of adult *A. virens*. Each symbol represents a comparison between two populations. Morphological divergence was estimated by the Euclidean distance between population means of normalized measurements of five characters. Forest-ecotone and forest-mountain comparisons generally show greater divergence than within-habitat comparisons for the same geographic distance. The data suggest that vicariance on mountains alone or between ecotone patches generates little morphological divergence. All mountain samples (sites 17 and 18) were located in ecotone, which may result in the low morphological divergence in mountain-ecotone comparisons. (B) Plot of morphological divergence (as estimated by the Euclidean distance between population means of normalized measurements of five characters) against geographic distance for populations of adult male olive sunbirds. Ecotone-forest comparisons tend to be morphologically more divergent than either ecotone-ecotone or forest-forest comparisons for populations the same geographic distance apart.

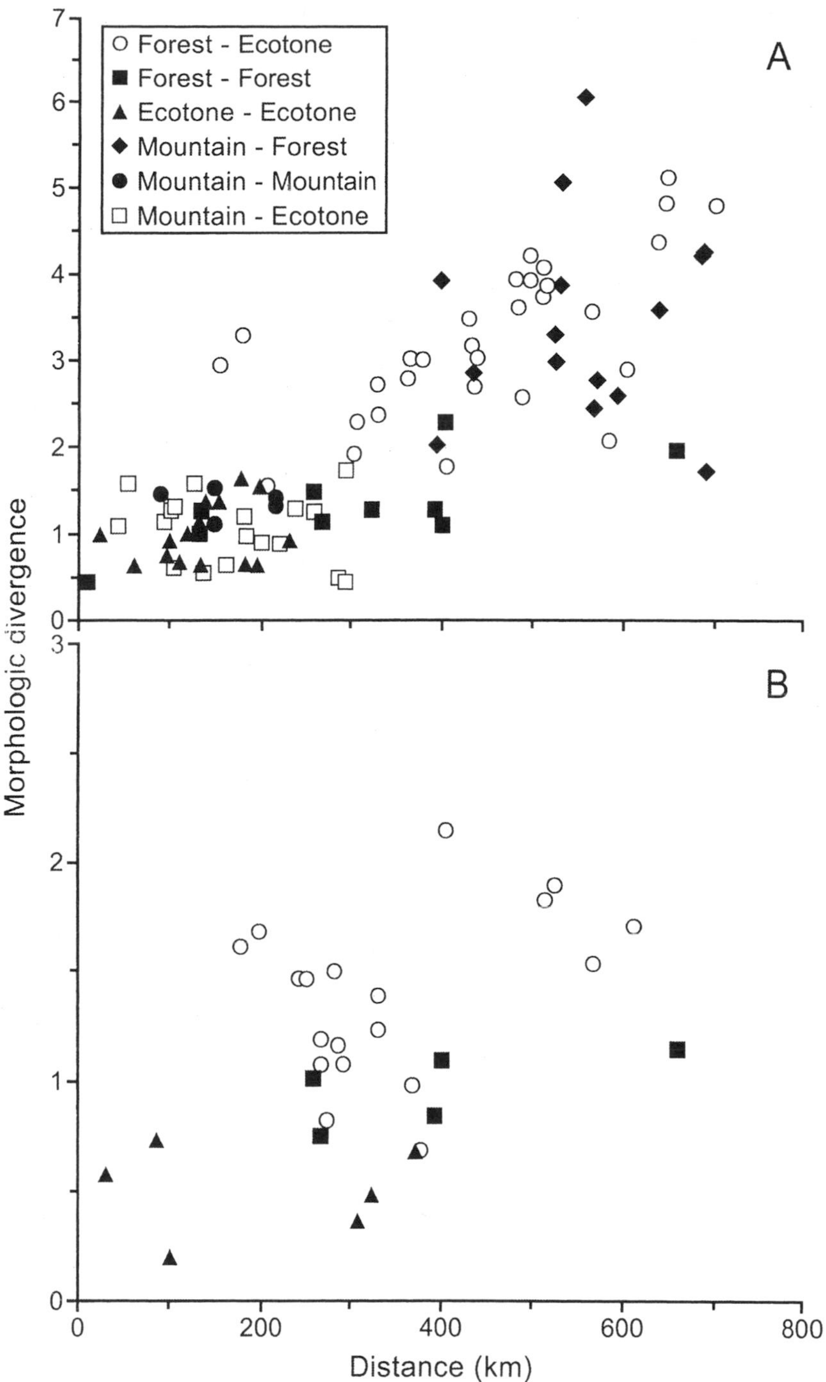

Forest - Ecotone
Forest - Forest
Ecotone - Ecotone
Mountain - Forest
Mountain - Mountain
Mountain - Ecotone
A
B
Morphologic divergence
Distance (km)
0
1
2
3
4
5
6
7
0
1
2
3
0
200
400
600
800

Table 9.1 Character sizes of adult *Andropadus virens* from forest and ecotone sites in Cameroon

Character	Forest		Ecotone DF		F		p
	No.	Mean ± SE	No.	Mean ± SE			
Weight (g)	45	22.4 ± 0.399	60	24.8 ± 0.335	102	21.9	< .001
Wing length (mm)	45	70.9 ± 0.453	61	76.8 ± 0.468	102	84.57	< .001
Tarsus length	45	19.2 ± 0.126	61	20.2 ± 0.112	102	31.19	< .001
Upper mandible length	45	12.1 ± 0.121	61	11.9 ± 0.121	102	1.26	.265
Bill depth	44	4.2 ± 0.037	61	4.3 ± 0.033	102	6.31	.014
Multivariate Wilk's Lambda					99	20.53	< .001

Note: Characters that differ significantly between forest sites include weight and wing length ($p < .01$, MANOVA), between ecotone sites only, tarsus length ($p < .001$). All measurements were taken by TBS using dial calipers (except mass, which was measured using a 50 g Pesola spring scale) (see Smith et al. 1997 for details). Analysis also showed significant differences for adult males and females when sexes were separated (Smith, Schneider, and Holder 2001; T. B. Smith, unpublished data).

bulbuls (Smith et al. 1997). In addition, ecotone-forest differences are greater than a third of the interspecific comparisons for wing length and a fifth for mass. When differences between species in tarsus length, upper mandible length, wing length, and weight were contrasted using principal components analysis, the results were similar. Using the differences in mean character size between species and between ecotone and forest populations of *A. virens,* we calculated principal components using a correlation matrix. Forest-ecotone comparisons of *A. virens* were greater than two and eleven of the interspecific comparisons, along PC1 and PC2, respectively (Smith et al. 1997).

Although we do not demonstrate evidence of reproductive isolation between populations of *A. virens,* significant differences in the frequencies of song elements and call rates were found between ecotone and forest males (Slabbekoorn and Smith 2002). Frequency differences were found to be related to differences between habitats in ambient noise levels (Slabbekoorn and Smith 2002). Thus, while mate choice experiments will be required to determine whether females choose mates based on differences in vocal characters, previous research suggests that when traits important in reproductive isolation and ecology are linked, they can become a powerful generator of reproductive divergence and isolation, and may eventually lead to speciation (Rice and Hostert 1993; Schluter 2000).

Olive Sunbirds

Comparisons of wing length and upper mandible length between four ecotone and six forest sites showed significant differences. We performed a MANOVA of four normalized morphological variables (wing length, tarsus length, upper mandible length, and cube root transformation of mass). Adult male olive sunbirds varied significantly between forest and ecotone (Wilks $\Lambda = 0.64$, $F = 7.87$, df $= 4$, $p = .0001$). As in *A. virens,* a trend toward larger characters in ecotone populations was in evidence. For example, populations of adult male olive sunbirds in ecotones had significantly longer wings and bills than forest populations (ecotone versus forest: wing length mm [mean ± SD] 62.2 ± 1.44, 60.41 ± 1.87, $t = 3.7$, $p < .001$; upper mandible length mm 23.2 ± 1.09, 21.7 ± 1.1, $t = 5.03$, $p < .0001$). Longer wings are consistent with the selective environment created by the more open habitats characteristic of forest-savanna mosaics or ecotones. However, the ecological correlates of longer bills will require further work. As in the little greenbul, morphological divergence is greater for between-habitat comparisons (i.e., ecotone-forest) than for within-habitat comparisons, regardless of the geographic distance separating populations (fig. 9.4B). For example, ecotone-forest comparisons of populations separated by only 200 km are more morphologically divergent than comparisons of forest populations separated by more than 600 km. Preliminary genetic analyses of sunbird populations, based on eight microsatellite loci, suggest that gene flow is not restricted within or between rainforest and ecotone habitats (T. B. Smith, R. K. Wayne, and N. Manoukis, unpublished data).

Black-bellied Seedcrackers

In contrast to the forest, where only small- and large-billed morphs are found (Smith 1987), a third, "mega"-bill form of the black-bellied seedcracker is found in ecotones (Smith 1997) (fig. 9.5). Mega-bills specialize on an extremely hard-seeded sedge, *S. racemosa,* found only in ecotonal areas. These sedge seeds are morphologically similar to the *S. verrucosa* seeds found in forests, but are considerably larger and over twice as hard (Smith 1997). Furthermore, the smallest and largest bill morphs appear to interbreed; of three nesting pairs found in ecotone regions of northern Cameroon, two were mega-billed pairs and one consisted of a small- and a mega-billed individual (Smith 1997). The latter pairing is remarkable, considering that the mega-billed form is 30% heavier and has a bill over 50% larger than the small-billed form, differences far exceeding those between many congeneric species (Smith 1997). Nuclear markers to estimate

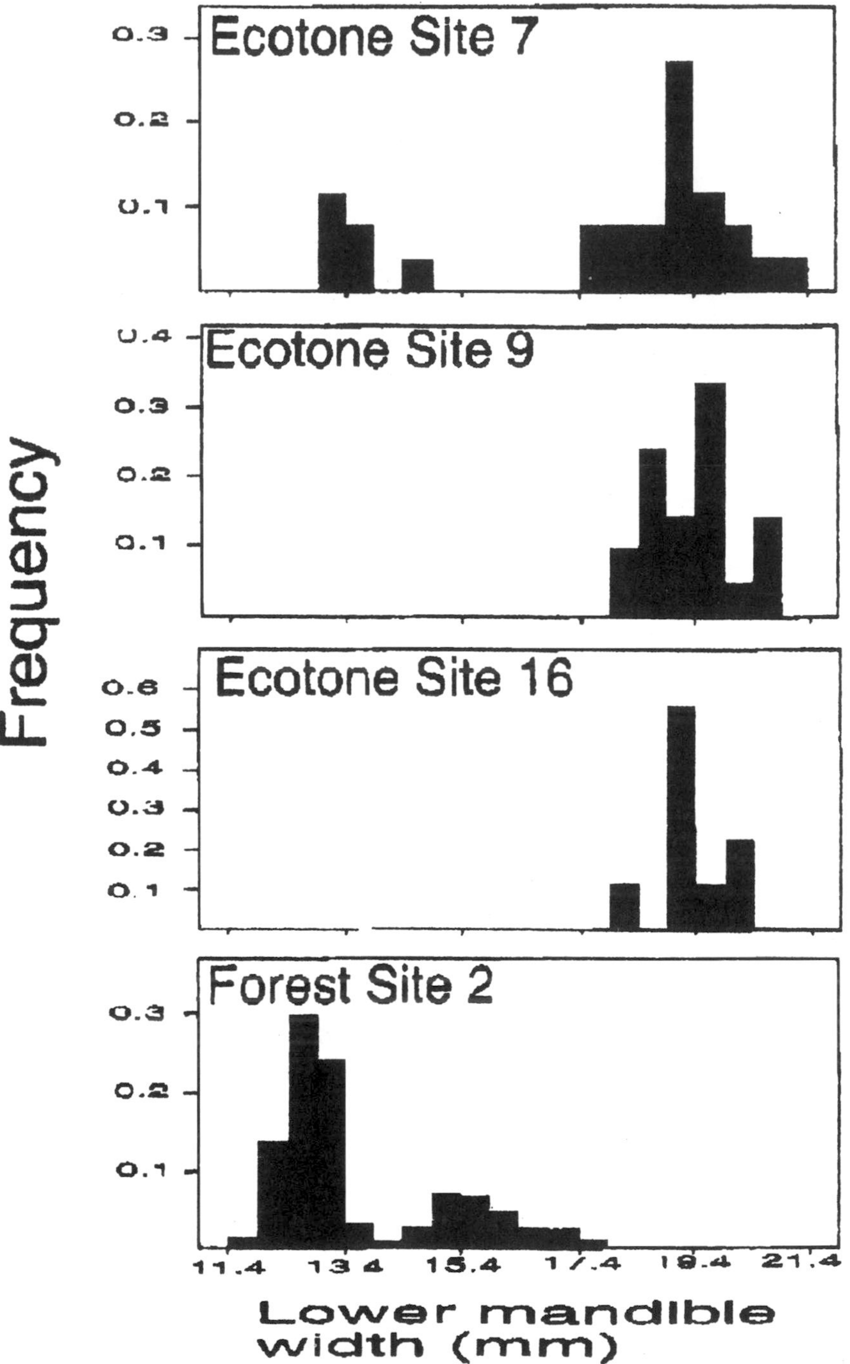

Figure 9.5 Frequency histograms for lower mandible width for adult male seedcrackers from selected sites in Cameroon (see fig. 9.3): 2 = Nidibi (main), 16 = Meiganga, 9 = Wrkwa, and 7 = Tibati.

gene flow are under development. However, in a study using mitochondrial control region, *Nm*s between habitats were found to exceed seven female migrants per generation (Smith and Girman 2000), indicating high levels of gene flow. Current research is focused on evidence for reproductive divergence in peripheral ecotone populations, where only the hardest seeds occur.

IMPORTANCE OF ECOLOGICAL GRADIENTS ON MOUNTAINS

Are ecological gradients other than those existing between rainforests and savannas potentially important in divergence and speciation in rainforests? Very likely they are. The possible importance of ecological gradients in rainforest divergence, and in speciation in general, was first raised by Endler (Endler 1982b, 1982c). However, evaluating the effects of ecological gradients on intraspecific differences, such as those between populations in lowland and in montane habitats, is difficult. This is because few bird species occur in both lowland and high elevational forests, and those that do are typically at low densities in one or both habitats.

Despite these difficulties, we were able to sample two mountains in the ecotonal region of Cameroon for *A. virens*. Results show that morphological divergence is high between central rainforest and mountain populations (see fig. 9.4A). Mountain-forest comparisons are in general much more divergent than forest-forest, ecotone-ecotone, or mountain-mountain comparisons of similar geographic distance. Therefore, isolation on mountains alone does not cause morphological divergence in *A. virens;* rather, it appears more likely that habitat shifts caused by ecological gradients are driving morphological divergence in this species. Finally, the reason why mountain-ecotone divergence was found to be low requires additional work; however, the fact that the mountain populations exist within ecotones is a possible explanation to be investigated (see fig. 9.3 and fig. 9.4A).

What is the relative importance of ecological gradients involving mountains and ecotones? Clearly, much more work is required to understand their relative importance in Africa. Moreover, there is a need to determine the influence of elevation generally. For example, the distinct shifts in morphology found in Cameroon above the ecotone forest borders do not seem to be found in the forest-ecotone transition of Cote D'Ivoire (Smith, Schneider, and Holder 2001). A main difference between these two regions is that the ecotone in Cameroon is also associated with an 800-meter change in elevation, while that in Cote D'Ivoire is not. Elevational gradients may be particularly important in South

America, where Fjeldså (1994) found the highest concentrations of new species in the Andes. The fact that the Andes are many thousands of kilometers long may provide unparalleled opportunities for gradient speciation. Phylogenetic analysis of species by habitat (Prychitko and Moore 1997) suggests an important role for mountains in speciation and supports the divergence-with-gene-flow model (see below).

The examination of divergence and gene flow across ecological gradients may prove valuable in temperate habitats as well. In North America, considerable debate has focused on the role of Pleistocene glacial refugia in speciation and whether isolation during this period is the likely cause of speciation (Bermingham et al. 1992; Klicka and Zink 1997; Avise and Walker 1998). Results of the ecotone model suggest that tests of alternative models of speciation and examination of morphological divergence and gene flow across major ecological boundaries in North America would be useful (Moritz et al. 2000). Divergence in neutral genes is often taken as evidence that a barrier promotes speciation, but such divergence may only indicate drift. If extrinsic barriers are ephemeral, intrinsic barriers must ultimately occur for populations to speciate. Intrinsic barriers are more likely to evolve rapidly under selection than under drift; thus, ecological differences, if they exist, will tend to quickly catalyze speciation in allopatry (Orr and Smith 1998; Rice and Hostert 1993).

REPRODUCTIVE ISOLATION INFERRED FROM INTERSPECIFIC COMPARISONS

Although the patterns of divergence in all three central African bird species support a central component of the divergence-with-gene-flow model, some degree of reproductive isolation needs to be documented to support the model. One method to assess reproductive isolation is to contrast traits important in reproductive isolation between populations in different habitats (Orr and Smith 1998). Indexes of reproductive divergence could be obtained from mate choice experiments. For example, the ecotone speciation hypothesis would be supported if a negative slope relating a measure of reproductive divergence to gene flow were greater for between-habitat (i.e., ecotone vs. forest) than within-habitat (i.e., forest vs. forest) comparisons. This approach can be applied to any taxon inhabiting more than one ecologically distinct environment (Orr and Smith 1998).

An alternative, interspecific method is to compare sister species using a phylogenetic analysis (Endler 1983; Orr and Smith 1998; Schluter and Nagel 1995). If sister species of forest species were commonly ecotone or mountain species, it would support the assertion that between-habitat differences are important in speciation. This kind of analysis is currently being applied to testing mechanisms of speciation in South America (Prychitko and Moore 1997). For example, for *Colaptes* woodpeckers, Prychitko and Moore found the closest sister taxa of mountain species to be lowland forest species, the predicted pattern under the divergence-with-gene-flow model of speciation. Here, results provide interspecific support for the hypotheses that speciation occurred between rather than within habitats and that ecological differences were important (for insects and fish, see Bernatchez and Wilson 1998; McMillan, Jiggins, and Mallet 1997; Spector 2002). Preliminary analysis of African sunbird phylogenies suggests that sister taxa are associated with differing habitats, supporting a gradient hypothesis (Smith et al., forthcoming). However, a complete phylogeny is necessary, gradients need to be examined in other regions, and further investigations are required. Furthermore, some studies provide little evidence for a role of gradients in divergence. For example, a phylogenetic examination of woodcreepers found across the várzea-terra firme ecotone in Brazil found no sister relationship across differing habitats (Aleixo 2002; da Silva and Bates 2002).

CONCLUSIONS

The evolutionary mechanisms responsible for generating the high biodiversity of tropical rainforests have been debated for decades (Endler 1982b; Erwin 1991b; Mayr 1963; Prance 1982a; Stebbins 1974). The most prominent hypothesized mechanisms of speciation in rainforests include the riverine barrier hypothesis, suggesting that major rivers are responsible for isolation (Ayres and Clutton-Brock 1992; Capparella 1992; Endler 1977; Patton, da Silva, and Malcolm 1994); the montane islands hypothesis, postulating that isolation on mountaintops during dry periods led to divergence and speciation (Fjeldså 1994; Joseph, Moritz, and Hugall 1995; Moreau 1966; Roy 1997; Wagner 1868); the ecological gradient hypothesis, maintaining that fragmentation of clines along ecological gradients gives rise to new taxa (Endler 1977, 1982b, 1982c); and the Pleistocene forest refuge hypothesis (Crowe and Crowe 1982; Haffer 1969, 1974; Mayr and O'Hara 1986; Vanzolini and Williams 1970; Whitmore and Prance 1987). The last is essentially a vicariance model of speciation that places little emphasis on natural selection, stressing instead the role of large isolated forest refugia in speciation (Haffer 1969; Mayr and O'Hara 1986). Empirical evidence provides little support for the view that speciation was actually tied to isolation in Pleistocene refugia or other periodically isolated areas (Capparella 1992; Colinvaux, De Oliveira et al. 1996; Flenley 1993; Mares 1992; Patton and Smith 1993; see also Fjeldså et al., chap. 8, and Colinvaux, chap. 6 in this volume). In fact, with the exception of the ecological gradient hypothesis, these theories reflect a historical trend toward equating centers of biodiversity with centers of species origin (Darwin 1958; Diels 1908; Takhtajan 1969, 1970; Willis 1922) (see also Latham and Ricklefs 1993 for other mechanisms).

In Africa, where hypotheses explaining patterns of biodiversity have received comparatively less study than in South America, the Pleistocene forest refuge hypothesis has received the majority of attention (Crowe and Crowe 1982; Diamond and Hamilton 1980; Endler 1982b; Jones 1987; Mayr and O'Hara 1986). In few cases have alternative speciation models that emphasize natural selection rather than drift been given a prominent role in speciation (Endler 1977, 1982b, 1982c; Smith et al. 1997). We suggest that natural selection in ecologically distinct habitats may be a major cause of speciation in rainforests. Ecological divergence, rather than vicariance events, could explain the high diversity of rainforest birds. The generality of our results is supported by the widespread occurrence of major contact zones between species and subspecies in ecotones (Chapin 1954; Crowe and Crowe 1982; Endler 1982b, 1982c).

Five additional observations lead to our conclusion. First, as we have shown for the little greenbul, divergent selection, rather than drift or other factors, most likely has caused morphological differentiation in ecotone populations, and the divergent traits can also be linked to traits important in mate choice and reproductive isolation (i.e., song). Second, concordant patterns of morphological variation are found in the two other species, the olive sunbird and black-bellied seedcracker. In seedcrackers, the ecological circumstances leading to a different selection regime in ecotones and rainforests can be identified. Third, laboratory experiments suggest that divergent selection may sometimes lead to reproductive divergence. Fourth, the magnitude of divergence in fitness-related characters is similar to that found between reproductively isolated species, suggesting that selection has caused divergence as large as that between species. Fifth, recent theoretical studies suggest that reproductive isolation can easily occur in parapatry in the presence of moderate levels of gene flow (Doebeli and Dieckmann 2003; Gavrilets, Li, and Vose 2000). Therefore, ecotones and other gradients, such as elevational gradients associated with mountains, may be integral to the production and maintenance of biodiversity in tropical rainforests. This idea contrasts with past theories of rainforest speciation that have focused on vicariance mechanisms (Haffer 1974; Mayr and O'Hara 1986). Our results imply that vicariance alone, without divergent natural selection, may not be a predominant force in rainforest speciation.

Centrally located rainforest areas are presently the main focus of conservation efforts, whereas ecotonal regions are rapidly being lost due to overgrazing, burning, and wood harvesting, with little or no effort toward their conservation (Smith et al., forthcoming). Ecotonal regions are implicitly assumed to be less important because they are mosaics of pure habitat types and may contain fewer species and smaller, less stable populations. The possibility that forest fragments located in the transitional zone between forest and savanna may be important sources of genetic and phenotypic diversity that contribute to rainforest biodiversity needs urgent consideration and further study. If these regions are found to be important centers of diversification, conservation efforts should be undertaken quickly to preserve them.

ACKNOWLEDGMENTS

We thank the government of the Republic of Cameroon for permission to conduct the field research and E. Bermingham, C. W. Dick, J. Endler, B. Larison, C. Moritz, and R. Ricklefs for helpful discussion and comments. This research was supported by grants from the National Geographic Society, National Environmental Research Council, Royal Society, and National Science Foundation (DEB-9726425 and IRCEB9977072).

10

Geologic, Evolutionary, and Ecological Bases of the Diversification of Neotropical Butterflies: Implications for Conservation

KEITH S. BROWN JR.

ABSTRACT

Communities of 300–1,800 species of diurnal forest Lepidoptera in forty-eight Neotropical sites from Mexico to southern Brazil are compared with each other and with twenty-four environmental variables, seeking correlations useful in evaluating the origins of biological diversity, endemism, and rarity and in setting priorities for effective landscape conservation in the region. Species endemism in Neotropical forests is concentrated in six regions, well separated by longstanding physiographic barriers (high mountains, dry regions, and the Caribbean). Subspecies and marker gene distributions plotted for more than 1,300 taxa indicate fifty smaller forest areas of endemism, closely corresponding to an independent geologic and statistical model for regions of forest persistence during the last glacial maximum, 18,000 years ago. Species richness in the Neotropical forests peaks near the peripheries of these subspecies endemism centers, and is adequately explained by environmental heterogeneity, unpredictability, and intermediate disturbance levels. Community richness and composition appear to be variably affected by climatic, topographic, soil, vegetation, and disturbance factors. Natural disturbance tends to increase heterogeneity, edge effects, and species richness, while anthropogenic disturbance above natural levels generally reduces biodiversity. Rare species are often concentrated in limited "paleoenvironments" in regions of complex topography. These correlations can be used in the selection, planning, and management of effective conservation units in the Neotropics, which should cover areas large enough to absorb the continual stochastic restructuring of the communities and involve local people in their monitoring and protection. Specific recommendations are offered for the effective choice and flexible management of forest landscapes to conserve the Neotropical biota.

INTRODUCTION

It has long been recognized that species richness in plants and animals is distributed unevenly among the world's biomes, tending to increase at lower latitudes (Lugo 1988). In the Neotropics, regional species lists for terrestrial and freshwater organisms tend to increase from the Tropic of Cancer south to well

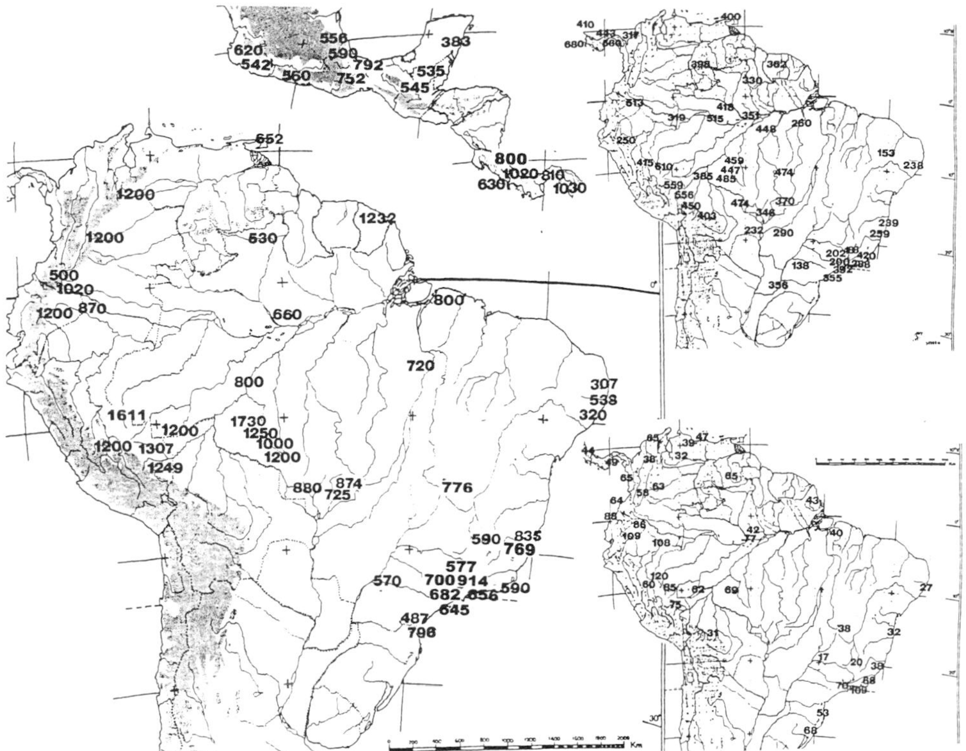

Figure 10.1 Numbers of species recorded at some well-studied Neotropical sites for butterflies (upper right map; see table 10.1), birds (lower left; see chapters in Remsen 1997), frogs (lower right; compiled by Moisés B. Souza and the late Adão J. Cardoso).

below the Equator. Peaks in most groups occur from 7° N to 15° S on the eastern Andean slopes, from 3° S to 15° S in the Amazon basin (due to richer soils and more water southward), and from 18° S to 26° S in the Atlantic forests (influenced by increasing rainfall and more complex topography southward to beyond the Tropic of Capricorn) (fig. 10.1, table 10.1). Genetic diversity typically shows more complex patterns at the local population or microhabitat level, while landscape diversity depends on ecological and geologic factors that still defy standardized measurement, varying with organisms, criteria, and scale. Although some patterns of biological diversity seem relatively clear based on the limited data now available, the proposed and possible causes for these patterns are myriad and confusing.

This is bad news, not only for the scientists who seek to discover, understand, and explain real patterns in nature, but also for the conservation planners and

Table 10.1 Significant environmental factors and butterfly species diversity in forty-eight Neotropical forest sites, including composite indices

Sites	Lat	Long	Area	Effort	Altit	AltVar	Topo	Temp	TVar	Rain	DryM	PWat	SCat	SBas	SMos	VegC	Vmos	Vine	Bamb	Dist	Pollu	SecV	TDis	Het	ResR	NDis	BDiv	Ithom	Mim	Bait	Nym	PaPi	Riod	Thecl	Ppoid	Pyrg	Hesp	Total	Refs[a]
Mexico/Guatemala																																							
Colima, CO	19	104	5	4	500	2000	4	20	10	1500	6	4	4	5	2	5	4	3	2	3	2	40	6.0	7	6	8	6	7	52	78	130	63	49	79	321	132	89	542	*15, 22*
Teocelo, VC	19	97	3	3	1000	700	5	19	6	3000	3	3	4	6	3	5	2	1	2	4	2	50	6.3	8	10	8	6	20	73	89	162	56	49	66	333	[154]	[103]	**590	*2*
Sierra de Juárez, OX*	18	96	4	3	1500	2500	5	15	10	5000	1	2	5	6	4	5	4	2	2	4	2	40	6.0	7	10	10	6	27	94	147	241	87	68	56	452	[150]	[150]	*752	*35, 22*
Sierra de Tuxtlas, VC	18	95	4	4	600	1000	4	24	7	4000	1	3	5	6	3	5	3	3	2	4	2	60	7.7	9	11	8	6	24	84	133	217	75	69	90	531	204	137	792	*4*
Sierra de Atoyac, GR	17	100	4	3	800	2000	5	22	6	1500	6	1	4	4	3	4	3	3	1	4	2	40	6.0	6	6	7	5	10	57	96	153	57	38	91	339	[110]	[111]	**560	*5*
Chajul, CH	16	91	3	4	150	100	3	25	4	3000	2	3	5	6	2	5	2	3	2	2	1	20	4.0	6	9	9	6	21	68	132	200	58	76	64	398	100	47	545	*6*
Tikal	17	90	4	3	250	300	3	25	4	3000	2	3	5	6	2	5	2	3	2	2	1	20	6.0	5	6	6	4	9	47	94	141	41	48	98	328	123	84	535	*7*
Costa Rica/Panama																																							
Turrialba	10	84	4	4	500	600	4	23	2	2000	1	2	5	5	2	5	2	3	3	4	2	60	8.0	9	10	10	9	35	77	142	219	42	117	[123]	[501]	[170]	[129]	**800	*9*
Corcovado	9	83	3	4	100	400	3	25	1	3000	4	4	5	5	2	5	2	3	2	2	1	30	5.7	6	8	5	7	27	65	109	174	43	79	[110]	[406]	[124]	[100]	**630	*9*
Chiriqui	9	82	4	4	1200	2000	5	18	1	3000	1	3	5	5	4	5	3	3	3	4	1	60	7.7	9	9	10	9	54	129	152	281	70	[120]	[160]	[631]	[180]	[209]	**1020	*9, 10*
Cerro Campana*	9	80	3	4	800	600	5	25	1	2000	4	2	4	4	3	4	3	2	3	4	1	50	6.7	9	8	6	8	38	88	134	222	44	[120]	140	[526]	[154]	[130]	**810	*10, 11*
Piña, Canal Zone*	9	80	4	4	100	300	3	27	0	3000	2	4	5	6	2	6	2	3	1	4	3	30	5.7	4	8	7	7	24	71	152	223	51	[120]	[120]	[514]	[170]	[126]	**810	*10*
Cerro Pirre	8	78	3	4	1000	1200	5	21	1	3000	1	2	4	4	2	5	3	3	2	2	1	10	3.3	8	9	10	10	57	109	175	284	54	[140]	[140]	[618]	[200]	[212]	**1030	*10*
Northern South America																																							
Trinidad*	11	61	5	4	200	900	3	26	2	2500	3	3	5	5	3	5	2	5	3	4	2	40	7.3	8	9	8	6	17	53	92	145	42	107	93	387	150	115	652	*8*
Ilha Maracá, RR	N3	61	3	3	150	30	2	26	2	2000	3	4	3	4	4	4	6	4	1	2	1	20	4.0	5	5	3	5	11	41	106	147	25	69	106	[347]	89	94	**530	*12*
Putumayo	N1	77	3	2	1500	1000	5	18	1	2000	0	2	4	5	2	5	3	2	4	1	1	10	3.3	9	8	8	7	24	40	98	138	58	49	100	[345]	[60]	[95]	**500	*13*
Mocoa	N1	77	4	4	600	500	4	24	2	4000	0	3	5	6	4	6	4	2	1	2	1	20	3.3	8	9	10	11	59	106	173	279	55	130	100	[664]	[240]	[216]	**1020	*13*
Jatun Sacha	S1	78	3	4	400	5	2	24	2	3700	0	4	6	5	3	5	3	3	2	2	1	30	4.7	10	8	7	10	58	104	203	307	53	194	59	613	111	87	811	*14*
Alto Rio Napo	S1	75	2	3	150	20	2	25	2	3000	0	4	5	5	4	5	4	3	2	1	1	10	4.0	7	6	6	9	52	85	154	239	49	153	100	[541]	[180]	[149]	**870	*15*
Manaus, AM*	S2	60	3	4	100	50	2	26	2	2000	2	2	4	2	2	3	2	2	1	2	1	30	4.0	3	4	3	3	20	46	135	181	19	180	94	474	[110]	[76]	**660	*16*
Southwest Amazonia																																							
Alto Juruá, AC*	9	72	4	3	300	200	3	25	4	2000	4	4	5	6	4	5	6	4	5	1	1	20	5.0	11	10	12	11	81	139	336	475	75	320	195	1065	274	272	1611	*17*
Cacaulândia, RO	10	63	4	4	200	250	3	25	5	2500	4	3	5	6	3	5	5	3	4	4	2	40	5.7	11	8	9	10	63	119	297	416	60	368	236	1080	378	272	1730	*21*
Jaru, RO*	10	62	3	3	300	200	3	25	5	2500	4	3	5	6	3	5	4	4	3	4	2	40	5.7	11	9	10	10	57	101	242	343	49	[225]	[150]	[767]	[283]	[200]	**1250	*15, 22*
Pakitza, Manu	12	71	4	3	400	150	3	25	4	2000	3	4	5	5	3	5	5	3	5	1	1	10	4.0	10	9	11	9	62	104	267	371	56	251	181	859	223	225	1307	*15, 23*
Tambopata	13	69	4	3	300	100	2	25	4	2500	3	4	5	5	3	5	5	3	3	1	1	10	4.0	10	9	10	9	42	90	251	341	53	242	172	808	220	221	1249	*5*
E.-So. Amazonia																																							
Serra dos Carajás, PA*	6	50	4	3	600	700	4	23	4	1500	3	2	3	4	4	4	5	5	3	5	3	50	8.7	11	8	7	8	33	78	120	198	41	[130]	86	[455]	[130]	[135]	**720	*17*
Cristalino, MT*	10	56	2	2	300	70	3	25	5	2500	4	3	5	5	4	5	4	4	3	1	1	10	4.7	10	8	6	9	34	72	219	291	15	121	27	490	67	63	620	*17*
Salto do Céu, MT*	15	58	3	2	350	200	3	24	7	1500	5	2	4	6	2	4	3	4	3	4	2	40	7.0	7	8	6	9	17	57	194	251	35	100	[160]	546	[170]	[164]	**880	*17, 24*
Chapada, MT*	15	56	4	4	400	300	3	23	7	1500	4	3	3	4	5	3	4	5	4	2	1	40	6.7	6	5	2	9	24	65	158	223	45	152	118	538	176	160	874	*24*
Brasilia, DE*	16	48	4	4	1000	700	3	22	7	1300	2	4	5	3	5	2	3	4	3	3	1	40	6.3	5	3	3	7	22	65	151	216	42	134	134	526	126	124	776	*25*
Northeast Brazil																																							
João Pessoa, PB*	7	35	2	4	20	50	2	25	1	1800	0	4	5	4	2	3	2	3	1	6	3	60	8.3	6	2	1	4	8	30	56	86	23	42	46	197	62	48	307	*18*
East Pernambuco*	8	35	3	3	100	200	3	25	1	2000	0	2	5	5	4	3	2	3	2	4	2	80	9.0	6	4	2	5	19	45	94	139	27	76	102	344	118	76	538	*19*

Maceió, AL	9	36	3	3	5	10	1	25	1	1500	0	5	5	3	2	3	2	1	2	6	4	90	10.3	3	2	2	4	11	34	52	86	20	[50]	[50]	[206]	[70]	[44]	**320	*20*
Linhares, ES*	19	40	4	3	20	40	2	23	6	1300	2	3	4	5	5	3	3	4	2	1	2	50	4.3	6	4	3	8	32	71	147	218	44	105	92	459	175	201	835	*17*
Santa Teresa, ES*	20	41	4	4	700	400	5	21	7	1500	2	2	4	2	3	6	5	5	4	2	1	50	7.3	8	5	4	9	36	84	160	244	53	[86]	[64]	[447]	[162]	[160]	**769	*17, 26*
Southeast Brazil, Interior																																							
Belo Horizonte, MG*	20	44	3	3	1000	500	5	22	6	1300	2	3	6	2	5	3	3	4	3	5	4	60	9.3	10	6	6	9	21	63	96	159	44	[57]	[120]	[380]	[110]	[100]	**590	*17, 27*
Poços de Caldas, MG*	22	47	3	2	1200	1000	5	18	5	1700	2	2	6	4	3	4	3	3	5	4	3	50	8.3	8	8	5	7	23	65	103	168	51	47	87	359	111	113	577	*19*
Serra de Itatiaia, RJ*	22	45	3	4	1400	2400	5	15	11	2000	3	3	4	2	3	5	5	3	6	1	1	20	5.0	9	9	9	8	27	81	147	228	60	116	144	548	166	200	914	*29*
Morro do Diabo, SP*	23	52	3	2	350	300	2	21	9	1100	5	4	4	3	3	3	3	5	4	4	2	40	7.7	6	6	7	5	21	50	106	156	34	[78]	[105]	[473]	100	97	**570	*30*
Campinas, SP*	23	47	2	4	600	40	2	21	6	1400	4	2	5	4	2	3	2	6	4	1	3	40	7.3	8	4	2	7	28	76	136	212	45	42	89	388	155	157	700	*17*
Serra do Japi, SP*	23	47	4	3	900	600	5	19	7	1500	3	3	4	3	2	4	3	5	6	4	1	30	7.3	8	7	7	7	31	80	128	208	55	54	112	429	131	122	682	*28*
Southeast Brazil, Coast																																							
Xerém, RJ*	23	43	3	2	100	200	5	24	5	1600	2	4	4	2	2	6	2	2	3	5	2	30	6.0	6	6	5	7	27	65	112	177	51	[90]	[110]	[428]	[118]	[110]	**656	*17*
Rio de Janeiro, RJ*	23	43	4	3	400	800	5	23	5	1300	2	1	4	5	4	6	3	2	2	6	3	80	9.7	7	6	4	6	23	66	103	169	54	80	103	406	124	126	656	*17*
Delta do São João, RJ*	23	42	2	3	10	10	1	23	5	1000	4	5	2	4	3	3	2	2	1	3	1	80	8.0	4	1	0	4	19	60	99	159	43	[70]	[107]	[379]	[101]	[110]	**590	*17*
Alto da Serra, SP*	24	47	3	2	900	350	5	18	8	2600	0	4	4	2	2	5	3	3	6	2	2	60	8.3	7	7	7	5	25	76	89	165	39	[45]	[105]	[354]	[110]	[136]	**600	*31*
São Vicente, SP*	24	47	4	4	50	400	5	21	7	2500	0	5	2	2	4	6	4	1	2	6	4	60	8.3	6	6	6	5	25	74	100	174	42	[80]	[110]	[406]	[110]	[129]	**645	*31*
Curitiba, PR	25	49	4	4	1000	400	3	15	6	1200	1	4	4	2	3	4	3	3	5	6	3	60	9.7	7	5	7	5	15	61	88	149	43	40	45	277	70	140	487	*32*
Joinville, SC*	26	49	4	4	100	200	3	20	5	1500	1	3	3	3	4	5	3	1	2	6	2	70	8.3	6	5	5	7	16	63	127	190	52	85	99	426	161	209	796	*33*

Source: Updated and expanded from Brown 1997a.

Note: Abbreviations at the tops of the columns, and norms for the calculation of values for each parameter, are as follows (almost all taken from Brown 1997a): **Lat** = Latitude from N to S; **Long** = Longitude W; **Area** = covered as $10^{(n+1)}$ hectares; **Effort** in days: 2 = 20–59, 3 = 60–200, 4 = > 200; **Altit**ude in meters above sea level; **Alt**itude **Var**iation covered in site; **Topo**graphy: 1 = level, 2 = gently rolling or depression, 3 = hilly, 4 = strongly folded, 5 = mountainous; **Temp**erature, annual mean in °C; Temperature **Var**iation between means of warmest and coldest months; **Rain**fall in mm, yearly average; Number of **Dry M**onths in the year (average); **P**ermanent **Wat**er in site: 1 = minimal, 2 = small ponds and streams, 3 = some larger rivers or lakes, 4 = many lakes, 5 = oceanside; **Soil Cat**egory averaged among those present: 1 = rock or hardpan, 2 = sandy or concretionary, 3 = cambisol or plinthic, 4 = moderate-texture latosol, 5 = moderate-texture podzolized, 6 = very argyllic or humic; **Soil Bas**es (fertility): 1 = laterite, rock, or coarse sand, 2 = alic, 3 = alic + dystrophic, 4 = dystrophic, 5 = dystrophic + eutrophic, 6 = eutrophic; **S**oil **Mos**aic, number of important different soil types in site; **Veg**etation **Cat**egory, corresponding to aspect diversity: 1 = principally anthropic or cleared systems, 2 = mangrove, restinga, savanna, scrub, white sand campina, 3 = poor dense forests, floodable or bamboo forests, 4 = open, palm, liana, or semi-deciduous forests, 5 = cloud forest or alluvial terrace, delta forest, 6 = rich mixture of dense and open forests; **V**egetation **Mos**aic, number of different vegetation types in site; **Vine** abundance from 1 = almost absent to 6 = dominant, covering up to half the basal area; **Bamb**oo abundance from 1 = essentially absent to 6 = present in many large patches, up to 30% of the mosaic; **Dist**urbance type: 1 = continuous forest, 2 = limited small clearings, 3 = larger converted areas, 4 = mosaic with human influence over 50%, 5 = strongly anthropic, including industrial use of land, 6 = urban landscape; **Pollu**tion (including agricultural) in site: 1 = negligible, 2 = light, 3 = moderate, 4 = heavy: **Sec**ondary **V**egetation in site as % of area. **Composite** indexes: Total **Dis**turbance as (Vine + Bamb + Dist + Poll + 0.2 × SecV)/3; **Het**erogeneity of environment, **Res**ource **R**ichness, and **N**atural **Dis**turbance calculated as the sums of relevant factors in topography, rainfall, dry months, soils, and vegetation as in Brown (1997a); **B**utterfly **Div**ersity as a sum of richness, daily list, genetic variation, and family balance of fauna, with values attributed as in Brown (1997a). Total species richness of **Ithom**iinae, **Mim**etic Nymphalidae (including Ithomiinae), **Bait**-attracted Nymphalidae, total of all **Nym**phalidae, **Pa**pilionidae + **Pi**eridae, **Riod**inine Lycaenidae, **Thecl**ine plus Polyommatine Lycaenidae, total **Papilionoid**ea (true butterflies), **Pyrg**ine and Pyrrhopygine skippers, **Hesp**eriine skippers (square brackets in the last five categories indicate estimated numbers for groups difficult to sample thoroughly), **Total** butterfly list.

*Localities censused by the author.

**Estimated total number of species, using the estimates in brackets for lycaenid and/or hesperiid species.

[a]References: 1 = Warren et al. 1998; 2 = Llorente-B., Garcez, and Luis-M, 1986; 3 = Luis-M., Vargas-F., and Llorente-B. 1991; 4 = Raguso and Llorente-B. 1991, 1997; 5 = Vargas-F., Llorente-B., and Luis-M 1991; 6 = Austin et al. 1996; de la Maza and de la Maza 1985; 7 = Austin et al. 1996; 8 = Barcant 1970; 9 = DeVries 1987, 1997; 10 = unpublished notes of Gordon Small on Panamanian butterflies; 11 = Robbins and Small 1981; 12 = Mielke and Casagrande 1992; 13 = Salazar-E. 1995; 14 = Murray 2000; 15 = Lamas, Robbins, and Harvey 1996; 16 = Brown and Hutchings 1997; 17 = Notes, lists, and personal observations of K. S. Brown Jr.; 18 = Kesselring and Ebert 1982; 19 = Ebert 1969; 20 = Cardoso 1949; 21 = G. Austin, list and personal communications; 22 = K. S. Brown Jr. 1984; 23 = Robbins et al. 1996; 24 = Brown 1987c; 25 = Brown and Mielke 1967; 26 = Brown and Freitas 2000b; 27 = Brown and Mielke 1968; 28 = Brown 1992; 29 = Zikán and Zikán 1968; 30 = Mielke and Casagrande 1998; 31 = R. B. Francini and A. V. L. Freitas, notes and lists; 32 = Mielke 1996; 33 = C. Mielke, unpublished lists and notes, 1998.

managers who struggle to effectively save or sustainably use biological diversity at all levels. It would be convenient to identify and quantify a few easily measured geologic or ecological factors that are important determinants of key ecosystem properties, such as those given, with their methods of measurement, in table 10.1. Whether the goal be rigorous protection of systems or their sustained use, planners and managers need to know which factors to evaluate, which species to watch, which phenomena to monitor, and which practices to emphasize in tropical ecosystems—preferably right now, while options are still available.

One approach to achieving these goals is to understand the major historical and ecological factors that influence or "determine" these system patterns and parameters (table 10.1, fig. 10.2), and take action to maintain these factors over both short and long time scales (Ricklefs and Schluter 1993b). What can geologic and biological studies contribute to this end? More specifically, where does geologic history appear in the local or landscape diversity picture? Can geologic history predict present-day population and community parameters and responses better than current ecological factors?

Many scientists seem to feel that landscape history is extremely important in limiting the options (if not in determining the detailed structure) of local populations and communities (Burnett et al. 1998; Nichols, Killingbeck, and August 1998). This is a reasonable assumption, given the continuous influences of climate and spatial compartments, the broad effects of ambient energy, hydrology, and resources, the pervasive consequences of major catastrophes, and the enormous time over which these factors have acted. Unfortunately, it is hard to experiment with or test the results of such factors, since few or no parallel controls are available, correlation does not guarantee causation, and biotic responses today do not necessarily reflect those in the distant past. The details of the history of a community are both dimly seen and untouchable, except perhaps by careful comparisons along diverse transects through time, space, and habitats.

Any field ecologist recognizes that the present-day composition and diversity of natural populations and communities are subject to many influences, from rock-hard geologic factors to current ephemeral and stochastic events, acting from the deep subsoil to the forest canopy (see fig. 10.2). While ecological influences have many effects that can be watched and followed, geologically determined factors such as topography, exposure, and microclimate are usually reflected in existing system characteristics. The less predictable and more rapid events are played out in the present on a stage set by the past. The medium-scale events (migrations, major natural disasters, or landscape restructuring by rivers and landslides, short-term climatic cycles such as "El Niño/La Niña," large tree

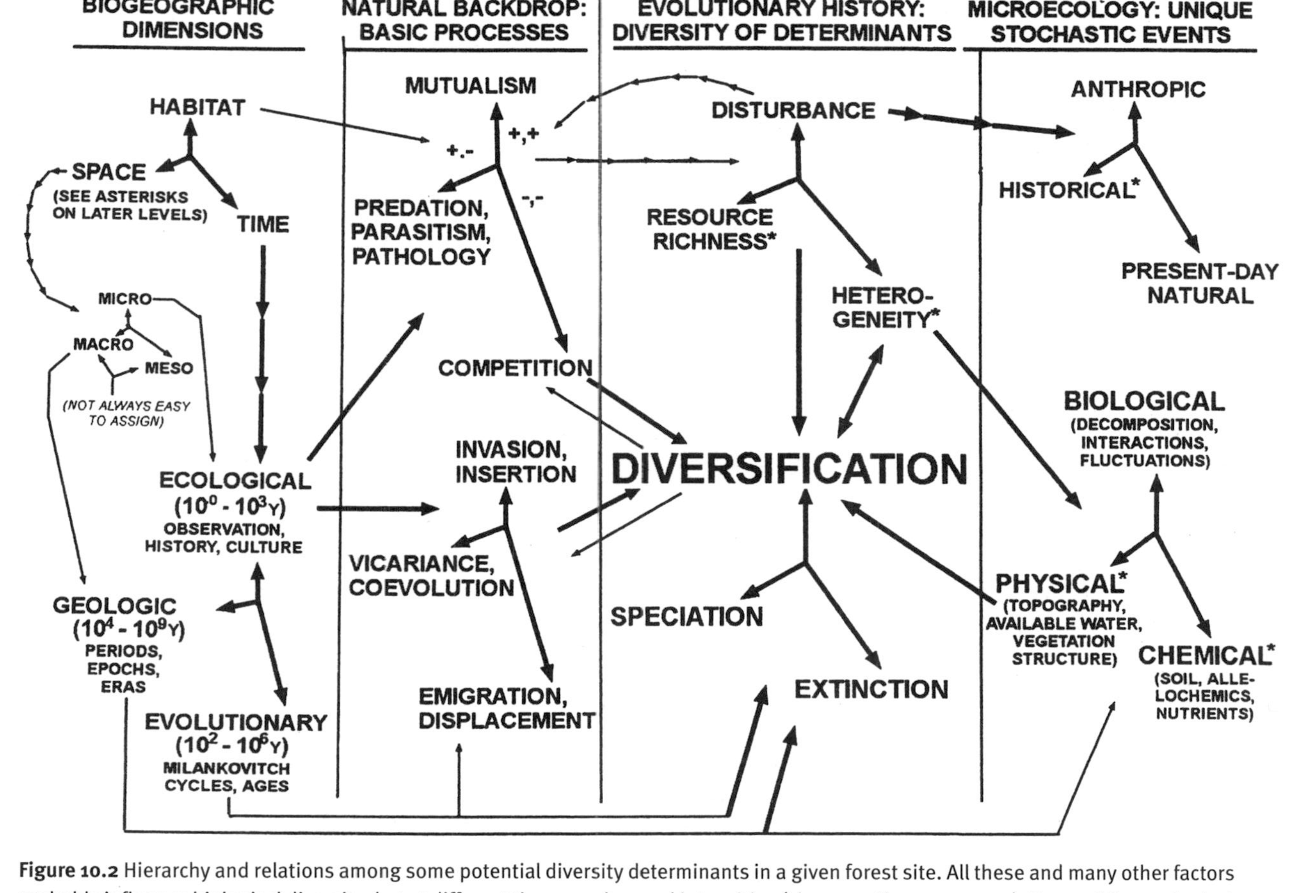

Figure 10.2 Hierarchy and relations among some potential diversity determinants in a given forest site. All these and many other factors probably influence biological diversity, but at different times, scales, and intensities (shown as three-way axes). Some of the ecological factors can be tested experimentally, while historical factors can be independently evaluated by geologic data or, in some cases, molecular sequences. (See also Terborgh 1992 for a much more complete discussion.)

or bamboo stand die-offs) affect a series of actors (the species now present) that were born, trained, and directed at the site (or elsewhere) through molecular, morphological, digestive, and behavioral peculiarities tied to long-standing genome capabilities and responses. Can general, orderly, and well-understood historical factors still have more weight than unique stochastic events in determining present-day biodiversity? Shall we continue the current pragmatic conservation strategy that covers all options simultaneously through the preservation of complete watersheds, including floodplain dynamics, unstable steep slopes, and all headwaters of a basin? Where do rich deltas, lacustrine systems, forested coastal plains, upland plateaus, and mountain ranges fit in? And how would we protect already existing conservation units limited to intermediate positions within river basins?

One point that few will contest is that the history of a population is partly accessible through the study of marker genes, proteins, or DNA sequences. Genetic diversity tends to accumulate with time and with historical options (see Ricklefs, chap. 3 in this volume), such that extinctions or bottlenecks seem to be more than balanced by opportunities for diversification at this level. Thus, genetic diversification is probably encouraged and preserved, rather than only reduced and destroyed, by all sorts of environmental changes through time and space.

Ecologists measure all these phenomena in the form of population and community characters and their variations across the landscape, with most experimental options suffering from the impossibility of controlling key factors. To avoid being "laughed out of court" by hard-nosed politicians and land managers, any historical correlations on which management suggestions are based need to be more than "just" theoretically probable or favorable to present policies. They must provide answers to long-standing problems, along with some indication of practical short-term tests for predictive ability and ways to follow the results of their applications, as well as to back out gracefully if they prove wrong or damaging in conservation practice.

Many chapters of this book provide fascinating insights into the effects of long-term climatic fluctuations, landscape-molding forces, and energy flow and resource availability on tropical biological communities. Sometimes the correlations that demonstrate these effects are supported by separate lines of evidence, including DNA sequences and predicted biodiversity values. Especially provocative are the chapters showing poor correlation among different lines of evidence, or the insidious effects of limited biological information or deficient sampling on the possibility of historical inference.

This chapter will examine some frequently proposed "determinants" of biological diversity in tropical forest systems to see whether or how they can be important general elements in monitoring and management plans or contribute to reserve design and location in the Neotropics. There are many possible approaches to the discovery and study of these factors (see fig. 10.2). Here, extensive data on Neotropical butterfly communities and landscapes (see table 10.1) will be used to address the following questions:

1. How important is the idiosyncratic *geologic history* of the local or regional biota to its biological richness?
2. Does the episodic restructuring of communities by *ecological factors* (physical, chemical, biological, and anthropogenic) contribute more to biological diversity patterns than historical factors do, or can it be relegated to "noise" in relation to evolutionary and geologic constraints? In particular, how do ecological factors act in tropical forest communities?
3. How can answers to these questions relate to *reserve design* and *management plans* for tropical forest systems and biological diversity? If the answer to question 2 shows a preponderance of unique or unpredictable ecological or stochastic factors, how can this finding be reconciled with conservation planning and action?

METHODS AND DATABASE FOR NEOTROPICAL FORESTS: BUTTERFLY LISTS

The empirical data used to seek answers to the above questions—standardized daily lists and cumulative site lists of butterflies (Ebert 1969; Brown 1972, 1997a; Brown and Hutchings 1997; Brown and Freitas 2000a; see table 10.1)—have been gathered over 45 years from several hundred sites in South American and Mesoamerican forests, under various regimes of human occupation (fig. 10.1A). Site sampling intensity varied from casual visits over less than 10 days to intensive regular transect censuses over decades (see table 10.1; see also Brown 1987a, fig. 4.2). In addition to lists in various seasons and in different primary vegetation or disturbance-influenced systems, most data sets include information on population biology (from mark-recapture study of select species), genetic variation (marker genes), resources used, various physical and chemical factors, and especially, the variation of all these within the site or along spatial and temporal transects (Brown 1979, 1982a, 1982b; see table 10.1). Methods for classification of climatic, topographic, soil, and vegetation characteristics at each site (mostly obtained from RADAMBRASIL 1973–1987) in relation to paleoecology, and of these characteristics and selected marker genes in relation to present-day endemicity and diversity patterns, are discussed in Brown (1979, 1982a, 1982b, 1987a,b, 1991; Brown and Prance 1987). Preliminary data and correlations among environmental indexes and species diversity have been presented for fifty-six sites from Mexico to southern Brazil by Brown (1997a; see also Brown and Freitas 2000a) and are also included here (in table 10.1), along with subspecies endemism (genotype) data for over 200 species and 5,000 sampling points (Brown 1979, 1982a, 1982b, 1987a), rarity data (by far the hardest to accumulate) for several dozen of these species and sites (Brown 1991, 1996a), and human use information (traditional and modern) for key systems (Brown 1996c, 1997a).

Daily butterfly censuses were made more efficient, complete, and comparable with baits of various sorts (pheromone precursors, fermenting fruit, rotting flesh, birdlime mimics, other excrement, flower patches, enriched sand and mud, edges and small clearings). Captures, being time-consuming, were limited to individuals not identifiable in the field; most were liberated after minimum handling, and less than 1% of the individuals observed were kept for sure identification or mounting of local reference collections and guides (specimens have been deposited locally and in the Museu de Historia Natural of UNICAMP). Daily checklists of species observed were entered each evening on previously prepared forms or in a notebook and included the number of individuals of each sex, genetic variations, behavior notes, and resources verified for each species. For maximum efficiency of data collection, each of two or more observers concentrated on one of several diverse subareas of the site, while a lone observer moved rapidly among all the subareas during the day. When the same subareas were censused on subsequent days, previously unrecorded species usually were fewer than 20% of those in the second census, a measure of the efficiency of the local inventory. Effort was measured as observer-hours of inventory on each list, with cloudy weather giving a 50% reduction in time counted and rainy periods not included (Brown and Hutchings 1997).

Similarities between lists of comparable effort at the same site were calculated with the simple Sørensen index, $2c/(a + b)$, where c represents species shared in the total lists a and b. Simple regressions and correlations were performed with Statistica (StatSoft 1995). Geographic coordinates (GPS) and topography, landform, soil, vegetation, and climatic data were obtained on site and checked against local or regional maps and compendia whenever available.

GEOLOGIC INFLUENCES ON THE EVOLUTION AND DIVERSIFICATION OF NEOTROPICAL BUTTERFLIES

Butterflies as an Optimum Taxonomic Group for Biogeographic Analyses

Butterflies may be one of the most efficient animal groups to use as indicators to compare values and changes in various ecosystem parameters (Brown 1972, 1982a, 1982b, 1991, 1996a, 1996b, 1996c, 1997a, 1997b; Wilcox et al. 1986; Kremen 1992, 1994; Sparrow et al. 1994; Beccaloni and Gaston 1995; New 1997; DeVries, Murray, and Lande 1997; Brown and Hutchings 1997; Brown and Freitas 2000a, 2000b; Horner-Devine et al. 2003). Butterflies are singularly useful for understanding and following natural communities in the Neotropics, due to a combination of well-developed systematics, facile field identification and marking, centrality in ecosystem processes (at the producer/consumer interface, often with high specificity), manageable diversity (sites show 300–1,800 species, of which half can be censused in 1 to 3 days: see Brown and Freitas 2000a, 2000b), a short life cycle (giving a rapidly recognizable response to environmental change), and popular appeal to local monitors.

The five to seven recognized butterfly families and a large majority of recognized subfamilies are cosmopolitan, typically most diversified in the tropics. One well-defined unit (Libytheinae or snout butterflies, presently regarded as the most primitive subfamily of Nymphalidae) is probably monogeneric, with one or two species on each continent or archipelago and a fossil from the Oligocene—a typical and trivial pattern. Like many widespread butterflies, its members are migratory in peak seasons (even in tropical forests), with individuals or swarms moving from tens to hundreds of kilometers through the landscape to find suitable host plants. This tendency and capability in the more mobile groups of butterflies (Robbins and Small 1981) not only adds diffusion and noise to their biogeographic patterns, but also makes the seasonal composition of local communities somewhat unstable and limits the number of "point endemic" species and alleles.

Neotropical butterflies are highly diversified at various levels. A few subfamilies, many tribes, most genera, and practically all species in the Neotropical region are endemic, with extensive geographic subspeciation and abundant and useful color pattern marker genes in local communities. Butterfly color patterns, derived from a very few stem cells, were already recognized in the nineteenth century as the writings of history and ecology in large letters across the easily read surfaces of the expanded wings (Bates 1864, 412–413).

Concepts of species and limits of intrapopulational variation are not uniform among active butterfly taxonomists, nor among populations of the species themselves, which can show variable hybridization or character displacement patterns along a single interface (Hammond 1991; Tyler, Brown, and Wilson 1994, 26). Even with a narrow "splitter" definition of species, however, only seven large regions of species endemism, obviously separated by major geographic barriers, can be seen in all families of Neotropical forest butterflies (fig. 10.3; see also Brown 1987a, 92, and Tyler, Brown, and Wilson 1994, 194). Three well-studied groups of common, mimetic, and sedentary forest butterflies (Nymphalidae, tribe Heliconiini and subfamily Ithomiinae, and Papilioninae, tribe Troidini) were examined for patterns of range restriction. Of the 300 species analyzed, only 75 are widespread; 18 are restricted to small areas, and 207 occupy a majority of the area in one of the seven regions of species endemism (Caribbean, 17; Central American, 16; Trans-Andean, 19; Andean, 40; Amazonian, 77; Atlantic, 32; Chaco-South Temperate, 6).

To measure diversification on a smaller geographic scale within each region of species endemism, data on the distributions of recognized subspecies in the same three groups were analyzed. Subspecies concepts accompanying extensive descriptions in the early 1900s underwent later revisions, based mostly on genetic studies (see Sheppard et al. 1985 for a summary and bibliography on the marker genes for well-differentiated geographic subspecies in *Heliconius*). Records were plotted from all over the Neotropics (over 5,000 sampling points in over 1,800 of the 4,650 quadrants of 30′ latitude and longitude, each about 55 × 55 km = 3,000 km² at the equator), from Mexico to central Argentina and Chile, including the Caribbean region and all elevations in the Andes. A total of 200 forest species (60 Heliconiini, 100 Ithomiinae, and 40 Troidini) with at least 1,290 geographically restricted subspecies showed sufficient geographic definition (table 10.2) to be useful in identification of patterns in this massive "spaghetti map." This map suggested at least forty-seven continental Neotropical regions of subspecies endemism, separated by regions of mixture coinciding with range limits for many of the subspecies. Thus, the regions of species

Figure 10.3 Seven large species endemism regions (CB, Caribbean; CA, Central American; TA, Trans-Andean; AN, Andean; AM, Amazonian; AT, Atlantic; CS, Chaco-South Temperate) for three groups of Neotropical forest butterflies and fifty smaller subspecies endemic centers, derived from quantitative analysis of color pattern marker genes. Separate subspecies endemism patterns for each of the three groups are shown below; note the almost total coincidence of position, but not of shape, in the different groups, reflecting their varying ecological preferences and a probable single predominant historical origin of the patterns. (Data and maps updated from Brown 1979, 1982a, 1982b, 1987a, 1991, and Tyler, Brown, and Wilson 1994.)

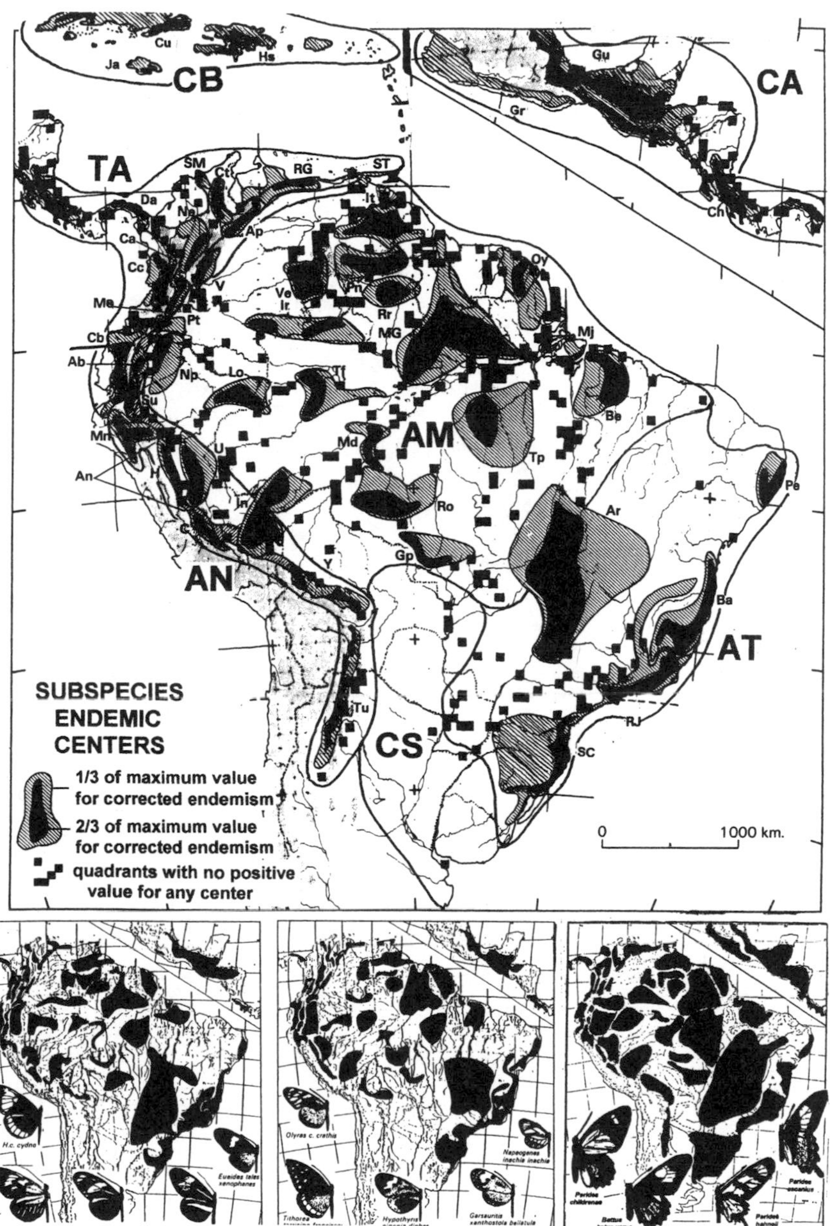

CB
CA
TA
AM
AN
AT
CS
Cu
Ja
Hs
Gu
Gr
Ch
SM
Ct
RG
ST
It
Da
Ne
Ap
Ca
Cc
Me
Cb
Ab
Pt
Np
Lo
Su
Mn
An
Ve
Ir
Pn
Rr
MG
Oy
Mj
Be
Md
Tp
U
Ro
In
Y
Gp
Ar
Pe
Ba
Tu
RJ
SC
SUBSPECIES ENDEMIC CENTERS
1/3 of maximum value for corrected endemism
2/3 of maximum value for corrected endemism
quadrants with no positive value for any center
0
1000 km.
H.c. cydno
Eueides tales xenophanes
Olyras c. crathis
Napeogenes inachia inachia
Garsauritis xanthostola bellatula
Parides childrenae
Parides ascanius
Parides hahneli

Table 10.2 Numbers of species or well-differentiated subspecies in each of three large groups of forest butterflies confined to centers of endemism within the various biogeographical regions of the Neotropics

		Number of subspecies[c]		
Region[a]	Center[b]	Heliconiini	Ithomiinae	Papilioninae
Caribbean	Cu = Cuba	3	1	10
	Hs = Hispaniola	3	*1	5
	Ja = Jamaica	2	1	3
Central American	Gr = Guerrero	1	2	14
	Gu = Guatemala	10	*11	*30
Trans-Andean	Ch = Chiriquí	11	16	17
	Da = Darién	3	11	6
	SM = Santa Marta	1	5	2
	Ct = Catatumbo	*8	5	2
	RG = Rancho Grande	9	12	7
	ST = Sucre/Trinidad	*8	6	4
	Ap = Apure	7	5	5
	V = Villavicencio	9	17	7
	Ne = Nechí	13	14	31
	Cc = Chocó	9	19	12
	Ca = Cauca	5	8	2
	Ma = Magdalena	*6	6	3
	Cb = Chimborazo	13	17	9
Amazonian-West (many combined with Andean)	Pt = Putumayo	8	18	4
	Np = Napo	11	18	15
	Ab = Abitagua	*9	*18	5
	Su = Sucúa	8	*18	2
	Mn = Marañón	*7	*16	7
	An = Andes (higher)	1	9	0
	H = Huallaga	*8	23	8
	U = Ucayali	*12	25	5
	C = Chanchamayo	4	22	8
	In = Inambari	*8	*27	7
	Y = Yungas	*14	*20	16
Amazonian-North (Tepuis, Guianas)	It = Imataca	*5	10	5
	Pn = Pantepui	2	13	1
	Ve = Ventuari	6	4	3
	Rr = Roraima	3	7	1
	Ir = Imerí	12	11	3
	MG = Manaus/Guiana	*19	*21	11
	Oy = Oyapock	11	15	7
Amazonian-South	Lo = Loreto	*6	*13	2
	Tf = Tefé	4	11	2
	Tp = Tapajós	*12	*27	9
	Mj = Marajó	5	3	3
	Be = Belém	6	14	9

(continued)

Table 10.2 *(continued)*

Region[a]	Center[b]	Number of subspecies[c]		
		Heliconiini	Ithomiinae	Papilioninae
	Md = Madeira	1	*10	3
	Ro = Rondônia	5	21	2
	Gp = Guaporé	5	9	2
	Ar = Araguaia (transitional)	*4	4	7
Atlantic	Pe = Pernambuco	1	6	2
	Ba = Bahia	*5	8	*8
	RJ = Rio de Janeiro	5	10	12
	SC = Santa Catarina	0	0	6
Chaco-South Temperate	Tu = Tucumán	0	0	2

Source: Brown 1979, 1982a, 1982b, 1987a; Tyler, Brown, and Wilson 1994.
[a]Regions of species endemism as shown in figure 10.3.
[b]Subspecies endemism centers as shown in figure 10.3. Possible endemism centers still incompletely studied (NW to SE): Ai = Apaporis, Jt = Jutaí, Jr = Juruá, Cj = Carajás, Ib = Ibiapaba, Dm = Diamantina, Sf = São Francisco, Bd = Bodoquena.
[c]Asterisk indicates further differentiation within center.

endemism were divided into various subregions defined by low-level (subspecific) differentiation in many of their inhabitants.

These "subspecies endemism centers" were further focused by calculating a corrected endemic value for the sum of all analyzed subspecies present in each 30′ × 30′ quadrant. Excluding seasonal or sexual variants and totally sympatric polymorphs, the presence of two or more different geographic subspecies of a single species in a quadrant gave a minus-one value in the total of subspecies endemism for any center represented there. The thus corrected values were organized into isoclines, producing forty-seven clearly defined endemism peaks separated by negative-value valleys (hybrid zones with at least half of the species present showing genetic mixture from two or more centers, thus with corrected endemism below 0) over the entire region (fig. 10.3). The patterns were different in shape, but not in general position, for the three groups analyzed (fig. 10.3, bottom), reflecting their different ecological preferences (climate, soils, topography, and vegetation) and dispersal capacities. This finding suggested that these patterns may have a historical origin, rather than depending on variation in ecological factors alone, which would lead to less coincident endemism patterns in each of the three groups. Each group clearly showed separate subspecies in a majority of the forty-six continental centers (table 10.2), most of which were not separated from adjacent centers by obvious physical or vegetation barriers, and included many members not mimetic of, nor otherwise dependent on, species in the other two groups. Identical differentiation patterns were observed in many other groups of forest Lepidoptera (Nymphalidae: Charaxinae, Acraeini, Nymphalinae; Lycaenidae: Riodininae; Pieridae; other Papilionidae; several moth groups—Arctiidae: Pericopinae; Notodontidae: Dioptidae; Castniidae), with widely divergent patterns of host plant use, behavior, preference for vegetation structure and topography, and lifestyles, mimetic or not of members of the analyzed groups.

Historical Influences on Biogeographic Patterns of Subspecies

This empirically derived pattern of low-level regional differentiation (subspeciation involving relatively few genes) might be a result of allopatric diversification associated with relatively recent episodes of cold, dry climate. These episodes could have affected the integrity of presently continuous tropical forest habitats within each region of species endemism, producing numerous isolated "paleoecological forest refugia" (hereafter abbreviated PFRs) within which the forest systems remained statistically more integrated than between them. This hypothesis was investigated by the construction of a spatially explicit and independent geologic model of the probability of PFRs 18,000 years ago, at the height of the last (Würm-Wisconsin) glacial episode, dated by pollen analyses throughout the Neotropics (van der Hammen 1992). This model was estimated by summation, for each of the quadrants, of paleoclimatic data favorable to continued orographic rainfall (such as along the base of the Andes), geomorphological data suggesting continued humid climate (polyconvex topography, with lack of paleopavements or angular landforms: Ab'Saber 1982), soil and subsoil characteristics that maintain forest facies under dryer seasonal climates today (fine-grained fertile soils), and vegetation structures suggesting long-term continuous organizational processes, such as high productivity in many layers. Negative characters of soils (hardpans, podzols, loose sands, and reworked gravel layers, all of these being signs of nonforest vegetation in the past) or of present-day vegetation (any type of savanna with much ancient endemicity) gave a subtraction from the sum. The resulting model (Brown 1979, 1982a, 1982b; Brown and Prance 1987) of conditions statistically favorable for the maintenance of tropical forest integrity during unfavorable climatic periods in the recent past (fig. 10.4, 60% or more likelihood) was superimposed on the corrected-endemism isocline for one-third of the maximum value for each subspecies endemism center (see fig. 10.3). Perhaps unsurprisingly, the overlap was highly significant, as almost all the subspecies endemism centers enclosed area(s) likely to have been PFRs, and little of the likely PFR area was not well known for

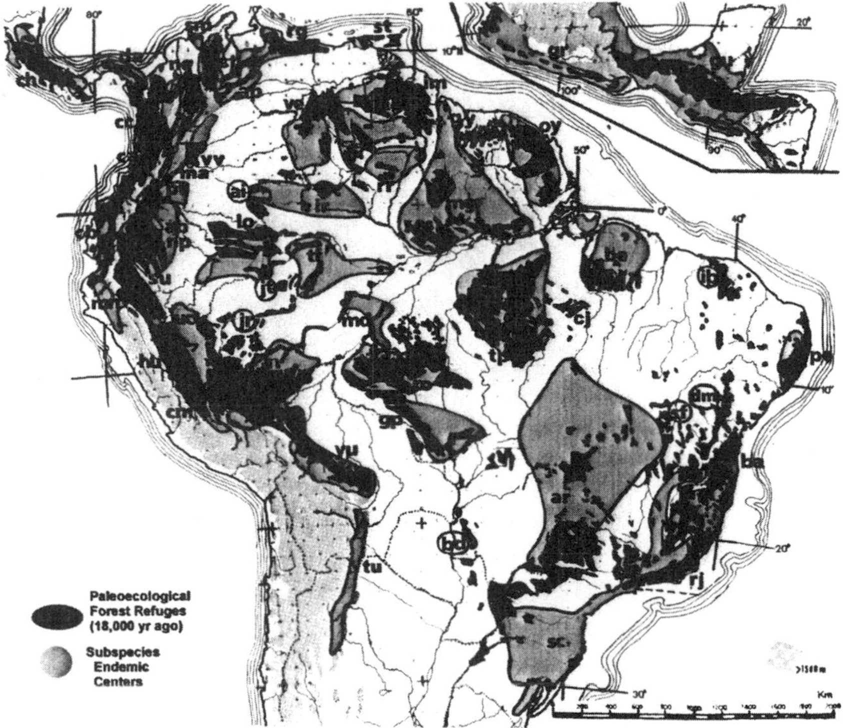

Figure 10.4 Butterfly subspecies endemic centers (shaded areas; see fig. 10.3) overlaid on probable paleoecological forest refugia (PFRs, black) derived not from biological data, but from a sum of independent data on paleoclimate (18,000 BP, peak of the most recent glaciation), geomorphology, soil characters, and vegetation structure. Probable "refuge" regions still incompletely sampled, but with various endemic subspecies already recognized in butterflies and other groups, include ai = Apaporis, bd = Bodoquena, cj = Carajás, dm = Diamantina, ib = Ibiapaba, jr = Juruá, jt = Jutaí, and sf = São Francisco.

subspecies endemism today. Both data sets also corresponded well to high-endemism regions defined in independent analyses of low-level differentiation (often regarded as species-level, however) in forest primates, mammals in general, birds, reptiles, frogs, scorpions, beetles, moths, flies, ants, bees, various groups of plants, and many other groups of Neotropical organisms, some of which were uncritically heaped onto the "PFR bandwagon," despite the highly variable quality and quantity of biogeographic and genetic information, in the 1980s (see discussion in Brown 1987b).

Even though this recent historical (PFR) model might still be regarded as useful (but see Colinvaux, chap. 6 in this volume) for explaining and predicting low-level endemism (an evolutionary phenomenon) and genetic diversity (locations of mixture or contact zones) in Neotropical forests, it is much less useful for predicting species richness, which in the butterflies analyzed is usually highest at the peripheries of the centers of endemism, away from PFR regions. Indeed, it seems probable that eventual restriction of forest species to PFRs may have led to more extinction than speciation, since the supersaturated and relatively isolated communities in these smaller areas would probably experience loss of metapopulations and species at a far greater rate than the development and accommodation of new genotypes (Turner 1982). Thus, geologic and historical factors might either increase or decrease biological diversity at different levels, and they are probably useful mostly for predicting endemism, and then only when systematic definition of ancestry is adequate (see Ricklefs, chap. 3 in this volume).

Paleoenvironments and Concentrations of Rare Primitive Taxa

Geologic and historical factors might also help predict sites of accumulation of rare and ancient species ("paleoenvironments" of Brown 1991), since these sites are often small "islands" within strongly reworked landscapes, where conditions have been neither so favorable as to promote massive dominance by younger widespread species with elimination of older endemics, nor so unfavorable as to directly eliminate the older residents themselves. Typically, these are sites with abundant but patchy resources, medium species richness (even though they are usually peripheral to endemic centers, like the high-richness areas), and complex topography, hydrology, and geologic history. They appear to meet the requirements of exaggerated stochasticity and a tightly organized local community that has "eaten up, folded into its genes" the effects of natural catastrophes (Wilson 1992, 15) by intensive coevolution of options and backup safeguards (such as highly variable periods of pupal diapause, large home ranges, and diverse basic behavior and resource options). In these sites, ancient species have been able to play cat-and-mouse with their better-adapted descendants and survive until today, however local, erratic, rare, and threatened they may be. Many probably have already gone extinct naturally, and others will do so in the future, independent of anthropogenic pressure, as today's common species—key elements in biological diversity—become likewise obsolete, confined to special environments, and finally replaced by others, perhaps better preadapted to coexist with Man the Destroyer.

The paleoenvironments that conserve rarity are unpredictable (and probably ephemeral) in space and time, easily recognized when found (Brown 1991, 1997a), and probably impossible to conserve indefinitely. Geologic factors may help us to understand these evolutionary relicts, but not always to confidently find them or predict their composition. Although they are unique in preserving archaeospecies and even archaeocommunities (hence the term "paleoenvironments"), they are not usually optimal in present-day diversity. How can we find, classify, and explain the places that are?

WHAT PROMOTES SPECIES DIVERSITY IN THE PRESENT TIME?

Correlates of Forest Species Richness in the Neotropics

When the quadrants of highest species richness in the three butterfly groups used for analysis of subspecies endemism were overlaid on four logical spatial models of factors proposed to generate and maintain diversity (Brown 1982a), only one model gave a broad positive correlation (fig. 10.5).

Very large-scale and important geologic factors, such as "moving bands" or deep arches across the Amazon basin from northwest to southeast, vast floodplains in ancient but still active sub-Andean basins between these "structural highs," and major Tertiary orogenies and embayments (fig. 10.5A), provided some help in understanding the detailed patterns of diversity in some regions, but were less applicable to topographically complex shield areas. In any case, these older forces are amply reflected in all later factors and phenomena up through today's floodplain dynamics, a major present source of landscape diversification (Räsänen, Salo, and Kalliola 1987; Räsänen et al. 1992).

Overlap of species richness with PFRs (see fig. 10.4) was small (fig. 10.5B), less than random, and overlap with environmental conditions known to provide favorable habitats in the present (climate, vegetation, and soils) was close to random (fig. 10.5C), with many high-diversity quadrants in regions favorable in only one or two of these factors.

A model based on rapid transitions in these environmental factors (thus representing high environmental heterogeneity: Endler 1982b; Benson 1982), combined with areas of unpredictably long dry seasons or winter cold snaps (representing intermediate system disturbance, enough to open up resources and niches), overlapped almost all the known high-diversity quadrants (fig. 10.5D). This finding corresponds with current theories about diversity generation and maintenance, as well as with empirical observations of large positive edge effects and high habitat turnover along transects in many diversified tropical systems (micro-beta diversity, see Ruokolainen et al., chap. 13, and Condit et al., chap. 14 in this volume). It also implies a preponderant action of ecology, especially environmental microcomplexity linked to both physical and biological factors, in providing positive feedback to diversity (see fig. 10.2), such as a wide range of soil

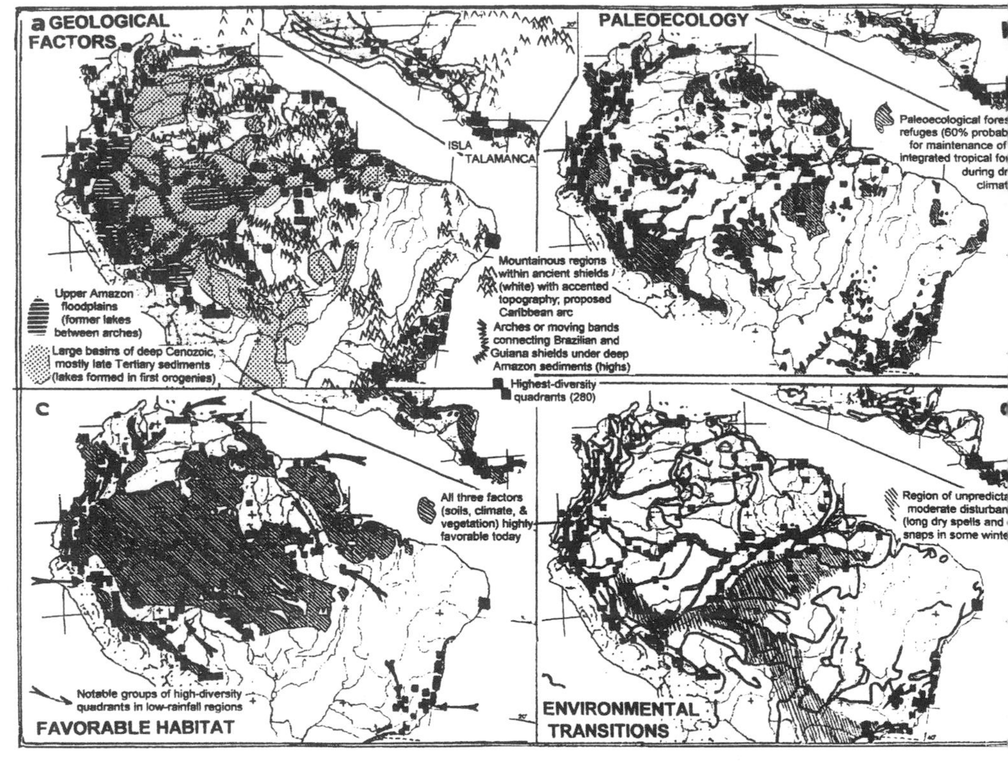

Figure 10.5 Quadrants of maximum regional species richness in butterflies superimposed on four different models for generation and maintenance of diversity: (A) important older geologic contributions, including regions of long-term floodplain dynamics due to eastward movement of major river courses in the upper Amazon basin during slow orogenies (see Räsänen, Salo, and Kalliola 1987; Räsänen et al. 1992) and arches underlying the sediments; (B) paleoecological forest refugia (from fig. 10.4); (C) areas favorable for high diversity today in three major environmental factors (climate, soils, vegetation); and (D) areas of maximum environmental heterogeneity, transition, and unpredictable disturbance today (variable dry season and unpredictable cold snaps). Only the last model shows a strong positive correlation between the two data sets. Note, however, that correlation is not causation, though it is still useful in landscape planning. Indeed, many sites in the upper Amazon are probably influenced by, and thus correlated with, the factors in all four models (see Colinvaux, chap. 6 in this volume).

types, plant species, or specific host plant interactions creating greater complexity and variation of the vegetation structure, and thereby more niches available per unit volume.

Ecological Correlates of the Variation in Structure and Richness in Forest Communities

Principal components analysis (PCA) of the importance of eighteen environmental factors in distinguishing the forty-eight sites (see table 10.1) revealed, in the first three composite axes, (explaining 54% of the variation: table 10.3A) highly significant contributions from ten factors, grouped logically into four altitude-related factors (including temperature and topography) dominating axis 1, three disturbance factors dominating axis 2, and three climatic and vegetation factors along axis 3. Humidity, vegetation, and especially soil factors dominated the next three axes. The forty-eight sites were well separated from each other and formed nine geographic and altitudinal groups along the first two axes (fig. 10.6A), corresponding to consistent differences in geologic (tectonic) history and present-day human occupation of the various biomes.

The first axis (climatic-topographic, 21% of the variance) was significantly correlated (by Pearson's r coefficient, using its square: table 10.3B) with the variation among the sites in the proportions of Papilionidae and Pieridae (many species in these families prefer low temperatures and higher altitudes). The second axis (disturbance-related, 18%) was significantly correlated with all groups except Theclinae, especially with the Ithomiinae, bait-attracted Nymphalidae, and metalmarks (Riodininae). This last group is time-consuming to sample adequately, but the first two are easily censused with pyrrolizidine alkaloids and fermented baits, respectively, and thus stand out as good indicator groups for following anthropogenic disturbance at a site (see Brown 1985 and DeVries, Murray, and Lande 1997). The variation in the total butterfly list was also sensitive (negatively) to anthropogenic disturbance (table 10.3B), with consistently higher richness in relatively well-preserved sites.

Detailed interactive correlation analysis within the context of canonical community ordination (CCA or CANOCO: Ter Braak and Smilauer 1999; the relatively small gradient in the first canonical axis for faunal data required redundancy analysis, RDA) readily identified a number of environmental factors as being quantitatively related to the proportions of certain groups at the sites (fig. 10.6B). Three significant factors (temperature, secondary vegetation, and annual rainfall, the first of these interchangeable with topography or altitude, the third with soil category) explained up to 31% of the variation in butterfly

Table 10.3 Statistics, composition, and importance of principal components derived from eighteen environmental factors in forty-eight Neotropical sites

(A) Importance of each environmental factor in the first six components (axes)

Environmental factors	Axis 1	Axis 2	Axis 3	Axis 4	Axis 5	Axis 6
Altitude	**0.449**	−0.067	0.092	−0.156	0.155	−0.182
Altitude variation	**0.393**	−0.058	0.173	−0.071	0.218	−0.091
Topography	**0.406**	−0.009	0.221	−0.001	0.064	−0.120
Temperature	**−0.442**	−0.118	−0.038	−0.066	0.183	−0.047
Temperature variation	***0.318***	0.076	−0.241	0.144	0.117	−0.067
Annual rainfall	−0.006	***−0.315***	**0.404**	0.106	0.026	0.164
Dry months in year	0.042	−0.094	**−0.367**	−0.175	***0.356***	**−0.433**
Permanent water	−0.202	0.067	−0.093	**0.467**	***−0.322***	0.098
Soil category	−0.055	−0.196	0.165	**−0.439**	−0.169	**0.434**
Soil bases (fertility)	−0.145	***0.322***	−0.192	−0.181	***0.365***	0.021
Soil mosaic	0.058	0.034	−0.131	0.246	**0.464**	**0.602**
Vegetation category	0.086	−0.234	***0.312***	***0.319***	0.009	−0.237
Vegetation mosaic	0.141	−0.229	−0.236	**0.414**	0.226	0.208
Vine abundance	0.036	−0.122	**−0.421**	***−0.336***	0.042	0.165
Bamboo abundance	0.290	−0.044	−0.267	−0.045	−0.400	0.114
Disturbance	0.020	**0.443**	0.204	−0.020	0.188	−0.034
Pollution	0.005	**0.415**	0.110	−0.092	0.086	0.138
Secondary vegetation	−0.011	**0.474**	0.105	−0.056	0.153	0.115
Predominant "flavor" of each axis in the PCA	Topography, temperature	Anthropogenic disturbance	Climate, vegetation	Vegetation, water, soils	Soils, vegetation	Soils, seasonality

Note: The most important factors are given in **bold,** less important factors in ***bold italic,*** including for axes 4–6 when similarly valued. The first axis (topographic-climatic) explained 21.1% of the variation in the environmental factors, the second axis another 17.6%, the third axis 14.9%, the fourth 8.4%, the fifth 7.4%, and the sixth 6.8% (total 76.1%).

(B) Variation (% corresponding to the square of Pearson's *r*) in eight butterfly groups and three combined groups among 48 Neotropical sites explained by the first three PCA axes

Taxonomic group	Axis 1	Axis 2	Axis 3	Comments
Ithomiinae (alone)	0.0	32.0	0.0	Sensitive to habitat change
Mimetic nymphalids (including the Ithomiinae)	5.1	25.6	0.1	Sensitive to disturbance; many prefer cooler mountain areas
Bait-attracted Nymphalidae	0.6	38.9	5.6	Very sensitive to disturbance
Nymphalidae (total)	0.0	38.5	2.3	
Papilionidae + Pieridae	28.1	22.5	6.5	Prefer higher and colder areas
Lycaenidae: Riodininae	5.0	23.2	4.0	Very local in intact vegetation
Lycaenidae: Theclinae	0.1	9.1	4.7	Myrmecophiles, very sensitive
Papilionoidea	0.2	32.3	2.7	
Hesperiidae: Pyrginae and Pyrrhopyginae	0.0	20.1	0.1	Sensitive to disturbance, but can migrate to new areas
Hesperiidae: Hesperiinae	5.7	12.0	2.3	Grass feeders, high altitudes
Total butterflies	0.1	27.3	2.2	**Respond clearly to disturbance**

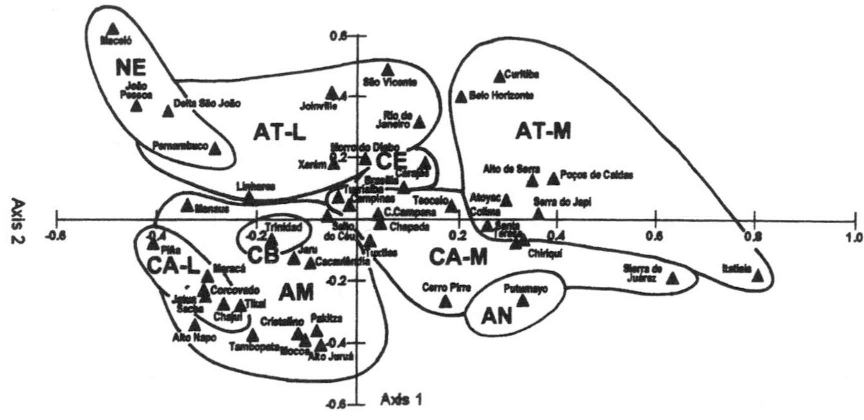

B C

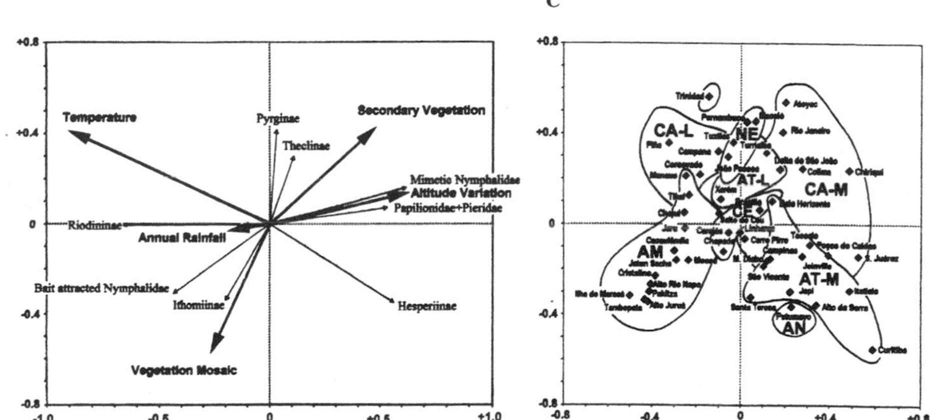

Figure 10.6 (A) Results of PCA analysis of eighteen environmental factors and butterfly species richness and proportions of eight different taxonomic/ecological groups and three groups combined to family level and above (superfamily and entire fauna) at forty-eight Neotropical sites (see table 10.1), as a map of site positions on the first two axes (corresponding to topographic and anthropogenic disturbance factors), showing logical geographic and altitudinal grouping of the sites. Codes: AM = Amazon basin, AN = Andes (Putumayo only), AT = Atlantic Forests (SE Brazil), CA = Central America, CB = Caribbean (Trinidad only), CE = Cerrado (central Brazil), L = lowland sites, M = montane sites, NE = extension of Atlantic forests into coastal northeastern Brazil. (B) Results of RDA analysis of the proportions of eight higher taxonomic groups of butterflies in the local community of the same sites; note relations between vectors of five main environmental factors and each butterfly group. (C) Grouping of the 48 sites in the RDA analysis; note similarity to that in the PCA ordination. Codes as in A, not using CB.

Table 10.4 Statistics of the principal vectors obtained in the RDA canonical analysis between eighteen environmental factors and the proportions of eight major butterfly groups in the community at forty-eight Neotropical sites

Factors	*F*	*P*	%
Temperature	11.54	.0001	20.1
Secondary vegetation	3.91	.0059	6.4
Annual rainfall	2.78	.0318	4.4
Vegetation mosaic	2.27	(.061)	3.5
Altitude variation	2.51	.0495	3.7
[Temperature variation	1.73	.1301 (n.s.)	2.5]
(Placing temperature as covariant)			
Topography	5.06	.0014	9.9
Secondary vegetation	4.69	.0023	8.5
Annual rainfall	2.69	.0314	4.7
Temperature variation	2.43	.049	4.1
Vegetation mosaic	2.87	.0247	4.7
[Altitude	1.71	.1384 (n.s.)	2.7]
(Placing topography also as covariant)			
Altitude	4.89	.0022	9.6
Secondary vegetation	5.60	.0006	10.0
Soil category	2.92	.021	5.0
Vegetation mosaic	2.33	.0536	3.9
Altitude variation	2.27	.0644 (n.s.)	3.7
Temperature variation	1.86	.1155 (n.s.)	2.9

community structure (table 10.4), and continued to order the sites logically (fig. 10.6C), though with more overlap than in the PCA.

In the RDA, the proportions of different subgroups in the same family showed near-opposite influences of climate, disturbance, and vegetation factors (fig. 10.6B: compare the vectors for bait-attracted vs. mimetic (flower-visiting) Nymphalidae, Theclinae vs. Riodininae, and Pyrginae vs. Hesperiinae). The simple correlation of many environmental factors with values for species richness or community structure (fig. 10.6B) was also easily verified (table 10.5), and was often observed directly at better-studied field sites (Brown and Freitas 2000a, 2000b).

Thus, with a constant geologic backdrop (topographic factors), changes in anthropogenic disturbance levels (three factors) should be most rapidly indicated by reductions in the richness of Ithomiinae, bait-attracted Nymphalidae, and Riodininae, the groups most highly correlated with these factors (see tables 10.3B and 10.4); the first two are readily censused with baits. Reduced rainfall

Table 10.5 Correlations between eighteen environmental factors and the richness of butterfly groups and total fauna in forty-eight Neotropical sites

Environmental factors	Ithomiinae	Mimetic (other)	Bait-attracted	**Nymphalidae**	Papilio-Pieridae	Lycaenidae: Riodinidae	Lycaenidae: Theclinae	**Papilionoidea**	Pyrginae	Hesperiinae	**Total fauna**
Mean altitude					**0.479**						
Altitude range					**0.574**						
Topography					**0.486**						
Temperature (annual mean)			*+		−0.379	0.40		*+			
Temperature Variation					0.325						
Rainfall (annual mean)	0.336	**0.432**		0.292	**0.474**			*+	*+		
Dry months (annual mean)							0.298				
Permanent water in site											
Soil category	0.293		*+	*+							
Soil fertility	0.314	0.317	0.398	0.392	0.401	0.309		0.375	**0.451**		0.365
Soil mosaic										*+	
Vegetation category	0.354	**0.422**		0.323	**0.536**			*+	0.309	0.307	0.298
Vegetation mosaic	**0.487**	0.472	0.591	0.588	0.334	**0.534**	0.391	**0.578**	0.448	0.563	0.579
Vines and lianas											
Bamboos				0.285			0.313			0.334	*+
Disturbance	−0.385	*−	**−0.446**	**−0.417**	−0.316		−0.355			−0.320	
Pollution	−0.371	−0.307	**−0.410**	**−0.402**		−0.335	*−	−0.383			−0.334
Secondary vegetation	−0.379	*−	**−0.481**	**−0.442**		−0.369	*−	−0.412			−0.356

Note: Only significant values are given ($P < .05$; underlined $P < .01$; **bold,** $P < .005$; **bold underlined** $P < .001$; * = near-significant correlation).

and changes in vegetation type should be reflected by scarcity of Papilionidae-Pieridae and model/mimetic Nymphalidae; bait-attracted species and Pyrginae respond strongly to soil fertility. All butterfly groups are tightly tied into rich vegetation mosaics.

In the end, composite environmental indexes (Brown 1997a) may best explain most of the variation in the species richness of the butterfly community or its components in a given site or season; these indexes combine favorable values in topography, climate, soils, vegetation structure, and disturbance regime, and represent essentially straight synthetic thinking rather than true tests of correlation (but see tables 10.3–10.5 and fig. 10.7A–D below).

Although all these factors may contribute to local diversity by multiplying resource richness and subtle habitat variation, fusing components of beta diversity to the point of being perceived as alpha-confusion, do they contribute to the large regional disparities mentioned in the introduction and shown in figure 10.1? In fact, the highest biological diversity occurs in regions where both historical disturbance (multiplying habitats as well as regional genetic diversity; peri- and interrefugial areas in fig. 10.4) and present-day ecological heterogeneity or unpredictable natural disturbance (figs. 10.5C and D); see Ruokolainen et al., chap. 13 in this volume) are at a maximum. These regions typically show complex topography, seasonal climate with rivers of varying volume constantly reworking the landscape and creating new habitat every year, subdominant plants on eutrophic soils (such as emergent Lecythidaceae trees or giant bamboo stands) flowering and/or dying simultaneously and leaving enormous spaces open to invasion, and abundant resources helping new species to settle in and join the system, at least for a while. Indeed, all these polydiverse and "polysuccessional" habitats share an important property: continual invasions, insertions, fluctuations, and extinctions of local populations of plants and animals, which redirect energy and mass flows, permit accumulation of "unused" resources (giving positive feedback to "scramble" contributions to biodiversity), and allow the arrival of transient (2–50 generations) species from all sides. This property is apparent in the genetic diversity seen, as well as in constant and apparently "supersaturated" species packing (seen in the daily lists) and exalted landscape complexity (Shmida and Wilson 1985). How can such chaotic systems be rationally studied and preserved so that evolution can continue its frenetic course of adapting species and systems to unpredictable disturbance at many scales of time and space?

LANDSCAPE COMPLEXITY, DISEQUILIBRIUM, AND LARGE TREE BUFFERING

Many ecological theories, models, and predictions presuppose that most communities are in relative equilibrium over observational and experimental time scales. Even in strongly seasonal climates, a regularly variable "dynamic" equilibrium is assumed, such that measurements in different years at the same season are comparable and usually combinable.

Long-term site studies in tropical systems do not confirm this assumption of equilibrium. This can be seen even in analyses of protective substances (dehydropyrrolizidine alkaloids) in distasteful Ithomiinae butterflies, which are prime models for large and diverse mimicry rings throughout the Neotropics as well as useful in biogeographic analyses. Great variation can be seen among individuals, populations, sites, and seasons (Brown 1985; Trigo et al. 1996), surely reflecting, and reflected in, the dynamics of dependent (mimetic) populations and host plants, and thereby influencing the local community. Populations of purportedly sedentary organisms, never before recorded, appear and then disappear with unsettling regularity and with nontrivial effects on the invaded or abandoned local communities (table 10.6).

Quantitative evidence for this lack of equilibrium tendencies comes from many sites with 10 or more years of intensive butterfly censuses (table 10.6–10.7; Brown 1972; Brown and Freitas 2000a). In the species-rich, high-productivity, variable-climate 250 ha Santa Genebra forest reserve near my house in Campinas, São Paulo, many species common on April blooms 5 to 10 years ago are rare or absent now on the same flowers, and vice versa. Composite indexes and richness numbers change continually and do not "settle back" to previous values after a year, or after 2 or 3 or 10 years, or at equivalent positions in sunspot cycles or El Niño-La Niña oscillations. Indexes of similarity between pairs of census lists, high (about 0.8) in adjacent weeks in the same habitat, diminish regularly with increasing time or habitat distance, swinging only part way back up at similar seasons (table 10.7A) or in similar-appearing ecological settings (see also Ruokolainen et al., chap. 13 in this volume). In a species-poor, low-productivity, Amazonian system with a more constant climate (the Biological Dynamics of Forest Fragments Project north of Manaus, Amazonas), the similarity indexes also diverge just as much with time as with change in habitat or "isolation" status with relation to nearby continuous forest (table 10.7B,; see Brown and Hutchings 1997, 100–101).

In both of these systems and all other ones followed, transient species appear and disappear at irregular intervals from days to decades, suggesting that all are

Table 10.6 Selection of "erratic" butterfly species (37) in the Santa Genebra Forest Reserve, Campinas, SP (neither rare residents, nor accidental tourists): Presence and syndromes, 1988–2000

FAMILY, Subfamily/tribe, *genus*, and *species*	Host plant (family)	Source: km, dir.	88–92: 89012[a] · 1997: apr my jn dz · 1998: jan fe mar apr my jn jl ag st nov dez · 1999: ja feb mar april my jn jul ag oc d · 2000: jf m ap m j	Syndrome[c]
List no.			1 5 10 15 20 25 30 35 40 45 50 55 60 65 70 75 80 85 90 95 100	
PAPILIONIDAE; PIERDAE				
Parides bunichus	Aristoloc	5 S	++ ++ ■+■ + + ■	seasonal
Protesilaus nigricornis	Lauraceae	50 S	■ +■● + ■ + +■ + +	multcol
Enantia melite clarissa	Leguminos	20 S	+ + + +■ +■+ + ■ +	erratic
Dismorphia thermesia	Leguminos	20 S	+■■■ + + + + ++ + + ■■■ + ■ +■■+ + ++■ + + +	coloniz
Dismorphia astyocha	Leguminos	50 S	+ + + + ■ ■ +++ ■	multpres
LYCAENIDAE, Theclinae				
Paiwarria venulius	Bignonia	60 N	■■ ■ ++ ■ ■ + ■■ ■ ++ + + ■ ■■ ■■ + ■ ■ ■ +	multcol
Ocaria ocrisia	Ochnaceae	60 N	+ ■ + + + ■■++ + + + + +	multcol
Michaelus jebus	Leguminos	60 N	+■ + + + ■ + +■	erratic
LYCAENIDAE, Riodininae				
Baeotis johannae	(Ants?)	60 N	■+■■■+ ■++ + + +++++■■+ ■■+ + ++ +	coloniz?
Adelotypa malca	(Ants)	0.1 E	+ + ■ ++ + ■■■ +	coloniz
NYMPHALIDAE, Danainae + Ithomiinae				
Danaus eresimus plexaure	Asclepiad	100 N	+ ■ + ■ ■	coloniz
Tithorea harmonia	Apocyn	60 N	+ ■ + + ■ ■ ■ ++ + ■■	multpres
Epityches eupompe	Solanac	50 S	■ ++ + + ■ ● ++■■■■+++ + ■+ + +	coloniz
Hypoleria plisthenes	Solanac	60 N	+ + ++ ■ +■ + ++	multcol
Heterosais edessa	Solanac	150 SE	■ + ■ ■+ ■■■■ ++ + ++ + +■+ +	coloniz
NYMPHALIDAE, Brassol. + Satyrinae + Charaxinae				
Opsiphanes cassiae	Musaceae	0.2 E	+ + +■ ■■ ■ ■+	erratic
Taygetis tripunctata	Bambuseae	100 W?	++++ + +■ ■+ +	resreduc
Pharneuptychia pharella	Gramineae	50 S	++++ ■+ + + +	disapunk
Splendeuptychia libitina	Bambuseae	3 SE	+ ++■ ■ ++ ■ ■■+■■ ++■+ +■	resreduc

Eteona tisiphone	Bambuseae	2 SE	■ +■ ■+ + ++ ■ + ■ ■ ■■ ■■■+ ■■+ +■ +■■	coloniz
Consul fabius drurii	Piperac	50 S	+ ■● +	migracol
Memphis otrere	Euphorbia	50 S	+ ■ + + ■ + + ■ + + + +	erratic
NYMPHALIDAE, Limenitidinae + Eurytelinae				
Adelpha syma	Rosaceae	50 S	+ + ■ + + + +■ +	erratic
Cybdelis phaesyla	Euphorbia	50 S	++ + ■■■ + + + + ++■+ +	multcol
Eunica tatila bellaria	Burserac	100 NW	+ +++ + +++ ■+ + +■■■■■++■+■ +■ + +■ + ■■■■■■ ++	multcol
NYMPHALIDAE, Nymph. + Acraeini + Heliconiini				
Phyciodes (Ortilia) velica	Acanthac	20 S	+ + + + ++ + + ■ +++ ■ +	multpres
Actinote genitrix	Composit	50 S	+ ++ + ■■ ■ + + ■■	wandflow
Philaethria wernickei	Passiflor	150 SE	+ ++ + ■	wandflow
Heliconius sara apseudes	Passiflor	150 SE	+ ■	wandflow
HESPERIIDAE, Eudaminae				
Urbanus velinus	Leguminos	400 E	■+■■++■■+++++ ++ + +■■ ■■■	migrflor
Astraptes alardus	Leguminos	200 NW	+ + + + + + + + +	erratic
HESPERIIDAE, Pyrginae				
Mylon pelopidas	Malvaceae	100 NW	+ + + + ■ + ■ +■+ ■ + + +■■■	wandflor
Antigonus nearchus	Malvaceae	50 S	++■ + + ■ + ++ + +■ + ■	seasonal
Anisochoria (3 species)	?	100 NW	+ ++ + + + ■ + + +++	erratic
HESPERIIDAE, Hesperiinae				
Naevolus orius	Gramineae	100 NW	+ + + + + + + ■ + + +	erratic
Tisias lesieur	Cannaceae	3 SE	+ + + ++ ++ + ■+ ■	erratic
Vacerra bonfilius	Arecaceae	50 S	+ + + + + + + +++ + ++ ++ ++++ + + ■+■ + ++	coloniz
Total day's list			c**b**d*ee*bbccccdd*eff*ddedddccccc**bbb**c**b**ccd*e*d*e*ddcc**b**cccddddced dddbcc**bbb**c**bb**<u>**aaaaa**</u>bccccdddccccc*eeee*ddcc**bb**<u>**a**</u>bcccc	
			1 5 10 15 20 25 30 35 40 45 50 55 60 65 70 75 80 85 90 95 100	

Note: Codes for records: + = presence of one or two males only, ■ = presence of many males, or females, and ● = presence of juvenile stages during the weekly census.

[a]Lists 4–5 were small due to overgrowth of border by large grasses.

[b]Species recorded: <u>**a**</u>, 300–340; **b**, 260–299; c, 220–259; d, 180–219; *e*, 140–179; *f*, 100–140.

[c]Suggested syndromes of erraticity: coloniz = successful colonization, with later broods (usually 1.5–3 month cycle); disapunk = disappeared for unknown reasons; erratic = erratic presence, no colonization; migracol = migratory and colonizes; migrflor = migratory seeking adult resources; multcol = multiple colonization attempts, one or more successful; multpres = multiple presence, probably unsuccessful in colonization; resreduc = reduction or elimination of key larval resource (bamboo) caused elimination; seasonal = seasonal colonization in some years, dies off; wandflor = wanders widely looking for floral resources.

Table 10.7 Similarity (as Sorenson's $S = 2c/a + b$) in species recorded between pairs of census lists of Neotropical butterflies

(A) "Complete" (10–14 h) weekly lists at various intervals in the Santa Genebra forest reserve, Campinas, São Paulo, 1988–1999

Lists[a] separated by:	*N*	Similarity (×100): mean and range of values		
		Nymphalidae-Pieridae-Papilionidae	Hesperiidae-Lycaenidae	Total list
5–11 days (1 week)	27	86 (80–90)	76 (67–81)	81 (75–84)
12–17 days (2 weeks)	26	85 (80–91)	73 (65–79)	79 (73–82)
18–24 days (3 weeks)	25	83 (78–88)	71 (64–79)	77 (71–82)
25–40 days (1 month)	28	82 (75–86)	69 (62–77)	75 (69–81)
41–75 days (2 months)	42	80 (71–88)	67 (57–75)	73 (64–78)
76–105 days (3 months)	50	77 (70–84)	60 (50–72)	68 (61–77)
106–166 days (4–5 months)	74	77 (69–84)	58 (47–70)	67 (62–72)
167–227 days (6–7 months)	43	77(69–85)	52 (37–70)	65 (55–76)
228–320 days (8–10 months)	44	75 (66–82)	56 (46–69)	65 (59–73)
Between years[b] (1998–1999)	55	83 (79–88)	72 (66–76)	77 (73–81)
(11–13 months, (others)	44	79 (73–86)	66 (59–72)	73 (69–79)
1 year)[c] (average)	(99)	81 (73–88)	69 (59–76)	75 (69–81)
23–25 months (2 years)	74	80 (74–84)	66 (57–72)	72 (64–76)
3, 4, and 5 years	14	80 (74–83)	63 (59–68)	71 (66–74)
6 and 7 years	19	73 (68–79)	60 (54–65)	67 (63–69)
95–97 months (8 years)	24	74 (69–79)	57 (49–64)	65 (61–70)
107–109 months (9 years)	24	75 (69–80)	58 (53–67)	66 (63–71)
119–121 months (10 years)	18	77 (73–83)	59 (53–64)	67 (65–70)
131–133 months (11 years)	18	77 (74–80)	60 (56–63)	68 (66–70)

[a]Peak season lists (March–May), almost always with over 210 species recorded, are represented in both lists compared, except in a few separated by 2 and 10 months and many by 3–9 months, where only one list is from the peak season.

[b]Excluded are comparisons with the abortive list of April 1992; values are also affected by the low list of 1991; both of these are due to excessive overgrowth of the reserve borders by large grasses.

[c]The first line (1998–1999) compares two years of exceptional butterfly abundance, separated by a wet winter, (1998–1999), which apparently increased by 0.02 (e.g., Nymphalidae-Pieridae-Papilionidae high extremes) to 0.07 (e.g., Hesperiidae-Lycaenidae low extremes) the previous average indices for separation of lists by 1 year ("others"). The third line gives the averages of the two periods.

(continued)

Table 10.7 *(continued)*

(B) Similarity indices in the Biological Dynamics of Forest Fragments Project, north of Manaus, Amazonas, Brazil

Category: Daily lists in same reserve	Compared between	*n*	Mean and SD		Comparison
Same environment	Less than a week apart	21	0.61	0.06	a
Same environment, semi-isolated	2–24 months apart	23	0.57	0.06	b
Same environment, intact forest	2–24 months apart	42	0.50	0.06	c ($t = 3.54, p < .001$)
Same environment, all types together	2–24 months apart	65	0.51	0.08	c
Same environment, intact forest	4–5 years apart	23	0.47	0.06	d ($t = 2.60, p < .01$)
Different environments	2–24 months apart	27	0.42	0.09	e ($p < .01$)

Source: Brown and Hutchings 1997, 100–101.

part of dynamic metapopulations spread across the landscape (Hanski and Gilpin 1997). Many such variations suggest a continual change in community composition, structure, and diversity, with no obvious directionality or points of short- or long-term equilibrium. Furthermore, the changes in diversity associated with these variations through seasons, years, and regional space may be greater than those measured between sites with very divergent geologic and evolutionary histories, again suggesting a lesser influence of history and a preponderant action of unpredictable ecological processes and rare, unique events in shaping the community and its richness in the present.

Among the strongest, most pervasive, and thus most influential of these ecological processes is the disturbance of system structure and energy and material flows by the death and toppling of a large tree. Others include landslides, bamboo forest die-offs, shifts in river courses (see Räsänen, Salo, and Kalliola 1987; Räsänen et al. 1992), flooding, flower or fruit resource failures (see Connell et al., chap. 23, and Wright, chap. 15 in this volume), and major fluctuations of or invasions by generalist or aggressive species, from tiny pathogens to large predators. These processes add further types of intense disturbance, most of which is neither frequently faced nor "eaten up" by microevolution of local populations. These strong, unpredictable natural disturbances tend to create, maintain, and impose a metapopulation/metacommunity model on vegetation, herbivores, predators, and decomposers. When this pattern becomes very fine-scaled, a highly diversified system comes to dominate the landscape, characterized by exalted micro-beta diversity and continual stochastic internal reorganizations. Most modern tropical forests seem to obey this model.

"First principles" can be applied to suggest and test probable relations between different kinds of diversity and different types of disturbance (see Brown and Brown 1992 and Brown 1996b, 1996c, 1997a). These relations were examined statistically by correlation analysis of a composite index for species richness in butterflies (including daily list, total site list, genetic diversity, and balance among different higher taxa; see table 10.1) with environmental heterogeneity (fig. 10.7A, positive, $r^2 = 0.53$, $P = 4 \times 10^{-9}$), resource richness (fig. 10.7B, $r^2 = .28$, $P = .0001$), and composite natural (fig. 10.7C, $r^2 = .28$, $P = .0001$, positive slope) and anthropogenic (fig. 10.7D, $r^2 = .148$, $P = .0069$, negative slope) environmental disturbance indexes (see table 10.1; Brown 1997a). The combination of the latter two indexes gave a scatter of points conforming to the left and right sections of a parabolic curve peaking near the upper limits of natural disturbances (fig. 10.7E, "Options for use" and "Species" curves; Brown and Brown 1992; Brown 1997a), such as major river course changes and extensive bamboo forest die-offs, or major fires, windthrows, and other spatially extensive and energetically intensive catastrophes. Natural systems in the Neotropics can thus become more diversified and thrive in energy and richness under moderate natural disturbance regimes that open up new niches, multiply positive edge effects, liberate resources, and redirect energy flows, especially on fertile soils (Brown 1979, 1982a, 1982b, 1987b). Even major disturbances can be accommodated in the local community by a proper mix of genetic variation and metapopulation organization, with boom-and-bust cycles interspersed with migration, invasion, and insertion of species in new microsites. Strong anthropogenic disturbance, however, leads to a reduction in diversity (fig. 10.7D, E).

This picture is primarily based on small herbivores with short life cycles (rapid responses), specialized plant resources, and appreciable natural diversification. Birds and frogs are rather similar, though with longer response times; both are very sensitive to disturbance (Bierregaard and Stouffer 1997; Cohn-Haft, Whittaker, and Stouffer 1997; Tocher, Gascon, and Zimmermann 1997; Pearman 1997). The picture can be quite different for long-lived trees and sedentary uniparous or oligoparous mammals, including primates, which tend to buffer the intensity of the effects of disturbance on the system without changing their basic pattern (and thus are not very useful as indicator organisms). Richness studies or environmental monitoring based only on such trees or large animals may give unstable results. Studies of seed banks in tropical forests reveal the tremendously diversified communities of small plants (some destined to

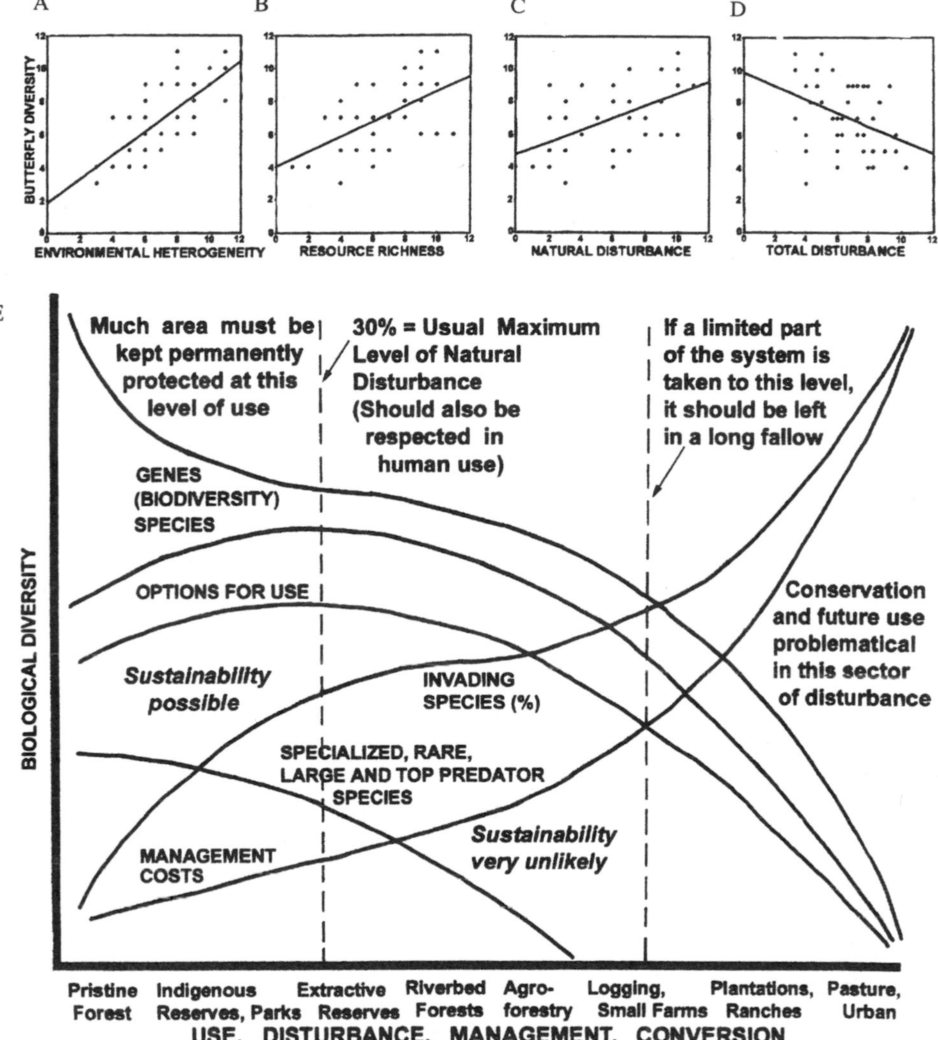

Figure 10.7 Environment and disturbance/diversity relationships in Neotropical forests (see Brown 1997a and data in table 10.1). (A–D) Linear regressions of the composite butterfly diversity index (DivInd; the original composite index in Brown 1997a, Bdiv, and even the total species list give essentially identical results; see table 10.1), against (A) environmental heterogeneity (slope near 1), (B) resource richness, (C) natural disturbance levels, and (D) total (mostly anthropogenic) disturbance (with negative slope −0.386). The summary graph (E) shows the relation between various types of diversity, options for use, management, and the intensity and type of disturbance in Neotropical forests (from Brown 1997a, combining figures 2 and 4 in that paper and simplifying the sum).

become large, most not) ready to sprout in treefall gaps or other natural clearings. Likewise, legions of usually rare small herbivores are always poised to occupy local resources relinquished by their predator-diminished competitors. Other important though small "engineers" in the system include the soil macro-, meso-, and microfaunas, insect defoliators and pollinators, flower and seed predators, and seed-dispersing ants, whose abundance may determine the population biology of many large trees. This dynamic picture of *disturbance-driven diversity* may be a major factor leading to the patterns shown in figures 10.6 and 10.7.

THE FUTURE: HOW CAN WE CONSERVE AND MANAGE NONEQUILIBRIUM LANDSCAPES COMPOSED OF MILLIONS OF SPECIES AND THEIR INTERACTIONS?

The above principles suggest some practical attitudes and actions in relation to the management of conservation areas in tropical forests. For example, while it is important to control and manage the sources and effects of human actions, it is not practical to try to discipline natural variations, fluctuations, or responses, or to attempt to force any equilibrium on the system. Disturbance should be confined to levels near or below natural levels to avoid the vicious cycle of progressively costly management (fig. 10.7E). Natural treefalls are to be studied, not "cleaned up" or, worse yet, prevented. A low optimum level of management will help to avoid the law of diminishing returns (reduced effects and options as more energy is invested; see fig. 10.7E and Brown 1997a, figures 2 and 4).

Indicators, keystones, facilitators, mutualists, and other unique kinds of species or groups need to be monitored and the processes that tie them into the system followed with zeal and continuity. Special areas (such as paleoenvironments, ravines, ridges and hilltops, river terraces and lakes, watersheds, and patches of rich soils) should be identified and maintained in a primitive state, even if they are not already "protected." Local peoples' knowledge should be used as much as possible in identifying such sites. A focus on conserving and maintaining natural processes (especially nutrient recycling in the soil), without neglecting genetic and landscape visions of diversity (such as species multiplications at persistent edges), can make an area much more effective in conservation. Great care should be taken to avoid the effective isolation of natural communities by concentrating on the maintenance of adequate humid, complex green corridors and connectivity in the landscape.

Flexibility needs to be built into protection and management instruments and policies so that one can get around unexpected reactions or strong disturbance events not included in the original planning. To aid in this strategy, a data bank for management and monitoring based on the empirical information accumulated by long-term residents and users of the system should be compiled. Most of these people will know by heart, by culture, and by genes more about the local systems that have sustained them, and about how best to manage them, than exogenous biologists (like us) can ever hope to understand. Many of them are anxious to serve as environmental monitors, usually already know how to do this work, and often are already doing it effectively, though they and we may not understand how or why.

Options to compensate for unexpected crashes in smaller or more fragmented communities must be kept open by maintenance of nearby subunits of metapopulations and metacommunities as well as corridors (such as gallery forests, valley bottoms and terraces, and ridgetops) and by avoidance of systemic poisons of any sort in the landscape. Most important is agility in following short-cycle indicators at key interfaces, knowing how to interpret their variations, and recognizing those that surpass natural responses to normal levels of disturbance, disequilibrium, destruction, and renewal. Local residents can often remember what happened after the last occurrence of such exceptional phenomena.

In his chapter in the book *Tropical Forest Remnants,* Francis Crome (1997) offered a number of additional suggestions for studying, using, and saving tropical forests under varying human occupation and use regimes. Especially important in light of the above steps are his recommendations to (1) live within the landscape you intend to study, (2) be suspicious of all but the most obvious generalities, and completely distrust these, (3) enjoy theory but don't let it substitute for good observation and common sense, (4) accept the fundamental importance of high-quality descriptive and deep-thinking natural history studies, (5) try diversified and holistic approaches to data gathering and analysis, (6) consider local people as a powerful functioning part of the system you study, and (7) use and compare diverse statistical packages to analyze your abundant data. His final recommendations are especially useful for managers: if a solution is easy, go ahead with it and do research on its details and veracity later, but first figure out the cost to people and the system if you are wrong.

To these I can add the following three lighter suggestions, based on experience:

1. Distrust your own best ideas, insights, and results, especially those that are convenient to your dearest hypotheses and well supported by your

data and statistics. Discuss them frequently with colleagues, co-workers, detractors, visionaries, and especially students.

2. Recognize the three stages of almost all data collection programs:

    Stage 1: Essentially all data collected conform magnificently with your hypotheses and the expected results. This stage can last for many sessions or seasons, and is the stage at which most work stops and gets put into a thesis, or published in coherent and popular papers or reports.

    Stage 2: Most new data collected contrast or conflict with data from stage 1, producing grave doubts about their validity, logic, or utility, as well as regrets for having published them already. This stage can last a few years or a lifetime, depending on your imagination and persistence in discovering new ways to combine, analyze, and interpret the data.

    Stage 3: New data collected are equally likely to support or confuse your interpretations or hypotheses—to add to the signal or the noise. At this point, if the sum of concordant data is an order of magnitude greater than that of discordant data, publish the former and rationalize the latter. If the two types are more equal in abundance, you are still in stage 2. Keep looking for novel directions, interpretations, combinations, and experimental ways to get more data; try tangential hypotheses to integrate a greater proportion of the data into different versions, models, or interpretations. Don't throw data away, but refine their collection as you go along.

3. Don't forget the Darwin-Murphy law, which states: "If Nature can find a way to tell you an outright lie, she will." Various corollaries change the second word to "a fossil," "a newly recognized species," "ecosystem analysis," "a GIS data bank," "a statistical approach," "a new host plant record," "an allele," "a GC-MS trace," "a natural molecule," "a local naturalist," "an evolutionary biologist," or "a landscape ecologist," with a concordant change of the penultimate pronoun. All this serious frivolity is an inevitable result of three natural facts: unimaginable natural variation, our gullibility and desire for harmony, and pressure to come up with simple predictions and answers, which lies especially heavily on conservers, protectors, and managers of complex natural systems. Disregard this law at your own risk—and happy data hunting in tropical forests.

ACKNOWLEDGMENTS

This chapter is dedicated to John Terborgh, who worked far longer and deeper into tropical rainforest reality than most anybody else, and published in a single place (1992) data on almost all aspects of their geology, history, ecology, and evolution, and enough interpretations and applications to chew on for many years hence. André Victor L. Freitas helped greatly in fieldwork and data analysis, and with figures; Márcio Uehara-Prado helped with the PCA and regression analyses. Many correlations were suggested by the late David R. Gifford (soils) and Ary Oliveira-Filho (climate, vegetation, and statistics). José Roberto Trigo and Silvana Henriques helped in chemical analyses. Butterfly identifications were graciously provided by Lee D. Miller (Satyrinae), Robert K. Robbins (Theclinae), Curtis J. Callaghan (Riodininae), Olaf H. H. Mielke (Hesperiidae), and Ronaldo B. Francini (Acraeini), all of whom ceded extensive unpublished information. The late Gordon Small, George Austin, Carlos Guilherme Mielke, and Gustavo M. Accacio provided unpublished lists for certain sites (see table 10.1). Other important contributions came from the Biological Dynamics of Forest Fragments Project in Manaus, often assisted by Roger W. Hutchings and encouraged by Richard O. Bierregaard. Financial support was received from the CNPq, the WWF-USA (including the USAID-supported Biodiversity Support Program), the MacArthur Foundation, CIFOR, CNPT-IBAMA, and FAPESP (including in the BIOTA-FAPESP Thematic Project "Lepidoptera of the State of São Paulo").

11

Dynamic Landscape Models for Tropical Rainforests

BRENDAN MACKEY AND WENGUI SU

ABSTRACT

This chapter proposes that tropical rainforest research will benefit from the development of dynamic landscape models based on conceptualizing tropical rainforests as complex adaptive systems. We first discuss methods used to examine the spatial and environmental dimensions of tropical forested landscapes. We consider the development of spatial analyses in terms of conventional vegetation mapping, the quantitative analysis of environmental relations, the simulation of forest succession, and the biotic regulation of the environment. We then propose a dynamic landscape modeling framework based on consideration of six principles: identifying a hierarchy of pattern and process, recognizing the role of bottom-up as well as top-down processes, identifying the critical behavior of individual agents, allowing for key biotic regulation effects, employing landscape-wide spatially distributed environmental modeling, and recognizing the ecosystem as an adaptive system. An example of a static landscape model is given from the rainforests of the Wet Tropics of Queensland, Australia, and an example of a dynamic landscape model is presented from cool temperate rainforest/wet sclerophyll forests in Tasmania, Australia. The chapter concludes with an assessment of research priorities for advancing the application of dynamic landscape models to tropical rainforests.

INTRODUCTION

It is axiomatic that tropical forests are landscape-scale phenomena and have a geographic distribution of many hundreds to many thousands of hectares. In the case of the Wet Tropics of Queensland, Australia, the tropical forests comprise a largely contiguous cover of about 11,000 square kilometers (Keto and Scott 1986). By contrast, most ecological studies conventionally record measurements at scales ranging from a few meters to a hectare. At the most, such observations might be taken at a few hundred such points scattered over the region. Generally, the more often measurements are repeated at a location, the fewer the ground survey points. Most ecological studies therefore are either nonspatial or have only a weak spatial component.

There are a number of reasons to include the spatial dimension in the study of tropical forest ecology. First, a long-standing question in ecology concerns the role of biological versus physical and environmental processes in structuring forest ecosystems. Second, the larger the geographic area, the more heterogeneous the environment in terms of conditions that affect plant ecophysiology and community organization. The composition, structure, and productivity of the vegetation at a site are influenced by processes that operate at a range of scales, many of which are unobservable in the field. Third, the biota does not merely passively respond to external physical environmental conditions; rather, it actively interacts with physical conditions to modify the environment. Fourth, disturbances operating at a range of space/time scales play an important role in structuring tropical forests.

CURRENT METHODS OF EXAMINING SPATIAL AND ENVIRONMENTAL DIMENSIONS OF TROPICAL RAINFORESTS

Mapping Vegetation Patterns

The spatial dimension of tropical rainforest ecology is conventionally seen as a mapping exercise based on patterns discerned by aerial photo interpretation (see Gunn et al. 1988) or by satellite-borne digital sensors such as Landsat Thematic Mapper (TM) (Harrison and Jupp 1990). Such mapping can take two approaches. First, vegetation units can be classified based on analysis of field survey plot data and mapped patterns then assigned to these predetermined vegetation classes. The second approach involves an initial landscape classification based on interpretation of the remotely sensed image and then vegetation labeling based on field surveys. In practice, some combination of the two approaches usually prevails. This conventional approach to vegetation mapping is exemplified by the work of Tracey and Webb (1975) in the Wet Tropics of Queensland (fig. 11.1).

As a way of dealing with the spatial dimension of tropical forests, this general approach has limitations. First, it assumes that there is a single classification of the vegetation that both exists and can be mapped using remotely sensed images; however, neither is necessarily true. Particular attributes of vegetation composition, structure, and productivity do not necessarily covary spatially, forming discrete spatial units. Key attributes may simply not be recognized in remotely sensed images that are dominated by canopy features. Hence, below-canopy attributes of interest may simply not register and may escape pattern recognition.

Second, conventional mapping exercises provide only static and descriptive

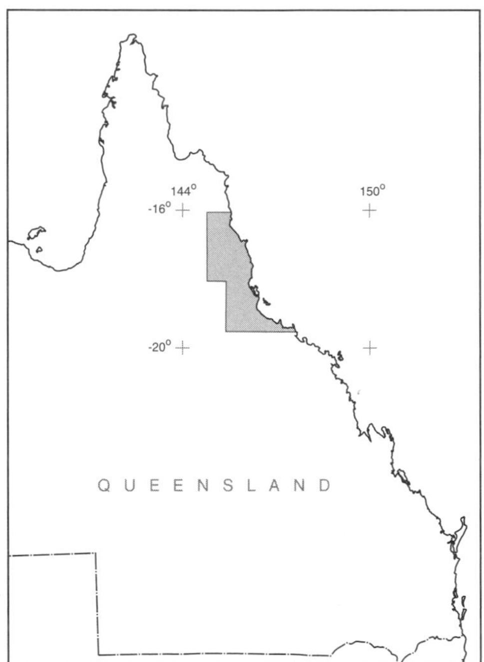

Figure 11.1 Location of the Wet Tropics of Queensland Study Region.

information about vegetation patterns, whereas tropical rainforests are dynamic ecosystems. At best, conventional mapping provides only a snapshot in time. But how temporally stable are these captured landscape patterns, and what is their ecological significance? To answer such questions requires the capacity to examine potential causal processes and to develop a predictive as well as a descriptive capability.

In addition to the use of remote sensing to map land cover classes, a diversity of satellite and airborne sensors are now routinely applied to sample and monitor specific forest attributes on a landscape-wide basis. Key sensors include MODIS (Moderate Resolution Imaging Spectroradiometer), a key instrument aboard the Terra (EOS AM) and Aqua (EOS PM) satellites, and JERS-1 SAR, the Japanese Earth Resources Satellite synthetic aperture radar. Such devices generate (albeit with varying degrees of accuracy) important forest attributes, including greenness indexes, leaf area index, and net primary productivity (NASA 2003) and woody biomass (Austin, Mackey, and Van Neil Kimberly 2003; Kasischke, Melack, and Dobson 1997).

Analysis of Environmental Relations

A second approach to examining the spatial dimension of tropical forests involves analysis of environmental relations. This approach was pioneered in Australia by Len Webb and colleagues (Webb 1968b; Webb, Tracey, and Williams 1976). Their analyses were based on field survey data that sampled the distribution of different rainforest types classified according to plant physiognomy and vegetation structure. Various analytical procedures were then applied to these data through a series of papers, including numerical taxonomic classification that identified clusters of spatially separated sites that shared similar vegetation and environmental conditions as defined by elevation, topographic position, and the relative potential nutrient status of the substrate. Nix (1991b) extended this analysis by using computer-based climate models to estimate "ex situ" long-term mean monthly climatic values at each of Webb and Tracey's field plots. Numerical classification procedures were then applied to examine the extent to which sites with similar vegetation attributes shared similar climatic conditions.

These data, along with new field survey data and improved estimates of climatic, substrate, and topographic variables, were reanalyzed by Mackey (1993, 1994) using a statistical modeling procedure called Algorithms for Mononotic Functions (AMF) (Bayes and Mackey 1991). The resulting correlations were coupled to raster-based environmental models developed by Mackey et al. (1988, 1989). Predictions of the potential distribution of mature rainforest structural types as a function of these environmental correlates were generated for the Wet Tropics of Queensland. In addition, Mackey (1991) generated predictive models of potential distribution for individual structural and physiognomic attributes such as dominant canopy leaf size, complexity, and canopy height. These potential distributions were masked by land cover data derived from Landsat TM imagery so that predictions were restricted to the current extent of rainforest in the region. Figure 11.2 shows an example of this analysis: a prediction of the potential distribution of rainforest canopies dominated by mesophyll-sized leaves, based on an AMF analysis of vegetation structure observed at 256 field plots as a function of climate and substrate nutrient status, masked by land cover data showing extant tropical rainforest.

These potential vegetation models are of interest in that they provide a quantification of plant-environment relations and enable a spatial prediction of those relations defined in environmental data space to be projected into geographic space. However, they represent only the environmental relations of mature rainforest structural types. In effect, they assume steady state conditions and are un-

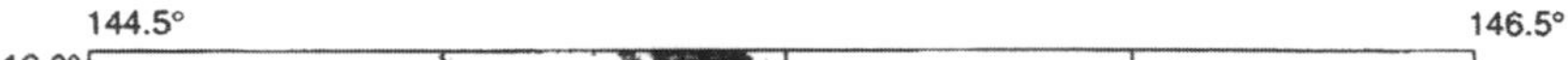

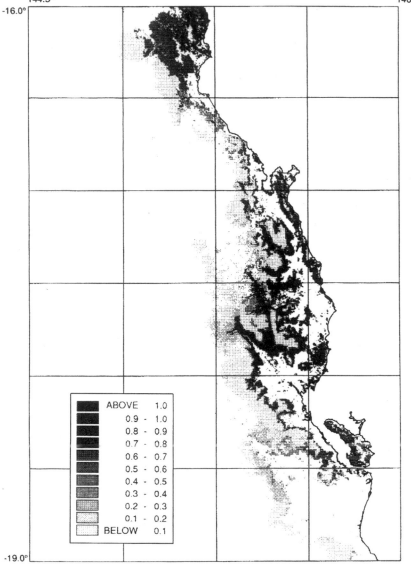

Figure 11.2 Prediction of the potential distribution of rainforest canopies dominated by mesophyll-sized leaves within extant forest in the Wet Tropics of Queensland, Australia. These predictions were based on environmental correlations derived from a statistical analysis of 256 survey plots. Values are maximum likelihood probabilities. The explanatory variables were minimum temperature of the coldest consecutive 3 months, precipitation of the driest consecutive 3 months, and a potential nutrient supply index. Rainforest structure and soil parent material were observed in situ, estimates of long-term mean monthly climate were generated ex situ using computer models, and extant rainforest cover was derived from analysis of Landsat remotely sensed data. The spatial resolution of the analysis was 400 m.

able to represent phase transitions following recovery from disturbance or other significant perturbations such as global climate change.

This approach to modeling also assumes that external physical environmental factors are the main determinant of biotic response. However, internal biotic factors also exert a major influence on vegetation distribution and pattern. This is apparent from the complex set of processes that determine the boundaries between rainforest and *Eucalyptus* forest in the Wet Tropics of Queensland. The spatial interplay between pyrophobic and pyrophytic vegetation is influenced by climate, substrate, and topography, together with negative and positive feedbacks from the vegetation (Hopkins et al. 1993; Ash 1988; also see discussion in Mackey et al. 2000, 2002).

Static spatial models based on correlation between extant vegetation and prevailing environmental conditions, while useful, have limited utility for predictive purposes. The danger lies in assuming that a spatial correlation indicates causality. Nonetheless, the methods used to model environmental variables related to the distribution and availability of heat, light, water, and mineral nutrients in a spatially explicit way are of interest here. Mathematical surfaces (derived from interpolation of data from a network of weather stations, using the method of Hutchinson [1987]) enabled the reliable estimation of various long-term mean monthly parameters. Using Geographic Information Systems, mapped geologic data were digitized and integrated with these spatial estimates of climate, together with land cover data from remotely sensed imagery. In addition, various environmental attributes were derived from terrain analysis using a digital elevation model. Terrain-based indexes used include radiation indexes that incorporate the effects of slope and aspect as well as indexes that relate to topographic controls on water flow. These indexes can be calculated using the TAPES suite of models (Moore, Grayson, and Ladson 1991; Wilson and Gallant 2000).

There is now the capacity to model key physical environmental resources on a landscape-wide basis using relatively widely available data, including climatic records from meteorological stations, topographic maps, and land cover data from satellite-based sensors. These tools provide the means to deal explicitly at a landscape scale with environmental heterogeneity that affects plant physiology and physiognomy, vegetation structure, and community dynamics.

Simulating Forest Succession

The vegetation modeling described above has the advantage of being spatially explicit, but the disadvantage of being temporally static. It can be contrasted with stand-level forest succession or gap-phase models (Botkin, James, and James 1972; Botkin 1993; Shugart 1984; 1991; Shugart and Noble 1981). These models emphasize both biological processes and environmental drivers. The biological processes are concerned with the birth, death, and growth of trees. The environmental drivers are based on functional relationships between tree growth and the effects of major environment constraints, but mainly on the competition for light between tree species in a (typically) 10 m^2 plot. Tree growth is modeled as a potential optimal DBH (diameter at breast height) increment modified to an actual DBH growth through indexes of the available environmental resources.

In the gap-phase models, the main process driving the growth of the tree is the available light above the tree canopy. Other factors, such as temperature, soil moisture conditions, and nutrient status, are introduced as a modifier of tree growth, but in a spatially implicit way. The light regime is attenuated as a function of leaf area index. The DBH increment is modeled as a function of available light, assimilation rate, and the species-specific response. The relative shade tolerance, life span, maximum height and diameter, and growth factor of a tree species are the key life history attributes needed to calibrate these models. Two versions of gap-phase models that have been developed for tropical forests are FORMIND (Koehler and Huth 1998; Kammesheidt, Koehler, and Huth 2001) and KIAMBRAM (Shugart et al. 1980).

In these models, the "gap" is the basic spatial building block, although the spatial distribution of the trees inside the gap is not explicitly modeled. Rather, the trees are simulated as an idealized single very large tree with a big leaf. Efforts have been made to try to take spatial effects into account in gap-phase models (Urban et al. 1991), but the basic assumptions remain. Generally, these models were not designed to capture, in a spatially explicit way, multi-scale landscape-wide processes.

Biotic Regulation of Environment

As noted above, the development of dynamic landscape models is complicated by the fact that the biota does not simply respond to external physical environmental conditions (Margulis, Mathews, and Haselton 2000; Gorshkov 1995). Rather, the biota has a capacity to modify the effective environment it experiences. This capacity for biotic environmental regulation is evident in all the primary environmental regimes and at all scales. For example, the biotic controls on the nutrient regime in the tropical forests of Central America were studied by Golley (1983), who demonstrated that the nutrient balance of target catchments is essentially in equilibrium for key chemicals such as phosphorous, with biological nutrient conservation mechanisms being the decisive factor. The work of Walker et al. (1981) in the Cooloola Sands of Queensland, Australia, also illustrated the role of vegetation at a landscape level in building up nutrients over time on inherently nutrient-poor substrates. The effective environment experienced by a plant is therefore a complex function of both external physical environmental conditions and internally generated biological processes.

The distribution and availability of the primary environmental resources (heat, light, water, mineral nutrients) are controlled by biophysical processes that operate over a hierarchy of space/time scales. Following the schema of Linacre (1992) and Mackey and Lindenmayer (2002), these processes can be considered in terms of at least five levels: global > meso > topo > canopy > micro. Global-scale processes refer to the variations in the solar flux as a function of latitude and time of year; mesoscale processes include the long-term climatic conditions experienced at a location as a function of the interaction between the prevailing weather conditions and elevation as well as major differences in geologic substrate. Topo-scale processes include the effect the local topography has in modifying surface radiation and in redistributing water. The dynamic noted above between rainforest and non-rainforest boundaries also plays out at the topo-scale (see Ash 1988; Mullen 1995). Canopy-scale processes include gap dynamics (Pickett 1983), and microscale processes include the biological nutrient recycling mechanisms mentioned above. Biotic regulation of the effective environment can take effect at any of these scales, though the larger the scale, the more the biotic feedbacks are a function of the aggregate effect of greater numbers of individual organisms operating over longer time scales. While such biotic effects have been well studied, their implications for predictive spatial modeling have not been so thoroughly considered.

In summary, new approaches to dynamic landscape modeling are needed that provide for the integration of environmental heterogeneity on a landscape-wide and temporally dynamic basis, the behaviors of individual species, and critical positive and negative feedbacks on the effective environment that stem from the aggregate behavior of large numbers of living organisms.

AN IMPROVED FRAMEWORK FOR DYNAMIC LANDSCAPE MODELING

The solution lies in conceptualizing tropical rainforests as complex adaptive systems. By "complex," we mean that they are composed of a very large number of components and interactions—too large for every component to be described by a single equation, but not large enough to be dealt with by the law of large numbers (*sensu* statistical thermodynamics: O'Neil et al. 1986; Gorshkov 1995). Given this assumption, the following suggestions constitute an improved framework for developing dynamic landscape models for tropical rainforests.

IDENTIFY A HIERARCHY OF PATTERN AND PROCESS

"Scale" refers to both the geographic extent of a phenomenon and the frequency or rate of change of its behavior. All environmental, biological, and ecological phenomena occur at a specifiable space/time scale. Certain phenomena are scale-specific in that they are observable only at certain scales. One tree does not a forest make—rather, the concept of a forest assumes a certain density of trees within a given area. It is possible to identify different hierarchically scaled levels in a forest ecosystem. We must therefore choose what levels in the system are to be examined (Allen and Hoekstra 1992).

In the context of forest landscapes, higher levels in the hierarchy can influence lower levels in two ways. First, larger-scale processes may contain smaller-scale processes; for example, a certain species may be found only in those locations that meet its niche specifications. Second, larger-scale processes may constrain smaller-scale processes; for example, the rate of primary production will be reduced as mesoscale temperatures decrease.

RECOGNIZE THAT BOTTOM-UP AS WELL AS TOP-DOWN PROCESSES ARE IMPORTANT IN DETERMINING SPATIAL PATTERNING

A traditional top-down analytical approach uses aggregate parameters to describe the large-scale factors controlling ecosystem dynamics and spatial patterns. Models developed using this approach break the system down into major components, develop partial differential equations or correlation functions to describe each component, and then combine these to gain an understanding of the system. A major disadvantage of this top-down modeling approach is that the influence of individual objects within the system can be suppressed. It is critical to recognize the importance of bottom-up processes based on spatially explicit local interactions between individual entities.

IDENTIFY THE CRITICAL BEHAVIOR OF INDIVIDUAL AGENTS

An important assumption is that the actions of individual entities, governed by a relatively small number of rules, are a key source of higher-level system behavior (i.e., spatially explicit local interactions produce larger-scale phenomena). Terms such as "agents" and "objects" are used to describe the smallest-scaled individual entities in a system that are involved in competitive interactions. In a tropical rainforest, agents can be defined in terms of plant and animal species or functional guilds. Identifying the behavioral responses of each (tree) agent (however defined) in terms of its potential environmental domain (i.e., the geographic distribution of its environmental niche), its seed production and dispersal, its post-disturbance response (e.g., methods of regeneration following gap creation), and other key life history attributes related to longevity and growth rates then becomes a critical task.

The environmental domain occupied by a taxon can be calculated empirically by analyzing the environmental correlation of survey records that sample its natural distribution. By matching this environmental envelope to a spatial database of equivalent environmental attributes, a spatial prediction of the taxon's potential domain can be generated (Austin, Cunningham, and Fleming 1984; Lindenmayer, Mackey, and Nix 1996; Mackey and Lindenmayer 2002). These kinds of output can in turn be used to model higher-level spatial constrains on tree-agent behavior (e.g., by specifying the geographic limits of a taxon's distribution).

ALLOW FOR KEY BIOTIC REGULATION EFFECTS

Having defined global, higher-level constraining processes and key agent behavior, it remains to identify feedbacks between the biotic and abiotic elements of the system. We can hypothesize that these feedbacks are a major source of spatial diversity and complexity in tropical rainforest landscapes. Feedbacks from lower to higher levels can take a number of forms, including spatial aggregation (e.g., catchment-level evapotranspiration, carbon retention, and nutrient recycling, as well as patterning of species assemblages), the kind and degree of spatial connectivity in the landscape (e.g., as promoted by seed dispersal, or as the result of land use activity) recovery abilities (e.g., the rate at which canopy closure occurs following disturbance), and the relationships between climate, topography, vegetation growth and succession, fuel loads, and the fire regime.

EMPLOY LANDSCAPE-WIDE SPATIALLY DISTRIBUTED ENVIRONMENTAL MODELING

Advances in climate interpolation, digital terrain analysis, and remote sensing provide the means to develop landscape-wide, spatially distributed models. Using these techniques, we can generate larger-scale, externally generated environmental constraints on lower-level (smaller-scale) phenomena.

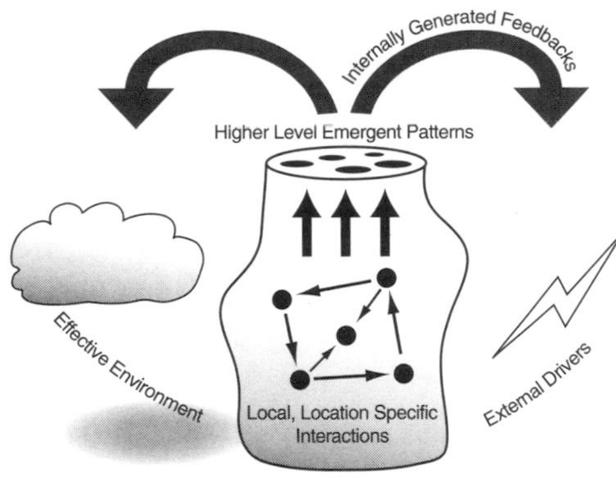

Figure 11.3 A conceptual model of complex adaptive systems. For tropical rainforests, the local, location-specific interactions refer to the distribution and interactions of individual trees. The higher-level emergent patterns are the spatial patterns of different forest types. An example of internally generated feedback is the influence of vegetation types on fuel loads and hence the fire regime experienced at a site. External drivers include mesoscale weather and climatic conditions. The effective environment is the environmental conditions as experienced by individual agents (trees).

RECOGNIZE THAT THE SYSTEM IS AN ADAPTIVE SYSTEM

Individual agents are not simply passive reactants to environmental perturbation, like floats bobbing in the sea. Rather, they are capable of receiving, storing, processing, and transmitting information, and in so doing change their behavior. Populations of living organisms also evolve as a result of genetic mutations and natural selection. To the extent that local behavior defines system conditions, when modeling tropical rainforest landscapes, we are dealing with adaptive systems.

In summary, the solution lies in conceptualizing tropical rainforests as complex adaptive systems that are to varying degrees self-regulating and self-organizing, operate under global (external) constraints, and within which can be recognized a hierarchy of patterns and processes. This conceptual framework is illustrated in figure 11.3. In adopting this conceptual framework, it follows that spatial patterns (such as the spatial patterning of species assemblages and stand structure in tropical forested landscapes) should be considered an emergent property of the system that arises at least partly as a result of the location-specific, competitive interactions of individual plants.

IMPLEMENTATION

The question now becomes what modeling and simulation techniques, programming tools, and data are required to make this framework operational. We suggest that the most appropriate computer environment is Object-Oriented Technology (OOT), which comprises Object-Oriented Modeling (OOM) and Object-Oriented Programming (OOP). OOM (also called Object-Oriented Analysis and Design in Software Development) is the phase of making assumptions and abstractions of the real-world problem, whereas OOP is the phase of implementation of the assumed abstractions with a specific programming language. OOT is not so much a formula for problem solving as a way of thinking. It is not new per se, but only relatively recently have the software and hardware been developed to the point that they can be readily applied to ecological problems. OOT is based on the idea that programs should represent the interaction between (virtual) representations of real objects, rather than the linear sequence of calculations associated with what is technically called *Procedural Programming* (see discussion in Silvert 1993).

The appeal of OOT is that its structure mimics our conceptualization of ecological systems as complex adaptive systems. As noted by Silvert, OOT promotes the idea that programs should not consist of lengthy procedures for manipulating the internal variables of objects; rather, objects should be sent messages that tell them how to use their internal "methods" to operate on these variables. The interactions between objects are driven by the flow of information. The implication is that the programmer is not responsible for instructing the virtual tree how to behave; rather, once the behavior has been encoded, it then becomes the responsibility of the tree to grow, compete, reproduce, and so forth.

In OOT an object contains a description of both its structure and, in a very integrated way, its behavior. Objects in OOT are hierarchically structured in that they can share inherited characteristics. OOT objects are therefore much more sophisticated than traditional type declarations such as "integer" and "real." The insight of OOT is to combine into a single entity data about the object and operations on those data. Hence, an OOP object contains both structural information and functional information. An object is both a group of related functions and a data structure that serves those functions. The functions are also known as the object's *methods*, and the fields of its data structure are its *instance variables*. The methods wrap around the instance variables and "hide" them from the rest of the program. With state and behavior combined in a single unit, an object becomes more than either alone; a synergistic relation is generated in which the whole is greater than the sum of the parts (Booch 1994; Rumbaugh 1991).

It is not surprising that OOT mimics ecological systems theory, as ecology was an early inspiration for structured programming theory. Any phenomenon defined as an agent can be similarly conceptualized as an OOT object (though an OOT object can be any class of phenomenon, such as a physical environ-

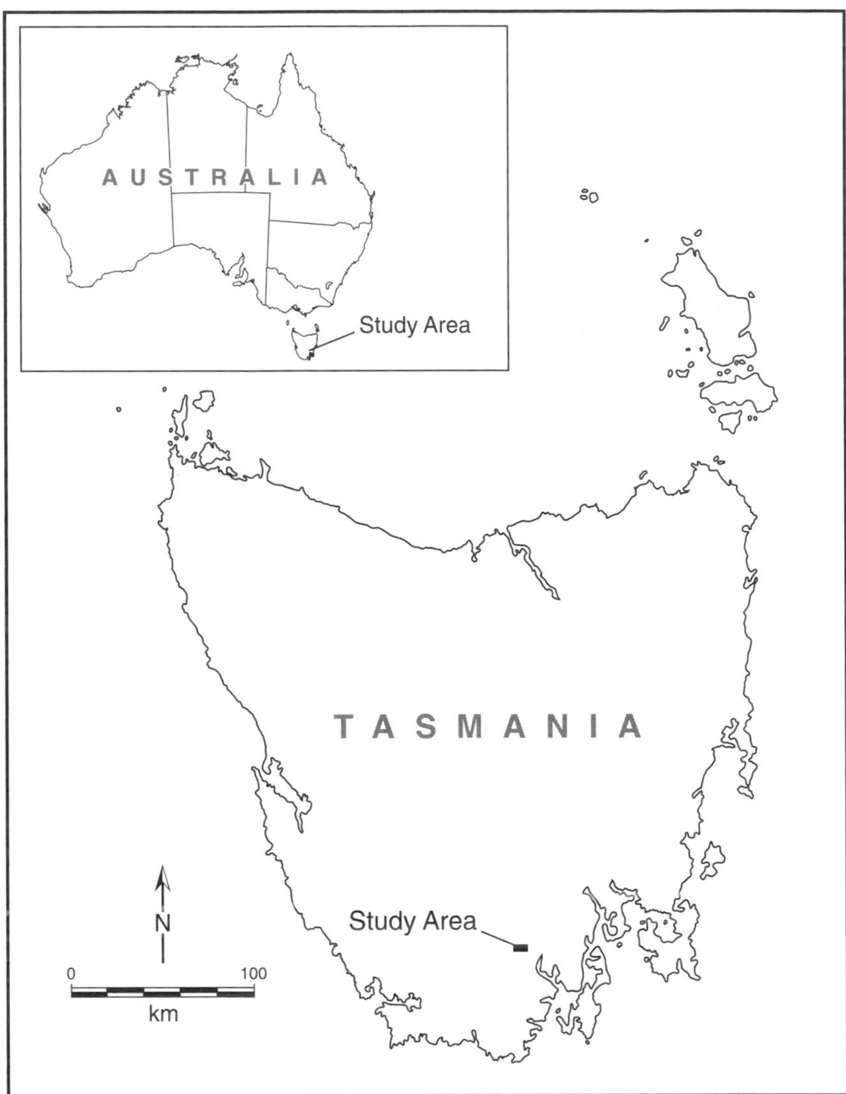

Figure 11.4 Location of the Warra Long Term Ecological Research Site, Tasmania, Australia.

mental space, in addition to an agent, such as a class of tree). So it is easy to imagine an individual organism as an object with its own properties (e.g., age, height) and a set of behaviors related to its establishment, growth, and death in response to its environment. In other words, these virtual agents have their own copies of behavioral code or genomes that let them individually perceive the local environment, evaluate the input, and choose how to act. These virtual objects can be let loose, so to speak, in a virtual landscape and allowed to exchange information with other objects. These interactions influence their effective environment and generate higher-level patterns. In this way, we can use such a landscape-wide simulation to explore how spatial and temporal patterns arise in complex, heterogeneous landscapes.

CASE STUDY: THE WARRA LTER SITE, TASMANIA, AUSTRALIAN

A dynamic landscape model based on the aforementioned framework and tools has been developed for a cool temperate rainforest/wet sclerophyll forest ecosystem at the Warra Long Term Ecological Research (LTER) site in Tasmania, Australia (fig. 11.4) (for further details on the computer model, see Su, Brown, and Mackey 2001; Su, Mackey, and Brown 2001; Su and Mackey 1997; Su 2003). The simulation model was written in the Java programming language, but utilized concepts originating in the SWARM simulation tool kit (Hiebeler 1994; Nelson et al. 1996; SWARM Development Group; NeXt Inc.). The case study area is 9 by 7 km, with an elevation range of 37–1,340 m, and is located in a humid cool climate zone. Annual rainfall is 1,200–1,500 mm, and mean monthly maximum and minimum temperatures range from 8.0°C to 16.0°C and from −0.5°C to 9.5°C, respectively. The topography is characterized by sharp relief and deep drainage lines, combined with a gradual transition of hills with various slope gradients. Fires are a major natural perturbation and driver of forest successional pathways.

A set of representative tree, shrub, and ground cover plant species was chosen as the individual agents for this simulation. The full suite of species modeled in this case study is detailed in table 11.1. Species were selected to represent the major functional guilds found in the landscape in terms of key life history attributes related to longevity and regeneration. The landscape is dominated by a mix of cool

Table 11.1 Species selected as representative of functional guilds for simulation modeling

Species name	Growth form	Longevity (years)
Eucalyptus oblique	Sclerophyll forest tree	350–400
Eucalyptus delegatensis	Sclerophyll forest tree	350–400
Nothofagus cunninghamii	Rainforest tree	400–600
Phyllocladus aspleniifolius	Rainforest tree	> 800
Pomaderris apetala	Broad-leaved understory shrub	60–80
Acacia melanoxylon	Forest tree	80–120
Gahnia grandis	Ground cover grass	15–25

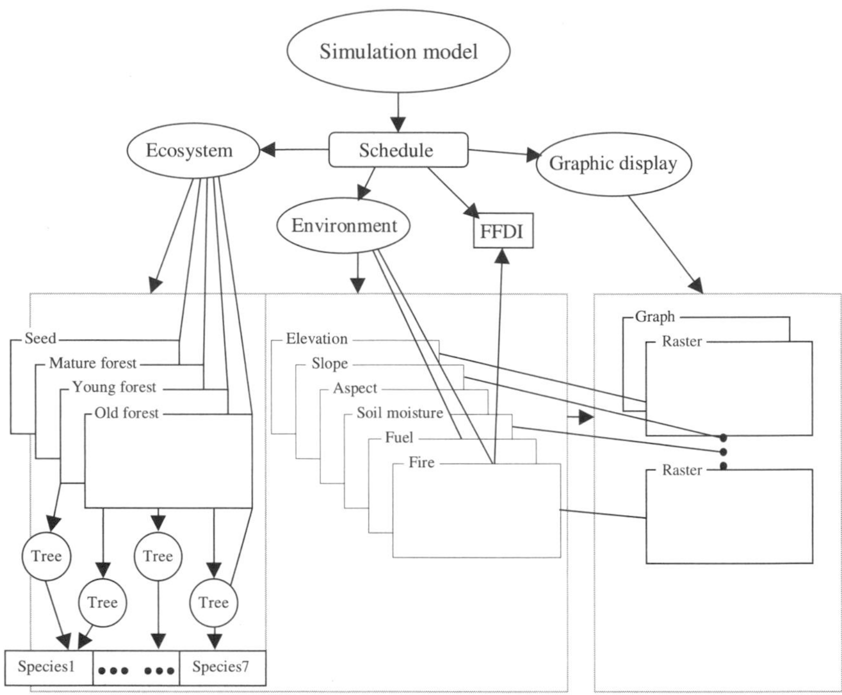

Figure 11.5 Overview of the structure of the computer model developed for the Warra case study.

temperate rainforest trees and *Eucalyptus* species. The rainforest trees are more shade-tolerant and can regenerate at low light levels, whereas the *Eucalyptus* species are less shade-tolerant and require high light levels for regeneration. In addition, the *Eucalyptus* species are adapted to fire regimes that are characterized by more intense and frequent fires. One of the dominant tree species in the landscape is *Eucalyptus obliqua,* which lives for 350–400 years. Regeneration occurs only after fire, when the canopy-stored seed is shed and germinates on the bare mineral soil. The dominant rainforest species in the landscape, *Nothofagus cunninghamii,* lives for 400–600 years. It can perpetuate itself without disturbance and is more likely to be killed than *Eucalyptus* species under the same fire intensity.

The physical environmental variables used in the simulation were generated from a 10 m resolution Digital Elevation Model (DEM). The DEM was used to calculate slope, aspect, an index of soil wetness based on terrain attributes, and topographically modified surface radiation. These environmental variables were used to model the environmental niche of each species and the topographic controls on litter, fuel loads, and fire behavior. Daily weather data from nearby weather stations were used to generate a characteristic temporal sequence of the Forest Fire Danger Index (MacArthur 1967). The FFDI was used to simulate the probability of fire, and its calculation involved a stochastic process to capture fire weather variability in each time step.

The spatial resolution of the virtual forest simulation was 10 m, as per the DEM. Forest growth was modeled as a function of age class on an annual time step. Separate objects were recognized for young, mature, and old forest, as these have different fire responses. Separate objects were also programmed for *seed space* (to keep track of seed availability for each species) and a *regeneration object* that controls each species' regeneration processes. The occurrence of fire (controlled by the *fire regime object*) depended on seasonal climatic and weather conditions, topographic effects, and vegetation. In addition to prevailing weather, fire events at a location depended on fuel loads, time since last fire, and the occurrence of lighting strike ignition (which was controlled by a randomizer variable). The overall structure of the computer model is shown in figure 11.5.

The simulation was commenced with a random distribution of tree agents (plate 2/fig. 11.6). After 500 years, the emergent landscape patterns in forest types

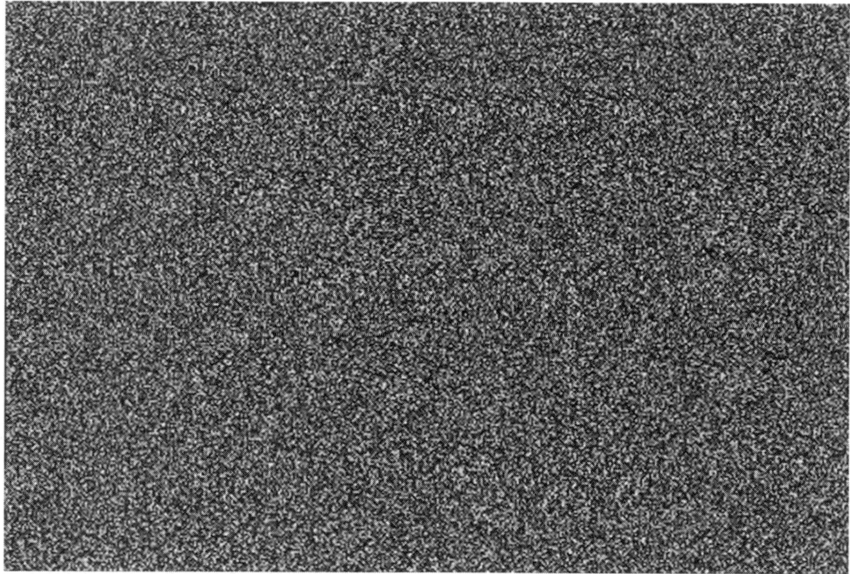

Figure 11.6 The simulation for the Warra Long Term Ecological Research Site was commenced with a set of randomly distributed tree agents. The different pixel colors represent the seven representative species listed in table 11.1 and graphed in figures 11.8 and 11.9: red, *Eucalyptus obliqua* ("obliqua" in figures 11.8 and 11.9); white, *E. delegatensis* ("delegatensis"); yellow, *Gahnia grandis* ("gahnia"); navy blue, *Nothofagus cunninghamii* ("myrtle"); sky blue, *Phyllocladus aspleniifolius* ("celerytop pine"); pink, *Acacia melanoxylon* ("blackwood"); and gray blue, *Pomaderris apetala* ("dogwood"). See plate 2.

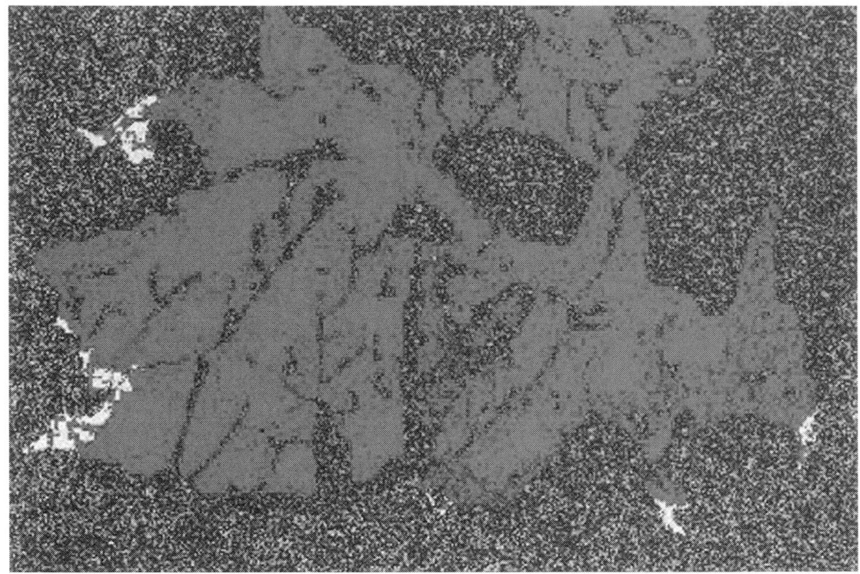

Figure 11.7 The emergent landscape patterns in forest types shown after 500 years of simulation. These patterns reflect the combined effects of individual tree behaviors, environmental constraints, and the history of fire regimes in the landscape. See plate 3; for description of pixel colors, see plate 2.

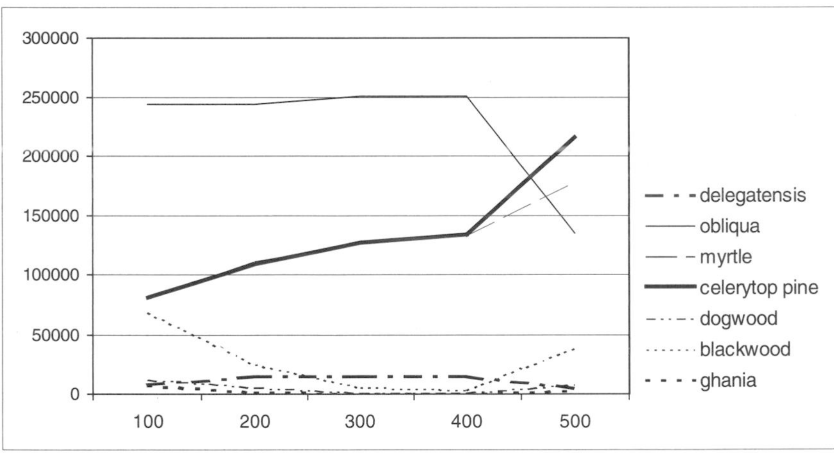

Figure 11.8 The change over time (no. of years) in the average number of individuals of each species in the virtual landscape (based on a number of simulation runs) when the simulation used the Forest Fire Danger Index calculated from actual weather data to drive the fire regime.

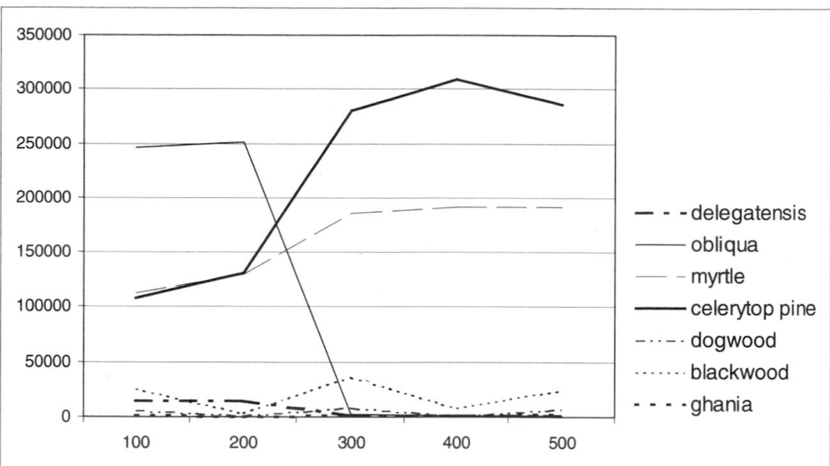

Figure 11.9 The change over time (no. of years) in the average number of individuals of each species in the virtual landscape (based on a number of simulation runs) when the simulation used the Forest Fire Danger Index calculated using a wetter climatic scenario to drive the fire regime.

shown in plate 3/figure 11.7 reflected the combined effects of individual species responses, environmental constraints, and the history of fire regimes in the landscape.

This model can be used to examine the potential effect of climate change scenarios on landscape-level forest patterns. Figure 11.8 shows the change over time in the average number of individuals of each species in the virtual landscape (based on a number of simulation runs) when the simulation uses FFDI calculated from actual weather data. This result can be contrasted with figure 11.9, which shows the results obtained using a wetter climatic scenario. Rainforest species can be seen to dominate in the landscape at the expense of *Eucalyptus* species due to climatically driven changes in the fire regime leading to an increase in mean fire interval and fire intensity.

RESEARCH PRIORITIES

Considerable development is needed before dynamic landscape modeling such as that described here can be routinely applied to tropical rainforest ecosystems. Indeed, its implementation will require a concerted research focus. Five research priorities can be identified.

Functional Guilds

An agent-based approach to dynamic landscape modeling presents difficulties when applied to tropical rainforests, with their high levels of local species diversity. Knowledge of niche responses and key life history attributes is often poor, except for a few commercially or culturally important species. One solution lies in clustering species into functional guilds and then identifying representative species for which some information is known. A functional classification could be based on common environmental requirements, growth rates, light tolerances, methods of regeneration, disturbance responses, or plant functional attributes (Gillison and Carpenter 1997). For example, Swaine and Whitmore (1988) proposed a functional classification for tropical rainforest tree species based on recognition of two groups: pioneer species, whose seeds can germinate only in gaps in the forest canopy open to the sky and in which full sunlight impinges at ground level for at least part of the day; and non-pioneer (climax) species, whose seeds can germinate under forest shade and whose seedlings can become established in forest shade and survive there. They also noted that pioneer species share a characteristic set of life history attributes, and that the two groups could be further subdivided based on height at maturity and life span.

Biotic Regulation and Feedbacks

Simulating forest ecosystems as complex adaptive systems assumes that higher constraints will emerge from the aggregate behavior of individual agents. A critical research issue relates to the limits of agent-driven environmental regulation and the extent to which spatial patterning is controlled by the externally driven distribution of the primary environmental regimes versus internally generated, agent-driven environmental regulation. Part of the answer lies in the extent to which the collective behavior of local agents can absorb, dampen, or modulate the larger-scale frequencies of higher-level, external drivers. This issue may be particularly important when considering the local water cycle in tropical rainforests, where deforestation can change the local precipitation regime (Henderson-Sellers, Zhang, and Howe 1996).

Defining the Hierarchy

While the concept of a hierarchically structured system is intuitively appealing to ecologists, in practice it can be difficult to identify objects and levels in an objective manner. Landscape ecosystems may be sufficiently well studied to enable the reliable identification of hierarchies and objects relevant to tropical rainforests. One key research question is the extent to which a generic set of hierarchies and objects for rainforests can be identified.

Disturbance Regimes

In the Warra case study, fire events were the main disturbance and driver of forest succession. Connell (1978) suggested that disturbances of various kinds tend to maintain tropical rainforests in a nonequilibrium state. Others have pointed to the key role of disturbances, including storms, lighting strikes, fires, treefalls, insect plagues, and landslides (Webb 1958; Hopkins 1990; Page et al. 2002), in tropical rainforest dynamics. The gaps created by these disturbances are a major catalyst of community dynamics in tropical rainforests (Pickett 1983), reflecting the differentiated response of tree species to the resultant environmental conditions. Spatially explicit analyses inclusive of fire regimes are difficult even in well-studied landscapes (Mackey et al. 2002). Tropical rainforests present a special challenge, given the influence of complex disturbance regimes comprising a suite of disturbance agents operating over a range of space/time scales.

Integrating Gap Models

In the Warra case study, tree age was an adequate surrogate for stand-level processes for model development and testing. However, in order to apply this approach to tropical rainforests characterized by high levels of species diversity and more complex age structures, it will be necessary to expand the simulation model to include an appropriate stand-level growth simulator, such as those based on the gap-phase model approach. This development is conceptually straightforward, but technically difficult, as it requires an order of magnitude increase in the number of computations.

CONCLUSIONS

Just as there now exists a global network of standard 1 ha permanent forest sample plots, we can envisage a global network of tropical rainforest virtual dynamic landscape models (VDLM) being established. Collaboration between researchers would be facilitated by the capacity of OOT to enable the decomposition of complex models into discrete modules for each agent or object. When a module is recognized as being sufficiently developed, it could then be considered a standard object or agent that any researcher can use to run on their virtual landscape. A similar proposal was made by Silvert (1993), who drew the analogy of an experimental biologist obtaining a standard mouse from a recognized supplier. The portability of OOT objects and modularization would therefore facilitate the ongoing development and sharing of objects by teams of research partners.

A VDLM network could serve as a repository for the current state of knowledge about tropical rainforests. As functions are derived from analysis of field data and experimentation, they could be programmed into the virtual landscape and their implications explored via simulation. They would provide a tool to investigate hypotheses about forest dynamics such as those discussed by Connell (1978). Furthermore, such an integrated modeling approach would help identify knowledge gaps and in turn set research agendas. A VDLM network could function as a focus and integrating platform for the multidisciplinary research needed to understand tropical forests in all their diversity and complexity.

We are not proposing that the aim of a virtual dynamic landscape exercise is to predict the location of all agents (however defined) in the landscape. Given the role of multi-scaled disturbance regimes and bottom-up processes, there is probably too much stochasticity in the system to achieve this goal. However, we should be able to accomplish a set of interrelated objectives, such as predicting the spatial domains within which certain phenomena are more or less likely to occur, replicating the characteristic spatial patterning found in a landscape, explaining current distributional patterns, and generating scenarios of future system response to external drivers.

Finally, we can also note the potential role of a VDLM network in providing a decision support tool for natural resource managers by allowing them to explore the implications of different management and global change scenarios. Such applications would extend the uses for which gap-phase models have been employed (e.g., Shugart et al. 1980; Kammesheidt, Koehler, and Huth 2001) and build on the kinds of databases and Geographic Information Systems currently being developed for many tropical landscapes (e.g., USGS 2002). Indeed, our proposal can be implemented only through the use of these kinds of spatial modeling tools, as they provide the geographic and environmental infrastructure on which the development of dynamic landscape models is based.

ACKNOWLEDGMENTS

The authors are grateful for the support and generous help received from Forestry Tasmania and, in particular, Dr. Mick Brown in facilitating access to the Warra LTER site, sharing his ecological expertise, and providing valuable comments on earlier drafts of this chapter.

12

Understanding and Conserving Tropical Diversity: Perspectives from Barro Colorado Island

EGBERT GILES LEIGH JR. AND IRA RUBINOFF

ABSTRACT

To understand and maintain tropical forest diversity, we must distinguish different species and learn what factors regulate different populations, how different species coexist, and how different species depend on one another. We must also learn how new species evolve and how different scales of environmental change influence speciation rate, as well as the diversity and species composition of ecological communities. These goals demand diverse approaches and a thorough understanding of natural history. For example, exclusion experiments in intertidal ecology suggest how the consequences of forest fragmentation can reveal the trophic organization of intact rainforest; field experiments with reef fish illustrate trade-offs inferred from the behavior of ant-following birds. Diversity reflects opportunities for coexistence; speciation with secondary overlap depends on the availability of a "niche opportunity." How much diversity a community maintains depends, in turn, on its trophic organization. Thus, high tree diversity may occur only where predators reduce the effect of generalist insect herbivores. The dynamism, trophic organization, and resistance to invaders of a forest ecosystem on a long-isolated landmass depend on that landmass's area. Ecological communities are organized for high productivity and species diversity, as economies are for high productivity and diversity of occupations. In both, high diversity depends on long freedom from major disruption.

INTRODUCTION

To understand why there are so many species in tropical forests, we must answer three questions:

1. How do tropical species originate?
2. What controls speciation rate and diversity buildup in tropical forest habitats?
3. How can so many species coexist in tropical forests?

It may seem premature to tackle these questions when we know so little about the patterns of tropical diversity we wish to explain. We know even less about species turnover—that is, how species composition changes as we pass from one area to another (Condit et al. 2001; Pitman et al. 2001). So many species remain undescribed (Stork 1988) that we know little about the numbers of species in regions of different sizes, even in "well-studied" groups of plants and animals. Moreover, our inability to tell species apart can obstruct research on how diversity is maintained. Understanding, for example, how different species of monkeys coexist presupposes the ability to distinguish not only the species of monkeys involved, but also the species of plants whose fruit and leaves they eat. Before Robin Foster learned the plants of Barro Colorado Island (BCI), in central Panama, well enough to teach others how to recognize them, or Croat (1978) had published his flora of that island, identifying the plants different animals used on BCI was a lengthy and uncertain business, which slowed all ecological work there and made some research impractical. Yet, even in our present state of ignorance, it is worth probing the origin and maintenance of tropical diversity.

The origin and the maintenance of diversity are related issues. Species diversity represents a balance between the origin and extinction of species. We understand mechanisms of coexistence better than mechanisms of diversification, so we discuss the former first.

HOW IS BIOLOGICAL DIVERSITY MAINTAINED?

The most obvious step we can take to preserve tropical diversity is to avoid disrupting those mechanisms that allow tropical species to exist, or to coexist. Therefore, we focus first, and at greatest length, on how tropical diversity is maintained. The first step toward this understanding is to learn what different species need in order to live and what factors regulate or limit their populations. In short, a good understanding of natural history is the beginning of wisdom.

Population Regulation

Knowing what factors limit populations provides crucial clues to understanding how those populations coexist. BCI's populations of giant damselflies, for example, are limited by the supply of mosquito wrigglers in the water-filled tree holes where their larvae grow (Fincke 1994). Food limitation of larvae governs the reproductive behavior of the largest giant damselfly, *Megaloprepus coerulatus,* and the means by which smaller species of giant damselflies coexist with it (Fincke 1992a, 1992b). Adult male *M. coerulatus* defend large tree holes, allowing only females they have mated with to lay eggs there (Fincke 1992a). Smaller species lay eggs earlier in the rainy season. In smaller tree holes, their larvae mature before *M. coerulatus* larvae grow big enough to eat them. On the other hand, BCI's most common canopy tree, *Trichilia tuberculata,* appears to be limited by a specialized pathogen that suppresses the survival of young *T. tuberculata* near their adults (Hubbell, Condit, and Foster 1990). Indeed, there may be so many kinds of tropical trees because each species is kept rare by a different pest (Janzen 1970).

Many means have been used to discover how populations are regulated. On BCI, behavioral ecologists have used the following criteria to infer that populations of vertebrate herbivores are limited by seasonal shortage of suitable food:

1. Mortality increases, especially among young animals, during the season of shortage, as in agoutis, pacas, howler monkeys, and sloths (Smythe 1978; Milton 1990).
2. Births are timed to coincide with the season when suitable food is most abundant, as among coatis (Russell 1982), fruit-eating bats (Bonaccorso 1979; Handley, Wilson, and Gardner 1991), and iguanas (Burghardt, Greene, and Rand 1977).
3. The growth of young animals slows or ceases entirely during the season of shortage, as in agoutis and pacas (Smythe 1978).
4. During the season of shortage, animals eat less preferred food items and range more widely and take more risks to find food, as do agoutis, pacas (Smythe 1978), howler monkeys (Milton 1982) and coatis (Russell 1982), and dispute more intensely for available food, as do howler monkeys (Milton 1982) and coatis.

Terborgh (1983) used similar criteria to infer limitation of monkeys by seasonal shortage of suitable food in Parque Nacional Manu, in Amazonian Peru. Predators or parasites may administer the coup de grace to ill-nourished animals (Smythe 1978; Milton 1982; Sinclair and Arcese 1995), but the fundamental limiting factor is seasonal shortage of food.

Stronger evidence of population limitation by seasonal shortage of suitable food comes from documenting a season when there is too little food of the appropriate type to feed the animals that depend on it. For example, African ruminants cannot survive on dry grass; they need green grass containing over 4% crude protein. Sinclair (1975) showed that grazers in the Serengeti are limited by seasonal shortage of green grass. In one to three dry-season months each year, the Serengeti has too little green grass to feed its ruminants. When green grass is in short supply, their fat reserves decline, and those with the most depleted fat reserves die (Sinclair 1975). Moreover, the greater the calculated dry-season deficit, the higher the dry-season mortality rate (Sinclair 1979, table 4.3). Sinclair's inferences have been abundantly confirmed by later work (Mduma, Sinclair, and Hilborn 1999).

Sinclair's (1975) paper sparked similar work on BCI. By measuring the amount of fruit falling to the ground each month, measuring the numbers and weights of each species of terrestrial frugivore, and using physiological regressions to estimate an animal's feeding rate from its body weight, Smythe, Glanz, and Leigh (1982) showed that in the season of shortage, too little fruit fell to feed the terrestrial frugivores. By measuring the numbers and weights of manakins—small fruit-eating birds—on a 19 ha island near BCI and the island's rate of production of fruit that manakins would eat, Worthington (1982) showed that the population was limited by seasonal shortage of suitable fruit.

Experiments can provide even clearer evidence of how populations are limited. The most familiar such experiment, though not the first, was Paine's (1966, 1974) removal of starfish (*Pisaster ochraceus*) from sections of rocky shore in the northeastern Pacific. Where starfish were removed, mussels (*Mytilus californianus*), the food most preferred by these starfish, spread much farther down the intertidal zone than elsewhere. Presumably, *Pisaster* had previously excluded these mussels from the lower intertidal zone. Such experiments have also been used in tropical forests. An exclusion experiment on BCI showed that birds limit the abundance of insects in aerial accumulations of litter in vine tangles (Gradwohl and Greenberg 1982). By supplementing the food supply of populations of fruit-eating spiny rats (*Proechimys semispinosus*) on selected 2 ha islands near BCI, Adler (1998) showed that these populations are food-limited even in the season of abundance.

The fragmentation of forest into island remnants by new reservoirs (Leigh et al. 1993, 2002; Terborgh et al. 1997, 2001; Cosson et al. 1999) is providing a multitude of "natural exclusion experiments" as various species of predators quickly disappear from the smaller islands and fragmentation disrupts other relationships. These exclusions are less adequately controlled than the human variety, but they occur on a more informative scale. A recent expansion of Venezuela's Guri reservoir has provided insights into how populations of howler monkeys are regulated. Some of Guri's newly created 1 ha islets support several howler monkeys apiece, a density many times higher than that on the mainland (Terborgh et al. 1997). Even on the mainland, howler monkeys must be relatively safe from predators. Mainland howler populations, however, are regulated socially, by the (enforced?) dispersal of subadults. Their social organization must ensure that, even in the season of shortage, the monkeys can eat enough to compete effectively with members of other troops. Terborgh et al. (1997) noticed that in the Guri reservoir, howler monkeys are never found on small islands visible from other land close enough to swim to. These monkeys attain unnatural densities, destructive of their food supply (Terborgh et al. 1997), only where landscape fragmentation disrupts the dispersal essential for normal population regulation.

Detecting regulation in populations of small animals often requires appropriate reckoning with spatial heterogeneity and study at appropriate spatial scales (Ray and Hastings 1996). Studies of mobile animals are much more likely to detect density dependence if the study plot is small enough that more than 10% of its population crosses its boundary each generation. Similarly, density dependence in the mortality of immobile eggs and pupae is usually detected in plots less than 0.1 ha in area, but seldom on larger plots. In both cases, larger plots tend to average out the density-dependent "signal" (Ray and Hastings 1996).

Coexistence

IS COEXISTENCE CAUSED?

Does coexistence require an explanation, or does species diversity simply represent a balance between speciation and random extinction, as Hubbell (1979, 1997b, 2001, and chap. 4 in this volume) suggests? Long-term monitoring is a useful tool for answering this question. During a 9-year mark-recapture study of BCI's bats, the relative numbers of different species caught, and the actual numbers caught of each species, varied relatively little from year to year (Kalko, Handley, and Handley 1996). As generation time is about two years for most species caught, much less than the duration of the study (Connell and Sousa 1983), it appears that the relative abundances of these populations are indeed regulated (Kalko, Handley, and Handley 1996), presumably by differences in the supplies of their respective foods (Bonaccorso 1979).

COEXISTENCE AND POPULATION REGULATION

Thus, to understand biological diversity, we must learn how so many species can coexist. Different species can coexist if each is limited by the availability of different habitats or resources or controlled by the activity of different predators or pathogens. Showing that two species differ in some aspect of their habitat or diet indicates that these differences allow the species in question to coexist only if the differences involve factors that are demonstrably limiting and if they render each species more sensitive to an increase in its own numbers than in those of competitors. Thus, understanding how species coexist hinges on knowing how their populations are regulated.

Seasonal changes in the amounts and types of food available sometimes reveal the role of niche differentiation in promoting the coexistence of different food-limited species (Zaret and Rand 1971; Rosenzweig and Abramsky 1986). On BCI, each of the many species of terrestrial frugivores that live on fruit when it is abundant falls back on a different specialty during the season of fruit shortage: coatis forage for invertebrates in the leaf litter, agoutis subsist on seeds buried during the season of abundance, pacas browse seedlings, and so on (Smythe 1978).

THE IMPORTANCE OF TRADE-OFFS

More generally, the world has many species because no one species does all things well: as MacArthur (1961) remarked, the jack-of-all-trades is master of none. Seedlings, or trees, that grow fast at high light levels survive poorly in shade (Kitajima 1994; Hubbell 1998). Bats adapted to hawking insects in the open air above the forest canopy cannot cope effectively with the cluttered environments inside the forest (Kalko 1995). Those robber flies (Asilidae) that are best suited to foraging in light gaps because their ability to warm quickly in sunlight allows a speedy takeoff and quicker, more maneuverable flight are the ones that are most torpid and ineffective when in the shade (Shelly 1984). Those fruit flies (*Drosophila* spp.) whose adults live longest, and thus have the most time to find suitable fallen fruit in which to lay eggs when fruit is scarce, have the slowest-growing larvae. Slow-growing larvae are less likely to have time to develop before faster-growing competitors eat all of their fruit (Sevenster and van Alphen 1993). Consequently, the *Drosophila* species best able to survive where fruit and fruit flies are scarce are the poorest competitors where fruit is abundant. In many guilds of competing species, there is a trade-off between dominance—the ability to drive competitors from rich resource patches—and the ability to survive where resources are scarce (Willis 1967, 1972, 1973).

One way to understand how biological diversity is maintained is to document the trade-offs enabling different species to coexist. The trade-off between the ability to defend rich resources and the capacity to survive where resources are scarce was first inferred from observations of animal behavior. Willis (1967, 1972, 1973) found an example of this type of trade-off among ant-following antbirds, which eat insects flushed by advancing swarms of army ants. The large ocellated antbird (*Phaenostictus mcleannani*) is dominant, and takes the best places at ant swarms, but it cannot forage away from swarms. Dominant competitors restrict the small spotted antbird (*Hylophylax naevioides*) to the poorest sites at ant swarms, but the spotted antbird can feed at least half as fast away from swarms as at them. The middle-sized bicolored antbird (*Gymnopithys leucaspis*) is intermediate in both respects. Experimental verification of this type of trade-off came from a field experiment with coral reef fish. Removing fish of a subordinate species from a coral reef had no effect on the numbers of the dominant competitor, but removing the dominant competitor caused marked increases in populations of subordinate species (Robertson and Gaines 1986; Robertson 1996).

On BCI, the trade-off between fast growth at high light levels and survival in shade was first inferred from Brokaw's (1987) discovery that the pioneer species whose saplings grew fastest in large gaps needed the largest gaps in order to survive at all, while the pioneer species that survived best in small gaps grew most slowly in large ones. This trade-off was later confirmed by experiments with seedlings of different species in a screened growing-house (Kitajima 1994), measurements of how light level influences the relation between total leaf area, leaf lifetime, and height and biomass growth of wild saplings of selected species (King 1994), and comparisons of mortality and maximum growth rates among the commoner species of BCI's 50 ha Forest Dynamics Plot (Hubbell 1998).

PEST PRESSURE AND THE DIVERSITY OF TROPICAL TREES

No one pest can penetrate the defenses of all plants, and no one plant can defend itself against all pests. Accordingly, trade-offs among the capacities of herbivores and pathogens to penetrate different plant defenses contribute to the diversity of tropical plants. Janzen (1970) and Connell (1971) proposed that there were many more kinds of trees in the tropics than in the temperate zone because:

1. Thanks to the absence of the winters that blight temperate-zone pests, pest pressure is much more intense in the tropics.
2. Thanks to the trade-offs pests face in penetrating different plant defenses, the bulk of the tropical plant matter consumed by pests is eaten by specialists on one or a few species.
3. Pests prevent any one tree species from become too common, making room for other species.

So far, most of the evidence for the role of pest pressure in maintaining the diversity of tropical trees is comparative. To begin with, pest pressure is indeed more intense in the tropics. Mature dicot leaves are more poisonous in the tropics than in the temperate zone (Coley and Aide 1991). In the tropics, but not in the temperate zone, young dicot leaves are more poisonous than their mature counterparts (Coley 1983). Despite being much more poisonous, young dicot leaves are eaten over three times more rapidly in the tropics than in the temperate zone (Coley and Barone 1996; Coley and Kursar 1996; Leigh 1999). Moreover, most of the damage to tropical plants is inflicted by pests specialized at least to particular genera of plants (Barone 1998; Novotny et al. 2002).

Warm temperatures have been associated with higher pest pressure and plant diversity in the past as well. In southern Wyoming, the mean annual temperature rose from 14°C in the late Paleocene to 21°C in the earliest Eocene. Humid swampy floodplain vegetation of the early Eocene was more diverse, and suffered a higher frequency of attack by more kinds of pests, than comparable Paleocene vegetation at a nearby site (Wilf and Labandeira 1999).

How do comparisons within the tropics bear on the relationship between pest pressure and tree diversity? Tree diversity is highest in everwet forest (Clinebell et al. 1995), where, thanks to the absence of a dry season, herbivorous insects are most uniformly present through the year (Wolda 1983, 96; Basset 2000, 121). Deciduous dry forest is less diverse, but more heavily eaten, than wetter forests (Leigh 1999): unlike everwet forest leaves, mature dry-forest leaves are too short-lived to pay for sufficient toughness to deter herbivores. Pest pressure, however, is better measured by the rate of herbivory on young, still expanding, leaves, which are roughly equally tender in all forests. Thus measured, pest pressure appears to be higher in wetter forest (Coley and Barone 1996). To test the pest pressure hypothesis more decisively, however, we must reckon with spatial heterogeneity.

SPATIAL HETEROGENEITY AND COEXISTENCE

Nothing could appear more random than the community of fruit flies that breed in fallen fruit on the forest floor. On BCI, however, distributions of individuals of each species of fruit fly over patches of fallen fruit are clumped in such a way that, for any pair of species *i* and *j*, the average individual of species *i* suffers less than one of species *j* from an increase in species *j*'s abundance (Sevenster and van Alphen 1996). The clumping of individuals of different species over resources is what allows these species to coexist—something that could be learned only by reckoning appropriately with the spatial heterogeneity of the system.

Testing the effect of pest pressure on tree diversity also requires reckoning with spatial heterogeneity. How can we tell whether each tree species is kept rare enough by its specialized pests to make room for other species limited by different pests? Pest pressure markedly influences the distribution and dynamics of saplings. In the absence of specialized pests, saplings should become established near their parents, but species with such "attracted" distributions, in which saplings cluster around conspecific adults, form a very small minority of the trees and shrubs on BCI (Condit, Hubbell, and Foster 1992). The same is true in a more diverse 50 ha plot at Pasoh Reserve, Malaysia (Okuda et al. 1997).

If one partitions BCI's 50 ha plot into 20 × 20 m subplots, then, for most species common enough to measure, the number of saplings greater than 1 cm in diameter appearing between successive censuses on a subplot, per reproductive adult of their species, is lower the higher the basal area (total cross-sectional area of trunks) of conspecifics on that subplot (Wills et al. 1997). This effect is local; it is equally apparent for 10 × 10 m subplots, both on BCI and in the 50 ha plot at Pasoh Reserve (Wills and Condit 1999). It is not detectable on 50 × 50 m subplots at BCI, as if these plots were large enough to "smooth out" the density-dependent signal (Wills et al. 1997). This effect is species-specific: for most species, recruitment rate per adult does not decline with total basal area of all species on the subplot.

Peters (2003) observed that quadrat analyses lost power because, for a tree close to a quadrat border, close neighbors across the border were ignored while more distant neighbors inside the quadrat were included. He thought it better to ask how a sapling's survival depended on the abundance of nearby conspecifics. Quadrat analyses had detected no effect on a tree's survival of the density of conspecifics on its quadrat. Ahumada et al. (2004), however, found that on BCI, a sapling alive in 1983 was more likely to have died the more conspecifics there were among its twenty nearest neighbors over 1 cm diameter at breast height (DBH). Moreover, the more the survival prospects of saplings of a particular species were injured by an additional conspecific among its nearest neighbors, the rarer that species was likely to be. Thus, at least on BCI, the intensity of pest pressure on a tree species was a significant influence on its abundance. Hubbell et al. (2001) found that the survival prospects of a sapling alive on BCI in 1983 were lower the higher the density of conspecifics nearby (the more conspecifics there were within 10 m). Peters (2003) found that at Pasoh Reserve, in most species common enough to study, saplings likewise died faster the higher the density of conspecifics nearby. Reckoning with spatial heterogeneity has revealed the most impressive evidence yet for the effect of pest pressure on tropical tree diversity.

Mutualisms and Tropical Diversity

Tropical forests illustrate competition at its most intense, yet they also represent the ultimate in mutualism. Mutualism plays an integral role in maintaining tropical diversity.

Many tropical plants need animals to pollinate their flowers or disperse their seeds (Corner 1964; Howe and Smallwood 1982), as well as root fungi (mycorrhizae) to extract nutrients from the soil (Janos 1980, 1983). These interdependences, in turn, create other interdependences (Leigh 1999). Most pollinators and seed dispersers depend on more than one species of plant to keep them fed during the year, so the pollination and seed dispersal of plants requiring animals for these services can be said to depend on the presence of other, potentially competing, plant species (see Forget 1994). Some of these pollinators and seed dispersers need other forests to keep them fed when food is short in one area. At La Selva, Costa Rica, many understory shrubs have their seeds dispersed by fruit-eating birds that migrate to nearby mountainsides when fruit is short at La Selva (Loiselle and Blake 1991). These interdependences are necessary conditions for maintaining tropical diversity.

We have far more to learn about the many ways in which plants may depend on animals. Smythe (1989) discovered that, on BCI, a fruit of the spiny palm, *Astrocaryum standleyanum,* has a future only if an agouti peels the flesh away and buries the seed. Ironically, this palm's regeneration depends on the activities of its major seed predator. Later, other tree species were discovered whose seeds escaped destruction by insects only if buried and forgotten by agoutis (Forget and Milleron 1991; Forget 1993, 1994). Some of the islets that were isolated around 1914 by the rising waters of Gatun Lake are too small to support resident mammals. On mammal-free islets forested since they were isolated, four tree species have been spreading. All of these species have large seeds, at least some of which escape insect attack even if not buried (Leigh et al. 1993). Did their large-seeded competitors need agoutis to bury their seeds out of reach of insect pests? Are agoutis keystone animals for the maintenance of tree diversity in central Panama?

The answer is not clear. Hunting has lowered mammal populations in many parts of central Panama. Wright et al. (2000) asked how hunting affected palm regeneration. Where hunting was heaviest, agoutis were six times rarer than on BCI; the proportion of seeds dispersed from parent palms was 10%, compared with 90% on BCI; and the proportion of dispersed seeds destroyed by bruchid beetles was 40%, compared with 5% on BCI. Yet the density of palm seedlings, and the number of juvenile palms per adult, was higher for *Astrocaryum* and *Attalea* in heavily hunted areas than on BCI, perhaps because on BCI, agoutis eat a much higher proportion of the dispersed seeds.

MUTUALISMS AS NECESSARY CONDITIONS FOR THE ORIGIN OF TROPICAL DIVERSITY

Using animals to pollinate their flowers was a crucial innovation that allowed weedy Cretaceous angiosperms to diversify in disturbed habitats (Crepet 1984);

using animals to disperse their seeds may have permitted angiosperm trees to diversify and dominate mature Cenozoic rainforests (Tiffney and Mazer 1995). These mutualisms are so essential because employing animals as pollinators and seed dispersers allows plant species to persist even when made rare by their pests (Regal 1977). Plants face a trade-off between fast growth and investment in anti-herbivore defenses (Coley, Bryant, and Chapin 1985). The ability to persist when rare allows a plant species to escape specialist pests (whose effect is lower the rarer their hosts) without sacrificing the capacity for rapid growth. Effective animal-mediated pollination and seed dispersal have accordingly allowed a diverse forest of fast-growing, productive, rare angiosperm species to replace a much less diverse, more heavily defended gymnosperm forest whose long-lasting defensive chemicals poisoned the soil and hindered nutrient recycling (Corner 1964; Regal 1977; Leigh 1994).

THE BENEFITS OF EFFECTIVE POLLINATION: FIG TREES

Fig trees illustrate the importance of effective pollinators. Each species of fig tree has its own species (sometimes more than one) of pollinating wasp (Corner 1940; Molbo et al. 2003). A fig "fruit" is a flower head turned outside in, so that the flowers line the inside of a ball with a hole at one end. One or more fertilized female wasps enter a fruit, pollinate its flowers, and lay eggs in about half of them. Each wasp larva matures within a single fig seed. When a fruit's wasps emerge as adults, they mate among themselves, and the fertilized females fly off, carrying pollen. In most fig species, a tree's fruits ripen all together, so the emerging wasps must find a different tree to pollinate. Some fig trees receive pollinators from 5 to 15 km away (Nason, Herre, and Hamrick 1996, 1998). Despite a density of only one adult per 10–100 ha, species such as *Ficus dugandii, Ficus popenoei,* and *Ficus obtusifolia* maintain extraordinary high genetic diversity (Hamrick and Murawski 1991; Nason, Herre, and Hamrick 1998).

Genetic diversity must benefit these plants. It has long been known that plants can defend themselves with fewer chemicals if they can vary the mix from one individual to the next (Dolinger et al. 1973). In some species of tropical trees, the seedlings that survive near a conspecific adult are those whose leaf chemistry differs most from that of the adult (Sánchez-Hidalgo, Martínez-Ramos, and Espinosa-García 1999). The ability to persist when rare also pays off. Leaves of two fig species have a photosynthetic capacity as high as that of any tree yet studied—indeed, closer to that of crop plants (Zotz et al. 1995; Zotz, Patiño, and Tyree 1997)—as if the capacity to persist when rare allowed them to shift resources from defense to fast growth. Therefore, "by leaf, fruit and easily rotted wood, fig plants supply an abundance of surplus produce" (Corner 1967, 24).

The benefits of domesticating pollinating wasps must be substantial, because fig trees pay handsomely for their pollinators. In each species, individuals must come into fruit at all times of year, regardless of how the time of fruiting affects the seeds' prospects. Large fig fruits must transpire abundantly to keep cool enough for their wasps to survive (Patiño, Herre, and Tyree 1994); therefore, large-fruited fig species must grow where they have ready and reliable access to water.

Biological Diversity and Ecosystem Organization

How an ecosystem's biological diversity is maintained depends on how that ecosystem is organized. Here we consider how mechanisms of coexistence depend on an ecosystem's trophic dynamics—what limits the community's primary production, its herbivory rates, and the like. We next explore how the size of a landmass might influence its ecosystem's characteristics. Finally, we show that ecosystems are organized for high diversity and productivity; unnatural disturbance is therefore likely to disrupt both.

DIVERSITY AND TROPHIC DYNAMICS

To understand how an ecological community maintains its diversity, we must understand its trophic dynamics. This proposition is obvious to marine biologists. They know that eliminating sea otters from a northern Pacific shore permits that shore's sea urchins, which the otters eat, to transform lush kelp beds that support a diversity of plants and animals into a barren pavement of coralline algae (Estes and Palmisano 1974; Estes et al. 1998). The experiments of marine biologists show how overharvesting of blue crabs permits the periwinkles those crabs eat to transform a lush salt marsh into a bare mud flat in 8 months (Silliman and Bertness 2002).

The long lives of trees have veiled the magnitude of the effect of predator removal from forest ecologists. Nonetheless, wolves and big cats formerly protected North American forests from deer and moose (McLaren and Peterson 1994; Terborgh et al. 1999). The elimination of these large predators has led to an exploding deer population and inexorable change in the species composition of North American forests (Alverson, Kuhlmann, and Waller 1994, 30).

The dependence of forests on predators for protection against herbivores is not restricted to the immature ecosystems of the temperate zone. When the Guri reservoir's rising water level created new 1 ha forested islets, leaf-cutter ant populations exploded on those islets. They must have been released from a predator—perhaps army ants—that could not survive on such small islets (Terborgh et al. 2001). The newly hyperabundant leaf-cutter ants sharply reduced the number and diversity of plant recruits (Terborgh et al. 2001). Their activities may lead to slower-growing, less productive vegetation.

Our understanding of the trophic dynamics of BCI illustrates the virtues of concentrating many different studies in one area. Together, these studies show that BCI's forest (like Guri's) depends on small predators for protection against insect herbivores. BCI's vertebrate herbivores, however, are limited by seasonal shortage of fruit and new leaves; they apparently do not need to be controlled by predators.

To learn whether birds help protect BCI's forest from insect herbivores, Leigh and Windsor (1982) estimated how much foliage insects eat by measuring the total area and dry weight of leaves falling into litter traps each week and the total area of holes and gaps in these leaves. About 7 tons dry weight of leaves fell per hectare per year, of which 7% of the surface area was eaten. If vertebrates and leaf-cutter ants eat their leaves whole, then other insects annually eat about 500 kg dry weight of foliage per hectare. Willis (1980) and Robinson (2001) censused BCI's birds in 1970 and 1995, respectively, providing data on their diets and weights. Using Nagy's (1987) regressions of a bird's feeding rate on its body weight, Leigh and Windsor (1982) and Leigh (1999) concluded that BCI's birds annually eat 24 kg dry weight of folivorous insects per hectare. If it takes 10 kg of leaf to make 1 kg of folivorous insect, then roughly half the foliage insects eat feeds insects that birds eat. Birds therefore eat enough insects to play a crucial role in protecting BCI's forest from insect pests. And indeed, many insect pests specialize on particular plants to avoid predators rather than plant defenses (Bernays 1998).

BCI does not need predators, however, to control its vertebrate herbivores. Robin Foster (1982a, 1982b) monitored seasonal variation in flower and fruit fall on BCI for 2 years, beginning in August 1969, as part of his graduate studies. He found fruiting peaks in September 1969 and in April and May, when the rainy season begins, in both 1970 and 1971. There was no fruiting peak in September 1970, and there was famine among the forest's fruit-eating mammals at that time (Foster 1982a). The dry season of 1970 was exceptionally wet. Foster concluded that BCI's populations of fruit-eating mammals are limited by seasonal shortage of fruit. His work inspired many further studies, which showed that BCI's various populations of vertebrate herbivores are indeed limited by seasonal shortage of suitable food, as mentioned above. Moreover, a failure of the fruit crop in September and October causes famine among fruit-eating mammals not only on BCI, but in nearby forests where hunting pressure is heavier (Wright, chap. 15 in this volume).

It appears that other Neotropical forests, like BCI, control vertebrate herbivores without predators. Big cats—jaguars and pumas—have been carefully studied in Peru's Parque Nacional Manu, which preserves one of the world's least disturbed tropical forest ecosystems. The Manu's big cats annually eat 250 g prey/ha (Emmons 1987), about 1/100 the annual consumption of folivorous insects by BCI's birds. Applying Nagy's (1987) regressions of feeding rate on body weight to the weights and abundances of the Manu's nonvolant mammals (Janson and Emmons 1990), Leigh (1999) calculated that herbivorous vertebrates weighing over 1 kg apiece eat 200,000 g dry weight/ha/yr of fruit and leaves in the Manu. This is 2/5 the amount of foliage eaten by insects other than leafcutter ants on BCI. The ratio of the big predators' to the herbivores' consumption is 40 times lower for the Manu's vertebrate herbivores than for BCI's folivorous insects; it seems most unlikely that big cats could limit the Manu's vertebrate herbivore populations.

ISLAND AREA AND ECOSYSTEM CHARACTERISTICS

Darwin (1859) knew that ecological communities on oceanic islands are easily invaded by exotics and are easily disrupted by such invasions. The devastation wrought by introduced brown tree snakes on Guam (Fritts and Rodda 1998) and by pigs, goats, rats, and invasive plants on other oceanic islands such as Hawaii, Réunion, and Mauritius (Carlquist 1980; Lorence and Sussman 1988; Macdonald et al. 1991) is a familiar story.

The smaller a long-isolated landmass, the lower the diversity of trees on a hectare of its rainforest (table 12.1). Opportunities for speciation may be rarer on small islands, and a population's risk of extinction is larger the smaller the island, the lower the ratio of speciation plus immigration to extinction, and the lower the island's equilibrium diversity (MacArthur and Wilson 1967).

The area of a long-isolated landmass also has a major effect on its trophic dynamics. The smaller such a landmass, the smaller its largest herbivore and its largest carnivore (table 12.1). Indeed, Burness, Diamond, and Flannery (2001) showed that the weight, W (kg), of the largest homeothermic herbivore on an isolated landmass of area A (km^2) could be estimated to within a factor of 2 by the equation $W = 0.47A^{0.52}$. The weight, w, of an isolated landmass's largest homeothermic carnivore is equally well predicted by the equation $w = 0.05A^{0.47}$.

The great continents all had herbivores capable of knocking down trees and expanding the limits of grassland, as well as aggressive secondary vegetation capable of restoring this damage. Despite their size, Madagascar's 400 kg elephant birds (*Aepyornis*) could not inflict such damage. Is this why Madagascar lacks a similarly aggressive secondary vegetation (Koechlin, Guillaumet, and Morat 1974)? Even South America did not evolve top predators capable of competing with those that crossed the land bridge from North America (Simpson 1980).

Table 12.1 Area, alpha diversity of trees, and weights of the largest homeothermic herbivore and largest homeothermic carnivore living 50,000 years ago on different isolated landmasses

Landmass	Land area (km^2)	Forest plot size (ha)	Tree diversity (Fisher's α)[a]	Largest herbivore (kg)	Largest carnivore (kg)
Eurasia	55,000,000	1.0	125	5500	380
South America	17,800,000	1.0	139	4200	390
Australia	7,700,000	1.7	32	1150	75
New Guinea	810,000	1.0	115	300	25
Madagascar	587,000	1.0	50	440	17
New Caledonia	16,648	0.25	25	40	—
Puerto Rico	9,104	1.0	9	50	1.0
Mauritius	1,874	1.0	10	19	0.6

Source: Data for landmass area and weights of largest herbivores and carnivores from Burness, Diamond, and Flannery (2001); tree data for Eurasia from Pasoh Reserve, Malaysia (Manokaran et al. 2004); tree data for South America from Yasuni (Pitman et al. 2002); data for Australia from Connell, Tracey, and Webb (1984); data for New Guinea from Wright et al. (1997); data for Madagascar from Rakotomalaza and Messmer (1999); data for New Caledonia from Jaffré and Veillon (1990); data for Puerto Rico from El Verde (Thompson et al. 2004); data for Mauritius from Vaughan and Wiehe (1941).

[a]Fisher's α is defined by the relation $S = \alpha \ln(1 + N/\alpha)$, where N is the number of trees $\geq$ 10 cm DBH on a plot and S is the number of species among them.

What effect do top predators have on the characteristics of a region's herbivores? Does an island's lack of large herbivores and large carnivores induce a lack of dynamism in its vegetation and a lack of energy or responsiveness among its animals that makes island ecosystems particularly easy to invade? Does the dynamism and responsiveness of continental biotas provide new niche opportunities, or the means to exploit them?

In Hawaii, Mauritius, and Réunion, the native vegetation is easily invaded and is seriously endangered by such introduced shrubs as *Psidium cattleianum* (Huenneke and Vitousek 1990; Lorence and Sussman 1988; Macdonald et al. 1991). On Madagascar, an island the size of France that separated from Africa 150 million years ago (Hay et al. 1999), *Psidium cattleianum* can become established and persist in large forest clearings, but cannot invade intact forest. In truly continental settings, plant invaders pose little danger (Rejmanek 1996). On small oceanic islands and even on New Zealand, which lacked native rodents, introduced rats and other human commensals caused widespread extinctions of ground-nesting birds (Strahan 1983; Steadman 1995). In Madagascar, introduced rats have spread through the native forest, threatening at least the more terrestrial of the native rodents (Goodman 1995), but no one has mentioned them as a cause of bird extinctions. In Australia, introduced rats have spread through the native forests, apparently without endangering native rodents (Strahan 1983). In continental settings, rats do not spread beyond manmade clearings (Charles-Dominique 1997, 26; Carleton and Schmidt 1990, 31–32).

ARE ECOSYSTEMS COMMONWEALTHS ORGANIZED FOR HIGH DIVERSITY?

Aristotle (*Physics* 199b1–3, translated in Barnes 1984, 340) argued that organisms are designed to grow and reproduce, since visibly mutant organisms usually do so less well than their normal counterparts. Similarly, Fisher (1930, 38) considered a species adapted to its environment if a slight change in either the organism or its environment usually reduced the organism's fitness. Such criteria can also be used to judge the adaptedness of ecosystems, and, indeed, unplanned or unprecedented human disturbance of an ecosystem can cause a catastrophic decline in diversity. In Indonesia and central Panama, careless farming or clearing ends in the replacement of diverse forest by a sterile monodominant grassland (Jacobs 1988, 252, 261; Dalling and Denslow 1998, 675–676). Even if, under natural conditions, the change would eventually favor increased diversity, as would global warming (Wilf and Labandeira 1999), its initial effect is adverse.

The threat a change poses to diversity depends crucially on whether or not the ecosystem has frequently experienced that change in the past—in other words, on whether or not the ecosystem is "designed" to cope with that change. The artificial reduction into 1 ha fragments of a forest that had previously long been a continuous expanse causes catastrophic declines in biomass (Laurance et al. 1997, 1998b) and tree diversity (Leigh et al. 1993). On the other hand, in the savannas of Belize or Venezuela, where forest has long been patchy, a natural 1 ha forest fragment is just as diverse as a hectare in extensive forest nearby (Kellman, Tackaberry, and Meave 1996). Thus foresters can preserve their forest's diversity by employing a cutting regime that mimics naturally occurring disturbances as closely as possible (Franklin et al. 1997). By cutting trees so as to open gaps of the sizes that favor the regeneration of the most desired tree species, managers of dipterocarp forest can preserve the forest's diversity, its soil, and its capacity to cope with the environmental stresses it would normally encounter (Bruenig 1996).

There are other reasons to believe that ecosystems are organized for high productivity and diversity (Leigh and Vermeij 2002). First, natural ecosystems have properties that humans desire, but must labor to attain. For example, good soil must be soft enough for roots to penetrate and porous enough to exchange gases with the atmosphere, yet cohesive enough to stay put. Good soil holds the rainwater and nutrients it receives tightly enough to keep them from draining or leaching away without preventing plant roots from acquiring them as needed (Bruenig 1996). Careless deforestation changes all these soil properties for the worse (Stallard, García, and Mitre 1999). Farmers labor to restore or maintain these same soil properties. Second, the diversity and productivity of the earth's ecosystems have increased over the course of evolution, and they have increased after every major biotic crisis.

How do ecosystems become adapted? Wilson (1980) and Leigh (1999) explore mechanisms that increase ecosystem productivity and diversity. Ecosystems are not units of selection, so their adaptedness cannot result from selection among ecosystems. Natural selection is driven primarily by individual advantage (Fisher 1930): plants and animals do not sacrifice for their ecosystem's good any more than humans sacrifice for the sake of their nation's economy. Instead, an ecosystem, like a free-market economy, is the joint achievement of interdependent participants, each acting for its own advantage. Competition among organisms has favored mechanisms that tap new sources of energy, such as photosynthesis, use available energy more efficiently, such as aerobic respiration, recycle others' wastes in profitable ways, as in respiration, nitrogen reduction, or decomposition of dead matter, or adapt to harsh conditions, as do C_4 or CAM metabolism. Competition has also enhanced resource turnover through the evolution of predators and herbivores, and it has favored cooperation between organisms of the same or different species to enhance the effectiveness of competition with others. Just as competition within human economies favors diversification of occupations as far as technology and economic and political stability allow, natural competition favors diversification. Finally, in natural systems, the tendency for poorly exploited energy sources to find users erodes unprofitable monopolies, which Adam Smith considered the greatest obstacle to enhancing the productivity of human economies (Leigh and Vermeij 2002).

The Changing Environments of Ecological Communities

How are ecological communities affected by different scales of environmental change? How do changes of different scale affect the maintenance of diversity? How rapidly can a community recover from protracted environmental disruption?

"NORMAL" CHANGE AND THE MAINTENANCE OF DIVERSITY

Insofar as "the jack of all trades is master of none," species can avoid being replaced by competitors only by specializing as much as the stability of their environment allows (MacArthur 1972; Leigh 1990). Thus, all else being equal, more stable habitats support more diverse communities. Tropical forests are free from winter, so their environments are more stable than those of temperate-zone forests. As we have seen, freedom from winter intensifies pressure on tropical plants from pathogens and insect pests, which presumably maintains the diversity of tropical trees (Janzen 1970). Moreover, the less seasonal the rainfall, the greater the tree diversity, even though such continual rainfall impoverishes the soil (Clinebell et al. 1995). Tropical forests also provide fruit, young leaves, and insects all through the year, although the supply varies with the season. This circumstance permits great diversity among a tropical forest's frugivorous and insectivorous bats, birds, and arboreal mammals (Emmons 1989).

Nonetheless, some aspects of biotic diversity depend on change. The opening of occasional clearings in a forest permits pioneers to coexist with mature forest tree species (Skellam 1951). If new clearings open up frequently enough to support pioneers but rarely enough that most of the forest is mature, the opening of these clearings increases the diversity of the forest as a whole (Horn 1974, 30). Temporal sorting of recruitment in response to environmental variation may also enable different species of tropical trees to coexist (Chesson and Warner 1981). Populations of different pollinators, seed dispersers, seed eaters, and seedling browsers presumably fluctuate differently from year to year, causing different trees to reproduce successfully in different years (Leigh 1982). If Chesson and Warner are right, the seemingly senseless variety of ways in which plants attract pollinators or dispersers allows a tree species to establish itself by finding a way to reproduce successfully in years when most of its competitors fail.

ADJUSTING TO UNFORESEEN CHANGE

Populations presumably recover best from disturbances their ancestors have frequently encountered. New types or patterns of disturbance are more likely to cause serious disruption. After all, an ecological community is adapted to the environmental context in which it evolved. This platitude raises two questions. First, did the ecological communities we study evolve in the environmental context we see today, and if not, what difference does that make? If we ignore past changes in community organization, are we deluding ourselves about the significance of what we are studying (Jackson 1997)? Second, how rapidly can the community recover from a protracted disruption of its context? It would be unwise to assess the effects of ongoing disturbances such as widespread deforestation or global warming without considering how ecological communities have responded to such events in the past. Answers to our questions depend largely on archaeological, paleontological, and geologic research.

When the Isthmus of Panama joined the Americas 3 million years ago, it allowed extensive interchange between long-separated terrestrial biotas (Simpson 1980). Plants and animals that did not evolve together now live in the same forest (Smythe 1986). Community composition has also changed more recently. Fifteen thousand years ago, when tropical forests were drier and 5°C cooler than today (Livingstone and Van der Hammen 1978; Bonnefille, Roeland, and Guiot 1990; Piperno, Bush, and Colinvaux 1991a; Adam 1994, 160–166; Colinvaux, De Oliveira et al. 1996; Colinvaux, De Oliveira, and Bush 2000; Piperno 1997), some Neotropical forests had species compositions with no modern parallel (Bush et al. 1992; Colinvaux, De Oliveira, and Bush 2000; Colinvaux, chap. 6 in this volume). Presumably, many of today's forests have species compositions that could not be found anywhere 15,000 years ago. What implications do these reassortments have for the degree of coadaptation—the effectiveness of mutual adjustment—among the members of a community?

The most striking change in Neotropical forest ecosystems during the last 50,000 years was the extinction of large mammals (Martin and Klein 1984). Human hunters swept through the Americas about 12,000 years ago, wiping out mammoths, mastodons, gomphotheres, ground sloths, wild horses, and the like, leaving no Neotropical mammal larger than a tapir (Janzen and Martin 1982). What was the effect of these mammals' disappearance? In the Ivory Coast, some tree species whose seeds are dispersed by elephants lack saplings in areas where elephants have disappeared (Alexandre 1978). How many plants disappeared from the Neotropics with their megafaunal dispersers? How many others have altered distributions and "dispersal ecologies"?

Webb and Rancy (1996, 353, 354) suggest that megaherbivores opened up Neotropical rainforest, or turned parts of it into savanna, as African elephants sometimes transform woodland into savanna today (Kingdon 1979). Probably it is wiser to say that the largest animals were most common in drier areas, as in Africa and India today (Karanth and Sunquist 1992). Malaysia's dipterocarp forest still has a few elephants and rhinoceros, and once had many more (Medway 1969), but, then as now, it was a splendid closed forest. African rainforest has its own species of forest elephant, smaller and less common than the open-country species, which leaves its forests intact.

During the Pleistocene, 10,000-year periods when the climate was much like today's alternated with 90,000-year periods when polar and mountain glaciers spread and the tropics were 5°C cooler and distinctly drier (Hays, Imbrie, and Shackleton 1976; Adam 1994, 160). During the last glacial maximum, areas of Guatemala 200–400 m above sea level, now supporting "primeval" seasonal evergreen forest, were covered with juniper scrub (Leyden 1984). The modern forest is less than 11,000 years old, and no one knows where its ancestors came from. The recovery of rainforest from glacial drought has also been tracked in Australia (Hopkins et al. 1993). As new pollen floras appear and climate models improve, the rate at which rainforest extends and tree diversity recovers when the climate becomes suitable can be traced more precisely. Nonetheless, tropical forest is most diverse where it was least disrupted by the climatic revolutions of the Pleistocene (Morley 2000).

In pre-Columbian times, Panama's Pacific side was thickly settled. Little forest was left (Piperno, Bush, and Colinvaux 1991b; Bush et al. 1992), and people were not eating forest animals such as agoutis or peccaries (Cooke and Ranere 1992). On the other hand, the wetter Caribbean side was less thickly settled, and people there were eating forest animals (Cooke and Ranere 1992). Parts of BCI have been forested for the last 2,500 years (Piperno 1990). The Spanish conquest of tropical America, about 400 years ago, nearly annihilated local peoples. Land in eastern Panama that was nearly all cornfield in 1600 now supports diverse, seemingly virgin, tropical forest (Piperno 1994; Bush and Colinvaux 1994). There is much more to be learned about the nature of the forest's recovery after the Spanish conquest (Bush et al. 1992).

THE ORIGINS OF TROPICAL BIOLOGICAL DIVERSITY

The first step in the origin of biological diversity is the origin of species. By and large, we know much less about how species form than how different species coexist. Indeed, it is truly remarkable how little we know about the mechanisms of speciation, given the vast literature devoted to the subject. Here, we show that common, widespread species that originated from marginal populations must be the product of natural selection: they must initially, at least, have had some advantage over their predecessors. Then we consider some mechanisms of speciation, how long speciation might take, and how constraints on speciation might limit the buildup of diversity.

Adaptation and the Mechanisms of Speciation

New species may originate by "accidents" irrelevant to their ability to coexist with their predecessors (Seehausen, van Alphen, and Lande 1999). An initially rare new species, however, is unlikely to spread quickly or widely by chance. In a constant population of N mature individuals, a neutral mutant allele with no influence on its bearers' reproductive success, which is now represented by

$n \ll N$ descendants, must have originated more than $n/3$ generations ago (Fisher 1930). The same holds for a new species with no advantage over its predecessors. Several non-pioneer species of tropical trees are, or were recently, represented by over 10 million reproductives apiece; these species originated far later than 3.3 million tree generations, or 100 million years, ago. To spread quickly or far, a new species must exploit a "niche opportunity" (Shea and Chesson 2002) by finding a better way than its predecessors to avoid natural enemies or use some source of energy.

In some cases, a population is sundered by a barrier, such as the isthmus that separated Pacific from Caribbean individuals in Panama. The separated populations become distinct species when alleles spread through each population, some of which are incompatible with alleles that have spread through the other, so that matings between members of the two populations cannot produce viable offspring (Fisher 1930; Orr and Turelli 2001). Fisher (1930) argued, however, that speciation is often a response to a trade-off: "Any environmental heterogeneity which requires special adaptations, which are either irreconcilable or difficult to reconcile, will exert upon the cohesive power of the species a certain stress" (Fisher 1930, 126). If two adaptations are mutually antagonistic, bearers of one may benefit by not mating with bearers of the other.

An example of speciation by mate choice driven by incompatible adaptations is provided by two butterfly species, *Heliconius melpomene* and *H. cydno*, which diverged less than a million years ago (Jiggins et al. 2001). These butterflies have brightly colored wings that advertise their distastefulness. Distasteful butterflies flying in the same habitat form "Mullerian mimicry rings," in which several distasteful species share the same wing colors, thus sharing the "load" of educating naive predators about their distastefulness. In Panama, *H. melpomene* is black with red crossbars on its forewings and yellow leading edges on its hindwings. It is a Mullerian mimic of the equally distasteful *H. erato*, and, like *H. erato*, *H. melpomene* flies in open country. *H. cydno* is black with white crossbars on its forewings and white borders on the rear of its hindwings. It is a Mullerian mimic of the distasteful *H. sappho*, and, like *H. sappho*, it tends to fly in the forest understory.

Apparently, *H. melpomene* and *H. cydno* diverged to take advantage of different habitats and different, preexisting mimicry rings (Jiggins et al. 2001). Hybrids between *H. cydno* and *H. melpomene* are much more likely to be eaten than their parental forms because birds do not recognize the hybrids' wing colors as denoting distastefulness. If given a choice between mating with a conspecific and hybridizing, Panamanian *melpomene* and *cydno* always mate with a member of their own species. Their refusal to hybridize may reflect selection to avoid bearing unfit offspring: *melpomene* from French Guiana, where *cydno* is not found, are less reluctant to mate with Panamanian *cydno*. The two species have been isolated long enough to accumulate some genetic incompatibility: female hybrids are sterile (although male hybrids are not).

Sometimes speciation occurs without genetic incompatibility, driven by the ecological unfitness of hybrids. In Ecuador, the distasteful dry-forest butterfly *Heliconius himera* diverged from its rainforest sister species, *H. erato*, 1.5 to 2 million years ago (Mallet, McMillan, and Jiggins 1998). These two butterflies are brightly but differently colored, advertising their distastefulness: the dry-forest butterfly's background color is blue and its rainforest counterpart's coal black (Jiggins et al. 1996). Hybrids of these species are fully viable and fertile in the laboratory. In nature, however, the unusual wing colors of the hybrids attract predators. Thus, where these two species overlap, a butterfly greatly prefers mates with the same colors. The width of a "hybrid zone" between overlapping populations with unfit hybrids is proportional to $\sqrt{(l^2/k)}$, where l^2 is the mean square distance of individuals from their birthplace and $1 - k$ is the reproductive success of hybrids relative to parental forms (Haldane 1948; Barton 1979). In most hybrid zones between differently colored races of *Heliconius*, unusual wing coloration halves hybrid reproduction, and the hybrid zone is 10 km wide. The hybrid zone between *himera* and *erato* is only 5 km wide, suggesting that very few hybrids reproduce. Jiggins et al. (1996) think that the extra hybrid disadvantage arises from physiological trade-offs between adaptations for life in wet and dry forest, and that the nearly complete reproductive failure of hybrids has helped transform these butterfly populations into distinct species.

Finally, Galápagos finches of sympatric species occasionally hybridize, although a female prefers to mate with a male singing her father's song, and both sexes prefer mates resembling their parents (P. R. Grant and B. R. Grant 1996, 1997). Before 1983, hybrid finches on Daphne Major almost never survived to reproduce, because there were so few seeds of sizes they could eat faster than their competitors could. When the heavy El Niño rains of 1983 changed the vegetation, making the seeds they needed available, hybrids flourished, reversing the speciation process, at least temporarily (B. R. Grant and P. R. Grant 1996, Grant and Grant 1997). A trade-off that rendered hybrids unfit was essential to keeping these finch "species" distinct.

Nearly all studies of the mechanisms of speciation, even polyploidy (Stebbins 1950; Ramsey and Schemske 1998, 2002) and pollinator shift (Bradshaw et al. 1995; Schemske and Bradshaw 1999), concern animals or herbs. We know little about the usual mechanisms of speciation among tropical trees. Yet tree diversity provides the foundation for animal diversity (Hutchinson 1959). Our ignorance of how trees speciate makes our supposed understanding of tropical diversity incomplete.

Yet the study of tree speciation is not impossible. Ehrendorfer (1982) used information on distributions of related tropical tree species to infer that speciation among them was usually allopatric. He used chromosome studies to show that polyploidy does not currently play a major role in speciation among tropical trees. Modern methods of phylogeography (Dick, Abdul-Salim, and Bermingham 2003) and genomic in situ hybridization (Leitch and Bennett 1997) can be used to refine these conclusions. If hybrids between different species or genera are far more likely to yield viable offspring in plants than in animals, mechanisms of mate choice, driven by the adaptiveness of diversification, must play a dominant role in plant speciation (Schluter 2000; Kay and Schemske 2003).

How Much Time Does Speciation Require?

How long does it take for one species to become two? Two sexual populations are called distinct species if, where they overlap, they do not interbreed, or, if they do interbreed, their hybrids are inviable or infertile (Fisher 1930). Estimating the lapse of time from the divergence between homologous proteins, Coyne and Orr (1997) found that in currently allopatric populations of *Drosophila* with no secondary contact, prezygotic and postzygotic isolation increased at roughly equal rates after the populations were separated. If proteins in *Drosophila* diverge at the same rate as proteins in mammals, such populations require an average of 2.7 million years to become distinct species, but the scatter around this average is enormous. Is it legitimate to use a mammalian "molecular clock"?

Useful insights into the time taken for speciation have come from comparisons of marine sister species separated by the Isthmus of Panama. The isthmus became a land bridge 3 million years ago. The rising isthmus divided some offshore populations long before it became a true land bridge (Knowlton et al. 1993); we assume that those nearshore populations that were most recently divided were split when the isthmus became a true land bridge. The degree of reproductive isolation between those "geminate pairs" last split by the isthmus is the best measure available of how long it takes two populations recently but completely divided from each other to become distinct species.

In sum, roughly half of the geminate populations split by the isthmus 3 million years ago have become distinct species. In the four geminate pairs of snapping shrimp (*Alpheus* spp.) most recently split by the isthmus, animals from the two populations of a geminate pair rarely produced viable young, although they often initiated courtship and sometimes paired (Knowlton et al. 1993). In experimental groups of gobies (*Bathygobius*) from both sides of Panama, a goby will spawn with one from the other coast about 18% of the time, producing fertile young (Rubinoff and Rubinoff 1971). Pacific *Diadema* spawn at full moon while Caribbean *Diadema* spawn just after new moon; these geminates appear to be good species even though they experienced no selection against hybrids (Lessios 1984). On the other hand, the Caribbean sea urchin *Echinometra viridis* can interbreed freely with its geminate *E. vanbrunti* when the two are placed together in the laboratory, even though they diverged earlier than the *Diadema* (Lessios 1998, 191, 194).

Controls on Speciation Rate

A central question concerning biotic diversity is whether speciation is limited primarily by shortage of ecological opportunities (unfilled niches) or by the rarity of circumstances that allow reproductive isolation to develop. This question is raised by Patton and da Silva's (chap. 7 in this volume) description of a boundary transverse to Amazonia's Rio Juruá that separates long-diverged clades in many species. Was this divergence the passive result of long separation by a ridge, since eroded away, or did "geminate clades" adapt to the different vegetation types that this boundary separates: "open forest" on one side, "dense forest" on the other? An answer to this question demands better understanding of the mechanisms of speciation. Let us, however, probe our ignorance.

Ehrlich and Raven (1969) argued that divergent selection, not absence of gene flow, is the primary engine of phenotypic divergence. Schneider and Moritz (1999) have presented evidence that, in itself, long-term isolation is unlikely to be the primary driver of phenotypic divergence and speciation among rainforest vertebrates. A skink, *Carlia rubrigularis,* lives in the leaf litter of closed rainforest and tall open forest in Australia's Wet Tropics. Skink populations on the two sides of the "Black Mountain Corridor" have been separated for 5 million years or more. There is little genetic differentiation among skink populations on the same side of the corridor, whatever their habitat (Schneider et al. 1999). Yet skinks from rainforests on opposite sides of the barrier resemble each other far more than either resembles an open-forest skink, and vice versa. Here, habitat dictates phenotype. This phenotypic divergence is partly driven by the much higher predation pressure in the open forest, which selects for skinks that mature when smaller (Schneider et al. 1999).

Speciation is particularly rapid in novel environments, tropical or temperate, such as remote archipelagoes or newly formed lakes (Schluter 1998), presumably because ecological opportunities are most abundant in such places. The twenty-eight species of the "silversword alliance" in Hawaii are descended from a single species of tarweed that colonized Kauai about 5 million years ago (Baldwin and Sanderson 1998). These species include trees, shrubs, rosette plants, cushion plants, and a vine. They occupy habitats ranging from sea level to alpine and from desert to everwet forest (Baldwin et al. 1991). The Hawaiian *Dubautia laevigata* of this alliance crosses as readily with *Raillardiopsis muiri,* one of its two closest Californian relatives, as with conspecifics (Baldwin et al. 1991), as if these two populations have not been separated long enough for genetic incompatibilities to develop. Crosses among the three genera of the silversword alliance are quite feasible (Carr and Kyhos 1986), but crosses among genera of their tarweed ancestors rarely work (Baldwin et al. 1991). Apparently, the many unfilled niches in Hawaii greatly accelerated this lineage's diversification. Other lineages have diversified as remarkably in Hawaii and on oceanic archipelagoes elsewhere (Carlquist 1965), some even more rapidly than the silversword alliance (Kim et al. 1996; Francisco-Ortega, Jansen, and Santos-Guerra 1996). As species sometimes diverge within an island (Kim et al. 1996), this rapid speciation cannot be ascribed entirely to the opportunities for reproductive isolation offered by occasional dispersal from one island to another.

If fruit flies are typical of most animals, then ecological opportunity must play a crucial role in many speciation events. If two *Drosophila* populations overlap after they first diverge, speciation is achieved ten times faster than if they remain separated (Coyne and Orr 1997), provided that the newly overlapping populations can coexist without merging. Speciation is hastened because overlap accelerates prezygotic isolation, increasing the flies' preference for mates from their own population; postzygotic isolation (as measured in the laboratory) is unaffected. As mate choice diverges so much more slowly in purely allopatric populations, the prezygotic isolation of overlapping *Drosophila* populations cannot reflect the capricious divergence of their mate preferences and sexually selected characteristics that Lande (1981) and Eberhard (1985) considered a principal engine of speciation. Since overlapping populations coexist only if they occupy different niches, individuals do better to mate with those like themselves, for hybrids will be unfit for the niche of either parent. Whatever caused the populations to diverge in the first place, the evolution of reproductive isolation in overlapping *Drosophila* populations seems to be driven by the incompatibility of their adaptations.

Speciation rate, however, is not controlled exclusively by ecological opportunity. Seehausen, van Alphen, and Lande (1999) report a case of incipient sympatric speciation by sexual selection among cichlid fishes in Lake Victoria with no apparent ecological divergence between the two populations. Moreover, when confronted by an ecological opportunity, some lineages diversify, but others do not. East African lakes offer an abundance of niches for fish, but haplochromine cichlids, in which sexual selection can isolate populations from each other in less than a thousand years, and in which a single invader's descendants can diversify to fill a new lake within 15,000 years (Seehausen, van Alphen, and Witte 1997; Seehausen, van Alphen, and Lande 1999), provide the lion's share of these lakes' fish diversity (Meyer 1993).

Finally, it takes time to diversify in response to ecological opportunities. When the Chicxulub bolide struck Yucatán, causing the wave of extinctions that ended the Cretaceous (Alvarez 1997), the "nuclear winter" it sparked extinguished 84% of the evergreen dicots and 33% of the deciduous dicots of northern New Mexico's Raton basin (Wolfe and Upchurch 1987), leaving a few species of ferns to cover the landscape. Although the impact replaced a rather dry climate with hot, everwet conditions (Wolfe 1990), a million years later plant diversity had not even recovered to pre-impact levels, and it was far from having attained "normal" rainforest diversity (Wolfe and Upchurch 1987).

Are the Tropics a Cradle of Speciation or a Museum of Diversity?

We have argued that a new species needs a niche opportunity in order to spread and multiply: diversity of species reflects diversity of ways of life. Nonetheless, niche opportunities are not filled immediately. Moreover, new opportunities appear as a community diversifies. Is speciation easier in the tropics? Are tropical species less likely to be eliminated by environmental catastrophe? Either circumstance would enhance tropical diversity relative to diversity at higher latitudes.

The traditional explanation for tropical diversity is that tropical conditions have always been present in the world, while, geologically speaking, "temperate" climates tend to be ephemeral. This explanation appeared less obvious when the severe effects of the climatic revolutions of the Pleistocene on many tropical settings became known (Livingstone and Van der Hammen 1978). Such rhythmic revolutions in tropical climates have happened before. In the late Triassic and early Jurassic, a chain of rift lakes in what is now the eastern United States stretched from 10° to 25° north paleolatitude. These lakes filled and emptied in a 22,000-year cycle for 40 million years (Olsen 1986). When the lakes were empty, the surrounding vegetation was depauperate, and when they were full, this vegetation was much more diverse (Olsen et al. 1978; Olsen 1986).

In light of these discoveries, Haffer (1969), Prance (1982a), and others suggested that the tropics were a cradle of speciation because the cyclic drying out of tropical regions for 90,000 of every 100,000 years fragmented and compressed rainforest populations into isolated "refugia," where they diverged. When forest reconnected the refugia during the next interglacial, the previously isolated populations would expand, overlap, and speciate. Refugia, however, do not appear to be effective species pumps. Forest diversity has apparently declined since the Miocene (Flenley, chap. 5 in this volume; Hooghiemstra and van der Hammen 1998). The highest tree diversity in the world is found in the western half of Amazonia (Gentry 1988b; De Oliveira and Mori 1999) and in parts of Malesia (Morley 2000); neither of these forests was fragmented during the Pleistocene (Piperno 1997; Hooghiemstra and van der Hammen 1998; Colinvaux, De Oliveira, and Bush 2000; Colinvaux et al. 2001; Morley 2000). In areas such as North America and tropical Australia, where habitats were fragmented during glacial periods, a single cycle of fragmentation did not cause speciation. Instead, speciation usually required several million years and many cycles of fragmentation (Klicka and Zink 1997; Avise and Walker 1998; Joseph, Moritz, and Hugall 1995; Moritz et al. 2000). The ridges that divided Amazonia into distinct regions a few million years ago contributed more to Amazonian speciation than did Pleistocene fragmentation (Patton and da Silva, chap. 7 in this volume).

As yet, there is no evidence that faster speciation contributes to tropical diversity (Avise and Walker 1998; Moritz et al. 2000). The freedom of certain tropical regions from major climate change during the Neogene, and especially during the Pleistocene, has, however, helped maintain tropical diversity (Morley 2000).

CONCLUDING REMARKS

To protect tropical diversity, we must understand how it evolves and how it is maintained. To understand how diversity is maintained, we must be able to distinguish the species involved, and we must learn what factors regulate different populations, how different species coexist, and the many and varied ways different species depend on one another. To understand how diversity evolves, we must learn what mechanisms allow one species to become two, and how different scales of environmental change influence speciation rates and the diversity and species composition of ecological communities.

These goals demand a thorough understanding of natural history. They also demand a diversity of approaches. Analyzing the consequences of the reduction of a forest to island fragments by a rising reservoir reveals the roles of the pollinators, seed dispersers, and predators that disappear from these islets in maintaining the diversity and trophic organization of intact forest. Comparing long-isolated landmasses of different sizes reveals the roles of large herbivores and large carnivores in maintaining an ecosystem's power to resist invaders and recover from disturbance. Study of the fossil record reveals that, in order to attain very high diversity, a forest must be free from major climatic disruptions for millions of years.

The tendency for biological diversity to increase over evolutionary time, within and among communities, and the adverse effects of new kinds of disruption on a community's diversity suggest that ecological communities are organized in ways that favor high diversity, just as a thriving economy supports a diversity of occupations. Biological diversity, like diversity of human occupations, develops in response to trade-offs in ability to exploit different resources under different conditions. Diversity develops, however, in a context of interdependence. Disrupt the links of interdependence by, for example, eliminating a forest's pollinators and seed dispersers, and diversity will collapse, even if the factors originally promoting its evolution are still operative.

ACKNOWLEDGMENTS

We are most grateful to the staff scientists and visitors at STRI for work that has revealed so much about the beauties of tropical nature, and to those agencies and individuals whose generous funding made this work possible. Egbert Leigh gives thanks to the plants and animals of Barro Colorado for their perpetual reminder about what we still need to learn. He is also grateful to Kathleen Kay and Douglas Schemske for offering hope that speciation among tropical plants is not beyond the bounds of human understanding.

13
Landscape Heterogeneity and Species Diversity in Amazonia

KALLE RUOKOLAINEN, HANNA TUOMISTO, AND RISTO KALLIOLA

ABSTRACT

Comparisons of local and regional vascular plant species counts in western Amazonia suggest that beta diversity (species turnover between sites) is exceptionally low in the area. We evaluate this conclusion by studying patterns of species richness and distribution in two plant groups, pteridophytes and the Melastomataceae, using published species lists for Peruvian and Ecuadorian Amazonia and our own field inventories. For three reasons, it appears that beta diversity must be higher than suggested by the species counts. First, intensive field inventories have uncovered several previously unreported species, which indicates that the existing regional species counts are underestimates. Second, geologic and climatic patterns and processes in the western Amazonian landscape are not compatible with the idea of low between-habitat diversity. Third, edaphic differences can be shown to affect species diversity and distributions. Even though it can be demonstrated that beta diversity is relevant in western Amazonia, it is clear that the present level of biogeographic, ecological, and taxonomic knowledge of Amazonian flora is inadequate for answering many elementary biological questions.

INTRODUCTION

In terms of taxonomy and biogeography, the vascular plants are fairly well known, at least in comparison with such other groups as nonvascular plants or insects. However, this does not necessarily mean that the level of taxonomic and biogeographic knowledge is satisfactory in tropical rainforest areas such as Amazonia. Indeed, there seem to be important gaps in our basic knowledge about the distribution and diversity of vascular plants in these areas, which may severely limit our ability to understand biogeography and species diversity in the tropics.

Biodiversity research in the tropics has a general problem: there are huge numbers of species, but few professionals, or even amateurs, studying them. In the temperate zones of the world, our knowledge of birds, butterflies, and plants has been to a large extent collected by volunteer enthusiasts, and professionals can count on a biogeographic data set that has been accumulated by a large number of people over a long period of time. For example, the bird atlas of Finland (Hyytiä, Kellomäki, and Koistinen 1983) includes presence-absence information for all bird species found in the country plotted on a 10 × 10 km grid. Such an effort could never have been finished and repeated (Väisänen, Lammi, and Koskimies 1998) without the input of thousands of amateur bird enthusiasts who screened the country (337,000 km^2) and returned their species lists to the coordinators of the project. Once published, such a volume is an invaluable source of information to anyone studying species distribution or diversity patterns, or monitoring temporal changes in those patterns.

In the tropics, the available information is a far cry from providing this degree of detail. Even at the scale of 1° latitude by 1° longitude (about 100 × 100 km), the observed species diversity is obviously biased by poor availability of data. Species richness data at this scale have been compiled from the specimen citations in *Flora Neotropica,* one of the very few sources of continent-wide species distribution information, by Wilfried Morawetz and his collaborators (Morawetz and Krügel 1996). They found that few 1° squares report more than a hundred plant species, while many report none (W. Morawetz, personal communication). Since floristic inventories in Amazonia as a rule yield far more than a hundred tree species in a single hectare (Gentry 1988a, 1988b; Valencia, Balslev, and Paz y Miño 1994; ter Steege et al. 2000), it is clear that the species diversity estimates and the species lists obtained from *Flora Neotropica* do not correspond to reality. This discrepancy is partly explained by the fact that not nearly all plant families have as yet been treated in *Flora Neotropica,* but still it gives food for thought.

Species lists are the basic units of information needed in most biodiversity studies; consequently, the availability, comprehensiveness, and quality of species lists have a great influence on our perception of nature. When the number of species present in a given area is estimated at any spatial scale (local, regional, or global), the result obviously depends on the available species lists. In order to estimate the degree of endemism in the biota of a given region, it is necessary to have access to species lists from both the area of interest and elsewhere. Species lists, ideally combined with species distribution maps, are needed to identify and understand biogeographic patterns and processes and to define biogeographic regions. Species lists, and conclusions based on them, have been elemental in the formulation of evolutionary and biogeographic hypotheses, such as the Pleistocene refuge theory (Haffer 1969; Prance 1982a), and in identifying priority areas for conservation (Workshop 90, 1991).

Amazonian forests have several characteristics that make studying and understanding regional patterns there rather challenging. Local species lists are laborious to produce, and field studies must be limited to small areas that are within practical reach from cities in order to keep the task manageable. Hence, systematic documenting of general large-scale patterns is rarely done. However, if species data are available from only a few scattered points, the conclusions drawn from them are likely to be rough generalizations and oversimplifications (for further discussion, see Nelson et al. 1990; Tuomisto and Ruokolainen 1997; Tuomisto 1998).

In Amazonia, comprehensive species lists are few and far between. At the local scale, tree inventories of 1–2 hectares in a few score sites have documented 100–300 tree species per hectare (Campbell et al. 1986; Balslev et al. 1987; Gentry 1988a; Maciel and Lisboa 1989; Phillips et al. 1994; Valencia, Balslev, and Paz y Miño 1994; Cerón and Montalvo 1997). In a 1 ha sample plot in Ecuador, 900 vascular plant species were found (Balslev et al. 1998). Compared with these values, the 4,000 plant species reported to occur in the entire Amazonian lowlands of Ecuador (ca. 7 million ha: Jørgensen and León-Yánez 1999) is a relatively small number. In other words, the reported level of beta diversity (site-to-site species turnover) appears remarkably low in relation to alpha diversity (species richness within a single site). This observation may reflect a situation in which most plant species are truly widespread and evenly distributed, but it may also be an indication of an inadequate exploration of the beta diversity component. If the latter is the case, then gamma diversity (the regional flora) in Amazonia could be significantly richer than has previously been thought.

Even though biological research in general is increasingly oriented toward modern experimental and laboratory methods, we argue that the traditional naturalist's approach is still very much needed, especially in the tropics. Careful observation of biological systems and their relationships with local environmental conditions, both present and past, is essential for understanding ecological and biogeographic patterns. It is also necessary to find out what is known about the species and their environment at the present time, and what is not known, in order to focus field studies so that important information gaps can be filled. The conclusions that can be drawn, for example, about biogeographic patterns or the distribution of species diversity are only as reliable as the field data on which they are based. New descriptive research may draw attention to previously neglected patterns that need to be analyzed in greater depth, or to other questions that deserve attention in future scientific studies.

This chapter examines the diversity of western Amazonia as an example of this approach. We review the available information on plant species distributions and environmental conditions in the Amazonian lowlands of Ecuador and

Peru in order to evaluate the currently available data, and we discuss the possible factors behind the observed diversity patterns.

THE QUESTION OF BETA DIVERSITY IN WESTERN AMAZONIA

The area from eastern Ecuador to northern Peru is often cited as being among the most species-rich areas in Amazonia, or even in the world. Reference in this context is usually made to the inventories that have produced amazingly high tree species richness numbers within small areas: about 300 species of trees (DBH > 10 cm) within a single hectare (Gentry 1988b; Valencia, Balslev, and Paz y Miño 1994). Only a single study has been conducted to obtain total plant species counts for a given hectare of forest: Balslev et al. (1998) have documented a total of about 900 vascular plant species in Cuyabeno, Ecuador.

These inventories, however, document species richness at a given point, not at the regional level. Attention has previously been drawn to the very high species numbers in small areas compared with the much less striking species numbers in larger areas (Tuomisto et al. 1995; Tuomisto 1998). Jørgensen and León-Yánez (1999) documented a total of 4,000 flowering plant species in the Amazonian lowlands of Ecuador (an area of about 70,000 km^2, using 500 m as the upper elevation limit). For Peruvian lowland Amazonia (approximately 550,000 km^2), Brako and Zarucchi (1993) list about 7,000 species. Other tropical lowland floras attain similar numbers for regional plant species richness. For example, Belize (23,000 km^2) has 2,500–3,000 species, and Bangladesh (144,000 km^2) has 5,000 species (World Conservation Monitoring Center 1992). Even low-elevation European countries, such as Hungary (93,000 km^2) and Belgium (30,500 km^2), do not fall far from these diversity levels, with their 2,150 and 1,500 plant species, respectively (World Conservation Monitoring Center 1992).

In summary, alpha diversity of plants appears extremely high in western Amazonia, whereas the existing data on regional or gamma diversity shows no spectacular values. These findings suggest that western Amazonian beta diversity is very low; a single hectare in Cuyabeno could contain a quarter of all the species known for an area 7 million times larger.

There are three possible ways to interpret these findings. First, the suggestion of low beta diversity may be true. Species in Amazonia are widespread and uniformly distributed (Pitman et al. 1999, 2001; Terborgh, Pitman et al. 2002), so any vegetation sample is likely to contain a high proportion of the total plant species pool. Second, the high alpha diversity may not be the general rule. The detailed inventories that have been done may have accidentally hit on hotspots

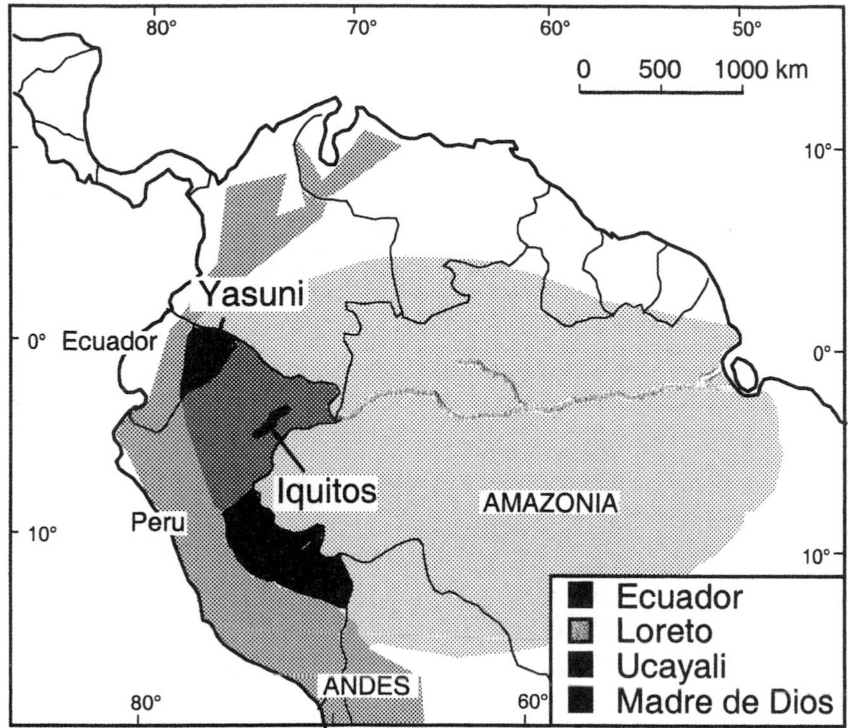

Figure 13.1 Map of northern South America with the study areas shown. The black areas labeled Yasuní and Iquitos contain our own field inventory sites.

of diversity, while the average local diversity in Amazonia is lower. Third, the suggestion of relatively low overall (gamma) diversity may not be true. There are large non-inventoried areas that may harbor plant species that have remained unknown to science so far.

In order to evaluate these three hypotheses, we have compiled species lists of pteridophytes and the Melastomataceae for different geographic regions within western Amazonia. We have chosen four regions for our analysis: the entire Amazonian lowlands of Ecuador ($<$ 500 m above sea level; 70,000 km^2), and the lowland parts ($<$ 500 m) of the departments Loreto (350,000 km^2), Ucayali (95,000 km^2), and Madre de Dios (80,000 km^2) in Peru (fig. 13.1). For these geographic regions, we have used species data from the available literature (Tryon and Stolze 1989–1994 and Brako and Zarucchi 1993 for Peru; Jørgensen and León-Yánez 1999 for Ecuador). In addition, we have used species data from our own field inventories within two of these regions.

The Iquitos data set from Loreto consists of inventories of thirty-two unflooded (terra firme) primary rainforest sites totaling 10.46 ha, and represents an area of about 2,000 km^2 in the area surrounding the city of Iquitos (for details on methods and localities, see Ruokolainen and Tuomisto 1998). The areas of the sampling units that were inventoried at each site varied between 0.1 and 0.8 ha. Generally, the species-area curves for the observed plant groups in the study area tended to level off within 0.25 ha (Tuomisto et al. 1995; Tuomisto and Poulsen 1996), so even if the sample sizes at different sites were not exactly the same, their results are roughly comparable, at least when averaged over several sites. The Yasuní data set from Ecuador includes the terra firme part of a larger data set collected within an area of about 500 km^2 in the Yasuní National Park (Tuomisto et al. 2002). Each of the twenty-five sites is represented by a sampling unit of 0.25 ha, totaling 6.25 ha.

REGIONAL DIVERSITY PATTERNS

The series *Pteridophyta of Peru* (Tryon and Stolze 1989–1994) reports a total of 290 pteridophyte species at elevations below 500 m from the three Amazonian departments in Peru. Loreto, which is the largest of them, harbors 243 of these species, Ucayali has 102 species, and Madre de Dios has 155 species. During our own fieldwork in the Iquitos area, we have encountered 149 pteridophyte species; at the present stage of identification, it seems that 38 of these are species new to Loreto and 35 are new to the entire Peruvian lowlands (fig. 13.2).

The *Catalogue of the Flowering Plants and Gymnosperms of Peru* (Brako and Zarucchi 1993) lists a total of 247 Melastomataceae for the Peruvian lowlands. Of these, 236 species are found in Loreto, 43 in Ucayali, and 69 in Madre de Dios. Our fieldwork in the Iquitos area has yielded 134 species of melastomes, of which 37 are new to Loreto and 36 are new to the Peruvian lowlands (fig. 13.2). Most (24) of these new species have not been identified to species, but they have been compared with the herbarium specimens (at U.S. National Herbarium and Missouri Botanical Garden) that represent the species cited by Brako and Zarucchi, and were found not to match any of them.

In Ecuador, 317 pteridophyte species are known from the Amazonian lowlands (Jørgensen and León-Yánez 1999). During our fieldwork in Yasuní we found 136 pteridophyte species, of which almost 30 were not previously known from Ecuador. As for melastomes, 162 species are listed in the *Catalogue of the Vascular Plants of Ecuador* (Jørgensen and León-Yánez 1999), and our own inventories include 86 species. Unfortunately, at this stage, it is not possible to estimate how many new melastome species we have found in Ecuador because our

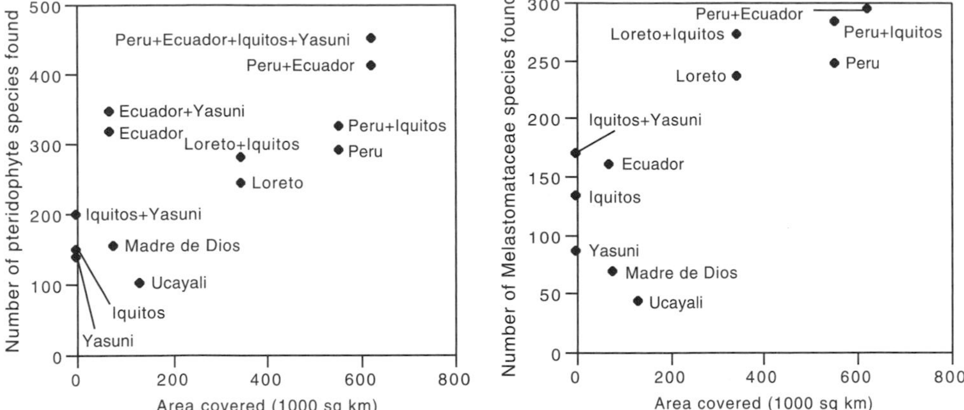

Figure 13.2 Number of pteridophyte and melastome species documented for different geographic regions in western lowland Amazonia (below 500 m elevation) plotted against geographic area. For Peru, species numbers are shown both for the entire region and for each of the departments Loreto, Ucayali, and Madre de Dios. The species numbers for Ecuador, Peru, and the Peruvian departments include only species listed in the literature. The numbers shown for Iquitos (which is situated in Loreto) and Yasuní (which is in Ecuador) include only species that we have found in our own inventories.

specimens have not yet been compared with specimens of those species that are listed by Jørgensen and León-Yánez.

For pteridophytes, the increment in species numbers due to our own collections is smaller in Ecuador than in Peru. This is probably because our inventory in Loreto was more comprehensive than our inventory in Ecuador (32 sites vs. 25 sites), and because the species list we used for Ecuador is more recent (i.e. more complete) than the species list we used for Peru. Both Yasuní and the Iquitos region are frequented by botanists, and they are therefore already well collected in comparison with other areas in Ecuador and Peru. This difference in collecting effort is probably the main factor behind the high species numbers for Ecuador and Loreto as compared with those for Madre de Dios and especially Ucayali. There are a few relatively well-collected sites in Madre de Dios, such as the Cocha Cashu biological station in the Manu National Park, but Ucayali does not have any comparable attractions, and its flora appears very much undercollected.

These examples demonstrate that the observed overall species richness of a given area is heavily influenced by collecting activity. Our quantitative surveys of very small areas in Loreto and Ecuador have revealed more than twice as many species as are presently known from the entire Ucayali department. We believe that once similar quantitative surveys or more active general collecting are extended to Ucayali, the number of species found there will increase dramatically. However, at this stage, it is impossible to guess how many of those species will already be known from other areas in Peru, and how many will be new to the country, or even new to science.

The species lists from our two different study areas can be used to estimate the extent to which beta diversity affects the total number of species in a larger region. If most of the species are found in both areas being compared, beta diversity at this scale is low, since neither of the areas contributes new species that are not already present in the other area.

Among the Peruvian departments, Loreto harbors almost all of the species that have been found in Peruvian Amazonia, and the two other departments contribute very little to the country's gamma diversity. Of the 241 melastome species that have been found in either Loreto or Ucayali, only 5 (2% of the combined flora) are not found in Loreto. With pteridophytes, Ucayali contributes only 11% of the 272 species found in either of the two departments (fig. 13.3). The situation is practically identical when Madre de Dios and Loreto are compared. The higher species richness of Madre de Dios as compared with Ucayali is not because new species have been discovered in Madre de Dios, but because a higher percentage of the species that are already known from Loreto have been encountered there. These observations may indicate that if there is beta diversity in Peruvian Amazonia, it is not apparent at such a wide geographic scale; rather, most of the beta diversity may already be represented in Loreto.

However, a different view emerges when Loreto (or all of Peruvian Amazonia) and Amazonian Ecuador are compared. Of the combined floras of Loreto and Ecuador, 37% of the pteridophyte species and 19% of the melastome species have not been found in Loreto (fig. 13.3). These contrasting results may reflect a real situation in which the floras of Madre de Dios and Ucayali are a subset of the Loreto flora, while Ecuadorian Amazonia is floristically different. However, this interpretation does not correspond well with what is known about environmental variation in the area: Loreto and Ecuadorian Amazonia share a perhumid aseasonal climate, while Madre de Dios and Ucayali receive far less precipitation, and in addition, have a distinct dry season.

Another possible explanation is that insufficient effort has been put into identifying the plant specimens collected in Madre de Dios and Ucayali, which is conceivable, since the general collecting effort in these areas has been lower than in Loreto and Ecuador. The species lists that we used for these analyses are lists of species names, so obviously they do not include information on specimens that have been collected in the area but not identified to species. When plant collections are identified, it is generally the widespread, common, and

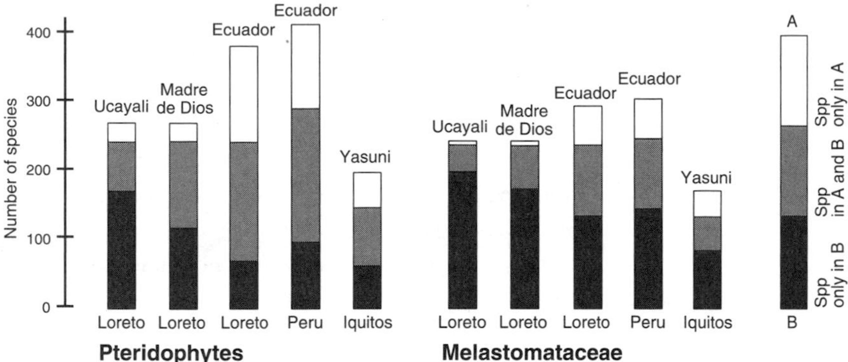

Figure 13.3 Number of pteridophyte and melastome species and the degree of species overlap in different geographic regions in western Amazonia.

easily recognizable species that are named first, either because the investigator is already familiar with them or because they are abundantly represented in herbaria and therefore a match is easy to find (Ruokolainen, Tuomisto, Vormisto, and Pitman 2002). As the work proceeds, the more difficult species can be identified, but the rare and undescribed species are the ones that are identified last. These latter species are not included in species lists that are produced before identification is complete; hence, even if there is a component of species unique to the area under study, this will not be apparent from the species list. To evaluate whether this has happened in the present case, it would be necessary to undertake surveys either in the field or in the sections for unidentified specimens in different herbaria.

A third interpretation is that the observed floristic difference between Loreto and Ecuador is an artifact. The Peruvian and Ecuadorian species lists were produced by different researchers, so it is possible that they have applied different names to the same species. However, in the case of Melastomataceae, this is not likely, as most of the specimens in the species lists were identified or revised by the same specialist, the late John Wurdack. Furthermore, our own field inventories in Loreto (Iquitos) and Ecuador (Yasuní) show about the same degree of floristic difference as the regional species lists do (see fig. 13.3).

ENVIRONMENTAL HETEROGENEITY

If Amazonian species are widely and uniformly distributed, then beta diversity should be insignificant compared with alpha diversity, and all species should be found more or less evenly throughout their biogeographic ranges. If, however, there are clear regional and local differences in the ecological characteristics of different sites, or the sites differ in their developmental histories, this uniformity model implies strong mechanisms that maintain homogeneous species distribution patterns despite such environmental variation.

An indirect way to consider the possible role of beta diversity is to look at the physical environment in order to evaluate how much potential habitat variation there is. The accumulating knowledge on western Amazonian environmental conditions suggests that beta diversity may indeed play an important role in determining overall species diversity in Amazonia.

The lowland rainforest area from Bolivia to Colombia presents considerable variation in climatic factors such as annual average rainfall, rainfall seasonality, and minimum temperature (Hoffmann 1975). For example, annual precipitation varies from 1,500 mm to over 4,000 mm, and the length of the dry season from zero to at least 4 months.

The difference between inundated and terra firme areas has long been recognized as ecologically important. Within inundated areas, considerable variation is found in the chemical properties of water and surface sediments (Sioli 1984; Kalliola et al. 1993). The terra firme can be equally heterogeneous. In the area surrounding Iquitos, soils with widely different textures and acidities are found, and their nutrient content can vary over an order of magnitude within a distance less than a kilometer (Ruokolainen, Linna, and Tuomisto 1997; Kauffman et al. 1998; Ruokolainen and Tuomisto 1998).

Knowledge of the geologic history of western Amazonia suggests that soil variation is the rule rather than the exception. The surface of western Amazonia is a mosaic of semi-marine to fluvial sediments, the ages of which vary from mid-Miocene (some 15 million years ago) to Holocene (Recent: Räsänen, Salo, and Kalliola 1987; Räsänen et al. 1995; Clapperton 1993; Hoorn 1993). These sediments may have had their origins in the eroding Andean slopes, in volcanic ash and lava, or in the old Guyanan or Brazilian shield areas (Räsänen 1993). Furthermore, the original physical and chemical characteristics of the sediments may have been altered in the process of recycling, in which once settled deposits are eroded and redeposited several times by rivers.

Historical processes may affect present species distribution patterns not only by affecting the environmental characteristics of habitats, but also by creating physical barriers to dispersal that promote speciation. Such barriers in the context of western Amazonia are thought to have been rather ephemeral on a geologic time scale, yet probably lasted long enough for speciation to take place. River channels and their floodplains are evident dispersal barriers (Hershkovitz

1969; Salo et al. 1986; Capparella 1988; Ayres and Clutton-Brock 1992), although their role in promoting speciation has been questioned (Haffer 1992; Patton and da Silva, chap. 7 in this volume). Savannas may have broken the continuous rainforest during phases of drier climate (Haffer 1969; Prance 1982a), although their existence has been severely questioned (Beven, Connor, and Beven 1984; Connor 1986; Colinvaux 1987, 1993, and chap. 6 in this volume; Salo 1987; Colinvaux, De Oliveira, and Bush 2000). It has been proposed that a long Miocene embayment traversed western Amazonia (Räsänen et al. 1995), but this may have occurred so long ago that its effects on species distributions are no longer evident.

On the basis of what we know or can deduce about environmental variation and landscape processes in western Amazonia, the region does not appear to be especially homogeneous, although it is not necessarily exceptionally heterogeneous either. Table 13.1 lists some examples of environmental factors that are often associated with the creation and maintenance of biogeographic patterns such as the distributions of individual species. In western Amazonia, both the actual landscape structure and the past environmental dynamics have varied to such a degree that it is conceivable that they have had biological consequences. Therefore, if one accepts that low beta diversity is a real phenomenon in Amazonia, one should also accept that more of its plants are generalists, in ecological terms, than elsewhere in the world. Unfortunately, there are rather few studies that have addressed this question in a quantitative way (Gentry 1988a; Clinebell et al. 1995; Duivenvoorden 1995; Tuomisto and Poulsen 1996; Ruokolainen, Linna, and Tuomisto 1997; Sollins 1998; Terborgh and Andresen 1998; Ruokolainen and Tuomisto 1998; Tuomisto, Ruokolainen, and Yli-Halla 2003). Consequently, opposing hypotheses exist about the role that environmental conditions play in explaining species distributions (Ashton 1969; Hubbell and Foster 1986; Gentry 1988a; Condit 1996; Pitman et al. 1999, 2001; Hubbell 2001 and chap. 4 in this volume; Condit et al. 2002; Condit et al., chap. 14 in this volume; Tuomisto, Ruokolainen, and Yli-Halla 2003).

INTERPRETING DIVERSITY AND SPECIES COMPOSITION

A general problem in interpreting regional species diversity numbers (gamma diversity) is that it is very difficult to separate the different factors that affect species diversity at such wide geographic scales. The same total number of species can be achieved by low local diversity combined with high site-to-site species turnover, or by high local diversity combined with low site-to-site

Table 13.1 Some environmental processes and their possible biological implications in western Amazonia

Environmental conditions	Possible biological implications	Should be addressed in research	Examples from western Amazonia
		Past	
Climate fluctuations	• Evolutionary processes • Species distribution patterns (gamma diversity)	• Time periods involved • Type and scale of change	• Climatic conditions during and after the Pleistocene (Clapperton 1993; Colinvaux 1993)
Geologic processes	• Evolutionary processes • Species distribution patterns (gamma diversity)	• Time periods involved • Type and scale of change	• Andean tectonics with sub- Andean sedimentation; weathering; marine transgressions (Räsänen et al. 1995)
		Present	
Climate patterns	• Species distribution patterns (gamma and beta diversity) • Landscape ecological phenomena	• Temperature and precipitation patterns • Seasonality and interannual variation	• Moist to seasonal forest formations (Pires and Prance 1985) • Influences of atypical weather conditions (friaje, El Niño)
Geologic patterns	• Species distribution patterns (gamma and beta diversity) • Landscape ecological phenomena	• Type and pattern of site conditions at different scales • Magnitude, direction, and rate of environmental change	• Biotopes related to geomorphology or physical and chemical soil properties (Ruokolainen, Linna, and Tuomisto 1997; Tuomisto, Ruokolainen, and Yli-Halla 2003) • Natural disturbance by fluvial activity (Salo et al. 1986)
Biological phenomena	• Biological interactions • Species distribution (alpha and beta diversity) • Population dynamics	• Energy flows and trophic interactions • Keystone species • Microsite conditions	• Dispersal ecology • Species interactions • Autecology of species

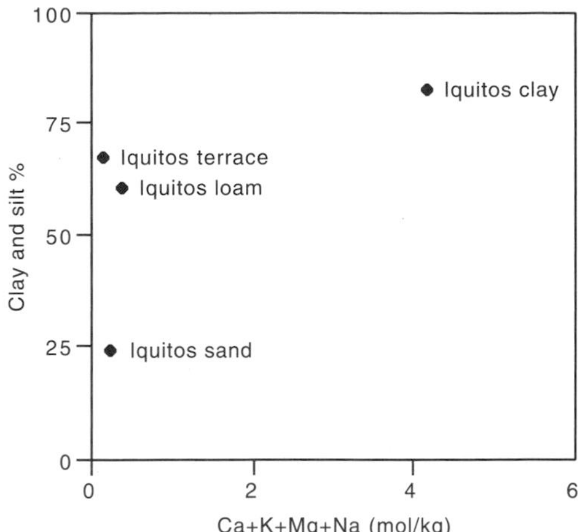

Figure 13.4 Mean soil characteristics in four geologically defined groups of study sites in the Iquitos region, Peru.

species turnover, or by any of numerous possible combinations of different alpha and beta diversity values (see also discussions in Condit et al., chap. 14 in this volume, and Tuomisto 1998). Furthermore, estimates of gamma diversity are distorted by unequal collecting activity. What does it mean to know that 200 species have been found in one area and 100 species in another, if we do not know how much effort has been put into looking for species in each area? The true species number could be anything above the reported number, and for all we know, the area that appears poorer in species could be the one that in reality is richer.

In view of the widely different regional species diversities reported above, and the problems in interpreting them, it would be interesting to know how species richness is distributed within those regions. Is the species richness of the forest relatively constant within a given region, or are there marked differences in the level of alpha diversity between sites? If the latter is the case, can the differences be explained by some ecological factors that characterize the sites?

To explore these questions, we have analyzed the floristic composition and species richness of our Iquitos and Yasuní data sets and compared them with what is known about the geologic background and soils of the study sites. In the Iquitos region, the thirty-two study sites can be classified into four groups according to their geologic background: (1) ten sites have clay soils mainly derived from the semi-marine Pebas formation, (2) nine sites have loamy soils in hilly terrain, (3) seven sites have loamy soils on river terraces, and (4) six sites have white sand soils. The fertility of the soils decreases in the same order (fig. 13.4).

In Yasuní, all twenty-five study sites are in hilly terrain with soil nutrient concentrations that are comparable to or higher than those in soils derived from the

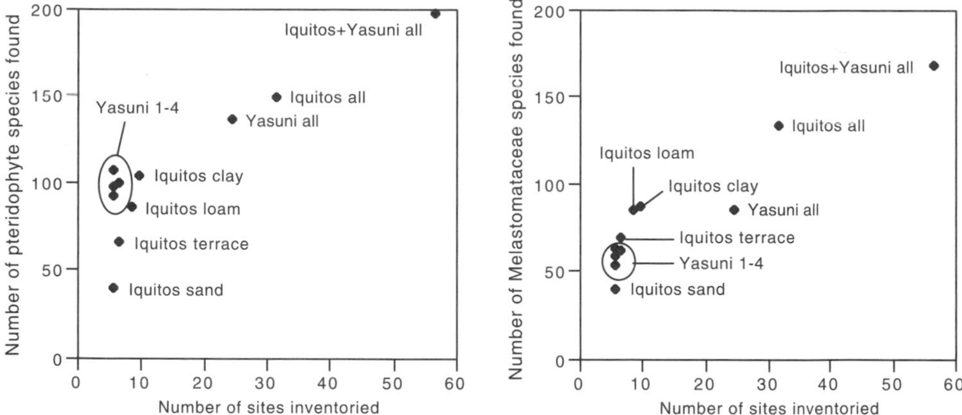

Figure 13.5 Number of pteridophyte and melastome species found in different sets of sites in Amazonian Ecuador and Peru. The Iquitos sites have been grouped into four categories on a geologic basis. The Yasuní sites, which have more uniform geology, have been randomly allocated to four sets in order to obtain comparable sample sizes.

Pebas formation. There are no obvious geologic differences among the sites inventoried in Yasuní, so for the purposes of data analysis in this chapter, the Yasuní sites were randomly allocated to four groups in order to obtain sets of sites comparable in size to those used for the geologic units in the Iquitos region.

In the case of pteridophytes, local species richness increases with soil fertility (fig. 13.5). With a comparable number of sites inventoried, the more fertile soils in Yasuní and Iquitos have clearly higher species numbers than the areas with poorer sandy and loamy soils. Consequently, variation in species richness among the samples is much more extensive in Iquitos than in Yasuní, although the difference in the total number of species found in the two areas is relatively small.

The diversity patterns of melastomes are clearly different from those of pteridophytes: the most species-rich groups of sites are those that have intermediate soil fertility levels, while the richest and the poorest soils harbor fewer species (fig. 13.5). It is noteworthy that the total number of melastome species found in Yasuní is about the same as that in either of the two most species-rich Iquitos landscapes, although the number of sites inventoried in Yasuní was much higher. The total number of melastome species found in the Iquitos region is almost twice as high as that in Yasuní.

With both pteridophytes and melastomes, there is a clear increase in the total species number when the species lists of Iquitos and Yasuní are combined (fig. 13.5). This increase is more pronounced with melastomes than with pterido-

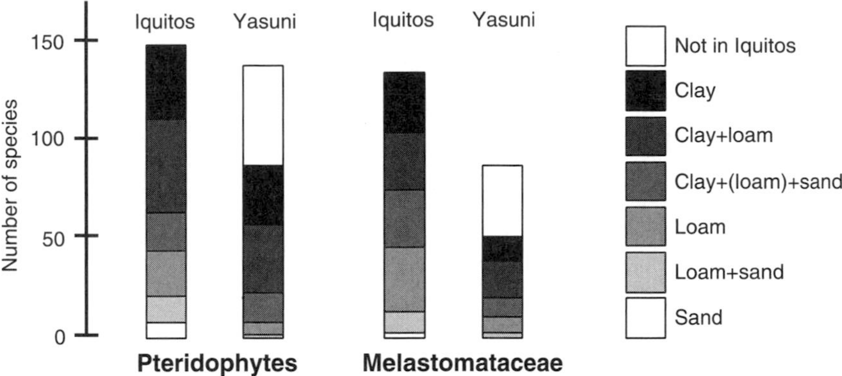

Figure 13.6 Frequencies of pteridophyte and melastome species with different edaphic distribution patterns in two study areas in western Amazonia. The edaphic classification of species is based on their occurrence at study sites with different geologic backgrounds in the Iquitos area, as indicated by the key at the right.

phytes. This pattern is also evident in figure 13.3, where it can be seen that, whereas the two areas share about 30% of their melastome species, they share almost 45% of their pteridophyte species.

On the basis of the edaphic characteristics of the study sites in Iquitos, it is possible to assign the observed plant species to several categories. For example, species that have been observed only on white sands can be considered specialists on poor sandy soils, and species that have been observed on either of the loamy soil categories, but not on sandy or clayey soils, can be considered specialists on intermediate loamy soils. Species with a wider ecological range can be found both on loamy soils and either sandy or clayey soils, and generalist species can be found on both of the extreme soil types, sand and clay.

Figure 13.6 shows the composition of the Iquitos and Yasuní floras in terms of these categories, and it can be observed that the spectra of the two areas are clearly different. Those species that in Iquitos are restricted to the poorest sandy and loamy soils are practically absent from Yasuní, while the proportion of species that prefer loamy to clayey soils is clearly higher in Yasuní than in Iquitos.

These results are in harmony with what is known about the soils in both regions. The Iquitos area has a wide variety of relatively poor soils, the like of which have not been found in Yasuní. On the other hand, the richest soils in Yasuní have clearly higher concentrations of cations than the richest soils of the Iquitos region (Tuomisto et al. 2003). If different substrates harbor different species, as has been indicated in earlier studies on pteridophytes and melastomes (Young and León 1989; van der Werff 1992; Tuomisto and Ruokolainen 1994;

Table 13.2 Matrix showing the similarities (measured with the Jaccard index) in the pteridophyte floras of eight sets of sites inventoried in Amazonian Ecuador (Yasuní) and Peru (Iquitos)

	Yas 2	Yas 3	Yas 4	Iqt cl	Iqt lo	Iqt te	Iqt sa
Yasuní 1	0.66	0.69	0.67	0.47	0.29	0.22	0.10
Yasuní 2		0.67	0.65	0.46	0.25	0.18	0.07
Yasuní 3			0.67	0.43	0.29	0.22	0.09
Yasuní 4				0.52	0.32	0.26	0.12
Iquitos clay					0.48	0.33	0.14
Iquitos loam						0.48	0.26
Iquitos terrace							0.38
Iquitos sand							

Table 13.3 Matrix showing the similarities (measured with the Jaccard index) in the Melastomataceae floras of eight sets of sites inventoried in Amazonian Ecuador (Yasuní) and Peru (Iquitos)

	Yas 2	Yas 3	Yas 4	Iqt cl	Iqt lo	Iqt te	Iqt sa
Yasuní 1	0.35	0.40	0.40	0.22	0.19	0.13	0.10
Yasuní 2		0.35	0.36	0.24	0.16	0.09	0.09
Yasuní 3			0.41	0.23	0.19	0.12	0.08
Yasuní 4				0.23	0.19	0.12	0.10
Iquitos clay					0.38	0.22	0.20
Iquitos loam						0.59	0.42
Iquitos terrace							0.45
Iquitos sand							

Tuomisto et al. 1995, 2002, 2003; Tuomisto, Poulsen, and Moran 1998; Tuomisto, Ruokolainen, and Yli-Halla 2003; Tuomisto and Poulsen 1996; Ruokolainen, Linna, and Tuomisto 1997; Tuomisto 1998; Ruokolainen and Tuomisto 1998), the floras of the Iquitos and Yasuní areas may differ simply for edaphic reasons.

This impression is strengthened when floristic similarity values calculated between pairs of samples are analyzed. Those samples with the most similar geologies are the ones that are also floristically most similar (tables 13.2 and 13.3). This finding is also reflected in the ordination diagrams, in which the increasing fertility gradient is clearly visible as an arc from left to right (fig. 13.7).

Spatial variations in the species compositions of pteridophytes, melastomes, and other trees (DBH $\geq$ 2.5 cm) have been shown to correlate with each other (Tuomisto et al. 1995; Ruokolainen, Linna, and Tuomisto 1997; Ruokolainen and Tuomisto 1998; Vormisto et al. 2000). Therefore, the floristic similarity and difference patterns among sites as indicated by pteridophytes and melastomes are

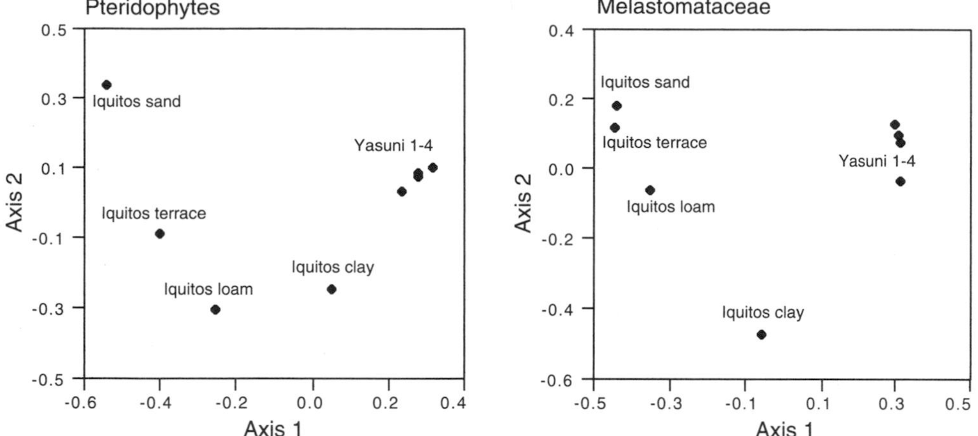

Figure 13.7 Floristic similarity map of eight geographic areas in Amazonia on the basis of their pteridophyte and melastome floras. The ordinations (principal coordinates analysis) are based on the similarity matrices shown in tables 13.2 (pteridophytes) and 13.3 (Melastomataceae).

probably directly transferable to the rest of the flora. However, patterns of species richness do not appear to be correlated between these plant groups, as the highest alpha diversities are found at different soil fertility levels. It can be postulated that since the local numbers of species of both pteridophytes and Melastomataceae seem to vary according to edaphic conditions, such variation is probably found among other plant groups as well. But since the species richness patterns are not correlated, knowledge of the alpha diversity of one plant group does not help in predicting the alpha diversity of another plant group (see also Tuomisto et al. 2002, 2003).

As these results draw attention to the importance of edaphic heterogeneity in plant distributions, they lend no support to the uniformity model. On the other hand, the observed variation in local species diversity makes it conceivable that the reported high alpha diversity values in western Amazonian forests represent rare exceptions. The number of local inventories in western Amazonia is so small in relation to the size of the area that it is possible that they give a biased estimate of average alpha diversity. Perhaps botanists have even deliberately sought for the most diverse forest patches for their inventories. There is certainly prestige in being able to report the most species-rich forest patch on earth, but it is rather difficult to estimate the number of tree species in a given hectare before the inventory has been finished. The only way to find out whether alpha diversity has been overestimated is to do more field inventories in such a way that the different edaphic conditions are well represented.

Not all aspects of species diversity and distribution can be explained by edaphic factors, however. Climate, especially the amount and seasonality of rainfall, is another important ecological factor, and the possibility that historical or biogeographic factors affect species diversity and distribution is always present. Unfortunately, these factors are much more difficult to study than edaphic variation (see discussion in Tuomisto and Ruokolainen 1997, and see Patton and da Silva, chap. 6 in this volume).

QUALITY OF ECOLOGY IS LIMITED BY QUALITY OF TAXONOMY

A temperate-zone botanist may take it for granted that vascular plant species can be identified with the help of field guides or other literature that provides species descriptions, illustrations, and identification keys. Not so in the tropics.

A lack of taxonomic literature leads to several kinds of problems in biodiversity research. First, species identification is laborious and expensive, as it has to be based on comparison of the specimens with vouchers in different herbaria. Second, identification errors accumulate when specimens that have been misidentified are used to identify later collections and there is no literature to check the identifications against. Third, usage of species names is not standardized, so researchers based in different herbaria may use the same name for different taxa, or different names for the same taxon. Fourth, a high percentage (commonly 20%–30% of trees: Campbell et al. 1986; Balslev et al. 1987; Maciel and Lisboa 1989; Cerón and Montalvo 1997) of the species in any inventory are likely to remain unidentified.

For all these reasons, lists of species names that have been produced by different researchers are not readily comparable. To obtain reliable comparisons of the floras of different areas, it is at present necessary to physically compare the specimens with each other, which of course is a rather laborious task and often quite difficult to arrange, as the specimens are scattered in different herbaria around the world. This situation leads to problems, for example, in estimating the degree of endemism in different areas, as species thought to be widespread may actually consist of a number of geographically separated species that have not been recognized simply because taxonomic revision has not been undertaken and the specimens have always been identified with the closest available name.

As an example of the importance of basic taxonomic work, the recent increase in the number of known *Danaea* species can be mentioned. *Danaea* is a fern genus that has not been monographed, so for a long time there has been uncertainty about the correct usage of names. In Peru, the genus has been reported to be represented by six species (Tryon and Stolze 1989). During our own field studies in Peru, we found two species that both key out to *D. nodosa* and three that key out to *D. elliptica.* A closer look at the material revealed that we had collected at least eight species of *Danaea* in Peru. Since only three of these were mentioned by Tryon and Stolze (1989), there are in reality at least eleven species of the genus in Peru.

The genus *Danaea* has also been treated in *Flora of Ecuador* (Tuomisto and Moran 2001); this treatment includes eighteen species, of which eight are described as new to science. Before this treatment, about thirty-five species of the genus had been recognized in the Neotropics. Since a monographic study has not been undertaken, it is not possible to estimate what the true number of species in this genus is. If other areas yield as many new species as Ecuador and Peru, the genus might be considerably richer in species than is commonly thought. On the other hand, a revision could reveal that some widespread species have been repeatedly described from different parts of their ranges. Resolving the synonymy of these species could again reduce the number of species, as has happened, for example, with some recent palm monographs (Barfod 1991; Henderson 1994).

CONCLUSIONS

In light of the above discussion, it is obvious that the level of current knowledge of plant species distribution and diversity patterns in Amazonia is far from adequate. Our Peruvian inventories, although covering only a small area, increased the number of species known in the department of Loreto by more than 15% over the recently published pteridophyte and Melastomataceae species lists. Our inventories included sites with different geologic histories and soil characteristics, and they clearly demonstrate that soil differences correspond to significant beta diversity, both locally and at the landscape level. However, the relative contributions of alpha and beta diversity to the regional or gamma diversity of western Amazonia remain uncertain.

The species diversity and compositions of different regions need to be compared for the purposes of developing ecological and evolutionary theory and planning landscape management and conservation. In order to be able to do meaningful comparisons, there should be at least a minimum amount of comparability in the sampling effort in the different regions, and the sampling should be such that the effects of the alpha and beta diversity components can be separated. Furthermore, if generalizations about regional species diversity are to be made, there should be some understanding of the degree of habitat heterogeneity and how it relates to beta diversity within the region. Until the full extent of beta diversity has been inventoried, estimates of gamma diversity must remain rather speculative. For all this work, basic taxonomic and nomenclature studies are a crucial prerequisite. There is a clear need to promote such studies in order to improve the basic knowledge of taxa on which the research of other disciplines depends.

Serious and extensive fieldwork is urgently needed if we want to be able to map correctly and understand even the most general biogeographic and biodiversity patterns in Amazonia. It is also imperative to take the limits of ecologically comparable patches into account when planning biological field research and extrapolating the results. Landscape ecological approaches can be used to focus fieldwork efforts on poorly inventoried areas and to evaluate the degree to which distribution and diversity patterns correspond to the predictions based on the available data. Until adequate knowledge of these basic aspects has been attained, it may not be relevant to concentrate too much on theories about the origin and dynamics of species diversity.

ACKNOWLEDGMENTS

We thank those numerous people who have participated in the fieldwork in Peru and Ecuador, as well as Universidad Nacional de la Amazonia Peruana and Pontificia Universidad Católica de Ecuador for logistic support. We are grateful to Peter Møller Jørgensen, who made the Ecuador checklist available to us before its publication.

14

Spatial Changes in Tree Composition of High-Diversity Forests: How Much Is Predictable?

RICHARD CONDIT, SALOMÓN AGUILAR, ANDRÉS HERNÁNDEZ, ROLANDO PÉREZ, SUZANNE LAO, AND CHRISTOPHER R. PYKE

ABSTRACT

Beta diversity refers to the change in species composition with distance. It is an important feature in theories of conservation biology, since it determines where protected areas must be located to include most species in a region. Yet it is poorly studied in tropical forests, where species' ranges are seldom known in much detail. In this chapter we report a study of the variation in species composition in tropical forest of central Panama, along a rainfall gradient and on a highly variable geologic background. Trees were censused in a total of thirty-six different plots, mostly 1 ha in size, but including three larger plots (4, 5, and 50 ha). The similarity in tree species composition between plot pairs declined with distance, both within the 50 ha plot, where distances were less than 1.2 km, and across the whole 55 km region. Plots more than 3 km apart nearly always had similarity scores less than 50%, and usually much lower. Thus, the only case in which two plots were similar in species composition was when they were close together. This decay with distance happened even when plots matched in geologic substrate, forest age, and total rainfall. Thus, geology, climate, and forest age all played some role in forest composition, but distance between plots was the strongest predictor of similarity. This finding suggests that forest composition is highly variable in central Panama, and is only partly predicted by substrate and climate. Abiotic features would be a poor surrogate on which to base conservation decisions in this area.

INTRODUCTION

Tropical forests are renowned for their alpha diversity. Very high numbers of species can coexist in small regions. Single hectares of forest can have three hundred tree species (Phillips et al. 1994; Valencia, Balslev, and Paz y Miño 1994), and 50 ha plots with over a thousand tree species have been censused (Romoleroux et al. 1997; Lee et al. 2002). Beta diversity is a much less studied aspect of tropical forests. How much does species composition change spatially? There is no necessary association between alpha diversity and beta diversity: there could be high numbers of species at any one site, but different sites could have the same complement of species. This is the pattern that Terborgh, Foster, and Nuñez (1996) described in tropical forest in Peru. Conversely, single sites could have few species, but adjacent sites completely different species. Forests of western North America are like this, with sites at different elevations having very different species, yet no one site having more than a handful of species.

Beta diversity is harder to document than alpha diversity because it requires many species inventories across a fairly large region. But from the perspective of conservation, beta diversity may be even more important than alpha diversity, because it speaks directly to which and how many natural areas should be protected. Moreover, beta diversity has much to say about the forces that organize community composition. Terborgh, Foster, and Nuñez (1996) used similarity in tree composition across sites to indicate that predictable, deterministic forces control species composition. Tuomisto and Ruokolainen (1994), Tuomisto et al. (1995), and Ruokolainen, Tuomisto, and Kalliola (chap. 13 in this volume) interpreted changes in species composition that were predicted by environmental features to support the notion that tree community composition is the result of predictable, niche-based forces. According to these views, within a given habitat, the same tree community will become established repeatedly and predictably, but in a different habitat, a different set of species will dominate. To the extent that habitat can be used as a predictor of species composition, conservation biologists can focus on preserving samples of each habitat to ensure maximum species protection.

Other views of tropical tree communities predict a different structure to beta diversity. If tree species are competitively similar, then their relative abundances will be determined entirely by dispersal limitation and by chance. Indeed, a quantitative community drift model predicts that all sites will differ in species composition, and that if dispersal is limiting, the difference will increase monotonically with the distance between sites (Hubbell 2001; Condit et al. 2002). If species composition changes independently of habitat change, then habitat preservation is a poor approach to conservation.

Condit et al. (2002) tested the dispersal model for beta diversity. Although dispersal alone predicted the qualitative form of the decay of similarity with distance in both Panama and in South America (Pitman et al. 1999, 2001; Condit et al. 2002), it was not adequate to predict differences among sites. In that analysis, and in that of Pyke et al. (2001), we inferred that climate or geology (and thus soil) must be at least partly responsible for the high species turnover in Panama relative to that in Amazonia. Here we examine explicitly how important geology, climate, and forest history are in predicting beta diversity. We compare species turnover across sites identical in habitat (geology, climate, forest age) to species turnover where habitat varies. In principle, with this kind of analysis, it should be possible to make quantitative statements about the relative contribution of deterministic and random forces in structuring the community. This, in turn, would let us judge how well a habitat preservation plan for conservation would protect the full complement of tree diversity in a region.

We carried out this study in central Panama, using three large plots (4, 5, and 50 ha) and thirty-one small (1 ha) plots. The 50 ha plot allowed detailed examination at a local scale of how forest composition changes with distance. The small plots were deliberately placed across geologic and climatic gradients (as in Gillison and Brewer 1985) in order to separate the effects of distance, geology, and climate on forest composition. Pyke et al. (2001) and Condit et al. (2002) analyzed the same data set.

STUDY SITE

The area of the Panama Canal is covered in substantial areas of natural vegetation: about half of the 300,000 ha of the canal's watershed is forested. Most of the remainder is grassland or cropland, including abandoned farms and active pastures mixed with sporadic tree cover. A strip of land on either side of the canal is forested, largely due to the presence of the U.S. military. On the east side of the canal, this strip forms two national parks, Camino de las Cruces and Soberania. There is also a large block of forest in Chagres National Park, a largely uninhabited and remote area east of the canal and east of Lake Alajuela (see Condit et al. 2001 and Ibáñez et al. 2002 for details on forest cover and park status).

Much of this forest, however, has been cleared and regrown over the past two centuries. Only a small area of forest near the canal is old growth, apparently standing in a relatively undisturbed state for more than 250 years. These patches of old growth are on Barro Colorado Island, where palynological evidence suggests there has been no human impact on the western half of the island for 600 years (Piperno 1990), and at Pipeline Road in Soberania National Park (between plots m20 and m16 in fig. 14.1). Chagres National Park is also mostly old growth, but most of the remaining forest near the canal is probably less than 150 years old, and some is much younger (Condit et al. 2000 and Ibáñez et al. 2002).

Annual rainfall even in the driest sites near the Panama Canal greatly exceeds evapotranspiration and is ample to sustain tall, moist, high-biomass forest.

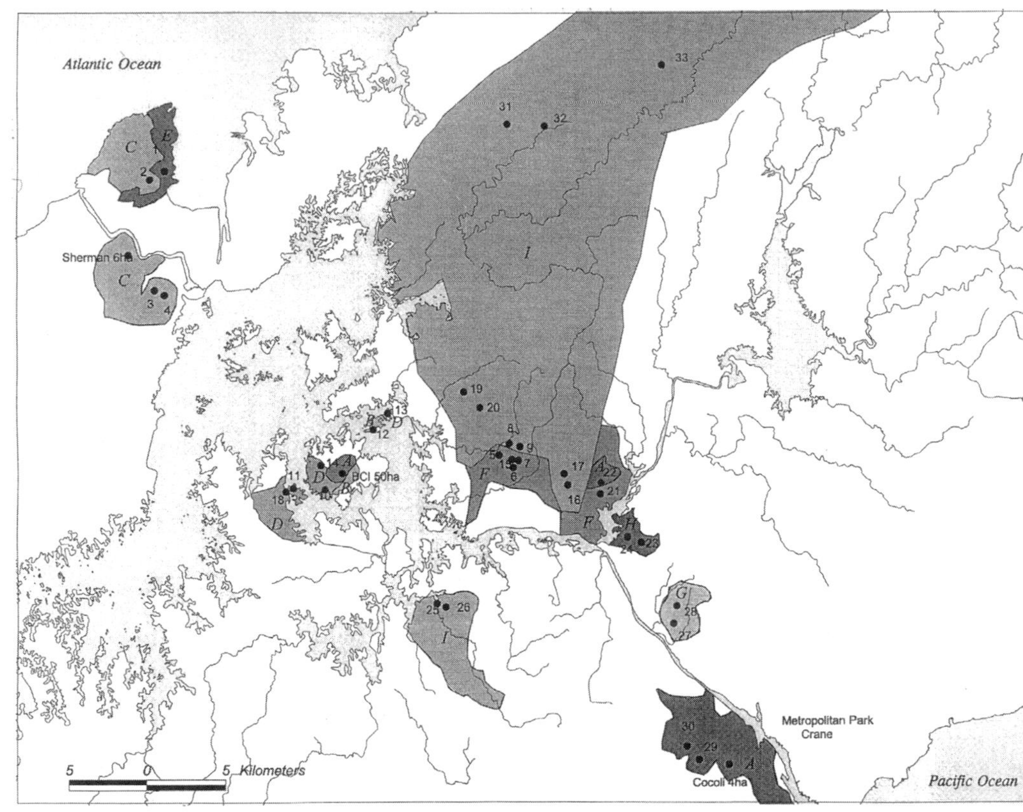

Figure 14.1 Map of plots and geology. The plot at Fort Sherman is 5 ha, and the separate hectares there are referred to as s0–s4 in the text and other figures. The plot at Cocoli is 4 ha, and these hectares are referred to as c1–c4. The six individual hectares from the 50 ha plot at Barro Colorado Island used in the landscape-scale analyses are designated b1–b6. The remaining plots are isolated hectares, and are designated L1–L4 and m5–m31; on this map, just the numbers 1–31 are used. Only geologic regions underlying plots are designated on this map: A = Miocene basalt; B = conglomerate of basalt and sandstone (Bohio Formation); C = Chagres sandstone; D = tuffaceous siltstone, sandstone, and limestone (Caimito Formation); E = Toro limestone; F = mudstone, siltstone, sandstone, limestone (Gatuncillo Formation); G = mudstone, siltstone, sandstone, tuff, limestone (La Boca Formation); H = agglomerate and fine-grained tuff (Las Cascadas Formation); I = pre-Tertiary basaltic and andesitic lavas and tuff (see Stewart, Stewart, and Woodring 1980 for further details). Lake Alajuela is the large lake east of the canal.

There is a long dry season, however, during which many trees lose all their leaves. Near the Pacific end of the canal, near Panama City, total annual rainfall is 2,000 mm, the dry season lasts 129 days, and more than 40% of the canopy is deciduous, but near the Atlantic, rainfall is 3,000 mm, the dry season is 102 days, and only 12% of the canopy is deciduous (Condit 1998a). A ridge 15–30 km east of the canal (around plot m31 in fig. 14.1) is far wetter, having a dry season of only 67 days and rainfall of 3,300 mm. The entire region is underlain by a complex geology, with a variety of rock formations in close proximity (fig. 14.1).

The forests of the canal area are well known floristically. According to the checklist for the flora of Panama (D'Arcy 1987, now computerized and updated), there are 863 tree species documented in the Panama Canal Zone, which covers about 125,900 hectares. A well-documented flora is a great advantage in studies of beta diversity, and we have been able to identify large numbers of trees over a wide area in a timely fashion.

METHODS

Forest inventories were done in thirty-one 100 × 100 m plots and two 80 × 40 m plots, censusing all trees 10 cm or greater in diameter at breast height (DBH). (Methods are described in detail in Condit 1998b.) If trees could not be named immediately, leaves were collected and compared with specimens in herbaria at the Smithsonian Tropical Research Institute and the University of Panama. In addition, we used data from a 50 ha plot on Barro Colorado Island (BCI) that was set up in 1981 (Hubbell and Foster 1983; Condit, Hubbell, and Foster 1995, 1996a, 1996b), a 5 ha plot near the Atlantic coast at Fort Sherman, and a 4 ha plot near the Pacific coast, on the Cocoli River (Condit et al., forthcoming). All stems of 1 cm DBH or greater were censused throughout these larger plots. In all plots, for all stems sizes, 286,829 individuals of 686 species were censused; 40,021 individuals of 517 species were 10 cm DBH or greater.

We report one set of analyses on forest composition within the 50 ha plot using all stems counted in the 1990 census (244,070 individuals of 1 cm DBH or greater). In the remaining analyses, we compare the composition of trees 10 cm DBH or greater across all 1 ha plots, plus six hectares of the BCI plot and individual hectares from Sherman and Cocoli (for a total of forty-six individual hectares). These forty-six hectares had 21,554 individuals and 493 species 10 cm DBH or greater.

Plots were located with the express purpose of examining how forest composition varies with distance, geology, climate, and human disturbance. To do so required estimates of forest age, a precipitation map, and a geologic map (Stewart, Stewart, and Woodring 1980). We categorized forest age as young secondary (largest trees < 50 cm DBH but with a canopy taller than 20 m), mature secondary (largest trees < 100 cm DBH), or old-growth (trees ≥ 100 cm DBH). We generated the precipitation map from data collected by the Panama Canal Commission at twenty-six meteorological stations, then estimated total annual rainfall at each plot by interpolating between the two nearest stations. Annual precipitation is highly correlated with the length of the dry season, which is probably the key limiting factor for tree distributions (Condit 1998a; Condit et al. 2000).

Plots were placed in local clusters, each of which served as one "experiment." Some clusters were placed so that all plots were in forest of approximately the same age, in close proximity so that rainfall did not vary, but on different geologic substrates. Other clusters were on a single rock formation at various distances from one another, or had different disturbance histories. This approach is similar to the "gradsect" design advocated by Gillison and Brewer (1985), since we positioned plots across gradients of precipitation, forest age, and geology.

Within the 50 ha plot, we also considered a finer habitat classification based on substrate. Each 20 × 20 m quadrat was classified as one of the following: swamp, a 1.2 ha region that is flooded with standing water most of the year; streamsides, regions within 20 m of small streams (1.9 ha); slopes, quadrats inclined by 7° or more (11.4 ha); and plateau, which is flat, nonflooded terrain. The plateau was subdivided into three sections: a 6.8 ha block in the eastern part of the plot that is at least 150 m above sea level, a 2.1 ha section of young forest, and a 24.8 ha western block that is less than 150 m in elevation. The remaining 1.8 ha of the 50 ha plot consisted of quadrats with a mixture of habitats, and these quadrats were not used in analyses. The habitats differ in soil moisture because of a perched water table that meets the surface along the slopes; the high plateau is farthest from the water table and thus driest (Condit, Hubbell, and Foster 1996a, 1996b; Harms et al. 2001). They also parallel geologic substrates: the plateau is a basalt cap at the summit of the island, which gives way to softer sedimentary rocks on the slopes.

One important shortcoming of the study is that the three independent variables—geology, climate, and forest age—often covary. Human agriculture is associated with drier climates and tends to avoid steep areas and rock formations that hold little water. Thus, forests on flatter areas closer to the Pacific side of the Isthmus of Panama are mostly young forests, with less than 100 years since major disturbances. Old growth occurs mainly on steep ridges and in wet sites. Also, the geology of the area is so complex that it is difficult to study sites at any great distance from one another that are on the same rock formation. Nevertheless, by deliberately placing plots near transitions in geology or forest age, we could test hypotheses about the effects of disturbance and geology on forest composition, and some clear results emerged.

Communities were compared using the Sørensen index of similarity calculated between pairs of square plots—either entire 1 ha plots, 1 ha quadrats within larger plots, or 20 × 20 m quadrats within the 50 ha plot. The Sørensen index is calculated as follows (Barbour, Burk, and Pitts 1987): Let x_i be the number of individuals of species i in plot 1, and y_i the number of individuals of the same species in plot 2. Call $\min_i$ the smaller of the two. Then the index is

$$\frac{\sum_i \min_i}{\sum_i (x_i + y_i)}$$

It is simply the proportion of individuals in each plot that can be matched (by species) with individuals in the other plot. All results presented here are very similar whether this similarity index or a version of the Sørensen index based only on presence-absence of species (Condit et al. 2002) is used.

RESULTS

Habitat and Distance Effects in the BCI Plot

Similarity between hectares in the 50 ha plot on BCI decayed with distance (fig. 14.2). Although there was scatter, the data are fit well by a logarithmic decay curve. Similarity between 20 × 20 m quadrats also declined logarithmically, and habitat differences were clear, although mostly very slight. Figure 14.3 shows similarity as a function of distance for quadrat pairs within the slope habitat as well as for pairs in which one quadrat was on the slope and one in a different habitat. (A graph based on plateau habitats was almost identical.) The swamp habitat stood out as very distinct from the slope, with similarities of less than 50% and with no distance effect. Differences between the slope and the other habitats were evident, but much less pronounced.

We can use figure 14.3 to make a quantitative assessment of the effects of habitat and distance on similarity, using the slope habitat as an example. When habitat was held constant—that is, when two quadrats on the slope were compared—mean similarity declined from 57% to 42% with distance. When distance was held constant, at 200–300 m, similarity between two slope quadrats was about 48%, while cross-habitat similarities were about 45%, except for the swamp, which had just 28% similarity to the slope. Thus, the distance effect on forest

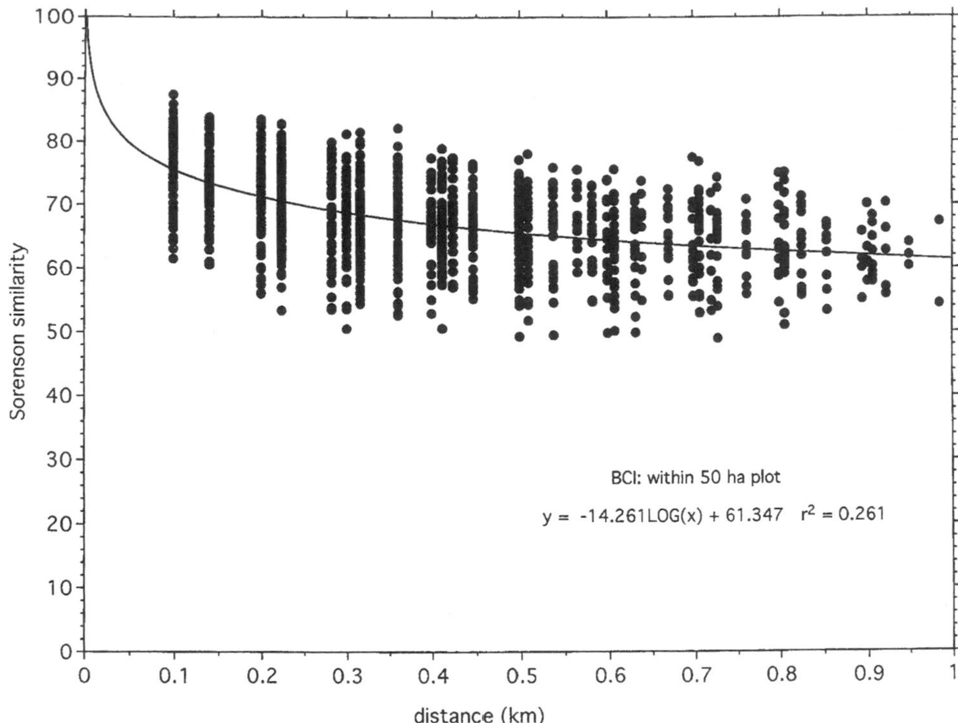

Figure 14.2 Similarity versus distance for all pairs of square hectares within the 50 ha plot at Barro Colorado Island, with only trees 10 cm DBH or greater included. There are 50 × 49/2 = 1,225 comparisons and thus 1,225 points on the graph. The curve through the points is the regression between similarity and the logarithm (base 10) of distance.

composition can be given as 15 similarity points—the change in similarity due to distance for a given habitat—while the habitat effect—the change in similarity with habitat at a given distance—was 20 points for the swamp, but only 3 points for the other habitats. Notice that most of the distance effect dissipated in less than 200 m, and that habitat effects were not evident beyond 500 m (except for the swamp).

Results comparing the plateau and streamsides to other habitats were quite similar to those shown for the slopes in figure 14.3; however, the swamp was qualitatively different. It had low similarity to other habitats, and to itself, and showed only very weak distance effects. We conclude that distance had a five times greater effect on tree species composition than habitat, at least for the slope and plateau habitats, which cover most of the plot. The swamp habitat was more distinct, however.

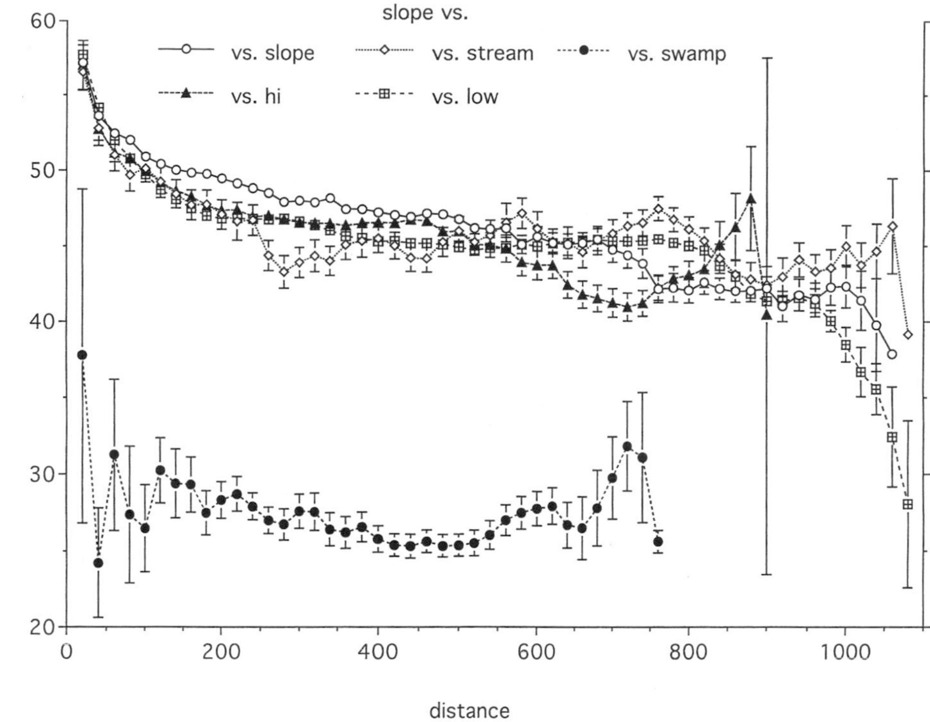

Figure 14.3 Similarity versus distance (m) for pairs of 20 × 20 m quadrats within the 50 ha plot, with all trees 1 cm DBH or greater included. Each point represents the mean similarity for a given habitat comparison, over a discrete distance range, starting with 20–39.9 m and continuing in 20 m brackets; confidence limits around each mean (calculated from a *t*-test) are given also. There are five curves on the graph, each for a different habitat comparison. The highest curve (open circles) is for comparisons of slope quadrats with other slope quadrats. The lowest curve (solid circles) is for comparisons of slope quadrats with swamp quadrats. Other curves are for slope quadrats versus streamside (stream), high plateau (hi), and low plateau (low) habitats.

Similarity and Sample Size

The mean similarity of adjacent 20 × 20 m quadrats, with all stems 1 cm DBH or greater included, was 57%. The mean similarity of adjacent 1 ha quadrats, with all stems 10 cm DBH or greater included, was 75%. Thus, similarity increased with the number of individuals sampled. We calculated the mean similarity for pairs of quadrats a fixed distance apart (500 m), but with varying quadrat size and DBH cutoff. Similarity increased with the logarithm of the number of individuals sampled. Thus, much larger samples yielded only slight increases in similarity; for example, while adjacent hectares were 75% similar, the two halves of the

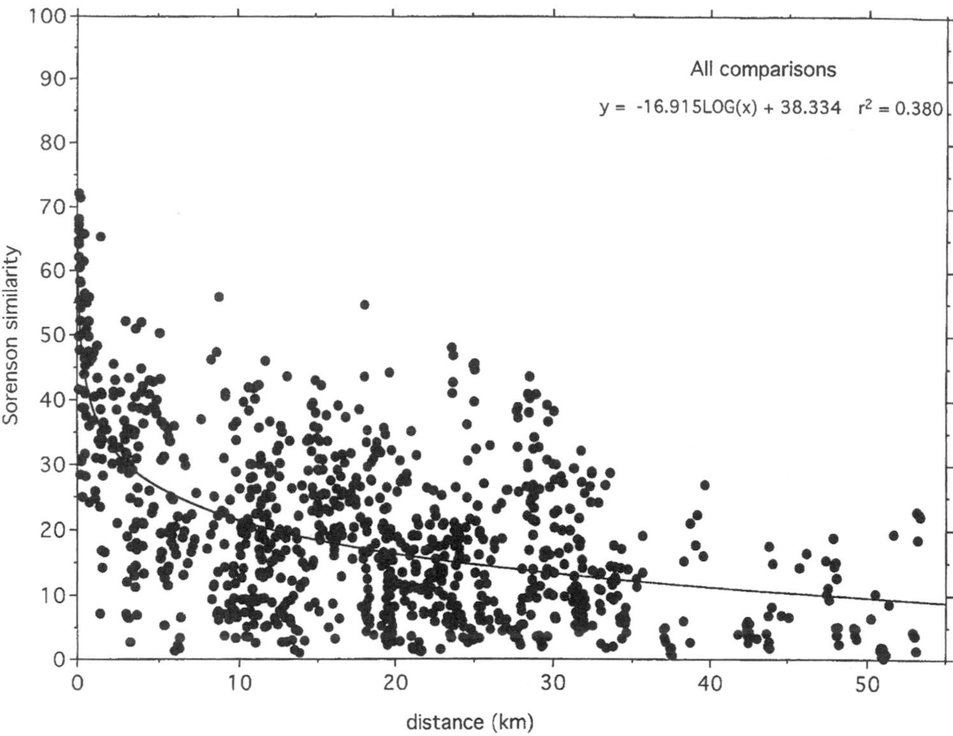

Figure 14.4 Similarity versus distance for pairs of square hectares, including thirty-one isolated hectares, four hectares at Cocoli, five hectares at Fort Sherman, and six of the fifty hectares at Barro Colorado Island, with only trees 10 cm DBH or greater included. There are 46 × 45/2 = 1,035 comparisons and thus 1,035 points on the graph. The curve through the points is the regression for similarity versus the logarithm (base 10) of distance.

50 ha plot had a similarity of 82%. Similarity was nearly independent of the DBH category used in the calculation when the number of individuals and distance were matched. For example, 20 × 20 m quadrats of stems 1 cm DBH or greater, 100 × 100 m quadrats of stems 10 cm or greater, and 250 × 250 m quadrats of stems 40 cm DBH or greater were roughly matched for stem number (195, 425, and 295 individuals, respectively). When separated by 500 m, the similarity indexes from pairs of each quadrat size were 45%, 53%, and 55%, respectively.

Similarity at a Landscape Scale

Similarity among 1 ha plots also decayed logarithmically with distance at much wider scales (fig. 14.4). Plots within 1 km of each other usually had simi-

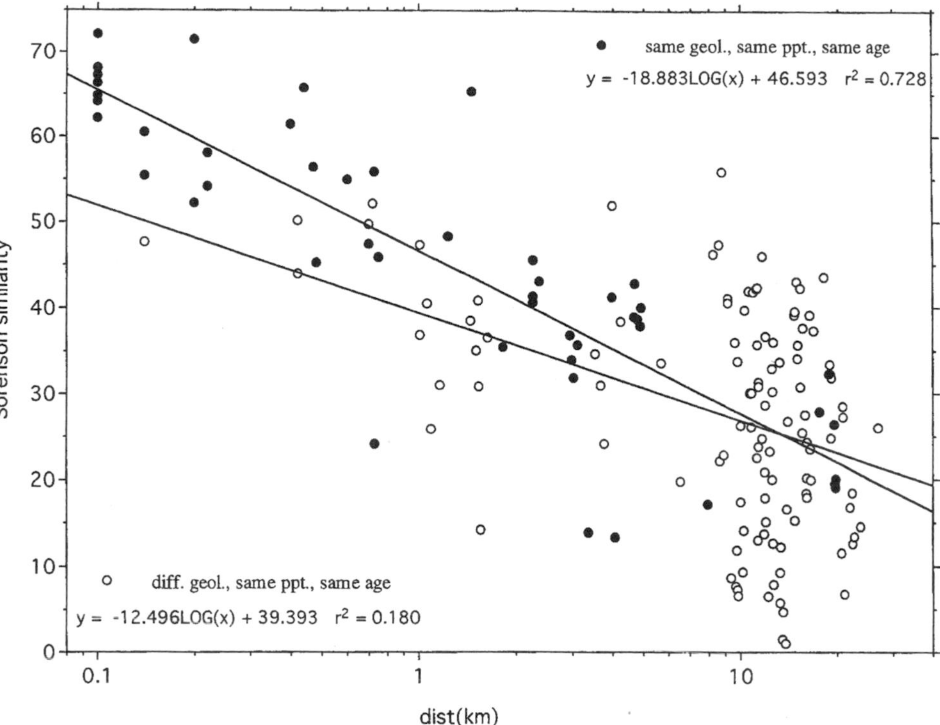

Figure 14.5 Similarity versus distance for some of the pairs from figure 14.4. Comparisons involving two plots, both of which are on identical geologic substrates, under the same climate (within 300 mm annual rainfall), and in the same forest age category, are shown with solid circles and fit by the upper regression line. Comparisons involving pairs of plots differing in geology but matching in climate and forest age are shown with open circles. The intercepts of the two regression lines do not differ significantly.

larities above 50%, but similarity declined quickly and was seldom above 50% in plots more than 2 km apart. Mean similarity fell below 30% at all distances beyond about 3 km.

How much of the decay with distance was due to habitat (geologic or climatic) differences? Figure 14.5 summarizes a test for geology. All pairwise comparisons involving two plots on the same geologic substrate, with the same precipitation (annual total within 300 mm of each other), and with the same forest age category are shown. Overlain are all pairwise comparisons of plots that differ in geology but match in precipitation and forest age. The regression for the first set is higher than for the second set, but the difference is not significant at the 5% level. The same test for forest age, however, did give a significant result (fig. 14.6),

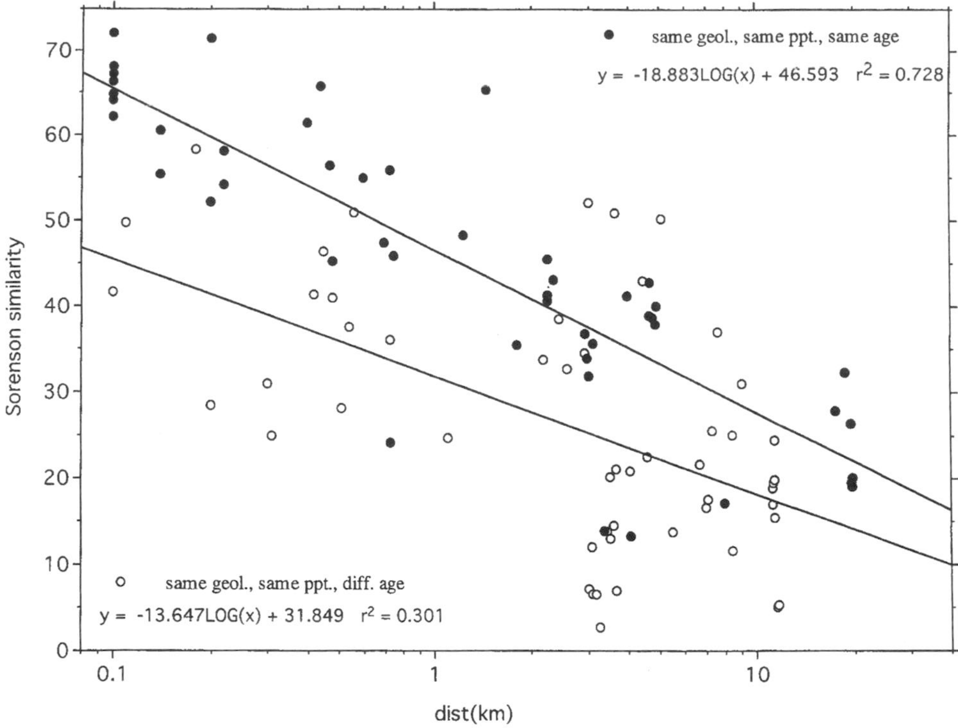

Figure 14.6 As in figure 14.5, but comparing pairs of plots in the same geology, climate, and forest age categories (solid circles) with pairs of plots that differ in forest age only (open circles). The intercepts for the two regression lines are significantly different ($p < .05$), with comparisons differing in forest age having a lower intercept. The four very low values within 1 km of distance are comparisons of plot s4 (young forest) with plots s0–s3 (old growth).

principally because young secondary forest was quite different in composition from mature forest.

A similar graph based on precipitation (not shown) showed that plots differing in rainfall (annual total differing $>$ 300 mm) were more different than plots with similar rainfall at distances of 10–20 km. It was impossible to assess a rainfall effect for plots less than 10 or more than 20 km apart, because in the former case, annual rainfall never differed by more than 300 mm, whereas in the latter case, other factors always differed. Regression lines for this test did not differ significantly, however.

Even if we accept the effects of geology, climate, or forest age as real, they are small effects. Plots separated by less than 3 km in matching habitat categories had similarity scores of 40%–70%. Plots separated by the same distance but differing in one of the three habitat characteristics had similarities of 30%–50%.

Plots differing in more than one habitat characteristic had similarities of 15%–40%. Moreover, even plots on identical habitat showed a decay of similarity with distance, and plots more than 7 km apart had similarity scores of less than 30% even when matching in all three habitat characteristics.

Local Plot Clusters

Examining all plot comparisons together mixes many different kinds of geology. Comparisons of local plot clusters offer a more powerful way to assess the importance of habitat characteristics because they were deliberately designed with that end in mind. Understanding the following examples requires close scrutiny of the geologic map and the plot locations (see fig. 14.1).

PLOTS M25 AND M26

Plots m25 and m26 were deliberately placed on a southern outcrop of pre-Tertiary lava, a rock formation that extends well to the north. The Pipeline Road plots (m8, m9, m16, m17, m19, m20) and plot m31 are on the same formation, but get much more rain, whereas plots m21–m24 get amounts of rainfall similar to m25 and m26, but are on a different geologic substrate. Plots on or near BCI (m10–m14 and m18, plus b1–b6 within the 50 ha plot on BCI) get more rain than m25 and m26 and are on different substrates.

Plots m25 and m26 were indeed more similar to the other plots on the same rock formation than to plots on different formations, even when distances were matched (fig. 14.7). Both plots were more similar to m8, m9, m16, m19, and m20 than they were to m21–m24, m13, m23, and b1–b6. There were some peculiarities that are not so easy to explain, however. Plots m25 and m26 were also quite similar to m6, m7, m15, and m16, even though the latter are on a different rock formation. And they were quite different from m17, even though m17 is on the same substrate as (and very close to) plots m16, m8, and m9.

Also striking in figure 14.7 is the similarity of plots m25 and m26 to the plots at Fort Sherman (s0–s3 and L2). In fact, except for their similarity to each other, m25 and m26 were more similar to s1–s3 than to any other plots, even though the Sherman sites are 30 km away. This finding suggests some sort of similarity in soils, but the Sherman sites are on a different substrate.

However, plots m25 and m26 were not particularly similar to any other plots. Their similarity to the Pipeline Road sites and the Sherman sites was less than 30%. Also, in this case, forest age and precipitation played no role in the similarities, or at least a minor role relative to geology. Plots m25 and m26 are on young secondary forest, yet were much more similar to older and wetter forest

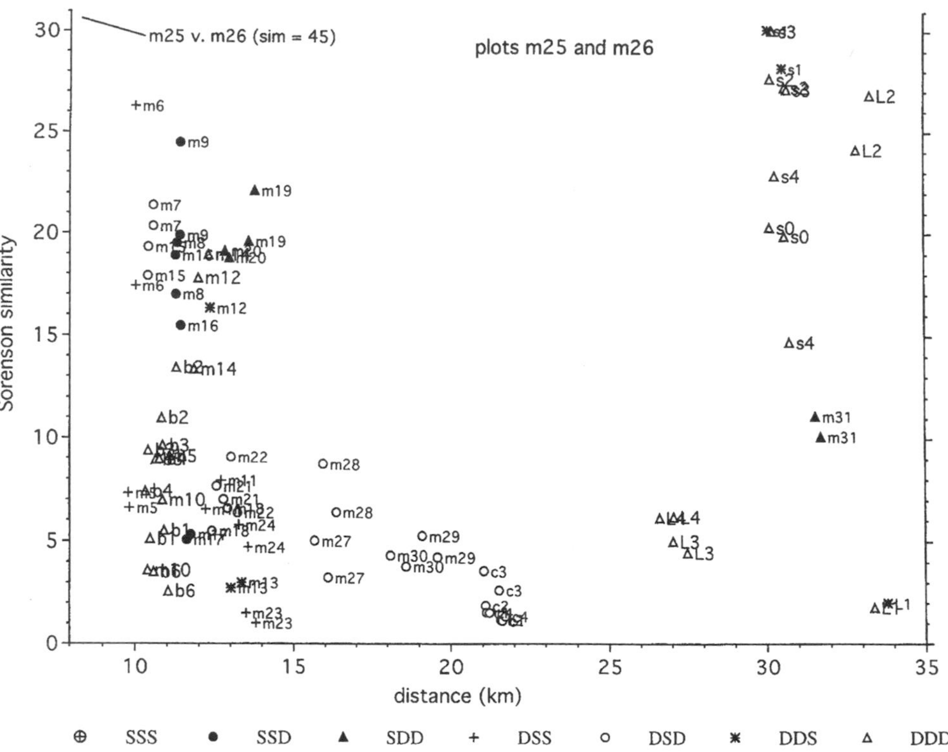

Figure 14.7 Similarity of plots m25 and m26 to all other 1 ha plots (including six from within the 50 ha plot on Barro Colorado Island). The different symbols indicate a habitat comparison for each plot, with the first of the three letters indicating whether geology is the same (S) or different (D), the second letter whether climate is the same or different, and the third letter whether forest age is the same or different: SSS = same geology, same climate (within 300 mm annual rainfall), same forest age category; SSD = same geology, same climate, different forest age; and so forth. Plots m25 and m26 are on pre-Tertiary lavas, which extend well north and also underlie plots m8, m9, m16, m17, m19, m20, and m31 (see fig. 14.1). They get 2,210 mm of rain annually and are in young secondary forest.

at Fort Sherman than they were to young forest on plots m21–m24, where rainfall is similar.

PLOTS M8 AND M9

Two plots at Pipeline Road, m8 and m9, are on the same rock formation as plots m25 and m26. But comparing them to other plots leaves a more equivocal picture (fig. 14.8). They were more similar to each other and to plots m19 and m20, on the same rock formation, than to any other plots (even though m19 and m20 are in mature secondary forest, whereas m8 and m9 are in old-growth forest). They were

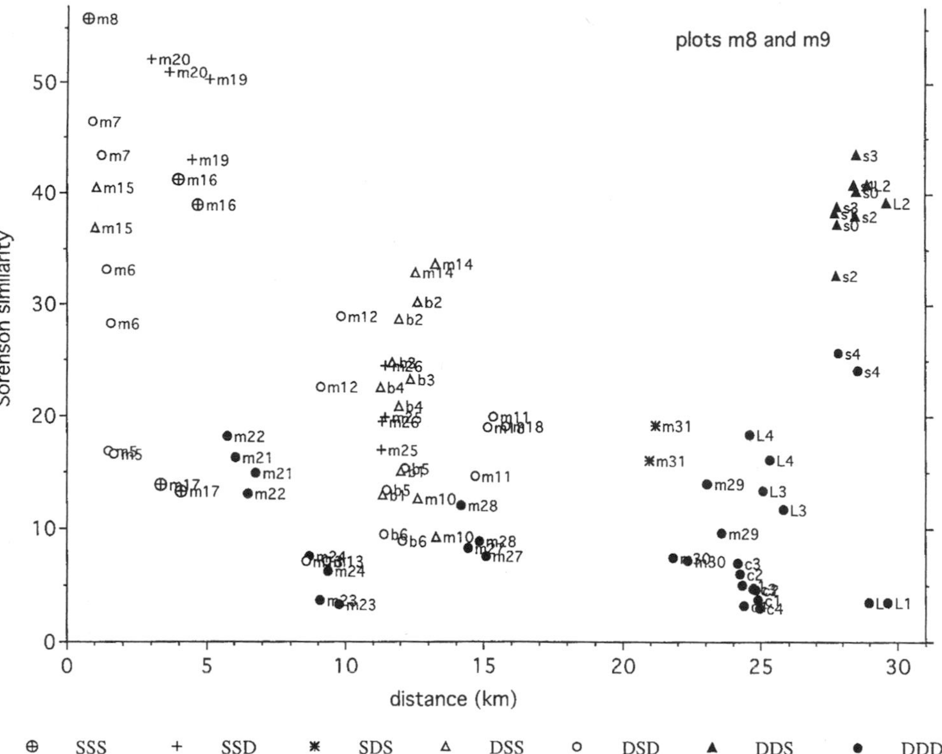

Figure 14.8 Similarity of plots m8 and m9 to other 1 ha plots. Abbreviations are as in figure 14.7. These two plots are on the same pre-Tertiary lavas as plots m25 and m26. They get 2,500 mm of rain annually and are in old-growth forest.

also similar to plot m16, on the same rock formation, but completely different from plot m17, m16's replicate. Plots m8 and m9 were quite similar to plots m7 and m15, even though they are on different rock formations. Beyond 10 km, plots m8 and m9 were more like plots on or near BCI, which have a similar climate but differ in geology, than plots m23, m24, m27, and m28, which get less rainfall. Plots m8 and m9 were remarkably similar to the plots at Fort Sherman, 30 km away—almost as similar as they were to sites within a couple of kilometers.

PLOT L1

Plot L1 was deliberately placed on a limestone formation near Fort Sherman because it is obvious that this formation carries a much different flora than anything around it. Large slabs of Toro limestone lie just at the surface, with virtually no soil. This site and several others like it in the canal area (but on different rock formations) are conspicuously deciduous in the dry season. Other plots at Fort Sherman have almost no deciduous species (Condit et al. 2000). Gentry (1982) commented on the limestone flora near the Panama Canal, although he worked on a rock formation near Lake Alajuela.

The similarity analysis bears out the distinctness of the forest on plot L1. Plot L2 is less than 2 km from L1, but the pair had a similarity of only 7%. Remarkably, L1 was more like the Cocoli forest, over 50 km away, than it was like any other plot. However, the latter comparison involved a similarity of only 23%, so L1 was also not much like anything else.

PLOTS M10 AND M14

Plots m10 and m14 are in old-growth forest on BCI, less than 2 km west of the 50 ha plot, but on a different rock formation. They were just as similar to the BCI plots on a different substrate, or in younger forest, as they were to each other (fig. 14.9). In this region, geologic substrate and forest age had no measurable effect on species composition.

Abundant Species

Variation in species composition can also be illustrated by examining the dominant species in the area, which were extremely variable from site to site. For example, *Faramea occidentalis* was the most abundant tree of 10 cm DBH or greater in the 50 ha plot on BCI (it ranked first in eighteen of the fifty hectares), but it was not top-ranking in any other plot and occurred in the top ten in just six out of thirty-eight hectares off BCI. *Quararibea asterolepis* ranked first in basal area in the 50 ha plot at BCI, and ranked in the top five in stems 10 cm DBH or greater in twenty-one of the fifty hectares, yet it did not reach the top ten ranks in any other plot. The top-ranking species in the 4 ha plot at Cocoli, *Calycophyllum candissimum*, was top-ranking at only one plot away from Cocoli (L1) and ranked in the top ten in just two others. No species ranked first in abundance in more than six of the forty-six hectares (only the palm *Socratea exorrhiza* ranked first in six plots), and no species appeared in the top ten ranks more than ten times (only *Socratea* made ten appearances).

Table 14.1 lists the top-ranking species in selected plots. For this comparison, we deliberately chose several plots that were most likely to be similar to one another: groups of plots that match in geology, climate, and forest age. In addition, plots m19, m20, s0, and s1 are compared because they had high similarity scores even though they are 30 km apart. It is clear that even at very nearby sites with

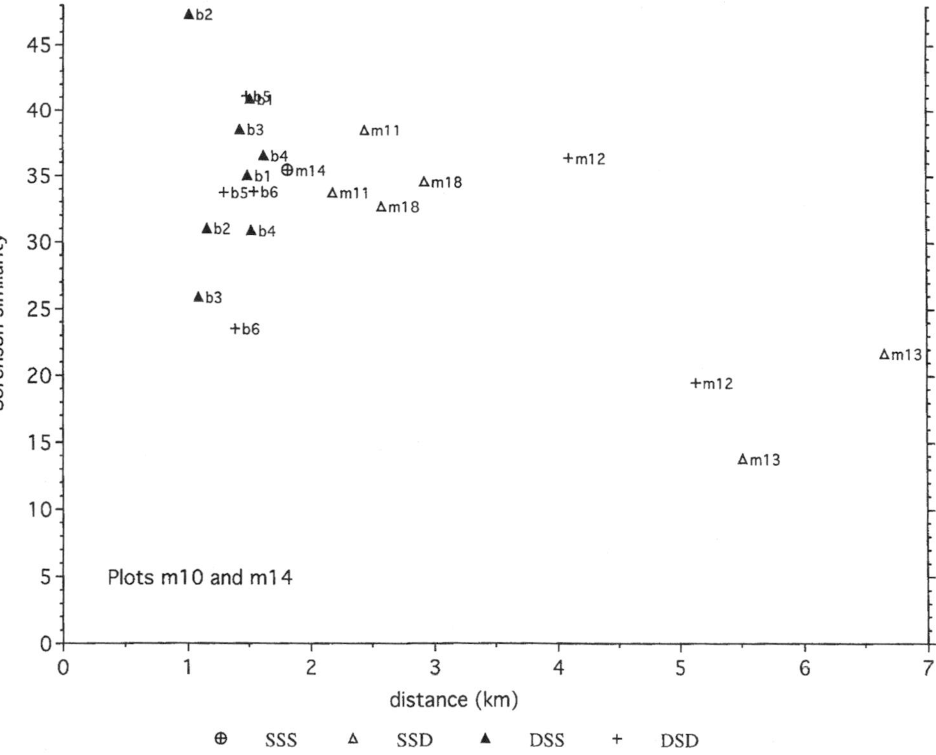

Figure 14.9 Similarity of plots m10 and m14 to other plots. Abbreviations are as in figure 14.7. Plots m10 and m14 are on Barro Colorado Island, west of the 50 ha plot, on the Caimito Formation. They get 2,580 mm of rain annually and are in old-growth forest.

the same geologic substrates and forest ages, the dominant species were not consistent in ranking. Indeed, only one pair of plots in table 14.1 shared more than half of their top ten species (s0 and s1 shared seven of ten). More typical are m29 and c3, only 2.3 km apart and on the same rock formation, but sharing just four of their top ten species. Plot m31 was included as the greatest contrast—the wettest site. The most abundant species there, the palm *Iriartea deltoidea*, did not occur in any other plot (though it is also the most abundant species of 10 cm DBH or greater in a large plot in Amazonian Ecuador: Romoleroux et al. 1997).

Range maps can summarize some key results, and figure 14.10 gives examples. *Tapirira guianensis* clearly shows the link among Fort Sherman and plots m19, m20, m8, m9, m25, and m26. *Bursera simaruba*, a familiar dry-forest species, appeared only in areas of less rain and on the limestone of plot L1.

Table 14.1 Top ten species (ranked by number of individuals ≥ 10 cm DBH) in selected plots

Plot	m22	m29	c3	m16	m19	m20	s0	s1	L2	m31
Precipitation	2,200 mm	2,030 mm	2,030 mm	2,330 mm	2,600 mm	2,600 mm	3,050 mm	3,050 mm	3,060 mm	3,350 mm
Forest age	Mature secondary	Mature secondary	Mature secondary	Old growth	Mature secondary	Mature secondary	Old growth	Old growth	Old growth	Old growth
Geologic substrate	Miocene basalt	Miocene basalt	Miocene basalt	Pre-Tertiary lavas	Pre-Tertiary lavas	Pre-Tertiary lavas	Chagres sandstone	Chagres sandstone	Chagres sandstone	Pre-Tertiary lavas
1.	*Swartzia*	*Heisteria*	*Anacardium*	*Poulsenia*	*Socratea*	*Perebea*	*Socratea*	*Socratea*	*Protium p.*	*Iriartea*
2.	*Astrocaryum*	*Anacardium*	*Calycophyllum*	*Gustavia*	*Perebea*	*Socratea*	*Brosimum u.*	*Marila*	*Morton iodendron*	*Socratea*
3.	*Faramea*	*Scheelia*	*Swartzia*	*Socratea*	*Malouetia*	*Dendropanax*	*Marila*	*Tovomita*	*Virola s.*	*Welfia*
4.	*Scheelia*	*Antirhea*	*Trichilia p.*	*Heisteria*	*Marila*	*Malouetia*	*Perebea*	*Perebea*	*Tetragastris*	*Pithecellobium*
5.	*Oenocarpus*	*Luehea*	*Protium t.*	*Oenocarpus*	*Virola s.*	*Tapirira*	*Theobroma*	*Brosimum u.*	*Perebea*	*Cassipourea*
6.	*Cryosophila*	*Calycophyllum*	*Brosimum a.*	*Perebea*	*Maranthes*	*Oxandra*	*Tapirira*	*Tapirira*	*Socratea*	*Eschweilera*
7.	*Protium t.*	*Guarea gl.*	*Posoqueria*	*Brosimum l.*	*Brosimum g.*	*Oenocarpus*	*Dendropanax*	*Aspidospermum*	*Heisteria*	*Tovomita*
8.	*Alseis*	*Oenocarpus*	*Scheelia*	*Trichilia t.*	*Tapirira*	*Poulsenia*	*Cespedezia*	*Vochysia*	*Brosimum g.*	*Cespedezia*
9.	*Cavanilesia*	*Coussarea*	*Antirrhea*	*Virola s.*	*Aspidospermum*	*Pourouma*	*Guatteria*	*Dendropanax*	*Hirtella*	*Pouteria*
10.	*Brosimum a.*	*Tetrathylacium*	*Faramea*	*Alseis*	*Brosimum l.*	*Marila*	*Tovomita*	*Manikara*	*Manikara*	*Virola k.*

Note: Plot locations are shown in figure 14.1. Only generic names are given except for *Brosimum, Guarea, Protium, Trichilia,* and *Virola,* which have multiple species in the table; their species' initials are included.

DISCUSSION

Beta diversity in Panama forest is high. Condit, Hubbell, and Foster (1996c) noticed that 50 ha of forest in Malaysia has three times as many tree species as 50 ha in Panama, but that the entire nation of Panama has about the same number of tree species as the Malay Peninsula (in about the same land area). Condit et al. (2002) documented elevated beta diversity in Panama relative to South America. Our current results give some insight into this beta diversity. A highly varied geology and climate in Panama certainly plays a role in species turnover, but we also see evidence of unexplained, apparently random, turnover in species composition.

The clearest indication of a habitat effect is the similarity between plots m25 and m26 and other plots on the same rock formation, but at some distance. Other examples of unusually high similarity at considerable distance are the plots at Fort Sherman (s0–s3) compared with those at Pipeline Road (m8, m9, m19, m20) and the limestone plot L1 compared with sites at Cocoli (c1–c4) across the isthmus. These two examples do not involve matched geology, but the similarity of these distant plots suggests that substrate is playing a role in community composition. Further knowledge about soils ought to support the substrate connections, and our vegetation data provide working hypotheses on which to base soil tests. We have two favored hypotheses: One is that soils on the pre-Tertiary basalt at Pipeline Road and at plots m25 and m26 are deeper, or hold water more effectively, than other soils in the area, and thus carry a number of species from wetter regions, even though they get no more rain than BCI. The second hypothesis is that the pre-Tertiary basalt produces a nutrient-poor soil, and the flora associated with it is not specialized for moisture, but rather for poor soil. A recent evaluation of the water-releasing capacities of soils (T. Kursar and B. Engelbrecht, personal communication) favors the former hypothesis: soils near plots m25 and m26 have more water available to trees at a given water volume than soils on BCI. Fort Sherman has a flora similar to that on the pre-Tertiary basalt; its water-releasing capacity and its nutrient status will also be important in distinguishing between the two hypotheses.

Aside from the Toro limestone supporting a deciduous forest and the pre-Tertiary basalt supporting a moisture-dependent flora, there is little indication of an effect of geology on forest composition. Different geologic formations around BCI and various formations south of plots m21 and m22 did not have any obvious effect on species composition. This is presumably why the overall test of the effect of geology gave an insignificant result.

Forest age showed a significant effect on species composition. Our impression

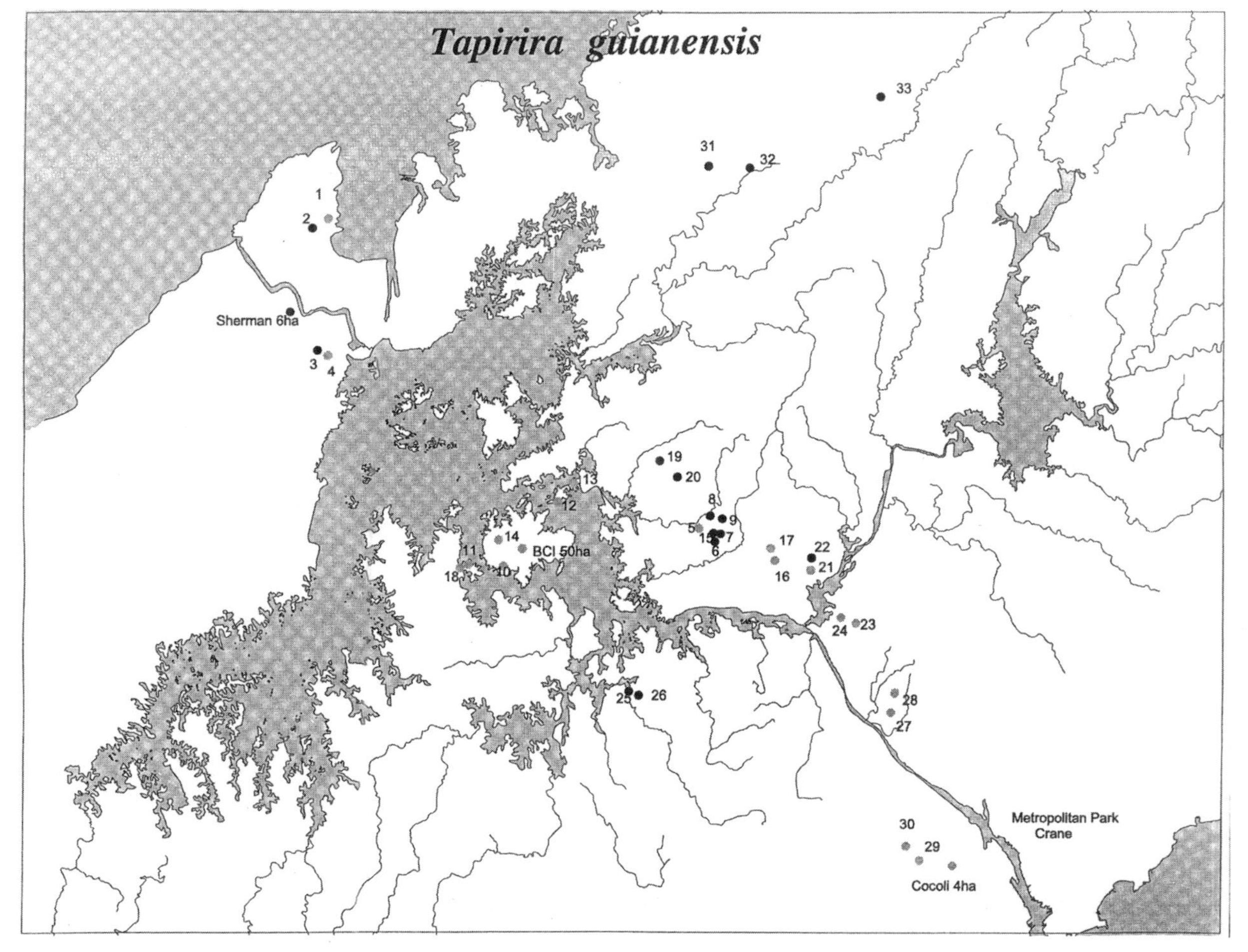
Tapirira guianensis
Sherman 6ha
BCI 50ha
Metropolitan Park
Crane
Cocoli 4ha

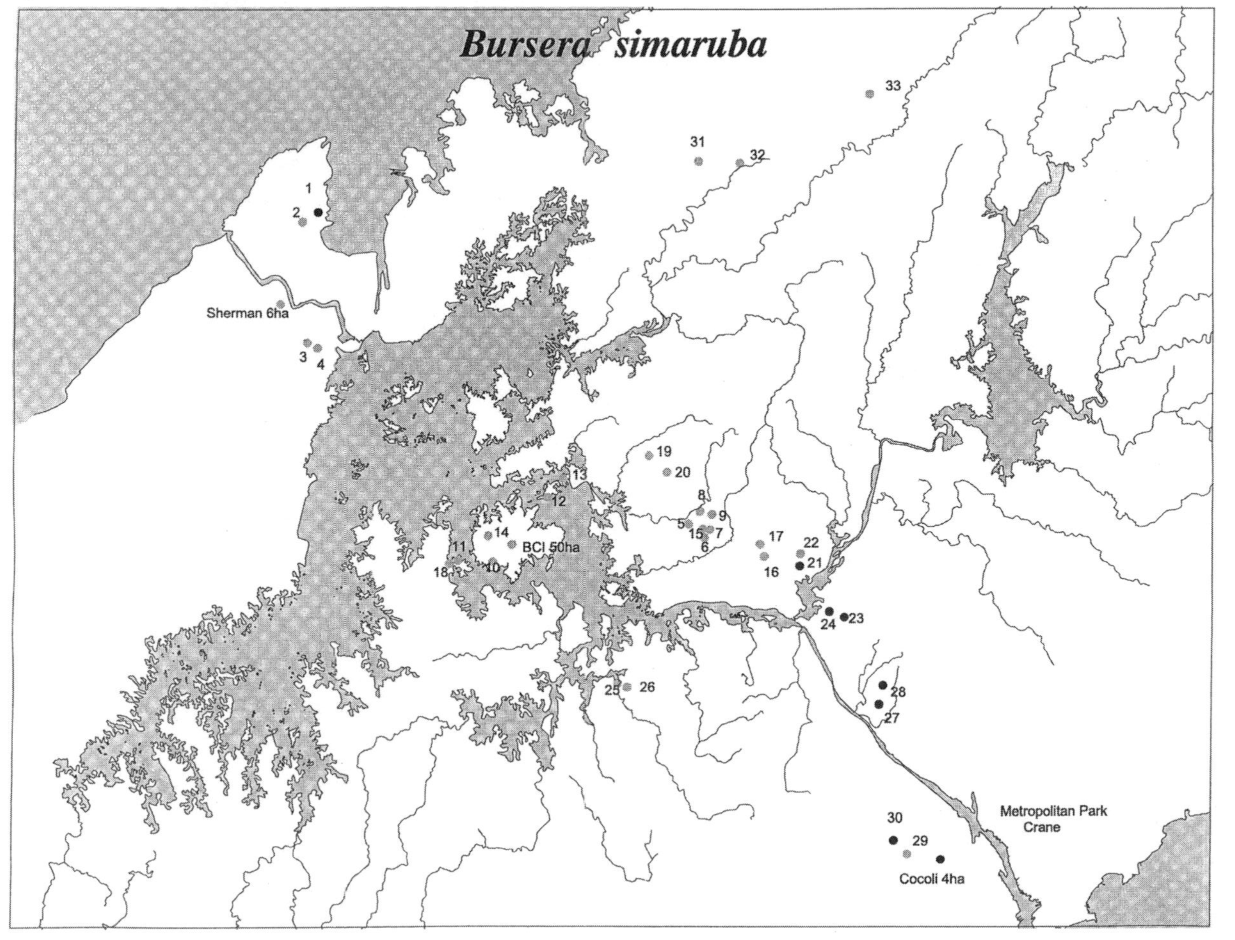

Figure 14.10 Range maps of selected species. Plots where a species was found are indicated by solid circles, and where it was not found by shaded circles.

is that this effect is mostly due to young forest having a distinct composition, especially in plots s4, m12, and m13. In comparisons involving mature secondary and old-growth forest (e.g., m10 and m14 versus nearby plots), forest age had no effect. Despite its distinctiveness, we doubt that young forest contributes much to beta diversity because it mostly harbors a consistent set of widespread invasive trees; however, we have not tested this hypothesis with the data.

The effect of climate was not clearly discernable in our data, probably because nearly all sites that differ in climate also differ in geology. In some conspicuous cases, the effect of geology overrode any effect of forest age or precipitation on species composition. But we certainly do not reject any role for climate. Indeed, one of our hypotheses is that the main effect of geology, and thus soils, on forest composition acts through moisture-holding capacity or soil depth, which obviously interacts with climate. Sollins (1998) reviewed eighteen studies on the importance of soils to tropical forest composition and found that edaphic factors—drainage and topography—had the greatest effects, as opposed to soil chemistry. In Pyke et al.'s (2001) ordination analysis of our data set, climate does prove to be an important factor predicting species composition. Ruokolainen, Tuomisto, Chave et al. (2002) offer more discussion of the effect of climate on tree species composition in this data set.

Despite these habitat effects on forest composition, we must emphasize that distance alone accounts for fairly high species turnover, and that the predictability of forest composition is low (but see Ruokolainen, Tuomisto, Chave et al. 2002). In fact, there is only one way to make a firm prediction about which species will be found at a new site: do an inventory next to the site. Nearby sites usually had forests of 60%–70% similarity. No sites more than a couple of kilometers apart had scores this high, and most had much lower similarity. Even plots with matching substrates, matching forest ages, and similar precipitation levels had low similarity when more than a few kilometers apart. Table 14.1 shows that dominant species were seldom the same, and is meant as a contrast to Terborgh, Foster, and Nuñez's (1996) table of abundant species for Peru. They found that plots 30 km apart in floodplain forest always shared six to eight of their ten most abundant tree species. Here in central Panama, even nearby sites seldom shared more than five of their top ten species. Forest composition in this part of Panama is evidently more variable than in Peru, even when fairly similar substrates and climates are deliberately selected (Pitman et al. 1999, 2001; Condit et al. 2002).

We recognize, though, that our analysis of substrate and other habitat variables is preliminary. We assumed that forests growing on the same rock formation experience similar soil conditions, and there are reasons to be cautious about this assumption. First, some of the formations are mixtures of rocks, and different sites within a formation may thus expose different rocks. Second, we have ignored topographic position and how it affects soil (Johnsson and Stallard 1989; Silver et al. 1994). We have topographic data for each plot, and a digital elevation map for the entire region is now done (R. Stallard, personal communication); T. Kursar and B. Engelbrecht (personal communication) have begun soil analyses. We intend to assemble this information, along with precipitation data, into a more complete model of tree species distributions. A similar approach has been used successfully for modeling forest structural types in the tropics (Mackey 1993; Mackey and Su, chap. 11 in this volume) and for modeling species distributions in other systems (Miller 1994; Cherrill et al. 1995; Sanderson et al. 1995).

At any rate, we feel that our results demand a pluralistic view about the forces that structure tree species composition in the tropics. Earlier studies seem to have emphasized what is predictable from simple habitat considerations, but have ignored what is not predictable (Hall and Swaine 1981; Baillie et al. 1987; ter Steege et al. 1993; Tuomisto and Ruokolainen 1994; Tuomisto et al. 1995; Terborgh, Foster, and Nuñez 1996). We believe that random forces and dispersal limitation are also important components of tree species composition in the tropics, along with niche differences among species and habitat differences.

Recently Ando et al. (1998), Pimm and Lawton (1998), and Van Jaarsveld et al. (1998) discussed the importance of species ranges and beta diversity in conservation. In the tropics, data on species ranges are scarce and usually have poor resolution. In central Panama, however, we now have sufficient information to examine how efficiently different arrangements of national parks would protect tree species. We know, for example, that plots L1, m25, m26, and m31 have unusual flora for the area, with species assemblages not seen elsewhere near the canal. Plots L1 and m31 were most unusual—their maximum Sørensen scores when compared with other plots were each 23%. In terms of localized species, however, plot m31 was by far the champion: it added 83 species to the data set (that is, the data set without m31, including all fifty hectares from the large plot on BCI, had 434 species, while with m31 added there were 517 species). Plot L1 added just three species, and plots m25 and m26 added five and seven species respectively. Since new parks may still be created in the canal area, we have an opportunity to influence conservation policy with good scientific information. Plot m31 is not currently in a protected area, and this part of the Santa Rita Ridge clearly merits some consideration in terms of plant species protection. Plots L1, m25, and m26 are also unprotected.

Perhaps more importantly, we would like to contribute to broader theories about beta diversity in species-rich forests in order to develop general policies for species preservation throughout the tropics. Results from the canal area of Panama suggest that the tree species composition of tropical forests can be predicted by abiotic features to only a limited extent, while much is unpredictable. This conclusion has important implications, for it suggests that conservation plans cannot simply be based on habitat designations. Because there is substantial species turnover within habitats, one cannot protect one section of a given habitat and hope to conserve most of the species found across that habitat. This conclusion is analogous to the growing concern about the use of "indicator" groups to designate conservation areas, since many studies to date show poor correlations between the distributions of species in one group, such as birds, and those in another group, such as plants (Wilcox et al. 1986; Kremen 1992; Balmford and Long 1995; Oliver, Beattie, and York 1998). Our parallel conclusion is that species distributions among tropical trees correlate poorly with abiotic habitat designations. If indicator groups or habitats do not work, conservation planning must be based on more empirical data on the ranges of individual species.

ACKNOWLEDGMENTS

The extensive botanical experience of R. Foster in Panama was crucial to this study, since most of us have trained with him in the field. We also thank S. Hubbell and R. Foster for initiating the 50 ha plot at BCI, the Smithsonian Tropical Research Institute and the National Science Foundation for supporting it, and dozens of field biologists for work in all the plots. The work in small plots was supported by the Department of Defense Legacy Program and the United States Agency for International Development, as well as the Smithsonian Tropical Research Institute. We also thank the organizers of the symposium "Tropical Rainforests: Past and Future" (C. Moritz and E. Bermingham) and the sponsoring bodies (STRI/CRC) for the opportunity to present this information.

15
The El Niño Southern Oscillation Influences Tree Performance in Tropical Rainforests

S. JOSEPH WRIGHT

ABSTRACT

The El Niño Southern Oscillation (ENSO) is the major cause of interannual climatic variation in the tropics (Ropelewski and Halpert 1987; Aceituno 1988; Kiladis and Diaz 1989). This chapter synthesizes the responses of tropical vegetation to ENSO-related climatic variation, with an emphasis on lowland rainforests in wet and superwet climates (*sensu* Walsh 1996a). The El Niño Southern Oscillation and its influence on global tropical climates are first described. Climatic factors limiting tropical vegetation are then reviewed. This discussion provides a framework for predicting the responses of tropical vegetation to ENSO-related climatic variation. Finally, these predictions are evaluated against plant performance observed during recent El Niño events. Indirect effects on animal herbivores are also considered.

INTRODUCTION

The El Niño Southern Oscillation

An understanding of the El Niño Southern Oscillation begins with the "normal" pattern of atmospheric circulation over the equatorial Pacific, known as the Walker Circulation (Glantz 1996). At sea level, westerly trade winds move warm surface waters across the Pacific. A large pool of warm water accumulates at the surface in the western Pacific, and cold subsurface waters upwell to the surface in the eastern Pacific. Warm surface waters heat the lower atmosphere in the western Pacific. The warm, moist air rises, causing high rainfall and low sea-level atmospheric pressures. The now dry air moves eastward. Cool, dry air finally descends or subsides in the eastern equatorial Pacific. Its descent suppresses rainfall and increases sea-level atmospheric pressures in the eastern Pacific. This "normal" pattern of atmospheric pressures oscillates with a pronounced 24-month periodicity (Rasmusson, Wang, and Ropelewski 1990). The Southern Oscillation Index (SOI), which quantifies this oscillation, equals the difference in standardized atmospheric pressures between Tahiti and Darwin, Australia.

Extreme values of the SOI occur at irregular multi-year intervals and are associated with El Niño (negative SOI) and La Niña (positive SOI) events.

The Walker Circulation is greatly altered during El Niño events. Initially, the westerly trade winds weaken and, in the west, even reverse direction. This shift permits the warm surface waters that are "normally" concentrated in the western Pacific to spread eastward. Sea surface temperatures become unusually warm in the central and eastern Pacific by April or May (or even as late as August) of an El Niño year. Convective activity increases with sea surface temperatures, and heavy rainfall soon affects the central Pacific, the Galápagos Islands, and coastal Peru and Ecuador. In the west, sea surface temperatures and convective activity decline, and drought affects Indonesia and Australia.

El Niño events also affect climates remote from the equatorial Pacific. Meteorologists use the term "teleconnection" to refer to an association between climatic anomalies at remote locations. El Niño teleconnections have been established by examining long-term climate records from thousands of meteorological stations (Ropelewski and Halpert 1987, 1989; Aceituno 1988; Kiladis and Diaz 1989; Diaz and Kiladis 1992). Teleconnections are probabilistic in the sense that the associated climatic anomalies co-occur with a prescribed probability. For example, Ropelewski and Halpert (1989) accepted a teleconnection when a remote climatic anomaly co-occurred with 70% of El Niño events. The probabilistic nature of teleconnections qualifies any evaluation of El Niño effects at sites remote from the equatorial Pacific. The occurrence of an El Niño event is insufficient. Rather, an El Niño event and the relevant teleconnection must co-occur to predict local vegetation responses at sites remote from the equatorial Pacific. This caveat holds throughout this chapter.

El Niño teleconnections influence most tropical climates. Temperatures increase by 0.5°C to 1°C throughout the tropics several months after sea surface temperatures peak in the central and eastern Pacific (fig. 15.1). Reduced cloudiness and increased solar inputs contribute to this small but widespread increase in temperature (Aceituno 1988; Kiladis and Diaz 1989; Diaz and Kiladis 1992). El Niño events bring below-average rainfall to southern Central America, northern South America, the Amazon, Malesia, New Guinea, northern Australia, equatorial west Africa, and parts of India (fig. 15.2). El Niño events also bring above-average rainfall to southeastern Brazil, northern Mexico, and arid parts of equatorial Africa (fig. 15.2). To summarize, El Niño events tend to bring reduced cloudiness and rainfall and increased solar irradiance to the wet and superwet equatorial tropics and increased rainfall to the subtropics and to some of the more arid areas within the equatorial tropics. The global teleconnections of La Niña events are generally opposite to those of El Niño events.

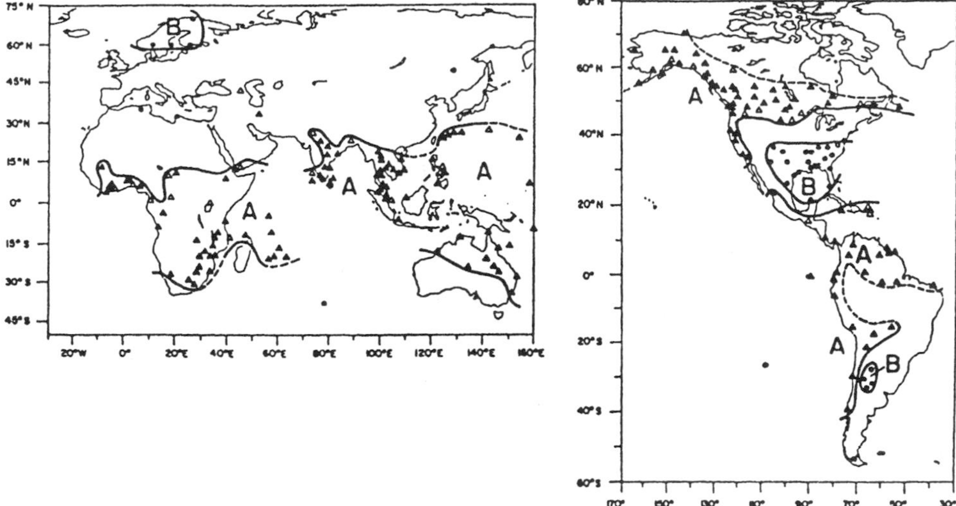

Figure 15.1 Global temperature anomalies for the December-January-February season following peak El Niño sea surface temperatures in the central and eastern Pacific. The letters A and B represent geographic areas with temperatures consistently above and below normal, respectively. Triangles and circles represent individual meteorological stations with positive and negative temperature differences (El Niño event minus La Niña event). Open and solid symbols represent significant differences at the 90% and 95% levels, respectively. (From Kiladis and Diaz 1989.)

El Niño events are unambiguously identified by extreme and persistent values of the SOI and sea surface temperature anomalies (Kiladis and Diaz 1989). There were twenty-two El Niño events in the twentieth century, in 1902, 1904, 1911, 1913, 1918, 1923, 1925, 1930, 1932, 1939, 1951, 1953, 1957, 1963, 1965, 1969, 1972, 1976, 1982, 1986, 1992 and 1997 (Kiladis and Diaz 1989; Trenberth and Hoar 1996). The El Niño events of 1982 and 1997 were particularly strong. There were also eighteen La Niña events in the twentieth century; however, there have been just two La Niña events in the past 20 years (1988 and 1998). For this reason, the remainder of this chapter focuses on El Niño conditions. It is important to recall, however, that ENSO variation is continuous and has a strong 24-month periodicity (Rasmussen, Wang, and Ropelewski 1990). This periodicity creates a strong tendency for dry, sunny, and warm years to alternate with wet, cloudy, and cool years over large parts of the equatorial tropics (Ropelewski and Halpert 1987; Aceituno 1988; Kiladis and Diaz 1989).

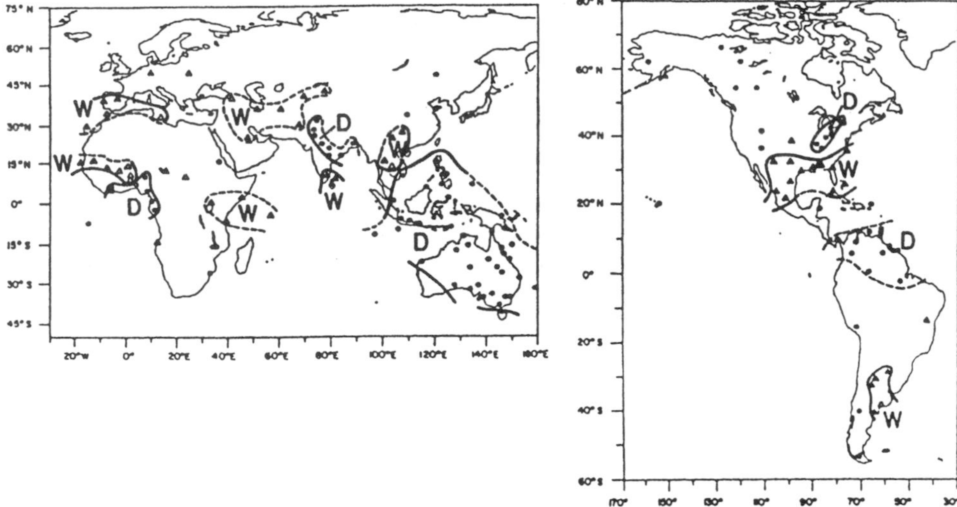

Figure 15.2 Global precipitation anomalies for the September-October-November season (Eastern Hemisphere) and December-January-February season (Western Hemisphere) following peak El Niño sea surface temperatures in the central and eastern Pacific. The letters W and D represent geographic areas with precipitation consistently above and below normal, respectively. Triangles and circles represent individual meteorological stations with positive and negative differences in precipitation (El Niño event minus La Niña event). Open and solid symbols represent significant differences at the 90% and 95% levels, respectively. (From Kiladis and Diaz 1989.)

Climatic Factors Limiting Net Primary Production in the Tropics

Temperature and the availabilities of water, light, and nitrogen largely determine net primary production in terrestrial ecosystems (Melillo et al. 1993). Nitrogen is widely believed to be available in excess in lowland tropical forests and will not be considered further here (Vitousek 1984; Silver 1994).

Water availability varies widely in the lowland tropics. Successful classifications of tropical vegetation emphasize seasonal drought and estimate the number of drought months from monthly mean values of rainfall and temperature (Koppen 1936; Walter 1971). Walsh (1996a) noted that mean monthly temperatures are aseasonal in the equatorial tropics and used mean monthly rainfall alone to calculate a perhumidity index to classify lowland tropical vegetation formations. The index ranges from +24 to −24 and is calculated by summing monthly values of +2, +1, −1, and −2 for very wet, wet, dry, and drought months with mean rainfall above 200 mm, between 100 and 200 mm, between

50 and 100 mm, and below 50 mm, respectively. Wet and dry months are separated at 100 mm rainfall because this amount balances monthly evapotranspiration. To capture soil water storage, 0.5 units are added each time a month with mean rainfall below 100 mm follows a month with mean rainfall above 100 mm. This simple perhumidity index successfully classifies lowland tropical vegetation (Walsh 1996a). Open thorn forests occur where the index falls below −12 with 8 or more dry months (annual rainfall typically < 700 mm). Deciduous seasonal forests occur where the index falls between −12 and −4.5 with 6 to 8 dry months. Semi-evergreen seasonal forests occur where the index falls between −4 and 4.5 with 4 to 6 dry months. Evergreen seasonal forests occur where the index has values between +5 and +9.5 with 3 to 5 dry months. Finally, rainforests occur in wet and superwet climates where the perhumidity index exceeds +10 or +20, respectively, with 0 to 3 dry months (annual rainfall > 2,000 mm). This chapter focuses on lowland tropical rainforests found in wet and superwet climates.

Moisture availability rarely limits plant performance in wet and superwet tropical climates. A forest irrigation experiment performed on Barro Colorado Island (BCI), Panama, is illustrative. BCI is at the margin of the lowland rainforest formation, with a perhumidity index of +10.5, 2,600 mm annual rainfall, and a single 4-month dry season. Irrigation maintained soil water content near wet-season levels (technically near field capacity) by adding 650 Mg of water to 4.5 ha of forest each week during five consecutive dry seasons. Herbs and shrubs showed limited responses to this massive manipulation, while trees and canopy lianas did not respond (Wright and Cornejo 1990a, 1990b; Wright 1991; Mulkey and Wright 1996; Cavelier, Wright, and Santamaria 1999). This difference between growth forms reflects different rooting depths. Herbs and shrubs with shallow roots are vulnerable to dry-season drought, while trees and lianas with deep roots are buffered (Wright 1992). Tree roots extract soil water reserves from depths to 12 m in similar forests (Nepstad et al. 1994). Only the most severe droughts cause stress among deeply rooted trees in wet and superwet tropical climates.

The potential for light limitation increases with the perhumidity index (*sensu* Walsh 1996a). The biomass of vegetation increases rapidly from arid to wetter environments. As a closed canopy develops, an ever greater proportion of leaves occupy shaded microenvironments, and the potential for light limitation increases rapidly. Radiant energy is extinguished exponentially with distance beneath forest canopies (Kira, Shinozaki, and Hozumi 1969). Global radiation was reduced by 53% just 6 m into the canopy of a lowland rainforest (Yoda 1974;

Aoki, Yabuki, and Koyama 1975). Photosynthetically active radiation (PAR, 400 to 700 nm) was reduced by 94% just 5 m into the canopy of a montane rainforest (Johnson and Atwood 1970). PAR is extinguished more rapidly than global radiation due to differential absorption by leaves. Photosynthesis by canopy leaves in tropical forests becomes saturated with light at photosynthetic photon flux densities (PPFD) of 450 to 600 µmol/m^2/s (Oberbauer and Strain 1986; Pearcy 1987); lower light levels limit leaf-level photosynthesis. PPFD varied by three orders of magnitude and was limiting in most determinations made between 0800 and 1000 hours for leaves from above 29 m in an Australian rainforest tree (Pearcy 1987). PPFD was less than 400 µmol/m^2/s in 71% of diurnal course measurements for canopy leaves of *Pentaclethra macroloba* in a rainforest in Costa Rica (Oberbauer and Strain 1986). Self-shading, lateral shading by neighbors, and shading by competing lianas potentially limit photosynthesis by all but the uppermost leaves in tropical forests.

Clouds and atmospheric water vapor further reduce the solar radiation received by tropical forests. This reduction is illustrated by a comparison of solar radiation at the equinoxes in central Panama. Dry-season conditions, with negligible cloud cover and reduced atmospheric water vapor concentrations, prevail during the March equinox, and wet-season conditions prevail during the September equinox. Global irradiance averaged 31% greater at the March equinox over a 17-year period (Wright 1996). Changes in solar radiation of this magnitude have profound effects on carbon uptake. Low light levels limit leaf-level photosynthesis in fully exposed leaves of the emergent tree *Ceiba pentandra* when cloud cover is heavy during the wet season in central Panama (Zotz and Winter 1994). Eddy correlation studies have detected a strong dependence of forest-level carbon uptake on cloud cover and irradiance in wet tropical regions (Fan et al. 1990; Grace et al. 1995; Loescher et al. 2003). Models of net primary productivity predict that low irradiance should limit forest-level carbon uptake during the wetter, cloudier season throughout the tropical wet forests of South America (Raich et al. 1991). ENSO-related changes in cloud cover should have similar effects.

Variable temperatures affect tropical plants in several ways. A short temperature drop of just 2°C or 3°C can cue reproduction (see the section on plant reproduction below). Small changes in temperature also affect carbon budgets. Plant respiration increases with temperature, and this increase reduces net primary production (Melillo et al. 1993; Grace et al. 1995; Clark et al. 2003).

Temperature, cloud cover, and solar irradiance are tightly correlated in the equatorial tropics, and data are required to resolve their net effect on carbon uptake (photosynthesis minus respiration). Net carbon uptake increases with irradiance and temperature on both day-to-day and seasonal time scales in lowland tropical forests (Fan et al. 1990; Raich et al. 1991; Grace et al. 1995). Year-to-year ENSO-related climatic variation is expected to have a similar effect.

Predicted Plant Responses to El Niño Teleconnections

Climatic anomalies may have different effects on different plant growth forms within a single forest. For example, susceptibility to drought is greatest among epiphytes, intermediate among shallowly rooted herbs and shrubs, and least among deeply rooted trees and lianas (Gentry and Dodson 1987; Wright 1992). The remainder of this chapter considers trees and, to a lesser extent, lianas because these growth forms dominate forest structure (and trees also dominate the tropical forest literature).

El Niño teleconnections alter cloud cover, rainfall, and temperature over a large portion of the tropics (see figs. 15.1 and 15.2). Plant responses to these anomalies are predicted to vary with the type of vegetation, the long-term mean climate, and the El Niño teleconnection. Two extremes are considered. Moisture availability limits plant performance during the dry season in strongly seasonal forests. Tree performance is predicted to improve when El Niño teleconnections bring anomalously heavy rainfall during the dry season to strongly seasonal forests and to more arid vegetation formations. Solar irradiance limits plant performance in rainforests in wet and superwet tropical climates (*sensu* Walsh 1996a). Tree performance is predicted to improve when El Niño teleconnections bring reduced cloud cover, mild drought, and increased irradiance and to decline when La Niña teleconnections bring increased cloud cover and reduced irradiance. Moisture rarely limits trees in rainforests in wet and superwet tropical climates (Wright and Cornejo 1990a, 1990b; Wright 1992; Nepstad et al. 1994). As drought becomes more severe, however, even deeply rooted trees may experience water stress.

To summarize, tree performance is predicted to increase in response to mild drought and to decrease in response to both anomalous heavy rainfall and severe drought in wet and superwet tropical climates. Experimental augmentation of light availability during a cloudy La Niña year demonstrated that heavy daytime cloud cover limits extension growth and reproduction by tall canopy trees in Panama (Graham et al. 2003). Experimental redirection of rainfall also demonstrated that extreme drought limits growth by Amazonian trees (Nepstad et al. 2002). It remains to evaluate the performance of tropical trees in response to natural climatic variation.

OBSERVED RESPONSES TO EL NIÑO TELECONNECTIONS IN ARID AND STRONGLY SEASONAL TROPICAL CLIMATES

El Niño events can bring dramatic increases in rainfall and productivity to arid tropical environments. The 1982–1983 El Niño brought more than 3 m of rain to the Darwin biological station in the Galápagos Islands, where annual rainfall averages just 406 mm. Plant productivity increased dramatically. Higher trophic levels responded, and Darwin's finches experienced a large pulse of recruitment (Grant 1986). The 1991–1992 El Niño event caused a similar chain of events on desert islands in the Gulf of California, leading to population irruptions in spiders and their parasitic wasps (Polis et al. 1998). Anomalous heavy rainfall associated with El Niño events increases productivity across trophic levels in otherwise arid tropical and subtropical environments.

Climatic anomalies associated with the El Niño Southern Oscillation also affect the radial growth of teak (*Tectona grandis*) in the strongly seasonal monsoon forests of Southeast Asia. Growth increments increase with the length of the monsoon in both Java and northern Thailand (table 15.1). The teleconnection between ENSO and Javanese rainfall is particularly strong for drought during El Niño events and heavy rainfall during La Niña events (Ropelewski and Halpert 1987, 1989). Teak growth increments increase with the SOI for Java (D'Arrigo, Jacoby, and Krusic 1994).

Radial growth increments also increase with rainfall in semi-evergreen seasonal forests in Costa Rica and Venezuela (table 15.1). ENSO teleconnections bring increased rainfall to both countries during El Niño events (Ropelewski and Halpert 1987, 1989), yet radial growth increments are unrelated to the SOI (Worbes 1999; Enquist and Leffler 2001). This observation may reflect the relatively weak ENSO teleconnections characteristic of the New World, where the expected climatic anomaly may occur in as few as 70% of El Niño events (Ropelewski and Halpert 1987). A reanalysis conditioned on those El Niño events with anomalously high rainfall may yet show a relationship between ENSO and tree performance in these forests.

OBSERVED RESPONSES TO EL NIÑO TELECONNECTIONS IN WET AND SUPERWET TROPICAL CLIMATES

Tree Growth

Radial growth increments for rainforest trees are generally consistent with the prediction that performance is enhanced during mild drought and reduced

Table 15.1 Tree responses to climatic variation in tropical forests

Type of response	Site	Range of climatic variation	Tree response	Source
		Semi-evergreen seasonal forests (−4 < perhumidity index ≤ 4.5)		
Radial growth	Java	65 yrs	Growth increases with rain days per yr	Berlage 1931; De Boer 1951
Radial growth	Thailand	40 yrs	Growth increases with length of monsoon	Buckley et al. 1995
Radial growth	Costa Rica	85 yrs	Growth increases with rainfall	Enquist and Leffler 2001
Radial growth	Venezuela	39 yrs	Growth increases with rainfall	Worbes 1999
		Rainforests in wet or superwet climates (perhumidity index > 10)		
		Mild drought		
Radial growth	Costa Rica	17 yrs	Greater growth in drier yrs (temperature effect greater)	Clark et al. 2003
Radial growth	Panama	Six mild El Niño events	5 of 7 largest growth increments observed in 33 yrs	Devall, Parresol, and Lê 1996
Seed set	Malaysia	Twofold range in sunshine hours per day	General flowering in yrs with ample sunshine	Van Schaik 1986
Seed set	Borneo	El Niño versus non-El Niño yrs	General flowering during El Niño yrs	Curran and Leighton 2000
Seed set	Panama	El Niño versus non-El Niño yrs	Elevated seed set during El Niño yrs	Wright et al. 1999
		Severe drought		
Radial growth	Panama	Severe drought during 1976 and 1982 El Niños	Smallest growth increment observed in 33 yrs in 1976	Devall, Parresol, and Lê 1996
Mortality	Guyana	Severe drought during 1925 El Niño	Elevated tree mortality	Davis and Richards 1933
Mortality	Borneo	Severe drought during 1982 El Niño	Elevated tree mortality	Leighton and Wirawan 1986
Mortality	Panama	Severe drought during 1982 El Niño	Elevated tree mortality	Condit, Hubbell, and Foster 1996c
Mortality	Brazil	Severe drought during 1997 El Niño	Elevated tree mortality	Williamson et al. 2000

Note: For rainforests in wet and superwet tropical climates (*sensu* Walsh 1996a), performance is predicted to improve during mild drought and to decline during severe drought. For more seasonal forests, performance is predicted to improve with rainfall in the drier season.

when rainfall is unusually heavy and when drought becomes severe (table 15.1). Growth increments were greater during drier years in a Costa Rican rainforest, although temperature had a greater effect on growth increments in this forest (Clark et al. 2003). Annual tree rings for *Cordia alliodora* (Boraginaceae) from the Barro Colorado Nature Monument (BCNM), Panama, spanning eight El Niño events and 33 years, were examined in another study (Devall, Parresol, and Lê 1996). El Niño events bring low rainfall, reduced cloudiness, and increased solar radiation to the BCNM. Six of the eight El Niño events were relatively mild, but the 1976 and 1982 El Niño events included the two most severe droughts recorded in 75 years for the BCNM (Windsor 1990). Five of the seven largest growth increments occurred during the six mild El Niño events, a statistically improbable coincidence (Fisher exact test, $p < .001$). In contrast, the smallest annual growth increment occurred in 1976. Mild drought enhanced tree growth, while severe drought did not.

Plant Reproduction

Climatic anomalies affect plant reproduction in at least three ways. First, unusual temperatures, low moisture availability, and low light levels may directly limit plant function and the resources available for reproduction. Second, a variable climate often provides the proximate cues that initiate reproduction. Known cues include changes in temperature and moisture availability as well as changes in day length. Finally, differential reproductive success may select for the timing of reproduction to coincide with favorable environmental conditions. ENSO-related climatic variation affects plant reproduction in all three ways.

General flowering in the dipterocarp forests of Malesia provides an example. This phenomenon involves hundreds of species from at least forty families that reproduce only at irregular, multi-year intervals in general flowering events (Appanah 1985). Many species that reproduce annually are also more successful in general flowering years (Sakai et al. 1999). Recently, it has been realized that general flowering events coincide with El Niño events, although this association is stronger to the east and weaker to the west within Malesia (Ashton, Givnish, and Appanah 1988; Yasuda et al. 1999; Curran and Leighton 2000; Wich and Van Schaik 2000). Earlier investigators noted an association between general flowering events and variable solar irradiance (Wycherley 1973; Van Schaik 1986). Specifically, a general flowering event is more likely when both the number of hours of sunshine in the previous few months and the number of years since the most recent general flowering event are large (fig. 15.3). Van Schaik (1986) hypothesized that general flowering species become more sensitive to some proxi-

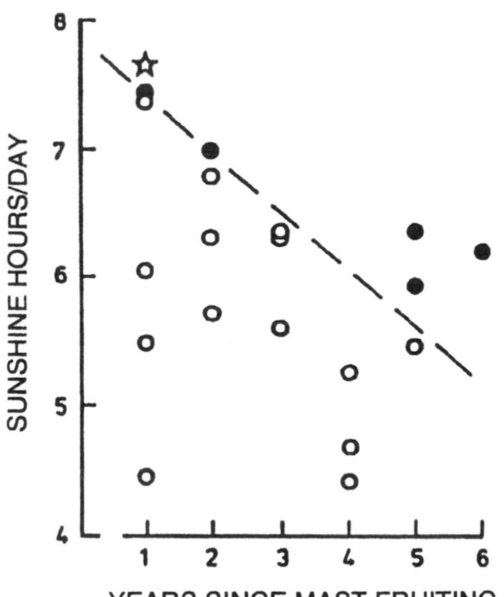

Figure 15.3 The dependence of mast fruiting in peninsular Malaysia on the number of hours of sunshine in the previous 3 months and the number of years since the most recent mast-fruiting event. Solid circles represent mast-fruiting years; open circles represent years without mast fruiting. The star represents a year without mast fruiting that followed two consecutive mast-fruiting years. (From Van Schaik 1986.)

mate cue as the level of carbohydrate reserves accumulated since the last reproductive event increases. The proximate cue turns out to be minimum temperatures just a few degrees below normal for several consecutive nights (Ashton, Givnish, and Appanah 1988; Sakai et al. 1999). The cold air masses from central Asia that provide this cue are most likely to descend into Malesia during El Niño events (Ashton, Givnish, and Appanah 1988; but see Yasuda et al. 1999). These observations may be summarized in the following hypothesis: General flowering plants evolved to reproduce in response to a proximate cue (brief cool temperature transgressions) associated with El Niño events because reduced cloudiness and the high irradiance that favors photosynthesis in rainforests are also associated with El Niño events. Any discussion of general flowering that omits animals is, however, incomplete, as we will see below.

Community-level fruit production also tracks El Niño events on Barro Colorado Island, Panama (Wright et al. 1999). As in Malesia, many mast-fruiting species concentrate reproduction in El Niño years, and many annually reproducing species set greater amounts of seed during El Niño events (fig. 15.4). Minimum temperatures are not the proximate cue (Wright et al. 1999), as cold air masses rarely reach BCI. The minimum temperature recorded just above the forest canopy was 20.3°C for 18 years beginning in 1981 (S. Paton, unpublished data). The proximate cue may instead be a relatively severe dry season. Threshold levels of drought enhance flowering success in a number of tropical forest

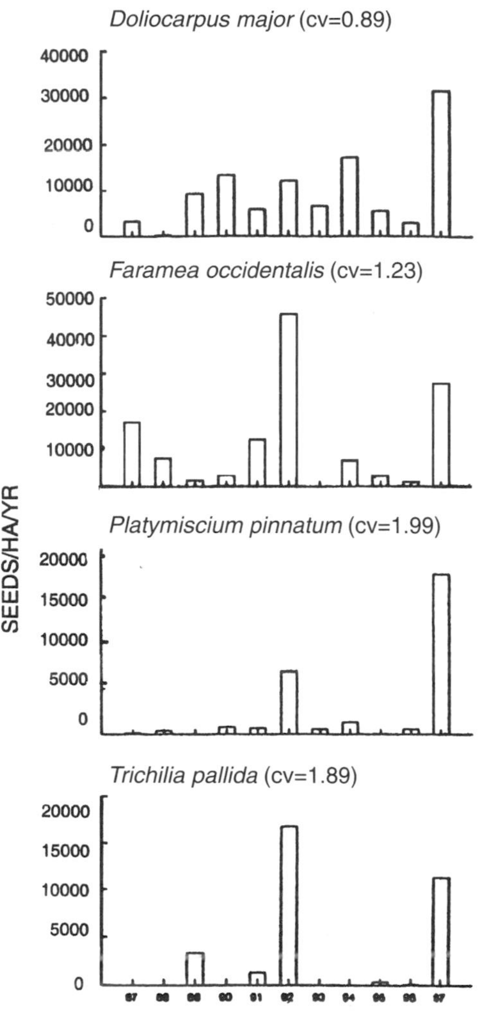

Figure 15.4 Annual seed production from 1987 through 1997 for four BCI plant species. Seed set was largely limited to the 1992 and 1997 El Niño years for the trees *Platymiscium pinnatum* and *Trichilia pallida*. *Doliocarpus major,* a liana, and *Faramea occidentalis,* a treelet, fruit annually, but had particularly heavy seed set during one or both of the El Niño years. This latter pattern is very common on BCI (Wright et al. 1999).

plant species (Alvim 1960, reviewed by Van Schaik, Terborgh, and Wright 1993). Such thresholds may be achieved only during relatively severe dry seasons. A drought cue is implicated by the timing of elevated irradiance, severe dry seasons, and elevated fruit production on BCI during three recent El Niño events (Foster 1982a; Wright et al. 1999). During the 1969 El Niño, the dry season was severe, and community-level fruit production was elevated (irradiance was not measured). In 1997, the dry season was again severe, and wet-season irradiance and fruit production were both elevated. Irradiance was also consistently elevated in 1989, 1990, 1991, and 1992; however, the dry seasons were relatively mild until the 1992 El Niño event. Elevated fruit production occurred only after the severe 1992 dry season. Severe dry seasons are often associated with El Niño events on BCI. As in Malesia, plants appear to have evolved to reproduce in response to a proximate cue (mild drought) associated with El Niño events because reduced cloudiness and the high irradiance that favors photosynthesis in rainforests are also associated with El Niño events. Once again, the role of animals must also be considered.

Elevated community-level fruit production and high irradiance were also observed in Cameroon during the 1992 El Niño event (Newbery, Songwe, and Chuyong 1998; Green and Newbery 2002). And community-level fruit production was elevated during 1997 in French Guyana, Roraima, and southeastern Peru (P. M. Forget, M. T. Nascimento, and M. Guariguata, personal communications). The pattern of elevated fruit production during El Niño events observed for Malesia and BCI may prove to be widespread in tropical rainforests.

Tree Mortality

Severe droughts coincide with the very strongest El Niño events in Borneo, Central America, and Amazonia (Leighton and Wirawan 1986; Leigh et al. 1990; Meggers 1994). There have been at least four reports of increased tree mortality in tropical rainforests following severe droughts associated with El Niño events. The 1925 El Niño brought severe drought to Guyana, and increased tree mortality followed (Davis and Richards 1933). The 1982–1983 El Niño brought severe drought to BCI, including six nearly rainless months (Leigh et al. 1990). Elevated tree mortality followed in old-growth forest (Condit, Hubbell, and Foster 1996c). The 1982–1983 El Niño also brought severe drought to eastern Borneo. Annual rainfall fell to as little as one-third of its long-term mean. Drought killed many canopy trees in primary forest, with the proportion killed ranging from 11% in a protected valley bottom to 37%–71% on steep slopes and exposed ridges (Leighton and Wirawan 1986). Finally, the 1997–1998 El Niño brought severe drought to the central Amazon, which again coincided with elevated tree mortality (Williamson et al. 2000) (table 15.1). This mortality is consistent with the prediction that severe drought associated with El Niño events can limit tree performance in wet and superwet climates.

Fire

The two most severe El Niño events of the twentieth century occurred in 1982 and 1997. Both brought severe drought and fire to rainforests in wet and superwet climates (Cochrane 2003). Thousands of square kilometers of selectively logged forests and secondary forests, along with smaller areas of adjacent primary forests, burned in eastern Borneo in 1983 (Leighton and Wirawan 1986). Fires also occurred in northern Borneo, southern peninsular Malaysia, and the Western Ghats of India in 1983 (Walsh 1996a). Fires were widespread in Indonesia and Brazil in 1997–1998 (Cochrane and Schulze 1998; Kinnaird and O'Brien 1998; Siegert et al. 2001). Once again, the fires were concentrated in selectively logged and secondary forests; however, primary rainforests were also involved. Forests on well-drained soils are particularly susceptible to fire during El Niño events in Guyana (Hammond and ter Steege 1998). Finally, extensive Amazonian charcoal deposits coincide with mega-El Niño events that occurred during the Quaternary (Meggers 1994; Piperno and Becker 1996). Severe drought associated with mega-El Niño events can have devastating effects on rainforests in wet and superwet climates.

Animals

Very few studies have evaluated direct effects of El Niño events on tropical forest animals. Terricolous arthropods delay their annual ascent into the canopies of Amazonian floodplain forests during El Niño events (Adis and Latif 1996). The severe 1982–1983 El Niño event had little direct effect on leaf-litter arthropods and other animals on BCI (Wheeler and Levings 1988; Leigh et al. 1990). Indirect effects on animals mediated by plant production are better known.

Variable community-level fruit production may induce population fluctuations in frugivores and granivores. Such fluctuations have recently been observed both on BCI and in Borneo. Elevated community-level fruit production during the 1992 El Niño permitted population increases among red-tailed squirrels (*Sciurus granatensis*), agoutis (*Dasyprocta punctata*), coatis (*Nasua narica*), collared peccaries (*Tayassu tajacu*), and deer (*Mazama americana*) on BCI. Community-level fruit production was extremely low in the following year, and famine reduced the populations of all five species (Wright et al. 1999). In Borneo, bearded pigs (*Sus scrofa*) are voracious seed predators. The nomadic adults migrated to a general flowering event and reproduced during the 1992 El Niño season. Juveniles, and eventually adults, starved during the long interval between general flowering events (Curran and Leighton 2000).

Evolution of Plant Reproductive Phenologies

The evolution of mast fruiting at multi-year intervals requires a selective agent that promotes the reproductive success of synchronous individuals and reduces the success of asynchronous individuals (Kelly 1994). Janzen (1974) hypothesized that generalist seed predators, especially mammals, played this role in the evolution of general flowering in Malesia. Seed predators are satiated and many seeds escape when community-level fruit production is elevated, and, seed predators are starved and their numbers are reduced during the long interval between general flowering events, when community-level fruit production is consistently low.

As mentioned above, the starvation of mammalian granivores during periods of low community-level fruit production has been observed both in Borneo, where general flowering occurs, and in Panama, where general flowering is unknown. This observation suggests two questions. First, what reduces community-level fruit production to levels that starve granivorous mammals? Famines were observed a year after the 1930, 1957, 1969, and 1992 El Niño events on BCI (Foster 1982a; Wright et al. 1999). Elevated community-level fruit production was also observed in 1969 and 1992 and was followed by extremely low community-level fruit production and famine one year later. Two factors may contribute to the alternation of elevated community-level fruit production during an El Niño year and extremely low community-level fruit production a year later. First, elevated fruit production consumes stored reserves and limits future production. This phenomenon is well known for many fruit and timber trees (Matthews 1963) and is likely to hold for many forest species. Second, the 24-month periodicity of the El Niño Southern Oscillation results in a strong tendency for sunny and cloudy years to alternate over many Neotropical forests (Aceituno 1988). High irradiance may favor fruit production during an El Niño year, and low irradiance may reduce fruit production a year later. Long-term radiation records are needed to evaluate this last hypothesis. Regardless of the mechanism involved, community-level variation in fruit production causes community-level fluctuations in the abundances of generalist mammals that consume seeds and seedlings. Therefore, the prerequisite for the evolution of mast fruiting appears to be in place in Panama.

The second question then becomes why general flowering has evolved in Malesia and not on BCI. Phylogenetic constraints and the natural histories of the dominant plant families probably favored the evolution of general flowering in Malesia (Wright et al. 1999). A very different pattern of climatic variation in the two regions may also be important. The El Niño Southern Oscillation directly controls tropical climates across the Pacific basin from Peru to Indonesia. El Niño events provide a predictable association between high irradiance and a low temperature cue in Malesia. This predictable association may have favored the evolution of general flowering. In contrast, the teleconnections that affect tropical climates remote from this core area are less predictable (Ropelewski and Harper 1987). High irradiance may favor fruit production in most tropical rainforests. However, the association between high irradiance, El Niño events, and a suitable proximate cue could be much weaker on BCI than in Malesia. The potential for evolutionary responses to El Niño conditions should therefore vary among the tropical continents.

CONCLUSIONS

This chapter evaluates the hypothesis that plant performance in tropical rainforests (*sensu* Walsh 1996a) is enhanced during mild El Niño events and reduced during very strong El Niño events. The hypothesis is supported by studies of community-level seed set, the radial growth of trees, tree mortality, and the occurrence of fire. Improved plant performance during mild El Niño events appears to be a very general phenomenon expressed in the tropical rainforests of Malesia, the Neotropics, and possibly Africa. The principal mechanisms affecting plant performance are hypothesized to be increased irradiance and photosynthesis during mild El Niño events and severe drought during strong El Niño events. Additional studies that span multiple El Niño events and complementary physiological studies will be required to evaluate this hypothesis more fully.

Models of both global climate change and regional deforestation predict decreased precipitation, increased temperatures, and more intense seasonality in the tropics (Shukla, Nobre, and Sellers 1990; Scholes and Breemen 1997). El Niño events share these attributes and may provide a window on the future for a large part of the tropics. Despite the frequent and widespread effects of El Niño on tropical climates and their relevance to global climate change, just a handful of studies have examined the effects of El Niño events on tropical rainforests. Even fewer studies report El Niño effects for more seasonal tropical forests. This situation must change.

ACKNOWLEDGMENTS

I thank Joe Connell and Egbert Leigh for thoughtful comments on this chapter. The Environmental Sciences Program of the Smithsonian Institution supported this research.

Part II

A MULTIDISCIPLINARY PERSPECTIVE ON AN ENTIRE RAINFOREST SYSTEM: THE AUSTRALIAN WET TROPICS

16 Overview: Rainforest History and Dynamics in the Australian Wet Tropics

CRAIG MORITZ

INTRODUCTION

From the preceding chapters, it is clear that both ecological and evolutionary processes shape diversity in rainforest biotas, but at different temporal and geographic scales. Ecological determinants such as productivity may limit local (alpha) diversity, whereas at a much larger spatial scale geographic turnover of species, resulting from the balance between speciation and extinction along with dispersal limitation and habitat specialization, contributes substantially to total diversity (Rosenzweig 1995; Hubbell 2001; Hubbell, chap. 4 in this volume). To get a better understanding of the relative contributions of these processes, we need to examine diversity across entire biogeographic regions for which we have evidence on rainforest history and high-quality information on the distribution and taxonomy of species. In such a situation, it should be possible to undertake the multidisciplinary studies, spanning paleoecological, phylogenetic, ecological, and biogeographic approaches, that are necessary to answer questions about macroecological patterns. Further, by understanding the historical and current determinants of diversity, we should be in a stronger position to offer practical advice about how to protect this diversity in the face of growing pressures from human populations and activities (see part III of this volume).

The rainforests of the Wet Tropics of northeastern Queensland, Australia, offer an unusual opportunity for such an analysis. These forests (fig. 16.1) are a major component of the "mesotherm archipelago" (Nix 1991a), a chain of upland isolates of tropical and subtropical rainforest surrounded by warmer and drier environments and representing remnants of rainforests that covered much of the continent until the mid-Miocene (Adam 1992; Greenwood and Christophel, chap. 18 in this volume). Indeed, Morley (2000) suggests that the Wet Tropics region could have sustained rainforests continuously since the Late Cretaceous. Although small in area (ca. 6,300 km^2 and $< 0.1\%$ of Australia), these forests have both high species diversity and high endemism (Rainforest Conser-

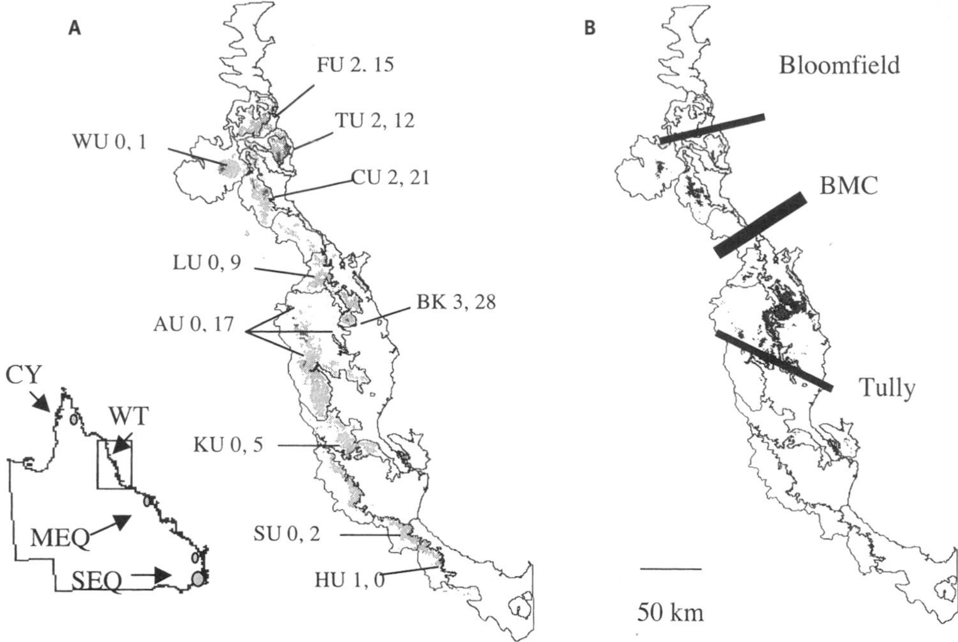

Figure 16.1 (A) Observed distribution of Wet Tropics (WT) rainforests across the upland (> 300 m) subregions associated with the Great Dividing Range and escarpment in northeastern Queensland, Australia (see also plate 4). This is the largest and most continuous area of rainforest within a chain of cool-adapted rainforest patches along the Queensland coast (see inset). The numbers after each subregion label refer to the number of single-subregion endemic species of vertebrates and low-vagility insects, respectively. Abbreviations: FU, Finnegan Uplands; TU, Thornton Uplands; WU, Windsor Uplands; CU, Carbine Uplands; LU, Lamb Uplands; AU Atherton Uplands; BK, Bellenden Ker Range; KU, Kirrima Uplands; SU, Spec Uplands; HU, Halifax Uplands. (After Yeates, Bouchard, and Monteith 2002). (B) Potential distribution of upland rainforest types at the last glacial maximum, predicted using a logistic regression model (C. Graham, S. Williams and C. Moritz, unpublished data). The major barriers observed using mtDNA phylogeography are indicated. BMC = Black Mountain Corridor (see Schneider and Williams, chap. 20 in this volume). Note the correspondence between inferred refugia and the areas of highest richness of narrowly endemic species.

vation Society of Queensland 1986; Adam 1992). The region includes some 25% of all plant genera found in Australia and thirty-six endemic plant genera, of which 78% are monotypic. As an indicator of the phylogenetic depth of this plant diversity, twelve of nineteen primitive angiosperm families occur here, and two of these are endemic. For animals, the region is similarly diverse, with over 30% of Australia's species of frogs, including most microhylid species, 62% of butterflies, 60% of bats, 23% of reptiles, and so on, with some seventy-three species of vertebrates endemic to these rainforests. While the Wet Tropics is remarkable for its endemism, its local plant species diversity is more similar to that in marginal areas than to that in the cores of the super-rich regions of Southeast Asia and the Neotropics (Connell et al., chap. 23 in this volume). In contrast, aquatic invertebrate diversity is among the highest recorded (Pearson, chap. 22 in this volume).

The combination of limited area, high but not unmanageable diversity, and intensive study over several decades (facilitated recently by a dedicated research center, the Cooperative Research Centre for Tropical Rainforest Ecology and Management: Stork, chap. 24 in this volume) has provided a rare opportunity for rainforest biologists to examine pattern and process at the scale of an entire biogeographic unit. Of particular note, surveys by curators of the Queensland Museum have resulted in an unusually detailed picture of the diversity and distributions of terrestrial snails and low-vagility insects across the region (Moritz et al. 2001; Yeates, Bouchard, and Monteith 2002; Bouchard et al., chap. 21 in this volume). The freshwater fauna has been documented across the region (Pusey and Kennard 1996; Pearson, chap. 22 in this volume), the vegetation has been classified structurally and mapped at 1:100,000 (Tracey and Webb 1975), there are rich environmental data at a fine spatial scale (Nix and Switzer 1991; Mackey and Su, chap. 11 in this volume), and there have been several detailed studies on vegetation history based on pollen cores (Kershaw, Moss, and Wild, chap. 19 in this volume) and subfossil charcoal remains (Hopkins et al. 1993, 1996). This rich spatial data provides a platform for introducing new methods for modeling biotic responses to past and future climate change (Hilbert and Ostendorf 2001; Hilbert, Ostendorf, and Hopkins 2001; Hugall et al. 2002; Williams, Bolitho, and Fox 2003) and for testing the efficiency of surrogates for biodiversity assessment (Moritz 2002; Moritz et al. 2001) that can be employed in less well known tropical regions.

Part II of this volume presents several perspectives on rainforest diversity for this single biogeographic region, including evidence on historical processes derived from geomorphology, paleobiology, and genetics and on patterns of species richness and abundance in relation to biogeographic history and ecological processes. Given the relatively stable geology of the region (see below), some key questions can be raised:

- How has climate change affected the long-term and recent history of the vegetation?
- How have the shifts in rainforest composition and distribution affected the richness and distribution of species?

- What can we learn from these patterns about the ecological and evolutionary processes that underlie the high diversity of the region?
- How can this knowledge inform conservation and management of this unique rainforest system?

THE HISTORICAL SETTING

In chapter 17, Nott provides a long-term perspective based on geomorphology of the region's key feature, the Great Dividing Range and the coincident escarpment, which runs close and parallel to the coast and thereby drives the substantial rainfall on which the forests depend. The range and its associated drainages have been in place and essentially stable for a long time, perhaps since the late Mesozoic. Although this general stability has been overlaid by localized volcanic activity and basalt flows, some recent (Willmott and Stephenson 1989), the antiquity of these highlands contrasts with more geologically active rainforest regions (e.g., the New Guinea highlands, the Neotropical Andes) and provides the setting for repeated climate-induced changes in rainforest distribution from the Tertiary to the present.

What do we know about the response of the vegetation to fluctuations in climate through the Tertiary and Quaternary? In Chapter 18, Greenwood and Christophel review the plant fossil (mostly macrofossil) evidence for changes in the nature and distribution of tropical forests across Australia from their origins in the Gondwanan early angiosperm forests of the Cretaceous. The major trend in the Tertiary was cooling, drying, and an increasing influence of dry seasonality. The record of macroflora fossils is relatively poor within the current, northeastern distribution of tropical rainforests. However, for much of the Tertiary, floras from the better-sampled regions in southeastern Australia bore a close resemblance to the mesothermal rainforests now characteristic of the Wet Tropics. Paleobotanical evidence from these regions suggests alternation between warm-wet phases (Early-Mid Eocene, Early Miocene, and possibly Early Pliocene) characterized by diversification and range expansion and cooler, drier conditions (Late Eocene to Early Miocene, Mid-Late Miocene, and Late Pliocene to Pleistocene), in which rainforest floras underwent extinction and continental-scale range contraction.

A combination of offshore palynological records and more detailed, but temporally restricted, pollen records from mostly upland terrestrial sites provides for a broad, unusually detailed synthesis of the Wet Tropics vegetation over the last 10 million years (Kershaw, Moss, and Wild, chap. 19). Rainforest was dominant for most of this time, although with extensive drier and gymnosperm-dominated rainforest surrounding complex angiosperm rainforest, the latter in the wetter regions. The long-term trend from the pollen record is toward decreasing diversity, particularly of cool-adapted species, with little contribution from the rainforests of New Guinea. The major transition in an otherwise stable system appears to have occurred from the mid-Pleistocene, over the last few hundred thousand years in particular, and may be related to increased climate variability and burning (natural and, from ca. 40,000 years ago, anthropogenic). The general consequence was an increase in fire-prone sclerophyllous woodlands at the expense of dry gymnosperm-dominated rainforest and, thus, loss of buffering of the angiosperm rainforests.

Effects of climatic variation on plant communities are also evident at a much smaller spatial and temporal scale. Connell and colleagues (chap. 23) review the results of one of the longest-running studies of plant community dynamics, located in the central Wet Tropics. This detailed 40-year study, combining observation and experiments, suggests that local forest composition is driven by recruitment dynamics, which, in turn, fluctuate (nonsynchronously) in response to climate, with major recruitment events following periods of drought (see also Wright, chap. 15 in this volume). This study also provides direct evidence for frequency dependence (rare-type advantage) of seedling survival and growth, supporting a key element of the Janzen-Connell hypothesis.

RESPONSES OF THE FAUNA

As is often the case in the tropics, there is essentially no fossil evidence from which we can infer the evolutionary and biogeographic history of the Wet Tropics fauna. The exception is the well-studied Mio-Pliocene fauna at Riversleigh, now in the arid zone some hundreds of kilometers to the west of the Wet Tropics. The Riversleigh fauna had many lineages in common with the current Wet Tropics fauna (Archer, Hand, and Godthelp 1994), but also had a much higher diversity. In a pattern now known to be common to several rainforest systems (Moritz et al. 2000), the great majority of vertebrates endemic to the Wet Tropics speciated long ago, at some time from the late Miocene to the Pliocene (Moritz et al. 1997), perhaps in association with the general drying and increased seasonality over that period (Greenwood and Christophel, chap. 18 in this volume). Despite clear evidence for contraction of rainforests to montane refugia (see fig. 16.1), there was no Pleistocene species pump!

So what, then, was the effect of the well-documented transformations and periodic contractions of rainforest during the mid- to late Pleistocene? Schneider and Williams (chap. 20) tackle this question through a combination of phylogeographic (genetic) analysis of widespread species and analysis of patterns of species richness and nestedness among subregions—an illustration of the powerful synergy between historical biogeography and community ecology. Their conclusion is that the major effect was local extinction, followed by some recolonization during a cool and mesic interval of the Holocene—thus, the rainforest contractions here acted as a filter of species. The spatial patterns of both genetic and species turnover are dominated by the same feature, the Black Mountain Corridor (BMC; see fig. 16.1), demonstrating the effect of long-term (Pliocene or earlier) isolation on community structuring and evolution within species. Further, both genetic and (endemic) species diversity are reduced in the southern upland areas, reflecting recolonization of these areas from Pleistocene refugia on the central Atherton Tableland (see also Moritz 2002; Yeates, Bouchard, and Monteith 2002).

Within these general patterns, there was substantial variation among species in how they responded to this history of habitat change. Responses were strongest for rainforest-dependent taxa and for those that are the most arboreal or, in the case of frogs, dependent on streams. For birds, species-level turnover across BMC is negligible; nonetheless, there is significant nesting of species distributions and, for species with narrower environmental ranges, significant (though small relative to reptiles and amphibians) genetic divergence (Joseph, Moritz, and Hugall 1995; J. Arnold, S. E. Williams, and C. Moritz, unpublished data). Species diversity analysis also revealed an intriguing connection between historical and recent extinction proneness. Guilds that show the strongest signals of historical extinction and recolonization—arboreal mammals and stream-breeding hylid frogs—are also those most vulnerable to recent habitat fragmentation (Laurance 1990) and disease-related declines (Williams and Hero 1998; Alford and Richards 1999).

The large area requirements of vertebrates and their concomitant history of local extinction followed by recolonization have, with one major exception (microhylid frogs of the genus *Cophixalus*), resulted in a coarse-grained pattern of distributions from which it is difficult to infer common biogeographic patterns or speciation processes. Indeed, for most genera, the sister taxa of species endemic to the Wet Tropics occur in mesic forests to the south (e.g., southeastern or central-eastern Queensland) or north (Papua New Guinea) of the region, consistent with ancient connections and speciation events (Moritz et al. 1997). By contrast, extensive surveys of low-vagility arthropods (especially bugs, beetles, and snails) by G. Monteith and colleagues from the Queensland Museum have revealed much higher levels of local endemism and diversity (Moritz et al. 2001; Yeates, Bouchard, and Monteith 2002), suggesting finer-grained distribution patterns that can be used to infer biogeographic history and speciation events. In relation to the former, detailed biogeographic analysis of an endemic snail species, employing a combination of mtDNA phylogeography and paleoclimatic distribution modeling, proved very effective at locating rainforest refugia (Hugall et al. 2002), and the same tools are illuminating biogeographic histories of sister taxa of endemic dung beetles (K. Bell, D. K. Yeates, and C. Moritz, unpublished data).

Bouchard et al. (chap. 21) have inferred geographic patterns of speciation by applying Brooks Parsimony Analysis (BPA: Brooks, Veller, and McLennan 2001) to distributional and phylogenetic evidence from eighty-seven species of arthropods across seventeen areas of endemism within the Wet Tropics. The results are intriguing: there is no single underlying history (area cladogram) or inferred mode of speciation. Rather, BPA suggests that all three modes of speciation explored—vicariant, peripheral, and sympatric—have made substantial contributions to arthropod diversity. The intersection of geographic history and mode of speciation is also of interest: the species present in the two centers of endemism, the Carbine Uplands and Bellenden Ker Range refugia, seem to have arisen via distinct mechanisms, more sympatric for the former and vicariant for the latter. By contrast, the species in the southern upland areas (Kirrima Uplands to Mount Elliot) are inferred to have arisen primarily via peripheral isolation following dispersal, consistent with the recent history of colonization inferred for vertebrates. Further insights are likely to come from additional phylogenetic analyses, preferably including molecular characters that allow for inferences about temporal patterns (Barraclough and Nee 2001), complemented by more intensive phylogeographic analyses of selected clades (e.g., Hugall et al. 2002; K. Bell, D. K. Yeates, and C. Moritz, unpublished data).

Relative to the terrestrial fauna, the aquatic diversity of the Wet Tropics is also high, but less is known of the effects of changes in rainforest distribution through the Quaternary on the aquatic fauna (but see McGlashan and Hughes 2000 and Hurwood and Hughes 2001 for examples of recent phylogeographic analyses). Pearson (chap. 22), therefore, takes a more local and ecological perspective on the factors that have shaped aquatic insect diversity at a local and regional scale, based on surveys of twenty sites across the altitudinal and latitudinal range of the Wet Tropics as well as long-term monitoring of single sites. Local diversity is very high, especially for certain families such as Trichoptera and Diptera, and there is some suggestion of higher endemism in the uplands. However, like fishes (Pusey and Kennard 1996), arthropods show little geographic structuring of species within an altitudinal zone; that is, high regional diversity is also reflected by high local diversity. Pearson points to the antiquity of the topography and stream flow patterns (see also Nott, chap. 17 in this volume) and the likelihood that stream discharge was maintained in upland areas even in dry periods of the Quaternary as causes of the high regional diversity. The high local diversity may be maintained by spatial and temporal patchiness of habitats, including the results of episodic disturbance due to cyclonic rains in the watersheds.

IMPLICATIONS FOR CONSERVATION AND MANAGEMENT

Together, the preceding analyses of the history and ecology of this rich biota sound some alarms for the present. It may be that much of the high diversity of the Wet Tropics rainforest is simply a reflection of its antiquity and its ability to survive historical contractions in well-buffered (though dissected: Hopkins et al. 1993) refugia and to expand rapidly from these refugia in more favorable times. However, the loss of the buffering drier rainforests during the last glacial maximum, combined with the creation of an inhospitable matrix (pastoral, agricultural, and urban) and human pressure on water resources, could threaten this diversity. In this context, it is crucial to develop a strong nexus between research and management, a topic reviewed by Stork (chap. 24).

People have interacted with the Wet Tropics rainforests for many thousands of years, with land use intensifying from European settlement in the early twentieth century to the present. With World Heritage listing in 1988, some sectors of the economy, notably timber production and mining, have become less important, while tourism, including rainforest-based ecotourism, have expanded. As Stork emphasizes, a major challenge is how to retain the high biological values of the region that support the new economy in the face of an expected 50% increase in the resident population over the next 20 years, as well as continued growth in tourist numbers, expansion of infrastructure, and influxes of invasive species.

If there is one message from the various studies on rainforest history and evolution reviewed above, it is that we cannot take a static approach to conserving biological diversity in the Wet Tropics, as conditions suitable for particular species move around the landscape. Managing this dynamic system will be a major challenge for management agencies and will require continual assessment of ecological and environmental trade-offs in land use planning (see also Moritz and McDonald, chap. 26 in this volume). A major challenge, and one that we are just beginning to perceive, is the effects of climate change. Recent modeling (Hilbert, Ostendorf, and Hopkins 2001; Williams, Bolitho, and Fox 2003) suggests substantial geographic shifts in climatic regimes suitable for specific forest types and the species they sustain, with potentially disastrous consequences for the montane endemics in particular. Protection and reforestation of strategically placed linkages is one possible solution, but for many high-elevation species the situation looks grim.

At best, the chapters in part II hint at the potential of multidisciplinary approaches for the integrated analysis of a single biogeographic system. As our data and analytical methods improve, so does our capacity to predict the spatial properties of diversity in this system under past, current, and perhaps future climates. Even in this relatively well protected system, there are continuing pressures on the rainforest fabric, and some species (e.g., amphibians: Alford and Richards 1999) have declined. The situation is now, or has the potential to become, much more dire in other rainforested areas with remarkably diverse biotas, such as Borneo and New Guinea (MacKinnon, chap. 27 in this volume). Aside from contributing to our knowledge of the ecological and evolutionary processes that shape diversity in rainforests, it is to be hoped that well-known areas such as the Wet Tropics can be used to test strategies for assessing diversity and prioritizing management (Margules and Pressey 2000; Ferrier 2002) that can be applied to regions for which we have less information.

17
The Origin and Evolution of Australia's Eastern Highlands

JONATHAN NOTT

ABSTRACT

The eastern Australian highlands (Great Dividing Range), incorporating the "continental divide," date back to at least the late Mesozoic. The vast majority of field evidence suggests that, apart from denudation, they have changed little in general morphological character since that time. Drainage disruption appears not to have been widespread and should not be automatically assumed to be the cause of variations in aquatic species between streams draining either side of the continental divide. Indeed, evidence in northeastern Queensland suggests that the continental divide has remained stationary since 180 MYA. Apart from the possible negating effects of global climate changes, the geomorphological setting provided by the eastern Australian highlands has been conducive for the growth of forests since at least the close of the Mesozoic. This is particularly so for rainforests, especially where the alignment of this mountain range enhances orographic uplift of moist, humid air masses.

INTRODUCTION

The existence of rainforest in eastern Australia is to a large degree a function of the Great Dividing Range (eastern Australian highlands), which extends 3,000 km from Cape York Peninsula in Queensland to Victoria (fig. 17.1). The role of these highlands, along with the generally humid climate, in controlling the distribution of rainforest is clearly exemplified in northeastern Queensland, where the orientation of the highlands and fronting escarpment, relative to the prevailing southeasterly trade winds, control the distribution of rainfall and, consequently, of rainforest. Near Townsville, for example, the escarpment runs parallel to the trades, and here the reduced orographic uplift results in drier, more open canopy forests. To the north, where the escarpment runs obliquely to the trades, orographic uplift is enhanced, rainfall increases markedly, and rainforest returns. However, the presence of these highlands and their significance for the existing climatic and ecological regime are probably the only undisputed aspects of our knowledge of this continental-scale landform. The origin and subsequent evolution of the eastern Australian highlands have been the focus of spirited debate for nearly a century.

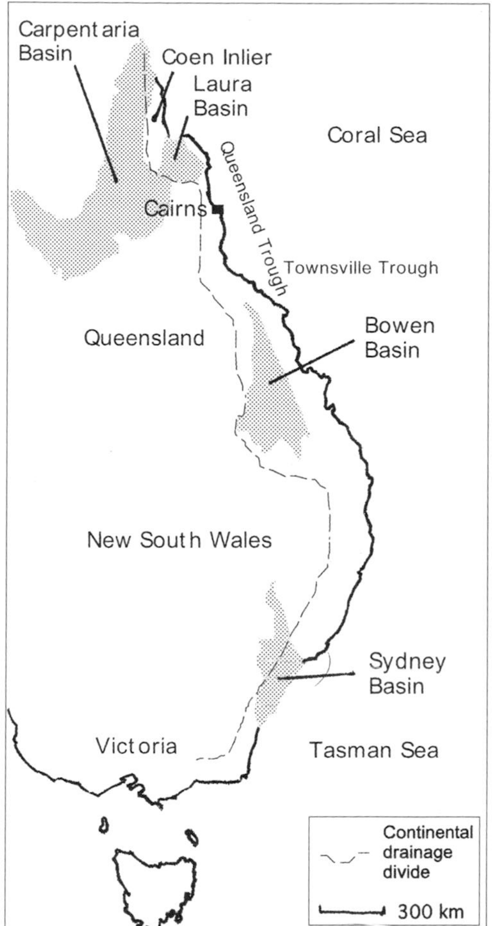

Figure 17.1 Location map showing some of the major sedimentary basins in eastern Australia, the continental drainage divide, and adjacent seas and offshore structures.

Despite the contention, studies of this mega-landform have provided useful insights into one of Earth's least understood geomorphological phenomena: the origin of highlands adjacent to continental passive margins. Mountain ranges proximal to convergent tectonic margins result from the collision and buckling of two continental margins, as is the case with the Himalaya, or the subduction and melting at depth of one plate beneath the other, resulting in volcanism and uplift, as with the Andes, or the sliding of adjacent plates along transform faults, as with the Southern Alps of New Zealand. Away from these zones of compression, there are numerous locations globally where mountain ranges occur adjacent to rifted continental margins, such as the Drakenburg of South Africa, the Ghats of India, and the Serra do Mar of South America. Of all these examples,

Australia's eastern highlands may offer the best opportunity to decipher the origin of passive margin mountain ranges. The geologic and geomorphological evidence throughout these highlands is unrivaled by that along any other passive margin because of its abundance and antiquity.

Three key questions need to be answered in order to fully understand the origin and evolution of the eastern Australian highlands:

1. When did these highlands come into existence, and what mechanisms were responsible?
2. What has been the nature of their subsequent evolution following uplift?
3. Have the highlands behaved, both during uplift and subsequently, as a single unit, or have the southern and northern segments behaved separately?

It is not the intention of this chapter to provide definitive answers to these questions, but rather to briefly summarize the state of knowledge. Such questions have relevance not only for the earth sciences, but also for the evolutionary ecology of rainforests and associated habitats in this region. This is particularly so with respect to the possibility of drainage disruption and the evolution of aquatic fauna on either side of the eastern Australian divide (see Pearson, chap. 22 in this volume). Understanding the longevity or initiation of conditions conducive to rainforest growth in eastern Australia, and contrasts between this system and others (e.g. Andes, New Guinea highlands), also depends on our knowledge of these highlands.

AGE OF THE EASTERN AUSTRALIAN HIGHLANDS

Virtually all of the research on the age of the eastern Australian highlands has been undertaken in southeastern Australia. Until the evolutionary unity of the entire highland chain is established, the results of this research will continue to pertain only to this region. However, some of the first detailed results on the origin and age of the northern component of the eastern Australian highlands are presented later in this section.

A considerable body of literature now exists on different aspects of the origin and subsequent development of Australia's southeastern highlands. Most of this literature discusses details of field investigations using geophysical, geologic, or geomorphological methods. In the first case, apatite fission track thermochronology (AFTT) has been the most recent and productive technique (Dimitru, Hill, and Coyle 1991; Kohn and Gleadow 1994; O'Sullivan et al. 1995), along with analyses of structural trends (Young 1977) and gravity studies (Young 1989). Geologic techniques have been used to examine the sedimentology (Bishop, Young, and McDougall 1985; Nott 1992) and stratigraphy of strata within the Paleozoic to Mesozoic sedimentary basins (Young 1977). Geomorphological studies have included analyses of river long-profiles (Bishop, Young, and McDougall 1985) and morphologies (Ollier and Pain 1994) and of the topographic relationships of late Mesozoic and Cenozoic basalts, sediments, and weathering profiles (Young 1977; Young and McDougall 1982, 1993; Bishop, Young, and McDougall 1985; Bishop 1988; Bishop and Goldrick 1998; Nott, Idnurm, and Young 1991; Nott 1992; Nott and Purvis 1995; Taylor et al. 1985).

One of the most striking conclusions to be drawn from the majority of these studies is that the southeastern Australian highlands appear to be considerably older than previously thought. Their exact age—that is, their time of uplift—is still not accurately known. The best estimate based on AFTT studies suggests that these highlands are at least of late Mesozoic age and are likely to be related to the formation of the adjacent Tasman Sea (see fig. 17.1) and southeastern Australian continental margin (Kohn and Gleadow 1994). According to this model, rifting of the then Australian landmass resulted in lithospheric thinning, allowing heating and updoming of the continental crust. Streams draining the newly created highlands gained considerable increase in potential and hence erosive energy, resulting in rapid denudation of the landmass and deposition of sediment into the newly formed Tasman Sea basin. The AFTT data suggest that, associated with rifting, there was rapid kilometer-scale denudation of the highlands during the Late Cretaceous. The geomorphological evidence suggests that, since the Paleocene, some 40 or so million years after the Late Cretaceous, denudation rates have slowed considerably to less than one-seventh the previous rate. During this time—that is, over the last 50–60 million years—denudation rates in this region have been among the lowest in the world.

Other lines of evidence also point toward the southeastern highlands having their origins as far back as the late Mesozoic. Bird and Chivas (1993) argued, based on the ^{18}O values of ancient regolith, that these highlands existed before the late Mesozoic. Young et al. (1996), also using oxygen isotope analysis, argued that the coastal plain on the seaward side of the highlands was in existence at this time. Likewise, Nott and Purvis (1995) suggested that the coastal plain is over 100 million years old, based on the presence of lavas of this antiquity at and close to modern sea level. These arguments assume that the coastal plain is an eroded feature cut from the highlands and that the eastern Australian escarpment, which, like the highlands, extends along the entire eastern side of the Australian continent, has receded through scarp retreat. A few authors have suggested that the coastal plain may have resulted from downwarping of a highland surface to its present position close to sea level (Ollier and Pain 1994). However, detailed stratigraphic analyses of basin strata, particularly in the Sydney Basin, have shown that, at least in this region, this cannot be the case (Young 1977; see also reviews by Nott and Purvis 1995 and Bishop and Goldrick 1998).

The age of the northeastern Australian highlands is much less well constrained, primarily because there have been fewer studies undertaken in this region. Like their southern counterparts, the highlands here are thought to have been uplifted in response to rifting of the continental margin and formation of the adjacent Coral Sea (see fig. 17.1). Rifting and seafloor creation appear to have been diachronous along the eastern Australian margin. Formation of the Tasman Sea began approximately 80–90 million years ago (MYA), as shown by magnetic striping across the seafloor. Coral Sea formation began approximately 50–60 MYA; for this reason, uplift of the northeastern highlands is thought to have occurred later than in the southeast. Recent research has suggested that although the Coral Sea developed between 50 and 60 MYA, rifting to form the Queensland and Townsville troughs (see fig. 17.1) began during the Jurassic to Early Cretaceous (~150–100 MYA), and uplift of the adjacent landmass may have occurred in response (Scott 1993; Struckmeyer and Symonds 1997).

It is not necessarily the case, however, that uplift must occur in association with seafloor formation. It is possible for uplift to occur many millions of years earlier as part of the initial rifting process. It is also possible that seafloor spreading results in another phase of uplift of an existing mountain chain. Indeed, as discussed later, some of the field evidence in northeastern Queensland suggests that the highlands there were in existence as long ago as the Jurassic, approximately 180 MYA, predating the formation of the Coral Sea and the Queensland and Townsville troughs.

HIGHLAND EVOLUTION FOLLOWING UPLIFT

Ollier and Pain (1994) suggested that the southeastern Australian highlands experienced substantial modification following uplift. This modification involved downwarping of the eastern flank of the highlands to form parts of the present coastal plain and widespread rearrangement of drainage patterns through either stream capture or reversal. According to this model, westward migration of the continental divide to its present position occurred concomitantly with downwarping and drainage disruption; prior to this, the divide was

A

Species richness of mammals and birds

Endemism of mammals and birds

B

Forest mammals and forest birds
Green; predominance of mammals. Blue; predominance of birds.

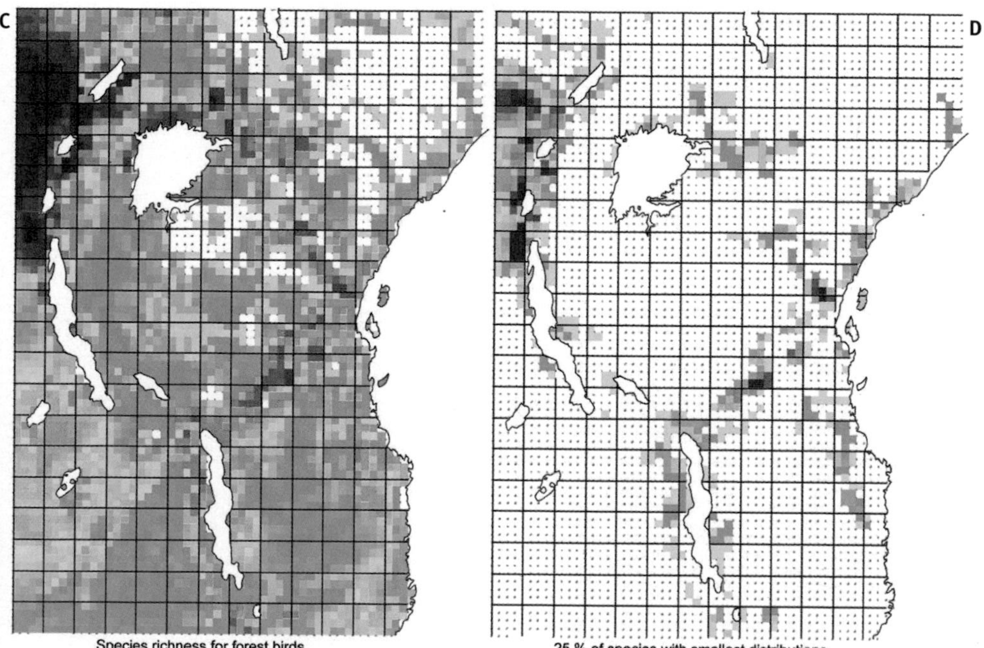

Plate 1 Species richness and endemism in Africa. Maps A and B compare patterns for forest birds and forest mammals, on a 1° spatial resolution. Species richness (A) and endemism (B) are expressed as brightness, with areas with the highest richness of both groups appearing white, a bias toward mammals shown in green, and a bias toward birds in blue (see Williams 1998). Maps C and D are focused on eastern Africa (15′ resolution) and show species richness and narrow (lower quartile) endemism (richness peaks are red, poor areas are blue).

Plate 2 The simulation for the Warra Long Term Ecological Research Site was commenced with a set of randomly distributed tree agents. The different pixel colors represent the seven representative species listed in table 11.1 and graphed in figures 11.8 and 11.9: red, *Eucalyptus obliqua* ("obliqua" in figures 11.8 and 11.9); white, *E. delegatensis* ("delegatensis"); yellow, *Gahnia grandis* ("gahnia"); navy blue, *Nothofagus cunninghamii* ("myrtle"); sky blue, *Phyllocladus aspleniifolius* ("celerytop pine"); pink, *Acacia melanoxylon* ("blackwood"); and gray blue, *Pomaderris apetala* ("dogwood").

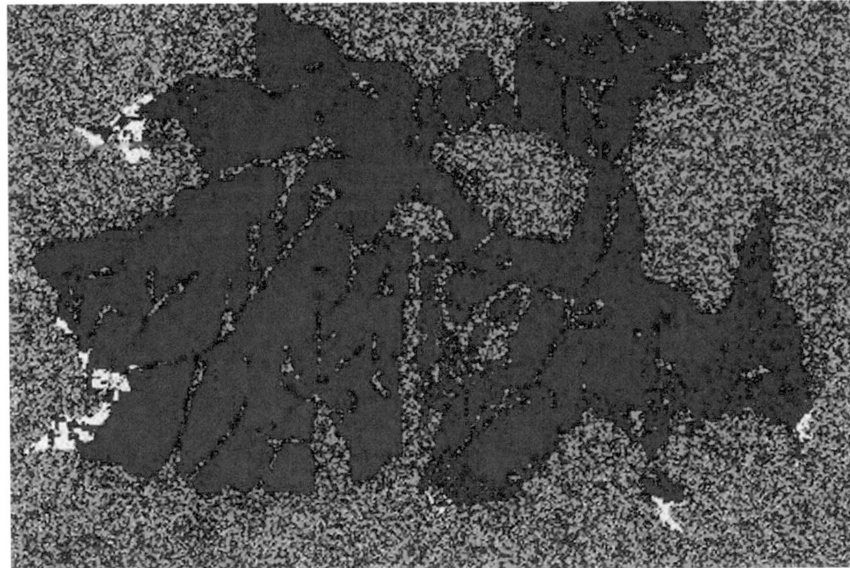

Plate 3 The emergent landscape patterns in forest types shown after 500 years of simulation. These patterns reflect the combined effects of individual tree behaviors, environmental constraints, and the history of fire regimes in the landscape. Pixel colors are described in plate 2.

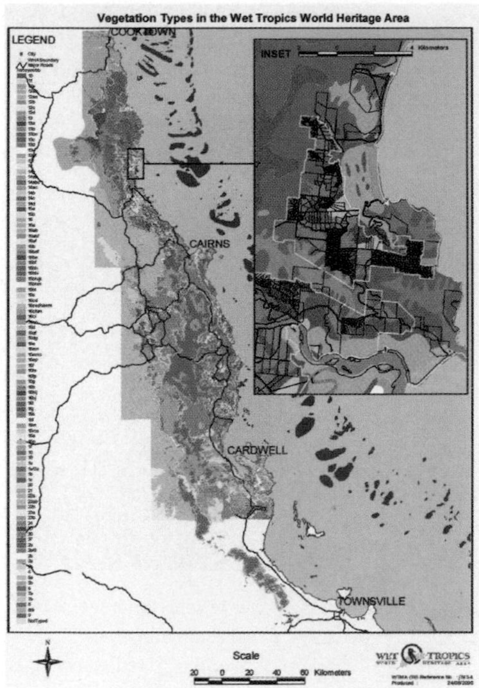

Plate 4 Distribution of major vegetation types (Webb and Tracey 1981) in and around the Wet Tropics of Queensland World Heritage Area.

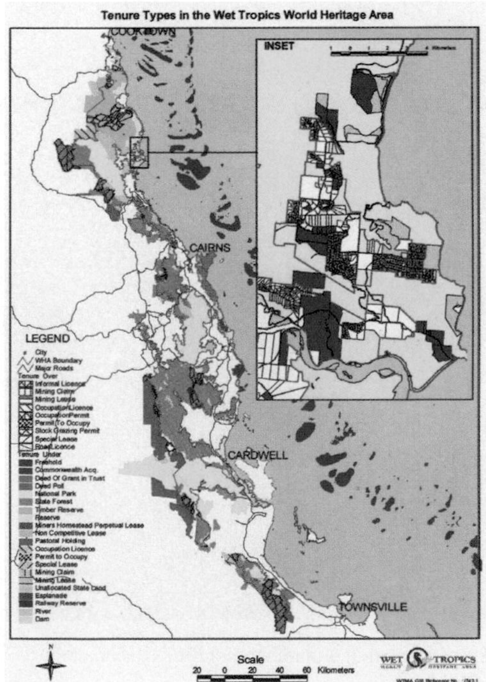

Plate 5 Distribution of land tenure types in the Wet Tropics of Queensland World Heritage Area.

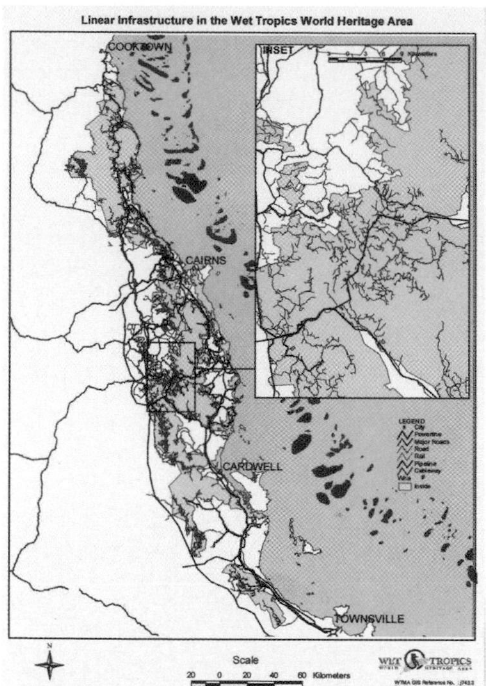

Plate 6 Distribution of major roads and powerlines in and around the Wet Tropics of Queensland World Heritage Area.

Plate 7 Industrial logging creates labyrinths of roads that promote forest colonization and overhunting. (Photograph by W. F. Laurance.)

east of the present coast. With the divide in this more easterly position, streams flowed westward across the highlands, where the divide now exists, into sedimentary basins in western New South Wales and Queensland and the region now occupied by the Gulf of Carpentaria. The downwarping of the eastern flank of the highlands resulted in a reversal of the headwaters of these streams, causing them to flow east into the newly formed or forming seas. Such ideas have been used to explain the phylogeography of freshwater fishes throughout northeastern Queensland (Hurwood and Hughes 1998) despite the absence of independent supporting geologic field evidence. Indeed, considerable geologic evidence exists to show that many major streams never flowed west across the position of the present continental divide.

Much of the debate on continental divide migration and stream alterations has centered on the southeastern highlands. Two principal schools of thought exist: one that argues that individual drainage lines, and hence the divide, have remained essentially stable since at least the early to mid-Tertiary (Young 1977; Young and McDougall 1982, 1985, 1993; Bishop 1988; Bishop, Young, and McDougall 1985; Taylor et al. 1985, 1990; Nott 1992), and one that suggests divide migration and stream alterations (Ollier and Pain 1994). The differences of opinion have occurred primarily because of the different methods used by the two groups. Those advocating stability base their arguments on evidence acquired from detailed field studies of generally quite large, individual stream catchments. Those proposing drainage disturbance rely not so much on field evidence, but primarily on the recognition of so-called irregularities of stream planform, such as "boat hook bends" and "barbed drainage," and the apparent alignment of streams on either side of the continental divide.

Ollier and Pain (1994) suggested that the two points of view are not necessarily in conflict because divide migration and drainage reorganization could have occurred prior to the Middle Eocene (45 MYA), this being the earliest age of much of the field evidence that clearly contradicts their hypothesis. However, there are other forms of evidence that discount the notion of downwarping and large-scale stream disruption in the southeastern highlands. Probably the clearest example comes from the southern part of the Sydney Basin, where horizontal to sub-horizontal Permo-Triassic strata overlie folded Paleozoic metasediments. The Permian strata dip at approximately 2° to the northeast (toward the coast), and this has been argued by several workers to be evidence for downwarping of the highland surface to form the coastal plain. However, as Young (1977) and Young and McDougall (1982) demonstrated, the inclining of these Permian strata must have occurred prior to the Triassic because the overlying

Triassic strata do not dip, but rather remain horizontal. If downwarping occurred during the Tertiary, or at any time after the Triassic, these strata would also dip toward the coast.

The stratigraphy of the southern Sydney Basin demonstrates that the coastal plain here is entirely erosional in origin. The highland surface at the southern extremity of the Sydney Basin is capped by Permian Nowra Sandstone. If downwarping had occurred, this stratum should crop out across the coastal plain. Rather, the coastal plain is carved into strata that sit approximately 500 m stratigraphically below the Nowra Sandstone. Weathering profiles dated by ^{18}O as late Mesozoic occur on this lowland surface, suggesting that at least 500 m of overlying Permian strata had been removed to expose the coastal plain by this time. Lavas older than 100 MYA, 150 km farther south along the coastal plain beyond the limits of the Sydney Basin, also highlight the antiquity of this feature (Nott and Purvis 1995).

The erosional origin of the coastal plain is further reinforced by AFTT studies (O'Sullivan et al. 1998). Fission track analysis measures denudation of the land surface or "rock uplift" relative to the land surface. It determines the depth below the land surface at which rocks now exposed at the surface occurred at a certain time in the past. As a result, it is possible to calculate the time taken for those rocks to reach the present land surface due to denudation. Fission track studies throughout southeastern Australia show much younger "ages" or "episodes of cooling" across the coastal plain and progressively older ages with distance inland. This pattern suggests that considerably more material was stripped from above the present coastal plain than across the present highlands. If downwarping had occurred, then the older fission track ages should also occur across the coastal plain; quite the opposite is true.

A similar situation exists in the northeastern highlands. Apatite fission track studies here also show that downwarping could not have occurred (O'Sullivan and Kohn 1998). Arguments concerning drainage reversal are also not supported by field evidence. Pain, Wilford, and Dohrenwend (1998) suggested that streams on Cape York Peninsula once had their headwaters east of the present coast, and that downwarping and divide migration resulted in stream reversal. They cited the Pascoe River catchment, where two apparent gaps through the continental divide give the appearance of former stream valleys. The southernmost gap is really a shallow col in the divide, rather than a gap. The northern valley does not extend to the divide. This valley is drained by a tributary creek to the Pascoe River, and the valley deepens downstream and contains a sedimentary unit of Miocene age that thickens in the downstream direction. These sediments also do not extend to the continental divide, and therefore cannot be as-

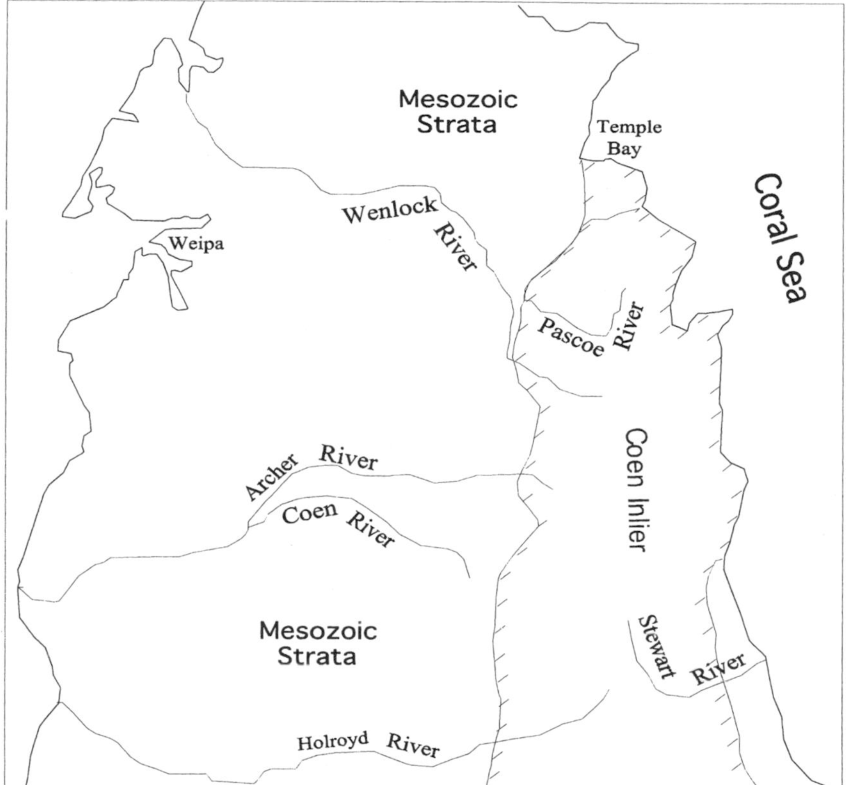

Figure 17.2 Streams of northern Queensland. Note the alignment of the north-flowing section of the Pascoe River with the boundary between the Coen Inlier and adjacent Mesozoic strata. The east-flowing section to the north is structurally controlled by a fault.

sociated with a prior stream course supposedly flowing west across the present divide. The location of this valley is structurally controlled, for it has formed along a fault along which numerous groundwater springs occur.

The planform of the Pascoe River also poses difficulties for the reversal hypothesis. The headwaters of the Pascoe rise to the east of the continental divide and flow west before turning north and then east to the Coral Sea (fig. 17.2). Prior to drainage reversal and turning toward the north, the now westerly-flowing section of the Pascoe supposedly continued west, joining with the Wenlock River, which flows into the Gulf of Carpentaria (Pain, Wilford, and Dohrenwend 1998). It is difficult to envisage why the headwaters of the Pascoe River should still be flowing west if downwarping and tilting of the land toward the east supposedly resulted in stream reversal. There is no need to invoke tectonic

Figure 17.3 The Barron River, showing the boat hook bend where the river turns sharply from its northward course toward the east. Note that the knickpoint (Barron Falls) is well downstream of the boat hook bend. Upstream of the knickpoint, the stream is graded to tableland surface; therefore, the upper Barron River could not have been captured by a stream draining eastward and advancing headward through the knickpoint retreat. Note also the two separate paleochannels of the Mitchell and Barron rivers.

events to explain the present course of the Pascoe River, for it too is structurally controlled (Forsyth and Nott 2003). The river turns north from its westerly course at the boundary of the Coen inlier (see fig. 17.1) and follows this boundary northward until it encounters a fault striking east, which it then follows to the sea.

A similar situation exists for the Barron River, which drains into the Coral Sea near Cairns (fig. 17.3). The Barron flows north, then turns sharply to the east. This sharp bend, known as a "boat hook bend," is often assumed to be a site of river capture. River capture, however, requires a steeper-gradient stream draining to a lower elevation to advance headward to the captured stream through a knickpoint retreat (a knickpoint can be a waterfall or very steep section of rapids). In this instance, the major knickpoint on the Barron River is the Barron Falls. These falls are located downstream of the boat hook bend, and therefore have not advanced sufficiently headward to have reached the bend and captured the river. The sharp easterly bend in the river has not resulted from capture. Further evidence in support of the stability of drainage patterns in this region comes from drill hole data within the Barron and adjacent Mitchell River catchments (Forsyth and Nott 2003). Here, the continental drainage divide has very low relief between the two catchments; indeed, in extreme floods, water from the Barron catchment flows into the Mitchell River system. Buried paleochannels of both the Mitchell and Barron rivers parallel each other in the region just upstream of the easterly bend in the Barron River (fig. 17.3). This finding shows that these two rivers have existed for a considerable time, and that the Mitchell River was not previously joined to the Barron River prior to any supposed capture or stream reversal.

Geologic evidence from Cape York Peninsula also suggests that the continental drainage divide has remained in its present position since the Jurassic (180 MYA), predating the time of postulated continental divide migration to its present position. The largely undeformed sandstones within the Laura Basin record paleocurrent flow directions prior to formation of the Coral Sea and the Queensland and Townsville troughs. The continental divide separates the Laura and Carpentaria basins and is here known geologically as the Kimba Arch, a Paleozoic granitic intrusion. Both of these basins have Jurassic strata as their basal sequences (fig. 17.4). The Dalrymple Sandstone, being the basal unit in the Laura Basin, does not extend across the Kimba Arch, but lenses onto the continental divide and thickens considerably eastward. Paleocurrent measurements from the Dalrymple Sandstone show that the streams that deposited this sequence flowed northeast and had their headwaters at the present divide (Nott and Horton 2000) (fig. 17.5). This finding, along with the lensing of the Dalrymple Sandstone onto the divide, suggests that the continental divide in this immediate region has remained in its present location since before initial deposition of this sandstone, about 180 MYA.

The stratigraphy of the Laura Basin shows that the continental divide there has experienced minimal denudation since the Jurassic. Exposures and drill logs show that approximately 58 m of Gilbert River Formation sits unconformably on Silurian granite and is overlain conformably by the Cretaceous marine Rolling Downs Group on the Kimba Arch (the continental divide: McConachie et al. 1998; see fig. 17.4). There is no obvious hiatus in deposition between the

Kimba Arch

A B

Rolling Downs Group
Gilbert River Formation
Dalrymple Sandstone

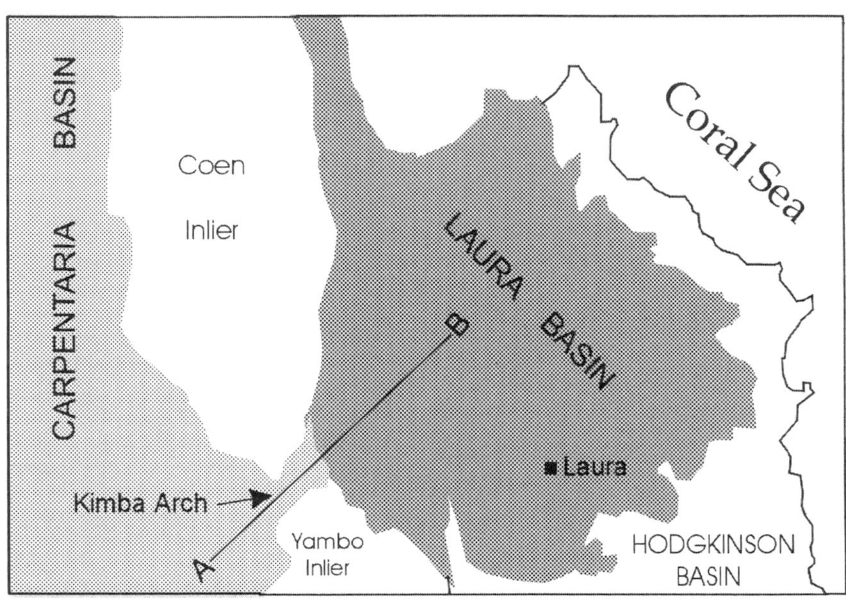

Figure 17.4 Cross-section through Kimba Arch of sedimentary units in the Laura and Carpentaria basins. Note the lensing of the Middle to Late Jurassic Dalrymple Sandstone onto Kimba Arch (the continental drainage divide). Note also its absence in Carpentaria Basin.

Gilbert River Formation and Rolling Downs Group, so in places, the Gilbert River Formation has remained totally preserved and represents the original depositional sequence. In these locations, only the Rolling Downs Group has been denuded. This unit is approximately 1,000 m thick in the center of the Laura Basin, presently below sea level. However, it is likely that this marine unit was less than 50 m thick when originally present across the continental divide. The rationale for this conclusion is as follows. The present height of the divide at the Kimba Arch, comprising a sedimentary cover (Mesozoic and Tertiary) 96 m thick above basement, is 212 m above sea level. Assuming that there has been minimal vertical movement of the divide since that time, the elevation of the site prior to deposition of the Gilbert River Formation would have been 116 m above

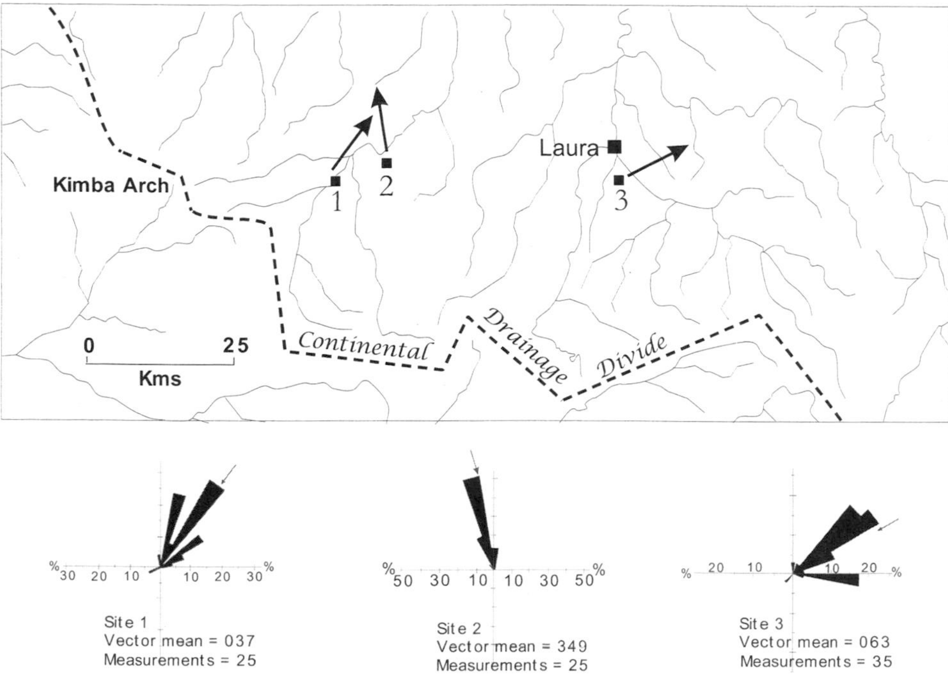

Figure 17.5 Location map of Dalrymple Sandstone paleocurrent measurement sites and results. Paleocurrent measurements are presented as rose diagrams below the location map. Results are in 10° segments, and arrows represent mean paleocurrent directions on the rose diagrams and on the location map. Note that stream flow was away from the continental divide during the Middle to Late Jurassic and in approximately the same direction as modern stream flow.

sea level. Sea levels reached a maximum height of 180 m above modern sea level during the Neocomian (when the Gilbert River Formation was deposited) (Haq, Hardenbol, and Vail 1987), which would have been sufficient to inundate the Kimba Arch and deposit the 58 m of Gilbert River Formation still preserved. Sea levels reached approximately 220 m above modern sea level during the middle Albian (Haq, Hardenbol, and Vail 1987), and at this time the Kimba Arch stood at 174 m above sea level (elevation of basement plus Gilbert River Formation). The land was still sufficiently low in elevation to have allowed the Kimba Arch to be inundated by the transgressing sea to a maximum height of approximately 50 m, and for deposition of the Rolling Downs Group. The unknown factor in this argument is the extent of vertical movement of the divide since the beginning of the Cretaceous. However, as is clearly shown by the paleocurrent directions within the Dalrymple Sandstone and its lensing onto the divide, the divide existed at that time. Therefore, it is reasonable to assume that the divide was at least 100 m above sea level by the Cretaceous, for it had sedimentary basins on either side, and it could not have been much higher, otherwise it would not have been inundated by the sea during the Neocomian and then later in the Albian. Only a few meters of Rolling Downs Group are presently preserved across the divide at the Kimba Arch; therefore, there must have been less than 50 m of denudation here since the Cretaceous (Albian).

The major tectonic events responsible for formation of the northeastern Australian continental margin were associated with extension of the continental crust to form the now offshore Queensland and Townsville basins (see fig. 17.1) (Scott 1993; Struckmeyer and Symonds 1997) during the Jurassic to Cretaceous. Uplift is suggested to have occurred adjacent to these rifts during the mid- to Late Cretaceous, predating formation of the Coral Sea basin during the Paleocene (Struckmeyer and Symonds 1997). The strata within the Laura and Carpentaria basins show that passive margin tectonics, at least in this immediate region, did not result in substantial migration of the divide westward or in grossly altered drainage patterns as a result of post-uplift subsidence of the highlands' eastern flank. This is not to say, however, that such events could not have occurred in other regions, for only similarly detailed investigations elsewhere throughout northeastern Australia will provide a comprehensive picture of the evolution of these highlands and their drainage patterns.

CONCLUSION

We are still far from an adequate understanding of the evolution of Australia's eastern highlands. The question of the evolutionary unity of the northern and southern segments of this highland chain remains unresolved. However, it now appears possible that these highlands, or at least substantial portions of them, were in existence during the late Mesozoic. Sections may have experienced subsequent uplift, and there may well have been substantial denudation since initial uplift. But extensive denudation in response to a new base level (i.e., opening of the Tasman and Coral seas) requires knickpoints to have first penetrated that section of the highlands; otherwise, streams would remain graded to a raised, not the new, base level. In other words, the fact that a new base level exists is communicated to the highlands only when streams adjust by altering their gradients. It is only after this that valley slopes steepen, relief increases, and, as a corollary, erosion rates increase. In the Laura Basin, knickpoints have not yet advanced headward to the continental divide; hence, denudation rates on the divide have remained low since before the late Mesozoic.

The evidence for widespread stability of drainage patterns throughout Australia's eastern highlands continues to mount. This evidence does not discount the possibility that in some locations, continental divide migration could have occurred and stream patterns altered. Furthermore, drainage disruption at a sub-catchment scale is also entirely possible. However, boat hook bends that occur upstream of knickpoints cannot be taken as evidence of stream capture or reversal.

18

The Origins and Tertiary History of Australian "Tropical" Rainforests

DAVID R. GREENWOOD
AND DAVID C. CHRISTOPHEL

ABSTRACT

In this chapter we use the plant macrofossil record, and in particular, the record from southeastern Australia as evidence of past ecosystems. We provide background information on the evolution of Australian tropical rainforests over the Tertiary period (65 to 1.8 million years ago), and we consider the origin of Australian tropical rainforests, how they responded to climatic and other environmental factors over geologic time, and the ecological processes that have shaped them in the crucible of continental drift and climatic deterioration.

INTRODUCTION

A number of events have been critical in the history of the Australian biota, and that of the tropical rainforests in particular (Truswell, Kershaw, and Sluiter 1987; Archer, Hand, and Godthelp 1994; Barlow 1994; Macphail et al. 1994; Crisp, West, and Linder 1999; Vadala and Greenwood 2001): the high southern latitude of the continent at the end of the Cretaceous period and its subsequent northward drift toward the equator (fig. 18.1) and contact with what is now the Indonesian archipelago (including the formation of the island of New Guinea); significant global climate change over the past 65 million years, essentially translating in the Australian context into significant drying more than any other climatic effect; and the evolution in situ from ancestral Gondwanan stock of much of the biota, but also significant immigration onto the continent by both plant and animal lineages from different geographic sources at several times.

The focus of this chapter will be the plant macrofossil record as evidence of past ecosystems, particularly the record from southeastern Australia. The microfossil and other geologic evidence of both climate change and significant geomorphological and tectonic events across the continent will also be reviewed. We deliberately focus on the macrofossil record from the southeast, as this record is the most detailed, and because macrofloras are to a large extent a

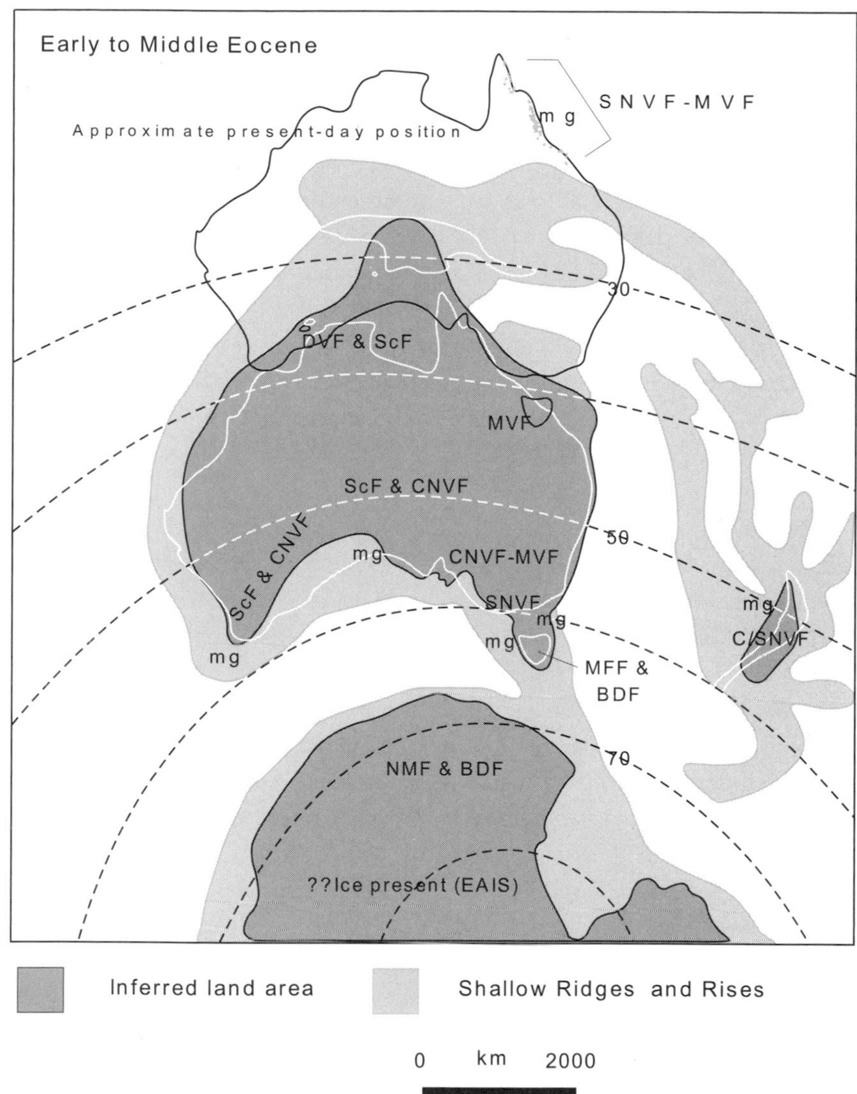

Figure 18.1 Sketch of the position of the Australian continent in the early Paleogene, showing vegetation types inferred from primarily macrofloral evidence. The present-day positions of Australia and of its tropical rainforests are shown for reference. BDF, broad-leaved deciduous forest and temperate mixed conifer; MVF, mesophyll vine forest (megathermal rainforest); DVF, deciduous vine forest (wet-dry deciduous forest); CNVF, complex notophyll vine forest (mesothermal-megathermal rainforest); SNVF, simple notophyll vine forest (mesothermal rainforest); MFF and NMF, microphyll fern forest and nanophyll mossy forest (microthermal rainforest); ScF, sclerophyllous forest; mg, mangroves with *Nypa* palms.

record of local communities (Spicer 1988; Greenwood 1991; Steart et al. 2002). Most importantly, the macrofossil record provides more than simple taxonomic analogy, as plant organs such as leaves provide strong evidence of paleoenvironments based on modern observations of relationships between climatic variables and leaf physiognomy (Wolfe 1985, 1993; Greenwood 1992, 2001; Greenwood and Wing 1995; Wilf 1997; Greenwood et al. 2003). Taxon-independent analogy also avoids the assumption that floristic associations ("communities") persist on the landscape and that they reflect fundamental units responding coherently to environmental influences (Kershaw and Bulman 1994; Colinvaux, chap. 6 in this volume). Microfloral (pollen and spores) evidence is used to provide a broader picture of regional vegetation and also to provide data on plant taxa poorly represented or not detected in the macrofloral record. By way of introduction, it is also important to set the scene and place the Australian tropical rainforest in biogeographic context.

The Australian continent today is dominated by two genera of woody plants, *Eucalyptus* s.l. (Myrtaceae) and *Acacia* (Mimosaceae). The forests, woodlands, and shrublands covering most of the continent are dominated by trees or tall shrubs of these genera, but also include significant representation of *Callitris* (Cupressaceae s.s.), *Casuarina* and *Allocasuarina* (Casuarinaceae), Proteaceae (e.g., *Banksia* and *Grevillea*), other Myrtaceae (e.g., *Leptospermum* and *Melaleuca*), Rutaceae, Epacridaceae, Fabaceae, and Goodeniaceae. These floristic associations range from the high-rainfall areas of southeastern, southwestern, and eastern Australia to the arid center and markedly wet-dry monsoonal north (Barlow 1994; Crisp, West, and Linder 1999). This vegetation is typically sclerophyllous, in the main a response to low soil fertility, but in part an adaptation to dry climate (i.e., xerophylly) and fire.

The marked sclerophylly of most Australian vegetation provides dramatic and sharp visual contrast with rainforest, so much so that any nonsclerophyllous forest is commonly termed "rainforest." Thus, in Australia, "rainforest" also encompasses deciduous monsoon forests and thickets (incongruously named "dry rainforests") on sites where annual rainfall may be as low as 600 mm, as well as seasonal evergreen tropical forests (Webb 1959; Greenwood 1996). Several authors have advocated alternative nomenclature to avoid this confusion (see discussion in Webb and Tracey 1994), referring to "closed forests" (i.e., with rain-green closed canopies) and "vine forests/thickets" (i.e., possessing plant synusiae lacking or poor in sclerophyllous vegetation). For the purposes of this chapter, "tropical rainforest" is considered to include all closed-canopy forests falling within Nix's (1982) humid mesothermal to megathermal* climates—that is, evergreen to semi-evergreen Mesophyll and Notophyll Vine Forests *sensu* Webb (1959) and Tracey (1982). We exclude from this definition the markedly dry-season deciduous monsoon forests and thickets (e.g., Semi-Deciduous Microphyll Vine Forest "Type 11" and Deciduous Microphyll Vine Thicket "Type 4" of Webb and Tracey [1994; Tracey 1982]: Greenwood 1996). Rainforest, however it is defined, occupies a small part of the present continent (less than 1% at the time of European colonization), reflecting primarily climatic restriction to an archipelago of suitable sites surrounded by a sea of fire-adapted *Eucalyptus*-dominated forest (fig. 18.2). This circumstance reflects the dynamic role wildfire plays in promoting the floristic and physiognomic character and mosaic nature of vegetation across the Australian landscape (Barlow 1994; Webb and Tracey 1994).

The prominent Australian woody plant families, Myrtaceae and Proteaceae, are richly represented taxonomically and numerically in mesothermal to megathermal notophyllous and mesophyllous vine forests (i.e., subtropical to tropical rainforests) and in sclerophyllous vegetation. In some instances these two forest types share some genera, such as *Grevillea* and *Lomatia* (Proteaceae), or sister taxa, such as the rainforest *Musgravea* and the sclerophyllous taxa *Banksia* and *Dryandra* (tribe Banksieae of Proteaceae). Other key families with one or more genera shared between rainforests and sclerophyllous vegetation include Capparidaceae, Casuarinaceae (e.g., *Gymnostoma* and *Allocasuarina/Casuarina*), Celastraceae, Combretaceae, Dilleniaceae, Ebenaceae, Euphorbiaceae, Fabaceae, Flindersiaceae, Meliaceae, Mimosaceae, Pittosporaceae, Rhamnaceae, Rubiaceae, Rutaceae, Sapindaceae, Solanaceae, Sterculiaceae, and Verbenaceae (Webb and Tracey 1994). The preeminent Australian genera, *Acacia* and *Eucalyptus*, are largely absent from tropical rainforests, however, occupying ecotonal or seral roles in some areas in response to disturbance.

At every taxonomic level, the tropical rainforests share floristic links with the drier and/or sclerophyllous vegetation types of the continent, reflecting a common evolutionary heritage and history. The interpretation of these phytogeographic patterns as reflecting a common origin for the sclerophyllous forests and tropical rainforests was not always accepted. Early narrative accounts of Australian phytogeography stressed the floristic similarities of the northern tropical

* Thermal nomenclature of Nix (1982): Megatherm dominant, mean annual temperature (MAT) > 24°C; mesothermal-megathermal interzone, MAT > 20°C < 24°C; mesotherm dominant, MAT > 14°C < 20°C; mesothermal-microtherm interzone, MAT > 12°C < 14°C; microtherm dominant, < 12°C.

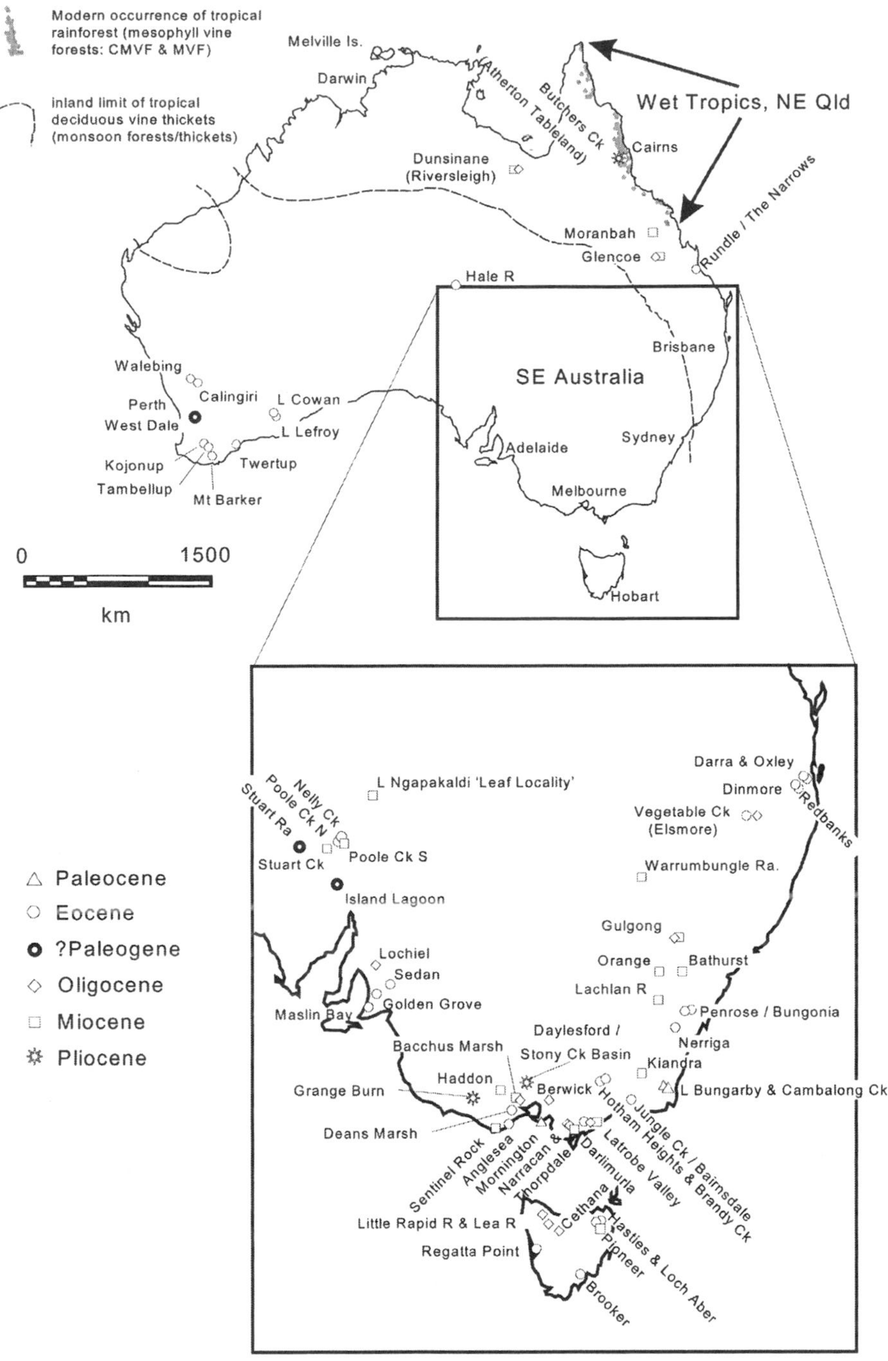

Modern occurrence of tropical rainforest (mesophyll vine forests: CMVF & MVF)
inland limit of tropical deciduous vine thickets (monsoon forests/thickets)
Melville Is.
Darwin
Atherton Tableland
Butchers Ck
Wet Tropics, NE Qld
Cairns
Dunsinane (Riversleigh)
Rundle / The Narrows
Moranbah
Glencoe
Hale R
Brisbane
SE Australia
Walebing
Calingiri
Perth
West Dale
L Cowan
L Lefroy
Kojonup
Tambellup
Twertup
Mt Barker
Adelaide
Sydney
Melbourne
Hobart
0
1500
km
△ Paleocene
○ Eocene
?Paleogene
◇ Oligocene
□ Miocene
Pliocene
Darra & Oxley
Dinmore
Redbanks
L Ngapakaldi 'Leaf Locality'
Nelly Ck
Poole Ck N
Stuart Ra
Vegetable Ck (Elsmore)
Stuart Ck
Poole Ck S
Warrumbungle Ra.
Island Lagoon
Gulgong
Lochiel
Orange
Bathurst
Sedan
Lachlan R
Maslin Bay
Golden Grove
Penrose / Bungonia
Daylesford / Stony Ck Basin
Nerriga
Bacchus Marsh
Kiandra
Haddon
Berwick
L Bungarby & Cambalong Ck
Grange Burn
Deans Marsh
Sentinel Rock
Anglesea
Mornington
Narracan & Thorpdale
Darlimurla
Latrobe Valley
Hotham Heights & Brandy Ck
Jungle Ck / Bairnsdale
Little Rapid R & Lea R
Cethana
Hasties & Loch Aber
Regatta Point
Pioneer
Brooker

rainforests to those on the island of New Guinea and in Southeast Asia, that of the temperate southern rainforests to those in New Zealand and Chile, and the high endemicity of the sclerophyllous flora as evidence, respectively, for an immigrant "Indomalayan" floristic element, an ancient "Antarctic" element, and an "autochthonous" element (Barlow 1994; Crisp, West, and Linder 1999). Phylogenetic phytogeographic analyses and the fossil record, however, testify to the essentially Gondwanan origin of Australia's tropical and temperate rainforests and the derivation of the sclerophyllous flora from the same ancestral stock (Webb, Tracey, and Jessup 1986; Truswell, Kershaw, and Sluiter 1987; Christophel and Greenwood 1989; R. S. Hill 1992, 1994, 1998; Barlow 1994; Macphail et al. 1994; Crisp, West, and Linder 1999; Vadala and Greenwood 2001). Accounts of the biogeographic implications of continental drift-mediated contact between Australia and its northern neighbors have promoted the idea of a complicated post-collision interaction with a bidirectional exchange of biota (limited by the inability of some biota to cross barriers) rather than invasion (Truswell, Kershaw, and Sluiter 1987; Vadala and Greenwood 2001). Macphail et al. (1994) suggest, however, that the role of long-distance dispersal to and from Australia by plants is perhaps understated.

Recent reviews of the evolution of the Australian flora have either been broad-brush portraits (e.g., Christophel and Greenwood 1989; R. S. Hill 1992; Christophel 1994) or histories of particular taxonomic groups (e.g., Christophel 1988; Hill 1994), or have focused on the microfloral record (e.g., Truswell 1990, 1993; Macphail et al. 1994; Martin 1998). Carpenter, Hill, and Jordan (1994) provided a macrofossil-based account of Tertiary vegetation evolution in Tasmania, including that of temperate rainforests, and Truswell (1990) presented a synthesis on the evolution of Australian rainforests based primarily on microfossil data. No previous discussion based primarily on macrofossils, to our knowledge, has focused on the evolution of Australia's tropical rainforests. Christophel (1981, 1988, 1994), Christophel and Greenwood (1987, 1988, 1989), and Greenwood (1996; Greenwood et al. 2003) discussed specific Tertiary macrofloras from southern and central Australia that provided some insight into the progenitors of the extant tropical rainforests and monsoon deciduous forests. This chapter builds on the analysis presented by Christophel (1981, 1988, 1994) and Christophel and Greenwood (1989) and includes more sites than these analyses,

Figure 18.2 Map of Australia, showing locations of macrofloras discussed in the text. Some sites are known from dispersed cuticle only. The main present-day occurrence of tropical rainforests and tropical deciduous vegetation, and the location of the Wet Tropics region, are shown for reference.

as well as new data and insights on other sites based on a significant increase in knowledge since the former works were written. The discussion here also builds on earlier spore-pollen (microfossil)-based accounts. Additional macro- and microfloral data presented in Greenwood et al. (2003) are not included here, as the latter work was completed after this chapter was finished. Readers are directed to Vickers-Rich (1991) and Archer, Hand, and Godthelp (1994, 1995) for recent syntheses on the evolution of the vertebrate fauna. The locations of the sites described in this chapter are shown in figure 18.2, and details of their macrofloras are given in table 18.1.

GEOLOGIC AND CLIMATIC FRAMEWORK

Continents in Motion

Australia has undergone significant latitudinal displacement during the Tertiary (see fig. 18.1), having been at high southern latitudes in the early Paleogene (Wilford and Brown 1994). Much of the continent was of low relief throughout the Tertiary, although sufficient relief has probably existed along the eastern margin at times, particularly in the southeast and Tasmania, to provide cooler climates than prevailed over much of the continent (Ollier 1986; Taylor 1994; Nott, chap. 17 in this volume). Limited volcanism occurred along the eastern margin throughout the Tertiary, producing large elevated plateaus in the northeastern Queensland area (e.g., the Atherton Tableland) and in New South Wales (e.g., Barrington Tops area). At times of global high sea level, the sea has inundated substantial low-lying areas of the continent (e.g., Murray Basin: Quilty 1994). Below we briefly review the major tectonic events that have provided the framework for the evolution of the Australian biota. In the following section we outline the sequence of climate change.

At the close of the Cretaceous and in the early Paleocene, 70–60 million years ago (MYA), the present-day Wet Tropics region of northeastern Queensland, which supports most of Australia's existing tropical rainforests, lay at 30°–40° S. Much of southern Australia lay at 50°–60° S and so would have experienced quite short days in winter and long days in summer. The island of New Guinea was probably a low-lying archipelago. At this time Australia retained a land connection to Antarctica (and thus via Antarctica to South America). This land connection directed ocean currents in north-south flows adjacent to the Australian continent, contributing to warm climates at this time (Quilty 1994). About 50 MYA, in the early Middle Eocene, the uplift of the Transantarctic Mountains may have provided the elevation necessary for the formation of snow and ice in Antarctica.

Table 18.1 Site details for principal macrofloras discussed in the text

Macroflora	Stratigraphic Age	Lat. (S)	Long. (E)	Taxa[a]																	
				1	2	3	4	5	6	7	8	9	10	11	12	13	14	15	16	17	18
Lake Bungarby	Late Paleocene	36°09′	149°08′						X				X		X		X				
Cambalong Ck	Late Paleocene	36°09′	149°08′			X	X			X			X		X		X				
Regatta Point	Early Eocene	42°10′	145°20′	X		X	X		X	X							?	X			
Hotham H'ts	Early Eocene	36°59′	147°09′		X		X		X		X		X				X	X	X		
Deans Marsh	Late Early to Middle Eocene	38°24′	144°11′					X			X		X				X		X		
Maslin Bay	Middle Eocene	35°30′	138°30′		X			X	X		X	X	X	X	X		X	X	X		
Golden Grove	Middle Eocene	34°47′	138°44′					X	X		X	X	X	X		X	X	X	X		
Nelly Creek	Middle Eocene	29°19′	137°18′		X				X	X			X				X	X	X		
Nerriga	Middle Eocene	35°07′	150°05′	X									?			X	X	X	X		
Anglesea	Late Middle Eocene	38°25′	144°11′	X			X	X	X		X	X	X	X		X	X	X	X		
Loch Aber	Middle-Late Eocene	41°02′	147°58′			X	X		X	X			X								
Hasties	Middle-Late Eocene	41°01′	147°53′			X	X		X	X					X		X	X			
Lochiel	Early Oligocene	33°56′	138°10′	X	X			X	X	X	X		X				X	X	X		
Cethana	Early-Late Oligocene	41°32′	146°07′	X	X	X	X	X	X		X		X		X		X	X	X		
Little Rapid R.	Early-Late Oligocene	41°09′	145°14′		X		X	X	X		X				X		X	X	X		
Narracan	Early Oligocene-Early Miocene	38°16′	141°46′				X				X			X	X		X	X			
Berwick	Late Oligocene-Early Miocene	37°06′	146°44′		X		X						X		X		X	X		X	
Pioneer	Late Oligocene-Early Miocene	41°05′	147°56′				X	X					X		X						

(continued)

Table 18.1 *(continued)*

Macroflora	Stratigraphic Age	Lat. (S)	Long. (E)	Taxa[a]																	
				1	2	3	4	5	6	7	8	9	10	11	12	13	14	15	16	17	18
Morwell Seam	Late Oligocene-Early Miocene	38°05′	146°05′	X	X	X	X		X	X	X	X	X	X		X	X	X	X		
Monpeelyata	Early Miocene	42°05′	146°45′			X	X								X						
Kiandra	Early Miocene	35°52′	148°30′			X	X		X						X		X		X		
Bacchus Marsh	Early Miocene	37°41′	144°26′		X	X	X						X		X				X		
Yallourn Clay	Late Early-early Middle Miocene	38°05′	146°05′	X	X	X	X			X	X	X	X		X	X	X	X	X		
Yallourn Seam	Middle Miocene	38°12′	146°21′	X	X	X	X		X	X	X	X	X	X		X	X	X	X		
Moranbah	Miocene	21°48′	147°58′	X	X			X			X			X			X	X	X		
Sentinel Rock	Miocene	38°48′	143°27′							X							X				X
Stuart Creek	Late Miocene	29°45′	136°45′			X					X	X	X	X				X	X	X	X
Leaf Locality	Late Miocene-Pliocene	28°17′	138°17′											X						X	
Grange Burn	Early Pliocene	37°42′	141°57′		X	X				X			X							X	

Source: Data from Duigan 1951; Greenwood et al. 2003; A. Vadala, Victoria University of Technology, personal communication; R. Barnes and R. S. Hill, University of Adelaide, personal communication; and sources cited herein.

[a]1, *Bowenia* or other rainforest cycads (Stangeriaceae/Zamiaceae); 2, *Agathis;* 3, *Araucaria* or other Araucariaceae; 4–7, Podocarpaceae (4, *Dacrycarpus;* 5, *Podocarpus;* 6, *Dacrydium, Nageia,* or *Acmopyle;* 7, *Phyllocladus*); 8, Cunoniaceae; 9–10, Proteaceae (9, Musgraveinaeor *Athertonia;* 10, *Banksieaephyllum/Banksieaeformis*); 11, Sterculiaceae (incl. *Brachychiton*); 12, *Nothofagus;* 13, *Diospyros;* 14, Lauraceae; 15, *Gymnostoma;* 16, Elaeocarpaceae (*Elaeocarpus* or *Sloanea*); 17, *Eucalyptus;* 18, *Acacia.*

Further cooling of southern latitudes by the Late Eocene (40–35 MYA) can be attributed to the formation of the circum-Antarctic ocean current, initiated by the breaking of the land connections between Australia and Antarctica and South America and Antarctica (Drake Passage), although the exact timing of the opening of Drake Passage is uncertain. The development of large-scale ice in East Antarctica by the Early Oligocene (38–36 MYA) initiated drier climates in central Australia at this time (Wilford and Brown 1994; Quilty 1994).

In the Late Oligocene and Early Miocene (30–20 MYA), northern Australia and New Guinea crossed into subtropical latitudes (30°–20° S), with southern Australia extending from still quite high (i.e., Tasmania at about 55° S) to middle latitudes. Mountain building in New Guinea was initiated during this interval due to the initial collision of the northern edge of the Australian plate with Sundaland, the tectonic region that today encompasses the Indonesian archipelago. From Late Miocene to Pliocene times (20–5 MYA), Australia's northern fringe entered tropical latitudes (20°–15° S), and by the close of the Pliocene, New Guinea was within the equatorial belt and had achieved high elevations in its interior (Wilford and Brown 1994).

Past Climates and Agents for Change

The evidence for past climates in Australia has been described in detail by Frakes, Francis, and Syktus (1992), Greenwood (1994), and Quilty (1994). A broad overview is given here to provide a framework for discussing the effect of the Tertiary climatic deterioration on rainforests in Australia. The Tertiary marine microfossil carbonate isotopic ($\delta^{18}O$) proxy record of sea surface temperatures documents shorter intervals of global warming and cooling within an overall Tertiary cooling trend (fig. 18.3; Shackleton and Kennett 1975; Stott et al. 1990; Feary et al. 1991; Frakes, Francis, and Syktus 1992; Zachos, Stott, and Lohmann 1994). Analyses of the paleobotanical record of climate indicate similar terrestrial trends, but these have only rarely been quantified (Wolfe 1994; Greenwood 1994, 1996, D. R. Greenwood, unpublished data; Greenwood and Wing 1995; Greenwood et al. 2003); more typically, analysis of the Australian terrestrial paleobotanical climate record has been qualitative (e.g., Christophel 1981; Nix 1982; Christophel and Greenwood 1988, 1989; Carpenter, Hill, and Jordan 1994; McLoughlin and Hill 1996). The Early Eocene represents the warmest global temperatures over the past 65 million years, with a cooling trend through the Eocene culminating in a significant global cooling episode in the Mid-Late Eocene-Early Oligocene. Global warming in the Early Miocene was followed by a cooling episode in the mid-Miocene (Stott et al. 1990; Frakes, Francis, and

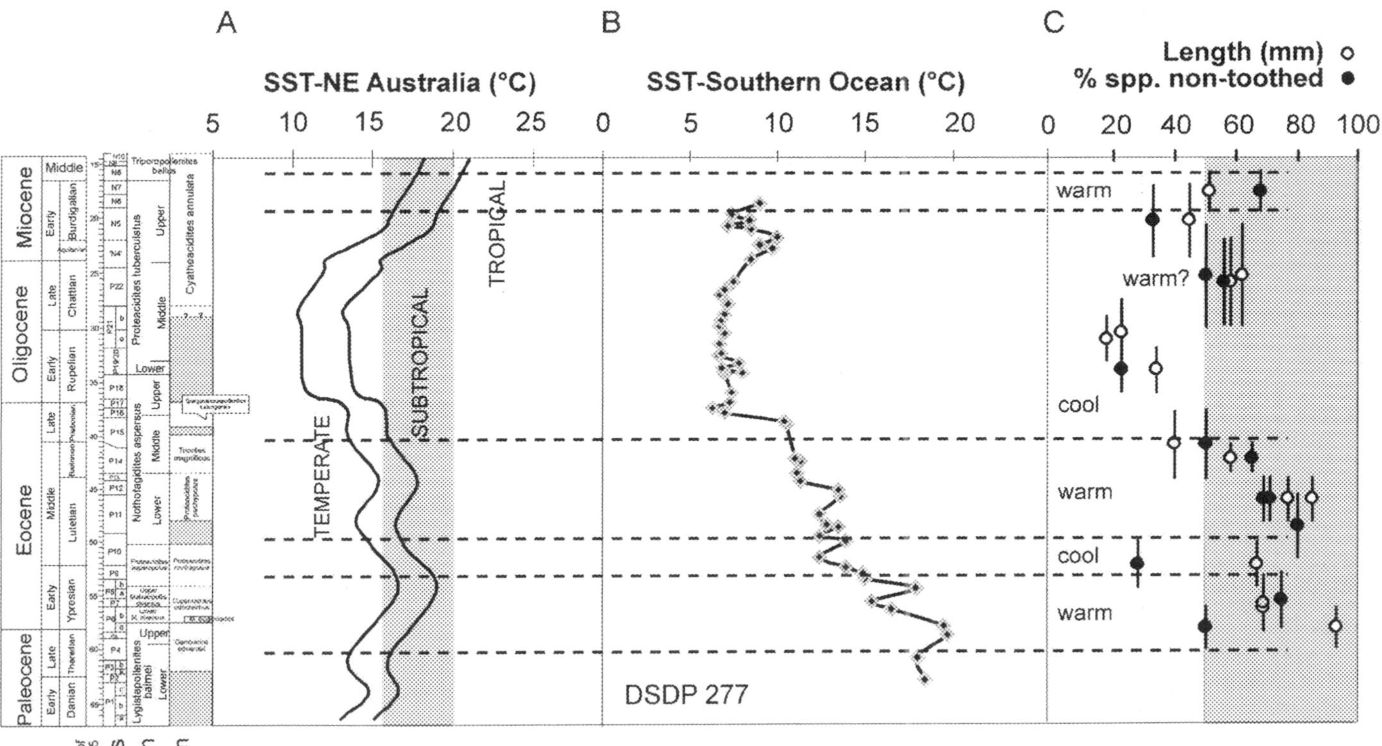

A
SST-NE Australia (°C)
5 10 15 20 25
TEMPERATE
SUBTROPICAL
TROPICAL
B
SST-Southern Ocean (°C)
0 5 10 15 20
DSDP 277
C
Length (mm)
% spp. non-toothed
0 20 40 60 80 100
warm
warm?
cool
warm
cool
warm
Paleocene
Eocene
Oligocene
Miocene
Early
Late
Middle
Danian
Thanetian
Ypresian
Lutetian
Bartonian
Priabonian
Rupelian
Chattian
Aquitanian
Burdigalian
Lygistepollenites balmei
Lower
Upper
Nothofagidites asperus
Proteacidites tuberculatus
Triporopollenites bellus
Cyatheacidites annulata
Proteacidites pachypolus
Geochronometric scale of Berggren et al. 1985
Marine biozones
Gippsland Basin
Otway Basin & other SE Aust.

Syktus 1992). Warm intervals during the Cenozoic are attributed to periods of high atmospheric concentrations of the greenhouse gas CO_2 (i.e., pCO_2 perhaps as high as 2,000 ppm, vs. ~260 ppm for much of the Holocene), although evidence for very high pCO_2 remains equivocal (Pearson and Palmer 2000; Royer et al. 2001). Sea surface temperatures off Australia's southern margin follow the global trends outlined above (fig. 18.3B). The record for northern Australia (Feary et al. 1991), however, documents a sustained warming event throughout the Miocene (fig. 18.3A), reflecting the regional amelioration of the global cooling trend due to Australia's position at lower latitudes at this time. Within Australia, the Tertiary terrestrial record documents a trend toward cooler, drier, and more seasonally dry climates (Kemp 1978, 1981; Quilty 1994; Greenwood 1994; Gallagher et al. 2003), a pattern of climatic change that has been linked to significant change in the Australian terrestrial biota (Martin 1978; Kemp 1981; Christophel and Greenwood 1989; Truswell 1993; Kershaw, Martin, and McEwen Mason 1994; Gallagher et al. 2003; Kershaw, Moss, and Wild, chap. 19 in this volume).

Based on the thermal responses of key Tertiary taxa, Nix (1982) suggested that during the Tertiary most of Australia's climate was mesothermal to megathermal, with only the southernmost margin being under dominant microthermal influence in the Oligocene and Miocene. Nix also noted that Paleogene thermal regimes need only be 2°–4°C warmer than present-day values in southern Australian to account for the oft-cited "subtropical" to "tropical" character of Paleogene floras. This "tropical character" was proposed on the basis of microfloras with meso-megathermal taxa such as *Anacolosa* or the presence of mangroves (Churchill 1973) and the Notophyll Vine Forest character of the Anglesea and Nerriga Eocene macrofloras (Christophel 1981). Global and regional syntheses of Paleogene climate have emphasized floristic evidence for the Australian region, noting northward-shifting bands of microtherm-mesotherm-dominated and mesotherm-dominated vegetation along the southern half of the Australian continent as it rafted northward from Antarctica (e.g., Wolfe 1985). However, Frakes, McGowran, and Bowler (1987) felt that the influence of Australia's northward drift had been overemphasized in explaining Tertiary climatic trends.

Figure 18.3 Stratigraphic analysis of temporal changes in climate estimated from Tertiary marine and terrestrial records contrasted for the Australian region. (A) Sea surface temperatures (SST) estimated from marine carbonate $\delta^{18}O$ for northeastern Australia (northern and southern Great Barrier Reef). (After Feary et al. 1991.) (B) SST estimated from marine carbonate $\delta^{18}O$ for the Southern Ocean. (After Shackleton and Kennett 1975.) (C) Mean variation in leaf length and leaf margin type through the Paleogene for southeastern Australia. (Data from Greenwood 1994; D. R. Greenwood, unpublished data; Carpenter, Hill, and Jordan 1994; data for some Eocene Australian sites from Greenwood and Wing 1995.)

In more recent studies (Christophel and Greenwood 1989; Greenwood 1994; Greenwood and Wing 1995; Greenwood, Vadala, and Banks 2000), broad-scale Australian Paleogene thermal regimes and mean annual temperatures (MAT) were reconstructed using foliar physiognomic correlations. These analyses suggested latitudinal thermal belts similar to those inferred by Nix (1982). Frakes, McGowran, and Bowler (1987) and Quilty (1994) noted that other proxy evidence, such as paleosols and sedimentary features, are consistent with Tertiary episodes of warm-wet climate and cooler-drier climate, within an overall cooling-drying trend associated with increasing seasonal dryness. The mosaic character of southern Australian Paleogene vegetation over the landscape has also been emphasized. Site-to-site differences probably reflect local climatic and edaphic influences due to local topography and soils (Kemp 1978, 1981; Christophel and Greenwood 1989; Truswell 1990, 1993; Macphail et al. 1994; McLoughlin and Hill 1996).

Macphail et al. (1994) analyzed Australian Tertiary microfloras and sea surface temperature (SST) trends inferred from the marine carbonate $\delta^{18}O$ record (e.g., Feary et al. 1991) and noted that significant ecological sifting of regional floras matched inferred regional cooling and warming. Carpenter, Hill, and Jordan (1994) and Greenwood (1994) noted climatically induced trends toward smaller leaf sizes in Oligocene than in middle Eocene macrofloras, and Hill (1994) noted similar trends within lineages of *Nothofagus* and other taxa for both mainland and Tasmanian localities. Key leaf attributes that are sensitive to climate, such as leaf size and leaf margin type, measured from southeastern Australian Tertiary macrofloras (fig. 18.3C) document responses that partly match the northeastern Australian sea surface temperature curve. Significant decreases in leaf size and in the proportion of non-toothed leaf species occur at times of cooling temperatures. That is, Oligocene floras have leaves less than 50 mm in mean length, and less than 50% of species are non-toothed, whereas Early to Middle Eocene and Early Miocene floras have leaves greater than 50 mm, and 50%–80% of species are non-toothed. Greenwood and colleagues (Greenwood, Vadala, and Banks 2000; Greenwood et al. 2003) have interpreted these data for the early Paleogene as indicating warm and cool intervals, with the Early and Middle Eocene having the highest temperatures for the Cenozoic.

THE TERTIARY MACROFLORAL RECORD

The Tertiary macrofloral record in Australia is primarily of leaves; however, a substantive record based on fruits and seeds is also available. Substantive seed floras were collected in the 1860s–1890s from "deep leads"—alluvial placer deposits that were mined for gold (Rozefelds and Christophel 1996a, 1996b; Greenwood, Vadala, and Douglas 2000). Seeds and fruits are also encountered in other facies, particularly the laterally extensive and thick brown Oligo-Miocene coal deposits of the Latrobe Valley in Victoria. Taxonomic studies of these floras continue, revealing strong links between the Tertiary rainforests of southern Australia and the present-day tropical rainforests (Vadala and Greenwood 2001). Leaf mats found in Tertiary fluviolacustrine clay plugs, often as overburden in coal or sand mines, provide valuable evidence not only of floristic associations, but also of the leaf physiognomy of the Tertiary vegetation (Christophel and Greenwood 1989; Greenwood 1992, 1994; Greenwood, Vadala, and Banks 2000). Leaf physiognomy provides evidence of both the structural type of a forest, as reflected in a fossil leaf assemblage, and of paleoclimate (Wolfe 1985, 1993; Greenwood 1992, 1994, 1996, 2001; Wilf 1997).

Tertiary macrofloras are known from most of the southern half of the Australian continent, but appear to be concentrated in the southeastern corner and in Tasmania (see fig. 18.2). In part, the apparent concentration of macrofloras in the southeast may reflect the concentration of research effort in that area (Greenwood, Vadala, and Douglas 2000), particularly the dramatic increase in knowledge about Tasmanian macrofloras over the last 15 years (e.g., Carpenter, Hill, and Jordan 1994). The abundance of macrofloras in Victoria and parts of New South Wales, however, probably reflects chance discoveries associated with early mining activity as much as fortuitous geology (Abele et al. 1988). The apparent scarcity of macrofloras from north of the present-day Tropic of Capricorn more than likely reflects climatic conditions that are not conducive to the preservation of organically preserved plant fossils. A number of largely undescribed macrofloras have been reported from sites along the Great Dividing Range (see fig. 18.2; Allen et al. 1960), and anecdotal evidence suggests that more Tertiary macrofloras will be discovered, especially in silicified sediments (e.g., Greenwood 1996; Pole and Bowman 1996; McLoughlin and Hill 1996).

The stratigraphic relationships of the macrofloras in this chapter (see figs. 18.2 and 18.3 and table 18.1) are based on published assignment to southern Australian spore-pollen zones (*sensu* Macphail et al. 1994) or other stratigraphic information published in papers dealing with specific macrofloras (e.g., Hill 1982; Pickett et al. 1990) and in regional accounts of Cenozoic geology (Harris 1971, 1985; Abele et al. 1988; Holdgate and Sluiter 1991; McGowran 1991; Macphail et al. 1994; Rowett and Sparrow 1994; Lindsay and Alley 1995). A recent palynostratigraphic reappraisal of some sites (Partridge 1998) is also used here. However, a recent recalibration of the Cenozoic time scale (Graciansky et al. 1998) and modifications to the Gippsland Basin spore-pollen zones (Partridge 1999) were not incorporated here, but were used by Greenwood et al. (2003). In some instances here, individual floras have been placed within spore-pollen zones rather than spanning the designated zone, based either on correlation with other biozonations or on correlation with transgression-regression cycles (e.g., Holdgate and Sluiter 1991). For example, according to Alley and co-workers (Alley 1987; Alley and Broadbridge 1992; Lindsay and Alley 1994), the Golden Grove clays (North Maslin Sands) are correlated with the Gippsland Basin Lower *Nothofagidites asperus* Zone (Stover and Partridge 1982) and with the boundary of the *Proteacidites pachypolus* and the *Proteacidites confragosus* zones of Harris (1971). McGowran (1991; B. McGowran, personal communication, April 6, 1994) considered the Golden Grove and Maslin Bay macrofloras late-Middle Eocene (Bartonian, Wilson Bluff transgression), whereas Lindsay and Alley (1995) placed these floras as mid-Middle Eocene age (Lutetian).

The uneven distribution of Tertiary macrofloras, both geographically across the Australian continent and temporally, presents difficulties for regional syntheses. However, the density of floras known and described from southeastern Australia and Tasmania provides a substantial database for the interpretation of climate change and vegetative evolution through the Tertiary. Much of this record is of rainforest vegetation, and as explained below, for significant intervals of the Tertiary, this vegetation was floristically and physiognomically closest to the tropical rainforests of northeastern Queensland.

THE CHARACTER OF PRESENT-DAY TROPICAL RAINFORESTS IN AUSTRALIA

The rainforests of the Wet Tropics region of northeastern Queensland are characterized by both high floristic diversity and high endemism. A large number of species, at least 103 genera, and even some families (e.g., Idiospermaceae) are endemic, and a number of these are viewed as highly primitive (e.g., *Austrobaileya, Idiospermum,* and *Noahadendron*). Floristic associations reflect climatic and edaphic factors such as soil nutrient status and drainage (Tracey 1982; Webb and Tracey 1994); typically these forests have high proportions of families such as Cunoniaceae (e.g., *Ceratopetalum* and *Geissois*), Elaeocarpaceae (e.g., *Elaeocarpus* and *Sloanea*), Flindersiaceae, Lauraceae (e.g., *Beilschmiedia, Cryptocarya,* and *Endiandra,* prominent in most rainforests), Myrtaceae (e.g., *Syzygium*), Proteaceae (very diverse), Rutaceae (e.g., *Acronychia*), Sapindaceae, and Sterculiaceae (e.g., *Argyrodendron* and *Brachychiton*). Deciduous canopy tree taxa, whose canopies are bare from days to months, are common in some families (e.g., *Toona australis* [Meliaceae] and *Brachychiton*), with the frequency of deciduous taxa and duration of the leafless interval in these forests depending on the length and severity of the dry season (Tracey 1982). Walking stick palms such as *Linospadix* and *Laccospadix* are characteristic of upland tropical rainforests, whereas *Livistona* spp. (Arecaceae) are well represented in lowland forests. *Linospadix minor*, however, is locally common in the lowland rainforests of the Daintree area of northeastern Queensland. Conifers such as Podocarpaceae (*Podocarpus* and *Prumnopitys*) and Araucariaceae (*Agathis* and *Araucaria*) are relatively widespread, as are cycads (*Bowenia* and *Lepidozamia*), but rarely are these gymnosperms a significant component of the vegetation. In contrast, Podocarpaceae (e.g., *Dacrycarpus, Dacrydium, Podocarpus*, and *Phyllocladus*) are important in New Guinean tropical montane forests (Paijmans 1976). *Nothofagus* subgenus *Brassospora* is absent from the Australian Wet Tropics, but appears to have become extinct relatively recently (Gallagher et al. 2003; Kershaw, Moss, and Wild, chap. 19 in this volume); it is an important canopy tree in mesothermal rainforests in New Guinea (Paijmans 1976).

Australian rainforests have been classified according to a physiognomic typology (loosely matching traditional classifications) (Webb 1959; Tracey 1982). This typology recognizes that structural complexity (i.e., number of tree strata and synusiae) and predominant tree canopy leaf size varies along major environmental gradients. In broad terms, leaf size in rainforest canopies varies proportionately with mean annual temperature, except where rainfall is limiting (Webb 1968a; Greenwood 1992, 1996). The Webb-Tracey rainforest types reflect primary environmental determinants and have definable climatic limits according to the Nix (1982) definitions (Mackey 1993). Australia's "tropical" rainforests occur primarily in mesothermal to marginal megathermal humid climates (i.e., MAT 14°–25°C; mean annual precipitation [MAP] >1,200 mm/yr), with the structurally most complex types (i.e., Complex Mesophyll Vine Forests) restricted to the warmest and wettest (MAT >20°C; MAP >1,800 mm/yr) and often most fertile sites (Tracey 1982). Greenwood (1992, 1996) found that each of the main rainforest types in the Webb-Tracey typology could be recognized in litter accumulations by its specific foliar physiognomic signature. Detection of similar signatures in fossilized leaf accumulations (i.e., leaf macrofloras) serves as evidence for the presence of the matching Webb-Tracey rainforest type. This approach is followed here to demonstrate the vegetation types for key sites over time (figs. 18.4 and 18.5), independent of taxonomic identifications. The floristic compositions of key floras are discussed to promote discussion of the biogeographic effects (extinction, diversification, and dispersal of taxa) of Tertiary climatic oscillations.

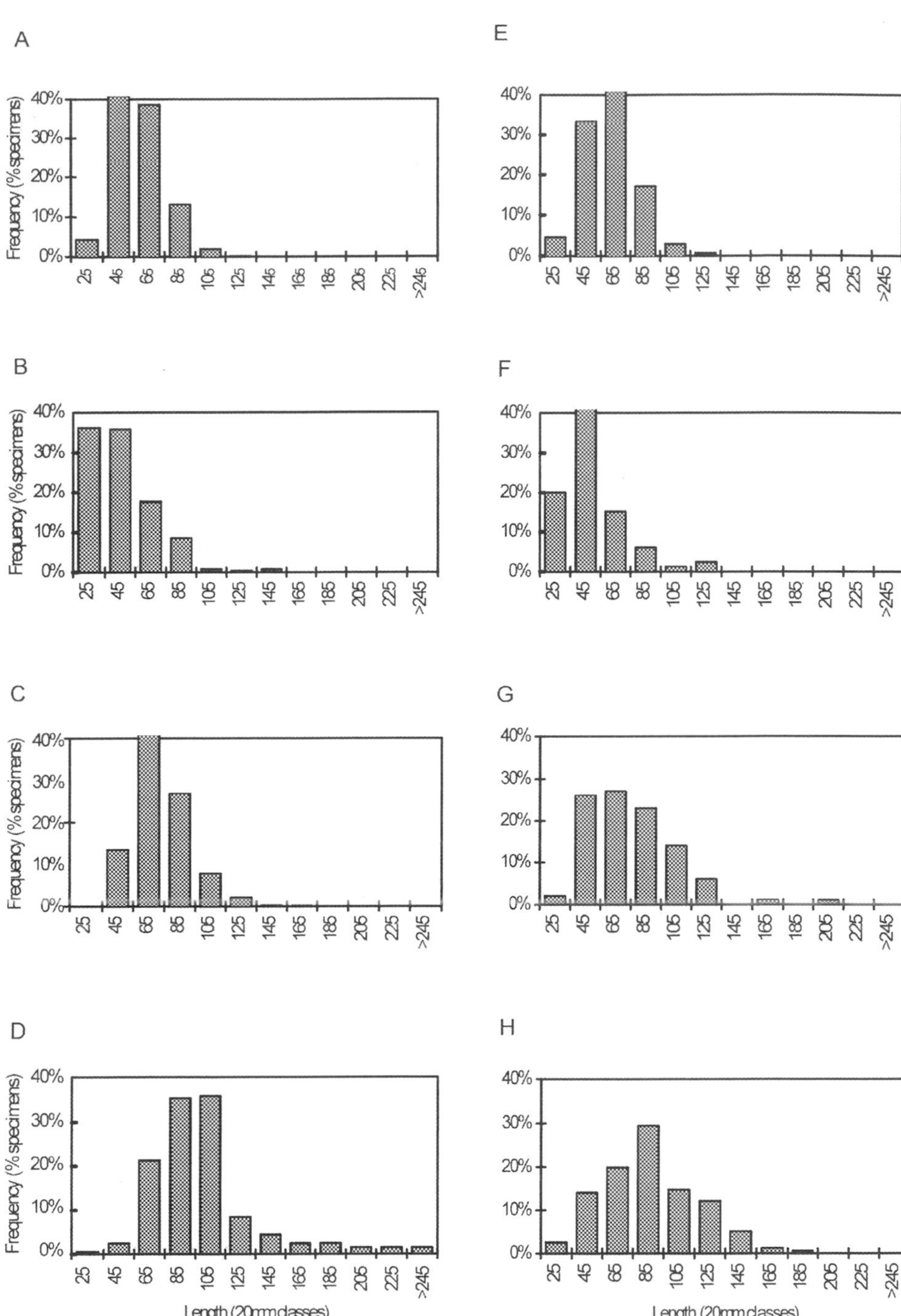
A
B
C
D
E
F
G
H
Frequency (% specimens)
40%
30%
20%
10%
0%
25
45
65
85
105
125
145
165
185
205
225
>245
Length (20mm classes)

ORIGINS AND EVOLUTION

Arrival and Diversification of the Proto-Tropical Rainforest Flora

The ultimate antecedents of Australia's rainforests can be traced to the early angiosperm forests of the Late Cretaceous (100–65 MYA). Climates in the Late Cretaceous were generally mild globally and were cool temperate at least in southern Australia (Frakes, Francis, and Syktus 1992; Quilty 1994). A mid-Cretaceous (Aptian) macroflora at Koonwarra in Victoria indicates conifer and Bennettalian-dominated forests with *Ginkgo,* cycads, and a minor angiosperm component; these angiosperms may have been understory shrubs, rather than canopy trees (Drinnan and Chambers 1986; Douglas 1994). Late Cretaceous (Cenomanian) macrofloras near Winton in western Queensland appear more "modern," however, with a small but significant angiosperm component and *Ginkgo,* Taxodiaceae (*Austrosequioa*), Araucariaceae, and Podocarpaceae conifers (Peters and Christophel 1978; Peters 1985; McLoughlin and Drinnan 1995). Many of the angiosperm leaves at Winton are quite broad and have marginal teeth, a physiognomy consistent with deciduous broad-leaved forests, which we interpret as a response to the short winter days experienced at the high southern latitude at this time. No Maastrichtian macrofloras are known from Australia (Douglas 1994); however, the microfloral record provides some insight into this age (Dettmann 1994).

Invasion of Australia by angiosperms occurred in several waves, with significant migration from northern Gondwana in the Turonian-Maastrichtian, but these invasions occurred concurrently with in situ evolution and diversification of austral plant taxa (Dettmann 1994). Migration pathways into Australia probably involved landmasses other than Southeast Asian elements, as Australia occupied a peripheral southern position in Gondwana. The area near the opening seaway between Australia and Antarctica was a focus of evolution and diversification for Proteaceae and possibly *Ilex* (Aquifoliaceae), whereas the South America-Antarctic Peninsular region (then still linked by land connection to Australia) was a center of diversification for *Nothofagus* (Dettmann 1994). Rainforest taxa known in the Australian record of this time (appearing sequentially over the interval) include Podocarpaceae (*Dacrycarpus, Dacrydium, Lagarostrobos,* and *Podocarpus*), early Proteaceae (including *Carnavonia,*

Figure 18.4 Foliar physiognomic signatures (*sensu* Greenwood 1992, 1996) of leaf size for modern and Tertiary rainforests: (A) MFF, mesotherm-microtherm; (B) DVF, wet-dry mesotherm-megatherm; (C) SNVF, mesotherm; (D) CNVF, mesotherm-megatherm; (E) Kiandra, Miocene; (F) Nelly Creek, Eocene; (G) Deans Marsh, Eocene; (H) Golden Grove, Eocene.

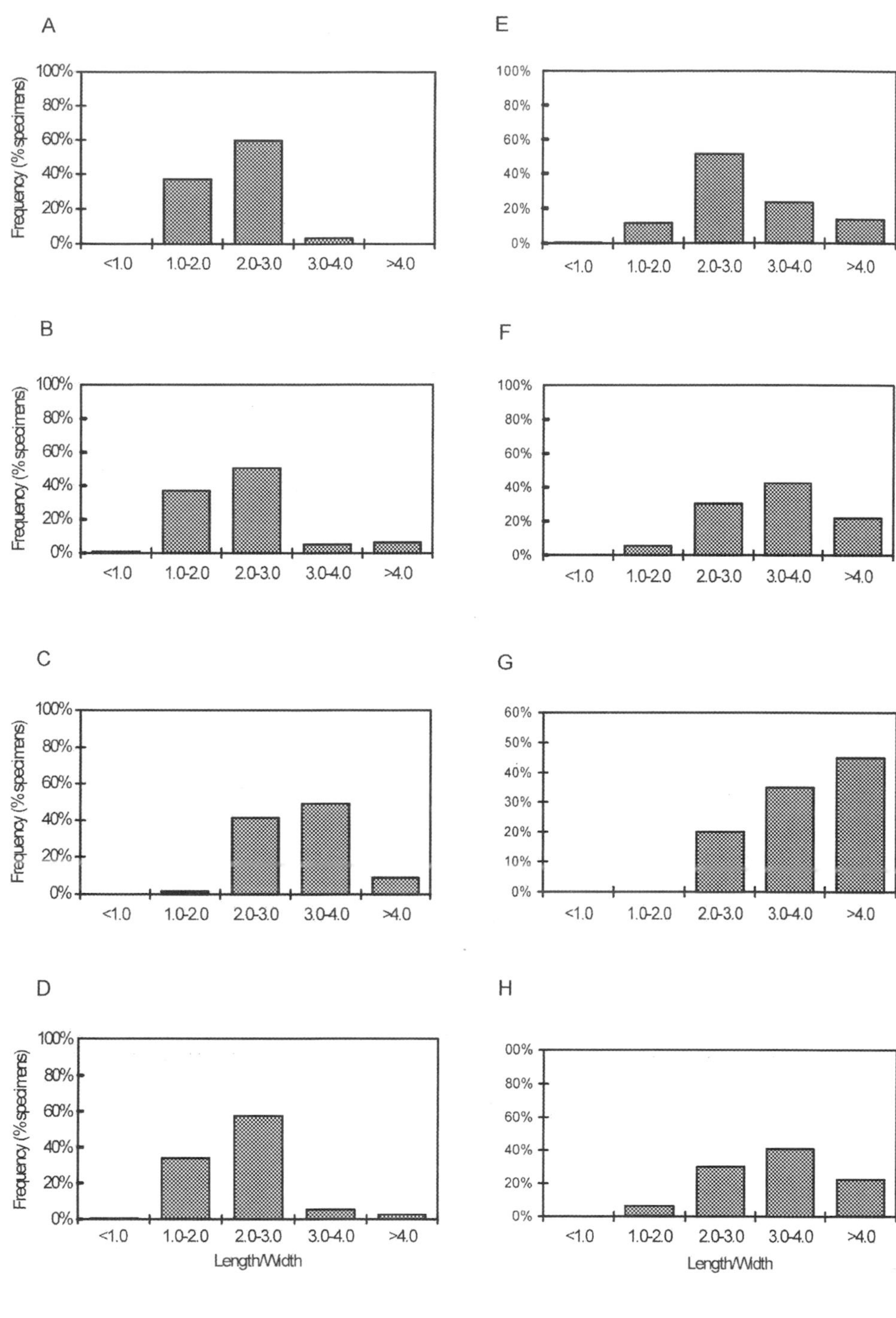

A
Frequency (% specimens)
100%
80%
60%
40%
20%
0%
<1.0
1.0-2.0
2.0-3.0
3.0-4.0
>4.0
B
Frequency (% specimens)
100%
80%
60%
40%
20%
0%
<1.0
1.0-2.0
2.0-3.0
3.0-4.0
>4.0
C
Frequency (% specimens)
100%
80%
60%
40%
20%
0%
<1.0
1.0-2.0
2.0-3.0
3.0-4.0
>4.0
D
Frequency (% specimens)
100%
80%
60%
40%
20%
0%
<1.0
1.0-2.0
2.0-3.0
3.0-4.0
>4.0
Length/Width
E
100%
80%
60%
40%
20%
0%
<1.0
1.0-2.0
2.0-3.0
3.0-4.0
>4.0
F
100%
80%
60%
40%
20%
0%
<1.0
1.0-2.0
2.0-3.0
3.0-4.0
>4.0
G
60%
50%
40%
30%
20%
10%
0%
<1.0
1.0-2.0
2.0-3.0
3.0-4.0
>4.0
H
00%
80%
60%
40%
20%
0%
<1.0
1.0-2.0
2.0-3.0
3.0-4.0
>4.0
Length/Width

Gevunia/Hicksbeachia, Grevillea, Lomatia, and *Macadamia*), *Ilex,* early *Nothofagus* (including *Brassospora* by the Santonian-Maastrichtian), and various fern groups (e.g., *Blechnum/Doodia* [Blechnaceae], Marattiaceae, and Schizeaceae). These forests were probably quite open-statured in response to the high southern latitudes, with many of the angiosperms best represented in the understory below a canopy of podocarps, Proteaceae, and rare *Nothofagus* (Specht, Dettmann, and Jarzen 1992). Many of the plant taxa known from these Late Cretaceous forests are today most diverse in or restricted to the cooler upland rainforests of the Australian Wet Tropics and of neighboring landmasses.

Beginnings: Paleocene to Early Eocene

While little is known in detail of Paleocene macrofloras, the Paleocene forests appear to have been more "modern" than those of the Late Cretaceous and include the first appearances of many taxa. The analysis of southeastern Australian microfloras by Macphail et al. (1994) points to significant shifts in regional vegetation composition and structure from the Danian to Thanetian, with microthermal-mesothermal podocarp conifers (e.g., *Lagarostrobos* and *Dacrydium*) declining, whereas Araucariaceae, *Nothofagus,* and some fern groups (e.g., Cyatheaceae, Gleicheniaceae) fluctuated in importance. Angiosperms with modern mesothermal-megathermal affinities (e.g., palms, *Anacolosa, Beauprea,* Cupanieae [Sapindaceae], and Polygalaceae) made first appearances or increased significantly during the Thanetian. Proteaceae are prominent and diverse in Paleocene microfloras. The microfloral record indicates that by the Early Eocene, the conifer-*Nothofagus* forests of the Early Paleocene had been replaced by diverse mesothermal-megathermal angiosperm multistratal rainforests with emergent Araucariaceae, including *Wollemia* (represented by *Dilwynites granulatus*). *Nothofagus* was present, but probably was a minor component of the vegetation, perhaps reflecting landscape mosaicism controlled by a compressed altitudinal vegetational zonation.

Leaves from the southeastern New South Wales Late Paleocene Cambalong Creek site and the nearby Lake Bungarby flora are typically broad and large. with about 50% of dicot taxa toothed at Cambalong Creek (Greenwood et al. 2003).

Figure 18.5 Foliar physiognomic signatures (*sensu* Greenwood 1992, 1996) of leaf shape (length/width) for modern and Tertiary rainforests: (A) MFF, mesotherm-microtherm; (B) DVF, wet-dry mesotherm-megatherm; (C) SNVF, mesotherm; (D) CNVF, mesotherm-megatherm; (E) Kiandra, Miocene; (F) Nelly Creek, Eocene; (G) Deans Marsh, Eocene; (H) Golden Grove, Eocene.

Fossil wood from Lake Bungarby has well-defined growth rings, indicating seasonality of growth, but with mild, favorable growing seasons (Taylor et al. 1990; R. S. Hill 1992). Cambalong Creek has moderate diversity, with Lauraceae dominant and *Nothofagus,* Proteaceae, and the conifers *Araucarioides* (Araucariaceae, probably representing the extant *Wollemia*), *Dacrycarpus,* and *Phyllocladus* (Vadala and Greenwood 2001) also present. The Lake Bungarby flora also contains a strongly sclerophyllous element (*Banksieaephyllum taylorii*), together with typical temperate rainforest taxa such as *Eucryphia,* and is rich in Podocarpaceae with imbricate foliage, including three species of *Acmopyle* (Hill 1991, 1994; Hill and Carpenter 1991). The pollen, wood, and limited leaf physiognomic evidence from these sites indicates that southern Australia, then at high southern latitudes, probably supported mixed conifer-angiosperm forest, which may have included a deciduous broad-leaved component. These forests have no structural-physiognomic analogue in present-day Australia.

Tasmanian Early Eocene floras have high conifer diversity, and microthermal lineages with small to medium-sized leaves appear to dominate the dicots (e.g., *Eucryphia:* Hill 1991). *Nothofagus* is known only from the Deloraine Early Eocene flora. The Early Eocene Regatta Point flora is floristically rich, containing palms (including *Nypa;* see below), cycads, conifers (e.g., *Araucaria, Dacrycarpus, Libocedrus,* and *Phyllocladus*), Lauraceae, Proteaceae (e.g., Banksieae), and other dicots (Hill 1992; Carpenter, Jordan, and Hill 1994). The Hotham Heights and Brandy Creek Early Eocene floras from Victoria are species-rich (> 30 and > 50 species as leaves, respectively) and contain Cunoniaceae, Elaeocarpaceae (including aff. *Sloanea*), Lauraceae (*Beilschmiedia, Cryptocarya, Endiandra,* and *Litsea*), rare Myrtaceae, Proteaceae (including *Banksieaephyllum* and cf. *Lomatia*), and a number of indeterminate taxa (Greenwood, Vadala, and Banks 2000; Greenwood, Vadala, and Douglas 2000; Greenwood et al. 2003; Keefe 2000; Vadala and Greenwood 2001). *Gymnostoma* has also been reported at Brandy Creek (Greenwood, Vadala, and Banks 2000; Greenwood, Vadala, and Douglas 2000). The conifers *Agathis, Dacrycarpus,* and *Dacrydium* occur at Hotham Heights (Banks 1999; Greenwood et al. 2003), and the microflora there is dominated by ferns, primarily tree ferns (Partridge 1998). The late Early Eocene Deans Marsh flora is moderately species-rich, with more than twenty-six species of broad-leaved angiosperms known from dispersed cuticles (eighteen known as macroscopic leaf remains) and only two species of conifers, including a broad-leaved species of *Podocarpus* (Rowett and Sparrow 1994; Greenwood et al. 2003). The foliar physiognomic signature of Deans Marsh matches those of modern Simple Notophyll Vine Forest from New South Wales (see figs. 18.4 and 18.5) and tropical montane rainforest (e.g., Microphyll Vine-

Fern Forest) from northeastern Queensland in most respects, but has a higher proportion of stenophylls (length/width > 4.0) and species with toothed margins than is typical of the modern forests.

Mangrove distribution is strongly controlled by temperature, and mangroves are generally considered indicative of "tropical" climates (Tomlinson 1986), although depauperate mangroves in southern Australia today occur as far south as Wilsons Promontory (36°45′ S). Microfloral evidence suggests that diverse mangroves (e.g., *Nypa, Acrostichum,* and *Sonneratia*-type) were prominent over much of the southern coastal margin of Australia in the Early Eocene (Churchill 1973; Truswell 1993; Macphail et al. 1994). These coastal communities included the mesothermal-megathermal to megathermal mangrove palm *Nypa,* which is recorded as both pollen (*Spinizonocolpites prominatus*) and macrofossils (e.g., Regatta Point).

Diversification and Modernization: The Middle Eocene "Tropical" Rainforests

Middle Eocene macrofloras from southeastern Australia are well known and generally are highly diverse (e.g., Christophel 1981, 1988, 1994; Christophel and Greenwood 1989; Hill 1992; Pole 1992; Greenwood et al. 2003). The foliar physiognomic signatures of these Middle Eocene macrofloras match those of Simple Notophyll Vine Forests (e.g., Anglesea) and Complex Notophyll Vine Forests (e.g., Nerriga, Golden Grove, and Maslin Bay) (see figs. 18.4 and 18.5). In most Middle Eocene floras, Lauraceae dominate, and there is significant representation of Elaeocarpaceae (*Elaeocarpus* and aff. *Sloanea*), Cunoniaceae, diverse Proteaceae and Myrtaceae, *Brachychiton* (Sterculiaceae), and *Gymnostoma* (figs. 18.6 and 18.7). A significant vine component (Menispermaceae, cf. *Legnephora*) is represented in the Nerriga flora (Hill 1989b). Lauraceous wood (aff. *Cryptocarya*) is known from Jungle Creek (Greenwood, Vadala, and Douglas 2000). These floras in general appear to have significantly lower diversity of conifers than older macrofloras in the region. Anglesea approaches the diversity of Paleocene and Early Eocene floras with at least six conifer taxa (Greenwood 1987; Christophel, Harris, and Syber 1987), and Hasties in Tasmania has a very high diversity of conifers (sixteen species, Pole 1992): perhaps reflecting climatically controlled latitudinal vegetational zonation in the Middle Eocene in southeastern Australia (e.g., Christophel and Greenwood 1989). Only a single leaf of *Nothofagus* has been reported from Maslin Bay; however, pollen of *Nothofagus* subgenus *Brassospora* is well represented and often dominant in Middle Eocene sediments (av. 50%–60% of the pollen sum), indicating at least an extralocal

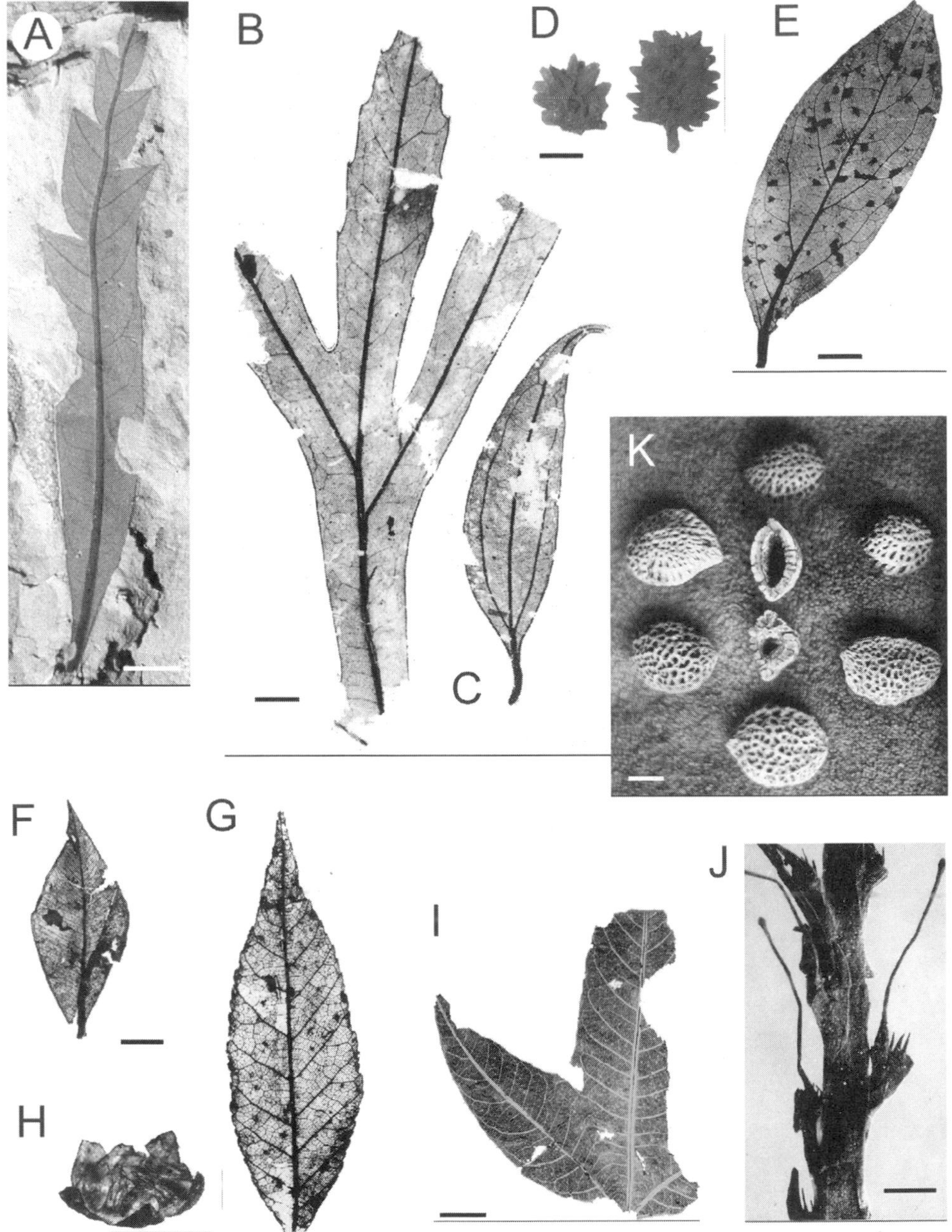
A
B
D
E
K
C
F
G
I
J
H

presence of this taxon in the forests (Truswell 1993; Macphail et al. 1994; Greenwood et al. 2003). The commonness of *Gymnostoma* in the Middle Eocene macrofloras is matched by consistent high values for Casuarinaceae in the microfloras.

Interpretation of Middle Eocene vegetation in southeastern Australia by palynologists is strongly influenced by the dominance of the microfloras by *Nothofagus* subgenus *Brassospora* and the nonpreservation of Lauraceae pollen. These discrepancies aside, there is actually a high degree of congruence in the interpretations of vegetation at this time based on the two fossil types. Macphail et al. (1994) noted that the Early Eocene can be viewed as the acme of lowland megathermal species-rich rainforest development in southeastern Australia (signified in part by the low representation of *Nothofagus* in Early Eocene microfloras). They stressed, however, the continuity of many taxa during much of the Eocene, and they suggested that mesothermal species-rich rainforests reached their maximum development in southeastern Australia during the Middle-Late Eocene, as expressed in part by a locally variable but very widespread expansion of *Nothofagus* subgenus *Brassospora* in microfloras.

Middle Eocene macrofloras from near Brisbane (e.g., Oxley, Redbanks, and Dinmore) and central Queensland (e.g., Rundle Shale), appear to represent mesothermal to perhaps megathermal forests (e.g., Complex Notophyll to Mesophyll Vine Forest). Taxa typical of the southeastern floras are known from these macrofloras (e.g., *Pterostoma, Agathis,* Ebenaceae, *Gymnostoma,* Lauraceae, Proteaceae: Rowett and Sparrow 1994), but with megathermal taxa such as *Nypa* (Arecaceae) and other tropical mangroves indicated in the microfloras (Macphail et al. 1994). The Nelly Creek and Poole Creek Middle Eocene macrofloras from central Australia, however, represent wet-dry Notophyllous Vine Forest with *Agathis, Dacrydium, Brachychiton,* and cf. *Dianella* (Hemerocallidaceae), and may have contained some deciduous and sclerophyllous elements (Christophel, Scriven, and Greenwood 1992; Greenwood 1996; Greenwood and Conran 2000; Hill and Christophel 2001). Microfloras also indicate differences between central and southeastern Australian vegetation (Macphail et al. 1994). A

Figure 18.6 Examples of key plant taxa known as macrofossils and from tropical rainforests: (A) *Banksieaephyllum decurrens* (Maslin Bay); (B) leaf aff. *Megahertzia* (Anglesea); (C) triplinerved Lauraceae leaf, aff. *Cryptocarya* (Anglesea); (D) *Gymnostoma* infructescences (Anglesea); (E) *Austrodiospyros cryptostoma* (Anglesea); (F) *Myrtaciphyllum douglasi* (Anglesea); (G) leaf of Elaeocarpaceae (Anglesea); (H) flower aff. *Basisperma* (Golden Grove); (I) leaf of *Brachychiton* (Golden Grove) showing natural fluorescence of venation under UV illumination (IR film); (J) inflorescence of *Musgraveinanthus alcoensis* (Anglesea); (K) fossil *Wilkinsonia* (lower) and extant *Athertonia* (upper) endocarps (Glencoe). Scale bar in all cases = 1 cm.

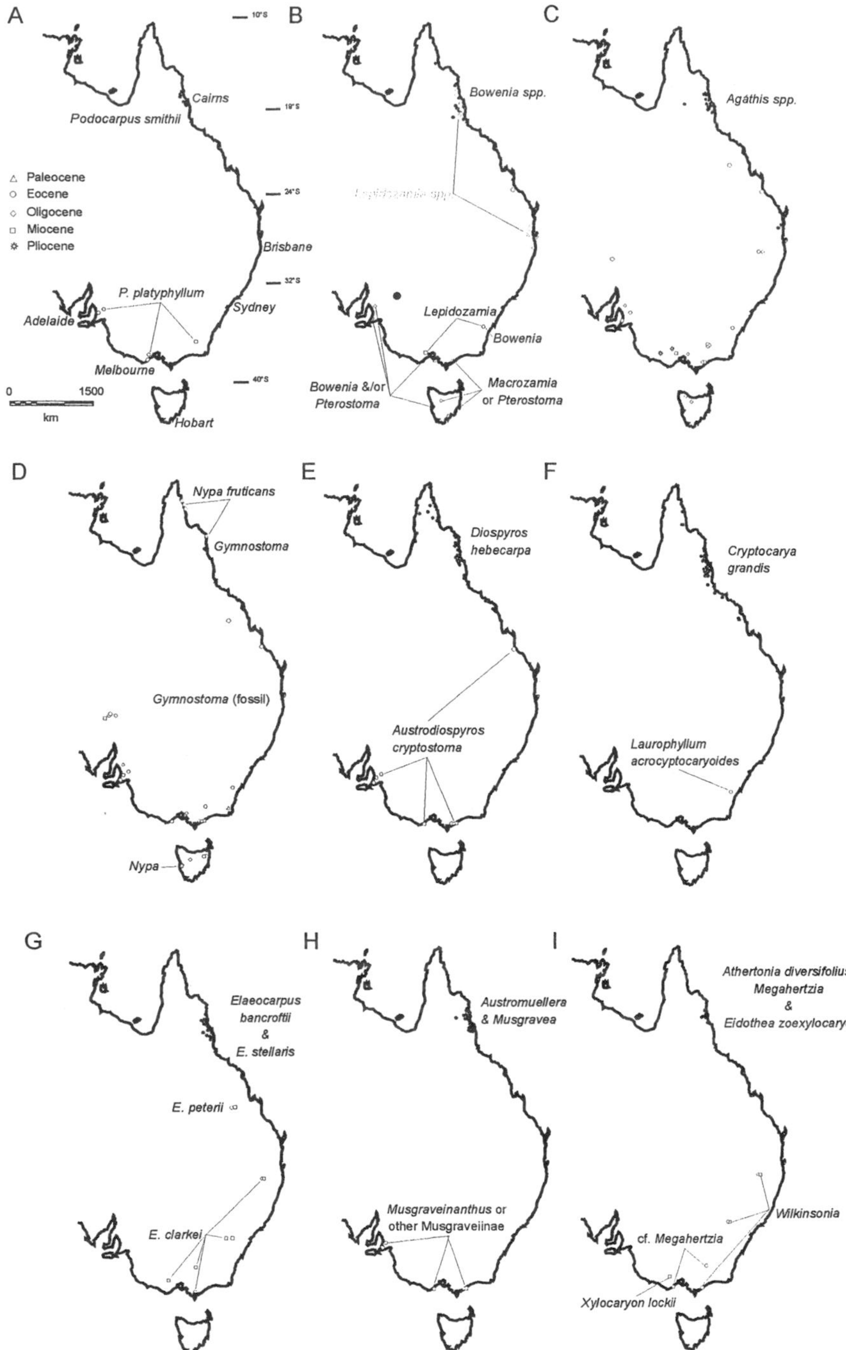
A
B
C
10°S
18°S
24°S
32°S
40°S
Cairns
Podocarpus smithii
Brisbane
Sydney
Adelaide
Melbourne
Hobart
P. platyphyllum
△ Paleocene
○ Eocene
◇ Oligocene
□ Miocene
✲ Pliocene
0
1500
km
Bowenia spp.
Lepidozamia
Bowenia
Bowenia &/or
Pterostoma
Macrozamia
or Pterostoma
Agathis spp.
D
E
F
Nypa fruticans
Gymnostoma
Gymnostoma (fossil)
Nypa
Diospyros
hebecarpa
Austrodiospyros
cryptostoma
Cryptocarya
grandis
Laurophyllum
acrocyptocaryoides
G
H
I
Elaeocarpus
bancroftii
&
E. stellaris
E. peterii
E. clarkei
Austromuellera
& Musgravea
Musgraveinanthus or
other Musgraveiinae
Athertonia diversifolius,
Megahertzia
&
Eidothea zoexylocarya
Wilkinsonia
cf. Megahertzia
Xylocaryon lockii

dispersed-cuticle flora from Hale River in central Australia appears to contain a significant rainforest element (Rowett and Sparrow 1994). Late Middle Eocene dispersed-cuticle floras from Western Australia (e.g., Lake Lefroy and Cowan) indicate diverse humid mesothermal rainforests there also, including *Spiraeanthemum* (Cunoniaceae), Elaeocarpaceae, *Gymnostoma*, highly diverse Lauraceae, Myrtaceae, *Nothofagus* (subgenus *Lophozonia*), diverse Proteaceae (e.g., Banksieae, *Darlingia*, Embothrieae, *Lomatia*, Macadamieae [Gevuininae-*Hicksbeachia*] and *Telopea*, and possibly also *Stenocarpus* and/or *Xylomelum* or *Orites*), and a prominent conifer element including species such as *Acmopyle*, *Dacrydium*, and *Dacrycarpus* (Podocarpaceae), as well as *Agathis* and Cupressaceae (Carpenter and Pole 1995). Late Middle Eocene to Late Eocene macrofloras in southwestern Australia (e.g., Westdale, Twertup, and Kojonup) exhibit mixtures of sclerophyllous and rainforest foliar physiognomy and taxa (Hill and Merrifield 1993; McLoughlin and Hill 1996).

A suite of taxa in the Middle Eocene macrofloras (see figs. 18.6 and 18.7) matches living taxa in the tropical rainforests of northeastern Queensland directly (e.g., *Podocarpus platyphyllum* cf. *P. smithii*, and an undescribed leaf from Anglesea cf. *Megahertzia*, fig. 18.6B). Other taxa in these Eocene floras closely match taxa in the tropical rainforests (e.g., *Lygodium* [Schizeaceae], *Bowenia* [Stangeriaceae], *Austrodiospyros cryptostoma* cf. *Diospyros hebecarpa* [Ebenaceae], *Musgraveinanthus* cf. *Musgravea* [Proteaceae] [Christophel 1981, 1984, 1988, 1994; D. C. Christophel, unpublished data; Basinger and Christophel 1985; Greenwood 1987; Christophel and Greenwood 1987, 1988, 1989; Christophel, Harris, and Syber 1987; Rozefelds, Christophel, and Alley 1992], and an undescribed *Linospadix* aff. *L. minor*). Significantly, some of the matched extant taxa have very restricted distributions or are endemic taxa in the northeastern Queensland and New Guinea tropical rainforests. For example, *Gymnostoma* today is common in New Guinea and Malesia, but in Australia it is relictual, whereas *Gymnostoma* was widespread in southern and central Australia throughout much of the Paleogene, but especially in the Middle Eocene (figs. 18.6D and 18.7D). Other ex-

Figure 18.7 Maps showing modern and known Tertiary records of key plant taxa. Solid symbols are modern herbarium records (Australian National Herbarium) and open symbols are Tertiary macrofossil records (see table 18.1 for sources). (A) *Podocarpus smithii*/*P. platyphyllum;* (B) *Bowenia, Pterostoma,* or other Zamiaceae; (C) *Agathis;* (D) *Gymnostoma* and *Nypa;* (E) *Diospyros hebecarpa*/*Austrodiospyros cryptostoma;* (F) *Cryptocarya grandis*/*Laurophyllum acrocryptocaryoides;* (G) *Elaeocarpus clarkei*/*E. bancroftii* and *E. stellaris*/*E. peterii;* (H) Musgraveinae; (I) *Athertonia diversifolia*/*Wilkinsonia, Megahertzia,* and *Eidothea zoexylocarya*/*Xylocaryon lockii.*

amples of these taxa are restricted to, or best represented in, upland (mesothermal) vegetation in northeastern Queensland. *Bowenia* (Stangeriaceae) and zamioid cycads (e.g., *Macrozamia*) are well represented in northeastern Queensland rainforests (fig. 18.7B), and these taxa (and/or the extinct *Pterostoma*) are known from the Eocene Regatta Point, Anglesea, Nerriga, and Sedan macrofloras (Rowett 1991; Hill 1994; Hill and Pole 1992). Other Middle Eocene taxa are extinct in Australia, but persist on neighboring landmasses; flowers from Golden Grove (fig. 18.6H), for example, most closely match *Basisperma lanceolata* (Myrtaceae) from the lower reaches of the Fly River in New Guinea (D. C. Christophel, unpublished data). Some Middle Eocene plant taxa, however, are most closely related to taxa found also or exclusively in subtropical rainforests in southern Queensland and northern New South Wales (e.g., *Petermanniopsis* cf. *Petermannia* and *Sloanea:* Christophel and Greenwood 1987; Christophel 1994; Conran, Christophel, and Scriven 1994). Oribatid mites collected from leaf domatia from fossil Elaeocarpaceae from Anglesea (fig. 18.6G) match species endemic to *Sloanea woolsii* (O'Dowd et al. 1991), a canopy tree species common in subtropical rainforests in New South Wales and southern Queensland.

Effects of Initial Cooling: Latest Eocene to Early Miocene Forests

Late Eocene to early Oligocene macrofloras from South Australia (e.g., Sedan and Lochiel) are known mainly from dispersed cuticles (Rowett 1991, 1992; Rowett and Sparrow 1994). These floras demonstrate the continuation of diverse humid mesothermal vegetation in low-lying areas, with sclerophyllous elements mixed with rainforest plants, including Cunoniaceae, Ebenaceae (cf. *Diospyros*), Elaeocarpaceae, highly diverse Lauraceae, Myrtaceae, and diverse Proteaceae (e.g., *Banksieaephyllum*, Embothrieae, and Macadamieae). A prominent conifer element in these floras included taxa known from Early to Middle Eocene floras, such as *Podocarpus platyphyllum* and *Acmopyle setiger, Dacrycarpus,* and other Podocarpaceae, as well as *Agathis* (Rowett and Sparrow 1994; Carpenter and Pole 1995). Mangrove pollen taxa also occur in some Late Eocene sediments in southeastern Australia (Macphail et al. 1994). The Late Eocene or early Oligocene West Dale macroflora from Western Australia also contains mixtures of sclerophyllous and rainforest elements, the latter including *Agathis* and Podocarpaceae (Hill and Merrifield 1993).

A diverse cool (but mild)-climate rainforest flora is indicated by the Early Oligocene Cethana macroflora. This flora contains fern allies (*Tmesipteris*), tree ferns (*Dicksonia*), cycads (*Pterostoma* and *Macrozamia*), Cunoniaceae (*Calli-*

coma, Schizomeria, Spiraeanthemum [as *Acsmithia*], and either *Weinmannia* or *Cunonia*), *Gymnostoma, Nothofagus* (*Lophozonia*), diverse Lauraceae, diverse Proteaceae (including rainforest and sclerophyllous taxa), and *Brachychiton* (Carpenter and Buchanan 1993; Carpenter, Hill, and Jordan 1994). Oligocene macrofloras from Tasmania include a number of taxa extinct in Australia today, such as *Nothofagus* subgenus *Brassospora* and the conifers *Fitzroya, Libocedrus,* and *Papuacedrus* (Cupressaceae) (Hill 1987; Carpenter, Hill, and Jordan 1994; Hill and Whang 1996). The Oligocene Darlimurla and Narracan macrofloras from southern Victoria are in urgent need of taxonomic revision; however, *Nothofagus* (subgenus *Lophozonia*), Lauraceae (cf. *Cinnamomum* and *Cryptocarya*), *Brachychiton,* Cunoniaceae (cf. *Geissois*), Proteaceae, Myrtaceae (?*Eucalyptus* and *Tristania* s.l.), Monimiaceae (*Hedycarya*), *Casuarina* s.l. (possibly *Gymnostoma*), and *Dacrycarpus* are recorded (Chapman 1926; Paterson 1935; Greenwood, Vadala, and Douglas 2000). Physiognomically, the Narracan flora matches Simple Notophyll Vine Forest. A small group of taxa, including *Acacia, Casuarina,* and *Eucalyptus,* are apparently not represented in the region prior to the Oligocene. The Late Oligocene Berwick macroflora in Victoria is of lower diversity than Eocene and Early Oligocene floras and contains *Nothofagus Lophozonia*-type leaves together with *Agathis* and *Eucalyptus,* suggesting a cooler and perhaps drier vegetation type than the warm-wet mesothermal rainforests of the Middle Eocene (Deane 1902; Pole et al. 1993).

Early Miocene macrofloras from Victoria (e.g., Bacchus Marsh) and southern New South Wales (e.g., Kiandra) physiognomically match cool forest types such as Microphyll Fern Forest (see figs. 18.4 and 18.5). *Nothofagus* (*Lophozonia*) is prominent in both floras, but the Bacchus Marsh flora is species-poor, being dominated by a Myrtaceae leaf type (cf. *Syzygium:* e.g., fig. 18.6F) together with *Elaeocarpus* endocarps and rare conifers, including *Araucaria* section Eutacta and *Dacrycarpus* (Christophel 1984; Greenwood 1994). Kiandra is rich in Lauraceae together with other taxa, including Podocarpaceae (*Dacrycarpus, Phyllocladus,* and *Podocarpus*), Cunoniaceae, Elaeocarpaceae, *Nothofagus* (*Lophozonia*), Monimiaceae (cf. *Doryphora*), Myrtaceae (cf. *Syzygium*), and Proteaceae. Both floras floristically match, in part, cool and warm temperate rainforest ecotones in New South Wales today, although the Bacchus Marsh association of *Nothofagus* and *Araucaria* was likened by Greenwood (1994) to the pattern seen in Chile, where these taxa commonly co-occur (Veblen and Schlegel 1982). The rich conifer element at Kiandra is found today in Tasmanian (but lacking *Dacrycarpus*) and New Zealand temperate rainforests and in highland forests in New Guinea, but not in Victoria or New South Wales.

A Short-Lived Recovery: The Latest Early Miocene Warm Phase

The late Early Miocene macro- and microfloras of the Yallourn Clays and Middle Miocene Yallourn Seam of the Latrobe Valley brown coal measures indicate diverse mesothermal rainforests in a mosaic with fire-adapted sclerophyllous vegetation (Greenwood 1994; Blackburn and Sluiter 1994; Kershaw 1996). These rainforests were rich in tropical rainforest taxa, including Lauraceae, Myrtaceae (e.g., *Acmena, Austromyrtus, Syzygium,* and *Tristania* s.l.), Proteaceae (e.g., *Darlingia, Orites, Stenocarpus* or *Oreocallis,* and *Xylomelum*), Cunoniaceae, Elaeocarpaceae (*Elaeocarpus* and aff. *Sloanea*), and *Diospyros,* as well as in various "temperate" (e.g., *Dacrydium, Dacrycarpus,* and *Phyllocladus*) and "tropical" conifers (e.g., *Agathis* and *Araucaria*) and zamioid cycads (*Bowenia* and *Macrozamia*), but also contained sclerophyllous taxa. *Nothofagus* (*Brassospora* and *Lophozonia*) is abundant as pollen, but *Nothofagus* subgenus *Lophozonia* leaves are known only from the interseam clays, where they may occur as extensive leaf mats (Greenwood 1994). Kershaw (1996) suggests that the forests of the Early Miocene coal seams grew under humid mesothermal climates. The character of these forests may not be generally indicative of regional vegetation, but as they are known in comparative detail (Blackburn and Sluiter 1994; Kershaw 1996), they are discussed here as an exemplar of regional processes and climatic effects on vegetation.

Carefully examined vertical stratigraphic sequences through the Yallourn and Morwell coal seams have revealed a stepwise shift in floristics between edaphically controlled communities (a hydroseral, fire-modified succession) at one temporal scale, as well as replacement of taxonomic sets by new sets over the Late Oligocene-Early Miocene (Morwell Seam) to Middle Miocene (Yallourn Seam) interval at a longer scale (Blackburn and Sluiter 1994). *Gymnostoma* is found throughout the two seams, but is most abundant in the upper part of the older Morwell Seam. In the younger Yallourn Seam *Gymnostoma* is less abundant, with its sclerophyllous sister taxon *Allocasuarina* (Casuarinaceae) appearing in small numbers. This pattern is also seen in central Australia, where *Gymnostoma* is common in Middle Eocene floras, whereas in the Late Miocene Stuart Creek and associated floras, *Gymnostoma* and *Casuarina* are found in association and may reflect local community ecological replacement (R. S. Hill 1990, 1994; Greenwood 1996). Evolution in leaf micromorphology within some Proteaceae (e.g., Banksieae) in the Latrobe Valley coal floras, as well as in other macrofloras, also indicates a shift from everwet to seasonally dry climates, but Hill (1998) urges that care be taken not to confound scleromorphy and xeromorphy in the fossil record. The younger floras contain both *Banksieaephyllum* species (and other Proteaceae) exhibiting adaptation to drought (i.e., narrow leaves with recurved margins, stomata in deep areolar pits with a dense indument) and species lacking such adaptations (i.e., broad, flat leaves with surficial stomata). The older floras contain *Banksieaephyllum* species and other Proteaceae lacking drought adaptations (Blackburn and Sluiter 1994; Hill 1998). It is likely that these plants reflect adaptation to low soil fertility as well as (in some cases) xeromorphic adaptation (Hill 1998).

Early Miocene seed floras from Victoria (e.g., Haddon, Eldorado), New South Wales (e.g., Bathurst, Elsmore, Gulgong, and Orange), and Queensland (Glencoe) contain taxa whose nearest living relatives are today found in the northeastern Queensland tropical rainforests, repeating patterns seen in the Middle Eocene floras. The fossil seed *Elaeocarpus clarkei* (F. Muell.) Selling, known from several sites in Victoria and New South Wales (fig. 18.7G), matches *Elaeocarpus bancroftii* endocarps (Rozefelds and Christophel 1996a, and 1996b). *Xylocaryon lockii* is known from Haddon and other sites in Victoria (Greenwood, Vadala, and Douglas 2000) and matches seeds of *Eidothea zoexylocarya,* a newly described primitive member of the Proteaceae from the tropical rainforests of northeastern Queensland assigned to its own subfamily (fig. 18.7I) (Douglas and Hyland 1995). The Glencoe seed flora (also named Capella: Rozefelds 1990) includes taxa such as *Elaeocarpus peterii,* which matches *E. stellaris,* and the form genus *Wilkinsonia* (figs. 18.6K and 18.7I), which represents fossil seeds indistinguishable from the endocarps of *Athertonia diversifolia* (Proteaceae). *Wilkinsonia* seeds are also reported from the base of the Miocene Yallourn Seam in Victoria (Rozefelds 1995). All of the matching living species in these examples are endemic to the present-day Wet Tropics region of northeastern Queensland (fig. 18.7).

The Neogene Aridification: Extinction and Final Contraction of Rainforests

Microfloral and faunal evidence supports the idea of a dramatic retreat of rainforest from sites in the continental interior and areas inland from the Great Dividing Range through the latter part of the Miocene and into the Pliocene (Archer, Hand, and Godthelp 1994; Martin 1994, 1998). Faunal and rare paleobotanical evidence from Miocene to Pleistocene sediments at Riversleigh in northern Australia indicates contracting rainforests there during the late Neogene (Archer, Hand, and Godthelp 1994). Abundant sedimentological and fossil evidence testifies to a significant shift toward much drier (but not yet arid) climates than in the Paleogene by the Late Miocene and Pliocene. A short recovery phase for rainforest was noted for the earliest part of the Early Pliocene in some areas of southeastern Australia (Martin 1991; Kershaw, Martin, and McEwen Mason 1994; Macphail 1997; Gallagher et al. 2003). Rainforests appear to have remained significant components of the landscape across southeastern Australia, but the significant tropical floristic element now endemic to northeastern Queensland appears to have been regionally extinct in southern Australia by the latest Pliocene or, in some cases, the early Pleistocene (see Kershaw, Moss, and Wild, chap. 19 in this volume). Diverse mesothermal rainforests were present in northeastern Queensland in the late Neogene, as Late Miocene to Pliocene sediments on the Atherton Tableland at Butchers Creek contain a diverse mesothermal rainforest microflora, and the limited macroflora includes Lauraceae (cf. *Neolitsea*). Evidence for this reconstruction is reviewed below.

The account by Macphail (1997) of the microfloral record of late Neogene vegetation for Australia included data on terrestrial plant spore-pollen assemblages from the offshore Gippsland Basin Hapuku-1 sediment core, as well as records from southern New South Wales (e.g., Martin 1991), Tasmania, and different areas in Victoria. Kershaw, Martin, and McEwen Mason (1994) provided additional data on Neogene environments, including a discontinuous record from the Latrobe Valley, and Gallagher et al. (2003) provided greater detail than provided by Macphail (1997) on the Hapuku-1 sediment core. In each of these records, rainforest declined in regional importance from the mid-Miocene, and a substantive influence from open-canopy sclerophyllous forests had been established by the Late Miocene-Early Pliocene. Pollen of *Acacia, Eucalyptus,* and Casuarinaceae (probably representing *Allocasuarina* or *Casuarina*), key taxa in present-day sclerophyllous forests and woodlands in eastern Australia, are absent or present in only trace amounts prior to the Early Pliocene. In the Hapuku-1 record, pollen of sclerophyllous taxa show marked increases through the Early Pliocene, concomitantly with rises in pollen of herbaceous taxa (Asteraceae, Chenopodiaceae, Poaceae, and Restionaceae) that are well represented in (while not exclusive to) present-day open-canopy sclerophyllous vegetation in eastern Australia. These changes in the regional importance of rainforest versus open-canopy sclerophyllous vegetation in each of the records were interpreted as indicating a shift from nonseasonal rainfall to a seasonal rainfall pattern (Martin 1991; Kershaw, Martin, and McEwen Mason 1994; Macphail 1997; Gallagher et al. 2003).

Two local terrestrial sites, Grange Burn and Stony Creek Basin, provide more detail on the history of "tropical rainforest" in southeastern Australia. The Grange Burn Early Pliocene site has a well-studied fauna that has a mixture of generalist marsupials (e.g., *Trichosurus,* the brush-tailed possum) or taxa from a wide range of open vegetation habitats (e.g., gliding possums such as *Petaurus*) and taxa from tropical rainforests (e.g., tree kangaroos, *Dendrolagus*, and cuscus, *Strigocuscus*: Archer, Hand, and Godthelp 1994). Macphail (1997) interpreted the Grange Burn microflora as indicating a local mosaic of araucarian rainforest (i.e., canopy with *Araucaria* and/or *Agathis* or with these trees as emergents, with *Nothofagus* and the tree fern family Cyatheaceae) and sclerophyllous open-canopy vegetation (e.g., *Acacia* and *Eucalyptus* with an understory including numerous graminoids and forbs, such as Asteraceae, Cyperaceae, Poaceae, and Restionaceae). Sclerophyllous vegetation (with *Eucalyptus*, *Casuarina* s.l., and cf. *Callitris*) was dominant throughout the latest Pliocene of Stony Creek Basin, alternating with relatively brief, discrete intervals of rainforest. The Stony Creek Basin rainforests were dominated by Podocarpaceae (predominantly *Podocarpus*, but also other genera), but also contained a taxonomically diverse assemblage of dicots that are today restricted to the northeastern Queensland tropical rainforests (Sniderman 1999; K. Sniderman, personal communication, August 2001). Consistent trace quantities of *Nothofagus* subgenus *Brassospora*, but almost no *Lophozonia*, in the Grange Burn and Stony Creek records suggest that the present-day temperate rainforests dominated by *Nothofagus cunninghamii* (i.e., subgenus *Lophozonia*) were not yet in place in the region.

There is an emerging picture of the Late Miocene and Pliocene macrofloral record (Hill 1994; Greenwood, Vadala, and Douglas 2000). A Miocene flora in the Warrumbungle Ranges in central New South Wales contains both sclerophyllous elements, such as *Eucalyptus*, and warm temperate or subtropical rainforest elements, such as *Ceratopetalum* (Holmes and Holmes 1992; Holmes, Holmes, and Martin 1983). Fossil *Acacia*, *Eucalyptus*, and *Nothofagus* wood is reported from Miocene beds at Lachlan River (Bishop and Bamber 1985). The Moranbah macroflora from near Emerald in central Queensland was once considered Eocene (based on a radiometric age for overlying basalts: Christophel and Greenwood 1989), but has a Miocene palynoflora (Partridge 1998). The Moranbah macroflora, which contains *Gymnostoma*, abundant Lauraceae, and rainforest Proteaceae, indicates the presence of humid mesothermal rainforests in the Miocene near the present-day humid tropical rainforest area. Its foliar physiognomy matches that of Complex Notophyll Vine Forest (Christophel 1994; Greenwood 1994).

The persistence of rainforest taxa, including *Phyllocladus* and *Agathis*, in southeastern Australia (e.g., Grange Burn and Stony Creek Basin or Daylesford) until about the end of the Pliocene is supported by the macrofloral record. Most mid-Miocene to Pliocene macrofloral sites in Victoria (e.g., Sentinel Rock and

Daylesford) contain not only sclerophyllous taxa, especially *Acacia, Banksia* (and other Proteaceae), *Casuarina,* and *Eucalyptus,* but also rainforest taxa such as *Phyllocladus* (Deane 1902, 1904; Cookson 1954; Greenwood, Vadala, and Douglas 2000).

In central Australia, the Late Miocene Stuart Creek and Poole Creek South floras, along with imprecisely dated floras in the Stuart Range and at Island Lagoon, provide evidence for mesothermal riparian gallery rainforests, with the interfluves vegetated by sclerophyllous plants. The floras include "rainforest taxa" such as *Brachychiton, Cochlospermum, Gymnostoma,* cf. *Papuacedrus, Araucaria,* Elaeocarpaceae, and *Callicoma* and other Cunoniaceae as well as sclerophyllous taxa such as *Banksia, Casuarina, Eucalyptus,* and other woody-fruited Myrtaceae (Lange 1978, 1982; Benbow et al. 1995; Greenwood 1996; Barnes and Hill 1999; Greenwood, Haines, and Steart 2001). *Eucalyptus* leaves dominate the Miocene-Pliocene Leaf Locality at Lake Ngakapaldi (Stirton, Tedford, and Woodburne 1967).

Overall, the emerging picture of the Late Miocene to Late Pliocene of central, eastern, and southeastern Australia is one of rainforests being restricted to edaphically or topographically wetter pockets in the regional vegetational mosaic. In general, these rainforests appear to have a floristic composition similar to that of present-day tropical rainforests of northeastern Queensland. At least in southeastern and central Australia, these "tropical rainforests" were in significant retreat by the Late Pliocene, being replaced primarily by sclerophyllous vegetation of modern aspect (i.e., open forests dominated by *Eucalyptus*). In southeastern Australia, temperate rainforests similar to those found today in the region (i.e., dominated by *Nothofagus* subgenus *Lophozonia*) were present by the latest Pliocene in the Gippsland region of Victoria (Kershaw, Martin, and McEwen Mason 1994; Gallagher et al. 2003).

OVERVIEW OF PATTERNS AND PROCESSES

A number of overriding trends can be seen in the presence and absence of key taxa over the Paleocene to Miocene in southeastern Australia. These trends are matched by shifts in diversity and canopy leaf size spectra (i.e., foliar physiognomic signatures: see figs. 18.4 and 18.5), which largely reflect climatic influences in the region (see fig. 18.3). Interpretation of Pliocene patterns is problematic, as the quality of the macrofloral database for this epoch is poor (Christophel 1981; Hill 1994; Gallagher et al. 2003), although, as discussed above, floristic patterns are apparent from microfloral data. Some taxa in the Paleocene forests may have been deciduous, reflecting latitudinal constraints in the seasonal light regime (Lange 1982; Carpenter, Hill, and Jordan 1994; Hill 1994; Scriven, McLoughlin, and Hill 1995; Greenwood et al. 2003), although few or no Australian extant relatives of these taxa are deciduous (e.g., Lauraceae, with one deciduous species in North America; *Nothofagus,* with one deciduous species of three in Australia and with deciduous species in South America). Carpenter, Hill, and Jordan (1994) suggest that the extinct Tertiary cycad *Pterostoma* may have been deciduous, a characteristic found in only one modern monsoonal Australian cycad, *Cycas armstrongii.*

A large number of taxa (e.g., *Nothofagus,* Banksieae, *Dacrycarpus, Gymnostoma, Agathis*) appear to maintain a presence in the local and regional vegetation throughout the Paleocene to Miocene, whereas other taxa (e.g., cycads, Lauraceae, *Araucaria,* and Ebenaceae cf. *Diospyros*) are absent or much less diverse during key intervals, reappearing subsequently, although in many cases different species in the same genus, or even different subgenera, are indicated for Paleogene and for Neogene floras (e.g., dominance by *Nothofagus* subgenus *Brassospora* in the Eocene, but by subgenus *Lophozonia* in the Late Pliocene to the present). In other cases the same species reoccurs. Some Paleogene taxa represent regionally or globally extinct lineages (e.g., *Pterostoma,* some conifers, some Proteaceae). Paleocene to Early Eocene floras (e.g., Cambalong Creek, Hotham Heights, Regatta Point) and Oligocene floras (e.g., Little Rapid River) are rich in conifers, whereas Middle Eocene floras (e.g., Golden Grove, Nerriga) often have low conifer diversity, although some latitudinal zonation was in place in the Middle Eocene (e.g., high conifer diversity at Hasties in Tasmania). In general, Late Paleocene and Early to Middle Eocene macrofloras and late Early Miocene floras have diverse Lauraceae components, whereas few or no species of Lauraceae are found in latest Eocene and Oligocene floras.

The pattern of high and low diversity for the Lauraceae is consistent with the inferred cool and warm phases, as Lauraceae in eastern Australian rainforests are much more species-rich in humid mesothermal vegetation than in mesothermal-microthermal wet or mesothermal-megathermal seasonally dry vegetation. A number of other taxa in southern Australia are largely restricted to the Paleocene to Eocene (e.g., *Eucryphia, Cordyline,* Musgraveinae [known as microfossils in the Miocene, however: Macphail et al. 1994; Blackburn and Sluiter 1994], and other "rainforest" Proteaceae) or appear to have their last regional representation in the Oligocene (e.g., *Acmopyle, Piper/Smilax,* and *Libocedrus*).

Despite a poorly documented monocot fossil record, endemic rainforest monocots such as Petermanniaceae, *Archontophoenix* and *Linospadix* (Arecaceae), and regional taxa such as *Calamus, Nypa* (Arecaceae), and *Cordyline* (Lomandraceae) were clearly present in Australia prior to the Miocene collision with Malesia. The pollen record shows palms (as *Arecipites*) to be significant elements since the Early Paleocene, perhaps revealing a late introduction of the Arecaceae into Australia, as the family is well represented in Late Cretaceous floras outside of Australia (Greenwood and Conran 2000).

The floristic links between present-day northeastern Queensland humid tropical rainforests (and those of neighboring landmasses) and southern Australian Tertiary rainforests are most strong in the warm phases of the Tertiary; namely, the Early to Middle Eocene (e.g., *Lygodium, Bowenia, Dacrycarpus* (New Guinea), *Podocarpus smithii*/*P. platyphyllum, Prumnopitys, Linospadix, Nypa, Basisperma* (New Guinea), *Diospyros hebecarpa*/*Austrodiospyros cryptostoma, Gymnostoma, Megahertzia,* Musgraveinae/*Musgraveinanthus, Nothofagus* subgenus *Brassospora,* and *Petermannia*/*Petermanniopsis*) and late Early to Middle Miocene (e.g., *Dacrycarpus, Phyllocladus hypophyllus*/*P. morwellensis, Athertonia diversifolia*/*Wilkinsonia* spp., *Eidothea zoexylocarya*/*Xylocaryon lockii, Elaeocarpus bancroftii*/*E. clarkei,* and *Gymnostoma*). The occurrence of several of these taxa at Early to Middle Eocene sites in Queensland (e.g., Dinmore) and of *Gymnostoma* and *Pterostoma* in the central Queensland Miocene Moranbah flora confirms that there was not necessarily a wholesale migration of taxa, but more than likely a contraction from a widespread base during cooler phases.

To what extent individual macrofossil taxa reflect ecological patterns, as opposed to taphonomic processes (including differential transport potential of the leaves of different taxa, incomplete systematic knowledge, and incomplete sampling: Greenwood 1991, 1994; Steart et al. 2002), is difficult to assess; however, the broad trends observed are consistent with floristic changes associated with cooling and warming trends through the Paleogene and early Neogene. The apparent absences and reappearances of taxa presented here probably reflect local extinctions and subsequent reinvasions from local or regional refugia, as well as southward migration into southeastern Australia from warmer areas to the north during warming intervals and from cooler southerly or montane sites during cooling intervals. Some taxa apparently restricted to the Eocene are still present in southeastern Australia today (e.g., *Brachychiton,* Arecaceae, and *Eucryphia*), and some of these taxa are known from Neogene microfloras from the region (Truswell 1993), implying a regional presence not indicated by the macrofloral record. Other taxa with restricted stratigraphic ranges occur more or less continuously throughout the region in microfloras (e.g., *Nothofagus Brassospora*), also suggesting a continual regional presence. Differential responses within the region may also influence the patterns observed. *Nothofagus Lophozonia*, for example, is primarily known from Tasmanian macrofloras of the pre-Oligocene, with only a single leaf recorded in the Maslin Bay Middle Eocene macroflora (Scriven, McLoughlin, and Hill 1995), and *Nothofagus Brassospora* is principally known from a limited set of Paleogene macrofloras from Tasmania, yet pollen of these taxa is known from microfloras throughout the region until the Late Pliocene (Truswell 1993; Macphail 1997; Gallagher et al. 2003). It is unclear whether these discrepancies between the macrofloral and microfloral records reflect differences in sampling effectiveness or an ecological pattern in which some taxa were absent from the habitats represented in the macrofloral record, but persisted in the regional vegetative mosaic (Christophel and Greenwood 1989; Greenwood 1991; Truswell 1993; Macphail et al. 1994).

As the discussion above indicates, little is actually known of the Tertiary history of the tropical rainforests of Australia within their current latitudinal occurrence. A mixed sclerophyllous and monsoon forest Tertiary macroflora from Melville Island (Pole and Bowman 1996) lacks key tropical rainforest taxa, and Tertiary macrofloras from Queensland remain systematically unknown (Allen et al. 1960; Rozefelds, Christophel, and Alley 1992; Christophel 1994). Nevertheless, the extensive record of vegetative evolution and of climate change during the Tertiary for southeastern Australia provides insight into the origins, evolution, and patterns of extinction and diversification experienced by the antecedents of the modern tropical rainforests. For much of the Tertiary, essentially temperate forest types (i.e., microthermal-mesothermal to mesothermal) prevailed over much of southern Australia, although these forests were more diverse than present-day southeastern Australian temperate rainforests. It seems likely that diverse mesothermal-megathermal rainforests occupied areas northward of these forests during the cold phases. During the Late Paleocene to Middle Eocene and late Early to Middle Miocene warm phases, the mesothermal-megathermal rainforests expanded southward at least as far as present-day Melbourne, and perhaps westward to near what is now Perth (e.g., Westdale, Lake Lefroy, and Kojonup floras), including the interior of the continent (e.g., Nelly Creek and Stuart Creek).

Periods of contraction from southeastern Australia (and perhaps central Australia) of the mesothermal-megathermal rainforests must have caused some taxa to become locally restricted or less species-rich at some times (e.g., Arecaceae and Lauraceae where MAT $< 10°C$ and coldest month mean temperature [CMM] $< 5°C$), and even to go locally extinct (e.g., *Acmopyle, Prumnopitys*, and Musgraveinae). During cool periods, temperate and sclerophyllous lineages probably expanded and diversified (particularly as scleromorphs may have been preadapted to seasonal drought), as evidenced by evolution within *Nothofagus* subgenus *Lophozonia* and Banksieae (Hill and Christophel 1987; Hill 1994) and by apparent ecological replacement within such families as Casuarinaceae (*Gymnostoma* by *Allocasuarina*). The later warm-phase expansions (e.g., late Early Miocene) must also have resulted in diversification within lineages, due to coalescence of formerly isolated refugia as well as the opportunities presented by increased areal cover and resultant heterogeneity of local environments. Neogene northward contractions may have left some of these evolutionary legacies in now isolated pockets of rainforest. Final extinctions in the Late Pliocene or perhaps early Pleistocene removed elements such as *Phyllocladus,* Araucariaceae, and many dicot groups from southern Australia, but the primary loss of the mesothermal rainforest biota appears to be a late Neogene event (possibly as late as the latest Pliocene in southeastern Australia), and must have extended throughout much of the continent. A second wave of extinction of mesothermal elements during the Pleistocene appears to have affected wet refugia in northeastern Australia (see Kershaw, Moss, and Wild, chap. 19 in this volume).

The lack of detection of the more noteworthy primitive angiosperms of the humid tropics (e.g., *Idiospermum*) in the fossil record is not necessarily significant, as "negative evidence" in the fossil record may reflect lack of data as much as it does real patterns. Some important endemic or otherwise biogeographically important taxa are known as fossils—some as macrofossils, others as microfossils (e.g., *Ilex*). What is perhaps surprising is the inherent conservatism of some plant lineages: taxa that appear to have remained morphologically unchanged since the Middle Eocene (e.g., *Podocarpus smithii* and *Megahertzia*) or Early Miocene (e.g., *Eidothea zoexylocarya* and *Elaeocarpus bancroftii*) are still found in the rainforests of northeastern Queensland. The realities of southeastern Australia's paleolatitude and climate in the Paleogene mean that the Tertiary forests are not truly analogous to modern Australian tropical rainforests (e.g., Lange 1982). The modern tropical rainforests, however, can be considered an evolutionary ark (an incongruous yet apt concept)—not a static "living fossil of a community," but rather a dynamic pool of taxa that has ebbed and flowed across the landscape, expanding and contracting with each climatic cycle between warm and wet and cool and dry, but now restricted to an archipelago of small, isolated pools. It is also evident that with successive expansions and contractions, some taxa have been left behind, diversifying or becoming isolated in suitable environments along the east coast of Australia (e.g., *Wollemia nobilis*) and even adapting to the newly dry environments of the interior.

In contrast, the rainforest floras in southeastern Australia appear to have experienced significant extinction since the Early Miocene, as they are depauperate in comparison to the Early Miocene rainforests, and probably in comparison to those of the Late Pliocene (Gallagher et al. 2003; K. Sniderman, unpublished data). Significant radiation, however, has occurred within major plant lineages into the expanding open-canopy vegetation that came to dominant the landscape in the late Neogene continental aridification. The overall patterns for Australia's "tropical" rainforests over the past 65 million years have thus been shaped by climate change, and initially by continental displacement from high to middle latitudes. These processes can be summarized as phases of diversification during range expansion in warm-wet intervals (Late Paleocene to Middle Eocene, Early Miocene and possibly the Early Pliocene) followed by phases of extinction or continental-scale range contraction (latest Eocene to Early Miocene, Late Miocene, and latest Pliocene to Pleistocene: see Kershaw, Moss, and Wild, chap. 19 in this volume).

ACKNOWLEDGMENTS

This work was made possible by funding from the Australian Research Council Large Grants Scheme to DRG (A39802019) and DCC (E8315626R) and by CRC-TREM funding to DCC. We would like to thank the following people for assistance at various phases of this project: Bernie Hyland, Stephen Gallagher, Bruce Gray, Peter Kershaw, Geoff Tracey, Len Webb, Mike Archer, Brian McGowran, and for their forbearance, Cathy Greenwood and Debbie Christophel. We would also like to thank Craig Moritz for inviting us to participate in this volume. Modern herbarium data were kindly made available by the Australian National Herbarium. We would also like to thank Alan Partridge and Kale Sniderman for sharing their unpublished work with us. The final draft benefited from useful reviews by Peter Kershaw and John Flenley. The revised work was completed in 1999; however, minor corrections and additions were made in mid-2001 and mid-2003. Due to time constraints and in order to retain essentially the original refereed work, some relevant literature published in 1999 and more recently could not be incorporated.

19

Patterns and Causes of Vegetation Change in the Australian Wet Tropics Region over the Last 10 Million Years

A. PETER KERSHAW, PATRICK T. MOSS, AND RUSSELL WILD

ABSTRACT

A generalized picture of the vegetation of the Wet Tropics of North Queensland, through the last 10 million years or the late Cenozoic era, is provided by well-dated marine palynological records. These records are supplemented by detailed, but temporally restricted, pollen studies of sections of the Pliocene, early Pleistocene, and mid-Pleistocene to Holocene periods from both marine or terrestrial sequences. Through most of the late Cenozoic era, rainforest was the dominant vegetation, with extensive drier araucarian rainforest surrounding core areas of complex rainforest within wetter areas. These complex rainforests, which may have had a distribution similar to those present prior to the impact of European people, became progressively impoverished floristically as temperatures increased in association with the northward movement of the Australian continent and as climate became more variable, and possibly drier, in line with global trends. However, losses were less than in most other parts of the continent. There is no evidence of any floristic gain, despite past claims for an invasion of Southeast Asian rainforest taxa into Australia with increasing proximity of the two landmasses. It is likely that a dry corridor in the northern Australian-Sahul Shelf region effectively prevented any major floristic interchange. Araucarian forest appears to have remained intact until it was progressively replaced by sclerophyllous vegetation as a result of increased burning over the last 200,000 years. The trigger may have been an acceleration in regional warming with the development of the West Pacific Warm Pool and the resulting increase in climatic variation through the establishment of the Southern Oscillation. Further increased levels of burning after the arrival of Aboriginal people would no doubt have contributed to this trend. It appears that rainforest has shown a high degree of resilience to environmental change over most of the last 10 million years, but recent events, both natural and the result of human activity, have had a disastrous effect on many component communities. The present rainforest patches, having lost their protective araucarian buffer, are now exposed to the ravages of a continuously evolving, fire-promoting sclerophyllous vegetation, and the lowland rainforests, at least, are probably feeling the stress of moving ever farther from their traditional, more temperate, latitudes.

INTRODUCTION

The late Cenozoic, covering the Late Miocene, Pliocene, Pleistocene, and Holocene geologic epochs, has witnessed substantial changes in global environments. These changes provide a basis for understanding the nature and distribution of present vegetation communities and their relationships. Over this time period there have been massive buildups of ice, first in Antarctica and then in high latitudes of the Northern Hemisphere, as the climate cooled, leading to substantial reductions in sea levels and marked changes in the amount and distribution of precipitation. The effects of the interaction between natural variation in incoming radiation and ice volume subsequently led, in the last few million years, to marked environmental variation, enhanced, within recent times, by the increasing effects of people. Associated with these changes have been the tectonic influences of mountain uplift and continental movement, which have had major effects on at least regional atmospheric and ocean circulation systems and may have been responsible for overall global cooling.

Despite the importance of the late Cenozoic, documentation of this period is poor, at least on land, largely because landscape instability has not been conducive to the continuous accumulation and preservation of fossil-bearing sediments. In addition, techniques have not generally been available to accurately date those generally discontinuous sequences that do exist.

The humid tropics is one region that is demonstrating some potential to provide a good record for the late Cenozoic, largely through the acquisition of offshore cores by the Ocean Drilling Program (ODP) for the purpose of documenting and understanding the evolution of carbonate platforms on the northeastern Australian margin (Davies et al. 1993). These offshore sediments contain pollen transported from land that provides some picture of regional vegetation.

Ocean sediments have several advantages for the construction of pollen records. They have accumulated under constantly waterlogged conditions, not directly affected by local hydrological conditions and changes in sea level, so that sedimentation is often continuous over long periods and pollen, once deposited, is not subject to oxidation. Furthermore, they can be dated from their paleomagnetic and isotope stratigraphy and from established biostratigraphies of wide-ranging marine fossils. Disadvantages often include substantial differential representation of pollen taxa due to a large degree of variation in dispersal ability, as well as coarse spatial resolution of vegetation due to the mixing of pollen from different communities and slow sedimentation rates. In North Queensland these disadvantages are offset, to some degree, by the nature and location of the marine cores and by knowledge of vegetation-pollen relationships from modern pollen studies and the construction of terrestrial and coastal pollen records.

In contrast to the majority of marine cores, those from this region include continental slope and trough sites, relatively close to land and with high sediment accumulation rates. However, these situations also increase the chances of sediment mixing through slumping and turbidite activity. Modern pollen studies include the analysis of spectra from rainforest (Kershaw and Bulman 1994; Kershaw and Hyland 1975; Kershaw and Strickland 1990), sclerophyllous vegetation (Kershaw 1976), coastal complexes (Crowley, Grindrod, and Kershaw 1994), and estuaries (Moss 1999) that provide information on the pollen production and dispersal characteristics of individual taxa and assemblages. There are terrestrial pollen records covering the later part of the Quaternary from volcanic crater lakes and swamps on the Atherton Tableland and from coastal swamps (Hiscock and Kershaw 1992), as well as one older Plio-Pleistocene record from the Tableland (Kershaw and Sluiter 1982).

THE SITES AND THEIR REGIONAL SETTING

All pollen sites considered in this chapter are within the Wet Tropics World Heritage Region or in the adjacent seas to the east (fig. 19.1). The Atherton Table-

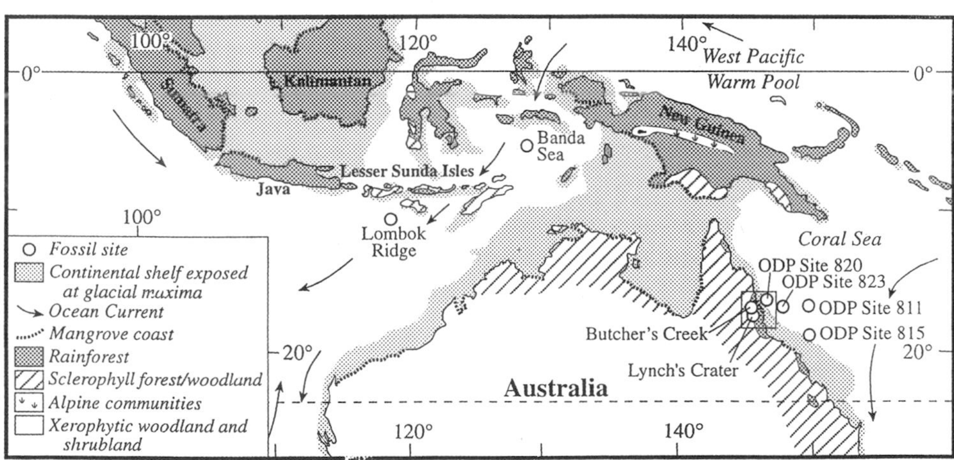

Figure 19.1 Location of fossil record sites mentioned in the text in relation to features of the geography of the northern Australian-southern Indonesian region. The limit of the continental shelf marks the approximate position of the coast during the height of late Quaternary glacial periods.

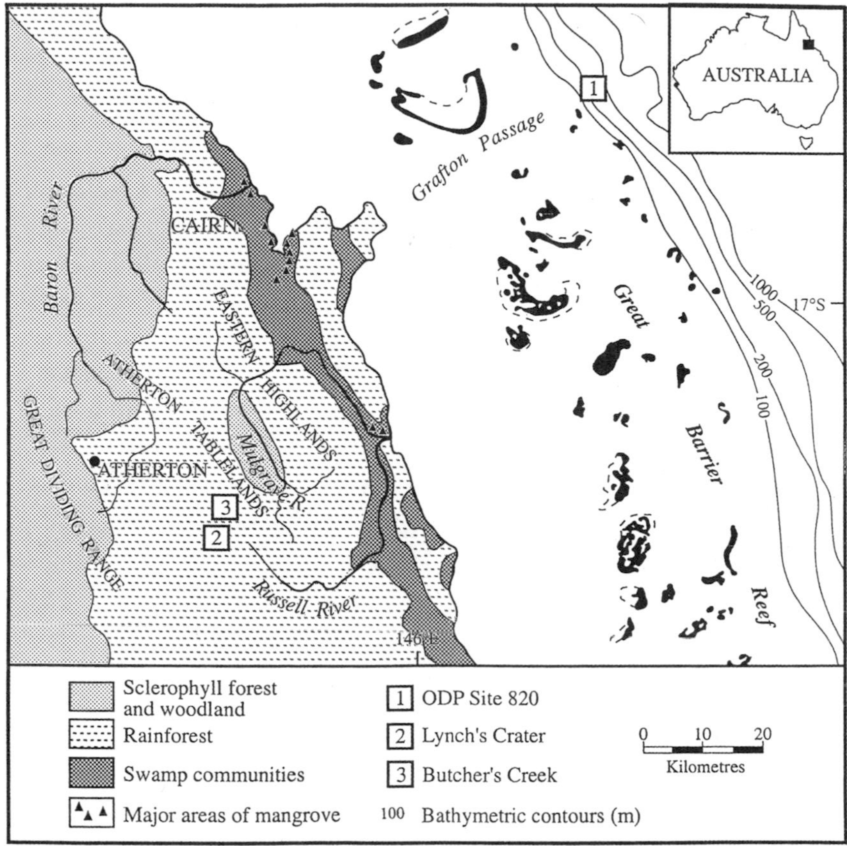

Figure 19.2 Location of sites of pollen records in and adjacent to the Wet Tropics region of northeastern Australia.

land sites are at an altitude of about 700 m, experience a mean annual rainfall in excess of 1,500 mm, with as much as 2,500 mm at Lynch's Crater, and occur within the pre-European extent of rainforest. They are separated from the coastal lowlands by the Bellenden Ker Ranges, which exceed 1,500 m in altitude. ODP Site 820 is located toward the top of the continental slope under about 200 m of water and about 50 km from the present coastline (fig. 19.2). As the predominant winds are from the east, it is likely that most pollen is derived by water rather than wind transport. The Barron and Mulgrave/Russell river systems are the most obvious sources. They drain much of the region and flow through the major vegetation types represented: rainforest, sclerophyllous woodland, coastal swamp vegetation, and mangroves. The pollen can then be channeled through the Grafton Passage within the Great Barrier Reef system to the site.

ODP Site 823, which lies about 120 km off the coast, was drilled in about 1,600 m of water in the Queensland Trough. The site probably derived most of its pollen from the Barron and Mulgrave/Russell river systems.

LATE CENOZOIC VEGETATION: AN OVERVIEW

A generalized picture of vegetation through much of the late Cenozoic is provided by a combination of the marine palynological records from ODP Sites 823 and 820. Major features of the original records, after recalculation of a common pollen sum based on pollen derived predominantly from terrestrial plants (i.e. rainforest gymnosperms, rainforest angiosperms, sclerophyllous trees and shrubs, and terrestrial herbs), are shown in figure 19.3, in which the spectra are also related to geologic ages derived from nanofossil (Wei and Gartner 1993) and benthic foraminiferal (Katz and Miller 1993) evidence from the cores and from the oxygen isotope records of Peerdeman (1993) and Peerdeman, Davies, and Chivas (1993) for the upper part of Site 820.

ODP Site 820 was sampled for pollen at 10 m intervals through the 400 m sequence. It is clear from the time scale that the sediment accumulation rate is generally higher in the basal part of the 1.4-million-year record, with some increase again in the very upper part. The large gaps between samples represent sections where pollen was too sparse to obtain the minimum count of 50 terrestrial grains. Thirty-seven samples were taken at approximately equidistant intervals through the 1,000 m of the ODP Site 823 core. The sedimentation rate is variable, but is fairly continuous from about 10.8 million years ago (MYA), although pollen is sparse or absent in sections, particularly through the Late Pliocene (and early Pleistocene, if the proposed date for the Plio-Pleistocene boundary of 2.6 MYA, rather than the current date of 1.81 MYA [Partridge 1997], is adopted) and from about 1.6 MYA to the present. At both sites, the effects on the pollen record of slumping and turbidite activity are a potential problem. In

Figure 19.3 Representation of major or indicator taxa in pollen records from ODP Site 823 (Martin and McMinn 1993) and ODP Site 820 (Kershaw, McKenzie, and McMinn 1993) in relation to the geologic time scale, the oxygen isotope records from ODP Site 820 (Peerdeman 1993) and from the combined ODP Sites 846 and 667 (Shackleton et al. 1995), and the inferred sea surface temperature records from ODP Sites 820 and 811. Total pollen of terrestrial plants, encompassing rainforest gymnosperms, rainforest angiosperms, rainforest-sclerophyllous taxa, and sclerophyllous taxa, makes up the pollen sum of each pollen spectrum on which all taxon percentages are based.

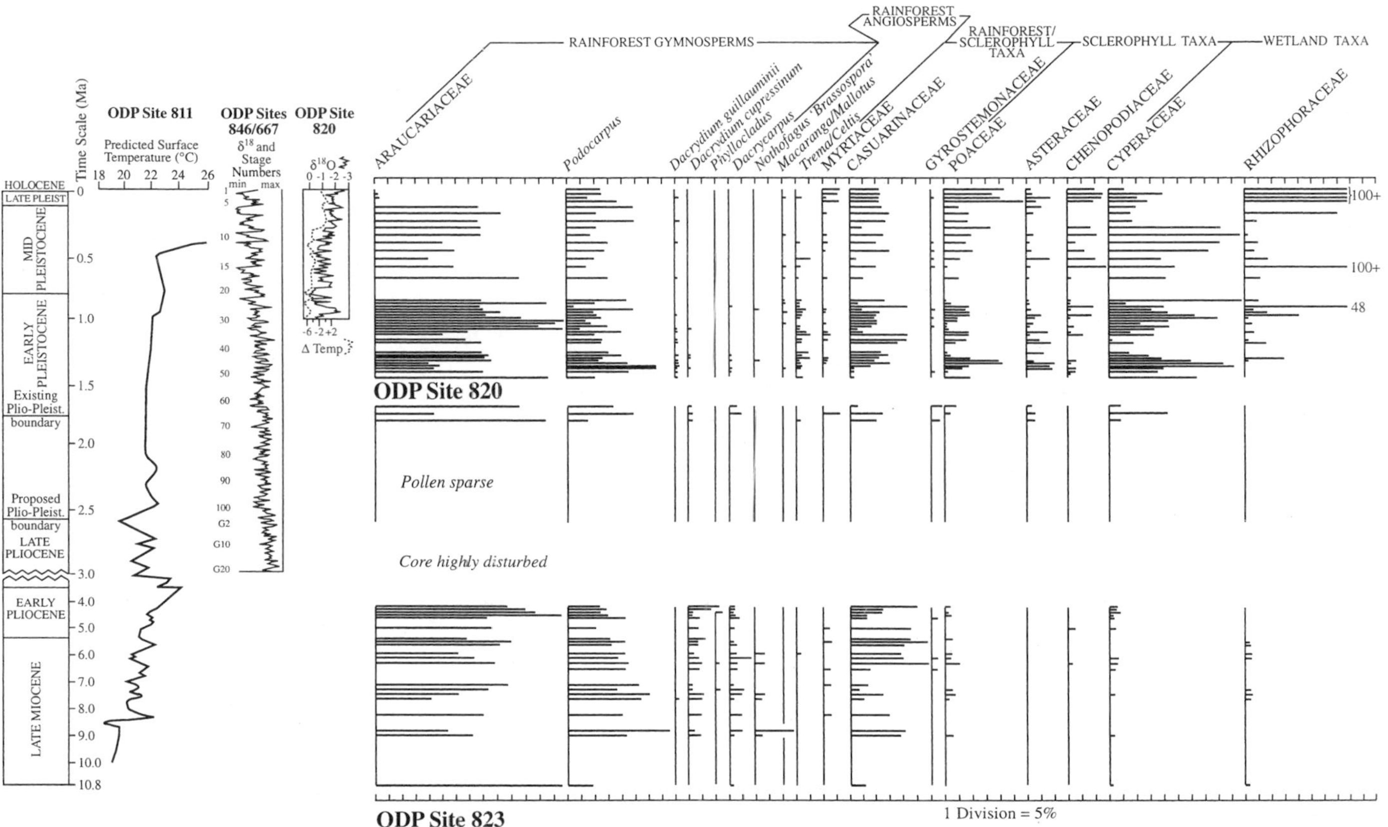

Time Scale (Ma)
ODP Site 811
Predicted Surface Temperature (°C)
ODP Sites 846/667
δ18 and Stage Numbers
min max
ODP Site 820
δ18O
Δ Temp.
HOLOCENE
LATE PLEIST
MID PLEISTOCENE
EARLY PLEISTOCENE
Existing Plio-Pleist. boundary
Proposed Plio-Pleist. boundary
LATE PLIOCENE
EARLY PLIOCENE
LATE MIOCENE
RAINFOREST GYMNOSPERMS
RAINFOREST ANGIOSPERMS
RAINFOREST/ SCLEROPHYLL TAXA
SCLEROPHYLL TAXA
WETLAND TAXA
ARAUCARIACEAE
Podocarpus
Dacrydium guillauminii
Dacrydium cupressinum
Phyllocladus
Dacrycarpus
Nothofagus 'Brassospora'
Macaranga/Mallotus
Trema/Celtis
MYRTACEAE
CASUARINACEAE
GYROSTEMONACEAE
POACEAE
ASTERACEAE
CHENOPODIACEAE
CYPERACEAE
RHIZOPHORACEAE
100+
100+
48
ODP Site 820
Pollen sparse
Core highly disturbed
ODP Site 823
1 Division = 5%

the ODP 820 core, where sediment loss is most likely, it is uncertain whether there are breaks in the record (Peerdeman, Davies, and Chivas 1993), but in the ODP 823 core, which would be a sediment sink, more than 2,000 such deposits have been recorded (Watts, Varga, and Feary 1993). However, these deposits have not affected the nanofossil stratigraphy (Wei and Gartner 1993), so at this gross scale, significant contamination from older material is unlikely.

The pollen data are shown against major environmental patterns derived from marine oxygen isotope records. The isotope sequence from ODP Sites 846/667 provides a standard global stratigraphy of predominantly ice volume with some temperature component (Shackleton et al. 1995). It illustrates a general cooling trend over the last 3 million years with a generally increasing amplitude and decreasing frequency of environmental variation through that time, particularly within the last 1 to 0.7 million years. In tropical areas such as North Queensland, the record can most usefully provide an indication of sea-level variation. From the beginning of the mid-Pleistocene, sea levels have been about 120 m lower than today during the height of glacial periods. The isotope record from Site 820 shows an interesting reversal of the overall trend in the global record, with the temperature component of the record suggesting a substantial increase in sea surface temperatures, especially about 300,000 years ago (Peerdeman 1993). The temperature component of the much longer isotope record from ODP Site 811 on the Queensland Plateau, east of the pollen sites, suggests that there has been a generally increasing sea surface temperature trend through the late Cenozoic, with a more substantial increase from about 500,000 years ago (Isern, McKenzie, and Feary 1996).

The combined pollen records indicate that gymnosperms have been a major component of the vegetation through most of the period. However, the values for the Podocarpaceae must be treated with some caution, as the possession of flotation bladders by the pollen grains allows wide dispersal by wind and water, and hence the potential for overrepresentation. With *Podocarpus,* overrepresentation is demonstrated by the maintenance of high values to the present day, despite the patchy occurrence of parent plants within the region. None of the other podocarps, which include *Dacrydium, Dacrycarpus,* and *Phyllocladus,* record substantial values, and hence they do not unduly influence the pollen spectra. Their disappearance from the record is also consistent with their present absence from the region. Araucariaceae, which embraces the genera *Araucaria* and *Agathis,* is likely to provide a better indication of parent plant abundance than *Podocarpus,* as the low values in the top samples reflect the restricted representation of the family within the Wet Tropics today. As *Araucaria* has the ability to dominate large areas of drier rainforest (Webb and Tracey 1967), it can be suggested that araucarian forest was a dominant forest type in the Wet Tropics landscape from at least the Mid-Miocene to the late Pleistocene.

Most of the rainforest angiosperms have relatively low representation, consistent with more limited dispersal and the general lack of dominance of taxa in complex rainforest vegetation. It is significant that the more notable rainforest genera include the *Macaranga/Mallotus* (Euphorbiaceae) and *Trema/Celtis* (Ulmaceae), which are wind-pollinated and can form monospecific stands under disturbed conditions. *Nothofagus* is an exception within the rainforest angiosperms and, in terms of stand domination and pollen dispersal, has the characteristics of a gymnosperm.

The Myrtaceae, Casuarinaceae, and Gyrostemonaceae are all taxa that have representatives in both rainforest and open vegetation, although the latter two are now predominantly confined to open vegetation. The history of Gyrostemonaceae is unclear, but Casuarinaceae, in the form of the rainforest genus *Gymnostoma*, was, judging from macrofossil remains, an important component of the vegetation of at least southeastern Australia until the Miocene epoch (Christophel 1980; Greenwood and Christophel, chap. 18 in this volume). Its demise may have been later in the northeast, as this region harbors small patches of the one remaining species of the genus on the continent. However, its presence cannot be determined from the records presented here, as the genera of Casuarinaceae are very difficult to separate by pollen morphological features (Kershaw 1970). Both Gyrostemonaceae and Casuarinaceae have well-dispersed pollen, which is likely to overrepresent the abundance of parent plants. The low values of Gyrostemonaceae are consistent with its generally more arid and southern Australian distribution. The values for Myrtaceae are surprisingly low, considering that it is well represented in rainforest, dominates present-day sclerophyllous vegetation in the form of *Eucalyptus*, and is a major component of most spectra from terrestrial assemblages on the Australian continent.

The terrestrial herbs and wetland taxa in these spectra generally provide realistic estimates of the abundance of parent plants, although the relative proximity of coastal vegetation to the marine sites is likely to overestimate the importance of lowland swamp Cyperaceae and the dominant mangrove family Rhizophoraceae. In addition to its predominant arid land source, Chenopodiaceae pollen is also likely to be derived from coastal salt marsh vegetation.

Stratigraphically, the combined record shows marked variation in taxon representation superimposed on some sustained changes. A component of the variation may be a reflection of relatively low pollen counts, although there is some suggestion of cyclicity in the abundance or presence of some taxa through parts of the diagram. Both variation and cyclicity may relate to climatic and sea-level change, particularly in the Quaternary, but resolution is too coarse to examine taxon patterns in relation to glacial-interglacial cycles.

Late Miocene vegetation in the humid tropics must have been composed predominantly of closed-canopy vegetation, as few herbaceous taxa are represented. The low values for Poaceae, Cyperaceae, and Chenopodiaceae may have been derived from localized disturbed environments along the coast, with perhaps some input from the drier interior of the continent. The lack of herbs has some bearing on the status of Casuarinaceae. Today, Casuarinaceae frequently shares the canopy of open sclerophyllous forest and woodland with *Eucalyptus* above a grassy understory. The apparent lack of such an understory could suggest that this family was represented mainly by rainforest members. However, in sclerophyllous communities where Casuarinaceae achieves dominance, the understory is often lacking grasses, suggesting that the grasses are predominantly associated with *Eucalyptus.* The low values for Myrtaceae, even if the family is underrepresented, suggest that there was no substantial presence of *Eucalyptus* during the Late Miocene.

The Late Miocene vegetation contained a number of essentially rainforest genera that are no longer present on mainland Australia. These include *Nothofagus* subgenus *Brassospora, Dacrydium, Phyllocladus,* and *Dacrycarpus.* All were important and widespread components of the dominant mesic rainforest in Australia within the mid-Tertiary period, but are now restricted to predominantly temperate, or more correctly microthermal (Nix 1982), environments in various geographic regions including New Guinea, New Caledonia, New Zealand, and Tasmania (Greenwood and Christophel, chap. 18 in this volume). It is likely that they achieved prominence in the cooler highland areas of the study region.

It is tempting to attribute the progressive demise of these taxa through the late Tertiary and Quaternary to the increasing temperature levels suggested by the ODP Site 811 isotope record. However, similar range reductions and extinctions in other parts of the Southern Hemisphere (Kershaw and McGlone 1995) that experienced temperature reductions, rather than increases, suggest that this explanation may be too simplistic. It is probable that a reduction in moisture levels and increasing climatic variation, at least in the Quaternary, may have been contributing factors. In attempting to assess the relative influence of these potential factors, it is unfortunate that evidence from the Late Pliocene to early Pleistocene is missing from the cores. However, limited pollen data for this period from ODP Site 815, just to the south of the humid tropics (Martin and McMinn 1993), suggest that there were no marked deviations from the trends evident in this record.

There is no clear evidence of any floral turnover associated with the decline in the more temperate elements. Rainforest angiosperms are certainly less well represented in the Tertiary than in the Quaternary, but this can be explained largely by the loss of high pollen producers that effectively diluted the angiosperm component. Even though there is no Tertiary record of *Macaranga/Mallotus* in the cores, this taxon is recorded as having been regionally present by Martin and McMinn (1993). However, the arrival of any tropical taxa, which are likely to have very limited pollen production and dispersal features and which may easily be hidden within the morphologies of diverse rainforest families or genera, may be difficult to detect in the marine records.

Open vegetation, both terrestrial and aquatic, expanded substantially in the late Tertiary and particularly the Quaternary. This expansion demonstrates a trend toward lower rainfall and/or greater climatic variation, although the extent of change may be exaggerated by greater exposure of the continental shelf with increased climatic variation, which would have provided more habitat for swamp communities, and the proximity to the coast of Site 820, which would favor representation of coastal communities. There may be a similar explanation for the large increase in mangrove pollen. Without a significant response in Myrtaceae through most of the Quaternary, it is difficult to postulate a broad regional expansion of sclerophyllous vegetation.

The largest change in regional vegetation within the last 10 million years occurred around the mid-late Pleistocene boundary, when there must have been a major reduction in the extent of araucarian forest. The increases in Myrtaceae and Poaceae suggest that the replacement was by eucalypt woodland. It has been proposed that, because there is no clear change in the climatic pattern at this time, some other factor must have been responsible, with the most likely factor being burning by early people, despite the fact that the replacement is dated around 130,000 years ago, some 80,000–90,000 years before the first archaeological evidence for people on the continent (Kershaw, McKenzie, and McMinn 1993). The massive and apparently sustained increase in mangrove pollen is consistent with major landscape disruption, as resultant soil erosion could have extended the substrate available for mangrove colonization.

LATE CENOZOIC VEGETATION: WINDOWS

Further insights into the nature of late Cenozoic vegetation are provided by more detailed analysis of particular periods. Two records have been constructed for critical parts of the ODP Site 820 core. One record covers the last 250,000 years and incorporates the major decline in Araucariaceae as well as providing information on the response of vegetation to Milankovitch forcing dominated by the 100,000-year eccentricity cycle. The other focuses on the transition from obliquity-dominated cyclicity, with a periodicity of about 40,000 years, to eccentricity-dominated cyclicity about a million years ago. This transition embraces several changes in the pollen record, including the last appearances of *Dacrycarpus* and *Nothofagus* and the first pronounced peak in Rhizophoraceae. Two other records, the Butcher's Creek and Lynch's Crater sequences, allow some comparison of pollen signatures from terrestrial sites with those derived from marine environments.

Pliocene

The Butcher's Creek sequence was constructed from a 1.5 m streamside exposure of oil shale and coal preserved beneath a basalt capping. The sequence represents sediment accumulation within a shallow lake succeeded by a swamp, probably over no more than a few thousand years. The initial impression of this pollen record (fig. 19.4), with its high values for both *Nothofagus* and Myrtaceae and its low Araucariaceae representation, is that it cannot be of late Cenozoic age. However, based on pollen stratigraphy and existing radiometric ages for basaltic material within the region, it was considered by Kershaw and Sluiter (1982) to date between 1 and 5 MYA. Using conventional pollen stratigraphic methods, a comparison with the combined ODP Site 820/823 pollen records does provide some support for this estimate and allow some refinement of it. One critical taxon is Asteraceae, which does not appear to have been present regionally until after 4 MYA. Considering that this site is within the heart of the Wet Tropics, the arrival of the opportunistic Asteraceae may have been much later than its first appearance regionally. The last occurrence of *Phyllocladus* in the ODP Site 815 record, between the nanofossil datum ages of 3.5 and 2.6 MYA (Gartner, Wei, and Shyu 1993), might provide a realistic upper age for the Butcher's Creek sequence of about 3 MYA.

Assuming that the true age of this sequence is between 3 and 4 MYA, it suggests that vegetation dominated by *Nothofagus* subgenus *Brassospora,* which covered much of Australia during the mid-Tertiary, must have survived in some abundance on the plateau and mountains of the Wet Tropics until at least the end of the Tertiary, long after it had disappeared or been relegated to relict status in other parts of the continent. Under these circumstances, it is perhaps surprising that the representation of *Nothofagus* is not more apparent in the ODP records. Its low values suggest that winds must have been predominantly from

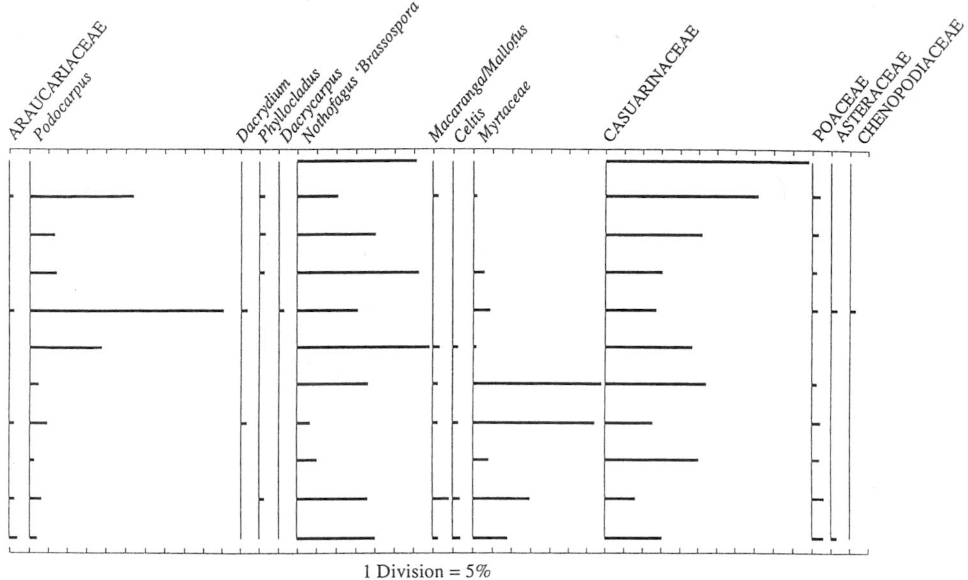

Figure 19.4 Representation of selected taxa from the Butcher's Creek pollen record of Kershaw and Sluiter (1982). Total pollen of terrestrial plants forms the pollen sum of each spectrum on which all taxon percentages are based.

the east, very much like today, and furthermore, that stream-borne pollen must have derived largely from lowland vegetation.

The lower part of the Butcher's Creek sequence is characterized by high values of Myrtaceae, of which almost all can be attributed to rainforest genera. In the upper part of the sequence, they give way to higher values of *Podocarpus* and *Nothofagus.* This pattern could simply reflect the colonization of the site by swamp forest as sediment filled the basin, or it could indicate a change in regional climate. As *Nothofagus* subgenus *Brassospora* is considered to have avoided poorly drained areas and would not have been a component of the swamp surface, a climatic cause is more likely. The change from higher levels of Myrtaceae and other rainforest angiosperms to increased representation of southern conifers and *Nothofagus* suggests cooling, while the hydroseral change may also indicate reduced precipitation. This pattern is consistent with a change from "interglacial" to "glacial" conditions and perhaps provides further evidence that the sequence is relatively young and within the grip of Late Pliocene or Quaternary climatic fluctuations. From comparisons of these spectra with modern samples from the region, Kershaw and Sluiter (1982) concluded that temperatures may have been some 3°C lower than today during the early part of the recorded period and even further reduced in the later part. These estimates are consistent with those from ODP Site 811 for about 3 MYA.

Despite the lower temperatures, the forests were still diverse. A total of 145 pollen morphological types were identified, similar to the number recorded in fourteen pollen spectra from a range of environments in Wet Tropics rainforests today (Kershaw 1973). Of these fossil types, 88 could be referred to extant taxonomic groups, with most still present within the region; community relationships were also consistent with those of today. This pattern suggests that the basic structure of many submontane-montane forests has remained intact despite the loss of a palynologically conspicuous "temperate" component.

Early Pleistocene

The pollen sequence from around the center of the ODP Site 820 core provides one of the few early Pleistocene records from Australia and the only one that is firmly dated (fig. 19.5). The record is considered to extend from the base of oxygen isotope stage 29 (about 945,000 years ago) to beyond the limit of the constructed isotope record (Peerdeman 1993), at least 1 million years ago. The pollen diagram has been divided into stages in relation to isotope stage boundaries to allow clear comparison between the isotope and pollen records. The odd-numbered stages represent times of low ice volume and high sea level, while the even-numbered stages reflect high ice volume and low sea level. For convenience, these stages will be referred to as interglacials and glacials, respectively, although, in contrast to the cyclicity in the mid-late Pleistocene, it is unlikely that variation in ice extent was sufficient to justify this distinction.

Looking at this record overall, there are some interesting differences from the generalized ODP record (see fig. 19.3). Values for Araucariaceae (here divided into the genera *Araucaria* and *Agathis*) and Casuarinaceae are lower, while the Myrtaceae have substantially increased percentages. There is also a greater representation of rainforest angiosperms, with *Elaeocarpus* and Cunoniaceae, not recorded in the generalized diagram, achieving some prominence. The major reason for these differences is that the method of sample preparation was changed from that traditionally used in stratigraphic palynology to one specifically designed for Quaternary marine sediments. A critical factor may have been the sieving process, in which a reduction in sieve size from 8 to 5 μm allowed the collection of small grains, which include Cunoniaceae and *Elaeocarpus* as well as some Myrtaceae.

Within the record, there is a general relationship between pollen representation and the isotope curve, with glacials generally showing higher values of gymnosperms and Poaceae and lower values of rainforest angiosperms than

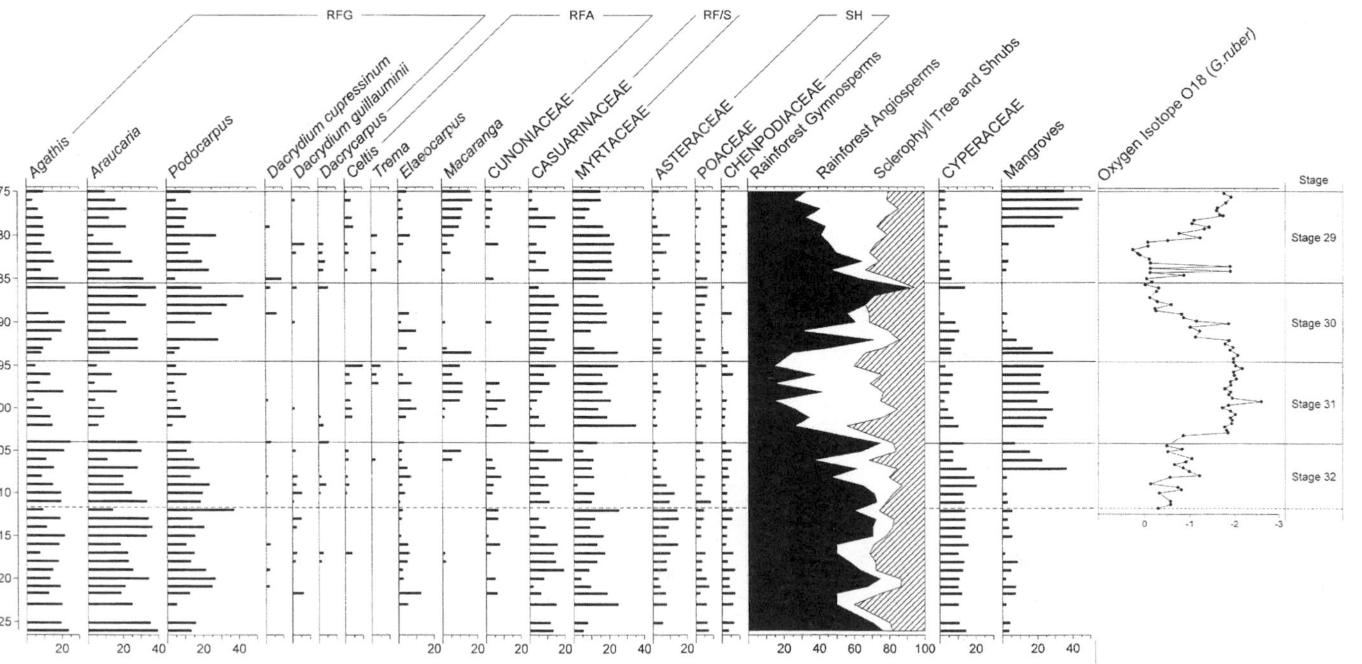

Figure 19.5 Representation of selected taxa from the early Pleistocene of ODP Site 820 (R. Wild, unpublished data) in relation to the oxygen isotope record of Peerdeman (1993). Total pollen of terrestrial plants forms the pollen sum of each spectrum on which all taxon percentages are based. RFG, rainforest gymnosperms; RFA, rainforest angiosperms; FR/S, rainforest or sclerophyllous trees; SH, sclerophyllous herbs.

interglacials. This observation suggests that the glacials were drier, as well as cooler, than the interglacials. Within the interglacials, there is some evidence of rainforest "succession," with Cunoniaceae peaking first, followed by *Elaeocarpus* and then *Macaranga/Mallotus* and *Celtis*. This pattern is characteristic of the late Quaternary, particularly the Holocene, for which sequences have been interpreted as initially indicating cool conditions giving way to a warm, wet climate, with a subsequent shift to a warm, drier and more variable climate (Hiscock and Kershaw 1992). The interglacials are also marked by increased values for Rhizophoraceae, indicating more favorable conditions for mangrove expansion when sea levels were high. A mangrove response is also evident toward the top of isotope stage 32, which appears to represent an interstadial, a suggestion supported by some representation of Cunoniaceae and *Elaeocarpus*.

There are differences as well as similarities between equivalent stages. Most obvious are the high values of Asteraceae and low values of Myrtaceae in inferred isotope stage 32 compared with stage 30. These differences could simply reflect the individuality of cycles, predictable from solar radiation forcing (Berger and Loutre 1991), but could also indicate a longer-term change in climate. As mentioned previously, this period in the ODP core was selected for study because of possible sustained changes in pollen representation that could reflect an alteration in the pattern of climatic variation within the record. It is not known whether the earlier part of the basal pollen stage can be accommodated in stage 32. Based on Peerdeman's estimates, the base of the sequence would extend to at least 1.1 MYA, long before the start of stage 32. If this were the case, it would suggest that marked cyclicity began in stage 31 and substantiate the proposal that this stage records the first substantial phase of mangrove expansion in the whole ODP record. Concerning the possible disappearance of temperate elements, there is no evidence of change within the pollen record. *Nothofagus* is not recorded, and *Dacrycarpus* appears to have survived. The record also demonstrates that *Dacrydium cupressinum* survived to at least this time. However, all gymnosperm taxa probably had much reduced ranges during the stage 31 "interglacial"; extension of the record will be critical to an assessment of whether increased cyclicity, particularly the attainment of high interglacial temperatures, contributed to their demise.

Mid-Late Pleistocene to Holocene

The period from the mid-late Pleistocene to the Holocene is most clearly documented by the detailed record from the upper part of ODP Site 820 and from Lynch's Crater. The Lynch's Crater diagram (fig. 19.6) has long provided a

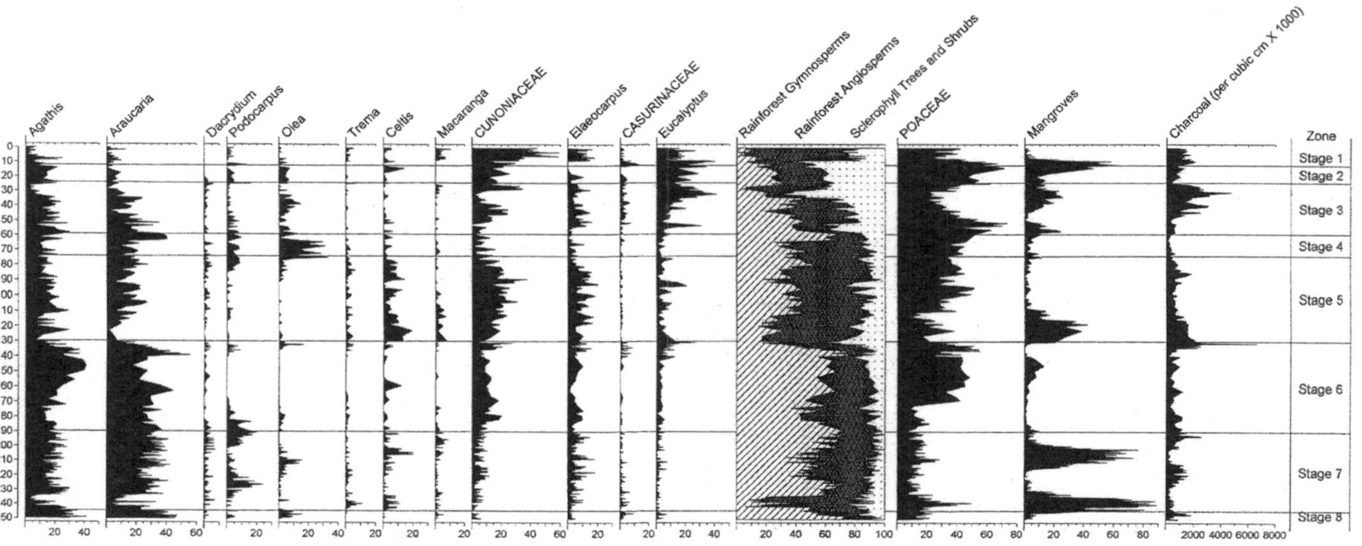

Figure 19.6 Representation of selected taxa and charcoal from Lynch's Crater (Kershaw 1985, 1986) in relation to the marine isotope stratigraphy. Total pollen of terrestrial arboreal taxa forms the pollen sum of each spectrum on which all taxon percentages are based. RFG, rainforest gymnosperms; RFA, rainforest angiosperms; ST, sclerophyllous trees.

picture of vegetation and climate from the Atherton Tableland through the late Quaternary period (Kershaw 1985, 1986). A major limitation of this record has been a lack of absolute time control beyond the limit of radiocarbon dating, about 40,000 years ago, which, it was hoped, would be rectified to some degree by comparison with the ODP record. Despite some uncertainty about details of dating of the ODP record, to be outlined shortly, the estimated time scale for Lynch's Crater has been supported and refined (Moss and Kershaw 2000). Consequently, the record is shown in relation to the established oxygen isotope chronology and is considered to cover about the last 215,000 years, or the last two glacial cycles.

The major distinction in the Lynch's Crater record is between the glacial pollen stages 2–4 and 6 and the predominantly interglacial stages 7, 5, and 1. The glacial stages are dominated by high values of *Araucaria*, Casuarinaceae, *Eucalyptus*, and Poaceae, which indicate the regional prominence of drier araucarian forest and sclerophyllous woodland under rainfall levels estimated to have been as low as half that experienced today. Temperatures are difficult to estimate due to the lack of modern analogues to the drier rainforest within northeastern Australia today and the insensitivity of sclerophyllous assemblages to temperature variation. Comparison with other diagrams previously presented for glacial phases is made difficult by the exclusion of Poaceae and other, very minor, herbaceous elements from the pollen sum. This was done to prevent distortion of terrestrial pollen values, as it is considered that Poaceae became an increasingly important part of local vegetation as swamp invaded the previous lake environment within Lynch's Crater beginning about 40,000 years ago.

Stages 7, 5, and 1 are distinguished by high values for rainforest angiosperms, very low *Araucaria* percentages, and reduced sclerophyllous representation. Interglacials proper—stages 7 and 1 and the early part of stage 5, known as substage 5e—have the highest percentages of angiosperms, particularly Cunoniaceae and *Elaeocarpus*, which are generally succeeded by peaks in *Trema*, *Celtis*, and *Macaranga*. Maximum expansion of complex rainforest probably occurred during substage 5e, consistent with the attainment of the warmest global temperatures and highest sea levels, as suggested by the isotope record, within the recorded period. Based on an analysis of the bioclimatic ranges of the recorded taxa, temperatures during substage 5e are estimated to have been about 3°C higher than today, and rainfall to have been similar to present levels (Kershaw and Nix 1989). Bioclimatic estimates suggest that the coolest conditions within these stages occurred in the middle part of stage 5, with temperatures annually and seasonally some 1°C–2°C lower than at present. Precipitation, however, was similar to that of today. Casuarinaceae and the conifers *Podocarpus* and *Dacry-*

dium guillauminii were prominent during this period, although *Dacrydium* was likely to have been restricted to swamp forest around the margin of the crater lake (Bohte and Kershaw 1999) rather than a component of the regional vegetation. Climatic conditions similar to those of the middle part of stage 5 may have occurred toward the end of stage 7, with the absence of *Dacrydium* perhaps best accounted for by deeper lake conditions inhibiting the establishment of marginal swamp.

Superimposed on the clear cyclicity of the record is a general increase in the proportion of sclerophyllous vegetation. The major contributor is *Eucalyptus,* which, between about 38,000 (possibly 45,000: Turney, Bird et al. 2001) and 26,000 years ago, clearly expands at the expense of the rainforest gymnosperms. In the absence of marked climate change at this time, these changes have been interpreted as indicating the replacement of dry araucarian forest by eucalypt woodland as a result of an increase in burning, a proposal supported by the first substantial representation of charcoal in the record. The most likely cause of increased burning is considered to be the activities of people, whose earliest presence throughout much of Australia, including southern Cape York Peninsula, is dated to somewhere between 55,000 and 40,000 years ago (David et al. 1997; Flood 1995; Roberts, Jones, and Smith 1990; Turney, Kershaw et al. 2001). The subsequent disappearance of *Dacrydium guillauminii* about 25,000 years ago is likely to be related to this increased burning, assisted perhaps by swamp drying toward the last glacial maximum. A subsequent reduction in charcoal representation may relate to reduced fuel as a result of very open vegetation around the height of the last glacial period or a reduction in human impact. The apparent abandonment of Ngarrabullgan cave, the closest Pleistocene archaeological site to Lynch's Crater, about 32,000 years ago is consistent with the latter suggestion (David et al. 1997).

The very high charcoal values from about 15,000 to 8,000 years ago could represent favorable climatic and fuel conditions for fire during the unstable transition from the last glacial maximum to the Holocene. This period of burning is reflected regionally in studies of soil charcoal (Hopkins et al. 1993). Burning was very much reduced after 8,000–7,000 years ago as rainforest expanded under high levels of precipitation. Although bioclimatic analyses indicate that maximum Holocene rainfall and temperatures were achieved between about 5,000 and 3,500 years ago at another site, Lake Euramoo, on the Atherton Tableland (Kershaw and Nix 1988), charcoal levels increase again markedly at Lynch's Crater around 4,500 years ago, largely as a result of burning on the crater swamp. Such burning could have been facilitated by the initiation of increased climatic variation, also noted in the Lake Euramoo record from about 5,000 years ago

(Kershaw and Nix 1988), which could be interpreted as indicating the latest onset of El Niño-Southern Oscillation (ENSO) activity, or an intensification of it (McGlone, Kershaw, and Markgraf 1992). However, the underlying cause of this burning, judging from its localized nature, was most likely the activities of people, and the date corresponds well with the first evidence for human habitation of complex rainforest within the humid tropics (Horsfall and Hall 1990) and with a sharp intensification of occupation within Australia as a whole (Lourandos and David 2002).

The sequence from the upper part of the ODP Site 820 record (fig. 19.7) equates with the Lynch's Crater record in both length of core (c. 65 m) and, through much of this core, sample resolution. There is some uncertainty about whether the ODP record is continuous when a detailed comparison to the reference isotope stratigraphy (Peerdeman, Davies, and Chivas 1993) is made, but it appears that the basic pattern of the isotope record is consistent with that covering pollen stages 8 to 1, or the last 250,000 years. This belief is strengthened by the mangrove evidence for major marine transgressions at the stage 8/7, 6/5, and 2/1 boundaries and within stage 7, the latter being characterized globally by its double interglacial pattern.

The representation of pollen in the late Quaternary ODP record shows many similarities with that in Lynch's Crater, despite differences in location and pollen catchment source and area. Rainforest pollen dominates terrestrial plant pollen throughout the record, with both gymnosperms and angiosperms contributing substantially. Perhaps most surprising are the higher *Eucalyptus* than Casuarinaceae values in the sclerophyllous component and the relatively low percentages for *Podocarpus*. These differences may be a reflection of temperature differences between sites, and they add support to a previous suggestion that the marine records reflect predominantly lowland vegetation. It is interesting to note that values for both Casuarinaceae and *Podocarpus* are much reduced in comparison with the generalized ODP record, illustrating again the value of the much improved pollen preparation technique. In the late Quaternary ODP record, the very small pollen grains of *Elaeocarpus* and Cunoniaceae generally dominate the rainforest angiosperm component and are largely responsible for reductions in the percentages of larger grains. The Myrtaceae are also well represented, but mainly by the larger eucalypt grains. Low representation of rainforest Myrtaceae in marine sediments is therefore considered to be mainly the result of poor dispersal rather than grain size.

Cyclic variation in pollen representation is evident, but not to the same degree as in the Lynch's Crater record. Rainforest angiosperms have the highest values in the early part of stages 7 and 5 and in stage 1, in which Araucariaceae

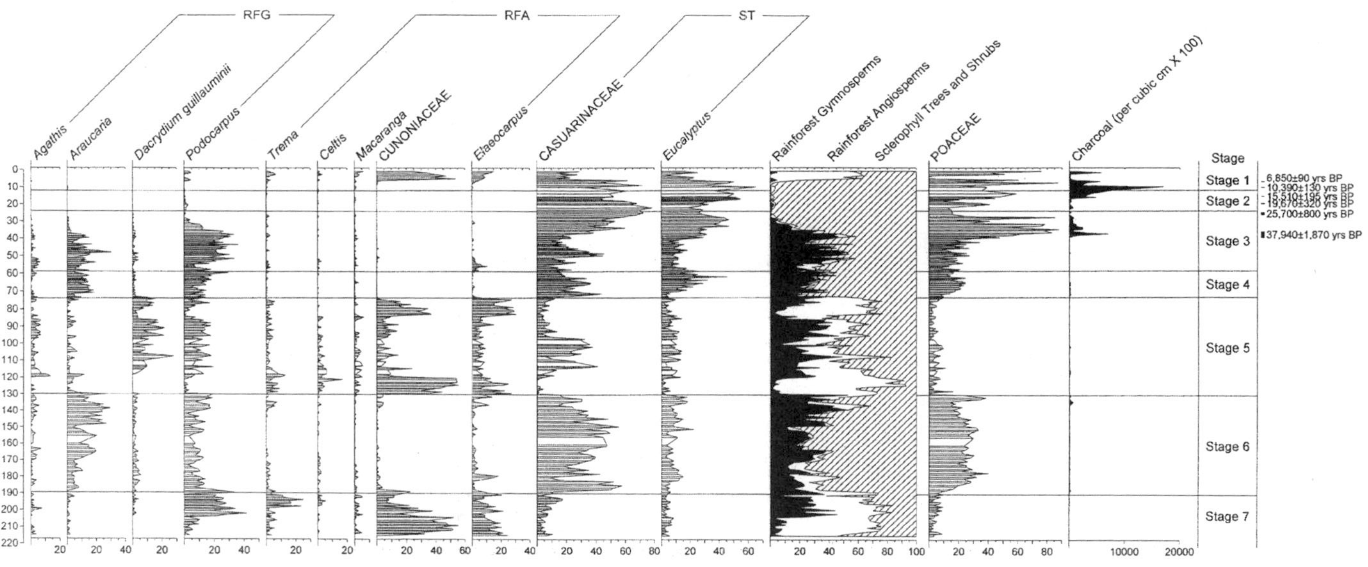

Figure 19.7 Representation of selected taxa and charcoal from the mid-Pleistocene to present of ODP Site 820 (Moss and Kershaw 2000; Moss 1999) in relation to the oxygen isotope record of Peerdeman, Davies, and Chivas (1993). Total pollen of terrestrial arboreal taxa forms the pollen sum of each spectrum on which all taxon percentages are based. RFG, rainforest gymnosperms; RFA, rainforest angiosperms; ST, sclerophyllous trees.

and particularly *Araucaria* percentages are very low. This pattern is in general agreement with the interpretation from Lynch's Crater and indicates the greatest expansion of complex rainforest over the whole region during interglacial periods. Substage 5e also stands out as the time of maximum complex rainforest expansion within the recorded period. Rainforest angiosperms maintain good representation, however, within intervening glacial phases, suggesting that complex rainforest was still widespread, at least in coastal areas. It is interesting to note that Cunoniaceae, in particular, achieves high values in glacial periods and in fact is better represented in stage 6 than in stage 7 and as well represented during the last glacial maximum (stage 2) as during the last interglacial (stage 5e). It would appear that this dominant of montane pollen assemblages was more abundant at lower altitudes during glacial periods and provides the best indication from the region of reduced glacial temperatures. Such a pattern is not evident in *Podocarpus* and Casuarinaceae, however, despite an expectation that they would have benefited from lower rainfall as well as lower temperatures during glacial periods. Reasons for their lack of response may include unsuitable substrates and poor migrational ability.

A more complete picture of the relative representation and distribution of communities can be gained from a consideration of the site characteristics of the ODP and Lynch's Crater records, in addition to their different locations. It might be inferred, due to an almost complete disappearance of complex rainforest taxa from the Lynch's Crater record and their strong presence in ODP Site 820 during glacial periods, that rainfall was reduced to below the limit for rainforest survival (i.e., about 1,500 mm), below present-day rainfall totals of about 2,500 mm, as around Lynch's Crater, but not below present-day levels of 3,000–4,000 mm, as recorded in much of the lowland catchment area of ODP Site 820. However, the bias toward riverine vegetation in the ODP core would have favored rainforest representation, and the extent of its distribution within interfluve areas would be difficult to calculate. Conversely, araucarian and sclerophyllous vegetation would have reduced representation relative to their importance in the landscape.

The late Quaternary ODP record, in common with Lynch's Crater, shows sustained trends in vegetation, and in this record these trends are at least as prominent as glacial cyclicity. The decrease in Araucariaceae, so pronounced in the generalized ODP 820 record, is evident, and its commencement refined to a date of about 135,000 years ago. This decline is accompanied by the first peak in *Eucalyptus*, high values for Poaceae, and substantial representation of charcoal. However, there is a further sustained decline in Araucariaceae, especially *Araucaria*, around 37,000 years ago (possibly 45,000 years ago: Moss and Kershaw

2000), which also corresponds with a peak in, and sustained higher levels of, *Eucalyptus* and a second major peak in charcoal. These changes most likely equate with those recorded in the Lynch's Crater record around this time. As in Lynch's Crater, the last appearance of *Dacrydium guillauminii* about 25,000 years ago indicates a substantial regional extinction. An earlier change in the record is registered around 170,000 years ago with a marked increase in Poaceae pollen, while throughout the diagram there is an increase in representation of Cunoniaceae.

This pattern of transformation of the landscape within the late Quaternary is clearly more complicated than suggested by either Lynch's Crater or the generalized ODP record. A previous interpretation of araucarian forest decline—that increased burning with the arrival of Aboriginal people began along the coastal plain and only later extended onto the Atherton Tableland (Kershaw, McKenzie, and McMinn 1993)—is unlikely, considering the two-tiered nature of the decline in the late Quaternary ODP record. Furthermore, the suggested relationship in the ODP core between the araucarian decline and increases in *Eucalyptus*, Poaceae, and mangroves is not really substantiated. The major increase in Poaceae occurred earlier, and the mangroves continue to reflect marine transgression phases in the main. However, there is a notable exception to the mangrove pattern around the phase of the decline that occurred about 40,000 years ago, but not the one 135,000 years ago: In the event 40,000 years ago there is a peak in mangroves although there is no evidence of a marine transgression or even a change in climate. Even the degree of correspondence between the araucarian decline and peaks in *Eucalyptus* and charcoal in the older event can be questioned, as the latter appear to lag somewhat behind the araucarian decline. The increase in eucalypt woodland, with its associated fire regime, may then simply be a response to the driest glacial conditions at the end of stage 6, rather than an active replacement of araucarian forest.

The increase in Poaceae is even more difficult to attribute to Aboriginal burning, due to its occurrence some 110,000–130,000 years before the first archaeological evidence for the presence of people and the fact that it is not associated with any response in the charcoal curve. The increase could indicate the regional expansion of grassland initially without a eucalypt canopy or some expansion of lowland swamp environments. It is perhaps surprising that charcoal values do not increase in a sustained fashion with the general rise in either Poaceae or *Eucalyptus* levels.

It would appear that this detailed ODP record has substantiated the evidence for a major vegetation change about 135,000 years ago, but not the proposed human cause. By contrast, the evidence for human impact about 40,000 years ago is enhanced, even though the two events share many features and contribute to the regional replacement, outside the complex rainforest core, of fire-sensitive araucarian forest by fire-tolerant or fire-promoting sclerophyllous vegetation. It is likely that human activities assisted an existing trend that demands an alternative explanation. The generalized ODP record suggests that this trend is probably confined to the period recorded in the late Quaternary record. However, the early Pleistocene sequence indicates a later extinction of some conifers than previously indicated. These conifers could have survived the early-late Pleistocene transition, and their eventual elimination could have been part of this late Quaternary transformation.

It has been noted that increased sea surface temperatures around the middle of the late Pleistocene have been suggested by the oxygen isotope records within the region, with an increase in the ODP Site 820 record of some 4°C between 400,000 and 275,000 years ago (Peerdeman, Davies, and Chivas 1993). This change coincides with lithological and geochemical changes within the core (Feary and Jarrard 1993) indicative of the growth of the Great Barrier Reef that is likely to have resulted from the temperature increase (Peerdeman, Davies, and Chivas 1993). The cause of the temperature increase has not been determined, but could well relate to changing land-sea configurations and accompanying volcanic activity within the Maritime Continent region as Australia continued its movement northward. Isern, McKenzie, and Feary (1996) relate the temperature increase to the development of the West Pacific Warm Pool.

The establishment of the Great Barrier Reef would have had a significant effect on coastal environments, particularly in the provision of protection against wave action. It is possible that such protection allowed an expansion of coastal swamp habitat, which could help explain the rise in Poaceae values, although there is no similar response in Cyperaceae, while mangrove values are as high in the mid-Pleistocene as they are in the late Pleistocene. Another influence of reef development could have been on patterns of pollen transport over the continental shelf to the core site. A progressive switch in pollen source from the higher-rainfall catchment of the Russell/Mulgrave river system to the lower-rainfall catchment of the Barron might account for increased sclerophylly in the ODP record. However, modern pollen samples from these rivers (Moss 1999) suggest that, today, the predominant source of ODP pollen is the Russell/Mulgrave. Consequently, it is difficult to use this changing local geography as an explanation of trends in the pollen record.

Concerning the rise in ocean temperature itself, it might be assumed that this change would lead to higher absolute and probably higher effective rainfall in the region. The maintenance of high levels of rainforest angiosperms, in an environment experiencing increased burning levels, might provide support for generally higher rainfall, but what about the increased burning itself? One explanation is that if the higher temperatures are related to the development of the West Pacific Warm Pool, this phenomenon could have created the strong temperature gradient across the Pacific Ocean that is a necessary prerequisite for the operation of ENSO. Consequently, even with generally increased precipitation, interannual variation may have resulted in periodic droughts conducive to burning and the replacement of drier araucarian rainforest by sclerophyllous vegetation. Once established, fire-promoting sclerophyllous vegetation could have continued to expand as a result of the process of ecological drift (Jackson 1968), particularly during the drier glacial periods.

This scenario might explain general trends within the record, but is limited in its prediction of those sharp changes that do not correspond clearly with times of major climate change. This is no problem around 40,000 years ago, as the additional source of fire from human activity is likely to have been important, but it is a problem for the Poaceae increase. No explanation can be given, but the fact that a similar change is recorded in a marine core from the eastern Indian Ocean between Australia and Indonesia, and at almost the same time (van der Kaars 1991; Wang et al. 1999), suggests that this may have been a regional phenomenon.

RAINFOREST STABILITY AND DIVERSITY

The vegetation of the Wet Tropics is composed of a variety of floristic elements and vegetation types, which have achieved dominance at various times during the Cenozoic within the Australian region as a whole. Many of the taxa that composed the highly diverse forests of the constantly wet and warm Mid-Eocene period are represented in today's lowland rainforests, while major components of the wet but cooler rainforests, characterized by *Nothofagus,* that had maximum geographic spread between the Late Eocene and Early Miocene (Macphail et al. 1994; Greenwood and Christophel, chap. 18 in this volume) are well represented in higher-altitude rainforests. The now very limited araucarian forests appear to have developed under drier climates with summer rainfall within inland parts of Australia in the Mid-Miocene and expanded coastward with continuing rainfall reduction to achieve greatest prominence during the Late Miocene and Pliocene (Kershaw 1988). Sclerophyllous vegetation, although present in the Miocene, greatly expanded during the Pliocene and particularly the Pleistocene, with greatest representation within the last glacial cycle (Kershaw, Martin, and McEwen Mason 1994). The Wet Tropics region is unusual in the degree to which the floristic characteristics of these different periods is represented. This phenomenon can, in general terms, be related to the region's local topography and coastal location, which provide a range of niches, including those suitable for high moisture-demanding components, and to its position on a drifting continent. Australia has been moving north throughout the Cenozoic, and northeastern Australia has managed to avoid the globally falling temperatures that have had such a disruptive effect on vegetation at high latitudes, including the southern part of Australia. As a consequence, the late Cenozoic history of the vegetation of the region is largely concerned with relative changes in the representation and distribution of these different components.

As suggested by the high "refugial" component of the vegetation, the region has been remarkably stable over most of the last 10 million years. Araucarian rainforest dominated the drier parts of the region until very recently, and, judging from present-day remnants, predominantly on offshore islands, would most likely have colonized continental shelf environments during lower sea-level phases. Too little is known about the associates of araucarian forest to determine whether there were any major changes in community composition over the recorded period.

It is unlikely that core areas of wetter rainforest, surrounded by the araucarian forests, were ever very much more extensive than today over the last 10 million years. However, their composition can be demonstrated to have changed through the recorded period. *Nothofagus* was still a significant component in the Late Miocene and, along with a number of podocarp taxa, most likely suggests cooler temperatures and less climatic variation than today. The presence of these taxa suggests the lowest temperatures for the record, consistent with sea surface temperature estimates from marine oxygen isotope data and patterns of carbonate deposition (Feary et al. 1991) in ocean cores off the coast of northeastern Australia.

The marine records indicate a temperature rise within the Early Pliocene, which broadly corresponds with the end of consistent *Nothofagus* representation in the ODP record. Occasional grains are recorded subsequently, which could indicate survival of the genus at least well into the Quaternary period. Higher-altitude survival until at least the Early Pliocene is clearly indicated in the Butcher's Creek record, which also demonstrates a degree of rainforest instability, perhaps resulting from Milankovitch cyclicity.

The most dramatic, sustained changes in vegetation composition occurred during the last million years, probably within the mid-Pleistocene. This is in contrast with most other parts of the world from which evidence is available, which show "modernization" of floras much earlier, and particularly around the

Plio-Pleistocene boundary. It is suggested that the pattern in northeastern Australia is a result of the effects of continued continental drift. Up until the mid-Pleistocene, continental movement allowed the maintenance of temperature and precipitation levels that may have also offset, to a large degree, the influence of increasing climatic cyclicity. In the mid-Pleistocene, dating from about 400,000 years ago, the effect of continental movement may have caused substantial changes in oceanic and atmospheric circulation patterns within the region, resulting in a further marked increase in temperature and the onset or intensification of an additional form of climatic variation in the form of ENSO. These climatic conditions, and an increase in fire activity associated with them, may have been the trigger for the replacement of araucarian forest by eucalypt woodland, although most activity took place within drier, glacial phases and, at least in the latter part of the process, Aboriginal burning was almost certainly a contributing factor. The final demise of podocarp taxa, which were most probably components of wetter forests, is poorly documented apart from *Dacrydium guillauminii,* which survived until the last glacial maximum, when it presumably succumbed to fire activity within drying swamp forest environments. The relict status of this species in swamp forests of New Caledonia subject to recent human burning is consistent with its presumed demise in the Australian Wet Tropics.

The decline in conifers is well documented due to their high pollen representation, distinct morphology, and the likelihood that individual genera or subgenera contained few species. It is probable that many angiosperms have also suffered, but their extinctions have not been identified because of poor representation and, frequently, a substantial degree of variation at species, genus, and sometimes even family levels within identified taxa. Exceptions include *Nothofagus* and the myrtaceous genus *Austromyrtus.* The former displays many characteristics of the conifers. The latter has been identified primarily from macrofossils rather than pollen. It was an associate of *Dacrydium* in the swamp forest of Lynch's Crater during stage 5 (Bohte and Kershaw 1999) and disappeared from this site—probably one of the last occurrences in Australia—during the last glacial period. There is no firm evidence for the appearance of new rainforest taxa within the region, suggesting that evolutionary change, at least at the higher taxonomic levels, has not been a significant factor. Consequently, it may be concluded that rainforest biodiversity has been decreasing throughout the recorded period.

The lack of new taxa also suggests rainforest isolation. The humid tropics region has been moving northward and becoming warmer, perhaps by as much as 8°C, throughout the late Cenozoic, yet the rainforest flora has remained essentially the same. Despite proximity to the Southeast Asian region and a long-held belief that a major component of the Australian tropical rainforest derived from this region (Burbidge 1960), particularly after continental contact in the Mid-Late Miocene (Raven and Axelrod 1972), the evidence presented here adds weight to the conclusion of Truswell, Kershaw, and Sluiter (1987) that there is no evidence of an influx from this source. It would appear that relatively low rainfall through the period of close proximity between Australia and Southeast Asia has maintained a gap too large for taxon dispersal.

This examination of the fossil record provides a basis for assessment of the present status, and prediction of the future status, of Wet Tropics rainforests. The prognosis is not encouraging. After a long period of relative stability, the rainforests have been severely affected by increased natural variation and human activities. The once dominant drier araucarian forests have almost disappeared and left the wetter rainforest patches isolated and exposed to the ravages of rapidly expanding fire-promoting sclerophyllous vegetation. Although, palynologically, the wetter rainforests appear to have maintained their representation and adapted to major glacial climatic oscillations, this may be, at least to some degree, a distortion of the pollen record resulting from the loss of high-pollen-producing Araucariaceae. Certainly it would appear that one component of the vegetation, peat swamp forest, all but disappeared from the landscape during the last glacial cycle, taking with it two of the three plant genera known to have become extinct within Australia during the last 10 million years. The other genus, *Dacrycarpus,* probably also had its last Australian representation in this region and disappeared within the last million years.

Of greatest concern for the future is the fate of the lowland rainforests. These forests, or what is left of them after the demands on their land by the sugar industry, are essentially high-latitude forests that, through continental drift, have found themselves experiencing a tropical lowland climate. They are not tropical rainforests, and must be suffering some stress, particularly under existing interglacial conditions. With further regard to increased temperatures, the Wet Tropics region takes on great significance, as it may have recently experienced a temperature rise greater than that proposed under a greenhouse climate and awaited by the rest of the world.

ACKNOWLEDGMENTS

We thank Gary Swinton for assistance with production of the illustrations and the Australian Research Council for supporting the North Queensland research. Paul Colinvaux and John Flenley provided valuable comments on a draft of the manuscript.

20

Effects of Quaternary Climate Change on Rainforest Diversity: Insights from Spatial Analyses of Species and Genes in Australia's Wet Tropics

CHRISTOPHER J. SCHNEIDER AND
STEPHEN E. WILLIAMS

ABSTRACT

Biogeographic patterns are often used to generate hypotheses concerning the evolutionary and ecological processes that structure patterns of species distribution and diversity. However, biogeographic patterns alone are often insufficient to infer historical processes. In this chapter we illustrate how analyses of molecular population genetic variation combined with spatial analyses of species distribution and diversity can provide strong inference of historical processes shaping current patterns of diversity at several hierarchical levels. The strengths of these analyses are multiplied when independent paleoecological data exist. We illustrate this approach using endemic vertebrate species from the Wet Tropics of Australia. We demonstrate that Quaternary climatic fluctuations, and associated changes in rainforest distribution and extent, have left an identifiable footprint on local, landscape, and regional patterns of genetic diversity, species distribution and diversity, and community composition.

INTRODUCTION

The role of Quaternary climate change in the evolution and biogeography of rainforest vertebrates remains a central question in tropical evolution and ecology. It has long been thought that tropical rainforests were severely fragmented by the cool, dry climates characteristic of Pleistocene ice ages and that this fragmentation had a large effect on the speciation and biogeography of rainforest animals (Haffer 1969; Vanzolini and Williams 1970; Mayr and O'Hara 1986; Whitmore and Prance 1987). Critics of the Pleistocene refuge model have raised several important issues. First, the biogeographic patterns from which the Pleistocene refuge model was derived are equally well explained by other evolutionary processes, such as parapatric diversification across ecological gradients (Endler 1982b). A generalization of this criticism is that biogeographic patterns alone provide little power to distinguish between alternative hypotheses concerning historical process (Endler 1982c). Second, Colinvaux and others (Colinvaux 1993; Colinvaux, Liu et al. 1996; Colinvaux, De Oliveira et al. 1996; Colinvaux et al. 2001; Colinvaux, chap. 6 in this volume) have questioned whether Pleistocene glacial periods resulted in fragmentation of lowland rainforest into isolated refugia. Palynological data from several sites in Amazonia indicate that rainforest was neither severely fragmented nor deeply dissected by savanna vegetation, and that closed forest, although different floristically from present rainforest, persisted throughout Pleistocene glacial periods. Finally, analyses of molecular divergence in a wide array of taxa indicate that most vertebrate species in rainforests are much older than expected from Pleistocene divergence (see Moritz et al. 2000 for review).

The gathering of direct evidence regarding the response of rainforest vegetation and vertebrate species to Quaternary climate change has been hindered by the lack of detailed paleobotanical data for most tropical regions (Colinvaux 1997) and by the incomplete knowledge of species taxonomy and distribution for most rainforest vertebrates (Patton et al. 1997). The Wet Tropics rainforest of Australia offers a striking exception. Because of its limited size, well-known endemic vertebrate fauna (Nix and Switzer 1991; Williams, Pearson, and Walsh 1996), and relatively complete paleoclimate and paleobotanical record (Kershaw 1983, 1994; Kershaw, McKenzie, and McMinn 1993), the Wet Tropics offers a unique opportunity to investigate the effects of Quaternary climate change on vertebrate species diversity and distribution across an entire rainforest system. Here we synthesize complementary information derived from spatial analyses of genetic variation and species distribution to examine the effects of Pleistocene climate-induced changes in rainforest.

THE AUSTRALIAN WET TROPICS

The Australian Wet Tropics rainforest exists as a series of naturally isolated rainforest blocks distributed along the coast and adjacent low mountains of northeastern Queensland. Endemic vertebrates in the Wet Tropics are largely confined to the cooler rainforest above 300 meters elevation and are part of what Nix (1991a) has called the "mesotherm archipelago," a series of isolated, cool rainforest blocks stretching from northern New South Wales to New Guinea. In the Wet Tropics, mesotherm rainforest exists as a series of semi-isolated islands separated by lower and warmer regions or deep river valleys (Nix 1991a). For analytical purposes, we divided the Wet Tropics into a number of biogeographic areas (figs. 16.1, 20.1), which reflect the topographic isolation and evolutionary

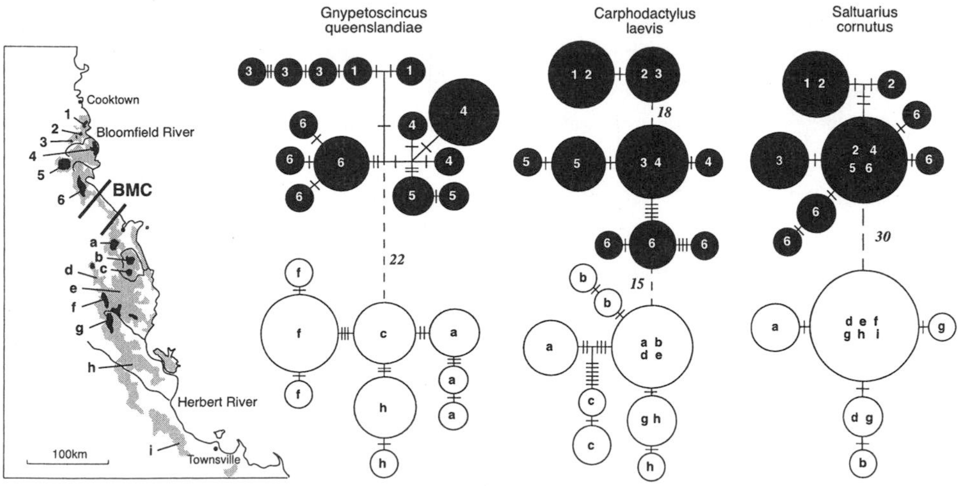

Figure 20.1 Map of the Wet Tropics region in northeastern Queensland, Australia, with unrooted parsimony trees of mtDNA haplotypes from three endemic lizard species.

distinctness of regions as revealed by biogeographic (Winter et al. 1984; McDonald 1992; Williams, Pearson, and Walsh 1996) and genetic (Schneider, Cunningham, and Moritz 1998) analyses of vertebrates.

Palynological and fossil charcoal evidence, together with paleoclimate models for the Wet Tropics rainforest of Australia, indicate that rainforest in the region was severely fragmented during Pleistocene glacial maxima (Kershaw 1983, 1994; Kershaw, McKenzie, and McMinn 1993; Nix 1991a), but the persistence of primitive rainforest angiosperms indicates that rainforest refugia persisted through glacial cycles (Webb and Tracey 1981a; Greenwood and Christophel, chap. 18 in this volume). The presence of fossil eucalyptus charcoal within some of these putative refugia (Hopkins et al. 1993, 1996) suggests that these areas were deeply dissected by fire-prone sclerophyllous vegetation and may have been even smaller and more convoluted than previously thought. Rainforest in the Wet Tropics appears to have gone through several cycles of expansion and contraction during the Quaternary (Kershaw 1983, 1994; Kershaw, McKenzie, and McMinn 1993; Kershaw, Moss, and Wild, chap. 19 in this volume), and paleoclimate models suggest that the most recent joining of currently disjunct rainforest regions may have occurred during a cool, wet period of the Holocene about 7,500–6,000 years ago (Nix 1991a).

There is abundant evidence from both palynology and paleoclimate models that Quaternary climate changes had a large effect on Australian rainforests, but how did these dramatic fluctuations in rainforest vegetation affect vertebrate species and their distributions? We approach this question through two complementary methods. The first is an analysis of genetic variation among populations of widespread endemic species in upland rainforest blocks, including nearly all putative Pleistocene refugia, to determine whether species experienced fragmentation and subsequent expansion in response to changes in rainforest distribution. The second is a spatial analysis of vertebrate species diversity and distribution among rainforest blocks to determine whether and how Quaternary climate changes structured current patterns of species diversity and community composition. The combined analysis of species distribution and molecular genetic variation overcomes many of the difficulties of inferring historical processes from biogeographic data alone and provides important insight into the historical determinants of the distribution and diversity of both species and genes.

MOLECULAR EVIDENCE FOR EFFECTS OF QUATERNARY CLIMATE CHANGE ON VERTEBRATE SPECIES IN THE WET TROPICS

The Question of Pleistocene Speciation

Molecular systematic analyses of several vertebrate taxa with representatives endemic to the Wet Tropics indicate that the great majority of speciation events predate the Pleistocene (Joseph and Moritz 1993; Joseph, Moritz, and Hugall 1995; Moritz et al. 1997, 2000; Schneider, Cunningham, and Moritz 1998) and, thus, that Pleistocene refugial speciation had little or no role in generating the high vertebrate species diversity in Australian rainforests. Rather than acting as species pumps, Pleistocene refugia appear to have acted as species filters, allowing some species to persist in the face of widespread extinction (Williams and Pearson 1997; Schneider, Cunningham, and Moritz 1998). These remnant populations are expected to have undergone periods of isolation and contraction during glacial maxima and subsequently expanded to occupy their current ranges in the Wet Tropics.

Predicted Population Genetic Effects of Pleistocene Climate Change

Most vertebrate species endemic to the Wet Tropics are widely distributed across the region, even among currently disjunct rainforest blocks (Nix and Switzer 1991; Williams, Pearson, and Walsh 1996). Therefore, the large-scale changes in rainforest extent and distribution during the Pleistocene are expected to be reflected in patterns of genetic variation within and among populations (Schneider, Cunningham, and Moritz 1998; Schneider and Moritz 1999). Our inferences regarding population history rely on variation in mitochondrial DNA (mtDNA) sequences because it is a reasonably sensitive indicator of recent changes in population size and distribution (Birky, Maruyama, and Fuerst 1983; Birky, Fuerst, and Maruyama 1989; Birky 1991; Rogers and Harpending 1992; Nielsen and Wakeley 2001) and because it can be easily measured in a diverse array of taxa (see also Patton and da Silva, chap. 7 in this volume). We have also focused on species of apparently low vagility, which allows us to detect patterns of isolation and fragmentation that might be obscured by recent gene flow in highly vagile species (Schneider, Cunningham, and Moritz 1998).

Several patterns of neutral genetic variation within and among populations are expected in species affected by Quaternary changes in rainforest distribution. Populations that experienced significant and sustained contraction in response to rainforest fragmentation are predicted to contain low levels of genetic variation, in this case measured by nucleotide diversity (π), the average number of nucleotide substitutions per nucleotide between sequences (Nei 1987). Pleistocene fragmentation is also predicted to result in strong geographic structuring of genetic variation, as indicated by high values of Φ_{st}, a measure of population genetic variation analogous to Wright's F_{st} (Excoffier, Smouse, and Quattro 1992). Furthermore, we expect monophyletic groups of very closely related alleles in each formerly isolated population. Population expansion is predicted to accompany recent rainforest expansion and should be detectable in the distribution of pairwise differences among individual mtDNA sequences (the mismatch distribution) (Rogers and Harpending 1992), in patterns of gene coalescence (Wakeley and Hey 1997; Nielsen and Wakeley 2001), and in the phylogeny of alleles (Slatkin and Hudson 1991; Templeton, Routman, and Phillips 1995).

The ecological characteristics of species are expected to affect species responses to Pleistocene rainforest contraction. On one end of the continuum of possible responses are species that are dependent on large tracts of mature rainforest and which experienced multiple local extinctions—in the extreme, being reduced to a single surviving population—in response to Pleistocene rainforest contraction. These species should show evidence of a severely reduced effective population size, as indicated by low genetic diversity over their entire current range. Expansion from a surviving population to the current distribution should be detectable by the presence of broadly distributed ancestral alleles (internal alleles in unrooted trees) (Templeton, Routman, and Phillips 1995), a star-like phylogeny of alleles (Slatkin and Hudson 1991), a Poisson mismatch distribution of pairwise differences among individuals (Rogers and Harpending 1992), significant departure from expected equilibrium patterns of neutral genetic variation (as revealed by various statistics: see Ramos-Onsins and Rozas 2002 for review), and low geographic population structure (indicated by low F_{st} values). By contrast, if species were able to maintain multiple refugial populations in small rainforest fragments through the Pleistocene, then we would expect exclusive (monophyletic) groups of closely related mtDNA haplotypes in each refugial area (assuming low recent gene flow), strong geographic structure (evident in high F_{st} values), a multimodal mismatch distribution, low within-population genetic diversity, and high nucleotide diversity overall.

Patterns of Genetic Variation in Endemic Vertebrates from the Australian Wet Tropics

Analyses of mtDNA variation in mammals, birds, frogs, and lizards across the Wet Tropics reveals the effects of Pleistocene and older historical events (Joseph and Moritz 1993; Joseph, Moritz, and Hugall 1995; Moritz et al. 1997; Schneider, Cunningham, and Moritz 1998; Schneider and Moritz 1999; Schneider et al. 1999). At a deep level, the Wet Tropics consists of two regions, separated by a well-known biogeographic gap: the Black Mountain Barrier or Black Mountain Corridor (BMC). Populations on either side of the BMC have been separated for several million years, as evidenced by deep mitochondrial divergence among populations north and south of the BMC. The deep historical isolation of regions north and south of the BMC provides two evolutionarily independent sets of populations in which to examine the effects of the more recent Quaternary climate changes.

The effects of Pleistocene climate change are apparent in the genetic structures of most species studied (references above and Hugall et al. 2002), with the exception of the more vagile and generalized species of birds (Joseph, Moritz, and Hugall 1995; J. Arnold, S. E. Williams, and C. Moritz, unpublished data). Here we restrict our discussion to three widespread, rainforest-endemic lizard species with limited dispersal ability, but varying life histories and ecologies, for which we have the most detailed sampling: the leaf-tail gecko (*Saltuarius cornutus*), the chameleon gecko (*Carphodactylus laevis*), and the prickly skink (*Gnypetoscincus queenslandiae*). Each species was examined over its full geographic range, including the majority of putative refugia (fig. 20.1), with sample sizes per locality varying from two to eight.

Like most widespread species in the Wet Tropics, the three species examined here exhibit a large disjunction in mtDNA variation across the BMC (fig. 20.1), and the magnitude of the genetic distance (d_{xy} in table 20.1) suggests pre-Pleistocene separation (Schneider, Cunningham, and Moritz 1998). On either

Table 20.1 Sequence variation and sample properties for each species

Area[a]	% nucleotide diversity within area (*n*/*p*)[b]		
	S. cornutus (49)	*C. laevis* (48)	*G. queenslandiae* (50)
FU (1,2,3)	0.60 (6/3)	0.12	0.71 (5/2)
TU (4)	0.00 (1/1)	0.11 (8/2)	0.26 (8/2)
WU (5)	0.00 (2/1)	0.11 (5/1)	0.19 (3/1)
CU (6)	0.20 (10/2)	0.44 (5/1)	0.19 (8/2)
LU (a)	0.00 (3/1)	0.47 (6/1)	0.46 (5/1)
AU (d,e,f)	0.14 (11/4)	0.37 (11/4)	0.13 (10/3)
BK (b,c)	0.00 (1/1)	0.27 (3/1)	0.00 (5/1)
TP (g,h,i)[c]	0.12 (9/3)	0.14 (4/2)	0.16 (6/2)
Mean per area	0.12	0.23	0.28
Total north of BMC	0.51 (19)	0.87 (28)	1.14 (24)
Total south of BMC	0.20 (26)	1.10 (26)	1.33 (30)
Φ_{st} N of BMC	0.247	0.828	0.830
Φ_{st} S of BMC	0.401	0.801	0.919
Φ_{st} Total	0.980	0.956	0.971
d_{xy} across BMC (±SE)[d]	9.0 ± 1.67	4.8 ± 1.24	6.6 ± 1.43

[a]Area abbreviations correspond to those of Williams, Pearson, and Walsh (1996); numbers in parentheses correspond to sampling localities in figure 20.1.
[b]n = number of individuals sampled; p = number of sampled populations within each area.
[c]The area "TP" used here extends from the Tully River to the Paluma Range and includes the Kirrama Uplands, Mt. Lee Uplands, and Mt. Spec Uplands of Williams, Pearson, and Walsh (1996).
[d]Estimates of genetic distance (d_{xy}) across the BMC were calculated using Kimura two-parameter distances. Standard errors reflect the maximum variance on these estimates (Takahata and Tajima 1991) and were calculated using a BASIC program originally written by Y. Satta and T. Ohta and modified by R. Slade.

side of the BMC, patterns of mtDNA sequence variation are remarkably consistent within species, but differ substantially among species.

North of the BMC, both *C. laevis* and *G. queenslandiae* show evidence of having maintained multiple refugial populations in each of the major rainforest blocks (Schneider and Moritz 1999). Both species show strong phylogeographic structure, with unique groups of mtDNA confined to each of the major upland rainforest blocks (fig. 20.1), levels of sequence divergence among blocks that, with one exception, are broadly consistent with expectations from late Pleistocene divergence, high Φ_{st} values (table 20.1), and multimodal mismatch distributions (fig. 20.2). In contrast, *S. cornutus* appears to have been reduced to

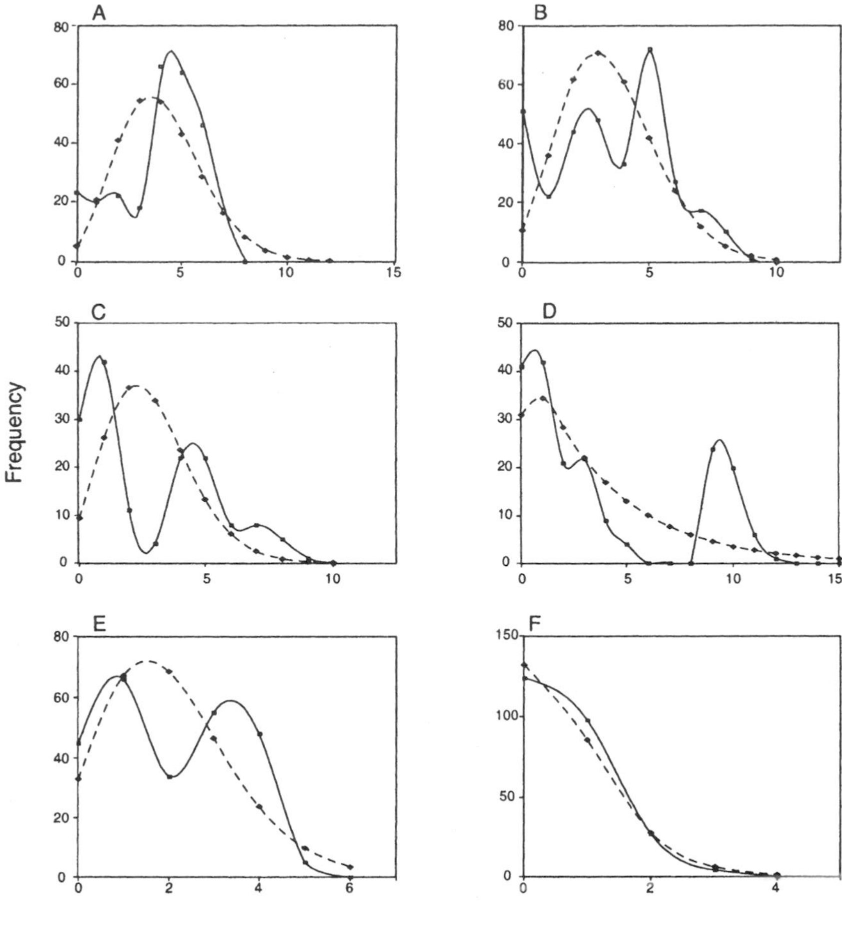

Figure 20.2 Observed mismatch distribution (solid lines) of pairwise differences among individuals and Poisson distribution (dashed lines) expected from an expanding population. Listed *p* values are the probability of the observed distribution fitting the Poisson expectation. (A) *Gnypetoscincus queenslandiae* north of the BMC and (B) *G. queenslandiae* south of the BMC. The multimodal mismatch distributions do not fit Poisson expectations of expansion from a single source ($p < .001$). (C) *Carphodactylus laevis* north of the BMC (excluding the divergent haplotypes found north of the Bloomfield River) and (D) *C. laevis* south of the BMC. The multimodal distributions do not fit the expectation of expansion from a single source ($p < .001$). (E) *S. cornutus* north of the BMC. The observed distribution does not fit the Poisson distribution ($p < .01$), however, if the relatively divergent haplotypes from north of the Bloomfield River are excluded, the observed distribution fits the Poisson ($0.50 > p > .10$). (F) *Saltuarius cornutus* south of the BMC. The observed distribution fits a Poisson distribution ($p = .50$) consistent with a recent population expansion.

two populations north of the BMC, probably one on either side of the Bloomfield River (fig. 20.1; Schneider and Moritz 1999). Extreme historical reduction in population size is indicated by low levels of nucleotide diversity overall, and the two groups apparent in the phylogeny of alleles (fig. 20.1) and the resulting bimodal mismatch distribution (fig. 20.2E) suggests two refugial populations. Recent expansion of one of the refugial populations (south of the Bloomfield River) is suggested by the low degree of population structure, the starlike phylogeny of alleles, and the presence of common, geographically widespread ancestral haplotypes (fig. 20.1).

Each species shows patterns of mtDNA variation south of the BMC that are similar to those in the north. South of the BMC, *G. queenslandiae* and *C. laevis* again show strong local phylogeographic structure, high Φ_{st} values, and high nucleotide diversity. The strong phylogeographic structure and consequent multimodal mismatch distribution of *G. queenslandiae* and *C. laevis* suggest that these species maintained multiple refugial populations south of the BMC. Interestingly, the distribution of divergent haplotype groups within each species is concordant with predicted refugia at locations a, c, and f in figure 20.1. By contrast, and as in the north, *S. cornutus* shows very low overall nucleotide diversity, a pattern that is consistent with severe population contraction. The low Φ_{st} value, unimodal mismatch distribution (fig. 20.2F), starlike phylogeny of alleles (fig. 20.1), and presence of widespread ancestral alleles are all consistent with contraction to a single refugial population, which subsequently expanded to cover the entire expanse of the southern Wet Tropics (Schneider and Moritz 1999).

Patterns in three species of hylid frogs (Schneider, Cunningham, and Moritz 1998; M. Cunningham, unpublished data) are similar to those of the endemic lizards in that patterns of mtDNA variation indicate multiple refugial populations in some species, severe contraction and recent expansion in others, and at least one case of recent dispersal across the BMC. Interestingly, the arboreal tree frog *Litoria genimaculata* shows a pattern of population reduction and recent expansion similar to that of *S. cornutus*, whereas the two stream-dwelling frogs, *L. nannotis* and *L. rheocola*, show patterns more similar to, but differing in important ways from, those of *G. queenslandiae* and *C. laevis* (discussed in Schneider, Cunningham, and Moritz 1998).

Reductions and Recolonizations

The patterns of genetic variation in the three rainforest endemic lizards are consistent with expectations based on fragmentation, reduction, and subsequent population expansion in response to late Pleistocene (and earlier) rainforest contraction and subsequent Holocene expansion. In these species, it appears that the major response to Pleistocene rainforest contraction was localized population reduction or extinction, followed by range expansion and mixing of formerly isolated populations (e.g., at locality 3 in fig. 20.1 for *C. laevis*). Range expansion was extensive in the case of *S. cornutus,* which appears to have (re)colonized the entire range of the Wet Tropics after having been reduced to perhaps single populations on either side of the BMC. The differences among species in response to historical rainforest contraction may reflect ecological differences among them, but apart from obvious differences in habit (*G. queenslandiae* is found at high density under logs and other cover in rainforest; *C. laevis* is found at low to moderate density on the ground or on low, narrow-diameter perches within 2 meters of the ground; and *S. cornutus* is arboreal, relatively uncommon, and associated with large rainforest trees), the ecology of these species is poorly known.

That the current ranges of *S. cornutus* and many other narrowly endemic vertebrate species extend across current barriers to dispersal indicates that these species expanded their ranges during a period when rainforest was more continuous than at present. This expansion may have occurred during a cool, wet phase of the Holocene about 7,500–6,000 years ago (Nix 1991a), when climate models indicate that mesothermal rainforest may have connected the currently disjunct rainforest blocks (Schneider, Cunningham, and Moritz 1998; Winter 1997; Hugall et al. 2002). Importantly, the southernmost regions of the Wet Tropics (south of the Herbert River) appear to have been recently colonized from source populations north of the Herbert River, as indicated by the fact that mtDNA sequences in southern populations are a nested subset of alleles found in populations north of the Herbert River (Schneider, Cunningham, and Moritz 1998).

Geographic patterns of molecular genetic variation indicate a clear response to Pleistocene and earlier rainforest contraction in the Wet Tropics. The response varied among species as a result of species-specific ecological differences, but the patterns of local extinction and subsequent expansion are clear. This turbulent history is expected to have far-reaching consequences for vertebrate species distribution and community composition, and, indeed, that appears to be the case (Williams and Pearson 1997). Spatial patterns of species distribution and assemblage structure reflect the effects of Quaternary climate changes on diversity at these levels as well.

SPATIAL ANALYSES OF ASSEMBLAGE STRUCTURE

The rainforest fauna of the Wet Tropics is considered to have once been widespread over much of northern Australia, but is now restricted to a relatively small and fragmented area (Winter 1988). Large-scale changes in the area, and probably in the type, of rainforest are expected to have had a profound effect on every level of community organization within the rainforest. The distributions of individual species have often been used as the basis for various hypotheses involving historical processes (Kikkawa, Monteith, and Ingram 1981; Winter et al. 1984; Winter 1988; 1997; see also the papers contained in Nix and Switzer 1991 and in McDonald 1992), especially when species distributions do not seem to fit habitat or bioclimatic models (i.e., the current distribution does not accord with the current ecology of the species). The failure of a species to occupy all of the suitable habitat in a region may result from past local extinctions, barriers to dispersal, or colonizations when habitat distribution was different from the current distribution. For example, in the Wet Tropics, many species of rainforest vertebrates do not occur south of the Herbert River, despite the presence of reasonably large areas of seemingly suitable habitat there.

The next level of community organization, assemblage structure (species composition, species richness, and ecological or guild structure), also shows evidence of structuring by Quaternary climatic fluctuations. We would expect that Quaternary fluctuations in rainforest area would affect patterns of assemblage similarity by influencing species composition through ecological sifting due to local extinction, barriers to dispersal and recolonization, geographic proximity, and periods of greater connectivity. Species richness should have been reduced during contraction episodes in a manner dependent on the degree of contraction, loss of habitat diversity, and the ecological characteristics of each species. Recolonization during expansion episodes would depend on the relative dispersal ability of each species, the quality of the connection (rainforest type, altitude, width, etc.) between major rainforest blocks, and the length of time that the connection persisted. Guilds (groups of species with similar ecological characteristics) that are most sensitive to fluctuations in habitat extent (i.e., species that are the most prone to extinction or have poor dispersal ability) would be expected to show the greatest degree of spatial structure. Guilds that are less affected or able to disperse easily within and between habitat patches would be expected to show little spatial structuring. If these factors have had major effects on assemblage structure, we would expect nonrandom spatial patterns of assemblage structure in accordance with these predictions.

All of the analyses conducted to date on spatial patterns of assemblage structure suggest that historical biogeography—specifically, the fluctuations in rainforest area during the Quaternary—has been the single largest determinant of current regional-scale patterns of vertebrate assemblage structure and biodiversity in the Wet Tropics. A range of different analyses have been used, which can be placed in three categories: (1) spatial patterns of similarity of assemblage composition; (2) the relationship between diversity at several scales (genes, species, ecological/functional groups) and environmental factors; and (3) the degree of nonrandom spatial nestedness in the subregional assemblages.

Similarity in Assemblage Composition

The similarity of assemblage composition in different geographic areas can be related to historical biogeography. Assemblage similarity, or lack thereof, may suggest sources of dispersal, recolonization, or vicariant assemblage development. High levels of assemblage similarity between subregions suggest a high degree of recent faunal interchange or convergent development of assemblage structure. Dissimilar assemblages suggest a relatively independent development of assemblage structure. Molecular data on specific species can differentiate between these alternatives.

The pattern of assemblage similarity exhibited by both frogs and mammals in the Wet Tropics indicates four assemblage types defined by geography and habitat type: northern, central, and southern upland rainforest subregions and the drier (predominantly non-rainforest) lowland subregions (Williams 1997). The largest split in assemblage similarity occurs between uplands and lowlands and between the northern and central/southern upland assemblages. This major split is the result of a number of species being restricted to either the northern uplands or the central/southern uplands, and is a striking feature of the biogeography of the Wet Tropics vertebrates (Winter et al. 1984; Winter 1988, 1997; Nix and Switzer 1991; Williams, Pearson, and Walsh 1996). This pattern is consistent with the dichotomy in within-species genetic structure across the Black Mountain Corridor as revealed by molecular studies (Joseph, Moritz, and Hugall 1995; Schneider, Cunningham, and Moritz 1998). The long historical isolation, demonstrated by the molecular data, of these two centers of endemism has resulted in the development of distinctly different assemblages.

Assemblages in the southern uplands (south of the Herbert River) tend to be very similar to one another (mammals: Williams 1997; Winter 1997; frogs: McDonald 1992; birds and reptiles: S. E. Williams, unpublished data), a finding that fits the hypothesis of recent faunal reconstitution from refugial areas on the Kirrama range in the central uplands. Recolonization probably occurred during cooler, wetter climatic periods of rainforest expansion (Winter 1997), reconstituting the rainforest assemblages in the southern uplands following episodes of local extinction during rainforest contractions (Williams and Pearson 1997). The drier lowlands contain a depauperate subset of Wet Tropics endemic species, presumably due to the limited and fragmented extent of rainforests in these subregions combined with the high probability that lowland specialists were more severely affected by periods of contraction. These patterns imply that the processes that produced them have had a profound effect at all levels of assemblage structure, from within-species genetic structure to the complete vertebrate assemblage.

Relationships between Species Richness and Environmental Variables

Spatial patterns of species richness within each subregion of the Wet Tropics were examined in relation to environmental variables in order to assess the proportion of the variance in these patterns that could be explained by straightforward habitat and climatic variables—that is, by current ecological interactions. Information describing the environmental characteristics of each subregion was compiled, including rainforest area, shape, vegetation diversity, altitudinal diversity, latitude, and a range of climatic variables (see Williams, Pearson, and Walsh 1996; Williams and Pearson 1997; Williams 1997 for detailed methodology). Shape is defined as the areographic shape of the habitat and can be quantified by the shape index (SI) (Patton 1975), which is dimensionless and is both theoretically and, in this study, empirically independent of area (log SI vs. log area, $r = .0780$, $P = .730$, $n = 22$). The shape index is a measure of the degree to which a shape differs from circular (SI = 1.0 for a circle; SI < 1.0 for all other shapes). It is important that shape be independent of area in order to separate the effects of shape and area so as to avoid collinearity in multiple regression models.

The relationships between the patterns of vertebrate species richness and environmental variables were examined using multiple regression techniques. When several environmental variables were strongly collinear, the variables with the lowest r^2 were not included in the multiple regression analyses. Bats and water birds were excluded from the analyses due to insufficient data on bats and the fact that water birds are dependent on a specific resource (water bodies) that is largely independent of rainforest. Multiple regression modeling (backward removal), with species richness as the dependent variable and the same set of ten environmental factors as the independent variables (area, shape, rainfall diversity, latitude, latitudinal range, altitudinal diversity, mean minimum winter temperature, annual rainfall, dry-season rainfall, number of rainforest structural vegetation types), was carried out for the total species richness of rainforest vertebrates and for mammals, birds, reptiles, and frogs separately.

ENVIRONMENTAL CORRELATES OF SPATIAL PATTERNS OF SPECIES RICHNESS

A relatively high amount of the variance (41%–83%) in species richness can be explained by a simple set of environmental variables (table 20.2), with habitat diversity (rainfall, vegetation, altitude) consistently explaining much of the variance. The number of rainfall regimes within a subregion accounted for approximately 61% of the variance in the species richness of rainforest vertebrates (table 20.2). None of the other environmental variables explained a significant amount of the variance beyond that already explained by the number of rainfall regimes. Similarly, the species richness of birds and reptiles in rainforest was

Table 20.2 Relationships between species richness and the environmental characteristics of subregions

Variable	Vertebrates	Mammals	Mammals (excl. area)[a]	Birds	Reptiles	Frogs	Frogs (excl. area)[a]
Rainfall diversity	0.0000	0.0173	0.0001	0.0018	0.0009	—	0.0054
Altitudinal diversity	—	—	—	—	—	0.0051	0.0570
Vegetation diversity	—	—	0.0582	—	—	—	0.0011
Rainforest area	—	0.0144	Excluded	—	—	0.0000	Excluded
Shape	—	(–)0.0001	(–)0.0001	—	—	—	—
Annual rainfall	—	—	—	—	—	—	0.0662
Latitude	—	—	—	—	—	(–)0.0036	—
Number of species	235	28	28	112	65	30	30
Overall F	29.26	23.46	19.53	13.19	15.54	26.71	19.51
df	1, 19	3, 17	3, 17	1, 19	1, 19	3, 17	4, 16
Overall P	0.0000	0.0000	0.0000	0.0018	0.0009	0.0000	0.0000
Overall r^2	0.6063	0.8055	0.7751	0.4098	0.4499	0.8250	0.8298

Note: Values in the upper part of the table are the probability that the factor is significant in the regression. The regression model uses backward removal of variables. Only variables that contributed significantly ($P < .1$) to at least one of the multiple regression models are included in the table. The lower part of the table details the final regression model (df = degrees of freedom) ($n = 21$ for all analyses; Elliot Uplands excluded due to an incomplete set of environmental data). An em dash indicates that the variable did not make a significant contribution to the model and was therefore removed from the analysis. Negative correlations are indicated by (–) in front of the probability value for the significance of that factor. $p = .0000$ indicates that $p < .0001$.

[a]Regressions in which area was excluded to examine the effects of habitat heterogeneity.

Table 20.3 Relationships between total species richness of rainforest terrestrial vertebrates, endemic species richness and endemism (dependent variables), and area and shape (independent variables, log-transformed) within subregions of the Australian Wet Tropics ($N = 22$) for each taxonomic group and the groups combined

	All vertebrates	Mammals	Arboreal mammals	Ground mammals	Birds	Reptiles	Frogs
			All species				
Area	0.0002	0.0000	0.0000	0.0000	0.0099	0.0111	0.0000
Shape	0.7917	0.0012	0.0016	0.1170	0.8296	0.4833	0.3213
Overall r^2	0.5252	0.7396	0.6580	0.6939	0.3066	0.3164	0.6396
			Endemic rainforest species				
Area	0.0000	0.0011	0.0017	0.0072	0.0000	0.0000	0.0000
Shape	0.0000	0.0051	0.0062	0.0335	0.0000	0.0023	0.0046
Overall r^2	0.8506	0.5491	0.5278	0.4119	0.8222	0.7407	0.7665

Source: After Williams and Pearson 1997.

best explained by the number of rainfall regimes, which explained 41% and 45% of the variance for these two groups, respectively (table 20.2). However, closer examination of meaningful ecological subsets is necessary to understand these patterns more fully. Restricting the analyses to regionally endemic species showed that the combination of rainforest area and areographic shape was highly significant to the richness of endemic species in all groups (Williams and Pearson 1997) (table 20.3).

The combination of rainforest shape, rainforest area, and rainfall diversity explains 81% of the variance in the species richness of rainforest mammals, while rainforest area, latitude, and altitudinal diversity explain 82% of the variance in patterns of frog species richness. Since most measures of habitat heterogeneity increase with area, the analyses were repeated for those groups in which area was significant (mammals and frogs) with area excluded from the analysis. Similar proportions of the variance in patterns of species richness could be explained by the combination of several indexes of habitat heterogeneity as by area (table 20.2). With the exclusion of area, vegetation diversity became significant for both mammals and frogs. Annual rainfall became significant in the regression of frog species richness, and latitude became nonsignificant when area was not included in the analysis. When the indexes of environmental heterogeneity (vegetation, altitude, rainfall) are not included in the analyses, rainforest area becomes highly significant in the explanation of patterns of species richness in all groups (Williams and Pearson 1997).

However, if we consider only the regionally endemic subset of vertebrates (all endemics or those in each separate taxonomic group), the only two variables of significance are rainforest area and shape (Williams and Pearson 1997). As shown in table 20.2, the only group for which shape was significant in explaining *total* species richness was arboreal mammals, although it was extremely significant in explaining the variance in species richness of *endemic* species in all groups (table 20.3). In fact, shape was more important than rainforest area in explaining the proportion of endemic species (endemism), although area explained more of the variance in species richness (Williams and Pearson 1997).

The significant influence of rainforest area on species richness is not surprising; however, the strong effect of shape on vertebrate endemism is very interesting. Shape does not influence the species richness of all rainforest vertebrates, but it is closely tied to the assemblage composition—specifically, to the proportion of the assemblage that is endemic. Areas that have a convoluted and fragmented shape have a greater proportion of more generalist species (nonendemics). Rainforest area remains the main factor in the pattern of species richness, while shape is the best predictor of the level of endemism. It is important to note that in all cases, it is the combination of rainforest area and shape that explains most of the variation in the spatial patterns of endemic species richness and proportion of endemism.

Having established that shape is related to patterns of endemism, it is important to consider what processes may be involved in producing this relationship. Habitat shape has been shown to be related to a number of processes that affect assemblage structure: dispersal between patches (Schonewald-Cox and Bayless 1986), within-patch dispersal or recolonization (Pickett and Thompson 1978), extinction (Schonewald-Cox and Bayless 1986), habitat heterogeneity (Noss 1983), and a variety of edge effects (Noss 1983). These factors are primarily landscape processes. Under current paradigms of landscape ecology, the significant effect of shape could be interpreted as a core area or edge effect, in which most endemic species are core rainforest species, diversity is strongly related to habitat area, and the area of the core habitat is related to both area and shape. However, this hypothesis predicts that shape should decrease in importance with area because the proportion of edge habitat decreases (Kupfer 1995). The fact that shape remains a significant factor, even when the analyses are restricted to large areas, suggests that the importance of shape in influencing regional patterns of endemism in the Wet Tropics rainforest is not due to an edge effect (Williams and Pearson 1997).

The hypothesis put forward by Williams and Pearson (1997) to explain the significance of shape was that the combination of current rainforest area and shape constitutes an index of the relative degree of historical contraction in rainforest area within each subregion, with the implication that historical fluctuation in rainforest area, coupled with the resultant nonrandom extinctions in each subregion (species sifting), has been an extremely important process in determining current patterns of distributions, species richness, and endemism in the vertebrates of Australian tropical rainforests. The number of extinctions within a specific subregion would be determined by the interaction of the degree of contraction, indexed by current area and shape, and the relative extinction-proneness of each species.

Although Pleistocene refugia are an integral part of this hypothesis, it should not be confused with the refugial hypothesis proposed by Haffer (1969) to explain high species diversity in the tropics. Here, we are suggesting that the Pleistocene refugia in the Australian Wet Tropics acted primarily as species filters, rather than the species pumps implied by Haffer's hypothesis, and that Quaternary fluctuations in rainforest area had a significant effect on patterns of diversity within the region.

Habitat diversity, at the rather coarse landscape scale, consistently explained large amounts of the variance in the species richness patterns of rainforest vertebrates for all classes combined and within each class separately (table 20.2). The relative effects of spatial heterogeneity in patterns of altitude, rainfall, and vegetation are difficult to untangle, since all three parameters are undoubtedly interrelated. The relative importance of each of these measures of habitat diversity varies between taxonomic groups, although the number of different rainfall regimes, which is probably an index of the number of broad habitat types, has the most consistent influence. The multiple regression results summarized in table 20.2 clearly show that habitat diversity, as expressed by the various combinations of rainfall diversity, altitudinal diversity, and vegetation diversity, explains large amounts of variance in spatial patterns of species richness. The similar r^2 values obtained from habitat diversity upon the removal of area suggest that the effect of habitat area on species richness patterns at this spatial scale is primarily an effect of the associated increase in habitat diversity with area, rather than an effect of area per se. A positive relationship between area and habitat heterogeneity has been observed many times in other studies (Southwood 1996); however, at this spatial scale, the indexes of habitat diversity used (spatial diversity of rainfall, altitude, and vegetation) are indexing the coarse number of habitat types, not the finer-scale habitat diversity usually related to niche partitioning. Therefore, the relationship is more likely to be indicating landscape-scale processes, such as movements between habitats and the spread of taxa within a region. That is, the presence of more habitat types within a subregion increases the number of generalist or nomadic/transient species that are likely to be recorded within the rainforest of that subregion due to movement within the subregion and long-term diversification in habitat preferences (Shmida and Wilson 1985; Ricklefs and Schluter 1993a; Southwood 1996).

GUILD STRUCTURE

Guilds, or groups of species that have similar ecological characteristics, are expected to respond in similar ways to a given process. Therefore, analyses of patterns of guild structure can add to our understanding of assemblage development in several ways. First, by examining relationships between environmental variables and within-guild species richness, it is possible to gain a much more detailed picture of what variables may be of importance to specific ecological guilds. It was shown clearly by Williams (1997) that analyses must consider ecologically meaningful subsets of the fauna; otherwise, the combination of different ecological groups can produce totally confounded patterns. Second, by determining exactly which guilds are responsible for most of the regional variation in total species richness, it is possible to construct more specific hypotheses on the determinants on regional patterns.

Much of the variation in the current patterns of mammal diversity within the Wet Tropics is explained by variation in just a few important guilds. The within-guild variation in the species richness of one guild (arboreal folivores) explains 73% of the regional variation in the species richness of rainforest mammals (Williams 1997). Similarly, 75% of the variation in the species richness of subregional frog assemblages is explained by the within-guild variation of just one guild (stream-dwelling hylids) (Williams and Hero 1998). In both of these examples, there is strong evidence that these functional guilds are the most extinction-prone subset of the class and that they have poor recolonization ability (Laurance 1991; Williams and Hero 1998). This finding supports the argument that extinctions during rainforest contractions and nonrandom recolonization patterns have been of major significance in structuring rainforest assemblages.

Nestedness

Nestedness is a measure of the degree to which the assemblages in subregions with low species richness are simply a subset of those in more diverse subregions. The implication is that archipelago systems, such as the Wet Tropics, with a high degree of nestedness are the result of nonrandom extinctions and recolonizations in the order of the specific extinction-proneness and dispersal ability of each species (Patterson and Atmar 1986). An index of nestedness called matrix temperature (t), calculated using a matrix of subregional presence/ab-

Table 20.4 Nestedness (*t*) of subregional assemblages of rainforest vertebrates for each taxonomic group and for the endemic subset of each group, listed in order of decreasing nestedness (increasing *t*)

Taxon	*t*	*p*
All endemics	15.1	3.81×10^{-64}
Mammals, rainforest	15.5	2.77×10^{-35}
Mammals, endemic	22.5	6.24×10^{-4}
Birds, rainforest	16.8	2.58×10^{-39}
Birds, endemic	7.1	1.34×10^{-11}
Frogs, rainforest	20.1	3.12×10^{-31}
Frogs, microhylid endemic[a]	21.6	4.72×10^{-5}
Frogs, non-microhylid endemic[a]	5.4	4.09×10^{-8}
Reptiles, rainforest	28.9	3.01×10^{-39}
Reptiles, endemic	16.3	3.53×10^{-14}

[a]Endemic frogs are also divided into microhylid and non-microhylid species due to the large differences between those two groups (Williams and Hero 1998).

sence data, was developed based on thermodynamic theories of order and disorder (Atmar and Patterson 1993). The degree to which the matrix temperature departs from randomness can be tested statistically using Monte Carlo simulations. Matrix temperature is used here to describe the degree of nestedness of the rainforest vertebrate assemblages in each subregion in the Wet Tropics. Matrix temperature and the probability of significant nestedness were calculated using the software developed by Atmar and Patterson (1995).

All subsets of the vertebrate fauna showed a significant degree of nonrandom nestedness (table 20.4). However, there were relatively large differences in the degree of nestedness exhibited by the different taxa and ecological subgroups. The high degree of assemblage nestedness exhibited by non-microhylid, regionally endemic frogs suggests that this group is either the most extinction-prone or the poorest colonizers. Schneider, Cunningham, and Moritz (1998) have shown that at least one species (*Litoria genimaculata*) in the southern uplands is a recent recolonization from more northern refugia on the Atherton Uplands, and that this species is one of the few to have crossed the Black Mountain corridor. However, this species is probably the least extinction-prone in its guild, or better at dispersal than the other species of stream hylids (Williams and Hero 1998). Reptiles seem to have been less structured by contractions than the other groups, possibly due to greater resilience or better postcontraction dispersal ability. Further analysis of reptile guilds and patterns of ecological similarity is needed here to allow a more detailed interpretation. The more detailed analyses on frog and mammal guilds clearly showed that in order to understand patterns of assemblage structure, the species had to be subdivided into meaningful ecological subsets or guilds (Williams and Hero 1998). The subset of endemic species was more nested than the whole species group in all cases except mammals. Mammals showed a higher degree of assemblage dissimilarity between the northern and southern rainforests than the other taxa (Williams 1997), and this pattern resulted in nesting within these two parts of the region, thereby reducing the nestedness of mammal assemblages over the region as a whole.

Except for a small number of species with highly restricted distributions, the species present in all of the subregions are almost entirely a nested subset of the two main centers of endemism within the region (the Thornton Uplands for the subregions north of the Daintree River and the Atherton Uplands for the rest of the region). The highly nested, nonrandom spatial structuring exhibited by rainforest vertebrate assemblages is indicative of a regional fauna that has been spatially structured by nonrandom extinction and recolonization (Patterson and Atmar 1986; Wright and Reeves 1992; Atmar and Patterson 1993). These analyses provide further evidence that the Quaternary fluctuations in rainforest area have had profound effects on the structure and development of vertebrate assemblages in the rainforests of the Australian Wet Tropics.

THE HISTORICAL FOOTPRINT OF QUATERNARY CLIMATE CHANGE

The observed spatial patterns of similarity in assemblage composition are consistent with a large influence from historical biogeography, as they are easily related to subregional extinctions and subsequent dispersal. Habitat diversity and area explain large amounts of the variation in regional patterns of vertebrate species richness; however, the patterns suggest that area is simply a surrogate for the combined expression of various forms of habitat diversity. The number of endemic species is best explained by the combination of rainforest shape and area. This relationship suggests that historical bottlenecks in rainforest area, and presumably habitat heterogeneity, during the Quaternary have had a large influence on the development of spatial patterns in assemblage structure. The results of this study suggest that current environmental variables (habitat area, habitat diversity, and climate) are the main determinant of overall species richness within any subregion; however, patterns of assemblage structure, especially the proportion of regional endemics, result primarily from the effects of Quaternary climatic fluctuations.

Further support for the influence of Quaternary climatic fluctuations on vertebrate assemblages is provided by the strong evidence (molecular data and nestedness analyses) for the assemblage in each subregion being a nonrandom subset of the regional fauna, structured by a history of extinctions and recolonizations dependent on the relative extinction-proneness and dispersal ability of the constituent species. Guild structure in those groups already examined is also in accordance with historical fluctuations in rainforest area. Those guilds that are the most extinction-prone or the least able to disperse across non-rainforest habitat are the guilds that drive most of the variation in regional patterns of species richness, again emphasizing the important influence of historical biogeography in this region. All of the analyses discussed above indicate that historical fluctuations in rainforest area have profoundly affected the structure and development of vertebrate assemblages, at all levels of community organization, throughout the Wet Tropics biogeographic region of Australia.

FUTURE DIRECTIONS

If, as we have hypothesized here, historical biogeography and the associated processes of extinction, dispersal, and recolonization have had such significant effects on the structure of the vertebrate assemblages of the Wet Tropics, then these findings have many implications pertaining to the development of ecological assemblages. Based on the discussions above, several predictions can be made, and could be tested by a combination of community surveys and genetic sampling over a range of nested spatial scales:

1. Local-scale diversity (within-species genetic diversity, species diversity, and ecological diversity) should decrease along a gradient from the areas that have had long-term rainforest refugia to the areas of most recent recolonization. Local-scale diversity should be lower in the areas most recently recolonized, due to founder effects resulting from local-scale bottlenecks in genetic diversity and species composition.
2. Associated with these founder effects, there should be an increase in the local-scale spatial patchiness of within-species genetic similarity and assemblage similarity (Hewitt 1996).
3. The strength of these patterns of diversity and spatial heterogeneity should vary depending on the relative ability of each species to disperse or cross non-rainforest habitat: it is expected that, in the areas of most recent recolonization, low-vagility species will show the strongest spatial patchiness and that their local populations will exhibit the lowest levels of

within-species genetic diversity (and the converse for highly vagile species).

4. Assemblage structure should be strongly affected by recolonization ability and habitat plasticity; that is, areas in the southern subregions, which have been recently recolonized, should be dominated by species that either have remained in situ due to high habitat plasticity or have high dispersal ability or ability to cross non-rainforest habitats. Geographic genetic analyses can differentiate between these alternative processes.
5. Niche breadth should be greater in the areas of recent recolonization due to the expansion of species into a relatively empty habitat with minimal initial competition and reduced numbers of interspecific competitors. This greater niche breadth may result in changes in species morphology or in an increase in the degree of morphological variation within species along the recolonization gradient. These morphological changes may represent important adaptive diversity that could be important in speciation.

More generally, patterns of genetic and phylogenetic variation are useful for addressing a wide variety of biogeographic hypotheses that are generated by analyses of species distribution and diversity in tropical areas. Spatial analyses of diversity across hierarchical levels, from genes to species and landscapes, provide a powerful means of inferring the historical component of current species distribution and diversity. Importantly for conservation biology, predictive models of species distribution in response to predicted climate change could be improved by testing them against patterns of genetic and species diversity in regions where the history of climate change and species response is well known. By looking backward in time, we may better hone the accuracy of models to predict the responses of species to future climate change.

SUMMARY AND CONCLUSIONS

Biogeographic patterns are often used to infer historical processes, but are often inadequate to distinguish between competing hypotheses. A combination of molecular phylogeographic analyses and spatial analyses of species distributions provides stronger inference of historical processes affecting distribution and diversity at all levels of the biological hierarchy.

Both spatial analyses of species distributions and mtDNA phylogeography provide evidence of large effects of Quaternary climate change on the distributions of rainforest endemic species in the Australian Wet Tropics. These patterns are consistent with the relatively well known palynological record for the region, which demonstrates large-scale contraction and expansion of rainforest in response to climatic fluctuations during the Quaternary.

Both the spatial distributions of species and the mtDNA phylogeography indicate that extinction is the primary historical process shaping current patterns of genetic and species diversity and community composition. However, the mtDNA data also indicate an important role for recent colonization, particularly in the southernmost regions of the Wet Tropics. This history of extinction and recolonization has important implications for understanding local diversity, community composition, and ecological processes. The importance of history to patterns of diversity and community composition is straightforward in that species presence or absence is largely a result of historical processes; however, the connection to current ecological processes may be more subtle. Extinction and recolonization may result in communities far from equilibrium, which may confound attempts to use equilibrium theories to explain current assemblage structure. Similarly, recently colonized areas may contain a preponderance of generalist species that are good dispersers. Again, this pattern may affect inferences regarding the current processes structuring local assemblages. It is clear that history plays an important role in shaping current community structure and ecological interactions (see Ricklefs and Schluter 1993a for review), and it is important to consider the relative importance of historical and current processes acting at different spatial and temporal scales.

The inference of historical process from spatial patterns of species distributions and assemblage structure is a "top-down" approach that uses comparative pattern analyses to generate hypotheses, rather than to test specific factors. These inferences and hypotheses can often be tested by a "bottom-up" approach utilizing analyses of spatial patterns of genetic variation within and among species. We believe that these approaches should not be seen as antagonistic, but as complimentary. Combined analyses of this type depend on a reasonably complete knowledge of species distributions and taxonomy and sufficient access for widespread genetic sampling. Neither of these conditions are likely to be met for many tropical systems in the near future, but targeted studies of well-known taxonomic groups are feasible for many regions.

ACKNOWLEDGMENTS

This work was supported by the Cooperative Research Centre for Tropical Rainforest Ecology and Management, Cairns, Australia. We are grateful to the CRC-TREM for organizing the conference that led to this volume, and we thank one anonymous reviewer and the volume editors for helpful comments and suggestions. This work benefited substantially from discussions with Michael Cunningham, Conrad Hoskins, Andrew Hugall, Marcia Lara, Keith McDonald, Richard Pearson, Jo Sumner, John Winter, and several others. CJS acknowledges the assistance of Keith McDonald, who shared his home, knowledge, and expertise and facilitated much of our research in the Wet Tropics.

21

Mosaic Macroevolution in Australian Wet Tropics Arthropods: Community Assemblage by Taxon Pulses

PATRICE BOUCHARD, DANIEL R. BROOKS, AND DAVID K. YEATES

ABSTRACT

This chapter represents the first attempt at studying patterns of speciation and community assemblage in arthropods of the Australian Wet Tropics. We divided the Australian Wet Tropics into seventeen areas of endemism (isolated patches of high-elevation rainforest) for our historical biogeographic analysis, which involved a combination of primary and secondary BPA (Brooks Parsimony Analysis). The results of the primary BPA determine whether the null hypothesis of simple vicariance is falsified. If the primary BPA analysis does not yield a single area cladogram that is supported by all of the taxon phylogenies used, then the null hypothesis must be rejected, and an a posteriori interpretation of the "noise" is necessary. The aim of secondary BPA is to find an explanation for the homoplasy found in the primary BPA. Phylogenetic and distributional data from the 87 species of arthropods included in our analysis yielded three most parsimonious area cladograms based on the primary BPA methodology. Conflicting area relationship data derived from fifteen taxon phylogenies resulted in a relatively well resolved but poorly supported strict area cladogram. In order to explain the homoplasy in the primary BPA, we looked for common patterns of area relationships among the fifteen initial phylogenies. Results from the secondary BPA show that there are no less than three general patterns of area relationships supported by the phylogenetic and distributional data. The results obtained in our historical biogeographic analysis indicate the following patterns of evolution: (1) there is no support for a single pattern of area relationships for the 87 species included in the analysis (tested using primary BPA); (2) three independent modules of area relationships are needed to explain the data (different clades support different patterns); (3) vicariance is not the principal mode of speciation; (4) within-area speciation (ecological differentiation) is common; (5) across-area peripheral isolate speciation accounts for a significant number of events; (6) all seventeen areas of endemism have reticulate histories (are uniquely assembled); (7) widespread species occupy between two and ten areas of endemism; and (8) in each of the three secondary BPA area cladograms, there is a single clade that becomes associated with other clades through colonization (sequential addition). These patterns of evolution support the "taxon pulse" model previously proposed by Erwin (1979, 1981, 1985; Erwin and Adis 1982).

INTRODUCTION

The origin of high species diversity in tropical rainforests has intrigued biologists for decades. Hypotheses to explain the current patterns of species richness in these habitats are varied (see Nores 1999 for summary). Although no single hypothesis can fully explain all patterns, it is generally agreed that historical factors have had a significant effect on the current diversity and community composition in tropical rainforests (Ricklefs and Schluter 1993a). An understanding of the processes of species diversification (speciation) is fundamental to explaining the diversity of life (Mayr 1963). Accumulation of phylogenetic information at the species and population levels has recently enabled biologists to test various hypotheses concerning the evolution of species richness and reveal factors that promote speciation (Barraclough, Vogler, and Harvey 1998; Barraclough and Nee 2001; Schneider, Cunningham, and Moritz 1998). In this chapter, we use phylogenetic and distributional data from arthropods endemic to the rainforests of tropical Australia to investigate the historical processes that have led to the current diversity patterns in this unique region.

The Wet Tropics World Heritage Area (henceforth Wet Tropics) is located between Cooktown and Townsville in northeastern Queensland, Australia (fig. 21.1). The main vegetation type in this region is tropical rainforest, but it is fringed and dissected by sclerophyllous forests, swamps, and mangrove forests (Wet Tropics Management Authority 2001). Isolated "montane blocks" of rainforest are found throughout the Wet Tropics (Joseph, Moritz, and Hugall 1995), usually in areas above 300 m in altitude (Rainforest Conservation Society of Queensland 1986). The Wet Tropics rainforests are floristically and structurally the most diverse in Australia (Rainforest Conservation Society of Queensland 1986; Crisp et al. 2001) and also support a major proportion of the continent's fauna (e.g., Nix and Switzer 1991; Williams, Pearson, and Walsh 1996).

The high levels of regional endemism and high species richness of the Wet Tropics biota make it especially well suited for studying the historical processes that may have led to this diversity (Schneider, Cunningham, and Moritz 1998). The most detailed studies on the evolution of Wet Tropics biota to date have been restricted to vertebrates. Recent evidence suggests that upland rainforests (above 300 m) support higher vertebrate species richness than lowland habitats (Williams 1997) and support a higher number of regional endemics (Nix and Switzer 1991; Williams and Pearson 1997), and that historical climatic fluctuations (during the Pleistocene and Tertiary) have promoted genetic diversity (through vicariance), but reduced local species diversity (through local extinc-

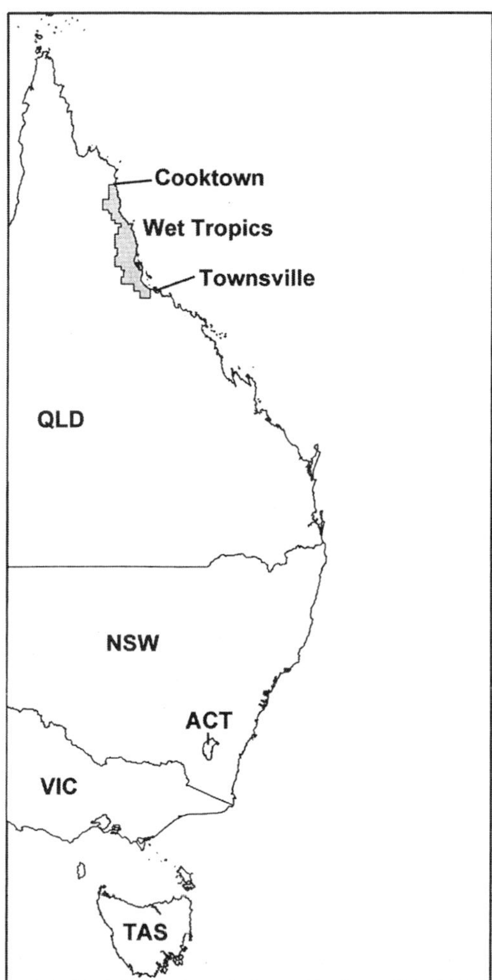

Figure 21.1 Map of eastern Australia, showing the area covered by the Wet Tropics World Heritage Area (in gray).

tion) of rainforest taxa (Joseph, Moritz, and Hugall 1995; Schneider, Cunningham, and Moritz 1998; Schneider and Williams, chap. 20 in this volume).

Compared with invertebrates, most vertebrate species are distributed over large areas within the Wet Tropics and are therefore less suitable for studies concerning the relationships of the various montane blocks within this region (Yeates, Bouchard, and Monteith 2002). On the other hand, a large number of rainforest-restricted arthropods (especially low-vagility taxa such as flightless insects) are known to be restricted to isolated patches of suitable habitat on a single or a few geographically adjacent mountains (Yeates, Bouchard, and Monteith 2002). Data from arthropods clearly have the potential to yield detailed information about the historical relationships of the various montane blocks within the Wet Tropics.

Over the last two decades, the arthropod fauna of the Wet Tropics has been extensively sampled. This was done primarily by staff of the Queensland Museum (Brisbane, Australia), G. Monteith in particular. Specimens obtained through these collecting efforts have served as the basis for numerous taxonomic publications (table 21.1). Although patterns of diversity in the Wet Tropics arthropod fauna have become clearer in recent times, the processes that have acted on this fauna since its first establishment in the region are still poorly understood.

Based on distributional data from over 250 flightless insect species restricted to the Wet Tropics, Yeates, Bouchard, and Monteith (2002) demonstrated that the main patches of upland tropical forest have acted as refugia for rainforest-adapted species during the glacial periods of the Pleistocene and Tertiary. Their results also indicate that a small number of montane blocks (e.g., Carbine Tableland, Mount Bellenden Ker) support a large percentage of these endemic flightless insects compared with other montane blocks (e.g., Seaview Range, Windsor Tableland). The reasons for this pattern are largely unknown. One of the most fundamental questions still to be addressed concerning the evolution of Wet Tropics arthropods concerns the historical processes that have led to the current patterns of diversity.

This chapter represents the first attempt at studying the patterns of speciation and community assemblage in arthropods of the Australian Wet Tropics. The null hypothesis that we are testing is that all arthropods present in the Wet Tropics have responded in the same way to vicariant events in the past and show a single pattern of speciation. Available species-level phylogenies of Wet Tropics arthropods are used in an attempt to find a general pattern of area relationships between the Wet Tropics' montane blocks. The historical biogeography technique called "Brooks parsimony analysis" or "BPA" (Brooks 1981; Wiley 1986, 1988a, 1988b; including recent improvements summarized in Brooks, Van Veller, and McLennan 2001; Brooks and McLennan 2002) is used here for this purpose.

AREAS OF ENDEMISM

For any biogeographic study, finding adequate areas of endemism is fundamental (Henderson 1991; Platnick 1991; Harold and Mooi 1994; Morrone 1994). An area of endemism is defined by the congruent distributional boundaries of

Table 21.1 List of beetle (Insecta: Coeloptera), bug (Insecta: Hemiptera), and spider (Arachnida: Araneae) genera that have at least one species endemic to the Wet Tropics of northeastern Australia

Taxon[a]	Distribution[b]	WT[c]	Other[d]	Source
COLEOPTERA				
Aderidae				
Megaxenus Lawrence	SEASIA, NG, WT	1	2	Lawrence, Kistner, and Pasteels 1990
Buprestidae				
Maoraxia Obenberger	EAUST, NZ, NCAL, PAC, SEASIA	1	7	Bellamy 1991
Carabidae				
Colasidia Basilewski	SEASIA, NG, WT	1	3	Baehr 1987
**Philipis* Erwin	EAUST	33	2	Baehr 1995
Rhysopleura Sloane	WT	1	0	McCairns et al. 1997
Cerylonidae				
Australiorylon Slipinski	EAUST, NG, PAC, SEASIA	2	20	Slipinski 1988
Cerylonopsis Heinze	AFR, ASIA, NG, NAUST, EAUST	1	50	Slipinski 1988
Philothermus AubE	COS	1	70	Slipinski 1988
Hypodacnella Slipinski	EAUST, NZ, NCAL	1	9	Slipinski 1988
Cerambycidae				
Psilomorpha Saunders	AUST	1	1	Scambler 1989
Chrysomelidae				
Aproida Pascoe	EAUST	1	2	Samuelson 1989
Cadmus Erichson[e]	EAUST	1	23	Reid 1999
Dytiscidae				
Carabhydrus Watts	EAUST	1	4	Watts 1978; Zwick 1981; Larson and Storey 1994
Terradessus Watts	WT	1	0	Watts 1982
Elateridae				
Austrelater Calder and Lawrence	EAUST	1	2	Calder, Lawrence, and Trueman 1993

(continued)

Table 21.1 *(continued)*

Taxon[a]	Distribution[b]	WT[c]	Other[d]	Source
Hydrophylidae				
Eurygmus Hansen	WT	1	0	Hansen 1990
Borborophorus Hansen	EAUST	1	2	Hansen 1990
Petasopsis Hansen	WT	1	0	Hansen 1990
Coelostomopsis Hansen	WT	2	0	Hansen 1990
Pilocnema Hansen	EAUST	1	1	Hansen 1990
Australocyon Hansen	EAUST	1	5	Hansen 1990
Chledocyon Hansen	WT, SWAUST	1	4	Hansen 1990
Pseudoosternum Hansen	NAUST	1	1	Hansen 1990
Ceronocyton Hansen	EAUST	1	2	Hansen 1990
Cenebriophilus Hansen	EAUST	1	1	Hansen 1990
Lampyridae				
Atyphella Olliff	NAUST, EAUST, NG	8	14	Calder 1998; Ballantyne and Lambkin 2000
Nitidulidae				
Cylindroramus Kirejtshuk & Lawrence	EAUST, NAUST	2	8	Kirejtshuk and Lawrence 1992
Ptilodactylidae				
Austrolichas Lawrence & Stribling	WT	1	0	Lawrence and Stribling 1992
Pyrochroidae				
Morpholycus Lea	EAUST	3	3	Pollock 1995
Rhysodidae				
Kaveinga Bell and Bell	EAUST	2	2	Bell and Bell 1991
Scarabaeidae				
Anomalomorpha Arrow	EAUST	1	2	Allsopp 2000
Aptenocanthon Matthews	EAUST, NAUST	5	3	Storey 1984; Storey and Monteith 2000
Aulacopris White	EAUST	1	2	Storey 1986
Australobalbus Howden & Cooper	NG, AUST	3	48	Howden 1992

Australoxenella Howden & Storey	NAUST	1	10	Storey and Howden 1996
Coptodactyla Burmeister	NG, EAUST, NAUST	2	15	Reid 2000
Daintreeola Howden & Storey	WT	1	0	Howden and Storey 2000
Gilletinus Boucomont	NG, EAUST	1	4	Howden 1992
Gongrolophus Stebnicka & Howden	WT	1	0	Stebnicka and Howden 1996
Homolotropus Macleay	EAUST	3	2	Britton 1987
Idanastes Britton	WT	1	0	Britton 1987
Neocorynophyllus Carne	WT	1	0	Carne 1985
Onthophagus Latreille	COS	4	>2000	Storey and Weir 1990
Protelura Britton	WT	2	0	Britton 1987
Pseudignambia Paulian	WT	20	0	T. A. Weir, pers. comm.
Sericesthis Boisduval	AUST	10	42	Britton 1987
**Temnoplectron* Westwood	NG, EAUST, NAUST	11	8	Reid and Storey 2000
Xyroa Britton	WT	4	0	Britton 1987
Tenebrionidae				
Apocryphodes Matthews	WT	5	0	Matthews 1998
**Apterotheca* Gebien	EAUST	42	2	Bouchard 2002
Atoreuma Gebien	EAUST	4	5	Matthews 1992; E. G. Matthews, pers. comm.
Bellendenum Matthews	WT	4	0	Matthews 1998
Blepegenes Pascoe	EAUST	1	7	Matthews 1998
Bluops Carter	WT	1	0	Matthews 1998
Bolusculus Matthews	WT	1	0	Matthews 1998
Coripera Pascoe	EAUST	4	9	Matthews 1998
Cuemus Bouchard	WT	2	0	Bouchard 2000
Cyphaleus Westwood	AUST	4	25	Matthews 1992; E. G. Matthews, pers. comm.
Diaspirus Matthews	EAUST	2	1	Matthews 1998
Dicyrtodes Matthews	WT	3	0	Matthews 1998

(continued)

Table 21.1 *(continued)*

Taxon[a]	Distribution[b]	WT[c]	Other[d]	Source
Ecnolagria Borchmann	AUST	2	6	Merkl 1987
Epomidus Matthews	WT	2	0	Matthews 1998
Leptogastrus Macleay	AUST	2	9	Matthews 1998
Monteithium Matthews	WT	2	0	Matthews 1998
Nolicima Matthews	AUST	2	13	Matthews 1998
Paraphanes Macleay	EAUST	1	1	Matthews 1992; E. G. Matthews, pers. comm.
Stenolagria Merkl	WT	2	0	Merkl 1987
HEMIPTERA				
Aradidae				
Aegisocoris Kormilev	WT	2	0	Monteith 1997
**Aellocoris* Kormilev	EAUST	10	3	Russell 1997
Chelonoderus Usinger	WT	4	0	Monteith 1997
Ctenoneurus Bergroth	AFR, SEASIA, NG, PAC, EAUST	2	43	Monteith 1997
Drakiessa Usinger & Matsuda	EAUST	3	11	Monteith 1997
Granulaptera Monteith	EAUST	6	1	Monteith 1997
Kumaressa Monteith	EAUST	1	2	Monteith 1980
Mesophloeobia Monteith	EAUST	1	3	Monteith 1997
Neophloeobia Usinger & Matsuda	EAUST	3	5	Monteith 1997
Coreidae				
Grosshygia Brailovsky	WT	3	0	Brailovsky 1993
Grosshygioides Brailovsky	WT	1	0	Brailovsky 1993
Delphacidae				
Kiambrama Donaldson	WT	2	0	Donaldson 1988
Notuchus Fennah	NCAL, NQLD, LHI	2	5	Donaldson 1988

Flatidae				
Siphanta Stål	SEASIA, NG, AUST	6	34	Fletcher 1985
Gerridae				
Tenagogonus Stål	AFR, ASIA, WT, PAC	1	14	Chen and Nieser 1992; Andersen and Weir 1997
Lygaeidae				
Lachnophoroides Distant	NCAL, EAUST	1	4	Woodward 1986
Mesoveliidae				
Austrovelia Malipatil and Monteith	NCAL, WT	1	1	Malipatil and Monteith 1983
Myerslopiidae				
Myerslopella Evans	WT	6	0	Hamilton 1999
Reduviidae				
Helonotus Amyot and Serville	NG, NAUST	1	app. 50	Malipatil 1986
Schizopteridae				
Duonota Hill	EAUST	4	4	Hill 1984
Lativena Hill	WT	2	0	Hill 1984
Ogeria Distant	SEASIA, PAC, EAUST	7	6	L. Hill 1990a
Pachyplagia Gross	SEASIA, EAUST	3	6	L. Hill 1990b
Pachyplagioides Gross	EAUST	4	3	L. Hill 1992
Tessaratomidae				
Tibiospina Sinclair	WT	1	0	Sinclair 2000
Veliidae				
Drepanovelia Andersen and Weir	EAUST	1	3	Andersen and Weir 2001
Microvelopsis Andersen and Weir	WT	3	0	Andersen and Weir 2001
ARANEAE				
Mygalomorphae				
Barychelidae				
Mandjelia Raven	AUST, NCAL	11	12	Raven 1994
Moruga Raven	NAUST	5	3	Raven 1994
Ozicrypta Raven	AUST	2	23	Raven 1994
Trittame Koch	EAUST	2	9	Raven 1990, 1994

(continued)

Table 21.1 *(continued)*

Taxon[a]	Distribution[b]	WT[c]	Other[d]	Source
Zophorame Raven	EAUST	2	2	Raven 1990, 1994
Dipluridae				
Cethegus Thorell	AUST	2	9	Raven 1984a
Ixamatus Simon	EAUST	1	7	Raven 1982a
Namea Raven	EAUST	3	12	Raven 1984b
Namirea Raven	EAUST	2	5	Raven 1984b, 1993
Xamiatus Raven	EAUST	1	4	Raven 1981, 1982b
Hexathelidae				
Hadronyche L. Koch	AUST	1	12	Raven 2000
Araneomorphae				
Amaurobiidae				
Bakala Davies	WT	1	0	Davies 1990
Malala Davies	EAUST	1	1	Davies 1993
Manjala Davies	EAUST	2	1	Davies 1990
Otira Forster and Wilton	NZ, TAS, WT	2	7	Davies 1986
Amaurobioidea (not assigned to families)				
**Carbinea* Davies	WT	4	0	Davies 1999
Jamara Davies	WT	1	0	Davies 1995a
Kababina Davies	WT	9	0	Davies 1995b
**Malarina* Davies	WT	4	0	Davies and Lambkin 2000a
Wabua Davies	EAUST	7	4	Davies and Lambkin 2000b
Amphinectidae				
Buyina Davies	WT	2	0	Davies 1998
Jalkaraburra Davies	WT	1	0	Davies 1998
Quemusia Davies	EAUST	1	3	Davies 1998

Ctenidae				
Amauropelma Raven and Stumkat	NEAUST	12	4	Raven, Stumkat, and Gray 2001
Lamponidae				
Centrina Platnick	EAUST	1	10	Platnick 2000
Centrothele L. Koch	NG, EAUST	5	5	Platnick 2000
Lampona Thorell	NG, AUST	6	51	Platnick 2000
Pseudolampona Platnick	AUST	1	11	Platnick 2000
Pholcidae				
Micromerys Bradley	NG, EAUST, NAUST	4	3	Huber 2001
Pholcus Walckenaer	COS	2	110	Huber 2000, 2001
Trichocyclus Simon	AUST	1	22	Huber 2001
Wugigarra Huber	AUST	10	12	Huber 2001
Pisauridae				
Inola Davies	WT	3	0	Davies 1982
Salticidae				
Pseudosynagelides Zabka	EAUST	2	4	Zabka 1991

Note: These three higher taxa have been the three most studied Wet Tropics invertebrate groups in the past 20 years because of available expertise and specialized methods used to collect them. Although this list is not exhaustive, it is representative of the information available for other taxa. Only studies that included detailed information about distribution and habitat preferences for all species within a genus were considered.

[a]Genera are listed in alphabetical order within each family. Phylogenies used in this chapter are identified by an asterisk.

[b]Distributions of genera: AFR = Africa; ASIA = includes the mainland of Asia as well as Southeast Asia; AUST = present on the Australian continent, with distribution more widespread than EAUST, NAUST, WT, or SWAUST; COS = cosmopolitan; EAUST = eastern Australia (restricted mostly east of the Great Divide); HOL = Holarctic; LHI = Lord Howe Island; NAUST = northern Australia (restricted mostly to the monsoonal forests along the northern coast of Australia); NCAL = New Caledonia; NG = New Guinea (includes Papua New Guinea and Irian Jaya); NQLD = northern Queensland (includes the Wet Tropics north to the tip of Cape York); NZ = New Zealand; PAC = Pacific Islands (east of Papua New Guinea, but excluding New Caledonia and New Zealand); SEASIA = Southeast Asia; SWAUST = restricted to the southwestern corner of Australia; TAS = Tasmania; WT = Australian Wet Tropics.

[c]Number of species restricted to the Wet Tropics.

[d]Number of species occurring outside of the Wet Tropics.

[e]Only the subgenus *Lachnabothra* Saunders was studied in this publication.

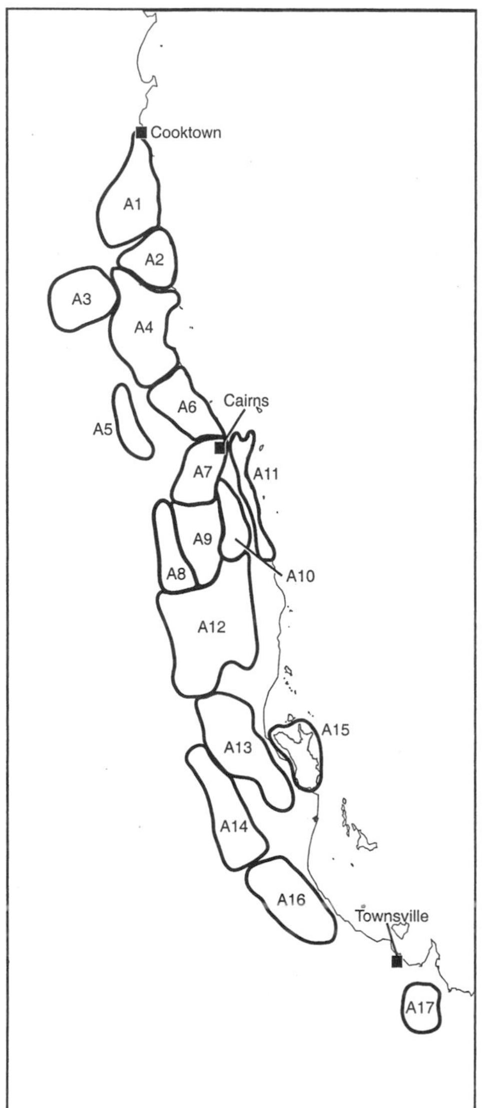

Figure 21.2 Map of the Australian Wet Tropics region, indicating the limits of the seventeen areas of endemism (montane blocks) used in this chapter: A1 = Mount Finnigan; A2 = Thornton Peak; A3 = Windsor Tableland; A4 = Carbine Tableland; A5 = Hann Tableland; A6 = Black Mountain; A7 = Lamb Range; A8 = Walsh/Hugh Nelson Ranges; A9 = Atherton Tableland; A10 = Mount Bellenden Ker; A11 = Malbon Thompson Range; A12 = Walter Hill Range; A13 = Kirrama/Cardwell Ranges; A14 = Seaview Range; A15 = Hinchinbrook Island; A16 = Paluma/Blue Water Ranges; A17 = Mount Elliot.

two or more species. Congruence does not demand complete agreement on those boundaries at all possible scales of mapping, but does require relatively extensive sympatry (Morrone and Crisci 1995). Oceanic islands and continental masses are easily defined areas of endemism because of their obvious isolation from one another. However, defining such areas on a continuous landscape is often more challenging (Morrone 1994).

The Australian Wet Tropics was originally divided into several "subregions" by Winter et al. (1984) based on mammal distributions. These subregions include lowland and upland (above 300 m) forest blocks and have recently been used as biogeographically distinct areas (Joseph, Moritz, and Hugall 1995; Williams, Pearson, and Walsh 1996; Williams 1997; Williams and Pearson 1997; Schneider, Cunningham, and Moritz 1998; Moritz et al. 2001). Most of the arthropod species included here occupy the upland rainforest blocks, which are separated from one another by corridors of dry sclerophyllous forest or deep river gorges (Williams 1997). Data from paleoclimatic reconstructions (Nix and Switzer 1991), as well as from distributions of more than 300 species of arthropods (Yeates, Bouchard, and Monteith 2002; D. K. Yeates and G. B. Monteith, unpublished data), indicate that seventeen areas (slightly modified from Winter et al. 1984) are likely to have contained at least small rainforest refugia during climatic fluctuations of the Pleistocene and Tertiary and can be considered "true" areas of endemism based on the restricted presence of two or more endemic arthropod species in each. These seventeen areas of endemism are listed and mapped in figure 21.2. The same seventeen areas were recently used to study patterns of species richness in the beetle genus *Apterotheca* Gebien (Bouchard 2002). One of these areas, the Seaview Range, contains small mountain peaks above 900 m (Nix and Switzer 1991). Although only one endemic insect species is known from this montane block to date (Yeates, Bouchard, and Monteith 2002), it is thought to have supported small rainforest refugia in the geologic past and is included in this analysis as an area of endemism.

TAXA

As mentioned in the introduction, recent intensive collecting of arthropods in the Australian Wet Tropics has led to a significant number of taxonomic publications (table 21.1). Unfortunately, hypotheses of relationships based on phylogenetic methodologies for species restricted to this region are available only in a handful of revisions. The monophyletic groups used in this chapter were selected based on the following criteria: availability of phylogenetic hypotheses at the species level obtained using parsimony, availability of detailed information on the distribution patterns of each species, and exclusive or predominant presence of the group in the Wet Tropics region (selection criteria from Turner, Hovenkamp, and Van Welzen 2001). The selected phylogenies (see table 21.1) were obtained from one genus of aradid bugs (*Aellocoris* Kormilev), three beetle genera (*Philipis* Erwin; *Temnoplectron* Westwood; *Apterotheca*), and two genera of spiders (*Malarina* Davies; *Carbinea* Davies). A total of fifteen clades containing three or more species restricted to the Wet Tropics were obtained from these publications (figs. 21.3–21.6). All phylogenies were based on morphological data except for the revision of the genus *Aellocoris,* for which a phylogeny based on combined molecular (16S) and morphological characters was selected for this study (Russell 1997). Distributions of the 87 arthropod species were derived from published records.

HISTORICAL BIOGEOGRAPHY: BROOKS PARSIMONY ANALYSIS

Hovenkamp (1997) noted that methods of historical biogeography comprise two areas of focus: the history of the areas in which species live (area-history methods) and the history of the species living in the areas (taxon-history methods). Area-history methods, better known as cladistic biogeography (Rosen 1978; Nelson and Platnick 1981; Humphries and Parenti 1999), are based on the principle that we can use the phylogenetic relationships of animals and plants to document relationships among the areas in which they live. These methods have been used extensively in recent years to try to find general global evolutionary patterns of biotic diversity using distributional data as well as phylogenetic information when available (see summary in Humphries and Parenti 1999). The most widely used techniques for implementing area-history methods are component analysis (Nelson and Platnick 1981; Page 1988, 1990a, 1990b, 1993a), reconciled tree analysis (Page 1993b, 1994), and three-area statement analysis (Nelson and Ladiges 1991a, 1991b). Unfortunately, as recently pointed out by Nelson and Ladiges (2001), these various techniques can yield different results when applied to a particular set of data. This situation has led to confusion among biologists, and the current lack of a unified methodology is undoubtedly a hindrance to the discovery of global patterns of biotic evolution. Van Veller, Kornet, and Zandee (2000) and Van Veller and Brooks (2001) termed area-history methods "a priori" methods because the sister relationships depicted in the taxon phylogenies can be altered prior to the biogeographic analysis in order to account for area reticulations.

Taxon-history methods, comprising the "parsimony" techniques Brooks parsimony analysis (BPA: Brooks 1981, 1985, 1990; Wiley 1986, 1988a, 1988b; Brooks and McLennan 1991, 2001, 2002; Brooks, Van Veller, and McLennan 2001) and component compatibility analysis (Zandee and Roos 1987), are based on the principle that we can use a combination of the phylogenetic relationships among species and their geographic distributions to understand complex histories of speciation and community assemblage. Van Veller, Kornet, and Zandee

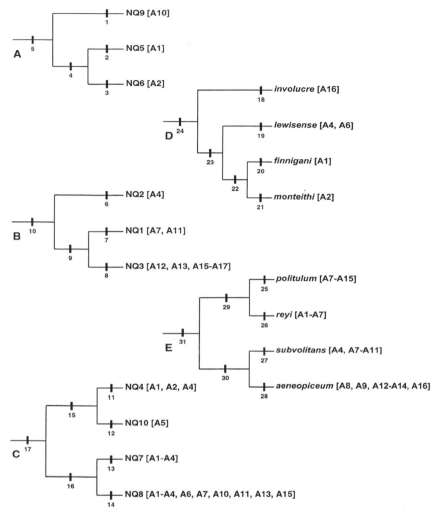

Figure 21.3 Taxon phylogenies used for the cladistic biogeographic analysis. Numbers on the phylogenies correspond to the characters coded for the primary and secondary BPA analyses. Numbers following the species names correspond to their distributions. (A) *Aellocoris* NQ9 clade. (B) *Ae.* NQ2 clade. (C) *Ae.* NQ4 clade. (D) *Temnoplectron involucre* Matthews clade. (E) *T. politulum* Macleay clade. See table 21.1 for references.

(2000) and Van Veller and Brooks (2001) described the taxon-history methods as "a posteriori" methods because the modification of sister-group relationships in the taxon phylogenies prior to the biogeographic analysis is forbidden. Brooks and McLennan (2001) suggested that this lack of a priori distortion of the input data made BPA a highly desirable discovery-based method.

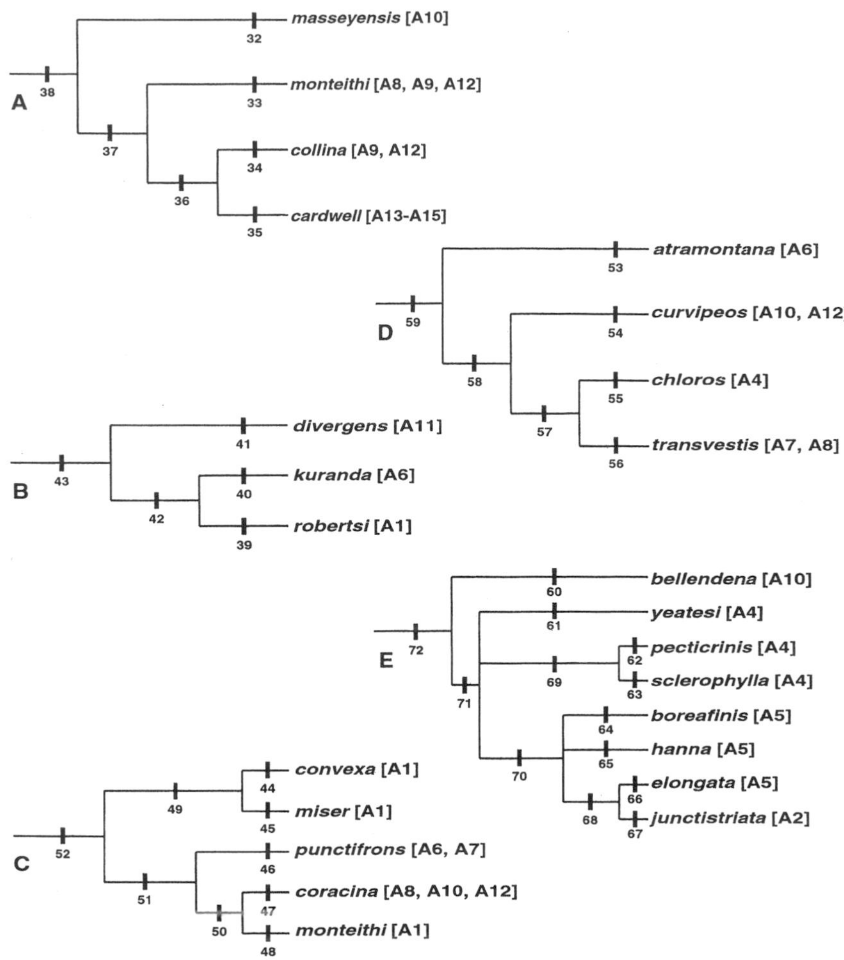

Figure 21.4 Taxon phylogenies used for the cladistic biogeographic analysis (continued). Numbers on the phylogenies correspond to the characters coded for the primary and secondary BPA analyses. Numbers following the species names correspond to their distributions. (A) *Malarina masseyensis* Davies clade. (B) *Apterotheca divergens* Bouchard clade. (C) *Ap. convexa* Bouchard clade. (D) *Ap. atramontana* Bouchard clade. (E) *Ap. bellendena* Bouchard clade. See table 21.1 for references.

We believe that the modification of BPA referred to as secondary BPA (Brooks, Van Veller, and McLennan 2001; Van Veller and Brooks 2001; Brooks and McLennan 2001, 2002) has improved the explanatory power of biogeographic analyses greatly by allowing evolutionary events of a complex nature to complement the a priori-assumed simplest explanation for the data. The combination of primary and secondary BPA (see Brooks, Van Veller, and McLennan

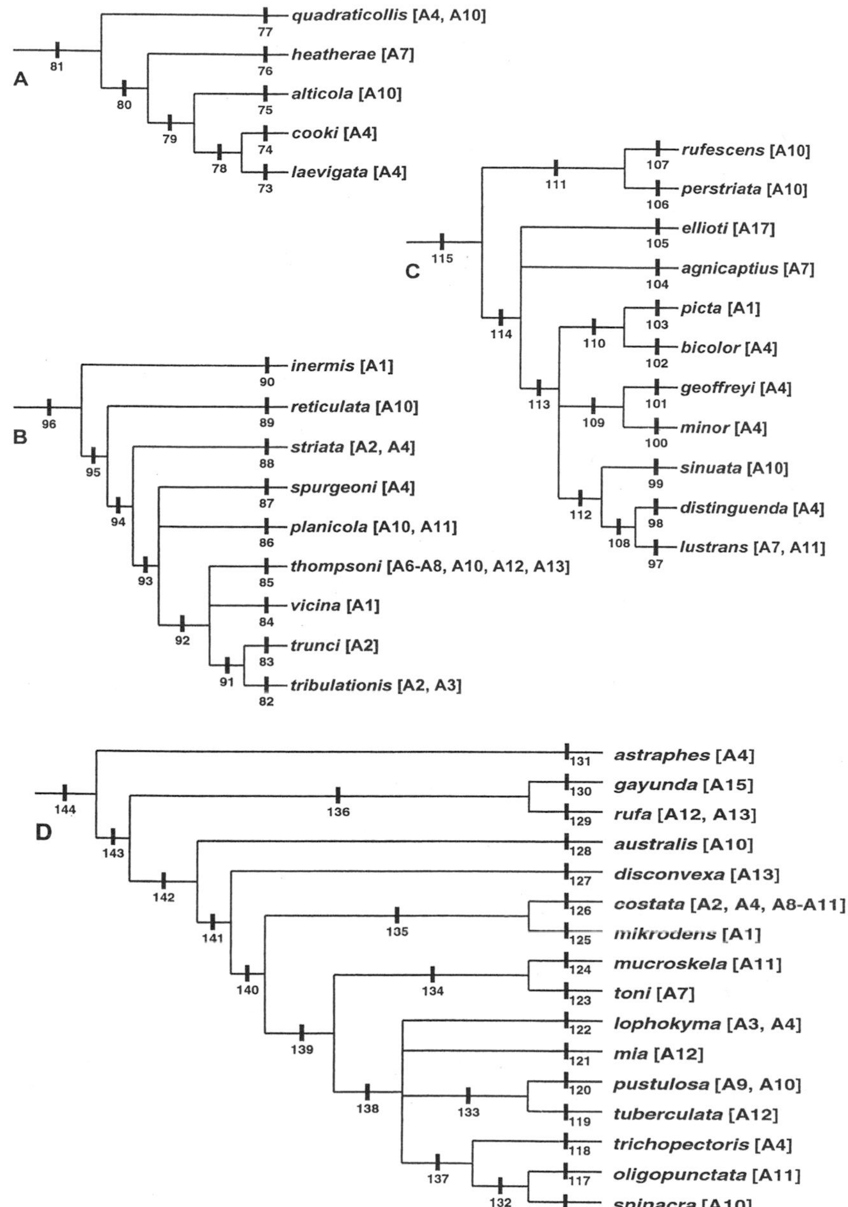

Figure 21.5 Taxon phylogenies used for the cladistic biogeographic analysis (continued). Numbers on the phylogenies correspond to the characters coded for the primary and secondary BPA analyses. Numbers following the species names correspond to their distributions. (A) *Philipis quadraticollis* Baehr clade. (B) *P. inermis* Baehr clade. (C) *P. rufescens* Baehr clade. (D) *Apterotheca astraphes* Bouchard clade. See table 21.1 for references.

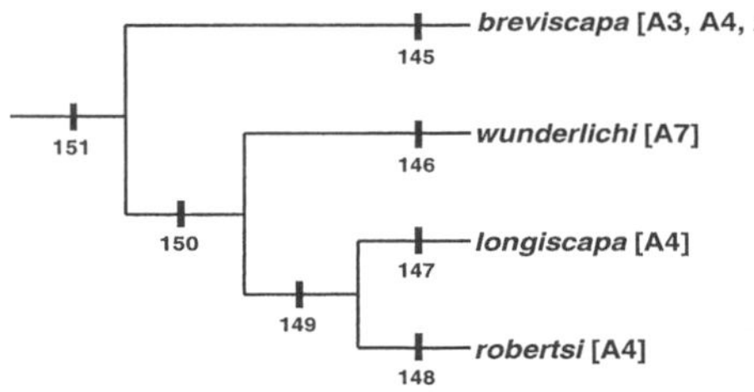

Figure 21.6 Taxon phylogenies used for the cladistic biogeographic analysis (continued): *Carbinea breviscapa* Davies clade. Numbers on the phylogenies correspond to the characters coded for the primary and secondary BPA analyses. Numbers following the species names correspond to their distributions. See table 21.1 for references.

2001) is used here to infer the relationships of seventeen areas of endemism (montane blocks) in the Australian Wet Tropics using available distributional and phylogenetic information from arthropods.

Primary BPA finds the most parsimonious general area cladogram possible given a set of phylogenetic relationships and geographic distributions (Wiley 1986, 1988a, 1988b; Brooks 1990; Brooks, Van Veller, and McLennan 2001; Van Veller and Brooks 2001). Primary BPA uses an area × taxon matrix obtained from binary coding of the terminal taxa and their hypothetical ancestors (Brooks 1981, 1985, 1990; Brooks and McLennan 1991; Morrone and Crisci 1995). The area × taxon matrix was derived using assumption 0, which minimizes the number of a priori decisions about widespread taxa by coding them as monophyletic (Marshall and Liebherr 2000; Van Veller, Kornet, and Zandee 2000; Brooks, Van Veller, and McLennan 2001; Van Veller and Brooks 2001). Assumption 0 uses unmodified individual taxon-area cladograms as the raw data for the pattern analysis, unlike assumptions 1 and 2 (Wiley 1986, 1988a, 1988b; Zandee and Roos 1987; Van Soest 1996; Van Veller and Brooks 2001; Brooks, Van Veller, and McLennan 2001; Brooks and McLennan 2002).

There are three possible reasons for the absence of a particular taxon from one or more areas of endemism: (1) the taxon never occurred in the sampled area, (2) the taxon became extinct in that area, or (3) the taxon is present, but has not yet been collected from that area (Myers and Giller 1988; Glasby and Alvarez 1999). Because it is often impossible to confidently determine the true reason for the absence of a taxon in a particular area, missing areas in BPA analyses are coded as "?" in order to minimize the number of a priori assumptions about distributions (Wiley 1986; Brooks 1990; Brooks and McLennan 1991, 2002; Brooks, Van Veller, and McLennan 2001).

The primary BPA data matrix was analyzed using the software PAUP*4.0b2a (Swofford 1999) for 100 random stepwise addition heuristic searches with tree-bisection-reconnection (TBR) branch swapping, MULPARS, and minimal length of zero collapsed to yield polytomies. Deltran optimization was employed, and a hypothetical ancestor coded with all zeros was used to root the cladograms. A strict consensus cladogram was used to summarize the information obtained from all equally parsimonious cladograms.

The results of the primary BPA determine whether the null hypothesis of simple vicariance in the data is falsified (Van Veller and Brooks 2001; Brooks, Van Veller, and McLennan 2001; Brooks and McLennan 2002). The null hypothesis proposed at the start of any biogeographic analysis is that the phylogenies will provide evidence of a "single" history in the relationships between the areas of endemism studied. However, reticulation in areas of endemism can be found in the form of widespread taxa (one species existing in more than one area), redundant distributions (more than one representative of a clade in an area), or missing species (one or more clades that do not have species in a particular area). If the primary BPA analysis does not yield a single area cladogram that is supported by all of the taxon phylogenies used, then the null hypothesis must be rejected, and a posteriori interpretation of the "noise" is necessary.

The aim of secondary BPA is to find an explanation for the homoplasy found in the primary BPA (Brooks 1990; Brooks, Van Veller, and McLennan 2001; Van Veller and Brooks 2001; Brooks and McLennan 2002). As first noted by Brooks (1990), single general area cladograms obtained from the phylogenetic and distributional data for unrelated taxa are unlikely to be found in nature, and therefore areas should be allowed to have several histories (see also Brooks and McLennan 1991, 2002; Van Soest 1996; Van Veller and Brooks 2001). The first step of secondary BPA is to look for potential vicariant pattern(s) that may be found in some or all of the taxon phylogenies and use this information as the "backbone" for the area cladogram(s). The next step involves the duplication of areas with redundant histories and the coding of all taxa into a new matrix. The last step involves reconstructing the historical relationships of the areas of endemism by allowing instances of post-speciation dispersal, peripheral isolate speciation, and sympatric speciation as well as extinction. Details on how to derive the different modes of speciation from the area cladogram obtained using secondary BPA can be found in Brooks, Van Veller, and McLennan (2001) and Brooks and McLennan (2002).

It should be emphasized that two fundamental principles must be observed when performing a secondary BPA analysis: assumption 0 (the resulting area cladograms need to reflect accurately each original taxon phylogeny) and parsimony (the resulting area cladograms need to include the smallest number of area duplications that explain all of the data). Several examples of empirical data analyzed using secondary BPA can be found in Brooks and McLennan (2002).

There are no software programs available to perform secondary BPA at this date, although such a tool is in the process of being constructed.

The raw input data used in the BPA analysis, in the form of species-level phylogenetic cladograms (figs. 21.3–21.6), are referred to as taxon phylogenies. Results of the biogeographic analyses, in the form of cladograms with areas as terminal taxa, are referred to as area cladograms. The following abbreviations are used throughout the text: Ae. (*Aellocoris*) and Ap. (*Apterotheca*).

Primary BPA

Distributional and phylogenetic information for 87 arthropod species was coded for the seventeen areas of endemism in the Australian Wet Tropics (appendix 21.1). A total of 59 species were each recorded from one area of endemism (67.8%). The remaining 28 species were each recorded from two to ten areas of endemism. All of the seventeen areas of endemism (see fig. 21.2) support at least two of the species for which phylogenetic information is available. A4 (Carbine Tableland) and A10 (Mount Bellenden Ker) support the highest number of species, with 27 and 20 respectively. The areas with the lowest diversity based on the present data are A17 (Mount Elliot), A14 (Seaview Range), and A16 (Paluma/Bluewater Ranges). These areas support two, three, and three species respectively.

Analysis of the primary BPA data matrix (appendix 21.1), containing 151 characters coded for seventeen areas of endemism, yielded three most parsimonious cladograms with a length of 206 steps (consistency index = 0.74). The resulting strict consensus cladogram (fig. 21.7) shows a mostly well resolved pattern of relationships except for A13–A17, which form a polytomy. The areas are separated into two main clades along the north-south axis. The larger northern clade includes A1–A12, whereas A13–A17 form the southern clade.

The pattern of relationships shown in figure 21.7 should, in theory, reflect the distributional input data from the various phylogenies used. However, the branching pattern in figure 21.7 shows that only the sister relationship between A1 and A2 is supported by at least two of the initial fifteen phylogenies (figs. 21.3–21.6; characters 4 and 22). All of the other clades on the strict consensus area cladogram are supported by homoplasious characters (shared non-endemic species or shared absence of species). Further investigation indicates that all of the areas of endemism have historically reticulate relationships.

Because of the apparent lack of agreement in the relationships between the areas of endemism in the available phylogenies (conflicting patterns of evolution within the Wet Tropics), it is impossible to obtain a well-supported general

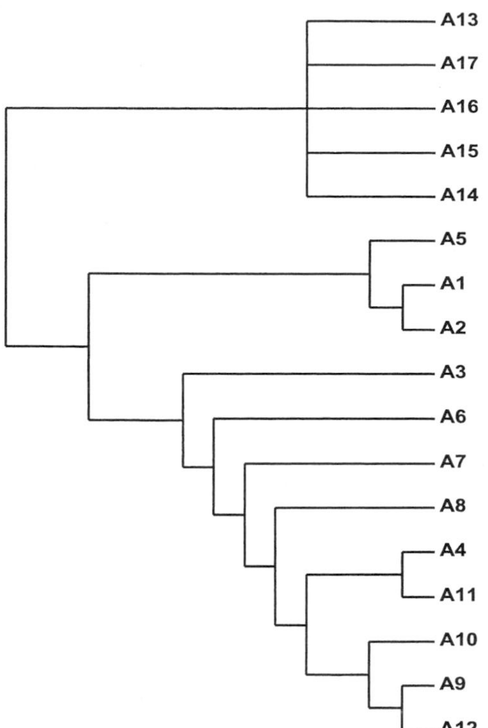

Figure 21.7 Strict consensus area cladogram of the three most parsimonious cladograms (length = 206, consistency index = 0.74). The analysis included a hypothetical ancestor coded "0" for all characters. The data matrix used is shown in appendix 21.1.

area cladogram using primary BPA. In other words, the null hypothesis that there is a single pattern of vicariance found in the Wet Tropics arthropod fauna is violated, and homoplasy, in the form of dispersal-based or ecologically mediated events, is necessary to explain the data.

Secondary BPA: Modes of Speciation

In order to explain the homoplasy in the primary BPA (based on the protocol outlined in Brooks, Van Veller, and McLennan 2001), we looked for common patterns of area relationships among the fifteen initial phylogenies. The results show that three general patterns (henceforth called "modules") of area relationships (figs. 21.8–21.10) are supported by Wet Tropics arthropods. Module I (fig. 21.8) has the vicariant backbone (A10 (A9, A12)) and is supported by the *T. politulum* Macleay (fig. 21.3E) and *M. masseyensis* Davies (fig. 21.4A) clades. Module II (fig. 21.9) has the vicariant backbone (A6 ((A1, A2) (A8, A10, A12))) and is supported by the *Ae.* NQ9 (fig. 21.3A), *Ae.* NQ4 (fig. 21.3C), *T. involucre* Matthews (fig. 21.3D), *Ap. divergens* Bouchard (fig. 21.4B), *Ap. convexa* Bouchard (fig. 21.4C), and

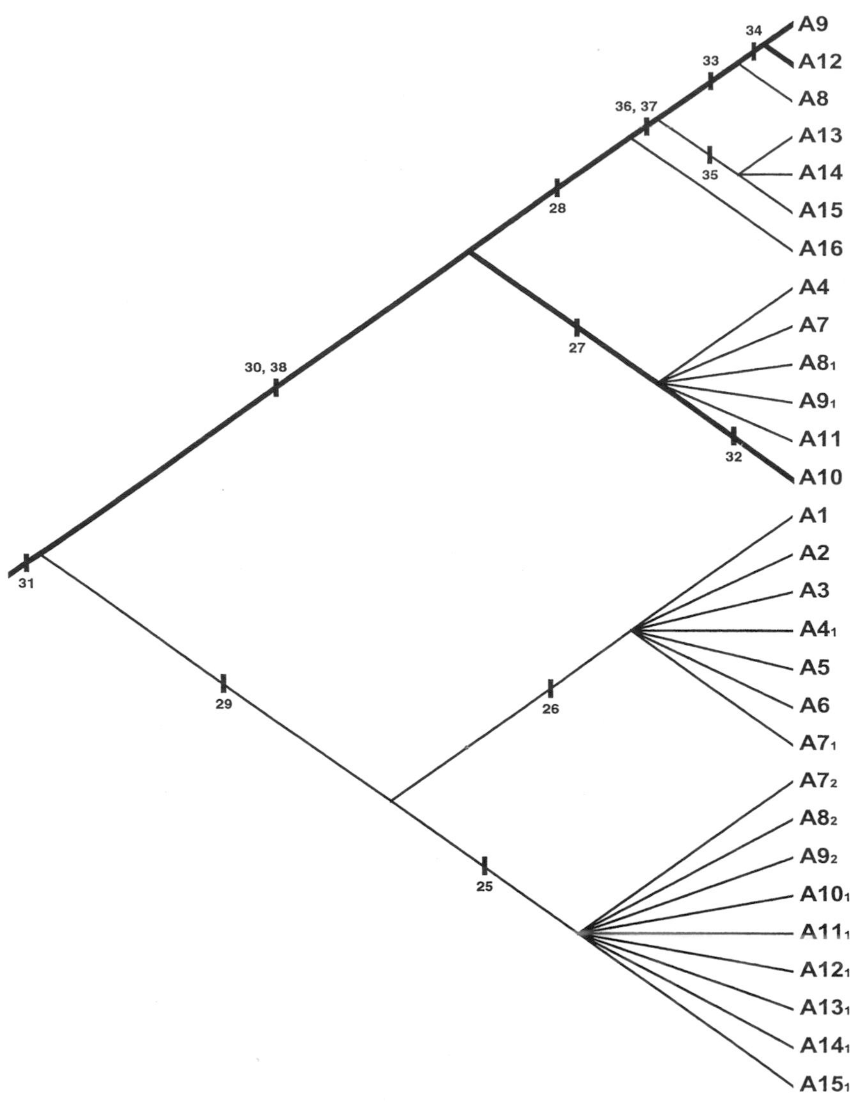

Figure 21.8 Area relationships (module I) derived from secondary BPA analysis supported by the *Temnoplectron politulum* Macleay and *Malarina masseyensis* Davies clades. Terminal nodes represent areas of endemism in figure 21.2. Numbers on the branches represent characters from the two supporting taxon phylogenies (figs. 21.3E and 21.4A). Modes of speciation for all species are summarized in table 21.2. The data matrix coded for all characters is given in appendix 21.2. Thicker branches indicate the vicariant backbone.

Table 21.2 Modes of speciation for taxa in the *Temnoplectron politulum* and *Malarina masseyensis* clades supporting the pattern of area relationships in module I (fig. 21.8)

Species	Vicariance	Sympatric speciation	Peripheral isolate	Post-speciation dispersal	Ancestor
25			A7–A15		?
26			A1–A7		?
27	A10			A4, A7–A9, A11	
28	A9, A12			A8, A13, A14, A16	
32	A10				
33		A9, A12		A8	
34		A9, A12			
35			A13–A15		?

Note: Numbers under "Species" refer to figures 21.3E and 21.4A. Numbers preceded by the letter "A" refer to the areas of endemism in figure 21.2.

P. inermis Baehr (fig. 21.5B) clades. Module III (fig. 21.10) has the vicariant backbone (A10 (A7 ((A3, A4) (A7 (A10, A4))))) and is supported by the *Ae.* NQ2 (fig. 21.3B), *Ap. atramontana* Bouchard (fig. 21.4D), *Ap. bellendena* Bouchard (fig. 21.4E), *P. quadraticollis* Baehr (fig. 21.5A), *P. rufescens* Baehr (fig. 21.5C), *Ap. astraphes* Bouchard (fig. 21.5D), and *C. breviscapa* Davies (fig. 21.6) clades.

In order to account for all of the redundant distributions in module I (fig. 21.8), seven areas have to be duplicated once (A4, A10, A11, A12, A13, A14, and A15) and three areas twice (A7, A8, and A9). All Wet Tropics areas of endemism are represented in the two taxon phylogenies supporting module I (figs. 21.3E and 21.4A) except for area 17. A data matrix coded using the duplicated areas is shown in appendix 21.2. The modes of speciation for species supporting module I are given in table 21.2. Both allopatric (*T. subvolitans* Matthews, *T. aeneopiceum* Matthews, and *M. masseyensis*) and sympatric (*M. monteithi* Davies and *M. collina* Davies) speciation events support the vicariant backbone, with three species (*T. subvolitans, T. aeneopiceum,* and *M. monteithi*) involved in post-speciation dispersal. The best explanation for the distribution patterns shown by species *T. politulum, T. reyi* Paulian, and *M. cardwell* Davies is episodes of peripheral isolation with the ancestor unknown.

Homoplasy in module II (fig. 21.9) can be explained only when A3, A11, and A13 are duplicated once, A2 and A7 twice, A1 and A6 three times, and A4 and A10 four times. Fourteen of the seventeen areas of endemism are represented by the six clades supporting this area cladogram (A9, A14, and A17 do not support any species). A data matrix coded using the duplicated areas is shown in appendix

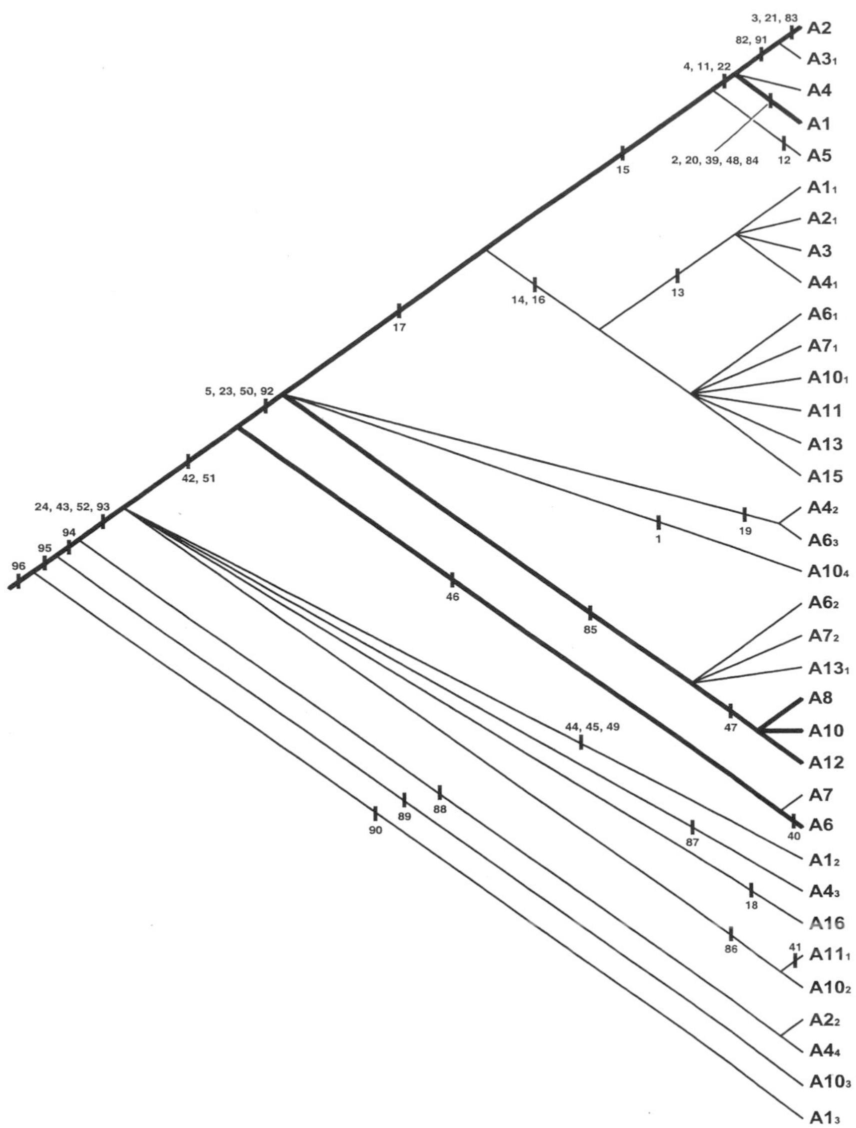

Figure 21.9 Area relationships (module II) derived from secondary BPA analysis supported by the *Aellocoris* NQ9, *Ae.* NQ4, *Temnoplectron involucre* Matthews, *Apterotheca divergens* Bouchard, *Ap. convexa* Bouchard, and *Philipis inermis* Baehr clades. Terminal nodes represent areas of endemism in figure 21.2. Numbers on the branches represent characters from the six supporting taxon phylogenies (figs. 21.3A, 21.3C, 21.3D, 21.4B, 21.4C, and 21.5B). Modes of speciation for all species are summarized in table 21.3. The data matrix coded for all characters is given in appendix 21.3. Thicker branches indicate the vicariant backbone.

Table 21.3 Modes of speciation for taxa in the *Aellocoris* NQ9, *Ae.* NQ4, *Temnoplectron involucre, Apterotheca divergens, Ap. convexa,* and *Philipis inermis* clades supporting the pattern of area relationships in module II (fig. 21.9)

Species	Vicariance	Sympatric speciation	Peripheral isolate	Post-speciation dispersal	Ancestor
1			A10		5
2	A1				
3	A2				
11		A1, A2, A4			
12			A5		15
13		A1, A2, A4		A3	
14		A1, A2, A4		A3, A6, A7, A10, A11, A13, A15	
18			A16		24
19			A4, A6		?
20	A1				
21	A2				
39	A1				
40	A6				
41			A11		43
44		A1			
45		A1			
46	A6			A7	
47	A8, A10, A12				
48	A1				
82		A2		A3	
83		A2			
84	A1				
85	A8, A10, A12			A6, A7, A13	
86			A10, A11		?
87			A4		93
88			A2, A4		?
89			A10		95
90			A1		96

Note: Numbers under "Species" and "Ancestor" refer to figures 21.3A, 21.3C, 21.3D, 21.4B, 21.4C, and 21.5B. Numbers preceded by the letter "A" refer to areas of endemism in figure 21.2.

21.3. Modes of speciation for the species in module II are given in table 21.3. Vicariance explains eleven of the twenty-eight speciation events in table 21.3 (*Ae.* NQ5, *Ae.* NQ6, *T. finnigani* Reid and Storey, *T. monteithi* Reid and Storey, *Ap. robertsi* Bouchard, *Ap. kuranda* Bouchard, *Ap. punctifrons* (Gebien), *Ap. coracina* Bouchard, *Ap. monteithi* Bouchard, *P. vicina* Baehr, and *P. thompsoni* Baehr). Sympatric speciation is involved in seven cases (*Ae.* NQ4, *Ae.* NQ7, *Ae.* NQ8, *Ap.*

convexa, Ap. miser Bouchard, *P. tribulationis* Baehr, and *P. trunci* (Darlington)), whereas peripheral isolate speciation accounts for the other ten events (*Ae.* NQ9, *Ae.* NQ10, *T. involucre, T. lewisense* Reid and Storey, *Ap. divergens, P. planicola* Baehr, *P. spurgeoni* Baehr, *P. striata* Baehr, *P. reticulata* Baehr, and *P. inermis*). The ancestors of the peripheral isolates *Ae.* NQ10, *T. involucre, Ap. divergens, P. spurgeoni, P. reticulata,* and *P. inermis* are 15, 24, 43, 93, 95, and 96 respectively. Ancestors of the peripheral isolates *P. planicola* and *P. striata* could not be determined based on our data. A total of five species demonstrate post-speciation dispersal (*Ae.* NQ7, *Ae.* NQ8, *Ap. punctifrons, P. tribulationis,* and *P. thompsoni*).

Module III (fig. 21.10) requires several area duplications in order to fully explain the data at hand. A1, A2, A6, A8, A9, A15, and A17 need to be duplicated once, A12 and A13 twice, A4 three times, and A7, A10, and A11 four times. All areas are represented except for A14. The data matrix coded using the duplicated areas for all taxa in the six clades supporting this module is given in appendix 21.4. Modes of speciation for the species in module III are given in table 21.4. Vicariant events in module III account for seventeen of the fifty-one species (*Ae.* NQ2, *Ae.* NQ1, *Ap. curvipeos* Bouchard, *Ap. chloros* Bouchard, *Ap. transvestis* Bouchard, *Ap. bellendena, P. alticola* Baehr, *P. heatherae* Baehr, *P. quadraticollis, P. distinguenda* Baehr, *P. sinuate* Baehr, *P. agnicaptius* Baehr, *Ap. spinacra* Bouchard, *Ap. trichopectoris* Bouchard, *Ap. pustulosa* (Carter), *Ap. lophokyma* Bouchard, and *C. breviscapa*). Sympatric speciation is the most likely explanation for seventeen of fifty-one species (*Ap. yeatesi* Bouchard, *Ap. pecticrinis* Bouchard, *Ap. sclerophylla* Bouchard, *Ap. boreafinis* Bouchard, *Ap. hanna* Bouchard, *Ap. elongata* Bouchard, *P. laevigata* Baehr, *P. cooki* Baehr, *P. minor* Baehr, *P. geoffreyi* Baehr, *P. bicolor* Baehr, *P. perstriata* Baehr, *P. rufescens, Ap. tuberculata* Bouchard, *Ap. mia* Bouchard, *C. longiscapa* Davies, and *C. robertsi* Davies). Speciation by peripheral isolation was found in species *Ae.* NQ3, *Ap. atramontana, Ap. junctistriata* Bouchard, *P. lustrans* Baehr, *P. picta* Baehr, *P. ellioti* Baehr, *Ap. oligopunctata* Bouchard, *Ap. mucroskela* Bouchard, *Ap. toni* Bouchard, *Ap. mikrodens* Bouchard, *Ap. costata* (Buck), *Ap. disconvexa* Bouchard, *Ap. australis* (Kulzer), *Ap. rufa* Bouchard, *Ap. gayunda* Bouchard, *Ap. astraphes,* and *C. wunderlichi* Davies. Ancestors of the peripheral isolates *Ap. atramontana, Ap. junctistriata, P. picta, P. ellioti, Ap. oligopunctata, Ap. toni, Ap. mucroskela, Ap. mikrodens, Ap. disconvexa, Ap. australis, Ap. gayunda, Ap. astraphes,* and *C. wunderlichi* were 59, 68, 110, 114, 132, 139, 139, 135, 141, 142, 143, 144, and 150 respectively. Ancestors of the remaining peripheral isolates in module III could not be identified. The species *Ae.* NQ1, *Ap. curvipeos, Ap. transvestis, P. quadraticollis, Ap. pustulosa,* and *C. breviscapa* were involved in post-speciation dispersal.

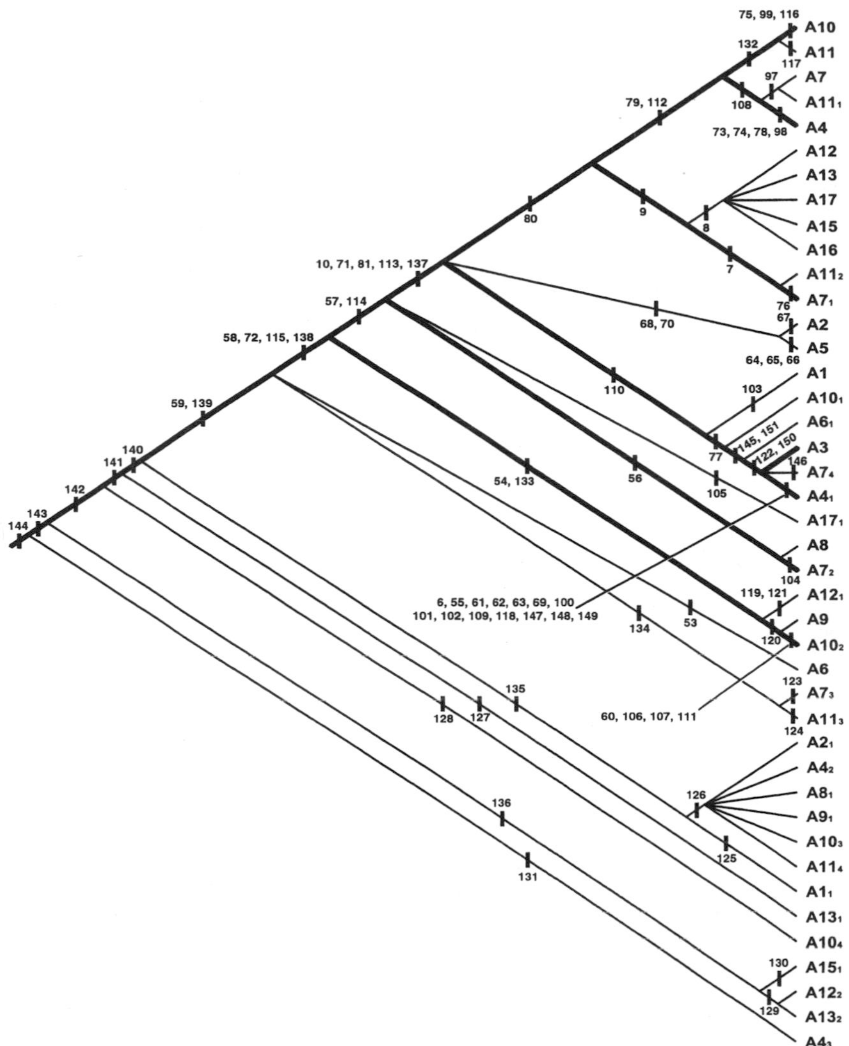

Figure 21.10 Area relationships (module III) derived from secondary BPA analysis supported by the *Aellocoris* NQ2, *Apterotheca atramontana* Bouchard, *Ap. bellendena* Bouchard, *Philipis quadraticollis* Baehr, *P. rufescens* Baehr, *Ap. astraphes* Bouchard, and *Carbinea breviscapa* Davies clades. Terminal nodes represent areas of endemism within the Australian Wet Tropics. Numbers on the branches represent characters from the seven supporting taxon phylogenies (figs. 21.3B, 21.4D, 21.4E, 21.5A, 21.5C, 21.5D, and 21.6). Modes of speciation for all species are summarized in table 21.4. The data matrix coded for all characters is given in appendix 21.4. Thicker branches indicate the vicariant backbone.

Table 21.4 Modes of speciation for taxa in the *Aellocoris* NQ2, *Apterotheca atramontana, Ap. bellendena, Philipis quadraticollis, P. refuescens, Ap. astraphes,* and *Carbinea breviscapa* clades supporting the pattern of area relationships in module III (fig. 21.10)

Species	Vicariance	Sympatric speciation	Peripheral isolate	Post-speciation dispersal	Ancestor
6	A4				
7	A7			A11	
8			A12, A13, A15–A17		?
53			A6		59
54	A10			A12	
55	A4				
56	A7			A8	
60	A10				
61		A4			
62		A4			
63		A4			
64		A5			
65		A5			
66		A5			
67			A2		68
73		A4			
74		A4			
75	A10				
76	A7				
77	A4			A10	
97			A7, A11		?
98	A4				
99	A10				
100		A4			
101		A4			
102		A4			
103			A1		110
104	A7				
105			A17		114
106		A10			
107		A10			
116	A10				
117			A11		132
118	A4				
119		A12			
120	A10			A9	
121		A12			
122			A3, A4		?
123			A7		139
124			A11		139
125			A1		135

(continued)

Table 21.4 *(continued)*

Species	Vicariance	Sympatric speciation	Peripheral isolate	Post-speciation dispersal	Ancestor
126			A2, A4, A8–A11		?
127			A13		141
128			A10		142
129			A12, A13		?
130			A15		143
131			A4		144
145	A3, A4			A6	
146			A7		150
147		A4			
148		A4			

Note: Numbers under "Species" and "Ancestor" refer to figures 21.3B, 21.4D, 21.4E, 21.5A, 21.5C, 21.5D, and 21.6. Numbers preceded by the letter "A" refer to areas of endemism in figure 21.2.

In summary, members of the fifteen initial phylogenies (87 species) evolved through vicariance (36%) as well as sympatric (30%) and peripheral isolate speciation (34%). Vicariance with post-speciation dispersal was found in ten species (*Ae.* NQ1, *T. subvolitans, T. aeneopiceum, Ap. punctifrons, Ap. curvipeos, Ap. transvestis, P. quadraticollis, P. thompsoni, Ap. pustulosa,* and *C. breviscapa*), whereas sympatric speciation with post-speciation dispersal accounted for four of the widespread distributions (*Ae.* NQ7, *Ae.* NQ8, *M. monteithi,* and *P. tribulationis*). Finally, three extinction events are required to explain all of the data. *Ap. robertsi* should have a sister species in A8, A10, and A12 as well as in A2. *Ap. monteithi* should have a sister species in A2.

Secondary BPA: Areas of Endemism

Overall arthropod diversity within each of the areas of endemism (table 21.5) is high (with 20 or more species) in A4 (Carbine Tableland) and A10 (Mount Bellenden Ker). A moderate number of arthropod species (between 10 and 19) were recorded from A1, A2, A7, A11, and A12. A low number of species (between 1 and 9) were recorded from A3, A5, A6, A8, A9, and A13–A17.

A summary of the modes of speciation observed in each of the seventeen areas of endemism is shown in table 21.5. Excluding the species that are present in an area because of post-speciation dispersal (columns II and IV in table 21.5), we can see that vicariant events (column I) account for part of the speciation pattern in only nine of the seventeen areas (A1, A2, A4, A6–A10, and A12). Of

Table 21.5 Summary of species diversity and modes of speciation in seventeen areas of endemism in the Australian Wet Tropics

Area	Number of species	Composition					
		I	II	III	IV	V	VI
A1	14	2, 20, 39, 48, 84		11, 13, 14, 44, 45		90, 103, 125	26
A2	11	3, 21		11, 13, 14, 82, 83			26, 88, 126
A3	6	122, 145			13, 14, 82		26
A4	27	6, 55, 77, 98, 118, 122, 145	27	11, 13, 14, 61, 62, 63, 73, 74, 100, 101, 102, 147, 148	87, 131	87, 131	19, 26, 88, 126
A5	5			64, 65, 66		12	26
A6	8	40, 46	85, 145		14	53	19, 26
A7	13	7, 56, 76, 104	27, 46, 85		14	123, 146	25, 26, 97
A8	8	47, 85	27, 28, 56		33		25, 126
A9	7	28	27, 120	33, 34			25, 126
A10	20	27, 32, 47, 54, 60, 75, 85, 99, 116, 120	77	106, 107	14	1, 89, 128	25, 86, 126
A11	10		7, 27		14	41, 117, 124	25, 86, 97, 126
A12	11	28, 47, 85	54	33, 34,		8, 25, 129	
A13	8		28, 85	119, 121	14	127	8, 25, 35, 129
A14	3		28				25, 35
A15	5				14	130	8, 25, 35
A16	3		28			18	8
A17	2					105	8

Note: The seventeen areas of endemism from figure 21.2 are listed in the first column. Numbers in the six "Composition" columns refer to the phylogenies in figures 21.3–21.6. The modes of speciation were recorded as follows: I, vicariant species in area of origin; II, vicariant species with dispersal; III, sympatric species in area of origin; IV, sympatric species with dispersal; V, peripheral isolates in area of origin; VI, peripheral isolate with area of origin unknown.

these areas, A10 is the only one where allopatric speciation is the dominant mode of speciation (with more vicariant events than sympatric and peripheral isolate speciation events combined). A total of eight areas (A3, A5, A11, A13–A17) were not involved in the allopatric speciation of any arthropod clades studied here.

Sympatric speciation (column III in table 21.5) is the most important mode of speciation for A2, A4, A5, and A12. Of these areas, A4 contains no less than thirteen episodes of sympatric speciation. A3, A6–A8, A11, and A13–A17 do not support any species that have speciated in situ. All areas show evidence of peripheral isolate speciation (columns V and VI in table 21.5). For A6, A7, A11, and A13–A17, this is the most important mode of speciation. A11 and A13–A17 support only peripheral isolate species according to our data.

Based on the results obtained from the secondary BPA analysis, several conclusions about speciation modes within the seventeen areas of endemism in the Australian Wet Tropics can be postulated. First, vicariant speciation accounts for about one-third of all speciation events. Second, there is evidence of substantial within-area diversification, dispersal along a broad front, and peripheral isolate speciation as a result of such dispersal. Third, non-vicariant episodes are recorded for all seventeen areas of endemism, whereas allopatric speciation occurs in only nine of those areas. Finally, there is little evidence of secondary extinction.

DISCUSSION

Origins of the Wet Tropics Arthropod Fauna

Intensive collecting of Wet Tropics arthropods during the past 20 years has provided much insight into the high diversity in this region. Recent taxonomic studies on beetles, bugs, and spiders (see table 21.1) indicate that the Wet Tropics supports a number of endemic genera, genera with the majority of species restricted to this region, and genera with only a small number of species restricted to this region compared with the number found in other regions of Australia and the world. The reasons why certain genera have more species restricted to the Wet Tropics than others are many. These reasons include the time of colonization of the region by the ancestor of the genus as well as the ways in which the genus has responded to historical events.

Before commenting on the processes that have led to the current patterns of arthropod diversity within the Australian Wet Tropics, let us first explore how the ancestral stocks for each clade are likely to have colonized this region. Crisp,

West, and Linder (1999) recently provided a synopsis of the origins of the Australian terrestrial flora. They used the panbiogeography approach (Croizat 1958, 1964) to identify four generalized tracks of colonization corresponding to components of the flora that are also present outside Australia: the South Pacific, Equatorial, Trans-Indian Ocean, and Pan-Temperate tracks. Here, we use Crisp, West, and Linder's four tracks to look at the origins of the Wet Tropics arthropod fauna.

The South Pacific track, which has also been referred to as the Southern, Antarctic, Gondwanan, or Austral component of the biota by other authors, is represented in the Wet Tropics arthropod fauna by taxa that are distributed in New Guinea, New Caledonia, monsoonal Australia, eastern Australia, New Zealand, and temperate South America. Based on the distributional data shown in table 21.1, the following arthropod genera are good examples of this track: *Hypodacnella* Slipinski, *Notuchus* Fennah, *Lachnophoroides* Distant, *Austrovelia* Malipatil and Monteith, *Otira* Forster, and *Mandjelia* Raven. Members of the tribe Adeliini (Coleoptera: Tenebrionidae), which have a well-documented Gondwanan distribution, are also quite diverse at the genus level in the Wet Tropics (e.g., *Apocryphodes* Matthews, *Bellendenum* Matthews, *Bluops* Carter, *Bolusculus* Matthews, *Dicyrtodes* Matthews: Matthews 1998).

Crisp, West, and Linder's Equatorial track is represented by genera that are distributed in Australia, New Guinea, Southeast Asia, India, Madagascar, Africa, and South America. Matthews (2000) recently mentioned that this track is the same as the Younger Northern, Indo-Malayan, and Asian Tertiary component used extensively in the literature previously. Based on distributional data (see table 21.1), the arthropod genera *Megaxenus* Lawrence, *Colasidia* Basilewski, *Australiorylon* Slipinski, *Cerylonopsis* Heinze, *Ctenoneurus* Bergroth, and *Tenagogonus* Stål are representatives of this track living in the Wet Tropics. It should be noted, however, that a significant number of genera of the Equatorial track that do not contain species endemic to the Wet Tropics, but have widespread species in the region, are not listed in table 21.1.

The third general track of Crisp and colleagues, the Trans-Indian Ocean track, contains taxa that have relatives in Africa, Madagascar, on Indian Ocean islands, and in Australia and New Zealand. These are taxa that cross the Indian Ocean but do not occur in Malesia, India, or Sri Lanka. Plant representatives of this track include Proteeae and Ehrharteae (Crisp, West, and Linder 1999). None of the arthropod genera listed in table 21.1 correspond closely to this track.

The last general track mentioned by Crisp and colleagues is the Pan-Temperate track. Terrestrial plant taxa that occupy temperate areas in both the Southern and Northern Hemispheres, such as *Rhododendron, Poa,* and *Festuca,* are included in this track. The best arthropod example of this component of the biota in the Wet Tropics is the blind, flightless, terrestrial water beetle *Terradessus caecus* (Watts 1982). The closest relative of this beetle is known only from high-altitude habitats of the Himalayas (Watts 1982; Rainforest Conservation Society of Queensland 1986).

The information above suggests that Wet Tropics arthropods originated from ancestors that invaded this region at various geologic times. For example, while members of the Equatorial track probably colonized the Wet Tropics within the last 15 million years, members of the Southern Pacific track have probably survived in this region for a much longer period of time. These data are of utmost importance when trying to understand the processes that have led to the current patterns of distribution and diversity within the Wet Tropics.

Can Vicariance Explain the Data?

In theory, species in unrelated clades have the potential to react differently to episodes of large-scale separation of populations based on several factors (e.g., vagility, ecological requirements, genetic variability). However, the existence of general historical biogeographic patterns argues that, despite this potential for clade-specific speciation, geologic evolution and large-scale climate changes through time have initiated vicariant speciation events in many co-occurring clades simultaneously, leading to the current patterns of diversity and distribution on the planet (Cracraft 1985). Based on this hypothesis, both area-history and taxon-history biogeography methods share the same initial null hypothesis: vicariant events are the predominant mode of diversification through allopatric speciation (Van Veller and Brooks 2001).

Our primary BPA analysis resulted in a well-resolved area cladogram (see fig. 21.7). However, the branching pattern obtained from this analysis was poorly supported by the initial taxon phylogenies, revealing a high degree of complexity in the input data and reticulate histories for the areas of endemism. Our secondary BPA analysis highlighted three different patterns of area relationships (see figs. 21.8–21.10) within the Wet Tropics. These three "modules" cannot be linked together based on the current information, even though members of the groups occur in the same areas.

Other empirical examples studied in the past using secondary BPA have yielded single area cladograms with a few area duplications necessary to account for all of the homoplasy (Brooks and McLennan 2001, 2002). However, there is one other instance known in which conflicting input data revealed more than one pattern of area relationships for a particular set of areas of endemism. In revisiting phylogenetic and distributional data from the Australian avifauna previously analyzed by Cracraft (1986, 1988, 1994), Brooks and McLennan (2002) recently demonstrated that two separate patterns of area relationships could be derived using secondary BPA. These two vicariance patterns of evolution for the Australian avifauna had been hypothesized previously by Cracraft (1986, 1988, 1994), but the techniques available to him at the time did not allow for more than one area cladogram. Brooks and McLennan (2002) showed that the two vicariant patterns involve three and five clades respectively. As for the results presented here, Brooks and McLennan's secondary BPA analysis showed that substantial biogeographic complexity needed to be accounted for and that looking for a single pattern of area relationships was not the most parsimonious solution.

Overall, our three modules of evolution (see tables 21.2–21.4) show that vicariance accounts for only 36% of all speciation events. Sympatric speciation and peripheral isolate speciation are also very important in explaining the data at hand (30% and 34% of all speciation events respectively). These findings show that vicariance alone cannot explain the current patterns of diversity in the Wet Tropics arthropod fauna. As pointed out earlier by Erwin (1981), there are a "multitude of biological processes and biological responses to climatic and geological processes," and "hypotheses that invoke single mechanism causal agents to explain distribution patterns of entire biotas . . . cannot do justice to the true complexity of patterns." The nature of the phylogenetic and distributional data for Australian Wet Tropics arthropods presented here, combined with the demonstrated reticulate histories of the areas they live in, confirms Erwin's claim that (at least some) biological systems are indeed extremely complex.

Area Relationships within the Australian Wet Tropics

The first pattern of area relationships obtained with secondary BPA (module I; fig. 21.8) shows that vicariant events involving A9, A10, and A12 are supported by two of the fifteen taxon phylogenies (figs. 21.3E and 21.4A). The vicariant backbone (A10 (A9, A12)) indicates that populations ancestral to the *T. politulum* and *M. masseyensis* clades became isolated in the Mount Bellenden Ker montane block (A10), as well as the Atherton Tableland (A9) plus Walter Hill Range (A12) blocks, during a single historical event. This separation eventually led to a single pattern of allopatric speciation.

The widespread distributions of all four species in the *T. politulum* clade (fig. 21.3E) and the presence of those species in the same areas of endemism require a large number of area duplications in order to explain all of the data. Reid and

Storey (2000) mention that the species pair *T. politulum* + *T. reyi* actually shows a pattern of allopatric speciation. According to these authors, the two species approach to within 10 km of each other in the Lamb Range block (A7), and this distribution pattern is consistent with the historical separation of two main populations by the dry corridor in the Black Mountain block (A6). The pattern shown by *T. subvolitans* + *T. aeneopiceum* was also thought by Reid and Storey (2000) to be associated with a vicariant event, although no clear indications as to the kind or location of a potential historical barrier were mentioned. The suspected involvement of *T. subvolitans* + *T. aeneopiceum* in a vicariant event was confirmed in our secondary BPA analysis. Our results show that *T. subvolitans* probably speciated in A10 and *T. aeneopiceum* in A9 and A12. Extensive post-speciation dispersal occurred in both species (see table 21.2).

The second pattern of area relationships supported by our data (module II; fig. 21.9) involves A1, A2, A6, A8, A10, and A12 in the following pattern: (A6 ((A1, A2) (A8, A10, A12))). This pattern can best be explained by the initial establishment of the *P. inermis* clade (fig. 21.5B) with sequential additions of the other five clades supporting this pattern through colonization. The first addition involved the simultaneous colonization of the *T. involucre* and *Ap. divergens* clades, followed by the *Ap. convexa* clade, then the *Ae.* NQ9 clade, and finally the *Ae.* NQ4 clade (see fig. 21.9).

As mentioned above, different ancestral stocks are likely to have colonized the Wet Tropics region at different geologic times, so it is logical that sequential colonization of the area by different clades could have occurred. This scenario is easier to imagine for groups that are unrelated and became established in the Wet Tropics at different periods. However, some of the clades mentioned above come from a single genus (e.g., *Apterotheca* and *Aellocoris*). This pattern reinforces the argument that different clades (even within a single genus) can be involved in independent histories even within the same areas of endemism.

The observation that montane block A6 (Black Mountain) seems to be involved in the same pattern of allopatric speciation in two taxon phylogenies (*Ap. convexa* and *Ap. divergens*) is somewhat surprising (see fig. 21.9). A6 supports only a very small number of endemic flightless insects compared with neighboring montane blocks (Yeates, Bouchard, and Monteith 2002), is not likely to have supported extensive rainforest refugia during the Pleistocene (Nix and Switzer 1991), and is often referred to as the "Black Mountain Barrier" in the literature (several vertebrates show distinct patterns of molecular diversity on either sides of this area: Joseph, Moritz, and Hugall 1995; Schneider, Cunningham, and Moritz 1998; Schneider and Williams, chap. 20 in this volume). The two clades supporting this pattern are restricted to the diverse beetle genus *Apterotheca* (Bouchard 2002).

The third major pattern of evolution in the Australian Wet Tropics (module III; fig. 21.10) involves A3, A4, A7, and A10 in the following pattern: (A10 (A7 ((A3, A4) (A7 (A10, A4))))). According to the results of the secondary BPA, the three areas A4, A7, and A10 were involved in sequential vicariant events. We hypothesize that A4, A7, and A10 were initially involved in a single vicariant event (probably as a result of habitat expansion and contraction), then subsequently reconnected and reseparated as the result of a different set of vicariant events, leading to the same pattern of area relationships in unrelated arthropod clades.

The pattern of evolution in module III can best be explained by the initial establishment of the *Ap. astraphes* clade (fig. 21.5D) with sequential additions of the other five clades supporting this pattern through colonization. The sequence is as follows: addition of the *Ap. atramontana* clade, then the *Ap. bellendena* clade, then the *P. rufescens* clade, then the *Ae.* NQ2 clade, and finally the *P. quadraticollis* clade.

Evidence for Taxon Pulses?

The results obtained in our historical biogeographic analysis of arthropods of the Australian Wet Tropics indicate the following patterns of evolution: (1) There is no support for a single pattern of area relationships for the 87 species included in the analysis (tested using primary BPA). (2) Three independent patterns of area relationships (modules) are needed to explain the data (different clades support different patterns). (3) Vicariance is not the principal mode of speciation (apart from montane block A10). (4) Within-area speciation (ecological differentiation) is common. (5) Across-area peripheral isolate speciation accounts for a significant number of speciation events. (6) All seventeen areas of endemism have reticulate histories (are uniquely assembled). (7) Widespread species occupy between two and ten areas of endemism. (8) In each of the three secondary BPA area cladograms, there is a single clade that becomes associated with other clades through colonization (sequential addition).

The conclusions above support the "taxon pulse" hypothesis previously proposed by Erwin (1979, 1981, 1985; Erwin and Adis 1982) to explain the general pattern of evolution in beetles of the family Carabidae. The taxon pulse hypothesis is similar to the hypothesis proposed by Darlington (1943) and named the "taxon cycle" by Wilson (1959, 1961; see also Ricklefs, chap. 3 in this volume). In broad terms, both models make two assumptions: that taxa and adaptations arise where the highest diversity for a taxon can be found, and that the distributional ranges of taxa periodically fluctuate around a more stable, continuously occupied habitat (Liebherr and Hajek 1990). During phases of habitat expansion, peripheral patches are colonized. Conversely, during habitat contractions, these patches become isolated (Liebherr and Hajek 1990).

The main difference between the two hypotheses is that taxon cycles are thought to occur over short periods of geologic time and involve active dispersal to colonize new areas. On the other hand, Erwin's taxon pulses may occur over long periods of time and are driven mostly by dispersal along a broad advancing front during expansion of suitable habitat, leading to significant peripheral isolate speciation as a result of such dispersal.

According to our data, the Carbine Tableland (A4) and Mount Bellenden Ker (A10) montane blocks seem to represent two areas of high diversity from which the more peripheral areas are colonized during habitat expansion phases. We believe that, as suggested by Yeates, Bouchard, and Monteith (2002), A4 and A10 have supported significant rainforest patches over a long geologic period (in the Pleistocene and Tertiary; see also Kershaw, Moss, and Wild, chap. 19 in this volume) and have acted as the source of much of the arthropod diversification in the Wet Tropics.

CONCLUSION

The historically contingent nature of taxon pulses means that at any given time, different clades constituting a complex biota are likely to form a mosaic of different stages in the process; thus, no single clade is likely to provide evidence of an entire taxon pulse cycle by itself. We believe that our results provide the best-documented case of insect communities being assembled as a result of taxon pulses because we analyzed multiple clades simultaneously. This analysis provided us with enough clades to see the entire taxon pulse process as envisioned by Erwin (1979, 1981, 1985; Erwin and Adis 1982).

Our study also corroborates others using BPA in suggesting that we cannot infer a simple relationship between degree of endemism and vicariant speciation (Brooks and McLennan 2001; Green, Van Veller, and Brooks, forthcoming). It is apparent that many areas of endemism have reticulated histories of speciation and community assemblage.

Future studies on the phylogenetic relationships, ecological requirements, and habitat partitioning of species within different arthropod clades, as well as the continuation of intensive collecting efforts in all habitat types within the Wet Tropics, will yield much-needed additional information about the processes that have led to the unparalleled diversity in this region.

ACKNOWLEDGMENTS

We would like to thank T. A. Weir, N. M. Anderson, G. B. Monteith, and S. E. Williams for their comments on previous versions of this chapter. V. T. Davies and R. J. Raven provided data on Wet Tropics spiders. Funding to PB was provided by FCAR (Fonds pour la formation de Chercheurs et l'Aide à la Recherche, Canada), OPRS (Overseas Postgraduate Scholarship, Australia), and UQPRS (University of Queensland Postgraduate Scholarship, Australia). PB and DKY were supported by the Cooperative Research Centre for Tropical Rainforest Ecology and Management, Australia.

Appendix 21.1 Data matrix used for the primary BPA analysis

	1	2	3	4	5	6	7	8	9	10	11	12	13	14	15	16	17	18	19	20	21	22	23	24	25	26	27	28	29	30	31	32	33	34	35	36	37	38	39	40	41	42	43	44	45	46	47	48	49	50	51	52	53	54	55
OG	0	0	0	0	0	0	0	0	0	0	0	0	0	0	0	0	0	0	0	0	0	0	0	0	0	0	0	0	0	0	0	0	0	0	0	0	0	0	0	0	0	0	0	0	0	0	0	0	0	0	0	0	0	0	0
A1	0	1	0	1	1	?	?	?	?	?	1	0	1	1	1	1	1	0	0	1	0	1	1	1	0	1	0	0	1	0	1	?	?	?	?	?	?	?	1	0	0	1	1	1	1	0	0	1	1	1	1	1	?	?	?
A2	0	0	1	1	1	?	?	?	?	?	1	0	1	1	1	1	1	0	0	0	1	1	1	1	0	1	0	0	1	0	1	?	?	?	?	?	?	?	?	?	?	?	?	?	?	?	?	?	?	?	?	?	?	?	?
A3	?	?	?	?	?	?	?	?	?	?	0	0	1	1	0	1	1	?	?	?	?	?	?	?	0	1	0	0	1	0	1	?	?	?	?	?	?	?	?	?	?	?	?	?	?	?	?	?	?	?	?	?	?	?	?
A4	?	?	?	?	?	1	0	0	0	1	1	0	1	1	1	1	1	0	1	0	0	0	1	1	0	1	1	0	1	1	1	?	?	?	?	?	?	?	?	?	?	?	?	?	?	?	?	?	?	?	?	?	0	0	1
A5	?	?	?	?	?	?	?	?	?	?	0	1	0	0	1	0	1	?	?	?	?	?	?	?	0	1	0	0	1	0	1	?	?	?	?	?	?	?	?	?	?	?	?	?	?	?	?	?	?	?	?	?	?	?	?
A6	?	?	?	?	?	?	?	?	?	?	0	0	0	1	0	1	1	0	1	0	0	0	1	1	0	1	0	0	1	0	1	?	?	?	?	?	?	?	0	1	0	1	1	0	0	1	0	0	0	0	1	1	1	0	0
A7	?	?	?	?	?	0	1	0	1	1	0	0	0	1	0	1	1	?	?	?	?	?	?	?	1	1	1	0	1	1	1	?	?	?	?	?	?	?	?	?	?	?	?	0	0	1	0	0	0	0	1	1	0	0	0
A8	?	?	?	?	?	?	?	?	?	?	?	?	?	?	?	?	?	?	?	?	?	?	?	?	1	0	1	1	1	1	1	0	1	0	0	0	1	1	?	?	?	?	?	0	0	0	1	0	0	1	1	1	0	0	0
A9	?	?	?	?	?	?	?	?	?	?	?	?	?	?	?	?	?	?	?	?	?	?	?	?	1	0	1	1	1	1	1	0	1	1	0	1	1	1	?	?	?	?	?	?	?	?	?	?	?	?	?	?	?	?	?
A10	1	0	0	0	1	?	?	?	?	?	0	0	0	1	0	1	1	?	?	?	?	?	?	?	1	0	1	0	1	0	1	1	0	0	0	0	0	1	?	?	?	?	?	0	0	0	1	0	0	1	1	1	0	1	0
A11	?	?	?	?	?	0	1	0	1	1	0	0	0	1	0	1	1	?	?	?	?	?	?	?	1	0	1	0	1	1	1	?	?	?	?	?	?	?	0	0	1	0	1	?	?	?	?	?	?	?	?	?	?	?	?
A12	?	?	?	?	?	0	0	1	1	1	?	?	?	?	?	?	?	?	?	?	?	?	?	?	1	0	0	1	1	1	1	0	1	1	0	1	1	1	?	?	?	?	?	0	0	0	1	0	0	1	1	1	0	1	0
A13	?	?	?	?	?	0	0	1	1	1	0	0	0	1	0	1	1	?	?	?	?	?	?	?	1	0	0	1	1	1	1	0	0	0	1	1	1	1	?	?	?	?	?	?	?	?	?	?	?	?	?	?	?	?	?
A14	?	?	?	?	?	?	?	?	?	?	?	?	?	?	?	?	?	?	?	?	?	?	?	?	1	0	0	1	1	1	1	0	0	0	1	1	1	1	?	?	?	?	?	?	?	?	?	?	?	?	?	?	?	?	?
A15	?	?	?	?	?	0	0	1	1	1	0	0	0	1	0	1	1	?	?	?	?	?	?	?	1	0	0	0	1	0	1	0	0	0	1	1	1	1	?	?	?	?	?	?	?	?	?	?	?	?	?	?	?	?	?
A16	?	?	?	?	?	0	0	1	1	1	?	?	?	?	?	?	?	1	0	0	0	0	0	1	0	0	0	1	0	1	1	?	?	?	?	?	?	?	?	?	?	?	?	?	?	?	?	?	?	?	?	?	?	?	?
A17	?	?	?	?	?	0	0	1	1	1	?	?	?	?	?	?	?	?	?	?	?	?	?	?	?	?	?	?	?	?	?	?	?	?	?	?	?	?	?	?	?	?	?	?	?	?	?	?	?	?	?	?	?	?	?

	56	57	58	59	60	61	62	63	64	65	66	67	68	69	70	71	72	73	74	75	76	77	78	79	80	81	82	83	84	85	86	87	88	89	90	91	92	93	94	95	96	97	98	99	100	101	102	103	104	105	106	107	108	109	110
OG	0	0	0	0	0	0	0	0	0	0	0	0	0	0	0	0	0	0	0	0	0	0	0	0	0	0	0	0	0	0	0	0	0	0	0	0	0	0	0	0	0	0	0	0	0	0	0	0	0	0	0	0	0	0	0
A1	?	?	?	?	?	?	?	?	?	?	?	?	?	?	?	?	?	?	?	?	?	?	?	?	?	?	0	0	1	0	0	0	0	0	1	0	1	1	1	1	1	0	0	0	0	0	0	1	0	0	0	0	0	0	1
A2	?	?	?	?	0	0	0	0	0	0	0	1	1	0	1	1	1	?	?	?	?	?	?	?	?	?	1	1	0	0	0	0	1	0	0	1	1	1	1	1	1	?	?	?	?	?	?	?	?	?	?	?	?	?	?
A3	?	?	?	?	?	?	?	?	?	?	?	?	?	?	?	?	?	?	?	?	?	?	?	?	?	?	1	0	0	0	0	0	0	0	0	1	1	1	1	1	1	?	?	?	?	?	?	?	?	?	?	?	?	?	?
A4	0	1	1	1	0	1	1	1	0	0	0	0	0	1	0	1	1	1	1	0	0	1	1	1	1	1	0	0	0	0	0	1	1	0	0	0	0	1	1	1	1	0	1	0	1	1	1	0	0	0	0	0	1	1	1
A5	?	?	?	?	0	0	0	0	1	1	1	0	1	0	1	1	1	?	?	?	?	?	?	?	?	?	?	?	?	?	?	?	?	?	?	?	?	?	?	?	?	?	?	?	?	?	?	?	?	?	?	?	?	?	?
A6	0	0	0	1	?	?	?	?	?	?	?	?	?	?	?	?	?	?	?	?	?	?	?	?	?	?	0	0	0	1	0	0	0	0	0	0	1	1	1	1	1	?	?	?	?	?	?	?	?	?	?	?	?	?	?
A7	1	1	1	1	?	?	?	?	?	?	?	?	?	?	?	?	?	0	0	0	1	0	0	0	1	1	0	0	0	1	0	0	0	0	0	0	1	1	1	1	1	1	0	0	0	0	0	0	1	0	0	0	1	0	0

Appendix 21.1 *(continued)*

	56	57	58	59	60	61	62	63	64	65	66	67	68	69	70	71	72	73	74	75	76	77	78	79	80	81	82	83	84	85	86	87	88	89	90	91	92	93	94	95	96	97	98	99	100	101	102	103	104	105	106	107	108	109	110
A8	1	1	1	1	?	?	?	?	?	?	?	?	?	?	?	?	?	?	?	?	?	?	?	?	?	?	0	0	0	1	0	0	0	0	0	0	1	1	1	1	1	?	?	?	?	?	?	?	?	?	?	?	?	?	?
A9	?	?	?	?	?	?	?	?	?	?	?	?	?	?	?	?	?	?	?	?	?	?	?	?	?	?	?	?	?	?	?	?	?	?	?	?	?	?	?	?	?	?	?	?	?	?	?	?	?	?	?	?	?	?	?
A10	0	0	1	1	1	0	0	0	0	0	0	0	0	0	0	0	1	0	0	1	0	1	0	1	1	1	0	0	0	1	1	0	0	1	0	0	1	1	1	1	1	0	0	1	0	0	0	0	0	0	1	1	0	0	0
A11	?	?	?	?	?	?	?	?	?	?	?	?	?	?	?	?	?	?	?	?	?	?	?	?	?	?	0	0	0	0	1	0	0	0	0	0	0	1	1	1	1	1	0	0	0	0	0	0	0	0	0	0	1	0	0
A12	0	0	1	1	?	?	?	?	?	?	?	?	?	?	?	?	?	?	?	?	?	?	?	?	?	?	0	0	0	1	0	0	0	0	0	0	1	1	1	1	1	?	?	?	?	?	?	?	?	?	?	?	?	?	?
A13	?	?	?	?	?	?	?	?	?	?	?	?	?	?	?	?	?	?	?	?	?	?	?	?	?	?	0	0	0	1	0	0	0	0	0	0	1	1	1	1	1	?	?	?	?	?	?	?	?	?	?	?	?	?	?
A14	?	?	?	?	?	?	?	?	?	?	?	?	?	?	?	?	?	?	?	?	?	?	?	?	?	?	?	?	?	?	?	?	?	?	?	?	?	?	?	?	?	?	?	?	?	?	?	?	?	?	?	?	?	?	?
A15	?	?	?	?	?	?	?	?	?	?	?	?	?	?	?	?	?	?	?	?	?	?	?	?	?	?	?	?	?	?	?	?	?	?	?	?	?	?	?	?	?	?	?	?	?	?	?	?	?	?	?	?	?	?	?
A16	?	?	?	?	?	?	?	?	?	?	?	?	?	?	?	?	?	?	?	?	?	?	?	?	?	?	?	?	?	?	?	?	?	?	?	?	?	?	?	?	?	?	?	?	?	?	?	?	?	?	?	?	?	?	?
A17	?	?	?	?	?	?	?	?	?	?	?	?	?	?	?	?	?	?	?	?	?	?	?	?	?	?	?	?	?	?	?	?	?	?	?	?	?	?	?	?	?	0	0	0	0	0	0	0	0	1	0	0	0	0	0

	111	112	113	114	115	116	117	118	119	120	121	122	123	124	125	126	127	128	129	130	131	132	133	134	135	136	137	138	139	140	141	142	143	144	145	146	147	148	149	150	151
OG	0	0	0	0	0	0	0	0	0	0	0	0	0	0	0	0	0	0	0	0	0	0	0	0	0	0	0	0	0	0	0	0	0	0	0	0	0	0	0	0	0
A1	0	0	1	1	1	0	0	0	0	0	0	0	0	0	1	0	0	0	0	0	0	0	0	0	1	0	0	0	0	1	1	1	1	1	?	?	?	?	?	?	?
A2	?	?	?	?	?	0	0	0	0	0	0	0	0	0	0	1	0	0	0	0	0	0	0	0	1	0	0	0	0	1	1	1	1	1	?	?	?	?	?	?	?
A3	?	?	?	?	?	0	0	0	0	0	0	1	0	0	0	0	0	0	0	0	0	0	0	0	0	0	0	1	1	1	1	1	1	1	1	?	?	?	?	?	1
A4	0	1	1	1	1	0	0	1	0	0	0	1	0	0	0	1	0	0	0	0	1	0	0	0	1	0	1	1	1	1	1	1	1	1	1	?	1	1	1	1	1
A5	?	?	?	?	?	?	?	?	?	?	?	?	?	?	?	?	?	?	?	?	?	?	?	?	?	?	?	?	?	?	?	?	?	?	?	?	?	?	?	?	?
A6	?	?	?	?	?	?	?	?	?	?	?	?	?	?	?	?	?	?	?	?	?	?	?	?	?	?	?	?	?	?	?	?	?	?	1	?	?	?	?	?	?
A7	0	1	1	1	1	0	0	0	0	0	0	0	1	0	0	0	0	0	0	0	0	0	0	1	0	0	0	0	1	1	1	1	1	1	?	1	?	?	?	1	1
A8	?	?	?	?	?	0	0	0	0	0	0	0	0	0	0	1	0	0	0	0	0	0	0	0	1	0	0	0	0	1	1	1	1	1	?	?	?	?	?	?	?
A9	?	?	?	?	?	0	0	0	0	1	0	0	0	0	0	1	0	0	0	0	0	0	1	0	1	0	0	1	1	1	1	1	1	1	?	?	?	?	?	?	?
A10	1	1	1	1	1	1	0	0	0	1	0	0	0	0	0	1	0	1	0	0	0	1	1	0	1	0	1	1	1	1	1	1	1	1	?	?	?	?	?	?	?
A11	0	1	1	1	1	0	1	0	0	0	0	0	0	1	0	1	0	0	0	0	0	1	0	1	1	0	1	1	1	1	1	1	1	1	?	?	?	?	?	?	?
A12	?	?	?	?	?	0	0	0	1	0	1	0	0	0	0	0	0	0	1	0	0	0	1	0	0	1	0	1	1	1	1	1	1	1	?	?	?	?	?	?	?
A13	?	?	?	?	?	0	0	0	0	0	0	0	0	0	0	0	1	0	1	0	0	0	0	0	0	1	0	0	0	0	1	1	1	1	?	?	?	?	?	?	?
A14	?	?	?	?	?	?	?	?	?	?	?	?	?	?	?	?	?	?	?	?	?	?	?	?	?	?	?	?	?	?	?	?	?	?	?	?	?	?	?	?	?
A15	?	?	?	?	?	0	0	0	0	0	0	0	0	0	0	0	0	0	0	1	0	0	0	0	0	1	0	0	0	0	0	0	1	1	?	?	?	?	?	?	?
A16	?	?	?	?	?	?	?	?	?	?	?	?	?	?	?	?	?	?	?	?	?	?	?	?	?	?	?	?	?	?	?	?	?	?	?	?	?	?	?	?	?
A17	0	0	0	1	1	?	?	?	?	?	?	?	?	?	?	?	?	?	?	?	?	?	?	?	?	?	?	?	?	?	?	?	?	?	?	?	?	?	?	?	?

Note: Numbers 1–151 refer to the phylogenies in figures 21.3–21.6. Area numbers (A1–A17) refer to the map in figure 21.2. 0, species absent; 1, species present; ?, clade absent.

Appendix 21.2 Coding for module I (fig. 21.8) supported by the *Temnoplectron politulum* and *Malarina masseyensis* clades

	25	26	27	28	29	30	31	32	33	34	35	36	37	38
A1	0	1	0	0	1	0	1	?	?	?	?	?	?	?
A2	0	1	0	0	1	0	1	?	?	?	?	?	?	?
A3	0	1	0	0	1	0	1	?	?	?	?	?	?	?
A4	0	0	1	0	0	1	1	?	?	?	?	?	?	?
A4_1	0	1	0	0	1	0	1	?	?	?	?	?	?	?
A5	0	1	0	0	1	0	1	?	?	?	?	?	?	?
A6	0	1	0	0	1	0	1	?	?	?	?	?	?	?
A7	0	0	1	0	0	1	1	?	?	?	?	?	?	?
A7_1	0	1	0	0	1	0	1	?	?	?	?	?	?	?
A7_2	1	0	0	0	1	0	1	?	?	?	?	?	?	?
A8	0	0	0	1	0	1	1	0	1	0	0	0	1	1
A8_1	0	0	0	1	0	1	1	0	1	0	0	0	1	1
A8_2	1	0	0	0	1	0	1	?	?	?	?	?	?	?
A9	0	0	0	1	0	1	1	0	1	1	0	1	1	1
A9_1	0	0	1	0	0	1	1	?	?	?	?	?	?	?
A9_2	1	0	0	0	1	0	1	?	?	?	?	?	?	?
A10	0	0	1	0	0	1	1	1	0	0	0	0	0	1
A10_1	1	0	0	0	1	0	1	?	?	?	?	?	?	?
A11	0	0	1	0	0	1	1	?	?	?	?	?	?	?
A11_1	1	0	0	0	1	0	1	?	?	?	?	?	?	?
A12	0	0	0	1	0	1	1	0	1	1	0	1	1	1
A12_1	1	0	0	0	1	0	1	?	?	?	?	?	?	?
A13	0	0	0	1	0	1	1	0	0	0	1	1	1	1
A13_1	1	0	0	0	1	0	1	?	?	?	?	?	?	?
A14	0	0	0	1	0	1	1	0	0	0	1	1	1	1
A14_1	1	0	0	0	1	0	1	?	?	?	?	?	?	?
A15	?	?	?	?	?	?	?	0	0	0	1	1	1	1
A15_1	1	0	0	0	1	0	1	?	?	?	?	?	?	?
A16	0	0	0	1	0	1	1	?	?	?	?	?	?	?

Note: Numbers in the first column refer to the areas of endemism in figure 21.2. Numbers in the first row correspond to terminal taxa in figures 21.3E and 21.4A. The two taxon phylogenies were coded using area duplications based on the secondary BPA methodology.

Appendix 21.3 Coding for module II (fig. 21.9) supported by the *Aellocoris* NQ9, *Ae.* NQ4, *Temnoplectron involucre*, *Apterotheca divergens*, *Ap. convexa*, and *Philipis inermis* clades

	1	2	3	4	5	11	12	13	14	15	16	17	18	19	20	21	22	23	24	39	40	41	42	43	44	45	46	47	48	49	50	51	52	82	83	84	85	86	87	88	89	90	91	92	93	94	95	96
A1	0	1	0	1	1	1	0	0	0	1	0	1	0	0	1	0	1	1	1	1	0	0	1	1	0	0	0	0	1	0	1	1	1	0	0	1	0	0	0	0	0	0	0	1	1	1	1	1
$A1_1$	?	?	?	?	?	0	0	1	1	0	1	1	?	?	?	?	?	?	?	?	?	?	?	?	?	?	?	?	?	?	?	?	?	?	?	?	?	?	?	?	?	?	?	?	?	?	?	?
$A1_2$	?	?	?	?	?	?	?	?	?	?	?	?	?	?	?	?	?	?	?	?	?	?	?	?	1	1	0	0	0	1	0	0	1	?	?	?	?	?	?	?	?	?	?	?	?	?	?	?
$A1_3$	?	?	?	?	?	?	?	?	?	?	?	?	?	?	?	?	?	?	?	?	?	?	?	?	?	?	?	?	?	?	?	?	?	0	0	0	0	0	0	0	0	1	0	0	0	0	0	1
A2	0	0	1	1	1	1	0	0	0	1	0	1	0	0	0	1	1	1	1	?	?	?	?	?	?	?	?	?	?	?	?	?	?	1	1	0	0	0	0	0	0	0	1	1	1	1	1	1
$A2_1$	?	?	?	?	?	0	0	1	1	0	1	1	?	?	?	?	?	?	?	?	?	?	?	?	?	?	?	?	?	?	?	?	?	?	?	?	?	?	?	?	?	?	?	?	?	?	?	?
$A2_2$	?	?	?	?	?	?	?	?	?	?	?	?	?	?	?	?	?	?	?	?	?	?	?	?	?	?	?	?	?	?	?	?	?	0	0	0	0	0	0	1	0	0	0	0	0	1	1	1
A3	?	?	?	?	?	0	0	1	1	0	1	1	?	?	?	?	?	?	?	?	?	?	?	?	?	?	?	?	?	?	?	?	?	?	?	?	?	?	?	?	?	?	?	?	?	?	?	?
$A3_1$	?	?	?	?	?	?	?	?	?	?	?	?	?	?	?	?	?	?	?	?	?	?	?	?	?	?	?	?	?	?	?	?	?	1	0	0	0	0	0	0	0	0	1	1	1	1	1	1
A4	?	?	?	?	?	1	0	0	0	1	0	1	?	?	?	?	?	?	?	?	?	?	?	?	?	?	?	?	?	?	?	?	?	?	?	?	?	?	?	?	?	?	?	?	?	?	?	?
$A4_1$	?	?	?	?	?	0	0	1	1	0	1	1	?	?	?	?	?	?	?	?	?	?	?	?	?	?	?	?	?	?	?	?	?	?	?	?	?	?	?	?	?	?	?	?	?	?	?	?
$A4_2$	?	?	?	?	?	?	?	?	?	?	?	?	0	1	0	0	0	1	1	?	?	?	?	?	?	?	?	?	?	?	?	?	?	?	?	?	?	?	?	?	?	?	?	?	?	?	?	?
$A4_3$	?	?	?	?	?	?	?	?	?	?	?	?	?	?	?	?	?	?	?	?	?	?	?	?	?	?	?	?	?	?	?	?	?	0	0	0	0	0	1	0	0	0	0	0	1	1	1	1
$A4_4$	?	?	?	?	?	?	?	?	?	?	?	?	?	?	?	?	?	?	?	?	?	?	?	?	?	?	?	?	?	?	?	?	?	0	0	0	0	0	0	1	0	0	0	0	0	1	1	1
A5	?	?	?	?	?	0	1	0	0	1	0	1	?	?	?	?	?	?	?	?	?	?	?	?	?	?	?	?	?	?	?	?	?	?	?	?	?	?	?	?	?	?	?	?	?	?	?	?
A6	?	?	?	?	?	?	?	?	?	?	?	?	?	?	?	?	?	?	?	0	1	0	1	1	0	0	1	0	0	0	0	1	1	?	?	?	?	?	?	?	?	?	?	?	?	?	?	?
$A6_1$	?	?	?	?	?	0	0	0	1	0	1	1	?	?	?	?	?	?	?	?	?	?	?	?	?	?	?	?	?	?	?	?	?	?	?	?	?	?	?	?	?	?	?	?	?	?	?	?
$A6_2$	?	?	?	?	?	?	?	?	?	?	?	?	?	?	?	?	?	?	?	?	?	?	?	?	?	?	?	?	?	?	?	?	?	0	0	0	1	0	0	0	0	0	0	1	1	1	1	1
$A6_3$	?	?	?	?	?	?	?	?	?	?	?	?	0	1	0	0	0	1	1	?	?	?	?	?	?	?	?	?	?	?	?	?	?	?	?	?	?	?	?	?	?	?	?	?	?	?	?	?
A7	?	?	?	?	?	?	?	?	?	?	?	?	?	?	?	?	?	?	?	?	?	?	?	?	0	0	1	0	0	0	0	1	1	?	?	?	?	?	?	?	?	?	?	?	?	?	?	?
$A7_1$	?	?	?	?	?	0	0	0	1	0	1	1	?	?	?	?	?	?	?	?	?	?	?	?	?	?	?	?	?	?	?	?	?	?	?	?	?	?	?	?	?	?	?	?	?	?	?	?
$A7_2$	?	?	?	?	?	?	?	?	?	?	?	?	?	?	?	?	?	?	?	?	?	?	?	?	?	?	?	?	?	?	?	?	?	0	0	0	1	0	0	0	0	0	0	1	1	1	1	1
A8	?	?	?	?	?	?	?	?	?	?	?	?	?	?	?	?	?	?	?	?	?	?	?	?	0	0	0	1	0	0	1	1	1	0	0	0	1	0	0	0	0	0	0	1	1	1	1	1
A10	?	?	?	?	?	?	?	?	?	?	?	?	?	?	?	?	?	?	?	?	?	?	?	?	0	0	0	1	0	0	1	1	1	0	0	0	1	0	0	0	0	0	0	1	1	1	1	1
$A10_1$	?	?	?	?	?	0	0	0	1	0	1	1	?	?	?	?	?	?	?	?	?	?	?	?	?	?	?	?	?	?	?	?	?	?	?	?	?	?	?	?	?	?	?	?	?	?	?	?
$A10_2$	?	?	?	?	?	?	?	?	?	?	?	?	?	?	?	?	?	?	?	?	?	?	?	?	?	?	?	?	?	?	?	?	?	0	0	0	0	1	0	0	0	0	0	0	1	1	1	1
$A10_3$	?	?	?	?	?	?	?	?	?	?	?	?	?	?	?	?	?	?	?	?	?	?	?	?	?	?	?	?	?	?	?	?	?	0	0	0	0	0	0	0	1	0	0	0	0	0	1	1

$A10_4$	1	0	0	0	1	?	?	?	?	?	?	?	?	?	?	?	?	?	?	?	?	?	?	?	?	?	?	?	?	?	?	?	?	?	?	?	?	?	?	?	?	?	?	?	?	?	?	?
A11	?	?	?	?	?	0	0	0	1	0	1	1	?	?	?	?	?	?	?	?	?	?	?	?	?	?	?	?	?	?	?	?	?	?	?	?	?	?	?	?	?	?	?	?	?	?	?	?
$A11_1$	?	?	?	?	?	?	?	?	?	?	?	?	?	?	?	?	?	?	?	0	0	1	0	1	?	?	?	?	?	?	?	?	?	0	0	0	0	1	0	0	0	0	0	0	1	1	1	1
A12	?	?	?	?	?	?	?	?	?	?	?	?	?	?	?	?	?	?	?	?	?	?	?	?	0	0	0	1	0	0	1	1	1	0	0	0	1	0	0	0	0	0	0	1	1	1	1	1
A13	?	?	?	?	?	0	0	0	1	0	1	1	?	?	?	?	?	?	?	?	?	?	?	?	?	?	?	?	?	?	?	?	?	?	?	?	?	?	?	?	?	?	?	?	?	?	?	?
$A13_1$	?	?	?	?	?	?	?	?	?	?	?	?	?	?	?	?	?	?	?	?	?	?	?	?	?	?	?	?	?	?	?	?	?	0	0	0	1	0	0	0	0	0	0	1	1	1	1	1
A15	?	?	?	?	?	0	0	0	1	0	1	1	?	?	?	?	?	?	?	?	?	?	?	?	?	?	?	?	?	?	?	?	?	?	?	?	?	?	?	?	?	?	?	?	?	?	?	?
A16	?	?	?	?	?	?	?	?	?	?	?	?	1	0	0	0	0	0	1	?	?	?	?	?	?	?	?	?	?	?	?	?	?	?	?	?	?	?	?	?	?	?	?	?	?	?	?	?

Note: Numbers in the first column refer to the areas of endemism in figure 21.2. Numbers in the first row correspond to terminal taxa in figures 21.3A, 21.3C, 21.3D, 21.4B, 21.4C, and 21.5B. The six taxon phylogenies were coded using area duplications based on the secondary BPA methodology.

Appendix 21.4 Coding for module III (fig. 21.10) supported by the *Aellocoris* NQ2, *Apterotheca atramontana, Ap. bellendena, Philipis quadraticollis, P. rufescens, Ap. astraphes*, and *Carbinea breviscapa* clades

	6	7	8	9	10	53	54	55	56	57	58	59	60	61	62	63	64	65	66	67	68	69	70	71	72	73	74	75	76	77	78	79	80	81
A1	0	?	?	?	?	?	?	?	?	?	?	?	?	?	?	?	?	?	?	?	?	?	?	?	?	?	?	?	?	?	?	?	?	?
$A1_1$	?	?	?	?	?	?	?	?	?	?	?	?	?	?	?	?	?	?	?	?	?	?	?	?	?	?	?	?	?	?	?	?	?	?
A2	?	?	?	?	?	?	?	?	?	?	?	?	0	0	0	0	0	0	0	1	1	0	1	1	1	?	?	?	?	?	?	?	?	?
$A2_1$	?	?	?	?	?	?	?	?	?	?	?	?	?	?	?	?	?	?	?	?	?	?	?	?	?	?	?	?	?	?	?	?	?	?
A3	?	?	?	?	?	?	?	?	?	?	?	?	?	?	?	?	?	?	?	?	?	?	?	?	?	?	?	?	?	?	?	?	?	?
A4	?	?	?	?	?	?	?	?	?	?	?	?	?	?	?	?	?	?	?	?	?	?	?	?	?	1	1	0	0	0	1	1	1	1
$A4_1$	1	0	0	0	1	0	0	1	0	1	1	1	0	1	1	1	0	0	0	0	0	1	0	1	1	0	0	0	0	1	0	0	0	1
$A4_2$	?	?	?	?	?	?	?	?	?	?	?	?	?	?	?	?	?	?	?	?	?	?	?	?	?	?	?	?	?	?	?	?	?	?
$A4_3$	?	?	?	?	?	?	?	?	?	?	?	?	?	?	?	?	?	?	?	?	?	?	?	?	?	?	?	?	?	?	?	?	?	?
A5	?	?	?	?	?	?	?	?	?	?	?	?	0	0	0	0	1	1	1	0	1	0	1	1	1	?	?	?	?	?	?	?	?	?
A6	?	?	?	?	?	1	0	0	0	0	0	1	?	?	?	?	?	?	?	?	?	?	?	?	?	?	?	?	?	?	?	?	?	?
$A6_1$	?	?	?	?	?	?	?	?	?	?	?	?	?	?	?	?	?	?	?	?	?	?	?	?	?	?	?	?	?	?	?	?	?	?
A7	?	?	?	?	?	?	?	?	?	?	?	?	?	?	?	?	?	?	?	?	?	?	?	?	?	?	?	?	?	?	?	?	?	?
$A7_1$	0	1	0	1	1	?	?	?	?	?	?	?	?	?	?	?	?	?	?	?	?	?	?	?	?	0	0	0	1	0	0	0	1	1
$A7_2$	?	?	?	?	?	0	0	0	1	1	1	1	?	?	?	?	?	?	?	?	?	?	?	?	?	?	?	?	?	?	?	?	?	?
$A7_3$	?	?	?	?	?	?	?	?	?	?	?	?	?	?	?	?	?	?	?	?	?	?	?	?	?	?	?	?	?	?	?	?	?	?
$A7_4$	?	?	?	?	?	?	?	?	?	?	?	?	?	?	?	?	?	?	?	?	?	?	?	?	?	?	?	?	?	?	?	?	?	?
A8	?	?	?	?	?	0	0	0	1	1	1	1	?	?	?	?	?	?	?	?	?	?	?	?	?	?	?	?	?	?	?	?	?	?
$A8_1$	?	?	?	?	?	?	?	?	?	?	?	?	?	?	?	?	?	?	?	?	?	?	?	?	?	?	?	?	?	?	?	?	?	?
A9	?	?	?	?	?	?	?	?	?	?	?	?	?	?	?	?	?	?	?	?	?	?	?	?	?	?	?	?	?	?	?	?	?	?
$A9_1$	?	?	?	?	?	?	?	?	?	?	?	?	?	?	?	?	?	?	?	?	?	?	?	?	?	?	?	?	?	?	?	?	?	?
A10	?	?	?	?	?	?	?	?	?	?	?	?	?	?	?	?	?	?	?	?	?	?	?	?	?	0	0	1	0	0	0	1	1	1
$A10_1$	?	?	?	?	?	?	?	?	?	?	?	?	?	?	?	?	?	?	?	?	?	?	?	?	?	0	0	0	0	1	0	0	0	1
$A10_2$	?	?	?	?	?	0	1	0	0	0	1	1	1	0	0	0	0	0	0	0	0	0	0	0	1	?	?	?	?	?	?	?	?	?
$A10_3$	?	?	?	?	?	?	?	?	?	?	?	?	?	?	?	?	?	?	?	?	?	?	?	?	?	?	?	?	?	?	?	?	?	?
$A10_4$	?	?	?	?	?	?	?	?	?	?	?	?	?	?	?	?	?	?	?	?	?	?	?	?	?	?	?	?	?	?	?	?	?	?
A11	?	?	?	?	?	?	?	?	?	?	?	?	?	?	?	?	?	?	?	?	?	?	?	?	?	?	?	?	?	?	?	?	?	?
$A11_1$	?	?	?	?	?	?	?	?	?	?	?	?	?	?	?	?	?	?	?	?	?	?	?	?	?	?	?	?	?	?	?	?	?	?
$A11_2$	0	1	0	1	1	?	?	?	?	?	?	?	?	?	?	?	?	?	?	?	?	?	?	?	?	?	?	?	?	?	?	?	?	?
$A11_3$	?	?	?	?	?	?	?	?	?	?	?	?	?	?	?	?	?	?	?	?	?	?	?	?	?	?	?	?	?	?	?	?	?	?

	97	98	99	100	101	102	103	104	105	106	107	108	109	110	111	112	113	114	115	116	117	118	119	120	121	122	123	124	125	126	127	128	129	130	131	132	133	134	135	136	137	138	139	140	141	142	143	144	145	146	147	148	149	150	151
A1	0	0	0	0	0	0	1	0	0	0	0	0	0	1	0	0	1	1	1	?	?	?	?	?	?	?	?	?	?	?	?	?	?	?	?	?	?	?	?	?	?	?	?	?	?	?	?	?	?	?	?	?	?	?	?
$A1_1$	?	?	?	?	?	?	?	?	?	?	?	?	?	?	?	?	?	?	?	0	0	0	0	0	0	0	0	0	1	0	0	0	0	0	0	0	0	0	1	0	0	0	0	1	1	1	1	1	?	?	?	?	?	?	?
A2	?	?	?	?	?	?	?	?	?	?	?	?	?	?	?	?	?	?	?	?	?	?	?	?	?	?	?	?	?	?	?	?	?	?	?	?	?	?	?	?	?	?	?	?	?	?	?	?	?	?	?	?	?	?	?
$A2_1$	?	?	?	?	?	?	?	?	?	?	?	?	?	?	?	?	?	?	?	0	0	0	0	0	0	0	0	0	0	1	0	0	0	0	0	0	0	0	1	0	0	0	0	1	1	1	1	1	?	?	?	?	?	?	?
A3	?	?	?	?	?	?	?	?	?	?	?	?	?	?	?	?	?	?	?	0	0	0	0	0	0	1	0	0	0	0	0	0	0	0	0	0	0	0	0	0	0	1	1	1	1	1	1	1	1	0	0	0	0	0	1
A4	0	1	0	0	0	0	0	0	0	0	0	1	0	0	0	1	1	1	1	?	?	?	?	?	?	?	?	?	?	?	?	?	?	?	?	?	?	?	?	?	?	?	?	?	?	?	?	?	?	?	?	?	?	?	?
$A4_1$	0	0	0	1	1	1	0	0	0	0	0	0	1	1	0	0	1	1	1	0	0	1	0	0	0	1	0	0	0	0	0	0	0	0	0	0	0	0	0	0	1	1	1	1	1	1	1	1	1	0	1	1	1	1	1
$A4_2$	?	?	?	?	?	?	?	?	?	?	?	?	?	?	?	?	?	?	?	0	0	0	0	0	0	0	0	0	0	1	0	0	0	0	0	0	0	0	1	0	0	0	0	1	1	1	1	1	?	?	?	?	?	?	?
$A4_3$	?	?	?	?	?	?	?	?	?	?	?	?	?	?	?	?	?	?	?	0	0	0	0	0	0	0	0	0	0	0	0	0	0	0	1	0	0	0	0	0	0	0	0	0	0	0	0	1	?	?	?	?	?	?	?
A5	?	?	?	?	?	?	?	?	?	?	?	?	?	?	?	?	?	?	?	?	?	?	?	?	?	?	?	?	?	?	?	?	?	?	?	?	?	?	?	?	?	?	?	?	?	?	?	?	?	?	?	?	?	?	?
A6	?	?	?	?	?	?	?	?	?	?	?	?	?	?	?	?	?	?	?	?	?	?	?	?	?	?	?	?	?	?	?	?	?	?	?	?	?	?	?	?	?	?	?	?	?	?	?	?	?	?	?	?	?	?	?
$A6_1$	?	?	?	?	?	?	?	?	?	?	?	?	?	?	?	?	?	?	?	?	?	?	?	?	?	?	?	?	?	?	?	?	?	?	?	?	?	?	?	?	?	?	?	?	?	?	?	?	1	0	0	0	0	0	1
A7	1	0	0	0	0	0	0	0	0	0	0	1	0	0	0	1	1	1	1	?	?	?	?	?	?	?	?	?	?	?	?	?	?	?	?	?	?	?	?	?	?	?	?	?	?	?	?	?	?	?	?	?	?	?	?
$A7_1$	?	?	?	?	?	?	?	?	?	?	?	?	?	?	?	?	?	?	?	?	?	?	?	?	?	?	?	?	?	?	?	?	?	?	?	?	?	?	?	?	?	?	?	?	?	?	?	?	?	?	?	?	?	?	?
$A7_2$	0	0	0	0	0	0	0	1	0	0	0	0	0	0	0	0	0	1	1	?	?	?	?	?	?	?	?	?	?	?	?	?	?	?	?	?	?	?	?	?	?	?	?	?	?	?	?	?	?	?	?	?	?	?	?
$A7_3$	?	?	?	?	?	?	?	?	?	?	?	?	?	?	?	?	?	?	?	0	0	0	0	0	0	0	1	0	0	0	0	0	0	0	0	0	0	1	0	0	0	0	1	1	1	1	1	1	?	?	?	?	?	?	?
$A7_4$	?	?	?	?	?	?	?	?	?	?	?	?	?	?	?	?	?	?	?	?	?	?	?	?	?	?	?	?	?	?	?	?	?	?	?	?	?	?	?	?	?	?	?	?	?	?	?	?	0	1	0	0	0	1	1
A8	?	?	?	?	?	?	?	?	?	?	?	?	?	?	?	?	?	?	?	?	?	?	?	?	?	?	?	?	?	?	?	?	?	?	?	?	?	?	?	?	?	?	?	?	?	?	?	?	?	?	?	?	?	?	?
$A8_1$	?	?	?	?	?	?	?	?	?	?	?	?	?	?	?	?	?	?	?	0	0	0	0	0	0	0	0	0	0	1	0	0	0	0	0	0	0	0	1	0	0	0	0	1	1	1	1	1	?	?	?	?	?	?	?
A9	?	?	?	?	?	?	?	?	?	?	?	?	?	?	?	?	?	?	?	0	0	0	0	1	0	0	0	0	0	0	0	0	0	0	0	0	1	0	0	0	0	1	1	1	1	1	1	1	?	?	?	?	?	?	?
$A9_1$	?	?	?	?	?	?	?	?	?	?	?	?	?	?	?	?	?	?	?	0	0	0	0	0	0	0	0	0	0	1	0	0	0	0	0	0	1	0	0	0	0	1	1	1	1	1	1	1	?	?	?	?	?	?	?
A10	0	0	1	0	0	0	0	0	0	0	0	0	0	0	0	1	1	1	1	1	0	0	0	0	0	0	0	0	0	0	0	0	0	0	0	1	0	0	0	0	1	1	1	1	1	1	1	1	?	?	?	?	?	?	?
$A10_1$	?	?	?	?	?	?	?	?	?	?	?	?	?	?	?	?	?	?	?	?	?	?	?	?	?	?	?	?	?	?	?	?	?	?	?	?	?	?	?	?	?	?	?	?	?	?	?	?	?	?	?	?	?	?	?
$A10_2$	0	0	0	0	0	0	0	0	0	1	1	0	0	0	1	0	0	0	1	0	0	0	0	1	0	0	0	0	0	0	0	0	0	0	0	0	1	0	0	0	0	1	1	0	0	0	1	1	?	?	?	?	?	?	?
$A10_3$	?	?	?	?	?	?	?	?	?	?	?	?	?	?	?	?	?	?	?	0	0	0	0	0	0	0	0	0	0	1	0	0	0	0	0	0	0	0	1	0	0	0	0	1	1	1	1	1	?	?	?	?	?	?	?
$A10_4$	?	?	?	?	?	?	?	?	?	?	?	?	?	?	?	?	?	?	?	0	0	0	0	0	0	0	0	0	0	0	0	1	0	0	0	0	0	0	0	0	0	0	0	0	0	1	1	1	?	?	?	?	?	?	?
A11	?	?	?	?	?	?	?	?	?	?	?	?	?	?	?	?	?	?	?	0	1	0	0	0	0	0	0	0	0	0	0	0	0	0	0	1	0	0	0	0	1	1	1	1	1	1	1	1	?	?	?	?	?	?	?
$A11_1$	1	0	0	0	0	0	0	0	0	0	0	1	0	0	0	1	1	1	1	?	?	?	?	?	?	?	?	?	?	?	?	?	?	?	?	?	?	?	?	?	?	?	?	?	?	?	?	?	?	?	?	?	?	?	?
$A11_2$	?	?	?	?	?	?	?	?	?	?	?	?	?	?	?	?	?	?	?	?	?	?	?	?	?	?	?	?	?	?	?	?	?	?	?	?	?	?	?	?	?	?	?	?	?	?	?	?	?	?	?	?	?	?	?
$A11_3$	?	?	?	?	?	?	?	?	?	?	?	?	?	?	?	?	?	?	?	0	0	0	0	0	0	0	0	1	0	0	0	0	0	0	0	0	0	1	0	0	0	0	1	1	1	1	1	1	?	?	?	?	?	?	?

A11$_4$	?	?	?	?	?	?	?	?	?	?	?	?	?	?	?	?	?	?	?	?	?	?	?	?	?	?	?	?	?	?	?	?	?	?	?	?	?	?	?	?	?	?	?	?	?	?	?	?	?	?	?	?	?	0	0	0	0	0	0	0	0	0	0	1	0	0	0	0	0	0	0	0	1	0	0	0	0	1	1	1	1	1	?	?	?	?	?	?	?
A12	0	1	0	1	1	?	?	?	?	?	?	?	?	?	?	?	?	?	?	?	?	?	?	?	?	?	?	?	?	?	?	?	?	?	?	?	?	?	?	?	?	?	?	?	?	?	?	?	?	?	?	?	?	?	?	?	?	?	?	?	?	?	?	?	?	?	?	?	?	?	?	?	?	?	?	?	?	?	?	?	?	?	?	?	?	?	?	?	?
A12$_1$	?	?	?	?	?	0	1	0	0	0	1	1	?	?	?	?	?	?	?	?	?	?	?	?	?	?	?	?	?	?	?	?	?	?	?	?	?	?	?	?	?	?	?	?	?	?	?	?	?	?	?	?	?	0	0	0	1	0	1	0	0	0	0	0	0	0	0	0	0	0	1	0	0	0	0	1	1	1	0	0	1	1	?	?	?	?	?	?	?
A12$_2$	?	?	?	?	?	?	?	?	?	?	?	?	?	?	?	?	?	?	?	?	?	?	?	?	?	?	?	?	?	?	?	?	?	?	?	?	?	?	?	?	?	?	?	?	?	?	?	?	?	?	?	?	?	0	0	0	0	0	0	0	0	0	0	0	0	0	1	0	0	0	0	0	0	1	0	0	0	0	0	0	1	1	?	?	?	?	?	?	?
A13	0	0	1	1	1	?	?	?	?	?	?	?	?	?	?	?	?	?	?	?	?	?	?	?	?	?	?	?	?	?	?	?	?	?	?	?	?	?	?	?	?	?	?	?	?	?	?	?	?	?	?	?	?	?	?	?	?	?	?	?	?	?	?	?	?	?	?	?	?	?	?	?	?	?	?	?	?	?	?	?	?	?	?	?	?	?	?	?	?
A13$_1$	?	?	?	?	?	?	?	?	?	?	?	?	?	?	?	?	?	?	?	?	?	?	?	?	?	?	?	?	?	?	?	?	?	?	?	?	?	?	?	?	?	?	?	?	?	?	?	?	?	?	?	?	?	0	0	0	0	0	0	0	0	0	0	1	0	0	0	0	0	0	0	0	0	0	0	0	0	0	1	1	1	1	?	?	?	?	?	?	?
A13$_2$	?	?	?	?	?	?	?	?	?	?	?	?	?	?	?	?	?	?	?	?	?	?	?	?	?	?	?	?	?	?	?	?	?	?	?	?	?	?	?	?	?	?	?	?	?	?	?	?	?	?	?	?	?	0	0	0	0	0	0	0	0	0	0	0	0	0	1	0	0	0	0	0	0	1	0	0	0	0	0	0	1	1	?	?	?	?	?	?	?
A15	0	0	1	1	1	?	?	?	?	?	?	?	?	?	?	?	?	?	?	?	?	?	?	?	?	?	?	?	?	?	?	?	?	?	?	?	?	?	?	?	?	?	?	?	?	?	?	?	?	?	?	?	?	?	?	?	?	?	?	?	?	?	?	?	?	?	?	?	?	?	?	?	?	?	?	?	?	?	?	?	?	?	?	?	?	?	?	?	?
A15$_1$	?	?	?	?	?	?	?	?	?	?	?	?	?	?	?	?	?	?	?	?	?	?	?	?	?	?	?	?	?	?	?	?	?	?	?	?	?	?	?	?	?	?	?	?	?	?	?	?	?	?	?	?	?	0	0	0	0	0	0	0	0	0	0	0	0	0	0	1	0	0	0	0	0	1	0	0	0	0	0	0	1	1	?	?	?	?	?	?	?
A16	0	0	1	1	1	?	?	?	?	?	?	?	?	?	?	?	?	?	?	?	?	?	?	?	?	?	?	?	?	?	?	?	?	?	?	?	?	?	?	?	?	?	?	?	?	?	?	?	?	?	?	?	?	?	?	?	?	?	?	?	?	?	?	?	?	?	?	?	?	?	?	?	?	?	?	?	?	?	?	?	?	?	?	?	?	?	?	?	?
A17	0	0	1	1	1	?	?	?	?	?	?	?	?	?	?	?	?	?	?	?	?	?	?	?	?	?	?	?	?	?	?	?	?	?	?	?	?	?	?	?	?	?	?	?	?	?	?	?	?	?	?	?	?	?	?	?	?	?	?	?	?	?	?	?	?	?	?	?	?	?	?	?	?	?	?	?	?	?	?	?	?	?	?	?	?	?	?	?	?
A17$_1$	?	?	?	?	?	?	?	?	?	?	?	?	?	?	?	?	?	?	?	?	?	?	?	?	?	?	?	?	?	?	?	?	?	?	0	0	0	0	0	0	0	0	1	0	0	0	0	0	0	0	0	1	1	?	?	?	?	?	?	?	?	?	?	?	?	?	?	?	?	?	?	?	?	?	?	?	?	?	?	?	?	?	?	?	?	?	?	?	?

Note: Numbers in the first column refer to the areas of endemism in figure 21.2. Numbers in the first row correspond to terminal taxa in figures 21.3B, 21.4D, 21.4E, 21.5A, 21.5C, 21.5D, and 21.6. The seven taxon phylogenies were coded using area duplications based on the secondary BPA methodology.

22

Biodiversity of the Freshwater Invertebrates of the Wet Tropics Region of Northeastern Australia: Patterns and Possible Determinants

RICHARD G. PEARSON

ABSTRACT

This chapter discusses the patterns of diversity and distribution of the stream invertebrates of the Wet Tropics and examines possible determinants of those patterns. The rainforest streams of tropical Queensland rise in mountains up to 1,600 m in elevation and descend across an ancient landscape of tablelands, gorges, and a coastal floodplain. These streams have probably remained permanent for millions of years. Physically, they are dominated by the flow regime, dictated by a summer wet season and a winter dry season, with mostly perennial flow. Increased wet-season flows are predictable, but cyclonic floods are not. Biologically, streams are characterized by high invertebrate diversity, despite climatic and habitat shifts probably causing historical extinctions of some species. Continuing descriptive and experimental studies are elucidating the determinants of this diversity, which include the geologic constancy of the streams, the equable temperatures, and the constancy of organic inputs, which facilitate constant breeding by many species and lead to evolutionary opportunities and increases in the species pool; seasonally and annually variable flows, which lead to sustained patchiness of habitats and species populations, providing maximum opportunities for colonization by a large proportion of the regional species pool; and random assemblages of species at the site or microhabitat scale, which allow for different assemblages on adjacent habitat patches.

INTRODUCTION

The Wet Tropics biogeographic region of Queensland is ancient and topographically varied, comprising mountains rising to about 1,600 m in elevation, tablelands, steep gorges, and narrow coastal floodplains. It has a seasonal tropical climate, and its rainfall is the highest in Australia. Streams are therefore a conspicuous feature of the region. The majority of streams, except for some of the smallest tributaries, are perennial (in contrast with streams in much of the rest of Australia) and contribute directly to the varied topography as the dominant geomorphological agents. Spectacular flooding occurs during the cyclonic storms that may hit the region in the summer.

Streams add unique biodiversity to the Wet Tropics, including a species-rich endemic invertebrate fauna (e.g., Walker et al. 1995; Pearson, Benson, and Smith 1986), fishes (Pusey and Kennard 1996), amphibians and reptiles (Cogger 1986), the more widely distributed platypus and water rat, and several bird species. The region's streams are also important for human activity, serving as agricultural, industrial, and domestic water supplies, drainage, and as a major focus for recreation and tourism, but they are under increasing pressure as water becomes the major constraint to development in the region. Scientifically, the fauna of these streams is of interest because of its diversity, because the taxonomic impediment that is so common in the tropics is either nonexistent (for fishes) or being surmounted (for invertebrates), and because the streams are probably ancient and enduring (Nott, chap. 17 in this volume).

METHODS

This chapter draws on several studies of streams in the Wet Tropics. Its assessment of broad distributions of invertebrate diversity is based on samples taken in the late dry season (October–November) of 1993 from twenty sites, which included second- to fourth-order streams across a broad latitudinal and altitudinal range of the Wet Tropics (table 22.1). Its description of habitat dynamics is based on benthic surveys in Birthday Creek before and after the wet season in 1991–1992. Temporal variation in the invertebrate assemblage of riffles at one site (Yuccabine Creek) is described from surveys undertaken through the 1980s and 1990s.

Invertebrates were collected by means of standardized replicated kick-sampling using a triangular-framed 200 μm mesh net and were preserved in alcohol for later processing in the laboratory. All invertebrates were identified as far as possible using current keys, with the exception of the Chironomidae, which were identified to subfamily level only. This chapter focuses in part on the Trichoptera. for which species identification of mature larvae is possible and which constitute a diverse group in the Wet Tropics and in Australia in general (Benson and Pearson 1988; Walker et al. 1995). Spatial and temporal variation in invertebrate composition were examined by ordination (nonmetric multidimensional scaling [MDS]).

Previous work has suggested that the high diversity of tropical streams is

Table 22.1 Locations of sampling sites and summary data for invertebrate samples from each site

Creek	Catchment[a]	Latitude (S)	Altitude (m)	No. of taxa per sample ± SE	Abundance per sample ± SE
Gap	Bloomfield*	15°49′	150	19.2 ± 2.2	109.8 ± 26.5
Woobadda	Bloomfield	15°57′	100	28.5 ± 2.5	795.2 ± 169.0
Baird 6	Bloomfield	16°01′	200	20.8 ± 4.8	372.5 ± 155.4
Emmagen	Daintree*	16°04′	200	13.7 ± 1.3	96.0 ± 7.1
Windmill	Mitchell	16°34′	900	13.5 ± 2.1	34.8 ± 7.1
Hartley	Daintree*	16°37′	350	24.2 ± 2.0	462.5 ± 116.7
Rifle	Mitchell	16°41′	550	31.7 ± 3.6	757.0 ± 146.8
Wallaby	Annan	16°47′	300	18.7 ± 2.6	111.3 ± 45.3
Shoteel	Barron	16°57′	450	31.5 ± 0.4	632.0 ± 92.4
Middle	Barron*	17°03′	40	3.8 ± 0.5	12.2 ± 5.2
Breach	Mulgrave	17°05′	700	27.5 ± 3.1	232.7 ± 56.2
Kauri	Barron	17°06′	900	15.0 ± 1.2	174.8 ± 21.8
Malbon Thompson	Mulgrave	17°11′	200	12.7 ± 1.2	88.8 ± 12.8
N. Johnstone (A)	N. Johnstone	17°25′	500	17.2 ± 2.7	93.2 ± 24.9
Charappa	S. Johnstone	17°43′	620	28.3 ± 2.1	316.8 ± 80.3
Pixies	Tully	17°47′	60	29.0 ± 2.9	169.0 ± 39.5
Yuccabine	Herbert	18°12′	600	18.2 ± 1.4	91.0 ± 13.2
Goddard	Murray	18°12′	500	19.5 ± 2.8	63.3 ± 11.5
Camp	Burdekin	19°58′	850	26.8 ± 2.0	183.2 ± 37.4
Birthday	Burdekin	19°58′	800	22.7 ± 3.8	148.2 ± 61.3

[a]An asterisk indicates the nearest major river.

partly due to a high turnover of species from habitat patch to habitat patch (e.g., from stone to stone) (Lake et al. 1994). This turnover may allow the larger species pool to be better represented at the site level. Patchiness of the fauna was examined in Birthday Creek by using individual sample units to determine whether each patch was inhabited by random or highly structured subsets of the species pool. Halved clay house bricks were used as the standard sample unit. These bricks had been found previously to be good surrogates for the natural stony substrate (Rosser and Pearson 1995) and had the advantage of being of fixed dimensions and of having similar histories. Bricks were placed in riffles in Birthday Creek and Camp Creek (a tributary of Birthday Creek, and with similar characteristics; the two sampling sites were about 2 km apart overland). Bricks were left in the stream for 2 months, which was ample time for a typical fauna to colonize (Rosser and Pearson 1995), and were then collected in a dip net. All attached animals were removed and preserved in alcohol for later processing in the laboratory. Samples were collected in February (summer wet season) and June (winter dry season). Numbers of bricks used were 40 at Birthday Creek in February and 44 in June, and 17 at Camp Creek in February and 37 in June. The variation in brick numbers was due to removal of bricks that were left high and dry or swamped by leaf litter, especially at Camp Creek.

RESULTS

Wet Tropics streams are characterized by discharge maxima in the summer wet season and minima in the winter (fig. 22.1). Most streams are perennial, although flow in some small headwater streams can cease in the dry season, leaving a series of unconnected pools; flow in lowland streams toward the periphery of the Wet Tropics can be similarly interrupted. Wet-season flooding is predictable, although the precise timing and magnitudes of floods are not. In particular, the incidence of cyclones, which bring high winds and torrential rainfall, is unpredictable both from year to year and within a summer. Cyclonic rains have dramatic effects on small streams such as Birthday Creek, in which floods substantially rearrange the substrate by moving rocks and sand, scouring rocks and bedrock, and removing leaf litter (fig. 22.2), which is a major habitat and the major input to the food web (Nolen and Pearson 1992).

The number of invertebrate taxa and abundance of invertebrates sampled from each site are shown in table 22.1. There was a substantial range in both richness and abundance, but there was no apparent correlation of either with latitude or altitude ($r < .15$, $P \ll .05$). The variation in number of taxa between sites was largely explained by the variation in abundance ($r = .85$, $p < .01$) (fig. 22.3).

The relationship between species richness of Trichoptera and number of samples is shown in figure 22.4. No asymptote for the number of species was reached, and species accumulated at a steady rate with increasing numbers of samples. Ordination revealed that spatial variation in trichopteran assemblage structure (on axis 1) was related most strongly to altitude (correlation coefficient, $r = .55$, $p < .05$) (fig. 22.5). Table 22.2 provides details of this relationship and shows that more trichopteran species occurred in the upland than the lowland streams. Moreover, samples from streams above 700 m included a greater number of exclusive species than the other altitudinal bands. It is probable that the difference in species richness between high- and low-altitude sites is even larger, given that trichopteran species richness was positively related to sampling effort and fewer samples were collected from the high-elevation sites.

Persistence of the invertebrate assemblage at Yuccabine Creek was examined

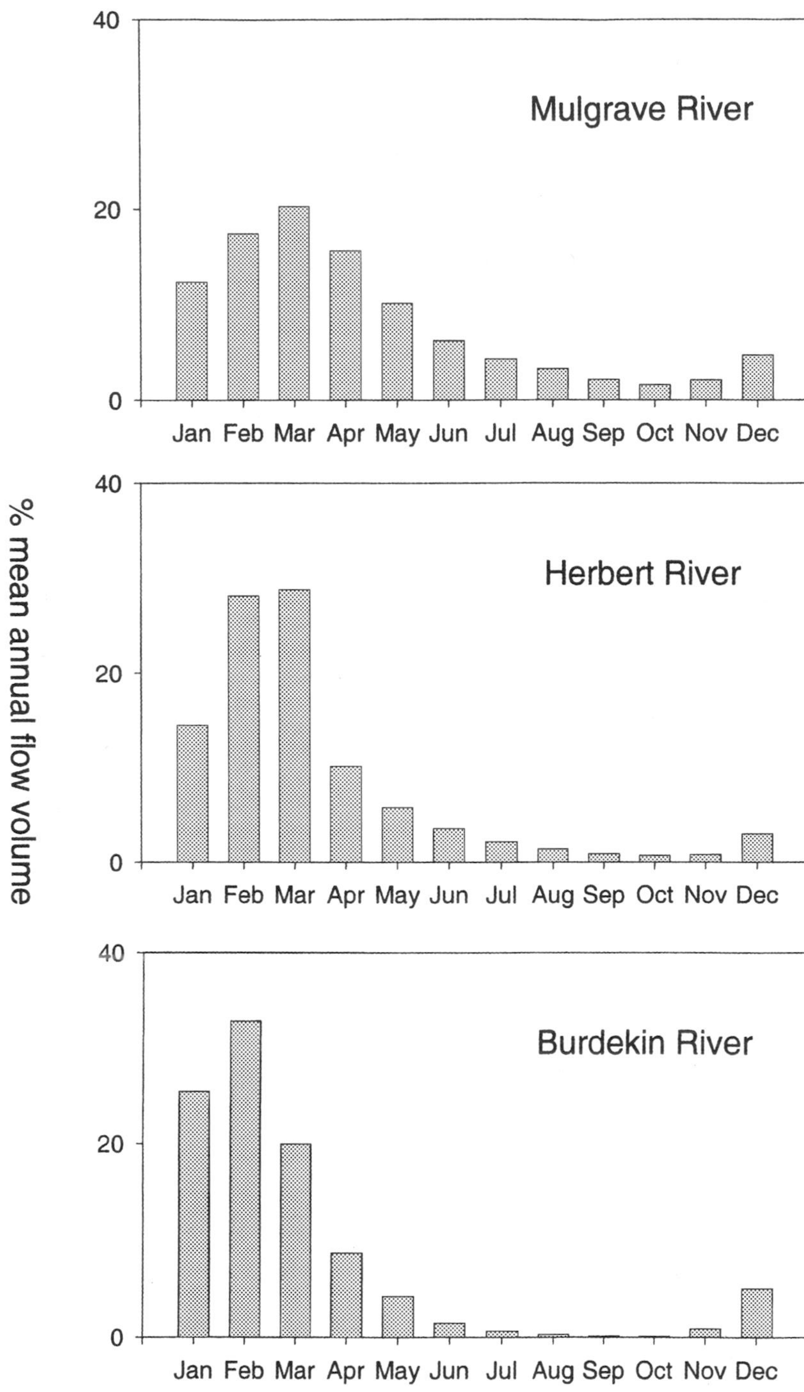

Figure 22.1 Mean monthly flow as a proportion of mean total annual flow in two Wet Tropics rivers (Mulgrave and Herbert) and a savanna river (Burdekin).

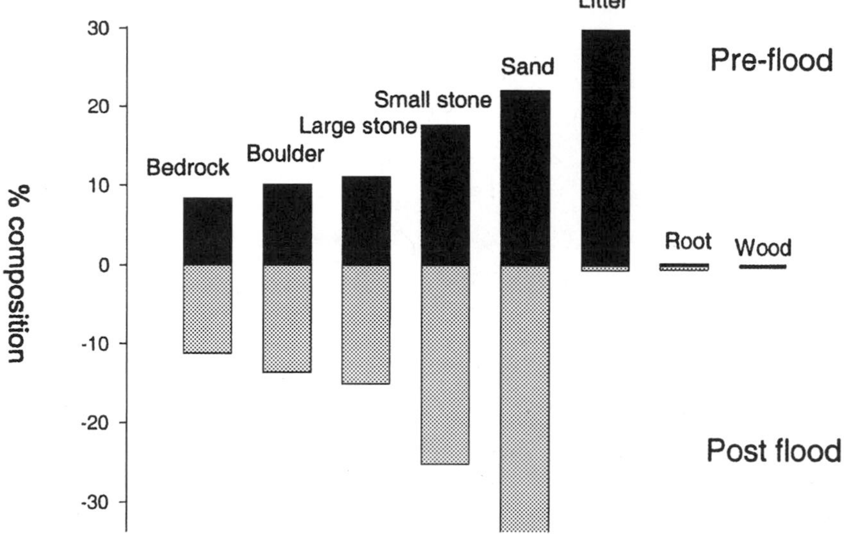

Figure 22.2 Composition of substrate in Birthday Creek before and after a cyclonic flood in March 1994.

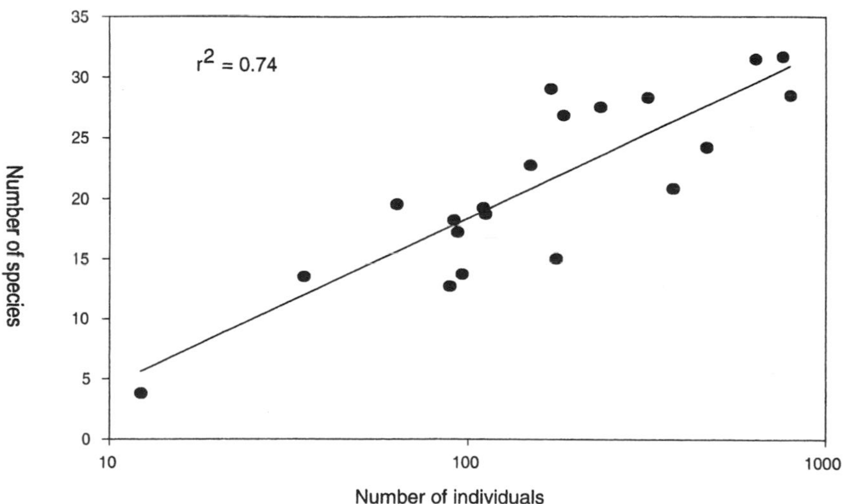

Figure 22.3 Number of invertebrate species versus number of individual invertebrates sampled.

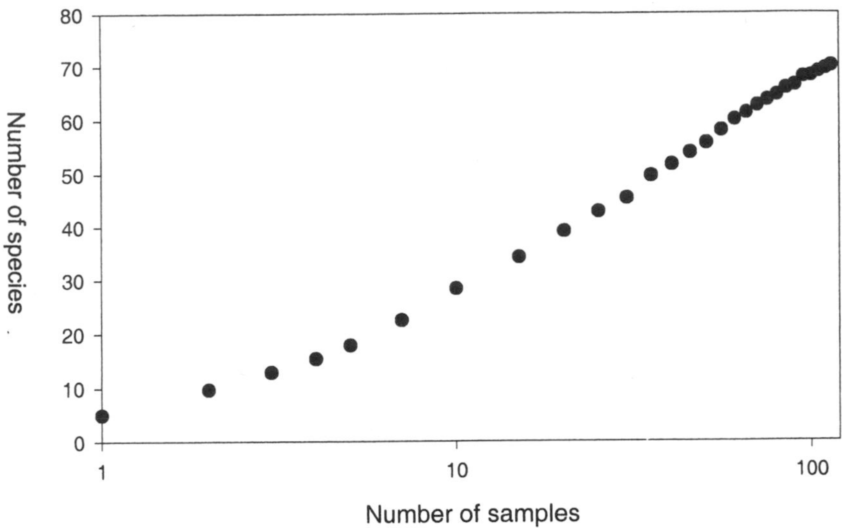

Figure 22.4 Species-area curve for Trichoptera from twenty sites (120 samples).

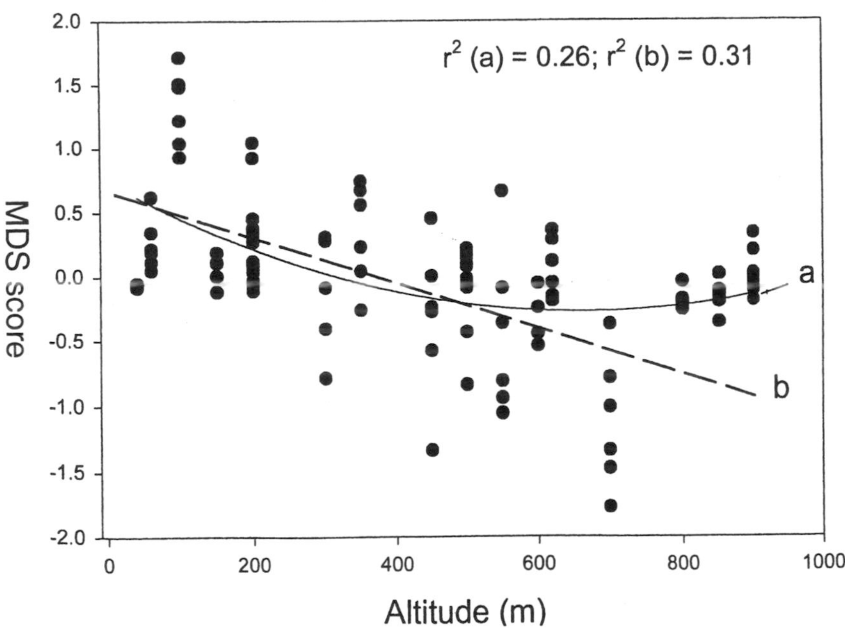

Figure 22.5 Plot of MDS axis 1 scores for 120 samples of Trichoptera versus altitude. Regression (a) includes all scores; regression (b) excludes scores for sites at 700 m altitude and above.

Table 22.2 Number of species of Trichoptera in different arbitrarily selected altitudinal bands

	Altitudinal band (m)			
	< 210	300–600	> 700	> 300
Number of sites	7	8	5	13
Number of species[a]	34	46	42	67
Number of species from total richness not recorded within altitudinal band	37	25	29	4
Number of species exclusive to altitudinal band	4	13	16	37

[a]Total number of species = 71.

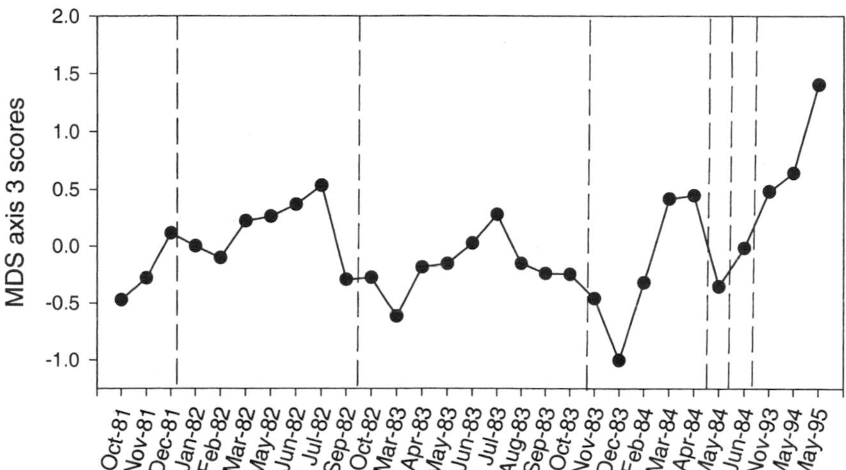

Figure 22.6 Plot of MDS axis 3 scores for invertebrate samples in Yuccabine Creek, 1981–1985. Note that tick intervals represent varying times. Vertical lines represent approximate breaks between years and decades.

using MDS ordination of samples. Temporal variation in the 1980s to 1990s was evident on axis 3 (fig. 22.6). Over the period from October 1981 to June 1984, an annual pattern of change in assemblage composition was evident, but by May 1995, a major change in composition had occurred. This shift was due largely to changes in the abundances of several families, with significant increases in Hydropsychidae and Psephenidae and decreases in Eustheniidae, Leptophlebiidae, Helicopsychidae, and larval Anura (MANOVA, $P < .05$).

The brick samples produced seventy-five taxa in total. The distribution of species abundances among all bricks pooled followed a lognormal distribution, as expected (fig. 22.7), except that two taxa were abundant outliers: the dipteran

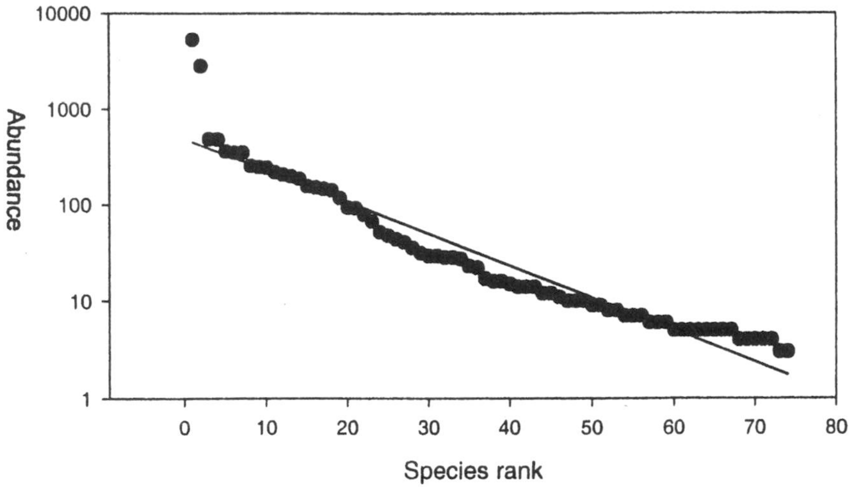

Figure 22.7 Abundances by rank of seventy-five species on all bricks pooled ($r^2 = .92$).

larvae *Simulium* sp. and the Chironomidae. *Simulium* is a rapid colonizer and was particularly abundant in February, when wet-season flows caused some disturbance (it constituted 63% of the fauna at Birthday Creek and 39% at Camp Creek in February, vs. 17% and 6%, respectively, in June). The Chironomidae includes several species, so its total numbers appear inflated because of its treatment as a single taxon.

Occurrences of species on bricks also followed a lognormal distribution (fig. 22.8), indicating that the bricks simply acted as sampling devices across the species pool, producing a pattern of species abundances characteristic of most communities. The incidence of occurrence of animals on bricks was clearly a simple function of abundance: more individuals in a species led to more bricks occupied (fig. 22.9). That is, species appeared not to be clumped on similar substrates. Across these brick samples, a total abundance of about 350 individuals led to greater than 80% of bricks being occupied by a particular species.

The relationship between species richness and abundance at the single-brick scale (fig. 22.10) indicates that maximum richness is achieved with a moderate number of individuals, suggesting that greater densities cause elimination of some species, presumably as a result mainly of competition for space. This relationship holds across seasons and sites, despite differences in overall abundance among them.

These data suggest that the species pool is sampled by bricks relatively randomly according to the relative abundance of the fauna. Such sampling might

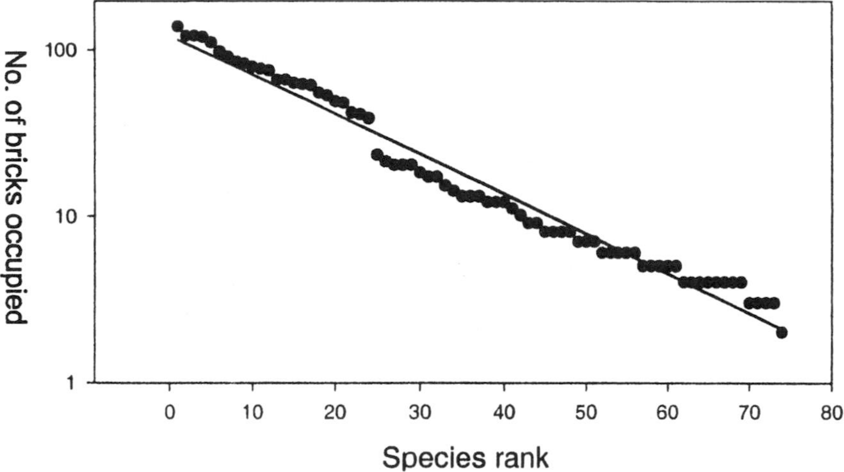

Figure 22.8 Number of bricks occupied by each of seventy-five species (r^2 = .97).

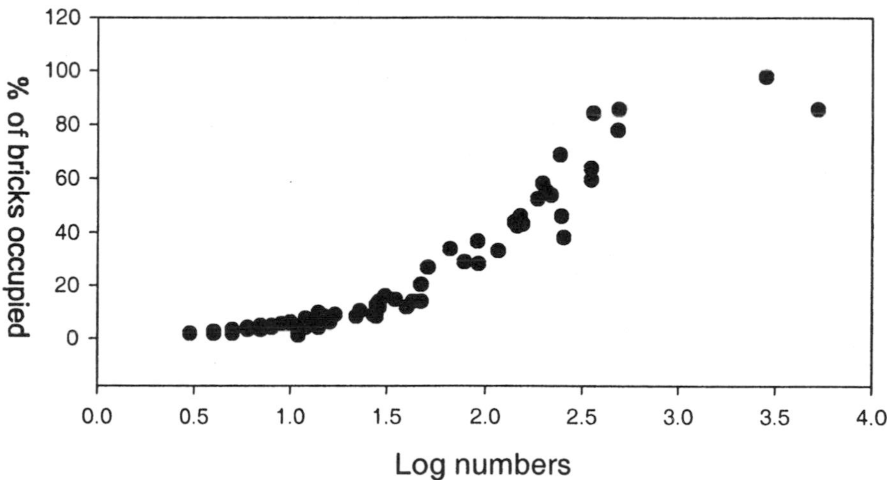

Figure 22.9 Proportion of bricks occupied by seventy-five species in relation to their overall abundances.

occur across trophic levels according to chance encounters leading to communities on each brick that may differ from one another, but in no standard way. This possibility was tested using a measure of nestedness, which essentially determines whether assemblages result from repeated sampling of a common pool or are derived independently (Atmar and Patterson 1993). The theory behind this measure relates to ideas of heat, entropy, and information theory, and the

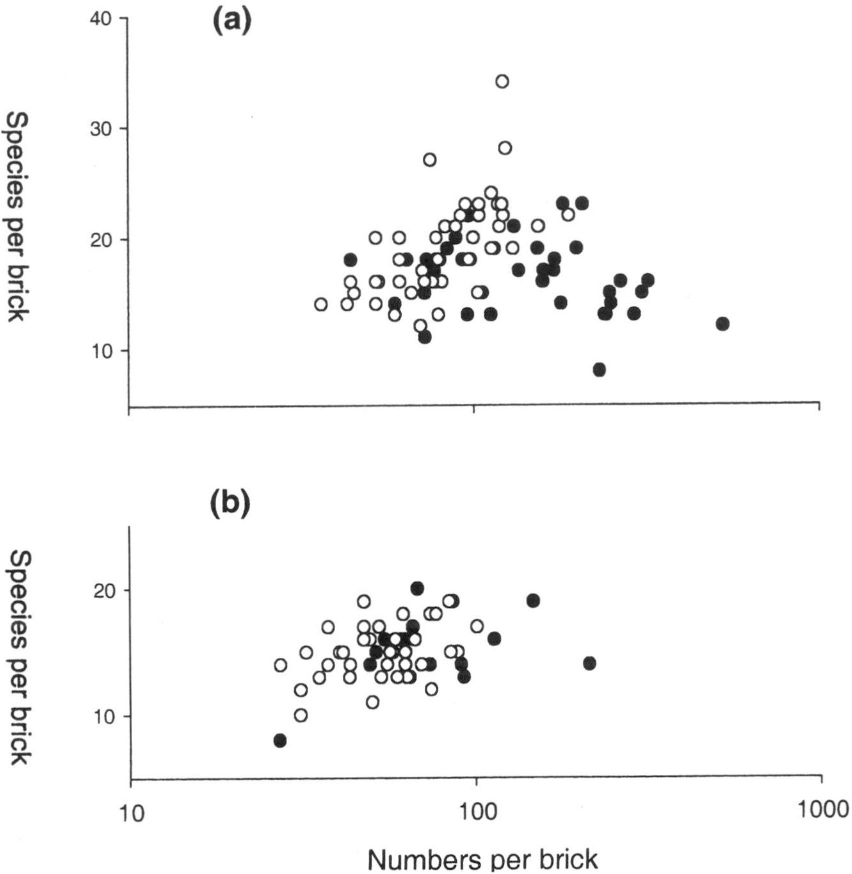

Figure 22.10 Relationship between species richness and total abundance of individuals per brick in (A) Camp Creek and (B) Birthday Creek, in February (solid circles) and June (open circles).

measure is quoted as a matrix temperature. Tests on all brick data pooled and on individual season and site samples revealed that the samples were indeed random, with no ordering to the brick assemblages (table 22.3).

DISCUSSION

Diversity of invertebrates in Wet Tropics streams is high in comparison with similar streams elsewhere in Australia (Lake et al. 1994) and globally (Pearson, Benson, and Smith 1986). A recent study by M. Vinson and C. Hawkins (per-

Table 22.3 Results of nestedness tests on brick samples

Sample	No. of bricks	Matrix temperature (°)	Monte Carlo mean ± SD (°)	*P*
All bricks	138	28.8	71.1 ± 1.6	9.8×10^{-88}
Birthday Ck Feb	40	30.4	68.0 ± 2.6	2.9×10^{-44}
Birthday Ck June	44	32.8	70.4 ± 2.4	2.4×10^{-47}
Camp Ck Feb	17	33.6	61.9 ± 4.8	1.7×10^{-9}
Camp Ck June	37	37.0	69.1 ± 3.1	2.6×10^{-25}

Note: Matrix temperature is a measure of nestedness and is compared with Monte-Carlo-generated temperature. *P* is the probability that the matrix was randomly generated.

sonal communication) revealed that Wet Tropics streams, compared with other tropical streams, have similar or greater local diversity, despite the fact that the Ephemeroptera and Plecoptera are apparently not especially diverse in the Wet Tropics, although current taxonomic work suggests that the Ephemeroptera have higher diversity than has so far been described (F. Christidis, personal communication). As in the rest of Australia, any lack of diversity in these taxa is made up for by high diversity in the Trichoptera and Diptera (Lake et al. 1985). In Wet Tropics streams, the Trichoptera are very diverse (Benson and Pearson 1988; Walker et al. 1995), as are the Chironomidae at the local scale (Pearson, Benson, and Smith 1986; B. McKie and P. Cranston, personal communication), despite the species richnesses of the Chironomidae being unremarkable at the regional scale (P. Cranston, personal communication).

Thus, high diversity in Wet Tropics streams is evident at the regional scale, but it is at the site scale that it is particularly noticeable. Lake et al. (1994) used identical sampling methods at similar temperate and tropical stream sites and showed a significantly greater number of species at the tropical sites. The sampling technique used individual stones as the replicates. The number of species per stone was much the same in the different regions; however, the cumulative species curve for the temperate streams reached an asymptote long before the curve for the tropical streams. That is, even though species richness per stone was much the same, the addition of new species with new stones continued for much longer in the tropics. This conclusion is supported by results from the brick samples, which showed that different units of the substrate essentially supported random samples of the invertebrate fauna, so that while alternative assemblages might occur on different bricks, there was little consistency to the alternatives.

Several possible reasons for high species richness in the tropics have been invoked, including greater constancy and a more equable climate (Begon, Harper, and Townsend 1986). Wet Tropics streams are probably very old systems (see Nott, chap. 17 in this volume), and some of them may have remained permanent throughout their long history (Willmott and Stephenson 1989). Coupled with relatively high temperatures, an almost constant supply of food, as the allochthonous base of the food web is supplied year-round (Benson and Pearson 1993), and continual feeding and breeding activity by insects (Nolen and Pearson 1992; Benson and Pearson 1988), this history has presumably allowed the development of many more generations per annum in the tropics, possibly enhancing opportunities for speciation. Further, while many species seem to be broadly distributed through the Wet Tropics, there appears to be significant restriction of some taxa to the uplands, and some endemics, such as crayfishes, are very restricted in their distributions. For some taxa, therefore, there are local endemics, while for others there is a regional pool of species apparently capable of colonizing new areas from time to time. Thus, in Yuccabine Creek, many chironomid species are transient members of the fauna, exploiting suitable microhabitats (both lotic and lentic) as they occur, as the stream goes through its seasonal cycle of flooding and drying (Pearson, Benson, and Smith 1986).

Maintenance of species diversity depends on ecological factors, and both biotic and abiotic variables may play a part. The streams of the Wet Tropics tend to be more predictable in their flow regime than those in most of the rest of Australia, and many of them maintain good base flows through the dry season. Predictability and constancy may allow for habitat specialization, as Pusey, Arthington, and Read (1995) and Pusey and Kennard (1996) have suggested for stream fishes. For the invertebrates, however, it is probable that habitat patchiness contributes more to the maintenance of high diversity. In many of the smaller streams of the Wet Tropics, although wet and dry seasons are predictable and associated disturbances are well accommodated (Pearson, Benson, and Smith 1986; Rosser and Pearson 1995), the extreme conditions of drought and cyclonic floods are unpredictable. Different scales of floods have different effects on the biota. Normal wet-season floods create some patchy disturbance by clearing out litter and fine particulate material, by rolling stones, and by mild abrasion of the epilithic layer on some stones, thereby opening up new habitats for colonization by a succession of species (Benson and Pearson 1987). Occasional (and unpredictable) large-scale floods may completely rearrange the substrate, causing severe rolling and abrasion, cleaning out all organic sediments (see fig. 22.2), and possibly depositing eroded material such as sand and clay, as happened in Birthday Creek in 1998 (R. G. Pearson, unpublished data). Such events lead to major losses of the biota, providing opportunities for colonization by the pool of available species and for exploitation by otherwise competitively inferior species. This scenario is, of course, somewhat speculative, and is the subject of current research in the Wet Tropics. However, the substantial changes in the community at Yuccabine Creek through a single year (Pearson, Benson, and Smith 1986) and over a decade (see fig. 22.6) demonstrate that there are major temporal changes in assemblages associated with seasonal factors (especially discharge) and medium-term climatic effects. Thus, the possible explanations for the shift in assemblages from the 1980s to the 1990s at Yuccabine Creek include a change in light regime as a result of treefall following Cyclone Winifred (in 1986) and the long drought experienced during the 1980s, when base flows were greatly reduced (R. G. Pearson, unpublished data).

Invertebrate distributions in streams of the Wet Tropics region are patchy at the reach and riffle scale, especially after floods and droughts (Pearson, Benson, and Smith 1986). At a larger scale, across the Wet Tropics, the distribution of invertebrate diversity also appears patchy, despite diversity being very similar from site to site (after correcting for abundance in the samples). The pattern of diversity in the Trichoptera provided detail at the species level that is not yet available for other important taxa. In this family, there was high diversity, which steadily increased with additional samples. The species number recorded from this survey (71 species) is less than that recorded at a single intensively sampled site (78 species at Yuccabine Creek: Pearson, Benson, and Smith 1986), but is still high compared with the average of 41.8 species recorded by Walker et al. (1995) from their ten most species-rich sites in the Wet Tropics. Moreover, the present data were collected from a single habitat type—riffles in second- to fourth-order streams—and therefore a species richness of up to 32 species per site compares very favorably with the richness described by Walker et al. (1995), collected from many different habitat types within each stream reach. This complement of species represents a substantial proportion of the Australian fauna (480 species: Neboiss 1991) from a very small area of the continent.

Patchiness of the stream fauna is a temporal as well as a spatial characteristic of Wet Tropics streams. At one site (Yuccabine Creek), invertebrate assemblages were variable both seasonally and over more than a decade. The longer-term changes involved shifts in feeding mode (Pearson, Benson, and Smith 1986), from fine-particle collector-gatherers to filterers (Leptophlebiidae to Hydropsychidae) and from one set of surface scrapers to another (Helicopsychidae and Anura to Psephenidae), with an attendant decline in some predators (Eustheniidae). Interestingly, it was during this period that general declines in stream-dwelling Anura were recorded in the Wet Tropics and globally (R. A. Alford, personal communication). It is probable that local factors driven by global weather patterns were responsible for the assemblage shifts in Yuccabine Creek, with drought during the 1980s and cyclone-driven treefall (Cyclone Winifred, 1986) being important factors affecting the site. This temporal patchiness contrasts with the greater consistency of discharge in equatorial streams (Yule and Pearson 1996), in which almost daily floods maintain constant physical conditions.

Hearnden and Pearson (1991) showed that the mayflies of Yuccabine Creek had distinct habitat preferences, even though most species could be found in most habitats. It is possible that each species has microhabitat/food refuges that sustain it through the most difficult times of the year, such as the late dry season, when stream discharge and habitat diminish substantially. At such times, biotic factors (competition and predation) may increase in importance. Such a period may provide the eye of the needle of survival for many species while providing a window of opportunity for selective processes and for some opportunistic species (Pearson, Benson, and Smith 1986).

Much of the pattern of patchy distribution and endemism currently observed for terrestrial vertebrates in the Wet Tropics region appears to be a result of extreme rainforest contractions during the Pleistocene (Winter 1988; Williams and Pearson 1997) due to greatly reduced rainfall (Kershaw 1978). However, the apparent similarity of the invertebrate fauna in streams across the Wet Tropics (within upper or lower latitudinal bands), including streams such as Birthday Creek, located in isolated rainforest areas where post-Pleistocene recolonization of many vertebrate species has not occurred (Williams and Pearson 1997), suggests that streams continued to be perennial across the region. The fact that rainforest persisted on mountains during the Pleistocene indicates that rainfall continued to be substantial on those mountains, and this situation would have kept the streams flowing. Biogeographic and geomorphological evidence (Willmott and Stephenson 1989) supports this conclusion. A contemporary view of how such streams might have appeared can be seen at the current periphery of the Wet Tropics. For example, streams at the southern end of the region near Townsville are intermittent in the lowlands, where rainfall is lower and vegetation is more xeric (mostly open woodlands), but perennial in the uplands, where they are fed by higher levels of orographic rainfall, which also sustains rainforest on the mountaintops (in the dry season, upland stream flow disappears underground before the streams reach the lowlands). It is possible, therefore, that extinctions have occurred in the lowlands, resulting in the altitudinal contrast in species richness seen in the Trichoptera.

The habitat and resource patchiness at the site scale mediated by fluctuations in the flow regime is important for invertebrates. A number of features of biodiversity and distribution within the Wet Tropics are common to both invertebrates and fishes. For example, both are diverse compared with elsewhere in Australia, and both are relatively homogeneously distributed across the Wet Tropics. Pusey and Kennard (1996) suggested that, for fishes, this pattern might have arisen because the rivers of the region contain a similar array of habitats and have similar flow regimes as a consequence of their similar spatial relationship to the Great Dividing Range. This suggestion probably holds true for aquatic invertebrates also. Pusey and Kennard (1996) proposed several mechanisms that might allow the dispersal of fishes from one drainage to another and thus maintain the observed faunistic homogeneity. For aquatic invertebrates that have a winged adult phase, such transfer between drainage basins is a simple matter of a short flight. The rate of dispersal from one basin to another, by whatever mechanism, need not have been rapid, given the extensive time that these rivers have been a feature of the landscape and the apparent absence of widespread historical reductions in stream flow.

It seems that a long history of developing diversity (Cranston and Naumann 1991) has helped to determine the current species pool, which is partly maintained and selected at the riffle or stream scale by a variety of ecological factors (Endler 1982c), especially factors involving discharge-related spatial and temporal patchiness. These mechanisms allow a large proportion of the species pool to exist at single sites; therefore, even if the species pool is not always exceptional, the site species richness is.

Since discharge-related habitat modification is of great importance in the Wet Tropics, and given the distinctive flow regime of rivers of the region and the intense pressure being put on streams in the Wet Tropics for water supply, the prospect of increasing stream flow regulation does not bode well for the maintenance of current ecological and ongoing evolutionary processes, especially in view of possible global warming effects on the local climate.

ACKNOWLEDGMENTS

I thank the following people for their contributions: Brad Pusey, Peter Cranston, and Niall Connolly for helpful discussion of this manuscript, and Marcel Bruyn, Jacqui Nolen, Faye Christidis, Niall Connolly, Andi Cairns, Linda Davis, Jeni Holt, and Michelle Reilly for services to invertebrate sampling and processing. The research was supported by grants from the Land and Water Resources Research and Development Corporation, the Australian Research Committee, and the Cooperative Research Centre for Tropical Rainforest Ecology and Management.

23 Dynamics of Seedling Recruitment in an Australian Tropical Rainforest

JOSEPH H. CONNELL, IGOR DEBSKI, CATHERINE A. GEHRING, LLOYD GOLDWASSER, PETER T. GREEN, KYLE E. HARMS, PETER JUNIPER, AND TAD C. THEIMER

ABSTRACT

We have measured seedling recruitment in all the common tree species, at several scales in time and space, over a 39-year period in a tropical rainforest in North Queensland, Australia. This forest has probably never been disturbed by humans. It has a higher tree density and basal area than most rainforest study plots in other regions. Among the factors determining the abundance, distribution, and diversity of trees in forests, initial seedling recruitment is important, because it determines the initial abundance of each species. We found that some common species produced few seedlings, while others produced enormous numbers at very long intervals, ranging up to a decade or more between bouts of recruitment. Few species produced seedlings regularly and evenly. Commoner species had more variable recruitment than did rarer species. To explain the enormous variation in recruitment that we have observed, we have begun to measure the dynamics of the stages preceding recruitment; for example, flowering, fruiting, germination, and initial seedling establishment. The greatest losses seem to occur between the initiation of fruit development and the germination of seeds, rather than earlier, during flowering and pollination, or later, during early survival of seedlings. A controlled field experiment indicated that ground-dwelling mammals and birds reduce rates of seed survival and of seedling recruitment and survival. Some of these effects may happen when these animals mix and move ground litter, as well as when they disperse seeds and feed on seeds and seedlings. Our analyses of long-term trends in population dynamics indicate that, during the period of growth to maturity, rates of growth and mortality rarely act in a frequency-dependent manner. This finding suggests that, if these rates do not change significantly over time, the species composition of the future generation of adult trees may be determined by the species composition of the present generation of seedling recruits: the adult community structure will be "recruitment-limited." Species diversity can be maintained if there is significant negative frequency dependence, with the commoner species having lower rates of recruitment, growth, or survival than the rarer species. Although negative frequency dependence was rare in older stages, it did occur during seedling recruitment. This finding suggests that species diversity may be maintained by forces acting during the very early life stages (flowering, fruiting, seed germination, or initial seedling establishment), which determine the species composition of the seedling recruits. We plan to investigate whether negative frequency dependence occurs during these younger life stages, or as a result of the activities of ground-dwelling vertebrates that affect the abundance of seeds and young seedling recruits.

INTRODUCTION

The abundance and distribution of tree populations is determined by rates of supply (seedling recruitment) and of loss (mortality). However, most studies of forest population dynamics have tended to neglect the supply side of the equation. Yet seedling recruitment determines the initial abundance of each species, setting the stage for all future events in the community dynamics of the trees. Over time, the surviving shade-tolerant seedlings create a mosaic of juveniles of various ages and sizes, known as "advanced regeneration," which serves as a template for the next generation of mature trees.

This idea is not new. Janzen (1970) and Connell (1971) proposed that, in mature tropical rainforests, spatial patterns of mortality of seeds and seedlings determine the species composition of the understory vegetation, which, under some circumstances, can determine that of the older stages. Evidence exists that supports this viewpoint: Uhl et al. (1988) found that 4 years after gap formation in an Amazonian rainforest, 97% of trees taller than 1 m in small gaps had existed as advanced regeneration before the gaps had formed; in a larger gap, 83% of trees taller than 2 m had originated as advanced regeneration. Brokaw and Scheiner (1989) observed that "creation of a gap in the canopy acts on patterns already established in the understory of the closed phase," and believed that these results "suggest the need to explore pervasive processes unrelated to discernible gaps." Connell (1989) observed that "the selection that takes place beneath the closed canopy has a great influence on the suite of species available to take advantage of the short burst of light in a gap."

Recognition of the paucity of studies of recruitment has stimulated an emphasis on "supply-side ecology" (Lewin 1986). Studies of supply-side ecology focus on the degree to which the distributions or abundances of species in a population or community are limited by dispersal or recruitment, relative to the degree to which they are limited by mortality. To date, most studies of supply-side ecology have dealt with limitation of abundance or distribution by recruitment in single-species populations of marine animals (Hjort 1914; Gulland 1982;

Warner and Chesson 1985; Warner and Hughes 1988; Underwood and Fairweather 1989; Caley et al. 1996), or with dispersal limitation of spatial patterns of seedlings in single-species populations of terrestrial plants (Augspurger 1983, 1984a, 1984b; DeSteven 1994; Clark, Macklin, and Wood 1998; Dalling and Wirth 1998; Silvera, Skillman, and Dalling 2003; Dalling, Swaine, and Garwood 1998). Some of the studies have analyzed several species at the same site, but have not compared their relative abundances.

In contrast to these studies of how dispersal limitation affects the spatial distribution of plants in single-species populations, this chapter addresses the question of the degree to which seedling recruitment affects the relative abundance of species in a multispecies assemblage of plants. Will the relative abundance of species of recruits in a community be passed on with little or no change to the future adult generation? It can be, if rates of growth and mortality during the period of growth to adulthood are not frequency-dependent (i.e., if growth or mortality rates do not vary as a function of the abundances of the different species). In that case, the relative abundances of species will probably not change as recruits grow to adulthood; the adult species composition of the community will be "recruitment-limited." In contrast, if growth and mortality in the period between recruitment and adulthood are frequency-dependent, then the relative abundances of adults of each species will probably not accurately reflect that of the recruits; the adult species composition of the community will not be recruitment-limited. (Such inferences require the assumption that rates of growth and mortality remain constant over time.) Apparently, few other studies have addressed the role of recruitment limitation at the community level. The only one we are aware of is that of Hubbell (1997a), who suggested that dispersal limitation might determine the diversity of the tree community in a Panamanian rainforest.

In this chapter we discuss the long-term patterns of variation in seedling recruitment of all tree species at a tropical rainforest study plot in North Queensland, Australia, over a period of 39 years. We also discuss some of the mechanisms underlying the observed variations in seedling recruitment. Finally, we describe two recent investigations of the life stages preceding the age at which the seedlings are first recorded in our long-term censuses and of the effects of vertebrate animals on the seedlings. We have carried out our study over a long period with the aim of documenting recruitment patterns that take place at both short and long time scales. The length of the study also increases the probability of assessing the effects on the tree populations of rare events (e.g., severe storms, droughts, fires, floods, population peaks of herbivores or pathogens, extremes of reproduction or recruitment), and of detecting gradual trends against the noisy background of short-term variations in environmental conditions or population fluctuations, which can have long-lasting effects on community structure and dynamics (e.g., Woods 1989; Hubbell and Foster 1992; Marshall and Swaine 1992; Meggers 1994; Nascimento and Proctor 1994; Nelson et al. 1994; Reader and Bricker 1994; Condit, Hubbell, and Foster 1995, 1996c; Newbery, Prins, and Brown 1996; Magnusson, Lima, and de Lima 1996; Swaine 1996; Walsh 1996b; Harms and Dalling 1997; Dalling, Swaine, and Garwood 1997; Dalling and Denslow 1998; Dalling, Swaine, and Garwood 1998; Schnitzer, Dalling, and Carson 2000; Dalling and Hubbell 2002; Dalling et al. 2002; Daws et al. 2002; DeSteven and Wright 2002; Pearson et al. 2002).

CHARACTERISTICS OF THE DAVIES CREEK FOREST PLOT

Since 1963 we have monitored tropical rainforest dynamics at Davies Creek, 17°05′ S, 145°34′ E, in North Queensland, Australia (Connell 1971, 1989; Connell, Tracey, and Webb 1984; Connell and Green 2000, 2001). The study area is a single plot 1.7 ha in area at 800 m elevation. Measurements at the plot indicate that it has an annual rainfall of about 300 cm. The means of the daily maximum and minimum air temperatures inside the forest over the past 3 years were 22.1°C and 15.2°C, respectively. The soils are relatively infertile and are derived from granite bedrock.

In 1963, all trees greater than 10 cm DBH on the entire 1.7 ha plot were mapped, tagged, measured, and identified; there were 1,426 such trees of 123 species. A similar census was done for all medium-sized trees between 2.5 and 10 cm DBH on permanently marked belt transects constituting 30% of the area of the plot and extending throughout it (see fig. 2 in Connell, Tracey, and Webb 1984 for a map of the transects).

This tropical rainforest site is unusual because it apparently has never been subject to cutting by humans. Our evidence for this is twofold: First, Australian aboriginal peoples were not farmers and entered these forests only to hunt and gather, so there was no cutting of trees for shifting cultivation, as occurred in many other tropical rainforests (Flood 1995). Second, many of the common large trees at Davies Creek are highly desirable timber species and would have been among the first to be cut if European timber cutters had logged the forest (R. Keenan, Queensland Department of Forestry [QDF], personal communication). The area has been protected by the QDF since 1952 as a plot for monitoring growth, surrounded by a buffer zone; it is now completely protected in a World Heritage Area.

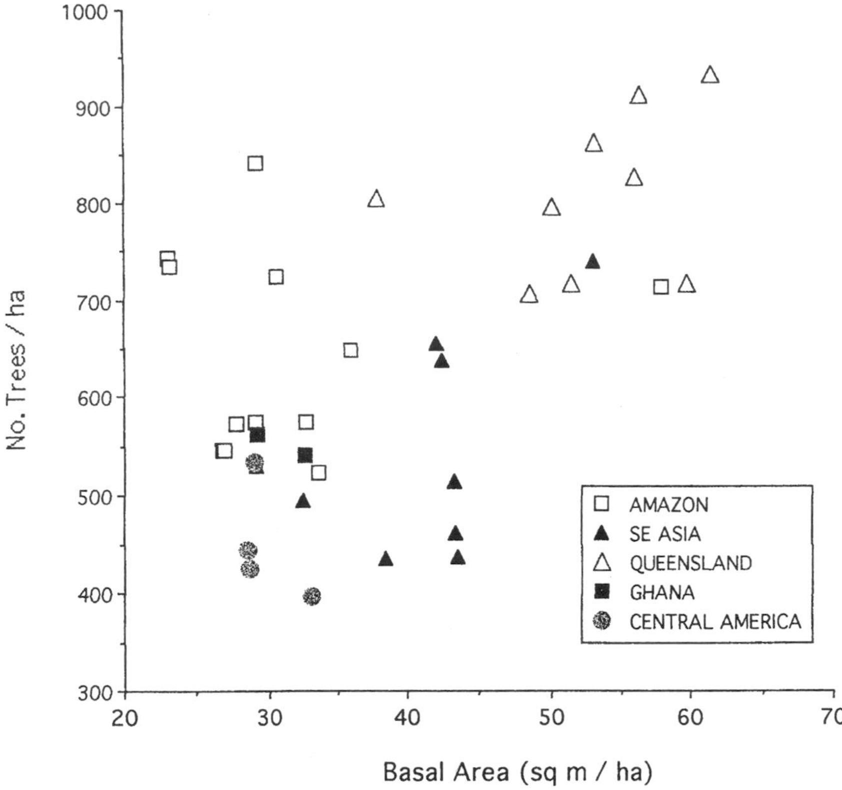

Figure 23.1 Density (no. of trees/ha) and basal area (m^2/ha) of trees greater than 10 cm DBH in study plots in various regions of the world. (Data from Nicholson, Henry, and Rudder 1988; Lieberman et al. 1990; Phillips et al. 1994; J. H. Connell, unpublished data.)

The abundance of trees greater than 10 cm in diameter at breast height (DBH) in most of the rainforests sampled in North Queensland is greater than that found elsewhere in the world, both in density (number/ha) and biomass (basal area/ha) (fig. 23.1, table 23.1). The species richness (number of species/ha) is less than that found in the large continuous rainforest regions of Southeast Asia, Africa, and South America, but similar to that of other regions on the fringes of those central regions, such as Central America and Ghana (fig. 23.2, table 23.1).

The dynamics of trees greater than 10 cm DBH at Davies Creek are slower than those at two other well-studied rainforest sites, at La Selva, Costa Rica (D. Lieberman et al. 1990; Lieberman and Lieberman 1987), and Gunung Palung,

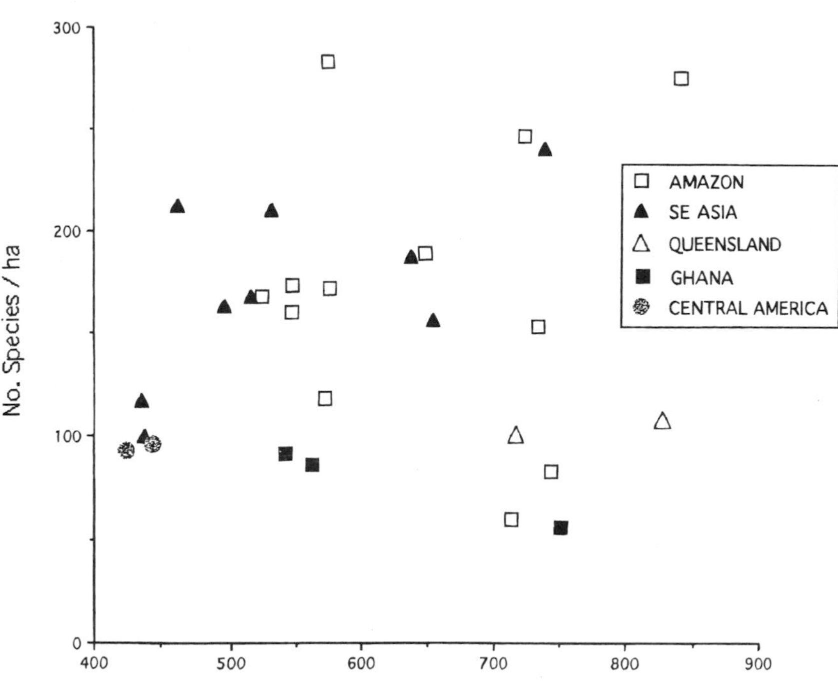

Figure 23.2 Species richness (no. species/ha) and density (no. trees/ha) of trees greater than 10 cm DBH in study plots in various regions of the world. (Data from Nicholson, Henry, and Rudder 1988; Foster and Hubbell 1990; Lieberman et al. 1990; Phillips et al. 1994; J. H. Connell, unpublished data.)

Borneo (C. Webb, unpublished data). The annual rates of mortality, stem growth, and opening of the canopy by treefalls are all lower at Davies Creek than at those two sites (table 23.1; canopy gaps as defined by Brokaw 1982).

It has been suggested that turnover of trees greater than 10 cm DBH has increased over the past 20–40 years in a high proportion of tropical rainforests of the world (Phillips and Gentry 1994). Phillips and Gentry estimated turnover as the mean of mortality and recruitment by growth; since mortality and recruitment were highly correlated in their analysis, either can suffice as a measure of turnover. We calculated the turnover in our tropical plot, measured as annual mortality rate of trees greater than 10 cm DBH, applying the equation used by Phillips and Gentry. Since we had measured mortality at fifteen censuses, but recruitment by growth at only three censuses, mortality was clearly the better

Table 23.1 Comparisons of abundance and diversity and rates of mortality, growth, and treefall gap formation for trees greater than 10 cm DBH in rainforest study plots at Davies Creek, Queensland, Australia, Barro Colorado Island, Panama, La Selva, Costa Rica, and Gunung Palung, Borneo

	Davies Creek	BCI	La Selva	Gunung Palung
	Statics			
1. No. stems/ha	716	536	450	638
2. Basal area (m^2/ha)	59.7	28.6	30.1	42.5
3. No. species/ha	101	92	92	187
4. No. species/500 stems	93		103	
	Dynamics			
5. % mortality/yr	0.69		2.03	1.1
6. Stem growth (DBH, mm/yr)	0.5		2.65	0.74
7. Gap formation rate (% area/yr)	0.4	0.73	0.96	

Sources: J. H. Connell, unpublished data, for Davies Creek; Lang and Knight 1983; Hubbell, Condit, and Foster 1990 for BCI; D. Lieberman et al. 1985, 1990; Lieberman and Lieberman 1987; Phillips et al. 1994 for La Selva; C. Webb, unpublished data, for Gunung Palung.

measure to investigate long-term trends in turnover in our study. In contrast to Phillips and Gentry, we found no evidence of a rising trend in turnover (as indicated by mortality) at our tropical plot from 1963 to 1996 (fig. 23.3).

SEEDLING RECRUITMENT

Long-Term Patterns of Variation

In 1965, all saplings and seedlings less than 2.5 cm DBH, including all sizes down to tiny, newly germinated seedlings, were mapped and tagged on permanently marked narrower transects, which constitute 9.6% of the total plot area and are nested within the transects for medium-sized trees. Thus, all woody plants except vines were mapped, the smaller size classes along transects located throughout the map of large trees. This arrangement ensured that the seedlings produced by the majority of adult trees on the plot would be adequately sampled in subsequent censuses. At intervals of 1 to 4 years thereafter, the survival of all previously mapped and tagged individuals was checked, and in addition, all newly recruited seedlings that had germinated and survived in the interval since the previous census were mapped, tagged, measured, and identified on precisely the same permanently marked transects used in the original mapping. These censuses of new recruits, which were done twenty-one times between 1965 and

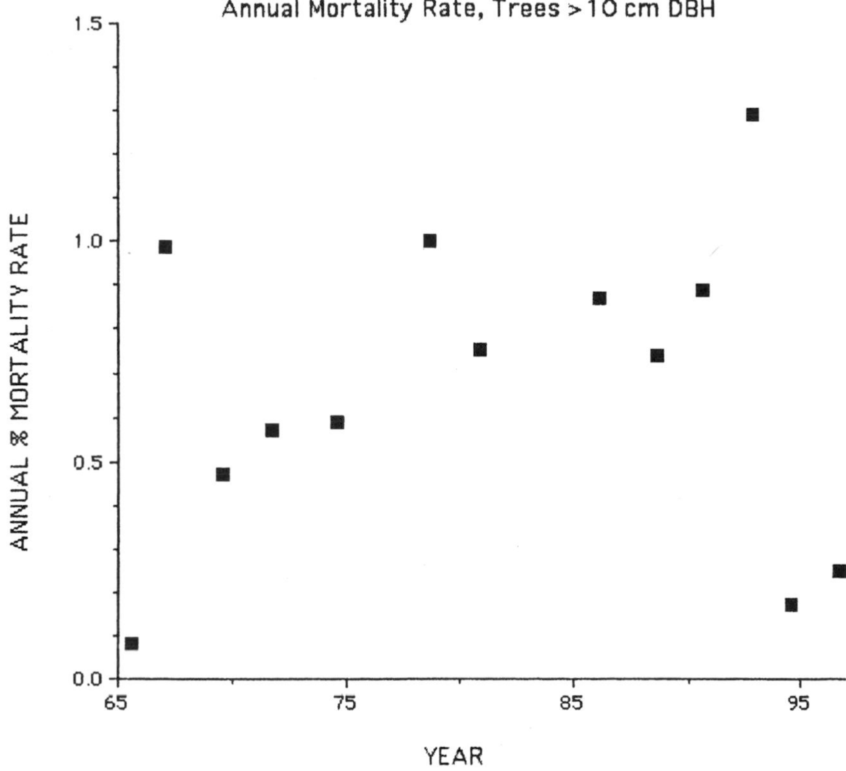

Figure 23.3 Changes over time in the annual mortality rates of trees greater than 10 cm DBH at the Davies Creek study plot. There was no significant correlation between the two variables.

2002, provide information about the temporal and spatial variation in seedling recruitment of all species of trees. In addition, all trees taller than 6 m on one portion of the plot have been censused by the QDF since 1952; this record of 45 years of continuous monitoring is one of the longest in any tropical forest (Phillips and Gentry 1994). Details of topography, census dates, and weather patterns are given in Connell, Tracey, and Webb (1984) and Connell and Green (2000).

Recruitment of seedlings in our standard periodic censuses was extremely variable within and among species. Of the 121 species that had at least two adults on the study plot in 1963, some have had little seedling recruitment over the past 31 years, while others have had high recruitment. For the 46 species for which we had a sufficient sample size (> 100 seedlings in all censuses combined), there was considerable temporal variation in recruitment within species: the coefficient of variation of the logarithm of the number of recruits per census ranged

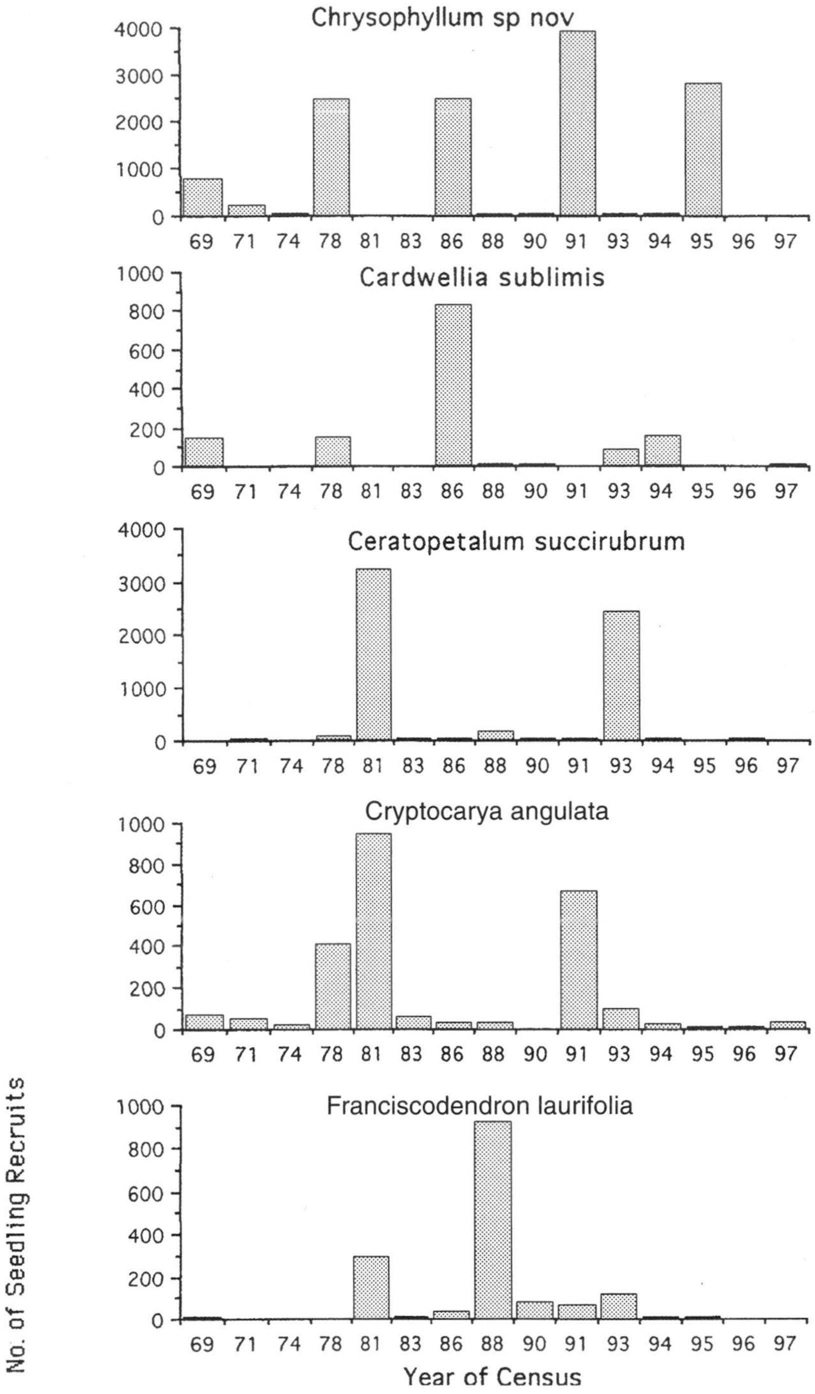

Chrysophyllum sp nov

4000
3000
2000
1000
0

69 71 74 78 81 83 86 88 90 91 93 94 95 96 97

Cardwellia sublimis

1000
800
600
400
200
0

69 71 74 78 81 83 86 88 90 91 93 94 95 96 97

Ceratopetalum succirubrum

4000
3000
2000
1000
0

69 71 74 78 81 83 86 88 90 91 93 94 95 96 97

Cryptocarya angulata

1000
800
600
400
200
0

69 71 74 78 81 83 86 88 90 91 93 94 95 96 97

Franciscodendron laurifolia

1000
800
600
400
200
0

69 71 74 78 81 83 86 88 90 91 93 94 95 96 97

Year of Census

No. of Seedling Recruits

from 21 to 387. This variation is especially evident in the commonest species (fig. 23.4).

To see whether the recruitment of different species was synchronized, we analyzed concordance of recruitment among the 46 species with more than 100 seedlings across the fourteen censuses from 1969 to 1996 (Connell and Green 2000). The analysis found that there was a low but statistically significant degree of synchrony (Kendall's coefficient of concordance, $N = 46$, $W = 0.09$, $p < .01$). The reason for this synchrony in recruitment may be that environmental conditions in some years are favorable for recruitment for the majority of species, while those in other years are not (see also Wright, chap. 15 in this volume).

This synchrony does not apply to all groupings of species. We assessed the synchrony of recruitment among the sixteen species with the highest variation in recruitment rate (i. e., a CV of > 100 and a range of > 50); no significant synchrony was found (Kendall's coefficient, $W = 0.08$, $N = 16$, $p > .05$). Also, the five species ranked highest in numbers of recruits recorded between 1965 and 1996 were not significantly synchronized (Kendall's coefficient, $N = 5$, $W = 0.33$, $p > .05$). For example, figure 23.4 shows that the first three seedling peaks in *Chrysophyllum* sp. nov. and *Cardwellia sublimis,* between 1965 and 1985, were clearly synchronized, but that their peaks were quite unsynchronized over the next 11 years. This change in synchrony across decades illustrates the value of long-term records.

Over 39 years, seedling numbers varied over three orders of magnitude. For the 121 species that had at least two adults in 1963, the number of new seedlings mapped and tagged since 1965 has ranged between 1 and 12,677. In one common species, *Chrysophyllum* sp nov., the seedling numbers per census ranged from 10 to 3,900; 98% appeared in five peaks spaced at 4- to 11-year intervals (Connell and Green 2000). Of the five species with the most seedlings, all showed a similar pattern of markedly episodic recruitment (fig. 23.4). This pattern of sporadic occurrences of very heavy seedling recruitment, separated by relatively long intervals with few seedlings, is analogous to the "mast seeding" seen in some forest trees (Appanah 1985; Ashton, Givnish, and Appanah 1988; Yap and Chan 1990; Sork, Bramble, and Sexton 1993; Newstrom et al. 1994; Koenig et al. 1994; Wright, chap. 15 in this volume). Figure 23.4 shows this extreme variation in the five species with the most recruits in the period 1965–1996.

Figure 23.4 Seedling recruitment rates (no./yr) of five species with high numbers of recruits recorded on the permanent transects at the Davies Creek study plot between 1965 and 1996. Each point represents the rate over the period since the previous census; the first census was in 1965.

The fact that these five masting species were also among the commonest in the community suggests that variation in recruitment might be related to a species' abundance. To test this hypothesis, we looked for a correlation between variation in recruitment and abundance. There were thirty-five species that had some trees greater than 10 cm DBH, as well as a total of more than 100 seedling recruits, between 1965 and 1997. For these species, the correlation between the logarithm of the CV of number of seedlings per census and the number of trees was positive and significant ($r^2 = .215$, $p < .01$), as it also was when tree abundance was measured as basal area ($r^2 = .123$, $p < .05$). Thus the commoner species have relatively more variable seedling recruitment.

Recruitment Limitation: The Influence of Seedling Recruitment on the Relative Abundance of Species in the Adult Community

To what degree do variations in seedling recruitment affect future adult abundance? How well does the relative abundance of species among the present seedling recruits predict future adult species composition and diversity? If growth and mortality rates during the period of growth to adulthood are not frequency-dependent, and if those rates remain constant during that period, then the relative abundance of species of seedlings will not be altered significantly as they grow to maturity, and recruitment will have determined the relative abundance of species in the future adult community.

We analyzed our data for the occurrence of frequency dependence of growth or mortality (Connell, Tracey, and Webb 1984), but found it only rarely. At a small spatial scale, we found that the recruits of species with abundant seedlings were likely to occur in single-species clumps, with a high proportion of nearest neighbors that were conspecific, whereas the recruits of species with few seedlings tended to be intermingled with other species, with a high proportion of nearest neighbors that were not conspecific. This observation suggested that frequency dependence would be occurring if seedlings performed more poorly when their nearest neighbors were conspecific (as was the case in abundant species) than when their neighbors were not conspecific (as was the case in rarer species). Our analyses found frequency dependence in growth in four of twelve seedling year classes analyzed, but not in the other eight. Survival was frequency-dependent in thirteen of twenty year classes, but not in the other seven (see tables 7 and 8 in Connell, Tracey, and Webb 1984). Overall, frequency dependence was demonstrated in about half of these instances of interactions between juveniles.

In contrast, at larger spatial scales, for both seedlings and older stages, we found no significant evidence for frequency dependence of growth or mortality. At the scale of the whole study plot, neither seedling growth nor mortality varied with the abundance of conspecific adults, measured either by numbers or basal area (see table 4 in Connell, Tracey, and Webb 1984). Also, neither growth nor mortality rates varied in relation to the abundance of conspecifics of the same size class for nine classes ranging from seedlings to large trees (see tables 5 and 6 in Connell, Tracey, and Webb 1984). This evidence is also weak at a smaller spatial scale: in quadrats (1.8 m × 12.2 m), five of forty-four regressions of growth rate versus abundance, and three of twenty-two regressions of mortality versus abundance, showed frequency dependence; however, at a significance level of 0.05, one or two would have occurred by chance in this many comparisons (Connell, Tracey, and Webb 1984). No density dependence in seed germination was found in field experiments in which seeds of two species were placed in dense and sparse patterns.

Last, we tested the hypothesis that seedlings and saplings in close proximity to conspecific adults would have higher mortality than those farther away (Janzen 1970; Connell 1971). Since juveniles of species whose adults were commoner would be more likely to occur closer to conspecific adults than would those of rarer species, agreement with this hypothesis would constitute evidence for frequency dependence. The result of the analysis showed that, of 28 species for which we had a sufficient sample size, 6 had higher mortality close to conspecific adults (in a zone within 1.5 times the crown radius of a conspecific adult) than at an equal distance farther away, suggesting frequency dependence. Increasing the zone of proximity to 3 times the crown radius gave a larger sample size. In this analysis, of 64 species, 10 showed frequency dependence in mortality and 54 did not (see table 10 in Connell, Tracey, and Webb 1984). Also, little evidence of frequency dependence in survival was found in field experiments in which seeds of two species were placed beneath the crowns of either conspecific or non-conspecific adults (see table 12 in Connell, Tracey, and Webb 1984). Overall, the evidence for frequency dependence in either growth rates or mortality rates during growth to maturity was weak.

Mechanisms Underlying Variation in Seedling Recruitment: Events during the Life Stages Preceding Recruitment

As described above, many species with mature adult trees on the study plot did not have seedlings at every census. Species with mature adults may not have seedlings in a particular census for one or more of the following reasons: (1) no flowers were produced in the period since the last census because the cues stimulating flowering were less strong than the factors inhibiting it (pathogens, predators, or deleterious environmental conditions); (2) flowers were produced, but did not develop into fruit with viable seeds, for reasons such as very unequal sex ratios of dioecious trees or floral sex organs, too few flowers or pollinators, fruits developed without seeds (parthenocarpic fruits), or abortion of developing fruits; (3) viable fruit and seeds were produced, but were either destroyed on the tree by frugivores or parasites before maturation or were dispersed away from the study plot; (4) after maturation, viable seeds arrived on our standard transects, but either they were all destroyed on the ground by predators or parasites, or the local physical conditions in that year were not suitable for germination or establishment of seedlings; (5) seedlings became established, but early mortality was so high that no seedlings survived to appear in our next census.

We began a long-term phenology study to investigate these possibilities in a variety of species, with the aim of estimating the losses among the different life stages leading up to seedling establishment. Monthly since January 1995, we have observed the reproductive activity of two to ten sexually mature individuals (mean 6.7 trees/species) of 103 species. We observe the trees with binoculars from the ground, scoring activity on a six-point scale from 0 (no flowers or fruits) to 5 (masses of flowers or fruits). The score is scaled to the size of the individual adult. Each individual is observed from the same location in each survey so that the monthly observations are comparable. In addition, we have measured the abundance of newly germinated seedlings in monthly surveys, from September 1994 onward, on twenty belt transects of 1 m × 100 m each on and around the study plot. All new seedling recruits that have appeared during the preceding month are counted, identified, and removed, except for those species in which large numbers of seedlings germinated in the same month; for these, all are removed except for a sample, which is mapped and its survival followed.

Analysis of our first 2.5 years of phenological observations shows that, of the 103 species, 15% never flowered; for example, the common species *Ceratopetalum succirubrum*, *Chrysophyllum* sp nov., *Macaranga subdentata*, and *Xanthopyllum octandrum* all failed to flower. A further 7% flowered, but did not initiate fruit; the remaining 78% had both flowers and fruit. Of the species that were observed to initiate some fruit development, 65% never had newly germinated seedlings on our transects. Examples of such species are *Beilschmedia bancroftii*, *Elaeocarpus elliffii*, *Guettardella tenuiflora*, *Halfordia scleroxyla*, and *Rapanea achradifolia*. Survival from the newly germinated seedling stage to the next regular census was high; of the 34 species of newly germinated seedlings recorded between September 1994 and September 1996, 82% (28 species) were also found in one or the other of the two next regular censuses, in October of 1995 and 1996.

These data provide an estimate of the degree to which losses in each of the life stages might influence the high annual variation in numbers of seedlings recruited. Our results show that the greatest proportion of the losses seem to occur between the start of fruit development and the time of germination, rather than at an earlier or a later stage. (All of the 103 species had produced seedlings at least once during the previous 29-year period before the phenology study began in 1995, so it is clear that records longer than 2.5 years are needed to adequately characterize the early stages of adult reproduction and seedling establishment.)

For some species, the reasons for such reproductive failure are known. For example, *Halfordia scleroxyla* produced masses of fruits in 1995, but failed to recruit any seedlings thereafter, and we found that virtually all of these fruits were seedless; such parthenocarpic behavior is apparently rare among the species in this forest. *Elaeocarpus* spp. regularly flowered and fruited, but many of their seeds appeared to be destroyed by insect predators while still on the tree. For *Hylandia dockrilli,* only two new seedling recruits have appeared since 1965. This species is monoecious, and we have evidence of variable sex expression from one year to the next. The trees that have flowered in the past 3 years have done so almost exclusively as males; however, some of these had masses of seed remnants on the ground beneath their crowns, indicating a female function in some previous years. These remnants may indicate intense seed predation, which, combined with predominately male functioning, might account for the lack of seedling recruitment.

Mechanisms Underlying the Variation in Seedling Recruitment: Precipitation

A likely environmental factor affecting reproduction and recruitment is precipitation. To investigate this possibility, we used long-term rainfall data from Atherton, which is the nearest standard meteorological station to the study site and close to the same elevation. Rainfall data gathered simultaneously at the Davies Creek plot and at Atherton were highly correlated: for 72 periods of 1 to 26 days between February 1995 and March 1996, when some rain was recorded at one or both stations, the regression equation was Davies Creek rain = 1.52 + (2.14 * Atherton rain) ($r^2 = .83$, df = 70, $p < .001$).

We regressed the total number of recruits per year against rainfall totals for three periods: the entire year immediately preceding the census date (which was usually in September–October), or only during the winter (May–September) or the summer (November–March) of that year. Because flowering and fruit development in many species was observed up to 2 years before the census date, we also repeated these analyses using rainfall from 1 and 2 years before the census date for each of the above three periods. In none of these analyses was there a statistically significant correlation ($N = 14$ for each, all r^2 ranging from 0 to .17).

Another aspect of precipitation that has been found to be of importance to reproduction and recruitment of trees is the length of relatively dry periods (Augspurger 1982; Wright, chap. 15 in this volume). Following the suggestion of Phillips et al. (1994), we tallied the number of consecutive "dry" months (when rainfall was less than 100 mm/month at Atherton) in each year. Since there was sometimes more than one such period in a year, we calculated the average number of consecutive dry months, and also the total number of dry months, in each year. We regressed the total number of recruits per year against each of these variables for each of the 3 years preceding the census. Of the six regressions, two were significantly positive: the total number of dry months in the year ending 1 year before the census ($N = 14$, $r^2 = .35$, $p < .05$) and the average number of consecutive dry months in the year ending 2 years before the census ($N = 14$, $r^2 = .38$, $p = .02$). Thus, seedling recruitment seems to be greater 1 to 2 years after a relatively long dry period. These lagged effects are consistent with the reproductive patterns that we have observed in our phenology study; some species take 1 to 1.5 years from flowering to seedling germination. Our analyses suggest that a relatively dry period is favorable for flowering, fruit development, or survival of fruit until germination, and that such a dry period may be more important than total precipitation, annually or seasonally (see also Wright, chap. 15 in this volume).

Effects of Ground-Dwelling Vertebrates on Recruitment and Survival of Seeds and Seedlings

Ground-dwelling vertebrates can act as seed dispersers, seed predators, litter disturbers, and herbivores. In Australian tropical rainforests, four species of native rodents (*Rattus fuscipes, R. leucopus, Uromys caudimaculatus,* and *Melomys cervinipes*), the musky rat kangaroo (*Hypsiprimnodon moschatus*), and the long-nosed bandicoot (*Parameles nasuta*) include fruits and seeds in their diet and so have the potential to act as seed dispersers or seed predators. The red-legged pademelon (*Thylogale stigmatica*) and the musky rat kangaroo may be important herbivores. Several ground-dwelling bird species have the potential to affect the rainforest understory through their activities as either seed dispersers (the cassowary, *Casuarius casuarius*) or litter disturbers (the chowchilla, *Orthonyx spaldingii;* the orange-footed scrubfowl, *Megapodius reinwardt;* and the brush turkey, *Alectura lathami*) (Theimer and Gehring 1999).

In some tree species, lack of seedling recruitment may be due to the seeds being completely destroyed by animals on the ground before germination. Several large individuals of *Prumnopitys amara* and *Beilschmedia bancroftii* have flowered and produced large fruit crops, but few new seedlings have appeared in the monthly seedling surveys. Seed predation by white-tailed rats (*Uromys caudimaculatus*) is an important source of seed mortality for *Beilschmedia bancroftii* in North Queensland (Harrington et al. 1997), and the seedlings that do arise on our plot apparently do so from seeds cached below the soil surface by white-tailed rats (Theimer 2001).

We set up the following field experiment to assess the overall effects of ground-dwelling birds and mammals on seeds and seedlings. Sixteen pairs of plots, each 6.5 m × 7.0 m in size, were established in the vicinity of the long-term study plot. One member of each pair was fenced to exclude vertebrates, while the other member of the pair was fenced only along the upper side to control for the effects of reduction of litter washing downhill during heavy rains. The growth, mortality, and recruitment of seedlings (< 30 cm height) within these plots have been measured at 6-month intervals since April of 1996, with ground-dwelling vertebrates excluded since November 1996. Live trapping has indicated that mammal access to the exclosure plots has been reduced to about 1/7 of that on the control plots. Measurements of the depth of litter at twenty locations in each exclosure and control plot indicate that the variance in depth in the controls was 1.75 times that in the exclosures. Neither seedling recruitment nor seedling survival differed between the exclosure and control plots in the 6 months (April to November 1996) prior to fence closing, nor during the first 6 months after fence closing (November 1996 to April 1997), but both were significantly higher in the exclosure plots than in the controls over the next 6 months (April to November 1997) (recruitment: Wilcoxon signed ranks test: $Z = 2.84$, $p = .004$; survival: paired *t*-test, $t = -5.74$, $p < .0001$; fig. 23.5). To measure the intensity of seed predation directly, we placed seeds of *Beilschmedia bancroftii* in both exclosures and controls; after 1 year, 64% of the seeds were still present in the exclosures, whereas all had disappeared in the controls after only 4 months.

DISCUSSION

Our study of rainforest trees greater than 2.5 cm DBH has been carried out for 34 years, and our study of saplings and seedlings for 32 years. Several other long-term studies of rainforest trees were reviewed by Swaine, Lieberman, and Putz (1987) and Phillips and Gentry (1994); these studies ranged from 6 to 38

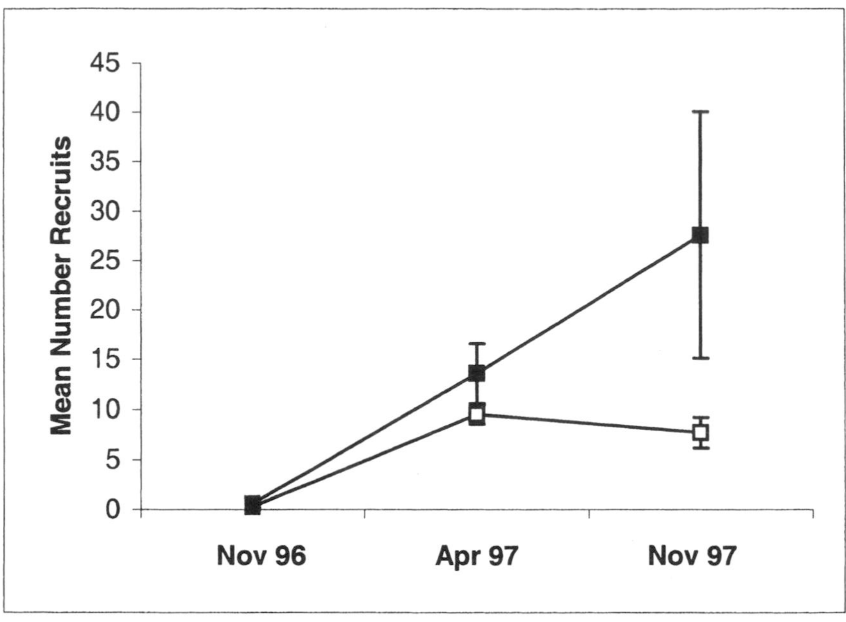

Figure 23.5 Rates of survival and recruitment of seedlings (mean ± 1 SE), in experimental plots at Davies Creek during the periods shown. The exclosures (represented by solid boxes) prevented entry by ground-dwelling mammals and birds; the adjacent controls (represented by open boxes) allowed entry. The exclosures were open for the first census period and closed for the last two.

years in length. Most of them used a minimum size of 10 cm DBH; three used minimum sizes of 3.2, 4.0, or 5.0 cm DBH. More recently, a few studies have established long-term plots that include smaller size classes (see reviews by Condit 1995; Lieberman 1996). To our knowledge, the present study has the longest record of dynamics of tropical rainforest trees less than 10 cm DBH.

The patterns of seedling recruitment among the many species on the study plot have been extremely complex during the past three decades. Most tree species did not produce seedlings every census, and sometimes there were long intervals of up to a decade between successive recruitments. Our phenological observations indicate that the absence of seedlings in a particular year could have been due to the an absence of flowering, or to flowering without subsequent fruit development. The largest proportion of the species began to develop fruit, but without seedlings subsequently appearing. Losses at this stage could have been due to fruits being destroyed on the tree at any stage in development, or to mature fruits never germinating after falling to the ground.

Many studies of phenology have been done (see review in Van Schaik, Ter-

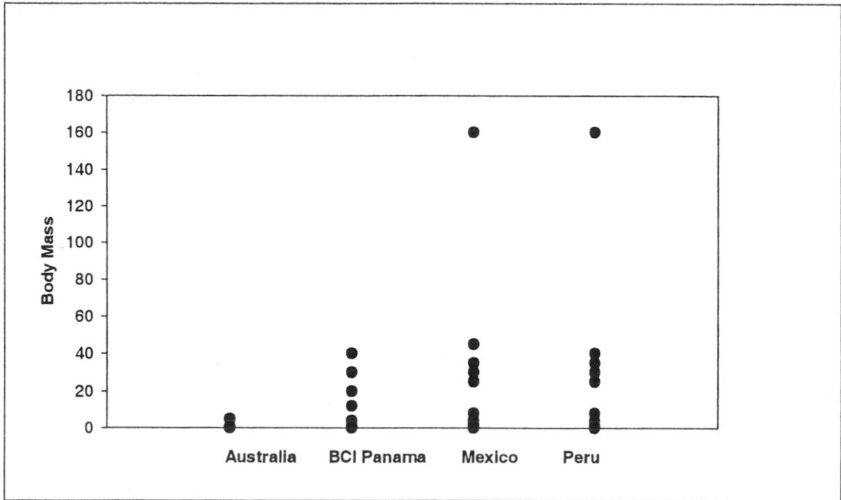

Figure 23.6 Body mass (kg) of ground-dwelling mammalian herbivores, seed predators, and seed dispersers that occur at four tropical rainforest sites: Davies Creek, Australia (T. C. Theimer and C. A. Gehring, unpublished data); Barro Colorado Island (BCI), Panama (Glanz 1990); Montes Azules, Mexico (Martinez-Gallardo and Sanchez-Cordero 1997); and Cocha Cashu, Peru (Janson and Emmons 1990).

borgh, and Wright 1993), and some have been long-term: Newstrom et al. (1994), for example, took 12 years of monthly phenological records in a Costa Rican rainforest. Two studies measured fruit fall (Foster 1982b) and seedling germination (Garwood 1983) in different years on Barro Colorado Island, Panama. However, the present study is, to our knowledge, the first to link phenological observations of flowering and fruiting to measurements of germination and early survival of seedlings during the same period on the same plot, with the aim of estimating losses among the different life stages leading up to seedling establishment.

Judging from the results of the field experiment designed to measure the effects of vertebrates, these losses may be due in part to attacks by vertebrates or to their disturbance of litter. Australian rainforest mammal communities have fewer large species than those in other regions (Eisenberg 1981); the absence of large ground-dwelling mammalian herbivores, such as tapirs, peccaries, and deer, is especially striking (fig. 23.6). Most of the smaller mammals act as seed dispersers and seed predators, with only the red-legged pademelon and the musky rat kangaroo feeding directly on seedlings. As a consequence of these differences, we predict that, in Australian tropical rainforests, vertebrate seed dispersers and seed predators should have a greater effect on the recruitment and mortality of tree seedlings than vertebrate herbivores. While seed-eating rodents consume the majority of fallen seeds, their scatter-hoarding behaviors may be the major avenue for the establishment of some seedling species in the face of heavy seed predation on our plot (Theimer 2001, 2003).

In addition to their roles as seed dispersers, rainforest vertebrates may also disperse mycorrhizal fungal spores, leading to indirect effects on seedling performance. Gehring, Wolff, and Theimer (2002) observed that vertebrate exclusion led to reductions in arbuscular mycorrhizal fungal diversity, which in turn reduced rates of seedling colonization by these fungal mutualists. Reductions in mycorrhizal inoculum are likely to influence seedling community dynamics because tree species in this rainforest vary in their dependence on mycorrhizal fungi for growth in the shaded understory (Gehring 2003).

Our field experiments suggest that litter-disturbing birds could have strong effects on seedling recruitment and mortality in Australian tropical rainforests. The effects of variation in litter depth on seedling establishment have often been demonstrated (Carson and Peterson 1990; Facelli and Pickett 1991; Facelli 1994; Molofsky and Augspurger 1992; Reader 1993; Cintra 1997). Since litter-disturbing animals increase the spatial heterogeneity of litter depth, they should promote the germination of a greater diversity of species of seeds than if they were absent. Theimer and Gehring (1999) documented that a common litter-disturbing bird on our plot, the chowchilla, created spatial variation in litter depth of magnitudes great enough to alter the germination success of three common tree species. Furthermore, seedling mortality due to litter disturbance by these birds was twofold to fivefold greater for two common species of seedlings than for two rarer species, suggesting that variation in susceptibility to this type of disturbance may affect plant community dynamics (Theimer and Gehring 1999).

Among the factors that determine the abundance, species composition, and diversity of trees in forests, we have concentrated on initial seedling recruitment, since it determines the initial abundance of each year's cohort. To measure the likelihood that the relative abundance of species in the seedling recruitment determines the relative abundance of species at the adult stage, we looked for evidence of frequency dependence during the period of growth from the seedling stage to adulthood. We found such evidence in about half the instances in which seedlings interacted with close neighbors (Connell, Tracey, and Webb 1984). However, in several other analyses of seedlings and older stages, growth and survival showed little relation to abundance of conspecific adults, density of individuals of the same size class, or proximity to conspecific adults. Given this evidence that growth and mortality in the period between recruitment and adulthood are only weakly frequency-dependent, we conclude that the species composition of older life stages may be determined by that of seedling recruitment.

Given the weakness of the evidence for frequency dependence in all stages from seedling to adult, could frequency dependence play a role in the maintenance of tree species diversity at our study site? It could, if the population dynamics of the early life stages that produce the initial recruits are frequency-dependent (in this context, we will use the term to refer only to negative frequency dependence; e.g., growth or survival rates that are lower in commoner than in rarer species). We found that the per capita recruitment rates of the group of species that reach maturity in the subcanopy and understory layers of the forest did exhibit negative frequency dependence (see fig. 5 in Connell, Tracey, and Webb 1984). In contrast, the group of species that mature only when they reach the canopy layer did not exhibit it. (This analysis used data from 1965–1980; a reanalysis using data from 1980–1997 reached similar conclusions: J. H. Connell et al., unpublished data.) In addition, some frequency dependence apparently occurs during later seedling growth and mortality due to interactions between the young seedlings.

Thus, the strongest evidence for frequency dependence at Davies Creek is confined to the earliest life stages. In contrast, in a plot on Barro Colorado Island, Panama, evidence of frequency dependence has been found in some older stages (Hubbell, Condit, and Foster 1990; Condit, Hubbell, and Foster 1992; Wills et al. 1997). The difference in these findings from the two sites could be due to differences in climate, tree species, tree abundance, and dynamics, as pointed out earlier (see figs. 23.1, 23.2, and table 23.1), or to the past history of the local forests. From our results at Davies Creek, we hypothesize that frequency dependence does occur in some species groups during the production of the initial seedling recruits—that is, during flowering, fruit development, seed dispersal, and seed germination—or during the early seedling period before the standard censuses are made. We plan to investigate these hypotheses, using the results from our phenology observations, as well as those from the field experiment measuring the effects of ground-dwelling vertebrates.

ACKNOWLEDGMENTS

We thank the many people who have helped us over the past 39 years. Special thanks are due to J. G. Tracey and L. J. Webb, who helped start the project and keep it running, and who, with M. D. Lowman in the later years, were responsible for most of the identifications. E. Volck of the Queensland Department of Forestry should be recognized for establishing this and other plots in rainforests in Queensland in 1952. I. R. Noble and I. Davies wrote the programs that have kept the database accurate and allowed it to be accessed for analysis and displayed in maps. M. J. Keough did the original analyses for frequency dependence cited here. Campbell Webb generously provided unpublished data from his study plots in Borneo. The research has been supported since 1962 by grants from the U.S. National Science Foundation; the most recent grants are DEB 92-20672, DEB 95-03217, and DEB 98-06310. It has also been supported through I. R. Noble of the Ecosystem Dynamics Group, Research School of Biological Sciences, Australian National University, Canberra, Australia.

24

The Theory and Practice of Planning for Long-Term Conservation of Biodiversity in the Wet Tropics Rainforests of Australia

NIGEL E. STORK

ABSTRACT

The Wet Tropics of Queensland World Heritage Area was established in 1988 to "protect, conserve, present, rehabilitate and transmit to future generations" the natural World Heritage values of the region—the evolutionary history of the rainforests, the superlative natural beauty of the area, and its unique and rich biological diversity. The region also has an important indigenous cultural heritage. The World Heritage Area was created against a preexisting set of land uses. Currently, there are more than 700 separate parcels of land within the World Heritage Area and many thousands of landholders whose land abuts it. Land uses varying from residential to agriculture, tourism, and forestry present many management problems and conflicting demands on the World Heritage Area. Creating short-term and long-term management goals for the conservation of biodiversity of the region is a complex task. Community consultation and support and expert and timely research are essential. Current problems include increasing demands for water from the World Heritage Area and continued forest clearing in adjacent lands. Immediate threats to biodiversity and other World Heritage values include feral animals, exotic weeds and other pests, and roadkills of cassowaries. In addition, globalization of trade is creating new problems with the unintentional transport of "hitchhiker" pest organisms. The consequences of climate change for different environments within the World Heritage Area are unknown. Determining the carrying capacities of particular areas and the limits of acceptable changes is fundamental to managing human uses. Research on the past and present dynamics of the Wet Tropics rainforests, on the current and past distribution of biodiversity, and new modeling of future scenarios should help managers to devise management plans to cope with future changes and threats.

INTRODUCTION

Sustainability had become the fundamental principle for decision making in natural resource management by the end of the twentieth century, but in reality it has been difficult to achieve, particularly in areas of the world that have only recently been developed. This is nowhere more true than in tropical forests, which so often are rich in a variety of valuable extractable resources, including timber, water, and minerals, but are located in countries with poor economies and in urgent need of revenues. Tropical rainforests in Australia have suffered a fate similar in many ways to that of rainforests elsewhere in the world, but considerable progress in safeguarding the future of what remains has been made.

The "Wet Tropics" or "Daintree" rainforests of northeastern Queensland were the subject of much controversy in the 1980s as tropical biologists and conservationists highlighted the need to conserve Australia's tropical rainforests. The designation of a large part of these rainforests as a World Heritage Area was a major step toward their conservation. The next, and most critical, step in achieving long-term sustainability is to integrate their conservation and sustainable use within a regional context. The fundamental challenge for researchers is to provide relevant information to decision makers so that they can achieve ecologically sustainable outcomes. Better resource management will increase economic benefits, employment, and human well-being.

This chapter considers those problems affecting the long-term sustainable use and management of the Wet Tropics World Heritage Area that need research-based solutions. Most of these problems also exist in other rainforest areas of the world that do not have the same level of protection and face a much less certain future. It is hoped that this review may provide a constructive assessment and model that can be used for other rainforest areas.

THE BIOLOGICAL AND EVOLUTIONARY SIGNIFICANCE OF THE WET TROPICS

Some 30 million years ago, tropical rainforests may have covered as much as half of Australia (Greenwood and Christophel, chap. 18 in this volume). For various reasons, some known, some unknown, the rainforests have contracted to a very tiny proportion of the Australian landscape. It is estimated that tropical, subtropical, and temperate rainforests today cover only 20,000 km^2—about 0.2% of Australia (Webb and Tracey 1981b). These remnant forests exist as a chain of discontinuous pockets extending more than 6,000 km from northern Australia along the east coast to Tasmania. Some 7,800 km^2 of tropical forests are located in northeastern Queensland, and of that area, about 90% is within the so-called Wet Tropics bioregion, a narrow coastal strip of land some 20–40 km wide that extends from Cooktown to Townsville (plate 4/fig. 24.1). These rainforests represent 0.01% of the world's tropical rainforests, and yet because of the

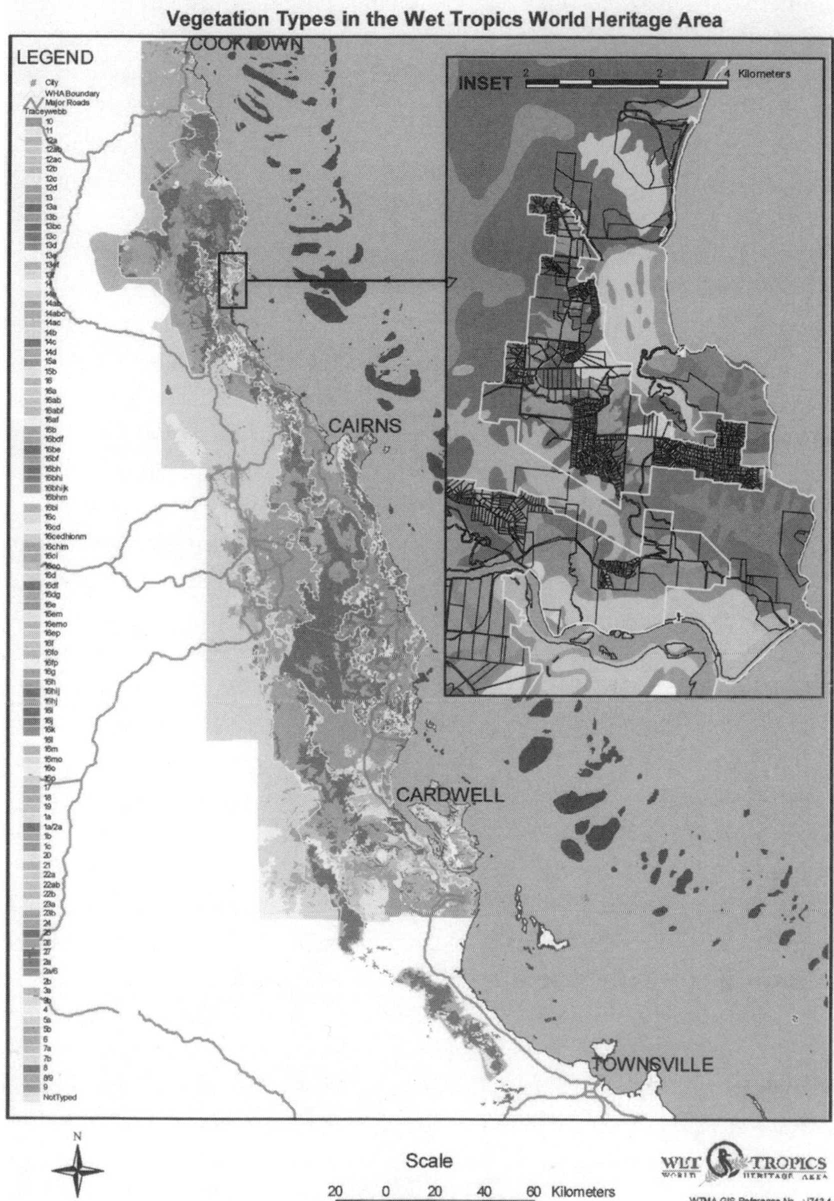

Figure 24.1 Distribution of major vegetation types (Webb and Tracey 1981) in and around the Wet Tropics of Queensland World Heritage Area. See also plate 4.

unique nature of the biota and its evolutionary significance, the Wet Tropics region is one of the world's top biodiversity hotspots (Myers 1988; Werren et al. 1995; but see Myers et al. 2000). Other smaller Australian tropical and subtropical rainforests are also of great importance, including those areas off-reserve, and rainforests farther north and south in Queensland, such as the Central Eastern Rainforests Reserves World Heritage Area and the Conondales and Eungella forests.

Although it represents a minute proportion of Australia's land surface (0.1%), the Wet Tropics region contains the richest variety of animals and plants in Australia, including two-thirds of the country's butterfly species, half of its birds, and a third of its mammals. Seventy species of vertebrate animals are found nowhere else in the world. A very high proportion of the fauna and flora are endemic to the Wet Tropics (Rainforest Conservation Society of Queensland 1986). More than 400 species of plants and 76 species of animals are officially listed as rare, vulnerable, or endangered (Wet Tropics Management Authority 1999). Without effective research, planning, and management, the biodiversity and ecosystem services of the Wet Tropics are likely to degrade or disappear over time.

The Wet Tropics also provides an unparalleled living record of the ecological and evolutionary processes that shaped the flora and fauna of Australia over the past 400 million years, since it was first part of the Pangaean landmass and then later the ancient continent Gondwana. As Gondwana split up some 100–120 million years ago, the landmass that now constitutes Australia began moving slowly northward, away from other landmasses, and only in the last 10–20 million years has it had contact with the Asian landmasses. Because the continent of Australia was isolated from other continents for 80 million years, it evolved its own unique biota. At the same time, it retains some of the most primitive examples of the biota of the ancient continents. For example, the rainforests of the Wet Tropics have more plant taxa with primitive characteristics than any other area on earth. Of the nineteen known families of primitive flowering plants (Takhtajan 1980), twelve are found in the Wet Tropics, and two (Idiospermaceae and Austrobaileyaceae) are found nowhere else in the world (Rainforest Conservation Society of Queensland 1986). For comparison, there are only nine primitive flowering plant families in the rainforests of South America, and none of them are endemic. Not surprisingly, the Wet Tropics region has been described as a key to the origins and ancient habitats of flowering plants and as a biological link with temperate and other tropical zones.

WORLD HERITAGE LISTING OF THE WET TROPICS RAINFORESTS

The unique nature of the Wet Tropics rainforests, their small size, and their inherent natural values led to their listing as a World Heritage Area in 1988. Responsibility for their management and safekeeping was placed in the hands of a newly established body, the Wet Tropics Management Authority. The Authority fulfils a planning, coordinating, funding, and monitoring role in ensuring that management activities contribute to implementing Australia's international World Heritage Convention obligations. The Wet Tropics fulfilled all four criteria set out by the IUCN: (1) an outstanding example representing the major stages in the earth's evolutionary history, (2) an outstanding example representing significant ongoing ecological and biological processes in ecosystem evolution and development, (3) containing superlative natural phenomena or exceptional natural beauty, (4) containing the most important significant habitats for the conservation of biodiversity. At the time of listing, only thirteen of the world's ninety-six natural World Heritage Areas fulfilled all four criteria.

The listing of the Wet Tropics was a long and complicated process (McDonald and Lane 2000), not least because of the complicated political landscape in Australia (Hundloe 2000), but also because it overlaid the existing land tenure and uses of the forests in the region. As plate 5/figure 24.2 show, there are more than 700 separate parcels of land of varying tenure within the World Heritage Area. Some are privately owned; others are state-owned and are the responsibility of different government departments. In addition, there are many thousands of other land blocks that abut the World Heritage Area, and the government is responsible for ensuring that these lands are managed in a way that will not negatively affect the area. Such has been the scale of the challenge to address the many conflicting demands on the World Heritage Area that the first Wet Tropics Management Plan came into force only on September 1, 1998, after more than 6 years of development (Hundloe 2000).

THE CHANGING SOCIOECONOMIC BASE OF THE WET TROPICS REGION

The socioeconomic face of the Wet Tropics has changed considerably over the last 150 years (see chapters in McDonald and Lane 2000). Prior to the earliest arrival of European settlers in the 1860s, a diverse range of Aboriginal groups lived for probably more than 10,000 years in the rainforest or at its edge, extracting food and shelter from the rainforest. It is probable that more than sixty clan

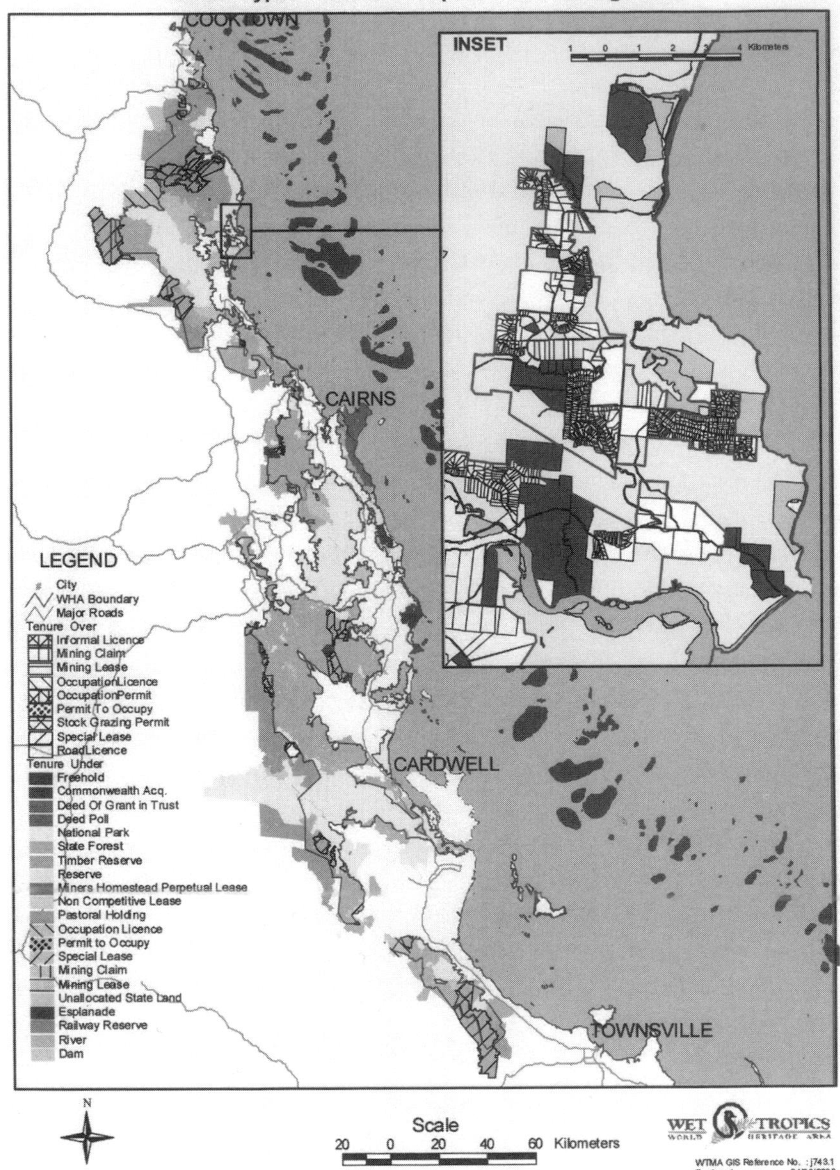

Figure 24.2 Distribution of land tenure types in the Wet Tropics of Queensland World Heritage Area. See also plate 5.

groups covered the area (Bottoms 2000). European settlers drove many of the Aborigines from their lands, and only recently have many traditional groups attempted to reclaim some of their former lands and a greater say in the management of the World Heritage Area. The issue of "native title" to land has been the subject of much legal and political controversy for the last 10 years in Australia, and many Aboriginal groups are seeking legal decisions about their rights to their former lands. Potentially, 80% or more of the World Heritage Area could be subject to native title. Some 15,000–20,000 Aboriginal people from sixteen distinct language groups have traditional and historical links with rainforest lands. Currently, Aboriginal people are negotiating greater involvement in management or co-management of rainforest areas. These negotiations involve a range of options, including some Aboriginal groups moving back into the World Heritage Area to continue their lives and traditions (Dale et al. 2000).

The economy of the Wet Tropics has developed considerably over the last hundred years through a mixture of timber production, agriculture, mining, and, more recently, tourism. European settlers cleared large areas of rainforest from the lowlands and the upland tablelands for agriculture and timber at the beginning of the twentieth century. Governments encouraged settlers to do this, and even as late as the 1950s, agricultural land was considered of no economic value until the forests had been cleared. A mixture of cattle and sugarcane currently predominates in the agricultural landscape, although a wide variety of other crops, particularly fruit and vegetables, are grown.

Timber production has been an important part of the economy for a hundred years. However, logging of rainforest timber ceased within the World Heritage Area upon listing in 1988, with large compensation payments for the industry. At the time of World Heritage listing, commercial forestry, the primary use of the state forests and timber reserves that cover 47% of the area, was worth A$20 million per year (Driml 1997). Almost all of the accessible rainforest areas of the Wet Tropics have been selectively logged, more recently using the Queensland Selective Logging System, which incorporates guidelines designed to reduce adverse effects of logging operations. Although timber extraction has ceased in the World Heritage Area, there is a rapidly developing small private farm-forestry industry supported by the state government, with the focus on growing mixed plantations of local endemic rainforest trees for timber and for biodiversity enhancement (Stork et al. 1997). Similarly, a mining industry based on a variety of metals, such as tin and gold, that developed in the first half of the twentieth century and was worth A$25 million per year (but see Driml 1994), has all but ceased. Mining leases still exist in the World Heritage Area, but are being phased out as they expire.

In the last 20 years, North Queensland has become internationally recognized for its tourism industry, largely based on the Great Barrier Reef World Heritage Area. At the same time, a rainforest tourism industry has rapidly developed, based on the neighboring Wet Tropics World Heritage Area.

FUTURE RESEARCH NEEDS

The Cooperative Research Centre for Tropical Rainforest Ecology and Management (Rainforest CRC), a partnership of all the major research providers and research users in the Wet Tropics region, undertook an intensive consultation process to identify the critical needs for research pertaining to the sustainable use and management of Australia's tropical rainforests. These critical research needs are discussed below.

The previous 150 years have seen such dramatic changes to the Wet Tropics region that it is hard for anyone to make firm predictions as to how the region may change in the future. However, in the last few years, many government and nongovernmental organizations in the region have worked together to produce and integrate strategic regional plans for environmental conservation, economic development, tourism, natural resources and water management, social planning and human services, urban growth and infrastructure, integrated transport, and solid waste (Far North Queensland Regional Planning Advisory Committee 1998a, 1998b). These plans, known as FNQ 2010, provide a set of integrated regional goals for the next 20 years. Achievement of these goals will require that the conflicting demands on the rainforests and the lands surrounding them be addressed. This will require multidisciplinary research to provide appropriate information for planning to minimize environmental problems.

Increasing Population Growth and Its Effect on the Wet Tropics

The population of North Queensland is projected to grow by about 50% in the next 20 years, and the number of visitors will probably increase in a similar fashion. For example, the population of Cairns, currently the largest town in the region, is projected to grow from 92,000 to 182,000. The increasing permanent and visiting population will place increasing demands on a range of finite resources such as water, landfill sites, and urban areas. Similarly, there is constant pressure to expand the areas currently under agriculture. Recently, for example, sugarcane has been introduced to the upland Tablelands region of the Wet Tropics, resulting in an increased demand for irrigation and water storage capacity.

Inevitably, the source for water is the streams and rivers that flow from the rainforest. For example, irrigation demand for water from the Barron River, which enters the sea just north of Cairns and is one of the major rivers on the Tablelands, is expected to increase by 60% by the year 2010. Predicted improvements in the management of water demand should reduce water consumption considerably. Changes in water extraction levels, and the dams and weirs that are often required, cause major changes in stream flow that may have severe negative effects on biodiversity in the rivers (Pearson and Connolly 2000). In some of the major rivers, flows have already been diverted through hydroelectric systems for the production of electricity. When flows are low in the dry season, water is released from the dams at peak whitewater rafting periods to enhance the visitor experience. These pulses or rapid changes in water levels also have considerable effects on rivers and their biota.

Water quality is also a serious issue for rivers that flow from agricultural lands through the rainforest because of the damaging effects of high nutrient levels, pollutants, and sediment loads not only on the rivers themselves, but also on the Great Barrier Reef (Productivity Commission 2002). Management of water flows and water quality is a key element of the FNQ 2010 regional strategy. However, if management is realistically to integrate the ecological and economic needs of rivers, rainforests, and the reef, these issues will require much greater research attention.

Evaluation of Trade-offs between Conservation and Development

Queensland's rainforests and other forests are a major economic asset to Australia because of the ecosystem goods and services they provide, such as clean water and air, flood mitigation, erosion control, pest control, and aesthetic, cultural, and spiritual values. And yet no sound estimate of the value of these assets has been made, nor have economic assessments been made of the consequences of land use changes in rainforest regions. The value of the ecosystem goods and services provided by all ecosystems worldwide was estimated at US$33 trillion a year—more than double the global Gross National Product (Costanza et al. 1997). So what is the value of the Wet Tropics region, and what resources are we prepared to invest to maintain and increase this value? The annual value per hectare for all tropical forests was estimated by Costanza and colleagues at US$2,007, which translates to A$2,676. Extrapolated over the 894,420 hectares of the Wet Tropics World Heritage Area, this gives an annual value of US$1,795 million, or A$2,895 million. This estimate suggests that the value of the ecosystem services of the Wet Tropics World Heritage Area may be greater than that of the entire economy of the region.

The main ecosystem services attributed by Costanza and colleagues to tropical forests were nutrient cycling (46%), raw materials (16%), erosion control (12%), climate regulation (11%), and recreation (6%). However, the value and relative importance of these and other ecosystem services to Australia will differ. For example, water is a rare resource in Australia, and therefore those ecosystem services associated with water will be of higher value. Developing sustainable management practices for the Wet Tropics rainforests is, therefore, of very significant economic importance to Australia, as the cost of replacing the services they provide far outweighs the cost of managing their sustainability (e.g., Chichilnisky and Geoffrey 1998). When one considers the replacement cost of some of the ecosystem goods and services the public relies on, the sustainable management and utilization of the environment makes sound economic as well as environmental sense. Increasingly, researchers are looking to the earth's biological diversity for new products of medicinal and other value. As yet I have seen no one place a value on this "public good," and yet a number of pharmaceutical companies are already investing in bioprospecting for new biological chemicals in Australian rainforest organisms.

The trade-offs between development and conservation of rainforest and the conflicts between protagonists on both sides are nowhere more acute than in the "Daintree" region of North Queensland. The lowland rainforest in this area is considered to be one of the most biologically diverse and significant regions of the Wet Tropics (Small et al. 1997). Prior to World Heritage listing, a large part of the lowland forest area in the Daintree was subdivided for residential and rural use. Although many of these subdivisions have not been developed, current and future potential development could add to the already highly fragmented nature of these biologically valuable forests. Some blocks have been purchased from private landowners through a government-funded buyback package. However, the conflict between development and conservation remains. A multifocused approach is needed to provide mutually acceptable compromises (McDonald 2000).

Maintaining a Diverse Regional Economy

The regional economy is heavily dependent on a few key industries, particularly sugarcane and tourism. The long-term success and survival of both industries will be influenced by many external factors. Who can predict at this stage the long-term future of rainforest tourism in North Queensland, as it is so dependent on a few critical markets, such as Japan, Korea, and Europe? Inevitably, if such key industries start to fail, there will be changing pressures on the Wet

Table 24.1 Results of a survey of 1,099 visitors looking at their reasons for visiting North Queensland

Attraction	Percentage of respondents
Great Barrier Reef	55.3
Rainforest	45.6
Climate	33.1
Natural environment	21.7
Visit friends and relatives	11.3
Visit named locations in NQ	10.1
Outdoor activities	9.5
New experience	8.5
Holiday, relax	7.5
On way around Australia	6.2
Temporary work	3.4
Enjoyed previous visit	3.3
Culture, lifestyle	3.2
Other	3.9

Source: Driml 1997.
Note: There is some overlap between categories, and total responses are greater than 100%, as multiple responses were possible.

Tropics rainforests. It is therefore sensible to seek to diversify the region's economic base to provide greater economic resilience.

The rainforest is one of the major attractions of the North Queensland region (table 24.1). Manidis Roberts Consulting (1994), which provide the most recent detailed information on visitors to the Wet Tropics World Heritage Area, estimated the number of visits to individual rainforest sites at 4.77 million per year in 1993. Driml (1997) converted this figure to 3.4 million visitor-days and calculated that these visitors bring more than A$753 million directly and indirectly to the region. In an economic study of the benefits of tourism to the Wet Tropics, almost 70% of tourists surveyed named the opportunity to visit the rainforest as "one of a number of important attractions to North Queensland," with 11% naming the rainforest as the most important attraction (Driml 1997).

The expansion and sustainable development of rainforest tourism can continue only if this is done in harmony with the conservation and management of the rainforest resource on which it depends. The tourism industry and park managers require new research and management guidelines on how to improve access to the rainforest and reduce the negative effects of tourism.

An increasingly important section of the domestic and international tourism market is concerned with the unique cultural connection of Aboriginal people to the country. Currently, this section contributes $200 million annually. The market for indigenous rainforest culture is as yet largely unexplored, and yet if exploited in a culturally sensitive manner, could provide a new direction for rainforest tourism as well as providing a boost to the economy of the indigenous population.

Incorporating Indigenous Interests into the Management of Tropical Rainforests

Australian Aboriginal rainforest culture is unique in the world. Rainforest Aboriginal people are distinctive physically, linguistically and culturally and have developed a unique material culture and economy adapted to the rainforest environment. Since most rainforest Aborigines have been displaced from their traditional lands, the survival of their culture, much of which is handed down by oral tradition, is seriously threatened in Australia.

The challenge facing management agencies, industry, researchers, and Aboriginal people is to develop a collaborative research and planning framework that equitably addresses each group's interests in the common goal of environmental, social, economic, and cultural sustainability. Cultural sustainability of the rainforest requires application of management, planning, and research frameworks that incorporate recognition of traditional ecological knowledge, rights, and interests in country, enabling indigenous people to maintain their culture and meet their obligations to country. Without the proper recognition of culture as equal to the considerations given to environmental and social impacts, Aboriginal rainforest culture will progressively diminish.

Threats to the Ecological Sustainability of the Wet Tropics

The Wet Tropics of Queensland World Heritage Area is threatened by a range of different forces and impacts. It is important to distinguish those threats that are localized and of a short-term nature from those that are more pervasive and long-term (tables 24.2–24.3). There is an obvious tendency for management bodies to place greater emphasis on shorter-term and more immediate concerns, as these are often the most tangible. Often these concerns are also of greatest community interest and are politically sensitive.

INVASIVE ORGANISMS

Australia has been severely affected over the last century by invasive organisms such as rabbits, cats, foxes, rodents, and many grasses. In fact, Australia has

Table 24.2 Human activities associated with pressures on the Wet Tropics of Queensland World Heritage Area at a range of scales

	Severity of pressure				
Extent of pressure	Cumulative minor effects		Interferes with natural processes		Transforms the landscape
Pervasive and/or permanent				Selection logging	Climate change
			Feral pigs	Powerlines, roads, dams	Mountaintop clearing
Widespread and/or long-term			Fire		
		Small clearings	Water extraction		
Local and/or ephemeral	Casual campsites	Walking tracks			

Source: After E. Saxon, personal communication.

Table 24.3 Consequences for the natural values and processes of the Wet Tropics of Queensland World Heritage Area of pressures at various scales

	Severity of pressure				
Extent of pressure	Cumulative minor impacts		Interferes with natural processes		Transforms the landscape
Pervasive and/or permanent				Loss of canopy cover and old-growth habitats	Disintegration of biotic communities
			Disease reservoir	Decline in biodiversity	Destruction of unique habitats
Widespread and/or long-term			Attenuated natural fire patterns		
		Establishment of exotic weeds and pests	Reduced dry-season stream flow		
Local and/or ephemeral	Site pollution and damage to local vegetation	Local disturbance of soil surface			

Source: After E. Saxon, personal communication.

the second largest number of introduced plant species of any country in the world (1,952 introduced species, 15,638 native species: Lövei 1997). These introduced species have had a devastating effect on the environment, causing the extinctions of many species of marsupials, native murid rodents, and plants and a reduction in the distributions of a great many others.

Australia's tropical rainforests are threatened by a large number of invasive plant species, which create a huge management problem. Most of these environmental weeds affect large areas of rainforest or former rainforest lands that have been converted to agriculture. A recent analysis of the 500 or more environmental weeds in the area (Werren 2001) suggested that the most serious threats come from pond apple (*Annona glabra*), thunbergia (*Thunbergia grandiflora*), harungana (*Harungana madagascarersis*), hymenachne (*Hymenachne amplexicaulia*), turbina (*Turbina corymbosa*), and lucaena (*Lucaena leucocephala*). The effect of these introduced weeds on the native fauna and flora is not always clear. The Cairns birdwing butterfly (*Troides prianus euphorion*—formerly known as *Ornithoptera prianus euphorion*) normally feeds on a native vine, *Aristolochia tagala*, and other native plants. However, it now appears to prefer to lay its eggs on the introduced ornamental species *A. elegans*, even though that plant is toxic to its caterpillars.

There are many feral vertebrates in the Wet Tropics, including pigs, cats, dogs, cattle, deer, some bird species, and numerous introduced fishes. In an analysis of the risk posed by feral animals, one species that has not yet been seen in the area, the fox, was identified as posing the greatest threat (Harrison and Congdon 2002). Recently, another introduced species, the rabbit, has moved north into agricultural areas, and it is expected that its main predator, the fox, will soon follow, presenting a major threat to many native vertebrates.

The most widely reported vertebrate threat to Australian rainforests is the feral pig (*Sus scrofa*), although the extent of the damage it causes is poorly understood (Johnson 2002). Feral pigs are believed to have come from European settlement in the last 150 years. In the Wet Tropics they disturb the soil and leaf litter in which they search for invertebrates and other food. There is some suggestion that they have aided the introduction of other invasive organisms, such as European earthworms, into the rainforests (J. Mitchell, personal communication). Exclosure experiments are under way to determine the nature and magnitude of disturbance caused by feral pigs. There is much concern in the agricultural community—particularly among sugarcane and banana growers—that the rainforest acts as a reservoir for feral pigs, and farmers would like to see the pigs removed from surrounding rainforests. Management bodies have instigated extensive pig-trapping programs to reduce pig numbers in the worst-affected areas. Other introduced mammals, such as feral cats, as yet have had little reported effect on rainforest species. Cane toads introduced from Hawaii are now very widespread in lowland rainforest, but little is known of their effects on native fauna.

Several exotic fish species are of concern in the Wet Tropics, including two naturalized live-bearers (the guppy, *Poecilia reticulata*, and the mosquito fish, *Gambusia holbrooki*) and two mouth-brooders (*Tilapia mariae* and *Oveochromis mossambicus*). These and other exotic fishes are becoming more common and are causing localized problems for endemic fish fauna (Harrison and Congdon 2002).

Introduced insect and mite species pose a special threat to the Wet Tropics, as many of them are difficult to detect. The papaya fruit fly (*Batrocera papayae*) was discovered in Cairns in October 1995, and a major eradication program costing more than A$10 million was implemented. The papaya fruit fly is endemic to Thailand, Indonesia, and Malaysia and feeds on a wide spectrum of rainforest fruits. Researchers were surprised and relieved to find that although it was widespread in agricultural areas of North Queensland, it was not breeding on any rainforest fruits in the Wet Tropics (Hadwen et al. 1998). Extensive use of male attractant (methyl eugenol) baits impregnated with malathion has seen the rapid and remarkable total eradication of this pest from the Wet Tropics.

The problem of pest species is likely to increase with the globalization of trade and the demand for access to more areas of rainforest by the tourism industry. It is therefore essential that research be carried out to examine the potential and real threats posed by some organisms. For example, *Phytophthora cinnamomi* is a major fungal pest of woody host plants on a worldwide basis. It has a broad host range and is responsible for losses amounting to tens of millions of dollars annually to Australian forestry and agriculture. In addition, it poses a serious threat to the conservation of native plant species. It is known to occur in some areas of rainforest in northeastern Queensland (Brown 1976; Brown and Sjolund 1987; Brown, Sjolund, and Tierney 1987), but its status has not been rigorously assessed for many years, during which time our understanding of its biology has greatly increased (Gadek 1999). At present, visitors are excluded from some of the most picturesque and biologically interesting montane areas of the Wet Tropics World Heritage Area based on the belief that visitation could cause the introduction of *Phytophthora* to rare plant communities. This organism is the subject of present and future research, the outcomes of which are of great interest to managers, conservationists, and the tourism industry.

INFRASTRUCTURE DEVELOPMENT

One of the threats to the integrity of rainforests is roads and other linear intrusions such as powerlines (Goosem 1997; Goosem and Marsh 1997). The Wet

Tropics bioregion has already been highly fragmented by clearing, particularly in the eastern lowlands and western tablelands. However, even the central escarpment, which has largely intact tracts of rainforest, is internally fragmented by a large and extensive network of roads, powerline clearings, and alterations of stream flow (plate 6/fig. 24.3). Internal fragmentation of a rainforest can disrupt the natural movements of many species, with a range of potential ecological and evolutionary effects. There are more than 1,400 km of major roads in use, and more than 5,000 km of unused roads or former logging tracks. The flagship species of the World Heritage Area, the Southern cassowary (*Casuarius casuarius johnsonii*), is a large flightless bird whose numbers are estimated at 2,000–4,000. Individuals are frequently killed by motorists, and there is a great deal of public concern about the effect of roads on this and other native species. Managing roads and traffic and encouraging habitat connectivity for ground and arboreal fauna through culverts and canopy bridges in order to reduce roadkill is a difficult task. Ecologists and engineers have collaborated in preparing a manual of best practices for road design, building, and maintenance in tropical forests (Queensland Main Roads 1997). The manual, which describes how to make roads more environmentally friendly through improved culvert design, erosion control, faunal crossings, and drainage techniques, has led to a greater research interaction between road designers and rainforest ecologists and should lead to more environmentally friendly rainforest roads.

RAINFOREST FRAGMENTATION AND CLEARING

The rainforests of northeastern Queensland are highly fragmented. Some of this fragmentation is natural, and some is due to forest clearing and use. As we have just seen, this fragmentation has been exacerbated by the extensive network of minor and major roads and old logging tracks. It is therefore not surprising that these forests have been the subject of extensive research on the effects of forest fragmentation (e.g. Laurance 1991, 1994; Laurance and Bierregaard 1997; Goosem 1997; Goosem and Marsh 1997). In reality, the core area of North Queensland rainforest, unaffected by human-induced edge effects, is surprisingly small. The most exhaustively studied of the North Queensland rainforests are those on mountaintops (Monteith and Davies 1990; Monteith 1994). Studies of more than 300 locations in the nineteen mountain rainforest zones of the Wet Tropics revealed a remarkably distinct and highly endemic fauna and flora, with many species endemic to individual mountain peaks or groups of peaks (Bouchard, Brooks, and Yeates, chap. 21, and Moritz and McDonald, chap 26 in this volume). In practice, these communities are under less threat than lowland communities, as development is unlikely to occur or be allowed on

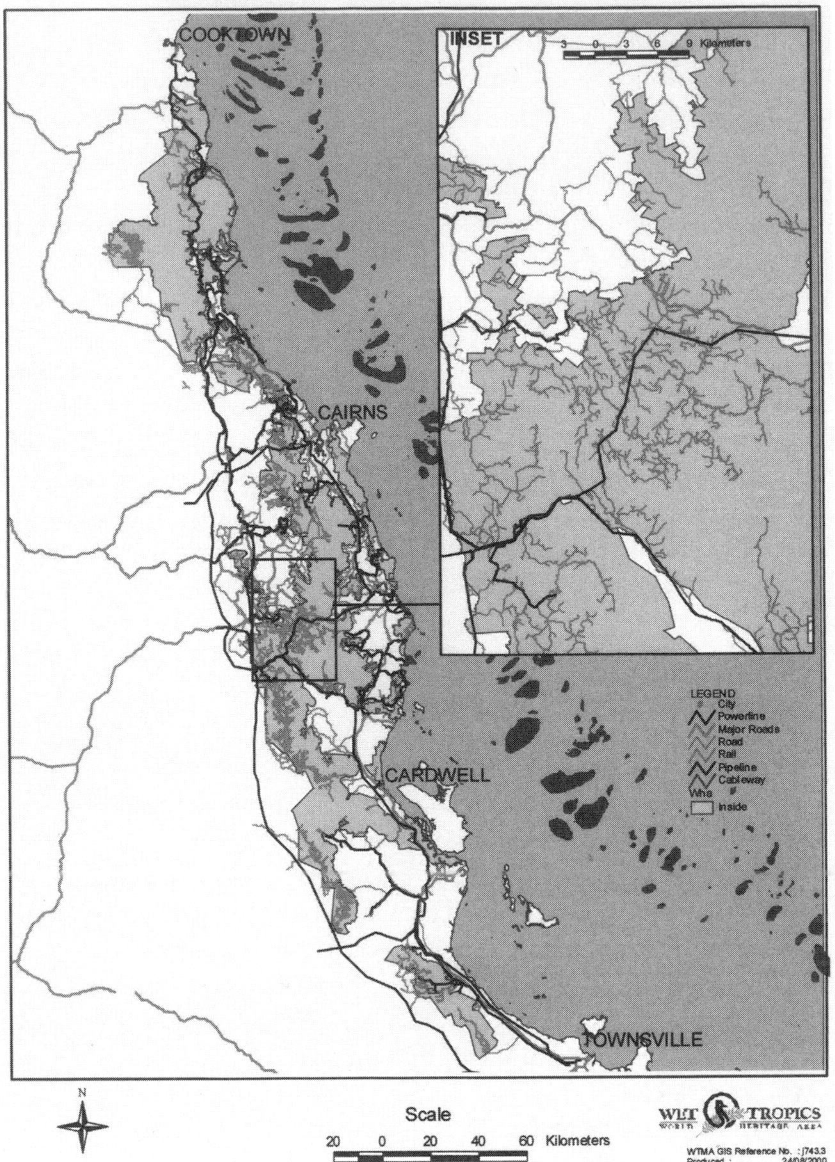

Figure 24.3 Distribution of major roads and powerlines in and around the Wet Tropics of Queensland World Heritage Area. See also plate 6.

these mountaintops. A great deal of research is still needed to determine the viability of rainforest fragments and the effect of fragmentation on communities. Inevitably, the focus of much future work will be on charismatic animals such as the northern bettong (*Bettongia tropica*), tree kangaroos, and tree possums, but the effect of fragmentation on invertebrates also needs to be determined. Numerous community groups are involved in tree planting to improve the connectivity of critical forest fragments, and the effectiveness of their actions also needs to be determined.

CLIMATE CHANGE

Perhaps the greatest threat to the viability of North Queensland's rainforests is climate change. Climate change is not something new, and Hopkins et al. (1993, 1996) have shown that these forests are highly dynamic, changing vegetation types from rainforest to dry forest and vice versa in response to changing climatic regimes over the last 20,000 years (see also Kershaw, Moss, and Wild, chap. 19 in this volume). However, land use changes mean that many areas of rainforest are now discontinuous and highly fragmented, and may therefore be less able to respond to climatic perturbations. We may also find that the scale and frequency of droughts or storms are different from those previously experienced in the region. Such extreme conditions could be critical in determining whether populations of individual species or whole communities survive. A combination of such climatic factors with the additional effects of introduced species or poor fire management could be catastrophic. Modeling of past, present, and future vegetation distributions for rainforest in the Wet Tropics using artificial neural network models (Hilbert and Ostendorf 2001) indicates that current land use patterns will severely affect potential future rainforest distributions in the Wet Tropics. Other modeling indicates that many of the seventy or more vertebrate species that are cool-adapted and endemic to the upland regions of the Wet Tropics may also disappear as temperatures rise over the next 50–100 years (Williams, Bolitho, and Fox, 2003).

LESSONS FOR OTHER COUNTRIES

The management issues for tropical rainforests in North Queensland are in many ways similar to those facing other tropical rainforest regions in other countries. The threats to those regions are sometimes of a different nature and on a different scale, but the dominant pressure is to "use" rainforests for short-term gain rather than with a view to long-term economic and ecological sustainability.

One lesson from the Wet Tropics experience is the necessity for multidisciplinary research to help guide management decisions. New data from such research has guided almost every step in the protection and sustainable use of the Wet Tropics World Heritage Area. Another critical factor is the involvement of many different organizations and communities in long-term decision making. Exclusion of particular sectors of the community only means that their interests will need to be considered at some time in the future and that true partnership agreements cannot be made. The long-term future of the Wet Tropics cannot be assured until the interests of rainforest Aboriginal people are considered alongside the interests of tourism, conservation, and other sectors. Integrating competing goals into regional planning processes that identify and resolve potential and real conflicts is vital.

Perhaps the most important lesson to be gained from the North Queensland experience over the last 10 years is the value of World Heritage listing as a mechanism for integrating the protection and conservation of rainforests and their sustainable use. This value was confirmed by the results of a meeting of many of those concerned with the conservation and sustainable use of tropical forests (CIFOR 1999). The World Heritage Convention provides a versatile mechanism for the conservation and sustainable use of tropical forests.

ACKNOWLEDGMENTS

I thank Craig Moritz, Steve Goosem, Miriam Goosem, Garry Werren, and Rosemary Hill for commenting on earlier versions of this chapter. I thank Earl Saxon for his suggestions on the effects of various pressures on tropical rainforests in North Queensland.

Part III

RAINFOREST FUTURES

25 Overview: Processes, People, and Prospects for Tropical Rainforests

CRAIG MORITZ, CHRISTOPHER W. DICK, AND ELDREDGE BERMINGHAM

The real future of tropical biology lies in whether, within our generation, the academic, social and commercial sectors can collaboratively preserve even small portions of tropical wildlands to be studied and used for understanding, material gain, and for intellectual development of the society in which the wildland is embedded.
—*D. H. Janzen (1986, 305)*

If a tree falls in the forest and there's no biologist there to hear it, it definitely doesn't make a sound.
—*Doug Daly* (New York Times, *May 7, 2002)*

From the fossil reconstruction of rainforest history to the unified theory of biodiversity and biogeography, our enthusiasm for understanding the origins and evolution of tropical rainforests is tempered by the fact that these forests are quickly disappearing. Because of human pressures, tropical forests may be experiencing the greatest challenge to their ecological resilience since the Cretaceous/Tertiary boundary (65 MYA), when the impact of a meteor decimated most tropical forests (Vajda, Raine, and Hollis 2001) and disrupted important plant-insect interactions for several million years (Labandeira, Johnson, and Wilf 2002). The tropical deforestation crisis has nearly run its course in several parts of the world, such as Indonesia (MacKinnon, chap. 27 in this volume) and the Atlantic forests of Brazil. Any biologist who has contemplated the future of tropical rainforests must be deeply concerned, and this concern has led, quite naturally, to an increasing effort to link the results of basic research to conservation.

EVOLUTIONARY PROCESSES AND CONSERVATION PLANNING

Biologists play a key role in determining which lineages and geographic regions need to be conserved, and how (Margules and Pressey 2000). A clearer understanding of evolutionary and ecological processes is essential if we are to develop strategies for conserving rainforests as the dynamic systems that they clearly are. The challenge is to integrate knowledge of pattern and process while developing efficient taxonomic and spatial surrogates for each (Cowling and Pressey 2001; Ferrier 2002). For many systems, our sampling of species diversity, particularly patterns of geographic turnover, is simply too limited to develop conservation plans with any confidence that designated areas will truly capture overall diversity or the ecological dynamics that maintain it (e.g., Patton and da Silva, chap. 7, and Ruokolainen, Tuomisto, and Kalliola, chap. 13 in this volume). Understanding of the biogeographic, paleoecological, and evolutionary history of rainforest areas should improve our capacity to predict spatial patterns of diversity and complementarity from available taxonomic and environmental data (Moritz et al. 2001).

Moritz and McDonald (chap. 26) develop a process-oriented approach to conservation, with particular reference to rainforest vertebrates of the Australian Wet Tropics. In the Wet Tropics and elsewhere (e.g., Patton and da Silva, chap. 7 in this volume), vicariant processes, often combined with local extinction and range expansion (Schneider and Williams, chap. 20 in this volume), have shaped both species and genetic diversity, so representation of the vicariant areas in a reserve network should protect both levels of diversity. However, to protect the evolutionary processes that promote phenotypic diversity, and potentially form new species, it is also crucial to include environmental gradients, such as rainforest-savanna ecotones (Smith et al., chap. 9 in this volume) and altitudinal gradients (Fjeldså et al., chap. 8 in this volume), within designated conservation areas. These latter areas are frequently under greater human pressure than large areas of intact rainforest and are likely to be underrepresented if efforts are focused exclusively on rainforests.

THE PROBLEM IS PEOPLE!

While biologists have the key role of defining the fundamental principles and requirements of an efficient conservation system, the larger challenge is to mesh this information with the political and socioeconomic forces that threaten biological diversity. MacKinnon (chapter 27) and Laurance (chapter 28) provide dispatches on the environmental threats facing Southeast Asia and the Amazon basin, respectively, the world's principal repositories of the species richness that is emblematic of tropical rainforests worldwide. In both cases there is substantial international investment in conservation, often targeted at capacity building and economic returns to local communities, but these efforts are swamped by larger-scale national development priorities, poorly regulated international trade, and, frankly, rampant corruption. This situation stands in stark contrast to the Australian Wet Tropics (Stork, chap. 24 in this volume), where there is agreement at national, state, and local government levels on maintaining biological diversity for both intrinsic and instrumental (e.g., ecosystem services, ecotourism) values, though even here there can be conflict with infrastructure and agricultural development. It follows that the recent trends toward increased logging, burning, and clearing of rainforest, as described for Indonesia and Brazilian Amazonia, are as much political as economic.

So how can biologists, immersed in their pursuit of knowledge of ecological and evolutionary processes, help to find solutions? Effective communication of research results, beyond the confines of traditional scientific publication, is one route. The reaction of the Brazilian media to the dire prognosis for the Amazon under current development plans (Laurance, Cochrane et al. 2001; Lawrence, chap. 28 in this volume) prompted an increase in funding from the Brazilian government for environmental impact assessments. Another route is to contribute to local understanding of the immediacy and scale of the issues, via data repatriation, training, and effective interpretation of research (e.g., Faith et al. 2001). One of the only rays of hope contained in MacKinnon's assessment of the Indonesian situation related to direct action taken by local communities in Papua. When it comes to the implementation of well-conceived, science-based strategies on the ground, we have a lot to learn.

26

Evolutionary Approaches to the Conservation of Tropical Rainforest Vertebrates

CRAIG MORITZ AND KEITH R. MCDONALD

ABSTRACT

Given continuing human pressures on rainforests worldwide, there is a need to bring our understanding of biological processes to bear on the question of how to prioritize areas for conservation and then how to manage them. We argue that maintaining evolutionary processes is a valid goal, and that a strategy to achieve this goal should build on our knowledge of the system in question. Evidence from evolutionary and biogeographic studies of rainforest vertebrates indicates that most extant species are old (Mio-Pliocene), the main effect of Pleistocene fluctuations being isolation of faunas and local extinction. Presently, there is strong phenotypic differentiation across habitat boundaries, but in some cases none between long-isolated (refugial) areas. These processes lead to geographic mosaicism in species richness, phylogenetic diversity, and phenotypic diversity. An appropriate conservation strategy for such regions is to first identify areas required to maintain endemic species and long-isolated populations. Second, within such areas, we should seek to maximize protection of habitat diversity across ecotones and other steep environmental gradients. This second step simultaneously maximizes retention and persistence of beta diversity of species, adaptive variation within species, and the potential for migratory responses to climate change. This approach was developed with the rainforests of the Wet Tropics of Queensland in mind and is illustrated for that region. Similar processes may underlie diversity in other rainforest systems characterized by steep environmental gradients and long-term vicariance. This process-oriented approach to conservation generally demands high-resolution data on species and phylogeographic diversity; however, it is possible that paleoclimatic distribution modeling may be reasonably effective as a surrogate for broad-scale assessments.

INTRODUCTION

There is irrefutable evidence that tropical rainforests are highly dynamic systems over both ecological and geologic time scales. This conclusion derives in part from studies of local transitions in pollen records, which, in combination, indicate broad-scale and repeated replacements of mesic warm-adapted rainforest with cool-adapted rainforest or xeric elements during the Quaternary glacial cycles (Flenley 1993; Kershaw 1994; Colinvaux, De Oliveira et al. 1996; Kershaw,

Moss, and Wild, chap. 19 in this volume) and earlier (Morley 2000). The effects of these fluctuations in rainforests on the diversity and distribution of rainforest-dependent vertebrates have been debated actively for over 30 years (Haffer 1969; Prance 1982a). Much of the attention has centered on Amazonia, in the form of a debate about whether hotspots of species richness and endemism represent locations of Quaternary refugia (Brown 1987b) and whether allopatric speciation occurred among these putative isolates (Haffer 1969; Endler 1982b; Mayr and O'Hara 1986; Bush 1994).

Three key questions about rainforest dynamics can be posed:

1. Did rainforests contract to isolated refugia during the Quaternary glacial cycles?
2. If so, was this contraction accompanied by local extinctions, rapid speciation, differential adaptation, or all three?
3. What was the effect of the ensuing expansion of rainforests during the early Holocene (Hopkins et al. 1993, 1996; Morley 2000) on species distributions, phenotypic evolution, and regional species diversity?

Whatever the answers to these questions, it must be recognized that in many systems, the current distributions of rainforests and their resident vertebrate species are recent phenomena, as are current associations among species. This dynamism represents a substantial challenge for conservation assessment and planning for both rainforests and other biomes.

Conservation planning for rainforests—in particular, the prioritization of areas for reserves or off-reserve management—has taken on increasing urgency as habitats worldwide are reduced in area or degraded and human pressures on remaining intact systems increase (Whitmore and Sayer 1992; Laurance and Bierregaard 1997; McKinnon, chap. 27, and Laurance et al., chap. 28 in this volume). Fortunately, in Australia, most major rainforest areas are now relatively well protected as a result of strong pressure from community organizations (e.g., Rainforest Conservation Society of Queensland 1986), although prioritization of these areas for management remains an issue. For broad-scale planning, a common approach is to identify sets of relatively undisturbed areas that maximize the total number of species or communities represented (Margules and Pressey 2000). Thus, attention has been given to areas of high species richness and endemism, although the correlation between these two characteristics can be poor within or across taxonomic groups (Prendergast et al. 1993; Kerr 1997). More recently, algorithms based on complementarity or irreplaceability of areas have been developed that seek to ensure the representativeness of reserve systems in relation to a defined conservation goal (Pressey et al. 1993;

Pressey, Johnson, and Wilson 1994; Lombard et al. 1997), although, again, correlation among taxa can be poor (van Jaarsveld et al. 1998), and even when correlated, some taxa are poor indicators for others (Moritz et al. 2001). In addition, consideration has been given to prioritizing divergent lineages in order to retain maximum phylogenetic diversity across species or intraspecific conservation units (Humphries, Williams, and Vane-Wright 1995; Crozier 1997), although this may not matter for a given region unless extinction risks (e.g., habitat loss) are strongly biased phylogenetically (Nee and May 1997).

These approaches, while increasingly explicit and efficient, suffer from their essentially static approach to biological diversity—they address the current distribution of communities, species, or genetic diversity, but fail to consider the historical processes that shaped that diversity (Margules and Pressey 2000; Cowling and Pressey 2001). It has been argued that conservation planning and assessment should incorporate information on evolutionary processes (Erwin 1991a; Brooks, Mayden, and McLennan 1992; Smith, Bruford, and Wayne 1993; Balmford, Mace, and Ginsburg 1998; Cowling and Pressey 2001), with the goal of protecting the processes that sustain diversity, rather than just their specific products (Brown and Brown 1992; Moritz 1995). Only by understanding these processes and incorporating them into planning can we devise conservation strategies that will protect diversity in the event of future changes, such as climate change and land use pressures. Key evolutionary processes that should be considered include speciation, phenotypic evolution and adaptation, range expansion, and genetic interactions within zones of secondary contact.

Given the fluctuations of rainforest distributions through time, it would seem important to recognize the effects of history on the current distributions, evolution, and associations of rainforest vertebrates for the purpose of conservation planning. One interesting attempt in this direction is the work of Fjeldså and colleagues (Fjeldså 1994; Fjeldså and Lovett 1997; Fjeldså et al., chap. 8 in this volume), who pointed out that some areas of high endemism represent concentrations of relatively ancient species (e.g., Amazonian lowlands), whereas others are dominated by young species (eastern Andean slopes). They went on to argue that the latter, as areas of active diversification, should receive more conservation attention, although a different view would be taken by proponents of maximizing phylogenetic diversity (Faith 1992; Humphries, Williams, and Vane-Wright 1995; Crozier 1997). Similarly, Smith et al. (1997; Smith et al., chap. 9 in this volume) pointed out the conservation significance of ecotones as sites of adaptive divergence and possibly speciation.

In this chapter we review briefly our current understanding of key evolutionary processes as they apply to rainforest vertebrates (see also Moritz et al.

2000; Moritz 2002) and then develop a strategy that seeks to maximize the representation of species and genetic diversity while also incorporating information on evolutionary processes and biogeographic history. Although drawing on examples from elsewhere, we focus on the vertebrates endemic to the "Wet Tropics" rainforests of northeastern Queensland, as we have a well-documented history of rainforest contractions during the Quaternary for this system (Kershaw 1994; Kershaw, Moss, and Wild, chap. 19 in this volume; Hopkins et al. 1993, 1996) and a growing appreciation of how those contractions have shaped the current pattern of vertebrate diversity (Schneider and Williams, chap. 20 in this volume).

EVOLUTIONARY PROCESSES

Speciation

Both the tempo and mode of speciation in tropical rainforest vertebrates have been actively debated in recent years. An early hypothesis (Haffer 1969), still advocated by some (e.g., Terborgh 1992; Haffer 1997; Roy 1997), is that the high species diversity of rainforest vertebrates stems from a (Plio-) Pleistocene "species pump," driven by allopatric divergence among refugia during periods of rainforest contraction. However, this view is challenged by a plethora of alternative speciation mechanisms (Bush 1994), increasing molecular evidence that most species of rainforest vertebrates predate the Pleistocene (Moritz et al. 2000, and see below), and the suggestion that climatic "flickers" were so rapid as to preclude speciation, with most species responding instead by migration (Roy et al. 1996).

The proposed alternative mechanisms of speciation can be broken down into three classes:

- *Allopatric divergence* due to drift, divergent selection, or both. This mechanism may have operated among rainforest refugia, across riverine barriers, or among montane isolates (e.g., Haffer 1969, 1997; Vanzolini and Williams 1970; Salo et al. 1986; Roy 1997; Patton and da Silva, chap. 7 in this volume).
- *Parapatric divergence,* wherein divergent selection pressures across a strong environmental gradient promote reproductive isolation even in the presence of gene flow (Endler 1977, 1982b; Smith et al. 1997; Smith et al., chap. 9 in this volume).
- *Sympatric divergence* (or "ecological speciation"), wherein disruptive

selection (e.g., trophic specialization) within a population, if genetically correlated with mate choice, can result in the formation of new species (Smith and Skulason 1996; Schluter 1998).

There have been few critical tests of these alternative hypotheses, although the work of Patton and colleagues is a notable exception. Phylogenetic analysis of Andean rodents supported allopatric over parapatric divergence in that sister species were allopatric rather than parapatric, indicating that divergence across steep altitudinal gradients had played little role in the diversification of this group (Patton and Smith 1992). In a further test of the effect of riverine barriers on codistributed lowland species, geographic patterns of genetic divergence were distributed predominantly across paleodrainages rather than across existing rivers (Patton, Silva, and Malcolm 1994, 2000; Patton and da Silva, chap. 7 in this volume). In support of the importance of allopatric divergence among montane isolates, Roy (1997) presented molecular phylogenetic evidence for Pleistocene divergence among allopatrically distributed subspecies of birds (*Andropanus*) endemic to East African mountains. In contrast, long-term (Plio-Pleistocene) isolation combined with marked range reductions has not resulted in detectable phenotypic divergence within species of birds, frogs, and lizards from the Australian Wet Tropics (Joseph, Moritz, and Hugall 1995; Schneider and Moritz 1999; M. Cunningham, unpublished data). These recent studies (see also Schneider and Williams, chap. 20 in this volume) illustrate the insights that can be derived from combining molecular phylogeographies and phylogenies with information on phenotypic variation and geographic distributions to investigate mechanisms of speciation in rainforest vertebrates.

One factor complicating interpretations of speciation mechanisms operating on tropical rainforest vertebrates is that divergences among most extant species appear to substantially predate the Quaternary climatic cycles. With few exceptions, estimates of mtDNA sequence divergences among sister species are more consistent with Pliocene or Miocene than with Pleistocene divergences (fig. 26.1), as also reported for temperate birds (Klicka and Zink 1997). This trend appears to be consistent across Neotropical, Australasian, and African vertebrate species (Moritz et al. 2000; Fjeldså et al., chap. 8 in this volume). For example, estimates of sequence divergence (16S rDNA) among microhylid frogs (*Cophixalus*), the only vertebrate genus with numerous narrowly endemic species in the Australian Wet Tropics, range from 5% to 19%, with a mean of 11%, whereas a value of less than 1% would be expected for Pleistocene separations (C. Hoskin, forthcoming).

The geographic patterns and causes of speciation in these old species are

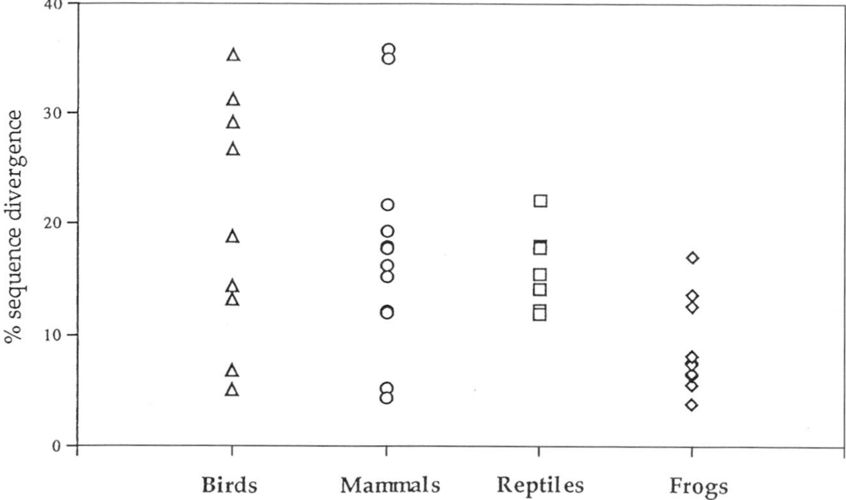

Figure 26.1 Estimates of mtDNA sequence divergence (Kimura two-parameter distances) among sister species of rainforest vertebrates. Estimates for birds, mammals, and reptiles are from protein-coding genes and are comparable at this level of divergence (data from Joseph, Moritz, and Hugall 1995; Roy 1997; Mustrangi and Patton 1997; Lara, Patton, and da Silva 1996; M. C. Lara, C. J. Schneider, and C. Moritz, unpublished data). Values for frogs are from 16S rDNA sequences for microhylid frogs (*Cophixalus*) from the Wet Tropics (data from C. Hoskin, forthcoming; C. Moritz, unpublished data), which evolve at approximately half the rate of the protein-coding sequences. Values of less than 2% and less than 1% would be expected for Quaternary divergences for the protein and rDNA sequences, respectively.

likely to be obscured by subsequent changes in geographic range. But, whatever the mechanism of diversification, the data conflict with the hypothesis that the high diversity of vertebrate species in rainforests is due to rapid speciation during the Pleistocene. With the possible exception, at least for birds, of geologically young montane regions (Fjeldså 1994; Roy 1997), it appears that rainforest systems essentially represent the remnants of species diversity attained at a time when rainforests were more geographically widespread (in Africa and Australia: Morley 2000; Greenwood and Christophel, chap. 18 in this volume). Interestingly, phylogenetic analyses of species-rich genera largely endemic to the Australian Wet Tropics rainforests (*Cophixalus:* C. Hoskin, forthcoming; beetles: Bell et al., forthcoming; Hemiptera: B. Russell et al., unpublished data; earthworms: C. Moritz, A. Hugall, and B. Jamieson, unpublished data) reveal a high frequency of probable sister species that are geographically adjacent despite their considerable age. These findings suggest that these taxa have diversified and survived in situ, rather than colonizing the region from a broader ancestral distribution. In turn, they imply that the long-term contraction of Australian rainforests was characterized by regional extinctions rather than migration of fauna to the East Coast refuge.

Adaptation and Phenotypic Divergence

Phenotypic divergence, reflecting the joint effects of selection and drift on underlying genes as well as environmental effects (plasticity), can be expected to occur among isolates and across environmental gradients in the presence of gene flow. Several recent experimental studies of natural populations have demonstrated that specific morphological or life history attributes can be generated repeatedly and rapidly (e.g., Malhotra and Thorpe 1991; Reznick et al. 1997; Losos, Warheit, and Schoener 1997; Losos et al. 1998). In a context of typically low rates of speciation, intraspecific phenotypic diversity, especially that which is genetically based, becomes an important component of biological diversity, whether it is transient or a stage in the formation of new species. An exhaustive review of patterns of phenotypic variation in rainforest vertebrates is beyond the scope of this chapter. Rather, we highlight two recent studies that may have broad implications for conservation.

The first is an analysis of morphological variation (in highly heritable traits) in greenbuls (*Andropanus*) from rainforest sites in ecotones and in continuous forest sites in West Africa (Smith et al. 1997; Smith et al., chap. 9 in this volume). Substantial morphometric divergence, similar to that observed among described species, was observed among different ecotonal populations despite gene flow, whereas similarly separated populations within continuous forests showed little or no differentiation. This finding was interpreted as evidence for the importance of environmental gradients in phenotypic diversification and possibly speciation.

The second study concerned morphological comparisons of populations of primarily rainforest-dwelling skink species (*Carlia*). Comparisons were made between populations in different historically isolated rainforest areas and between populations in rainforest and adjacent wet sclerophyllous habitats within historical rainforest areas (Schneider et al. 1999). This study revealed substantial differences in size at maturity and other size-related characters across habitats, again despite gene flow, but not between rainforest areas probably isolated from one another since the Pliocene. This finding is all the more remarkable because the skink populations within each area appear to have undergone dramatic range reductions and subsequent expansions during the late Pleistocene and early Holocene. The lack of morphological divergence among historically isolated populations of vertebrates from the Australian Wet Tropics (Schneider and Moritz 1999) may reflect their survival in ecologically similar rainforest refugia, and hence a lack of divergent selection pressures.

Together, these studies lead to two conclusions. First, long-term isolation, even when combined with population bottlenecks, is neither sufficient nor necessary to generate substantial phenotypic diversity. Second, divergent selection pressures across environmental gradients appear to be important in promoting variation in phenotypes and life histories within species.

Extinction and Colonization

Recent studies of the Australian Wet Tropics provide a clear picture of the effects of late Pleistocene rainforest contractions and Holocene expansions on vertebrate species richness and distributions (Schneider and Williams, chap. 20 in this volume). This clarity derives from several features of the system: (1) it is relatively small (less than 1 million ha; fig. 26.2A), yet contains a large number (~ 73) of endemic vertebrate species or subspecies; (2) most of these endemic vertebrates are found in upland areas of mesothermal rainforest; (3) the taxonomy is reasonably stable, and distributions are reasonably well known; (4) the system has a well-documented history of rainforest contraction, and there are independent estimates of the locations of major refugia based on plant biogeography and paleoclimatic modeling (Webb and Tracey 1981a; Nix 1991a; fig. 26.2B); and (5) geographic patterns of genetic (mtDNA sequence) diversity have been examined in several bird, reptile, and frog species (e.g., Joseph, Moritz, and Hugall 1995; Schneider, Cunningham, and Moritz 1998) and combined quantitatively with paleobioclimatic modeling for a snail species (Hugall et al. 2002).

The overwhelming signature is one of local extinctions and associated reorganization of communities, probably during the most severe contraction some 26,000–10,000 years ago, and possibly during the previous glacial period (150,000–120,000 years ago) as well (Kershaw 1994; Kershaw, Moss, and Wild, chap. 19 in this volume). This history is suggested by a significant association between the extent of convolution of rainforest blocks, independent of area, and the local richness of endemic species, a correlation that is specific to endemic species and which holds across frogs, reptiles, birds, and mammals (Williams 1997; Williams and Pearson 1997). Confirmation comes from patterns of mtDNA phylogeography, wherein most rainforest herpetofauna examined show a major genetic break across a historical (but not current) disjunction in rainforest called the "Black Mountain Corridor" (BMC), and several species appear

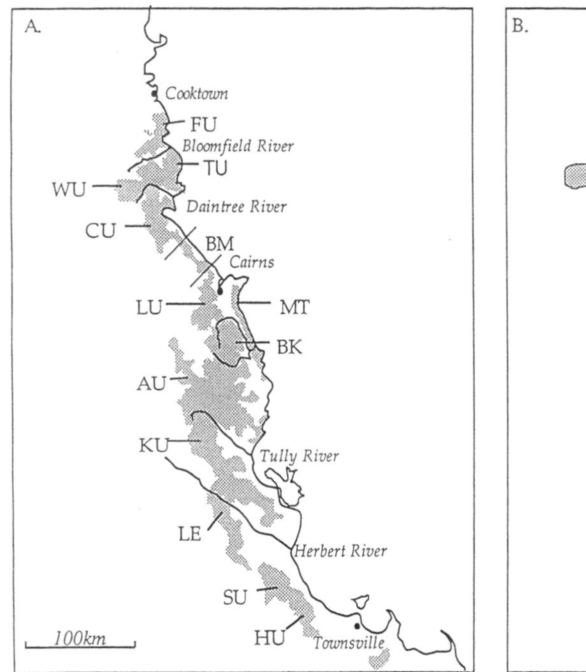

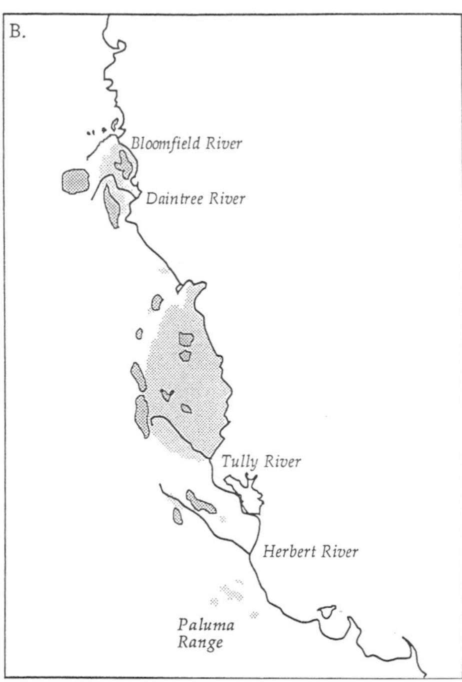

Figure 26.2 (A) Current distribution of Wet Tropics rainforests, with locations mentioned in text labeled. (B) Predicted refugia at 10,000 years ago, showing refugial areas predicted from angiosperm distributions (dark shading: Webb and Tracey 1981a) and from paleoclimatic modeling (light shading: Nix 1991a). (After Schneider, Cunningham, and Moritz 1998.)

to have undergone dramatic range reductions on each side of this barrier (Joseph, Moritz, and Hugall 1995; Schneider, Cunningham, and Moritz 1998; Schneider and Moritz 1999; M. Cunningham, unpublished data). In some cases, the data are consistent with survival in single refugia on either side of the BMC, but other species appear to have survived in multiple geographic refugia on either side, perhaps because of differences in habitat or area requirements.

Subsequently, rainforests expanded rapidly across the upland areas about 8,000 years ago, although expansion in the lowlands occurred much later (Hopkins et al. 1993, 1996). A period of cooler and wetter climates approximately 7,500–6,000 years ago appears to have created conditions suitable for colonization by upland-restricted rainforest species, even across areas that are currently isolated (Nix 1991a; Winter 1997; fig. 26.3). The genetic data support recolonizations in that locations predicted to have had rainforest areas too small to sustain vertebrate populations, such as the southernmost block (HU in fig. 26.2A), have a subset of the alleles found in adjacent predicted refugia and presumably were

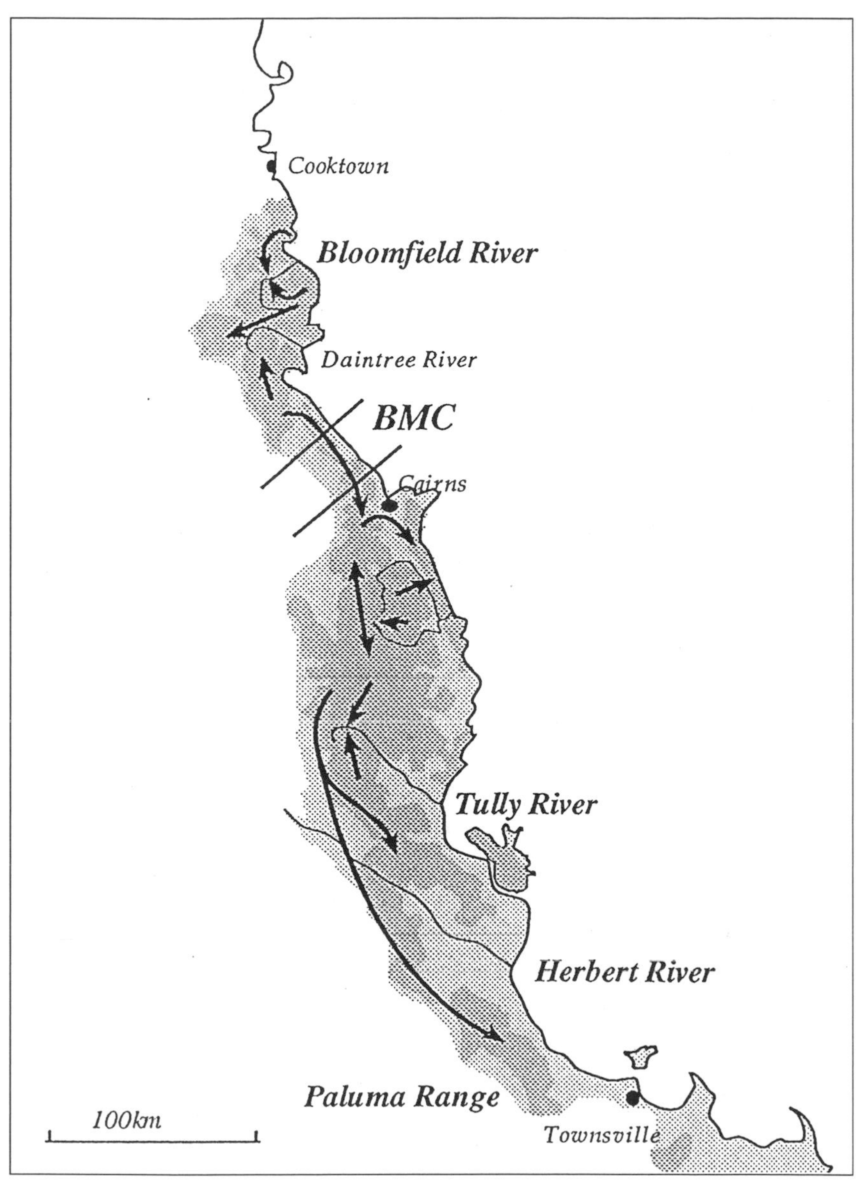

Figure 26.3 Inferred pattern of population expansions during the relatively cool, wet period 7,500–6,000 years ago. The area predicted by paleoclimatic modeling (Nix 1991a) to have been suitable for cool-adapted rainforest species is represented by light shading; the current distribution of rainforest is represented by dark shading. (Redrawn with minor modifications from Schneider, Cunningham, and Moritz 1998.)

colonized from there (Joseph, Moritz, and Hugall 1995; Schneider, Cunningham, and Moritz 1998). Further secondary contacts, identified from overlapping distributions of divergent and otherwise geographically restricted mtDNA clusters, are observed between putative refugia at three sites (fig. 26.3): north of the Bloomfield River, in the southern BMC-LU area, and across the Tully River Gorge.

Our suggestion, although it is speculative, is that these areas of secondary contact or range expansion may represent significant foci for future evolution (adaptation or speciation) of rainforest vertebrates. In the former areas, introgression between historically isolated populations may increase local genetic and phenotypic variance (Grant and Grant 1992; DeMarias et al. 1992) and possibly generate new evolutionary lineages (Arnold 1997; Rieseberg and Wendel 1993) or create conditions favoring reinforcement of genetic isolation and thus speciation. The evidence obtained so far from genetic analyses of zones of secondary contact in the Wet Tropics provides little indication of assortative mating (*Bettongia tropica:* Pope, Estoup, and Moritz 2000; *Carlia rubrigularis:* B. Phillips, S. Baird, and C. Moritz, unpublished data; *Litoria nannotis:* M. Cunningham, unpublished data), but for *C. rubrigularis* there is evidence for strong selection against hybrids (B. Phillips, S. Baird, and C. Moritz, unpublished data). Range expansions may be accompanied by increased phenotypic variation due to ecological release, but this remains to be tested. Areas such as the southern uplands of the Wet Tropics represent novel, reconstituted communities in which local ecological interactions may differ from those in refugial areas (Ricklefs and Schluter 1993a).

Because of its unusually long isolation (Morley 2000) and relatively small area, the Wet Tropics system may not be representative of evolutionary dynamics in other rainforest areas, such as those with widespread lowland rainforests, although potential parallels include climatically restricted, mid- to high-elevation rainforest areas such as the East African and Cameroon mountains (Fjeldså et al., chap 8 in this volume; Smith et al. 2000; Smith et al., chap. 9 in this volume), the Atlantic forests of Brazil, and the highlands of Madagascar, New Caledonia, and New Guinea. One intriguing difference is between upland refugial (presumably ecologically stable) areas adjacent to extensive lowlands versus those that are more isolated. All have high species richness and endemicity. However, in the former areas, exemplified by the East African rift mountains and the eastern flank of the Andes, there appears to be a higher proportion of young species (Fjeldså 1994; Fjeldså et al., chap. 8 in this volume; Moritz et al. 2000), whereas the more isolated Australian and Atlantic forest systems are, to a first approximation, dominated by old taxa, often with sister taxa in geographically distant locations (Moritz et al. 1997; Patton, da Silva, and Malcolm 2000; Lara and Patton 2000). This emerging pattern may reflect higher speciation rates, lower extinction rates, or both in areas with adjacent uplands and lowlands, and it should be evaluated further by more precise phylogeographic analyses within these regions and their extension to other regions.

Evolutionary Consequences of Historical Rainforest Contraction

The preceding brief review of evolutionary processes operating on rainforest vertebrates during the Quaternary (see also Moritz et al. 2000) leads to the following conclusions relevant to conservation assessments and planning:

- Speciation of rainforest vertebrates, by whatever mechanism, is rare, such that most extant species are of Pliocene or greater age. One possible exception is birds in geologically recent montane areas.
- Phenotypic divergence can occur repeatedly across environmental gradients due to selection pressures, but appears unaffected by long-term isolation and range reduction per se.
- The primary effect of late Pleistocene contractions of rainforest, where these occurred, was localized extinction, rather than phenotypic divergence or speciation.
- Subsequent to the contractions, rainforest expansions during the early Holocene resulted in substantial range expansions of vertebrate species and, in some cases, secondary contact between genetically (but not necessarily phenotypically) distinct lineages.
- As a consequence, rainforest landscapes that underwent severe contractions during the late Pleistocene are now of three types: areas with long histories of occupation and high species endemism, but little, if any, phenotypic uniqueness (refugia), expansion areas with recently reconstituted communities or secondary contacts, and strong environmental gradients that promote phenotypic diversity and perhaps speciation.

PRINCIPLES FOR CONSERVATION PLANNING

The overall goal of a conservation strategy should be to protect the processes, both ecological and evolutionary, that sustain diversity at the ecosystem, species, and genetic levels. In order to achieve this goal, is it essential to retain viable populations of species within a landscape that permits dynamic ecological and evolutionary responses to environmental change. The core principles for meeting this objective are simple: preserve the unique products of evolution—that is, "keep all the pieces"—and maintain the viability of landscapes necessary for their continued evolution. All this must be done in the context of human pressures on the system. Below, we elaborate on these two principles and suggest a strategy for conservation planning that is consistent with them. It should be noted that, whereas the above goals and principles are general, this strategy is specific to the Wet Tropics and other systems with analogous evolutionarily and biogeographic histories.

Keep All the Pieces

The diversity present among rainforest vertebrates, as in any system, covers a wide spectrum, potentially from endemic monotypic higher taxa through individual genotypes in widespread species. In order to prioritize areas for conservation, the elements that are to protected must be defined explicitly (Margules and Pressey 2000). Although alternatives could be proposed (e.g., species with essential ecological functions: L. E. Gilbert 1980), it makes sense to focus on elements of diversity that are unique to the system and which cannot be replaced readily. These elements are endemic species and, within species, historically isolated sets of populations (also termed evolutionarily significant units, or ESUs: Moritz 1994).

For rainforest vertebrates, we have inferred that species are formed rarely, so that loss of any one species is unlikely to be reversed within any time frame relevant to managers. Likewise, we argue that ESUs should be protected, despite the lack of obvious phenotypic divergence among historically isolated populations (at least in the Wet Tropics), because their underlying genotypic combinations cannot be replaced if they are extinguished, and because they could represent nascent species (Avise, Walker, and Johns 1998). How best to protect adaptive genetic diversity within species is still debated, with some arguing that phenotypically distinct populations should be protected, regardless of the level of historical isolation (e.g., Crandall et al. 2000). An alternative approach, based on the concept of recoverability (Moritz 1999, 2002), suggests that we should consider historical isolation and adaptive evolution as separate processes. The former can be conserved by recognizing distinct conservation units and areas and the latter through a landscape approach—that is, by protecting the context for continued evolution: viable populations distributed across spatially heterogeneous landscapes.

Maintain Landscape Elements Necessary for Continued Evolution

To maintain active evolutionary processes across rainforest landscapes, two elements that should be protected are environmental gradients and areas of range expansion, especially those in which multiple species have zones of secondary contact between previously isolated (refugial) populations. Protection of environmental gradients, especially in relation to topography, achieves several objectives, including allowing migratory responses to climate change, maintaining areas of recent diversification (where this applies: e.g., Fjeldså 1994; Fjeldså et al., chap. 8 in this volume), and retaining among-habitat (beta) diversity of species. Other significant gradients include transitions between geologic and rainfall thresholds, especially as they control the distribution of plant communities (e.g., Tuomisto et al. 1995; Ruokolainen, Tuomisto, and Kalliola, chap. 13 in this volume) and thereby influence selection on vertebrate species. The rationale for protecting areas of expansion and secondary contact was given above.

Conservation Strategy

In practice, allocating areas for reservation or priority off-reserve conservation requires compromises in relation to other land uses, economic considerations, and consideration of the viability of the areas selected in a landscape context (Margules and Pressey 2000). Inevitably, these decisions have a strong social and political component. It may be that most of a given rainforest system is perceived to be of significance in relation to one or more of the above criteria; however, greater flexibility in management should ensue if the reasons for protecting each area are explicit.

Given adequate information on distributions, the selection of areas to maximize the representation of endemic species is relatively straightforward (Margules and Pressey 2000), although it needs to be borne in mind that the outcome for vertebrates may not predict conservation priorities for taxa distributed at smaller spatial scales (Moritz et al. 2001). There may also be sufficient information from molecular data on relationships and approximate divergence times to weight species and areas according to their phylogenetic distinctiveness (Vane-Wright, Humphries, and Williams 1991; Crozier 1997), if so desired. However, it should be noted that there is very little data with which to assess concordance across taxonomic groups in such weighting schemes.

More difficult to implement is the notion of protecting historically isolated populations, or ESUs. One criterion for recognizing these populations is the presence of geographically bounded, reciprocally monophyletic groups of mtDNA alleles, with supporting evidence from allele frequency differences at nuclear genes (Moritz 1994; Moritz, Lavery, and Slade 1995). However, the number of species that can be assayed in this way inevitably is restricted. Another option is to attempt to identify historically isolated areas (Avise 1992; Moritz and Faith 1998) by assaying a range of widely distributed species that are expected a priori to be affected by historical contractions of rainforest (i.e., low-vagility rainforest specialists). This approach has the potential to predict patterns of historical isolation for other similarly affected species, although the geographic scale over which species survived or recolonized will vary (Hugall et al. 2002; Schneider and Williams, chap. 20 in this volume).

We propose the following strategy to identify areas for protection according to the above principles (Moritz 2002):

1. Select areas that maximize representation of historically isolated communities and of viable populations of endemic species.
2. Add areas with secondary contact among historical isolates, giving highest priority to those involving multiple species.
3. Within the areas selected in steps (1) and (2), maximize representation of environmental gradients and diversity of forest types.
4. Ensure that the selected areas constitute an ecologically viable landscape following traditional reserve design principles (minimize edges, isolation, etc.: e.g., Lombard et al. 1997).

APPLICATION OF CONSERVATION STRATEGY

In the following analysis we apply the conservation strategy outlined above to the endemic vertebrates of the Australian Wet Tropics. This area has been listed as a World Heritage Area and is mostly protected, although land tenure types vary from National Park through State Forest to Unallocated State Land. Rather than selecting areas for reserves, the challenge is deciding which areas should receive maximum protection (even if already in National Parks), which should be targeted for rehabilitation, and which should have priority for conversion from other tenure types to National Park land.

The vertebrate species distribution data used in this analysis come from Williams, Pearson, and Walsh (1996; S. E. Williams, unpublished data), and have been modified according to recent observations and changes in taxonomy. Nonetheless, ongoing and intensive surveys and genetic analyses are still turning up new species and refining distributions, so that the results presented here are illustrative, rather than definitive. Genetic (mtDNA) data are derived from Joseph, Moritz, and Hugall (1995) and Schneider and colleagues (Schneider, Cunningham, and Moritz 1998; Schneider et al. 1999). The analysis is restricted to upland regions, which represent the stronghold of virtually all of the endemic rainforest vertebrates (Williams, Pearson, and Walsh 1996). These regions are divided into a series of topographically defined units identified in previous species-biogeographic analyses (see fig. 26.2A: Winter 1984; Nix 1991a; Williams and Pearson 1997).

Biogeographic units were prioritized in relation to the distribution of endemic vertebrate species using the concept of irreplaceability: the extent to which a given site contributes to a specific conservation goal or, conversely, the extent to which options for a representative reserve system are foreclosed if that area is excluded (Pressey, Johnson, and Wilson 1994; Ferrier 2002). The algorithm used is based on complementarity: the units containing the most geographically restricted species are selected first, then those with the next most restricted species not represented in the first group are added, and so on. The values assigned are in relation to a target of encompassing 15% or 50% of the occurrences of endemic species, with each species occurring in at least one unit. As units are added to the protected area (e.g., on the basis of current levels of protection), the calculations are repeated to take account of changes in irreplaceability. The calculations were made using C-PLAN conservation planning software (NSW NPWS 1996).

The mtDNA data were considered in three ways. First, the distributions of areas showing discrete clusters of mtDNA alleles (putative ESUs) were compared across all species assayed to identify congruent patterns (see also Schneider, Cunningham, and Moritz 1998). Second, an index of isolation for each area was constructed using the total branch length (number of substitutions) defining monophyletic clusters of alleles, averaged across all species examined (those without monophyletic groups scoring zero). Third, the Phylogenetic Diversity (PD) measure introduced by Faith (1992) and developed for comparative genetic (mtDNA) data by Moritz and Faith (1998) was applied. The total branch length of alleles represented by combinations of areas was estimated from neighbor-joining trees for each species and summed across species. For this purpose, only the lizard and frog species were included, as these groups have the best geographic coverage. To allow for missing data for some species-area combinations, the PD values are presented as averages across the species included. Under the assumptions of the approach (see Moritz and Faith 1998), higher values are expected to predict higher feature diversity.

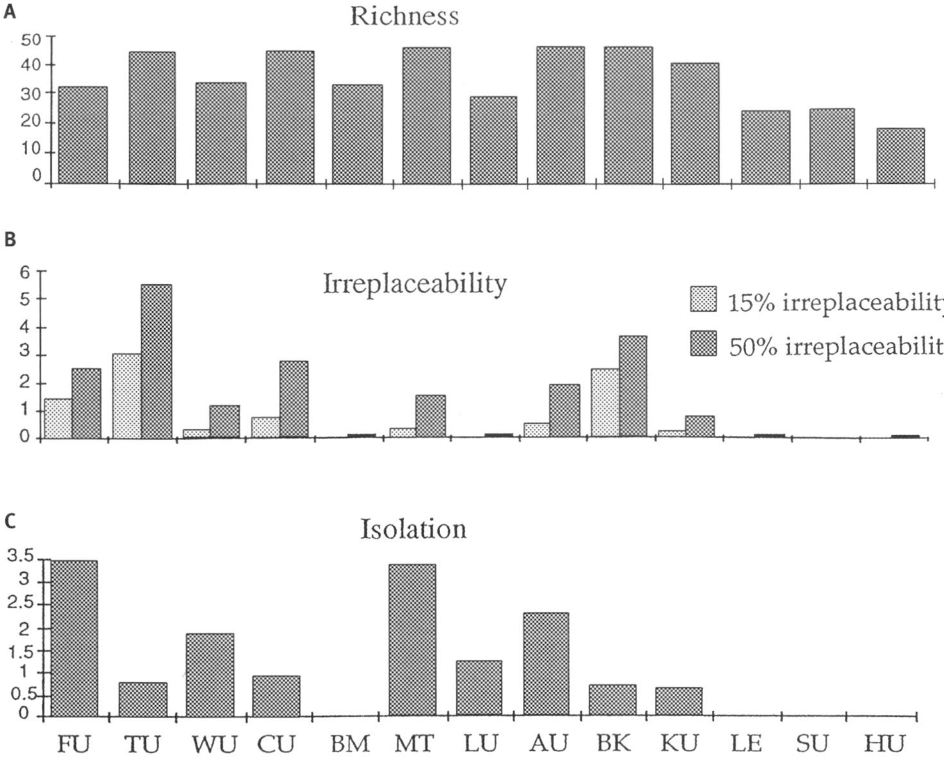

Figure 26.4 Comparison of different measures of conservation value for endemic vertebrates of thirteen upland areas in the Wet Tropics (see fig. 26.2). (A) Richness of endemic species. (B) Irreplaceability values at targets of 15% (light shading) and 50% (dark shading) of areas occupied by each species. (C) The genetic uniqueness of each area averaged across species that showed discrete mtDNA clusters (isolation).

Species Irreplaceability and Genetic Divergence

The estimates of species richness and irreplaceability (at targets of 15% and 50% of areas occupied by each species) across thirteen upland biogeographic units are shown in figure 26.4. The number of endemic species is highest for the Thornton, Carbine, Lamb, and Atherton Uplands (TU, CU, LU and AU, respectively) and the Bellenden Ker Range (BK), declines rapidly in the southern blocks (KU, LE, SU, HU), and is also relatively low in the northern Windsor and Finnegan Uplands (WU, FU), the Black Mountain corridor (BM), and the Malbon Thompson Range (MT). By contrast, the irreplaceability values (15% target) are highest for the Thornton Uplands, followed by the Bellenden Ker Range and the Finnegan Uplands, because of the presence of complementary endemic species restricted to each of these locations. No endemic vertebrate species are restricted to the species-rich Atherton Uplands. At a 50% target, the significance of the Finnegan Uplands is accentuated further, but the irreplaceability of the Carbine Uplands becomes greater than that of the Finnegan Uplands because of its high species richness. This result differs somewhat from that of a separate analysis (Moritz et al. 2001) that included snails, insects, and plants in addition to vertebrates; here, the Atherton and Carbine Uplands had high irreplaceability in addition to BK, FU, and TU.

The extent of protection by National Park status varies widely among biogeographic units in the Wet Tropics. To identify those areas most important for conversion from other land tenure types to National Park status (and appropriate management), we defined six areas with substantial National Park land—BK, FU, TU, KU, SU, and HU—as being adequately protected and examined rankings of irreplaceability among the remaining seven biogeographic units. This analysis identified the Lamb Uplands as being the most important biogeographic unit for the expansion of protected areas, although this expansion was not identified as having a positive value until a 25% target was invoked. With adequate protection of LU, the next units warranting additional protected areas were the Carbine and Windsor Uplands. Despite its high richness of endemic species, the relatively less protected Atherton Uplands ranks low when irreplaceability is used as a criterion because most of its endemic vertebrate species are shared with adjacent units (BK, LU, and KU). As noted above, including invertebrate species, with their more fine-grained diversity, increased the conservation significance of the Atherton Uplands (Moritz et al. 2001).

The geographic distribution of putative ESUs across ten species surveyed for mtDNA variation is summarized in figure 26.5 as both primary (deep divergences) and secondary (shallow divergence) clusters. Four features of these patterns of divergence are notable. First, these patterns reflect a common history of separation by the Black Mountain Corridor (see fig. 26.2A), although both the Lamb Uplands and the Malbon Thompson Range have been colonized from both directions (see also Joseph, Moritz, and Hugall 1995; Schneider, Cunningham, and Moritz 1998). Second, the species vary in the geographic scale over which ESUs occur, and some have additional deep genetic breaks (e.g., the gecko *C. laevis* north of the Bloomfield River and at Malbon Thompson Range, and *L. nannotis* south of the Tully River. Third, in all cases examined, the southernmost locations (HU, SU) are undifferentiated from areas farther to the north (KU, AU), suggesting that the vertebrate assemblages in the former areas are dominated by recent range expansion. Fourth, areas of secondary contact have been defined for three species, and more are predicted to occur across the BMC and Lamb Uplands and possibly the Tully River as well.

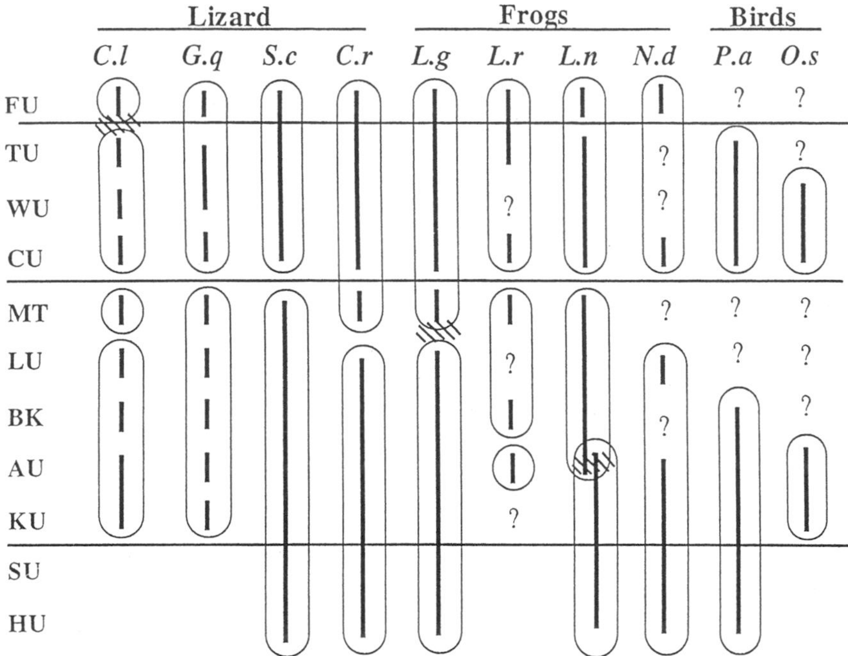

Figure 26.5 Summary of distribution of ESUs for ten vertebrate species sampled from multiple upland areas in the Wet Tropics. Putative ESUs (diagnosed as having reciprocally monophyletic mtDNA clusters) are indicated by bars, and higher-level clusters of ESUs are bounded by lines. Cross-hatched areas indicate locations of secondary contacts. A question mark indicates that a species is present but has not yet sampled. Species abbreviations: lizards: *C.l., Carphodactylus laevis; G.q., Gnypetoscincus queenslandiae; S.c., Saltuarius cornutus; C.r., Carlia rubrigularis;* frogs: *L.g., Litoria genimaculata; L.r., Litoria rheocola; L.n., Litoria nannotis; N.d., Nyctimistes dayi;* birds: *P.a., Poecilodryas albispecularis; O.s., Orthonyx spaldingii.*

The isolation indexes and pairwise PD values derived from the mtDNA data for the eight species of reptiles and amphibians shown in figure 26.5 are summarized in table 26.1, and an ordination of the latter (using multidimensional scaling) is shown in figure 26.6. In contrast to both species richness and irreplaceability, the highest isolation values are seen at FU and MT, reflecting substantial mtDNA divergence for two and three species, respectively, in those units (see Schneider, Cunningham, and Moritz 1998 for details). The lowest values (reflecting the combinations predicted to capture feature diversity most poorly) occur among KU, SU, and HU, areas thought to have been involved in a recent colonization event, whereas the highest values are between regions at the geographic extremes of the range. On the basis of maximizing the area spanned by the ordination (Faith and Walker 1996), the best strategy would be to select a

Table 26.1 PD estimates for Wet Tropics biogeographic zones for eight species of herpetofauna

	Species[a]	FU	TU	WU	CU	MT	LU	AU	BK	KU	SU	HU
							← BMC →					
FU	8	**3.375**	12.57	13	12.63	26.25	45.33	44.13	42	52.67	57	59
TU	7		**0.714**	4.8	7.286	22	40.5	40.86	36.71	42.67	58.67	53
WU	5			**1.8**	8.4	20.2	41.2	44.4	41.8	42	65	54
CU	8				**0.875**	23.43	43.33	41.63	39.29	43.29	62.33	51.2
MT	7					**3.286**	26.67	28.71	34.5	34.5	60.67	47
LU	6						**1.167**	7.833	5	12.83	23	18.5
AU	8							**2.25**	9.429	13	20.3	21.3
BK	8								**0.625**	12.67	22	17.5
KU	7									**0.571**	4	5
SU	5										**0**	2
HU	4											**0**

Note: Diagonal (boldfaced) indicates mean % sequence divergence of monphyletic clades across species. Numbers above the diagonal indicate mean PD estimates across pairwise comparisons of areas.

[a]Number of species from each biogeographic zone for which mtDNA data are available.

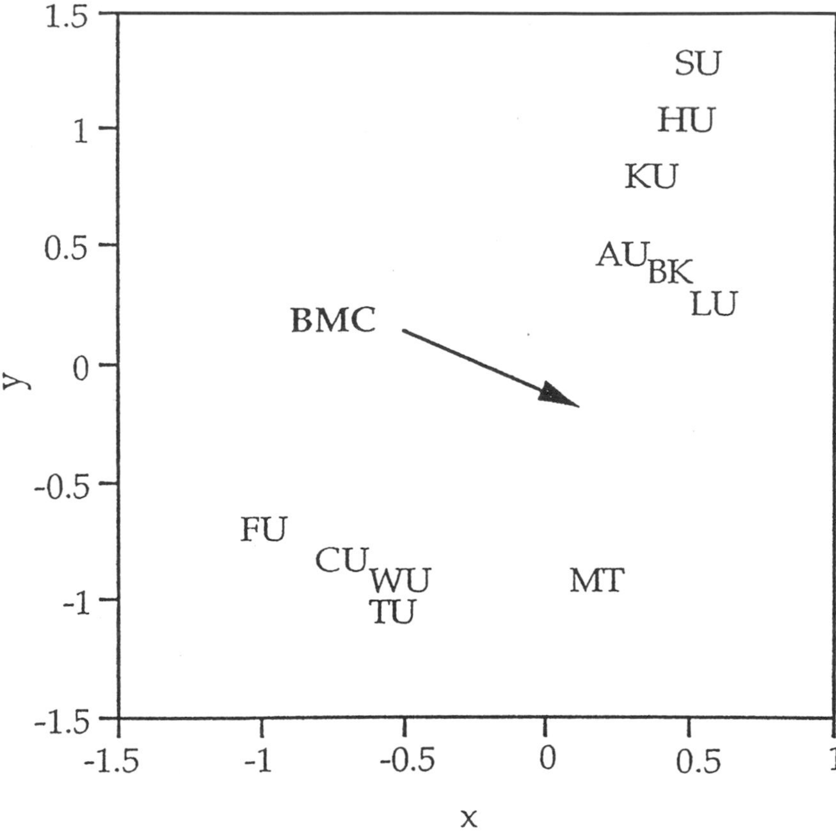

Figure 26.6 Multidimensional scaling ordination of mean PD values among upland areas in the Wet Tropics. Note the sharp distinction between the northern and southern regions and the intermediate position of MT. The arrow indicates the geographic location of the Black Mountain Corridor.

combination of MT and one area from each of the northern and southern groups of biogeographic units (for additional analyses, see Moritz 2002).

Conservation priorities according to historical isolation (genetic irreplaceability) and species irreplaceability (15% target) are contrasted in figure 26.7. The eleven areas assessed using both approaches fall into four quadrats. Rainforest areas in quadrat I have high conservation values by virtue of their high species irreplaceability, but have relatively low genetic isolation from adjacent areas. The interpretation is that each of these refugial areas harbors (complementary) geographically restricted species, but other more widespread endemic species found there have experienced recent expansions to adjacent areas (see

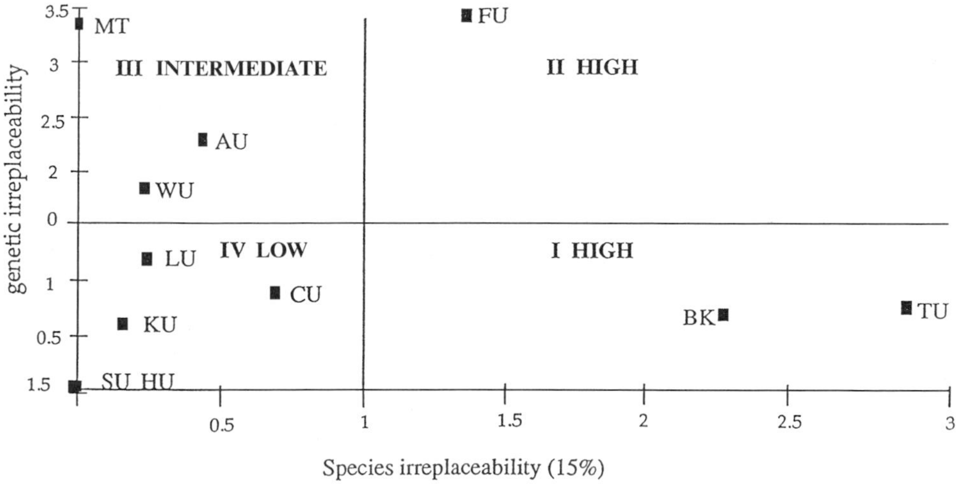

Figure 26.7 Bivariate plot of isolation index (mean divergence of ESUs) and species irreplaceability at a 15% target. Upland areas have been divided into four categories of conservation value on the basis of these two dimensions (see text).

fig. 26.3). In quadrat II, FU has both high genetic irreplaceability and species irreplaceability, representing the presence of some narrow endemic species and long-term isolation of some widely distributed endemics. This area is also a predicted refuge, but does not appear to have been the source for colonization of adjacent areas. Quadrat III includes areas with moderate to substantial genetic isolation, but relatively low value as assessed by species irreplaceability, with MT having among the highest values for genetic uniqueness, but no geographically restricted endemic species. Quadrat IV includes the recently colonized areas that are accorded low value according to both criteria; on current evidence these areas have neither geographically restricted endemic species nor localized ESUs.

Synthesis

Based on the foregoing analysis of the distributions of species and historically isolated units (step 1 in the conservation strategy), the three areas with highest conservation significance appear to be TU, BK, and FU, and those with the lowest values are LU, CU, KU, SU, and HU (fig. 26.8). Although genetic data are too sparse for formal analysis, it is likely that BM and LE would also be included in this low-priority group. The iterative analyses of areas requiring additional protection identified LU, followed by CU and WU, and additional consideration should be given to MT because of the presence of genetically divergent lineages within some

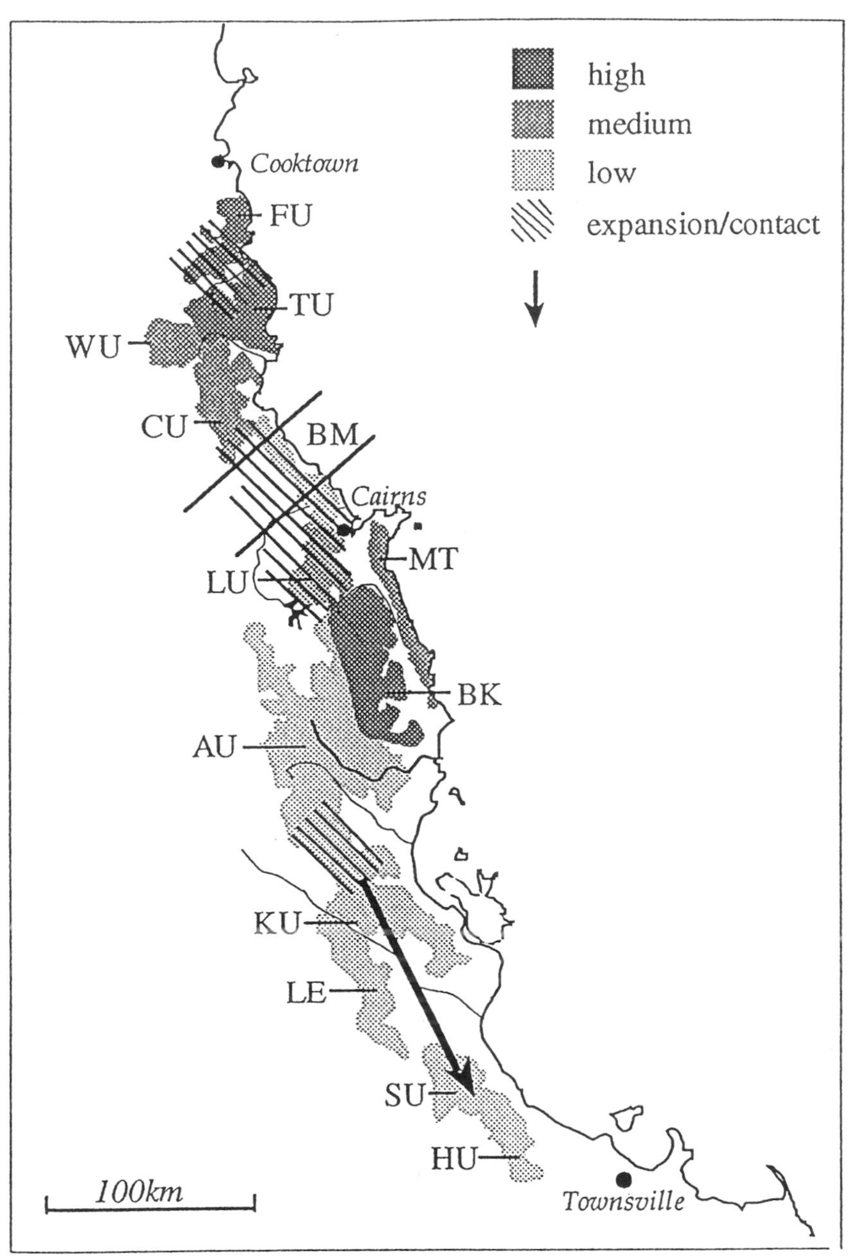

Figure 26.8 Map of upland areas in the Wet Tropics indicating conservation values for vertebrate species derived from genetic distinctiveness and species irreplaceability (low, medium, high; see fig. 26.7) and processes of secondary contact (diagonal hatching) and congruent range expansions (arrow to HU).

species. We also reiterate that both AU and CU are accorded high conservation status when insect and snail species are included in the analysis (Moritz et al. 2001; see also Bouchard, Brooks, and Yeates, chap. 21 in this volume).

Step 2 is to add areas of expansion, with particular emphasis on multispecies contact zones (fig. 26.8). In this context, the key areas are LU and the southern section of FU, both of which have multispecies secondary contacts, and SU-HU, representing a reconstituted assemblage of vertebrates. Notably, two of these areas (LU and SU-HU) were accorded relatively low priority on the basis of step 1.

The final steps in the strategy would be to identify major environmental gradients in each selected area—in this case most likely altitudinal transects—and then to make sure that the selected areas are configured in a landscape likely to ensure the ecological viability of populations and habitats in the region (e.g., Lombard et al. 1997).

The above analysis is, inevitably, based on our knowledge of current patterns of diversity, integrated with spatial surrogates for key evolutionary processes. However, as shown by the extensive paleoecological record (Hopkins et al. 1993, 1996; Kershaw, Moss, and Wild, chap. 19 in this volume) and analyses of genetic and species diversity (Schneider and Williams, chap. 20 in this volume), distributions of the endemic vertebrates of the Wet Tropics have been affected directly by past climate change. So what of future climate change? Our capacity to predict shifts in spatial distributions is limited by inadequate knowledge of the constraints imposed by physiology and ecological interactions. However, spatial modeling of both the critical habitats (especially notophyll and microphyll forest types: Hilbert and Ostendorf 2001) and the endemic vertebrate species (Williams, Bolitho, and Fox 2003) suggests marked reductions in areas of potentially suitable environment for mid- to upper montane species, especially in the major historical refugia on the coast: FU, TU, and BK, and to a lesser extent, CU. That areas that have persisted as core habitat though the climatic oscillations of the Quaternary and earlier, and which now harbor numerous narrow endemic species, many with deep evolutionary histories, should now be under threat is of great concern and underscores the potentially unique nature of the coming climates in tropical biomes.

IMPLICATIONS FOR MANAGEMENT

As areas of intact rainforest are depleted worldwide, there is an urgent need to protect additional areas, either through dedicated reserves or effective off-reserve management. Ultimately, these efforts will come down to management of people and socioeconomic conditions (Laurance et al., chap. 28, MacKinnon, chap. 27, and Stork, chap. 24 in this volume), but it remains essential for biologists to identify and prioritize areas with the aim of securing the maximum possible proportion of the remaining diversity.

In this chapter, we have illustrated how an understanding of the tempo and pattern of speciation, adaptation and phenotypic divergence, and historical biogeography can help to identify a conservation strategy that is consistent with the goal of maintaining evolutionary processes and the nonrecoverable products of those processes. The actual strategy suggested should not be viewed as prescriptive, as it was constructed with the idiosyncrasies of the Australian Wet Tropics in mind, although a similar process may prove effective in analogous topographically complex systems dominated by old species, such as the Atlantic forests of Brazil (Brown and Brown 1992; Mustrangi and Patton 1997; Lara and Patton 2000) and possibly the montane areas of Papua New Guinea. However, the principle of inferring and protecting key evolutionary processes is generally applicable (e.g., Fjeldså 1994; Cowling and Pressey 2001).

Although mostly contained within a World Heritage Area, the Wet Tropics rainforests cover a variety of land tenure types, and the effects of various land uses such as agriculture, population expansion, and tourism vary widely across the region (Stork, chap. 24 in this volume). Based on our analysis of patterns and processes for endemic vertebrates (see Moritz et al. 2001 for consideration of other taxa), we make the following recommendations:

1. The Thornton Uplands (TU) should receive the highest level of protection available under current legislation (National Park Scientific) by virtue of its extraordinarily high irreplaceability for endemic species. This status would preclude development of access for tourism.
2. Given adequate protection (and management) of BK, TU, and FU, the most significant area for conversion of State Forest to National Park is the Lamb Uplands. This area has a high richness of endemic species and is also important as a zone of secondary integration of historically isolated populations (ESUs) for several species (Pope, Estoup, and Moritz 2000; Phillips, Baird, and Moritz 2004), as well as representing core habitat for some others (e.g., the threatened tropical bettong, *Bettongia tropica*).
3. Two other areas with little or no formal protection (as National Parks) that warrant additional attention are the Carbine Uplands and the Malbon Thompson Range. The former has a high richness of endemic species and high irreplaceability, especially when insects and snails are

included (Moritz et al. 2001; see also Bouchard, Brooks, and Yeates, chap. 21 in this volume), and the latter contains multiple genetically divergent lineages.

4. As a matter of urgency, we need to improve our ability to predict the effects of future climate change on sensitive biota and regions—particularly the narrow endemics occupying the evolutionarily unique coastal refugia (FU, TU, BK), but also ecologically sensitive taxa such as folivorous mammals (Williams, Bolitho, and Fox 2003)—and to develop management responses (where possible).

One obvious limitation of the general strategy outlined above is that it is a rare luxury to have detailed comparative data on patterns of genetic diversity, let alone a thorough understanding of species taxonomy and biogeography (Patton and da Silva, chap. 27, and Ruokolainen, Tuomisto, and Kalliola, chap. 13 in this volume). However, one prospect to emerge from the Wet Tropics system is that paleobioclimatic modeling of habitats, when combined with information on species distributions and a crude assessment of ecology (vagility, degree of specialization to rainforests), can provide reasonable predictions of the geographic patterns of major isolation and expansion events (Schneider, Cunningham, and Moritz 1998; Hugall et al. 2002). In large part, the good performance of paleomodels (relative to independent molecular data) in the Wet Tropics is due to its very steep environmental gradients, which serve to minimize spatial errors in the face of imprecise estimates of historical climates. Whether this predictive ability holds across other systems where climate-driven vicariance events have dominated the historical dynamics of rainforests remains to be seen (e.g., McGuigan et al. 1998), but it does suggest the possibility of using predictive paleomodels of either species or their habitats (Nix 1991a; Hilbert et al. 2001) as surrogates to infer the underlying historical biogeography. Also, where such retrospective models are shown to perform well relative to independent data, we can have more confidence in predictions of spatial changes in biodiversity patterns under future climate change scenarios (e.g., Williams, Bolitho, and Fox 2003).

ACKNOWLEDGMENTS

Thanks to M. Cunningham, C. Hoskin, C. Schneider, M. Lara, and L. Pope for access to data, assistance with analyses, and vigorous discussions about the meaning of it all. K. Richardson conducted the analyses of species irreplaceability, and we are grateful to R. Pressey and colleagues for access to, and assistance with, C-PLAN software. L. Pope and A. Hugall assisted with figures and preparation of the manuscript and provided yet more insights.

27
Parks, People, and Policies: Conflicting Agendas for Forests in Southeast Asia

KATHY MACKINNON

ABSTRACT

Humankind has had a long history in Asia, and several Southeast Asian nations are among the world's most densely populated countries. Nevertheless, the region still supports some of the globe's most extensive, diverse, and species-rich forests. Over the last 30 years, however, there has been an unprecedented rise in habitat loss and degradation, fueled by exploitation of forests for timber and conversion to agriculture. Destruction of these tropical forests can be expected to lead to losses of species and biodiversity. Throughout the region, countries have established parks and protected areas for biodiversity conservation, but many habitat types, especially lowland forests, are underprotected, and many conservation areas are "paper" parks only. Conflicts between production and conservation are bound to continue in a policy context that favors increased exploitation and unsustainable development. Case studies from the region illustrate the challenges and opportunities for integrating conservation and development in Southeast Asian forests for the benefit of both biodiversity and local communities.

INTRODUCTION

Tropical Forests and Biodiversity Loss

The five principal causes of biodiversity loss and species extinction are habitat loss and fragmentation, habitat degradation, overexploitation, secondary extinctions, and the impact of alien species (Kramer, van Schaik, and Johnson 1997). Almost all natural habitats throughout the world are being modified, degraded, or converted to anthropogenic landscapes. The tropical rainforests that harbor roughly 50% of all terrestrial biodiversity are among some of the most threatened habitats. In 1990 it was estimated that some 170,000 km^2 (17,000,000 ha) of rainforest was being cleared every year globally, an area equivalent to the size of Cambodia (FAO 1993). Given recent deforestation figures for Indonesia of 18 million hectares of forest lost between 1985 and 1997 (World Bank 2001; Holmes 2002), this global total is probably a gross underestimate. Of the world's three major tropical forest regions, Southeast Asia has the highest rate of forest destruction and logging (Laurance 1999).

Since the Earth Summit in Rio de Janeiro in 1992, biodiversity conservation in general, and tropical rainforests in particular, have received an unprecedented amount of attention and funding. Nevertheless, there is no indication that the rate of rainforest loss or degradation is slowing, either globally (Whitmore and Sayer 1992; Terborgh and van Schaik 1997) or regionally (J. MacKinnon 1997). In densely populated Southeast Asia, forest loss is continuing at an unprecedented rate, both to meet the needs of a land-hungry and growing population and to fuel economic development. The estimated figures for forest loss in the Indonesian archipelago alone have almost trebled over the last 12 years, from 900,000 hectares annually in 1990 to at least 1.7 million hectares by 1997 (Holmes 2002) and probably closer to 2.5 million hectares by 2003, according to recent estimates. Clearly such rates of loss will have an enormous impact on biodiversity and future development options.

Logging plays a major role in forest destruction. In some areas forests are clear-cut prior to land conversion for agriculture, plantations, and transmigration settlements. More usually, however, it is not logging activities per se that cause forest loss, but the land clearance afterward when logging roads and poor management of logging concessions provide access for illegal loggers and migrant farmers. Agricultural conversion, both by small farmers and for large-scale plantations, contributes to habitat loss both directly, through forest clearance, and indirectly, through out-of-control fires that begin as deliberate burning to clear land.

Destruction and degradation of tropical forests leads to habitat fragmentation and ultimately to loss of species and genetic resources. Fragmentation restricts plants and animals to "islands" of habitat, often too small to support viable breeding populations. A much-quoted rule of thumb holds that a 90% reduction of habitat will result in the almost immediate loss of about half of the species found in an area (Wilson 1992). Once fragments have become isolated from sources of colonization, however, species loss continues, often rapidly, through the process of secondary extinction. Depending on the size of the remaining fragment, 90% or more of the initial species complement can ultimately disappear (Diamond 1984). Very small fragments lose species rapidly, especially larger mammals and predators at the head of the food chain (Lovejoy et al. 1983). The relationships between animals and plants and their role in forest dynamics are complex and poorly understood, but it is clear that the loss of key species from an ecosystem can have far-reaching effects (Crooks and Soulé 1999; Leigh and Rubinoff, chap. 12 in this volume). As well as reducing the total area of available habitat, forest fragmentation results in a dramatic increase in the amount of habitat edge and magnifies edge effects, thus altering ecological processes over large areas and even deep inside apparently undisturbed forest

(Laurance 2000). For example, studies in the 90,000-hectare Gunung Palung National Park in western Borneo show that recruitment of canopy trees has collapsed, mainly because of a dramatic increase in seed predation as a result of vertebrate seed predators that have flooded into the park from surrounding degraded areas (Curran et al. 1999).

Tropical forest species are especially prone to extinction, since species richness is linked to species rareness (Whitmore 1984). The greatest richness of plant and animal species is concentrated in lowland forests, so it should be of particular concern that the old-growth lowland tropical forests of the Philippines, Thailand, Vietnam, Sumatra, and Borneo, all rich in endemics, have already been reduced to less than 10% of their original areas (J. MacKinnon 1997; Terborgh and van Schaik 1997). Yet the rate of forest loss and degradation continues apace (Jepson et al. 2001; Kinnaird et al. 2003). Throughout Southeast Asia, forest loss and fragmentation is so extensive, especially in lowland areas, that several countries include ecoregions where further habitat loss will certainly lead to species extinctions. It has been predicted, for example, that all non-swamp lowland forest outside protected areas will be lost by 2005 in Sumatra, and by 2010 in Kalimantan (Indonesian Borneo) (Holmes 2002). This forecast emphasizes the importance of securing those areas already designated for conservation.

All the countries of Southeast Asia have ratified the Convention on Biological Diversity, but very few have succeeded in establishing and managing an adequate and representative protected area network to safeguard their national biological heritage (J. MacKinnon 1997). The concept of sustainable forest management, though universally endorsed, is rarely even attempted. Forest destruction is proceeding so fast that this decade probably represents the last chance to protect viable areas of tropical forests; indeed for some countries it is already too late. The fate of Asian forests will depend on reconciling the often conflicting needs and agendas of people, parks, and government policies and promoting economic development and growth consistent with wise natural resource management and maintenance of forest cover. It has also become increasingly obvious that forest management is linked to good governance (EIA 1998; Jepson et al. 2001; FWI/GFW 2002).

Protected Areas: Cornerstones of Biodiversity Protection

For most species, protecting adequate and connected habitat will be the single most important way to ensure their long-term survival. Protected areas

Table 27.1 Country data for forest cover and protected areas (PAs) in Southeast Asia

Country	Area (1,000 km^2)	% forest cover	% deforested (per annum)	Area in PAs (1,000 ha)	% PA cover
Brunei	5.8	81	0.4	115	20.0
Cambodia	182	60	1.4	3,267	18.0
Indonesia	1,905	57	1.1[a]	18,230	9.5
Laos	237	56	1.0	2,756	11.6
Malaysia	330	53	2.3	1,504	4.5
Myanmar	677	43	1.4	173	1.0
Papua New Guinea	463	78	0.3	82	0.2
Philippines	300	26	1.0	597	2.0
Singapore	0.6	7	0.5	3	4.5
Thailand	513	25	4.0	7,939	12.1
Vietnam	332	25	1.6	1,330	4.0

Source: Adapted from J. MacKinnon 1997.
[a]Over 20 million hectares of forest were lost in Indonesia between 1985 and 1997; most of this loss was in the lowland forests of western Indonesia (Sumatra, Kalimantan, and Sulawesi).

are the cornerstones of biodiversity and species conservation (Kramer, van Schaik, and Johnson 1997; Bruner et al. 2001). Conservationists have long debated how much habitat needs to be protected to conserve all species and where, and how large, conservation areas should be. Biodiversity is not distributed uniformly; centers of biological richness or endemism can be recognized in setting conservation priorities (MacKinnon and MacKinnon 1986; Johnson 1995; Dinerstein et al. 1995; J. MacKinnon 1997). It has been suggested that a very high proportion of the world's biodiversity could be preserved by focusing conservation efforts on twenty-five biodiversity hotspots, a mere 1.4% of the earth's land surface (Myers et al. 2000). Nevertheless, since we do not know the distribution, value, or even identity of all species, conservation efforts cannot be restricted to these hotspots alone, but must be focused more widely on representative samples of habitat throughout all biogeographic regions.

The World Conservation Union (IUCN) proposed that nations allocate 10% of their land for conservation areas. Several countries have achieved this overall target (Groombridge 1992), including a few in Southeast Asia (table 27.1). But very few national protected area networks protect 10% of all major habitat types within that country. Some habitats, such as montane forests, are generally better protected (or under less pressure for development), whereas the species-rich lowland forests, including swamp forests and coastal mangroves, are generally poorly represented in protected area networks (MacKinnon and MacKinnon 1986; J. MacKinnon 1997).

Lowland rainforests contain the greatest richness of plant and animal species. More than half the mammals of Peninsular Malaysia are confined below elevations of 350 m, and 81% are restricted to below 660 m (Stevens 1968). This observation emphasizes the importance of areas such as the Taman Negara conservation area (4,643 km^2) of West Malaysia, which encompasses a large block of lowland rainforest, hill, and montane habitats. The park supports 60% of the endemic mammal species of the entire Sunda Shelf region as well as more than 70% of the lowland bird species recorded for Peninsular Malaysia (Medway 1971; Wells 1971). Similarly, on Borneo, 78% of all resident birds depend on some form of closed woodland, and 244 species (61%) are confined to mixed lowland forests; 60% of these lowland birds (146 species) are Sunda endemics. Mammal and bird lists for Bornean reserves confirm the richness of lowland forest habitats, with 274 birds, half the Bornean list, recorded in the lowland forests of Kutai National Park, East Kalimantan (MacKinnon et al. 1996). In addition to their species richness, lowland forests play an important role as sources of colonists for higher elevations; loss or fragmentation of lowland forests can lead to the impoverishment of nearby montane island avifaunas (MacKinnon and Phillipps 1993).

The size of protected areas and their connectedness to other areas of natural habitat are important if they are to maintain viable populations of all their constituent species over the long term. Large, wide-ranging mammals such as tigers (*Panthera tigris*), Sumatran rhinos (*Dicerorhinus sumatrensis*), and elephant families (*Elephas maximus*) require large core areas of 60 km^2 or more (K. MacKinnon 1997; Kinnaird et al. 2003). Predators and large herbivores play a key role in ecosystem health and forest dynamics. Carnivores regulate densities of herbivores, seed predators, and seed dispersers within the available food supply. Large herbivores influence seed dispersal and forest regeneration. Losses of carnivores and large ungulates will ultimately be reflected in a change in forest species composition (Crooks and Soulé 1999; Connell et al., chap. 23 in this volume), but maintaining viable populations of such species requires that protected areas be large. Moreover, large forest mammals such as tigers, elephants, and rhinoceros are disproportionately affected by habitat reduction because they tend to avoid forest boundaries where human activities increase disturbance (Kinnaird et al. 2003). Smaller reserves not only support fewer large mammals, including predators, but those present are more likely to come into conflict with, and be killed by, surrounding human residents (Woodroffe and

Ginsberg 1998). Since few protected areas are very large, it is important to look at other solutions for protecting extensive areas of habitat. Increasingly, conservationists are proposing a landscape approach to species conservation, linking protected areas via biological corridors and promoting transboundary cooperation. Thus, large tiger conservation units have been proposed to include one or more protected areas and adjacent wildlands, including areas that straddle international boundaries (Dinerstein et al. 1997).

Establishing a protected area network that includes representation of all major habitat types, either in large habitat blocks or in a series of smaller reserves along altitudinal and environmental gradients, may be the most effective strategy for ensuring more complete protection of all native flora and fauna. Several protected area systems in Southeast Asia seem to be achieving this goal. A review of the distribution of Bornean birds and mammals (other than bats) shows that almost all are represented in at least one of the island's protected areas (MacKinnon et al. 1996). Other island, national, and regional reviews give a similar picture (Petocz and de Fretes 1983; Round 1988; MacKinnon and MacKinnon 1986; Wells 1984). Even in Indochina, where protected area networks are among the least adequate in Asia, most large mammals, including endemics and threatened species, are recorded from at least one reserve (MacKinnon and MacKinnon 1986, 1987).

From Planning to Protection

Scientific planning to establish a representative network of protected areas is merely the first step in effective biodiversity conservation. Rainforest reserves require very little manipulative management, but they do need effective protection to prevent encroachment, illegal logging, poaching, and overexploitation, activities that disrupt the natural forest cycles. Effective protection requires a strong commitment from government and other agencies. Protected areas are often perceived as opportunities forgone, since the ecological and environmental services they provide are poorly recognized. Yet the benefits of many conservation areas (watershed protection, flood control, genetic reservoirs, research and recreation potential) far outweigh their costs (staff salaries, loss of agricultural opportunities). Most protected areas can be justified according to traditional cost-benefit criteria (MacKinnon et al. 1986; McNeely 1988). Table 27.2 illustrates some of the economic and environmental benefits of some national parks in Indonesia.

While most national protected area systems within Southeast Asia are still imperfect in their representation and overall habitat coverage, there is an even

Table 27.2 Economic and environmental benefits of national parks in Indonesia

Region	Park	Total area (km^2)	Benefits[a]								
			Watershed protection	Agriculture	Fisheries	Water supply to industry	Tourism potential	Biodiversity	Genetic resources	Research/ education	Soil or coastal protection
Sumatra	Barisan Selatan	1,900	**		***		**	***	**	***	***
	Berbak	3,650	***	***	*		*	***	**	**	***
	Kerinci Seblat	14,846	***	***	*	**	**	***	**	*	***
	Way Kambas	1,235	**	**	***		***	***	*	**	**
	Gunung Leuser	8,080	***	***	**	**	***	***	***	***	***
	Siberut	1,900	*		*		**	***	***	***	**
Java and Bali	Gede/Pangrango	150	***	***	*	***	***	***	**	***	***
	Ujung Kulon	761	**	**	***		***	***	**	***	***
	Baluran	250	**	**	**		***	***	*	***	*
	Bromo Tengger/Ijen	576	***	***	*	*	***	**		**	**
	Meru Betiri	580	***	**	**	*	**	***	**	*	**
	Alas Purwo	620	**	**	**		***	***	**	*	*
	Bali Barat	570	*	*	***		***	***	*	**	**
	P. Seribu	1,100			***		***	***	***	***	**
	Karimun Jawa	1,116			***		***	***	***	**	**
Kalimantan	Gunung Palung	900	***	**	**		*	***	***	***	**
	Tanjung Putting	3,050	***	**	**		**	***	**	***	*
	Kutai	2,000	***	**	*	***	***	***	**	**	*
Nusa Tenggara	Rinjani Gunung	1,170	***	***	*		***	***	**	*	***
	Komodo	340	**		***		***	***	**	**	*
Sulawesi	Lore Lindu	2,310	***	**	**	*	**	***	**	*	**
	Rawa Aopa	1,500	***	**	*		*	***	*	*	*
	Dumoga Bone	3,000	***	***	**	*	**	***	***	***	***
	Bunaken	890			***		***	***	**	***	**
Maluku	Manusela	1,890	***	***	**		*	***	***	***	***
Irian Jaya	Wasur	4,262	**	*	***		**	***	***	*	**
	Teluk Cenderawasih	14,500			***		**	***	***	*	***

[a]*, some benefits; **, substantial benefits; ***, large benefits.

Table 27.3 Biological richness and protected area management in Southeast Asia

Country[a]	EBAs[b]	Endangered species[c] Mammal	Bird	Plant	Priority "A" sites	Protection enforcement	Total staff/ 1,000 km²	Budget ($/km²)
Brunei*	1	17	13	27	2	Good	165	2,771
Cambodia*		28	18	15	6	Poor	0	1
Indonesia*	24	77	123	509	58	Poor	10–100	6–100
Laos*	1	33	23	10	7	Poor	—	1
Malaysia*	2	32	35	510	9	Good	109	500
Myanmar*	4	29	40	56	7	Medium	186	69
Papua New Guinea+	12	38	22	103	10	Poor	14	229
Philippines*	9	31	43	604	6	Poor	—	—
Singapore		7	5	84	0	Good	—	—
Thailand*		33	38	454	5	Medium	36	667
Vietnam*	3	35	40	642	10	Poor	201	n/a

Source: Data from J. MacKinnon 1997; World Bank 2001.
Note: The range for Indonesia reflects the fact that some of the smaller parks are better resourced, with more staff; several parks and reserves have virtually no staff.
[a]An asterisk indicates countries including or within biodiversity hotspots; a plus sign indicates major tropical wilderness areas.
[b]EBA: Endemic Bird Area.
[c]Numbers of endangered species from IUCN Red Lists.
[d]Based on total protected area staff—field staff considerably less.

more urgent need: to turn many of the region's "paper" parks into well-managed entities on the ground (K. MacKinnon 1997). Although there is some speculation that simply declaring an area a national park or reserve will increase its protection (Bruner et al. 2001), its long-term survival will depend on effective management, including adequate staff and equipment for patrols and law enforcement. Even in the most biologically rich countries of Asia, funding for management of protected areas is often low (table 27.3).

Even with adequate budgets, however, parks may still be threatened unless there is political commitment and local support for conservation. The recent economic crisis in Indonesia, combined with political upheaval, decentralization, and breakdown of law and order, is leading to unprecedented pressures on national parks. Illegal logging is rampant in several national parks as locals seize the opportunity to grab land and resources. Two of the worst affected parks are Tanjung Puting, Kalimantan, and Gunung Leuser, Sumatra (EIA 1998, 1999; EIA/Telapak 2000). Ironically, both are relatively well resourced, with the Leuser ecosystem receiving substantial donor assistance under a project financed by the European Union. Nevertheless, local governments are not supporting park staff in their battle against illegal logging. Without political support at the provincial and local levels, the future for the parks and conservation looks bleak.

PEOPLE AND PARKS: ENGAGING LOCAL SUPPORT FOR PROTECTED AREA MANAGEMENT

While parks are created for their biological values, their long-term survival, protection, and management depend on a whole host of other factors: political, social, and economic (Brandon 1997; K. MacKinnon 1997; Brandon, Redford, and Sanderson 1998). Declaring an area protected, marking the boundary, and employing a guard force are all essential steps in conservation area establishment, but they are unlikely to achieve effective protection without additional support measures that take into account local land tenure and the needs and aspirations of local people. Some adjoining communities may have derived part of their livelihood from the designated conservation area and are now likely to see their rights curtailed; others may be recent immigrants, exploiting forest resources and clearing land for agriculture. In both cases, their legitimate needs for land and livelihoods must be addressed. Indeed, many in the conservation community believe that wildlife conservation and protected areas in poorer countries are doomed unless local communities become an integral part of conservation efforts and benefit economically from those efforts. As a result, a whole generation of integrated conservation and development projects (ICDPs) was born.

Reconciling the needs of conservation and local communities is a complex and difficult task, whether at the local community level or in the regional context. ICDPs aim to link the conservation of biological diversity in parks with local social and economic development (Wells and Brandon 1992; Wells et al. 1999). The concept is appealing, but often such initiatives have met with only limited success, satisfying neither the conservation nor the rural development agenda (Noss 1997; Brandon, Redford, and Sanderson 1998; Hackel 1999; Oates 1999; Wells et al. 1999; MacKinnon 2001; Terborgh, van Schaik et al. 2002). Case studies from Indonesia illustrate the opportunities and challenges inherent in ICDP design and implementation.

Empowering Local Communities in Irian Jaya (Papua)

Involvement of local communities and endorsement of their traditional resource management systems is working effectively for biodiversity conservation in the Arfak Mountains Nature Reserve in the Bird's Head of Irian Jaya. The reserve's montane forests harbor at least 110 species of mammals (53 of them New Guinea endemics) and 320 species of birds, half of the avifauna recorded for Irian Jaya (Craven and de Fretes 1987). The area was gazetted as a strict nature reserve, but all the land was traditionally owned by the Hatam people, who collected forest resources. The World Wide Fund for Nature (WWF) worked with local Hatam villagers to develop a management strategy that would enable them to continue their traditional lifestyle, but engage them as guardians of the area against outsiders.

The reserve and adjacent outlying lands were divided into sixteen nature reserve management areas (NRMAs). The size and boundary of each NRMA were defined by the extent to which each collective group of landowners was willing to work together. A committee of influential people, such as village heads and church leaders, was assigned to manage each NRMA in accordance with tribal customs and community decisions. The committee was responsible for identifying the official landowners and overseeing the correct marking of the boundary. The Hatam were allowed to retain enough land outside the reserve for future subsistence needs. The Hatam worked unpaid to mark the western boundary of the reserve, to which all villagers had agreed. At the same time, the Indonesian authorities were planting concrete markers along the eastern border of the reserve, without village consultation and with maps that included some village lands and gardens within the reserve. The government's markers have since been removed or ignored, while the Hatam villagers still respect the western boundary (Mandosir and Stark 1993).

The management system developed with the Hatam works because the boundary falls under multiple jurisdictions and allows rapid identification of violators as either landowners or outsiders. No one is allowed to establish permanent houses or gardens in the reserve, but the indigenous people are allowed to collect firewood and timber for home use and hunt with traditional weapons such as bows and arrows. Members of one community may not take forest resources belonging to another community without permission of the owners. Fires may be built for cooking and comfort, but not to aid hunting. The regulations allow the continuation of the Hatam's traditional lifestyles, but outsiders face much stricter regulations. They are not allowed to hunt, to make temporary shelters from forest materials, or to remove plants, trees, or animals. Infringements are initially dealt with by the committees, which have government-sanctioned powers to enforce reserve regulations. Usually violations cease after warnings and fines at the community level, but options exist to pass the matter higher, to the reserve management authority or to the district government officer (*camat*), if necessary. The local communities have seized the opportunity to play an active role in protecting their own traditional lands and resources.

As well as promoting local stewardship of the reserve, WWF also worked with the local communities to provide alternative income-generating activities to reduce the need to extend gardens within the reserve. One such project involves farming of the *Ornithoptera* birdwing butterflies for which the area is renowned (Mandosir and Stark 1993). Gardens of butterfly food plants, such as the *Aristolochia* vine, have been established in secondary forest areas outside the reserve. Wild butterflies lay their eggs on the vines; larvae feed and pupate high on the plants. The villagers harvest the live pupae, which are then sold to a marketing center. No adult butterflies can be caught or sold. Since only a proportion of the live pupae are found and harvested, wild populations are continually being replenished. With careful control of collection and marketing by the committees and a local nongovernmental organization (NGO), the butterfly farming should be sustainable. This activity is directly linked to protection of the nature reserve, where wild butterflies spend most of their lives, yet it provides local people with a cash "crop" that is light to transport and yields high returns ($1.50 to $60 according to species) without damaging the natural forest.

This successful model, involving community participation and enfranchisement as well as provision of economic incentives, has since been replicated in Wasur National Park in southeastern Irian Jaya. Wasur's 420,000 hectares adjoin the Tonda wildlife management area in Papua New Guinea; together, the two reserves protect a vast expanse of monsoon forest and savanna habitats rich in wildlife. All land within Wasur National Park is traditionally owned and used for shifting gardens. WWF is working with local community groups and government agencies to recognize the park as a traditional use area where indigenous people and long-term residents are allowed to continue shifting agriculture and hunting of the introduced rusa deer (*Cervus timorensis*) (Craven and Wardojo 1993). The management strategy has stopped illegal hunting by outsiders while allowing local people to continue hunting traditionally with bows and arrows. By protecting park wildlife from overexploitation and ensuring that park benefits now accrue to the indigenous inhabitants, WWF and the park authorities have cultivated good local support for the park.

The Irian Jaya programs have worked well through a mixture of acknowledgment and extension of traditional rights and customs and the provision of small-scale economic activities. They offer some simple lessons and ingredients for success: close consultation with local people; identification of key players; understanding of community dependence on resources; provision of alternative income-generating or social benefits that come "on stream" quickly; strict enforcement of agreed boundaries and regulations, with the communities themselves engaged in guarding the reserve; employment opportunities for local people; flexibility to adapt management strategies to local needs and situations; and clear linkages between economic benefits and park conservation.

Integrating Conservation with Regional Development in Sumatra

Most ICDPs have been local efforts, like the Arfak example, to relieve pressure on reserves by offering small-scale economic activities to surrounding communities. The ICDP for Kerinci Seblat National Park in Sumatra originated as a much more ambitious attempt to enlist support from provincial and national governments so that the conservation area was a fully integrated, and valued, part of regional development.

The Kerinci Seblat National Park (KSNP) is one of the largest and most important conservation areas in Southeast Asia. Extending south along the Barisan range, the park straddles four provinces and covers more than 1.4 million hectares. The park and its environs encompass a range of habitats, from species-rich lowland forests through hill forests and unique highland wetland systems to montane forests and subalpine habitats on Mount Kerinci, at 3,805 m Sumatra's highest mountain. The park is remarkable for its species richness, with records of more than 4,000 plants, more than 350 birds, including 14 of the 20 Sumatran mainland endemics, and 144 mammals (73% of the Sumatran mammal fauna and one-thirtieth of the world total). It harbors some of the last viable populations of rare and endangered mammals such as the endemic Sumatran hare (*Nesolagus netscheri*), small Sumatran rhinoceros, clouded leopard (*Neofelis nebulosa*), Sumatran tiger, Malay tapir (*Tapirus indicus*), and elephant. Many of the wide-ranging large herbivores and predators, including the tiger and its ungulate prey, require large areas of lowland forest to provide adequate feeding grounds and access to vital mineral licks. The park also provides watershed protection for two of Sumatra's major rivers, the Batanghari and Musi, as well as millions of hectares of downstream farmlands. The integrity of the park and its biodiversity values are threatened by agricultural encroachment and cinnamon plantations, mining concessions that overlap park lands, poaching of tigers and rhinos, and logging (legal and illegal) in the lowland and hill forests (K. MacKinnon 1997; Jepson et al. 2001).

The park was declared in 1982, but almost immediately the Ministry of Forestry excised the dipterocarp-rich lowland forests for logging, a policy decision with major implications for conservation efforts. The ICDP began in 1997, financed with a World Bank loan and a grant from the Global Environment

Facility (GEF), with the stated objective of protecting forests and biodiversity both within and beyond park boundaries (World Bank 1996). In 1999, after lengthy consultations with adjacent communities, the boundaries were agreed upon and the park was legally gazetted, the first national park in Indonesia to achieve this status. The project provided financing to strengthen park management, spatial planning tools for development planning, and grants to adjacent communities to support alternative livelihoods and rural development in return for commitment to conservation agreements. Considerable resources were provided for village facilitators to work with local communities to agree upon boundaries, map resources, and decide upon reciprocal conservation commitments. More than seventy-five boundary villages eventually received some kind of development assistance under the ICDP after entering into conservation agreements with local government and conservation authorities.

After 6 years and millions of dollars of investment, the ICDP achieved mixed results. Although the park was gazetted, the project failed to achieve its conservation objectives. Today, KSNP is under threat from continued agricultural encroachment and illegal logging, both within the park and in the adjacent forest concessions. It was always unrealistic to expect that provision of development options alone would induce local communities to reduce their impact on KSNP's forests, especially since much of the agricultural encroachment is not driven by poverty, but is forest clearance to plant a valuable cash crop, cassiavera (*Cinnamomum burmanni*). Although it was clear that strong enforcement and protection measures would be needed, park staff have been unable to stop land clearance and illegal logging, even with generous resources for patrolling, training, and equipment. There was no clear linkage between development activities and conservation, and few of the beneficiary communities maintained their reciprocal commitments to respect park boundaries. Some beneficiaries continued incursions into the forest, and were often a greater threat than villages that received no benefits. At least one local bupati (regent) still complains of the park as an opportunity cost, even though in recent months his constituents have suffered floods, landslides, losses of rice crops, and severe hardship as a result of heavy rains washing away logged hillsides. The substantial investments in expensive technical assistance, facilitation, and development grants could probably have been more effectively used for strengthened enforcement, including prosecution of known offenders, and a more aggressive outreach campaign to raise local awareness of the park's values and linkages to ecosystem services, such as flood control. Ironically, the major NGO involved, funded to undertake community facilitation because of its long-term commitment to the area, walked away at the end of the project just like other contracted technical assistance.

In spite of the establishment of an interprovincial planning committee, regional development strategies continue to threaten park integrity. World Bank teams had to repeatedly intervene to stop a proposed road development from Muara Labuh to Kambang in the province of West Sumatra, which would have bisected the park and provide further access for agricultural expansion and poaching. Several other roads are also planned that would fragment park habitats. Three mining companies have exploration concessions that overlap park boundaries. Park management authorities continue to challenge transport and mining plans that conflict with park management plans.

In addition to protecting biodiversity within the park, the project sought to minimize losses of biodiversity in the adjacent lowland forests and to ensure that natural forest cover was maintained after logging. Plans to provide training for reduced-impact logging were abandoned due to extensive illegal logging within concessions. Rapid ecological assessment surveys identified areas of high biodiversity and importance for wildlife or watershed protection within the forest concessions. Proposals have been prepared to return these high-value forests, such as the Sipurak Hook, to the park, but the Ministry of Forestry has been slow to process these requests, even though the concessionaires are in flagrant violation of logging contracts and in some cases are no longer active. The current forest anarchy within Sumatra, with illegal logging operations extending even into national parks, further complicates the situation. Local authorities are both unable and unwilling to close down illegal sawmills, which often have the backing of highly placed political and military figures (Jepson et al. 2001).

Both the donor and the government agree that the ICDP was too ambitious, with too many objectives and too much funding over too short a time. Would the park have been in the same condition without the project? Although illegal logging is a serious threat and park patrols are met with increasing violence, KSNP appears to have suffered less deforestation, both within the park and in the broader ecosystem, than other Sumatran parks such as Barisan Selatan and Leuser (Kinnaird et al. 2003; Y. Robertson, personal communication). There is still hope that areas important for biodiversity and endangered species, such as the Sipurak Hook and RKI Finger, will be returned to the park and that adjacent concessions will be closed to stop logging roads from reaching park boundaries. Small, dedicated tiger and rhino patrols continue to work effectively with NGO support. At least partly due to the project, a newly formed consortium of local NGOs has built capacity and become an effective force for conservation and change in the region. KSNP is still one of the most important conservation areas in Southeast Asia, but will only remain so if further forest loss can be prevented.

POLICIES AND DISINCENTIVES: THE ROOT CAUSES OF BIODIVERSITY LOSS

The KSNP case study highlights the greatest challenge facing parks and reserves in Southeast Asia and elsewhere in the tropics: the conflict between conservation and economic development. Most conservation efforts seek to reduce local pressures on parks and species, but there is an increasing awareness that it is not always the small-scale illegal activities of local communities that are the greatest threat. Often forest degradation and forest loss are also the result of actions and development agendas that are driven by policies generated far away from the site of conservation concern (Brandon 1997).

A variety of policies are affecting the rate of tropical forest loss in Southeast Asia: land use, resettlement and transmigration policies that encourage opening up of frontier regions; provincial and national transport and communication policies that encourage road building through primary forests; energy policies that promote the flooding of lowland valleys for hydroelectric power schemes; pricing policies for timber and agricultural products; subsidies for agricultural plantations and wood and pulp processing ventures; and land tenure policies that encourage colonists to settle frontier areas or promote land uses that lead to soil degradation and the need to open new farming land. In many countries in Southeast Asia, agriculture and forestry policies deliberately encourage the opening up of remote forest areas; construction of new roads then leads to further agricultural encroachment and greater hunting and harvesting efforts. Even global markets influence rates of forest loss. Recent studies in Barisan Selatan National Park show that rates of forest clearance in the park increase when global coffee prices rise as local farmers expand their holdings to plant more coffee (Kinnaird et al. 2003). Rapid population growth and expanding settlements will continue to fuel the expansion of the agricultural frontier into Asia's forests.

Indonesia has some of the most extensive and biodiversity-rich forests in the region. The liquidation of these forest resources began under Suharto's government (1966–1998) with the declaration of all Indonesian forests as state property and the allocation of forest and mining concessions to powerful conglomerates and politico-business families. The short concession periods, lack of regulation, levy system, and other perverse incentives all encouraged poor logging practices (Repetto 1988). Weak concession management further contributed to forest loss by failing to prevent pioneer farmers from illegally clearing logged stands. During the 1990s forest loss in Indonesia continued apace, fueled by the timber industry's rapacious demand for wood, the growing pulp and paper industry, the surging demand for land on which to establish oil palm and other estate crops, and plans to increase the mining of the vast deposits of coal, gold, and other minerals that lie beneath the archipelago's forests (Barber 1998; FWI/GFW 2002). The development of oil palm plantations exploded in the 1990s, with the total area under the crop growing from 1.8 million hectares in 1994 to an estimated 2.4 million hectares in 1997. More than 6 million hectares of forest have been allocated and cleared for oil palm plantations. The plantation owners have profited from clearing and selling the wood, yet only one-third of this area has so far been planted with oil palm. Even so, companies are still demanding that more forest be converted for plantations (FWI/GFW 2002).

The devastating fires that have periodically raged through forests in Indonesia over the last 20 years are also attributable to policy failures that promote exploitation and land conversion. The 1982–1983 fires in East Kalimantan were an ecological and economic disaster, damaging an estimated 46,000 km^2 of forest across the whole island of Borneo (MacKinnon et al. 1996), The most visible culprits were the shifting cultivators and pioneer farmers who lit the fires, but the conditions that made the forests vulnerable were the direct result of two decades of deforestation, encouraged by government land use policies intended to open a frontier region to large-scale commercial exploitation (Mackie 1984). Kalimantan and Sumatra have suffered subsequent large-scale fires, especially when the monsoon rains came late. The 1997–1998 fires were the worst yet, with more than 5.3 million hectares of forestland damaged in one province, East Kalimantan, and approximately 9 million hectares for all of Indonesia (Holmes 2002).

These fires were not natural disasters, but the result of deliberate burning by logging concessionaires, plantation owners, and small farmers, all intent on clearing more land for agricultural production (and often subsidized by the government to do so!). One of the affected sites was the location of a much-criticized scheme to convert 1 million hectares of Central Kalimantan peat swamp forest to rice production, even though these lands are less than optimal for agriculture. As well as affecting degraded lands, the fires nibbled into more than seventeen reserves and national parks, destroyed fruit trees, and increased threats to endangered species such as orangutans (*Pongo pygmaeus*) and other forest primates and large mammals (Kinnaird and O'Brien 1998). The economic costs of the 1997–1998 fires have been conservatively estimated at $10 billion in terms of burned timber, lost tourism revenue, and human health in Indonesia, and may be billions higher if one considers the whole of Southeast Asia, where 20 million people were blanketed in smoke for months on end (Barber and Schweithelm 2000).

In such a context, the small-scale activities initiated through ICDPs are unlikely to achieve conservation success beyond the most local scale. Even among the poorest communities, livelihood opportunities may be supplementary rather than replacing more damaging activities. Moreover, the proponents of ICDPs have often ignored the inherent conflict between development and conservation, especially when dealing with marginalized communities in remote forest areas or on poor soils where agricultural opportunities are limited. Rather than using conservation areas and conservation funds to support rural livelihoods in such areas, a better alternative for reducing pressure on biodiversity and forests may be to promote development elsewhere (Kramer and van Schaik 1997).

FOREST CONSERVATION BEYOND PARK BOUNDARIES

Most countries in Southeast Asia have less than 10% of their land area designated for conservation, but adjacent production forests could play a key role in conservation of biodiversity. By the mid-1990s the area of tropical forests worldwide allocated to logging concessions exceeded the area in reserves by a factor of 8:1 (Johns 1997). In Indonesia alone, half of the total forest estate (more than 35% of the country) is scheduled to be logged. As primary forest continues to decline, logged forests will have to play an increasingly important role in the conservation of many rainforest animals and plants. Selectively logged forests, especially when large and only lightly disturbed, can support a high proportion of mature forest species, including most mammals and many species that are unable to survive in isolated forest reserves (Johns 1988, 1997). Production forests can also serve as buffers and corridors between strictly protected areas, effectively increasing the conservation estate. Although they can never replace the conservation role of fully protected areas, production forests could be a useful supplement to existing reserves.

Since the conservation value of production forests will depend on the degree of disturbance to habitats and wildlife during and after logging operations, it is imperative that forest management practices (including rotation cycles) be improved and revised to minimize disturbance and to maintain biodiversity. Policy changes may be required, but in many cases stricter application and enforcement of existing regulations would greatly improve forestry practice. A key element in maintaining a permanent forest estate is to stop migrant farmers and hunters from moving in along logging roads and colonizing and clearing newly logged areas.

Innovative solutions to conserve biodiversity in production forests are already being tested in Malaysia. In Sabah, the parastatal organization Yayasan Sabah holds a timber concession of almost a million hectares. Within this concession area are two important blocks of lowland and hill forest, designated as conservation areas, which will remain intact while the rest of the concession is worked. As yet Danum Valley (43,800 ha) and Maliau Basin (39,000 ha) have no official legal status as protected areas; they can be regarded as privately established conservation areas, managed by Yayasan Sabah. In cooperation with the British Royal Society, Yayasan Sabah has established a research station at Danum Valley, where Malaysian and international scientists are engaged in a long-term scientific research program. Research topics include forest regeneration studies and the effects of logging on watersheds, forest dynamics, and plant and animal communities (Marshall and Swaine 1992). The scientific presence and international attention have convinced the Malaysian authorities of the value of the conservation areas. Yayasan Sabah is also exploring the possibilities of income-generating activities other than logging within the concession and establishing a lodge for wildlife tourism. The success of the tourism venture will depend on the maintenance of substantial tracts of lowland rainforest and healthy populations of interesting wildlife such as orangutans, flying squirrels, and elephants. This, in turn, should encourage better forest management to minimize disturbance to forests and wildlife during logging operations.

The sustainable management and retention of a permanent forest estate is important both for biodiversity conservation and for human welfare, especially for those native communities that are most dependent on forests for subsistence and income. Many tropical rainforests are harvested for much more than their timber. Non-timber forest products (NTFPs), including wild game and fish, may have a value to local and national economies far in excess of the value of standing timber (Caldecott 1988b, Peters, Gentry, and Mendelsohn 1989). Plant products can include valuable foods, palm oils, fodder for livestock, fiber, fuel, beverages, horticultural plants, antioxidants, sources of chlorophyll, enzymes, food colorings, sweeteners, spices, vitamins, and medicinal plants. Throughout Southeast Asia many non-timber forest resources have been harvested for hundreds of years, both for subsistence and for sale (Burkill 1935; de Beer and McDermott 1989; MacKinnon 1998). Many ICDPs promote harvesting of non-timber forest products, often in park buffer zones, as a way of providing sustainable livelihoods. In Laos the Sustainable Non-timber Forest Project was established with primarily social and development objectives, yet contributes to forest conservation (Chape 2001).

Because of the long history of human use, it is often assumed that commercial harvesting of non-timber plant products has little or no ecological impact on tropical forests. In fact, there is a very high probability that intensive extraction will gradually lead to depletion of these resources over time (Browder 1992; Robinson 1993; Southgate, Coles-Ritchie, and Salazar-Canalos 1996). Sustainable harvesting depends on the selection of species, resource, and sites and adjustment of harvest levels to allow regeneration and growth of the species being harvested. Ecology and forest management are key to sustainable resource exploitation in tropical forests; it is critical to understand what happens to the plant populations being exploited and what levels of harvesting they can sustain (Peters 1996). Much of the exploitation of non-timber forest products throughout Southeast Asia is no longer sustainable, including harvesting of rattans (Caldecott 1988a, Peluso 1983). The valuable manau rattan (*Calamus manan*), prized for furniture, has been virtually wiped out in Kerinci Seblat National Park (MacKinnon 1998).

Within tropical forests, there are mosaics of different habitats, some more uniform and less diverse in species composition than others (Whitmore 1984). Sustainable harvesting is more likely in habitats where there is relatively low species diversity and a high density of commercial species. The overall ecological impact of harvesting non-timber forest products will depend on the floristic composition of the forest, the nature and intensity of the harvesting, and the species or type of resource being harvested. Some plant species and populations will be more susceptible to overexploitation than others. In general, forest species that occur at high densities, exhibit high regeneration rates, and are pollinated by either insects or wind should be able to tolerate more harvesting. It is interesting to note that both wild durian in Borneo and Brazil nuts in Amazonia, both heavily harvested, occur at low densities and have obligate relationships with seed or fruit dispersers, characteristics that make them more susceptible to overexploitation (Peters 1996).

Hunting and harvesting of forest animals can also be a serious threat to forest integrity. For wildlife populations already threatened and stressed by forest fragmentation and habitat conversion, hunting can be the last straw, causing local extinctions of some species. Even where forests seem intact and healthy, those forests may be empty of large mammals and birds, their main predators, frugivores, and seed dispersers (Redford 1992). The forests of Laos and other parts of Indochina are being hunted out to feed the wildlife trade in neighboring China (Duckworth, Salter, and Khounboline 1999). Wildlife surveys in Sarawak hill forests showed that in areas with high hunting pressure, the numbers of species of primates, hornbills, and total birds were lower than in areas with no or little hunting, and that some local populations of gibbons, langurs, and macaques had been greatly reduced or even extirpated (Bennett, Nyaoi, and

Sompud 1999). Throughout Southeast Asia, continued hunting at current levels will drive animals to extinction, disrupt forest ecology, and deprive local people of a major source of protein. With loss of these key animal species, forest ecosystems could start to collapse and decay (Crooks and Soulé 1999). From a conservation viewpoint, the message is clear. To preserve forest diversity, it will be necessary not only to protect large areas of forest but to direct hunting effort away from more vulnerable species, such as primates, toward species with higher reproductive outputs, such as pigs and deer, which are more able to withstand the offtake (Redford 1992; Bennett, Nyaoi, and Sompud 1999; Bennett and Robinson 2000).

GOVERNANCE AND POLITICAL COMMITMENT

Under the current policy environment, many conservation efforts in Southeast Asia are unlikely to achieve their long-term objectives; most will, at best, simply hold the line. The economic crisis that rocked the region in the late 1990s put additional pressures on the region's forests. So too did the devastating floods in China, which led to a moratorium on logging in that country's upper watersheds. To meet its domestic needs for timber, China has increased its imports of timber from neighboring countries, including Southeast Asia. Logging companies have expanded their activities, and all accessible forests in the region are under threat from logging, even where timber stock levels are low. Under pressure from multinational and bilateral donors, both Papua New Guinea and Cambodia have undertaken review and revision of their forest policies in exchange for fiscal support and structural adjustment lending. For Papua New Guinea, forest reform offers opportunities for more sustainable forest management and greater benefits for local landowners (box 27.1).

In Indonesia, the economic crisis led to political upheaval and the downfall of the Suharto regime, but the exploitation and unsustainable management of forests continued and expanded. The interim government of President Habibe (1998–1999) responded to demands for reform by pushing through legislation on regional autonomy, with decentralization and devolution of decision making to the district (*kabupaten*) level. With little capacity for development planning, but a need to generate their own revenues, many *kabupaten* governments have encouraged forest clearance for plantations. Forest conversion provides a source of rents for local governments as well as an excuse to harvest natural forests to feed the pulp and paper industries (FWI/GFW 2002). Threats to remaining forests are further compounded by new exploitation permits for min-

BOX 27.1 Conservation and Forest Management in Papua New Guinea

Papua New Guinea (PNG) occupies the eastern half of the island of New Guinea and still boasts 33 million hectares of closed natural forest (77% of the country). New Guinea's extensive forest tracts are famous for their species richness and endemism, harboring some 15,000–20,000 plant species, 1,500 trees, 200 mammals, and 750 birds; 53% of the birds are endemic to the island, including 90% of the world's birds of paradise. Overall, PNG is sparsely populated, with some 700 distinct cultural/language groups. Economic growth over the past two decades has been spurred by large-scale mining, petroleum, and logging operations, though the majority of the population continues to rely on subsistence agriculture (swidden) and collection and utilization of forest products. Some 15 million hectares of forests are accessible for logging, of which 1.5 million hectares have already been logged. Annually, about 25,000 hectares of natural forest are cleared for logging, agriculture, and infrastructure; another 125,000 hectares are selectively logged, generally in an unsustainable manner. Of the over 6 million hectares of approved timber blocks, more than 1.5 million hectares are located in areas of high biological value. Forest loss and degradation is now becoming a serious problem.

Papua New Guinea has very few protected areas under government management, just 0.2% of the total land area. Almost all land, including forests, is recognized as belonging to local communities and landowners. Although the Department of Forestry identifies and allocates logging concessions, concessionaires must then enter into timber rights agreements with local clan groups, and royalties must be paid to landowner groups. Opportunities to expand the conservation estate will, therefore, depend on encouraging local landowners to adopt land use practices that are consistent with conservation objectives. A new method, called BioRap, has been used to identify priority areas for the conservation of biodiversity. An iterative process determines a range of options for "capturing" maximum biodiversity at different costs in terms of agricultural and forestry opportunities forgone (Nix et al. 2000).

A World Bank/GEF project will work with the government of PNG to improve current forestry practices and strengthen forest management to promote harvesting that is ecologically and socially sustainable. Changes in forestry policy were initiated as a prerequisite for Bank support for a structural adjustment loan. In addition to policy dialogue, the project will help the Forestry Department to strengthen its planning and monitoring role so as to encourage sustainable forestry management, including the initiation of independent auditing of logging operations. It will also support strengthening of the environmental institutions responsible for requiring and monitoring environmental impact assessments of new and existing developments. In addition, there will be a comprehensive effort to improve landowner access to information and technical advice for more informed decision making. This effort includes the identification of alternatives to logging and the setting up of the Mama Graun Conservation Trust Fund to finance such options, including clan conservation areas, if landowners choose to follow a conservation rather than a full-scale development path.

Livelihood opportunities that offer alternatives to commercial logging are limited; ecotourism, for instance, has only limited potential in PNG rainforests. Some international NGOs have therefore decided to move ahead with programs that promote logging, but on a more ecologically sustainable and socially fair basis than that practiced by the commercial logging companies. Already they are experiencing some of the challenges and difficulties of logging forests to "save" them (MacKinnon 1998). The issue is particularly complex because while walk-about sawmills and other "lighter" logging techniques may promote more equitable distribution of wealth and development benefits to local communities, such activities will still affect forest biodiversity to some extent.

Because of its land tenure arrangements, PNG is probably one of the most difficult countries in Southeast Asia in which to establish and retain a conservation area network. It will be an ongoing challenge to encourage clans to adopt a conservation approach in the most biologically important areas while they watch their neighbors reap instant rewards from logging agreements. Conservation of PNG's forests will depend on a mix of clan conservation areas, better regulation of commercial concessions, and promotion of best practices for more sustainable logging and forest harvesting, including community management.

eral deposits and pressure from the Ministry of Mining to release protection forests, and even national parks, for mining.

Today, Indonesia is a society in transition, riven by economic, political, and social crises, and the gap between sustainable development and the reality of current forest mismanagement could hardly be wider. Illegal logging networks are seizing control of Indonesia's forests (McCarthy 1999). Timber plunder, followed by forest clearance, is rampant in the lowland forests of the Sunda Shelf. Corruption is pervasive, with civilian and military officials involved in harvesting and marketing illegal timber. Legal companies buy illegal timber from their own concessions to exceed their legal annual allowable cut. Conflicting laws on land and cutting rights, as well as failures in enforcement, allow both legal and illegal loggers to cut without hindrance.

Illegal logging is fast becoming the de facto institutional arrangement governing Indonesia's forests. In 1998, less than 26 million of the 58 million cubic meters of Indonesia's timber supply came from legal production (Brown 1999). By 2000, even the Indonesian Plywood Association (APKINDO) was complaining that illegal sources from Kalimantan and Sumatra were supplying at least 1 million m^3 of Indonesia's 7 million m^3 timber market share in China (FWI/GFW 2002). Illegal logging is occurring throughout Indonesia, even within national parks, with networks of "entrepreneurs" and state bureaucrats apparently immune from prosecution (EIA/Telapak 2000; Jepson et al. 2001). Forest mismanagement and exploitation have social as well as environmental consequences. Deals brokered between village leaders and illegal logging interests threaten the stability of village governance institutions, create more intervillage disputes, and increase distrust of those community leaders who act only in their own self-interest.

BOX 27.2 Indonesia's Commitments Concerning Forest Policy and Management

By July 1999, the Consultative Group of Donors for Indonesia (CGI) were so concerned about the fate of the country's forests that they placed forestry issues high on the agenda for discussion with the government, along with governance, poverty alleviation, and corruption. In 2000 the Ministry of Forestry made three groups of commitments:

1. Establish an Interdepartmental Committee on Forestry
2. Formulate a National Forest Program (NFP)
3. Take the following immediate actions to address urgent issues raised by the CGI:
    - Cooperation and coordination with other ministries to stop illegal logging, especially within national parks, and close illegal sawmills
    - Speed up forest resource assessment as a basis for NFP formulation
    - Put a moratorium on conversion of natural forests until the NFP is agreed upon
    - Downsize and restructure the wood-based industry to balance supply of and demand for raw materials and increase competitiveness
    - Close heavily indebted wood industries and link proposed debt writeoffs to capacity reduction
    - Link the reforestation program to existing forest industries
    - Recalculate the real value of timber
    - Use decentralization as a tool to enhance sustainable forest management

Progress on most of these issues has been disappointingly slow to date, with illegal logging continuing unabated, even within conservation areas. Biodiversity-rich forests are still being felled to feed the overcapacity in the wood processing and pulp and paper industries.

Source: World Bank 2001.

So far, the central government has proved unable or unwilling to stem this illegal activity, in spite of repeated commitments to multilateral donors to develop a new National Forest Program and take action to improve forest management, including stopping further conversion of forests to oil palm plantations, reducing mill overcapacity, and stopping illegal logging in national parks (box 27.2). Early in 2002 the Navy seized three ships exporting illegal timber from Central Kalimantan, but they were later released after considerable internal, and external, political pressure. The destruction of forest ecosystems and globally important biodiversity continues with no concerted plan of action to stop the losses, even though indiscriminate logging will result in long-term damage to watershed forests and increase fire risks. The recent export ban on Indonesian timber will be meaningless without concerted action to enforce closures of illegal sawmills and stop illegal logging operations. Sadly, whereas the nation's political and economic situation may rebound, the forests will not.

Indonesia is a megadiversity country in megacrisis. If the current state of resource anarchy prevails, the lowland forests of western Indonesia will be totally destroyed within the decade. Such forest losses will have serious environmental and social consequences. This situation is a regional and global emergency, but its resolution depends on the interplay between political realities, government policies, and the needs and aspirations of local people. Protection and sustainable management of forest lands and resources will be a key determinant of Indonesia's short-term economic recovery and the long-term future of her people. From a conservation perspective, priority must be given to stopping illegal logging in Tanjung Puting and Gunung Palung national parks in Kalimantan and in the major Sumatran parks (Gunung Leuser, Kerinci Seblat, and Barisan Selatan). One of the few encouraging recent developments is the declaration of the Sembilang National Park to protect the lowland swamp forests of South Sumatra, an action encouraged by a supportive provincial government. As Indonesia's lowland forests vanish, it becomes increasingly important to secure conservation status for those remaining tracts, such as Sebuku-Sembakung in East Kalimantan, where irreplaceable and globally important biodiversity is under imminent threat. Such actions would send a clear message that decentralized government can also mean responsible government.

A TIME FOR ACTION

Management of Southeast Asian forests is entering a critical phase. In the past, small areas of forest were often cleared for shifting agriculture, then allowed to lie fallow; vegetation regenerated and animals returned. Increasingly, land use is changing, moving in one direction from closed forest to swidden agriculture to intensively used croplands and degraded lands. At each step of this cascade, biodiversity is reduced (Terborgh and van Schaik 1997). As the region's population increases, land use intensifies, and forest areas are reduced and fragmented, we can expect to see greater attrition of biodiversity. Protected areas will be critical to stemming this loss.

With increasing populations and pressures on land, it is probably unrealistic to hope that many more large protected areas will be established, so conservationists must look for innovative opportunities in the production landscape outside park boundaries. Production forests are useful habitat for wildlife, but only so long as they remain forests and are not converted to other uses. Habitat corridors through agricultural lands and protection of watersheds can also benefit conservation. So too can development decisions that draw farmers away from marginal lands or route roads away from wilderness areas. Slowing agricultural expansion into forests, mountains, and other habitats that are marginal for agriculture, and rehabilitating degraded lands for sustainable production, should become a priority for the future.

An important first step would be for each nation to define areas to be maintained as permanent forest estate and identify and implement appropriate management systems for those forests, whether for conservation, production, or protection of watersheds. Local communities, with local knowledge of soil fertility and forest regeneration cycles, have an important role to play. Many Asian forests are mosaics of mature, secondary, and regenerating forest—areas that have been cleared for swidden agriculture, then allowed to lie fallow. Yet other areas are actively managed by local communities as part of sophisticated agroforestry systems. Often these agroforestry systems involve intensive management of secondary vegetation after forest clearing for agriculture. Elsewhere, indigenous communities implement silvicultural management in areas of primary forest under their control (Padoch and Peters 1993). The greatest need, however, is for the trade-offs and conflicts between conservation and development to be fully recognized to allow for more consistent land use planning and better valuation of forest services in national accounting.

The financial crisis in Southeast Asia and the ensuing increase in pressure on forests and other natural resources has reemphasized the importance of good governance and political commitment to ensure sound conservation and forestry practices. The greatest challenge of all will be to address the root causes of biodiversity loss: the land use strategies, policies, programs, and perverse economic incentives that fail to recognize that biodiversity conservation is key to sustainable development. Conservationists, policymakers, government officers, the scientific community, NGOs, and local communities need to work together, and with the private sector, to ensure that biodiversity issues, options, and concerns are integrated into sectoral policies and sustainable national and regional development programs, promoting conservation within the production landscape.

ACKNOWLEDGMENTS

This chapter was first drafted in 1998, but has been revised to take account of later developments and their impacts on forests in Southeast Asia, especially in Indonesia. The author is grateful to Bill Laurance for comments on an earlier draft and to the many colleagues and friends with whom she has worked on conservation projects throughout Southeast Asia.

28

The Future of the Amazon

WILLIAM F. LAURANCE, SCOTT BERGEN, MARK A. COCHRANE, PHILIP M. FEARNSIDE, PATRICIA DELAMÔNICA, SAMMYA AGRA D'ANGELO, CHRISTOPHER BARBER, AND TITO FERNANDES

ABSTRACT

What is happening to the forests of the Amazon today? What will the region be like in another 20 years? Which areas are most vulnerable, and which stand a chance of surviving the coming decades largely intact? In this chapter we grapple with these thorny questions. If you are interested in the Amazon, but are not up to date on all the development issues, trends, and controversies, then this chapter was written for you. Parts of this chapter are speculative; in developing our predictions it was necessary to adopt a coarse-grained approach. Here we are predicting broad, basin-wide patterns of forest conversion, not specific, local-scale patterns, because such fine-scale predictions would undoubtedly prove rife with errors. We begin by summarizing the principal threats to the Amazon today: deforestation, logging, forest fragmentation, and wildfires. We then attempt to predict the pattern and scale of forest conversion over the next two decades based on current trends in deforestation, human migration, and planned and existing highways, roads, and infrastructure projects.

INTRODUCTION

The Amazon contains nearly 60% of the world's remaining tropical rainforest (Whitmore 1997). Closed-canopy forests in the Amazon basin encompass about 5.3 million square kilometers, an area the size of western Europe (Sarre, Sobral Filho, and Reis 1996). By far the largest forest type is *terra firme*—forest that is not seasonally flooded. There also are extensive areas of seasonally flooded forest along rivers and in floodplains (termed *várzea* if they are flooded by relatively nutrient-rich white waters and *igapó* if inundated by nutrient-poor black waters), as well as limited areas of bamboo forest and vine forest. In addition, there are scattered savannas and open forests in drier areas of the basin, where narrow strips of rainforest vegetation (termed "gallery forest") often persist along permanent rivers and streams (IBGE 1997).

Most of the Amazon is flat or undulating, occurs at low elevations (< 300 m), and has poor soils. About four-fifths of the Amazon's soils are classified as latosols (Brown and Prance 1987; Sarre, Sobral Filho, and Reis 1996), which are typically heavily weathered, acidic, high in toxic aluminum, and poor in nutrients such as phosphorus, calcium, and potassium. In these soils, clay particles can form tight aggregations, giving the soils poor water-holding characteristics, even with high clay contents (Richter and Babbar 1991). The most productive soils in the Amazon are concentrated along the basin's western margin, in the Andean foothills and their adjoining floodplains. These areas are much more recent geologically than the rest of the basin (see Ruokolainen, Tuomisto, and Kalliola, chap. 13 in this volume) and thus their soils are far less heavily weathered.

There is a strong gradient of rainfall and seasonality in the Amazon. In general, forests in the basin's eastern and southern portions are driest, with the strongest dry season. Although evergreen, these forests are near the physiological limits of tropical rainforest and can persist only by having deep root systems that can take up groundwater during the dry season (Nepstad et al. 1994). The wettest and least seasonal forests are in the northwestern Amazon, with the central Amazon being intermediate; forests in these areas do not require deep roots.

CURRENT THREATS TO THE AMAZON

Deforestation

In the past, Amazonian development has been limited by the basin's poor soils, its remoteness from major population centers, and diseases such as malaria and yellow fever. This situation is rapidly changing. More of the Brazilian Amazon's forest has been destroyed over the last 30 years than in the previous 450 years since European colonization (Lovejoy 1999). Losses of Amazonian forests in Bolivia, Ecuador, Colombia, and Peru have also risen dramatically in recent decades (Sarre, Sobral Filho, and Reis 1996; Viña and Cavalier 1999; Steininger, Tucker, Ersts et al. 2001; Steininger, Tucker, Townshend et al. 2001).

Deforestation rates in the Amazon probably average 3–4 million ha per year—larger than the total area of Belgium. The most reliable deforestation statistics are those for the Brazilian Amazon, which have been produced annually since 1990 (except 1993) based on Landsat TM images (INPE 1996, 1998, 2000). Despite various initiatives to slow forest loss, deforestation in the Brazilian Amazon (fig. 28.1) rose significantly ($P = .02$, Mann-Whitney U-test) from 1990–1994 to 1995–2002) (Laurance, Albernaz, and Da Costa 2001). (Economic conditions influenced these trends; 1991 was an exceptionally low year because Brazilian bank accounts were frozen, while 1995 was an exceptionally high year be-

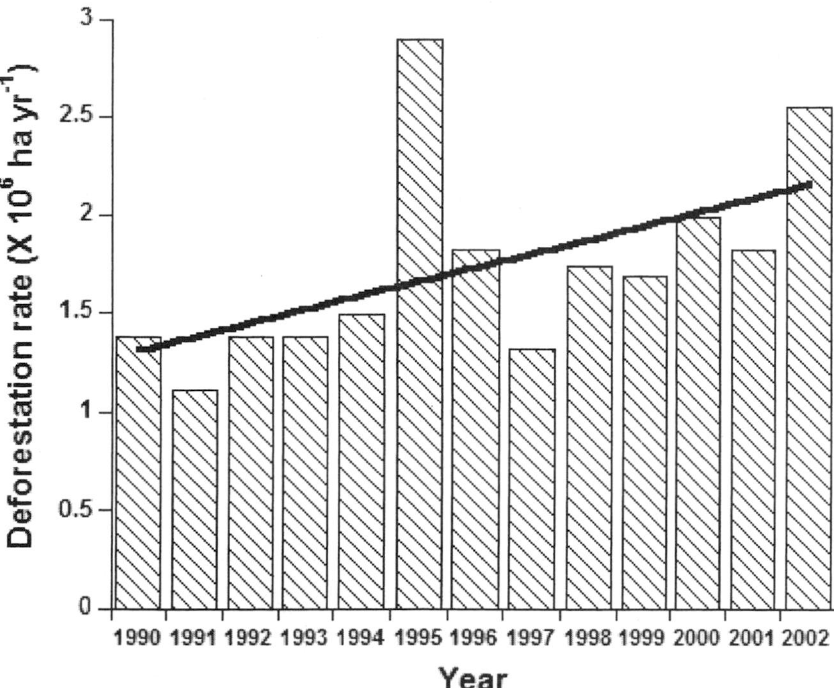

Figure 28.1 Annual deforestation rates in the Brazilian Amazon since 1990. The regression line shows the overall trend. These estimates do not include small clearings (< 6.25 ha) or the extensive areas affected by logging or ground fires.

cause available investment funds increased following government economic reforms: Fearnside 1999.)

There are two main causes of deforestation in the Amazon today. The first is large-scale cattle ranching, typically by relatively wealthy landowners. Ranchers commonly use bulldozers to extract timber prior to felling and burning the forest (Uhl and Buschbacher 1985). Large- and medium-scale ranchers are estimated to cause 70%–75% of all deforestation in the Brazilian Amazon (Fearnside 1993; Nepstad, Moreira, and Alencar 1999) and account for much forest loss elsewhere in Latin America (e.g., Viña and Cavalier 1999).

The second major cause of deforestation is slash-and-burn farming, typically conducted by small landowners who clear small (1–2 ha) areas of forest each year. The forest's understory is slashed with machetes, and the debris is ignited during the dry season. The ash from the burned vegetation provides a brief pulse of plant nutrients, which supports crops for a few years before the area is left fallow and the farmer is forced to clear more forest. Slash-and-burn farming occurs both opportunistically (often illegally) and as a result of government-sponsored colonization programs that allocate small forest tracts (50–200 ha) to individual families. Brazil has hundreds of Amazonian colonization projects involving millions of people, initiated in part to help divert population flows that would otherwise further overcrowd Brazil's major cities (Fearnside 1990, 1993).

A third cause of deforestation, industrial agriculture, is increasing rapidly in importance along the drier southern margins of the Amazon (and also in drier areas in the east-central Amazon near Santarém) and in adjoining transitional forests and *cerrado* woodlands and savannas. Most of these farms are devoted to soybeans, the production of which involves clearing large expanses of flat land (Fearnside 2001; Steininger, Tucker, Ersts et al. 2001; Steininger, Tucker, Townshend et al. 2001).

Logging

Industrial logging is increasing dramatically in the Amazon. Tropical logging is usually selective, in that only a small percentage of trees are harvested, although the number of harvested species varies considerably among regions. In new Amazonian frontiers, for example, only 5–15 species are typically harvested (1–3 trees/ha), but 100–150 species are harvested in older frontiers (5–10 trees/ha; Uhl et al. 1997). Valuable timbers such as mahogany (*Swietenia* spp.) are often overexploited and play a key role in making logging operations profitable (Fearnside 1997).

Most of the direct effects of logging arise from the networks of roads, tracks, and small clearings created during cutting operations (plate 7/fig. 28.2), which cause collateral tree mortality, soil erosion and compaction, vine and grass invasions, and microclimatic changes associated with disruption of the forest canopy (Uhl and Guimarães Vieira 1989; Verissimo et al. 1992, 1995; Johns 1997). In addition, logging has important indirect effects. By creating labyrinths of forest roads, logging opens up areas for colonization by migrant settlers who often use destructive slash-and-burn farming methods (Uhl and Buschbacher 1985; Verissimo et al. 1995; Laurance 2001). Logging also allows a sharp increase in hunting, which can dramatically affect some wildlife species. In the Malaysian state of Sarawak, for example, one logging camp was estimated to consume over 30,000 kg of wildlife meat each year (Bennett and Gumal 2001).

In recent years, multinational timber companies from Malaysia, Indonesia, South Korea, and other Asian countries have moved rapidly into the Brazilian Amazon by buying large forest tracts, often obtained by purchasing interests in local timber firms. In Guyana, Suriname, and Bolivia, Asian corporations have

Figure 28.2 Industrial logging creates labyrinths of roads that promote forest colonization and overhunting. (Photograph by W. F. Laurance.) See also plate 7.

obtained long-term forest leases (termed "concessions": Colchester 1994; Sizer and Rice 1995). In 1996 alone, Asian companies invested more than $500 million in the Brazilian timber industry (Muggiati and Gondim 1996). Asian multinationals now control at least 13 million ha of Amazonian forest (Laurance 1998).

A striking feature of the Amazonian timber industry is that illegal logging is rampant (see also MacKinnon, chap. 27 in this volume). A 1997 study by the Brazilian government concluded that 80% of Amazonian logging was illegal, and recent raids have netted massive stocks of stolen timber (Abramovitz 1998). Aside from widespread illegal cutting, most legal operations of the hundreds of domestic timber companies in the Amazon are poorly managed. A government inspection of thirty-four operations in Paragominas, Brazil, for example, concluded that "the results were a disaster," and that not one was using accepted practices to limit forest damage (Walker 1996). In a controversial effort to gain better control over logging operations, Brazil opened thirty-nine of its National Forests (totaling 14 million ha) to logging in 1997, arguing that logging concessions would not be granted to companies with poor environmental records (*Critica* 1997). Much larger areas of the Brazilian Amazon are likely to be designated as logging reserves in the future (Verissimo, Cochrane, and Souza 2002).

Forest Fragmentation

The rapid pace of deforestation is leading to widespread forest fragmentation. Habitat fragmentation has myriad effects on Amazonian forests, such as altering the diversity and composition of fragment biotas and changing ecological processes such as pollination, nutrient cycling, and carbon storage (Lovejoy et al. 1986; Bierregaard et al. 1992; Didham et al. 1996; Laurance and Bierregaard 1997; Laurance, Lovejoy et al. 2002). Edge effects—ecological changes associated with the abrupt, artificial edges of forest fragments—penetrate at least 300 m into Amazonian forests (Laurance et al. 1997, 1998a, 2000) and possibly much farther (Skole and Tucker 1993; Laurance 2000).

One key study found that by 1988, the area of forest in the Brazilian Amazon that was fragmented (< 100 km^2 in area) or prone to edge effects (< 1 km from forest edge) was over 150% larger than the area that had actually been deforested (Skole and Tucker 1993). Because over 15% of the region's forest has now been cleared (INPE 1996, 1998, 2000), the total area affected by fragmentation, deforestation, and edge effects could constitute a third of the Brazilian Amazon today (Laurance 1998). This figure would probably rise if the extensive areas affected by logging and ground fires were included, but such changes are difficult to detect (Stone and Lefebvre 1998) and have not been quantified in the satellite images used to map Amazonian deforestation (Nepstad, Verissimo et al. 1999).

Forest fragmentation is occurring at many spatial scales. On a regional scale, the once remote interior of the Amazon is being dissected by major highways, powerlines, and transportation projects, which inevitably lead to rapid deforestation. On a local scale, different land uses tend to generate characteristic patterns of fragmentation. Cattle ranchers, for example, typically destroy large, rectangular blocks of forest, and habitat fragments that persist in such landscapes are somewhat regular in shape (fig. 28.3A). Forest colonization projects, however, result in more complex patterns of fragmentation, creating very irregularly shaped fragments and a high proportion of forest edge (Dale and Pearson 1997; Laurance et al. 1998b). The resulting spatial pattern has been likened to the ribs of a fish (fig. 28.3B).

Wildfires

Under natural conditions, large-scale fires are very rare in Amazonian rainforests, occurring perhaps once or twice every thousand years during exceptionally severe El Niño droughts (Sanford et al. 1985; Saldariagga and West 1986; Meggers 1994; Piperno and Becker 1996). (However, some drier Amazonian for-

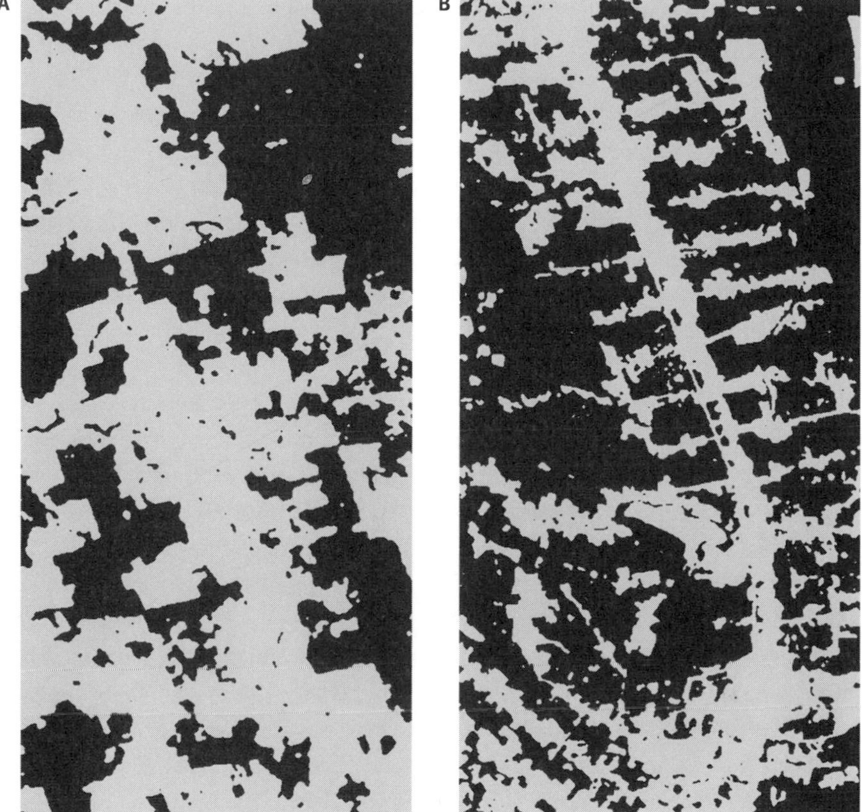

Figure 28.3 Different land uses produce characteristic patterns of forest loss and fragmentation. (A) Deforestation by large-scale cattle ranching (near Paragominas, Pará). (B) "Fishbone" deforestation pattern associated with forest colonization projects (near Tailândia, Pará). Each rectangle shows an area of 570 km^2. (From Cochrane and Laurance 2002.)

est formations, such as sandy-soil campinaranas, apparently burned more frequently than did primary rainforest: B. W. Nelson, personal communication.) Closed-canopy tropical forests are poorly adapted to fire (Uhl and Kauffman 1990), and even light ground fires can cause high tree mortality (Kauffman 1991; Barbosa and Fearnside 1999; Cochrane and Schulze 1999; Cochrane et al. 1999; Nepstad, Moreira, and Alencar 1999).

Fire is used commonly in the Amazon today to clear forests, destroy slash piles, and help control weeds in pastures. Over a 4-month period in 1997, satellite images revealed nearly 45,000 separate fires in the Amazon (P. Brown 1998), virtually all of them human-caused. During drought years, smoke from forest burning becomes so bad that regional airports must be closed and hospitals report dramatic increases in the incidence of respiratory problems (Laurance 1998).

Human land uses dramatically increase the incidence of fire in tropical forests. Logged forests are far more susceptible to fires, especially during droughts. Logging increases forest desiccation and woody debris (Uhl and Kauffman 1990) and greatly increases access by slash-and-burn farmers and ranchers, which are the main sources of ignition (Uhl and Buschbacher 1985). The combination of logging, migrant farmers, and drought was responsible for the massive fires that destroyed millions of hectares of Southeast Asian forests in 1982–1983 and 1997–1998 (Leighton and Wirawan 1986; Woods 1989; N. Brown 1998; MacKinnon, chap. 27 in this volume).

Fragmented forests are also vulnerable to fire because fragment edges are prone to desiccation (Kapos 1989) and because forest remnants are juxtaposed with fire-prone pastures, farmlands, and regenerating forests. Ground fires (fig. 28.4) originating in nearby pastures can penetrate hundreds to thousands of meters into fragmented forests (Kauffman 1991; Cochrane and Laurance 2002). These low-intensity fires kill many trees and increase canopy openings and fuel loads, making the forest far more prone to catastrophic wildfires in the future (Cochrane et al. 1999; Cochrane and Schulze 1999). During the 1997–1998 El Niño drought, wildfires lit by farmers and ranchers swept through an estimated 3.4 million ha of fragmented and natural forest, savanna, regenerating forest, and farmland in the northern Amazonian state of Roraima (Barbosa and Fearnside 1999), and there were many large fires in other locations (Cochrane and Schulze 1998).

Available evidence suggests that there might be a "deforestation threshold" above which landscapes become far more prone to fires. This could potentially occur as a result of positive feedbacks among deforestation, regional drying, smoke, and fire (Cochrane and Schulze 1999; Cochrane et al. 1999; Nepstad, Moreira, and Alencar 1999; Nepstad, Verissimo et al. 1999; Laurance and Williamson 2001). Amazonian forests recycle at least half of all rainfall back into the atmosphere, helping to maintain frequent rains, lower surface temperatures, and moderate dry seasons (Salati and Vose 1984). Regional deforestation can reduce rainfall (IPCC 1996), making forests more fire-prone and, in turn, promoting additional deforestation and fires. Smoke particles from fires further reduce rainfall by trapping microdroplets of water in the atmosphere, precluding the formation of raindrops (Rosenfeld 1999). Such positive feedbacks are most likely in the drier eastern, southern, and north-central areas of the Amazon, where rainforests are already near their physiological limits (Nepstad et al. 1998).

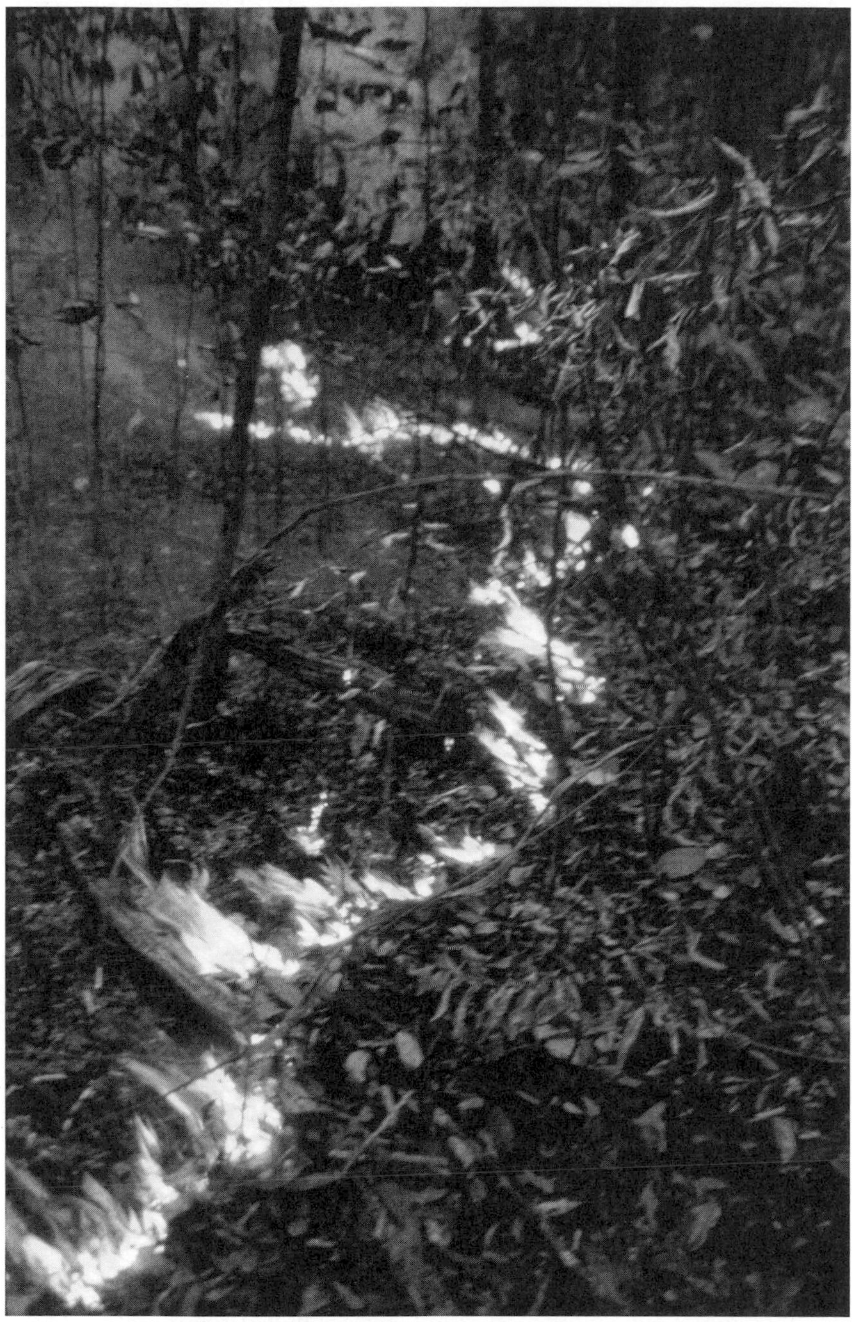

Figure 28.4 Low-intensity ground fires can penetrate considerable distances into forests, killing many trees and making the forests vulnerable to devastating wildfires in the future. (Photograph by M. A. Cochrane.)

Ancillary Threats

Today, even the remotest areas of the Amazon are being influenced by human activities. Illegal gold mining is widespread, with wildcat miners polluting streams with mercury (used to separate gold from sediments) and degrading stream basins with pressure hoses. Illegal miners also threaten indigenous Indians through intimidation and introductions of new diseases (Christie 1997). In addition, increasing numbers of major oil, natural gas, and mineral developments are being sanctioned by Amazonian governments (Nepstad et al. 1997; Laurance 1998). Finally, hunting pressure is growing throughout the Amazon because of greater access to forests and markets and the common use of shotguns (Peres 2001). Intensive hunting can dramatically alter the structure of animal communities, extirpate species with low reproductive rates, and exacerbate the effects of habitat fragmentation on exploited species (Robinson and Redford 1991).

FUTURE THREATS TO THE AMAZON

In this section we highlight several proximate and ultimate factors that will affect future development trends in the Amazon. These factors relate mainly to projected changes in population size, infrastructure development, and spatial patterns of forest conversion (see Laurance, Cochrane et al. 2001; Laurance, Fearnside et al. 2001).

Population Growth

The human population of the Amazon is increasing rapidly, for two reasons. First, populations have been growing throughout Latin America, nearly tripling (from 166 to 448 million) between 1950 and 1990 (Mahar and Schneider 1994). Although the traditionally high fertility rates of Latin American women have declined in recent decades, the momentum of population growth will continue for some time because a large proportion of the population is young or still in their child-bearing years. In addition, Amazonian residents often begin bearing children early—in their late teens or early twenties—which contributes substantially to rapid population growth.

Second, there is much immigration into the Amazon. In Brazil, poor economic conditions and droughts in the northeast, limited opportunities in large cities, the displacement of agricultural workers by mechanized farming, and government colonization programs designed to reduce urban overcrowding and help secure the Amazonian frontier have all contributed to a major influx of immigrants into the Amazon (Fearnside 1987, 1990, 1993). As a result of immigration and rapid growth, the population of the Brazilian Amazon has increased twice as fast as in the rest of Brazil, rising from 2 million in the 1960s to over 20 million today (Laurance, Albernaz, and Da Costa 2001).

Changing Patterns of Deforestation

The spatial patterns of Amazonian forest conversion are changing in alarming ways. Historically, large-scale deforestation has been most intensive in the eastern and southern areas of the Amazon (the "arc of deforestation"), in the Brazilian states of Pará, Maranhão, Rondônia, Acre, and Mato Grosso and in northern Bolivia (Skole and Tucker 1993). Since the 1960s, forest conversion has risen dramatically in these areas as a result of large-scale ranching, logging, international development projects, government-sponsored colonization schemes, mining, hydroelectric dams, and land speculation (Fearnside 1987, 1990, 1995; Dale and Pearson 1997; Nepstad et al. 1997; Steininger, Tucker, Ersts et al. 2001, Steininger, Tucker, Townshend et al. 2001). There has also been considerable forest clearing along rivers and in parts of the northern and western Amazon—in Ecuador, Colombia, Peru, and Roraima (Brazil).

But this picture is rapidly changing. Major new highways, roads, and transportation projects are now dissecting the heart of the basin, providing access to areas once considered too remote for development. One of the most ambitious new highways, BR-174, runs from the city of Manaus in the central Amazon northward to the Venezuelan border, spanning a distance of over 1,000 km. Almost fully graded and paved, it was initially promoted as a surgical cut through the forest to provide direct access to Caribbean ports and markets in Venezuela. In 1997, however, Brazilian President Fernando Henrique Cardoso announced that 6 million ha of land along the highway would be opened to settlement, and boasted that the area to be farmed would be "so colossal that it would double the nation's agricultural production" (Cassia 1997). This highway is already promoting rapid forest clearing, especially within 100 km of Manaus.

As a result of logging booms and rapidly increasing development, central and northern Amazonian cities such as Manaus, Santarém, and Boa Vista are burgeoning. Ongoing construction to link Manaus to Rondônia in the southern Amazon by paving highway BR-319 will provide greatly increased access to the region for migrant settlers, and raises the alarming prospect that over the next decade Amazonian forests could be bisected by an expanding swath of deforestation and logging (Laurance 1998).

New Infrastructure Projects

Amazonian countries have ambitious short-term plans to develop major infrastructure projects encompassing large expanses of the basin. These projects are intended to accelerate economic development and exports, especially in the agriculture, timber, and mining sectors of the economy. In the Brazilian Amazon, massive investments, on the order of $40 billion in the years 2000–2007, are being implemented to fast-track the construction of dozens of major infrastructure projects—highways, railroads, gas lines, hydroelectric projects, powerlines, and river channelization projects (Friends of the Earth 1999; Avança Brasil 1999). The Amazonian road network is being rapidly expanded and upgraded, with many unpaved sections being converted to paved, all-weather highways. Key environmental agencies, such as the Ministry of the Environment, are being largely excluded from the planning of these projects (Laurance and Fearnside 1999; Laurance, Cochrane et al. 2001).

One indicator of the scale of planned development is the rapidly expanding network of hydroelectric dams. At least nineteen major (100–13,000 megawatt) dams are planned in the Brazilian Amazon over the next 10–20 years, nearly all in forested areas (Eletrobrás 1998). These new dams will vastly increase the 600,000 ha of forest that is currently inundated by reservoirs (because the region is quite flat, Amazonian hydroelectric reservoirs are often very large: Fearnside 1995). Most of these dam sites are in tributaries flowing northward into the Amazon River from Brazil's central plateau (the Tocantins, Araguaia, Xingu, and Tapajós Rivers), a region with a high concentration of indigenous peoples (Fearnside 1990). In addition to destroying forests and degrading aquatic systems, hydroelectric dams require networks of access roads and powerline clearings, which promote further forest loss and fragmentation.

New infrastructure projects will dissect vast expanses of the Amazon. The northern Amazon, for example, has already been bisected by BR-174, and will soon be cut by a road linking the rapidly growing city of Boa Vista to Guyana and by a major powerline corridor linking Guri Dam in Venezuela with Boa Vista. These projects will affect large expanses of forest as well as many indigenous groups in the northern Amazon (Soltani and Osborne 1994), and will greatly increase access to the region for loggers, ranchers, miners, and colonists. Paving of the BR-163 highway between Cuiabá and Santarém could create a large swath of degraded forest through the south-central part of Amazonia.

Other projects are equally ambitious. When completed, the massive Ferronorte Railway will be the largest transportation project in Brazil, traversing over 4,000 km of Amazonian forest while linking the cities of Santarém (along the

Amazon River) and Porto Velho (in Rondônia) to those in southern Brazil. In the central and eastern Amazon, the Madeira, Tocantins, and Araquaia rivers are being channelized in order to allow deep-water river barges to transport soybeans from rapidly expanding agricultural areas in central Brazil (Fearnside 2001). In the southern Amazon, planned road projects will traverse large expanses of forest and ascend the Andes to reach the Pacific coast, passing through Bolivia, Peru, and northern Chile. In addition, a 3,000 km natural gas line currently under construction will run from Santa Cruz, Bolivia, to São Paulo, Brazil (Soltani and Osborne 1994).

Logging and Mining Booms

Increasingly, logging and mining activities are becoming important driving forces in the exploitation of the Amazonian frontier. Timber, petroleum, natural gas, and mineral resources (iron ore, bauxite, gold, copper: Sarre, Sobral Filho, and Reis 1996) provide the economic impetus for construction of roads, highways, and transportation networks, which greatly increase access to forests for colonists, ranchers, and land speculators. Roads created for oil exploration and development in Amazonian Ecuador have caused a drastic increase in forest colonization, land speculation, and commercial hunting (Holmes 1996). Similar trends are likely in the Peruvian Amazon, much of which is currently being opened for oil and gas concessions (fig. 28.5). Logging operations also greatly increase access to frontier areas; it has been estimated that 10,000 to 15,000 km^2 of forest are being logged each year in the Brazilian Amazon alone, a figure nearly as large as the area being deforested each year (Nepstad, Moreira, and Alencar 1999; Nepstad, Verissimo et al. 1999).

PREDICTING THE FUTURE OF THE BRAZILIAN AMAZON

In this section we attempt to predict the scale and pattern of Amazonian forest degradation over the next two decades. We confine our predictions to the Brazilian Legal Amazon, which constitutes about two-thirds of the basin (ca. 4.9 million km^2), because accurate spatial data on deforestation, transportation networks, and planned infrastructure projects for the other Amazonian and Guianan countries were very difficult to acquire on a consistent basis. Our analysis is based on a GIS (Geographic Information Systems) model that integrates spatial data on existing and planned development activities.

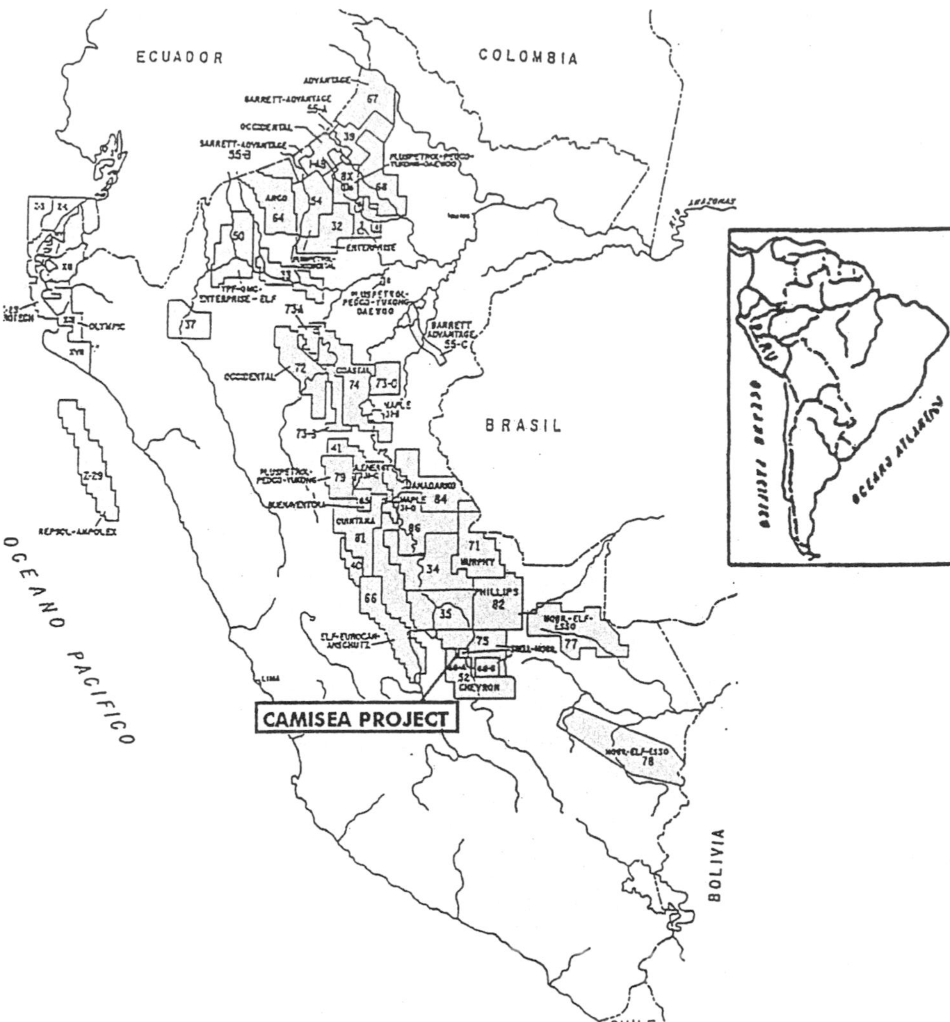

Figure 28.5 Much of the Peruvian Amazon is being opened up for oil and gas exploration and development. Shaded areas show current oil and gas concessions, mostly owned by multinational corporations.

GIS Data Layers

To develop our model, we used the best and most recent available information on forest cover, rivers, planned and existing roads and infrastructure projects, fire-proneness of forests, logging and mining intensity, and various conservation units (table 28.1). Principal data sources for forest cover, current roads

Table 28.1 Data layers used in analysis of land use trends in the Brazilian Amazon. Infrastructure projects include railroads, hydroelectric reservoirs, powerlines, gas lines, and river-channelization projects.

Layer	Data sources
Current forest cover and rivers	Forest/non-forest coverage produced by the Basic Science and Remote Sensing Initiative, Michigan State University, based on 1995 Landsat TM imagery
Existing highways (paved) and roads (unpaved)	1995 map of Brazilian Legal Amazon (1:3,000,000 scale) produced by Brazilian Institute for Geography and Statistics (IBGE); supplemented by 1999 map of Amazonian protected areas (1:4,000,000 scale, Instituto Socioambiental, São Paulo, Brazil), JERS-1 radar imagery for 1999, and personal knowledge
Planned roads and highways	Maps and information provided by the Avança Brasil and highway upgrades program (Avança Brasil 1999)
Existing infrastructure projects[a]	1995 IBGE map of Brazilian Legal Amazon, supplemented by personal knowledge
Planned infrastructure projects[a]	Maps and information provided by Avança Brasil (1999), Eletrobrás (1998), and personal knowledge
Fire-proneness of forests	Map of areas with high, medium, and low fire vulnerability produced by Nepstad et al. (1998, Nepstad, Morerra, and Alencar 1999), based on analyses of forest cover, seasonal soil moisture, logging activity, and recent fires during the 1998 dry season
Logging and mining activity	1998 map of estimated legal and illegal logging, wildcat gold mining, and industrial mining, produced by IBAMA, Brazil's national environmental agency
Federal and state parks and reserves, national forests, extractive reserves, and indigenous lands and reserves	1995 IBGE map of Brazilian Legal Amazon, supplemented by 1999 map of Amazonian protected areas and personal knowledge

[a]Infrastructure projects include railroads, hydroelectric reservoirs, powerlines, gas lines, and river channelization projects.

and highways, and conservation units were 1:3,000,000- and 1:4,000,000-scale maps produced by Brazilian agencies and conservation organizations, augmented with remote-sensing (Landsat TM and JERS-1 radar) images and personal knowledge. The maps and remote-sensing images were produced from 1995 to late 1999.

Data on new highways and road upgrades and planned infrastructure projects (fig. 28.6) were gleaned from recent sources, principally reports and Internet data prepared for international investors by Avança Brasil (1999), as well as the 1998–2007 development plan for Eletrobrás (1998), Brazil's federal electricity

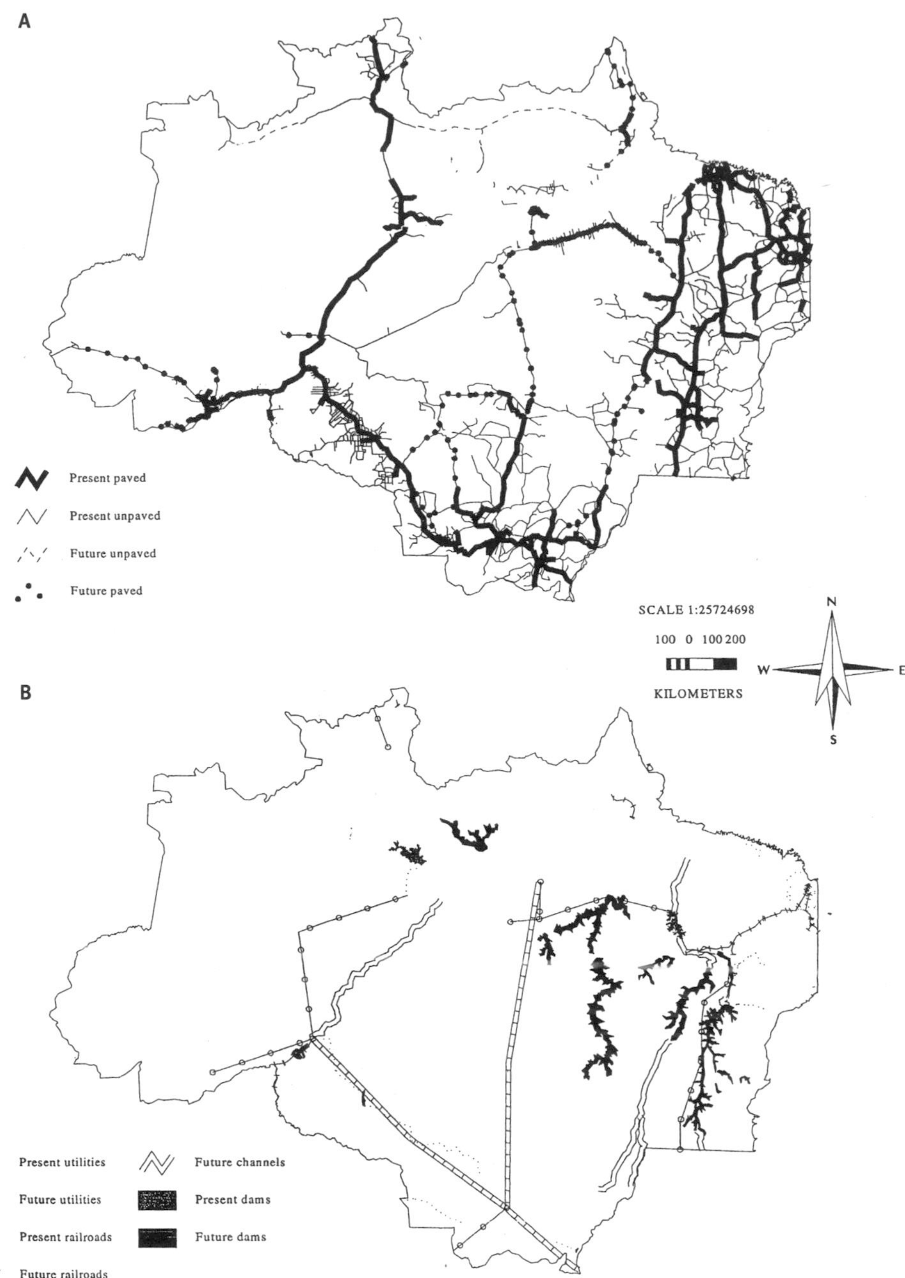

Figure 28.6 Existing and planned highways and infrastructure projects in the Brazilian Amazon. (A) Highways and roads. (B) Major infrastructure projects. "Utilities" are gas lines and powerlines, while "channels" are river channelization projects.

utility. The probability of forest fires was based on the map of Nepstad et al. (1998; Nepstad, Moreira, and Alencar 1999), who integrated extensive data on forest cover, seasonal soil water availability, recent fires, and logging activity in order to predict areas of high, moderate, and low fire vulnerability during the 1998 dry season. Maps of the estimated extent of logging (both legal and illegal), industrial mining, and illegal gold mining were produced by IBAMA (Brazil's national environmental agency) in 1998.

The Brazilian Amazon has a variety of federal and state conservation units that vary considerably in their degree of environmental protection. We identified thirteen major types of reserves and parks, which we placed into three general categories (table 28.2). Areas with nominally high protection include National Parks, Ecological Stations, and Ecological Reserves, which nominally receive strong protection. Sanctioned activities in such areas include research, education, and often, recreation and tourism.

Areas with moderate protection are National Forests, Extractive Reserves, and Sustainable Development Reserves, among others, which may be legally subjected to nominally "sustainable" levels of industrial logging, agriculture, livestock grazing, hunting, fishing, tourism, and extraction of non-timber products (e.g., rubber, fuelwood, fruits, seeds, fibers). Mining is usually prohibited, although illegal gold mining certainly occurs in some of these reserves.

The final category, areas with uncertain protection, includes the extensive indigenous lands and reserves that collectively constitute about 18% of the Brazilian Legal Amazon. In some areas, these lands may be more effectively protected than National Parks, especially where indigenous people are territorial and repel illegal colonists, loggers, and gold miners. In other areas, however—particularly where indigenous people have frequent contact with outsiders—a corruption of traditional lifestyles can occur. In a number of cases, indigenous groups in Brazil have sold their timber to commercial loggers, permitted wildcat mining, overhunted wildlife, illegally cleared protected lands, invaded national parks, impeded firefighters, and even assaulted government inspectors attempting to control illegal logging (Redford and Stearman 1993; Alvard et al. 1997; Margolis 2000). Hence, environmental protection in indigenous lands and reserves is likely to be highly variable, and will tend to decline as contact with outsiders increases.

Buffer Zones

Roads and infrastructure projects promote forest degradation by greatly increasing human access, and in some cases (such as hydroelectric reservoirs) by

Table 28.2 Legally permitted activities within conservation areas in the Brazilian Amazon

Type of area	Recreation & tourism	Agriculture & livestock	Logging	Non-timber harvests	Hunting	Mining
Areas with nominally high protection						
National/state parks	Yes	No	No	No	No	No
Ecological reserves	Yes	No	No	No	No	No
Biological reserves	No	No	No	No	No	No
Ecological stations	No	No	No	No	No	No
Areas with moderate protection						
National/state forests	Yes	Yes	Yes	Yes	Yes[a]	No
National forest reserves	Yes	Yes	Yes	Yes	Yes[a]	No
Extractive reserves	Yes	Yes	Yes	Yes	Yes[a]	No
State extractive forests	Yes	Yes	Yes	Yes	Yes[a]	No
Sustainable use forests	Yes	Yes	Yes	Yes	Yes[a]	No
Sustainable development reserves	Yes	Yes	Yes	Yes	Yes[a]	No
Environmental protection areas	Yes	Yes[b]	Yes[b]	Yes[b]	No	Yes[b]
Areas of relevant ecological interest	Yes	Yes[b]	No	Yes[b]	No	No
Areas with uncertain protection						
Indigenous lands and reserves	No	Yes	Yes	Yes	Yes	No

Sources: Silva 1996; Olmos, Queiroz Filho, and Lisboa 1998; Rylands and Pinto 1998; Borges et al. 2001; Web sites of IBAMA, Instituto Socioambiental, and IBGE; personal communication with Luciene Pohl of Brazil's National Indian Foundation (FUNAI).

[a]Hunting is allowed in some areas; for others information was unavailable.

[b]These activities are not expressly permitted, but because people are allowed to live in these reserves they will certainly occur, at least on a limited scale.

destroying large areas of forest directly. To predict the future effects of planned roads and other infrastructure projects, we assessed the past effects of existing highways and roads on primary forest cover in the Amazon.

To do this, we overlaid the existing road network on the Landsat TM-based Pathfinder map of the Brazilian Amazon for 1992. Many of the region's major highways (e.g., Belém-Brasília, Transamazon, BR-364) were constructed in the 1960s and 1970s, and thus had been in existence for 15–25 years by 1992—roughly comparable to the 20-year time frame for our predictions. Initially, five "buffer zones" were created around all paved highways (0–10, 11–25, 26–50, 51–75, and 76–100 km on each side of the highway), and the percentage loss of primary forest cover within each zone was determined. This analysis was then repeated using the entire network of highways and unpaved roads. Clouds, cloud shadows, and rivers were removed from the analyses (< 5% of total area). Buffers were truncated if they passed outside the Brazilian Legal Amazon. Deforestation was registered only for closed-canopy forests; losses of other habitats (e.g., savanna) were not included. Analyses were run on a Silicon Graphics Origin supercomputer at the Basic Science and Remote Sensing Initiative, Michigan State University.

As expected, the analyses (fig. 28.7) revealed that deforestation strongly increased near highways and roads. Both averaged about 30% forest loss within the 0–10 km buffer zone, but highways had more far-reaching effects than roads, averaging about 20% and 15% forest loss in the 11–25 and 26–50 km zones, respectively. Roads tended to generate more localized deforestation, with average forest loss declining below 15% beyond 25 km from the road.

Networks of roads tend to proliferate near highways, as is evident, for example, along the Belém-Brasília and eastern Transamazon highways. The most far-reaching effect we observed was the construction of 200–300 km long state and local roads ramifying laterally from highways in Pará, Mato Grosso, and Amazonas states (see fig. 28.6). Road networks are also generated by infrastructure projects, as it is nearly impossible to construct hydroelectric dams, powerlines, gas lines, and other major facilities without road access.

Model Assumptions

We used the buffer zone analyses to help generate two alternative predictions—termed the "optimistic" and "non-optimistic" scenarios—for the future of the Brazilian Amazon. Our models predict the spatial distribution of four broad land use categories. The first category is heavily degraded areas, regions in which primary forest cover is likely to be absent or markedly reduced and

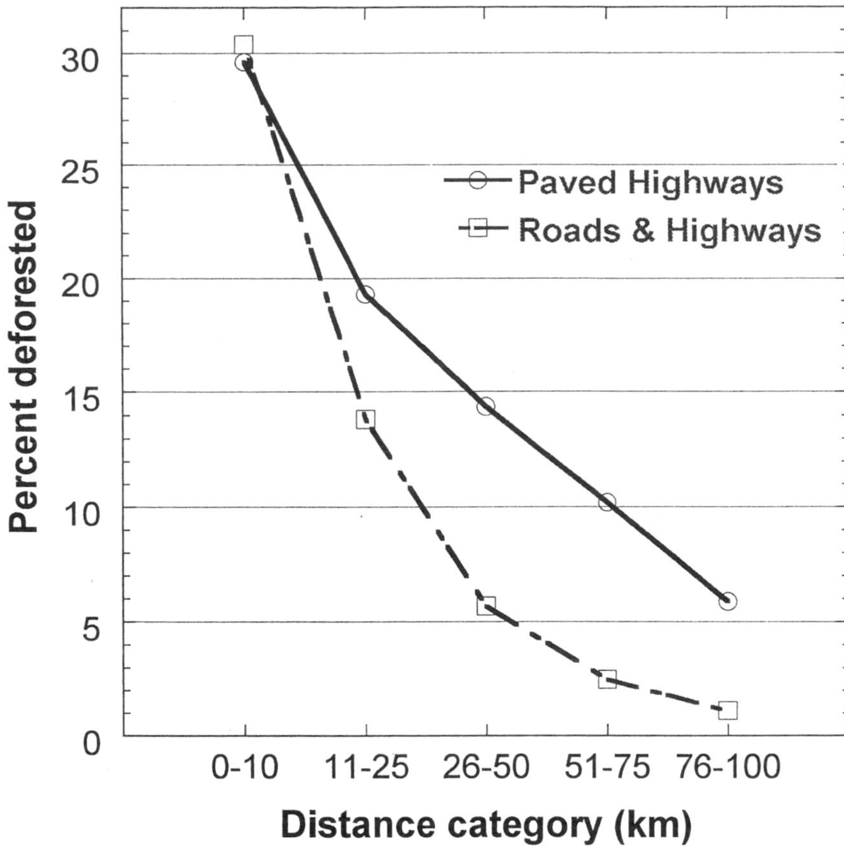

Figure 28.7 Percentage of closed-canopy forest destroyed by 1992 as a function of distance from paved highways, and from all roads and highways, in the Brazilian Amazon.

heavily fragmented. Such areas are highly vulnerable to edge effects, fires, logging, and overhunting and are severely degraded ecologically. Moderately degraded areas have mostly intact primary forest cover (> 85%), but contain localized forest clearings and some roads and may be affected by logging, mining, hunting, and oil and gas exploration. Lightly degraded areas have nearly intact primary forest cover (> 95%), but can experience illegal gold mining, small-scale farming, hunting, hand logging, and non-timber resource extraction (e.g., rubber tapping). "Pristine areas" have fully intact primary forest cover and are free from anthropogenic impacts aside from limited hunting, fishing, and swidden farming by traditional indigenous communities.

The optimistic and non-optimistic models differ in that the former assumes that highways, roads, and infrastructure projects will generate more localized

Table 28.3 Explicit assumptions of "optimistic" and "non-optimistic" GIS models used to predict forest degradation in the Brazilian Amazon

	Optimistic scenario	Non-optimistic scenario
Buffers around paved highways (current and planned)		
Heavily degraded zone	0–25 km	0–50 km
Moderately degraded zone	26–50 km	51–100 km
Lightly degraded zone	51–75 km	101–200 km
Pristine zone	> 75 km	> 200 km
Buffers around unpaved roads, railroads, powerlines, gas lines, industrial mines, and river channelization projects (current and planned)		
Heavily degraded zone	0–10 km	0–25 km
Moderately degraded zone	11–25 km	26–50 km
Lightly degraded zone	26–50 km	51–100 km
Pristine zone	> 50 km	> 100 km
Buffers around hydroelectric reservoirs		
Heavily degraded zone	Area inundated	Area inundated
Moderately degraded zone	0–5 km	0–10 km
Lightly degraded zone	6–10 km	11–25 km
Pristine zone	> 10 km	> 25 km
Areas prone to logging	Moderately degraded	Moderately degraded
Areas prone to wildcat mining	Lightly degraded	Lightly degraded
Areas prone to fires		
High vulnerability	Moderately degraded	Heavily degraded
Moderate vulnerability	Lightly degraded	Moderately degraded
Conservation areas		
High-protection areas outside buffers	Pristine	Pristine
High-protection areas inside buffers	Pristine	Lightly degraded
Moderate-protection areas outside buffers	Lightly degraded	Lightly degraded
Moderate-protection areas inside buffers	Lightly degraded	Moderately degraded
Indigenous areas outside buffers	Pristine	Lightly degraded
Indigenous areas inside buffers	Lightly degraded	Moderately degraded

effects and that conservation areas will be less prone to disturbances (table 28.3). The sizes of the buffer zones used in the models were necessarily somewhat arbitrary, but have an empirical basis in our analyses of past deforestation. In the non-optimistic model, for example, we assumed that paved highways would create a 50 km wide zone of heavily degraded forest on each side because our analysis suggested that these areas averaged less than 85% forest cover (see fig. 28.7). Such areas would be prone to logging, fragmentation, fires, edge effects, and other ecological changes that could affect much of the remaining forest cover (see Skole and Tucker 1993; Nepstad, Verissimo et al. 1999, Cochrane et al. 1999; Gascon, Williamson, and da Fonseca 2000; Laurance 2000). Likewise, we conservatively assumed that the lightly degraded zone would extend 100–200 km from paved highways because we observed a number of roads stretching at least 200 km from existing highways.

In both scenarios, logging and wildcat mining were assumed to cause moderate and light forest degradation, respectively. However, the models differed in terms of the viability of protected areas. The optimistic model assumed that all reserves would remain pristine or only lightly degraded, whereas the non-optimistic model assumed that indigenous lands and reserves with moderate protection (or parts thereof) would be moderately degraded within 50 km of roads or 100 km of highways; otherwise they would be pristine or lightly degraded. The non-optimistic model also assumed that reserves with high protection would be lightly degraded near roads and highways.

GIS Analyses

All maps and spatial data were georeferenced to a geographic coordinate system, using Imagine 8.3 software (ERDAS 1998). Subsequently, georeferenced digital images were used for vector data layer construction, using Arc/Info 7.2.1 (ESRI 1999) via heads-up digitizing methods. Road and infrastructure buffers were created with Arc/Info software for the appropriate distances. Data layers were integrated with overlay methodology. Most analyses were performed on a Silicon Graphics Indigo2 workstation at Biological Dynamics of Forest Fragments Project (BDFFP) headquarters in Manaus, Brazil.

Results

The optimistic scenario (fig. 28.8A) suggests that by the year 2020 there will be continued deforestation in the southern and eastern portions of the Brazilian Amazon and considerable large-scale fragmentation of forests in the central and southern parts of the basin. The Brazilian Amazon will be nearly bisected by heavily to moderately degraded areas along a north-south axis running from Rondônia to Manaus and northward to Venezuela. Pristine and lightly degraded forests will be fragmented into several blocks, with the largest tract surviving in the western Brazilian Amazon. According to this scenario, pristine forests will constitute just 28.0% of the region, and lightly degraded forests will constitute another 28.0%. Almost 27% of the region will be deforested or heavily degraded (fig. 28.9).

Figure 28.8 Projected forest degradation in the Brazilian Amazon by the year 2020: (A) optimistic scenario; (B) non-optimistic scenario. Gray areas = deforested or heavily degraded, including savannas and other nonforested areas; crosshatched areas = moderately degraded; single-hatched areas = lightly degraded; white areas = pristine.

A

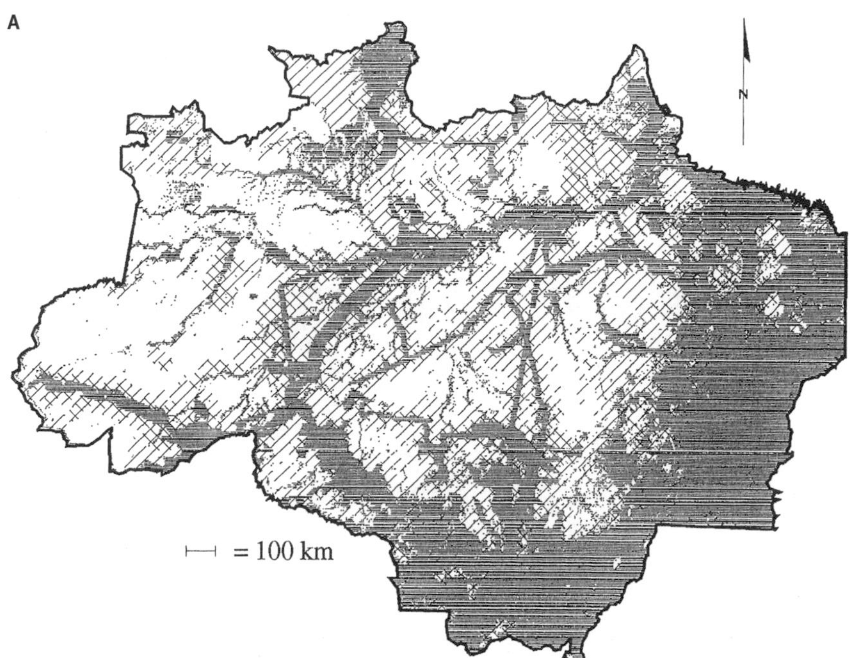

B

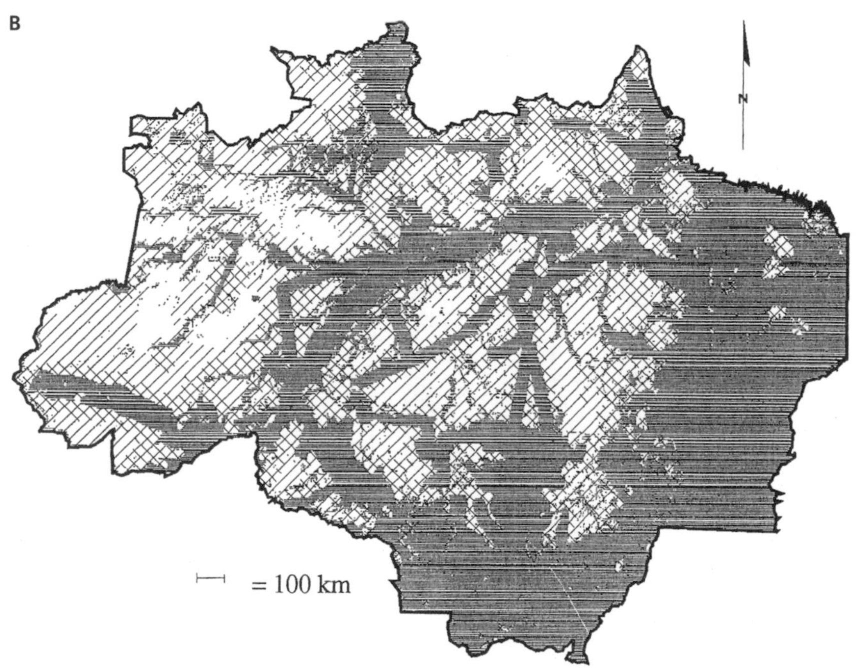

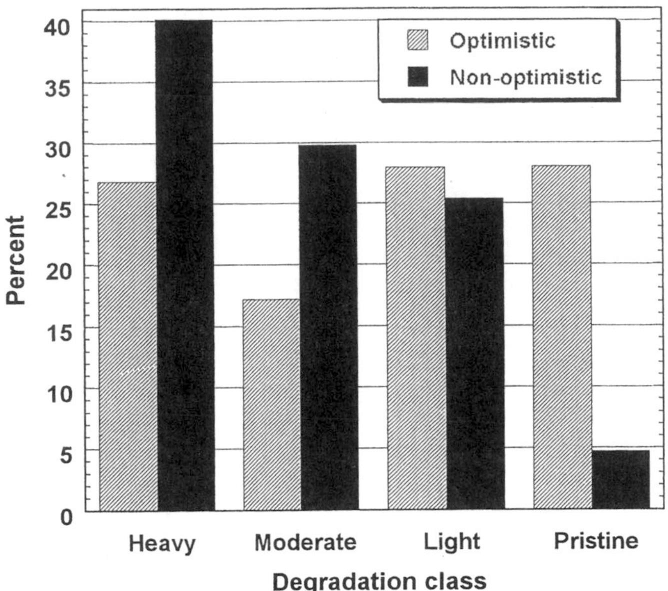

With new highways and infrastructure
Optimistic
Non-optimistic
Percent
40
35
30
25
20
15
10
5
0
Heavy
Moderate
Light
Pristine
Degradation class

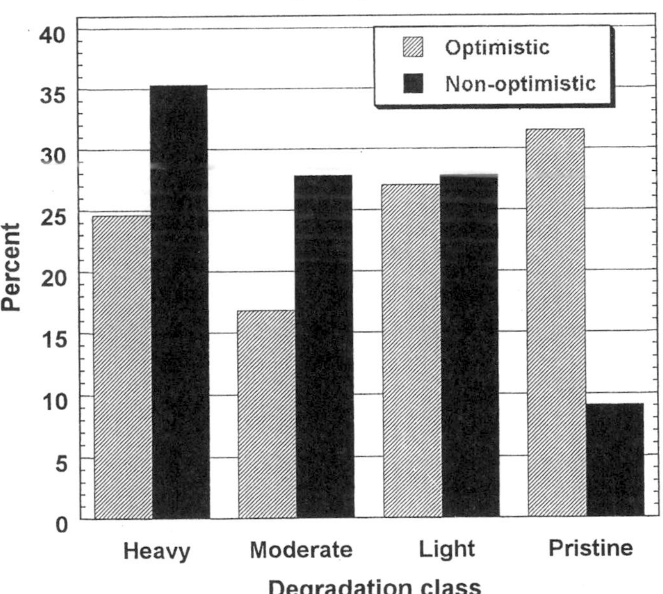

Without new highways and infrastructure
Optimistic
Non-optimistic
Percent
40
35
30
25
20
15
10
5
0
Heavy
Moderate
Light
Pristine
Degradation class

The non-optimistic scenario (fig. 28.8B) projects an even more dramatic loss of forests along the southern and eastern areas of the basin. Large-scale fragmentation is also more extensive, with much forest in the central, northern, and southeastern areas persisting only in isolated tracts. The basin is almost completely bisected by a swath of heavily degraded lands along the north-south axis running from Rondônia to Venezuela. There are very few areas of pristine forest aside from those in the western quarter of the region. This scenario predicts that pristine forests will constitute just 4.9% of the region, with lightly degraded forests constituting another 25.4%. Over 40% of the region will be heavily degraded.

Discussion and Implications

Both of our models suggest that the Brazilian Amazon will be drastically altered by current development plans and prevailing land use trends over the next 20 years. The principal differences between the models are in the extent of forest loss and fragmentation (see fig. 28.8) and the relative proportions of heavily degraded versus pristine forests (see fig. 28.9).

Some degree of oversimplification in our models was inevitable. For example, we did not incorporate the effect of population density into our models, in part because we observed that local road density in the Amazon seemed to be a reasonably good surrogate for local population density. It is also apparent that the buffer zones around roads, highways, and infrastructure projects will be more variable spatially than is indicated in our models. While we have incorporated many of the factors that are likely to influence local deforestation (e.g., distance to roads, road quality [paved vs. unpaved], presence and type of protected areas, vulnerability to forest fires, logging and mining activity), it is impossible to include every potentially relevant factor (see Laurance, Albernaz et al. 2002 for further analyses of factors that influence Amazonian deforestation).

The optimistic and non-optimistic scenarios vary considerably, and it is therefore important to ask which is the most realistic. At least two considerations suggest that the non-optimistic scenario may better approximate reality. First, the non-optimistic model realistically assumes that forests with high fire vulnerability will become heavily degraded, while those of moderate vulnerability will become moderately degraded. The model of fire vulnerability we used

Figure 28.9 Predicted percentages of Brazilian Amazon forest in four degradation classes by the year 2020 according to the optimistic and non-optimistic scenarios.

(Nepstad et al. 1998) was produced for a normal dry season and is therefore conservative, in the sense that much larger areas of the Amazon will become vulnerable to fires during periodic El Niño droughts (Nepstad et al. 1998; Cochrane and Schulze 1998, 1999).

Second, the non-optimistic model assumes that protected areas within 50 km of highways and roads will be lightly to moderately degraded. In fact, many protected areas in the Amazon are little more than "paper parks" with inadequate protection. Ferreira et al. (1999) evaluated eighty-six federal parks and protected areas in Brazil and found that 43% were at high to extreme risk because of illegal deforestation, colonization, hunting, isolation of the reserve from other forest areas, and additional forms of encroachment. More than half of all reserves (54.6%) were judged to have nearly nonexistent management. For some reserves, even our non-optimistic scenario may be overly optimistic.

The fates of indigenous lands and reserves will have an important effect on forest conservation. In many of these areas, the quality of environmental protection has declined markedly as indigenous groups come into more frequent contact with outsiders and traditional lifestyles are lost (Margolis 2000). In this sense, reducing construction of new roads and highways near indigenous lands may be one of the most effective measures to ensure that traditional management systems are not corrupted.

Other investigators have also attempted to predict spatial patterns of Amazonian deforestation. Recent studies by a Brazilian nongovernmental organization attempted to predict the extent of deforestation that will be caused by new highway construction under the Avança Brasil program (Nepstad et al. 2000, 2001; Carvalho et al. 2001), but did not consider the effects of other infrastructure projects (hydroelectric reservoirs, powerlines, gas lines, railroads, river channelization projects, and their associated road networks) on forests (see Fearnside 2002). In addition, an ongoing study by C. Souza Jr. (personal communication) is using data on existing road networks, logging, and recent fires in order to assess conversion pressure on Brazilian Amazonian forests. Earlier studies, such as those of Kangas (1990) and Bryant, Nielsen, and Tangley (1997), did not incorporate the effects of massive planned highway and infrastructure developments under Avança Brasil, and hence are seriously out of date.

Obviously, our models illustrate only two of a potentially infinite number of possible futures for the Brazilian Amazon. While we believe our approach is based on realistic assumptions, it has two limitations. First, our model predictions are somewhat difficult to test and verify, especially for lightly degraded forests. Low-intensity selective logging and illegal gold mining, for example, are nearly impossible to detect with remote sensing, although technological improvements could change this in the future. Second, our models rely on specific assumptions about the future drivers of forest degradation (see table 28.3). Perhaps the most crucial assumption is that current infrastructure projects will proceed as planned and that there will be no major new development initiatives. The unforeseen construction of a new highway, for example, could alter the scale and spatial pattern of forest degradation, reducing the accuracy of our predictions.

In the Amazon, hundreds of millions of dollars are currently being expended on efforts to promote conservation planning via international programs such as the Pilot Program to Protect the Brazilian Rainforest, bilateral initiatives, and the activities of nongovernmental organizations (Laurance and Fearnside 1999; Laurance, Cochrane et al. 2001). The most important conclusion of our study is that current domestic and international efforts to promote conservation planning in the Brazilian Amazon are likely to be swamped by short-term plans to invest over US$40 billion in Amazonian transportation and infrastructure projects. The environmental impacts of these projects will be further magnified by population increases, forest colonization projects, and rapidly expanding logging and mining industries. If our models provide even a rough approximation of the future, the forests of the Amazon will be profoundly altered over the next two decades. We conclude that a fundamental reevaluation of the criteria used in selecting, planning, and licensing large-scale development projects is urgently needed (see Fearnside 2002). Without major policy changes, current development schemes are likely to have dire effects on Amazonian forests.

ACKNOWLEDGMENTS

We thank Bruce Nelson, Heraldo Vasconcelos, and Rita Mesquita for discussion and reviewing the manuscript. Support was provided by the NASA-LBA program, Andrew W. Mellon Foundation, World Wildlife Fund-U.S., MacArthur Foundation, National Institute for Amazonian Research, and the Smithsonian Institution. This chapter is publication number 316 in the BDFFP technical series.

REFERENCES

Abele, C., C. S. Gloe, G. Hocking, G. Holdgate, P. R. Kenley, C. R. Lawrence, D. Ripper, W. F. Threlfall, and P. F. Bolger. 1988. Tertiary. Pages 251–350 in J. G. Douglas and J. A. Ferguson, eds., *Geology of Victoria.* Geological Society of Australia (Victorian Division), Melbourne.

Abramovitz, J. 1998. *Taking a stand: Cultivating a new relationship with the world's forests.* Worldwatch Institute, Washington, DC.

Ab'Saber. A. N. 1982. The paleoclimate and paleoecology of Brazilian Amazonia. Pages 41–59 in G. T. Prance, ed., *Biological diversification in the tropics.* Columbia University Press, New York.

Absy, M. L. 1979. A palynological study of Holocene sediments in the Amazon Basin. Ph.D. thesis, University of Amsterdam.

Absy, M. L., A. Cleef, M. Fornier, M. Servant, A. Siffedine, M. N. F. Da Silva, F. Soubies, K. Suguio, B. Turcq, and T. van der Hammen. 1991. Mise en evidence de quatre phases d'ouverture de la foret dense dans le sud-est de l'Amazonie au cours des 60 000 dernieres annees. Premiere comparaison avec d'autres regions tropicales. *Comptes Rendus de L'Académie des Sciences, Paris* 313:673–678.

Absy, M. L., and T. van der Hammen. 1976. Some palaeoecological data from Rondonia, southern part of the Amazon Basin. *Acta Amazonica* 6:293–299.

Accacio, G. M. 1997. Borboletas em parques urbanos: Estudos na cidade de São Paulo. M.Sc. Thesis, Universidade de São Paulo, São Paulo, Brazil.

Aceituno, P. 1988. On the functioning of the Southern Oscillation in the South American sector. Part I: Surface climate. *Monthly Weather Review* 116:505–524.

Adam, P. 1994. *Australian rainforests.* Oxford University Press, Oxford.

Adis, J., and M. Latif. 1996. Amazonian arthropods respond to El Niño. *Biotropica* 28:403–407.

Adler, G. H. 1994. Tropical forest fragmentation and isolation promote asynchrony among populations of a frugivorous rodent. *Journal of Animal Ecology* 63:903–911.

———. 1998. Impacts of resource abundance on populations of a tropical forest rodent. *Ecology* 79:242–254.

Agapow, P. M., and A. Purvis. 2002. Power of eight tree shape statistics to detect nonrandom diversification: A comparison by simulation of two models of cladogenesis. *Systematic Biology* 51:866–872.

Ahumada, J. A., S. P. Hubbell, R. Condit, and R. B. Foster. 2004. Long-term tree survival in a Neotropical forest: The influence of local biotic neighborhood. Pages 408–432 in E. Losos and E. G. Leigh Jr., eds., *Tropical diversity and dynamism: Findings from a network of tropical forest plots.* University of Chicago Press, Chicago.

Aleixo, A. 2002. Molecular systematics and the role of the "várzea"-"terra-firme" ecotone in the diversification of *Xiphorhynchus* woodcreepers (Aves: Dendtocolaptidae). *Auk* 119:621–640.

Alexandre, D.-Y. 1978. Le rôle disséminateur des éléphants en forêt de Tai, Côte d'Ivoire. *La Terre et la Vie* 32:47–72.

Alford, R. A., and S. J. Richards. 1999. Global amphibian declines: A problem in applied ecology. *Annual Review of Ecology and Systematics* 30:133–165.

Allen, R. J., H. G. S. Cribb, R. F. Isbell, T. B. H. Jenkins, N. R. McTaggart, W. D. Mott, H. R. E. Staines, P. J. Stephenson, N. C. Stevens, D. M. Traves, and G. W. Tweedale. 1960. Lower Cainozoic. Pages 341–455 in D. Hill and A. K. Denmead, eds., *The geology of Queensland.* Melbourne University Press and Geological Society of Australia, Adelaide.

Allen, T. F. H., and T. W. Hoekstra. 1992. *Toward a unified ecology.* Columbia University Press, New York.

Alley, N. F. 1987. Middle Eocene age of the megafossil flora at Golden Grove, South Australia: Preliminary report, and comparison with the Maslin Bay flora. *Transactions of the Royal Society of South Australia* 111(3):211–212.

Alley, N. F., and L. M. Broadbridge. 1992. Middle Eocene palynofloras from the One Tree Hill area, St Vincent Basin, South Australia. *Alcheringa* 16:241–267.

Allsopp, P. G. 2000. Revision of the Australian genus *Anomalomorpha* Arrow (Coleoptera: Scarabaeidae: Dynastinae) with a new species from the Wet Tropics of Queensland. *Memoirs of the Queensland Museum* 46:1–7.

Alvard, M. S., J. G. Robinson, K. H. Redford, and H. Kapland. 1997. The sustainability of subsistence hunting in the Neotropics. *Conservation Biology* 11:977–982.

Alvarez, W. 1997. T. rex *and the Crater of Doom.* Princeton University Press, Princeton, NJ.

Alverson, W. S., W. Kuhlmann, and D. M. Waller. 1994. *Wild forests: Conservation biology and public policy.* Island Press, Washington, DC.

Alvim, P. de T. 1960. Moisture stress as a requirement for flowering of coffee. *Science* 132:354.

Amadon, D., and L. L. Short. 1992. Taxonomy of lower categories: Suggested guidelines. *Bulletin of British Ornithologists Club* 112A:11–38.

Ambrose, G. J., R. A. Callen, R. B. Flint, and R. T. Lange. 1979. *Eucalyptus* fruits in stratigraphic context in Australia. *Nature* 280(5721):387–389.

American Ornithologists' Union. 1998. *Check-list of North American birds.* American Ornithologists' Union, Washington, DC.

Andersen, N. M., and T. A. Weir. 1997. The gerrine water striders of Australia (Hemiptera: Gerridae): Taxonomy, distribution and ecology. *Invertebrate Taxonomy* 11:203–299.

———. 2001. New genera of Veliidae (Hemiptera: Heteroptera) from Australia, with notes on generic classification of the subfamily Microveliinae. *Invertebrate Taxonomy* 15:217–258.

Anderson, J. A. L., and J. Muller. 1975. Palynological study of a Holocene peat and a Miocene coal deposit from N.W. Borneo. *Review of Palaeobotany and Palynology* 19:291–351.

Ando, A., J. Camm, S. Polasky, and A. Solow. 1998. Species distributions, land values, and efficient conservation. *Science* 279:2126–2128.

Aoki, M., K. Yabuki, and H. Koyama. 1975. Micrometeorology and assessment of primary production of a tropical rain forest in West Malaysia. *Journal of Agricultural Meteorology* 31:115–124.

Appanah, S. 1985. General flowering in the climax rain forests of Southeast Asia. *Journal of Tropical Ecology* 1:225–240.

Arbogast, B. S., S. V. Edwards, J. Wakeley, and P. Beerli. 2002. Estimating divergence times from molecular data on phylogenetic and population genetic timescales. *Annual Review of Ecology and Systematics* 33:707–740.

Archer, M., S. J. Hand, and H. Godthelp. 1994. Patterns in the history of Australia's mammals and inferences about palaeohabitats. Pages 80–103 in R. S. Hill, ed., *The history of Australian vegetation: Cretaceous to Recent.* Cambridge University Press, Cambridge.

———. 1995. Tertiary environmental and biotic change in Australia. Pages 77–90 in E. S. Vrba, G. H. Denton, T. C. Partridge, and C. Burckle, eds., *Paleoclimate and evolution, with emphasis on human origins.* Yale University Press, New Haven, CT.

Arctander, P., and J. Fjeldså. 1994. Andean tapaculos of the genus *Scytalopus* (Aves, Rhinocryptidae): A study of speciation using DNA sequence data. Pages 205–225 in V. Loeschcke, J. Tomiuk, and S. K. Jain, eds., *Conservation genetics.* Birkhäuser, Basel.

Arnold, M. L. 1997. *Natural hybridization and evolution.* Oxford series in evolution and ecology. Oxford University Press, Oxford.

Arrhenius, O. 1921. Species and area. *Journal of Ecology* 9:95–99.

Ash, J. 1988. The location and stability of rainforest boundaries in north-eastern Queensland, Australia. *Journal of Biogeography* 15:619–630.

Ashton, P. S. 1969. Speciation among tropical forest trees: Some deductions in the light of recent evidence. *Biological Journal of the Linnean Society* 1:155–196.

Ashton, P. S., T. J. Givnish, and S. Appanah. 1988. Staggered flowering in the Dipterocarpaceae: New insights into floral induction and the evolution of mast fruiting in the aseasonal tropics. *American Naturalist* 132:44–66.

Atmar, W., and B. D. Patterson. 1993. The measure of order and disorder in the distribution of species in fragmented habitat. *Oecologia* 96:373–382.

———. 1995. The nestedness temperature calculator: A Visual Basic program, including 294 presence-absence matrices. AICS Research, University Park, NM; Field Museum of Natural History, Chicago.

Augspurger, C. K. 1982. A cue for synchronous flowering. Pages 133–150 in E. G. Leigh Jr., A. S. Rand, and D. M. Windsor, eds., *The ecology of a tropical forest.* Smithsonian Institution Press, Washington, DC.

———. 1983. Offspring recruitment around tropical trees: Changes in cohort distance with time. *Oikos* 40:189–196.

———. 1984a. Pathogen mortality of tropical tree seedlings: Experimental studies of the effects of dispersal distance, seedling density and light conditions. *Oecologia* 61:211–217.

———. 1984b. Seedling survival of tropical tree species: Interactions of dispersal distance, light gaps and pathogens. *Ecology* 65:1705–1712.

Austin, G. T., N. M. Haddad, C. Méndez, T. D. Sisk, D. D. Murphy, A. Launer, and P. R. Ehrlich. 1996. Annotated checklist of the butterflies of the Tikal National Park area of Guatemala. *Tropical Lepidoptera* 7:21–37.

Austin, J. M., B. G. Mackey, and P. Van Neil Kimberly. 2003. Estimating forest biomass using satellite radar: An exploratory study in a temperate Eucalyptus forest. *Forest Ecology and Management* 176:575–583.

Austin, M. P., C. B. Cunningham, and P. M. Fleming. 1984. New approaches to direct gradient analysis using environmental scalars and statistical curve-fitting procedures. *Vegetatio* 55:11–27.

Avança Brasil. 1999. *Avança Brasil: Development structures for investment.* Ministry for Development, Industry, and Foreign Trade, Brasília, Brazil.

Ávila-Pires, T. C. S. 1995. *Lizards of Brazilian Amazonia (Reptilia: Squamata).* Zoologisches Verhandelingen, Leiden.

Avise, J. C. 1989a. Gene trees and organismal histories: A phylogenetic approach to population biology. *Evolution* 43:1192–1208.

———. 1989b. A role for molecular genetics in the recognition and conservation of endangered species. *Trends in Ecology and Evolution* 4:279–281.

———. 1992. Molecular population structure and the biogeographic history of a regional fauna: A case history with lessons for conservation biology. *Oikos* 63:62–76.

———. 1994. *Molecular markers, natural history and evolution.* Chapman & Hall, New York.

———. 1996. Towards a regional conservation genetics perspective. Pages 431–470 in J. C. Avise and J. Hamrick, eds., *Conservation genetics: Case histories from nature.* Chapman & Hall, New York.

———. 2000. *Phylogeography: The history and formation of species.* Harvard University Press, Cambridge, MA.

Avise, J. C., J. Arnold, R. M. Ball, E. Bermingham, T. Lamb, J. E. Neigel, C. A. Reeb, and N. C. Saunders. 1987. Interspecific phylogeography: The mitochondrial DNA bridge between population genetics and systematics. *Annual Review of Ecology and Systematics* 18:489–522.

Avise, J. C., and D. Walker. 1998. Pleistocene phylogeographic effects on avian populations and the speciation process. *Proceedings of the Royal Society of London* B 265:457–463.

Avise, J. C., D. Walker, and G. C. Johns. 1998. Speciation durations and Pleistocene effects on vertebrate phylogeography. *Proceedings of the Royal Society of London* B 265:1707–1712.

Axelrod, D. I., and P. H. Raven. 1978. Late cretaceous and tertiary vegetation history of Africa. Pages 77–130 in M. J. A. Werger, ed., *Biogeography and ecology of southern Africa.* Dr. W. Junk, The Hague.

Ayres, J. M., and T. H. Clutton-Brock. 1992. River boundaries and species range size in Amazonian primates. *American Naturalist* 140:531–537.

Badgley, C., and D. L. Fox. 2000. Ecological biogeography of North American mammals: Species density and ecological structure in relation to environmental gradients. *Journal of Biogeography* 27:1437–1467.

Baehr, M. 1987. Revision of the Australian Zuphiinae. 2. *Colasidia monteithi* sp. nov. from North Queensland, first record of the tribe Leleupidiini in Australia (Insecta: Coleoptera: Carabidae). *Memoirs of the Queensland Museum* 25:135–140.

———. 1995. Revision of *Philipis* (Coleoptera: Carabidae: Bembidiinae), a genus of arboreal tachyine beetles from the rainforests of eastern Australia: Taxonomy, phylogeny and biogeography. *Memoirs of the Queensland Museum* 38:315–381.

Baillie, I. C., P. S. Ashton, M. N. Court, J. A. R. Anderson, E. A. Fitzpatrick, and J. Tinsley. 1987. Site characteristics of tree species in mixed dipterocarp forest on tertiary sediments in central Sarawak, Malaysia. *Journal of Tropical Ecology* 3:201–220.

Bains, S., R. M. Corfield, and R. D. Norris. 1999. Mechanisms of climate warming at the end of the Paleocene. *Science* 285:724–727.

Baldwin, B. G., D. W. Kyhos, J. Dvorak, and G. D. Carr. 1991. Chloroplast DNA evidence for a North American origin of the Hawaiian silversword alliance (Asteraceae). *Proceedings of the National Academy of Sciences USA* 88:1840–1843.

Baldwin, B. G., and M. J. Sanderson. 1998. Age and rate of diversification of the Hawaiian silversword alliance. *Proceedings of the National Academy of Sciences USA* 95:9402–9406.

Ballantyne, L. A., and C. L. Lambkin. 2000. Lampyridae of Australia (Coleoptera: Lampyridae: Luciolinae: Luciolini). *Memoirs of the Queensland Museum* 46:15–93.

Balmford, A., and A. Long. 1995. Across-country analysis of biodiversity congruence and current conservation efforts in the tropics. *Conservation Biology* 9:1539–1547.

Balmford, A., G. M. Mace, and J. R. Ginsburg. 1998. The challenges to conservation in a changing world: Putting processes on the map. Pages 1–28 in G. M. Mace, A. Balmford, and J. R. Ginsburg, eds., *Conservation in a changing world: Integrating processes into priorities for action.* Cambridge University Press, Cambridge.

Balmford, A., J. L. Moore, T. Brooks, N. Burgess, L. A. Hansen, P. Williams, and C. Rahbek. 2001. Conservation conflict across Africa. *Science* 291:2616–2619.

Balslev, H., J. Luteyn, B. Øllgaard, and L. B. Holm-Nielsen. 1987. Composition and structure of adjacent unflooded and floodplain forest in Amazonian Ecuador. *Opera Botanica* 92:37–57.

Balslev, H., R. Valencia, G. Paz y Miño, H. Christensen, and I. Nielsen. 1998. Species count of vascular plants in one hectare of humid lowland forest in Amazonian Ecuador. Pages 585–594 in F. Dallmeier, and J. A. Comiskey, eds., *Forest Biodiversity in North, Central and South America, and the Caribbean: Research and Monitoring.* Man and the Biosphere Series, vol. 21. UNESCO, Paris; Parthenon Publishing Group, New York.

Banks, M. 1999. The Early Eocene macroflora of Hotham Heights. B.Sc.(Hons.) thesis, Victoria University of Technology, Melbourne.

Barber, C. 1998. Forest resource scarcity and social conflict in Indonesia. *Environment* 40(4):4–37.

Barber, C. V., and J. Schweithelm. 2000. *Trial by fire.* World Resources Institute, Washington, DC.

Barbosa, R. I., and P. M. Fearnside. 1999. Incêndios na Amazônia brasileira: Estimativa da emissão de gases do efeito estufa pela queima de diferentes ecossistemas de Roraima na passagem do evento "El Niño" (1997/98). *Acta Amazonica* 29:513–534.

Barbour, M. G., J. H. Burk, and W. D. Pitts. 1987. *Terrestrial plant ecology.* Benjamin/Cummings, Menlo Park, CA.

Barcant, M. 1970. *Butterflies of Trinidad and Tobago.* Collins, London.

Bard, E. 2001. Comparison of alkenone estimates with other paleotemperature proxies. Geochemistry, Geophysics, Geosystems vol. 2, no. 1. Paper number 2000GC000050.

Barfod, A. 1991. A monographic study of the subfamily Phytelephantoideae. *Opera Botanica* 105:1–73.

Barlow, B. A. 1994. Phytogeography of the Australian region. Pages 3–36 in R. H. Groves, ed., *Australian Vegetation,* 2nd ed. Cambridge University Press, Cambridge.

Barnes, J., ed. 1984. *The complete works of Aristotle.* Vol. 1. Princeton University Press, Princeton, NJ.

Barnes, R. W., and R. S. Hill. 1999. Macrofossils of *Callicoma* and *Codia* (Cunoniaceae) from Australian Cainozoic sediments. *Australian Systematic Botany* 12:647–670.

Barone, J. A. 1998. Host-specificity of folivorous insects in a moist tropical forest. *Journal of Animal Ecology* 67(3):400–409.

Barraclough, T. G., P. H. Harvey, and S. Nee. 1995. Sexual selection and taxonomic diversity in passerine birds. *Proceedings of the Royal Society of London* B 259:211–215.

Barraclough, T. G., and S. Nee. 2001. Phylogenetics and speciation. *Trends in Ecology and Evolution* 16:391–399.

Barraclough, T. G., S. Nee, and P. H. Harvey. 1998. Sister group analysis in identifying correlates of diversification. *Evolutionary Ecology* 12:751–754.

Barraclough, T. G., A. P. Vogler, and P. H. Harvey. 1998. Revealing the factors that promote speciation. *Philosophical Transactions of the Royal Society of London* B 353:241–249.

Barthlott, W., W. Lauer, and A. Placke. 1996. Global distribution of species diversity in vascular plants: Towards a world map of phytodiversity. *Erdkunde* 50:317–327.

Barton, N. H. 1979. Gene flow past a cline. *Heredity* 43:333–339.

Basinger, J. F., and D. C. Christophel. 1985. Fossil flowers and leaves of the Ebenaceae from the Eocene of southern Australia. *Canadian Journal of Botany* 63:1825–1843.

Basset, Y. 2000. Insect herbivores foraging on seedlings in an unlogged rain forest in Guyana: Spatial and temporal considerations. *Studies in Neotropical Fauna and Environment* 35:115–129.

Bates, H. W. 1864. *The naturalist on the River Amazons.* Abridged ed. John Murray, London. Reprinted in 1962 by the University of California Press, Los Angeles.

Bates, J. M., S. J. Hackett, and J. Goerck. 1999. High levels of mitochondrial DNA differentiation in two lineages of antbirds (*Drymophila* and *Hypocnemis*). *Auk* 116:1093–1106.

Bayes, A. J., and B. G. Mackey. 1991. Algorithms for monotonic functions and their application to ecological studies in vegetation science. *Ecological Modelling* 56:135–159.

Bayes, M. K. 1998. A molecular phylogenetic study of the galagos, strepsirrhine primates and archontan mammals. Ph.D. thesis, Oxford Brookes University, Oxford.

Bearder, S. K., P. E. Honess, and L. Ambrose. 1995. Species diversity among galagos with special reference to mate recognition. Pages 331–352 in L. Alterman, M. K. Izard, and G. A. Doyle, eds., *Creatures of the dark: The nocturnal prosimians.* Plenum Press, New York.

Beccaloni, G. W., and K. J. Gaston. 1995. Predicting the species richness of Neotropical forest butterflies: Ithomiinae (Lepidoptera: Nymphalidae) as indicators. *Biological Conservation* 71:77–86.

Begon, M., J. L. Harper, and C. R. Townsend. 1986. *Ecology: Individuals, populations and communities.* Blackwell, Oxford.

Bell, K., D. K. Yeates, C. Moritz, and G. B. Monteith. 2004. Molecular phylogeny and biogeography of the dung beetle genus *Temnoplectron* Westwood (Scarabaeidae: Scarabaeinae) from Australia's wet tropics. *Molecular Phylogenetics and Evolution* 31(2): 741–53.

Bell, R. T., and J. R. Bell. 1991. The Rhysodini of Australia (Insecta: Coleoptera: Carabidae or Rhysodidae). *Annals of the Carnegie Museum* 60:179–210.

Bellamy, C. L. 1991. Further review of the genus *Maoraxia* Obenberger (Coleoptera: Buprestidae). *Invertebrate Taxonomy* 5:457–468.

Belt, T. 1874. *The naturalist in Nicaragua.* John Murray, London.

Benbow, M., N. F. Alley, M. Lindsay, and D. R. Greenwood. 1995. Geological history and palaeoclimate. Pages 208–217 in J. H. Drexel and W. V. Preiss, eds., *The geology of South Australia,* vol. 2, *The Phanerozoic.* South Australian Geological Survey, Bulletin 54. South Australian Geological Survey, Adelaide.

Benkman, C. W. 1991. Predation, seed size partitioning and the evolution of body size in seed-eating finches. *Evolutionary Ecology* 5:118–127.

Bennett, E. L., and M. T. Gumal. 2001. The interrelationships of commercial logging, hunting, and wildlife in Sarawak: Recommendations for forest management. Pages 359–274 in R. Fimbel, A. Grajal, and J. G. Robinson, eds., *The cutting edge: Conserving wildlife in logged tropical forests.* Columbia University Press, New York.

Bennett, E. L., A. J. Nyaoi, and J. Sompud. 1999. Saving Borneo's bacon: The sustainability of hunting in Sarawak. Pages 305–324 in J. G. Robinson and E. L. Bennett, eds., *Hunting for sustainability in tropical forests.* Columbia University Press, New York.

Bennett, E. L., and J. G. Robinson. 2000. Hunting of wildlife in tropical forests: Implications for biodiversity and forest peoples. Environment Department Papers, 76. World Bank, Washington, DC.

Bennett, K. D. 1983. Devensian Late-glacial and Flandrian vegetational history at Hockham Mere, Norfolk, England. *New Phytologist* 95:457–487.

Benson, L. J., and R. G. Pearson. 1987. The role of drift and effect of season in colonization of implanted substrata in a tropical Australian stream. *Freshwater Biology* 18:109–116.

———. 1988. Diversity and seasonality of adult Trichoptera captured in a light trap at Yuccabine Creek, a tropical Australian rainforest stream. *Australian Journal of Ecology* 13:337–344.

———. 1993. Litter inputs to a tropical Australian upland rainforest stream. *Australian Journal of Ecology* 18:377–383.

Benson, W. W. 1982. Alternative models for infrageneric differentiation in the humid tropics: Tests with passion vine butterflies. Pages 608–640 in G. T. Prance, ed., *Biological diversification in the tropics.* Columbia University Press, New York.

Beresford, P. 2002. Molecular systematics and biogeography of certain Guineo-Congolian passerines. Ph.D. thesis, City University of New York.

Berger, A., J. Imbrie, J. Hays, G. Kukla, and B. Salzman, eds. 1984. *Milankovitch and climate.* Reidel, Dordrecht.

Berger, A., and M. F. Loutre. 1991. Insolation values for the climate of the last 10 m.y. *Quaternary Science Reviews* 10:297–317.

Berggren, W. A., D. V. Kent, J. J. Flynn, and J. A. Van Couvering. 1985. Cenozoic geochronology. *Geological Society of America Bulletin* 96:1407–1418.

Berlage, H. P. 1931. On the relationship between thickness of tree-rings of Djati (teak) trees and rainfall on Java. *Tectona* 24:939–953.

Bermingham, E., and C. Dick. 2001. The *Inga:* Newcomer or museum antiquity. *Science* 293:2214–2216.

Bermingham, E., and A. P. Martin. 1998. Comparative mtDNA phylogeography of Neotropical freshwater fishes: Testing shared history to infer the evolutionary landscape of lower Central America. *Molecular Ecology* 7:499–517.

Bermingham, E., S. Rohwer, S. Freeman, and C. Wood. 1992. Vicariance biogeography in the Pleistocene and speciation in North American wood warblers: A test of Mengel's model. *Proceedings of the National Academy of Sciences USA* 89:6624–6628.

Bernatchez, L., and C. C. Wilson. 1998. Comparative phylogeography of Nearctic and Paleoarctic fishes. *Molecular Ecology* 7:431–452.

Bernays, E. A. 1998. The value of being a resource specialist: Behavioral support for a neutral hypothesis. *American Naturalist* 151:451–464.

Beven, S., E. F. Connor, and K. Beven. 1984. Avian biogeography in the Amazon basin and the biological model of diversification. *Journal of Biogeography* 11:383–399.

Bierregaard, R. O. Jr., T. E. Lovejoy, V. Kapos, A. dos Santos, and R. W. Hutchings. 1992. The biological dynamics of tropical rainforest fragments. *BioScience* 42:859–866.

Bierregaard, R. O. Jr., and P. C. Stouffer. 1997. Understory birds and dynamic habitat mosaics in Amazonian rainforests. Pages 138–155 in W. E. Laurance and R. O. Bierregaard Jr., eds., *Tropical forest remnants: Ecology, management, and conservation of fragmented communities.* University of Chicago Press, Chicago.

Bird, M., and A. Chivas. 1993. Geomorphic and palaeoclimatic implications of an oxygen-isotope chronology for Australian deeply weathered profiles. *Australian Journal of Earth Sciences* 40:345–358.

Birky, C. W. 1991. Evolution and population genetics of organelle genes: Mechanisms and models. Pages 112–134 in R. K. Selander, A. G. Clark, and T. S. Whittam, eds., *Evolution at the molecular level.* Sinauer Associates, Sunderland, MA.

Birky, C. W., P. Fuerst, and T. Maruyama. 1989. Organelle gene diversity under migration, mutation, and drift: Equilibrium expectations, approach to equilibrium, effects of heteroplasmic cells, and comparison to nuclear genes. *Genetics* 121:613–627.

Birky, C. W. Jr., T. Maruyama, and P. Fuerst. 1983. An approach to population and evolutionary genetic theory for genes in mitochondria and chloroplasts, and some results. *Genetics* 103:513–527.

Bishop, P. 1988. The eastern highlands of Australia: The evolution of an intraplate highland belt. *Progress in Physical Geography* 12:159–182.

Bishop, P., and R. K. Bamber. 1985. Silicified wood of Early Miocene *Nothofagus, Acacia* and Myrtaceae (aff. *Eucalyptus* B) from the Upper Lachlan Valley, New South Wales. *Alcheringa* 9:221–228.

Bishop, P., and G. Goldrick. 1998. Eastern Australia. Pages 227–255 in M. Summerfield, ed., *Geomorphology and global tectonics.* Wiley, Chichester.

Bishop, P., R. W. Young, and I. McDougall. 1985. Stream profile change and long-term landscape evolution: Early Miocene and modern rivers of the east Australian highland crest, central New South Wales, Australia. *Journal of Geology* 93:455–474.

Blackburn, D. T., and I. R. K. Sluiter. 1994. The Oligo-Miocene coal floras of southeastern

Australia. Pages 328–367 in R. S. Hill, ed., *The history of Australian vegetation: Cretaceous to Recent.* Cambridge University Press, Cambridge.

Bock, W. J. 1986. Species concepts, speciation, and macroevolution. Pages 31–57 in D. Iwatsuki, P. H. Raven, and W. J. Bock, eds., *Modern aspects of species.* University of Tokyo Press, Tokyo.

Bohte, A., and A. P. Kershaw. 1999. Taphonomic influences on the interpretation of the palaeoecological record from Lynch's Crater, northeastern Australia. *Quaternary International* 57:49–59.

Bonaccorso, F. J. 1979. Foraging and reproductive ecology in a Panamanian bat community. *Bulletin of the Florida State Museum, Biological Sciences* 24:359–408.

Bonnefille, R., J. C. Roeland, and J. Guiot. 1990. Temperature and rainfall estimates for the past 40,000 years in equatorial Africa. *Nature* 346:347–349.

Booch, G. 1994. *Object-oriented analysis and design with applications.* Benjamin/Cummings, Redwood City, CA.

Borges, S. H., M. Pinheiro, A. Murchie, and C. Durigan. 2001. Preservação do Rio Negro: As unidades de conservação. Pages 303–329 in A. Oliveira and D. Daly, eds., *As florestas do Rio Negro.* Universidade Paulista Press, São Paulo, Brazil.

Botkin, D. B. 1993. *Forest dynamics: An ecological model.* Oxford University Press, Oxford.

Botkin, D. B., F. J. James, and R. W. James. 1972. Some ecological consequences of a computer model of forest growth. *Journal of Ecology* 60:849–872.

Bottoms, T. 2000. Bama Country: Aboriginal Homelands. Pages 32–47 in G. T. McDonald and M. B. Lane, eds., *Securing the Wet Tropics?* Federation Press, Leichhardt, Australia.

Bouchard, P. 2000. *Cuemus,* a new genus of Tenebrionidae (Coleoptera) from the northern Queensland Wet Tropics. *Memoirs of the Queensland Museum* 46:95–100.

———. 2002. Phylogenetic revision of the flightless Australian genus *Apterotheca* Gebien (Coleoptera: Tenebrionidae: Coelometopinae). *Invertebrate Systematics* 16:449–554.

Bowie, R. C. K. 2003. Birds, molecules and evolutionary processes among Africa's Islands in the Sky. Ph.D. thesis, University of Cape Town, South Africa.

Bradshaw, H. D. Jr., S. M. Wilbert, K. G. Otto, and D. W. Schemske. 1995. Genetic mapping of floral traits associated with reproductive isolation in monkeyflowers (*Mimulus*). *Nature* 376:762–765.

Brailovsky, H. 1993. A revision of the tribe Colpurini from Australia (Hemiptera: Heteroptera: Coreidae). *Memoirs of the Queensland Museum* 34:35–60.

Brako, L., and J. L. Zarucchi. 1993. *Catalogue of the flowering plants and gymnosperms of Peru.* Monographs in Systematic Botany from the Missouri Botanical Garden, no. 45. Missouri Botanical Garden, St. Louis.

Brandon, K. 1997. Policy and practical considerations in land-use strategies for biodiversity conservation. Pages 90–114 in R. Kramer, C. van Schaik, and J. Johnson, eds., *Last stand: Protected areas and the defense of tropical biodiversity.* Oxford University Press, New York.

Brandon, K., K. H. Redford, and S. E. Sanderson, eds. 1998. *Parks in peril: People, politics and protected areas.* The Nature Conservancy and Island Press, Washington, DC.

Britton, E. B. 1987. A revision of the Australian chafers (Coleoptera: Scarabaeidae: Melolonthinae). Vol. 5. Tribes Scitalini and Comophorinini. *Invertebrate Taxonomy* 1:685–799.

Broecker, W. S., and G. H. Denton. 1989. The role of ocean-atmosphere reorganizations in glacial cycles. *Geochemica et Cosmochemica Acta* 53:2465–2501.

Brokaw, N. V. L. 1982. The definition of treefall gap and its effect on measures of forest dynamics. *Biotropica* 14:158–160.

———. 1987. Gap-phase regeneration of three pioneer tree species in a tropical forest. *Journal of Ecology* 75:9–19.

Brokaw, N. V. L., and S. M. Scheiner. 1989. Species composition in gaps and structure of a tropical forest. *Ecology* 70:538–540.

Brooks, D. R. 1981. Hennig's parasitological method: A proposed solution. *Systematic Zoology* 30:229–249.

———. 1985. Historical ecology: A new approach to studying the evolution of ecological associations. *Annals of the Missouri Botanical Garden* 72:660–680.

———. 1990. Parsimony analysis in historical biogeography and coevolution: Methodological and theoretical update. *Systematic Zoology* 39:14–30.

Brooks, D. R., R. L. Mayden, and D. A. McLennan. 1992. Phylogeny and biodiversity: Conserving our evolutionary legacy. *Trends in Ecology and Evolution* 7:55–59.

Brooks, D. R., and D. A. McLennan. 1991. *Phylogeny, ecology and behavior: A research program in comparative biology.* University of Chicago Press, Chicago.

———. 2001. A comparison of a discovery-based and an event-based method of historical biogeography. *Journal of Biogeography* 28:757–767.

———. 2002. *The nature of diversity: An evolutionary voyage of discovery.* University of Chicago Press, Chicago.

Brooks, D. R., M. G. P. Van Veller, and D. A. McLennan. 2001. How to do BPA, really. *Journal of Biogeography* 28:345–358.

Brooks, T., A. Balmford, N. Burgess, J. Fjeldså, L. A. Hansen, J. Moore, C. Rahbek, and P. Williams. 2001. Towards a blueprint for conservation in Africa. *BioScience* 51:613–624.

Browder, J. 1992. The limits of extractivism. *BioScience* 42:174–181.

Brown, B. N. 1976. *Phytophthora cinnamomi* associated with patch death in tropical rain forests in Queensland. *Australian Plant Pathology Society Newsletter* 5(1):1–4.

Brown, B. N., and T. U. Sjolund. 1987. *Phytophthora* species in Queensland forests: Species other than *Phytophthora cinnamomi* in tropical forests. Unpublished report, Queensland Department of Forestry, Brisbane.

Brown, B. N., T. U. Sjolund, and J. W. Tierney. 1987. *Phytophthora* species in Queensland forests. Unpublished report, Queensland Department of Forestry, Brisbane.

Brown, D. G. 1999. *Addicted to rent: Corporate and spatial distribution of forest resources in Indonesia.* DFID/ITFMP, Jakarta.

Brown, J. H. 1981. Two decades of homage to Santa Rosalia: Toward a general theory of diversity. *American Zoologist* 21:877–888.

———. 1984. On the relationship between the abundance and distribution of species. *American Naturalist* 124:255–279.

Brown, J. W., and P. A. Opler. 1990. Patterns of butterfly species density in peninsular Florida. *Journal of Biogeography* 17:615–622.

Brown, K. S. Jr. 1972. Maximizing daily butterfly counts. *Journal of the Lepidopterists' Society* 26:183–196.

———. 1979. *Ecologia geográfica e evolução nas florestas Neotropicais.* Universidade Estadual de Campinas, Campinas, São Paulo, Brazil.

———. 1982a. Historical and ecological factors in the biogeography of aposematic Neotropical Lepidoptera. *American Zoologist* 22:453–471.

———. 1982b. Paleoecology and regional patterns of evolution in Neotropical forest butterflies. Pp. 255–308 in G. T. Prance, ed., *Biological diversification in the tropics.* Columbia University Press, New York.

———. 1984. Species diversity and abundance in Jaru, Rondônia (Brazil). *News of the Lepidopterists' Society* 1984 (3), 45–47.

———. 1985. Chemical ecology of dehydropyrrolizidine alkaloids in adult Ithomiinae (Lepidoptera: Nymphalidae). *Revista Brasileira de Biologia* 44:435–460.

———. 1987a. Biogeography and evolution of Neotropical butterflies. Pages 66–104 in T. C. Whitmore and G. T. Prance, eds., *Biogeography and Quaternary history in tropical America.* Clarendon Press, Oxford.

———. 1987b. Conclusions, synthesis, and alternative hypotheses. Pages 175–196 in T. C. Whitmore and G. T. Prance, eds., *Biogeography and Quaternary history in tropical America.* Clarendon Press, Oxford.

———. 1987c. Zoogeografia da região do Pantanal Matogrossense. Pages 137–178 in *Anais do 1º Simpósio sobre Recursos Naturais e Sócio-Econômicos do Pantanal (Corumbá, Mato Grosso).* EMBRAPA, Brasília, Distrito Federal, Brazil.

———. 1991. Conservation of Neotropical environments: Insects as indicators. Pages 349–404 in N. M. Collins and J. A. Thomas, eds., *The conservation of insects and their habitats.* Royal Entomological Society, Symposium 15. Academic Press, London.

———. 1992. Borboletas da Serra do Japi: Diversidade, habitats, recursos alimentares e variação temporal. Pages 142–186 in L. P. C. Morellato, ed., *História natural da Serra do Japi: Ecologia e Preservação de uma Área Florestal no Sudeste do Brasil.* Editora da UNICAMP, Campinas, São Paulo, Brazil.

———. 1993. Neotropical Lycaenidae: An overview. Pages 45–61 in T. R. New, ed., *Conservation biology of Lycaenidae.* IUCN, Gland, Switzerland.

———. 1996a. The conservation of threatened Brazilian butterflies. Pages 45–62 in S. A. Ae, T. Hirowatari, M. Ishii, and L. P. Brower, eds., *Decline and conservation of butterflies in Japan,* vol. 3. Lepidopterological Society of Japan, Osaka, Japan.

———. 1996b. Diversity of Brazilian Lepidoptera: History of study, methods for measurement, and use as indicator for genetic, specific, and system richness. Pages 121–154 in C. E. M. Bicudo and N. A. Menezes, eds., *Biodiversity in Brazil: A first approach.* CNPq/Instituto de Botânica, São Paulo, Brazil.

———. 1996c. The use of insects in the study, inventory, conservation and monitoring of biological diversity in the Neotropics, in relation to land use models. Pages 128–149 in S. A. Ae, T. Hirowatari, M. Ishii, and L. P. Brower, eds., *Decline and conservation of butterflies in Japan,* vol. 3. Lepidopterological Society of Japan, Osaka, Japan.

———. 1997a. Diversity, disturbance, and sustainable use of Neotropical forests: Insects as indicators for conservation monitoring. *Journal of Insect Conservation* 1:25–42.

———. 1997b. Insetos como rápidos e sensíveis indicadores de uso sustentável de recursos naturais. Pages 143–155 in H. L. Martos and N. B. Maia, eds., *Indicadores Ambientais.* PUCC/Shell Brasil, Sorocaba, São Paulo, Brazil.

Brown, K. S. Jr., and G. G. Brown. 1992. Habitat alteration and species loss in Brazilian forests. Pages 119–142 in T. C. Whitmore and J. A. Sayer, eds., *Tropical deforestation and species extinction.* Chapman & Hall, London.

Brown, K. S. Jr., A. J. Damman, and P. Feeny. 1981. Troidine swallowtails (Lepidoptera: Papilionidae) in southeastern Brazil: Natural history and foodplant relationships. *Journal of Research on the Lepidoptera* 19:199–226.

Brown, K. S. Jr., and A. V. L. Freitas. 2000a. Atlantic Forest butterflies: Indicators for landscape conservation. *Biotropica* 32:934–956.

———. 2000b. Diversidade de Lepidoptera em Santa Teresa, Espírito Santo. *Boletim do Museu Biologia Mello Leitão* (N. Ser.) 11/12:71–118.

Brown, K. S. Jr., and R. W. Hutchings. 1997. Disturbance, fragmentation, and the dynamics of diversity in Amazonian forest butterflies. Pages 99–110 in W. F. Laurance and R. O. Bierregaard Jr., eds., *Tropical forest remnants: Ecology, management, and conservation of fragmented communities.* University of Chicago Press, Chicago.

Brown, K. S. Jr., and O. H. H. Mielke. 1967. Lepidoptera of the Central Brazil Plateau. 1. Preliminary list of *Rhopalocera. Journal of the Lepidopterists' Society* 21:77–106, 145–168.

———. 1968. Lepidoptera of the Central Brazil Plateau. 3. Partial list for the Belo Horizonte area, showing the character of the southeastern "blend zone." *Journal of the Lepidopterists' Society* 22:147–157.

Brown, K. S. Jr., and G. T. Prance. 1987. Soils and vegetation. Pages 19–45 in T. C. Whitmore and G. T. Prance, eds., *Biogeography and Quaternary history in tropical America.* Clarendon Press, Oxford.

Brown, N. 1998. Out of control: Fires and forestry in Indonesia. *Trends in Ecology and Evolution* 13:41.

Brown, P. 1998. Forest fires: Setting the world ablaze. *The Guardian,* London, March 20.

Bruenig, E. F. 1996. *Conservation and management of tropical rainforests.* CAB International, Wallingford, U.K.

Bruner, A. G., R. E. Gullison, R. E. Rice, and G. A. B. da Fonseca. 2001. Effectiveness of parks in protecting tropical biodiversity. *Science* 291:125–128.

Bryant, D., D. Nielsen, and L. Tangley. 1997. *The last frontier forests: Ecosystems and economies on the edge.* World Resources Institute, Washington, DC.

Buckley, B. M., M. Barbetti, M. Watanasak, R. D'Arrigo, S. Boonchirdchoo and S. Sarutanon. 1995. Dendrochronological investigations in Thailand. *International Association of Wood Anatomists Journal* 16:393–409.

Burbidge, N. T. 1960. The phytogeography of the Australian region. *Australian Journal of Botany* 8:75–212.

Burgess, N., H. de Klerk, J. Fjeldså, and C. Rahbek, C. 2000. A preliminary assessment of congruence between biodiversity patterns in Afrotropical forest birds and forest mammals. *Ostrich* 71:286–290.

Burghardt, G. M., H. W. Greene, and A. S. Rand. 1977. Social behavior in hatchling green iguanas: Life in a reptile rookery. *Science* 195:689–691.

Burkill, I. H. 1935. *A dictionary of the economic products of the Malay Peninsula.* 2 vols. Government Printing Office, Singapore.

Burness, G. P., J. M. Diamond, and T. Flannery. 2001. Dinosaurs, dragons and dwarfs: The evolution of maximal body size. *Proceedings of the National Academy of Sciences USA* 98:14518–14523.

Burnett, M. R., P. V. August, J. H. Brown Jr., and K. T. Killingbeck. 1998. The influence of geomorphological heterogeneity on biodiversity. 1. A patch-scale perspective. *Conservation Biology* 12:363–370.

Burnham, R. J., and A. Graham. 1999. The history of Neotropical vegetation: New developments and status. *Annals of the Missouri Botanical Garden* 86:546–589.

Burslem, D. F. R. P., and T. C. Whitmore. 1999. Species diversity, susceptibility to disturbance and tree population dynamics in tropical rain forest. *Journal of Vegetation Science* 10:767–776.

Busack, S. D., and S. B. Hedges. 1984. Is the peninsula effect a red herring? *American Naturalist* 123:266–275.

Bush, M. B. 1991. Modern pollen rain data from South and Central America: A test of the feasibility of fine-resolution lowland tropical palynology. *Holocene* 1:162–167.

———. 1994. Amazonian speciation: A necessarily complex model. *Journal of Biogeography* 21:5–17.

———. 2000. Deriving response matrices from Central American modern pollen rain. *Quaternary Research* 54:132–143.

Bush, M. B., and P. A. Colinvaux. 1990. A pollen record of a complete glacial cycle from lowland Panama. *Journal of Vegetation Science* 1:105–118.

———. 1994. Tropical forest disturbance: Paleoecological records from Darien, Panama. *Ecology* 75:1761–1768.

Bush, M. B., P. A. Colinvaux, M. C. Wiemann, D. R. Piperno, and K-b. Liu. 1990. Late Pleistocene temperature depression and vegetation change in Ecuadorian Amazonia. *Quaternary Research* 34:330–345.

Bush, M. B., P. E. De Oliveira, P. A. Colinvaux, M. C. Miller, and J. E. Moreno. 2004. Amazonian paleoecological histories: One hill, three watersheds. *Palaeogeography, Palaeoclimatology, Palaeoecology* 214:359–393.

Bush, M. B., M. C. Miller, P. E. De Oliveira, and P. A. Colinvaux. 2002. Orbital forcing signal in sediments of two Amazonian lakes. *Journal of Paleolimnology* 27:341–352.

Bush, M. B., E. Moreno, P. E. De Oliveira, E. Asanza, and P. A. Colinvaux. 2001. The influence of biogeographic and ecological heterogeneity on Amazonian pollen spectra. *Journal of Tropical Ecology* 17:729–744.

Bush, M. B., D. R. Piperno, P. A. Colinvaux, P. E. De Oliveira, L. A. Krissek, M. C. Miller, and W. E. Rowe. 1992. A 14,300-yr paleoecological profile of a lowland tropical lake in Panama. *Ecological Monographs* 62:251–275.

Bush, M. B., and R. S. Rivera. 1998. Pollen dispersal and representation in a Neotropical forest. *Global Ecology and Biogeography Letters* 7:379–392.

Caldecott, J. 1988a. Climbing towards extinction. *New Scientist* (June 9):62–66.

———. 1988b. Hunting and wildlife management in Sarawak. IUCN Tropical Forest Programme, Gland, Switzerland and Cambridge, U.K.

Calder, A. A. 1998. *Coleoptera: Elateroidea.* CSIRO Publishing, Melbourne.

Calder, A. A., J. F. Lawrence, and J. W. H. Trueman. 1993. *Austrelater,* gen. nov. (Coleoptera: Elateridae), with a description of the larva and comments on elaterid relationships. *Invertebrate Taxonomy* 7:1349–1394.

Caley, M. J. 1997. Local endemism and the relationship between local and regional diversity. *Oikos* 79:612–615.

Caley, M. J., M. H. Carr, M. A. Hixon, T. P. Hughes, G. P. Jones, and B. A. Menge. 1996. Recruitment and local dynamics of open marine populations. *Annual Review of Ecology and Systematics* 27:477–500.

Campbell, D. G., D. C. Daly, G. T. Prance, and U. N. Maciel. 1986. Quantitative ecological inventory of terra firme and várzea tropical forest on the Rio Xingu, Brazilian Amazon. *Brittonia* 38:369–393.

Capparella, A. P. 1988. Genetic variation in Neotropical birds: Implications for the speciation process. *Acta Congressus Internationalis Ornithologici* 19:1658–1664.

———. 1992. Neotropical avian diversity and riverine barriers. *Acta Congressus Internationalis Ornithologici* 20:307–316.

Cardillo, M. 1999. Latitude and rates of diversification in birds and butterflies. *Proceedings of the Royal Society of London* B 266:1221–1225.

Cardoso, A. 1949. Lepidópteros de Alagoas. *Revista de Entomologia* 20:427–436.

Carleton, M. D., and D. F. Schmidt. 1990. Systematic studies of Madagascar's endemic rodents (Muroidea: Nesomyinae): An annotated gazetteer of collecting localities of known forms. *American Museum Novitates* 2987:1–36.

Carlquist, S. 1965. *Island life.* Natural History Press, Garden City, NY.

———. 1980. *Hawaii: A natural history.* Pacific Tropical Botanical Garden, Lawai, Hawaii.

Carne, P. B. 1985. A new genus and species of Dynastinae from North Queensland (Coleoptera: Scarabaeidae). *Journal of the Australian Entomological Society* 24:75–76.

Carpenter, R. J., and A. M. Buchanan. 1993. Oligocene leaves, fruit and flowers of the Cunoniaceae from Cethana, Tasmania. *Australian Systematic Botany* 6:91–109.

Carpenter, R. J., R. S. Hill, and G. Jordan. 1994. Cenozoic vegetation in Tasmania: Macrofossil evidence. Pages 276–298 in R. S. Hill, ed., *The history of Australian vegetation: Cretaceous to Recent.* Cambridge University Press, Cambridge.

Carpenter, R. J., G. J. Jordan, and R. S. Hill. 1994. *Banksieaephyllum taylorii* (Proteaceae) from the Late Paleocene of New South Wales and its relevance to the origin of Australia's scleromorphic flora. *Australian Systematic Botany* 7:385–392.

Carpenter, R. J., and M. Pole. 1995. Eocene plant fossils from the Lefroy & Cowan Paleodrainages, Western Australia. *Australian Systematic Botany* 8:1107–1154.

Carr, G. D., and D. W. Kyhos. 1986. Adaptive radiation in the Hawaiian silversword alliance (Compositae-Madiinae). 2. Cytogenetics of artificial and natural hybrids. *Evolution* 40:959–976.

Carson, W. P., and C. J. Peterson. 1990. The role of litter in an old-field community: Impact of litter quantity in different seasons on plant species richness and abundance. *Oecologia* 85:8–13.

Carvalho, G., A. C. Barros, P. Moutinho, and D. C. Nepstad. 2001. Sensitive development could protect the Amazon instead of destroying it. *Nature* 409:131.

Cassia, R. de. 1997. BR-174: FHC anuncia abertura de nova fronteira agrícola no Norte. *Amazonas em Tempo* (Manaus, Brazil), 25 June, A-4.

Caswell, H. 1976. Community structure: A neutral model analysis. *Ecological Monographs* 46:327–364.

Cavagnetto, C., and P. Anadón. 1995. Une mangrove complexe dans le Bartonien du Bassin de l'Erbe (NE de l'Espagne). *Paleontographica* B 236:147–165.

Cavelier, J., S. J. Wright, and J. Santamaria. 1999. Effects of irrigation on fine root biomass and production, litterfall and trunk growth in a semideciduous lowland forest in Panama. *Plant and Soil* 211:207–213.

Cavender-Bares, J., and N. M. Holbrook. 2001. Hydraulic properties and freezing-induced cavitation in sympatric evergreen and deciduous oaks with contrasting habitats. *Plant, Cell and Environment* 24:1243–1256.

Cerón, C. E., and C. A. Montalvo. 1997. Composición y estructura de una hectárea de bosque en la Amazonía Ecuatoriana—con información etnobotánica de los Huaorani. Pages 153–172 in R. Valencia and H. Balslev, eds., *Estudios sobre diversidad y ecología de plantas.* Pontificia Universidad Católica del Ecuador, Quito.

Chan, K. M. A., and B. R. Moore. 2002. Whole-tree methods for detecting differential diversification rates. *Systematic Biology* 51:855–865.

Chape, S. 2001. An overview of integrated approaches to conservation and community development in the Lao People's Democratic Republic. *Parks* 11 (2):24–32.

Chapin, J. P. 1924. Size-variation in *Pyrenestes,* a genus of weaver-finch. *Bulletin of the American Museum of Natural History* 49:415–441.

———. 1932. The birds of the Belgian Congo. *Bulletin of the American Museum of Natural History* 65:756.

———. 1954. The birds of the Belgian Congo. *Bulletin of the American Museum of Natural History* 75:1–846.

Chapman, F. 1926. New or little-known fossils in the National Museum. Part 29. On some Tertiary plant remains from Narracan, South Gippsland. *Proceedings of the Royal Society of Victoria,* n.s., 38:183–191.

Charles-Dominique, P. 1977. *Ecology and behaviour of nocturnal primates.* Columbia University Press, New York.

Charles-Dominique, P., P. Blanc, D. Larpin, M. P. Ledru, B. Riera, C. Sarthou, M. Servant, and C. Tardy. 1998. Forest perturbations and biodiversity during the last ten thousand years in French Guiana. *Acta Oecologica* 19:295–302.

Chave, J., H. C. Muller-Landau, and S. A. Levin. 2002. Comparing classical community models: Theoretical consequences for patterns of diversity. *American Naturalist* 159:1–23.

Chen, P., and N. Nieser. 1992. Gerridae, mainly from Sulawesi and Pulau Buton (Indonesia). 3. Notes on Melanesian aquatic and semiaquatic bugs (Heteroptera). *Tijdschrift voor Entomologie* 135:145–162.

Cherrill, A. J., C. McClean, P. Watson, K. Tucker, S. P. Rushton, and R. A. Sanderson. 1995. Predicting the distributions of plant species at the regional scale: A hierarchical matrix model. *Landscape Ecology* 10:197–207.

Cherry, J. L., F. R. Adler, and K. P. Johnson. 2002. Islands, equilibria, and speciation. *Science* 296:975a.

Chesson, P. L., and R. R. Warner. 1981. Environmental variability promotes coexistence in lottery competitive systems. *American Naturalist* 117:923–943.

Chichilnisky, G., and H. Geoffrey. 1998. Economic returns from the biosphere. *Nature* 391:629–630.

Christie, M. 1997. Yanomami Indians appeal for help against invaders. Reuters News Service, 31 August.

Christophel, D. C. 1980. Occurrence of *Casuarina* megafossils in the Tertiary of southeastern Australia. *Australian Journal of Botany* 28:249–259.

———. 1981. Tertiary megafossil floras as indicators of floristic associations and palaeoclimate. Pages 379–390 in A. Keast, ed., *Ecological biogeography of Australia.* Dr. W. Junk, The Hague.

———. 1984. Early Tertiary Proteaceae: The first floral evidence for the Musgraveinae. *Australian Journal of Botany* 32:177–186.

———. 1988. Evolution of the Australian flora through the Tertiary. *Plant Systematics and Evolution* 162:63–78.

———. 1994. The early Tertiary macrofloras of continental Australia. Pages 262–275 in R. S. Hill, ed., *The history of Australian vegetation: Cretaceous to Recent.* Cambridge University Press, Cambridge.

Christophel, D. C., and D. R. Greenwood. 1987. A megafossil flora from the Eocene of Golden Grove, South Australia. *Transactions of the Royal Society of South Australia* 111(3):155–162.

———. 1988. A comparison of Australian tropical rainforest and Tertiary fossil leaf-beds. Pages 139–148 in R. Kitching, ed., *The ecology of Australia's Wet Tropics.* Proceedings of the Ecological Society of Australia, vol. 15. Surrey Beatty and Sons, Sydney.

———. 1989. Changes in climate and vegetation in Australia during the Tertiary. *Review of Palaeobotany and Palynology* 58:95–109.

Christophel, D. C., W. K. Harris, and A. K. Syber. 1987. The Eocene flora of the Anglesea locality, Victoria. *Alcheringa* 11:303–323.

Christophel, D. C., L. J. Scriven, and D. R. Greenwood. 1992. The Middle Eocene megafossil flora of Nelly Creek (Eyre Formation), Southern Lake Eyre Basin, South Australia. *Transactions of the Royal Society of South Australia* 116(2):65–76.

Churchill, D. M. 1973. The ecological significance of tropical mangroves in the early Tertiary floras of southern Australia. Pages 79–85 in J. E. Glover and G. Playford, eds., *Mesozoic and Cainozoic palynology: Essays in honour of Isabell Cookson.* Special Publication no. 4. Geological Society of Australia, Canberra.

CIFOR. 1999. World Heritage Forests: The World Heritage Convention as a mechanism for conserving tropical forest biodiversity. CIFOR/UNESCO, Bogor, Indonesia.

Cintra, R. 1997. Leaf litter effects on seed and seed predation of the palm *Astrocaryum murumuru* and the legume tree *Dipteryx micrantha* in Amazonian forest. *Journal of Tropical Ecology* 13:709–725.

Clapperton, C. 1993. *Quaternary geology and geomorphology of South America.* Elsevier, Amsterdam.

Clark, D. A., S. C. Piper, C. D. Keeling, and D. B. Clark. 2003. Tropical rain forest tree growth and atmospheric carbon dynamics linked to interannual temperature variation during 1984–2000. *Proceedings of the National Academy of Sciences USA* 100:5852–5857.

Clark, J. S., E. Macklin, and L. Wood. 1998. Stages and spatial scales of recruitment limitation in southern Appalachian forests. *Ecological Monographs* 68:213–235.

Clark, J. S., and J. S. McLachlan. 2003. Stability of forest biodiversity. *Nature* 423:635–638.

CLIMAP. 1976. The surface of the ice-age earth. *Science* 191:1131–1144.

Clinebell, R. R. II, O. L. Phillips, A. H. Gentry, N. Stark, and H. Zuuring. 1995. Prediction of Neotropical tree and liana species richness from soil and climatic data. *Biodiversity and Conservation* 4:56–90.

Cochrane, M. A. 2003. Fire science for rainforests. *Nature* 421:913–919.

Cochrane, M. A., A. Alencar, M. D. Schulze, C. M. Souza, D. C. Nepstad, P. Lefebvre, and E. Davidson. 1999. Positive feedbacks in the fire dynamics of closed canopy tropical forests. *Science* 284:1832–1835.

Cochrane, M. A., and W. F. Laurance. 2002. Fire as a large-scale edge effect in Amazonian forests. *Journal of Tropical Ecology* 18:311–325.

Cochrane, M. A., and M. D. Schulze. 1998. Forest fires in the Brazilian Amazon. *Conservation Biology* 12:948–950.

———. 1999. Fire as a recurrent event in tropical forests of the eastern Amazon: Effects on forest structure, biomass, and species composition. *Biotropica* 31:2–16.

Cody, M. L. 1975. Towards a theory of continental species diversities. Pages 214–257 in M. L. Cody and J. M. Diamond, eds., *Ecology and evolution of communities.* Harvard University Press, Cambridge, MA.

Cogger, H. G. 1986. *Reptiles and amphibians of Australia.* Reed Books, Chatswood, N.S.W.

Cohn-Haft, M., A. Whittaker, and P. C. Stouffer. 1997. A new look at the "species-poor" central Amazon: The avifauna north of Manaus, Amazonas, Brazil. Pages 205–235 in J. V. Remsen Jr., ed., *Studies in Neotropical ornithology honoring Ted Parker.* Ornithological Monographs, no. 48. American Ornithologists' Union, Washington, DC.

Colchester, M. 1994. The new sultans: Asian loggers move in on Guyana's forests. *Ecologist* 24:45–52.

Coley, P. D. 1983. Herbivory and defensive characteristics of tree species in a lowland tropical forest. *Ecological Monographs* 53:209–233.

Coley, P. D., and T. M. Aide. 1991. Comparisons of herbivory and plant defenses in temperate and tropical broad-leaved forests. Pages 25–49 in P. W. Price, T. M. Lewinsohn, G. W. Fernandes, and W. W. Benson, eds., *Plant-animal interactions: Evolutionary ecology in tropical and temperate regions.* Wiley, New York.

Coley, P. D., and J. A. Barone. 1996. Herbivory and plant defenses in tropical forests. *Annual Review of Ecology and Systematics* 27:305–335.

Coley, P. D., J. P. Bryant, and F. S. Chapin III. 1985. Resource availability and plant antiherbivore defense. *Science* 230:895–899.

Coley, P. D., and T. A. Kursar. 1996. Anti-herbivore defenses of young tropical leaves: Physiological constraints and ecological trade-offs. Pages 305–336 in S. S. Mulkey, R. L. Chazdon, and A. P. Smith, eds., *Tropical forest plant ecophysiology.* Chapman & Hall, New York.

Colinvaux, P. A. 1973. *Introduction to ecology.* Wiley, New York.

———. 1978. *Why big fierce animals are rare.* Princeton University Press, Princeton, NJ.

———. 1981. Historical ecology in Beringia: The South Land Bridge Coast at St Paul Island. *Quaternary Research* 16:18–36.

———. 1987. Amazon diversity in the light of the paleoecological record. *Quaternary Science Reviews* 6:93–114.

———. 1993. Pleistocene biogeography and diversity in tropical forests of South America. Pages 473–499 in P. Goldblatt, ed., *Biological relationships between Africa and South America.* Yale University Press, New Haven, CT.

———. 1996. Quaternary environmental history and forest diversity in the Neotropics. Pages 359–405 in J. B. C. Jackson, A. F. Budd, and A. G. Coates, eds., *Evolution and environment in tropical America.* University of Chicago Press, Chicago.

———. 1997. *The ice-age Amazon and the problem of diversity.* Nederlandse Organisatie voor Wetenschappelijk Onderzoek, Rotterdam.

Colinvaux, P. A., P. E. De Oliveira, and M. B. Bush. 2000. Amazonian and Neotropical plant communities on glacial time-scales: The failure of the aridity and refuge hypotheses. *Quaternary Science Reviews* 19:141–169.

Colinvaux, P. A., P. E. De Oliveira, and J. E. Moreno. 1999. *Amazon pollen manual and atlas.* Harwood, Amsterdam.

Colinvaux, P. A., P. E. De Oliveira, J. E. Moreno, M. C. Miller, and M. B. Bush. 1996. A long pollen record from lowland Amazonia: Forest and cooling in glacial times. *Science* 274:85–88.

Colinvaux, P. A., G. Irion, M. Räsänen, M. B. Bush, and J. A. S. Nunes de Mello. 2001. A paradigm to be discarded: Geological and paleoecological data falsify the Haffer and Prance refuge hypothesis of Amazonian speciation. *Amazoniana* 16:609–646.

Colinvaux, P. A., K-b. Liu, P. E. De Oliveira, M. B. Bush, M. C. Miller, and M. Steinitz-Kannan. 1996. Temperature depression in the lowland tropics in glacial times. *Climatic Change* 32:19–33.

Condit, R. 1995. Research in large, long-term tropical forest plots. *Trends in Ecology and Evolution* 10:18–22.

———. 1996. Defining and mapping vegetation types in mega-diverse tropical forests. *Trends in Ecology and Evolution* 11:4–5.

———. 1998a. Ecological implications of changes in drought patterns: Shifts in forest composition in Panama. *Climatic Change* 39:413–427.

———. 1998b. *Tropical forest census plots.* Springer-Verlag, Berlin; R. G. Landes, Georgetown, TX.

Condit, R., S. Aguilar, A. Hernández, R. Pérez, S. Lao, G. Angehr, S. P. Hubbell, and R. B. Foster. 2004. Tropical forest dynamics across a rainfall gradient and the impact of an El Niño dry season. *Journal of Tropical Ecology* 20(1):51–72.

Condit, R., S. P. Hubbell, and R. B. Foster. 1992. Recruitment near conspecific adults and the maintenance of tree and shrub diversity in a Neotropical forest. *American Naturalist* 140:261–286.

———. 1995. Mortality rates of 205 Neotropical tree and shrub species and the impact of a severe drought. *Ecological Monographs* 65:419–439.

———. 1996a. Assessing the response of plant functional types in tropical forests to climatic change. *Journal of Vegetation Science* 7:405–416.

———. 1996b. Changes in a tropical forest with a shifting climate: Results from a 50 ha permanent census plot in Panama. *Journal of Tropical Ecology* 12:231–256.

———. 1996c. Changes in tree species abundance in a Neotropical forest: Impact of climate change. *Journal of Tropical Ecology* 12:231–256.

Condit, R., S. P. Hubbell, J. V. LaFrankie, R. Sukumar, N. Manokaran, R. B. Foster, and P. S. Ashton. 1996. Species-area and species-individual relationships for tropical trees: A comparison of three 50-ha plots. *Journal of Ecology* 84:549–562.

Condit, R., N. Pitman, E. G. Leigh Jr., J. Chave, J. Terborgh, R. B. Foster, P. Nuñez V., S. Aguilar, R. Valencia, G. Villa, H. C. Muller-Landau, E. Losos, and S. P. Hubbell. 2002. Beta-diversity in tropical forest trees. *Science* 295:666–669.

Condit, R., W. D. Robinson, R. Ibáñez, S. Aguilar, A. Sanjur, R. Martínez, R. Stallard, T. García, G. Angehr, L. Petit, S. J. Wright, T. R. Robinson, and S. Heckadon. 2001. Maintaining the canal while conserving biodiversity around it: A challenge for economic development in Panama in the 21st century. *BioScience* 51:135–144.

Condit, R., K. Watts, S. A. Bohlman, R. Pérez, S. P. Hubbell, and R. B. Foster. 2000. Quantifying the deciduousness of tropical forest canopies under varying climates. *Journal of Vegetation Science* 11:649–658.

Connell, J. H. 1971. On the role of natural enemies in preventing competitive exclusion in some marine animals and in rain forest trees. Pages 298–312 in P. J. den Boer and G. Gradwell, eds., *Dynamics in populations.* Centre for Agricultural Publishing and Documentation, Wageningen, The Netherlands.

———. 1978. Diversity in tropical rainforests and coral reefs. *Science* 199:1302–1310.

———. 1989. Some processes affecting the species composition in forest gaps. *Ecology* 70:560–562.

Connell, J. H., and P. T. Green. 2000. Seedling dynamics over thirty-two years in a tropical rainforest tree. *Ecology* 81:568–584.

———. 2001. Seedling regeneration over 35 years in Australian tropical and subtropical rainforests. Pages 268–269 in K. N. Ganeshaiah, R. U. Shaanker, and K. S. Bawa, eds., *Tropical ecosystems: Structure, diversity and human welfare.* Science Publishers, Enfield, NH.

Connell, J. H., and E. Orias. 1964. The ecological regulation of species diversity. *American Naturalist* 98:387–414.

Connell, J. H., and W. P. Sousa. 1983. On the evidence needed to judge ecological stability or persistence. *American Naturalist* 121:789–824.

Connell, J. H., J. G. Tracey, and L. J. Webb. 1984. Compensatory recruitment, growth, and mortality as factors maintaining rain forest tree diversity. *Ecological Monographs* 54:141–164.

Connor, E. F. 1986. The role of Pleistocene forest refugia in the evolution and biogeography of tropical biotas. *Trends in Ecology and Evolution* 1:165–168.

Connor, E. F., and E. D. McCoy. 1979. The statistics and biology of the species-area relationship. *American Naturalist* 113:791–833.

Connor, E. F., and D. Simberloff. 1979. The assembly of species communities: Chance or competition. *Ecology* 60:1132–1140.

Conran, J. G., D. C. Christophel, and L. J. Scriven. 1994. *Petermanniopsis anglesäensis:* An Australian fossil net-veined monocotyledon from Eocene Victoria. *International Journal of Plant Science* 155:816–827.

Cooke, R. G., and A. J. Ranere. 1992. Precolumbian influences on the zoogeography of Panama: An update based on archaeofaunal and documentary data. *Tulane Studies in Zoology and Botany,* suppl. 1:21–58.

Cookson, I. C. 1954. The Cainozoic occurrence of *Acacia* in Australia. *Australian Journal of Botany* 2(1):52–59.

Corbet, C. B. 1997. The species in mammals. Pages 341–356 in M. F. Claridge, H. A. Dawah, and M. R. Wilson, eds., *The units of biodiversity.* Chapman & Hall, London.

Cordeiro, N. 1998. Preliminary analyses of the nestedness patterns of montane forest birds in the Eastern Arc Mountains. *Journal of East African Natural History Society* 87:101–119.

Cornell, H. V. 1993. Unsaturated patterns in species assemblages: The role of regional processes in setting local species richness. Pages 243–252 in R. E. Ricklefs and D. Schluter, eds., *Species diversity in ecological communities: Historical and geographical perspectives.* University of Chicago Press, Chicago.

Cornell, H. V., and J. H. Lawton. 1992. Species interactions, local and regional processes, and limits to the richness of ecological communities: A theoretical perspective. *Journal of Animal Ecology* 61:1–12.

Corner, E. J. H. 1940. *Wayside trees of Malaya.* Government Printer, Singapore.

———. 1964. *The life of plants.* World Press, Cleveland, OH.

———. 1967. *Ficus* in the Solomon Islands and its bearing on the post-Jurassic history of Melanesia. *Philosophical Transactions of the Royal Society of London* B 253:23–159.

Cortés-Ortiz, L., E. Bermingham, C. Rico, E. Rodríguez-Luna, I. Sampaio, and M. Ruiz-García. 2003. Molecular systematics and biogeography of the Neotropical monkey genus, *Alouatta. Molecular Phylogenetics and Evolution* 26:64–81.

Cosson, J. F., S. Ringuet, O. Claessens, J. C. de Massary, A. Dalecky, J. F. Villiers, L. Granjon, and J. M. Pons. 1999. Ecological changes in recent land-bridge islands in French Guiana, with emphasis on vertebrate communities. *Biological Conservation* 91:213–222.

Costanza, R., R. d'Arge, R. de Groot, S. Farber, M. Grasso, B. Hannon, K. Limburg, S. Naeem, R. V. O'Neil, J. Paruelo, T. G. Raskin, P. Sutton, and M. van den Belt. 1997. The value of the world's ecosystem services and natural capital. *Nature* 387:253–260.

Coventry, R. J., P. J. Stephenson, and A. W. Webb. 1985. Chronology of landscape evolution and soil development in the upper Flinders River area, Queensland, based on isotopic dating of Cainozoic basalts. *Australian Journal of Earth Sciences* 32:433–447.

Cowling, R. M., and R. L. Pressey. 2001. Rapid plant diversification: Planning for an evolutionary future. *Proceedings of the National Academy of Sciences USA* 98:5452–5457.

Coyne, J. A., and H. A. Orr. 1997. "Patterns of speciation in *Drosophila*" revisited. *Evolution* 51:295–303.

Cracraft, J. 1982. A nonequilibrium theory for the rate-control of speciation and extinction and the origin of macroevolutionary patterns. *Systematic Zoology* 31:348–365.

———. 1985. Biological diversification and its causes. *Annals of the Missouri Botanical Garden* 72:794–822.

———. 1986. Origin and evolution of continental biotas: Speciation and historical congruence within the Australian avifauna. *Evolution* 40:977–996.

———. 1988. Deep-history biogeography: Retrieving the historical pattern of evolving continental biotas. *Systematic Zoology* 37:221–236.

———. 1994. Species diversity, biogeography, and the evolution of biotas. *American Zoologist* 34:33–47.

Crandall, K. A., O. R. P. Bininda-Emonds, G. M. Mace, and R. K. Wayne. 2000. Considering evolutionary processes in conservation biology. *Trends in Ecology and Evolution* 15:290–295.

Crane, P. R., and S. Lidgard. 1990. Angiosperm diversification and paleolatitudinal gradients in Cretaceous floristic diversity. *Science* 246:675–678.

Cranston, P. S., and I. D. Naumann. 1991. Biogeography. Pages 180–197 in Division of Entomology, CSIRO, *The insects of Australia: A textbook for students and research workers.* 2nd ed. Melbourne University Press, Carleton, Victoria.

Craven, I., and Y. de Fretes. 1987. Arfak Mountains Nature Conservation Area, Irian Jaya. Management Plan 1988–1982. World Wildlife Fund, Bogor, Indonesia.

Craven, I., and W. Wardojo. 1993. Gardens in the forest. Pages 22–28 in E. Kemf, ed., *The law of the mother.* Sierra Club Books, San Francisco.

Crepet, W. L. 1984. Advanced (constant) insect pollination mechanisms: Pattern of evolution and implications vis-á-vis angiosperm diversity. *Annals of the Missouri Botanical Garden* 71:607–630.

Crisp, M. D., S. Laffan, H. P. Linder, and A. Monro. 2001. Endemism in the Australian flora. *Journal of Biogeography* 28:183–198.

Crisp, M. D., J. G. West, and H. P. Linder. 1999. Biogeography of the terrestrial flora. Pages 321–367 in A. E. Orchard and H. S. Thompson, eds., *Flora of Australia,* vol. 1, *Introduction.* 2nd ed. ABRS/CSIRO Australia, Melbourne.

Critica (Manaus, Brazil). 1997. Controle sobre florestas exige a reforma do IBAMA. January 19.

Croat, T. B. 1978. *The flora of Barro Colorado Island.* Stanford University Press, Stanford, CA.

Croizat, L. 1958. *Panbiogeography.* Vols. I, IIa, IIb. Published by the author, Caracas.

———. 1964. *Space, time, form: The biological synthesis.* Published by the author, Caracas.

Crome, F. H. J. 1997. Researching tropical forest fragmentation: Shall we keep on doing what we're doing? Pages 485–501 in W. F. Laurance and R. O. Bierregaard Jr., eds., *Tropical forest remnants: Ecology, management, and conservation of fragmented communities.* University of Chicago Press, Chicago.

Crooks, R., and M. E. Soulé. 1999. Mesopredator release and avifaunal extinctions in a fragmented system. *Nature* 400:563–566.

Crow, J. F., and M. Kimura. 1970. *An introduction to population genetics theory.* Harper & Row, New York.

Crowe, T. M., and A. A. Crowe. 1982. Patterns of distribution, diversity and endemism in Afrotropical birds. *Journal of Zoology* 198:417–442.

Crowley, G. M., J. Grindrod, and A. P. Kershaw. 1994. Modern pollen deposition in the tropical lowlands of northeast Queensland, Australia. *Review of Palaeobotany and Palynology* 83:299–327.

Crozier, R. H. 1997. Preserving the information content of species: Genetic diversity, phylogeny, and conservation worth. *Annual Review of Ecology and Systematics* 28:243–268.

Curran, L. M., I. Caniago, G. D. Paoli, D. Astianti, M. Kusneti, M. Leighton, C. E. Nirarita, and H. Haeruman. 1999. Impact of El Nino and logging on canopy tree recruitment in Borneo. *Science* 286:2184–2188.

Curran, L. M., and M. Leighton. 2000. Vertebrate responses to spatio-temporal variation in seed production of mast-fruiting Dipterocarpaceae. *Ecology* 70:101–128.

Currie, D. J. 1991. Energy and large scale patterns of animal and plant species richness. *American Naturalist* 137:27–49.

Curry, W. B., and D. W. Oppo. 1997. Synchronous, high frequency oscillations in tropical sea surface temperature and North Atlantic deep water production during the last glacial cycle. *Paleoceanography* 12:1–14.

Dale, A., M. B. Lane, D. Yarrow, and A. Bigelow. 2000. Aboriginal participation in management: Reconciling local interests with World Heritage. Pages 187–199 in G. T. McDonald and M. B. Lane, eds., *Securing the Wet Tropics?* Federation Press, Leichhardt, Australia.

Dale, V. H., and S. M. Pearson. 1997. Quantifying habitat fragmentation due to land-use change in Amazonia. Pages 400–409 in W. F. Laurance and R. O. Bierregaard Jr., eds., *Tropical forest remnants: Ecology, management, and conservation of fragmented communities.* University of Chicago Press, Chicago.

Dalling, J. W., and J. S. Denslow. 1998. Soil seed bank composition along a forest chronosequence in seasonally moist tropical forest, Panama. *Journal of Vegetation Science* 9:669–678.

Dalling, J. W., and S. P. Hubbell. 2002. Seed size, growth rate and gap microsite conditions as determinants of recruitment success for pioneer species. *Journal of Ecology* 90:557–568.

Dalling, J. W., S. P. Hubbell, and K. Silvera. 1998. Seed dispersal, seedling emergence and gap partitioning in gap-dependent tropical tree species. *Journal of Ecology* 86:674–689.

Dalling, J. W., H. C. Muller-Landau, S. J. Wright, and S. P. Hubbell. 2002. Role of dispersal in the recruitment limitation of Neotropical pioneer species. *Journal of Ecology* 90:714–727.

Dalling, J. W., M. D. Swaine, and N. C. Garwood. 1997. Soil seed bank community dynamics in seasonally moist lowland forest, Panama. *Journal of Tropical Ecology* 13:659–680.

———. 1998. Dispersal patterns and seed bank dynamics of pioneer tree species in moist tropical forest, Panama. *Ecology* 79:564–578.

Dalling, J. W., and R. Wirth. 1998. Dispersal of *Miconia argentea* seeds by the leaf-cutting ant, *Atta columbica. Journal of Tropical Ecology* 14:705–710.

Daly, D. C., and G. T. Prance. 1989. Brazilian Amazon. Pages 401–426 in D. G. Campbell and H. D. Hammond, eds., *Floristic inventory of tropical countries: The status of plant systematics, collections, and vegetation, plus recommendations for the future.* New York Botanical Gardens, New York.

Danielsen, F. 1997. Stable environments and fragile communities: Does history determine the resilience of avian rain-forest communities to habitat degradation. *Biodiversity and Conservation* 13:423–434.

D'Arcy, W. G. 1987. *Flora of Panama: Checklist and index.* Vols. 1–4. Missouri Botanical Garden, Saint Louis.

Darlington, P. J. 1943. Carabidae of mountains and islands: Data on the evolution of isolated faunas, and on atrophy of wings. *Ecological Monographs* 13:38–61.

D'Arrigo, D. R., G. C. Jacoby, and P. J. Krusic. 1994. Progress in dendroclimatic studies in Indonesia. *Terrestrial, Atmospheric and Oceanic Sciences* 5:349–363.

Darwin, C. R. 1859. *On the origin of species.* John Murray, London.

———. 1958. *The autobiography of Charles Darwin.* Collins, London.

da Silva, J. M. C., and J. M. Bates. 2002. Biogeographic patterns and conservation in the South American Cerrado: A tropical savanna hotspot. *BioScience* 52:225–233.

da Silva, M. N. F., and J. L. Patton. 1993. Amazonian phylogeography: mtDNA sequence variation in arboreal echimyid rodents (Caviomorpha). *Molecular Phylogenetics and Evolution* 2:243–255.

———. 1998. Molecular phylogeography and the evolution and conservation of Amazonian mammals. *Molecular Ecology* 7:475–486.

David, B., R. Roberts, C. Tuniz, R. Jones, and J. Head. 1997. New optical and radiocarbon dates from Ngarrabullgan cave, a Pleistocene archaeological site in Australia: Implications for the comparability of time clocks and for the human colonisation of Australia. *Antiquity* 71:183–188.

Davies, P. J., J. A. McKenzie, A. Palmer-Julson, C. Betzler, T. C. Brachert, M.-P. P. Chen, J.-P. Crumiere, and others, eds. 1993. *Proceedings of the Ocean Drilling Program: Initial Reports.* Vol. 133. Ocean Drilling Program, College Station, TX.

Davies, V. T. 1982. *Inola* nov. gen., a web-building pisaurid (Araneae: Pisauridae) from northern Australia with descriptions of three species. *Memoirs of the Queensland Museum* 20:479–487.

———. 1986. New Australian species of *Otira* Forster & Wilton, 1973 and *Storenosoma* Hogg, 1900 (Araneae: Amaurobiidae). *Memoirs of the Queensland Museum* 22:237–251.

———. 1990. Two new spider genera (Araneae: Amaurobiidae) from rainforests of Australia. *Acta Zoologica Fennica* 190:95–102.

———. 1993. A new spider genus (Araneae: Amaurobioidea) from rainforests of Queensland, Australia. *Memoirs of the Queensland Museum* 33:483–489.

———. 1995a. A new genus (Araneae: Amaurobioidea: Amphinectidae) from the Wet Tropics of Australia. *Memoirs of the Queensland Museum* 38:463–469.

———. 1995b. A tiny cribellate spider, *Jamara* gen. nov (Araneae: Amaurobioidea: Midgeeinae) from northern Queensland. *Memoirs of the Queensland Museum* 38: 93–96.

———. 1998. A revision of the Australian metaltellines (Araneae: Amaurobioidea: Amphinectidae: Metaltellinae). *Invertebrate Taxonomy* 12:211–243.

———. 1999. A new spider genus from North Queensland, Australia (Araneae: Amaurobioidea: Kababinae). *Journal of Arachnology* 27:25–36.

Davies, V. T., and C. L. Lambkin. 2000a. *Malarina,* a new spider genus (Araneae: Amaurobioidea: Kababininae) from the Wet Tropics of Queensland, Australia. *Memoirs of the Queensland Museum* 45:273–283.

———. 2000b. *Wabua,* a new spider genus (Araneae: Amaurobioidea: Kababinae) from North Queensland, Australia. *Memoirs of the Queensland Museum* 46:129–147.

Davis, M. B. 1986.Vegetation-climate equilibrium. *Vegetatio* 67:1–141.

Davis, M. B., R. E. Moeller, and J. Ford. 1984. Sediment focussing and pollen influx. Pages 261–293 in E. Y. Haworth and J. W. G. Lund, eds., *Lake sediments and environmental history.* University of Minnesota Press, Minneapolis.

Davis, T. A. W., and P. W. Richards. 1933. The vegetation of Moraballi Creek, British Guiana: An ecological study of a limited area of tropical rain forest. Part 1. *Journal of Ecology* 21:350–384.

Daws, M. I., D. F. R. P. Burslem, L. M. Crabtree, P. Kirkman, C. E. Mullins, and J. W. Dalling. 2002. Differences in seed germination responses may promote coexistence of four sympatric *Piper* species. *Functional Ecology* 16:258–267.

Deane, H. 1902. Preliminary report on the fossil flora of Pitfield, Mornington, Sentinel Rock (Otway coast), Berwick, and Wonwron. *Records of the Geological Survey of Victoria* 1:13–14.

———. 1904. Further notes on the Cainozoic flora of Sentinel Rock, Otway Coast. *Records of the Geological Survey of Victoria* 1:212–216.

de Beer, J. H., and M. J. McDermott. 1989. *The economic value of non-timber forest products in Southeast Asia.* Netherlands Committee for IUCN, Amsterdam.

De Boer, H. J. 1951. Tree-ring measurements and weather fluctuations in Java from AD 1514. *Proceedings of the Koniklijke Nederlandse Akademie van Wetenschappen* B54:194–209.

de Klerk, H. M., T. M. Crowe, J. Fjeldså, and N. D. Burgess. 2002. Patterns of species richness and narrow endemism of terrestrial bird species in the Afrotropical Region. *Journal of Zoology* 256:327–342.

de la Maza-E., J., and R. de la Maza-E. La fauna de mariposas de "Boca de Chajul," Chiapas, Mexico. Partes 1 y 2. *Revista de la Sociedade Mexicana de Lepidopterologia* 9:23–44; 10:1–25.

DeMarias, B. D., T. E. Dowling, M. E. Douglas, W. L. Minckley, and P. C. Marsh. 1992. Origin of *Gila seminuda* (Teleostei: Cyprinidae) through introgressive hybridisation: Implications for evolution and conservation. *Proceedings of the National Academy of Sciences USA* 89:2747–2751.

deMenocal, P. B. 1995. Plio-Pleistocene African climate. *Science* 270:53–58.

De Oliveira, A. A., and S. A. Mori. 1999. A central Amazonian terra firme forest. 1. High tree species richness on poor soils. *Biodiversity and Conservation* 8:1219–1244.

De Oliveira, P. E. 1992. A palynological record of Late Quaternary vegetation and climatic change in Southeastern Brazil. Ph.D. thesis, Ohio State University, Columbus.

De Oliveira, P. E., A. M. F. Barreto, and K. Suguio. 1999. Late Pleistocene/Holocene climatic and vegetational history of the Brazilian Caatinga: The fossil dunes of the middle São Francisco River. *Palaeogeography, Palaeoclimatology, Palaeoecology* 152:319–337.

DeSteven, D. 1994. Tropical tree seedling dynamics: Recruitment patterns and their population consequences. *Journal of Tropical Ecology* 10:369–382.

DeSteven, D., and S. J. Wright. 2002. Consequences of species coexistence. *Oecologia* 130:1–14.

Dettmann, M. E. 1994. Cretaceous vegetation: The microfossil record. Pages 143–169 in R. S. Hill, ed., *The history of the Australian vegetation: Cretaceous to Recent.* Cambridge University Press, Cambridge.

Devall, M. S., B. R. Parresol, and K. Lê. 1996. Dendroecological analysis of laurel (*Cordia alliodora*) and other species from a lowland moist tropical forest in Panamá. *Radiocarbon* 1996:395–404.

DeVries, P. J. 1987. *The butterflies of Costa Rica and their natural history.* Princeton University Press, Princeton, NJ.

———. 1997. *The butterflies of Costa Rica and their natural history.* Vol. 2, *Riodinidae.* Princeton University Press, Princeton, NJ.

DeVries, P. J., D. Murray, and R. Lande. 1997. Species diversity in vertical, horizontal, and temporal dimensions of a fruit-feeding butterfly community in an Ecuadorian rainforest. *Biological Journal of the Linnaean Society* 62:343–364.

Diamond, A. W., and A. C. Hamilton. 1980. The distribution of forest passerine birds and Quaternary climatic change in Africa. *Journal of Zoology* 191:379–402.

Diamond, J. M. 1972. Biogeographic kinetics: Estimation of relaxation times for avifaunas of Southwest Pacific Islands. *Proceedings of the National Academy of Sciences USA* 69: 3199–3203.

———. 1984. "Normal" extinction patterns of isolated populations. Pages 193–246 in M. H. Nitecki, ed., *Extinctions.* University of Chicago Press, Chicago.

Diaz, H. F., and G. N. Kiladis. 1992. Atmospheric teleconnections associated with the extreme phase of the Southern Oscillation. Pages 8–27 in H. F. Diaz and V. Markgraf, eds., *El Niño: Historical and paleoclimatic aspects of the Southern Oscillation.* Cambridge University Press, Cambridge.

Dick, C. W., K. Abdul-Salim, and E. Bermingham. 2003. Molecular systematics reveals cryptic Tertiary diversification of a widespread tropical rainforest tree. *American Naturalist* 160:691–703.

Didham, R. K., J. Ghazoul, N. E. Stork, and A. J. Davis. 1996. Insects in fragmented forests: A functional approach. *Trends in Ecology and Evolution* 11:255–260.

Diels, L. 1908. *Pfanzengeographie.* Borntraeger, Berlin.

Dimitru, T. A., K. C. Hill, and D. A. Coyle. 1991. Fission track thermochronology: Application to continental rifting of southeast Australia. *APEA Journal* 31:131–142.

Dinerstein, E., D. M. Olson, D. J. Graham, A. L. Webster, S. A. Primm, M. P. Bookbinder, and G. Ledec. 1995. *A conservation assessment of the terrestrial ecoregions of Latin America and the Caribbean.* The World Wildlife Fund and World Bank, Washington, DC.

Dinerstein, E., E. Wikramanayake, J. G. Robinson, U. Karanth, A. Rabinowitz, D. Olson, T. Mathew, P. Hedao, and M. Connor. 1997. *A framework for identifying high priority areas and actions for the conservation of tigers in the wild.* World Wildlife Fund-US and Wildlife Conservation Society, Washington, DC.

Dinesen, L. 1995. Seasonal variation in feeding ecology of Shelley's greenbul in subtropical evergreen forests. *African Journal of Ecology* 33:420–425.

Dodd, M. E., J. Silvertown, and M. W. Chase. 1999. Phylogenetic analysis of trait evolution and species diversity variation among angiosperm families. *Evolution* 53:732–744.

Doebeli, M., and U. Dieckmann. 2003. Speciation along environmental gradients. *Nature* 421:259–264.

Dolinger, P. M., P. R. Ehrlich, W. L. Fitch, and D. E. Breedlove. 1973. Alkaloid and predation patterns in Colorado lupine populations. *Oecologia* 13:191–204.

Donaldson, J. F. 1988. Further studies on Asiracinae (Homoptera: Delphacidae) in Australia and New Caledonia. *Journal of the Australian Entomological Society* 27:133–141.

Douglas, A. W., and B. P. M. Hyland. 1995. Subfam. 3. Eidotheoideae. Pages 127–129 in A. E. Orchard, ed., *Flora of Australia,* vol. 16, *Elaeganaceae,* Proteaceae 1. Australian Government Publishing Service, Canberra.

Douglas, J. G. 1994. Cretaceous vegetation: The macrofossil record. Pages 171–188 in R. S. Hill, ed., *The history of Australian vegetation: Cretaceous to Recent.* Cambridge University Press, Cambridge.

Dowsett, R. J., and F. Dowsett-Lemaire. 1997. *Flore et fauna du Parc National D'odzala, Congo.* Tauraco Research Report 6. Tauraco Press, Liege, Belgium.

Driml, S. 1994. Protection for profit: Economic and financial values of the Great Barrier Reef World Heritage Area and other protected areas. Research Publication no. 35. Great Barrier Reef Marine Park Authority, Townsville, Queensland.

———. 1997. Towards sustainable tourism in the Wet Tropics World Heritage Area. Wet Tropics Management Authority Information Paper. WTMA, Cairns.

Drinnan, A. N., and T. C. Chambers. 1986. Flora of the Lower Cretaceous Koonwarra Fossil Bed (Korumburra Group), South Gippsland, Victoria. *Memoirs of the Association of Australasian Palaeontologists* 3:1–77.

Duckworth, J. W., R. E. Salter, and K. Khounboline. 1999. *Wildlife in Lao PDR.* IUCN, WCS, and CPAWMN, Vientiane.

Duigan, S. L. 1951. A catalogue of the Australian Tertiary flora. *Proceedings of the Royal Society of Victoria* 63:41–56.

Duivenvoorden, J. F. 1995. Tree species composition and rain forest-environment relationships in the middle Caqueta area, Colombia, NW Amazonia. *Vegetatio* 120:91–113.

Duke, N. C. 1992. Mangrove floristics and biogeography. Pages 63–100 in A. I. Robertson and D. M. Alongi, eds., *Tropical mangrove ecosystems.* Coastal and estuarine studies, 41. American Geophysical Union, Washington, DC.

Duke, N. C., J. A. H. Benzie, J. A. Goodall, and E. R. Ballment. 1998. Genetic structure and evolution of species in the mangrove genus *Avicennia* (Avicenniaceae) in the Indo-West Pacific. *Evolution* 52:1612–1626.

Durrett, R., and S. A. Levin. 1996. Spatial models of species-area curves. *Journal of Theoretical Biology* 179:119–127.

Eberhard, W. G. 1985. *Sexual selection and animal genitalia.* Harvard University Press, Cambridge, MA.

Ebert, H. 1969. On the frequency of butterflies in eastern Brazil, with a list of the butterfly fauna of Poços de Caldas, Minas Gerais. *Journal of the Lepidopterists' Society* 23, suppl. 3:1–48.

Edwards, S. V., and P. Beerli. 2000. Perspective: Gene divergence, population divergence, and the variance in coalescence time in phylogeographic studies. *Evolution* 54:1839–1854.

Ehrendorfer, F. 1982. Speciation in woody angiosperms of tropical origin. Pages 479–509 in C. Barigozzi, ed., *Mechanisms of speciation.* Liss, New York.

Ehrlich, P. R., and P. H. Raven. 1969. Differentiation of populations. *Science* 165:1228–1232.

EIA. 1998. *The politics of extinction.* Environmental Investigation Agency (EIA), London.

———. 1999. *The final cut.* Environmental Investigation Agency, London.

EIA/Telapak. 2000. *Illegal logging in Tanjung Puting National Park: An update on the Final Cut report.* Environmental Investigation Agency, London; Telapak, Bogor, Indonesia.

Eisenberg, J. F. 1981. *The mammalian radiations: An analysis of trends in evolution, adaptation, and behavior.* University of Chicago Press, Chicago.

Elenga, H., A. Vincens, and D. Schwartz. 1991. Presence d'elements forestiers montagnards sur les Plateaux Bateke (Congo) au Pleistocene superieur: Nouvelles donnees palynologiques. *Palaeoecology of Africa* 22:239–252.

Eletrobrás. 1998. *Eletrobrás: The ten-year expansion plan, 1998–2007.* Centrais Elétricas do Brasil, Rio de Janeiro, Brazil.

Ellison, A. M., E. J. Farnsworth, and R. E. Merkt. 1999. Origins of mangrove ecosystems and the mangrove biodiversity anomaly. *Global Ecology and Biogeography Letters* 8:95–115.

Emmons, L. H. 1987. Comparative feeding ecology of felids in a Neotropical rainforest. *Behavioral Ecology and Sociobiology* 20:271–283.

———. 1989. Tropical rain forests: Why they have so many species and how we may lose this biodiversity without cutting a single tree. *Orion Nature Quarterly* 8(3):8–14.

Endler, J. A. 1977. *Geographic variation, speciation, and clines.* Monographs in Population Biology, no. 10. Princeton University Press, Princeton, NJ.

———. 1982a. Alternative hypotheses in biogeography: Introduction and synopsis of the symposium. *American Zoologist* 22:349–354.

———. 1982b. Pleistocene forest refuges: Fact or fancy? Pages 641–657 in G. T. Prance, ed., *Biological diversification in the tropics.* Columbia University Press, New York.

———. 1982c. Problems in distinguishing historical from ecological factors in biogeography. *American Zoologist* 22:441–452.

———. 1983. Testing causal hypotheses in the study of geographical variation. Pages 424–443 in J. Felsenstein, ed., *Numerical taxonomy.* Springer-Verlag, New York.

Enquist, B. J., and A. J. Leffler. 2001. Long-term tree ring chronologies from sympatric tropical dry-forest trees: Individualistic responses to climatic variation. *Journal of Tropical Ecology* 17:41–60.

ERDAS. 1998. Environmental research data analysis system. ERDAS, Atlanta, GA.

Erwin, T. L. 1979. Thoughts on the evolutionary history of ground beetles: Hypotheses generated from comparative faunal analyses of lowland forest sites in temperate and tropical regions. Pages 539–592 in L. Erwin, G. E. Ball, and D. R. Whitehead, eds., *Carabid beetles: Their evolution, natural history, and classification.* Dr. W. Junk, The Hague.

———. 1981. Taxon pulses, vicariance, and dispersal: An evolutionary synthesis illustrated by carabid beetles. Pages 159–196 in G. Nelson and D. E. Rosen, eds., *Vicariance biogeography: A critique.* Columbia University Press, New York.

———. 1985. The taxon pulse: A general pattern of lineage radiation and extinction among carabid beetles. Pages 437–472 in G. E. Ball, ed., *Taxonomy, phylogeny and zoogeography of beetles and ants.* Dr. W. Junk, Dordrecht.

———. 1991a. An evolutionary basis for conservation strategies. *Science* 253:750–752.

———. 1991b. How many species are there? Revisited. *Conservation Biology* 5:330–333.

Erwin, T. L., and J. Adis. 1982. Amazonian inundation forests: Their role as short-term refuges and generators of species richness and taxon pulses. Pages 358–371 in G. T. Prance, ed., *Biological diversification in the tropics.* Columbia University Press, New York.

ESRI. 1999. Arc/Info 7.2.1. Environmental Systems Research Institute, Redlands, CA.

Estes, J. A., and J. F. Palmisano. 1974. Sea otters: Their role in structuring nearshore communities. *Science* 185:1058–1060.

Estes, J. A., M. T. Tinker, T. M. Williams, and D. F. Doak. 1998. Killer whale predation on sea otters linking oceanic and nearshore ecosystems. *Science* 282:473–476.

Ewens, W. J. 1972. The sampling theory of selectively neutral alleles. *Theoretical Population Biology* 3:87–112.

———. 1979. *Mathematical population genetics.* Springer-Verlag, Berlin.

Excoffier, L., P. E. Smouse, and J. M. Quattro. 1992. Analysis of molecular variance inferred from metric distances among DNA haplotypes: Application to human mitochondrial DNA restriction data. *Genetics* 131:479–491.

Facelli, J. M. 1994. Multiple indirect effects of plant litter affect the establishment of woody seedlings in old fields. *Ecology* 75:1727–1735.

Facelli, J. M., and S. T. A. Pickett. 1991. Plant litter: Its effects on plant community structure. *Botanical Review* 57:1–32.

Faegri, K., and L. van der Pilj. 1979. *The principles of pollination ecology.* 3rd ed. Munksgaard, Copenhagen.

Faith, D. 1992. Systematics and conservation: On predicting the feature diversity of subsets of taxa. *Cladistics* 8:361–373.

Faith, D., H. A. Nix, C. R. Margules, M. F. Hutchinson, P. A. Walker, J. West, J. L. Stein, J. L. Kestevan, A. Allison, and G. Natera. 2001. The BioRap biodiversity assessment and planning study for Papua New Guinea. *Pacific Conservation Biology* 6:279–288.

Faith, D., and P. Walker. 1996. How do indicator groups provide information about the relative biodiversity for different sets of areas?: On hotspots, complementarity and pattern-based approaches. *Biodiversity Letters* 3:18–25.

Fan, S.-M., S. C. Wofsy, P. S. Bakwin, and D. J. Jacob. 1990. Atmosphere-biosphere exchange of CO_2 and O_3 in the Central Amazon forest. *Journal of Geophysical Research* 95:16851–16864.

FAO. 1993. Forest resources assessment 1990: Tropical countries. FAO Forestry Paper 112. Food and Agriculture Organization of the United Nations, Rome.

Far North Queensland Regional Planning Advisory Committee. 1998a. FNQ 2010: Regional planning project: Integrated regional strategies for Far North Queensland. Queensland Department of Local Government and Planning, Cairns.

———. 1998b. FNQ 2010: Regional planning project: Strategic directions and regional priorities for Far North Queensland. Queensland Department of Local Government and Planning, Cairns.

Farrell, B. D., D. E. Doussourd, and C. Mitter. 1991. Escalation of plant defense: Do latex and resin canals spur plant diversification? *American Naturalist* 138:881–900.

Farrell, B. D., and C. Mitter. 1993. Phylogenetic determinants of insect/plant community diversity. Pages 253–266 in R. E. Ricklefs and D. Schluter, eds., *Species diversity in ecological communities: Historical and geographical perspectives.* University of Chicago Press, Chicago.

Farrell, B. D., C. Mitter, and D. J. Futuyma. 1992. Diversification at the insect-plant interface. *BioScience* 42:34–42.

Fearnside, P. M. 1987. Causes of deforestation in the Brazilian Amazon. Pages 37–61 in R. F. Dickinson, ed., *The geophysiology of Amazonia: Vegetation and climate interactions.* John Wiley, San Francisco.

———. 1990. Environmental destruction in the Amazon. Pages 179–225 in D. Goodman and A. Hall, eds., *The future of Amazonia: Destruction or sustainable development?* Macmillan, London.

———. 1993. Deforestation in the Brazilian Amazon: The effect of population and land tenure. *Ambio* 8:537–545.

———. 1995. Hydroelectric dams in the Brazilian Amazon as sources of "greenhouse" gases. *Environmental Conservation* 22:7–19.

———. 1997. Protection of mahogany: A catalytic species in the destruction of rain forests in the American tropics. *Environmental Conservation* 24:303–306.

———. 1999. Biodiversity as an environmental service in Brazil's Amazonian forests: Risks, value and conservation. *Environmental Conservation* 26:305–321.

———. 2001. Soybean cultivation as a threat to the environment in Brazil. *Environmental Conservation* 28:23–38.

———. 2002. Avança Brasil: Environmental and social consequences of Brazil's planned infrastructure in Amazonia. *Environmental Management* 30:735–747.

Feary, D. A., P. J. Davies, C. J. Pigram, and P. A. Symonds. 1991. Climatic evolution and control on carbonate deposition in northeast Australia. *Palaeogeography, Palaeoclimatology, Palaeoecology* (Global and Planetary Change Section) 89:341–361.

Feary, D. A., and R. D. Jarrard. 1993. Sedimentology and downhole log analysis of Site 820, central Great Barrier Reef outer shelf: The factors controlling Pleistocene progradational and aggradational seismic geometry. *Proceedings of the Ocean Drilling Program, Scientific Results* 133:315–326.

Ferraz-Vicentini, K. R., and M. L. Salgado-Labouriau. 1996. Palynological analysis of a palm swamp in central Brazil. *Journal of South American Earth Sciences* 9:207–219.

Ferreira, L. V., R. M. L. de Sá, R. Buschbacher, G. Batmanian, B. R. Bensuran, and K. L. Costa. 1999. *Áreas protegidas ou espaços ameaçados?* World Wide Fund for Nature, Brasília, Brazil.

Ferrier, S. 2002. Mapping spatial pattern in biodiversity for regional planning: Where to from here? *Systematic Biology* 51:331–363.

Fincke, O. M. 1992a. Consequences of larval ecology for territoriality and reproductive success of a Neotropical damselfly. *Ecology* 73:449–462.

———. 1992b. Interspecific competition for tree holes: Consequences for mating systems and coexistence in Neotropical damselflies. *American Naturalist* 139:80–101.

———. 1994. Population regulation of a tropical damselfly in the larval stage by food limitation, cannibalism, intraguild predation, and habitat drying. *Oecologia* 100:118–127.

Fischer, A. G. 1960. Latitudinal variation in organic diversity. *Evolution* 14:64–81.

Fisher, R. A. 1930. *The genetical theory of natural selection.* Clarendon Press, Oxford.

Fisher, R. A., A. S. Corbet, and C. B. Williams. 1943. The relation between the number of species and the number of individuals in a random sample of an animal population. *Journal of Animal Ecology* 12:42–58.

Fjeldså, J. 1994. Geographical patterns of relict and young species of birds in Africa and South America and implications for conservation priorities. *Biodiversity and Conservation* 3:107–226.

———. 1999. The impact of human forest disturbance on the endemic avifauna of the Udzungwa Mountains, Tanzania. *Bird Conservation International* 9:47–62.

———. 2003. Patterns of endemism in African birds: How much does taxonomy matter? *Ostrich* 74:30–38.

Fjeldså, J., D. Ehrlich, E. Lambin, and E. Prins. 1997. Are biodiversity "hotspots" correlated with current ecoclimatic stability? A pilot study using the NOAA-AVHRR remote sensing data. *Biodiversity and Conservation* 6:401–422.

Fjeldså, J., E. Lambin, and B. Mertens. 1999. The relationship of species richness and endemism to ecoclimatic stability: A case study comparing distribution of Andean birds with remotely sensed environmental data. *Ecography* 22:63–78.

Fjeldså, J., and J. C. Lovett. 1997. Geographical patterns of old and young species in African forest biota: The significance of specific montane areas as evolutionary centres. *Biodiversity and Conservation* 6:325–346.

Fjeldså, J., and C. Rahbek. 1998. Continent-wide diversification processes and conservation priorities. Pages 139–160 in G. M. Mace, A. Balmford, and J. R. Ginsberg, eds., *Conservation in a changing world: Integrating processes into priorities for action.* Cambridge University Press, Cambridge.

Flenley, J. R. 1979. *The equatorial rain forest: A geological history.* London: Butterworths.

———. 1993. The origins of diversity in tropical rain forests. *Trends in Ecology and Evolution* 8:119–120.

———. 1996. The tropical rain forest. Pages 573–598 in I. Douglas, R. Huggett, and M. Robinson, eds., *Companion encyclopaedia of geography, the environment and humankind.* Routledge, London.

———. 1998. Tropical forests under the climates of the last 30,000 years. *Climatic Change* 39:177–197.

———. 2003. Some prospects for lake sediment analysis in the 21st century. *Quaternary International* 105:77–80.

Flenley, J. R., and K. R. Butler. 2001. Evidence for continued disturbance of upland rain forest in Sumatra for the last 7,000 years of an 11,000 year record. *Palaeogeography, Palaeoclimatology, Palaeoecology* 171:289–305.

Fletcher, M. J. 1985. Revision of the genus *Siphanta* Stål (Homoptera: Fulgoroidea: Flatidae). *Australian Journal of Zoology,* suppl. ser. 110:1–94.

Flood, J. 1995. *Archaeology of the dreamtime.* Rev. ed. Angus and Robertson, Sydney.

Flood, R. D., D. J. W. Piper, A. Klaus, and L. C. Peterson, eds. 1997. *Proceedings of the Ocean*

Drilling Program, Scientific Results. Vol. 155. Ocean Drilling Program, College Station, TX.

Forget, P.-M. 1993. Post-dispersal predation and scatterhoarding of *Dipteryx panamensis* (Papilionaceae) seeds by rodents in Panama. *Oecologia* 94:255–261.

———. 1994. Recruitment pattern of *Vouacapoua americana* (Caesalpinaceae), a rodent-dispersed tree species in French Guiana. *Biotropica* 26:408–419.

Forget, P.-M., and T. Milleron. 1991. Evidence for secondary seed dispersal by rodents in Panama. *Oecologia* 87:596–599.

Forsyth, A., and J. Nott. 2003. Evolution of drainage patterns on Cape York Peninsula, northeast Queensland. *Australian Journal of Earth Sciences* 50:145–155.

Foster, R. B. 1982a. Famine on Barro Colorado Island. Pages 201–212 in E. G. Leigh Jr., A. S. Rand, and D. M. Windsor, eds., *The ecology of a tropical forest.* Smithsonian Institution Press, Washington, DC.

———. 1982b. The seasonal rhythm of fruitfall on Barro Colorado Island. Pages 151–172 in E. G. Leigh Jr., A. S. Rand, and D. M. Windsor, eds., *The ecology of a tropical forest.* Smithsonian Institution Press, Washington, DC.

Foster, R. B., and S. P. Hubbell. 1990. The floristic composition of the Barro Colorado forest. Pages 85–98 in A. H. Gentry, ed., *Four Neotropical rainforests.* Yale University Press, New Haven, CT.

Frakes, L. A., J. E. Francis, and J. I. Syktus. 1992. *Climate modes of the Phanerozoic: The history of the Earth's climate over the past 600 million years.* Cambridge University Press, Cambridge.

Frakes, L. A., B. McGowran, and J. M. Bowler. 1987. Evolution of Australian environments. Pages 1–16 in G. R. Dyne and D. W. Walton, eds., *Fauna of Australia.* v. 1A. *General Articles.* Australian Government Publishing Service, Canberra.

Francis, A. P., and D. J. Currie. 1998. Global patterns of tree species richness in moist forest: Another look. *Oikos* 81:598–602.

Francisco-Ortega, J., R. K. Jansen, and A. Santos-Guerra. 1996. Chloroplast DNA evidence of colonization, adaptive radiation, and hybridization in the evolution of the Macronesian flora. *Proceedings of the National Academy of Sciences USA* 93:4085–4090.

Franklin, J. F., D. R. Berg, D. A. Thornburgh, and J. C. Tappeiner. 1997. Alternative silvicultural approaches to timber harvesting: Variable retention harvest systems. Pages 111–139 in K. A. Kohm and J. F. Franklin, eds., *Creating a forestry for the 21st century.* Island Press, Washington, DC.

Friends of the Earth. 1999. *O debate sobre políticas públicas para Amazônia na imprensa brasileira.* Vol. 4. Friends of the Earth, Amazonia Program, Brasília, Brazil.

Fritts, T. H., and G. H. Rodda. 1998. The role of introduced species in the degradation of island ecosystems: A case history of Guam. *Annual Review of Ecology and Systematics* 29:113–140.

FWI/GFW. 2002. *The state of the forest: Indonesia.* Forest Watch Indonesia and Global Forest Watch, Washington, DC.

Gadek, P. 1999. Patch deaths in tropical Queensland rainforests: Association and impact of *Phytophthora cinnamomi* and other soil borne organisms. Technical Report. Cooperative Research Centre for Tropical Rainforest Ecology and Management, Cairns.

Gallagher, S. J., D. R. Greenwood, D. Taylor, A. J. Smith, M. W. Wallace, and G. R. Holdgate. 2003. The Pliocene climatic and environmental evolution of southeastern Australia: Evidence from the marine and terrestrial realm. *Palaeogeography, Palaeoclimatology, Palaeoecology* 194:1–34.

Gallant, J. C., and W. P. Wilson. 1996. TAPES-G: Grid-based terrain analysis program for the environmental sciences. *Computers and Geosciences* 22(7):713–722.

Ganopolski, A., S. Rahmstorf, V. Petoukhov, and M. Claussen. 1998. Simulation of modern and glacial climates with a coupled global model of intermediate complexity. *Nature* 391:351–356.

García-Moreno, J., and J. Fjeldså. 1999. Re-evaluation of species limits in the genus *Atlapetes* based on mtDNA sequence data. *Ibis* 141:199–207.

Gartner, S., W. Wei, and J. P. Shyu. 1993. Neogene calcareous nanofossil biostratigraphy at Sites 812 through 818, northeastern Australian margin. *Proceedings of the Ocean Drilling Program, Scientific Results* 133:3–18.

Garwood, N. C. 1983. Seed germination in a seasonal tropical forest in Panama: A community study. *Ecological Monographs* 53:159–181.

Gascon, C., S. C. Lougheed, and J. P. Bogart. 1996. Genetic and morphologic variation in *Vanzolinius discodactylus:* A test of the river hypothesis of speciation. *Biotropica* 28: 376–387.

———. 1998. Patterns of genetic population differentiation in four species of Amazonian frogs: A test of the riverine barrier hypothesis. *Biotropica* 30:104–119.

Gascon, C., J. R. Malcolm, J. L. Patton, M. N. F. da Silva, J. P. Bogart, S. C. Lougheed, C. A. Peres, S. Neckel, and P. T. Boag. 2000. Riverine barriers and the geographic distribution of Amazonian species. *Proceedings of the National Academy of Sciences USA* 97:13672–13677.

Gascon, C., G. B. Williamson, and G. A. B. da Fonseca. 2000. Receding forest edges and vanishing reserves. *Science* 288:1356–1358.

Gaston, K. J. 1998. Species-range size distributions: Products of speciation, extinction and transformation. *Philosophical Transactions of the Royal Society of London* B 353:219–230.

Gates, D. M. 1968. Energy exchange between organisms and environment. *Australian Journal of Science* 31:67–74.

Gause, G. F. 1934. *The struggle for existence.* Williams and Wilkins, Baltimore.

Gavrilets, S., H. Li, and M. D. Vose. 2000. Patterns of parapatric speciation. *Evolution* 54:1126–1134.

Gehring, C. A. 2003. Growth responses to arbuscular mycorrhizae by rain forest seedlings vary with light intensity and tree species. *Plant Ecology* 167:127–139.

Gehring, C. A., J. Wolff, and T. C. Theimer. 2002. Terrestrial vertebrates increase fungal spore abundance and diversity and the mycorrhizal innoculum potential of a rainforest soil. *Ecology Letters* 5:1–9.

Gentry, A. H. 1982. Patterns of Neotropical plant species diversity. *Evolutionary Biology* 15:1–84.

———. 1988a. Changes in plant community diversity and floristic composition on environmental and geographic gradients. *Annals of the Missouri Botanical Garden* 75: 1–34.

———. 1988b. Tree species richness of upper Amazonian forests. *Proceedings of the National Academy of Sciences USA* 85:156–159.

Gentry, A. H., and C. Dodson. 1987. Contribution of nontrees to species richness of a tropical rain forest. *Biotropica* 19:149–156.

Gilbert, F. S. 1980. The equilibrium theory of biogeography: Fact or fiction? *Journal of Biogeography* 7:209–235.

Gilbert, L. E. 1980. Food web organization and conservation of Neotropical diversity. Pages 11–34 in M. E. Soulé and B. A. Wilcox, eds., *Conservation biology: An evolutionary-ecological perspective.* Sinauer Associates, Sunderland, MA.

Gill, F. B. 1998. Hybridization in birds. *Auk* 115:281–283.

Gillett, J. B. 1962. Pest pressure, an underestimated factor in evolution. Pages 37–46 in D. Nichols, ed., *Taxonomy and Geography.* Publication no. 4. Systematics Association, London.

Gillison, A. N., and K. R. W. Brewer. 1985. The use of gradient directed transects or gradsects in natural resource surveys. *Journal of Environmental Management* 20:103–127.

Gillison, A. N., and G. Carpenter. 1997. A generic plant functional attribute set and grammar for dynamic vegetation description and analysis. *Functional Ecology* 11:775–783.

Givnish, T. J. 1997. Adaptive radiation and molecular systematics: Issues and approaches. Pages 1–54 in T. J. Givnish and K. J. Sytsma, eds., *Molecular evolution and adaptive radiation.* Cambridge University Press, Cambridge.

———. 1999. On the causes of gradients in tropical tree diversity. *Journal of Ecology* 87:193–210.

Glantz, M. H. 1996. *Currents of change: El Niño's impact on climate and society.* Cambridge University Press, Cambridge.

Glanz, W. E. 1990. Neotropical mammal densities: How unusual is the community on Barro Colorado Island, Panama? Pages 287–313 in A. H. Gentry, ed., *Four Neotropical rainforests.* Yale University Press, New Haven, CT.

Glasby, C. J., and B. Alvarez. 1999. Distribution patterns and biogeographic analysis of Austral Polychaeta (Annelida). *Journal of Biogeography* 26:507–533.

Gleason, H. A. 1926. The individualistic concept of the plant association. *Torrey Botanical Club Bulletin* 53:7–26.

Glor, R. E., L. J. Vitt, and A. Larson. 2001. A molecular phylogenetic analysis of diversification in Amazonian *Anolis* lizards. *Molecular Ecology* 10:2661–2668.

Golley, F. B. 1983. Nutrient cycling and nutrient conservation. Pages 137–156 in F. B. Golley, ed., *Ecosystems of the world. 14A. Tropical rainforest ecosystems: Structure and function.* Elsevier, Amsterdam.

Goodman, S. M. 1995. *Rattus* on Madagascar and the dilemma of protecting the endemic rodent fauna. *Conservation Biology* 9:450–453.

Goosem, M. 1997. Internal fragmentation: The effects of roads, highways, and powerline clearings on movements and mortality of rainforest vertebrates. Pages 241–255 in W. F. Laurance and R. O. Bierregaard Jr., eds., *Tropical forest remnants: Ecology, management, and conservation of fragmented communities.* University of Chicago Press, Chicago.

Goosem, M., and H. Marsh. 1997. Fragmentation of a small-mammal community by a powerline corridor through tropical rainforest. *Wildlife Research* 24:613–629.

Gorshkov, V. G. 1995. *Physical and biological bases of life stability: Man, biota, and environment.* Springer-Verlag, New York.

Gotelli, N. J., and G. R. Graves, eds. 1996. *Null models in ecology.* Smithsonian Institution Press, Washington, DC.

Gould, S. J., D. M. Raup, J. J. Sepkoski, T. J. M. Schopf, and D. S. Simberloff. 1977. The shape of evolution: A comparison of real and random clades. *Paleobiology* 3:23–40.

Grace, J., J. Lloyd, J. McIntyre, A. C. Miranda, P. Meir, H. S. Miranda, C. Nobre, J. Moncrieff, J. Massheder, Y. Malhi, I. Wright, and J. Gash. 1995. Carbon dioxide uptake by an undisturbed tropical rain forest in southwest Amazonia, 1992 to 1993. *Science* 270:778–780.

Graciansky, P.-C. de, J. Hardenbol, T. Jacquin, and P. R. Vail. 1998. Mesozoic and Cenozoic sequence stratigraphy of European basins. SEPM Special Publication no. 60. Society for Sedimentary Geology, Tulsa, OK.

Gradwohl, J., and R. Greenberg. 1982. The effect of a single species of avian predator on the arthropods of aerial leaf litter. *Ecology* 63:581–583.

Graham, A. 1985. Studies in Neotropical paleobotany. 4. The Eocene communities of Panama. *Annals of the Missouri Botanical Garden* 72:504–534.

Graham, E. A., S. S. Mulkey, K. Kitajima, N. G. Phillips, and S. J. Wright. 2003. Cloud cover limits net CO_2 uptake and growth of a rainforest tree during tropical rainy seasons. *Proceedings of the National Academy of Sciences USA* 100:572–576.

Grant, B. R., and P. R. Grant. 1996. High survival of Darwin's finch hybrids: Effects of beak morphology and diets. *Ecology* 77:500–509.

Grant, P. R. 1986. *Ecology and evolution of Darwin's finches.* Princeton University Press, Princeton, NJ.

Grant, P. R., and B. R. Grant. 1992. Hybridization of bird species. *Science* 256:193–197.

———. 1996. Speciation and hybridization in island birds. *Philosophical Transactions of the Royal Society of London* B 351:765–772.

———. 1997. Genetics and the origin of bird species. *Proceedings of the National Academy of Sciences USA* 94:7768–7775.

Green, J. J., and D. M. Newbery. 2002. Reproductive investment and seedling survival of the mast-fruiting rain forest tree, *Microberlinia bisulcata* A. chev. *Plant Ecology* 162:169–183.

Green, M., M. Van Veller, and D. R. Brooks. Forthcoming. Assessing modes of speciation: Range asymmetry and biogeographical congruence. *Cladistics* 18:112–124.

Greenwood, D. R. 1987. Early Tertiary Podocarpaceae: Megafossils from the Eocene Anglesea locality, Victoria, Australia. *Australian Journal of Botany* 35(2):111–134.

———. 1991. The taphonomy of plant macrofossils. Pages 145–169 in S. K. Donovan, ed., *Fossilization: The processes of taphonomy.* Belhaven Press, London.

———. 1992. Taphonomic constraints on foliar physiognomic interpretations of Late Cretaceous and Tertiary palaeoclimates. *Review of Palaeobotany and Palynology* 71:142–194.

———. 1994. Palaeobotanical evidence for Australian Tertiary climates. Pages 44–59 in R. S. Hill, ed., *The history of Australian vegetation: Cretaceous to Recent.* Cambridge University Press, Cambridge.

———. 1996. Eocene monsoon forests in central Australia? *Australian Systematic Botany* 9(2):95–112.

———. 2001. Climate—wood and leaves. Section 4.3.6. Pages 480–483 in D. E. G. Briggs and P. R. Crowther, eds., *Palaeobiology II*. Blackwell Scientific, London.

Greenwood, D. R., and J. Conran. 2000. The Australian Cretaceous and Tertiary monocot fossil record. Pages 52–62 in K. L. Wilson and D. A. Morrison, eds., *Monocots: Systematics and evolution*. CSIRO Publishing, Melbourne.

Greenwood, D. R., P. W. Haines, and S. C. Steart. 2001. New species of *Banksieaeformis* and a *Banksia* "Cone" (Proteaceae) from the Tertiary of central Australia. *Australian Systematic Botany* 14(6):870–890.

Greenwood, D. R., P. T. Moss, A. I. Rowett, A. J. Vadala, and R. L. Keefe. 2003. Plant communities and climate change in southeastern Australia during the early Paleogene. Pages 365–380 in S. L. Wing, P. D. Gingerich, B. Schmitz, and E. Thomas, eds., *Causes and consequences of globally warm climates in the early Paleogene*. Special Paper 369. Geological Society of America, Boulder, CO.

Greenwood, D. R., A. J. Vadala, and M. Banks. 2000. Climates and changes in forest floristics during the Paleocene and Eocene in southeastern Australia. *GFF* (Geologiska Föreningens i Stockholm Förhandlingar) 122:65–66.

Greenwood, D. R., A. J. Vadala, and J. G. Douglas. 2000. Victorian Paleogene and Neogene macrofloras: A conspectus. *Proceedings of the Royal Society of Victoria* 112(1):65–92.

Greenwood, D. R., and S. L. Wing. 1995. Eocene continental climates and latitudinal gradients. *Geology* 23(11):1040–1048.

Groombridge, B., ed. 1992. *Global biodiversity: Status of the Earth's living resources*. Chapman & Hall, London.

Grove, A. T. 1978. *Africa south of the Sahara*. 3rd ed. Oxford University Press, Oxford.

Guilderson, T. P., R. G. Fairbanks, and J. L. Rubenstone. 1994. Tropical temperature variations since 20,000 years ago: Modulating interhemispheric climate change. *Science* 263:663–665.

Gulland, J. A. 1982. Why do fish numbers vary? *Journal of Theoretical Biology* 97:69–75.

Gunn, R. H., J. A. Beattie, A. M. H. Riddler, and L. A. Lowrie. 1988. Mapping. Pages 90–110 in R. H. Gunn, J. A. Beattie, R. E. Reid, and van de Graaff, eds., *Australian soil and land survey handbook: Guidelines for conducting surveys*. Inkata Press, Melbourne.

Guo, Q., and R. E. Ricklefs. 2000. Species richness in plant genera disjunct between temperate eastern Asia and North America. *Botanical Journal of the Linnean Society* 134: 401–423.

Guo, Q., R. E. Ricklefs, and M. L. Cody. 1998. Vascular plant diversity in eastern Asia and North America: Historical and ecological explanations. *Botanical Journal of the Linnean Society* 128:123–136.

Haberle, S. G. 1997. Upper Quaternary vegetation and climate history of the Amazon basin: Correlating marine and terrestrial pollen records. *Proceedings of the Ocean Drilling Program, Scientific Results* 155:381–396.

Haberle, S. G., and M. A. Maslin. 1999. Late Quaternary vegetation and climate change in the Amazon Basin based on a 50,000 year pollen record from the Amazon fan, PDP site 932. *Quaternary Research* 51:27–38.

Hackel, J. D. 1999. Community conservation and the future of Africa's wildlife. *Conservation Biology* 13:726–734.

Hadwen, W. L., A. Small, R. L. Kitching, and R. A. I. Drew. 1998. Potential suitability of North Queensland rainforest sites as habitat for the Asian papaya fruit fly, *Bactrocera papayae* Drew and Hancock (Diptera: Tephritidae). *Australian Journal of Entomology* 37:219–227.

Haffer, J. 1969. Speciation in Amazonian forest birds. *Science* 165:131–137.

———. 1974. Avian speciation in tropical South America, with a systematic survey of the toucans (Ramphastidae) and jacamars (Galbulidae). Publications of the Nuttall Ornithological Club, no. 14. Nuttall Ornithological Club, Cambridge, MA.

———. 1978. Distribution of Amazon forest birds. *Bonner Zoologische Beiträge* 29:38–78.

———. 1992. On the "river effect" in some forest birds of southern Amazonia. *Boletim do Museu Paraense Emilio Goeldi*, ser. Zool. 8:217–245.

———. 1993. Time's cycle and time's arrow in the history of Amazonia. *Biogeographica* 69:15–45.

———. 1997. Alternative models of vertebrate speciation in Amazonia: An overview. *Biodiversity and Conservation* 6:451–476.

———. 2001. Hypotheses to explain the origin of species in Amazonia. Pages 45–118 in I. C. Guimarães Vieira, J. M. Cardoso da Silva, D. C. Oren, and M. Â. D'Incao, eds., *Diversidade de Amazônia*. Museu Paraense Emílio Goeldi, Belém, Pará, Brazil.

Haffer, J., and G. T. Prance. 2001. Climatic forcing of evolution in Amazonia during the Cenozoic: On the refuge theory of biotic differentiation. *Amazoniana* 16:579–608.

Haldane, J. B. S. 1948. The theory of a cline. *Journal of Genetics* 48:277–284.

Hall, B. P., and R. E. Moreau. 1970. *An atlas of speciation in African passerine birds*. London: British Museum.

Hall, J. B., and M. D. Swaine. 1981. *Distribution and ecology of vascular plants in a tropical rain forest: Forest vegetation in Ghana*. Dr. W. Junk Publishers, The Hague.

Hamer, K. C., and J. K. Hill. 2000. Scale-dependent effects of habitat disturbance on species richness in tropical forests. *Conservation Biology* 14:1435–1440.

Hamilton, K. G. A. 1999. The ground-dwelling leafhoppers Myerslopiidae, new family, and Stagmatiini, new tribe (Homoptera: Membracoidea). *Invertebrate Taxonomy* 13:207–235.

Hammond, D. S., and H. ter Steege. 1998. Propensity for fire in Guianan rainforests. *Conservation Biology* 12:944–947.

Hammond, P. C. 1991. Patterns of geographic variation and evolution in polytypic butterflies. *Journal of Research on the Lepidoptera* 29:54–76.

Hamrick, J. L., and D. A. Murawski. 1991. Levels of allozyme diversity in populations of uncommon Neotropical tree species. *Journal of Tropical Ecology* 7:395–399.

Handley, C. O. Jr., D. E. Wilson, and A. L. Gardner, eds. 1991. *Demography and natural history of the common fruit bat,* Artibeus jamaicensis, *on Barro Colorado*. Smithsonian Contributions to Zoology, no. 511. Smithsonian Institution Press, Washington, DC.

Hansen, M. 1990. Australian Sphaeridiinae (Coleoptera: Hydrophilidae): A taxonomic outline with descriptions of new genera and species. *Invertebrate Taxonomy* 4:317–395.

Hanski, I. 1997. Metapopulation dynamics: From concepts and observations to predictive models. Pages 69–91 in I. Hanski and M. E. Gilpin, eds., *Metapopulation biology: Ecology, genetics, and evolution*. Academic Press, San Diego.

Hanski, I., and M. E. Gilpin, eds. 1997. *Metapopulation biology: Ecology, genetics, and evolution.* Academic Press, London.

Haq, B. U., J. Hardenbol, and P. R. Vail. 1987. Chronology of fluctuating sea levels since the Triassic. *Science* 235:1156–1167.

Harms, K. E., R. Condit, S. P. Hubbell, and R. B. Foster. 2001. Habitat associations of trees and shrubs in a Neotropical forest. *Journal of Ecology* 89:947–959.

Harms, K. E., and J. W. Dalling. 1997. Damage and herbivory tolerance through resprouting as an advantage of large seed size in tropical trees and lianas. *Journal of Tropical Ecology* 13:481–490.

Harold, A. S., and R. D. Mooi. 1994. Areas of endemism: Definitions and recognition criteria. *Systematic Biology* 43:261–266.

Harpending, H. C., M. A. Batzer, M. Gurven, L. B. Jorde, A. R. Rogers, and S. T. Sherry. 1998. Genetic traces of ancient demography. *Proceedings of the National Academy of Sciences USA* 95:1961–1967.

Harrington, G. N., A. K. Irvine, F. H. J. Crome, and L. A. Moore. 1997. Regeneration of large-seeded trees in Australian rainforest fragments: A study of higher order interactions. Pages 292–303 in W. F. Laurance and R. O. Bierregaard Jr., eds., *Tropical forest remnants: Ecology, management, and conservation of fragmented communities.* University of Chicago Press, Chicago.

Harris, W. K. 1971. Tertiary stratigraphic palynology. Pages 67–87 in H. Wopfner and J. C. Douglas, eds., *The Otway Basin of Southeastern Australia.* Special bulletin. Geological Surveys of South Australia and Victoria, Melbourne.

———. 1985. Middle to Late Eocene depositional cycles and dinoflagellate zones in southern Australia. Pages 133–144 in J. M. Lindsay, ed., *Stratigraphy, Palaeontology, Malacology: Papers in honour of Dr Nell Ludbrook.* Special publication, no. 5. South Australian Department of Mines and Energy.

Harrison, B. A., and D. L. B. Jupp. 1990. *Introduction to image processing.* CSIRO, Melbourne.

Harrison, D. A., and B. C. Congdon. 2002. *Wet Tropics vertebrate pest risk assessment scheme.* Cooperative Research Centre for Tropical Rainforest Ecology and Management, Cairns.

Harrison, R. 1991. Molecular changes at speciation. *Annual Review of Ecology and Systematics* 22:281–308.

Harvey, P. H., R. M. May, and S. Nee. 1994. Phylogenies without fossils. *Evolution* 48:523–529.

Hasegawa, M., H. Kishino, and T. A. Yano. 1985. Dating of the human-ape splitting by a molecular clock of mitochondrial DNA. *Journal of Molecular Evolution* 22:160–174.

Hay, W. W., R. M. DeConto, C. N. Wold, K. M. Wilson, S. Voigt, M. Schulz, A. Rossby Wold, W.-C. Dullo, A. B. Ronov, A. N. Balukhovsky, and E. Söding. 1999. Alternative global Cretaceous paleogeography. Pages 1–47 in E. Barrera and C. C. Johnson, eds., *Evolution of the Cretaceous ocean-climate system.* Special Paper 332. Geological Society of America, Boulder, CO.

Hays, J. D., J. Imbrie, and N. J. Shackleton. 1976. Variations in the Earth's orbit: Pacemaker of the ice ages. *Science* 194:1121–1132.

Heard, S. B., and D. L. Hauser. 1995. Key evolutionary innovations and their ecological mechanisms. *Historical Biology* 10:151–173.

Heard, S. B., and A. O. Mooers. 2002. Signatures of random and selective mass extinctions in phylogenetic tree balance. *Systematic Biology* 51:889–897.

Hearnden, M. R., and R. G. Pearson. 1991. Habitat partitioning among mayflies (Insecta: Ephemeroptera) in an Australian tropical stream. *Oecologia* 87:91–101.

Heilbuth, J. C. 2000. Lower species richness in dioecious clades. *American Naturalist* 156:221–241.

Henderson, A. 1994. *The palms of the Amazon.* Oxford University Press, New York.

Henderson, I. M. 1991. Biogeography without area? *Australian Journal of Botany* 4:59–71.

Henderson-Sellers, A., H. Zhang, and W. Howe. 1996. Human and physical aspects of tropical deforestation. Pages 359–292 in T. W. Giamelluca and A. Henderson-Sellers, eds., *Climate change: Developing Southern Hemisphere perspectives.* John Wiley and Sons, Chichester.

Hershkovitz, P. 1969. The Recent mammals of the Neotropical region: A zoogeographic and ecological review. *Quarterly Review of Biology* 44:1–70.

———. 1977. *Living New World monkeys (Platyrrhini) with an introduction to primates.* Vol. 1. University of Chicago Press, Chicago.

Hewitt, G. M. 1996. Some genetic consequences of ice ages, and their role in divergence and speciation. *Biological Journal of the Linnean Society* 58:247–276.

———. 2000. The genetic legacy of the Quaternary ice ages. *Nature* 405:907–913.

Hiebeler, D. 1994. The Swarm simulation system and individual-based modelling. Pages 474–494 in J. M. Power, M. Strome, and T. C. Daniel, eds., *Decision support 2001: Advanced technology for natural resource management. 17th Annual Geographic Information Seminar and the Resource Technology '94 Symposium,* American Society for Photogrammetry and Remote Sensing.

Hilbert, D. W., and B. Ostendorf. 2001. The utility of empirical, artificial neural network approaches to modeling the distribution of regional to global vegetation in past, present, and future climates. *Ecological Modelling* 146:311–327.

Hilbert, D. W., B. Ostendorf, and M. S. Hopkins. 2001. Sensitivity of tropical forests to climate change in the humid tropics of north Queensland. *Austral Ecology* 26:590–603.

Hill, J. L., and R. A. Hill. 2001. Why are tropical rain forests so species rich? Classifying, reviewing and evaluating theories. *Progress in Physical Geography* 25:326–354.

Hill, L. 1984. New genera of Hypselosomatinae (Heteroptera: Schizopteridae) from Australia. *Australian Journal of Zoology,* suppl. ser. 103:1031–1055.

———. 1990a. Australian *Ogeria* Distant (Heteroptera: Schizopteridae). *Invertebrate Taxonomy* 4:697–720.

———. 1990b. A revision of Australian *Pachyplagia* Gross (Heteroptera: Schizopteridae). *Invertebrate Taxonomy* 3:605–617.

———. 1992. A revision of *Pachyplagioides* Gross (Heteroptera: Schizopteridae). *Invertebrate Taxonomy* 6:245–260.

Hill, R. S. 1982. The Eocene megafossil flora of Nerriga, New South Wales, Australia. *Palaeontographica* B 181:44–77.

———. 1986. Lauraceous leaves from the Eocene of Nerriga, New South Wales. *Alcheringa* 10:327–351.

———. 1987. Discovery of *Nothofagus* fruits of an important Tertiary pollen type. *Nature* 327:56–58.

———. 1988. A re-investigation of *Nothofagus muelleri* (Ett.) Paterson and *Cinnamomum nuytsii* Ett. from the Late Eocene of Vegetable Creek. *Alcheringa* 12:221–231.

———. 1989a. Early Tertiary leaves of the Menispermaceae from Nerriga, New South Wales. *Alcheringa* 13:37–44.

———. 1989b. New species of *Phyllocladus* (Podocarpaceae) macrofossils from southeastern Australia. *Alcheringa* 13:193–208.

———. 1990. Evolution of the modern high latitude Southern Hemisphere flora: Evidence from the Australian macrofossil record. Pages 31–42 in J. C. Douglas and D. C. Christophel, eds., *3rd IOP Conference, 1988, Proceedings.* IOP Publication no. 2. A-Z Printers and International Organisation of Palaeobotanists, Melbourne.

———. 1991. Leaves of *Eucryphia* (Eucryphiaceae) from Tertiary sediments in south-eastern Australia. *Australian Systematic Botany* 4:481–497.

———. 1992. Australian vegetation during the Tertiary: Macrofossil evidence. *The Beagle, Records of the Northern Territory Museum of Arts and Sciences* 9(1):1–10.

———. 1994. The history of selected Australian taxa. Pages 390–420 in R. S. Hill, ed., *The history of Australian vegetation: Cretaceous to Recent.* Cambridge University Press, Cambridge.

———. 1998. Fossil evidence for the onset of xeromorphy and scleromorphy in the Australian Proteaceae. *Australian Systematic Botany* 11:391–400.

Hill, R. S., and A. J. Bigwood. 1987. Tertiary gymnosperms from Tasmania: Araucariaceae. *Alcheringa* 11:325–335.

Hill, R. S., and R. J. Carpenter. 1991. Evolution of *Acmopyle* and *Dacrycarpus* (Podocarpaceae) foliage as inferred from macrofossils in south-eastern Australia. *Australian Systematic Botany* 4:449–479.

Hill, R. S., and D. C. Christophel. 1987. Tertiary leaves of the tribe Banksieae (Proteaceae) from south-eastern Australia. *Botanical Journal of the Linnean Society* 97:205–227.

———. 2001. Two new species of *Dacrydium* (Podocarpaceae) Based on vegetative fossils from Middle Eocene sediments at Nelly Creek, South Australia. *Australian Systematic Botany* 14:193–205.

Hill, R. S., and H. E. Merrifield. 1993. An early Tertiary macroflora from Westdale, south-western Australia. *Alcheringa* 17:285–326.

Hill, R. S., and M. Pole. 1992. Leaf and shoot morphology of extant *Afrocarpus, Nageia* and *Retrophyllum* (Podocarpaceae) species, and species with similar leaf arrangement, from Tertiary sediments in Australasia. *Australian Systematic Botany* 5:337–358.

Hill, R. S., and S. S. Whang. 1996. A new species of *Fitzroya* (Cupressaceae) from Oligocene sediments in north-western Tasmania. *Australian Systematic Botany* 9:867–875.

Hill, W. C. O. 1953. *Primates: Comparative anatomy and taxonomy.* Vol. 1, *Strepsirrhini.* University of Edinburgh Press, Edinburgh.

Hillis, D. M., B. K. Mable, and C. Moritz. 1996. Applications of molecular systematics:

The state of the field and a look at the future. Pages 515–543 in D. M. Hillis, C. Moritz, and B. K. Mable, eds., *Molecular systematics,* 2nd ed. Sinauer Associates, Sunderland, MA.

Hiscock, P., and A. P. Kershaw. 1992. Palaeoenvironments and prehistory of Australia's top end. Pages 43–75 in J. R. Dodson, ed., *The naive lands: Human/environment interactions in Australia and Oceania.* Longman Cheshire, Melbourne.

Hjort, J. 1914. *Fluctuations in the great fisheries of northern Europe viewed in the light of biological research.* Rapports et Procès-verbaux des Réunions, conseil international pour l'exploration de la Mer 20:1–228.

Hodges, S. A. 1997. Floral nectar spurs and diversification. *International Journal of Plant Sciences* 158:S81–S88.

Hodges, S. A., and M. L. Arnold. 1995. Spurring plant diversification: Are floral nectar spurs a key innovation? *Proceedings of the Royal Society of London* B 262:343–348.

Hoffmann, J. A. J. 1975. *Climatic atlas of South America.* WMO, UNESCO, Cartographia, Budapest, Hungary.

Holdgate, G. R., and I. R. K. Sluiter. 1991. Oligocene-Miocene marine incursions in the Latrobe Valley depression, onshore Gippsland Basin: Evidence, facies relationships and chronology. Pages 137–157 in M. A. J. Williams, P. DeDeckker, and A. P. Kershaw, eds., *The Cainozoic in Australia: A reappraisal of the evidence.* Special Publication no. 18. Geological Society of Australia, Sydney.

Holdridge, L. R. 1967. *Life zone ecology.* Tropical Science Center, San Jose, Costa Rica.

Holmes, B. 1996. The low-impact road. *New Scientist* (September 21):43.

Holmes, D. 2002. Where have all the forests gone? EASES Discussion Paper, World Bank, Washington, DC.

Holmes, W. B. K., and F. M. Holmes. 1992. Fossil flowers of *Ceratopetalum* Sm. (Family Cunoniaceae) from the Tertiary of eastern Australia. *Proceedings of the Linnean Society of New South Wales* 113:265–270.

Holmes, W. B. K., F. M. Holmes, and H. A. Martin. 1983. Fossil *Eucalyptus* remains from the Middle Miocene Chalk Mountain Formation, Warrumbungle Mountains, New South Wales. *Proceedings of the Linnean Society of New South Wales* 106:299–310.

Honess, P. E. 1996. Speciation among galagos (Primates, Galagidae) in Tanzanian forests. Ph.D. dissertation, Oxford Brooks University, Oxford.

Honess, P. E., and S. Bearder. 1998. Descriptions of the dwarf galago species of Tanzania. *African Primates* 2:75–78.

Hooghiemstra, H., and T. van der Hammen. 1998. Neogene and Quaternary development of the Neotropical forest: The forest refugia hypothesis, and a literature overview. *Earth-Science Reviews* 44:147–183.

Hoorn, C. 1993. Marine incursions and the influence of Andean tectonics on the Miocene depositional history of northwestern Amazonia: Results of a palynostratigraphic study. *Palaeogeography, Palaeoclimatology, Palaeoecology* 105:267–309.

———. 1994a. An environmental reconstruction of the palaeo-Amazon River system (Middle-Late Miocene, NW Amazonia). *Palaeogeography, Palaeoclimatology, Palaeoecology* 112:187–238.

———. 1994b. Fluvial palaeoenvironments in the intracratonic Amazonas Basin (Early Miocene-early Middle Miocene, Colombia). *Palaeogeography, Palaeoclimatology, Palaeoecology* 109:1–54.

Hopkins, M. S. 1990. Disturbance: The forest transformer. Pages 40–55 in L. J. Webb and J. Kikkawa, eds., *Australian tropical rainforests: Science-values-meaning.* CSIRO, Melbourne.

Hopkins, M. S., J. Ash, A. W. Graham, J. Head, and R. K. Hewett. 1993. Charcoal evidence of the spatial extent of *Eucalyptus* woodland expansions and rainforest contractions in North Queensland during the late Pleistocene. *Journal of Biogeography* 20:357–372.

Hopkins, M. S., J. Head, J. E. Ash, R. K. Hewett, and A. W. Graham. 1996. Evidence of a Holocene and continuing recent expansion of lowland rainforest in humid tropical North Queensland. *Journal of Biogeography* 23:737–745.

Horn, H. S. 1974. The ecology of secondary succession. *Annual Review of Ecology and Systematics* 5:25–37.

Horner-Devine, M. C., G. C. Daily, P. R. Ehrlich, and C. L. Boggs. 2003. Countryside biogeography of tropical butterflies. *Conservation Biology* 17:168–177.

Horsfall, N., and J. Hall. 1990. People and the rainforest: An archaeological perspective. Pages 33–39 in L. J. Webb and J. Kikkawa, eds., *Australian tropical rainforests: Science-values-meaning.* CSIRO, Melbourne.

Hoskin, C. J. Forthcoming. Australian microhylid frogs (*Cophixalus* and *Austrochaperina*): Phylogeny, new species, species redescription, new calls, distributional data and breeding notes. *Australian Journal of Zoology.*

Hovenkamp, P. 1997. Vicariance events, not areas, should be used in biogeographical analysis. *Cladistics* 13:67–79.

Howden, H. F. 1992. A revision of the Australian beetle genera *Eucanthus* Westwood, *Bolbobaineus* Howden & Cooper, *Australobolbus* Howden & Cooper and *Gilletinus* Boucomont (Scarabaeidae: Geotrupinae). *Invertebrate Taxonomy* 6:605–717.

Howden, H. F., and R. I. Storey. 2000. New Stereomerini and Rhyparini from Australia, Borneo and Fiji (Coleoptera: Scarabaeidae: Aphodiinae). *Memoirs of the Queensland Museum* 46:175–182.

Howe, H. F., and J. Smallwood. 1982. Ecology of seed dispersal. *Annual Review of Ecology and Systematics* 12:201–228.

Hubbell, S. P. 1979. Tree dispersion, abundance and diversity in a tropical dry forest. *Science* 203:1299–1309.

———. 1995. Towards a theory of biodiversity and biogeography on continuous landscapes. Pages 173–201 in G. R. Carmichael, G. E. Folk, and J. L. Schnoor, eds., *Preparing for global change: A Midwestern perspective.* Academic Publishing, Amsterdam.

———. 1997a. Niche assembly, dispersal limitation, and the maintenance of diversity in tropical tree communities and coral reefs. *Proceedings of the Eighth International Coral Reef Symposium* 1:387–396.

———. 1997b. A unified theory of biogeography and relative species abundance and its application to tropical rain forests and coral reefs. *Coral Reefs* 16, suppl.: S9–S21.

———. 1998. The maintenance of diversity in a Neotropical tree community: Conceptual issues, current evidence, and challenges ahead. Pages 17–44 in F. Dallmeier and J. A. Comiskey, eds., *Forest biodiversity research, monitoring and modeling: Conceptual issues and Old World case studies.* UNESCO, Paris, and Parthenon Publishing, Pearl River, NY.

———. 2001. *The unified neutral theory of biodiversity and biogeography.* Princeton University Press, Princeton, NJ.

———. 2003. Modes of speciation and the lifespans of species under neutrality: A response to the comment of Robert E. Ricklefs. *Oikos* 100:193–199.

Hubbell, S. P., J. A. Ahumada, R. Condit, and R. B. Foster. 2001. Local neighborhood effects on long-term survival of individual trees in a Neotropical forest. *Ecological Research* 16:859–875.

Hubbell, S. P., R. Condit, and R. B. Foster. 1990. Presence and absence of density dependence in a Neotropical tree community. *Philosophical Transactions of the Royal Society of London* B 330:269–281.

Hubbell, S. P., and R. B. Foster. 1983. Diversity of canopy trees in a Neotropical forest and implications for conservation. Pages 25–41 in S. L. Sutton, T. C. Whitmore, and A. C. Chadwick, eds., *Tropical rain forest: Ecology and management.* Blackwell Scientific Publications, Oxford.

———. 1986. Biology, chance, and history and the structure of tropical rain forest tree communities. Pages 314–329 in J. M. Diamond and T. J. Case, eds., *Community ecology.* Harper & Row, New York.

———. 1992. Short-term population dynamics of a Neotropical forest: Why ecological research matters to tropical conservation and management. *Oikos* 63:48–61.

Huber, B. A. 2000. *New World pholcid spiders (Araneae: Pholcidae): A revision at generic level.* Bulletin of the American Museum of Natural History, no. 254. American Museum of Natural History, New York.

———. 2001. *The pholcids of Australia (Araneae; Pholcidae): Taxonomy, biogeography, and relationships.* Bulletin of the American Museum of Natural History, no. 260. American Museum of Natural History, New York.

Huenneke, L. F., and P. M. Vitousek. 1990. Seedling and clonal recruitment of the invasive tree *Psidium cattleianum:* Implications for management of native Hawaiian forests. *Biological Conservation* 53:199–211.

Hugall, A., C. Moritz, A. Mousalli, and J. Stanisic. 2002. Reconciling paleodistribution models and comparative phylogeography in the Wet Tropics rainforest land snail *Gnarosophia bellendenkerensis. Proceedings of the National Academy of Sciences USA* 99 (9):6112–6117.

Humphries, C. J., and L. R. Parenti. 1999. *Cladistic biogeography.* 2nd ed. Academic Press, London.

Humphries, C. J., P. H. Williams, and R. I. Vane-Wright. 1995. Measuring biodiversity value for conservation. *Annual Review of Ecology and Systematics* 26:93–111.

Hundloe, T. 2000. Behind the Wet Tropics: Politics, institutions and sustainable development. Pages 150–167 in G. T. McDonald and M. B. Lane, eds., *Securing the Wet Tropics?* The Federation Press, Leichhardt, Australia.

Hunter, J. P. 1998. Key innovations and the ecology of macroevolution. *Trends in Ecology and Evolution* 13:31–36.

Huntley, B., and T. Webb, eds. 1988. *Vegetation history.* Kluwer, Dordrecht.

Hurwood, D. A., and J. M. Hughes. 2001. Historical interdrainage dispersal of eastern rainbowfish from the Atherton Tableland, north-eastern Australia. *Journal of Fish Biology* 58:1125–1136.

Hutchings, P., and P. Saenger. 1987. *Ecology of mangroves.* University of Queensland Press, St. Lucia, Australia.

Hutchinson, G. E. 1959. Homage to Santa Rosalia, or, Why are there so many kinds of animals? *American Naturalist* 93:145–159.

Hutchinson, M. F. 1987. Methods of generating weather variables. Pages 149–157 in A. H. Bunting, ed., *Agricultural environments: Characterisation, classification and mapping.* CAB International, Wallingford, U.K.

Hyland, B. P. M. 1989. A revision of Lauraceae in Australia (excluding *Cassytha*). *Australian Systematic Botany* 2:135–367.

Hyvärinen, H., and J. C. Ritchie. 1975. Pollen stratigraphy of Mackenzie pingo sediments, N.W.T., Canada. *Arctic and Alpine Research* 7:261–272.

Hyytiä, K., E. Kellomäki, and J. Koistinen, eds. 1983. *Suomen lintuatlas.* Lintutieto Oy, Helsinki, Finland.

Ibáñez, R., R. Condit, G. Angehr, S. Aguilar, T. Garcia, R. Martínez, A. Sanjur, R. Stallard, S. J. Wright, A. S. Rand, and S. Heckadon. 2002. An ecosystem report on the Panama Canal: Monitoring the status of the forest communities and the watershed. *Environmental Monitoring and Assessment* 80:65–95.

IBGE. 1997. Diagnóstico ambiental da Amazônia Legal. CD-ROM with GIS version of RADAM maps. Brazilian Institute for Geography and Statistics (IBGE), Brasília, Brazil.

INPE. 1996. *Deforestation estimates in the Brazilian Amazon, 1992–1994.* National Institute for Space Research (INPE), São Jose dos Campos, Brazil.

———. 1998. *Deforestation estimates in the Brazilian Amazon, 1995–1997.* National Institute for Space Research (INPE), São Jose dos Campos, Brazil.

———. 2000. *Deforestation estimates in the Brazilian Amazon, 1998–1999.* National Institute for Space Research (INPE), São Jose dos Campos, Brazil.

IPCC. 1996. *Climate change 1995: Impacts, adaptations and mitigation of climate change: Scientific technical analyses.* Intergovernmental Panel on Climate Change, Cambridge University Press, Cambridge.

Irion, G. 1978. Soil infertility in the Amazonian rain forest. *Naturwissenschaften* 65:515–519.

Irion, G., J. Müller, J. Nunes de Mello, and W. J. Junk. 1995. Quaternary geology of the Amazonian lowland. *Geo-Marine Letters* 15:172–178.

Irwin, D. M., T. D. Kocher, and A. C. Wilson. 1991. Evolution of the cytochrome *b* gene in mammals. *Journal of Molecular Evolution* 32:128–144.

Isawa, Y., T. Kubo, and K. Sato. 1995. Maintenance of forest species diversity and latitudinal gradient. *Vegetatio* 121:127–134.

Isern, A. R., J. A. McKenzie, and D. A. Feary. 1996. The role of sea-surface temperature as a control on carbonate platform development in the western Coral Sea. *Palaeogeography, Palaeoclimatology, Palaeoecology* 124:247–272.

Jablonski, D. 1998. Geographic variation in the molluscan recovery from the end-Cretaceous extinction. *Science* 279:1327–1330.

———. 2002. Survival without recovery after mass extinctions. *Proceedings of the National Academy of Sciences USA* 99:8139–8144.

Jackson, J. B. C. 1997. Reefs since Columbus. *Coral Reefs* 16, suppl.:S23–S32.

Jackson, W. D. 1968. Fire, air, water and earth: An elemental ecology of Tasmania. *Proceedings of the Ecological Society of Australia* 3:9–16.

Jacobs, M. 1988. *The tropical rain forest.* Springer, Berlin.

Jacobs, S. C., A. Larson, and J. M. Cheverud. 1995. Phylogenetic relationships and orthogenetic evolution of coat color among tamarins (genus *Saguinus*). *Systematic Biology* 44:515–532.

Jaffré, T., and J.-M. Veillon. 1990. Étude floristique et structurale de deux forêts denses humides sur roches ultrabasiques en Nouvelle-Calédonie. *Bulletin du Muséum National d'Histoire Naturelle,* 4th sér., sect. B. Adansonia 12:243–275.

Janos, D. P. 1980. Mycorrhizae influence tropical succession. *Biotropica,* suppl. 12(2):56–64.

———. 1983. Tropical mycorrhizas, nutrient cycles and plant growth. Pages 327–345 in S. L. Sutton, T. C. Whitmore, and A. C. Chadwick, eds., *Tropical rain forest: Ecology and management.* Blackwell Scientific Publications, Oxford.

Janson, C. H., and L. H. Emmons. 1990. Ecological structure of the nonflying mammal community at Cocha Cashu Biological Station, Manu National Park, Peru. Pages 314–338 in A. H. Gentry, ed., *Four Neotropical rainforests.* Yale University Press, New Haven, CT.

Janssen, C. R. 1967. A postglacial pollen diagram from a small *Typha* swamp in northwestern Minnesota, interpreted from pollen indicators and surface samples. *Ecological Monographs* 37:145–172.

Jansson, R., and M. Dynesius. 2002. The fate of clades in a world of recurrent climatic change: Milankovitch oscillations and evolution. *Annual Review of Ecology and Systematics* 33:741–777.

Janzen, D. H. 1970. Herbivores and the number of tree species in tropical forests. *American Naturalist* 104:501–528.

———. 1974. Tropical blackwater rivers, animals and mast fruiting by the Dipterocarpaceae. *Biotropica* 4:69–103.

———. 1986. The future of tropical biology. *Annual Review of Ecology and Systematics* 17:305–324.

Janzen, D. H., and P. S. Martin. 1982. Neotropical anachronisms: The fruits the gomphotheres ate. *Science* 215:19–27.

Jepson, P., J. Jarvie, K. MacKinnon, and K. A. Monk. 2001. The end for Indonesia's lowland forests? *Science* 292:859–861.

Jetz, W., and C. Rahbek. 2001. Geometric constraints explain much of the species richness pattern in African birds. *Proceedings of the National Academy of Sciences USA* 98:5661–5666.

———. 2002. Geographic range size and determinants of avian species richness. *Science* 297:1548–1551.

Jiggins, C. D., W. O. McMillan, W. Neukirchen, and J. Mallet. 1996. What can hybrid zones tell us about speciation? The case of *Heliconius erato* and *H. himera* (Lepidoptera: Nymphalidae). *Biological Journal of the Linnean Society* 59:221–242.

Jiggins, C. D., R. E. Naisbit, R. L. Coe, and J. Mallet. 2001. Reproductive isolation caused by color pattern mimicry. *Nature* 411:302–305.

Johansson, L. 2001. *Ten million trees later.* Deutsche Gesellschaft für Technische Zusammenarbeit, Eschborn, Germany.

Johns, A. D. 1988. Effects of selective timber extraction on rainforest structure and composition and some consequences for frugivores and folivores. *Biotropica* 20 (1):31–37.

Johns, A. G. 1997. *Timber production and biodiversity conservation in tropical rain forests.* Cambridge University Press, Cambridge.

Johnson, C. N. 1998. Species extinction and the relationship between distribution and abundance. *Nature* 384:272–274.

———, ed. 2002. *Feral pigs: Pest status and prospects for control.* Proceedings of a feral pig workshop, James Cook University, Cairns, March 1999. Cooperative research Centre for Tropical Rainforest Ecology and Management, Cairns.

Johnson, K. P., F. R. Adler, and J. L. Cherry. 2000. Genetic and phylogenetic consequences of island biogeography. *Evolution* 54:387–396.

Johnson, M. P., and P. H. Raven. 1973. Species number and endemism: The Galapagos archipelago revisited. *Science* 179:893–895.

Johnson, N. 1995. *Biodiversity in the balance: Approaches to setting geographic conservation priorities.* Biodiversity Support Program, Washington, DC.

Johnson, N. K., J. V. Remsen, and C. Cicero. 1999. Resolution of the debate over species concepts in ornithology: A new comprehensive biological species concept. Pages 1470–1482 in N. J. Adams and R. H. Slotow, eds., Proceedings XXII International Ornithological Congress, Durban. BirdLife South Africa, Johannesburg.

Johnson, P. L., and D. M. Atwood. 1970. Aerial sensing and photographic study of the El Verde rain forest. Pages B63–78 in H. T. Odum, ed., *A tropical rain forest.* Division of Technical Information, U.S. Atomic Energy Commission, Washington, DC.

Johnsson, M. J., and R. F. Stallard. 1989. Physiographic controls on the composition of sediments derived from volcanic and sedimentary terrains on Barro Colorado Island, Panama. *Journal of Sedimentary Petrology* 59:768–781.

Jolly, D., and A. Haxeltine. 1997. Effect of low glacial atmospheric CO_2 on tropical African montane vegetation. *Science* 276:786–788.

Jones, C. B. 1987. Evidence supporting the Pleistocene forest refuge hypothesis for primates. *Biotropica* 19:373–375.

Jørgensen, P. M., and S. León-Yánez. 1999. Catalogue of the vascular plants of Ecuador. Missouri Botanical Garden Press, St. Louis.

Joseph, L., and C. Moritz. 1993. Phylogeny and historical aspects of the ecology of eastern Australian scrubwrens: Evidence from mitochondrial DNA. *Molecular Ecology* 2:161–170.

Joseph, L., C. Moritz, and A. Hugall. 1995. Molecular support for vicariance as a source of diversity in rainforest. *Proceedings of the Royal Society of London* B 260:177–182.

Judd, W. S., R. W. Sanders, and M. J. Donoghue. 1994. Angiosperm family pairs: Preliminary phylogenetic analyses. *Harvard Papers in Botany* 5. Harvard University Herbaria, Cambridge, MA.

Kahn, J. R., and J. A. McDonald. 1997. The role of economic factors in tropical deforestation. Pages 13–28 in W. F. Laurance and R. O. Bierregaard Jr., eds., *Tropical forest remnants: Ecology, management, and conservation of fragmented communities.* University of Chicago Press, Chicago.

Kalko, E. K. V. 1995. Echolocation signal design, foraging habitats, and guild structure in six Neotropical sheath-tailed bats (Emballonuridae). Pages 259–273 in P. A. Racey and S. M. Swift, eds., *Ecology, evolution and behaviour of bats.* Symposia of the Zoological Society of London, no. 67. Oxford: Clarendon Press.

Kalko, E. K. V., C. O. Handley Jr., and D. Handley. 1996. Organization, diversity, and long-term dynamics of a Neotropical bat community. Pages 503–553 in M. Cody and J. Smallwood, eds., *Long-term studies of vertebrate communities.* Academic Press, San Diego.

Kalliola, R., A. Linna, M. Puhakka, J. Salo, and M. Räsänen. 1993. Mineral nutrients from fluvial sediments in the Peruvian Amazon. *Catena* 20:333–349.

Kammesheidt, L., P. Koehler, and A. Huth. 2001. Sustainable timber harvesting in Venezuela: A modeling approach. *Journal of Applied Ecology* 38:756–770.

Kangas, P. 1990. Deforestation and diversity of life zones in the Brazilian Amazon: A map analysis. *Ecological Modeling* 49:267–275.

Kapos, V. 1989. Effects of isolation on the water status of forest patches in the Brazilian Amazon. *Journal of Tropical Ecology* 5:173–185.

Karanth, K. U., and M. E. Sunquist. 1992. Population structure, density and biomass of large herbivores in the tropical forests of Nagarahole, India. *Journal of Tropical Biology* 8:21–35.

Kareiva, P., and U. Wennergren. 1995. Connecting landscape patterns to ecosystem and population processes. *Nature* 373:299–302.

Karlin, S., and J. MacGregor. 1972. Addendum to a paper by W. Ewens. *Theoretical Population Biology* 3:113–116.

Karr, J. R. 1976. Within- and between-habitat avian diversity in African and Neotropical lowland habitats. *Ecological Monographs* 46:457–481.

Kasischke, E. S., J. M. Melack, and M. C. Dobson. 1997. The use of imaging radars for ecological applications: A review. *Remote Sensing of the Environment* 59:141–156.

Kastner, T. P., and M. A. Goñi. 2003. Constancy in the vegetation of the Amazon Basin during the late Pleistocene: Evidence from the organic matter composition of Amazon deep sea fan sediments. *Geology* 31:291–294.

Katz, M. E., and K. G. Miller. 1993. Neogene subsidence along the northeastern Australian margin: Benthic foraminiferal evidence. *Proceedings of the Ocean Drilling Program, Scientific Results* 133:75–92.

Kauffman, J. B. 1991. Survival by sprouting following fire in tropical forests of the eastern Amazon. *Biotropica* 23:219–224.

Kauffman, S., G. Paredes Arce, and R. Marquina. 1998. Suelos de la zona de Iquitos. Pages 139–229 in R. Kalliola and S. Flores Paitán, eds., *Geoecología y desarrollo Amazónico: Estudio integrado en la zona de Iquitos, Perú.* Annales Universitatis Turkuensis Ser A II, vol. 114. University of Turku, Finland.

Kay, K. M., and D. W. Schemske. 2003. Pollinator assemblages and visitation rates for 11 species of Neotropical *Costus* (Costaceae). *Biotropica* 35:198–207.

Keefe, R. L. 2000. Windows on an ancient forest: The palaeoecology of the Early Eocene flora of Brandy Creek Mine, Eastern Highlands, Victoria. B.Sc. (Hons.) thesis, Victoria University of Technology, Melbourne.

Keith, S., E. K. Urban, and C. H. Fry. 1992. *The birds of Africa.* Vol. 4. Academic Press, New York.

Kellman, M., R. Tackaberry, and J. Meave. 1996. The consequences of prolonged fragmentation: Lessons from tropical gallery forests. Pages 37–57 in J. Schelhas and R. Greenberg, eds., *Forest patches in tropical landscapes.* Island Press, Washington, DC.

Kelly, D. 1994. The evolutionary ecology of mast seeding. *Trends in Ecology and Evolution* 9:465–470.

Kemp, E. M. 1978. Tertiary climatic evolution and vegetation history in the southeast Indian Ocean region. *Palaeogeography, Palaeoclimatology, Palaeoecology* 24:169–208.

———. 1981. Tertiary palaeogeography and the evolution of Australian climate. Pages 31–50 in A. Keast, ed., *Ecological Biogeography of Australia.* Dr. W. Junk, The Hague.

Kendall, R. L. 1969. An ecological history of the Lake Victoria Basin. *Ecological Monographs* 39:121–176.

Kennett, J. P. 1995. A review of polar climatic evolution during the Neogene, based on the marine sediment record. Pages 49–64 in E. S. Vrba, G. H. Denton, T. C. Partridge, and C. Burckle, eds., *Paleoclimate and evolution with emphasis on human origins.* Yale University Press, New Haven, CT.

Kerr, J. T. 1997. Species richness, endemism and the choice of areas for conservation. *Conservation Biology* 11:1094–1100.

Kershaw, A. P. 1970. Pollen morphological variation in the Casuarinaceae. *Pollen et Spores* 12:145–161.

———. 1973. The numerical analysis of modern pollen spectra from north-east Queensland rainforests. Pages 191–199 in J. E. Glover and G. Playford, eds., *Mesozoic and Cainozoic palynology: Essays in honour of Isabell Cookson.* Special Publication no. 4. Geological Society of Australia, Canberra.

———. 1976. A late Pleistocene and Holocene pollen diagram from Lynch's Crater, northeastern Queensland, Australia. *New Phytologist* 77:469–498.

———. 1978. Record of the last interglacial-glacial cycle from north-eastern Queensland. *Nature* 272:159–161.

———. 1983. A Holocene pollen diagram from Lynch's crater, north-eastern Queensland, Australia. *New Phytologist* 94:669–682.

———. 1985. An extended late Quaternary vegetation record from northeastern Queensland and its implications for the seasonal tropics of Australia. Pages 179–189 in M. G. Ridpath and L. K. Corbett, eds., *Ecology of the Wet-Dry Tropics.* Proceedings of the Ecological Society of Australia, vol. 13. Ecological Society of Australia, Canberra.

———. 1986. Climatic change and Aboriginal burning in north-east Australia during the last two glacial/interglacial cycles. *Nature* 322:47–49.

———. 1988. Australasia. Pages 237–306 in B. Huntley and T. Webb III, eds., *Vegetation history.* Kluwer, New York.

———. 1994. Pleistocene vegetation of the humid tropics of northeastern Queensland, Australia. *Palaeogeography, Palaeoclimatology, Palaeoecology* 109:399–412.

———. 1996. A bioclimatic analysis of Early to Middle Miocene brown coal floras, Latrobe Valley, southeastern Australia. *Australian Journal of Botany* 45(3):373–383.

Kershaw, A. P., and D. Bulman. 1994. The relationship between modern pollen samples and environment in the humid tropics region of northeastern Australia. *Review of Palaeobotany and Palynology* 83:83–96.

Kershaw, A. P., and B. P. M. Hyland. 1975. Pollen transfer and periodicity in a rainforest situation. *Review of Palaeobotany and Palynology* 19:129–138.

Kershaw, A. P., H. A. Martin, and J. McEwen Mason. 1994. The Neogene: A period of transition. Pages 435–462 in R. Hill, ed., *Australian vegetation history: Cretaceous to Recent.* Cambridge University Press, Cambridge.

Kershaw, A. P., and M. S. McGlone. 1995. The Quaternary history of the Southern conifers. Pages 30–63 in N. Enright and R. S. Hill, eds., *The ecology of the southern conifers.* Melbourne University Press, Melbourne.

Kershaw, A. P., G. M. McKenzie, and A. McMinn. 1993. A Quaternary vegetation history of northeastern Queensland from pollen analysis of ODP site 820. *Proceedings of Ocean Drilling Program, Scientific Results* 133:107–114.

Kershaw, A. P., and H. A. Nix. 1988. Quantitative palaeoclimatic estimates from pollen data using bioclimatic profiles of extant taxa. *Journal of Biogeography* 15:589–602.

———. 1989. The use of climatic envelopes for estimation of quantitative palaeoclimatic estimates. Pages 78–85 in T. H. Donnelly and R. J. Wasson, eds., CLIMANZ 3. CSIRO Division of Water Resources, Canberra.

Kershaw, A. P., and I. R. Sluiter. 1982. Late Cainozoic pollen spectra from the Atherton Tableland, northeastern Australia. *Australian Journal of Botany* 30:279–295.

Kershaw, A. P., and K. M. Strickland. 1990. A 10 year pollen trapping record from northeastern Australia. *Review of Palaeobotany and Palynology* 64:281–288.

Kesselring, J., and H. Ebert. 1982. Relação das borboletas encontradas na "Mata do Buraquinho," João Pessoa, Estado da Paraíba, Brasil. *Revista nordestina de Biologia* 2:105–118.

Kikkawa, J., G. B. Monteith, and G. Ingram. 1981. Cape York Peninsula: Major region of faunal interchange. Pages 1697–1736 in A. Keast, ed., *Ecological biogeography of Australia.* Dr. W. Junk, London.

Kiladis, G. N., and H. F. Diaz. 1989. Global climatic anomalies associated with extremes in the Southern Oscillation. *Journal of Climate* 2:1069–1090.

Kilburn, P. D. 1966. Analysis of the species-area relation. *Ecology* 47:831–843.

Kim, S.-C., D. J. Crawford, J. Francisco-Ortega, and A. Santos-Guerra. 1996. A common origin for woody *Sonchus* and five related genera in the Macronesian islands: Molecular evidence for extensive radiation. *Proceedings of the National Academy of Sciences, USA* 93:7743–7748.

Kimura, M., and T. Ohta. 1971. *Theoretical aspects of population genetics.* Princeton University Press, Princeton, NJ.

King, D. A. 1994. Influence of light level on the growth and morphology of saplings in a Panamanian forest. *American Journal of Botany* 81:948–957.

Kingdon, J. 1971. *East African mammals.* Vol. 1. Academic Press, London.

———. 1979. *East African mammals.* Vol. 3B, *Large mammals.* University of Chicago Press, Chicago.

———. 1989. *Island Africa: The evolution of Africa's rare animals and plants.* Princeton University Press, Princeton, NJ.

———. 1997. *African mammals.* Academic Press, San Diego.

Kingsland, S. E. 1985. *Modeling nature: Episodes in the history of population ecology.* University of Chicago Press, Chicago.

Kinnaird, M. F., and T. G. O'Brien. 1998. Ecological effects of wildfire on lowland rainforest in Sumatra. *Conservation Biology* 12 (5):954–956.

Kinnaird, M. F., E. W. Sanderson, T. G. O'Brien, H. T. Wibisono, and G. Woolmer. 2003. Deforestation trends in a tropical landscape and implications for endangered large mammals. *Conservation Biology* 17 (1):245–257.

Kira, T., K. Shinozaki, and K. Hozumi. 1969. Structure of forest canopies as related to their primary productivity. *Plant and Cell Physiology* 10:129–142.

Kirejtshuk, A. G., and J. F. Lawrence. 1992. Cychramptodini, a new tribe of Nitidulidae (Coleoptera) from Australia. *Journal of the Australian Entomological Society* 31:29–46.

Kitajima, K. 1994. Relative importance of photosynthetic rates and allocation patterns as correlates of seedling shade tolerance of 13 tropical trees. *Oecologia* 98:419–428.

Klicka, J., and R. M. Zink. 1997. The importance of recent ice ages in speciation: A failed paradigm. *Science* 277:1666–1669.

Knowlton, N., L. A. Weigt, L. A. Solórzano, D. K. Mills, and E. Bermingham. 1993. Divergence in proteins, mitochondrial DNA, and reproductive compatibility across the isthmus of Panama. *Science* 260:1629–1632.

Koechlin, J., J.-L. Guillaumet, and P. Morat. 1974. *Flore et Végétation de Madagascar.* Cramer, Vaduz, Liechtenstein.

Koehler, P., and A. Huth. 1998. The effects of tree species grouping in tropical rainforest modelling: Simulations with the individual-based model FORMIND. *Ecological Modelling* 109:301–321.

Koenig, W. D., R. L. Mumme, W. J. Carmen, and M. T. Stanback. 1994. Acorn production by oaks in central coastal California: Variation within and among years. *Ecology* 75:99–109.

Kohler, P., T. Ditzer, R. C. Ong, and A. Huth. 2001. Comparison of measured and simulated growth on permanent plots in Sabah's rain forests. *Forest Ecology and Management* 144:101–111.

Kohn, B. P., and A. J. W. Gleadow. 1994. Thermo-tectonic evolution of the Snowy Mountains: An apatite fission track study. *Geological Society of Australia Abstracts* 36:8.

Koppen, W. 1936. Das geographische system der Klimate. In W. Koppen and W. Geiger, eds., *Handbuch der Klimatologie,* Vol. 1, Teil C. Gebruder Borntraeger, Berlin.

Koppen, W., and W. Geiger, eds. 1936. *Handbuch der Klimatologie.* Vol. 1, Teil C. Gebruder Borntraeger, Berlin.

Kovach Computing Services. 1995–2000. *Multi-Variate Statistical Package.* Version 3.12a. Pentraeth, Anglesey, Wales.

Kramer, R. A., and C. P. van Schaik. 1997. Preservation paradigms and tropical rain forests. Pages 3–14 in R. A. Kramer, C. P. van Schaik, and J. Johnson, eds., *Last stand: Protected areas and the defense of tropical biodiversity.* Oxford University Press, New York.

Kramer, R. A., C. P. van Schaik, and J. Johnson, eds. 1997. *Last stand: Protected areas and the defense of tropical biodiversity.* Oxford University Press. New York.

Kremen, C. 1992. Assessing the indicator properties of species assemblages for natural areas monitoring. *Ecological Applications* 2:203–217.

———. 1994. Biological inventory using target taxa: A case study of the butterflies of Madagascar. *Ecological Applications* 4:407–422.

Kupfer, J. A. 1995. Landscape ecology and biogeography. *Progress in Physical Geography* 19:18–34.

Labandeira, C. C., K. R. Johnson, and P. Wilf. 2002. Impact of the terminal Cretaceous event on plant-insect associations. *Proceedings of the National Academy of Sciences USA* 99:2061–2066.

Lake, P. S., L. A. Barmuta, A. J. Boulton, I. C. Campbell, and R. M. St. Clair. 1985. Australian streams and Northern Hemisphere stream ecology: Comparisons and problems. Pages 61–82 in J. R. Dodson and M. Westoby, eds., *Are Australian ecosystems different?* Proceedings of the Ecological Society of Australia, vol. 14. Ecological Society of Australia, Canberra.

Lake, P. S., E. S. G. Schreiber, B. J. Milne, and R. G. Pearson. 1994. Species richness in streams: Patterns over time, with stream size and with latitude. *Verhandlungen International Verein Limnologie* 25:1822–1826.

Lamas, G., R. K. Robbins, and D. J. Harvey. 1996. Mariposas del Alto Rio Napo, Loreto, Peru (Lepidoptera: Papilionoidea y Hesperioidea). *Revista Peruana de Entomologia* 39:63–74.

Lande, R. 1981. Models of speciation by sexual selection on polygenic traits. *Proceedings of the National Academy of Sciences USA* 78:3721–3725.

Lang, G. E., and D. H. Knight. 1983. Tree growth, mortality, recruitment and canopy gap formation during a 10-year period in a tropical forest. *Ecology* 64:1075–1080.

Lange, R. T. 1978. Carpological evidence for fossil *Eucalyptus* and other Leptospermeae (subfamily Leptospermoideae of Myrtaceae) from a Tertiary deposit in the South Australian arid zone. *Australian Journal of Botany* 26:221–233.

———. 1982. Australian Tertiary vegetation, evidence and interpretation. Pages 44–89 in J. M. G. Smith, ed., *A history of Australasian vegetation.* McGraw Hill, Sydney.

Lara, M. C., and J. L. Patton. 2000. Evolutionary diversification of spiny rats (genus *Trinomys,* Rodentia, Echimyidae) in the Atlantic Forest of Brazil. *Zoological Journal of the Linnean Society* 130:661–686.

Lara, M. C., J. L. Patton, and M. N. F. da Silva. 1996. The simultaneous diversification of South American echimyid rodents (Hystricognathis) based on complete cytochrome *b* sequence. *Molecular Phylogenetics and Evolution* 5:403–413.

Larson, D. J., and R. I. Storey. 1994. *Carabhydrus mubboonus,* a new species of rheophilic water beetle (Coleoptera: Dytiscidae) from Queensland, Australia. *Canadian Entomologist* 126:895–906.

Latham, R. E., and R. E. Ricklefs. 1993a. Continental comparisons of temperate-zone tree species diversity. Pages 294–314 in R. E. Ricklefs and D. Schluter, eds., *Species diversity: Historical and geographical perspectives.* University of Chicago Press, Chicago.

———. 1993b. Global patterns of tree species richness in moist forests: Energy-diversity theory does not account for variation in species richness. *Oikos* 67:325–333.

Laurance, W. F. 1990. Comparative responses of five arboreal marsupials to tropical forest fragmentation. *Journal of Mammalogy* 71:641–653.

———. 1991. Ecological correlates of extinction proneness in Australian tropical rainforest mammals. *Conservation Biology* 5:79–89.

———. 1994. Rainforest fragmentation and the structure of small mammal communities in tropical Queensland. *Biological Conservation* 69:23–32.

———. 1998. A crisis in the making: Responses of Amazonian forests to land use and climate change. *Trends in Ecology and Evolution* 13:411–415.

———. 1999. Reflections on the tropical deforestation crisis. *Biological Conservation* 91:109–117.

———. 2000. Do edge effects occur over large spatial scales? *Trends in Ecology and Evolution* 15:134–135.

———. 2001. Tropical logging and human invasions. *Conservation Biology* 15:4–5.

Laurance, W. F., A. Albernaz, and C. Da Costa. 2001. Is deforestation accelerating in the Brazilian Amazon? *Environmental Conservation* 28:305–311.

Laurance, W. F., A. K. M. Albernaz, G. Schroth, P. M. Fearnside, E. Ventincinque, and C. Da Costa. 2002. Predictors of deforestation in the Brazilian Amazon. *Journal of Biogeography* 29:737–748.

Laurance, W. F., and R. O. Bierregaard Jr., eds. 1997. *Tropical forest remnants: Ecology, management, and conservation of fragmented communities.* University of Chicago Press, Chicago.

Laurance, W. F., M. A. Cochrane, S. Bergen, P. M. Fearnside, P. Delamonica, C. Barber, S. D'Angelo, and T. Fernandes. 2001. The future of the Brazilian Amazon. *Science* 291: 438–439.

Laurance, W. F., P. Delamonica, S. G. Laurance, H. Vasconcelos, and T. E. Lovejoy. 2000. Rainforest fragmentation kills big trees. *Nature* 404:836.

Laurance, W. F., and P. M. Fearnside. 1999. Amazon burning. *Trends in Ecology and Evolution* 14:457.

Laurance, W. F., P. M. Fearnside, M. A. Cochrane, S. D'Angelo, S. Bergen, and P. Delamonica. 2001. Development of the Brazilian Amazon. *Science* 292:1652–1654.

Laurance, W. F., L. V. Ferreira, J. M. Rankin-de Merona, and S. G. Laurance. 1998a. Rain forest fragmentation and the dynamics of Amazonian tree communities. *Ecology* 79:2032–2040.

Laurance, W. F., L. V. Ferreira, J. M. Rankin-de Merona, S. G. Laurance, R. W. Hutchings, and T. E. Lovejoy. 1998b. Effects of forest fragmentation on recruitment patterns in Amazonian tree communities. *Conservation Biology* 12:460–464.

Laurance, W. F., S. G. Laurance, and P. Delamonica. 1998. Tropical forest fragmentation and greenhouse gas emissions. *Forest Ecology and Management* 110:173–180.

Laurance, W. F., S. G. Laurance, L. V. Ferreira, J. Rankin-de Merona, C. Gascon, and T. E. Lovejoy. 1997. Biomass collapse in Amazonian forest fragments. *Science* 278:1117–1118.

Laurance, W. F., T. E. Lovejoy, H. L. Vasconcelos, E. M. Bruna, R. K. Didham, P. C. Stouffer, C. Gascon, R. O. Bierregaard, S. G. Laurance, and E. Sampaio. 2002. Ecosystem decay of Amazonian forest fragments: A 22-year investigation. *Conservation Biology* 16:605–618.

Laurance, W. F., and G. B. Williamson. 2001. Positive feedbacks among forest fragmentation, drought, and climate change in the Amazon. *Conservation Biology* 15:1529–1535.

Laurance, W. F., G. B. Williamson, P. Delamônica, A. Oliveira, T. E. Lovejoy, C. Gascon, and L. Pohl. 2001. Effects of a strong drought on Amazonian forest fragments and edges. *Journal of Tropical Ecology* 17:771–785.

Lawrence, J. F., D. H. Kistner, and J. M. Pasteels. 1990. A new genus and three new species of termitophilous Aderidae (Coleoptera) from Australia, Papua New Guinea and the Philippines, with notes on their biology. *Invertebrate Taxonomy* 4:643–654.

Lawrence, J. F., and J. B. Stribling. 1992. A new genus of Ptilodactylidae (Coleoptera: Elateriformia) from North Queensland, with description of the presumed larva. *Journal of the Australian Entomological Society* 31:19–27.

Ledru, M. P. 1993. Late Quaternary environmental and climatic changes in central Brazil. *Quaternary Research* 39:90–98.

Ledru, M. P., J. Bertaux, A. Sifeddine, and K. Suguio. 1998. Absence of last glacial maximum records in lowland tropical forests. *Quaternary Research* 49:233–237.

Ledru, M. P., R. C. Cordeiro, J. M. Landim, L. Martin, P. Mourguiart, A. Sifeddine, and B. Turcq. 2001. Late-glacial cooling in Amazonia inferred from pollen at Lagoa do Caçó, Northern Brazil. *Quaternary Research* 55:47–56.

Lee, H. S., S. J. Davies, J. V. LaFrankie, S. Tan, T. Yamakura, A. Itoh, and P. S. Ashton. 2002. Floristic and structural diversity of 52 hectares of mixed dipterocarp forest in Lambir Hills National Park, Sarawak, Malaysia. *Journal of Tropical Forest Science* 14:379–400.

Lee, N. S., T. Sang, D. J. Crawford, S. H. Yeau, and S.-C. Kim. 1996. Molecular divergence between disjunct taxa in eastern Asia and eastern North America. *American Journal of Botany* 83:1373–1378.

Leigh, E. G. Jr. 1982. Introduction: Why are there so many kinds of tropical trees? Pages 63–66 in E. G. Leigh Jr., A. S. Rand, and D. M. Windsor, eds., *The ecology of a tropical forest.* Smithsonian Institution Press, Washington, DC.

———. 1990. Community diversity and environmental stability: A re-examination. *Trends in Ecology and Evolution* 5:340–344.

———. 1994. Do insect pests promote mutualism among tropical trees? *Journal of Ecology* 82:677–680.

———. 1999. *Tropical forest ecology.* Oxford University Press, New York.

Leigh, E. G. Jr., J.-F. Cosson, J.-M. Pons, and P.-M. Forget. 2002. En quoi l'étude des îlots forestiers permet-elle de mieux connaître le fonctionnement de la forêt tropicale? *Revue d'Écologie* (*La Terre et la Vie*) 57:181–194.

Leigh, E. G. Jr., and G. J. Vermeij. 2002. Does natural selection organize ecosystems for the maintenance of high productivity and diversity? *Philosophical Transactions of the Royal Society of London* B 357:709–718.

Leigh, E. G. Jr., S. J. Wright, F. E. Putz, and E. A. Herre. 1993. The decline of tree diversity on newly isolated tropical islands: A test of a null hypothesis and some implications. *Evolutionary Ecology* 7:76–102.

Leigh, E. G. Jr., and D. M. Windsor. 1982. Forest production and regulation of primary consumers on Barro Colorado Island. Pages 111–122 in E. G. Leigh Jr., A. S. Rand, and D. M. Windsor, eds., *The ecology of a tropical forest.* Smithsonian Institution Press, Washington, DC.

Leigh, E. G. Jr., D. M. Windsor, A. S. Rand, and R. B. Foster. 1990. The impact of the "El

Niño" drought of 1982–83 on a Panamánian semideciduous forest. Pages 473–486 in P. W. Glynn, ed., *Global ecological consequences of the 1982–83 El Niño-Southern Oscillation.* Elsevier, Amsterdam.

Leighton, M., and N. Wirawan. 1986. Catastrophic drought and fire in Borneo tropical rain forest associated with the 1982–1983 El Niño Southern Oscillation Event. Pages 75–102 in G. T. Prance, ed., *Tropical rain forests and the world atmosphere.* American Association for the Advancement of Science Selected Symposium 101. Westview Press, Boulder, CO.

Leitch, I. J., and M. D. Bennett. 1997. Polyploidy in angiosperms. *Trends in Plant Science* 2:470–476.

Lessios, H. A. 1984. Possible prezygotic reproductive isolation in sea urchins separated by the isthmus of Panama. *Evolution* 38:1144–1148.

———. 1998. The first stages of speciation as seen in organisms separated by the isthmus of Panama. Pages 186–201 in D. J. Howard and S. H. Berlocher, eds., *Endless forms: Species and speciation.* Oxford University Press, New York.

Letouzey, R. 1968. *Etude phytogeographique du Cameroun.* Lechevalier, Paris.

Levin, S. A. 1992. The problem of pattern and scale in ecology. *Ecology* 73:1943–1967.

Lewin, R. 1986. Supply-side ecology. *Science* 234:25–27.

Lewontin, R. C. 1974. *The genetic basis of evolutionary change.* Columbia University Press, New York.

Leyden, B. W. 1984. Guatemalan forest synthesis after Pleistocene aridity. *Proceedings of the National Academy of Sciences USA* 81:4856–4859.

Leyden, B. W., M. Brenner, D. A. Hodell, and J. H. Curtis. 1993. Late Pleistocene climate in the Central American lowlands: Climate change in continental isotope records. Pages 165–178 in P. K. Swart et al., eds., *Climate change in continental isotopic records.* Geophysical Monographs, 78. American Geophysical Union, Washington, DC.

Li, H. L. 1952. Floristic relationships between eastern Asia and eastern North America. *Transactions of the American Philosophical Society,* n.s., 42:371–429.

Li, S., and K. T. Adair. 1994. Species pools in eastern Asia and North America. *Sida* 16:281–299.

Lieberman, D. 1996. Demography of tropical tree seedlings: A review. Pages 131–138 in M. D. Swaine, ed., *The ecology of tropical forest tree seedlings.* Man and the Biosphere Series, vol. 17. UNESCO, Paris; Parthenon, New York.

Lieberman, D., G. S. Hartshorn, M. Lieberman, and R. Peralta. 1990. Forest dynamics at the La Selva biological station, 1969–1985. Pages 509–521 in A. Gentry, ed., *Four Neotropical rainforests.* Yale University Press, New Haven, CT.

Lieberman, D., and M. Lieberman. 1987. Forest tree growth and dynamics at La Selva, Costa Rica (1969–1982). *Journal of Tropical Ecology* 3:347–358.

Lieberman, D., M. Lieberman, G. S. Hartshorn, and R. Peralta. 1985. Growth rates and age-size relationships of tropical wet forest trees in Costa Rica. *Journal of Tropical Ecology* 1:97–100.

Lieberman, M., D. Lieberman, G. Hartshorn, and R. Peralta. 1985. Small-scale altitudinal variation in lowland tropical forest vegetation. *Journal of Ecology* 73:505–516.

Liebherr, J. K., and A. E. Hajek. 1990. A cladistic test of the taxon cycle and taxon pulse hypotheses. *Cladistics* 6:39–59.

Linacre, E. 1992. *Climate data and resources: A reference and guide.* Routledge, London.

Lindenmayer, D. L., B. G. Mackey, and H. A. Nix. 1996. The bioclimatic domains of four species of commercially important eucalypts from south-eastern Australia. *Australian Forestry* 59(2):74–89.

Lindsay, J. M., and N. F. Alley. 1995. St Vincent Basin. Pages 208–217 in J. H. Drexel and W. V. Preiss, eds., *The geology of South Australia,* vol. 2, *The Phanerozoic.* Bulletin 54. South Australian Geological Survey, Adelaide.

Liu, K-b., and P. A. Colinvaux. 1985. Forest changes in the Amazon Basin during the last glacial maximum. *Nature* 318:556–557.

Livingstone, D. A. 1975. Late Quaternary climatic change in Africa. *Annual Review of Ecology and Systematics* 6:249–280.

———. 1993. Evolution of African climate. Pages 455–472 in P. Goldblatt, ed., *Biological relationships between Africa and South America.* Yale University Press, New Haven, CT.

Livingstone, D. A., and T. Van der Hammen. 1978. Palaeogeography and palaeoclimatology. Pages 61–90 in *Tropical forest ecosystems: A state-of-knowledge report,* UNESCO, Paris.

Llorente-B., J., A. Garcez, and A. Luis-M. 1986. El Paisaje Teoceleno. 4. Las mariposas de Jalapa-Teocelo, Veracruz. *Teocelo* 3:14–37.

Lloyd, P. J., and A. P. Kershaw. 1997. Late Quaternary vegetation and Early Holocene quantitative climate estimates from Morwell Swamp, Latrobe Valley, South-eastern Australia. *Australian Journal of Botany* 45:549–563.

Loescher, H. W., S. F. Oberbauer, H. L. Gholz, and D. B. Clark. 2003. Environmental controls on net ecosystem-level carbon exchange and productivity in a Central American tropical wet forest. *Global Change Biology* 9:396–412.

Loiselle, B. A., and J. G. Blake. 1991. Temporal variation in birds and fruits along an elevational gradient in Costa Rica. *Ecology* 73:180–193.

Lombard, A. T., R. M. Cowling, R. L. Pressey, and P. J. Mustart. 1997. Reserve selection in a species rich and fragmented landscape on the Agulhas plain, South Africa. *Conservation Biology* 11:1101–1116.

Longman, K. A., and J. Jenik. 1992. Forest-savanna boundaries: General considerations. Pages 3–20 in P. A. Furley, J. Proctor, and J. A. Ratter, eds., *Nature and dynamics of forest-savanna boundaries.* Chapman & Hall, New York.

Loreau, M. 2000. Are communities saturated? On the relationship between a, b, and g diversity. *Ecology Letters* 3:73–76.

Lorence, D. H., and R. W. Sussman. 1988. Diversity, density and invasion in a Mauritian wet forest. Pages 187–204 in P. Goldblatt and P. P. Lowry II, eds., *Modern systematic studies in African botany.* Missouri Botanical Garden, St. Louis.

Losos, J. B. 1996. Phylogenetic perspectives on community ecology. *Ecology* 77:1344–1354.

Losos, J. B., T. R. Jackman, A. Larson, K. de Queiroz, and L. Rodriguez-Schettino. 1998. Contingency and determinism in replicated adaptive radiations of island lizards. *Science* 279:2115–2118.

Losos, J. B., K. I. Warheit, and T. W. Schoener. 1997. Adaptive radiation following experimental island colonisation in *Anolis* lizards. *Nature* 387:70–73.

Louette, M. 1981. *The birds of Cameroon: An annotated checklist.* Verhandelingen van de

Koniklijke Academie voor Wetenschappen, Letteren Schone Kunsten van Belgie, Klasse de Wetenschappen 43:1–295.

Lougheed, S. C., C. Gascon, D. A. Jones, J. P. Bogart, and P. T. Boag. 1999. Ridges and rivers: A test of competing hypotheses of Amazonian diversification using a dart-poison frog (*Epipedobates femoralis*). *Proceedings of the Royal Society of London* B 266:1829–1835.

Lourandos, H., and B. David. 2002. Long-term archaeological and environmental trends: A comparison from Late Pleistocene-Holocene Australia. Pages 307–338 in A. P. Kershaw, B. David, N. J. Tapper, D. Penny, and J. Brown, eds., *The environmental and cultural history and dynamics of the Southeast Asian-Australian region.* Catena Verlag, Reiskirchen, Germany.

Lövei, G. L. 1997. Global change through invasion. *Nature* 388 (14):627–628.

Lovejoy, T. E. 1999. Preface. *Biological Conservation* 91:100.

Lovejoy, T., R. O. Bierregaard Jr., J. Rankin, and H. O. R. Schubart. 1983. Ecological dynamics of tropical forest fragments. Pages 337–386 in S. L. Sutton, T. C. Whitmore, and A. C. Chadwick, eds., *Tropical rain forest: Ecology and management.* Blackwell Scientific Publications, Oxford.

Lovejoy, T. E., R. O. Bierregaard Jr., A. Rylands, J. R. Malcolm, C. Quintela, L. Harper, K. Brown, A. Powell, G. Powell, H. Schubart, and M. Hays. 1986. Edge and other effects of isolation on Amazon forest fragments. Pages 257–285 in M. E. Soulé, ed., *Conservation biology: The science of scarcity and diversity.* Sinauer Associates, Sunderland, MA.

Lovett, J. C., and S. K. Wasser. 1993. *Biogeography and ecology of the rainforests of eastern Africa.* Cambridge University Press, Cambridge.

Lovette, I. J., and E. Bermingham. 1999. Explosive speciation in the New World *Dendroica* warblers. *Proceedings of the Royal Society of London* B 266:1629–1636.

Lugo, A. 1988. Diversity of tropical species: Questions that elude answers. Special issue, *Biology International* 19:1–37.

Luis-M., A., I. Vargas-F., and J. Llorente-B. 1991. Lepidoptera de Oaxaca. 1. Distribución y fenologia de los Papilionoidea de la Sierra de Juárez. Publicaciones Especiales del Museo de Zoologia, Facultad de Ciencias, UNAM, Mexico 3: i-iii, 1–119.

Lundberg, J. G., L. G. Marshall, J. Guerrero, B. Horton, M. C. Malabarba, and F. Wesselingh. 1998. The stage for Neotropical fish diversification: A history of tropical South American rivers. Pages 13–48 in L. R. Malabarba, R. E. Reis, R. P. Vari, C. A. S. Lucena, and Z. M. S. Lucena, eds., *Phylogeny and classification of Neotropical fishes.* Museu de Ciências e Tecnologia, PUCRS, Porto Alegre, Brazil.

Lynch, J. D. 1988. Refugia. Pages 311–342 in A. A. Myers and P. S. Giller, eds., *Analytical biogeography.* Chapman & Hall, London.

MacArthur, R. H. 1961. Population effects of natural selection. *American Naturalist* 95:195–199.

———. 1965. Patterns of species diversity. *Biological Reviews of the Cambridge Philosophical Society* 40:510–533.

———. 1972. *Geographical ecology: Patterns in the distribution of species.* Harper & Row, New York.

MacArthur, R. H., and E. O. Wilson. 1963. An equilibrium theory of insular zoogeography. *Evolution* 17:373–387.

———. 1967. *The theory of island biogeography.* Princeton University Press, Princeton, NJ.

Macdonald, I. A. W., C. Thébaud, W. Strahm, and D. Strasberg. 1991. Effects of alien plant invasions on native vegetation remnants on La Réunion (Mascarene Islands, Indian Ocean). *Environmental Conservation* 18:51–61.

Maciel, U. N., and P. L. B. Lisboa. 1989. Estudo floristico de 1 hectare de mata de terra firme no km 15 da rodovia Presidente Medici-Costa Marques (RO-429), Rondônia. *Boletim do Museu Paraense Emílio Goeldi,* Serie Botanica 5:25–37.

Mackey, B. G. 1991. The spatial extension of vegetation site data: A case study in the rainforests of the Wet Tropics of Queensland, Australia. Ph.D. thesis, Australia National University, Canberra.

———. 1993. A spatial analysis of the environmental relations of rainforest structural types. *Journal of Biogeography* 20:303–336.

———. 1994. Predicting the potential distribution of rain-forest structural characteristics. *Journal of Vegetation Science* 5:43–54.

Mackey, B. G., and D. B. Lindenmayer. 2002. Towards a hierarchical framework for modelling the distribution of animals. *Journal of Biogeography* 28:1147–1166.

Mackey, B. G., D. B. Lindenmayer, A. M. Gill, A. M. McCarthy, and J. A. Lindesay. 2002. *Wildlife, fire and future climate: A forest ecosystem analysis.* CSIRO Publishing, Collingwood, Victoria.

Mackey, B. G., I. Mullen, R. Sims, K. Baldwin, J. Gallant, and D. W. McKenney. 2000. Towards a spatial model of boreal forest ecosystems: The role of digital terrain analysis. Pages 391–422 in J. Wilson and J. Gallant, eds., *Digital terrain analysis: Theory and applications.* John Wiley and Sons, New York.

Mackey, B. G., H. A. Nix, M. F. Hutchinson, and J. P. McMahon. 1988. Assessing the representativeness of places for conservation reservation and heritage listing. *Environmental Management* 12(4):501–514.

Mackey, B. G., H. A. Nix, J. A. Stein, and S. E. Cork. 1989. Assessing the representativeness of the Wet Tropics of Queensland World Heritage Property. *Biological Conservation* 50:279–303.

Mackie, C. 1984. The lessons behind East Kalimantan's forest fires. *Borneo Research Bulletin* 16:63–74.

MacKinnon, J. 1997. *Protected areas systems review of the Indomalayan Realm.* The World Bank, Asian Bureau for Conservation (ABC) and World Conservation Monitoring Centre (WCMC), Cambridge.

MacKinnon, J., and K. MacKinnon. 1986. *Review of the protected areas system in the Indo-Malayan Realm.* IUCN, Gland.

———. 1987. Conservation status of the primates of the Indochinese subregion. *Primate Conservation* 8:187–195.

MacKinnon, J., K. MacKinnon, G. Child, and J. Thorsell. 1986. *Managing protected areas in the tropics.* IUCN, Gland.

MacKinnon, J., and K. Phillipps. 1993. *A field guide to the birds of Borneo, Sumatra, Java and Bali.* Oxford University Press, Oxford.

MacKinnon, K. 1997. The ecological foundations of biodiversity protection. Pages 36–63 in

R. Kramer, C. van Schaik, and J. Johnson, eds., *Last stand: Protected areas and the defense of tropical biodiversity.* Oxford University Press, New York.

———. 1998. Sustainable use as a conservation tool in the forests of South East Asia. Pages 174–192 in E. J. Millner-Gulland and R. Mace, eds., *Conservation of biological resources.* Blackwell Science, Oxford.

———. 2001. Integrated conservation and development projects: Can they work? *Parks* 11 (2):1–5.

MacKinnon, K., G. Hatta, H. Halim, and A. Mangalik. 1996. *The ecology of Kalimantan.* Periplus, Singapore.

Mackworth-Praed, C. W., and C. H. B. Grant. 1973. *Birds of west and west-central Africa.* Vol. 2. Longman, London.

Macphail, M. K. 1997. Late Neogene climates in Australia: Fossil pollen- and spore-based estimates in retrospect and prospect. *Australian Journal of Botany* 45:425–464.

Macphail, M. K., N. F. Alley, E. M. Truswell, and I. R. K. Sluiter. 1994. Early Tertiary vegetation: Evidence from spores and pollen. Pages 189–261 in R. S. Hill, ed., *The history of Australian vegetation: Cretaceous to Recent.* Cambridge University Press, Cambridge.

Maddison, W. P., and D. R. Swofford. 1992. *MacClade: Analysis of phylogeny and character evolution.* Sinauer Associates, Sunderland, MA.

Magnusson, W. E., A. P. Lima, and O. de Lima. 1996. Group lightning mortality of trees in a Neotropical forest. *Journal of Tropical Ecology* 12:899–903.

Magurran, A. E. 1988. *Ecological diversity and its measurement.* Princeton University Press, Princeton, NJ.

Mahar, D., and R. Schneider. 1994. Incentives for tropical deforestation: Some examples from Latin America. Pages 159–171 in K. Brown and D. W. Pearce, eds., *The causes of tropical deforestation: The economic and statistical analysis of factors giving rise to the loss of tropical forests.* University College London Press, London.

Malhotra, A., and R. S. Thorpe. 1991. Experimental detection of rapid evolutionary response in natural lizard populations. *Nature* 353:347–348.

Malipatil, M. B. 1986. Revision of Australian *Helonotus* Amyot and Serville (Heteroptera: Reduviidae). *Journal of the Australian Entomological Society* 25:171–175.

Malipatil, M. B., and G. B. Monteith. 1983. One new genus and four new species of terrestrial Mesoveliidae (Hemiptera: Gerromorpha) from Australia and New Caledonia. *Australian Journal of Zoology* 31:943–955.

Mallet, J., W. O. McMillan, and C. D. Jiggins. 1998. Mimicry and warning color at the boundary between races and species. Pages 390–403 in D. J. Howard and S. H. Berlocher, eds., *Endless forms: Species and speciation.* Oxford University Press, New York.

Mandosir, S., and M. Stark. 1993. Butterfly ranching. Pages 114–120 in E. Kemf, ed., *The law of the mother.* Sierra Club Books, San Francisco.

Manidis Roberts Consultants and Taylor Environmental Consulting. 1994. Data summary: 1993 visitor use survey: Wet Tropics World Heritage Area. Report to the Wet Tropics Management Authority, Cairns.

Manokaran, N., E. S. Quah, P. S. Ashton, J. V. LaFrankie et al. 2004. Pasoh Forest Dynamics Plot, Malaysia. Chapter 7.13 (Pages 585–598) in E. Losos and E. G. Leigh Jr., eds.,

Tropical diversity and dynamism: Findings from a network of tropical forest plots. University of Chicago Press, Chicago.

Mares, M. A. 1992. Neotropical mammals and the myth of Amazonian biodiversity. *Science* 255:976–979.

Margolis, M. 2000. Not as green as they seem. *Newsweek International,* 27 March, 10–14.

Margules, C. R., and R. L. Pressey. 2000. Systematic conservation planning. *Nature* 405: 243–253.

Margulis, L., C. Mathews, and A. Haselton, eds. 2000. *Environmental evolution: Effects of the origin and evolution of life on Planet Earth.* 2nd ed. MIT Press, Cambridge, MA.

Marshall, A. G., and M. D. Swaine. 1992. *Tropical rain forest: Disturbance and recovery.* The Royal Society, London.

Marshall, C. J., and J. K. Liebherr. 2000. Cladistic biogeography of the Mexican transition zone. *Journal of Biogeography* 27:203–216.

Martin, H. A. 1978. Evolution of the Australian flora and vegetation through the Tertiary: Evidence from pollen. *Alcheringa* 2:181–202.

———. 1990. Tertiary climate and phytogeography in southeastern Australia. *Review of Palaeobotany and Palynology* 65:47–55.

———. 1991. Tertiary stratigraphic palynology and palaeoclimate of the inland river systems in New South Wales. Pages 181–194 in M. A. J. Williams, P. DeDeckker, and A. P. Kershaw, eds., *The Cainozoic in Australia: A reappraisal of the evidence.* Special Publication no. 18. Geological Society of Australia, Sydney.

———. 1994. Australian Tertiary phytogeography: Evidence from palynology. Pages 104–142 in R. S. Hill, ed., *The history of Australian vegetation: Cretaceous to Recent.* Cambridge University Press, Cambridge.

———. 1998. Tertiary climatic evolution and the development of aridity in Australia. *Proceedings of the Linnean Society of New South Wales* 119:115–136.

Martin, H. A., and A. McMinn. 1993. Palynology of sites 815 and 823: The Neogene vegetation history of coastal northeastern Australia. *Proceedings of the Ocean Drilling Program, Scientific Results* 133:115–125.

Martin, P. S., and R. G. Klein, eds. 1984. *Quaternary extinctions.* University of Arizona Press, Tucson.

Martinez-Gallardo, R., and V. Sanchez-Cordero. 1997. Lista de mamiferos terrestres. Pages 625–628 in E. G. Soriano, R. Dirzo, and R. C. Vogt, eds., *Historia natural de Los Tuxtlas.* Universidad Nacional Autonoma de Mexico, Mexico City.

Matocq, M. D., J. L. Patton, and M. N. F. da Silva. 2000. Population genetic structure of two ecologically distinct Amazonian spiny rats: Separating history and current ecology. *Evolution* 54:1423–1432.

Matthews, E. G. 1992. Classification, relationships and distribution of the genera of Cyphaleini (Coleoptera: Tenebrionidae). *Invertebrate Taxonomy* 6:437–522.

———. 1998. Classification, phylogeny and biogeography of the genera of Adeliini (Coleoptera: Tenebrionidae). *Invertebrate Taxonomy* 12:685–824.

———. 2000. Origins of Australian arid-zone tenebrionid beetles. *Invertebrate Taxonomy* 14:941–951.

Matthews, J. D. 1963. Factors affecting the production of seed by forest trees. *Forestry Abstracts* 24:1–13.

May, R. M. 1975a. Patterns of species abundance and diversity. Pages 81–120 in M. L. Cody and J. M. Diamond, eds., *Ecology and evolution of communities.* Belknap Press of Harvard University Press, Cambridge, MA.

———. 1975b. *Stability and complexity in model ecosystems.* Princeton University Press, Princeton, NJ.

Mayle, F. E., R. Burbridge, and T. J. Killeen. 2000. Millennial-scale dynamics of southern Amazonian rain forests. *Science* 290:2291–2294.

Mayr, E. 1963. *Animal species and evolution.* Harvard University Press, Cambridge, MA.

———. 1982. *The growth of biological thought: Diversity, evolution, and inheritance.* Belknap Press of Harvard University Press, Cambridge, MA.

Mayr, E., and R. J. O'Hara. 1986. The biogeographical evidence supporting the Pleistocene forest refuge hypothesis. *Evolution* 40:55–67.

McArthur, A. G. 1967. *Fire behaviour in eucalypt forests.* Commonwealth Forestry and Timber Bureau Leaflet 107.

McCairns, R. F., R. Freitag, H. A. Rose, and F. J. D. Mcdonald. 1997. Taxonomic revision of the Australian Cicindelidae (Coleoptera), excluding species of *Cicindela. Invertebrate Taxonomy* 11:599–687.

McCarthy, J. F. 1999. "Wild logging": The rise and fall of logging networks and biodiversity conservation projects on Sumatra's rainforest frontier. CIFOR Occasional Paper 31. CIFOR, Bogor, Indonesia. Available at www.cifor.cgiar.org.

McConachie, B. A., J. N. Dunster, P. Wellman, T. J. Denaro, C. F. Pain, M. A. Habermehl, and J. J. Draper. 1998. Carpentaria lowlands and Gulf of Carpentaria region. Pages 365–397 in J. Bain and J. J. Draper, eds., *North Queensland Geology.* AGSO Bulletin 240. Australian Geological Survey Organisation, Canberra.

McDonald, G. T. 2000. *Daintree futures studies.* Cooperative Research Centre for Tropical Rainforest Ecology and Management, Cairns.

McDonald, G. T., and M. B. Lane, eds. 2000. *Securing the Wet Tropics?* The Federation Press, Leichhardt, Australia.

McDonald, K. R. 1992. *Distribution patterns and conservation status of North Queensland rainforest frogs.* Conservation technical report no.1. Queensland Department of Environment and Heritage, Brisbane.

McGill, B. J. 2003. A test of the unified neutral theory of biodiversity. *Nature* 422:881–885.

McGlashan, D. J., and J. M. Hughes. 2000. Reconciling patterns of genetic variation with stream structure, earth history and biology in the Australian freshwater fish *Craterocephalus stercusmuscarum* (Atherinidae). *Molecular Ecology* 9:1737–1751.

McGlone, M. S., A. P. Kershaw, and V. Markgraf. 1992. El Nino/Southern Oscillation climatic variability in Australasian and South American palaeoenvironmental records. Pages 435–462 in H. F. Diaz and V. Markgraf, eds., *El Niño: Historical and Palaeoclimatic Aspects of the Southern Oscillation.* Cambridge University Press, Cambridge.

McGowran, B. 1991. Maastrichtian and early Cainozoic, southern Australia: Planktonic and foraminiferal biostratigraphy. Pages 79–98 in M. A. J. Williams, P. DeDeckker, and

A. P. Kershaw, eds., *The Cainozoic in Australia: A reappraisal of the evidence.* Special Publication no. 18. Geological Society of Australia, Sydney.

McGowran, B., G. Moss, and A. Beecroft. 1992. Late Eocene and Early Oligocene in southern Australia: Local neritic signals of global oceanic changes. Pages 178–201 in D. R. Prothero and W. A. Berggren, eds., *Eocene-Oligocene climatic and biotic evolution.* Princeton University Press, Princeton, NJ.

McGuigan, K., K. McDonald, K. Parris, and C. Moritz. 1998. Mitochondrial DNA diversity and historical biogeography of a wet forest restricted frog (*Litoria pearsoniana*) from mid-east Australia. *Molecular Ecology* 7:175–186.

McGuinness, K. A. 1984. Equations and explanations in the study of species-area curves. *Biological Reviews* 59:423–440.

McLaren, B. E., and R. O. Peterson. 1994. Wolves, moose and tree rings on Isle Royale. *Science* 266:1555–1558.

McLoughlin, S., and A. N. Drinnan. 1995. A Cenomanian flora from the Winton Formation, Eromanga Basin, Queensland, Australia. *Memoirs of the Queensland Museum* 38 (1):273–313.

McLoughlin, S., and R. S. Hill. 1996. The succession of Western Australian Phanerozoic terrestrial floras. Pages 61–80 in S. D. Hopper et al., eds., *Gondwanan Heritage: Past, Present and Future of the Western Australian Biota.* Surrey Beatty and Sons, Sydney.

McMillan, W. O., C. D. Jiggins, and J. Mallet. 1997. What initiates speciation in passion-vine butterflies? *Proceedings of the National Academy of Sciences USA* 94:8628–8633.

McNeely, J. A. 1988. *Economics and biological diversity: Developing and using economic incentives to conserve biological resources.* IUCN, Gland, Switzerland.

Mduma, S. A. R., A. R. E. Sinclair, and R. Hilborn. 1999. Food regulates the Serengeti wildebeest: A 40-year record. *Journal of Animal Ecology* 68:1101–1122.

Means, D. B., and D. Simberloff. 1987. The peninsula effect: Habitat correlated species decline in Florida's herpetofauna. *Journal of Biogeography* 14:551–568.

Medway, Lord. 1969. *The wild mammals of Malaya.* Oxford University Press, Kuala Lumpur.

———. 1971. The importance of Taman Negara in the conservation of mammals. *Malayan Nature Journal* 24 (2):212–214.

Meggers, B. J. 1994. Archeological evidence for the impact of mega-Niño events on Amazonian during the past two millennia. *Climatic Change* 28:321–338.

Melillo, J. M., A. D. McGuire, D. W. Kicklighter, B. Moore III, C. J. Vorosmarty, and A. L. Schloss. 1993. Global climate change and terrestrial net primary production. *Nature* 363:234–239.

Mengel, R. M. 1964. The probable history of species formation in some northern wood warblers (Parulidae). *Living Bird* 3:9–43.

Merkl, O. 1987. A review of the Australian species of the subtribe Lagriina (Coleoptera, Tenebrionidae: Lagriini). *Annales Historico-Naturales Musei Nationalis Hungarici* 79: 121–166.

Meyer, A. 1993. Phylogenetic relationships and evolutionary processes in East African cichlid fishes. *Trends in Ecology and Evolution* 8:279–284.

Meyer de Schauensee, R. 1966. *The species of birds of South America and their distribution.* Academy of Natural Sciences, Philadelphia.

Mielke, C. G. C. 1996. Papilionoidea e Hesperioidea (Lepidoptera) de Curitiba e seus arredores, Paraná, Brasil, com notas taxonômicas sobre Hesperiidae. *Revista Brasileira de Zoologia* 11:759–776.

Mielke, O. H. H., and M. M. Casagrande. 1992. Lepidoptera: Papilionoidea e Hesperioidea coletados na Ilha de Maracá, Alto Alegre, Roraima, parte do Projeto Maracá, com uma lista complementar de Hesperiidae de Roraima. *Acta Amazonica* 21:175–210.

———. 1998. Papilionoidea e Hesperioidea (Lepidoptera) do Parque Estadual do Morro do Diabo, Teodoro Sampaio, São Paulo, Brasil. *Revista Brasileira de Zoologia* 14:967–1001.

Miller, R. I., ed. 1994. *Mapping the diversity of nature.* Chapman & Hall, London.

Millington, A. C., P. J. Styles, and R. W. Critchley. 1992. Mapping forests and savannas in sub-Saharan Africa from advanced very high resolution radiometer (AVHRR) imagery. Pages 37–62 in P. A. Furley, J. Proctor, and J. A. Ratter, eds., *Nature and dynamics of forest-savanna boundaries.* Chapman & Hall, New York.

Milton, K. 1982. Dietary quality and demographic regulation in a howler monkey population. Pages 273–289 in E. G. Leigh Jr., A. S. Rand, and D. M. Windsor, eds., *Ecology of a tropical forest.* Smithsonian Institution Press, Washington, DC.

———. 1990. Annual mortality patterns of a mammal community in central Panama. *Journal of Tropical Ecology* 6:493–499.

Mitra, S., H. Landel, and S. Pruett-Jones. 1996. Species richness covaries with mating system in birds. *Auk* 113:544–551.

Mitter, C., B. Farrell, and B. Weigmann. 1988. The phylogenetic study of adaptive zones: Has phytophagy promoted insect diversification? *American Naturalist* 132:107–128.

Mohammed, M. U., R. Bonnefille, and T. C. Johnson. 1995. Pollen and isotopic records in Late Holocene sediments from Lake Turkana, Kenya. *Palaeogeography, Palaeoclimatology, Palaeoecology* 119:371–383.

Molbo, D., C. Machado, J. G. Sevenster, L. Keller, and E. A. Herre. 2003. Cryptic species of fig-pollinating wasps: Implications for the evolution of the fig-wasp mutualism, sex allocation and precision of adaptation. *Proceedings of the National Academy of Sciences USA* 100 (10):5867–5872.

Møller, A. P., and J. J. Cuervo. 1998. Speciation and feather ornamentation in birds. *Evolution* 52:859–869.

Molofsky, J., and C. Augspurger. 1992. The effect of leaf litter on early seedling establishment in a tropical forest. *Ecology* 73:68–77.

Monteith, G. B. 1980. Relationships of the genera of Chinamyersiinae, with description of a relict species from mountains of North Queensland (Hemiptera: Heteroptera: Aradidae). *Pacific Insects* 21:275–285.

———. 1994. Distribution and altitudinal zonation of low vagility insects of the Queensland Wet Tropics: A report to the Wet Tropics Management Authority. Parts 1 and 2. Queensland Museum, Brisbane.

———. 1997. Revision of the Australian flat bugs of the subfamily Mezirinae (Insecta: Hemiptera: Aradidae). *Memoirs of the Queensland Museum* 41:1–169.

Monteith, G. B., and V. T. Davies. 1990. Preliminary account of a survey of arthropods (insects and spiders) along an altitudinal rainforest transect in tropical Queensland. Pages

345–413 in G. Werren and P. Kershaw, eds., *The rainforest legacy,* vol. 2, *Flora and fauna of the rainforests.* Australian Heritage Commission, special publication no. 7 Australian Government Publishing Service, Canberra.

Mooers, A. Ø., and S. B. Heard. 1997. Inferring evolutionary process from the phylogenetic tree shape. *Quarterly Review of Biology* 72:31–54.

Mooers, A. Ø., and A. P. Møller. 1996. Colonial breeding and speciation in birds. *Evolutionary Ecology* 10:375–385.

Moore, I. D., R. B. Grayson, and A. R. Ladson. 1991. Digital terrain modelling: A review of hydrological, geomorphological and biological applications. *Hydrological Processes* 5:3–30.

Moore, J. L., L. Manne, T. Brooks, N. D. Burgess, R. Davies, C. Rahbek, P. Williams, and A. Balmford. 2002. The distribution of cultural and biological diversity in Africa. *Proceedings of the Royal Society of London* B 269:1645–1653.

Moore, M. E., A. J. Gleadow, and J. F. Lovering. 1986. Thermal evolution of rifted continental margins: New evidence from fission tracks in basement apatites from southeastern Australia. *Earth and Planetary Science Letters* 34:359–365.

Moore, W. S. 1995. Inferring phylogenies from mtDNA variation: Mitochondrial-gene trees versus nuclear gene trees. *Evolution* 49:718–726.

Moore, W. S., and V. R. DeFilippis. 1997. The window of taxonomic resolution for phylogenies based on mitochondrial cytochrome *b.* Pages 83–119 in D. Mindell, ed., *Avian molecular evolution and systematics.* Academic Press, San Diego.

Morawetz, W., and P. Krügel. 1996. Computer-aided comparative chorology of Neotropical plants. Pages 217–227 in J.-L. Guillaumet, M. Belin, and H. Puig, eds., *Phytogéographie tropicale: Réalités et perspectives.* Actes du colloque international de Phytogéographie tropicale, Paris, July 6–8, 1993. ORSTOM, Paris.

Moreau, R. E. 1963. Vicissitudes of the African biomes in the Late Pleistocene. *Proceedings of the Linnaean Society of London* 165:35–46.

———. 1966. *The bird faunas of Africa and its islands.* Academic Press, New York.

Moritz, C. 1994. Defining evolutionarily significant units for conservation. *Trends in Ecology and Evolution* 9:373–375.

———. 1995. Uses of molecular phylogenies for conservation. *Philosophical Transactions of the Royal Society of London* B 349:113–118.

———. 1999. A molecular perspective on the conservation of diversity. Pages 21–34 in M. Kato, ed., *The biology of biodiversity.* Springer Verlag, Tokyo.

———. 2002. Strategies to protect biological diversity and the evolutionary processes that sustain it. *Systematic Biology* 51(2):238–254.

Moritz, C., and D. Faith. 1998. Comparative phylogeography and the identification of genetically divergent areas for conservation. *Molecular Ecology* 7:419–429.

Moritz, C., L. Joseph, and M. Adams. 1993. Cryptic diversity in an endemic rainforest skink (*Gnypetoscincus queenslandiae*). *Biodiversity and Conservation* 2:412–425.

Moritz, C., L. Joseph, C. Cunningham, and C. J. Schneider. 1997. Molecular perspectives on historical fragmentation of Australian tropical and subtropical rainforest: Implications for conservation. Page 442–454 in W. Laurance and R. Bierregaard Jr., eds., *Tropical for-*

est remnants: Ecology, management, and conservation of fragmented communities. University of Chicago Press, Chicago.

Moritz, C., S. Lavery, and R. Slade. 1995. Using allele frequency and phylogeny to define units for conservation and management. *American Fisheries Society Symposium* 17:249–262.

Moritz, C., J. L. Patton, C. J. Schneider, and T. B. Smith. 2000. Diversification of rainforest faunas: An integrated molecular approach. *Annual Review of Ecology and Systematics* 31:533–563.

Moritz, C., K. S. Richardson, S. Ferrier, G. B. Monteith, J. Stanistic, S. E. Williams, and T. Whiffin. 2001. Biogeographic concordance and efficiency of taxon indicators for establishing conservation priority in a tropical rainforest biota. *Proceedings of the Royal Society of London* B 268:1875–1881.

Morley, R. J. 2000. *Origin and evolution of tropical rain forests.* John Wiley and Sons, Chichester.

Morrone, J. J. 1994. On the identification of areas of endemism. *Systematic Biology* 43:438–441.

Morrone, J. J., and J. V. Crisci. 1995. Historical biogeography: Introduction to methods. *Annual Review of Ecology and Systematics* 26:373–401.

Moss, P. T. 1999. Late Quaternary environments of the humid tropics of northeastern Australia. Ph.D. thesis, Monash University, Melbourne.

Moss, P. T., and A. P. Kershaw. 2000. The last glacial cycle from the humid tropics of northeastern Australia: Comparison of terrestrial and marine records. *Palaeogeography, Palaeoclimatology, Palaeoecology* 155:155–176.

Muggiati, A., and A. Gondim. 1996. Madeireiras. *O Estado de S. Paulo* (São Paulo, Brazil), September 16.

Mulkey, S. S., and S. J. Wright. 1996. Influence of seasonal drought on the carbon balance of tropical forest plants. Pages 187–216 in S. S. Mulkey, R. L. Chazdon, and A. P. Smith, eds., *Tropical forest plant ecophysiology.* Chapman & Hall, New York.

Mullen, I. 1995. Environmental process and landscape pattern: Rainforests of the south coast of New South Wales. B.Sc. (Hons) thesis, Australian National University, Canberra.

Muller, J. 1981. Fossil pollen records of extant angiosperms. *Botanical Reviews* 47:1–142.

Murray, D. L. 2000. Survey of the butterfly fauna of Jatun Sacha, Ecuador (Lepidoptera: Hesperioidea and Papilionoidea). *Journal of Research on the Lepidoptera* 35:42–60.

Mustrangi, M. A., and J. L. Patton. 1997. Phylogeography and systematics of the slender mouse opossum *Marmosops* (Marsupialia, Didelphidae). *University of California Publications in Zoology* 130:1–86.

Myers, A. A., and P. S. Giller. 1988. Biogeographic reconstruction. Introduction. Pages 301–310 in A. A. Myers and P. S. Giller, eds., *Analytical biogeography: An integrated approach to the study of animal and plant distributions.* Chapman & Hall, New York.

Myers, N. 1988. Threatened biotas: "Hotspots" in tropical forests. *Environmentalist* 8:187–208.

Myers, N., R. A. Mittermeier, C. G. Mittermeier, G. A. B. da Fonseca, and J. Kent. 2000. Biodiversity hotspots for conservation priorities. *Nature* 403:853–858.

Nagy, K. A. 1987. Field metabolic rate and food requirement scaling in mammals and birds. *Ecological Monographs* 57:111–128.

NASA. 2003. MODIS (or Moderate Resolution Imaging Spectroradiometer) Web site. National Space and Aeronautics and Space Administration. http://modis.gsfc.nasa.gov/about/index.html.

Nascimento, M. T., and J. Proctor. 1994. Insect defoliation of a monodominant Amazonian rainforest. *Journal of Tropical Ecology* 10:633–636.

Nason, J. D., E. A. Herre, and J. L. Hamrick. 1996. Paternity analysis of the breeding structure of strangler fig populations: Evidence for substantial long-distance wasp dispersal. *Journal of Biogeography* 23:501–512.

———. 1998. The breeding structure of a tropical keystone plant resource. *Nature* 391:685–687.

Neboiss, A. 1991. Trichoptera. Pages 787–816 in Division of Entomology, CSIRO, *The insects of Australia: A textbook for students and research workers.* 2nd ed. Melbourne University Press, Carleton, Victoria.

Nee, S. 2001. Inferring speciation rates from phylogenies. *Evolution* 55:661–668.

Nee, S., T. G. Barraclough, and P. H. Harvey. 1996. Temporal changes in biodiversity: Detecting patterns and identifying causes. Pages 230–252 in K. Gaston, ed., *Biodiversity.* Oxford University Press, Oxford.

Nee, S., and R. M. May. 1997. Extinction and the loss of evolutionary history. *Science* 278:692–694.

Nee, S., R. M. May, and P. H. Harvey. 1994. The reconstructed evolutionary process. *Philosophical Transactions of the Royal Society of London* B 344:305–311.

Nee, S., A. Ø. Mooers, and P. H. Harvey. 1992. Tempo and mode of evolution revealed from molecular phylogenies. *Proceedings of the National Academy of Sciences USA* 89:8322–8326.

Nee, S., and G. Stone. 2003. The end of the beginning for neutral theory. *Trends in Ecology and Evolution* 18(9):433–434.

Neftel, A., H. Oeschger, J. Schwander, B. Stauffer, and A. H. Zumbrunn. 1982. Ice core sample measurements give atmospheric CO_2 content during the past 40,000 years. *Nature* 295:220–223.

Nei, M. 1987. *Molecular evolutionary genetics.* Columbia University Press, New York.

Neigel, J. E., and J. C. Avise. 1986. Phylogenetic relationships of mitochondrial DNA under various demographic models of speciation. Pages 515–534 in E. Nevo and S. Karlin, eds., *Evolutionary processes and theory.* Academic Press, New York.

Nelson, B. W., C. A. C. Ferreira, M. N. F. Da Silva, and M. L. Kawaski. 1990. Endemism centres, refugia and botanical collection density in Brazilian Amazonia. *Nature* 345:714–716.

Nelson, B. W., V. Kapos, J. B. Adams, W. J. Oliveira, O. P. G. Braun, and I. Do Amaral. 1994. Forest disturbance by large blowdowns in the Brazilian Amazon. *Ecology* 75:853–858.

Nelson, G., and P. Y. Ladiges. 1991a. Standard assumptions for biogeographic analysis. *Systematic Botany* 4:41–58.

———. 1991b. Three-area statements: Standard assumptions for biogeographic analysis. *Systematic Biology* 40:470–485.

———. 2001. Gondwana, vicariance biogeography and the New York school revisited. *Australian Journal of Botany* 49:389–409.

Nelson, G., and N. I. Platnick. 1981. *Systematics and biogeography: Cladistics and vicariance.* Columbia University Press, New York.

Nelson, M., R. Burkhart, C. Langton, and M. Askenazi. 1996. The SWARM simulation system: A toolkit for building multi-agent simulation. Santa Fe Institute Working Paper, 96–04–2.

Nepstad, D. C., J. P. Capobianco, A. C. Barros, G. Carvalho, P. Moutinho, P. Lefebvre, and U. Lopes. 2000. *Avança Brasil: Cenários futuros para a Amazônia.* Institute for Environmental Research in the Amazon (IPAM), Belém, Brazil.

Nepstad, D. C., G. Carvalho, A. Barros, A. Alencar, J. Capobianco, J. Bishop, P. Moutinho, P. Lefebvre, and U. Silva Jr. 2001. Road paving, fire regime feedbacks, and the future of Amazon forests. *Forest Ecology and Management* 154:295–407.

Nepstad, D. C., C. Carvalho, E. Davidson, P. Jipp, P. Lefebvre, G. Negreiros, E. Silva, T. Stone, S. Trumbore, and S. Vieira. 1994. The role of deep roots in the hydrological cycles of Amazonian forests and pastures. *Nature* 372:666–669.

Nepstad, D. C., C. Klink, C. Uhl, I. C. Guimarães Vieira, P. Lefebvre, M. Pedlowski, E. Matricardi, G. Negreiros, I. Brown, E. Amaral, A. Homma, and R. Walker. 1997. Land-use in Amazonia and the cerrado of Brazil. *Ciencia e Cultura* 49:73–86.

Nepstad, D. C., A. G. Moreira, and A. A. Alencar. 1999. *Flames in the rain forest: Origins, impacts, and alternatives to Amazonian fires.* Pilot Program to Conserve the Brazilian Rain Forest, Brasília, Brazil.

Nepstad, D. C., A. Moreira, A. Verissimo, P. Lefebvre, P. Schlesinger, C. Potter, C. Nobre, A. Setzer, T. Krug, A. Barros, A. Alencar, and J. Pereira. 1998. Forest fire prediction and prevention in the Brazilian Amazon. *Conservation Biology* 12:951–955.

Nepstad, D. C., P. Moutinho, M. B. Dias, E. Davidson, G. Cardinot, D. Markewitz, R. Figueiredo, N. Vianna, J. Chambers, D. Ray, J. B. Guerreiros, P. Lefebvre, L. Sternberg, M. Moreira, L. Barros, F. Y. Ishida, I. Tohlver, E. Belk, K. Kalif, and K. Schwalbe. 2002. The effects of partial throughfall exclusion on canopy processes, aboveground production, and biogeochemistry of an Amazon forest. *Journal of Geophysical Research-Atmospheres* 107 (D20): art. no. 8085.

Nepstad, D. C., A. Verissimo, A. Alencar, C. Nobre, E. Lima, P. Lefebvre, P. Schlesinger, C. Potter, P. Moutinho, E. Mendoza, M. Cochrane, and V. Brooks. 1999. Large-scale impoverishment of Amazonian forests by logging and fire. *Nature* 398:505–508.

New, T. R. 1997. Are Lepidoptera an effective "umbrella group" for biodiversity conservation? *Journal of Insect Conservation* 1:5–12.

Newbery, D. M., H. H. T. Prins, and N. Brown, eds. 1996. *Dynamics of tropical communities.* British Ecological Society Symposium no. 37. Blackwell Science, Oxford.

Newbery, D. M., N. C. Songwe, and G. B. Chuyong. 1998. Phenology and dynamics of an African rainforest at Korup, Cameroon. Pages 267–308 in D. M. Newbery, H. H. T. Prins, and N. D. Brown, eds., *Dynamics of tropical communities.* Blackwell Scientific, London.

Newmark, W. D. 1991. Tropical forest fragmentation and the local extinction of understory birds in the East Usambara Mountains, Tanzania. *Conservation Biology* 5:67–78.

Newsome, J., and J. R. Flenley. 1988. Late Quaternary vegetational history of the Central

Highlands of Sumatra. 2. Palaeopalynology and vegetational history. *Journal of Biogeography* 15:555–578.

Newstrom, L. E., G. W. Frankie, H. G. Baker, and R. K. Colwell. 1994. Diversity of long-term flowering patterns. Pages 142–160 in L. A. McDade, K. S. Bawa, H. A. Hespenheide, and G. S. Hartshorn, eds., *La Selva: Ecology and natural history of a Neotropical rainforest.* University of Chicago Press, Chicago.

NeXT Inc. Object-oriented programming and the Objective-C language. http://www.next.com/Pubs/Documents/OPENSTEP/ObjectiveC/objctoc.html.

Nichols, W. F., K. T. Killingbeck, and P. V. August. 1998. The influence of geomorphological heterogeneity on biodiversity. 2. A landscape perspective. *Conservation Biology* 12:371–379.

Nicholson, D. I., N. Henry, and J. Rudder. 1988. Stand changes in North Queensland rainforests. Pages 61–80 in R. Kitching, ed., *The ecology of Australia's Wet Tropics.* Proceedings of the Ecological Society of Australia, vol. 15. Surrey Beatty and Sons, Sydney.

Nicholson, S. E. 1994. Recent rainfall fluctuations in Africa and their relationship to past conditions over the continent. *Holocene* 4:121–131.

Nielsen, R., and J. Wakeley. 2001. Distinguishing migration from isolation: A Markov chain approach. *Genetics* 158:885–896.

Nix, H. A. 1982. Environmental determinants of biogeography and evolution in Terra Australia. Pages 47–66 in W. R. Barker and P. J. M. Greenslade, eds., *Evolution of the flora and fauna of arid Australia.* Peacock, Adelaide.

———. 1991a. Biogeography: Patterns and process. Pages 11–39 in H. A. Nix and M. Switzer, eds., *Rainforest animals: Atlas of vertebrates endemic to Australia's Wet Tropics.* Australian National Parks and Wildlife Service, Canberra.

———. 1991b. An environmental analysis of Australian rainforests. Pages 1–26 in G. L. Werren and A. K. Kershaw, eds., *Australian National Rainforests Study,* vol. 2, *Flora and fauna of the rainforests.* Australian Government Publishing Service, Canberra.

Nix, H. A., D. P. Faith, M. F. Hutchinson, C. R. Margules, J. West, A. Allison, J. L. Kesteven, G. Natera, W. Slater, J. L. Stein, and P. Walker. 2000. *The BioRap toolbox: A national study of biodiversity assessment and planning for Papua New Guinea.* CSIRO Press, Melbourne.

Nix, H. A., and M. A. Switzer. 1991. *Rainforest animals: Atlas of vertebrates endemic to Australia's Wet Tropics.* Australian National Parks and Wildlife Service, Canberra.

Nolen, J. A., and R. G. Pearson. 1992. Life history studies of *Anisocentropus kirramus* Neboiss (Trichoptera: Calamoceratidae) in a tropical Australian rainforest stream. *Aquatic Insects* 14:213–221.

Nores, M. 1999. An alternative hypothesis for the origin of Amazonian bird diversity. *Journal of Biogeography* 26:475–485.

Noss, A. J. 1997. Challenges to nature conservation with community development in central African forests. *Oryx* 31:180–188.

Noss, R. F. 1983. A regional landscape approach to maintain diversity. *BioScience* 33:700–706.

Nott, J. F. 1992. Long-term drainage evolution in the Shoalhaven catchment, southeast highlands, Australia. *Earth Surface Processes and Landforms* 17:361–374.

———. 1995. Discussion: Tectonics and landscape evolution in southeast Australia. *AGSO Journal of Australian Geology and Geophysics* 16:319–321.

Nott, J. F., and S. Horton. 2000. 180 Ma continental drainage divide in northeast Australia: Role of passive margin tectonics. *Geology* 28:763–766.

Nott, J. F., M. Idnurm, and R. W. Young. 1991. Sedimentology, weathering age and geomorphological significance of Tertiary sediments on the far south coast of New South Wales. *Australian Journal of Earth Sciences* 38:357–373.

Nott, J. F., and A. C. Purvis. 1995. Geomorphic and tectonic significance of Early Cretaceous lavas on the coastal plain, southern New South Wales. *Australian Journal of Earth Sciences* 42:145–149.

Nott, J. F., R. W. Young, and I. McDougall. 1996. Back-wearing versus down-wearing versus gorge extension in the long-term denudation of a highland mass: Quantitative evidence from the Shoalhaven catchment, southeastern Australia. *Journal of Geology* 104: 224–233.

Novotny, V., S. E. Miller, Y. Basset, L. Cizek, P. Drozd, K. Darrow, and J. Leps. 2002. Predictably simple: Assemblages of caterpillars (Lepidoptera) feeding on rainforest trees in Papua New Guinea. *Proceedings of the Royal Society of London* B 269:2337–2344.

NSW NPWS. 1996. C-PLAN Conservation Planning Software. New South Wales National Parks and Wildlife Service.

Oates, J. F. 1999. *Myth and reality in the rainforest: How conservation strategies are failing in West Africa.* University of California Press, Berkeley.

Oberbauer, S. F., and B. R. Strain. 1986. Effects of canopy position and irradiance on the leaf physiology and morphology of *Pentaclethra macroloba* (Mimosaceae). *American Journal of Botany* 73:409–416.

O'Brien, E. M., R. Field, and R. J. Whittaker. 2000. Climatic gradients in woody plant (tree and shrub) diversity: Water-energy dynamics, residual variation, and topography. *Oikos* 89:588–600.

Odgaard, B. V. 1999. Fossil pollen as a record of past biodiversity. *Journal of Biogeography* 26:7–17.

O'Dowd, D. J., C. R. Brew, D. C. Christophel, and R. A. Norton. 1991. Mite-plant associations from the Eocene of southern Australia. *Science* 252:99–101.

Okuda, T., N. Kachi, S. K. Yap, and N. Manokaran. 1997. Tree distribution pattern and fate of juveniles in a lowland tropical rain forest: Implications for regeneration and maintenance of species diversity. *Plant Ecology* 131:155–171.

Oldfield, F. 1968. The Quaternary vegetational history of the French Pays Basque. 1. Stratigraphy and Pollen Analysis. *New Phytologist* 67:677–731.

Oliver, I., A. J. Beattie, and A. York. 1998. Spatial fidelity of plant, vertebrate, and invertebrate assemblages in multiple-use forest in eastern Australia. *Conservation Biology* 12:822–835.

Ollier, C. D. 1986. The origin of alpine landforms in Australasia. Pages 3–26 in B. A. Barlow, ed., *Flora and fauna of alpine Australia: Ages and origins.* CSIRO, Melbourne.

Ollier, C. D., and C. F. Pain. 1994. Landscape evolution and tectonics in southeastern Australia. *AGSO Journal of Australian Geology and Geophysics* 15:335–345.

Olmos, F., A. P. Queiroz-Filho, and C. A. Lisboa. 1998. As unidades de conservação de Rondônia. Secretariat for Planning (SEPLAN), Rondônia, Brazil.

Olsen, P. E. 1986. A 40-million-year lake record of early Mesozoic orbital climatic forcing. *Science* 234:842–848.

Olsen, P. E., C. L. Remington, B. Cornet, and K. S. Thomson. 1978. Cyclic changes in late Triassic lacustrine communities. *Science* 201:729–733.

Olson, T. R. 1979. Studies on aspects of the morphology and systematics of the genus *Otolemur* Coquerel, 1859 (Primates: Galagidae). Ph.D. thesis, University of London.

O'Neil, R. V., D. L. DeAngelis, J. B. Waide, and T. F. H. Allen. 1986. *A hierarchical concept of ecosystems.* Princeton University Press, Princeton, NJ.

Orians, G. H., and R. T. Paine. 1983. Convergent evolution at the community level. Pages 431–458 in D. J. Futuyma and M. Slatkin, eds., *Coevolution.* Sinauer Associates, Sunderland, MA.

Orr, M. R., and T. B. Smith. 1998. Ecology and speciation. *Trends in Ecology and Evolution* 13:502–506.

Orr, H. A., and M. Turelli. 2001. The evolution of postzygotic isolation: Accumulating Dobzhansky-Miller incompatibilities. *Evolution* 55:1085–1094.

O'Sullivan, P. B., D. A. Foster, B. P. Kohn, A. J. W. Gleadow, and A. Raza. 1995. Constraints on the dynamics of rifting and denudation on the eastern margin of Australia: Fission track evidence for two discrete causes of rock cooling. *PACRIM* 95:441–446.

O'Sullivan, P. B., and B. P. Kohn. 1998. Episodic late Palaeozoic to Cainozoic cooling/denudation along the northeastern Queensland margin. 14th Australian Geological Convention, July 1998, Townsville. *Geological Society of Australia Abstracts* 49:345.

O'Sullivan, P. B., B. P. Kohn, A. J. W. Gleadow, and R. W. Brown. 1998. The palaeoplain model does not work for the southeast Australian passive margin: Evidence from AFT Thermochronology. 14th Australian Geological Convention, July 1998, Townsville. *Geological Society of Australia Abstracts* 49:346.

Owens, I. P. F., P. M. Bennett, and P. H. Harvey. 1999. Species richness among birds: Body size, life history, sexual selection or ecology? *Proceedings of the Royal Society of London* B 266:933–939.

Padoch, C., and C. M. Peters. 1993. Managed forest gardens in West Kalimantan, Indonesia. Pages 167–176 in J. J. Cohen and C. S. Potter, eds., *Perspectives on biodiversity: Case studies of genetic resource conservation.* American Association for the Advancement of Science, Washington, DC.

Page, R. D. M. 1988. Quantitative cladistic biogeography: Constructing and comparing area cladograms. *Systematic Zoology* 37:254–270.

———. 1990a. Component analysis: A valiant failure? *Cladistics* 6:119–136.

———. 1990b. Temporal congruence and cladistic analysis of biogeography and cospeciation. *Systematic Zoology* 39:205–226.

———. 1993a. COMPONENT: Tree comparison software for Microsoft Windows. Version 2.0. Natural History Museum, London.

———. 1993b. Genes, organisms, and areas: The problem of multiple lineages. *Systematic Biology* 42:77–84.

———. 1994. Maps between trees and cladistic analysis of historical associations among genes, organisms and areas. *Systematic Biology* 43:58–77.

Page, S. E., F. O. Siegert, J. Rieley, V. Boehm Hans-Dieter, A. Jayak, and S. Limin. 2002. The amount of carbon released from peat and forest fires in Indonesia during 1997. *Nature* 420:61–64.

Paijmans, K. 1976. *New Guinea vegetation.* CSIRO and Australian National University Press, Canberra.

Pain, C. F., J. R. Wilford, and J. C. Dohrenwend. 1998. Regolith of Cape York Peninsula. Pages 419–439 in J. H. C. Bain and J. J. Draper, eds., *North Queensland geology.* AGSO Bulletin 240. Australian Geological Survey Organisation, Canberra.

Paine, R. T. 1966. Food web complexity and species diversity. *American Naturalist* 100:65–75.

———. 1974. Intertidal community structure. *Oecologia* 15:93–120.

Pamilo, P., and M. Nei. 1988. Relationships between gene trees and species trees. *Molecular Biology and Evolution* 5:568–583.

Parkes, A., J. T. Teller, and J. R. Flenley. 1992. Environmental history of the Lake Vaihiria drainage basin, Tahiti, French Polynesia. *Journal of Biogeography* 19:431–437.

Partridge, A. 1998. Report on palynology of Tertiary sediment samples. BIOSTRATA, Melbourne.

Partridge, A. D. 1999. Late Cretaceous to Tertiary geological evolution of the Gippsland Basin, Victoria. Ph.D. thesis, La Trobe University, Melbourne.

Partridge, T. C. 1997. Reassessment of the position of the Plio-Pleistocene boundary: Is there a case for lowering it to the Gauss-Matuyama paleomagnetic reversal? *Quaternary International* 40:5–10.

Paterson, H. T. 1935. Notes on plant remains from Narracan and Darlimurla, South Gippsland. *Proceedings of the Royal Society of Victoria,* n.s., 48(1):67–74.

Patiño, S., E. A. Herre, and M. T. Tyree. 1994. Physiological determinants of *Ficus* fruit temperature and implications for survival of pollinator wasp species: Comparative physiology through an energy budget approach. *Oecologia* 100:13–20.

Patterson, B. D., and W. Atmar. 1986. Nested subsets and the structure of insular mammalian faunas and archipelagos. *Biological Journal of the Linnean Society* 28:65–82.

Patton, D. R. 1975. A diversity index for quantifying habitat edge. *Wildlife Society Bulletin* 3:171–173.

Patton, J. L., and L. P. Costa. 2003. Molecular phylogeography and species limits in rainforest didelphid marsupials of South America. Pages 63–81 in M. Jones, C. Dickman, and M. Archer, eds., *Predators with pouches: The biology of carnivorous marsupials.* CSIRO Publishing, Collingwood, Victoria, Australia.

Patton, J. L., and M. N. F. da Silva. 1998. Rivers, refuges, and ridges: The geography of speciation of Amazonian mammals. Pages 203–213 in S. Berlocher and D. J. Howard, eds., *Endless forms: Species and speciation.* Oxford University Press, Oxford.

———. 2001. Molecular phylogenetics and the diversification of Amazonian mammals. Pages 139–164 in I. C. Guimarães Vieira, J. M. Cardoso da Silva, D. C. Oren, and M. Â. D'Incao, eds., *Diversidade de Amazônia.* Museu Paraense Emílio Goeldi, Belém, Pará, Brazil.

Patton, J. L., M. N. F. da Silva, M. C. Lara, and M. A. Mustrangi. 1997. Diversity, differentiation, and the historical biogeography of non-volant mammals of the Neo-tropical forests. Pages 455–465 in W. F. Laurance and R. O. Bierregaard Jr., eds., *Tropical forest remnants: Ecology, management, and conservation of fragmented communities.* University of Chicago Press, Chicago.

Patton, J. L., M. N. F. da Silva, and J. R. Malcolm. 1994. Gene genealogy and differentiation among arboreal spiny rats (Rodentia: Echimyidae) of the Amazon Basin: A test of the riverine barrier hypothesis. *Evolution* 48:1314–1323.

———. 1996. Hierarchical genetic structure and gene flow in three sympatric species of Amazonian rodents. *Molecular Ecology* 5:229–238.

———. 2000. *Mammals of the Rio Juruá and the evolutionary and ecological diversification of Amazonia.* Bulletin of the American Museum of Natural History, no. 244. American Museum of Natural History, New York.

Patton, J. L., and M. F. Smith. 1992. mtDNA phylogeny of Andean mice: A test of diversification across ecological gradients. *Evolution* 46:174–183.

———. 1993. The diversification of South American murid rodents: Evidence from mitochondrial DNA sequence data for the akodontine tribe. *Biological Journal of the Linnean Society* 50:149–177.

Pearcy, R. W. 1987. Photosynthetic gas exchange responses of Australian tropical forest trees in canopy, gap and understory micro-environments. *Functional Ecology* 1:169–178.

Pearman, P. B. 1997. Correlates of amphibian diversity in an altered landscape of Amazonian Ecuador. *Conservation Biology* 11:1211–1225.

Pearson, D. L. 1977. A pantropical comparison of bird community structure on six lowland forest sites. *Condor* 79:232–244.

———. 1982. Historical factors and bird species richness. Pages 441–452 in G. T. Prance, ed., *Biological diversification in the tropics.* Columbia University Press, New York.

Pearson, P. N., and M. R. Palmer. 2000. Atmospheric carbon dioxide concentrations over the past 60 million years. *Nature* 406:695–699.

Pearson, R. G., L. J. Benson, and R. E. W. Smith. 1986. Diversity and abundance of the fauna in Yuccabine Creek, a tropical rainforest stream. Pages 329–342 in P. de Deckker and W. D. Williams, eds., *Limnology in Australia.* CSIRO, Melbourne.

Pearson, R. G., and N. M. Connolly. 2000. Nutrient enhancement, food quality and community dynamics in a tropical rainforest stream. *Freshwater Biology* 43:31–42.

Pearson, T. R. H., D. F. R. P. Burslem, C. E. Mullins, and J. W. Dalling. 2002. Germination ecology of Neotropical pioneers: Interacting effects of environmental conditions and seed size. *Ecology* 83:2798–2807.

Peerdeman, F. M. 1993. The Pleistocene climatic and sea-level signature of the northeastern Australian continental margin. Ph.D. thesis, Australian National University, Canberra.

Peerdeman, F. M., and P. J. Davies. 1993. Sedimentological response of an outer-shelf, upper-slope sequence to rapid changes in Pleistocene eustatic sea level: Hole 820A, northeastern Australian margin. *Proceedings of the Ocean Drilling Program, Scientific Results* 133:303–313.

Peerdeman, F. M., P. J. Davies, and A. R. Chivas. 1993. The stable oxygen isotope signal in shallow-water, upper-slope sediments off the Great Barrier Reef (Hole 820A). *Proceedings of the Ocean Drilling Program, Scientific Results* 133:163–173.

Peluso, N. 1983. Networking in the commons: A tragedy for rattan? *Indonesia* 35:95–108.

Pennington, R. T., D. E. Prado, and C. A. Pendry. 2000. Neotropical seasonally dry forests and Quaternary vegetation changes. *Journal of Biogeography* 27:261–273.

Perdices, A., E. Bermingham, A. Montilla, and I. Doadrio. 2002. Evolutionary history of the genus *Rhamdia* (Teleostei: Pimelodidae) in Central America. *Molecular Phylogenetics and Evolution* 25:172–189.

Peres, C. A. 2001. Synergistic effects of subsistence hunting and habitat fragmentation on Amazonian forest vertebrates. *Conservation Biology* 15:1490–1505.

Peres, C. A., J. L. Patton, and M. N. F. da Silva. 1996. Riverine barriers and gene flow in Amazonian saddle-back tamarins. *Folia Primatologica* 67:113–124.

Peters, C. M. 1996. *The ecology and management of non-timber forest resources.* World Bank Technical Paper no. 322. World Bank, Washington, DC.

Peters, C. M., A. Gentry, and R. Mendelsohn. 1989. Valuation of an Amazonian rainforest. *Nature* 339:655–656.

Peters, H. A. 2003. Neighbour-regulated mortality: The influence of positive and negative density dependence on tree populations in species-rich tropical forests. *Ecology Letters* 6:757–765.

Peters, M. D. 1985. A taxonomic analysis of a mid-Cretaceous megaplant assemblage from Queensland. Ph.D. thesis, University of Adelaide, Adelaide.

Peters, M. D., and D. C. Christophel. 1978. *Austrosequioa wintonensis,* a new taxodiaceous cone from Queensland, Australia. *Canadian Journal of Botany* 56(24):3119–3128.

Petocz, R., and Y. de Fretes. 1983. *Mammals of the reserves of Irian Jaya.* WWF/IUCN, Jayapura.

Phillips, B. L., S. J. E. Baird, and C. Moritz. 2004. When vicars meet: A narrow contact zone between phylogeographic lineages of the rainforest skink *Carlia rubrigularis. Evolution* 58(7):1536–1548.

Phillips, O. L., and A. H. Gentry. 1994. Increased turnover through time in tropical forests. *Science* 263:954–958.

Phillips, O. L., P. Hall, A. H. Gentry, S. A. Sawyer, and R. Vásquez. 1994. Dynamics and species richness of tropical rain forests. *Proceedings of the National Academy of Sciences USA* 91:2805–2809.

Pianka, E. R. 1966. Latitudinal gradients in species diversity: A review of concepts. *American Naturalist* 100:33–46.

Pickett, J. W., N. Smith, P. M. Bishop, R. S. Hill, M. K. Macphail, and W. B. K. Holmes. 1990. A stratigraphic evaluation of Ettingshausen's New England Tertiary plant localities. *Australian Journal of Earth Science* 37:293–303.

Pickett, S. T. A. 1983. Differential adaptation of tropical tree species to canopy gaps and its role in community dynamics. *Tropical Ecology* 24(1):68–84.

Pickett, S. T. A., and J. N. Thompson. 1978. Patch dynamics and the design of nature reserves. *Biological Conservation* 13:27–37.

Pimm, S. L., and J. H. Lawton. 1998. Planning for biodiversity. *Science* 279:2068–2069.

Piperno, D. R. 1990. Fitolitos, arqueología y cambios prehistóricos de la vegetación en un lote de cincuenta hectáreas de la isla de Barro Colorado. Pages 153–156 in E. G. Leigh Jr., A. S. Rand, and D. M. Windsor, eds., *Ecología de un bosque tropical.* Smithsonian Tropical Research Institute, Balboa, Panama.

———. 1994. Phytolith and charcoal evidence for prehistoric slash-and-burn agriculture in the Darien rain forest of Panama. *Holocene* 4:321–325.

———. 1997. Phytoliths and microscopic charcoal from leg 155: A vegetational and fire history of the Amazon Basin during the last 75,000 K.Y. *Proceedings of the Ocean Drilling Program, Scientific Results* 155:411–418.

Piperno, D. R., and P. Becker. 1996. Vegetational history of a site in the central Amazon Basin derived from phytolith and charcoal records from natural soils. *Quaternary Research* 45:202–209.

Piperno, D. R., M. B. Bush, and P. A. Colinvaux. 1991a. Paleoecological perspectives on human adaptation in central Panama. 1. The Pleistocene. *Geoarchaeology* 6:201–226.

———. 1991b. Paleoecological perspectives on human adaptation in central Panama. 2. Holocene. *Geoarchaeology* 6:227–250.

Pires, J. M., and G. T. Prance. 1985. The vegetation types of the Brazilian Amazon. Pages 109–145 in G. T. Prance, and T. E. Lovejoy, eds., *Key environments: Amazonia.* Pergamon Press, Oxford.

Pitman, N. C. A., J. Terborgh, M. R. Silman, and P. Nuñez V. 1999. Tree species distributions in an upper Amazonian forest. *Ecology* 80:2651–2661.

Pitman, N. C. A., J. W. Terborgh, M. R. Silman, P. Nuñez V., D. A. Neill, C. E. Cerón, W. A. Palacios, and M. Aulestia. 2001. Dominance and distribution of tree species in upper Amazonian terra firme forests. *Ecology* 82:2101–2117.

———. 2002. A comparison of tree diversity in two upper Amazonian forests. *Ecology* 83:3210–3224.

Platnick, N. I. 1991. On areas of endemism. Pages xi–xii in P. Y. Ladiges, C. J. Humphries, and L. W. Martinelli, eds., *Austral Biogeography.* CSIRO, Melbourne.

———. 2000. *A relimitation and revision of the Australasian ground spider family Lamponidae (Araneae: Gnaphosidea).* Bulletin of the American Museum of Natural History, no. 245. American Museum of Natural History, New York.

Plaziat, J.-C., C. Cavagnetto, J. C. Koeniguer, and F. Baltzer. 2001. History and biogeography of the mangrove ecosystem, based on a critical reassessment of the paleontological record. *Wetlands Ecology and Management* 9:161–179.

Pole, M. 1992. Eocene vegetation from Hasties, north-eastern Tasmania. *Australian Systematic Botany* 5:431–475.

Pole, M., and D. M. J. S. Bowman. 1996. Tertiary plant fossils from Australia's "Top End." *Australian Systematic Botany* 9:113–126.

Pole, M. S., R. S. Hill, N. Green, and M. K. Macphail. 1993. The Oligocene Berwick Quarry flora: Rainforest in a drying environment. *Australian Systematic Botany* 6:399–427.

Polis, G. A., S. D. Hurd, C. T. Jackson, and F. Sanchez-Piñero. 1998. Multifactor population limitation: Variable spatial and temporal control of spiders on Gulf of California islands. *Ecology* 79:490–502.

Pollock, D. A. 1995. Classification, reconstructed phylogeny and geographical history of genera of Pilipalpinae (Coleoptera: Tenebrionidea: Pyrochroidae). *Invertebrate Taxonomy* 9:563–708.

Pope, L., A. Estoup, and C. Moritz. 2000. Phylogeography and population structure of an ecotonal marsupial, *Bettongia tropica*, determined using mtDNA and microsatellites. *Molecular Ecology* 9:2041–2054.

Prance, G. T. 1973. Phytogeographic support for the theory of Pleistocene forest refuges in the Amazon Basin, based on evidence from distribution patterns in Caryocaraceae, Chrysobalanaceae, Dichapetalaceae and Lecythidaceae. *Acta Amazonica* 3 (3):5–28.

———, ed. 1982a. *Biological diversification in the tropics.* Columbia University Press, New York.

———. 1982b. Forest refuges: Evidence from woody angiosperms. Pages 137–157 in G. T. Prance, ed., *Biological diversification in the tropics.* Columbia University Press, NY.

Prendergast, J. R., R. M. Quinn, J. H. Lawton, B. C. Eversham, and D. W. Gibbons. 1993. Rare species, the coincidence of hotspots and conservation strategies. *Nature* 365:335–337.

Prentice, I. C., P. J. Bartlein, and T. Webb. 1991. Vegetation and climate change in eastern North America since the last glacial maximum. *Ecology* 72:2038–2056.

Pressey, R. L., C. J. Humphries, C. R. Margules, R. I. Vane-Wright, and P. H. Williams. 1993. Beyond opportunism: Key principles for systematic reserve selection. *Trends in Ecology and Evolution* 8:124–128.

Pressey, R. L., I. R. Johnson, and P. D. Wilson. 1994. Shade of irreplaceability: Towards a measure of the contribution of sites to a reservation goal. *Biodiversity and Conservation* 3:242–262.

Pressey, R. L., and S. L. Tully. 1994. The cost of ad hoc reservation: A case study in western New South Wales. Australian Journal of Ecology 19:375–384.

Preston, F. W. 1948. The commonness, and rarity, of species. *Ecology* 29:254–283.

———. 1962. The canonical distribution of commonness and rarity. *Ecology* 43:185–215, 410–432.

Price, T., I. J. Lovette, E. Bermingham, H. L. Gibbs, and A. D. Richman. 2000. The imprint of history on communities of North American and Asian warblers. *American Naturalist* 156:354–367.

Prigogine, A. 1987. Disjunctions of montane forest birds in the Afrotropical region. *Bonner Zoologische Beiträge* 38:195–207.

Productivity Commission. 2003. *Industries in the Great Barrier Reef catchment and measures to address declining water quality.* Research report. Productivity Commission, Canberra.

Prychitko, T. M., and W. S. Moore. 1997. The utility of DNA sequences of an intron from the beta-fibrinogen gene in phylogenetic analysis of woodpeckers (Aves: Picidae). *Molecular Phylogenetics and Evolution* 8:193–204.

Pumijumnong, N., D. Eckstein, and U. Sass. 1995. Tree-ring research on *Tectona grandis* in northern Thailand. *International Association of Wood Anatomists Journal* 16:385–392.

Purvis, A. 1995. A composite estimate of primate phylogeny. *Philosophical Transactions of the Royal Society of London* B 348:405–421.

Pusey, B. J., A. H. Arthington, and M. G. Read. 1995. Species richness and spatial variation in fish assemblage structure in two rivers of the Wet Tropics of North Queensland. *Environmental Biology of Fishes* 42:181–199.

Pusey, B. J., and M. J. Kennard. 1996. Species richness and geographical variation in assemblage structure of the freshwater fish fauna of the Wet Tropics region of northern Queensland. *Marine and Freshwater Research* 47:563–573.

Putzer, H. 1984. The geological evolution of the Amazon basin and its mineral resources. Pages 15–46 in H. Sioli, ed., *The Amazon: Limnology and landscape ecology of a mighty tropical river and its basin.* Dr. W. Junk, Dordrecht.

Pyke, C. R., R. Condit, S. Aguilar, and S. Lao. 2001. Floristic composition across a climatic gradient in a Neotropical lowland forest. *Journal of Vegetation Science* 12:553–566.

Qian, H., and R. E. Ricklefs. 1999. A comparison of the taxonomic richness of vascular plants in China and the United States. *American Naturalist* 154:160–181.

———. 2000. Large-scale processes and the Asian bias in species diversity of temperate plants. *Nature* 407:180–182.

Qiu, Y.-L., C. R. Parks, and M. W. Chase. 1995. Molecular divergence in the eastern Asia-eastern North America disjunct section *Rytidospermum* of *Magnolia* (Magnoliaceae). *American Journal of Botany* 82:1589–1598.

Queensland Main Roads. 1997. *Roads in the Wet Tropics.* Technology and Environment Division, Queensland Main Roads, Brisbane.

Quilty, P. G. 1994. The background: 144 million years of Australian palaeoclimate and palaeogeography. Pages 14–43 in R. S. Hill, ed., *The history of Australian vegetation: Cretaceous to Recent.* Cambridge University Press, Cambridge.

RADAMBRASIL, Projeto. 1973–1987. *Levantamento de recursos naturais.* Vols. 1–34. Ministério de Minas e Energia, Departamento Nacional de Produção Mineral and Instituto Brasileiro de Geografia e Estatística, Rio de Janeiro, Brazil.

RADAMBRASIL. 1977. *Levantamento de Recursos naturais.* Folha SB. 19, *Juruá.* Departamento Nacional da Produção Mineral, Rio de Janeiro, Brasil.

Raguso, R. A., and J. Llorente-B. 1991. The butterflies (Lepidoptera) of the Tuxtlas mountains, Veracruz, Mexico, revisited: Species richness and habitat disturbance. *Journal of Research on the Lepidoptera* 29:105–133.

———. 1997. Papilionoidea. Pages 257–291 in E. S. González, R. Dirzo, and R. C. Vogt, eds., *Historia natural de los Tuxtlas.* Instituto de Biologia, UNAM, México City, Mexico.

Raich, J. W., E. B. Rastetter, J. M. Melillo, D. W. Kicklighter, P. A. Steudler, B. J. Peterson, A. L. Grace, B. Moore, and C. J. Vorosmarty. 1991. Potential net primary productivity in South America: Application of a global model. *Ecological Applications* 1:399–429.

Rainforest Conservation Society of Queensland. 1986. *Tropical rainforests of North Queensland: Their conservation significance: A report to the Australian Heritage Commission.* Special Australian Heritage Publication Series, no. 3. Australian Government Publishing Service, Canberra.

Rakotomalaza, P. J., and N. Messmer. 1999. Structure and floristic composition of the vegetation in the Réserve Naturelle Integrale d'Andohahela, Madagascar. *Fieldiana: Zoology* 94:51–96.

Ramos-Onsins, S. E., and J. Rozas. 2002. Statistical properties of new neutrality tests against population growth. *Molecular Biology and Evolution* 19:2092–2100.

Ramsey, J., and D. W. Schemske. 1998. Pathways, mechanisms, and rates of polyploid formation in flowering plants. *Annual Review of Ecology and Systematics* 29:467–501.

———. 2002. Neopolyploidy in flowering plants. *Annual Review of Ecology and Systematics* 33:589–639.

Rapoport, E. H. 1994. Remarks on marine and continental biogeography: An areographical viewpoint. *Philosophical Transactions of the Royal Society of London* B 343:71–78.

Räsänen, M. 1993. La geohistoria y geología de la Amazonia peruana. Pages 43–67 in R. Kalliola, M. Puhakka, and W. Danjoy, eds., *Amazonia Peruana: Vegetación húmeda tropical en el llano subandino.* PAUT and ONERN, Jyväskylä, Finland.

Räsänen, M., A. M. Linna, J. C. R. Santos, and F. R. Negri. 1995. Late Miocene tidal deposits in the Amazonian foreland basin. *Science* 269:386–390.

Räsänen, M., R. Neller, J. Salo, and H. Jungner. 1992. Recent and ancient fluvial deposition systems in the Amazonian foreland basin, Peru. *Geological Magazine* 129:293–306.

Räsänen, M., J. Salo, H. Jungner, and L. R. Pittman. 1990. Evolution of the Western Amazon Lowland Relief: Impact of Andean foreland dynamics. *Terra Research* 2:320–332.

Räsänen, M., J. Salo, and R. J. Kalliola. 1987. Fluvial perturbance in the western Amazon Basin: Regulation by long-term sub-Andean tectonics. *Science* 238:1398–1401.

Rasmusson, E. M., X. Wang, and C. F. Ropelewski. 1990. The biennial component of ENSO variability. *Journal of Marine Systems* 1:71–96.

Raup, D. M., S. J. Gould, T. J. M. Schopf, and D. S. Simberloff. 1973. Stochastic models of phylogeny and the evolution of diversity. *Journal of Geology* 81:525–542.

Raven, P. H., and D. I. Axelrod. 1972. Plate tectonics and Australasian biogeography. *Science* 176:1379–1386.

Raven, R. J. 1981. A review of the Australian genera of the mygalomorph spider subfamily Diplurinae (Dipluridae: Chelicerata). *Australian Journal of Zoology* 29:321–363.

———. 1982a. On the mygalomorph spider genus *Xamiatus* Raven (Diplurinae: Dipluridae) with the description of a new species. *Memoirs of the Queensland Museum* 20:473–478.

———. 1982b. Systematics of the Australian mygalomorph spider genus *Ixamatus* Simon (Diplurinae: Dipluridae: Chelicerata). *Australian Journal of Zoology* 30:1035–1067.

———. 1984a. A new diplurid genus from eastern Australia and a related *Aname* species (Diplurinae: Dipluridae: Araneae). *Australian Journal of Zoology*, suppl. ser. 96:1–51.

———. 1984b. Systematics of the Australian curtain-web spiders (Ischnothelinae: Dipluridae: Chelicerata). *Australian Journal of Zoology*, suppl. ser. 93:1–102.

———. 1990. A revision of the Australian spider genus *Trittame* Koch (Mygalomorphae: Barychelidae) and a new related genus. *Invertebrate Taxonomy* 4:21–54.

———. 1993. The biodiversity of Australian mygalomorph spiders. 1. Two new species of *Namirea* (Araneae: Dipluridae). *Memoirs of the Queensland Museum* 34:81–88.

———. 1994. Mygalomorph spiders of the Barychelidae in Australia and the western Pacific. *Memoirs of the Queensland Museum* 35:291–706.

———. 2000. A new species of funnel-web spider (Hadronyche: Hexathelidae: Mygalomorphae) from North Queensland. *Memoirs of the Queensland Museum* 46:225–230.

Raven, R. J., K. Stumkat, and M. R. Gray. 2001. Revisions of Australian ground-hunting spiders: 1. *Amauropelma* gen. nov. (Araneomorphae: Ctenidae). *Records of the Western Australian Museum* 64:187–227.

Ray, C., and A. Hastings. 1996. Density dependence: Are we searching at the wrong spatial scale? *Journal of Animal Ecology* 65:556–566.

Reader, R. J. 1993. Control of seedling emergence by ground cover and seed predation in relation to seed size for some old-field species. *Journal of Ecology* 81:169–175.

Reader, R. J., and B. D. Bricker. 1994. Barriers to establishment of invading, non-forest plants in deciduous forest nature reserves. *Environmental Conservation* 21:62–66.

Redford, K. H. 1992. The empty forest. *BioScience* 42:412–422.

Redford, K. H., and A. M. Stearman. 1993. Forest-dwelling native Amazonians and the conservation of biodiversity. *Conservation Biology* 7:248–255.

Regal, P. J. 1977. Ecology and evolution of flowering plant dominance. *Science* 196:622–629.

Reid, C. A. M. 1999. Revision of leaf-beetles of the genus *Cadmus* Erichson, subgenus *Lachnabothra* Saunders (Coleoptera: Chrysomelidae: Cryptophalinae). *Invertebrate Taxonomy* 13:1–66.

———. 2000. A complex of cryptic species in the genus *Coptodactyla* Burmeister (Coleoptera: Scarabaeidae: Coprini). *Memoirs of the Queensland Museum* 46:231–251.

Reid, C. A. M., and R. I. Storey. 2000. Revision of the dung beetle genus *Temnoplectron* Westwood (Coleoptera: Scarabaeidae: Scarabaeini). *Memoirs of the Queensland Museum* 46:253–297.

Rejmanek, M. 1996. Species richness and resistance to invasions. Pages 153–171 in G. H. Orians, R. Dirzo, and J. H. Cushman, eds., *Biodiversity and ecosystem processes in tropical forests.* Springer, Berlin.

Remsen, J. V. Jr., ed. 1997. *Studies in Neotropical ornithology honoring Ted Parker.* Ornithological Monographs, no. 48. American Ornithologists' Union, Washington, DC.

Renner, S. S., H. Balslev, and L. B. Holm-Nielsen. 1990. Flowering plants of Amazonian Ecuador: A checklist. *AAU Reports* 24:1–241.

Repetto, R. 1988. *The forest for the trees: Government policies and misuse of forest resources.* Cambridge University Press, Cambridge.

Reznick, D. N., F. H. Shaw, F. H. Rodd, and R. G. Shaw. 1997. Evaluation of the rate of evolution in natural populations of guppies (*Poecilia reticulata*). *Science* 275:1934–1937.

Rice, R. R., and E. E. Hostert. 1993. Laboratory experiments on speciation: What have we learned in 40 years? *Evolution* 47:1637–1653.

Richards, P. 1952. *The tropical rain forest: An ecological study.* Cambridge University Press, Cambridge,

Richards, P. W. 1973. Africa, the "Odd Man Out." Pages 21–6 in B. J. Meggers, E. S. Ayensu, and W. D. Duckworth, eds., *Tropical forest ecosystems in Africa and South America.* Smithsonian Institution Press, Washington, DC.

Richman, A. D. 1996. Ecological diversification and community structure in the Old World leaf warblers (genus *Phylloscopus*): A phylogenetic perspective. *Evolution* 50:2461–2470.

Richter, D. D., and L. I. Babbar. 1991. Soil diversity in the tropics. *Advances in Ecological Research* 21:315–389.

Ricklefs, R. E. 1973. *Ecology.* Nelson, London.

———. 1987. Community diversity: Relative roles of local and regional processes. *Science* 235:167–171.

———. 1989. Speciation and diversity: Integration of local and regional processes. Pages 599–622 in D. Otte and J. A. Endler, eds., *Speciation and its consequences.* Sinauer Associates, Sunderland, MA.

———. 2000. The relationship between local and regional species richness in birds of the Caribbean Basin. *Journal of Animal Ecology* 69:1111–1116.

———. 2002. Splendid isolation: Historical ecology of the South American passerine fauna. *Journal of Avian Biology* 33:207–211.

———. 2003. A comment on Hubbell's zero-sum ecological drift model. *Oikos* 100:185–192.

Ricklefs, R. E., and E. Bermingham. 1999. Taxon cycles in the Lesser Antillean avifauna. *Ostrich* 70:49–59.

———. 2001. Nonequilibrium diversity dynamics of the Lesser Antillean avifauna. *Science* 294:1522–1524.

———. 2002a. The concept of the taxon cycle in biogeography. *Global Ecology and Biogeography* 11:353–361.

———. 2002b. Islands, equilibria, and speciation: Response. *Science* 296:975a.

Ricklefs, R. E., and G. W. Cox. 1972. Taxon cycles in the West Indian avifauna. *American Naturalist* 106:195–219.

———. 1978. Stage of taxon cycle, habitat distribution, and population density in the avifauna of the West Indies. *American Naturalist* 112:875–895.

Ricklefs, R. E., and R. E. Latham. 1993. Global patterns of diversity in mangrove floras. Pages 215–229 in R. E. Ricklefs and D. Schluter, eds., *Species diversity in ecological communities: Historical and geographical perspectives.* University of Chicago Press, Chicago.

Ricklefs, R. E., and S. S. Renner. 1994. Species richness within families of flowering plants. *Evolution* 48:1619–1636.

———. 2000. Evolutionary flexibility and flowering plant familial diversity: A comment on Dodd, Silvertown and Chase. *Evolution* 54:1061–1065.

Ricklefs, R. E., and D. Schluter, eds. 1993a. *Species diversity in ecological communities: Historical and geographical perspectives.* University of Chicago Press, Chicago.

———. 1993b. Species diversity: Regional and historical influences. Pages 350–363 in R. E. Ricklefs and D. Schluter, eds., *Species diversity in ecological communities: Historical and geographical perspectives.* University of Chicago Press, Chicago.

Riddle, B. R. 1996. The molecular phylogeographic bridge between deep and shallow history in continental biotas. *Trends in Ecology and Evolution* 11:207–211.

Rieseberg, L. H., and J. F. Wendel. 1993. Introgression and its consequences in plants. Pages 70–109 in R. G. Harrison, ed., *Hybrid zones and the evolutionary process.* Oxford University Press, New York.

Rind, D., and D. Peteet. 1985. Terrestrial conditions at the last glacial maximum and CLIMAP sea-surface temperature estimates: Are they consistent? *Quaternary Research* 24:1–22.

Ritchie, J. C. 1977. The modern and Late Quaternary vegetation of the Campbell-Dolomite uplands, near Inuvik, N.W.T., Canada. *Ecological Monographs* 47:401–423.

Robbins, R. K., G. Lamas, O. H. H. Mielke, D. J. Harvey, and M. M. Casagrande. 1996. Taxonomic composition and ecological structure of the species-rich butterfly community at Pakitza, Parque Nacional del Manu, Peru. Pages 217–252 in D. E. Wilson and A. Sandoval, eds., *Manu: The biodiversity of southeastern Peru.* Smithsonian Institution Press, Washington, DC.

Robbins, R. K., and G. B. Small. 1981. Wind dispersal of Panamanian hairstreak butterflies (Lepidoptera: Lycaenidae) and its evolutionary significance. *Biotropica* 13:308–315.

Roberts, R. G., R. Jones, and M. A. Smith. 1990. Thermoluminescence dating of a 50,000-year-old human occupation site in northern Australia. *Nature* 345:153–156.

Robertson, D. R. 1996. Interspecific competition controls abundance and habitat use of territorial Caribbean damselfishes. *Ecology* 77:885–899.

Robertson, D. R., and S. D. Gaines. 1986. Interference competition structures habitat use in a local assemblage of coral reef surgeonfishes. *Ecology* 67:1372–1383.

Robinson, J. G. 1993. The limits to caring: Sustainable living and the loss of biodiversity. *Conservation Biology* 7:20–28.

Robinson, J. G., and K. Redford, eds. 1991. *Neotropical wildlife use and conservation.* University of Chicago Press, Chicago.

Robinson, W. D. 2001. Changes in abundance of birds in a Neotropical forest fragment over 25 years: A review. *Animal Biodiversity and Conservation* 24(2):51–65.

Rogers, A. R., and H. Harpending. 1992. Population growth makes waves in the distribution of pairwise genetic differences. *Molecular Biology and Evolution* 9:552–569.

Rohde, K. 1992. Latitudinal gradients in species diversity: The search for the primary cause. *Oikos* 65:514–527.

Romoleroux, K., R. Foster, R. Valencia, R. Condit, H. Balslev, and E. Losos. 1997. Especies leñosas (dap ≥ 1 cm) encontradas en dos hectáreas de un bosque de la Amazonía ecuatoriana. Pages 189–215 in R. Valencia and H. Balslev, eds., *Estudios sobre diversidad y ecología de plantas.* Pontificia Universidad Católica del Ecuador, Quito.

Ron, S. R. 2001. Biogeographic area relationships of lowland Neotropical rainforest, based on raw distributions of vertebrate groups. *Biological Journal of the Linnean Society* 71:379–402.

Ropelewski, C. F., and M. S. Halpert. 1987. Global and regional scale precipitation patterns associated with the El Niño/Southern Oscillation. *Monthly Weather Review* 115:1606–1626.

———. 1989. Precipitation patterns associated with the high index phase of the Southern Oscillation. *Journal of Climate* 2:268–284.

Rosen, D. E. 1978. Vicariant patterns and historical explanation in biogeography. *Systematic Zoology* 27:159–188.

Rosenfeld, D. 1999. TRMM observed first direct evidence of smoke from forest fires inhibiting rainfall. *Geophysical Research Letters* 26:3105–3108.

Rosenzweig, M. L. 1995. *Species diversity in space and time.* Cambridge University Press, Cambridge.

Rosenzweig, M. L., and Z. Abramsky. 1986. Centrifugal community organization. *Oikos* 46:339–348.

———. 1993. How are diversity and productivity related? Pages 52–65 in R. E. Ricklefs and D. Schluter, eds., *Species diversity in ecological communities: Historical and geographical perspectives.* University of Chicago Press, Chicago.

Rosser, Z., and R. G. Pearson. 1995. Responses of rock fauna to physical disturbance in two Australian tropical rainforest streams. *Journal of the North American Benthological Society* 14:183–196.

Round, P. D. 1988. *Resident forest birds in Thailand: Their status and conservation.* ICBP Monograph no. 2. International Council for Bird Preservation, Cambridge.

Rowett, A. I. 1991. The dispersed cuticular floras of South Australian Tertiary coalfields. Part 1: Sedan. *Transactions of the Royal Society of South Australia* 115(1):21–36.

———. 1992. The dispersed cuticular floras of South Australian Tertiary coalfields. Part 2: Lochiel. *Transactions of the Royal Society of South Australia* 116(3):95–107.

Rowett, A. I., and A. D. Sparrow. 1994. Multivariate analysis of Australian Eocene dispersed cuticle floras: Influence of age, geography and taphonomy on biozonation. *Review of Palaeobotany and Palynology* 81:165–183.

Roy, K., D. Jablonski, and J. W. Valentine. 2000. Dissecting latitudinal diversity gradients: Functional groups and clades of marine bivalves. *Proceedings of the Royal Society of London* B 267:293–299.

Roy, K., J. W. Valentine, D. Jablonski, and S. M. Kidwell. 1996. Scales of climate variability and time averaging in Pleistocene biotas: Implications for ecology and evolution. *Trends in Ecology and Evolution* 11:458–463.

Roy, M. S. 1997. Recent diversification in African greenbuls (*Andropadus:* Pycnonotidae) supports montane speciation model. *Proceedings of the Royal Society of London* B 278:1–8.

Roy, M. S., P. Arctander, and J. Fjeldså. 1998. Speciation and taxonomy of montane greenbuls of the genus *Andropadus* (Aves: Pycnonotidae). *Steenstrupia* 24:51–66.

Roy, M. S., J. M. C. da Silva, P. Arctander, J. Garcia-Moreno, and J. Fjeldså. 1997. The role of montane regions in the speciation of South American and African birds. Pages 325–343 in D. Mindell, ed., *Avian molecular evolution and systematics.* Academic Press, San Diego.

Royer, D. L., S. L. Wing, D. J. Beerling, D. W. Jolley, P. L. Koch, L. J. Hickey, and R. A. Berner. 2001. Paleobotanical evidence for near present-day levels of atmospheric CO_2 during part of the Tertiary. *Science* 292:2310–2313.

Rozefelds, A. C, 1990. A new Mid-Tertiary rainforest flora from Capella, in central Queensland. Pages 123–136 in J. G. Douglas and D. C. Christophel, eds., *Proceedings of the 3rd IOP Conference, 1988.* IOP Publication no. 2. A-Z Printers and International Organisation of Palaeobotanists, Melbourne.

———. 1995. Miocene *Wilkinsonia* fruits (Hicksbeachiinae, Proteaceae) from the base of the Yallourn Formation, Latrobe valley, Victoria. *Papers and Proceedings of the Royal Society of Tasmania* 129:59–62.

Rozefelds, A. C., and D. C. Christophel. 1996a. *Elaeocarpus* (Elaeocarpaceae) endocarps from the Early to Middle Miocene Yallourn Formation. *Muelleria* 9:229–237.

———. 1996b. *Elaeocarpus* (Elaeocarpaceae) endocarps from the Oligo-Miocene of eastern Australia. *Papers and Proceedings of the Royal Society of Tasmania* 130:41–48.

Rozefelds, A. C., D. C. Christophel, and N. F. Alley. 1992. Tertiary occurrence of the fern *Lygodium* (Schizaeaceae) in Australia and New Zealand. *Memoirs of the Queensland Museum* 32:203–222.

Rubinoff, R. W., and I. Rubinoff. 1971. Geographic and reproductive isolation in Atlantic and Pacific populations of Panamanian *Bathygobius*. *Evolution* 25:88–97.

Rumbaugh, J. 1991. *Object-oriented modelling and design*. Prentice Hall, Englewood Cliffs, NJ.

Rundle, H. D., L. Nagel, J. W. Boughman, and D. Schluter. 2000. Natural selection and parallel speciation in sympatric sticklebacks. *Science* 287:306–308.

Ruokolainen, K., A. Linna, and H. Tuomisto. 1997. Use of Melastomataceae and pteridophytes for revealing phytogeographic patterns in Amazonian rain forests. *Journal of Tropical Ecology* 13:243–256.

Ruokolainen, K., and H. Tuomisto. 1998. Vegetación natural de la zona de Iquitos. Pages 253–365 in R. Kalliola and S. Flores Paitán, eds., *Geoecología y desarrollo Amazónico: Estudio integrado en la zona de Iquitos, Perú*. Annales Universitatis Turkuensis Ser A II, vol. 114. University of Turku, Finland.

Ruokolainen, K., H. Tuomisto, J. Chave, H. C. Muller-Landau, R. Condit, N. Pitman, J. Terborgh, S. P. Hubbell, E. G. Leigh Jr., J. F. Duivenvoorden, J.-C. Svenning, and S. J. Wright. 2002. Beta-diversity in tropical forests. *Science* 297:1439.

Ruokolainen, K., H. Tuomisto, J. Vormisto, and N. Pitman. 2002. Potential effects of two biases on estimating Amazonian plant distributions. *Journal of Tropical Ecology* 18:935–942.

Russell, B. L. 1997. Systematics of an aradid flat bug, *Aellocoris* Kormilev, inhabiting rainforest blocks in the Wet Tropics. Honours thesis, University of Queensland, Brisbane.

Russell, J. K. 1982. Timing of reproduction by coatis (*Nasua narica*) in relation to fluctuations in food resources. Pages 413–431 in E. G. Leigh Jr., A. S. Rand, and D. M. Windsor, eds., *Ecology of a tropical forest*. Smithsonian Institution Press, Washington, DC.

Rylands, A. B. 1991. *The status of conservation areas in the Brazilian Amazon*. World Wildlife Fund, Washington, DC.

Rylands, A. B., and L. P. Pinto. 1998. *Conservação da biodiversidade na Amazônia Brasiliera: Uma análise do sistema de unidades de conservação*. Brazilian Foundation for Sustainable Development, Brasília, Brazil.

Saatchi, S. S., B. W. Nelson, E. Podest, and J. Holt. 2000. Mapping land cover types in the Amazon using 11-km JERS-1 mosaic. *International Journal of Remote Sensing* 21:1201–1234.

Saenger, P., E. J. Hegerl, and J. D. S. Davie. 1983. Global status of mangrove ecosystems. *Environmentalist* 3:1–88.

Sakai, S., K. Momose, T. Yumoto, T. Nagamitsu, H. Nagamasu, A. A. Hamid, and T. Nakashizuka. 1999. Plant reproductive phenology over four years including an episode of general flowering in a lowland dipterocarp forest, Sarawak, Malaysia. *American Journal of Botany* 86:1414–1436.

Salati, E., and P. B. Vose. 1984. Amazon Basin: A system in equilibrium. *Science* 225:129–138.

Salazar-E., J. A. 1995. Lista preliminar de las mariposas diurnas Lepidoptera: *Rhopalocera* que habitan el Departamento de Putumayo: Notas sobre la distribución en la zona andina. *Colombia Amazonica* 8:11–69.

Saldariagga, J., and D. C. West. 1986. Holocene fires in the northern Amazon Basin. *Quaternary Research* 26:358–366.

Sale, P. F. 1977. Maintenance of high diversity in coral reef fish communities. *American Naturalist* 111:337–359.

Salo, J. 1987. Pleistocene forest refuges in the Amazon: Evaluation of the biostratigraphical, lithostratigraphical and geomorphological data. *Annales Zoologici Fennici* 24:203–211.

———. 1988. Rainforest diversification in the western Amazon basin: The role of river dynamics. Report no. 16. Department of Biology, University of Turku, Finland.

Salo, J., R. Kalliola, I. Häkkinen, Y. Mäkinen, P. Niemelä, M. Puhakka, and P. D. Coley. 1986. River dynamics and the diversity of Amazon lowland forest. *Nature* 322:254–258.

Samuelson, G. A. 1989. A review of the hispine tribe Aproidini (Coleoptera: Chrysomelidae). *Memoirs of the Queensland Museum* 27:599–604.

Sánchez-Hidalgo, M. E., M. Martínez-Ramos, and F. J. Espinosa-García. 1999. Chemical differentiation between leaves of seedlings and spatially close adult trees from the tropical rainforest species *Nectandra ambigens* (Lauraceae): An alternative test of the Janzen-Connell model. *Functional Ecology* 13:725–732.

Sanders, H. L. 1968. Marine benthic diversity: A comparative study. *American Naturalist* 102:243–282.

Sanderson, R. A., S. P. Rushton, A. T. Pickering, and J. P. Byrne. 1995. A preliminary method of predicting plant species distributions using the British national vegetation classification. *Journal of Environmental Management* 43:265–288.

Sanford, R. L., J. Saldariagga, K. Clark, C. Uhl, and R. Herrera. 1985. Amazon rain-forest fires. *Science* 227:53–55.

Sarre, A., M. Sobral Filho, and M. Reis. 1996. The amazing Amazon. *ITTO Tropical Forest Update* 6(4):3–7.

Sauer, J. D. 1988. *Plant migration: The dynamics of geographic patterning in seed plant species.* University of California Press, Berkeley.

Saunders, H. L. 1968. Benthic marine diversity: A comparative study. *American Naturalist* 102:243–282.

Savolainen, V., S. B. Heard, M. P. Powell, T. J. Davies, and A. O. Mooers. 2002. Is cladogenesis heritable? *Systematic Biology* 51:835–843.

Sayer, J. A., C. S. Harcourt, and N. M. Collins. 1992. *The conservation atlas of tropical forests: Africa.* World Conservation Monitoring Centre, Cambridge.

Scambler, D. J. 1989. A revision of the genus *Psilomorpha* Saunders (Coleoptera: Cerambycidae: Cerambicinae). *Invertebrate Taxonomy* 3:163–173.

Schemske, D. W., and H. D. Bradshaw. 1999. Pollinator preference and the evolution of floral traits in monkeyflowers (*Mimulus*). *Proceedings of the National Academy of Sciences USA* 96:11910–11915.

Schlesinger, W. H. 1991. *Biogeochemistry: An analysis of global change.* Academic Press, San Diego.

Schluter, D. 1998. Ecological causes of speciation. Pages 114–129 in D. J. Howard and S. H.

Berlocher, eds., *Endless forms: Species and speciation.* Oxford University Press, New York.

———. 2000. *The ecology of adaptive radiation.* Oxford: Oxford University Press.

Schluter, D., and J. D. McPhail. 1992. Ecological character displacement and speciation in sticklebacks. *American Naturalist* 140:85–108.

Schluter, D., and L. M. Nagel. 1995. Parallel speciation by natural selection. *American Naturalist* 146:292–301.

Schluter, D., and R. R. Repasky. 1991. Worldwide limitation of finch densities by food and other factors. *Ecology* 72:1763–1774.

Schluter, D., and R. E. Ricklefs. 1993a. Convergence and the regional component of species diversity. Pages 230–242 in R. E. Ricklefs and D. Schluter, eds., *Species diversity in ecological communities: Historical and geographical perspectives.* University of Chicago Press, Chicago.

———. 1993b. Species diversity: An introduction to the problem. Pages 1–10 in R. E. Ricklefs and D. Schluter, eds., *Species diversity in ecological communities: Historical and geographical perspectives.* University of Chicago Press, Chicago.

Schneider, C. J., M. Cunningham, and C. Moritz. 1998. Comparative phylogeography and the history of endemic vertebrates in the Wet Tropics rainforests of Australia. *Molecular Ecology* 7:487–498.

Schneider, C. J., and C. Moritz. 1999. Rainforest refugia and evolution in Australia's Wet Tropics. *Proceedings of the Royal Society of London* B 266:191–196.

Schneider, C. J., T. B. Smith, B. Larison, and C. Moritz. 1999. A test of alternative models of diversification in tropical rainforests: Ecological gradients vs. rainforest refugia. *Proceedings of the National Academy of Sciences USA* 96:13869–13873.

Schnitzer, S. A., J. W. Dalling, and W. P. Carson. 2000. The impact of lianas on tree regeneration in tropical forest canopy gaps: Evidence for an alternative pathway of gap phase regeneration. *Journal of Ecology* 88:655–666.

Scholes, R. J., and N. van Breemen. 1997. The effects of global change on tropical ecosystems. *Geoderma* 79:9–24.

Schonewald-Cox, C. M., and J. W. Bayless. 1986. The boundary model: A geographical analysis of design and conservation of nature reserves. *Biological Conservation* 38:305–322.

Schwarzbach, A. E., and R. E. Ricklefs. 2000. Systematic affinities of Rhizophoraceae and Anisophyllaceae, and intergeneric relationships with the Rhizophoraceae, based on chloroplast DNA, nuclear ribosomal DNA, and morphology. *American Journal of Botany* 87:547–564.

Scott, D. L. 1993. Architecture of the Queensland Trough: Implications for the structure and tectonics of the northeastern Australian margin. *AGSO Journal of Australian Geology and Geophysics* 14:21–34.

Scriven, L. J., S. McLoughlin, and R. S. Hill. 1995. *Nothofagus plicata* (Nothofagaceae), a new deciduous Eocene macrofossil species, from southern continental Australia. *Review of Palaeobotany and Palynology* 86:199–209.

Seehausen, O., J. J. M. van Alphen, and R. Lande. 1999. Color pattern and sex ratio distortion in a cichlid fish as an incipient stage in sympatric speciation by sexual selection. *Ecology Letters* 2:367–378.

Seehausen, O., J. J. M. van Alphen, and F. Witte. 1997. Cichlid fish diversity threatened by eutrophication that curbs sexual selection. *Science* 277:1808–1811.

Seiffert, E. R., E. L. Simons, and Y. Attia. 2003. Fossil evidence for an ancient divergence of lorises and galagos. *Nature* 422:421–424.

Serle, W., G. J. Morel, and W. Hartwig. 1977. *A field guide to the birds of West Africa.* Collins, London.

Servant, M., J. Maley, B. Turcq, M. L. Absy, P. Brenac, M. Fournier, and M. P. Ledru. 1993. Tropical forest changes during the late Quaternary in African and South American lowlands. *Global and Planetary Change* 7:25–40.

Sevenster, J. G., and J. J. M. van Alphen. 1993. A life history trade off in *Drosophila* species and community structure in variable environments. *Journal of Animal Ecology* 62:720–736.

———. 1996. Aggregation and coexistence. 2. A Neotropical *Drosophila* community. *Journal of Animal Ecology* 65:308–324.

Shackleton, N. J., A. Berger, and W. R. Peltier. 1990. An alternative astronomical calibration of the lower Pleistocene timescale based on ODP Site 677. *Transactions of the Royal Society of Edinburgh: Earth Sciences* 81:251–261.

Shackleton, N. J., S. Crowhurst, T. Hagelberg, N. Pisias, and D. A. Schneider. 1995. A new late Neogene timescale: Applications to leg 138 sites. *Proceedings of Ocean Drilling Program, Scientific Results* 138:73–101.

Shackleton, N. J., and J. P. Kennett. 1975. *Paleotemperature history of the Cenozoic and the initiation of Antarctic glaciation: Oxygen and carbon isotope analyses in DSDP sites 277, 279, and 281.* Initial Reports of the Deep Sea Drilling Project, 29. U.S. Government Printing Service, Washington, DC.

Shea, K., and P. Chesson. 2002. Community ecology theory as a framework for biological invasions. *Trends in Ecology and Evolution* 17:170–176.

Shelly, T. E. 1984. Comparative foraging behavior of Neotropical robber flies (Diptera: Asilidae). *Oecologia* 62:188–195.

Sheppard, P. M., J. R. G. Turner, K. S. Brown Jr., W. W. Benson, and M. C. Singer. 1985. Genetics and the evolution of Muellerian mimicry in *Heliconius* butterflies. *Philosophical Transactions of the Royal Society of London* B 308:433–613.

Shmida, A., and M. V. Wilson. 1985. Biological determinants of species diversity. *Journal of Biogeography* 12:1–20.

Shugart, H. H. 1984. *A theory of forest dynamics.* Springer Verlag, New York.

———. 1991. Spatial application of gap models. *Forest Ecology and Management* 42:95–110.

Shugart, H. H., M. S. Hopkins, I. P. Burgess, and A. T. Mortlock. 1980. The development of a succession model for subtropical rain forest and its application to assess the effects of timber harvest at Wiangaree State Forest. *Journal of Environmental Management* 11:243–265.

Shugart, H. H., and I. R. Noble. 1981. A computer model of succession and fire response of the high altitude *Eucalyptus* forest of the Brindabella Range, Australian Capital Territory. *Australian Journal of Ecology* 6:149–164.

Shukla, J., C. Nobre, and P. Sellers. 1990. Amazon deforestation and climate change. *Science* 247:1322–1325.

Sibley, C. G., and J. E. Ahlquist. 1990. *Phylogeny and classification of the birds of the world: A study in molecular evolution.* Yale University Press, New Haven, CT.

Siegert, F., G. Ruecker, A. Hinrichs, and A. A. Hoffmann. 2001. Increased damage from fires in logged forests during droughts caused by El Niño. *Nature* 414:437–440.

Silliman, B. R., and M. D. Bertness. 2002. A trophic cascade regulates salt marsh primary production. *Proceedings of the National Academy of Sciences USA* 99:10500–10505.

Silva, L. L. 1996. *Ecologia: Manejo de áreas silvestres.* Ministry of the Environment, Brasília, Brazil.

Silver, W. L. 1994. Is nutrient availability related to plant nutrient use in humid tropical forests? *Oecologia* 98:336–343.

Silver, W. L., F. N. Scatena, A. H. Johnson, T. G. Siccama, and M. J. Sanchez. 1994. Nutrient availability in a montane wet tropical forest: Spatial patterns and methodological considerations. *Plant and Soil* 164:129–145.

Silvera, K., J. B. Skillman, and J. W. Dalling. 2003. Seed germination, seedling growth and habitat partitioning in two morphotypes of the tropical pioneer tree *Trema micrantha* in a seasonal forest in Panama. *Journal of Tropical Ecology* 19:27–34.

Silvert, W. 1993. Object-orientated ecosystem modelling. *Ecological Modelling* 68:91–118.

Simpson, B. B., and J. Haffer. 1978. Speciation patterns in the Amazonian forest biota. *Annual Review of Ecology and Systematics* 9:497–518.

Simpson, G. G. 1964. Species density of North American Recent mammals. *Systematic Zoology* 13:57–73.

———. 1980. *Splendid isolation: The curious history of South American mammals.* Yale University Press, New Haven, CT.

Simpson, K., and N. Day. 1984. *The birds of Australia.* Tanager Books, Dover, NH.

Sinclair, A. R. E. 1975. The resource limitation of trophic levels in tropical grassland ecosystems. *Journal of Animal Ecology* 44:497–520.

———. 1979. The eruption of the ruminants. Pages 82–103 in A. R. E. Sinclair and M. Norton-Griffiths, ed., *Serengeti: Dynamics of an ecosystem.* University of Chicago Press, Chicago.

Sinclair, A. R. E., and P. Arcese. 1995. Population consequences of predation-sensitive foraging: The Serengeti wildebeest. *Ecology* 76:882–891.

Sinclair, D. P. 2000. Two new genera of Tessaratomidae (Hemiptera: Heteroptera: Pentatomoidea). *Memoirs of the Queensland Museum* 46:299–305.

Sioli, H. 1984. *The Amazon: Limnology and landscape ecology of a mighty tropical river and its basin.* Dr. W. Junk, The Hague.

Sizer, N., and R. Rice. 1995. *Backs to the wall in Suriname: Forest policy in a country in crisis.* World Resources Institute, Washington, DC.

Skellam, J. G. 1951. Random dispersal in theoretical populations. *Biometrika* 38:196–218.

Skole, D., and C. J. Tucker. 1993. Tropical deforestation and habitat fragmentation in the Amazon: Satellite data from 1978 to 1988. *Science* 260:1905–1910.

Slabbekoorn, H., and T. B. Smith. 2002. Habitat-dependent song divergence in the little greenbul: An analysis of environmental selection pressures on acoustic signals. *Evolution* 56:1849–1858.

Slatkin, M. 1987. Gene flow and the geographic structure of natural populations. *Science* 236:787–792.

———. 1993. Isolation by distance in equilibrium and non-equilibrium populations. *Evolution* 47:264–279.

———. 1994. Cladistic analysis of DNA sequence data from subdivided populations. Pages 18–34 in L. A. Real, ed., *Ecological genetics.* Princeton University Press, Princeton, NJ.

Slatkin, M., and R. R. Hudson. 1991. Pairwise comparisons of mitochondrial DNA sequences in stable and exponentially growing populations. *Genetics* 129:555–562.

Slatkin, M., and W. P. Maddison. 1989. A cladistic measure of gene flow from the phylogenies of alleles. *Genetics* 123:603–613.

Slipinski, S. A. 1988. Revision of the Australian Cerylonidae (Coleoptera: Cucujoidea). *Annales Zoologici* 42:1–74.

Slowinski, J. B., and C. Guyer. 1993. Testing whether certain traits have caused amplified diversification: An improved method based on a model of random speciation and extinction. *American Naturalist* 142:1019–1024.

Small, A., J. Playford, G. Werren, and A. Shapcott. 1997. Vegetation studies in the Daintree lowlands: A community approach to biodiversity conservation. Pages 452–457 in P. Hale and D. Lamb, eds., *Conservation outside nature reserves.* University of Queensland Press, Brisbane.

Smith, A. G., D. G. Smith, and B. M. Funnell. 1994. *Atlas of Mesozoic and Cenozoic coastlines.* Cambridge University Press, Cambridge.

Smith, T. B. 1987. Bill size polymorphism and intraspecific niche utilization in an African finch. *Nature* 329:717–719.

———. 1990a. Natural selection on bill characters in the two bill morphs of the African finch *Pyrenestes ostrinus. Evolution* 44:832–842.

———. 1990b. Resource use by bill morphs of an African finch: Evidence for intraspecific competition. *Ecology* 71:1246–1257.

———. 1991. Inter- and intra-specific diet overlap during lean times between *Quelea erythrops* and bill morphs of *Pyrenestes ostrinus. Oikos* 60:76–82.

———. 1993. Disruptive selection and the genetic basis of bill size polymorphism in the African finch, *Pyrenestes. Nature* 363:618–620.

———. 1997. Adaptive significance of the mega-billed form in the polymorphic black-bellied seedcracker *Pyrnestes ostrinus. Ibis* 139:382–387.

Smith, T. B., M. W. Bruford, and R. K. Wayne. 1993. The preservation of process: The missing element of conservation programs. *Biodiversity Letters* 1:164–167.

Smith, T. B., and D. J. Girman. 2000. Reaching new adaptive peaks: Evolution of alternative bill forms in an African finch. Pages 139–156 in T. A. Mousseau, B. Sinervo, and J. A. Endler, eds., *Adaptive genetic variation in the wild.* Oxford University Press, New York.

Smith, T. B., K. Holder, D. Girman, K. O'Keefe, B. Larison, and Y. Chan. 2000. Comparative avian phylogeography of Cameroon and Equatorial Guinea mountains: Implications for conservation. *Molecular Ecology* 9:1505–1516.

Smith, T. B., and D. McNiven. 1993. Preliminary survey of the avifauna of Mt. Tchabal Mbabo, west-central Cameroon. *Bird Conservation International* 3:13–19.

Smith, T. B., S. Saatchi, C. Graham, H. Slabbekoorn, and G. Spicer. Forthcoming. Putting process on the map: Why ecotones are important for preserving biodiversity. In A. Purvis, J. Gittleman, and T. Brooks, eds., *Phylogeny and conservation.* Cambridge University Press, Cambridge.

Smith, T. B., C. J. Schneider, and K. Holder. 2001. Refugial isolation vs. ecological gradients: Testing alternative mechanisms of evolutionary divergence in four rainforest vertebrates. *Genetica* 112:383–398.

Smith, T. B., and S. Skulason. 1996. Evolutionary significance of resource polymorphism in fish, amphibians and birds. *Annual Review of Ecology and Systematics* 27:111–133.

Smith, T. B., R. K. Wayne, D. J. Girman, and M. W. Bruford. 1997. A role for ecotones in generating rainforest biodiversity. *Science* 276:1855–1857.

Smythe, N. 1978. *The natural history of the Central American agouti.* Smithsonian Contributions to Zoology, no. 257. Smithsonian Institution Press, Washington, DC.

———. 1986. Competition and resource partitioning in the guild of Neotropical terrestrial frugivorous mammals. *Annual Review of Ecology and Systematics* 17:169–188.

———. 1989. Seed survival in the palm *Astrocaryum standleyanum:* Evidence for dependence upon its seed dispersers. *Biotropica* 21:50–56.

Smythe, N., W. E. Glanz, and E. G. Leigh Jr. 1982. Population regulation in some terrestrial frugivores. Pages 227–238 in E. G. Leigh Jr., A. S. Rand, and D. M. Windsor, eds., *Ecology of a tropical forest.* Smithsonian Institution Press, Washington, DC.

Sniderman, J. M. K. 1999. Early Pleistocene vegetation and climate change at Stony Creek Basin, western uplands of Victoria, Australia. B.Sc. (Hons) thesis, Monash University, Melbourne.

Sollins, P. 1998. Factors influencing species composition in tropical lowland rain forest: Does soil matter? *Ecology* 79:23–30.

Soltani, A., and T. Osborne. 1994. *Arteries for global trade, consequences for Amazonia.* Amazon Watch, Malibu, CA.

Soltis, D. E., P. S. Soltis, and M. W. Chase, et al. 2000. Angiosperm phylogeny inferred from 18S rDNA, rbcL, and atpB sequences. *Botanical Journal of the Linnean Society* 133:381–461.

Sork, V. L., J. Bramble, and O. Sexton. 1993. Ecology of mast-fruiting in three species of North American deciduous oaks. *Ecology* 74:528–541.

Soubies, F., K. Suguio, and L. Martin. 1991. The Quaternary lacustrine deposits of the Serra dos Carajás (State of Para, Brazil): Ages and other preliminary results. *Boletim IG-USP, Publicação Especial* 8:233–243.

Southgate, D., M. Coles-Ritchie, and P. Salazar-Canalos. 1996. Can tropical forests be saved by harvesting non-timber products? CSERGE Working Paper GEC 96–02. Norwich, U.K.

Southwood, T. R. E. 1996. Natural communities: Structure and dynamics. *Philosophical Transactions of the Royal Society of London* 351:1113–1129.

Sparrow, H. R., T. D. Sisk, P. R. Ehrlich, and D. D. Murphy. 1994. Techniques and guidelines for monitoring Neotropical butterflies. *Conservation Biology* 8:800–9.

Specht, R. L., M. E., Dettmann, and D. M. Jarzen. 1992. Community associations and structure in the Late Cretaceous vegetation of southeast Australasia and Antarctica. *Palaeogeography, Palaeoclimatology, Palaeoecology* 94:283–309.

Spector, S. 2002. Biogeographic crossroads as priority areas for biodiversity conservation. *Conservation Biology* 16:1480–1487.

Spicer, R. A. 1988. The formation and interpretation of plant fossil assemblages. *Advances in Botanical Research* 16:96–191.

Srivastava, D. 1999. Using local-regional richness plots to test for species saturation: Pitfalls and potentials. *Journal of Animal Ecology* 68:1–16.

Stallard, R., T. García, and M. Mitre. 1999. Hidrologia y suelos. Pages 57–83 in S. Heckadon-Moreno, R. Ibáñez, and R. Condit, eds., *La Cuenca del Canal: Deforestación, Urbanización y Contaminación.* Smithsonian Tropical Research Institute, Panamá.

StatSoft, Inc. 1995. *Statistica for Windows.* StatSoft, Inc., Tulsa, Oklahoma.

Stattersfield, A. J., M. J. Crosby, A. J. Long, and D. C. Wege. 1998. *Endemic bird areas of the world: Priorities for biodiversity conservation.* BirdLife International, Cambridge.

Steadman, D. W. 1995. Prehistoric extinctions of island birds: Biodiversity meets zooarchaeology. *Science* 267:1123–1131.

Steart, D. C., P. I. Boon, D. R. Greenwood, and N. T. Diamond. 2002. Transport of leaf litter in upland streams of *Eucalyptus* and *Nothofagus* forests in south-eastern Australia. *Archiv für Hydrobiologie* 156:43–61.

Stebbins, G. L. 1950. *Variation and evolution in plants.* Columbia University Press, New York.

———. 1974. *Flowering plants: Evolution above the species level.* Harvard University Press, Cambridge, MA.

Stebnicka, Z. T., and H. F. Howden. 1996. Australian genera and species in the tribes Odontolochini, Psammodiini, Rhyparini, Stereomerini and part of the Eupariini (Coleoptera: Scarabaeoidea: Aphodiinae). *Invertebrate Taxonomy* 10:97–170.

Steininger, M. K., C. Tucker, P. Ersts, T. Killeen, and S. Hecht. 2001. Clearance and fragmentation of semi-deciduous tropical forest in the Tierras Bajas zone, Santa Cruz, Bolivia. *Conservation Biology* 15:856–866.

Steininger, M. K., C. Tucker, J. Townshend, V. Bell, A. Desch, P. Ersts, and T. Killeen. 2001. Tropical Deforestation in the Bolivian Amazon. *Environmental Conservation* 28:127–134.

Stevens, G. C. 1989. The latitudinal gradient in geographical range: How so many species coexist in the tropics. *American Naturalist* 133:240–256.

Stevens, W. E. 1968. *The conservation of wildlife in West Malaysia.* Office of the Warden, Federal Game Department, Ministry of Lands and Mines, Serembang.

Stewart, R. H., J. L. Stewart, and W. P. Woodring. 1980. Geologic map of the Panama Canal and vicinity, Republic of Panama. United States Geological Survey, Reston, VA.

Stirton, R. A., R. H. Tedford, and M. O. Woodburne. 1967. A new Tertiary formation and fauna from the Tirari Desert, South Australia. *Records of the South Australian Museum* 15:427–462.

Stone, T., and P. Lefebvre. 1998. Using multi-temporal satellite data to evaluate selective logging in Pará, Brazil. *International Journal of Remote Sensing* 19:2517–2526.

Storey, R. I. 1984. A new species of *Aptenocanthon* Matthews from North Queensland. (Coleoptera: Scarabaeidae: Scarabaeinae). *Memoirs of the Queensland Museum* 21:387–390.

———. 1986. A new flightless species of *Aulacopris* White from North Queensland (Coleoptera: Scarabaeidae: Scarabaeinae). *Memoirs of the Queensland Museum* 22:197–203.

Storey, R. I., and H. F. Howden. 1996. Revision of *Australoxenella* Howden & Storey in Australia (Coleoptera: Scarabaeidae: Aphodiinae). *Memoirs of the Queensland Museum* 39: 365–380.

Storey, R. I., and G. B. Monteith. 2000. Five new species of *Aptenocanthon* Matthews (Coleoptera: Scarabaeidae: Scarabaeinae) from tropical Australia, with notes on distribution. *Memoirs of the Queensland Museum* 46:349–358.

Storey, R. I., and T. A. Weir. 1990. New species of *Onthophagus* Latreille (Coleoptera: Scarabaeidae) from Australia. *Invertebrate Taxonomy* 3:783–815.

Stork, N. E. 1988. Insect diversity: Facts, fiction and speculation. *Biological Journal of the Linnean Society* 35:321–337.

Stork, N. E., S. R. Harrison, J. L. Herbohn, and R. Keenan. 1997. Biodiversity conservation and sustainable management of forests: Socioeconomic problems with farm-forestry in rainforest timber production in North Queensland. Pages 159–168 in J. Kikkawa, P. Dart, D. Doley, K. Ishii, D. Lamb, and K. Juzuki, eds., *Overcoming Impediments to Reforestation: Tropical Forest Rehabilitation in the Asia-Pacific Region.* Proceedings of the 6th International Workshop for BIO-REFOR, Brisbane, 2–5 December 1997. BIO-REFOR, Tokyo.

Stott, L. D., J. P. Kennett, N. J. Shackleton, and R. M. Corfield. 1990. *Proceedings of the Ocean Drilling Program, Scientific Results* 113:849–863.

Stover, L. E., and A. D. Partridge. 1982. Eocene spore-pollen from the Werrilup Formation, Western Australia. *Palynology* 6:69–95.

Strahan, R., ed. 1983. *The Australian Museum complete book of Australian mammals.* Angus and Robertson, Sydney.

Street, F. A., and A. T. Grove. 1979. Global maps of lake level fluctuations since 30,000 yr BP. *Quaternary Research* 12:83–118.

Street-Perrott, A. 1994. Palaeo-perspectives: Changes in terrestrial ecosystems. *Ambio* 23:37–43.

Street-Perrott, F. A., Y. Huang, R. A. Perrot, G. Eglinton, P. Barker, L. B. Khelifa, D. D. Harkness, and D. O. Olago. 1997. Impact of lower atmospheric carbon dioxide on tropical mountain ecosystems. *Science* 278:1422–1426.

Strong, D. R., D. Simberloff, L. G. Abele, and A. B. Thistle, eds. 1984. *Ecological communities: Conceptual issues and the evidence.* Princeton University Press, Princeton, NJ.

Struckmeyer, H. I. M., and P. A. Symonds. 1997. Tectonostratigraphic evolution of the Townsville Basin, Townsville Trough, offshore northeastern Australia. *Australian Journal of Earth Sciences* 44:799–817.

Stuart, S. N., R. J. Adams, and M. D. Jenkins. 1990. *Biodiversity in sub-Saharan Africa and its islands: Conservation, management, and sustainable use.* IUCN, Gland.

Stute, M., M. Forster, H. Frischkorn, A. Serejo, J. F. Clark, P. Schlosser, W. S. Broecker, and

G. Bonani. 1995. Cooling of tropical Brazil (5°C) during the last glacial maximum. *Science* 269:379–383.

Su, W. 2003. The design and implementation of an agent-based dynamic landscape simulation model: A case study in tall wet sclerophyll forest in Southern Tasmania. Ph.D. thesis, Australian National University.

Su, W., M. J. Brown, and B. G. Mackey. 2001. Agent-based dynamic modeling of forest ecosystem at Warra LTER Site. *Tasforests* 13(2):129–140.

Su, W., and B. G. Mackey. 1997. A spatially explicit and temporal dynamic simulation model of forested landscape ecosystems. Pages 1635–1640 in A. D. McDonald and M. McAleer, eds., Proceedings: MODSIM 97 International Congress on Modelling and Simulation, Vol. 4. Modeling and Simulation Society of Australia.

Su, W., B. G. Mackey, and M. J. Brown. 2001. Landscape dynamic modelling: Report to Forest and Wood Product Research and Development Council. PN97.102.

Sugihara, G. 1981. $S = cA^z$, $z = 1/4$: A reply to Connor and McCoy. *American Naturalist* 117:790–793.

Sugihara, G., L.-F. Bersler, T. R. E. Southwood, S. L. Pimm, and R. M. May. 2003. Predicted correspondence between species abundances and dendrograms of niche similarities. *Proceedings of the National Academy of Sciences USA* 100:5246–5251.

Sundquist, E., and W. S. Broecker, eds. 1985. *The carbon cycle and atmospheric CO_2: Natural variations Archean to present.* Geophysical monographs, 32. American Geophysical Union, Washington, DC.

Swaine, M. D. 1996. *The ecology of tropical forest tree seedlings.* Man and the Biosphere Series, vol. 17, UNESCO, Paris; Parthenon, New York.

Swaine, M. D., D. Lieberman, and F. E. Putz. 1987. The dynamics of tree populations in tropical forest. *Journal of Tropical Ecology* 3:359–366.

Swaine, M. D., and T. C. Whitmore. 1988. On the definition of ecological species groups in tropical rainforests. *Vegetatio* 75:81–86.

Swarm Development Group. SWARM Web site. http://www.santafe.edu/projects/swarm/.

Swofford, D. L. 1991. *PAUP: Phylogenetic analysis using parsimony.* Version 3.1. Center for Biodiversity of the Illinois Natural History Survey, Champaign, Illinois.

———. 1999. *PAUP*: Phylogenetic analysis using parsimony.* Version 4.0b2a. Sinauer Associates, Sunderland, MA.

Tajima, F. 1983. Evolutionary relationships of DNA sequences in finite populations. *Genetics* 105:437–460.

Takahata, N., and F. Tajima. 1991. Sampling errors in phylogeny. *Molecular Biology and Evolution* 8:494–502.

Takhtajan, A. L. 1969. *Flowering plants: Origin and dispersal.* Edinburgh: Oliver and Boyd.

———. 1970. *Proiskhdenie i Rasselenie Tsvekowykh Rastenii.* Leningrad: Akademia Nauk, Bot. Inst. im V. L. Komarova.

———. 1980. Outline of the classification of flowering plants (Magnoliophyta). *Botanical Review* 46:225–359.

Tansley, A. G. 1935. The use and abuse of vegetational concepts and terms. *Ecology* 16:284–307.

Taylor, G. 1994. Landscapes of Australia: Their nature and evolution. Pages 60–79 in R. S.

Hill, ed., *The history of Australian vegetation: Cretaceous to Recent.* Cambridge University Press, Cambridge.

Taylor, G., G. R. Taylor, M. Bink, C. Foudoulis, I. Gordon, J. Hedstrom, J. Minello, and F. Whippy. 1985. Pre-basaltic topography of the northern Monaro and its implications. *Australian Journal of Earth Sciences* 32:65–71.

Taylor, G., E. M. Truswell, K. G. McQueen, and M. C. Brown. 1990. Early Tertiary palaeogeography, landform evolution, and palaeoclimates of the Southern Monaro, N.S.W., Australia. *Palaeoclimatology, Palaeoecology, Palaeogeography* 78:109–134.

Templeton, A. R. 1987. Species and speciation. *Evolution* 41:233–235.

Templeton, A. R., E. Routman, and C. A. Phillips. 1995. Separating population structure from population history: A cladistic analysis of the geographical distribution of mitochondrial DNA haplotypes in the tiger salamander, *Ambystoma tigrinum. Genetics* 140:767–782.

Terborgh, J. 1974. Preservation of natural diversity: The problem of species extinction. *BioScience* 24:715–722.

———. 1983. *Five New World primates.* Princeton University Press, Princeton, NJ.

———. 1992. *Diversity and the tropical rainforest.* New York: Scientific American Library.

Terborgh, J., and E. Andresen. 1998. The composition of Amazonian forests: Patterns at local and regional scales. *Journal of Tropical Ecology* 14:645–664.

Terborgh, J., J. A. Estes, P. Paquet, K. Ralls, D. Boyd-Heger, B. J. Miller, and R. F. Noss. 1999. The role of top carnivores in regulating terrestrial ecosystems. Pages 39–64 in M. E. Soulé and J. Terborgh, eds., *Continental conservation.* Island Press, Washington, DC.

Terborgh, J. W., and J. Faaborg. 1980. Saturation of bird assemblages in the West Indies. *American Naturalist* 116:178–195.

Terborgh, J., R. B. Foster, and P. Nuñez V. 1996. Tropical tree communities: A test of the nonequilibrium hypothesis. *Ecology* 77:561–567.

Terborgh, J., L. Lopez, P. Nuñez V., M. Rao, G. Shahabuddin, G. Orihuela, M. Riveros, R. Ascanio, G. H. Adler, T. D. Lambert, and L. Balbas. 2001. Ecological meltdown in predator-free forest fragments. *Science* 294:1923–1926.

Terborgh, J., L. Lopez, J. Tello, D. Yu, and A. R. Bruni. 1997. Transitory states in relaxing ecosystems of land bridge islands. Pages 256–274 in W. F. Laurance and R. O. Bierregaard Jr., eds., *Tropical forest remnants: Ecology, management, and conservation of fragmented communities.* University of Chicago Press, Chicago.

Terborgh, J., N. C. A. Pitman, M. R. Silman, H. Schichter, and P. Nuñez V. 2002. Maintenance of tree diversity in tropical forests. Pages 1–17 in D. J. Levey, W. R. Silva, and M. Galetti, eds., *Seed dispersal and frugivory: Ecology, evolution, and conservation.* CABI Publishing, New York.

Terborgh, J., and C. P. van Schaik. 1997. Minimizing species loss: The imperative of protection. Pages 15–35 in R. Kramer, C. van Schaik, and J. Johnson, eds., *Last stand: Protected areas and the defense of tropical biodiversity.* Oxford University Press, New York.

Terborgh, J., C. P. van Schaik, L. Davenport, and M. Rao. 2002. *Making parks work: Strategies for preserving tropical nature.* Island Press, Washington, DC.

Ter Braak, C. J. F., and D. Smilauer. 1999. *Canoco for Windows, version 4.02.* Centre for Biometry, Wageningen, the Netherlands.

ter Steege, H., V. G. Jetten, P. A. Marcel, and M. J. A. Werger. 1993. Tropical rain forest types and soil factors in a watershed in Guyana. *Journal of Vegetation Science* 4:705–716.

ter Steege, H., D. Sabatier, H. Castellanos, T. van Andel, J. Duivenvoorden, A. Adalardo de Oliveira, R. Ek, R. Lilwah, P. Maas, and S. Mori. 2000. An analysis of the floristic composition and diversity of Amazonian forests including those of the Guiana Shield. *Journal of Tropical Ecology* 16:801–828.

Theimer, T. C. 2001. Seed scatterhoarding by white-tailed rats: Consequences for seedling recruitment by an Australian rain forest tree. *Journal of Tropical Ecology* 17:177–189.

———. 2003. Intraspecific variation in seed size affects scatterhoarding behaviour of an Australian tropical rain-forest rodent. *Journal of Tropical Ecology* 19:95–98.

Theimer, T. C., and C. A. Gehring. 1999. Effects of a litter-disturbing bird species on tree seedling germination and survival in an Australian tropical rain forest. *Journal of Tropical Ecology* 15:737–749.

Thompson, J., N. Brokaw, J. K. Zimmerman, R. B. Waide, E. M. Everham III, and D. A. Schaefer. 2004. Luquillo Forest Dynamics Plot, Puerto Rico. Pages 540–550 in E. Losos and E. G. Leigh Jr., eds., *Tropical diversity and dynamism: Findings from a network of tropical forest plots.* University of Chicago Press, Chicago.

Thompson, J. D., D. G. Higgins, and T. J. Gibson. 1994. CLUSTAL W: Improving the sensitivity of progressive multiple sequence alignment through sequence weighting, position-specific gap penalties and weight matrix choice. *Nucleic Acids Research* 22:4673–4680.

Tiffney, B. H., and S. J. Mazer. 1995. Angiosperm growth habit, dispersal and diversification reconsidered. *Evolutionary Ecology* 9:93–117.

Tocher, M. D., C. Gascon, and B. I. Zimmermann. 1997. Fragmentation effects on a central Amazonian frog community: A ten-year study. Pages 124–137 in W. F. Laurance and R. O. Bierregaard Jr., eds., *Tropical forest remnants: Ecology, management, and conservation of fragmented communities.* University of Chicago Press, Chicago.

Tomlinson, P. B. 1986. *The botany of mangroves.* Cambridge University Press, Cambridge.

Tracey, J. G. 1982. *The vegetation of the humid tropics of North Queensland.* CSIRO, Melbourne.

Tracey, J. G., and L. J. Webb. 1975. *Vegetation of the humid tropical region of North Queensland.* 15 maps at 1:100 000 scale + key. CSIRO, Long Pockets Labs, Indooroopily, Queensland.

Tranquillini, W. 1979. *Physiological ecology of the alpine timberline.* Springer-Verlag, New York.

Trenberth, K. E., and T. J. Hoar. 1996. The 1990–1995 El Niño-Southern Oscillation event: Longest on record. *Geophysical Research Letters* 23:57–60.

Trigo, J. R., K. S. Brown Jr., S. A. Henriques, and L. E. S. Barata. 1996. Qualitative patterns of pyrrolizidine alkaloids in Ithomiinae butterflies. *Biochemical Systematics and Ecology* 24:181–8.

Truswell, E. M. 1990. Australian rainforests: The 100 million year record. Pages 7–22 in L. J. Webb and J. Kikkawa, eds., *Australian tropical rainforests: Science-values-meaning.* CSIRO, Melbourne.

———. 1993. Vegetation changes in the Australian Tertiary in response to climatic and phytogeographic forcing factors. *Australian Systematic Botany* 6(5):533–558.

Truswell, E. M., A. P. Kershaw, and I. R. Sluiter. 1987. The Australian-Southeast Asian connection: Evidence from the palaeobotanical record. Pages 32–49 in T. C. Whitmore, ed., *Biogeography of the Malay Archipelago.* Clarendon Press, Oxford.

Tryon, R. M., and R. G. Stolze. 1989–1994. Pteridophyta of Peru. *Fieldiana Botany,* n.s., 20, 22, 27, 29, 32, 34.

Tuomisto, H. 1998. What satellite imagery and large-scale field studies can tell about biodiversity patterns in Amazonian forests. *Annals of the Missouri Botanical Garden* 85: 48–62.

Tuomisto, H., and R. C. Moran. 2001. Marattiaceae. *Flora of Ecuador* 66:23–68.

Tuomisto, H., and A. D. Poulsen. 1996. Influence of edaphic specialization on pteridophyte distribution in Neotropical rain forests. *Journal of Biogeography* 23:283–293.

Tuomisto, H., A. D. Poulsen, and R. C. Moran. 1998. Edaphic distribution of some species of the fern genus *Adiantum* in Western Amazonia. *Biotropica* 30:392–399.

Tuomisto, H., A. D. Poulsen, K. Ruokolainen, R. C. Moran, C. Quintana, J. Celi, and G. Cañas. 2003. Linking floristic patterns with soil heterogeneity and satellite imagery in Ecuadorian Amazonia. *Ecological Applications* 13(2):352–371.

Tuomisto, H., and K. Ruokolainen. 1994. Distribution of Pteridophyta and Melastomataceae along an edaphic gradient in an Amazonian rain forest. *Journal of Vegetation Science* 5:25–34.

———. 1997. The role of ecological knowledge in explaining biogeography and biodiversity in Amazonia. *Biodiversity and Conservation* 6:347–357.

Tuomisto, H., K. Ruokolainen, R. Kalliola, A. Linna, W. Danjoy, and Z. Rodriguez. 1995. Dissecting Amazonian biodiversity. *Science* 269:63–66.

Tuomisto, H., K. Ruokolainen, A. D. Poulsen, R. C. Moran, C. Quintana, G. Cañas, and J. Celi. 2002. Distribution of pteridophytes and Melastomataceae along edaphic gradients in Yasuni National Park, Ecuadorian Amazonia. *Biotropica* 34:516–533.

Tuomisto, H., K. Ruokolainen, and M. Yli-Halla. 2003. Dispersal, environment, and floristic variation of western Amazonian forests. *Science* 299:241–244.

Turner, H., P. Hovenkamp, and P. C. Van Welzen. 2001. Biogeography of Southeast Asia and the West Pacific. *Journal of Biogeography* 28:217–230.

Turner, J. R. G. 1982. How do refuges produce biological diversity? Allopatry and parapatry, extinction and gene flow in mimetic butterflies. Pages 309–335 in G. T. Prance, ed., *Biological diversification in the tropics.* Columbia University Press, New York.

Turner, M. G. 1989. Landscape ecology: The effect of pattern on process. *Annual Review of Ecology and Systematics* 20:171–197.

Turney, C. S. M., M. I. Bird, L. K. Fifield, R. G. Roberts, M. Smith, C. E. Dorch, R. Grün, E. Lawson, L. K. Ayliffe, G. H. Miller, J. Dorch, and R. G. Creswell. 2001. Early human occupation at Devil's Lair, southwestern Australia, 50,000 years ago. *Quaternary Research* 55:3–13.

Turney, C. S. M., A. P. Kershaw, P. Moss, M. I. Bird, L. K. Fifield, R. G. Cresswell, G. M. Santos, M. L. di Tada, P. A. Hausladen, and Z. Youping. 2001. Redating the onset of burning at Lynch's Crater (North Queensland): Implications for human settlement in Australia. *Journal of Quaternary Science* 16:767–771.

Tyler, H. A., K. S. Brown Jr., and K. H. Wilson. 1994. *Swallowtail butterflies of the Americas:*

A study in biological dynamics, ecological diversity, biosystematics, and conservation. Scientific Publishers, Gainesville, FL.

Uhl, C., P. Barreto, A. Verissimo, E. Vidal, P. Amaral, A. C. Barros, C. Souza, J. Johns, and J. Gerwing. 1997. Natural resource management in the Brazilian Amazon. *BioScience* 47:160–168.

Uhl, C., and R. Buschbacher. 1985. A disturbing synergism between cattle ranch burning practices and selective tree harvesting in the eastern Amazon. *Biotropica* 17:265–268.

Uhl, C., K. Clark, N. Dezzeo, and P. Maquirino. 1988. Vegetation dynamics in Amazonian treefall gaps. *Ecology* 69:751–763.

Uhl, C., and I. C. Guimarães Vieira. 1989. Ecological impacts of selective logging in the Brazilian Amazon: A case study from the Paragominas region of the state of Pará. *Biotropica* 21:98–106.

Uhl, C., and J. B. Kauffman. 1990. Deforestation, fire susceptibility, and potential tree responses to fire in the eastern Amazon. *Ecology* 71:437–449.

Underwood, A. J., and P. Fairweather. 1989. Supply-side ecology and benthic marine ecology. *Trends in Ecology and Evolution* 4:16–20.

Urban, D. L., G. B. Bonan, T. M. Smith, and H. H. Shugart. 1991. Spatial application of gap models. *Forest Ecology and Management* 42:95–110.

USGS. 2002. U.S. Geological Service. Global GIS Web site. http://webgis.wr.usgs.gov/globalgis/.

Vadala, A. J., and D. R. Greenwood. 2001. Australian Paleogene vegetation and environments: Evidence for palaeo-Gondwanic elements in the fossil records of Lauraceae and Proteaceae. Pages 196–221 in I. Metcalfe, J. M. B. Smith, and I. Davidson, eds., *Faunal and floral migrations and evolution in SE Asia-Australasia.* Swets & Zeitlinger Publishers, Lisse.

Väisänen, R. A., E. Lammi, and P. Koskimies. 1998. *Muuttuva pesimälinnusto.* Kustannusosakeyhtiö Otava, Helsinki, Finland.

Vajda, V., J. I. Raine, and C. J. Hollis. 2001. Indication of global deforestation at the Cretaceous-Tertiary Boundary by New Zealand fern spike. *Science* 294:1700–1703.

Valencia, R., H. Balslev, and G. Paz y Miño. 1994. High tree alpha-diversity in Amazonian Ecuador. *Biodiversity and Conservation* 3:21–28.

Van der Hammen, T. 1992. *Historia, ecología y vegetación.* Corporación Colombiana para la Amazonia "Araracuara," Bogotá, Colombia.

van der Hammen, T., and M. L. Absy. 1994. Amazonia during the last glacial. *Palaeogeography, Palaeoclimatology, Palaeoecology* 109:247–261.

van der Hammen, T., and H. Hooghiemstra. 2000. Neogene and Quaternary history of vegetation, climate, and plant diversity in Amazonia. *Quaternary Science Reviews* 19: 725–742.

van der Kaars, W. A. 1991. Palynology of eastern Indonesian marine piston-cores: A late Quaternary vegetational and climatic record for Australasia. *Palaeogeography, Palaeoclimatology, Palaeoecology* 85:239–302.

Vandermeer, J. 1972. Niche theory. *Annual Review of Ecology and Systematics* 3:107–132.

van der Werff, H. 1992. Substrate preference of Lauraceae and ferns in the Iquitos area, Peru. *Candollea* 47:11–20.

Vane-Wright, R. I., C. J. Humphries, and P. H. Williams. 1991. What to protect: Systematics and the agony of choice. *Biological Conservation* 55:235–254.

Van Jaarsveld, A. S., S. Freitag, S. L. Chown, C. Muller, S. Koch, H. Hull, C. Bellamy, M. Kruger, S. Endrö-Younga, M. W. Mansell, and C. H. Scholtz. 1998. Biodiversity assessment and conservation strategies. *Science* 279:2106–2108.

Van Schaik, C. P. 1986. Phenological changes in a Sumatran rain forest. *Journal of Tropical Ecology* 2:327–347.

Van Schaik, C. P., J. W. Terborgh, and S. J. Wright. 1993. The phenology of tropical forests: Adaptive significance and consequences for primary consumers. *Annual Review of Ecology and Systematics* 24:353–377.

Van Soest, R. W. M. 1996. Recoding widespread distributions in general area cladogram construction. *Vie et Milieu* 46:155–161.

van Steenis, C. G. G. J. 1934–1936. On the origin of the Malaysian mountain flora. Bulletin du Jardin Botanique Buitenzorg Series 3, Part 1, 13:135–262; Part 2, 13:289–417, Part 3, 14:56–72.

Van Veller, M. G. P., and D. R. Brooks. 2001. When simplicity is not parsimonious: A priori and a posteriori methods in historical biogeography. *Journal of Biogeography* 28:1–11.

Van Veller, M. G. P., D. J. Kornet, and M. Zandee. 2000. Methods in vicariance biogeography: Assessment of the implementations of assumptions 0, 1 and 2. *Cladistics* 16:319–345.

van Zeist, W., and M. R. van der Spoel-Walvius. 1980. A palynological study of the Lateglacial and the postglacial in the Paris Basin. *Palaeohistoria* 27:67–109.

van Zeist, W., and H. Woldring. 1980. Holocene vegetation and climate of northwestern Syria. *Palaeohistoria* 22:111–125.

Vanzolini, P. E., and E. E. Williams. 1970. South American anoles: Geographic differentiation and evolution of *Anolis chrysolepis* species group (Sauria: Iguanidae). Arquivos de Zoologia, São Paulo, 19:1–298.

Vargas-F., I., J. Llorente-B., and A. Luis-M. 1991. Lepidopterofauna de Guerrero. 1. Distribución y fenologia de los Papilionoidea de la Sierra de Atoyac. Publicaciones Especiales del Museo de Zoologia, Facultad de Ciencias, UNAM, Mexico 2:1–127.

Vaughan, R. E., and P. O. Wiehe. 1941. Studies on the vegetation of Mauritius. 3. The structure and development of the upland climax forest. *Journal of Ecology* 29:127–160.

Veblen, T. T., and F. M. Schlegel. 1982. Reseña ecològica de los bosques del sur de Chile. *Bosque* 4:73–115.

Veríssimo, A., P. Barreto, M. Mattos, R. Tarifa, and C. Uhl. 1992. Logging impacts and prospects for sustainable forest management in an old Amazonian frontier: The case of Paragominas. *Forest Ecology and Management* 55:169–199.

Verissimo, A., P. Barreto, R. Tarifa, and C. Uhl. 1995. Extraction of a high-value natural resource in Amazonia: The case of mahogany. *Forest Ecology and Management* 72:39–60.

Veríssimo, A., M. A. Cochrane, and C. Souza Jr. 2002. National forests in the Amazon. *Science* 297:1478.

Vermeij, G. J. 1991. When biotas meet: Understanding biotic interchange. *Science* 253:1099–1104.

Vickers-Rich, P. 1991. The Mesozoic and Tertiary history of birds on the Australian Plate.

Pages 721–808 in P. Vickers-Rich, J. M. Monaghan, R. F. Baird, T. H. Rich, E. M. Thompson, and C. Williams, eds., *Vertebrate palaeontology of Australasia.* Pioneer Design Studios and Monash University Publishing Committee, Melbourne.

Viña, A., and J. Cavalier. 1999. Deforestation rates (1938–1988) of tropical lowland forests on the Andean foothills of Colombia. *Biotropica* 31:31–36.

Vitousek, P. M. 1984. Litterfall nutrient cycling and nutrient limitation in tropical forests. *Ecology* 65:285–298.

Volkov, I., J. R. Banavar, S. P. Hubbell, and A. Maritan. 2003. Neutral theory and relative species abundance in ecology. *Nature* 424:1035–1037.

Vormisto, J., O. L. Phillips, K. Ruokolainen, H. Tuomisto, and R. Vásquez. 2000. A comparison of fine-scale distribution patterns of four plant groups in an Amazonian rainforest. *Ecography* 23:349–359.

Voss, R. S., and L. H. Emmons. 1996. *Mammalian diversity in Neotropical rainforests: A preliminary assessment.* Bulletin of the American Museum of Natural History, no. 230. American Museum of Natural History, New York.

Wagner, M. 1868. *Die Darwin'sche theorie und das migrationsgesgesetz der organismen.* Leipzig: Dunker and Humblot.

Wakeley, J., and J. Hey. 1997. Estimating ancestral population parameters. *Genetics* 145:847–855.

Walker, D. 1966. The Late Quaternary history of the Cumberland Lowland. *Philosophical Transactions of the Royal Society* B 251:1–210.

Walker, G. 1996. Kinder cuts. *New Scientist* (September 21):40–42.

Walker, J., C. H. Thompson, I. F. Fergus, and B. R. Tunstall. 1981. Plant succession and soil development in coastal sand dunes of subtropical eastern Australia. Pages 107–131 in D. C. West, H. H. Shugart, and D. B. Botkin, eds., *Forest succession: Concepts and application.* Springer-Verlag, New York.

Walker, K., A. Neboiss, J. Dean, and D. Cartwright. 1995. A preliminary investigation of the caddis-flies (Trichoptera) of the Queensland Wet Tropics. *Australian Entomologist* 22:19–31.

Wallace, A. R. 1852. On the monkeys of the Amazon. *Proceedings of the Zoological Society of London* 20:107–110.

———. 1876. *The geographical distribution of animals.* Macmillan, London. Reprinted in 1963 by Hafner, New York.

———. 1878. *Tropical nature and other essays.* Macmillan, London.

Walsh, R. P. D. 1996a. Climate. Pages 159–205 in P. W. Richards, ed., *The tropical rain forest.* Cambridge University Press.

———. 1996b. Drought frequency changes in Sabah and adjacent parts of northern Borneo since the late nineteenth century and possible implications for tropical rain forest dynamics. *Journal of Tropical Ecology* 12:385–407.

Walter, G. H. 1988. Competitive exclusion, coexistence and community structure. *Acta Biotheoretica* 37:281–313.

Walter, H. 1971. *Ecology of tropical and subtropical vegetation.* D. Mueller-Dombois, trans.; J. H. Burnett, ed. Oliver & Boyd, Edinburgh.

Wang, X., S. van der Kaars, A. P. Kershaw, M. Bird, and F. Jansen. 1999. A record of fire, vegetation and climate through the last three glacial cycles from Lombok Ridge core G6–4, eastern Indian Ocean, Indonesia. *Palaeogeography, Palaeoclimatology, Palaeoecology* 147:241–256.

Warner, R. R., and P. L. Chesson. 1985. Coexistence mediated by recruitment fluctuations: A field guide to the storage effect. *American Naturalist* 125:769–787.

Warner, R. R., and T. P. Hughes. 1988. The population dynamics of reef fishes. *Proceedings of the Sixth International Coral Reef Symposium, Townsville* 1:149–155.

Warren, A. D., I. Vargas-F., A. Luiz-M., and J. Llorente-B. 1998. Butterflies of the State of Colima, México. *Journal of the Lepidopterists' Society* 52:40–72.

Watterson, G. A. 1974. Models for the logarithmic species abundance distributions. *Theoretical Population Biology* 7:256–276.

Watts, C. H. S. 1978. A revision of the Australian Dytiscidae. *Australian Journal of Zoology,* suppl. ser. 57:1–166.

———. 1982. A blind terrestrial water beetle from Australia. *Memoirs of the Queensland Museum* 20:527–531.

Watts, K. F., L. L. Varga, and D. A. Feary. 1993. Origins, timing, and implications of Miocene to Pleistocene turbidites, debris flows, and slump deposits of the Queensland Trough, northeastern Australia (Site 823). *Proceedings of the Ocean Drilling Program, Scientific Results* 133:379–446.

Watts, W. A. 1969. A pollen diagram from Mud lake, Marion County, North-Central Florida. *Geological Society of America Bulletin* 80:631–642.

———. 1970. The full-glacial vegetation of northwestern Georgia. *Ecology* 51:17–33.

Webb, C. O., D. D. Ackerly, M. A. McPeek, and M. J. Donoghue. 2002. Phylogenies and community ecology. *Annual Review of Ecology and Systematics* 33:475–505.

Webb, L. J. 1958. Cyclones as an ecological factor in tropical lowland rainforest, North Queensland. *Australian Journal of Botany* 6:220–8.

———. 1959. A physiognomic classification of Australian rainforests. *Journal of Ecology* 47:551–570.

———. 1968a. Environmental determinants of the structural types of Australian rain forest vegetation. *Ecology* 49:296–311.

———. 1968b. Environmental relations of the structural types of Australian rainforests. *Journal of Ecology* 47:551–570.

Webb, L. J., and J. G. Tracey. 1967. An ecological guide to new planting areas and site potential for Hoop Pine. *Australian Forestry* 31:224–239.

———. 1981a. Australian rainforests: Pattern and change. Pages 605–694 in J. A. Keast, ed., *Ecological biogeography of Australia.* Dr. W. Junk, The Hague.

———. 1981b. The rainforests of northern Australia. Pages 67–101 in R. H. Groves, ed., *Australian vegetation.* Cambridge University Press, Cambridge.

———. 1994. The rainforests of northern Australia. Pages 87–130 in R. H. Groves, ed., *Australian vegetation,* 2nd ed. Cambridge University Press, Cambridge.

Webb, L. J., J. G. Tracey, and L. W. Jessup. 1986. Recent evidence for autochthony of Australian tropical and subtropical rainforest floristic elements. *Telopea* 2:575–589.

Webb, L. J., J. G. Tracey, and W. T. Williams. 1976. The value of structural features in tropical forest ecology. *Australian Journal of Ecology* 1:3–28.

Webb, R. S., D. H. Rind, S. J. Lehman, R. J. Healy, and D. Sigman. 1997. Influence of ocean heat transport on the climate of the last glacial maximum. *Nature* 385:695–699.

Webb, S. D. 1991. Ecogeography and the Great American Interchange. *Paleobiology* 17:266–280.

Webb, S. D., and A. Rancy. 1996. Late Cenozoic evolution of the Neotropical mammal fauna. Pages 335–358 in J. B. C. Jackson, A. F. Budd, and A. G. Coates, eds., *Evolution and environment in tropical America.* University of Chicago Press, Chicago.

Webb, T. 1987. The appearance and disappearance of major vegetational assemblages: long term vegetational dynamics in eastern North America. *Vegetatio* 69:177–188.

Wei, W., and S. Gartner. 1993. Neogene calcareous nanofossils from Sites 811 and 819 through 825, offshore northeastern Australia. *Proceedings of the Ocean Drilling Program, Scientific Results* 133:19–38.

Weiher, E., and P. A. Keddy. 1999. *The search for assembly rules in ecological communities.* Cambridge University Press, Cambridge.

Wells, D. R. 1971. Survival of the Malaysian bird fauna. *Malayan Nature Journal* 24:248–256.

———. 1984. The forest avifauna of western Malesia and its conservation. Pages 213–222 in A. W. Diamond and T. E. Lovejoy, eds., *Conservation of tropical birds.* International Council for Bird Preservation, Cambridge.

Wells, M., and K. Brandon. 1992. *People and parks: Linking protected area management with local communities.* World Bank, WWF-US and USAID.

Wells, M., S. Guggenheim, A. Khan, W. Wardojo, and P. Jepson. 1999. *Investing in biodiversity: A review of Indonesia's integrated conservation and development projects.* World Bank, Washington, DC.

Wen, J. 1999. Evolution of eastern Asian and eastern North American disjunct distributions in flowering plants. *Annual Review of Ecology and Systematics* 30:421–455.

Wen, J., R. K. Jansen, and K. Kilgore. 1996. Evolution of the eastern Asian and eastern North American disjunct genus *Symplocarpus* (Araceae): Insights from chloroplast DNA restriction site data. *Biochemical Systematics and Ecology* 24:735–747.

Werren, G. L. 2001. *Environmental weeds of the Wet Tropics bioregion: Risk assessment and priority ranking.* Cooperative Research Centre for Tropical Rainforest Ecology and Management, Cairns.

Werren, G. L., S. Goosem, J. G. Tracey, and J. P. Stanton. 1995. The Australian Wet Tropics centre of plant diversity. Pages 500–506 in S. D. Davies, V. H. Heywood, and A. C. Hamilton, eds., *World's centres of plant diversity,* vol. 2. Oxford University Press, Oxford.

Westoby, M. 1993. Biodiversity in Australia compared with other continents. Pages 170–177 in R. E. Ricklefs and D. Schluter, eds., *Species diversity in ecological communities: Historical and geographic perspectives.* University of Chicago Press, Chicago.

Wet Tropics Management Authority. 1999. Annual Report 1998–1999. WTMA, Cairns.

Wet Tropics Management Authority. 2001. Wet Tropics. Protected Areas Programme. Accessed on May 13, 2001. http://www.wcmc.org.uk/protected_areas/data/wh/-wttropi.html.

Wheeler, D. E., and S. C. Levings. 1988. Impact of El Niño on litter arthropods. Pages 309–326 in J. C. Trager, ed., *Advances in myrmecology.* Flora and Fauna, Gainesville, FL.

White, F. 1983. *The vegetation of Africa.* UNESCO, Paris.

White, P. S. 1983. Eastern Asian-North American floristic relations: The plant community level. *Annals of the Missouri Botanical Garden* 70:734–747.

Whitlock, M. C., and D. E. McCauley. 1999. Indirect measures of gene flow and migration: FST does not equal 1/(4Nm + 1). *Heredity* 82:117–125.

Whitmore, T. C. 1984. *Tropical rain forests of the Far East.* 2nd ed. Clarendon Press, Oxford.

———. 1997. Tropical forest disturbance, disappearance, and species loss. Pages 3–12 in W. F. Laurance and R. O. Bierregaard Jr., eds., *Tropical forest remnants: Ecology, management, and conservation of fragmented communities.* University of Chicago Press, Chicago.

Whitmore, T. C., and G. T. Prance, eds. 1987. *Biogeography and Quaternary history of tropical America.* Clarendon Press, Oxford.

Whitmore, T. C., and J. A. Sayer, eds. 1992. *Tropical deforestation and species extinction.* Chapman & Hall, London.

Whittaker, R. H. 1953. A consideration of climax theory: The climax as a population and pattern. *Ecological Monographs* 23:41–78.

———. 1956. Vegetation of the Great Smoky Mountains. *Ecological Monographs* 26:1–80.

———. 1969. Evolution of diversity in plant communities. Pages 178–260 in G. Woodwell, ed., *Diversity and stability in ecological systems.* Brookhaven Symposia in Biology, 22. Brookhaven National Laboratory, Upton, NY.

———. 1972. Evolution and measurement of diversity. *Taxon* 21:213–251.

———. 1977. Evolution of species diversity in land communities. *Evolutionary Biology* 10:1–67.

Whittaker, R. J., K. J. Willis, and R. Field. 2001. Scale and species richness: Towards a general, hierarchical theory of species diversity. *Journal of Biogeography* 28:453–470.

Wich, S. A., and C. P. Van Schaik. 2000. The impact of El Nino on mast fruiting in Sumatra and elsewhere in Malesia. *Journal of Tropical Ecology* 16:563–577.

Wiens, J. A. 1997. Metapopulation dynamics and landscape ecology. Pages 43–62 in I. Hanski and M. E. Gilpin, eds., *Metapopulation biology: Ecology, genetics, and evolution.* Academic Press, San Diego.

Wilcox, B. A. 1978. Supersaturated island faunas: A species-area relationship for lizards on post-Pleistocene land-bridge islands. *Science* 199:996–998.

Wilcox, B. A., D. D. Murphy, P. R. Ehrlich, and G. T. Austin. 1986. Insular biogeography of the montane butterfly faunas in the Great Basin: Comparison with birds and mammals. *Oecologia* 69:188–194.

Wiley, E. O. 1986. Methods in vicariance biogeography. Pages 283–306 in P. Hovenkamp, ed., *Systematics and evolution: A matter of diversity.* University of Utrecht Press, Utrecht.

———. 1988a. Parsimony analysis and vicariance biogeography. *Systematic Zoology* 37: 271–290.

———. 1988b. Vicariance biogeography. *Annual Review of Ecology and Systematics* 19:513–542.

Wilf, P. 1997. When are leaves good thermometers? A new case for Leaf Margin Analysis: *Paleobiology* 23:373–390.

Wilf, P., and C. Labandeira. 1999. Response of plant-insect associations to Paleocene-Eocene warming. *Science* 284:2153–2156.

Wilford, G. E., and P. J. Brown. 1994. Maps of late Mesozoic-Cenozoic Gondwana break-up: Some palaeogeographical implications. Pages 5–13 in R. S. Hill, ed., *The history of Australian vegetation: Cretaceous to Recent.* Cambridge University Press, Cambridge.

Wilkinson, L. 1986. SYSTAT: The System for Statistics. SYSTAT, Inc., Evanston, IL.

Williams, C. B. 1964. *Patterns in the balance of nature.* Academic Press, London.

Williams, P. H. 1998. Biodiversity indicators: Graphical techniques, smoothing and searching for what makes relationships work. *Ecography* 21:1–10.

Williams, P. H., K. J. Gaston, and C. J. Humphries. 1994. Do conservationists and molecular biologists value differences between organisms in the same way? *Biodiversity Letters* 2:67–78.

Williams, P. H., D. Gibbons, C. Margules, A. Rebelo, C. Humphries, and R. Pressey. 1996. A comparison of richness hotspots, rarity hotspots and complementary areas for conserving diversity using British birds. *Conservation Biology* 10:155–174.

Williams, S. E. 1997. Patterns of mammalian species richness in the Australian tropical rainforests: Are extinctions during historical contractions of the rainforest the primary determinants of current regional patterns in biodiversity? *Wildlife Research* 24: 513–530.

Williams, S. E., E. E. Bolitho, and S. Fox. 2003. Climate change in Australian tropical rainforests: An impending environmental catastrophe. *Proceedings of the Royal Society London* B 270:1887–1892.

Williams, S. E., and J.-M. Hero. 1998. Rainforest frogs of the Australian Wet Tropics: Guild classification and the ecological similarity of declining species. *Proceedings of the Royal Society of London* B:265:597–602.

Williams, S. E., and R. G. Pearson. 1997. Historical rainforest contractions, localized extinctions and patterns of vertebrate endemism in the rainforests of Australia's Wet Tropics. *Proceedings of the Royal Society of London* B 264:709–716.

Williams, S. E., R. G. Pearson, and P. J. Walsh. 1996. Distribution and biodiversity of the terrestrial vertebrates of Australia's Wet Tropics: A review of current knowledge. *Pacific Conservation Biology* 2:327–362.

Williamson, G. B., W. F. Laurance, A. A. Oliveira, P. Delamonica, C. Gascon, T. E. Lovejoy, and L. Pohl. 2000. Amazonian tree mortality during the 1997 El Nino drought. *Conservation Biology* 14:1538–1542.

Williamson, M. 1988. Relationship of species number to area, distance, and other variables. Pages 91–115 in A. A. Myers and G. S. Giller, eds., *Analytical biogeography.* Chapman & Hall, New York.

Willis, E. O. 1967. The behavior of bicolored antbirds. *University of California Publications in Zoology* 79:1–132.

———. 1972. *The behavior of spotted antbirds.* Ornithological Monographs, no. 10. American Ornithologists' Union, Washington, DC.

———. 1973. *The behavior of ocellated antbirds.* Smithsonian Contributions to Zoology, no. 144. Smithsonian Institution Press, Washington, DC.

———. 1980. Ecological roles of migratory and resident birds on Barro Colorado Island, Panama. Pages 205–225 in A. Keast and E. S. Morton, eds., *Migrant birds in the Neotropics.* Smithsonian Institution Press, Washington, DC.

Willis, J. C. 1922. *Age and area: A study in geographical distribution and origin in species.* Cambridge University Press, Cambridge.

Willmott, W. F., and P. J. Stephenson. 1989. *Rocks and landscapes of the Cairns district.* Queensland Department of Mines, Brisbane.

Wills, C., and R. Condit. 1999. Similar non-random processes maintain diversity in two tropical rainforests. *Proceedings of the Royal Society of London* B 266:1445–1452.

Wills, C., R. Condit, R. B. Foster, and S. P. Hubbell. 1997. Strong density- and diversity-related effects help to maintain tree species diversity in a Neotropical forest. *Proceedings of the National Academy of Sciences USA* 94:1252–1257.

Wilson, D. E., and D. M. Reeder, eds. 1993. *Mammal species of the world.* 2nd ed. Smithsonian Institution Press, Washington, DC.

Wilson, D. S. 1980. *The natural selection of populations and communities.* Benjamin/Cummings, Menlo Park, CA.

Wilson, E. O. 1959. Adaptive shift and dispersal in a tropical ant fauna. *Evolution* 13:122–144.

———. 1961. The nature of the taxon cycle in the Melanesian ant fauna. *American Naturalist* 95:169–193.

———. 1992. *The diversity of life.* Harvard University Press, Cambridge, MA.

Wilson, J. P., and J. C. Gallant. 2000. *Terrain analysis: Principles and applications.* John Wiley and Sons, New York.

Windsor, D. M. 1990. *Climate and moisture variability in a tropical forest: Long-term records from Barro Colorado Island, Panamá.* Smithsonian Contributions to the Earth Sciences, no. 29. Washington, DC: Smithsonian Institution Press.

Winter, J. W. 1984. Conservation studies of tropical rainforest possums. Pages 469–481 in A. P. Smith and I. D. Hume, eds., *Possums and gliders.* Australian Mammal Society, Sydney.

———. 1988. Ecological specialization of mammals in Australian tropical and sub-tropical rainforest: Refugial or ecological determinism? Pages 127–138 in R. Kitching, ed., *The ecology of Australia's Wet Tropics.* Proceedings of the Ecological Society of Australia, vol. 15. Surrey Beatty and Sons, Sydney.

———. 1997. Responses of non-volant mammals to late Quaternary climatic changes in the Wet Tropics region of north-eastern Australia. *Wildlife Research* 24:493–511.

Winter, J. W., F. C. Bell, L. I. Pahl, and R. G. Atherton. 1984. *The specific habitats of selected northeastern Australian rainforest mammals.* Report to the World Wide Fund for Nature, Sydney.

Wolda, H. 1983. Spatial and temporal variation in abundance in tropical animals. Pages 93–105 in S. L. Sutton, T. C. Whitmore, and A. C. Chadwick, eds., *Tropical rain forest: Ecology and management.* Blackwell Scientific Publications, Oxford.

Wolfe, J. A. 1985. The distribution of major vegetational types during the Tertiary. Pages 357–375 in E. T. Sundquist and W. S. Broecker, eds., *The carbon cycle and atmospheric* CO_2: Natural variations Archean to present. Geophysical Monographs, 32. American Geophysical Union, Washington, DC.

———. 1990. Palaeobotanical evidence for a marked temperature increase following the Cretaceous/Tertiary boundary. *Nature* 343:153–156.

———. 1993. *A method of obtaining climatic parameters from leaf assemblages.* U.S. Geological Survey Bulletin 2040.

———. 1994. Tertiary climatic changes at middle latitudes of western North America. *Palaeogeography, Palaeoclimatology, Palaeoecology* 108:195–205.

Wolfe, J. A., and G. R. Upchurch Jr. 1987. Leaf assemblages across the Cretaceous-Tertiary boundary in the Raton Basin, New Mexico and Colorado. *Proceedings of the National Academy of Sciences USA* 84:5096–5100.

Woodroffe, R., and J. R. Ginsberg. 1998. Edge effects and the extinction of populations inside protected areas. *Science* 280:2126–2128.

Woods, P. 1989. Effects of logging, drought, and fire on tropical forests in Sabah, Malaysia. *Biotropica* 21:290–298.

Woodward, T. E. 1986. A new flightless montane species of Lachnophoroides Distant (Heteroptera: Lygaeidae) from North Queensland. *Memoirs of the Queensland Museum* 22:189–195.

Worbes, M. 1999. Annual growth rings, rainfall-dependent growth and long-term growth patterns of tropical trees from the Caparo Forest Reserve in Venezuela. *Journal of Ecology* 87:391–403.

Workshop 90. 1991. Biological priorities for conservation in Amazonia. Map produced by Conservation International, Washington, DC.

World Bank. 1996. *Kerinci-Seblat Integrated Conservation and Development Project.* World Bank, Washington, DC.

———. 2001. *Indonesia: Environment and natural resource management in a time of transition.* World Bank, Washington, DC.

World Conservation Monitoring Center. 1992. *Global biodiversity: Status of the earth's living resources.* Chapman & Hall, London.

Worthington, A. 1982. Population sizes and breeding rhythms of two species of manakins in relation to food supply. Pages 213–225 in E. G. Leigh Jr., A. S. Rand, and D. M. Windsor, eds., *Ecology of a tropical forest.* Smithsonian Institution Press, Washington, DC.

Wright, D. D., J. H. Jessen, P. Burke, and H. G. de Silva Garza. 1997. Tree and liana enumeration and diversity on a one-hectare plot in Papua New Guinea. *Biotropica* 29:250–260.

Wright, D. H., D. J. Currie, and B. A. Maurer. 1993. Energy supply and patterns of species richness on local and regional scales. Pages 66–74 in R. E. Ricklefs and D. Schluter, eds., *Species diversity in ecological communities: Historical and geographical perspectives.* University of Chicago Press, Chicago.

Wright, D. H., and J. H. Reeves. 1992. On the meaning and measurement of nestedness of species assemblages. *Oecologia* 92:416–428.

Wright, S. J. 1991. Seasonal drought and the phenology of shrubs in a tropical moist forest. *Ecology* 72:1643–1657.

———. 1992. Seasonal drought, soil fertility and the species density of tropical forest plant communities. *Trends in Ecology and Evolution* 7:260–263.

———. 1996. Phenological responses to seasonality in tropical forest plants. Pages 440–460 in S. S. Mulkey, R. L. Chazdon, and A. P. Smith, eds., *Tropical forest plant ecophysiology.* Chapman & Hall, New York.

Wright, S. J., C. Carrasco, O. Calderon, and S. Patton. 1999. The El Niño Southern Oscillation, variable fruit production and famine in a Neotropical forest. *Ecology* 80:1632–1647.

Wright, S. J., and F. H. Cornejo. 1990a. Seasonal drought and leaf fall in a tropical forest. *Ecology* 71:1165–1175.

———. 1990b. Seasonal drought and the timing of flowering and leaf fall in a Neotropical forest. Pages 49–61 in K. S. Bawa and M. Hadley, eds., *Reproductive ecology of tropical forest plants.* Man and the Biosphere Series, vol. 17. UNESCO, Paris, and Parthenon Publishing Group, Carnforth, U.K.

Wright, S. J., H. Zeballos, I. Domínguez, M. M. Gallardo, M. C. Moreno, and R. Ibáñez. 2000. Poachers alter mammal abundance, seed dispersal and seed predation in a Neotropical forest. *Conservation Biology* 14:227–239.

WWF. 1997. *The year the world caught fire.* WWF International Discussion Paper. WWF, Gland, Switzerland.

Wycherley, P. R. 1973. The phenology of plants in the humid tropics. *Micronesica* 9:75–96.

Yap, S. K., and H. T. Chan. 1990. Phenological behaviour of some *Shorea* species in peninsular Malaysia. Pages 21–35 in K. S. Bawa and M. Hadley, eds., *Reproductive ecology of tropical forest plants.* Man and the Biosphere Series, vol. 17. UNESCO, Paris, and Parthenon Publishing Group, Carnforth, U.K.

Yasuda, M., J. Matsumoto, N. Osada, S. Ichikawa, N. Kachi, M. Tani, T. Okuda, A. Furudawa, A. R. Nik, and N. Manokaran. 1999. The mechanism of general flowering in Dipterocarpaceae in the Malay Peninsula. *Journal of Tropical Ecology* 15:437–449.

Yeates, D. K., P. Bouchard, and G. B. Monteith. 2002. Patterns and levels of endemism in the Australian Wet Tropics rainforest: Evidence from flightless insects. *Invertebrate Systematics* 16:605–619.

Yoda, K. 1974. Three-dimensional distribution of light intensity in a tropical rain forest of west Malaysia. *Japanese Journal of Ecology* 24:247–254.

Yoder, A. D. 1997. Back to the future: A synthesis of Strepsirrhine systematics. *Evolutionary Anthropology* 6(1):11–22.

Young, K. R., and B. León. 1989. Pteridophyte species diversity in the central Peruvian Amazon: Importance of edaphic specialization. *Brittonia* 41:388–395.

Young, R. W. 1977. Landscape development in the Shoalhaven catchment in southeastern New South Wales. *Zeitschrift für Geomorphologie* 21:262–283.

———. 1989. Crustal constraints on the evolution of the continental divide of Eastern Australia. *Geology* 17:528–530.

Young, R. W., S. Cope, D. M. Price, A. R. Chivas, and B. E. Chenhall. 1996. Character and age of lateritic weathering at Jervis Bay, southern New South Wales, Australia. *Australian Geographic Studies* 34(2):237–246.

Young, R. W., and I. McDougall. 1982. Basalts and silcretes on the coast near Ulladulla, southern new South Wales. *Journal of the Geological Society of Australia* 29:425–430.

———. 1985. The age, extent and geomorphological significance of the Sassafras basalt, south-eastern New South Wales. *Australian Journal of Earth Sciences* 32:323–331.

———. 1993. Long-term landscape evolution: Early Miocene and modern rivers in southern New South Wales, Australia. *Journal of Geology* 101:35–49.

Yule, C. M., and R. G. Pearson. 1996. Aseasonality of benthic invertebrates in a tropical stream on Bougainville Island, Papua New Guinea. *Archiv für Hydrobiologie* 137:95–117.

Zabka, M. 1991. Salticidae (Arachnida: Araneae) of Oriental, Australian and Pacific regions, 7. *Mopsolodes, Abracadabrella* and *Pseudosynagelides:* New genera from Australia. *Memoirs of the Queensland Museum* 30:621–644.

Zachos, J. C., L. D. Stott, and K. C. Lohmann. 1994. Evolution of early Cenozoic marine temperatures. *Paleoceanography* 9(2):353–387.

Zandee, M., and M. C. Roos. 1987. Component-compatibility in historical biogeography. *Cladistics* 3:305–332.

Zaret, T. M., and A. S. Rand. 1971. Competition in tropical stream fishes: Support for the competitive exclusion principle. *Ecology* 52:336–342.

Zeh, D. W., J. A. Zeh, and R. L. Smith. 1989. Ovipositors, amnions, and eggshell architecture in the diversification of terrestrial arthropods. *Quarterly Review of Biology* 64:147–168.

Zikán, J. F., and W. Zikán. 1968. Inseto-fauna do Itatiaia e da Mantiqueira, 3: Lepidoptera. *Pesqisas agropecuarias Brasil* 3:45–109.

Zimmermann, E. 1990. Differentiation of vocalisations in bushbabies (Galaginae, Prosimae, Primates) and the significance for assessing phylogenetic relationships. *Journal of Zoological Systematics and Evolution* 28:217–239.

Zobel, M. 1992. Plant species coexistence: The role of historical, evolutionary and ecological factors. *Oikos* 65:314–320.

Zotz, G., G. Harris, M. Königer, and K. Winter. 1995. High rates of photosynthesis in the tropical pioneer tree, *Ficus insipida* Willd. *Flora* 190:265–272.

Zotz, G., S. Patiño, and M. T. Tyree. 1997. CO_2 gas exchange and the occurrence of CAM in tropical woody hemiepiphytes. *Flora* 192:143–150.

Zotz, G., and K. Winter. 1994. Photosynthesis of a tropical canopy tree, *Ceiba pentandra,* in a lowland forest in Panama. *Tree Physiology* 14:1291–1301.

Zwick, P. 1981. *Carabhydrus andreas,* a new Australian dytiscid (Coleoptera, Dytiscidae). *Aquatic Insects* 3:167–170.

CONTRIBUTORS

Sammya Agra D'Angelo
Biological Dynamics of Forest Fragments Project
Instituto Nacional de Pesquisas da Amazônia
Caixa Postal 478
Manaus, AM 69011-970, Brazil
Salomón Aguilar
Center for Tropical Forest Science
Smithsonian Tropical Research Institute
Unit 0948, APO AA 34002-0948 USA
Christopher Barber
Center for Global Change and Earth Observations
Michigan State University
East Lansing, MI 48823, USA
Michelle K. Bayes
Biology Department
Royal Holloway University
Egham, Surrey TW20 0EX, Great Britain
Scott Bergen
Center for Environmental Literacy
Mt. Holyoke College
Talcott 100
South Hadley, MA 01075, USA
Eldredge Bermingham
Smithsonian Tropical Research Institute
Unit 0948, APO AA 34002-0948 USA
Patrice Bouchard
Agriculture and Agri-Food Canada
K. W. Nearby Building
960 Carling Avenue
Ottawa, ON K1A 0C6, Canada
Daniel R. Brooks
Department of Zoology
University of Toronto
25 Harbord Street
Toronto, Ontario, M5S 1A1, Canada
Keith S. Brown Jr.
Departamento de Zoologia
Instituto de Biologia, UNICAMP
C.P. 6109
Campinas, São Paulo, 13.083-970, Brazil

Michael W. Bruford
School of Biosciences
Cardiff University
P.O. Box 915, Main Building, Cathays Park
Cardiff CF10 3TL, Wales, UK
David C. Christophel
Department of Biological Sciences
University of Denver
Room 102 Olin Building
2190 E. Iliff Avenue
Denver, CO 80208, USA
Mark A. Cochrane
Center for Global Change and Earth Observations
Michigan State University
1405 S. Harrison Road, Room 101
East Lansing, MI 48823-5243, USA
Paul Colinvaux
Marine Biological Laboratory
7 MBL Street
Woods Hole MA 02543, USA
Richard Condit
Center for Tropical Forest Science
Smithsonian Tropical Research Institute
Unit 0948, APO AA 34002-0948 USA
Joseph H. Connell
Department of Ecology, Evolution and Marine Biology
University of California
Santa Barbara, CA 93107, USA
Igor Debski
Flat 4, 371 Hereford St.
Christchurch, New Zealand
Patricia Delamônica
P.O. Box 12486
Gainesville, FL 32604, USA
Christopher W. Dick
Department of Ecology and Evolutionary Biology
University of Michigan
Ann Arbor, MI 48104, USA
Maria Nazareth F. da Silva
Department of Zoology
Instituto Nacional de Pesquisas da Amazônia
Caixa Postal 478
Manaus, AM 69011-970, Brazil

Philip M. Fearnside
Department of Ecology
Instituto Nacional de Pesquisas da Amazônia
Caixa Postal 478
Manaus, AM 69011-970, Brazil
Tito Fernandez
Biological Dynamics of Forest Fragments Project
Instituto Nacional de Pesquisas da Amazônia
Caixa Postal 478
Manaus, AM 69011-970, Brazil
Jon Fjeldså
Zoological Museum
University of Copenhagen
Vertebrate Department, Universitetsparken 15
DK-2100 Copenhagen Ø, Denmark
John R. Flenley
School of People, Environment and Planning
Massey University
Palmerston North, New Zealand
Catherine A. Gehring
Department of Biological Sciences
Northern Arizona University
Flagstaff, AZ 86011, USA
Derek Girman
Department of Biology
Sonoma State University
1808 E. Cotati Avenue
Rohnert Park, CA 94928, USA
Lloyd P. Goldwasser
Department of Demography
University of California
Berkeley, CA 94720-2120, USA
Peter T. Green
Tropical Forest Research Centre
P.O. Box 780
Atherton, QLD 4883, Australia
David R. Greenwood
Coordinator, Environmental Science Program
Brandon University
Brodie Science Building Rm. 4-14
270 18th Street
Brandon, MB R7A 6A9, Canada

Kyle E. Harms
Department of Biological Sciences
Louisiana State University
202 Life Sciences Building
Baton Rouge, LA 70803, USA
Andrés Hernández
Center for Tropical Forest Science
Smithsonian Tropical Research Institute
Unit 0948, APO AA 34002-0948 USA
Stephen P. Hubbell
Department of Plant Biology
University of Georgia
Athens, GA 30602, USA
and
Smithsonian Tropical Research Institute
Unit 0948, APO AA 34002-0948 USA
Peter Juniper
Tropical Forest Research Centre, CSIRO
P.O. Box 780
Atherton, QLD 4883, Australia
Risto Kalliola
Department of Geography
University of Turku
FIN-20014 Turku, Finland
A. Peter Kershaw
Centre for Palynology and Palaeoecology
School of Geography and Environmental Science
Monash University, VIC 3800, Australia
Suzanne Lao
Center for Tropical Forest Science
Smithsonian Tropical Research Institute
Unit 0948, APO AA 34002-0948 USA
William F. Laurance
Smithsonian Tropical Research Institute
Unit 0948, APO AA 34002-0948 USA
and
Biological Dynamics of Forest Fragments Project
Instituto Nacional de Pesquisas da Amazônia
Caixa Postal 478
Manaus, AM 69011-970, Brazil
Egbert Giles Leigh Jr.
Smithsonian Tropical Research Institute
Unit 0948, APO AA 34002-0948 USA

Brendan Mackey
School of Resources, Environment and Society
The Australian National University
Canberra, ACT 0200, Australia
Kathy MacKinnon
Environment Department
World Bank
1818 H Street
Washington, D.C. 20433, USA
Keith R. McDonald
Queensland Parks and Wildlife Service
Northern Region
Atherton, QLD 4883, Australia
Craig Moritz
Museum of Vertebrate Zoology
3101 Valley Life Sciences Building
University of California
Berkeley, CA 94720-3160, USA
Patrick T. Moss
Department of Geography
University of Wisconsin
Madison, WI 53706, USA
Jonathan Nott
School of Tropical Environmental Studies and Geography
James Cook University
P.O. Box 6811
Cairns, QLD 4870, Australia
James L. Patton
Museum of Vertebrate Zoology
3101 Valley Life Sciences Building
University of California
Berkeley, CA 94720, USA
Richard G. Pearson
School of Tropical Biology
James Cook University
Townsville, QLD 4811, Australia
Rolando Pérez
Center for Tropical Forest Science
Smithsonian Tropical Research Institute
Unit 0948, APO AA 34002-0948 USA
Christopher R. Pyke
National Center for Ecological Analysis and Synthesis
735 State Street, Suite 300
Santa Barbara, CA 93101, USA

Robert E. Ricklefs
Department of Biology
University of Missouri at St. Louis
8001 Natural Bridge Road
St. Louis, MO 63121-4499, USA
Michael S. Roy
Smithsonian Tropical Research Institute
Unit 0948, APO AA 34002-0948, USA
Ira Rubinoff
Smithsonian Tropical Research Institute
Unit 0948, APO AA 34002-0948 USA
Kalle Ruokolainen
Department of Biology
University of Turku
FIN-20014 Turku, Finland
Christopher J. Schneider
Department of Biology
Boston University
5 Cummington St.
Boston, MA 02215, USA
Thomas B. Smith
Center for Tropical Research, Institute of the Environment and
Department of Organismic Biology, Ecology, and Evolution
1609 Hershey Hall, Box 951496
University of California, Los Angeles
Los Angeles, CA 90095-1496, USA
Nigel E. Stork
Cooperative Research Centre for Tropical Rainforest Ecology and Management
James Cook University
P.O. Box 6811
Cairns, QLD 4870, Australia
Wengui Su
GIS Section, Integrated Policy & Strategy Branch, Resource Management and
Conservation (RMC)
Department of Primary Industry, Water and Environment (DPIWE)
134 Macquarie Street, P.O. Box 44
Hobart, TAS 7001, Australia
Tad C. Theimer
Department of Biological Sciences
Box 5640
Northern Arizona University
Flagstaff, AZ 86011, USA

Hanna Tuomisto
Department of Biology
University of Turku
FIN-20014 Turku, Finland
Robert K. Wayne
Department of Organismic Biology, Ecology, and Evolution
2312 Life Sciences Building
Box 951606
University of California, Los Angeles
Los Angeles, CA 90095-1606, USA
Russell Wild
Centre for Palynology and Palaeoecology
School of Geography and Environmental Science
Monash University
Clayton, VIC 3800, Australia
Stephen E. Williams
School of Tropical Biology / Rainforest CRC
James Cook University
Townsville, QLD 4811, Australia
S. Joseph Wright
Smithsonian Tropical Research Institute
Apartado 2072, Balboa, Ancon, Republic of Panama
David K. Yeates
CSIRO Entomology
P.O. Box 1700
Canberra, ACT 2601, Australia

INDEX

Page numbers in italics refer to tables and figures.